Students Get Results with McGraw-Hill Connect® Sociology

Connect strengthens the link between faculty, students, and coursework, helping everyone accomplish more in less time. Innovative, adaptive technology engages students in the course content so they are better prepared, are more active in discussion, and achieve better results.

connect INSIGHT™

Instructors Get Results with McGraw-Hill Connect Insight™

The first and only analytics tool of its kind, *Connect Insight* is a series of visual data displays, each framed by an intuitive question (How are my students doing? How is my section doing?) that provides at-a-glance information regarding how your class is doing. *Connect Insight* is accessible at a moment's notice from your tablet device or desktop.

sociology

in modules

sociology
in modules

third edition

Richard T. Schaefer

DEPAUL UNIVERSITY

Mc
Graw
Hill
Education

SOCIOLOGY IN MODULES

ISBN 978-1-259-25446-8
MHID 1-259-25446-1

dedication

To my grandchildren, Tillie and Reuben. May they enjoy exploring life's possibilities.

www.mhhe.com

about the author

Richard T. Schaefer: Professor, DePaul University
BA Northwestern University; MA, PhD University of Chicago

Growing up in Chicago at a time when neighborhoods were going through transitions in ethnic and racial composition, Richard T. Schaefer found himself increasingly intrigued by what was happening, how people were reacting, and how these changes were affecting neighborhoods and people's jobs. His interest in social issues caused him to gravitate to sociology courses at Northwestern University, where he eventually received a BA in sociology.

"Originally as an undergraduate I thought I would go on to law school and become a lawyer. But after taking a few sociology courses, I found myself wanting to learn more about what sociologists studied, and fascinated by the kinds of questions they raised." This fascination led him to obtain his MA and PhD in sociology from the University of Chicago. Dr. Schaefer's continuing interest in race relations led him to write his master's thesis on the membership of the Ku Klux Klan and his doctoral thesis on racial prejudice and race relations in Great Britain.

Dr. Schaefer went on to become a professor of sociology at DePaul University in Chicago. In 2004 he was named to the Vincent DePaul professorship in recognition of his undergraduate teaching and scholarship. He has taught introductory sociology for over 35 years to students in colleges, adult education programs, nursing programs, and even a maximum-security prison. Dr. Schaefer's love of teaching is apparent in his interaction with his students. "I find myself constantly learning from the students who are in my classes and from reading what they write. Their insights into the material we read or current events that we discuss often become part of future course material and sometimes even find their way into my writing."

Dr. Schaefer is the author of the thirteenth edition of *Sociology* (McGraw-Hill, 2012), *Sociology: A Brief Introduction,* 11th edition (McGraw-Hill, 2015), and the sixth edition of *Sociology Matters* (McGraw-Hill, 2014). He is also the author of *Racial and Ethnic Groups,* now in its fourteenth edition (2014), *Racial and Ethnic Diversity in the USA* (first edition, 2014), and *Race and Ethnicity in the United States,* seventh edition (2013), all published by Pearson. Together with William Zellner, he coauthored the ninth edition of *Extraordinary Groups,* published by Worth in 2011. Dr. Schaefer served as the general editor of the three-volume *Encyclopedia of Race, Ethnicity, and Society,* published by Sage in 2008. These books have been translated into Chinese, Japanese, Portuguese, and Spanish, as well as adapted for use in Canadian colleges.

Dr. Schaefer's articles and book reviews have appeared in many journals, including *American Journal of Sociology; Phylon: A Review of Race and Culture; Contemporary Sociology; Sociology and Social Research; Sociological Quarterly;* and *Teaching Sociology.* He served as president of the Midwest Sociological Society in 1994–1995.

Dr. Schaefer's advice to students is to "look at the material and make connections to your own life and experiences. Sociology will make you a more attentive observer of how people in groups interact and function. It will also make you more aware of people's different needs and interests—and perhaps more ready to work for the common good, while still recognizing the individuality of each person."

brief contents

contents

4 Socialization and the Life Course 76

5 Social Interaction, Social Structure, and Groups 97

6 The Mass Media 125

7 Deviance, Crime, and Social Control 150

8 Stratification and Social Mobility in the United States 177

9 Global Inequality 205

10 Racial and Ethnic Inequality 225

chapter-opening excerpts

Every chapter in this textbook begins with an excerpt from one of the works listed here. These excerpts convey the excitement and relevance of sociological inquiry and draw readers into the subject matter of each chapter.

boxed features

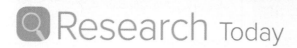

⊕ Sociology in the Global Community

⊗ Our Wired World

⊛ Sociology on Campus

⊗ Taking Sociology to Work

social policy sections

maps

tracking sociological perspectives tables

summing up tables

Modules Work for Instructors & Students

Modules allow you to assign the content you want in the order you prefer, and the format promotes student learning and success by presenting content in small, manageable chunks.

Modules Work for you

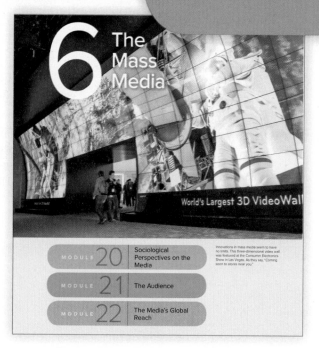

Create, Because Customization Matters.

Finally you have the ability to customize your introductory Sociology course materials to align with your course goals.

- Prefer to cover Deviance in the first few weeks of class? No problem. Just click and rearrange the modules.
- Want additional coverage on Family Relationships? **Easy.** Just search our database to find the best content for your students.
- Don't cover Research Methods in your course? **Simple.** Just omit those modules.

You can also upload your syllabus or any other content you have written to tailor your McGraw-Hill Sociology materials just how you want them, in a snap. Register today at www.mcgrawhillcreate.com and craft your course resources to match the way you teach!

A Revision Informed by Student Data

Over the course of two years, data points showing concepts that caused students the most difficulty were collected anonymously from Connect Sociology's LearnSmart for *Sociology in Modules,* Second Edition. This student performance data provided a new source of information that could be used together with instructor reviews to inform plans for the Third Edition.

The data from LearnSmart were presented in the form of a **Heat Map,** which graphically illustrated "hot spots" in the text that impacted student learning. The data were analyzed and used to guide the revision of core content, as well as questions and other auto-gradable activities in **Connect Sociology** and **LearnSmart,** to further support student success.

reference group is binge drinking. On the one hand, we can view binge drinking as *deviant*, as violating a school's standards of conduct and endangering a person's health. On the other hand, we can see it as *conforming*, or complying with peer culture. In the United States, people are socialized to have mixed feelings about both conforming and nonconforming behavior. The term *conformity* can conjure up images of mindless imitation of a peer group—whether a circle of teenagers wearing "phat pants" or a group of business executives all dressed in gray suits. Yet the same term can also suggest that an individual is cooperative, or a "team player." What about those who do not conform? They may be respected as individualists, leaders, or creative thinkers who break new ground. Or they may be labeled as "troublemakers" and "weirdos."

This chapter examines the relationships among deviance and conformity, crime and social control. What is deviance, and what are its consequences? What causes crime? How does society control people's behavior, convincing us to conform to both unwritten rules and formal laws? We will begin by defining deviance

and describing the stigma that is associated with it. Then we will distinguish between conformity and obedience, and examine a surprising experiment on obedience to authority. We will study the mechanisms societies use, both formal and informal, to encourage conformity and discourage deviance, paying particular attention to the law and how it reflects our social values.

Next, we will focus on theoretical explanations for deviance, including the functionalist approach employed by Émile Durkheim and Robert Merton; interactionist-based theories; labeling theory, which draws on both the interactionist and the conflict perspectives; and conflict theory. In the last part of the chapter we will focus on crime, a specific type of deviant behavior. As a form of deviance that is subject to official, written norms, crime has been a special concern of both policymakers and the public in general. We will look at various types of crime found in the United States, the ways crime is measured, and international crime rates. Finally, the Social Policy section considers the controversial topic of the death penalty.

What Is Deviance?

For sociologists, the term *deviance* does not mean perversion or depravity. **Deviance** is behavior that violates the standards of conduct or expectations of a group or society. In the United States, alcoholics, compulsive gamblers, and the mentally ill would all be classified as deviants. Being late for class is categorized as a deviant act; the same is true of wearing jeans to a formal wedding. On the basis of the sociological definition, we are all deviant from time to time. Each of us violates common social norms in certain situations (Best 2004).

Is being overweight an example of deviance? In the United States and many other cultures, unrealistic standards of appearance and body image place a huge strain on people—especially

women and girls—based on how they look. Journalist Naomi Wolf (1992) has used the term *beauty myth* to refer to an exaggerated ideal of beauty, beyond the reach of all but a few females, which has unfortunate consequences. In order to shed their "deviant" image and conform to unrealistic societal norms, many women and girls become consumed with adjusting their appearances. Yet what is deviant in one culture may be celebrated in another.

Deviance involves the violation of group norms, which may or may not be formalized into law. It is a comprehensive concept that includes not only criminal behavior but also many actions that are not subject to prosecution. The public official who takes a bribe has defied social norms, but so has the high school student who refuses to sit in an assigned seat or cuts class. Of course, deviation from norms is not always negative, let alone criminal. A member of an exclusive social club who speaks out against a traditional policy of not admitting women, Blacks, and Jews is deviating from the club's norms. So is a police officer who blows the whistle on corruption or brutality within the department.

From a sociological perspective, deviance is hardly objective or set in stone. Rather, it is subject to social definition within a particular society and at a particular time. For that reason, what is considered deviant can shift from one social era to another. In most instances, those individuals and groups with the greatest status and power define what is acceptable and what is deviant. For example, despite serious medical warnings against the dangers of tobacco, made since 1964, cigarette smoking continued to be accepted for decades—in good part because of the power of tobacco farmers and cigarette manufacturers. Only after a long campaign led by public health and anticancer activists did cigarette smoking become more of a deviant activity. Today, many state and local laws limit where people can smoke.

Deviance and Social Stigma

A person can acquire a deviant identity in many ways. Because of physical or behavioral characteristics, some people are

In 2009, baseball fans were shocked by the revelation that, like several other baseball greats, superstar Alex Rodriguez had used banned substances and lied about it.

Think about It
If your friends or teammates violate a social norm, is their behavior deviant?

151

An Analytics Tool That Provides Classroom Performance Data

Connect INSIGHT

The first and only analytics tool of its kind, **Connect Insight™** is a series of visual data displays, each framed by an intuitive question (How are my students doing? How effective are my assignments?), to provide at-a-glance information regarding how your class is doing. **Connect Insight** is accessible at a moment's notice from your tablet device or desktop.

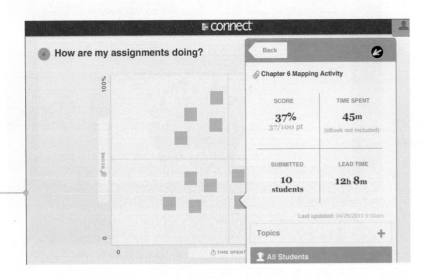

Improve Student Performance with LearnSmart

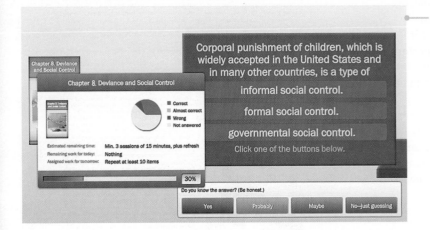

||LEARNSMART®

LearnSmart is an adaptive learning system that helps students study efficiently and effectively for greater success. **LearnSmart** intelligently pinpoints concepts students do not understand and maps out personalized study plans that ground students in the fundamentals of sociology, allowing instructors to focus valuable class time on higher-level concepts.

Offer Your Students a More Personalized Reading Experience with SmartBook

||SMARTBOOK™

SmartBook creates a personalized reading experience by highlighting the most important concepts a student needs to learn based on what that student does and doesn't know. **SmartBook** adds value to every minute a student spends studying *Sociology in Modules*.

Help Your Students to Succeed with Connect Sociology

Connect Sociology includes assignable and assessable quizzes, exercises, and interactive activities, all associated with learning objectives for *Sociology in Modules,* Third Edition. Videos, interactive assessments, and scenario-based activities engage students and add real-world perspective to the introductory sociology course. In addition, printable, exportable reports show how well each student or section is performing on each course segment.

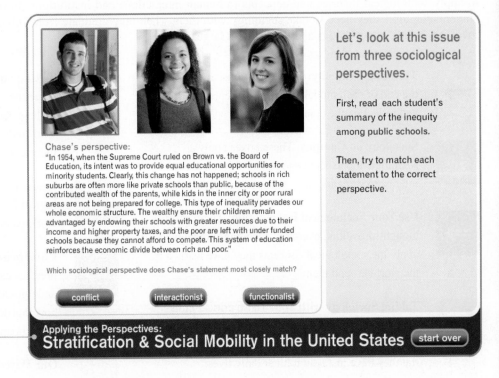

Chase's perspective:
"In 1954, when the Supreme Court ruled on Brown vs. the Board of Education, its intent was to provide equal educational opportunities for minority students. Clearly, this change has not happened; schools in rich suburbs are often more like private schools than public, because of the contributed wealth of the parents, while kids in the inner city or poor rural areas are not being prepared for college. This type of inequality pervades our whole economic structure. The wealthy ensure their children remain advantaged by endowing their schools with greater resources due to their income and higher property taxes, and the poor are left with under funded schools because they cannot afford to compete. This system of education reinforces the economic divide between rich and poor."

Which sociological perspective does Chase's statement most closely match?

conflict   interactionist   functionalist

Let's look at this issue from three sociological perspectives.

First, read each student's summary of the inequity among public schools.

Then, try to match each statement to the correct perspective.

Applying the Perspectives:
Stratification & Social Mobility in the United States start over

Investigate Sociology These engaging, interactive, scenario-based activities challenge students to delve into issues of race, class, gender, and culture, giving them the experience of *doing* sociology.

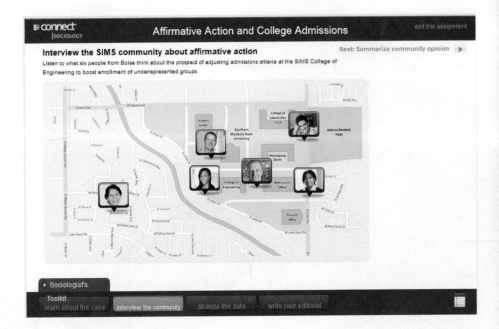

Affirmative Action and College Admissions   exit this assignment

Interview the SiMS community about affirmative action   Next: Summarize community opinion

Listen to what six people from Boise think about the prospect of adjusting admissions criteria at the SiMS College of Engineering to boost enrollment of underrepresented groups.

Sociologist's Toolkit
learn about the case   interview the community   analyze the data   write your editorial

Take Sociology with You

Sociology in Modules highlights the distinctive ways in which sociologists examine human social behavior, as well as the ways in which research findings contribute to our understanding of society. In doing so, it helps students to think like sociologists and to apply sociological theories and concepts to human interactions and institutions. In other words, *Sociology in Modules* gives students the tools they need to take sociology with them when they graduate from college, begin to pursue careers, and become involved in their communities and the world at large.

 Thinking Critically: These questions, appearing at the end of each module, prompt students to review and reflect on the content.

 Sociology on Campus: These boxes apply a sociological perspective to issues of immediate interest to students.

 Use Your Sociological Imagination: These short, thought-provoking exercises encourage students to apply the sociological concepts they have learned to the world around them.

 Taking Sociology with You: These critical thinking questions and reflection prompts at the end of each chapter encourage students to apply the material they have just read to their daily lives.

 Taking Sociology to Work: These boxes underscore the value of an undergraduate or community college degree in sociology by profiling individuals who studied sociology and now use its principles in their work.

 Research Today: These boxes present new sociological findings on topics such as sports, social networks, and transracial adoption.

 Careers in Sociology: This appendix to Chapter 1 presents career options for students who have their undergraduate degree in sociology and explains how this degree can be an asset in a wide variety of occupations.

 Our Wired World: These boxes describe the Internet's effect on social activities such as lying, love, and politicking.

 Sociology in the Global Community: These boxes provide a global perspective on topics such as stratification, marriage, and the women's movement.

 Social Policy Sections: The end-of-chapter social policy sections apply sociological concepts and theories to important social issues currently being debated by policymakers and the general public.

Maps: Mapping Life Nationwide and Mapping Life Worldwide maps show social trends in the United States as well as in the global community.

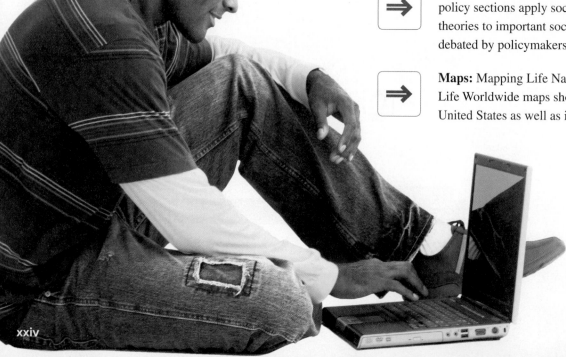

What's New

Chapter 1: Understanding Sociology

- Opening excerpt from *Alone Together* by Sherry Turkle
- Discussion of the Atlanta Sociological Laboratory, founded by W. E. B. DuBois, and its contributions to applied sociology
- Subsection on queer theory, with key term treatment
- Research Today box, "Looking at Sports from Five Sociological Perspectives"

Chapter 2: Sociological Research

- Inclusion of a written report with executive summary as the final task in the scientific method
- Updated figure on educational level and household income, based on 2013 census release
- Discussion of the reliability and validity of the American Community Survey
- Updated figure on the impact of a college education on income
- Updated coverage of the U.S. Army's Human Terrain System as an example of ethnographic research
- Coverage of the use of content analysis of children's books to assess children's environmental awareness
- Section on queer theory and methodology
- In the section on the data-rich future, discussion of researchers' use of a government database to map housing conditions in Boston, with figure, "Seeing Boston's Housing Issues"
- Updated coverage of public opinion research on the legalization of marijuana

Chapter 3: Culture

- Updated figure, "Life Goals of First-Year College Students in the United States, 1966–2012"
- In the Sociology on Campus box "A Culture of Cheating?" discussion of two recent cases of high-achieving students caught cheating on exams
- Example of the culture shock a Westerner might experience in Japan
- Use of the culture wars that arise out of regional political differences in the United States as an illustration of the development of subcultures
- In the Social Policy section, opening example of the role of language differences in increasing the risk of clinical errors in emergency rooms
- In the Social Policy section, discussion of the current trend toward linguistic diversity in the United States
- Updated Mapping Life Nationwide map, "Percentage of People Who Speak a Language Other Than English at Home, by State"

Chapter 4: Socialization and the Life Course

- Opening excerpt, "The Challenge," by military journalist Jim Garamone
- Updated and expanded coverage of Romanian orphans, with photo
- Updated discussion of the effect of young people's use of social media on their socialization
- Sociology on Campus box, "Unplugging the Media: What Happens?" with figure, "Responses to a Day without Media"
- Discussion of the cost and availability of broadband Internet service in developing countries
- Updated discussion of the life events marking the passage to adulthood, with new Use Your Sociological Imagination exercise
- Discussion of the pressing need for day care in Japan
- Expanded discussion of the public policy perspective on day care

Chapter 5: Social Interaction, Social Structure, and Groups

- Opening excerpt from "Pathology of Imprisonment" by Philip Zimbardo
- Taking Sociology to Work box, "Sarah Levy, Owner, S. Levy Foods"
- Discussion of research on the importance of group solidarity following the shootings at Virginia Tech in 2007
- Explanation of the difference between social networks and social media
- Discussion of the perceived need to reform the process of bureaucratization in China
- Thinking Critically exercise
- Sociology in the Global Community box, "Disney World: A Postmodern Theme Park," with key term treatment of Jean Baudrillard's concept of hyperconsumerism
- Social Policy section, "The State of the Unions Worldwide," with figure, "Labor Union Membership Worldwide"

Chapter 6: The Mass Media

- Opening excerpt from *Electronic Media* by Lynne S. Gross
- Inclusion of IMDb in table, "Status Conferred by the Media"
- Description of the Chinese government's efforts to minimize online dissent
- Discussion of the portrayal of homosexuality (or the lack of it) in the mass media from the perspective of queer theory
- Discussion of hyper-local media, with key term treatment
- Discussion of Rwanda's effort to develop its economy by encouraging investment in information and communications technologies
- Discussion of the mass media as a form of social capital

- Discussion of crowdsourcing as a way to encourage mobile giving, with key term treatment
- Revised figure, "Who's on the Internet"
- Revised figure, "Media Penetration in Selected Countries," including cell phones, the Internet, and social networking
- Discussion of the monitoring of text messages by public health researchers in Kenya to track the spread of malaria
- Thoroughly revised Social Policy section, "The Right to Privacy," including discussion of (a) Edward Snowden's revelations about the National Security Agency's collection of massive amounts of data on ordinary citizens, with key term treatment of Charles Tilly's concept of *big data;* (b) the approval of "tower dumps," or the indiscriminate collection of information from all cell phones in an area, by subpoena only; and (c) the installation of data-recording sensors on appliances, security badges, and other objects

Chapter 7: Deviance, Crime, and Social Control

- Discussion of the stigmatization of people with mental illness as potentially violent and criminal, despite evidence to the contrary
- Updated Mapping Life Nationwide map, "The Status of Medical Marijuana"
- Updated table, "National Crime Rates and Percentage Change"
- Figure, "Victimization Rates, 1993–2012"
- Social Policy section on gun control, including (a) recent shootings in Aurora, Colorado, and Newtown, Connecticut; (b) statistics on gun ownership in the United States compared to other countries; (c) expanded coverage of the cutoff of funding for research on gun violence; and (d) the public health perspective on gun control
- Thinking Critically exercise

Chapter 8: Stratification and Social Mobility in the United States

- Opening excerpt from "Cost of Homelessness" by the National Alliance to End Homelessness
- Expanded subsection on the supposed existence of class warfare in the United States, with discussion of the Occupy Wall Street movement
- Expanded discussion of conspicuous consumption, including ostentatious displays on Facebook, with key term treatment
- Discussion of the growing inequality in household wealth
- Discussion of precarious workers' use of social media to gain political recognition
- Updated coverage of the impact of race and ethnicity on intergenerational mobility
- Social Policy section, "Minimum Wage Laws," including discussions of (a) wage theft; (b) President Obama's proposal to raise the minimum wage; and (c) the concept of a living wage, with key term treatment

Chapter 9: Global Inequality

- Expanded coverage of the Millennium Project
- Revised figure, "Foreign Aid Per Capita in Nine Countries"
- Sociology in the Global Community box, "Walking the Last Mile in Uganda: The Avon Approach"
- Revised figure, "Multinational Corporations Compared to Nations"

Chapter 10: Racial and Ethnic Inequality

- Opening excerpt from "Iyeska: Notes from Mixed-Blood Country" by Charles Trimble
- Updated figure, "U.S. Median Income by Race, Ethnicity, and Gender"
- Research Today box, "Institutional Discrimination in the Voting Booth," with map, "Voter ID Requirements"
- Expanded coverage of residential segregation in the United States, with table, "Segregated Metropolitan America"
- Mapping Life Nationwide map, "Minority Population by County"

Chapter 11: Stratification by Gender

- Opening excerpt from Azadeh Moaveni, *Lipstick Jihad: A Memoir of Growing Up Iranian in America and American in Iran*
- Sociology in the Global Community box, "Women in Combat Worldwide"
- Discussion of the glass escalator, with key term treatment
- Updated discussion of feminism
- Updated Social Policy section, "The Battle over Abortion from a Global Perspective," with discussion of recent changes in state and local policies regarding abortion clinics and Mapping Life Nationwide double map, "State Abortion-Related Policies, 2000–2014"

Chapter 12: Stratification by Age

- Opening excerpt from Jill Quadagno, *Aging and the Life Course: An Introduction to Social Gerontology*
- Discussion of the recent reversal of the trend toward early retirement and the reasons for it
- Updated statistics on aging worldwide and updated figure, "World's 'Oldest' Countries Compared to the United States"
- Updated "Aging, Japanese Style" box to include results of a 2014 survey
- Discussion of how the worldwide recession has complicated trends in retirement age
- Addition of Navajo customs to "Native Americans and Death" box
- Updated figure, "Minority Population Age 65 and Older: 2012–2050"

- Addition of figure, "Labor Force by Age, 2000–2050"
- Updated information about legality of assisted suicide in Social Policy section

Chapter 13: The Family and Human Sexuality

- Discussion of how the gay marriage debate has revived the polygamous marriage debate
- Our Wired World box, "Love Is in the Air and on the Web"
- Discussion of the Healthy Marriage and Responsible Fatherhood Initiative under the Obama Administration
- Mapping Life Nationwide map, "Same-Sex Couple Households as Percent of All Households"
- Coverage of increased acceptance of LGBT people, especially by businesses and federal agencies
- Thoroughly revised Social Policy section on gay marriage, including (a) discussion of queer theorists' perspective on gay marriage; (b) the Supreme Court decision in *United States v. Windsor,* which invalidated a key section of the Defense of Marriage Act; (c) local resistance to gay marriage; (d) dissenting LGBT views of same-sex marriage; and (e) Mapping Life Nationwide map, "Gay Marriage Recognition by State"

Chapter 14: Education

- Discussion of the persistence of school segregation in the United States, despite recent suburbanization of African American and Hispanic families
- Updated figure, "Tuition Costs, 1981–2011"
- Updated Mapping Life Nationwide map, "Average Salary for Teachers"
- Social Policy section, "Charter Schools"

Chapter 15: Religion

- Research Today box, "Mormons: A Controversial Denomination"
- Thinking Critically question

Chapter 16: Government and the Economy

- Opening excerpt from *Who Rules America? The Triumph of the Corporate Rich,* Seventh Edition, by G. William Domhoff
- Our Wired World box, "Politicking Online"
- Subsection on the temporary workforce
- Discussion of "reshoring," a countertrend to offshoring of U.S. manufacturing and service centers
- Thinking Critically question

Chapter 17: Health, Population, and Environment

- Opening excerpt from Andrew Szasz, *Shopping Our Way to Safety: How We Changed from Protecting the Environment to Protecting Ourselves*

- Figure, "AIDS by the Numbers Worldwide"
- Section on mental Illness, with subsections on (a) theoretical models of mental disorders, including the medical model and labeling theory, and (b) patterns of care; and Use Your Sociological Imagination exercise
- Subsection on climate change, with key term treatment of climate change and global warming
- Discussion of migrations caused by climate change in the western United States
- Module 55, "Population," with sections on (a) demography, (b) world population patterns, (c) fertility patterns in the United States, and (d) population and migration; three figures; one table; and Sociology in the Global Community box, "Population Policy in China"

Chapter 18: Social Movements and Social Change in the Global Community

- Opening excerpt, "The Information Revolution's Broken Promises," by Karl Albrecht
- Our Wired World box, "Organizing for Controversy via Computer-Mediated Communication"
- Discussion of the possibility that technological advances may eliminate people's jobs, with table, "Jobs Projected to Be Eliminated by Computerization"
- Our Wired World box, "The Internet's Global Profile"
- Discussion of transnationals' participation in social movements
- Thinking Critically exercise
- Module 57, "Collective Behavior," with sections on (a) theories of collective behavior and (b) forms of collective behavior; Summing Up table, "Forms of Collective Behavior"

Teaching Resources

Instructor's Manual. The Instructor's Manual includes detailed chapter outlines and chapter summaries; learning objectives; a chapter-by-chapter bulleted list of new content; key terms; essay questions; and critical thinking questions.

PowerPoint Slides. The PowerPoint Slides include bulleted lecture points, figures, and maps. They can be used as is or modified to meet the instructor's individual needs.

Test Bank. The Test Bank includes multiple-choice, true-false, and essay questions for every chapter. McGraw-Hill's computerized EZ Test allows the instructor to create customized exams using either publisher-supplied test items or the instructor's own questions.

These instructor resources can be accessed through the Library tab in Connect.

Campus

McGraw-Hill Campus is a first-of-its-kind institutional service that provides faculty with true, single sign-on access to all of McGraw-Hill's course content, digital tools, and other high-quality learning resources from any learning management system (LMS). This innovative offering allows secure, deep integration and seamless access to any of our course solutions, including McGraw-Hill Connect, McGraw-Hill LearnSmart, McGraw-Hill Create, and Tegrity. McGraw-Hill Campus covers our entire content library, including eBooks, assessment tools, presentation slides, and multimedia content, among other resources. This open and unlimited service allows faculty to quickly prepare for class, create tests or quizzes, develop lecture material, integrate interactive content, and much more.

CourseSmart
Learn Smart. Choose Smart.

CourseSmart offers thousands of the most commonly adopted textbooks across hundreds of courses from a wide variety of higher education publishers. It is the only place for faculty to review and compare the full text of a textbook online, providing immediate access without the environmental impact of requesting a printed exam copy. At CourseSmart, students can save up to 50% off the cost of a printed book, reduce their impact on the environment, and gain access to powerful Web tools for learning, including full text search, notes and highlighting, and e-mail tools for sharing notes among classmates. Learn more at www.coursesmart.com

Acknowledgments

As with the first two editions, Elaine Silverstein has played a significant role in the development of my sociology book in the module format. I have received strong support and encouragement from Gina Boedeker, managing director of products and markets, and Susan Trentacosti, content project manager. Additional guidance and support were provided by Carolyn Arcabascio, photo researcher, and Carey Lange, copyeditor. This edition continues to reflect many insightful suggestions made by reviewers of the eleven hardcover and paperback brief editions. I also continued to benefit from the creative ideas of Rhona Robbin, lead product developer.

Additional guidance and support were provided by Briana Porco, product developer for the digital program; Phil Weaver and Kimberli Brownlee, marketing managers; Diane Grayson, brand coordinator; Trevor Goodman, designer; John Leland, content licensing specialist; Carol Bielski, manufacturing; and Leonard Behnke, content licensing manager.

As is evident from these acknowledgments, the preparation of a textbook is truly a collaborative effort. The most valuable member of this effort continues to be my wife, Sandy. She provides the support so necessary in my creative and scholarly activities.

I have had the good fortune to introduce students to sociology for many years. These students have been enormously helpful in spurring on my sociological imagination. In ways I can fully appreciate but cannot fully acknowledge, their questions in class and queries in the hallway have found their way into this work.

Richard T. Schaefer
www.schaefersociology.net
schaeferrt@aol.com

Academic Reviewers

This project has benefited from constructive and thorough evaluations provided by sociologists from both two-year and four-year institutions.

Jennifer Altman, *Middlesex County College*
Erin K. Anderson, *Washington College*
Michelle Bentz, *Central Community College, Columbus*
Cathy Blair, *Minnesota West Community and Technical College*
Marshall Botkin, *Frederick Community College*
Judith Brake, *Ozarks Technical Community College*
Matthew Cazessus, *Greenville Technical College*
Susan R. Cody, *Georgia Perimeter College*
Richard Deutsch, *John A Logan College*
Jessica Halperin, *Metropolitan Community College, Maple Woods*

Rose Hunte, *Metro Community College, Fort Omaha*
Bethany Johnson, *Gordon College*
Keith Kerr, *Quinnipiac University*
Joan Luxenburg, *University of Central Oklahoma*
Carla Newman, *El Paso Community College, Valle Verde*
Douglas O'Neill, *South Dakota State University*
Trish Ramirez, *El Paso Community College, Valle Verde*
Lucia Rodriguez, *El Paso Community College, Valle Verde*
David Schjott, *Northwest Florida State College*
Denise Shuster, *Owens Community College*
Monica Sosa, *Tarrant County College, Southeast*
Frank Stanford, *Blinn College, Bryan*
Megan G. Swindal, *University of Alabama*
Gerald Titchener, *Des Moines Area Community College*
Glen Tolle, *Blinn College, Bryan*
Jonathan Treas, *Wichita State University*
Brent Ur, *Blinn College, Bryan*
Jay Vargas, *Minnesota West Community and Technical College*
Shonda Whetstone, *Blinn College, Bryan*

Connect Consultants

The creation of *Connect Sociology* has been a highly collaborative effort. Thank you to the following for their guidance, insight, and innovative suggestions.

Douglas Adams, *University of Arkansas*
Paul Calarco, *Hudson Valley Community College*
Susan Ciriello, *Northern Virginia Community College*
Susan Cody-Rydzewski, *Georgia Perimeter College*
Lisa Coole, *Bridgewater College*
Gianna Durso Finley, *Mercer County Community College*
Ike Eberstein, *Florida State University*
Erica Hunter, *University at Albany*
Terina Lathe, *Central Piedmont Community College*
Royal Loresco, *South Texas College*

Michael Loukinen, *Northern Michigan University*
Melinda Messineo, *Ball State University*
Narayan Persaud, *Florida A&M University*
Olga Rowe, *Oregon State University*
Alan Rudy, *Central Michigan University*
Megan Seely, *Sierra College*
Tomecia Sobers, *Fayetteville Tech Community College*
Karrie A. Snyder, *Northwestern University*
Margaret Taylor, *Greenville Technical College*

Connect Contributors

These instructors contributed their time, thought, and creativity to make our vision for *Connect Sociology* a reality. Thank you to the following content authors.

Russell Davis, *University of West Alabama*
Shelly Dutchin, *Western Technical College*
Lois Easterday, *Onondaga Community College*
Samuel Echevarria-Cruz, *Austin Community College*
Tammie Foltz, *Des Moines Area Community College*
Kimberly K. Hennessee, *Ball State University*
Curt Hosier, *Indiana University–Purdue University, Fort Wayne*
Marjorie Jolles, *Roosevelt University*
Thomas Kersen, *Jackson State University*
Jenny Kosinski, *Rock Valley College*
Laura Johnson, *Southeast Missouri State University*
David Locher, *Missouri Southern State University*
Linda Lombard, *Embry-Riddle Aeronautical University*
Kevin Parent, *Point Park University*
Tommy Sadler, *Union University*
Denise Shuster, *Owens Community College*
Rachel Stehle, *Cuyahoga Community College*
John C. Tenuto, *College of Lake County*
Marie Wallace, *Pima Community College*
Sally Vyain, *Ivy Tech Community College*

1

Understanding Sociology

No matter where you're going—to work, to study abroad, or just on vacation—you can take sociology and its insights with you.

1

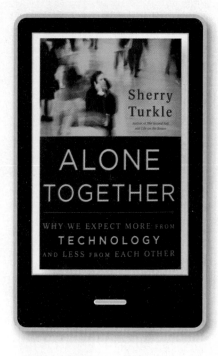

Did you ever suspect that you were hiding from people while you were online with them?

MIT sociologist and psychologist Sherry Turkle thinks that the web may actually distance us from others.

" Technology proposes itself as the architect of our intimacies. These days, it suggests substitutions that put the real on the run. The advertising for Second Life, a virtual world where you get to build an avatar, a house, a family, and a social life, basically says, "Finally, a place to love your body, love your friends, and love your life." In Second Life, a lot of people, as represented by their avatars, are richer than they are in first life and a lot younger, thinner, and better dressed. And we are smitten with the idea of sociable robots, which most people first meet in the guise of artificial pets. Zhu Zhu pet hamsters, the "it" toy of the 2009–2010 holiday season, are presented as "better" than any real pet could be. We are told they are lovable and responsive, don't require cleanup, and will never die.

Technology is seductive when what it offers meets our human vulnerabilities. And as it turns out, we are very vulnerable indeed. We are lonely but fearful of intimacy. Digital connections and the sociable robot may offer the illusion of companionship without the demands of friendship. Our networked life allows us to hide from each other, even as we are tethered to each other. We'd rather text than talk.

From the start, people used interactive and reactive computers to reflect on the self and think about the difference between machines and people. Were intelligent machines alive? If not, why not?

Digital connections and the sociable robot may offer the illusion of companionship without the demands of friendship.

Computers no longer wait for humans to project meaning onto them. Now, sociable robots meet our gaze, speak to us, and learn to recognize us. They ask us to take care of them; in response, we imagine that they might care for us in return. Indeed, among the most talked about robotic designs are in the area of care and companionship. In summer 2010, there are enthusiastic reports in the *New York Times* and the *Wall Street Journal* on robotic teachers, companions, and therapists. And Microsoft demonstrates a virtual human, Milo, that recognizes the people it interacts with and whose personality is sculpted by them. Tellingly, in the video that introduces Milo to the public, a young man begins by playing games with Milo in a virtual garden; by the end of the demonstration, things have heated up—he confides in Milo after being told off by his parents.

We are challenged to ask what such things augur. Some people are looking for robots to clean rugs and help with the laundry. Others hope for a mechanical bride. As sociable robots propose themselves as substitutes for people, new networked devices offer us machine-mediated relationships with each other, another kind of substitution. We romance the robot and become inseparable from our smartphones.

As this happens, we remake ourselves and our relationships with each other through our new intimacy with machines. People talk about web access on their Black-Berries as "the place for hope" in life, the place where loneliness can be defeated. A woman in her late sixties describes her new iPhone: "It's like having a little Times Square in my pocketbook. All lights. All the people I could meet." People are lonely. The network is seductive. But if we are always on, we may deny ourselves the rewards of solitude. "

(Turkle 2011:1–3)

Think about your life before you owned a cell phone: How did you connect with others then? How do you connect with them now? In this excerpt from *Alone Together: Why We Expect More from Technology and Less from Each Other,* Sherry Turkle writes that modern technology—especially communications technology—is changing the way we relate to others. Today, our digital communications devices tend to preoccupy us, often burying us in a deluge of information, both audio and video. Yet in the end, they cannot substitute for the ties that bind, the face-to-face relationships that hold family and friends together. Ironically, in an effort

to dig out from the communications overflow, we are constantly seeking new networking gadgets (Turkle 2011:280).

We've come a long way from the days when home entertainment meant black-and-white television, and "reaching out" involved a land-line telephone and voice messages. Today, we not only carry the telephone with us; we use it to watch television and movies delivered over the Internet. Social life is being impacted by and carried out through an object we hold in our hand.

As a field of study, sociology is extremely broad in scope. You will see throughout this book the range of topics sociologists investigate—from suicide to TV viewing habits, from

Amish society to global economic patterns, from peer pressure to genetic engineering. Sociology looks at how others influence our behavior; how major social institutions like the government, religion, and the economy affect us; and how we ourselves affect other individuals, groups, and even organizations.

How did sociology develop? In what ways does it differ from other social sciences? These modules will explore the nature of sociology as both a field of inquiry and an exercise of the "sociological imagination." In Module 1, we'll look at the discipline as a science and consider its relationship to other social sciences. In Modules 2 and 3, we'll meet four pioneering thinkers—Émile Durkheim, Max Weber, Karl Marx, and W. E. B. DuBois—and examine the theoretical perspectives that grew out of their work. In Module 4, we'll note some of the practical applications for sociological theory and research. Finally, we'll see how sociology helps us to develop a sociological imagination. For those students interested in exploring career opportunities in sociology, the chapter closes with a special appendix.

MODULE 1 | What Is Sociology?

"What has sociology got to do with me or with my life?" As a student, you might well have asked this question when you signed up for your introductory sociology course. To answer it, consider these points: Are you influenced by what you see on television? Do you use the Internet? Did you vote in the last election? Are you familiar with binge drinking on campus? Do you use alternative medicine? These are just a few of the everyday life situations described in this book that sociology can shed light on. But as the opening excerpt indicates, sociology also looks at large social issues. We use sociology to investigate why thousands of jobs have moved from the United States to developing nations, what social forces promote prejudice, what leads someone to join a social movement and work for social change, how access to computer technology can reduce social inequality, and why relationships between men and women in Seattle differ from those in Singapore.

Sociology is, simply, the scientific study of social behavior and human groups. It focuses on social relationships; how those relationships influence people's behavior; and how societies, the sum total of those relationships, develop and change.

The Sociological Imagination

In attempting to understand social behavior, sociologists rely on a particular type of critical thinking. A leading sociologist, C. Wright Mills, described such thinking as the **sociological imagination**—an awareness of the relationship between an individual and the wider society, both today and in the past (Mills [1959] 2000a). This awareness allows all of us (not just sociologists) to comprehend the links between our immediate, personal social settings and the remote, impersonal social world that surrounds and helps to shape us.

A key element in the sociological imagination is the ability to view one's own society as an outsider would, rather than only from the perspective of personal experiences and cultural biases. Consider something as simple as sporting events. On college campuses in the United States, thousands of students cheer well-trained football players. In Bali, Indonesia, dozens of spectators gather around a ring to cheer on roosters trained in cockfighting. In both instances, the spectators debate the merits of their favorites and bet on the outcome of the events. Yet what is considered a normal sporting event in one part of the world is considered unusual in another part.

The sociological imagination allows us to go beyond personal experiences and observations to understand broader public issues. Divorce, for example, is unquestionably a personal hardship for a husband and wife who split apart. However, C. Wright Mills advocated using the sociological imagination to view divorce not as simply an individual's personal problem but rather as a societal concern. Using this perspective, we can see that an increase in the divorce rate actually redefines a major social institution—the family. Today's households frequently include stepparents and half-siblings whose parents have divorced and remarried. Through the complexities of the blended family, this private concern becomes a public issue that affects schools, government agencies, businesses, and religious institutions.

The sociological imagination is an empowering tool. It allows us to look beyond a limited understanding of human behavior to see the world and its people in a new way and through a broader lens than we might otherwise use. It may be as simple as understanding why a roommate prefers country music to hip-hop, or it may open up a whole different way of understanding other populations in the world. For example, in the aftermath of the terrorist attacks on the United States on September 11, 2001, many citizens wanted to understand how Muslims throughout the world perceived their country, and why. From time to time this textbook will offer you the chance to exercise your sociological imagination in a variety of situations.

use your **sociological imagination**

You are walking down the street in your city or hometown. In looking around you, you can't help noticing that half or more of the people you see are overweight. How do you explain your observation? If you were C. Wright Mills, how do you think you would explain it?

Sociology and the Social Sciences

Is sociology a science? The term **science** refers to the body of knowledge obtained by methods based on systematic observation. Just like other scientific disciplines, sociology involves the

Sociology is the scientific study of social behavior and human groups.

organized, systematic study of phenomena (in this case, human behavior) in order to enhance understanding. All scientists, whether studying mushrooms or murderers, attempt to collect precise information through methods of study that are as objective as possible. They rely on careful recording of observations and accumulation of data.

Of course, there is a great difference between sociology and physics, between psychology and astronomy. For this reason, the sciences are commonly divided into natural and social sciences. **Natural science** is the study of the physical features of nature and the ways in which they interact and change. Astronomy, biology, chemistry, geology, and physics are all natural sciences. **Social science** is the study of the social features of humans and the ways in which they interact and change. The social sciences include sociology, anthropology, economics, history, psychology, and political science.

These social science disciplines have a common focus on the social behavior of people, yet each has a particular orientation. Anthropologists usually study past cultures and preindustrial societies that continue today, as well as the origins of humans. Economists explore the ways in which people produce and exchange goods and services, along with money and other resources. Historians are concerned

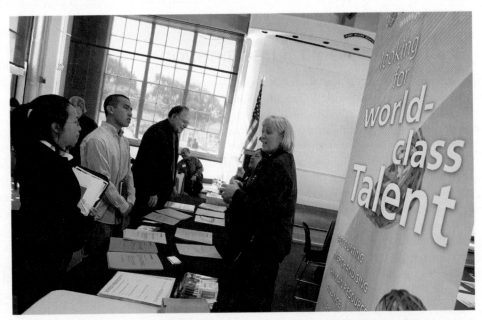

with the peoples and events of the past and their significance for us today. Political scientists study international relations, the workings of government, and the exercise of power and authority. Psychologists investigate personality and individual behavior. So what do *sociologists* focus on? They study the influence that society has on people's attitudes and behavior and the ways in which people interact and shape society. Because humans are social animals, sociologists examine our social relationships scientifically. The range of the relationships they investigate is vast, as the current list of sections in the American Sociological Association suggests (Table 1-1).

Let's consider how different social scientists might study the impact of the global recession that began in 2008. Historians would stress the pattern of long-term fluctuations in world markets. Economists would discuss the roles played by government, the private sector, and the world monetary system. Psychologists would study individual cases of emotional stress among workers, investors, and business owners. And political scientists would study the degree of cooperation among nations—or lack of it—in seeking economic solutions.

What approach would sociologists take? They might note a change in marital patterns in the United States. Since the recession began, the median age of first marriage has risen to

As the nation struggled to recover from a deep and lengthy recession, recently laid-off workers jostled the long-term unemployed at a crowded job fair in San Francisco. Sociologists use a variety of approaches to assess the full impact of economic change on society.

TABLE 1-1   SECTIONS OF THE AMERICAN SOCIOLOGICAL ASSOCIATION

Aging and the Life Course	Emotions	Organizations, Occupations, and Work
Alcohol, Drugs, and Tobacco	Environment and Technology	Peace, War, and Social Conflict
Altruism, Morality, and Social Solidarity	Ethnomethodology and Conversation Analysis	Political Economy of the World-System
Animals and Society	Evolution, Biology, and Society	Political Sociology
Asia and Asian America	Family	Population
Body and Embodiment	Global and Transnational Sociology	Race, Gender, and Class
Children and Youth	History of Sociology	Racial and Ethnic Minorities
Collective Behavior and Social Movements	Human Rights	Rationality and Society
Communication and Information Technologies	International Migration	Religion
Community and Urban Sociology	Inequality, Poverty, and Mobility	Science, Knowledge, and Technology
Comparative and Historical Sociology	Labor and Labor Movements	Sex and Gender
Consumers and Consumption	Latino/a Sociology	Sexualities
Crime, Law, and Deviance	Law	Social Psychology
Culture	Marxist Sociology	Sociological Practice and Public Sociology
Development	Mathematical Sociology	Teaching and Learning
Disability and Society	Medical Sociology	Theory
Economic Sociology	Mental Health	
Education	Methodology	

Think about It Which of these topics do you think would interest you the most? Why?

The range of sociological issues is very broad. For example, sociologists who belong to the Animals and Society section of the ASA may study the animal rights movement; those who belong to the Sexualities section may study global sex workers or the gay, bisexual, and transgendered movements. Economic sociologists may investigate globalization or consumerism, among many other topics.

Source: American Sociological Association 2014.

28.7 years for men and 26.7 years for women. Sociologists might also observe that today, fewer people are making that trip to the altar than in the past. If the U.S. marriage rate had remained the same as it was in 2006, about 4 million more Americans would have married by 2010.

Similarly, sociologists might evaluate the recession's impact on education. In the United States, private school enrollment from elementary through high school declined from 13.6 percent in 2006 to 12.8 percent in 2010 as families cut back on nonessential expenditures. Sociologists might even consider the recession's effect on environmental actions, such as carpooling. In all but 1 of the 50 largest metropolitan areas in the United States (New Orleans), the percentage of working people aged 16 to 64 dropped significantly during the recession. When friends and co-workers are laid off, carpools shrink and more people end up driving to work alone (El Nasser and Overberg 2011).

Sociologists would take a similar approach to studying episodes of extreme violence. In April 2007, just as college students were beginning to focus on the impending end of the semester, tragedy struck on the campus of Virginia Tech. In a two-hour shooting spree, a mentally disturbed senior armed with semi-automatic weapons killed a total of 32 students and faculty at Virginia's largest university. Observers struggled to describe the events and place them in some social context. For sociologists in particular, the event raised numerous issues and topics for study, including the media's role in describing the attacks, the presence of violence in our educational institutions, the gun control debate, the inadequacy of the nation's mental health care system, and the stereotyping and stigmatization of people who suffer from mental illness.

Besides doing research, sociologists have a long history of advising government agencies on how to respond to disasters. Certainly the poverty of the Gulf Coast region complicated the challenge of evacuating New Orleans in 2005. With Hurricane Katrina bearing down on the Gulf Coast, thousands of poor inner-city residents had no automobiles or other available means of escaping the storm. Added to that difficulty was the high incidence of disability in the area. New Orleans ranked second among the nation's 70 largest cities in the proportion of people over age 65 who are disabled—56 percent. Moving wheelchair-bound residents to safety requires specially equipped vehicles, to say nothing of handicap-accessible accommodations in public shelters. Clearly, officials must consider these factors in developing evacuation plans (Bureau of the Census 2005b).

Sociological analysis of the disaster did not end when the floodwaters receded. Long before residents of New Orleans staged a massive anticrime rally at City Hall in 2007, researchers were analyzing resettlement patterns in the city. They noted that returning residents often faced bleak job prospects. Yet families who had stayed away for that reason often had trouble enrolling their children in schools unprepared for an influx of evacuees. Faced with a choice between the need to work and the need to return their children to school, some displaced families risked sending their older children home alone. Meanwhile, opportunists had arrived to victimize unsuspecting homeowners. And the city's overtaxed judicial and criminal justice systems, which had been understaffed before Katrina struck, had been only partially restored. All these social factors led sociologists and others to anticipate the unparalleled rise in reported crime the city experienced in 2006 and 2007 (Jervis 2008; Kaufman 2006).

Throughout this textbook, you will see how sociologists develop theories and conduct research to study and better understand societies. And you will be encouraged to use your sociological imagination to examine the United States (and other societies) from the viewpoint of a respectful but questioning outsider.

Sociology and Common Sense

Sociology focuses on the study of human behavior. Yet we all have experience with human behavior and at least some knowledge of it. All of us might well have theories about why people become homeless, for example. Our theories and opinions typically come from common sense—that is, from our experiences and conversations, from what we read, from what we see on television, and so forth.

In our daily lives, we rely on common sense to get us through many unfamiliar situations. However, this commonsense knowledge, while sometimes accurate, is not always reliable, because it rests on commonly held beliefs rather than on systematic analysis of facts. It was once considered common sense to accept that the earth was flat—a view rightly questioned by Pythagoras and Aristotle. Incorrect commonsense notions are not just a part of the distant past; they remain with us today.

Contrary to the common notion that women tend to be chatty compared to men, for instance, researchers have found little difference between the sexes in terms of their talkativeness. Over a five-year period they placed unobtrusive microphones on 396 college students in various fields, at campuses in Mexico as well as the United States. They found that both men and women spoke about 16,000 words per day (Mehl et al. 2007).

Similarly, common sense tells us that today, violent crime holds communities on the border between the United States and Mexico in a kind of death grip, creating an atmosphere of lawlessness reminiscent of the old Wild West. Based on televised news stories and on concerns expressed by elected officials throughout the southwestern United States, this assertion may sound reasonable; however, it is not true. Although some communities in Mexico have fallen under the control of drug cartels, the story is different on the U.S. side of the border. All available crime data—including murder, extortion, robbery, and kidnapping rates, whether reported or documented in victim surveys—show that in the hundred-mile-deep border area stretching from San Diego to Brownsville, Texas, crime rates are significantly lower than in similar U.S. cities outside the area. Furthermore, the crime rate has been dropping faster near the border than in other similar-size U.S. communities for at least the last 15 years (Gillum 2011; Gomez et al. 2011).

Like other social scientists, sociologists do not accept something as a fact because "everyone knows it." Instead, each piece of information must be tested and recorded, then analyzed in relation to other data. Sociologists rely on scientific studies in order to describe and understand a social environment. At times, the findings of sociologists may seem like common sense, because they deal with familiar facets of everyday life. The difference is that such findings have been *tested* by researchers. Common sense now tells us that the earth is round, but this particular commonsense notion is based on centuries of scientific work that began with the breakthroughs made by Pythagoras and Aristotle.

What Is Sociological Theory?

Why do people commit suicide? One traditional commonsense answer is that people inherit the desire to kill themselves. Another view is that sunspots drive people to take their lives. These explanations may not seem especially convincing to contemporary researchers, but they represent beliefs widely held as recently as 1900.

Sociologists are not particularly interested in why any one individual commits suicide; they are more concerned with identifying the social forces that systematically cause some people to take their own lives. In order to undertake this research, sociologists develop a theory that offers a general explanation of suicidal behavior.

We can think of theories as attempts to explain events, forces, materials, ideas, or behavior in a comprehensive manner. In sociology, a **theory** is a set of statements that seeks to explain problems, actions, or behavior. An effective theory may have both explanatory and predictive power. That is, it can help us to see the relationships among seemingly isolated phenomena, as well as to understand how one type of change in an environment leads to other changes.

The World Health Organization (2010) estimates that almost a million people die from suicide every year. More than a hundred years ago, a sociologist tried to look at suicide data scientifically. Émile Durkheim ([1897] 1951) developed a highly original theory about the relationship between suicide and social factors. Durkheim was primarily concerned not with the personalities of individual suicide victims, but rather with suicide rates and how they varied from country to country. As a result, when he looked at the number of reported suicides in France, England, and Denmark in 1869, he also noted the total population of each country in order to determine the rate of suicide in each nation. He found that whereas England had only 67 reported suicides per million inhabitants, France had 135 per million and Denmark had 277 per million. The question then became "Why did Denmark have a comparatively high rate of reported suicide?"

Durkheim went much deeper into his investigation of suicide rates. The result was his landmark work *Suicide,* published in 1897. Durkheim refused to accept unproved explanations regarding suicide, including the beliefs that inherited tendencies or cosmic forces caused such deaths. Instead, he focused on social factors, such as the cohesiveness or lack of cohesiveness of religious, social, and occupational groups.

Durkheim's research suggested that suicide, although it is a solitary act, is related to group life. He found that people without religious affiliations had a higher suicide rate than those who were affiliated; the unmarried had much higher rates than married people; and soldiers had a higher rate than civilians. In addition, there seemed to be higher rates of suicide in times of peace than in times of war and revolution, and in times of economic instability and recession rather than in times of prosperity. Durkheim concluded that the suicide rates of a society reflected the extent to which people were or were not integrated into the group life of the society.

Émile Durkheim, like many other social scientists, developed a theory to explain how individual behavior can be understood within a social context. He pointed out the influence of groups and societal forces on what had always been viewed as a highly personal act. Clearly, Durkheim offered a more *scientific* explanation for the causes of suicide than that of inherited tendencies or sunspots. His theory has predictive power, since it suggests that suicide rates will rise or fall in conjunction with certain social and economic changes.

Of course, a theory—even the best of theories—is not a final statement about human behavior. Durkheim's theory of suicide is no exception. Sociologists continue to examine factors that contribute to differences in suicide rates around the world and to a particular society's rate of suicide. In Las Vegas, for example, sociologists have observed that the chances of dying by suicide are strikingly high—twice as high as in the United States as a whole. Noting Durkheim's emphasis on the relationship between suicide and social isolation, researchers have suggested that Las Vegas's rapid growth and constant influx of tourists have undermined the community's sense of permanence, even among longtime residents. Although gambling—or more accurately, losing while gambling—may seem a likely precipitating factor in suicides there, careful study of the data has allowed researchers to dismiss that explanation. What happens in Vegas may stay in Vegas, but the sense of community cohesiveness that the rest of the country enjoys may be lacking (Wray et al. 2008, 2011).

MODULE 1 | Recap and Review

Summary

Sociology is the scientific study of social behavior and human groups. In this module, we examine the nature of sociological theory and the work of some of the founders of the discipline.

1. The **sociological imagination** is an awareness of the relationship between an individual and the wider society. It is based on the ability to view our own society as an outsider might, rather than from the perspective of our limited experiences and cultural biases.

2. In contrast to other **social sciences,** sociology emphasizes the influence that groups can have on people's behavior and attitudes and the ways in which people shape society.

3. Knowledge that relies on common sense is not always reliable. Sociologists must test and analyze each piece of information they use.

4. Sociologists employ **theories** to examine relationships between observations or data that may seem completely unrelated.

Thinking Critically

1. What aspects of the social and work environment in a fast-food restaurant would be of particular interest to a sociologist? How would the sociological imagination help in analyzing the topic?

2. Can you think of any explanation, other than lack of community, for the high suicide rate in Las Vegas? Does that explanation agree with Durkheim's theory?

3. Think about the sociologists profiled in this module, Mills and Durkheim. Whose work seems most relevant to today's social problems? Why did you choose that thinker, and which social problems were you thinking of?

Key Terms

Natural science

Science

Social science

Sociological imagination

Sociology

Theory

People have always been curious about sociological matters—how we get along with others, what we do for a living, whom we select as our leaders. Philosophers and religious authorities of ancient and medieval societies made countless observations about human behavior. They did not test or verify those observations scientifically; nevertheless, their observations often became the foundation for moral codes. Several of these early social philosophers correctly predicted that a systematic study of human behavior would emerge one day. Beginning in the 19th century, European theorists made pioneering contributions to the development of a science of human behavior.

Early Thinkers

Auguste Comte

The 19th century was an unsettling time in France. The French monarchy had been deposed in the revolution of 1789, and Napoleon had suffered defeat in his effort to conquer Europe. Amid this chaos, philosophers considered how society might be improved. Auguste Comte (1798–1857), credited with being the most influential of the philosophers of the early 1800s, believed that a theoretical science of society and a systematic investigation of behavior were needed to improve society. He coined the term *sociology* to apply to the science of human behavior.

Writing in the 1800s, Comte feared that the excesses of the French Revolution had permanently impaired France's stability. Yet he hoped that the systematic study of social behavior would eventually lead to more rational human interactions. In Comte's hierarchy of the sciences, sociology was at the top. He called it the "queen," and its practitioners "scientist-priests." This French theorist did not simply give sociology its name; he presented a rather ambitious challenge to the fledgling discipline.

Harriet Martineau

Scholars learned of Comte's works largely through translations by the English sociologist Harriet Martineau (1802–1876). But Martineau was a pathbreaker in her own right: she offered insightful observations of the customs and social practices of both her native Britain and the United States. Martineau's book *Society in America* ([1837] 1962) examined religion, politics, child rearing, and immigration in the young nation. It gave special attention to social class distinctions and to such factors as gender and race. Martineau ([1838] 1989) also wrote the first book on sociological methods.

Martineau's writings emphasized the impact that the economy, law, trade, health, and population could have on social problems. She spoke out in favor of the rights of women, the emancipation of slaves, and religious tolerance. Later in life, deafness did not keep her from being an activist. In Martineau's ([1837] 1962) view, intellectuals and scholars should not simply

Harriet Martineau, an early pioneer of sociology who studied social behavior both in her native England and in the United States. Martineau proposed some of the methods still used by sociologists, including systematic observation.

offer observations of social conditions; they should *act* on their convictions in a manner that will benefit society. That is why Martineau conducted research on the nature of female employment and pointed to the need for further investigation of the issue (Deegan 2003; Hill and Hoecker-Drysdale 2001).

Herbert Spencer

Another important early contributor to the discipline of sociology was Herbert Spencer (1820–1903). A relatively prosperous Victorian Englishman, Spencer (unlike Martineau) did not feel compelled to correct or improve society; instead, he merely hoped to understand it better. Drawing on Charles Darwin's study *On the Origin of Species,* Spencer applied the concept of evolution of the species to societies in order to explain how they change, or evolve, over time. Similarly, he adapted Darwin's evolutionary view of the "survival of the fittest" by arguing that it is "natural" that some people are rich while others are poor.

Spencer's approach to societal change was extremely popular in his lifetime. Unlike Comte, Spencer suggested that since societies are bound to change eventually, one need not be highly critical of present social arrangements or work actively for social change. This viewpoint appealed to many influential people in England and the United States who had a vested interest in the status quo and were suspicious of social thinkers who endorsed change.

Émile Durkheim

Émile Durkheim made many pioneering contributions to sociology, including his important theoretical work on suicide. The son of a rabbi, Durkheim (1858–1917) was educated in both France and Germany. He established an impressive academic reputation and was appointed one of the first professors of sociology in France. Above all, Durkheim will be remembered for his insistence that behavior must be understood within a larger social context, not just in individualistic terms.

To give one example of this emphasis, Durkheim ([1912] 2001) developed a fundamental thesis to help explain all forms of society. Through intensive study of the Arunta, an Australian tribe, he focused on the functions that religion performed and underscored the role of group life in defining what we consider to be religion. Durkheim concluded that like other forms of group behavior, religion reinforces a group's solidarity.

Another of Durkheim's main interests was the consequences of work in modern societies. In his view, the growing division of labor in industrial societies, as workers became much more specialized in their tasks, led to what he called "anomie." **Anomie** refers to the loss of direction felt in a society when social control of individual behavior has become ineffective. Often, the state of anomie occurs during a time of profound social change, when people have lost their sense of purpose or direction. In a period of anomie, people are so confused and unable to cope with the new social environment that they may resort to suicide.

Durkheim was concerned about the dangers that alienation, loneliness, and isolation might pose for modern industrial societies. He shared Comte's belief that sociology should provide direction for social change. As a result, he advocated the creation of new social groups—mediators between the individual's family and the state—that would provide a sense of belonging for members of huge, impersonal societies. Unions would be an example of such groups.

Like many other sociologists, Durkheim did not limit his interests to one aspect of social behavior. Later in this book we will consider his thinking on crime and punishment, religion, and the workplace. Few sociologists have had such a dramatic impact on so many different areas within the discipline.

Max Weber

Another important early theorist was Max Weber (pronounced VAY-ber). Born in Germany, Weber (1864–1920) studied legal and economic history, but gradually developed an interest in sociology. Eventually, he became a professor at various German universities. Weber taught his students that they should employ *verstehen* (pronounced fair-SHTAY-en), the German word for "understanding" or "insight," in their intellectual work. He pointed out that we cannot analyze our social behavior by the same type of objective criteria we use to measure weight or temperature. To fully comprehend behavior, we must learn the subjective meanings people attach to their actions—how they themselves view and explain their behavior.

For example, suppose that a sociologist was studying the social ranking of individuals in a fraternity. Weber would expect the researcher to employ *verstehen* to determine the significance of the fraternity's social hierarchy for its members. The researcher might examine the effects of athleticism or grades or social skills or seniority on standing within the fraternity. He or she would seek to learn how the fraternity members relate to other members of higher or lower status. While investigating these questions, the researcher would take into account people's emotions, thoughts, beliefs, and attitudes (L. Coser 1977).

We also owe credit to Weber for a key conceptual tool: the ideal type. An **ideal type** is a construct or model for evaluating specific cases. In his works, Weber identified various characteristics of bureaucracy as an ideal type (discussed in detail in Module 19). In presenting this model of bureaucracy, Weber was not describing any particular organization, nor was he using the term *ideal* in a way that suggested a positive evaluation. Instead, his purpose was to provide a useful standard for measuring how bureaucratic an actual organization is (Gerth and Mills 1958). Later in this book, we will use the concept of *ideal type* to study the family, religion, authority, and economic systems, as well as to analyze bureaucracy.

Although their professional careers coincided, Émile Durkheim and Max Weber never met and probably were unaware of each other's existence, let alone ideas. Such was not true of the work of Karl Marx. Durkheim's thinking about the impact of the division of labor in industrial societies was related to Marx's writings, while Weber's concern for a value-free, objective sociology was a direct response to Marx's deeply held convictions. Thus, it is not surprising that Karl Marx is viewed as a major figure in the development of sociology, as well as several other social sciences (Figure 2-1).

Karl Marx

Karl Marx (1818–1883) shared with Durkheim and Weber a dual interest in abstract philosophical issues and the concrete reality of everyday life. Unlike them, however, Marx was so critical of existing institutions that a conventional academic career was impossible. He spent most of his life in exile from his native Germany.

Marx's personal life was a difficult struggle. When a paper he had written was suppressed, he fled to France. In Paris, he met Friedrich Engels (1820–1895),

FIGURE 2-1 CONTRIBUTORS TO SOCIOLOGY

	Émile Durkheim 1858–1917	**Max Weber 1864–1920**	**Karl Marx 1818–1883**	**W. E. B. DuBois 1868–1963**
Academic training	Philosophy	Law, economics, history, philosophy	Philosophy, law	Sociology
Key works	1893—*The Division of Labor in Society* 1897—*Suicide: A Study in Sociology* 1912—*Elementary Forms of Religious Life*	1904–1905—*The Protestant Ethic and the Spirit of Capitalism* 1921—*Economy and Society*	1848—*The Communist Manifesto* 1867—*Das Kapital*	1899—*The Philadelphia Negro* 1903—*The Negro Church* 1903—*Souls of Black Folk*

Source: Developed by author.

with whom he formed a lifelong friendship. The two lived at a time when European and North American economic life was increasingly dominated by the factory rather than the farm.

While in London in 1847, Marx and Engels attended secret meetings of an illegal coalition of labor unions known as the Communist League. The following year they prepared a platform called *The Communist Manifesto,* in which they argued that the masses of people with no resources other than their labor (whom they referred to as the *proletariat*) should unite to fight for the overthrow of capitalist societies. In the words of Marx and Engels:

> The history of all hitherto existing society is the history of class struggles. . . . The proletarians have nothing to lose but their chains. They have a world to win. WORKING MEN OF ALL COUNTRIES, UNITE! (Tucker 1978:473, 500).

After completing *The Communist Manifesto,* Marx returned to Germany, only to be expelled. He then moved to England, where he continued to write books and essays. Marx lived there in extreme poverty; he pawned most of his possessions, and several of his children died of malnutrition and disease. Marx clearly was an outsider in British society, a fact that may well have influenced his view of Western cultures.

In Marx's analysis, society was fundamentally divided between two classes that clashed in pursuit of their own interests. When he examined the industrial societies of his time, such as Germany, England, and the United States, he saw the factory as the center of conflict between the exploiters (the owners of the means of production) and the exploited (the workers). Marx viewed these relationships in systematic terms; that is, he believed that a system of economic, social, and political relationships maintained the power and dominance of the owners over the workers. Consequently, Marx and Engels argued that the working class should overthrow the existing class system. Marx's influence on contemporary thinking has been dramatic. His writings inspired those who would later lead communist revolutions in Russia, China, Cuba, Vietnam, and elsewhere.

Even apart from the political revolutions that his work fostered, Marx's significance is profound. Marx emphasized the *group* identifications and associations that influence an *individual's* place in society. This area of study is the major focus of contemporary sociology. Throughout this textbook, we will consider how membership in a particular gender classification, age group, racial group, or economic class affects a person's attitudes and behavior. In an important sense, we can trace this way of understanding society back to the pioneering work of Karl Marx.

W. E. B. DuBois

Marx's work encouraged sociologists to view society through the eyes of those segments of the population that rarely influence decision making. In the United States, some early Black sociologists, including W. E. B. DuBois (1868–1963), conducted research that they hoped would assist in the struggle for a racially egalitarian society. DuBois (pronounced doo-BOYSS) believed that knowledge was essential in combating prejudice and achieving tolerance and justice. Sociologists, he contended, needed to draw on scientific principles to study social problems such as those experienced by Blacks in the United States. To separate opinion from fact, he advocated research on the lives of Blacks. Through his in-depth studies of urban life, both White and Black, in cities such as Philadelphia and Atlanta, DuBois ([1899] 1995) made a major contribution to sociology.

Like Durkheim and Weber, DuBois saw the importance of religion to society. However, he tended to focus on religion at the community level and on the role of the church in the lives of its members ([1903] 2003). DuBois had little patience with theorists such as Herbert Spencer, who seemed content with the status quo. He believed that the granting of full political rights to Blacks was essential to their social and economic progress.

Through what became known as the Atlanta Sociological Laboratory, DuBois also promoted groundbreaking research by other scholars. While investigating religion, crime, and race relations, these colleagues trained their students in sociological research. The extensive interviews conducted by students in Atlanta still enrich our understanding of human behavior (Earl Wright II 2012).

Because many of his ideas challenged the status quo, DuBois did not always find a receptive audience within either the government or the academic world. As a result, he became increasingly involved with organizations whose members questioned the established social order. In 1909 he helped to found the National Association for the Advancement of Colored People, better known today as the NAACP (Wortham 2008).

DuBois's insights have been lasting. In 1897 he coined the term **double consciousness** to refer to the division of an individual's identity into two or more social realities. He used the term to describe the experience of being Black in White America. Today, an African American holds the most powerful office in the nation, President of the United States. Yet for millions of African Americans, the reality of being Black in the United States typically is not one of power (DuBois [1903] 1961).

Twentieth-Century Developments

Sociology today builds on the firm foundation developed by Émile Durkheim, Max Weber, Karl Marx, and W. E. B. DuBois. However, the field certainly has not remained stagnant over the past hundred years. While Europeans have continued to make contributions to the discipline, sociologists from throughout the world and especially the United States have advanced sociological theory and research. Their new insights have helped us to better understand the workings of society.

Charles Horton Cooley

Charles Horton Cooley (1864–1929) was typical of the sociologists who came to prominence in the early 1900s. Born in Ann Arbor, Michigan, Cooley received his graduate training in economics but later became a sociology professor at the University of Michigan. Like other early sociologists, he had become interested in this new discipline while pursuing a related area of study.

Cooley shared the desire of Durkheim, Weber, and Marx to learn more about society. But to do so effectively, he preferred to use the sociological perspective to look first at smaller units—intimate, face-to-face groups such as families, gangs, and friendship networks. He saw these groups as the seedbeds of society, in the sense that they shape people's ideals, beliefs, values, and social nature. Cooley's work increased our understanding of groups of relatively small size.

Jane Addams

In the early 1900s, many leading sociologists in the United States saw themselves as social reformers dedicated to systematically studying and then improving a corrupt society. They were genuinely concerned about the lives of immigrants in the nation's growing cities, whether those immigrants came from Europe or from the rural American South. Early female sociologists, in particular, often took active roles in poor urban areas as leaders of community centers known as *settlement houses.* For example, Jane Addams (1860–1935), a member of the American Sociological Society, cofounded the famous Chicago settlement house called Hull House.

Addams and other pioneering female sociologists commonly combined intellectual inquiry, social service work, and political activism—all with the goal of assisting the underprivileged and creating a more egalitarian society. For example, working with the Black journalist and educator Ida Wells-Barnett, Addams successfully prevented racial segregation in the Chicago public schools. Addams's efforts to establish a juvenile court system and a women's trade union reveal the practical focus of her work (Addams 1910, 1930; Deegan 1991; Lengermann and Niebrugge-Brantley 1998).

By the middle of the 20th century, however, the focus of the discipline had shifted. Sociologists for the most part restricted themselves to theorizing and gathering information; the aim of transforming society was left to social workers and activists. This shift away from social reform was accompanied by a growing commitment to scientific methods of research and to value-free interpretation of data. Not all sociologists were happy with

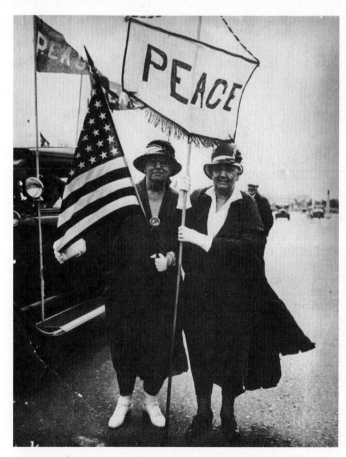

Jane Addams (right) was an early pioneer both in sociology and in the settlement house movement. She was also an activist for many causes, including the worldwide campaign for peace.

this emphasis. A new organization, the Society for the Study of Social Problems, was created in 1950 to deal more directly with social inequality and other social problems.

Robert Merton

Sociologist Robert Merton (1910–2003) made an important contribution to the discipline by successfully combining theory and research. Born to Slavic immigrant parents in Philadelphia, Merton won a scholarship to Temple University. He continued his studies at Harvard, where he acquired his lifelong interest in sociology. Merton's teaching career was based at Columbia University.

Merton (1968) produced a theory that is one of the most frequently cited explanations of deviant behavior. He noted different ways in which people attempt to achieve success in life. In his view, some may deviate from the socially approved goal of accumulating material goods or the socially accepted means of achieving that goal. For example, in Merton's classification scheme, *innovators* are people who accept the goal of pursuing material wealth but use illegal means to do so, including robbery, burglary, and extortion. Although Merton based his explanation of crime on individual behavior that has been influenced by society's approved goals and means, it has wider applications. His theory helps to account for the high crime rates among the nation's poor, who may see no hope of advancing themselves through traditional roads to success. Module 24 discusses Merton's theory in greater detail.

Merton also emphasized that sociology should strive to bring together the *macro-level* and *micro-level* approaches to the study of society. **Macrosociology** concentrates on large-scale phenomena or entire civilizations. Émile Durkheim's cross-cultural study of suicide is an example of macro-level research. More recently, macrosociologists have examined international crime rates (see Module 25) and the stereotype of Asian Americans as a "model minority" (see Module 33). In contrast, **microsociology** stresses the study of small groups, often through experimental means. Sociological research on the micro level has included studies of how divorced men and women disengage from significant social roles (see Module 10) and of how a teacher's expectations can affect a student's academic performance (see Module 42).

Pierre Bourdieu

Increasingly, scholars in the United States have been drawing on the insights of sociologists in other countries. The ideas of the French sociologist Pierre Bourdieu (1930–2002) have found a broad following in North America and elsewhere. As a young man, Bourdieu did fieldwork in Algeria during its struggle for independence from France. Today, scholars study Bourdieu's research techniques as well as his conclusions.

Bourdieu wrote about how capital in its many forms sustains individuals and families from one generation to the next. To Bourdieu, *capital* included not just material goods, but cultural and social assets. **Cultural capital** refers to noneconomic goods, such as family background and education, which are reflected in a knowledge of language and the arts. Not necessarily book knowledge, cultural capital refers to the kind of education that is valued by the socially elite. Though a knowledge of Chinese cuisine is culture, for example, it is not the prestigious kind of culture that is valued by the elite. In the United States, immigrants—especially those who arrived in large numbers and settled in ethnic enclaves—have generally taken two or three generations to develop the same level of cultural capital enjoyed by more established groups. In comparison, **social capital** refers to the collective benefit of social networks, which are built on reciprocal trust. Much has been written about the importance of family and friendship networks in providing people with an opportunity to advance. In his emphasis on cultural and social capital, Bourdieu's work extends the insights of early social thinkers such as Marx and Weber (Bourdieu and Passerson 1990; Poder 2011).

Today sociology reflects the diverse contributions of earlier theorists. As sociologists approach such topics as divorce, drug addiction, and religious cults, they can draw on the theoretical insights of the discipline's pioneers. A careful reader can hear Comte, Durkheim, Weber, Marx, DuBois, Cooley, Addams, and many others speaking through the pages of current research. Sociology has also broadened beyond the intellectual confines of North America and Europe. Contributions to the discipline now come from sociologists studying and researching human behavior in other parts of the world. In describing the work of these sociologists, it is helpful to examine a number of influential *theoretical perspectives,* also known as *approaches* or *views.*

MODULE 2 | **Recap and Review**

Summary

The thinkers who founded the discipline of sociology and developed it in the 19th and 20th centuries were reacting to the social world in which they lived.

1. Nineteenth-century thinkers who contributed sociological insights included Auguste Comte, a French philosopher; Harriet Martineau, an English sociologist; and Herbert Spencer, an English scholar.

2. Other important figures in the development of sociology were Émile Durkheim, who pioneered work on suicide; Max Weber, who taught the need for insight in intellectual work; Karl Marx, who emphasized the importance of the economy and social conflict; and W. E. B. DuBois, who advocated for the usefulness of basic research in combating prejudice and fostering racial tolerance and justice.

3. In the 20th century, the discipline of sociology was indebted to the U.S. sociologists Charles Horton Cooley and Robert Merton, as well as to the French sociologist Pierre Bourdieu.

4. **Macrosociology** concentrates on large-scale phenomena or entire civilizations; **microsociology** stresses the study of small groups.

Thinking Critically

1. Consider the work of early sociologists such as Comte and Martineau. What social problems were they reacting to? To what extent have those problems been rectified today?

2. How is 19th-century industrialization related to the development of sociological thought?

3. What are some examples of social and cultural capital that you possess?

Key Terms

Anomie

Cultural capital

Double consciousness

Ideal type

Macrosociology

Microsociology

Social capital

Verstehen

MODULE 3 | **Major Theoretical Perspectives**

Sociologists view society in different ways. Some see the world basically as a stable and ongoing entity. They are impressed with the endurance of the family, organized religion, and other social institutions. Other sociologists see society as composed of many groups in conflict, competing for scarce resources. To still other sociologists, the most fascinating aspects of the social world are the everyday, routine interactions among individuals that we sometimes take for granted. These three views, the ones most widely used by sociologists, are the functionalist, conflict, and interactionist perspectives. Together, these approaches will provide an introductory look at the discipline.

■ Functionalist Perspective

Think of society as a living organism in which each part of the organism contributes to its survival. This view is the **functionalist perspective,** which emphasizes the way in which the parts of a society are structured to maintain its stability. In examining any aspect of society, then, functionalists emphasize the contribution that it makes to overall social stability.

Talcott Parsons (1902–1979), a Harvard University sociologist, was a key figure in the development of functionalist theory. Parsons was greatly influenced by the work of Émile Durkheim, Max Weber, and other European sociologists. For more than four decades, he dominated sociology in the United States with his advocacy of functionalism. Parsons saw any society as a vast network of connected parts, each of which helps to maintain the system as a whole. His approach, carried forward by German sociologist Niklas Luhmann (1927–1998), holds that if an aspect of social life does not contribute to a society's stability or survival—if it does not serve some identifiably useful function or promote value consensus among members of society—it will not be passed on from one generation to the next (Joas and Knöbl 2009; Knudsen 2010).

Let's examine an example of the functionalist perspective. Many Americans have difficulty understanding the Hindu prohibition against slaughtering cows (specifically, zebu). Cattle browse unhindered through Indian street markets, helping themselves to oranges and mangoes while people bargain for the little food they can afford. What explains this devotion to the cow in the face of human deprivation—a devotion that appears to be dysfunctional?

The simple explanation is that cow worship is highly functional in Indian society, according to economists, agronomists, and social scientists who have studied the matter. Cows perform two essential tasks: plowing the fields and producing milk. If eating beef were permitted, hungry families might be tempted to slaughter their cows for immediate consumption, leaving themselves without a means of cultivation. Cows also produce dung, which doubles as a fertilizer and a fuel for cooking. Finally, cow meat sustains the neediest group in society, the *Dalit,* or untouchables, who sometimes resort to eating beef in secrecy. If eating beef were socially acceptable, higher-status Indians would no doubt bid up its price, placing it beyond the reach of the hungriest.

Manifest and Latent Functions

A college catalog typically states various functions of the institution. It may inform you, for example, that the university intends to "offer each student a broad education in classical and contemporary thought, in the humanities, in the sciences, and in the arts." However, it would be quite a surprise to find a catalog that declared, "This university was founded in 1895 to assist people in finding a marriage partner." No college catalog will declare this as the purpose of the university. Yet societal institutions serve many functions, some of them quite subtle. The university, in fact, *does* facilitate mate selection.

Robert Merton (1968) made an important distinction between manifest and latent functions. **Manifest functions** of institutions are open, stated, and conscious functions. They involve the intended, recognized consequences of an aspect of society, such as the university's role in certifying academic competence and excellence. In

Cows (zebu), traditionally considered sacred in India, wander freely through this city, respected by all who encounter them. The sanctity of the cow is still functional in India, where plowing, milking, and fertilizing are far more important to subsistence farmers than a diet that includes beef.

contrast, **latent functions** are unconscious or unintended functions that may reflect hidden purposes of an institution. One latent function of universities is to hold down unemployment. Another is to serve as a meeting ground for people seeking marital partners.

Dysfunctions

Functionalists acknowledge that not all parts of a society contribute to its stability all the time. A **dysfunction** refers to an element or process of a society that may actually disrupt the social system or reduce its stability.

We view many dysfunctional behavior patterns, such as homicide, as undesirable. Yet we should not automatically interpret them in this way. The evaluation of a dysfunction depends on one's own values, or as the saying goes, on "where you sit." For example, the official view in prisons in the United States is that inmate gangs should be eradicated because they are dysfunctional to smooth operations. Yet some guards have come to view prison gangs as a functional part of their jobs. The danger posed by gangs creates a "threat to security," requiring increased surveillance and more overtime work for guards, as well as requests for special staffing to address gang problems (G. Scott 2001).

● Conflict Perspective

Where functionalists see stability and consensus, conflict sociologists see a social world in continual struggle. The **conflict perspective** assumes that social behavior is best understood in terms of tension between groups over power or the allocation of resources, including housing, money, access to

services, and political representation. The tension between competing groups need not be violent; it can take the form of labor negotiations, party politics, competition between religious groups for new members, or disputes over the federal budget.

Throughout most of the 1900s, the functionalist perspective had the upper hand in sociology in the United States. However, the conflict approach has become increasingly persuasive since the late 1960s. The widespread social unrest resulting from battles over civil rights, bitter divisions over the war in Vietnam, the rise of the feminist and gay liberation movements, the Watergate political scandal, urban riots, confrontations at abortion clinics, and shrinking economic prospects for the middle class have offered support for the conflict approach—the view that our social world is characterized by continual struggle between competing groups. Currently, the discipline of sociology accepts conflict theory as one valid way to gain insight into a society.

The Marxist View

As we saw earlier, Karl Marx viewed struggle between social classes as inevitable, given the exploitation of workers that he perceived under capitalism. Expanding on Marx's work, sociologists and other social scientists have come to see conflict not merely as a class phenomenon but as a part of everyday life in all societies. In studying any culture, organization, or social group, sociologists want to know who benefits, who suffers, and who dominates at the expense of others. They are concerned with the conflicts between women and men, parents and children,

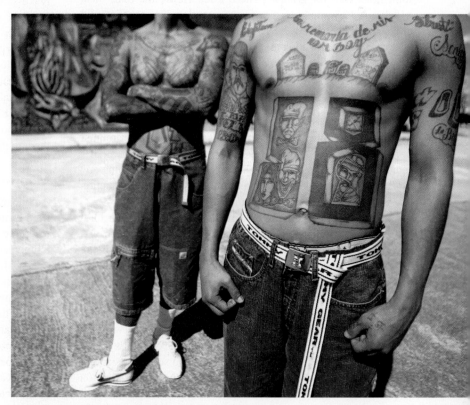

Sociologists who take the Marxist view ask "Who benefits, who suffers, and who dominates?" What might these tattoos suggest to a Marxist theorist?

Ida Wells-Barnett explored what it meant to be female and Black in the United States. Her work established her as one of the earliest feminist theorists.

cities and suburbs, Whites and Blacks, to name only a few. Conflict theorists are interested in how society's institutions—including the family, government, religion, education, and the media—may help to maintain the privileges of some groups and keep others in a subservient position. Their emphasis on social change and the redistribution of resources makes conflict theorists more radical and activist than functionalists (Dahrendorf 1959).

The Feminist Perspective

Sociologists began embracing the feminist perspective only in the 1970s, although it has a long tradition in many other disciplines. The **feminist perspective** sees inequity in gender as central to all behavior and organization. Because it focuses clearly on one aspect of inequality, it is often allied with the conflict perspective. Proponents of the feminist view tend to focus on the macro level, just as conflict theorists do. Drawing on the work of Marx and Engels, contemporary feminist theorists often view women's subordination as inherent in capitalist societies. Some radical feminist theorists, however, view the oppression of women as inevitable in *all* male-dominated societies, whether capitalist, socialist, or communist.

An early example of this perspective (long before the label came into use by sociologists) can be seen in the life and writings of Ida Wells-Barnett (1862–1931). Following her groundbreaking publications in the 1890s on the practice of lynching Black Americans, she became an advocate in the women's rights campaign, especially the struggle to win the vote for women. Like feminist theorists who succeeded her, Wells-Barnett used her analysis of society as a means of resisting oppression. In her case, she researched what it meant to be Black, a woman in the United States, and a Black woman in the United States (Giddings 2008; Wells-Barnett 1970).

Queer Theory

Traditionally, sociologists and other researchers have assumed that men and women are heterosexual. They either ignored other sexual identifications or treated them as abnormal. Yet as French social theorist Michel Foucault (1978) has pointed out, what is regarded as normal or even acceptable human sexuality varies dramatically from one culture to another, as well as from one time period to another. Today, in *queer theory*, sociologists have moved beyond narrow assumptions to study sexuality in all its forms.

Historically, the word *queer* was used in a derogatory manner, to stigmatize a person or behavior. Beginning in the early 1970s, however, gay and lesbian activists began to use the word as a term of empowerment. They dismissed the notion of heterosexuality as the only normal form of sexuality, along with the belief that people must be either heterosexual or homosexual. Instead, they recognized multiple sexual identities, including bisexuality. **Queer theory** is the study of society from the perspective of a broad spectrum of sexual identities, including heterosexuality, homosexuality, and bisexuality.

Queer theorist Eve Sedgwick (1990) argues that any analysis of society is incomplete if it does not include the spectrum of sexual identities that people embrace. Consider, for example, the reelection of President Obama in 2012. Political scientists have often noted the overwhelming support the president received from African Americans, Latinos, and women voters. Yet most have ignored the huge support—76 percent—that the president enjoyed among gay, lesbian, and bisexual voters. In comparison, heterosexual voters split evenly (49 percent to 49 percent nationwide) between Obama and his running mate, Mitt Romney. In the three battleground states of Florida, Ohio, and Virginia, support from gay, lesbian, and bisexual voters alone was enough to put Obama over the top. If Romney had carried just 51 percent of the gay, lesbian, and bisexual vote nationwide, he would have become the next president of the United States (Gates 2012).

 use your **sociological imagination**

You are a sociologist who takes the conflict perspective. How would you interpret the practice of prostitution? How would your view of prostitution differ if you took the functionalist perspective? The feminist perspective? The perspective of queer theory?

Interactionist Perspective

Workers interacting on the job, encounters in public places like bus stops and parks, behavior in small groups—all these aspects of microsociology catch the attention of interactionists. Whereas functionalist and conflict theorists both analyze large-scale, society-wide patterns of behavior, theorists who take the **interactionist perspective** generalize about everyday forms of social interaction in order to explain society as a whole. Today, given rising concern over the cost and availability of gas, interactionists have begun to study a form of commuter behavior called "slugging." To avoid driving to work, commuters gather at certain preappointed places to seek rides from complete strangers. When a driver pulls into the parking area or vacant lot and announces his destination, the first slug in line who is headed for that destination jumps in. Rules of etiquette have emerged to smooth the social interaction between driver and passenger: neither the driver nor the passenger may eat or smoke; the slug may not adjust the windows or radio or talk on a cell phone. The presence of the slugs, who get a free ride, may allow the driver to use special lanes reserved for high-occupancy vehicles (Slug-Lines.com 2011).

Interactionism (also referred to as *symbolic interactionism*) is a sociological framework in which human beings are viewed as living in a world of meaningful objects. Those "objects" may include material things, actions, other people, relationships, and even symbols. Interactionists see symbols as an especially important part of human communication (thus the term *symbolic interactionism*). Symbols have a shared social meaning that is understood by all members of a society. In the United States, for example, a salute symbolizes respect, while a clenched fist signifies defiance. Another culture might use different gestures to convey a feeling of respect or defiance. These types of symbolic interaction are classified as forms of **nonverbal communication,** which can include many other gestures, facial expressions, and postures (Masuda et al. 2008).

Manipulation of symbols can be seen in dress codes. Schools frown on students who wear clothes displaying messages that appear to endorse violence or drug and alcohol consumption. Businesses stipulate the attire employees are allowed to wear on the job in order to impress their customers or clients. In 2005, the National Basketball Association (NBA) adopted a new dress code for the athletes who play professional basketball—one that involved not the uniforms they wear on court, but the clothes they wear off court on league business. The code requires "business casual attire" when players are representing the league. Indoor sunglasses, chains, and sleeveless shirts are specifically banned (Crowe and Herman 2005:A23).

While the functionalist and conflict approaches were initiated in Europe, interactionism developed first in the United States. George Herbert Mead (1863–1931) is widely regarded as the founder of the interactionist perspective. Mead taught at the University of Chicago from 1893 until his death. As his teachings have become better known, sociologists have expressed greater interest

in the interactionist perspective. Many have moved away from what may have been an excessive preoccupation with the macro (large-scale) level of social behavior and have redirected their attention toward behavior that occurs on the micro (small-scale) level.

Erving Goffman (1922–1982) popularized a particular type of interactionist method known as the **dramaturgical approach,** in which people are seen as theatrical performers. The dramaturgist compares everyday life to the setting of the theater and stage. Just as actors project certain images, all of us seek to present particular features of our personalities while we hide other features. Thus, in a class, we may feel the need to project a serious image; at a party, we may want to look relaxed and friendly.

● The Sociological Approach

Which perspective should a sociologist use in studying human behavior? Functionalist? Conflict? Interactionist? Feminist? Queer theorist? We simply cannot squeeze all sociological thinking into 4 or 5 theoretical categories—or even 10, if we include several other productive approaches. However, by studying the three major frameworks, we can better grasp how sociologists seek to explore social behavior. Table 3-1 summarizes these three broad approaches to sociological study.

Although no one approach is correct by itself, and sociologists draw on all of them for various purposes, many sociologists tend to favor one particular perspective over others. A sociologist's theoretical orientation influences his or her approach to a research problem in important ways—including the choice of what to study, how to study it, and what questions to pose (or not to pose). Box 3-1 shows how researchers would study sports from different sociological perspectives.

TABLE **3-1** MAJOR SOCIOLOGICAL PERSPECTIVES

Tracking Sociological Perspectives

	Functionalist	Conflict	Interactionist
View of Society	Stable, well integrated	Characterized by tension and struggle between groups	Active in influencing and affecting everyday social interaction
Level of Analysis Emphasized	Macro	Macro	Micro, as a way of understanding the larger macro phenomena
Key Concepts	Manifest functions Latent functions Dysfunctions	Inequality Capitalism Stratification	Symbols Nonverbal communication Face-to-face interaction
View of the Individual	People are socialized to perform societal functions	People are shaped by power, coercion, and authority	People manipulate symbols and create their social worlds through interaction
View of the Social Order	Maintained through cooperation and consensus	Maintained through force and coercion	Maintained by shared understanding of everyday behavior
View of Social Change	Predictable, reinforcing	Change takes place all the time and may have positive consequences	Reflected in people's social positions and their communications with others
Example	Public punishments reinforce the social order	Laws reinforce the positions of those in power	People respect laws or disobey them based on their own past experience
Proponents	Émile Durkheim Talcott Parsons Robert Merton	Karl Marx W. E. B. DuBois Ida Wells-Barnett	George Herbert Mead Charles Horton Cooley Erving Goffman

BOX 3-1

Research Today

Looking at Sports from Five Sociological Perspectives

We watch sports. Talk sports. Spend money on sports. Some of us live and breathe sports. Because sports occupy much of our time and directly or indirectly consume and generate a great deal of money, it should not be surprising that sports have sociological components that can be analyzed from various theoretical perspectives. In this section we will look at sports from five major sociological perspectives.

Functionalist View

In examining any aspect of society, functionalists emphasize the contribution it makes to overall social stability. Functionalists regard sports as an almost religious institution that uses ritual and ceremony to reinforce the common values of a society. For example:

- Sports socialize young people into such values as competition and patriotism.
- Sports help to maintain people's physical well-being.
- Sports serve as a safety valve for both participants and spectators, who are allowed to shed tension and aggressive energy in a socially acceptable way.
- Sports bring together members of a community (who support local athletes and teams) or even a nation (during World Cup matches and the Olympics) and promote an overall feeling of unity and social solidarity.

Conflict View

Conflict theorists argue that the social order is based on coercion and exploitation. They emphasize that sports reflect and even exacerbate many of the divisions of society:

- Sports are a form of big business in which profits are more important than the health and safety of the workers (athletes).
- Sports perpetuate the false idea that success can be achieved simply through hard work, while failure should be blamed on the individual alone (rather than on injustices in the larger social system).
- Professional athletes' behavior can promote violence and the use of performance-enhancing drugs.
- Communities divert scarce resources to subsidize the construction of professional sports facilities.
- Sports maintain the subordinate role of Blacks and Latinos, who toil as athletes but are less visible in supervisory positions as coaches, managers, and owners.

- Team logos and mascots (like the Washington Redskins) disparage American Indians.

Feminist View

Feminist theorists consider how watching or participating in sports reinforces the roles that men and women play in the larger society:

- Although sports generally promote fitness and health, they may also have an adverse effect on participants' health. Men are more likely to resort to illegal steroid use (among bodybuilders and baseball players, for example); women, to excessive dieting (among gymnasts and figure skaters, for example).
- Gender expectations encourage female athletes to be passive and gentle, qualities that do not support the emphasis on competitiveness in sports. As a result, women find it difficult to enter sports traditionally dominated by men, such as Indy or NASCAR.
- Although professional women athletes' earnings are increasing, they typically trail those of male athletes.

> Despite their differences, functionalists, conflict theorists, feminists, queer theorists, and interactionists would all agree that there is much more to sports than exercise or recreation.

Queer Theory

Proponents of queer theory emphasize the ways in which sports promote heterosexuality as the only acceptable sexual identity for athletes:

- Coaches and players routinely use slurs based on negative stereotypes of homosexuals to stigmatize athletes whose performance is inadequate.
- As a group, professional athletes are highly reluctant to display any sexual identity other than heterosexuality in

Professional golfer Stacy Lewis won $1.9 million in 2013, making her the 3rd most successful woman on the pro golf circuit that year. Among men, her winnings would have put her in 36th place.

public, for fear of damaging their careers and losing their fans and commercial sponsors.

- Parents who are not heterosexual encounter hostility when they try to register their children for sports or scouting programs, and are often rejected from coaching and other support roles.

Interactionist View

In studying the social order, interactionists are especially interested in shared understandings of everyday behavior. Interactionists examine sports on the micro level by focusing on how day-to-day social behavior is shaped by the distinctive norms, values, and demands of the world of sports:

- Sports often heighten parent–child involvement; they may lead to parental expectations for participation, and sometimes unrealistically, for success.
- Participation in sports builds the friendship networks that permeate everyday life.
- Despite class, racial, and religious differences, teammates may work together harmoniously and may even abandon common stereotypes and prejudices.

—Continued

—Continued

- Relationships in the sports world are defined by people's social positions as players, coaches, and referees—as well as by the high or low status that individuals hold as a result of their performances and reputations.

Despite their differences, functionalists, conflict theorists, feminists, queer theorists, and interactionists would all agree that there is much more to sports than exercise or recreation. They would also agree that sports and other popular forms of culture are worthy subjects of serious study by sociologists.

LET'S DISCUSS

1. Have you experienced or witnessed discrimination in sports based on gender, race, or sexual identity?

If so, how did you react? Has the representation of Blacks, women, or gays on teams been controversial on your campus? If so, in what ways?

2. Which of the five sociological perspectives seems most useful to you in analyzing sports? Why?

Sources: Acosta and Carpenter 2001; Eitzen 2009; Fine 1987; Sefiha 2012; Sharp et al. 2013; Young 2004; Zirin 2008.

Whatever the purpose of sociologists' work, their research will always be guided by their theoretical viewpoints. For example, sociologist Elijah Anderson (1990) embraces both the interactionist perspective and the groundbreaking work of W. E. B. DuBois. For 14 years Anderson conducted fieldwork in Philadelphia, where he studied the interactions of Black and White residents who lived in adjoining neighborhoods. In particular, he was interested in their public behavior, including their eye contact—or lack of it—as they passed one another on the street. Anderson's research tells us much about the everyday social interactions of Blacks and Whites in the United States, but it does not explain the larger issues behind those interactions. Like theories, research results illuminate one part of the stage, leaving other parts in relative darkness.

MODULE 3 | Recap and Review

Summary

Sociologists make use of five major perspectives, all of which offer unique insights into the same issues.

1. The **functionalist perspective** emphasizes the way in which the parts of a society are structured to maintain its stability.

2. The **conflict perspective** assumes that social behavior is best understood in terms of conflict or tension between competing groups.

3. The **interactionist perspective** is concerned primarily with fundamental or everyday forms of interaction, including symbols and other types of nonverbal communication.

4. The **feminist perspective,** which is often allied with the conflict perspective, sees inequity in gender as central to all behavior and organization.

5. **Queer theory** stresses that to fully understand society, scholars must study it from the perspective of a range of sexual identities, rather than exclusively from a "normal" heterosexual point of view.

Thinking Critically

1. Describe an aspect of contemporary society that you consider to be a dysfunction.

2. Describe a symbol or object that has particular meaning on your campus.

3. Relate the toys on display in your local store to issues of race, class, and gender.

Key Terms

Conflict perspective

Dramaturgical approach

Dysfunction

Feminist perspective

Functionalist perspective

Interactionist perspective

Latent function

Manifest function

Nonverbal communication

Queer theory

You've seen how sociologists employ the major sociological perspectives in their research. How does sociology relate to *you,* your own studies, and your own career? In this section you'll learn about *applied* and *clinical sociology,* two growing fields that allow sociology majors and those with advanced degrees in sociology to apply what they have learned to real-world settings. You'll also see how to develop your sociological imagination, one of the keys to thinking like a sociologist. See the appendix at the end of Module 4 for more information on careers in sociology.

Applied and Clinical Sociology

Many early sociologists—notably, Jane Addams, W. E. B. DuBois, and George Herbert Mead—were strong advocates for social reform. They wanted their theories and findings to be relevant to policymakers and to people's lives in general. For instance, Mead was the treasurer of Hull House, where he applied his theory to improving the lives of those who were powerless (especially immigrants). He also served on committees dealing with Chicago's labor problems and public education. DuBois led the Atlanta Sociological Laboratory from 1895 to 1924, supporting scholars in their applied research on business, criminal justice, health care, and philanthropy (Earl Wright II 2012).

Today, **applied sociology** is the use of the discipline of sociology with the specific intent of yielding practical applications for human behavior and organizations. By extension, Michael Burawoy (2005), in his presidential address to the American Sociological Association, endorsed what he called *public sociology,* encouraging scholars to engage a broader audience in bringing about positive outcomes. In effect, the applied sociologist reaches out to others and joins them in their efforts to better society.

Often, the goal of applied or public sociology is to assist in resolving a social problem. For example, in the past 50 years, eight presidents of the United States have established commissions to delve into major societal concerns facing our nation. Sociologists are often asked to apply their expertise to studying such issues as violence, pornography, crime, immigration, and population. In Europe, both academic and government research departments are offering increasing financial support for applied studies.

One example of applied sociology is the growing interest in learning more about local communities. Since its founding in 1994, the Northeast Florida Center for Community Initiatives (CCI), based at the University of North Florida in Jacksonville, has conducted several community studies, including a homeless census and survey, an analysis of the economic impact of the arts in Jacksonville, and a long-term survey of the effects of Hurricane Katrina. Typical of applied sociology, these outreach efforts are collaborative, involving faculty, undergraduate and graduate students, volunteers, and community residents (Center for Community Initiatives 2012a).

Another of CCI's applications of sociology, the Magnolia Project, is based in a storefront clinic in an underprivileged area of Jacksonville. Part of the federal Healthy Start initiative, which aims to decrease high infant mortality rates, the project serves women of childbearing age who have little or no regular access to health care. CCI's responsibilities include (1) interviewing and surveying key community participants, (2) coordinating data collection by the project's staff, (3) analyzing data, and (4) preparing progress reports for funding agencies and community partners. Through March 2012, not a single infant death had occurred among the 293 participants in the program (Center for Community Initiatives 2012b).

Growing interest in applied sociology has led to such specializations as *medical sociology* and *environmental sociology.* The former includes research on how health care professionals and patients deal with disease. To give one example, medical sociologists have studied the social impact of the AIDS crisis on families, friends, and communities (see Module 53). Environmental sociologists examine the relationship between human societies and the physical environment. One focus of their work is the issue of "environmental justice" (see Module 55), raised when researchers and community activists found that hazardous waste dumps are especially likely to be situated in poor and minority neighborhoods (M. Martin 1996).

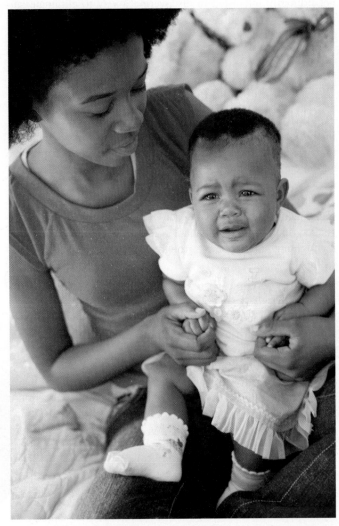

The Center for Community Initiatives' Magnolia Project, an example of applied sociology, aims to decrease high rates of infant mortality.

The growing popularity of applied sociology has led to the rise of the specialty of clinical sociology. Louis Wirth (1931) wrote about clinical sociology more than 75 years ago, but the term itself has become popular only in recent years. While applied sociology may simply evaluate social issues, **clinical sociology** is dedicated to facilitating change by altering social relationships (as in family therapy) or restructuring social institutions (as in the reorganization of a medical center).

Applied sociologists generally leave it to policymakers to act on their evaluations. In contrast, clinical sociologists take direct responsibility for implementation and view those with whom they work as their clients. This specialty has become increasingly attractive to graduate students in sociology because it offers an opportunity to apply intellectual learning in a practical way. A shrinking job market in the academic world has made such alternative career routes appealing.

Applied and clinical sociology can be contrasted with **basic sociology** (also called *pure sociology*), which seeks a more profound knowledge of the fundamental aspects of social phenomena. This type of research is not necessarily meant to generate specific applications, although such ideas may result once findings are analyzed. When Durkheim studied suicide rates, he was not primarily interested in discovering a way to eliminate suicide. In this sense, his research was an example of basic rather than applied sociology.

Developing a Sociological Imagination

In this book, we will be illustrating the sociological imagination in several different ways—by showing theory in practice and in current research; by noting the ways in which electronic devices and apps are changing our social behavior; by thinking globally; by exploring the significance of social inequality; by speaking across race, gender, and religious boundaries; and by highlighting social policy throughout the world.

Theory in Practice

We will illustrate how the major sociological perspectives can be helpful in understanding today's issues, from capital punishment to abortion. Sociologists do not necessarily declare, "Here I am using functionalism," but their research and approaches do tend to draw on one or more theoretical frameworks, as will become clear in the pages to follow.

Research Today

Sociologists actively investigate a variety of issues and social behavior. We have already seen that research can shed light on the social factors that affect suicide rates. Sociological research often plays a direct role in improving people's lives, as in the case of increasing the participation of African Americans in diabetes testing. Throughout the rest of the book, the research performed by sociologists and other social scientists will shed light on group behavior of all types.

Our Wired World

"What is the news today?" For many people, "the news" means the latest comments, pictures, and videos posted online by friends and acquaintances. For some, such up-to-the-minute connectivity has become addictive. During the superstorm that hit New Jersey and New York in October 2012, more than a few people missed their wireless connections more than they did their electrical service.

Throughout this book we will frequently touch on our ever-expanding wired world. The impact of these changes was the focus of Sherry Turkle's attention in the opening excerpt of this chapter. More and more, the electronic gadgets and applications we now depend on for almost everything in our lives are altering our social behavior.

Thinking Globally

Whatever their theoretical perspective or research techniques, sociologists recognize that social behavior must be viewed in a global context. **Globalization** is the worldwide integration of government policies, cultures, social movements, and financial markets through trade and the exchange of ideas. Although public discussion of globalization is relatively recent, intellectuals have been pondering both its negative and positive social consequences for a long time. Karl Marx and Friedrich Engels warned in *The Communist Manifesto* (written in 1848) of a world market that would lead to production in distant lands, sweeping away existing working relationships.

Today, both the positive and negative aspects of globalization are receiving increased scrutiny from sociologists.

Your Morning Cup of Coffee

When you drink a cup of coffee, do you give much thought to where the coffee beans came from, or do you think more about the pleasure you get from the popular beverage? Coffee certainly is popular—as an import, it is second only to petroleum, the most traded commodity in the world.

Although the coffee trade has been globalized, the customs of coffee drinking still vary from place to place. Starbucks now has 17,000 locations in 55 countries. Managers find that in European countries, where the coffeehouse culture originated, 80 percent of customers sit down to drink their coffee. Europeans want to get to know their baristas, so in 2012 Starbucks introduced nametags. In the United States, by contrast, 80 percent of Starbucks customers leave the store immediately, taking their coffee with them.

Today, the coffee trade relies on the exploitation of cheap labor. Coffee is a labor-intensive crop: there is little that technology can do to ease the coffee picker's burden. The typical coffee picker works in a developing nation near the equator, receiving for a day's wages an amount that matches the price of a single cup of coffee in North America. In the 1940s, advocacy

> The typical coffee picker works in a developing nation near the equator, receiving for a day's wages an amount that matches the price of a single cup of coffee in North America.

groups began to promote the sale of certified *fair trade coffee*, which gives a living wage to those who harvest the crop, allowing them to become economically self-sufficient. As of 2012, fair trade coffee accounted for a small percentage of all the coffee bought and sold in the United States, and perhaps 10 percent of the coffee consumed at Starbucks. Recently, a similar movement has begun to promote fair trade in the global clothing industry, reported on by Kelsey Timmerman in his book *Where Am I Wearing?*

Ecological activists have drawn attention to what they see as the coffee industry's contribution to the trend toward global warming. The need to make room for more coffee fields, they charge, has encouraged the destruction of rain forests. The same criticism can be aimed at much of the consumption in industrial nations. Of all the products that emerge from developing nations, however, few have as singular a place in many people's daily ritual as that morning cup of joe. The drink in your hand is your tangible link to rural workers in some of the poorest areas of the world.

LET'S DISCUSS

1. Do you enjoy coffee? Would you willingly pay more for a cup of coffee if you knew that the worker who picked the beans would benefit from the higher price?

2. The coffee trade has been blamed for perpetuating social inequality and global warming. Can you think of any positive effects of the coffee trade? Who benefits most from this economic activity?

Sources: Alderman 2012; Fieser 2009; Jaffee 2012; Luttinger and Dicum 2006; E. Marx 2009; Ritzer 2013:171–177; Timmerman 2009.

Today, developments outside a country are as likely to influence people's lives as changes at home. For example, though much of the world was already in recession by September 2001, the terrorist attacks on New York City and Washington, D.C., caused an immediate economic decline, not just in the United States, but throughout the world. One example of the massive global impact was the downturn in international tourism, which lasted for at least two years. The effects have been felt by people far removed from the United States, including African game wardens and Asian taxi drivers. Some observers see globalization and its effects as the natural result of advances in communications technology, particularly the Internet and satellite transmission of the mass media. Others view it more critically, as a process that allows multinational corporations to expand unchecked. We examine the impact of globalization on our daily lives and on societies throughout the world in Box 4-1 and throughout this book (Fiss and Hirsch 2005).

The Significance of Social Inequality

Who holds power? Who doesn't? Who has prestige? Who lacks it? Perhaps the major theme of analysis in sociology today is **social inequality,** a condition in which members of society have differing amounts of wealth, prestige, or power. For example, the disparity between what coffee bean pickers in developing nations

are paid and the price you pay for a cup of coffee underscores global inequality (see Box 4-1). And the impact of Hurricane Katrina on residents of the Gulf Coast drew attention to social inequality in the United States. Predictably, the people who were hit the hardest by the massive storm were the poor, who had the greatest difficulty evacuating before the storm and have had the most difficulty recovering from it.

Some sociologists, in seeking to understand the effects of inequality, have made the case for social justice. W. E. B. DuBois ([1940] 1968:418) noted that the greatest power in the land is not "thought or ethics, but wealth." As we have seen, the contributions of Karl Marx, Jane Addams, and Ida Wells-Barnett also stressed this belief in the overarching significance of social inequality, and by extension, social justice. In this book, social inequality will be the central focus of Modules 26 through 30, and sociologists' work on inequality will be highlighted throughout.

Speaking across Race, Gender, and Religious Boundaries

Sociologists include both men and women, who come from a variety of ethnic, national, and religious origins. In their work, sociologists seek to draw conclusions that speak to all people—not just the affluent or powerful. Doing so is not always easy.

Insights into how a corporation can increase its profits tend to attract more attention and financial support than do, say, the merits of a needle exchange program for low-income inner-city residents. Yet today more than ever, sociology seeks to better understand the experiences of all people.

Sociologists have noted, for example, that the huge tsunami that hit South Asia in 2004 affected men and women differently. When the waves hit, mothers and grandmothers were at home with the children; men were outside working, where they were more likely to become aware of the impending disaster. Moreover, most of the men knew how to swim, a survival skill that women in these traditional societies usually do not learn. As a result, many more men than women survived the catastrophe—about 10 men for every 1 woman. In one Indonesian village typical of the disaster area, 97 of 1,300 people survived; only 4 were women. The impact of this gender imbalance will be felt for some time, given women's primary role as caregivers for children and the elderly (BBC News 2005).

Social Policy throughout the World

One important way we can use a sociological imagination is to enhance our understanding of current social issues throughout the world. Beginning with Chapter 2, each chapter will conclude with a discussion of a contemporary social policy issue. In some cases we will examine a specific issue facing national governments. For example, government funding of child care centers will be discussed in Chapter 4, Socialization and the Life Course; global immigration in Chapter 10, Racial and Ethnic Inequality; and religion in the schools in Chapter 13, Religion and Education. These Social Policy sections will demonstrate how fundamental sociological concepts can enhance our critical thinking skills and help us to better understand current public policy debates taking place around the world.

In addition, sociology has been used to evaluate the success of programs or the impact of changes brought about by policymakers and political activists. For example, Module 29 includes a discussion of research on the effectiveness of welfare programs. Such discussions underscore the many practical applications of sociological theory and research.

Sociologists expect the next quarter century to be perhaps the most exciting and critical period in the history of the discipline. That is because of a growing recognition—both in the United States and around the world—that current social problems must be addressed before their magnitude overwhelms human societies. We can expect sociologists to play an increasing role in government by researching and developing public policy alternatives. It seems only natural for this textbook to focus on the connection between the work of sociologists and the difficult questions confronting policymakers and people in the United States and around the world.

MODULE | **Recap and Review**

Summary

Studying sociology allows you many ways to exercise your sociological imagination.

1. **Applied** and **clinical sociology** use the discipline of sociology to solve practical problems in human behavior and organizations. In contrast, **basic sociology** is sociological inquiry that seeks only a deeper knowledge of the fundamental aspects of human phenomena.

2. This textbook makes use of the sociological imagination by showing theory in practice and in current research: by thinking globally; by focusing on the significance of social inequality; by speaking across racial, gender, and religious boundaries; and by highlighting social policy around the world.

Thinking Critically

1. What issues facing your local community would you like to address with applied sociological research? Do you see any global connections to these issues?

2. In what specific ways does globalization affect your everyday life? Do you think the impact of globalization is primarily positive or negative?

Key Terms

Applied sociology

Basic sociology

Clinical sociology

Globalization

Social inequality

For the past two decades the number of U.S. college students who have graduated with a degree in sociology has risen steadily. In this appendix we'll consider some of the options these students have after completing their education.

How do students first learn about the sociological perspective on society? Some may take a sociology course in high school. Others may study sociology at community college, where 40 percent of all college students in the United States are enrolled. Indeed, many future sociology majors first develop their sociological imaginations at a community college.

An undergraduate degree in sociology doesn't just serve as excellent preparation for future graduate work in sociology. It also provides a strong liberal arts background for entry-level positions in business, social services, foundations, community organizations, not-for-profit groups, law enforcement, and many government jobs. A number of fields—among them marketing, public relations, and broadcasting—now require investigative skills and an understanding of the diverse groups found in today's multiethnic and multinational environment. Moreover, a sociology degree requires accomplishment in oral and written communication, interpersonal skills, problem solving, and critical thinking—all job-related skills that may give sociology graduates an advantage over those who pursue more technical degrees.

Consequently, while few occupations specifically require an undergraduate degree in sociology, such academic training can be an important asset in entering a wide range of occupations. To emphasize this point, a number of chapters in this book highlight a real-life professional who describes how the study of sociology has helped in his or her career. For example, in Module 20 a Taking Sociology to Work box explains how a college graduate uses her training in sociology as a social media manager for nonprofit organizations. And in Module 48, another Taking Sociology to Work box shows how a recent graduate uses the skill set he acquired as a sociology major in his role as a government analyst.

Figure A-1 summarizes the sources of employment for those with BA or BS degrees in sociology. It shows that fields including nonprofit organizations, education, business, and government offer major career opportunities for sociology graduates. Undergraduates who know where their career interests lie are well advised to enroll in sociology courses and specialties best suited to those interests. For example, students hoping to become health

Did you know that as a student at Princeton University, Michelle Obama majored in sociology? She used that degree as a stepping-stone to Harvard Law School. Read her senior thesis at www.politico.com/news/stories/0208/8642.html.

planners would take a class in medical sociology; students seeking employment as social science research assistants would focus on courses in statistics and methods. Internships, such as placements at city planning agencies and survey research organizations, afford another way for sociology students to prepare for careers. Studies show that students who choose an internship placement have less trouble finding jobs, obtain better jobs, and enjoy greater job satisfaction than students without internship placements. Finally, students should expect to change fields during their first five years of employment after graduation—for example, from sales and marketing to management (American Sociological Association 2009; Salem and Grabarek 1986; Spalter-Roth et al. 2013).

Many college students view social work as the field most closely associated with sociology. Traditionally, social workers received their undergraduate training in sociology and allied fields such as psychology and counseling. After some practical experience, social workers would generally seek a master's degree in social work (MSW) to be considered for supervisory or administrative positions. Today, however, some students choose (where it is available) to pursue a bachelor's degree in social work (BSW). This degree prepares graduates for direct service positions, such as caseworker or group worker.

Many students continue their sociological training beyond the bachelor's degree. More than 250 universities in the United States have graduate programs in sociology that offer PhD and/or master's degrees. These programs differ greatly in their areas of specialization, course requirements, costs, and the research and teaching opportunities available to graduate students. About 71 percent of the graduates are women (American Sociological Association 2005; National Center for Education Statistics 2012).

Higher education is an important source of employment for sociologists with graduate degrees. About 83 percent of recent PhD recipients in sociology seek employment in colleges and universities. These sociologists teach not only majors who are committed to the discipline but also students hoping to become doctors, nurses, lawyers, police officers, and so forth (American Sociological Association 2005). Sociologists who teach in colleges and universities may use their knowledge and training to influence public policy. For example, sociologist Andrew Cherlin (2003) has commented on the debate over proposed federal funding to promote marriage among welfare recipients. Citing the results of two of his studies, Cherlin questioned the potential effectiveness of such a policy in strengthening low-income families. Because many single mothers choose to marry someone other than the father of their children—sometimes for good reason—their children often grow up in stepfamilies.

FIGURE A-1 Occupations of Graduating Sociology Majors

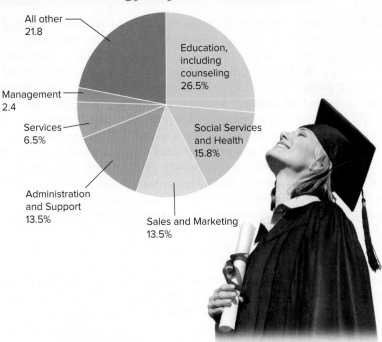

All other
21.8

Education, including counseling
26.5%

Management
2.4

Services
6.5%

Social Services and Health
15.8%

Administration and Support
13.5%

Sales and Marketing
13.5%

Note: Based on a national survey of current occupation in 2013 of 763 graduates with a sociology major in the Class of 2005.
Source: Spalter-Roth et al. 2013:Table 7.

Cherlin's research shows that children who are raised in stepfamilies are no better off than those in single-parent families. He sees government efforts to promote marriage as a politically motivated attempt to foster traditional social values in a society that has become increasingly diverse.

For sociology graduates who are interested in academic careers, the road to a PhD (or doctorate) can be long and difficult. This degree symbolizes competence in original research; each candidate must prepare a book-length study known as a dissertation. Typically, a doctoral student in sociology will engage in four to seven years of intensive work, including the time required to complete the dissertation. Yet even this effort is no guarantee of a job as a sociology professor.

The good news is that over the next 10 years, the demand for instructors is expected to increase because of high rates of retirement among faculty from the baby boom generation, as well as the anticipated slow but steady growth in the college student population in the United States. Nonetheless, anyone who launches an academic career must be prepared for considerable uncertainty and competition in the college job market (American Sociological Association 2009).

Of course, not all people who work as sociologists teach or hold doctoral degrees. Take government, for example. The Census Bureau relies on people with sociological training to interpret data for other government agencies and the general public. Virtually every agency depends on survey research—a field in which sociology students can specialize—in order to assess everything from community needs to the morale of the agency's workers. In addition, people with sociological training can put their academic knowledge to effective use in probation and parole, health sciences, community development, and recreational services. Some people working in government or private industry have a master's degree (MA or MS) in sociology; others have a bachelor's degree (BA or BS).

Currently, about 15 percent of the members of the American Sociological Association use their sociological skills outside the academic world, whether in social service agencies or in marketing positions for business firms. Increasing numbers of sociologists with graduate degrees are employed by businesses, industry, hospitals, and nonprofit organizations. Studies show that many sociology graduates are making career changes from social service areas to business and commerce. For an undergraduate major, sociology is excellent preparation for employment in many parts of the business world (Spalter-Roth et al. 2013).

Whether you take a few courses in sociology or complete a degree, you will benefit from the critical thinking skills developed in this discipline. Sociologists emphasize the value of being able to analyze, interpret, and function within a variety of working situations—an asset in virtually any career. Moreover, given rapid technological change and the expanding global economy, all of us will need to adapt to substantial social change, even in our own careers. Sociology provides a rich conceptual framework that can serve as a foundation for flexible career development and assist you in taking advantage of new employment opportunities.

Mastering This Chapter

taking sociology with you

1 Research! Time your daily activities. How much time do you spend communicating with others via electronic media, compared to speaking with them directly? How many different people do you converse with in person and how many via digital devices?

2 In what ways have you been affected by the recent recession? Has the widespread loss of jobs and homes made you and others more aware of the problem of homelessness, or has it pushed the issue out of sight?

3 Consider some group or organization that you participate in. Using Robert Merton's concepts, list its manifest and latent functions.

key terms

Anomie The loss of direction felt in a society when social control of individual behavior has become ineffective.

Applied sociology The use of the discipline of sociology with the specific intent of yielding practical applications for human behavior and organizations.

Basic sociology Sociological inquiry conducted with the objective of gaining a more profound knowledge of the fundamental aspects of social phenomena. Also known as *pure sociology*.

Clinical sociology The use of the discipline of sociology with the specific intent of altering social relationships or restructuring social institutions.

Conflict perspective A sociological approach that assumes that social behavior is best understood in terms of tension between groups over power or the allocation of resources, including housing, money, access to services, and political representation.

Cultural capital Noneconomic goods, such as family background and education, which are reflected in a knowledge of language and the arts.

Double consciousness The division of an individual's identity into two or more social realities.

Dramaturgical approach A view of social interaction in which people are seen as theatrical performers.

Dysfunction An element or process of a society that may disrupt the social system or reduce its stability.

Feminist perspective A sociological approach that views inequity in gender as central to all behavior and organization.

Functionalist perspective A sociological approach that emphasizes the way in which the parts of a society are structured to maintain its stability.

Globalization The worldwide integration of government policies, cultures, social movements, and financial markets through trade and the exchange of ideas.

Ideal type A construct or model for evaluating specific cases.

Interactionist perspective A sociological approach that generalizes about everyday forms of social interaction in order to explain society as a whole.

Latent function An unconscious or unintended function that may reflect hidden purposes.

Macrosociology Sociological investigation that concentrates on large-scale phenomena or entire civilizations.

Manifest function An open, stated, and conscious function.

Microsociology Sociological investigation that stresses the study of small groups, often through experimental means.

Natural science The study of the physical features of nature and the ways in which they interact and change.

Nonverbal communication The sending of messages through the use of gestures, facial expressions, and postures.

Queer theory The study of society from the perspective of a broad spectrum of sexual identities, including heterosexuality, homosexuality, and bisexuality.

Science The body of knowledge obtained by methods based on systematic observation.

Social capital The collective benefit of social networks, which are built on reciprocal trust.

Social inequality A condition in which members of society have differing amounts of wealth, prestige, or power.

Social science The study of the social features of humans and the ways in which they interact and change.

Sociological imagination An awareness of the relationship between an individual and the wider society, both today and in the past.

Sociology The scientific study of social behavior and human groups.

Theory In sociology, a set of statements that seeks to explain problems, actions, or behavior.

Verstehen The German word for "understanding" or "insight"; used to stress the need for sociologists to take into account the subjective meanings people attach to their actions.

Read each question carefully and then select the best answer.

1. Sociology is
   a. very narrow in scope.
   b. concerned with what one individual does or does not do.
   c. the systematic study of social behavior and human groups.
   d. an awareness of the relationship between an individual and the wider society.

2. Which of the following thinkers introduced the concept of the sociological imagination?
   a. Émile Durkheim
   b. Max Weber
   c. Karl Marx
   d. C. Wright Mills

3. Émile Durkheim's research on suicide suggested that
   a. people with religious affiliations had a higher suicide rate than those who were unaffiliated.
   b. suicide rates seemed to be higher in times of peace than in times of war and revolution.
   c. civilians were more likely to take their lives than soldiers.
   d. suicide is a solitary act, unrelated to group life.

4. Max Weber taught his students that they should employ which of the following in their intellectual work?
   a. anomie
   b. *verstehen*
   c. the sociological imagination
   d. microsociology

5. Robert Merton's contributions to sociology include
   a. successfully combining theory and research.
   b. producing a theory that is one of the most frequently cited explanations of deviant behavior.
   c. an attempt to bring macro-level and micro-level analyses together.
   d. all of the above

6. Which sociologist made a major contribution to society through his in-depth studies of urban life, including both Blacks and Whites?
   a. W. E. B. DuBois
   b. Robert Merton
   c. Auguste Comte
   d. Charles Horton Cooley

7. In the late 19th century, before the term *feminist view* was even coined, the ideas behind this major theoretical approach appeared in the writings of
   a. Karl Marx.
   b. Ida Wells-Barnett.
   c. Charles Horton Cooley.
   d. Pierre Bourdieu.

8. Thinking of society as a living organism in which each part of the organism contributes to its survival is a reflection of which theoretical perspective?
   a. the functionalist perspective
   b. the conflict perspective
   c. the feminist perspective
   d. the interactionist perspective

9. Karl Marx's view of the struggle between social classes inspired the contemporary
   a. functionalist perspective.
   b. conflict perspective.
   c. interactionist perspective.
   d. dramaturgical approach.

10. Erving Goffman's dramaturgical approach, which postulates that people present certain aspects of their personalities while obscuring other aspects, is a derivative of what major theoretical perspective?
    a. the functionalist perspective
    b. the conflict perspective
    c. the feminist perspective
    d. the interactionist perspective

11. While the findings of sociologists may at times seem like common sense, they differ because they rest on _____ analysis of facts.

12. Within sociology, a(n) _____ is a set of statements that seeks to explain problems, actions, or behavior.

13. In _____ _____'s hierarchy of the sciences, sociology was the "queen," and its practitioners were "scientist-priests."

14. In *Society in America,* originally published in 1837, English scholar _____ _____ examined religion, politics, child rearing, and immigration in the young nation.

15. _____ _____ adapted Charles Darwin's evolutionary view of the "survival of the fittest" by arguing that it is "natural" that some people are rich while others are poor.

16. Sociologist Max Weber coined the term _____ _____ in referring to a construct or model that serves as a measuring rod against which actual cases can be evaluated.

17. In *The Communist Manifesto,* _____ _____ and _____ _____ argued that the masses of people who have no resources other than their labor (the proletariat) should unite to fight for the overthrow of capitalist societies.

18. _____ _____, an early female sociologist, cofounded the famous Chicago settlement house called Hull House and also tried to establish a juvenile court system.

19. The university's role in certifying academic competence and excellence is an example of a(n) _____ function.

20. The _____ _____ draws on the work of Karl Marx and Friedrich Engels in that it often views women's subordination as inherent in capitalist societies.

2 Sociological Research

On a busy street in Toronto, a researcher interviews a man about his views on contemporary social issues. Surveys are just one of the methods sociologists use to collect data.

MODULE 5 | What Is the Scientific Method?

MODULE 6 | Major Research Designs

MODULE 7 | Ethics of Research

MODULE 8 | Developments of Methodology

Did you ever wonder how researchers study behaviors that are private and personal?

Sociologists Patricia Adler and Peter Adler went on the Internet to study people who injure themselves. Read on to see what they learned.

66 Self-injury has existed for nearly all of recorded history. Although it has been defined and regarded in various ways over time, its rise in the 1990s and early 2000s has taken a specific, although contested, form and meaning. We focus in this book on the deliberate, non-suicidal destruction of one's own body tissue, incorporating practices such as self-cutting, burning, branding, scratching, picking at skin. . . .

Our goal here is to discuss the form of this latest incarnation of self-injury, now often regarded as a typical behavior among adolescents, describing and analyzing it through the voices and from the perspective of those who practice it. . . .

Many self-injurers were driven to this behavior by nothing more serious than the minor stresses typically associated with normal adolescence. . . . People cited upsets with their friends, romantic relationships, and family members as having led them to self-injury. Mike was a scruffy-looking college student who always wore a stocking cap. He started cutting and burning himself between the ages of 12 and 14. When he was in high school Mike's girlfriend broke up with him, leaving him devastated. He reflected, "Yeah, I thought every relationship was the end of the world. I kept getting further and further depressed, and I just needed something to where I could vent and rage without having any outward signs so that anybody could tell anything was wrong." He turned to cutting to assuage his feelings of sadness. . . .

Over the years that we were actively involved in the self-injury cyber world, it took several twists and turns. The earliest of the sites we discovered probably originated during the late 1990s. At that time, most sites were privately owned and unmonitored. Participants often used the term *self-mutilation*, and it was not uncommon to find graphic details and pictures of injuries. Sites had names such as "bleed me," "ruin your life," "bioetchings," "bleeding to ease the pain," "cut it out," and "gallery of pain." Their main purpose, it appeared, was to offer fellowship to self-harmers so they would know they were not alone. . . .

Over the course of our research we also collected tens of thousands (in the range of 30,000–40,000) of Internet messages and emails, including those posted publicly and those written to and by us. In 2006 we enlisted the aid of three student coders to help us sort and analyze the emails and postings from the Internet groups. At this time we were working on one paper, and the students helped us find posts and emails pertinent to our specific focus. We repeated this process again in 2008 with ten more student coders, expanding the project greatly. Each student took one set of emails we had collected from a group, board, or chat room and poured [sic] through the years of postings we had assembled. We divided the students into groups of five and met with each group biweekly. At each session the students submitted notes and memos about the material they had scanned, and we brainstormed for sociological codes, categories, concepts, trends, and patterns. 99

Mike was a scruffy-looking college student who always wore a stocking cap. He started cutting and burning himself between the ages of 12 and 14.

(P. Adler and P. Adler 2011:1, 43, 44, 54–55)

I n this excerpt from Patricia A. Adler and Peter Adler's book *The Tender Cut: Inside the Hidden World of Self-Injury,* the authors describe their extensive research on a little-known behavior and its social underpinnings. Over a six-year period, the Adlers conducted lengthy, emotionally intense interviews with self-injurers, becoming friends with many. They met others in virtual space, through Internet-based support groups and web postings. "Rather than remaining strictly detached from our subjects, we became involved in their lives, helping them and giving voice to their experiences and beliefs," the Adlers admit (2007:542; 2011).

The Adlers' work on self-injury reflects all three major sociological approaches. For self-injurers, who rarely come into contact with others like themselves, the Internet functions as a meeting place, a refuge from their self-imposed social isolation. As conflict theorists would point out, their unconventional behavior marginalizes them, preventing them from receiving assistance even when they would welcome it. Interactionists would recognize the critical nature of self-injurers' interpersonal contacts, in person and often online. And feminist and queer theorists would look for gender or sexual orientation differences in self-injurers' behavior.

Though many people would like to ignore the phenomenon of self-injury, believing that those who practice it will eventually "grow out of it," the Adlers' research allows us to consider it intelligently and scientifically, within the social context. Self-injurers, the Adlers found, are a diverse group, whose behavior is carefully planned and considered. Surprisingly, members often begin to injure themselves in the company of others rather than in secret. They have recently begun to coalesce as a subculture (2007:559–560).

Effective sociological research can be quite thought-provoking. It may suggest many new questions that require further study, such as why we make assumptions about people who engage in atypical behaviors like self-injury. In some cases, rather than raising additional questions, a study will simply confirm previous beliefs and findings. Sociological research can also have practical applications. For instance, research results that disconfirm accepted beliefs about marriage and the family may lead to changes in public policy.

These modules will examine the research process used in conducting sociological studies. How do sociologists go about setting up a research project? How do they ensure that the results of the research are reliable and accurate? Can they carry out their research without violating the rights of those they study?

We will look first at the steps that make up the scientific method used in research. Then we will look at various techniques commonly used in sociological research, such as experiments, observations, and surveys. We will pay particular attention to the ethical challenges sociologists face in studying human behavior, and to the debate raised by Max Weber's call for "value neutrality" in social science research. We will also examine feminist and queer theorists' methodologies and the role technology plays in research today.

Though sociological researchers can study almost any subject, in this chapter we will concentrate on two in particular. The first is the relationship of education to income, which we will use as an example in the module on the scientific method. The second is the controversial subject of human sexual behavior. Like self-injury, sexual behavior is private and personal, and therefore hard to study. The Social Policy section that closes this chapter describes the difficulties and challenges of researching closely guarded sexual behaviors.

Whatever the area of sociological inquiry and whatever the perspective of the sociologist—whether functionalist, conflict, feminist, queer theorist, interactionist, or any other—there is one crucial requirement: imaginative, responsible research that meets the highest scientific and ethical standards.

MODULE 5 | **What Is the Scientific Method?**

Like all of us, sociologists are interested in the central questions of our time: Is the family falling apart? Why is there so much crime in the United States? Can the world feed a growing population? Such issues concern most people, whether or not they have academic training. However, unlike the typical citizen, the sociologist has a commitment to use the **scientific method** in studying society. The scientific method is a systematic, organized series of steps that ensures maximum objectivity and consistency in researching a problem.

Many of us will never actually conduct scientific research. Why, then, is it important that we understand the scientific method? The answer is that it plays a major role in the workings of our society. Residents of the United States are constantly bombarded with "facts" or "data." A television news report informs us that "one in every two marriages in this country now ends in divorce," yet as Module 41 will show, that assertion is based on misleading statistics. Almost daily, advertisers cite supposedly scientific studies to prove that their products are superior. Such claims may be accurate or exaggerated. We can better evaluate such information—and will not be fooled so easily—if we are familiar with the standards of scientific research.

These standards are quite stringent, and they demand as strict adherence as possible. The scientific method requires precise preparation in developing research. Otherwise, the research data collected may not prove accurate. Sociologists and other researchers follow five basic steps in the scientific method: (1) defining the problem, (2) reviewing the literature, (3) formulating the hypothesis, (4) selecting the research design and then collecting and analyzing data, and (5) developing the conclusion (Figure 5-1). After reaching the conclusion, researchers write a report on their study. Often the report will begin with an *executive summary* of the

FIGURE 5-1 The Scientific Method

The scientific method allows sociologists to objectively and logically evaluate the data they collect. Their findings can suggest ideas for further sociological research.

method they followed and their conclusion. In the sections that follow, we'll use an actual example to illustrate the scientific method.

Defining the Problem

Does it "pay" to go to college? Some people make great sacrifices and work hard to get a college education. Parents borrow money for their children's tuition. Students work part-time jobs or even take full-time positions while attending evening or weekend classes. Does it pay off? Are there monetary returns for getting that degree?

The first step in any research project is to state as clearly as possible what you hope to investigate—that is, *define the problem.* In this instance, we are interested in knowing how schooling relates to income. We want to find out the earnings of people with different levels of formal schooling.

Early on, any social science researcher must develop an operational definition of each concept being studied. An **operational definition** is an explanation of an abstract concept that is specific enough to allow a researcher to assess the concept. For example, a sociologist interested in status might use membership in exclusive social clubs as an operational definition of status. Someone studying prejudice might consider a person's unwillingness to hire or work with members of minority groups as an operational definition of prejudice. In our example, we need to develop two operational definitions—education and earnings—in order to study whether it pays to get an advanced educational degree. We'll define *education* as the number of years of schooling a person has achieved and *earnings* as the income a person reports having received in the past year.

Initially, we will take a functionalist perspective (although we may end up incorporating other perspectives). We will argue that opportunities for more earning power are related to level of schooling, and that schools prepare students for employment.

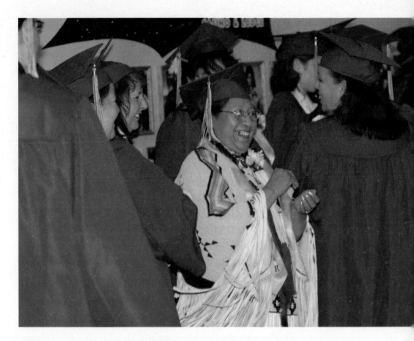

It seems reasonable that these graduates of Fort Bethold Community College on the Fort Bethold Reservation, North Dakota, will earn more income than high school graduates. How would you go about testing that hypothesis?

⬤ Reviewing the Literature

By conducting a *review of the literature*—relevant scholarly studies and information—researchers refine the problem under study, clarify possible techniques to be used in collecting data, and eliminate or reduce avoidable mistakes. In our example, we would examine information about the salaries for different occupations. We would see if jobs that require more academic training are better rewarded. It would also be appropriate to review other studies on the relationship between education and income.

The review of the literature would soon tell us that many factors besides years of schooling influence earning potential. For example, we would learn that the children of rich parents are more likely to go to college than those of poor parents, so we might consider the possibility that rich parents may later help their children to secure better-paying jobs.

We might also look at macro-level data, such as state-by-state comparisons of income and educational levels. In one macro-level study based on census data, researchers found that in states whose residents have a relatively high level of education, household income levels are high as well (Figure 5-2). This finding suggests that schooling may well be related to income, though it does not speak to the micro-level relationship we are interested in. That is, we want to know whether *individuals* who are well educated are also well paid.

⬤ Formulating the Hypothesis

After reviewing earlier research and drawing on the contributions of sociological theorists, the researchers may then *formulate the hypothesis.* A **hypothesis** is a speculative statement about the relationship between two or more factors known as variables. Income, religion, occupation, and gender can all serve as variables in a study. We can define a **variable** as a measurable trait or characteristic that is subject to change under different conditions.

Researchers who formulate a hypothesis generally must suggest how one aspect of human behavior influences or affects another. The variable hypothesized to cause or influence another is called the **independent variable.** The other variable is termed the **dependent variable** because its action *depends* on the influence of the independent variable. In other words, the researcher believes that the independent variable predicts or causes change in the dependent variable. For example, a researcher in sociology might anticipate that the availability of affordable housing (the independent variable, *x*) affects the level of homelessness in a community (the dependent variable, *y*).

Our hypothesis is that the higher one's educational degree, the more money one will earn. The independent variable that is to be measured is the level of education. The variable that is thought to depend on it—income—must also be measured.

Identifying independent and dependent variables is a critical step in clarifying cause-and-effect relationships. As shown in Figure 5-3, **causal logic** involves the relationship between a condition or variable and a particular consequence, with one leading to the other. For instance, being less integrated into society may be directly related to, or produce a greater likelihood of, suicide. Similarly, the time students spend reviewing material for a quiz may be directly related to, or produce a greater likelihood of, getting a high score on the quiz.

A **correlation** exists when a change in one variable coincides with a change in the other. Correlations are an indication that causality *may* be present; they do not necessarily indicate causation. For example, data indicate that people who prefer

FIGURE 5-2 **Educational Level and Household Income in the United States**

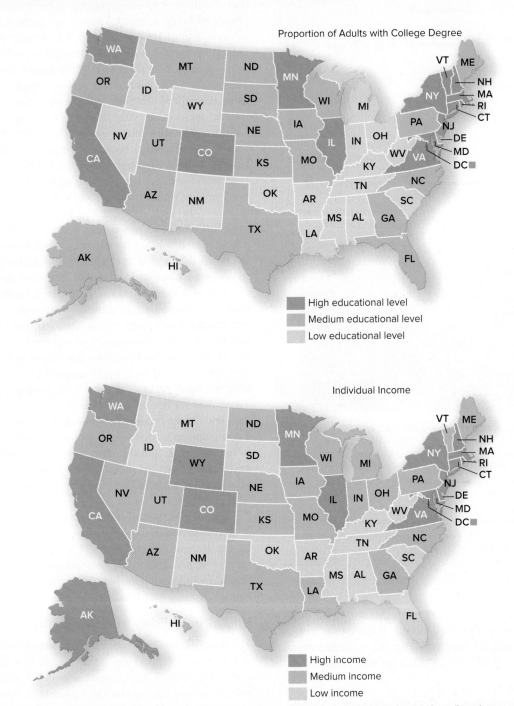

Proportion of Adults with College Degree

■ High educational level
■ Medium educational level
□ Low educational level

Individual Income

■ High income
■ Medium income
□ Low income

Notes: Cutoffs for high/medium and medium/low educational levels in 2012 were 31 percent and 25.7 percent of the population with a college degree, respectively; median for the entire nation was 29.1 percent. Cutoffs for high/medium and medium/low individual income levels in 2011 were $54,000 and $45,000, respectively; national median income was $51,371 in 2011.
Source: American Community Survey in Bureau of the Census 2013a:Table 80201.

to watch televised news programs are less knowledgeable than those who read newspapers and newsmagazines. This correlation between people's relative knowledge and their choice of news media seems to make sense, because it agrees with the common belief that television dumbs down information. But the correlation between the two variables is actually caused by a third variable, people's relative ability to comprehend large amounts of information. People with poor reading skills are much more likely than others to get their news from television, while those who are more educated or skilled turn more often to the print

FIGURE 5-3 Causal Logic

Independent variable		Dependent variable
x	→	y
Level of educational degree	→	Level of income
Degree of lack of integration into society	→	Likelihood of suicide
Availability of affordable housing	→	Level of homelessness
Parents' church attendance	→	Children's church attendance
Time spent preparing for quiz	→	Performance on quiz
Parents' income	→	Likelihood of children's enrolling in college

In *causal logic,* an independent variable (often designated by the symbol *x*) influences a dependent variable (often designated as *y*); thus, *x* leads to *y*. For example, parents who attend church regularly (*x*) are more likely to have children who are churchgoers (*y*). Notice that the first two pairs of variables are taken from studies already described in this textbook.

Think about It Identify two or three dependent variables that might be influenced by this independent variable: number of alcoholic drinks ingested.

Source: Developed by author.

media. Though television viewing is *correlated* with lower news comprehension, then, it does not *cause* it. Sociologists seek to identify the *causal* link between variables; the suspected causal link is generally described in the hypothesis (Neuman 2009).

● Collecting and Analyzing Data

How do you test a hypothesis to determine if it is supported or refuted? You need to collect information, using one of the research designs described in Module 6. The research design guides the researcher in collecting and analyzing data.

Selecting the Sample

In most studies, social scientists must carefully select what is known as a sample. A **sample** is a selection from a larger population that is statistically representative of that population. There are many kinds of samples, but the one social scientists use most frequently is the random sample. In a **random sample**, every member of an entire population being studied has the same chance of being selected. Thus, if researchers want to examine the opinions of people listed in a city directory (a book that, unlike the telephone directory, lists all households), they might use a computer to randomly select names from the directory. The results would constitute a random sample. The advantage of using specialized sampling techniques is that sociologists do not need to question everyone in a population (Igo 2007).

In some cases, the subjects researchers want to study are hard to identify, either because their activities are clandestine or because lists of such people are not readily available. How do researchers create a sample of illegal drug users, for instance, or of women whose husbands are at least 10 years younger than they are? In such cases, researchers employ what are called *snowball* or *convenience samples*—that is, they recruit participants through word of mouth or by posting notices on the Internet. With the help of special statistical techniques, researchers can draw conclusions from such nonrandom samples.

It is all too easy to confuse the careful scientific techniques used in representative sampling with the many *nonscientific* polls that receive much more media attention. For example, website viewers are often encouraged to register their views on headline news or political contests. Such polls reflect nothing more than the views of those who happened to visit the website and took the time, perhaps at some cost, to register their opinions. These data do not necessarily reflect (and indeed may distort) the views of the broader population. Not everyone has access to a computer on a regular basis, or the means and/or inclination to register their opinions. Even when these techniques include answers from tens of thousands of people, they will be far less accurate than a carefully selected representative sample of 1,500 respondents.

For the purposes of our research example, we will use information collected in the American Community Survey conducted by the Bureau of the Census. Each year, the Census Bureau surveys approximately 77,000 households across the United States. Technicians at the bureau then use the data to estimate the nation's entire population.

Ensuring Validity and Reliability

The scientific method requires that research results be both valid and reliable. **Validity** refers to the degree to which a measure or scale truly reflects the phenomenon under study. A valid measure of income depends on the gathering of accurate data. Various studies show that people are reasonably accurate in reporting how much money they earned in the most recent year. If a question is written unclearly, however, the resulting data might not be accurate. For example, respondents to an unclear question about income might report their parents' or spouse's income instead of their own.

Reliability refers to the extent to which a measure produces consistent results. Some people may not disclose accurate information, but most do. In the American Community Survey, about 98 percent of the households that researchers approach participate

FIGURE 5-4 Impact of a College Education on Income

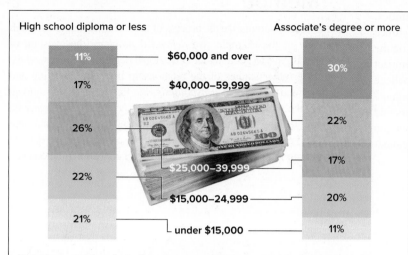

High school diploma or less		Associate's degree or more
11%	**$60,000 and over**	30%
17%	**$40,000–59,999**	22%
26%	**$25,000–39,999**	17%
22%	**$15,000–24,999**	20%
21%	**under $15,000**	11%

Forty-three percent of people with a high school diploma or less (left) earn under $25,000 a year, while only 28 percent earn $40,000 or more. In contrast, only 31 percent of those with an associate's degree or higher (right) earn less than $25,000, while 52 percent earn $40,000 or more.

Think about It What kinds of knowledge and skills do people with an associate's degree or higher possess, compared to those with a high school education or less? Why would employers value those kinds of knowledge and skills?

Source: Author's analysis of DeNavas-Walt et al. 2013, Detailed Table PINC-03. Only people with earnings included.

more than high school graduates. The relationship continues through more advanced levels of schooling, so that those with graduate degrees earn the most.

The relationship is not perfect, however. Some people who drop out of high school end up with high incomes, and some with advanced degrees earn modest incomes, as shown in Figure 5-4. A successful entrepreneur, for example, might not have much formal schooling, while the holder of a doctorate may choose to work for a low-paying nonprofit institution. Sociologists are interested in both the general pattern that emerges from their data and exceptions to the pattern.

Sociological studies do not always generate data that support the original hypothesis. Many times, a hypothesis is refuted, and researchers must reformulate their conclusions. Unexpected results may also lead sociologists to reexamine their methodology and make changes in the research design.

Controlling for Other Factors

A **control variable** is a factor that is held constant to test the relative impact of an independent variable. For example, if researchers wanted to know how adults in the United States feel about restrictions on smoking in public places, they would probably attempt to use a respondent's smoking behavior as a control variable. That is, how do smokers versus nonsmokers feel about smoking in public places? The

in the survey. The Census Bureau checks their responses against those of similar households, to ensure that the data do not differ significantly from other known responses. The bureau also checks their responses for reliability, since more and more data are being collected online (American Community Survey 2013b).

Developing the Conclusion

Scientific studies, including those conducted by sociologists, do not aim to answer all the questions that can be raised about a particular subject. Therefore, the conclusion of a research study represents both an end and a beginning. Although it terminates a specific phase of the investigation, it should also generate ideas for future study.

Supporting Hypotheses

In our example, we find that the data support our hypothesis: people with more formal schooling *do* earn more money than others. Those with a high school diploma earn more than those who failed to complete high school, but those with an associate's degree earn

How would researchers study our attitudes toward people who smoke cigarettes in public? They would likely use respondents' past smoking behavior as a control variable. In that case, they might hypothesize that respondents who smoke may be more tolerant of smoking in public than respondents who don't smoke. Another interesting question would be whether people who have quit smoking feel differently about lighting up in public than other nonsmokers. What do you think?

researchers would compile separate statistics on how smokers and nonsmokers feel about antismoking regulations.

Our study of the influence of education on income suggests that not everyone enjoys equal educational opportunities, a disparity that is one of the causes of social inequality. Since education affects a person's income, we may wish to call on the conflict perspective to explore this topic further. What impact does a person's race or gender have? Is a woman with a college degree likely to earn as much as a man with similar schooling? Later in this textbook we will consider these other factors and variables. That is, we will examine the impact that education has on income while controlling for variables such as gender and race.

In Summary: The Scientific Method

Let us briefly summarize the process of the scientific method through a review of the example. We *defined a problem* (the question of whether it pays to get a higher educational degree). We *reviewed the literature* (other studies of the relationship between education and income) and *formulated a hypothesis* (the higher one's educational degree, the more money one will earn). We *collected and analyzed the data,* making sure the sample was representative and the data were valid and reliable. Finally, we *developed the conclusion:* the data do support our hypothesis about the influence of education on income.

MODULE 5 | Recap and Review

Summary

Sociologists are committed to the use of the **scientific method** in their research efforts. In this module we examine the basic principles of the scientific method.

1. There are five basic steps in the scientific method: define the problem, review the literature, formulate a hypothesis, collect and analyze data, and develop the conclusion.

2. Whenever researchers wish to study abstract concepts, such as intelligence or prejudice, they must develop workable **operational definitions.**

3. A hypothesis states a possible relationship between two or more **variables.**

4. By using a **sample,** sociologists avoid having to test everyone in a population.

5. According to the scientific method, research results must possess both **validity** and **reliability.**

Thinking Critically

1. What might be the effects of a college education on society as a whole? Think of some potential effects on the family, government, and the economy.

2. Suppose that two researchers used different operational definitions for the same term. Could both researchers' results be reliable and valid? Explain your answer.

Key Terms

Causal logic

Control variable

Correlation

Dependent variable

Hypothesis

Independent variable

Operational definition

Random sample

Reliability

Sample

Scientific method

Validity

Variable

MODULE 6 | Major Research Designs

An important aspect of sociological research is deciding *how* to collect the data. A **research design** is a detailed plan or method for obtaining data scientifically. Selection of a research design is often based on the theories and hypotheses the researcher starts with (Merton 1948). The choice requires creativity and ingenuity, because it directly influences both the cost of the project and the amount of time needed to collect the data. Research designs

that sociologists regularly use to generate data include surveys, ethnography, experiments, and existing sources.

Surveys

Almost all of us have responded to surveys of one kind or another. We may have been asked what kind of detergent we use, which presidential candidate we intend to vote for, or what our favorite television program is. A **survey** is a study, generally in the form of an interview or questionnaire, that provides researchers with information about how people think and act. As anyone who watches the news during presidential campaigns knows, surveys have become a staple of political life.

When you think of surveys, you may recall seeing online polls that offer instant results. Although such polls can be highly interesting, they reflect only the opinions of those who visit the website and choose to respond online. As we have seen, a survey must be based on precise, representative sampling if it is to genuinely reflect a broad range of the population. In our wired world, more and more people can be reached only through their cell phones. Box 6-1 describes the challenges of conducting a public opinion survey on a cell phone.

In preparing to conduct a survey, sociologists must not only develop representative samples; they must also exercise great care in the wording of questions. An effective survey question must be simple and clear enough for people to understand. It must also be specific enough so that there are no problems in interpreting the results. Open-ended questions ("What do you think of the programming on educational television?") must be carefully phrased to solicit the type of information desired. Surveys can be indispensable sources of information, but only if the sampling is done properly and the questions are worded accurately and without bias.

In wording questions, researchers must also pay careful attention to changes in society. In December 2010, officials at the Bureau of Labor Statistics recognized the effects of an extended recession by changing a decades-old practice. In the past, multiple-choice questions about how long a respondent had been unemployed had ended with a maximum of "99 weeks or over." By the end of 2010, joblessness had become so chronic that the bureau increased the number of choices, ending with "290 weeks or longer."

There are two main forms of the survey: the **interview,** in which a researcher obtains information through face-to-face, phone, or online questioning, and the **questionnaire,** in which the researcher uses a printed or written form to obtain information from a respondent. Each of these has its own advantages. An interviewer can obtain a higher response rate, because people find it more difficult to turn down a personal request for an interview than to throw away a written questionnaire. In addition, a skillful interviewer can go beyond written questions and probe for a subject's underlying feelings and reasons. Patricia and Peter Adler conducted 139 in-depth interviews for their book on the sensitive subject of self-injury (see the chapter-opening excerpt). On the other hand, questionnaires have the advantage of being cheaper, especially in large samples.

Why do people have sex? A straightforward question, but until recently it was rarely investigated scientifically, despite its significance to public health, marital counseling, and criminology. To find the answer, researchers interviewed nearly 2,000 undergraduates at the University of Texas at Austin. In developing the question for the interview, they first asked a random sample of 400 students to list all the reasons why they had ever had sex. The explanations were highly diverse, ranging from "I was drunk" to "I wanted to feel closer to God." The team then asked another sample of 1,500 students to rate the importance of each of the 287 reasons given by the first group. Table 6-1 ranks the

results. Nearly every reason was rated most important by at least some respondents. Though there were some gender differences in the replies, there was significant consensus between men and women on the top 10 reasons (Meston and Buss 2007).

Studies have shown that the characteristics of the interviewer have an impact on survey data. For example, female interviewers tend to receive more feminist responses from female subjects than do male interviewers, and Black interviewers tend to receive more detailed responses about race-related issues from Black subjects than do White interviewers. The possible impact of gender and race indicates again how much care social research requires (D. W. Davis and Silver 2003).

The survey is an example of **quantitative research,** which collects and reports data primarily in numerical form. Most of the survey research discussed so far in this book has been quantitative. While this type of research can make use of large samples, it can't offer great depth and detail on a topic. That is why researchers also make use of **qualitative research,** which relies on what is seen in field and naturalistic settings, and often focuses on small groups and communities rather than on large groups or whole nations. The most common form of qualitative research is ethnography, or observation, which we consider next. Throughout this book you will find examples of both quantitative and qualitative research, since both are used widely. Some sociologists prefer one type of research to the other, but we learn most when we draw on many different research designs and do not limit ourselves to a particular type of research.

Ethnography

Investigators often collect information or test hypotheses through firsthand studies. **Ethnography** is the study of an entire social setting through extended systematic fieldwork. **Observation,** or direct participation in closely watching a group or organization, is the basic technique of ethnography. However, ethnographic research also includes the collection of historical information and the conduct of in-person interviews. Although ethnography may seem a relatively informal method compared to surveys or experiments, ethnographic researchers are careful to take detailed notes while observing their subjects.

In some cases, the sociologist actually joins a group for a period, to get an accurate sense of how it operates. This approach is called *participant observation.* In Barbara Ehrenreich's widely read book *Nickel and Dimed: On (Not) Getting By in America,* the author was a participant observer. Disguising herself as a divorced, middle-aged housewife without a college degree, Ehrenreich set out to see what life was like for low-wage workers. Her book chronicles her own and others' experiences trying to make ends meet on a minimum wage (Ehrenreich 2001).

During the late 1930s, in a classic example of participant-observation research, William F. Whyte moved into a low-income Italian neighborhood in Boston. For nearly four years he was a member of the social circle of "corner boys" that he describes in *Street Corner Society.* Whyte revealed his identity to these men and joined in their

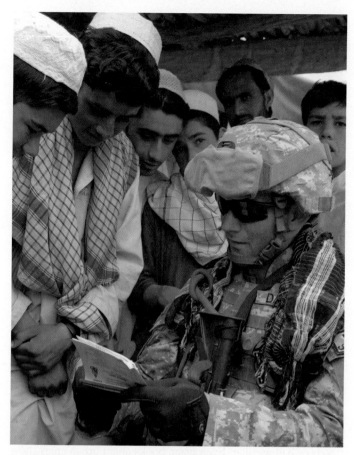

Sergeant Britt Damon, a social scientist on the U.S. Army Human Terrain Team, chats with Afghani children during a search operation. The participation of social scientists in the Army program, which some see as a violation of scholarly detachment, has proved controversial.

the events taking place around them. This raises a delicate issue. If the research is to be successful, the observer cannot allow the close associations or even friendships that inevitably develop to influence the subjects' behavior or the conclusions of the study. Even while working hard to gain acceptance from the group being studied, the participant observer *must* maintain some degree of detachment.

The U.S. Army's Human Terrain System (HTS) illustrates the challenges of observation research. In locations such as Iraq and Afghanistan, social scientists embedded with the U.S. military have been identifying local customs, family structures, and internal social conflicts in order to help the Army gain citizens' trust. Although the idea of scholars cooperating with warriors struck many people as inappropriate, others countered that the information they contributed would help soldiers to avoid needless violence. The program has been scaled back as U.S. troops have withdrawn, but in 2013 the military still funded 20 different HTS teams at a cost of $58 million (Forte 2010; Vanden Brook 2013).

Experiments

When sociologists want to study a possible cause-and-effect relationship, they may conduct experiments. An **experiment** is an artificially created situation that allows a researcher to manipulate variables.

In the classic method of conducting an experiment, two groups of people are selected and matched for similar characteristics, such as age or education. The researchers then assign the subjects to one of two groups: the experimental or the control group. The **experimental group** is exposed to an independent variable; the **control group** is not. Thus, if scientists were testing a new type of antibiotic, they would administer the drug to an experimental group but not to a control group.

In some experiments, just as in observation research, the presence of a social scientist or other observer may affect the behavior of the people being studied. Sociologists have used the term **Hawthorne effect** to refer to the unintended influence that observers of experiments can have on their subjects. The term originated as the result of an experiment conducted at the Hawthorne plant of the Western Electric Company during the 1920s and 1930s. Researchers found that *every* change they made in working conditions—even reduced lighting—seemed to have a positive effect on workers' productivity. They concluded that workers had made a special effort to impress their observers. Though the carefully constructed study did identify some causes for changes in the workers' behavior that did not have to do with their being observed, the term *Hawthorne effect* has become synonymous with a placebo or guinea pig effect (Franke and Kaul 1978).

Use of Existing Sources

Sociologists do not necessarily need to collect new data in order to conduct research and test hypotheses. The term **secondary analysis** refers to a variety of research techniques that make use of previously collected and publicly accessible information and data. Generally, in conducting secondary analysis, researchers use data in ways that were unintended by the initial collectors of information.

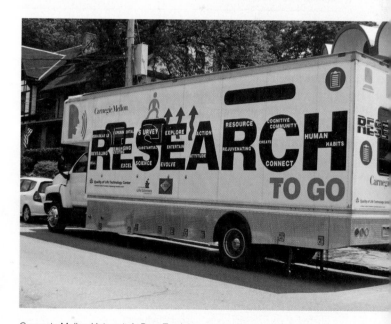

Carnegie Mellon University's Data Truck lets researchers go where their subjects are—from nightclubs to marathon races. Equipped with the latest technology, the truck allows social scientists to enter the responses to their community surveys into their databases on-site. It also gives them access to online social networks in the area, and even lets them videotape street activity.

TABLE 6-2 EXISTING SOURCES USED IN SOCIOLOGICAL RESEARCH

Most Frequently Used Sources

Census data

Crime statistics

Birth, death, marriage, divorce, and health statistics

Other Sources

Newspapers and periodicals

Personal journals, diaries, e-mail, and letters

Records and archival material of religious organizations, corporations, and other organizations

Transcripts of radio programs

Motion pictures and television programs

Web pages, blogs, and chat rooms

Song lyrics

Scientific records (such as patent applications)

Speeches of public figures (such as politicians)

Votes cast in elections or by elected officials on specific legislative proposals

Attendance records for public events

Videos of social protests and rallies

Literature, including folklore

Think about It Which of these sources do you access to collect information?

Source: Developed by author.

For example, census data are compiled for specific uses by the federal government but are also valuable to marketing specialists in locating everything from bicycle stores to nursing homes.

Sociologists consider secondary analysis to be *nonreactive*—that is, it does not influence people's behavior. For example, Émile Durkheim's statistical analysis of suicide neither increased nor decreased human self-destruction. Researchers, then, can avoid the Hawthorne effect by using secondary analysis.

There is one inherent problem, however: the researcher who relies on data collected by someone else may not find exactly what is needed. Social scientists who are studying family violence can use statistics from police and social service agencies on *reported* cases of spouse abuse and child abuse, but how many cases are not reported? Government bodies have no precise data on *all* cases of abuse.

Many social scientists find it useful to study cultural, economic, and political documents, including newspapers, periodicals, radio and television tapes, the Internet, scripts, diaries, songs, folklore, and legal papers (Table 6-2). In examining these sources, researchers employ a technique known as **content analysis**, which is the systematic coding and objective recording of data, guided by some rationale. Box 6-2 describes a recent content study of gender differences in the way Boy Scouts and Girl Scouts earn merit badges.

Content analysis can be revealing. Following a recent increase in devastating hurricanes, floods, and prolonged droughts, many people have expressed the need to educate future generations about climate change. To assess children's awareness of the environment, sociologists conducted a content analysis of award-winning picture books over the last 70 years. Their work revealed a noticeable *decline* in depictions of the natural environment and animals. Today, when children's books do address environmental events, they are more likely to portray volcanic eruptions than floods or bad weather. Even when books about urban areas show smokestacks emitting huge quantities of black smoke, the story line does not identify air pollution as a problem (J. Williams et al. 2012).

Table 6-3 summarizes the major research designs, along with their advantages and limitations.

 use your **sociological imagination**

Imagine you are a legislator or government policymaker working on a complex social problem. What might happen if you were to base your decision on faulty research?

TABLE 6-3 MAJOR RESEARCH DESIGNS

Method	Examples	Advantages	Limitations
Survey	Questionnaires Interviews	Yields information about specific issues	Can be expensive and time-consuming
Ethnography	Observation	Yields detailed information about specific groups or organizations	Involves months if not years of labor-intensive data
Experiment	Deliberate manipulation of people's social behavior	Yields direct measures of people's behavior	Ethical limitations on the degree to which subjects' behavior can be manipulated
Existing sources/Secondary analysis	Analysis of census or health data Analysis of films or TV commercials	Cost-efficiency	Limited to data collected for some other purpose

Gender Messages in Scouting

Nearly 5 million children in the United States participate in scouting. What gender messages do these young people receive during their time as Scouts?

A key form of guidance not just for Scouts but for their leaders is the Scouts' handbook. Sociologist Kathleen Denny did a content analysis of the Boy Scouts' *Webelos Handbook* and the *Junior Girl Scout Handbook.* Focusing specifically on material for Scouts in the fourth and fifth grades, she found that both handbooks delivered traditional gender messages. Girl Scout activities were more likely

Merit badges for boys (left) and girls (right)

> The most gender-specific aspect of the Girl Scout handbook is the subjects of the badges themselves.

than Boy Scout activities to be communal or other-oriented; Boy Scout activities were more likely to be solo undertakings.

Denny found that the names of merit badges also conveyed traditional gender messages. Girl Scout badge names often include puns or other forms of word play; Boy Scout badges do not. For example, the Boy Scout badge for studying rocks and geology is called simply the Geologist badge; the comparable Girl Scout badge

is called the Rocks Rock badge. Boy Scout badges more often have career-oriented names—Engineer, Craftsman, Scientist; Girl Scout badge names have less of a career orientation—Sky Search instead of Astronomer, Car Care instead of Mechanic.

The most gender-specific aspect of the Girl Scout handbook is the subjects of the badges themselves. Many refer to stereotypically feminine activities: Caring for Children, Looking Your Best, Sew Simple. Besides personal hygiene and healthy eating, the Looking Your Best badge includes an "Accessory Party," which requires Scouts to "experiment to see how accessories highlight your features and your outfit." Needless to say, such badges are not

offered in the Boy Scouts. The most nearly comparable one in the Boy Scout handbook is the Fitness badge, which includes activities such as keeping a food diary and warning a relative about the dangers of drugs and alcohol.

Denny acknowledges that Scout handbooks are not the only influence on gender roles in scouting. How are gender messages communicated in person during troop or pack meetings and ceremonies, for example? How do parents reinforce or mediate the gender themes in scouting? And how do children adjust to, accept, or rebel against the gender messages they receive as Scouts? Denny's research suggests the need for further research on gender socialization in the Boy Scouts and Girl Scouts.

LET'S DISCUSS

1. Did you participate in scouting as a child? If so, were you aware of the gender messages you were receiving as part of the scouting experience? How did you react?

2. If you were a Scout leader yourself, what kind of gender model would you attempt to be? How would you become that kind of model?

Sources: Boy Scouts of America 2010; K. Denny 2011; Girl Scouts of the USA 2001:39; World Association of Girl Guides and Girl Scouts 2011.

MODULE 6 | **Recap and Review**

Summary

In this module we focus on **research designs,** or the types of plans sociologists use to collect data.

1. Sociologists use four major research designs: surveys, observation, experiments, and existing sources.

2. The two principal forms of **survey** research are the **interview** and the **questionnaire.**

3. **Ethnography** allows sociologists to study certain behaviors and communities that cannot be investigated through other research methods.

4. When sociologists wish to study a cause-and-effect relationship, they may conduct an **experiment.**

5. Sociologists may also make use of existing sources in **secondary analysis** and **content analysis.**

Thinking Critically

1. How would you set up an experiment to measure the effect of playing video games on school-age children's grades?

2. Suppose your sociology instructor has asked you to study homelessness in your community. Which research technique would you find most useful? How would you use that technique?

Key Terms

Content analysis

Control group

Ethnography

Experiment

Experimental group

Hawthorne effect

Interview

Observation

Qualitative research

Quantitative research

Questionnaire

Research design

Secondary analysis

Survey

MODULE 7 | Ethics of Research

A biochemist cannot inject a drug into a human being unless it has been thoroughly tested and the subject agrees to the shot. To do otherwise would be both unethical and illegal. Sociologists, too, must abide by certain specific standards in conducting research, called a **code of ethics**. The professional society of the discipline, the American Sociological Association (ASA), first published the society's *Code of Ethics* in 1971 and reviewed it most recently in 1997. It puts forth the following basic principles:

1. Maintain objectivity and integrity in research.

2. Respect the subject's right to privacy and dignity.

3. Protect subjects from personal harm.

4. Preserve confidentiality.

5. Seek informed consent when data are collected from research participants or when behavior occurs in a private context.

6. Acknowledge research collaboration and assistance.

7. Disclose all sources of financial support (American Sociological Association 1999).

These basic principles probably seem clear-cut. How could they lead to any disagreement or controversy? Yet many delicate ethical questions cannot be resolved simply by reading these seven principles. For example, should a sociologist who is engaged in participant-observation research always protect the confidentiality of subjects? What if the subjects are members of a religious cult allegedly involved in unethical and possibly illegal activities? What if the sociologist is interviewing political activists and is questioned by government authorities about the research?

Because most sociological research uses *people* as sources of information—as respondents to survey questions, subjects of ethnography, or participants in experiments—these sorts of questions are important. In all cases, sociologists need to be certain they are not invading their subjects' privacy. Generally, they do so by assuring subjects of anonymity and by guaranteeing the confidentiality of personal information. In addition, research proposals that involve human subjects must now be overseen by a review board, whose members seek to ensure that subjects are not placed at an unreasonable level of risk. If necessary, the board may ask researchers to revise their research designs to conform to the code of ethics.

We can appreciate the seriousness of the ethical problems researchers confront by considering the experience of sociologist Rik Scarce, described in the next section. Scarce's vow to protect his subjects' confidentiality got him into considerable trouble with the law.

Confidentiality

Like journalists, sociologists occasionally find themselves subject to questions from law enforcement authorities because of knowledge they have gained in the course of their work. This uncomfortable situation raises profound ethical questions.

In May 1993, Rik Scarce, a doctoral candidate in sociology at Washington State University, was jailed for contempt of court. Scarce had declined to tell a federal grand jury what he knew—or even whether he knew anything—about a 1991 raid on a university research laboratory by animal rights activists. At the time, Scarce was conducting research for a book about environmental protesters and knew at least one suspect in the break-in. Curiously, although he was chastised by a federal judge, Scarce won respect from fellow prison inmates, who regarded him as a man who "wouldn't snitch" (Monaghan 1993:A8).

The American Sociological Association supported Scarce's position when he appealed his sentence. Scarce maintained his silence. Ultimately the judge ruled that nothing would be gained by further incarceration, and Scarce was released after serving 159 days in jail. In January 1994, the U.S. Supreme Court declined to hear Scarce's case on appeal. The Court's failure to consider his case led Scarce (2005) to argue that federal

Taking Sociology to Work

Dave Eberbach, *Associate Director, Iowa Institute for Community Alliances*

Dave Eberbach is a people person who has been working with computers most of his career. In 1994 he was hired as a research coordinator by the United Way of Central Iowa. In that position he helped to create and implement Iowa's Homeless Management Information System (HMIS), which coordinates data on housing and homeless service providers. Eberbach also collaborated with the Human Service Planning Alliance to create and maintain a "data warehouse" of social statistics from diverse sources. As a research coordinator, he found that the data helped him to identify small pockets of poverty that were generally hidden in state and county statistics.

Today, Eberbach works at the Iowa Institute for Community Alliances, a small nonprofit organization that offers computerized client management and on-site program monitoring to homeless and housing service providers. As Associate Director, Eberbach oversees a staff of seven and meets with clients who are working to improve service delivery to vulnerable people. "As fewer resources are being spent on social programs, it has been imperative to make sure that the focus of programs is on client success, not maintaining systems," he explains.

Eberbach went to Grinnell College, where he took a variety of social science courses before settling on sociology as a major. While there, he benefited from the presence of several visiting professors, who exposed him to a variety of racial and cultural perspectives. He found that his personal acquaintance with them complemented the concepts he was learning in his sociology classes. Today, Eberbach draws on his college experiences in his work, which brings him into contact with a diverse group of people.

As a student, Eberbach recalls, he never thought he would use statistics in his career, and didn't work very hard in the course. "As it turned out," he says, "I use it nearly every day. Understanding data and statistics and being able to explain numbers to others has been very important in my job." The reverse has also been true, however: having a background in sociology has been helpful to him in systems design. "Understanding that systems need to work for a variety of groups of people, not just folks that grew up like I did," he explains, has been very helpful. "The world is not a computer problem or a math problem to be solved," he continues, "but rather a complex environment where groups of people continually bump into one another."

LET'S DISCUSS

1. Do you know what you want to be doing 10 years from now? If so, how might a knowledge of statistics help you in your future occupation?

2. What kinds of statistics, specifically, might you find in the Human Service Planning Alliance's data warehouse? Where would they come from?

legislation is needed to clarify the right of scholars and members of the press to preserve the confidentiality of those they interview.

Conflict of Interest

Sometimes disclosing all the sources of funding for a study, as required in principle 7 of the ASA's *Code of Ethics,* is not a sufficient guarantee of ethical conduct. Especially in the case of both corporate and government funding, money given ostensibly for the support of basic research may come with strings attached. Accepting funds from a private organization or even a government agency that stands to benefit from a study's results can call into question a researcher's objectivity and integrity (principle 1). The controversy surrounding the involvement of social scientists in the U.S. Army's Human Terrain System is one example of this conflict of interest.

Another example is the Exxon Corporation's support for research on jury verdicts. In 1989, the Exxon oil tanker *Valdez* hit a reef off the coast of Alaska, spilling more than 11 million gallons of oil into Prince William Sound. Five years later a federal court ordered Exxon to pay $5.3 billion in damages for the accident. Exxon appealed the verdict and began approaching legal scholars, sociologists, and psychologists who might be willing to study jury deliberations. The corporation's objective was to develop academic support for its lawyers' contention that the punitive judgments in such cases result from faulty deliberations and do not have a deterrent effect.

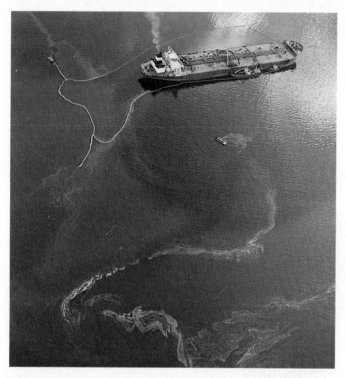

A floating containment barrier (or boom) encircles the Exxon oil tanker *Valdez* after it was grounded on a reef off the coast of Alaska. Exxon was found negligent in the environmental disaster and was ordered to pay $5.3 billion for the cleanup. On appeal, the company managed to reduce the damages to $500 million based on academic research that it had funded—research that some scholars believe involved a conflict of interest.

Some scholars have questioned the propriety of accepting funds under these circumstances, even if the source is disclosed. In at least one case, an Exxon employee explicitly told a sociologist that the corporation offers financial support to scholars who have shown the tendency to express views similar to its own. An argument can also be made that Exxon was attempting to set scholars' research agendas with its huge war chest. Rather than funding studies on the improvement of cleanup technologies or the assignment of long-term environmental costs, Exxon chose to shift scientists' attention to the validity of the legal awards in environmental cases.

The scholars who accepted Exxon's support deny that it influenced their work or changed their conclusions. Some received support from other sources as well, such as the National Science Foundation and Harvard University's Olin Center for Law, Economics, and Business. Many of their findings were published in respected academic journals after review by a jury of peers. Still, at least one researcher who participated in the studies refused monetary support from Exxon to avoid even the suggestion of a conflict of interest.

Exxon has spent roughly $1 million on the research, and at least one compilation of studies congenial to the corporation's point of view has been published. As ethical considerations require, the academics who conducted the studies disclosed Exxon's role in funding them. Nevertheless, the investment appears to have paid off. In 2006, drawing on these studies, Exxon's lawyers succeeded in persuading an appeals court to reduce the corporation's legal damages from $5.3 to $2.5 billion. In 2008 Exxon appealed that judgment to the Supreme Court, which further reduced the damages to $500 million. The final award, which is to be shared by about 32,000 plaintiffs, will result in payments of about $15,000 to each person (Freudenburg 2005; Liptak 2008).

● Value Neutrality

The ethical considerations of sociologists lie not only in the methods they use and the funding they accept, but also in the way they interpret their results. Max Weber ([1904] 1949) recognized that personal values would influence the questions that sociologists select for research. In his view, that was perfectly acceptable, but under no conditions could a researcher allow his or her personal feelings to influence the *interpretation* of data. In Weber's phrase, sociologists must practice **value neutrality** in their research.

As part of this neutrality, investigators have an ethical obligation to accept research findings even when the data run counter to their personal views, to theoretically based explanations, or to widely accepted beliefs. For example, Émile Durkheim challenged popular conceptions when he reported that social (rather than supernatural) forces were an important factor in suicide.

Although some sociologists believe that neutrality is impossible, ignoring the issue would be irresponsible. Let's consider what might happen if researchers brought their own biases to the investigation. A person investigating the impact of intercollegiate sports on alumni contributions, for example, might focus only on the highly visible revenue-generating sports of football and basketball and neglect the so-called minor sports, such as tennis or soccer, which are more likely to involve women athletes. Despite the early work of W. E. B. DuBois and Jane Addams, sociologists still need to be reminded that the discipline often fails to adequately consider all people's social behavior.

In her book *The Death of White Sociology* (1973), Joyce Ladner called attention to the tendency of mainstream sociology to treat the lives of African Americans as a social problem. More recently, feminist sociologist Shulamit Reinharz (1992) has argued that sociological research should be not only inclusive but also open to bringing about social change and to drawing on relevant research by nonsociologists. Both Ladner and Reinharz maintain that researchers should always analyze whether women's unequal social status has affected their studies in any way. For example, one might broaden the study of the impact of education on income to consider the implications of the unequal pay status of men and women. The issue of value neutrality does not mean that sociologists can't have opinions, but it does mean that they must work to overcome any biases, however unintentional, that they may bring to their analysis of research.

Sociologist Peter Rossi (1987) admits to having liberal inclinations that direct him to certain fields of study. Yet in line with Weber's view of value neutrality, Rossi's commitment to rigorous research methods and objective interpretation of data has sometimes led him to controversial findings that are not necessarily supportive of his liberal values. For example, his measure of the extent of homelessness in Chicago in the mid-1980s fell far below the estimates of the Chicago Coalition for the Homeless. Coalition members bitterly attacked Rossi for hampering their social reform efforts by minimizing the extent of homelessness. Rossi (1987:79) concluded that "in the short term, good social research will often be greeted as a betrayal of one or another side to a particular controversy."

MODULE 7 | **Recap and Review**

Summary

Sociologists must abide by certain ethical principles when conducting research.

1. The *Code of Ethics* of the American Sociological Association calls for objectivity and integrity in research, confidentiality, and disclosure of all sources of financial support.

2. Max Weber urged sociologists to practice value neutrality in their research by ensuring that their personal feelings do not influence their interpretation of data.

Thinking Critically

1. If you were planning to do research on human sexuality, which of the seven principles in the ASA's *Code of Ethics* would particularly concern you? What ethical problems might arise in such a study, and how would you attempt to prevent them?

2. Why did Max Weber specify the need for neutrality in the interpretation of data? Is complete value neutrality possible in sociological research? To what extent should researchers try to overcome their own biases?

Key Terms

Code of ethics

Value neutrality

MODULE 8 | **Developments of Methodology**

Feminist Methodology

Of the five theoretical perspectives introduced in Module 3, the feminist perspective has had the greatest impact on the current generation of social researchers. How might this perspective influence research? Although researchers must be objective, their theoretical orientation may influence the questions they ask—or just as important, the questions they fail to ask. Until recently, for example, researchers frequently studied work and the family separately. Yet feminist theorists see the two spheres of activity as being closely integrated. Similarly, work and leisure, paid and unpaid domestic work may be seen not as two separate spheres, but as two sides of the same coin.

Recently, feminist scholars have become interested in self-injury, a practice described at the beginning of this chapter. Research shows that 85 percent of self-injurers are female; feminist researchers seek to explain why women predominate in this population. Rather than treat the behavior as a medical disorder, they note that society encourages women much more than men to attend to their bodies through hair removal,

skin treatments, and depigmentation. Given this heightened attention to the female body, feminists suggest that specific instances of victimization can lead women to self-injure. They also seek to better understand male self-injurers, and are testing the hypothesis that among men, self-injury is a manifestation of hypermasculinity in the tolerance of pain (P. Adler and P. Adler 2011:25–27, 35–36).

The feminist perspective has also had an impact on global research. To feminist theorists, the traditional distinction between industrial nations and developing nations overlooks the close relationship between these two supposedly separate worlds. Feminist theorists have called for more research on the special role that immigrant women play in maintaining their households; on the use of domestic workers from less developed nations by households in industrial nations; and on the global trafficking of sex workers (Cheng 2003; Cooper et al. 2007; Sprague 2005).

Feminist researchers tend to involve and consult their subjects more than other researchers, and they are more oriented toward seeking change, raising the public consciousness, and influencing policy. They are particularly open to a multidisciplinary approach, such as making use of historical evidence or legal studies (T. Baker 1999; Lofland 1975; Reinharz 1992).

Feminist theorists see the global trafficking of sex workers as a sign of the close relationship between the supposedly separate worlds of industrial nations and dependent developing nations.

Queer Theory and Methodology

If researchers wish to generalize about society, their findings must be representative of all people. Over the last generation, feminist theorists have insisted that women deserve as much attention from researchers as men. Similarly, exponents of queer theory ask whether researchers consider gays and lesbians in their studies, or simply assume that the generalizations they make apply to everyone, whether heterosexual or gay?

According to the National Bureau of Economic Research, most research significantly underreports the proportion of gays and lesbians in the population; it also underestimates the percentage of people who hold anti-gay views. The bureau suggests using a "veiled reporting" technique, in which respondents are asked whether they consider themselves to be heterosexual in the context of other much less sensitive questions, such as "Did you spend a lot of time playing video games as a child?"

FIGURE 8-1 Seeing Boston's Housing Issues

Housing Issues in Boston
Highest

Lowest

More and more data are available to researchers. Boston scholars identified a link between citizen requests for city services and housing conditions. The areas with darker color registered more complaints and had lower-quality housing overall.

Source: Based on citizen complaints data summarized in Boston Area Research Initiative 2013.

In one study, when respondents were asked about their sexual orientation within a group of such questions, 19 percent of them reported that they were nonheterosexual; when the question was asked more directly, the proportion was 11 percent (Coffman et al. 2013).

This study suggests that if researchers want to generalize about *both* heterosexuals and homosexuals, they should be extremely careful in wording questions about respondents' sexual orientation—compared even to other sensitive topics, such as political and religious affiliations.

The Data-Rich Future

Advances in technology have affected all aspects of our lives, and sociological research is no exception. Massive increases in available data have allowed sociologists to undertake research

Lying for Love Online

Today, about 40 million people seek love online, and according to one estimate, 21 percent of heterosexual couples and 61 percent of same-sex couples meet online. But do these people tell the truth in their online postings? Not always, and not often.

Data gathered from online dating sites like Match.com, OkCupid, and Yahoo reveal both truthfulness and deception in people's online postings:

- In their profiles, people often describe an idealized self—for example, "I rock climb."
- Women typically describe themselves as 8.5 pounds heavier than they really are; men, as 2 pounds lighter.
- Men are more likely than women to say they are younger, taller, and wealthier than they really are.
- Less attractive people often post enhanced or retouched photos.
- Women post photos that are an average of 1.5 years old; men post photos that are 6 months old.
- Men are more likely than women to lie about their occupation, education, and relationship status.

Although much of the time these deceptions may be small, their widespread nature has made them an almost expected part of the game. In one study, a man who

> Men are more likely than women to say they are younger, taller, and wealthier than they really are.

posted a five-year-old photograph said he looked the "same" now except that he had a beard. In another case, a woman saw no problem in listing her occupation as "marketing" rather than retail sales. After all, she explained, "it's not like me saying I'm a janitor, and then lying and saying that I'm a CEO." That, she concluded, would be unacceptable.

Little wonder that research shows daters like the personalities they meet online better than the ones they meet in person.

LET'S DISCUSS

1. Have you tried using an online dating service? If so, were you truthful in describing yourself online? Did the people you were matched with turn out to be truthful?

2. Why do you think online daters engage in deception if they are hoping eventually to meet someone face-to-face?

Sources: N. Ellison et al. 2012; R. Epstein 2009; Gelles 2011; Rosenbloom 2011; Toma et al. 2008; Toma and Hancock 2010.

---

that was virtually impossible just a decade ago. In the recent past, only people with grants or major institutional support could work easily with large amounts of data. Now anyone with a computer can access huge amounts of data and learn more about social behavior.

Across the United States, cities and towns of all sizes receive and record citizens' complaints. Sometimes those complaints are acted on; sometimes, for a variety of reasons, they are merely recorded into a database. In Boston, researchers found a treasure trove of data on housing complaints, covering everything from poor heating and chronic dampness to the presence of pests, such as bedbugs. Hundreds of thousands of calls had been recorded along with specific addresses, allowing researchers to compare housing conditions from one neighborhood to another.

Researchers soon realized that the data could be mapped to show the relative seriousness of the city's housing problems at a glance. Figure 8-1 presents a map of Boston's neighborhoods,

color-coded based on the distribution of requests for city services made over a more than two-year period. The darker the color, the greater the number of complaints. As the team noted, the data are not an exact indication of "problem housing areas," because homeowners are much more likely than renters to call for government assistance, regardless of their income. Conversely, problems often go unreported in neighborhoods where renters dominate, whether tenants are rich or poor (O'Brien et al. 2013; Scharfenberg 2013).

In foreign countries, data are sometimes as available as they are in the United States. From 2009 through fall 2013, countries around the world experienced intense bursts of influenza. How did medical researchers track the virus's spread across a nation, much less the world? Epidemiologists typically rely on reports that originate in doctors' offices and are funneled through government agencies. Data collection is a time-consuming process, with many days passing between the detection of symptoms and the publication of official statistics. However, public health researchers may have found a way to track contagious diseases using Google. By monitoring the topics people search for and compensating for the relative access to computers in different countries (high in Sweden and low in Nigeria, for example), they can monitor the spread of disease almost in real time. Although their first efforts at online data tracking overestimated the outbreak, their accuracy improves with each passing year (Dukić et al. 2011; D. Lazer et al. 2014).

Similarly, in the past sociologists had to rely on victims' complaints or police reports to understand crime patterns. Now they are beginning to access real-time, geocoded (that is, location-specific) incident reports. These new data will offer sociologists much more information, which they can interpret and relate to other aspects of the social environment (G. King 2011). Box 8-1 describes some new opportunities the Internet offers to researchers who study dating and mate selection (and who once were confined to surveying undergraduates).

One ethical concern raised by all these data involves individual privacy. Sociologists now have access to information about people's real estate transactions, campaign contributions, online product purchases, and even travel along tollways. What steps should they take to protect the privacy of the individuals whose data they are using? This is not an academic question. Today, 87 percent of the people in the United States can be personally identified given only their gender, date of birth, and ZIP code (G. King 2011).

We have seen that researchers rely on a number of tools, from time-tested observational research and use of existing sources to the latest in computer technologies. The Social Policy section that follows will describe researchers' efforts to survey the general population about a controversial aspect of social behavior: human sexuality. This investigation was complicated by its potential social policy implications. Because in the real world, sociological research can have far-reaching consequences for public policy and public welfare, each of the following chapters in this book will close with a Social Policy section.

social policy and Sociological Research|
Studying Human Sexuality

How can researchers study human sexual behavior? Neuroscientists Ogi Ogas and Sai Gaddam (2011) studied millions of web searches, websites, and videos related to sex. They found that women and men differ decidedly in their preferences, but found very little (if any) distinction between heterosexuals and homosexuals, other than their sexual orientation. This type of research has significant limitations, however. Ogas and Gaddam could not distinguish between online fantasies and rational desires, or between a single search and one of many repeated searches by the same person. Nevertheless, this cyber study is a step forward in the effort to understand human sexual behavior (Bartlett 2011).

Looking at the Issue

In this age of devastating sexually transmitted diseases, there is no time more important to increase our scientific understanding of human sexuality. As we will see, however, this is a difficult topic to research, not only because of privacy concerns but because of all the preconceptions, myths, and beliefs people bring to the subject of sexuality. Many people actively oppose research on human sexuality. How does one carry out scientific research on such a controversial and personal topic?

Applying Sociology

Sociologists have little reliable national data on patterns of sexual behavior in the United States. Until the 1990s, the only comprehensive study of sexual behavior was the famous two-volume *Kinsey Report,* prepared in the 1940s (Kinsey et al. 1948, 1953; see also Igo 2007). Although the *Kinsey Report* is still widely quoted, the volunteers interviewed for the report were not representative of the nation's adult population.

In part, we lack reliable data on patterns of sexual behavior because it is difficult for researchers to obtain accurate information about this sensitive subject. Moreover, until AIDS emerged in the 1980s, there was little scientific demand for data on sexual behavior, except for specific concerns such as contraception. And even though the AIDS crisis has reached dramatic proportions, government funding for studies of sexual behavior is still controversial and therefore difficult to obtain.

The controversy surrounding research on human sexual behavior raises the issue of value neutrality, which becomes especially delicate when one considers the relationship of sociology to the government. The federal government has become the major source of funding for sociological research. Yet Max Weber urged that sociology remain an autonomous discipline and not become unduly influenced by any one

—Continued

Sex may sell, but persuading legislators to fund research on human sexual behavior is still a challenge.

segment of society. According to Weber's ideal of value neutrality, sociologists must remain free to reveal information that is embarrassing to the government, or for that matter, supportive of government institutions.

Initiating Policy

In 1987 the National Institute of Child Health and Human Development sought proposals for a national survey of sexual behavior. Sociologists responded with various plans that a review panel of scientists approved for funding. However, in 1991, the U.S. Senate voted to forbid funding any survey of adult sexual practices. Despite the vote, sociologists developed the National Health and Social Life Survey (NHSLS) to better understand the sexual practices of adults in the United States. The researchers raised $1.6 million of *private* funding to make their study possible (Laumann et al. 1994a, 1994b).

The authors of the NHSLS believe that their research is important. They argue that data from their survey allow interest groups to more easily address public policy issues such as AIDS, sexual harassment, welfare reform, sex discrimination, abortion, teenage pregnancy, and family planning. Moreover, the research findings help to counter some commonsense notions. For instance, contrary to the popular beliefs that women regularly use abortion for birth control and that poor teens are the most likely socioeconomic group to have abortions, researchers found that three-fourths of all abortions are the first for the woman, and that well-educated and affluent women are more likely to have abortions than poor teens (Sweet 2001).

The usefulness of the NHSLS in addressing public policy issues has proved influential. As Figure 8-2 shows, scholars around the world are now studying human sexual behavior, in an effort to reduce the occurrence of HIV/AIDS.

FIGURE 8-2 Median Age of First Sex

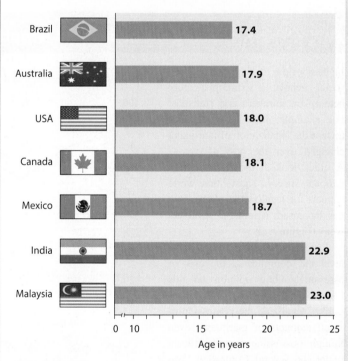

Source: Durex 2007.

TAKE THE ISSUE WITH YOU

1. Do you see any merit in the position of those who oppose government funding for research on sexual behavior? Explain your reasoning.

2. Exactly how could the results of research on human sexual behavior be used to control sexually transmitted diseases?

3. Compare the issue of value neutrality in government-funded research to the same issue in corporate-funded research. Are concerns about conflict of interest more or less serious in regard to government funding?

Summary

Feminist theory and technological change have had important impacts on sociological research.

1. The feminist perspective has affected the questions sociologists ask, what groups they choose to study, the methods they use, and how globalization influences research.

2. Technology plays an important role in sociological research, whether it be a computer database or information obtained from the Internet.

3. Despite failure to obtain government funding, researchers developed the National Health and Social Life Survey (NHSLS) to better understand the sexual practices of adults in the United States.

Thinking Critically

1. Even if women are represented in a study, could the researcher's gender influence the data that are collected? If so, how? How might the problem be prevented?

2. Male sociologists once overlooked women in their studies of city life. What other groups could easily be overlooked in today's research, and why?

3. Suppose that you are a sociologist. You are trying to obtain funding for a study of adult sexual behavior from a government source. What arguments would you make to convince the government to fund your study?

Appendix | Using Statistics and Graphs

In their effort to better understand social behavior, sociologists rely heavily on numbers and statistics. For example, how have attitudes toward the legalization of marijuana changed over the past 45 years? A quick look at the results of 14 national surveys shows that while support for legalization of the drug has increased, it remains relatively weak (Figure A-2).

Recent legislation on the state level has complicated the task of assessing public opinion on this issue. Some states have passed initiatives legalizing the possession of small amounts of marijuana, even though possession remains illegal under the federal Controlled Substances Act. Researchers now must track how public opinion may differ from the national trend in states where marijuana use is both tolerated and legal.

FIGURE A-2 **Changing Attitudes toward the Legalization of Marijuana**

Do you think the use of marijuana should be made legal, or not?

Source: Gallup 2012; see Newport 2012 in references.

Using Statistics

The most common summary measures used by sociologists are percentages, means, modes, and medians. A **percentage** is a portion of 100. Use of percentages allows us to compare groups of different sizes. For example, if we were comparing financial contributors to a town's Baptist and Roman Catholic churches, the absolute numbers

of contributors in each group could be misleading if there were many more Baptists than Catholics in the town. By using percentages, we could obtain a more meaningful comparison, showing the proportion of persons in each group who contribute to churches.

The **mean,** or *average,* is a number calculated by adding a series of values and then dividing by the number of values. For example, to find the mean of the numbers 5, 19, and 27, we would add them together (for a total of 51), divide by the number of values (3), and discover that the mean is 17.

The **mode** is the single most common value in a series of scores. Suppose we were looking at the following scores on a 10-point quiz:

10 10 9 9 8 8 7 7 7 6 5

The mode—the most frequent score on the quiz—is 7. While the mode is easier to identify than other summary measures, it tells sociologists little about all the other values. Hence, you will find much less use of the mode in this book than of the mean and the median.

The **median** is the midpoint or number that divides a series of values into two groups of equal numbers of values. For the quiz just discussed, the median, or central value, is 8. The mean, or average, would be 86 (the sum of all scores) divided by 11 (the total number of scores), or 7.8.

Some of these statistics may seem confusing at first. But think how difficult it is to comb through an endless list of numbers to identify a pattern or central tendency. Percentages, means, modes, and medians are essential time-savers in sociological research and analysis.

Reading Graphs

Tables and figures (that is, graphs) allow social scientists to display data and develop their conclusions more easily. In December 2012, the Gallup poll interviewed 1,015 people in the United States age 18 and over, by both cell phone and landlines. Each respondent was asked, "Do you think the use of marijuana should be made legal, or not?" Without some type of summary, there is no way that analysts could examine the hundreds of individual responses to this question and reach firm conclusions. One type of summary sociologists use, a **cross-tabulation,** shows the relationship between two or more variables. Through the cross-tabulations presented graphically in Figure A-3, we can quickly see that older people are less likely to favor the legalization of marijuana than younger people, and that Republicans are less supportive of legalization than Democrats.

Graphs, like tables, can be quite useful to sociologists. And illustrations are often easier for the general public to understand, whether in newspapers or in PowerPoint presentations. Still, as with all data, we need to be careful how they are presented.

FIGURE A-3 **People Who Favor Legalization of Marijuana by Political Affiliation and Age**

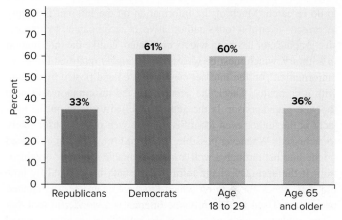

Source: Gallup 2012; see Newport 2012 in references.

Appendix II **Writing a Research Report**

Let's say you have decided to write a report on cohabitation (unmarried couples living together). How do you go about doing the necessary library research? Students must follow procedures similar to those used by sociologists in conducting original research. For your first step you must define the problem that you wish to study—perhaps in this case, how much cohabitation occurs and what its impact is on later marital happiness. The next step is to review the literature, which generally requires library research.

Finding Information

The following steps will be helpful in finding information:

1. Don't forget to begin with the materials closest at hand. Check this textbook and other textbooks that you own.

2. Use the library's online catalog. Computerized library systems now access not only the college library's collection but also books and magazines from other libraries, available through interlibrary loans. These systems allow you to search for books by author or title. You can use title searches to locate books by subject as well. For example, if you search the title base for the keyword *cohabitation,* you will learn where books with that word in the title are located in the library's stacks. Near those books will be other works on cohabitation, which may not happen to have that word in the title. You may also want to search other, related keywords, such as *unmarried couples.*

3. Investigate using computerized periodical indexes, if they are available in your library. *Sociological Abstracts* online covers most sociological writing since 1952. In 2014, a search of just this one database found exactly 2,438 documents having either *cohabitation* or *unmarried couples* as keywords. Some dealt with laws about cohabitation, while others focused on trends in other countries. If you limited your topic to same-sex couples, you would find 137 citations. Other electronic databases cover general-interest periodicals (*Time, Ms., National Review, Atlantic Monthly,* and so forth), reference materials, or newspapers. These electronic systems may be connected to a printer, allowing you to produce a printout complete with bibliographic information, and sometimes even complete copies of articles.

4. Examine government documents. The U.S. government, states and cities, and the United Nations publish information on virtually every subject of interest to social science researchers. Publications of the Census Bureau, for example, include tables showing the number of unmarried couples living together and some social characteristics of those households.

5. Use newspapers. Major newspapers publish annual or even weekly indexes that are useful in locating information about specific events or issues. Lexis-Nexis is an electronic index to U.S. and international newspapers.

6. Ask people, organizations, and agencies concerned with the topic for information and assistance. Be as specific as possible in making requests. You might receive very different information on the issue of cohabitation from talking with marriage counselors and with clergy from different religions.

7. If you run into difficulties, consult the instructor or the reference librarian at your college library.

A word of caution: be extremely careful in using the Internet to do research. Much of the information on the Internet is simply incorrect—even if it looks authoritative, is accompanied by impressive graphics, or has been widely circulated. Unlike the information in a library, which must be screened by a highly qualified librarian, "information" on the Internet can be created and posted by anyone with a computer. Check the sources for the information and note the web page sponsor. Is the author qualified to write on the subject? Is the author even identified? Is the web page sponsor likely to be biased? Whenever possible, try to confirm what you have read on the Internet through a well-known, reputable source or organization. If the accuracy of the information could be affected by how old it is, check the date on which the page or article was created or updated. Used intelligently, the Internet is a wonderful tool that offers students access to many of the reliable print sources noted earlier, including government documents and newspaper archives extending back over a century.

Writing the Report

Once you have completed all your research, you can begin writing the report. Here are a few tips:

- Be sure the topic you have chosen is not too broad. You must be able to cover it adequately in a reasonable amount of time and a reasonable number of pages.

- Develop an outline for your report. You should have an introduction and a conclusion that relate to each other, and the discussion should proceed logically throughout the paper. Use headings within the paper if they will improve clarity and organization.

- Do not leave all the writing until the last minute. It is best to write a rough draft, let it sit for a few days, and then take a fresh look before beginning revisions.

- If possible, read your paper aloud. Doing so may be helpful in locating sections or phrases that don't make sense.

Remember that you *must* cite all information you have obtained from other sources, including the Internet. Plagiarism is a serious academic offense, for which the penalties are severe. If you use an author's exact words, it is essential that you place them in quotation marks. Even if you reworked someone else's ideas, you must indicate the source of those ideas.

Mastering This Chapter

taking sociology with you

1 Think about a job you are interested in. How can you see yourself using research techniques—surveys, observation, experiments, or existing sources—in that occupation?

2 How can a sociologist genuinely maintain value neutrality while studying a group that he or she finds repugnant (for example, a White supremacist organization, a satanic cult, or a group of convicted rapists)?

3 New technologies have benefited sociological research by facilitating surveys and statistical analysis. Can you think of any potential drawbacks these new technologies might have for sociological investigation?

Causal logic The relationship between a condition or variable and a particular consequence, with one leading to the other.

Code of ethics The standards of acceptable behavior developed by and for members of a profession.

Content analysis The systematic coding and objective recording of data, guided by some rationale.

Control group The subjects in an experiment who are not introduced to the independent variable by the researcher.

Control variable A factor that is held constant to test the relative impact of an independent variable.

Correlation A relationship between two variables in which a change in one coincides with a change in the other.

Cross-tabulation A table or matrix that shows the relationship between two or more variables.

Dependent variable The variable in a causal relationship that is subject to the influence of another variable.

Ethnography The study of an entire social setting through extended systematic fieldwork.

Experiment An artificially created situation that allows a researcher to manipulate variables.

Experimental group The subjects in an experiment who are exposed to an independent variable introduced by a researcher.

Hawthorne effect The unintended influence that observers of experiments can have on their subjects.

Hypothesis A speculative statement about the relationship between two or more variables.

Independent variable The variable in a causal relationship that causes or influences a change in another variable.

Interview A face-to-face, phone, or online questioning of a respondent to obtain desired information.

Mean A number calculated by adding a series of values and then dividing by the number of values.

Median The midpoint or number that divides a series of values into two groups of equal numbers of values.

Mode The single most common value in a series of scores.

Observation A research technique in which an investigator collects information through direct participation, by closely watching a group or community.

Operational definition An explanation of an abstract concept that is specific enough to allow a researcher to assess the concept.

Percentage A portion of 100.

Qualitative research Research that relies on what is seen in field or naturalistic settings more than on statistical data.

Quantitative research Research that collects and reports data primarily in numerical form.

Questionnaire A printed or written form used to obtain information from a respondent.

Random sample A sample for which every member of an entire population has the same chance of being selected.

Reliability The extent to which a measure produces consistent results.

Research design A detailed plan or method for obtaining data scientifically.

Sample A selection from a larger population that is statistically representative of that population.

Scientific method A systematic, organized series of steps that ensures maximum objectivity and consistency in researching a problem.

Secondary analysis A variety of research techniques that make use of previously collected and publicly accessible information and data.

Survey A study, generally in the form of an interview or questionnaire, that provides researchers with information about how people think and act.

Validity The degree to which a measure or scale truly reflects the phenomenon under study.

Value neutrality Max Weber's term for objectivity of sociologists in the interpretation of data.

Variable A measurable trait or characteristic that is subject to change under different conditions.

Read each question carefully and then select the best answer.

1. The first step in any sociological research project is to
   a. collect data.
   b. define the problem.
   c. review previous research.
   d. formulate a hypothesis.

2. An explanation of an abstract concept that is specific enough to allow a researcher to measure the concept is a(n)
   a. hypothesis.
   b. correlation.
   c. operational definition.
   d. variable.

3. The variable hypothesized to cause or influence another is called the
   a. dependent variable.
   b. hypothetical variable.
   c. correlation variable.
   d. independent variable.

4. A correlation exists when
   a. one variable causes something to occur in another variable.
   b. two or more variables are causally related.
   c. a change in one variable coincides with a change in another variable.
   d. a negative relationship exists between two variables.

5. Through which type of research technique does a sociologist ensure that data are statistically representative of the population being studied?
   a. sampling
   b. experiments
   c. ethnography
   d. control variables

6. In order to obtain a random sample, a researcher might
   a. administer a questionnaire to every fifth woman who enters a business office.
   b. examine the attitudes of residents of a city by interviewing every 20th name in the city's telephone book.
   c. study the attitudes of registered Democratic voters by choosing every 10th name found on a city's list of registered Democrats.
   d. do all of the above.

7. A researcher can obtain a higher response rate by using which type of survey?
   a. an interview
   b. a questionnaire
   c. representative samples
   d. ethnographic techniques

8. In the 1930s, William F. Whyte moved into a low-income Italian neighborhood in Boston. For nearly four years, he was a member of the social circle of "corner boys" that he describes in *Street Corner Society*. His goal was to gain greater insight into the community established by these men. What type of research technique did Whyte use?
   a. experiment
   b. survey
   c. secondary analysis
   d. participant observation

9. When sociologists want to study a possible cause-and-effect relationship, they may engage in what kind of research technique?
   a. ethnography
   b. survey research
   c. secondary analysis
   d. experiment

10. Émile Durkheim's statistical analysis of suicide was an example of what kind of research technique?
   a. ethnography
   b. observation research
   c. secondary analysis
   d. experimental research

11. Unlike the typical citizen, the sociologist has a commitment to use the _____ method in studying society.

12. A(n) _____ is a speculative statement about the relationship between two or more factors known as variables.

13. _____ refers to the degree to which a measure or scale truly reflects the phenomenon under study.

14. In order to obtain data scientifically, researchers need to select a research _____.

15. If scientists were testing a new type of toothpaste in an experimental setting, they would administer the toothpaste to a(n) _____ group, but not to a(n) _____ group.

16. The term _____ _____ refers to the unintended influence that observers of experiments can have on their subjects.

17. Using census data in a way unintended by its initial collectors would be an example of _____ _____.

18. Using _____ _____, researchers conducted a study of gender-stereotyped behavior in children's coloring books.

19. The American Sociological Association's *Code of* _____ requires sociologists to maintain objectivity and integrity and to preserve the confidentiality of their subjects.

20. As part of their commitment to _____ neutrality, investigators have an ethical obligation to accept research findings even when the data run counter to their personal views or to widely accepted beliefs.

Answers

1 (b); 2 (c); 3 (d); 4 (c); 5 (a); 6 (c); 7 (a); 8 (d); 9 (d); 10 (c); 11 scientific; 12 hypothesis; 13 Validity; 14 design; 15 experimental, control; 16 Hawthorne effect; 17 secondary analysis; 18 content analysis; 19 *Ethics*; 20 value

3
Culture

In Kenya, Maasai tribesmen ride bicycles through Masai Mara National Park. Shared learned behavior—what we call culture—can move across international borders to become part of other societies.

What do you think of the society described here by anthropologist Horace Miner?

Could you live in such a culture?

❝ Nacirema culture is characterized by a highly developed market economy which has evolved in a rich natural habitat. While much of the people's time is devoted to economic pursuits, a large part of the fruits of these labors and a considerable portion of the day are spent in ritual activity. The focus of this activity is the human body, the appearance and health of which loom as a dominant concern in the ethos of the people. While such a concern is certainly not unusual, its ceremonial aspects and associated philosophy are unique.

The fundamental belief underlying the whole system appears to be that the human body is ugly and that its natural tendency is to debility and disease. Incarcerated in such a body, man's only hope is to avert these characteristics through the use of the powerful influences of ritual and ceremony. Every household has one or more shrines devoted to this purpose. The more powerful individuals in the society have several shrines in their houses and, in fact, the opulence of a house is often referred to in terms of the number of such ritual centers it possesses. Most houses are of wattle and daub construction, but the shrine rooms of the more wealthy are walled with stone. Poorer families imitate the rich by applying pottery plaques to their shrine walls.

The focal point of the shrine is a box or chest which is built into the wall. In this chest are kept the many charms and magical potions without which no native believes he could live.

While each family has at least one such shrine, the rituals associated with it are not family ceremonies but are private and secret. The rites are normally only discussed with children, and then only during the period when they are being initiated into these mysteries. I was able, however, to establish sufficient rapport with the natives to examine these shrines and to have the rituals described to me.

The focal point of the shrine is a box or chest which is built into the wall. In this chest are kept the many charms and magical potions without which no native believes he could live. These preparations are secured from a variety of specialized practitioners. The most powerful of these are the medicine men, whose assistance must be rewarded with substantial gifts. However, the medicine men do not provide the curative potions for their clients, but decide what the ingredients should be and then write them down in an ancient and secret language. This writing is understood only by the medicine men and by the herbalists who, for another gift, provide the required charm.

The charm is not disposed of after it has served its purpose, but is placed in the charm-box of the household shrine. As these magical materials are specific for certain ills, and the real or imagined maladies of the people are many, the charm-box is usually full to overflowing. The magical packets are so numerous that people forget what their purposes were and fear to use them again. While the natives are very vague on this point, we can only assume that the idea in retaining all the old magical materials is that their presence in the charm-box, before which the body rituals are conducted, will in some way protect the worshipper. ❞

(Miner 1956:503–504)

In this excerpt from his journal article "Body Ritual among the Nacirema," Horace Miner casts an anthropologist's observant eye on the intriguing rituals of an exotic culture. If some aspects of this culture seem familiar to you, you are right, for what Miner is describing is actually the culture of the United States ("Nacirema" is "American" spelled backward). The "shrine" Miner writes of is the bathroom; he correctly informs us that in this culture, one measure of wealth is how many bathrooms one's home has. In their bathroom rituals, he goes on, the Nacirema use charms and magical potions (beauty products and prescription drugs) obtained from specialized practitioners (such as hair stylists), herbalists (pharmacists), and medicine men (physicians). Using our sociological imaginations, we could update Miner's description of the Nacirema's charms, written in 1956, by adding tooth whiteners, anti-aging creams, Waterpiks, and hair gel.

When we step back and examine a culture thoughtfully and objectively, whether it is our own culture in disguise or another less familiar to us, we learn something new about society. Take Fiji, an island in the Pacific where a robust, nicely rounded body has always been the ideal for both men and women. This is a society in which traditionally, "You've gained weight" has been considered a compliment, and "Your legs are skinny," an insult. Yet a recent study shows that for the first time, eating disorders have been showing up among young people in Fiji. What has happened to change their body image? Since the introduction of cable television in 1995, many Fiji islanders, especially young women, have begun to emulate not their mothers and aunts, but the small-waisted stars of television programs currently airing there, like *Gossip Girl* and *Modern Family*. Studying culture in places like Fiji, then, sheds light on our society as well (A. Becker 2007; Fiji TV 2012).

In these four modules we will see just how basic the study of culture is to sociology. Our discussion will focus both on general cultural practices found in all societies and on the wide variations that can distinguish one society from another. We will define and explore the major aspects of culture, including language, norms, sanctions, and values. We will see how cultures develop a dominant ideology, and how functionalist and conflict theorists view culture. And we'll study the development of culture around the world, including the cultural effects of the worldwide movement toward globalization. Finally, in the Social Policy section, we will look at the conflicts in cultural values that underlie current debates over bilingualism.

MODULE 9 | What Is Culture?

Culture is the totality of learned, socially transmitted customs, knowledge, material objects, and behavior. It includes the ideas, values, and artifacts (for example, DVDs, comic books, and birth control devices) of groups of people. Patriotic attachment to the flag of the United States is an aspect of culture, as is a national passion for the tango in Argentina.

Sometimes people refer to a particular person as "very cultured" or to a city as having "lots of culture." That use of the term *culture* is different from our use in this textbook. In sociological terms, culture does not refer solely to the fine arts and refined intellectual taste. It consists of *all* objects and ideas within a society, including slang words, ice-cream cones, and rock music. Sociologists consider both a portrait by Rembrandt and the work of graffiti spray painters to be aspects of culture. A tribe that cultivates soil by hand has just as much culture as a people that relies on computer-operated machinery. Each people has a distinctive culture with its own characteristic ways of gathering and preparing food, constructing homes, structuring the family, and promoting standards of right and wrong.

The fact that you share a similar culture with others helps to define the group or society to which you belong. A fairly large number of people are said to constitute a **society** when they live in the same territory, are relatively independent of people outside their area, and participate in a common culture. Metropolitan Los Angeles is more populous than at least 150 nations, yet sociologists do not consider it a society in its own right. Rather, they see it as part of—and dependent on—the larger society of the United States.

A society is the largest form of human group. It consists of people who share a common heritage and culture. Members of the society learn this culture and transmit it from one generation to the next. They even preserve their distinctive culture through literature, art, video recordings, and other means of expression.

Sociologists have long recognized the many ways in which culture influences human behavior. Through what has been termed a tool kit of habits, skills, and styles, people of a common culture construct their acquisition of knowledge, their interactions with kinfolk, their entrance into the job market—in short, the way in which they live. If it were not for the social transmission of culture, each generation would have to reinvent television, not to mention the wheel (Swidler 1986).

Having a common culture also simplifies many day-to-day interactions. For example, when you buy an airline ticket, you know you don't have to bring along hundreds of dollars in cash. You can pay with a credit card. When you are part of a society, you take for granted many small (as well as more important) cultural patterns. You assume that theaters will provide seats for the audience, that physicians will not disclose confidential information, and that parents will be careful when crossing the street with young children. All these assumptions reflect basic values, beliefs, and customs of the culture of the United States.

Today, when text, sound, and video can be transmitted around the world instantaneously, some aspects of culture transcend

Cultural practices vary across societies. In China, married couples rarely wear wedding rings. To signify their commitment, couples who appear in public often sport matching or complementary outfits.

national borders. The German philosopher Theodor Adorno and others have spoken of the worldwide **culture industry** that standardizes the goods and services demanded by consumers. Adorno contends that globally, the primary effect of popular culture is to limit people's choices. Yet others have shown that the culture industry's influence does not always permeate international borders. Sometimes the culture industry is embraced; at other times, soundly rejected (Adorno [1971] 1991:98–106; Horkheimer and Adorno [1944] 2002).

Cultural Universals

All societies have developed certain common practices and beliefs, known as **cultural universals.** Many cultural universals are, in fact, adaptations to meet essential human needs, such as the need for food, shelter, and clothing. Anthropologist George Murdock (1945:124) compiled a list of cultural universals, including athletic sports, cooking, dancing, visiting, personal names, marriage, medicine, religious ritual, funeral ceremonies, sexual restrictions, and trade.

The cultural practices Murdock listed may be universal, but the manner in which they are expressed varies from culture to culture. For example, one society may let its members choose their marriage partners; another may encourage marriages arranged by the parents.

Not only does the expression of cultural universals vary from one society to another; within a society, it may also change dramatically over time. Each generation, and each year for that matter, most human cultures change and expand.

Ethnocentrism

Many everyday statements reflect our attitude that our culture is best. We use terms such as *underdeveloped, backward,* and *primitive* to refer to other societies. What "we" believe is a religion; what "they" believe is superstition and mythology.

It is tempting to evaluate the practices of other cultures on the basis of our perspectives. Sociologist William Graham Sumner (1906) coined the term **ethnocentrism** to refer to the tendency to assume that one's own culture and way of life represent the norm or are superior to all others. The ethnocentric person sees his or her group as the center or defining point of culture and views all other cultures as deviations from what is "normal." Westerners who think cattle are to be used for food might look down on India's Hindu religion and culture, which view the cow as sacred. Or people in one culture may dismiss as unthinkable the mate selection or child-rearing practices of another culture. In sum, our view of the world is dramatically influenced by the society in which we were raised.

Ethnocentrism is hardly limited to citizens of the United States. Visitors from many African cultures are surprised at the disrespect that children in the United States show their parents. People from India may be repelled by our practice of living in the same household with dogs and cats. Many Islamic fundamentalists in the Arab world and Asia view the United States as corrupt, decadent, and doomed to destruction. All these people may feel comforted by membership in cultures that in their view are superior to ours.

Cultural Relativism

While ethnocentrism means evaluating foreign cultures using the familiar culture of the observer as a standard of correct behavior, **cultural relativism** means viewing people's behavior from the perspective of their own culture. It places a priority on understanding other cultures, rather than dismissing them as "strange" or "exotic." Unlike ethnocentrists, cultural relativists employ the kind of value neutrality in scientific study that Max Weber saw as so important.

Cultural relativism stresses that different social contexts give rise to different norms and values. Thus, we must examine practices such as polygamy, bullfighting, and monarchy within the particular contexts of the cultures in which they are found. Although cultural relativism does not suggest that we must unquestionably accept every cultural variation, it does require a serious and unbiased effort to evaluate norms, values, and customs in light of their distinctive culture.

Consider the practice of children marrying adults. Most people in North America cannot fathom the idea of a 12-year-old girl marrying. The custom, which is illegal in the United States, is common in West Africa and South Asia. Should the United States respect such marriages? The apparent answer is no. In 2006 the U.S. government spent $623 million to discourage the practice in many of the countries with the highest child-marriage rates (Figure 9-1).

From the perspective of cultural relativism, we might ask whether one society should spend its resources to dictate the norms of another. However, federal officials have defended the government's actions. They contend that child marriage deprives girls of education, threatens their health, and weakens public health efforts to combat HIV/AIDS (Jain and Kurz 2007; B. Slavin 2007).

Sociobiology and Culture

While sociology emphasizes diversity and change in the expression of culture, another school of thought, sociobiology, stresses the universal aspects of culture. **Sociobiology** is the systematic study of how biology affects human social behavior. Sociobiologists assert that many of the cultural traits humans display, such as the almost universal expectation that women will be nurturers and men will be providers, are not learned but are rooted in our genetic makeup.

Sociobiology is founded on the naturalist Charles Darwin's (1859) theory of evolution. In traveling the world, Darwin had noted small variations in species—in the shape of a bird's beak, for example—from one location to another. He theorized that over hundreds of generations, random variations in genetic makeup had helped certain members of a species to survive in a particular environment. A bird with a differently shaped beak might have been better at gathering seeds than other birds, for instance. In reproducing, these lucky individuals had passed on their advantageous genes to succeeding generations. Eventually, given their advantage in survival, individuals with the variation began to outnumber other members of the species. The species was slowly adapting to its environment. Darwin called this process of adaptation to the environment through random genetic variation *natural selection.*

FIGURE 9-1 **Countries with High Child-Marriage Rates**

Percentage of women
age 20 to 24 who were
married or in union before
age 18

- More than 60 percent
- 41–60 percent
- 21–40 percent
- 20 percent or less
- Data not available or
  child marriage not
  widely practiced

Note: Data are the most recent available, ranging from 1987 to 2006.
Source: UNICEF 2010.

In 21 countries, 40 percent or more of the women under 18 are married.

Sociobiologists apply Darwin's principle of natural selection to the study of social behavior. They assume that particular forms of behavior become genetically linked to a species if they contribute to its fitness to survive (van den Berghe 1978). In its extreme form, sociobiology suggests that *all* behavior is the result of genetic or biological factors, and that social interactions play no role in shaping people's conduct.

Sociobiologists do not seek to describe individual behavior on the level of "Why is Fred more aggressive than Jim?" Rather, they focus on how human nature is affected by the genetic composition of a *group* of people who share certain characteristics (such as men or women, or members of isolated tribal bands). In general, sociobiologists have stressed the basic genetic heritage that *all* humans share and have shown little interest in speculating

about alleged differences between racial groups or nationalities. A few researchers have tried to trace specific behaviors, like criminal activity, to certain genetic markers, but those markers are not deterministic. Family cohesiveness, peer group behavior, and other social factors can override genetic influences on behavior (Guo et al. 2008; E. Wilson 1975, 1978).

Certainly most social scientists would agree that there is a biological basis for social behavior. Like interactionists, however, conflict theorists and functionalists believe that people's behavior rather than their genetic structure defines social reality. Conflict theorists fear that the sociobiological approach could be used as an argument against efforts to assist disadvantaged people, such as schoolchildren who are not competing successfully (Freese 2008; Machalek and Martin 2010; E. Wilson 2000).

MODULE | **Recap and Review**

Summary

Culture is the totality of learned, socially transmitted customs, knowledge, material objects, and behavior. This module examines the social practices common to all cultures.

1. A shared culture helps to define the group or **society** to which we belong.

2. Anthropologist George Murdock compiled a list of **cultural universals,** or common practices found in

every culture, including marriage, sports, cooking, medicine, and sexual restrictions.

3. People who assume their own culture is superior to other cultures engage in **ethnocentricism.** In contrast, **cultural relativism** is the practice of viewing other people's behavior from the perspective of their own culture.

Thinking Critically

1. Select three cultural universals from George Murdock's list and analyze them from a functionalist perspective. Why are these practices found in every culture? What functions do they serve?

2. What are some problems with looking at social behavior from a sociobiological point of view? What are some benefits? How useful do you find this perspective?

Key Terms

Cultural relativism

Cultural universal

Culture

Culture industry

Ethnocentrism

Society

Sociobiology

Role of Language

Language is one of the major elements of culture. It is also an important component of cultural capital. Recall from Module 2 that Pierre Bourdieu used the term *cultural capital* to describe noneconomic assets, such as family background and past educational investments, which are reflected in a person's knowledge of language and the arts.

Members of a society generally share a common language, which facilitates day-to-day exchanges with others. When you ask a hardware store clerk for a flashlight, you don't need to draw a picture of the instrument. You share the same cultural term for a small, portable, battery-operated light. However, if you were in England and needed this item, you would have to ask for an electric torch. Of course, even within the same society, a term can have a number of different meanings. In the United States, *pot* signifies both a container that is used for cooking and an intoxicating drug. In this section we will examine the cultural influence of language, which includes both the written and spoken word and nonverbal communication.

Language: Written and Spoken

Seven thousand languages are spoken in the world today—many more than the number of countries. For the speakers of each one, whether they number 2,000 or 200 million, language is fundamental to their shared culture.

The English language, for example, makes extensive use of words dealing with war. We speak of "conquering" space, "fighting" the "battle" of the budget, "waging war" on drugs, making a "killing" on the stock market, and "bombing" an examination; something monumental or great is "the bomb." An observer from an entirely different and warless culture could gauge the importance that war and the military have had in our lives simply by recognizing the prominence that militaristic terms have in our language. Similarly, the Sami people of northern Norway and

Sweden have a rich diversity of terms for snow, ice, and reindeer (Haviland et al. 2008; Magga 2006).

Language is, in fact, the foundation of every culture. **Language** is an abstract system of word meanings and symbols for all aspects of culture. It includes speech, written characters, numerals, symbols, and nonverbal gestures and expressions. Because language is the foundation of every culture, the ability

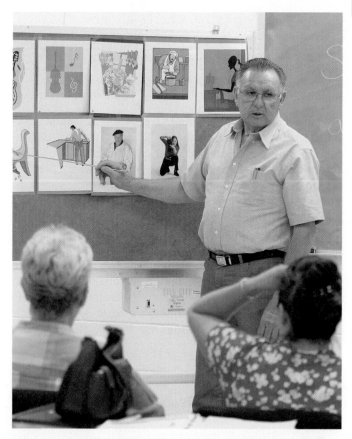

A native speaker trains instructors from the Oneida Nation of New York in the Berlitz method of language teaching. As of 2012, there were 527 speakers of the Oneida language. Many Native American tribes are taking similar steps to recover their seldom used languages, realizing that language is the essential foundation of any culture.

to speak other languages is crucial to intercultural relations. Throughout the Cold War era, beginning in the 1950s and continuing well into the 1970s, the U.S. government encouraged the study of Russian by developing special language schools for diplomats and military advisers who dealt with the Soviet Union. And following September 11, 2001, the nation recognized how few skilled translators it had for Arabic and other languages spoken in Muslim countries. Language quickly became a key not only to tracking potential terrorists, but also to building diplomatic bridges with Muslim countries willing to help in the war against terrorism.

Language does more than simply describe reality; it also serves to *shape* the reality of a culture. For example, most people in the United States cannot easily make the verbal distinctions concerning snow and ice that are possible in the Sami culture. As a result, they are less likely to notice such differences.

The **Sapir-Whorf hypothesis,** named for two linguists, describes the role of language in shaping our interpretation of reality. According to Sapir and Whorf, because people can conceptualize the world only through language, language *precedes* thought. Thus, the word symbols and grammar of a language organize the world for us. The Sapir-Whorf hypothesis also holds that language is not a given. Rather, it is culturally determined, and it encourages a distinctive interpretation of reality by focusing our attention on certain phenomena (Sapir 1929).

For decades, the Navajo have referred to cancer as *lood doo na'dziihii.* Now, through a project funded by the National Cancer Institute, the tribal college is seeking to change the phrase. Why? Literally, the phrase means "the sore that does not heal," and health educators are concerned that tribal members who have been diagnosed with cancer view it as a death sentence. Their effort to change the Navajo language, not easy in itself, is complicated by the Navajo belief that to talk about the disease is to bring it on one's people (Fonseca 2008).

Similarly, feminist theorists have noted that gender-related language can reflect—although in itself it does not determine—the traditional acceptance of men and women in certain occupations. Each time we use a term such as *mailman, policeman,* or *fireman,* we are implying (especially to young children) that these occupations can be filled only by males. Yet many women work as *mail carriers, police officers,* and *firefighters*—a fact that is being increasingly recognized and legitimized through the use of such nonsexist language.

Language can shape how we see, taste, smell, feel, and hear. It also influences the way we think about the people, ideas, and objects around us. Language communicates a culture's most

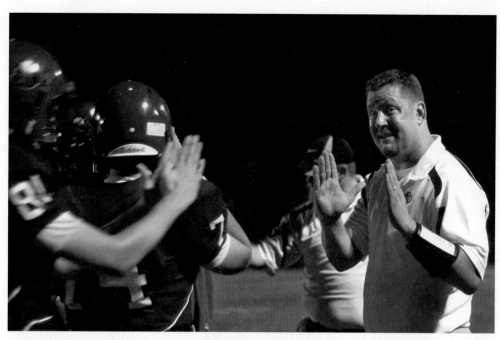

Using American Sign Language, a form of nonverbal communication, a football coach discusses a play with his team. The Silent Warriors, four-time national champions and the pride of the Alabama School for the Deaf, have defeated both hearing and nonhearing teams.

important norms, values, and sanctions. That's why the decline of an old language or the introduction of a new one is such a sensitive issue in many parts of the world (see the Social Policy section at the end of this chapter).

Nonverbal Communication

If you don't like the way a meeting is going, you might suddenly sit back, fold your arms, and turn down the corners of your mouth. When you see a friend in tears, you may give a quick hug. After winning a big game, you probably high-five your teammates. These are all examples of *nonverbal communication,* the use of gestures, facial expressions, and other visual images to communicate.

We are not born with these expressions. We learn them, just as we learn other forms of language, from people who share our same culture. This statement is as true for the basic expressions of happiness and sadness as it is for more complex emotions, such as shame or distress (Fridlund et al. 1987).

Like other forms of language, nonverbal communication is not the same in all cultures. For example, sociological research done at the micro level documents that people from various cultures differ in the degree to which they touch others during the course of normal social interactions. Even experienced travelers are sometimes caught off guard by these differences. In Saudi Arabia, a middle-aged man may want to hold hands with a partner after closing a business deal. In Egypt, men walk hand in hand in the street; in cafés, they fall asleep while lounging in each other's arms. These gestures, which would shock an American businessman, are considered compliments in those cultures. The meaning of hand signals is another form of nonverbal communication that can differ from one culture to the next. In Australia, the thumbs-up sign is considered rude (Passero 2002; Vaughan 2007).

A related form of communication is the use of symbols to convey meaning to others. **Symbols** are the gestures, objects, and words that form the basis of human communication. The thumbs-up gesture, a gold star sticker, and the smiley face in an e-mail are all symbols. Often deceptively simple, many symbols are rich in meaning and may not convey the same meaning in all social contexts. Around someone's neck, for example, a cross can symbolize religious reverence; over a grave site, a belief in everlasting life; or set in flames, racial hatred. Box 10-1 describes the delicate task of designing an appropriate symbol for the 9/11 memorial at New York's former World Trade Center—one that would have meaning for everyone who lost loved ones there, regardless of nationality or religious faith.

Norms and Values

"Wash your hands before dinner." "Thou shalt not kill." "Respect your elders." All societies have ways of encouraging and enforcing what they view as appropriate behavior while discouraging and punishing what they consider to be inappropriate behavior. They also have a collective idea of what is good and desirable in life—or not. In this section we will learn to distinguish between the closely related concepts of norms and values.

Norms

Norms are the established standards of behavior maintained by a society. For a norm to become significant, it must be widely

Sociology in the Global Community

BOX 10-1

Symbolizing 9/11

On September 11, 2001, the World Trade Center's twin towers took only minutes to collapse. Nearly a decade later, the creator of the memorial to those lost that day was still perfecting the site plan. Thirty-four-year-old architect Michael Arad, the man who submitted the winning design, had drawn two sunken squares, measuring an acre each, in the footprints left by the collapsed towers. His design, "Reflecting Absence," places each empty square in a reflecting pool surrounded by cascading water. Today, as visitors to the massive memorial stand at the edge of the site, they are struck by both the sound of the thundering water and the absence of life.

The memorial does not encompass the entire area destroyed in the attack, as some had wanted. In one of the great commercial capitals of the world, economic forces demanded that some part of the property produce income. Others had argued against constructing a memorial of any kind on what they regarded as hallowed ground. "Don't build on my sister's grave," one of them pleaded. They too had to compromise. On all sides of the eight-acre memorial site, new high rises have been and continue to be built. When construction is finished, the site will also accommodate a new underground transit hub.

Originally, the architect's plans called for the 2,982 victims of the attack to be listed elsewhere on the site. Today, in a revised plan, the names are displayed prominently along the sides of the reflecting pool. Arad had suggested that they be placed randomly, to symbolize the "haphazard brutality of life." Survivors objected, perhaps because they worried about locating their loved ones' names. In a compromise, the names were chiseled into the bronze walls of the memorial in groups that Arad calls "meaningful adjacencies": friends and co-workers;

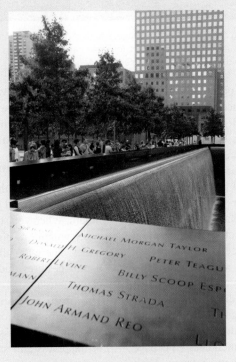

fellow passengers on the two downed aircraft, arranged by seat number; and first responders, grouped by their agencies or fire companies. Suggestions that would give first responders special recognition were set aside. The list includes victims of the simultaneous attack on the Pentagon in Washington, D.C., and passengers on the flight headed for the White House, who were attempting to thwart the attack when the plane crashed in a field in Pennsylvania. The six people who perished in the 1993 truck bombing at the World Trade Center are also memorialized.

Away from Ground Zero, symbols of 9/11 abound. Numerous small monuments and simple plaques grace intersections throughout metropolitan New York, particularly those that had a direct line of sight to the twin towers. In hundreds of cities worldwide, scraps of steel from the twisted buildings and remnants of destroyed emergency vehicles have been incorporated into memorials. And the USS *New York*, whose bow was forged from seven and a half tons of steel debris salvaged from the towers, has served as a working symbol of 9/11 since its commissioning in 2009.

> Numerous small monuments and simple plaques grace intersections throughout metropolitan New York, particularly those that had a direct line of sight to the twin towers.

LET'S DISCUSS

1. What does the 9/11 memorial symbolize to you? Explain the meaning of the cascading water, the reflecting pools, and the empty footprints. What does the placement of the victims' names suggest?

2. If you were designing a 9/11 memorial, what symbol or symbols would you incorporate? Use your sociological imagination to predict how various groups would respond to your design.

Sources: Blais and Rasic 2011; Kennicott 2011; Needham 2011.

shared and understood. For example, in movie theaters in the United States, we typically expect that people will be quiet while the film is shown. Of course, the application of this norm can vary, depending on the particular film and type of audience. People who are viewing a serious artistic film will be more likely to insist on the norm of silence than those who are watching a slapstick comedy or horror movie.

One persistent social norm in contemporary society is that of heterosexuality. As sociologists, and queer theorists especially, note, children are socialized to accept this norm from a very young age. Overwhelmingly, parents describe adult romantic relationships to their children exclusively as heterosexual relationships. That is not necessarily because they consider same-sex relationships unacceptable, but more likely because they see heterosexuality as the norm in marital partnerships. According to a national survey of mothers of three- to six-year-olds, one in five mothers teaches her young children that homosexuality is wrong. The same survey showed that parenting reflects the dominant ideology, in which homosexuality is treated as a rare exception. Most parents assume that their children are heterosexual; only one in four has even considered whether his or her child might grow up to be gay or lesbian (K. Martin 2009).

Types of Norms   Sociologists distinguish between norms in two ways. First, norms are classified as either formal or informal. **Formal norms** generally have been written down and specify strict punishments for violators. In the United States, we often formalize norms into laws, which are very precise in defining proper and improper behavior. Sociologist Donald Black (1995) has termed **law** "governmental social control," meaning that laws are formal norms enforced by the state. Laws are just one example of formal norms. Parking restrictions and the rules of a football or basketball game are also considered formal norms.

In contrast, **informal norms** are generally understood but not precisely recorded. Standards of proper dress are a common example of informal norms. Our society has no specific punishment, or *sanction,* for a person who shows up at school or work wearing inappropriate clothing. Laughter is usually the most likely response.

Norms are also classified by their relative importance to society. When classified in this way, they are known as *mores* and *folkways.* **Mores** (pronounced "MOR-ays") are norms deemed highly necessary to the welfare of a society, often because they embody the most cherished principles of a people. Each society demands obedience to its mores; violation can lead to severe penalties. Thus, the United States has strong mores against murder, treason, and child abuse, which have been institutionalized into formal norms.

Folkways are norms governing everyday behavior. Folkways play an important role in shaping the daily behavior of members of a culture. Society is less likely to formalize folkways than mores, and their violation raises comparatively little concern. For example, walking up a down escalator in a department store challenges our standards of appropriate behavior, but it will not result in a fine or a jail sentence.

use your **sociological imagination**

You are a high school principal. What norms would you want to govern the students' behavior? How might those norms differ from norms appropriate for college students?

Norms and Sanctions   Suppose a football coach sends a 12th player onto the field. Imagine a college graduate showing up in shorts for a job interview at a large bank. Or consider a driver who neglects to put money in a parking meter. These people have violated widely shared and understood norms. So what happens? In each of these situations, the person will receive sanctions if his or her behavior is detected.

Sanctions are penalties and rewards for conduct concerning a social norm. Note that the concept of *reward* is included in this definition. Conformity to a norm can lead to positive sanctions such as a pay raise, a medal, a word of gratitude, or a pat on the back. Negative sanctions include fines, threats, imprisonment, and stares of contempt.

Table 10-1 summarizes the relationship between norms and sanctions. As you can see, the sanctions that are associated with formal norms (which are written down and codified) tend to be formal as well. If a college football coach sends too many players onto the field, the team will be penalized 15 yards. The driver who fails to put money in the parking meter will receive a ticket and have to pay a fine. But sanctions for violations of informal norms can vary. The college graduate who goes to the bank interview in shorts will probably lose any chance of getting the job; on the other hand, he or she might be so brilliant that bank officials will overlook the unconventional attire.

The entire fabric of norms and sanctions in a culture reflects that culture's values and priorities. The most cherished values will be most heavily sanctioned; matters regarded as less critical will carry light and informal sanctions.

Summing Up

TABLE 10-1   NORMS AND SANCTIONS

Norms	Sanctions	
	Positive	**Negative**
Formal	Salary bonus	Demotion
	Testimonial dinner	Firing from a job
	Medal	Jail sentence
	Diploma	Expulsion
Informal	Smile	Frown
	Compliment	Humiliation
	Cheers	Bullying

Acceptance of Norms People do not follow norms, whether formal or informal, in all situations. In some cases, they can evade a norm because they know it is weakly enforced. It is illegal for U.S. teenagers to drink alcoholic beverages, yet drinking by minors is common throughout the nation. (In fact, teenage alcoholism is a serious social problem.)

In some instances, behavior that appears to violate society's norms may actually represent adherence to the norms of a particular group. Teenage drinkers are conforming to the standards of their peer group when they violate norms that condemn underage drinking. Similarly, business executives who use shady accounting techniques may be responding to a corporate culture that demands the maximization of profits at any cost, including the deception of investors and government regulatory agencies.

Norms are violated in some instances because one norm conflicts with another. For example, suppose that you live in an apartment building and one night hear the screams of the woman next door, who is being beaten by her husband. If you decide to intervene by ringing their doorbell or calling the police, you are violating the norm of minding your own business, while following the norm of assisting a victim of violence.

Acceptance of norms is subject to change as the political, economic, and social conditions of a culture are transformed. Until the 1960s, for example, formal norms throughout much of the United States prohibited the marriage of people from different racial groups. Over the past half century, however, such legal prohibitions were cast aside. The process of change can be seen today in the increasing acceptance of single parents and growing support for the legalization of marriage between same-sex couples.

When circumstances require the sudden violation of long-standing cultural norms, the change can upset an entire population. In Iraq, where Muslim custom strictly forbids touching by strangers for men and especially for women, the war that began in 2003 brought numerous daily violations of the norm. Outside important mosques, government offices, and other facilities likely to be targeted by terrorists, visitors had to be patted down and have their bags searched by Iraqi security guards. To reduce the discomfort caused by the procedure, women were searched by female guards and men by male guards. Despite that concession, and the fact that many Iraqis admitted or even insisted on the need for such measures, people still winced at the invasion of their personal privacy. In reaction to the searches, Iraqi women began to limit the contents of the bags they carried or simply to leave them at home (Rubin 2003).

Values

Though we each have a personal set of values—which may include caring or fitness or success in business—we also share a general set of values as members of a society. Cultural **values** are these collective conceptions of what is considered good, desirable, and proper—or bad, undesirable, and improper—in a culture. They indicate what people in a given culture prefer as well as what they find important and morally right (or wrong). Values may be specific, such as honoring one's parents and owning a home, or they may be more general, such as health, love, and democracy. Of course, the members of a society do not uniformly share its values. Angry political debates and billboards promoting conflicting causes tell us that much.

Values influence people's behavior and serve as criteria for evaluating the actions of others. The values, norms, and sanctions of a culture are often directly related. For example, if a culture places a high value on the institution of marriage, it may have norms (and strict sanctions) that prohibit the act of adultery or make divorce difficult. If a culture views private property as a basic value, it will probably have stiff laws against theft and vandalism.

The values of a culture may change, but most remain relatively stable during any one person's lifetime. Socially shared, intensely felt values are a fundamental part of our lives in the United States. Sociologist Robin Williams (1970) has offered a list of basic values. It includes achievement, efficiency, material comfort, nationalism, equality, and the supremacy of science and reason over faith. Obviously, not all 314 million people in this country agree on all these values, but such a list serves as a starting point in defining the national character.

Each year more than 200,000 entering college students at nearly 300 of the nation's four-year colleges fill out a questionnaire about their values. Because this survey focuses on an array of issues, beliefs, and life goals, it is commonly cited as a barometer of the nation's values. The respondents are asked what values are personally important to them. Over the past half century, the value of "being very well-off financially" has shown the strongest gain in popularity; the proportion of first-year college students who endorse this value as "essential" or "very important" rose from 42 percent in 1966 to 81 percent in 2012 (Figure 10-1).

During the 1980s and 1990s, support for values having to do with money, power, and status grew. At the same time, support for certain values having to do with social awareness and altruism, such as "helping others," declined. According to the 2011 nationwide survey, only 42 percent of first-year college students stated that "influencing social values" was an "essential" or "very important" goal. The proportion of students for whom "helping to promote racial understanding" was an essential or very important goal reached a record high of 46 percent in 1992, then fell to 35.3 percent in 2012. Like other aspects of culture, such as language and norms, a nation's values are not necessarily fixed.

Whether the slogan is "Think Green" or "Reduce Your Carbon Footprint," students have been exposed to values associated with environmentalism. How many of them accept those values? Poll results over the past 40 years show fluctuations, with a high of nearly 46 percent of students indicating a desire

FIGURE 10-1 **Life Goals of First-Year College Students in the United States, 1966–2012**

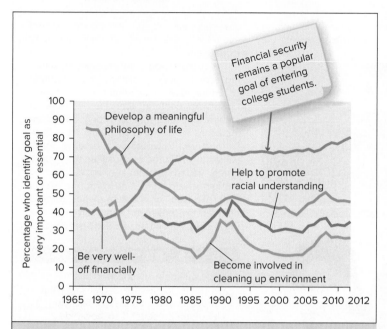

Financial security remains a popular goal of entering college students.

Think about It Why do you think values have shifted among college students in the past few decades? Which of these values is important to you?

Sources: Pryor et al. 2007, 2013.

to become involved in cleaning up the environment. By the 1980s, however, student support for embracing this objective had dropped to around 20 percent or even lower (see Figure 10-1). Even with recent attention to global warming, the proportion remains level at only 26.5 percent of first-year students in 2012.

Recently, cheating has become a hot issue on college campuses. Professors who take advantage of computerized services that can identify plagiarism, such as the search engine Google, have been shocked to learn that many of the papers their students hand in are plagiarized in whole or in part. Box 10-2 examines the shift in values that underlies this decline in academic integrity.

Values can also differ in subtle ways not just among individuals and groups, but from one culture to another. For example, in Japan, young children spend long hours working with tutors, preparing for entrance exams required for admission to selective schools. No stigma is attached to these services, known

as "cram schools"; in fact, they are highly valued. Yet in South Korea, people have begun to complain that cram schools give affluent students an unfair advantage. Since 2008, the South Korean government has regulated the after-school tutoring industry, limiting its hours and imposing fees on the schools. Some think this policy has lowered their society's expectations of students, describing it as an attempt to make South Koreans "more American" (Ramstad 2011; Ripley 2011).

Another example of cultural differences in values is public opinion regarding the treatment of different racial and ethnic groups. As Figure 10-2 shows, opinion on the need for equal treatment of different racial and ethnic groups varies dramatically from one country to another.

Global Culture War

For almost a generation, public attention in the United States has focused on **culture war,** or the polarization of society over controversial cultural elements. Originally, in the 1990s, the term referred to political debates over heated issues such as abortion, religious expression, gun control, and sexual orientation. Soon, however, it took on a global meaning—especially after 9/11, as Americans wondered, "Why do they hate us?" Through 2000, global studies of public opinion had reported favorable views of the United States in countries as diverse as Morocco and Germany. But after the United States established a military presence in Iraq and Afghanistan, foreign opinion of the United States became quite negative (J. Hunter 1991; Kohut et al. 2005, 2007).

In the past 30 years, extensive efforts have been made to compare values in different nations, recognizing the challenges

FIGURE 10-2 **Valuing Ethnicity by Country**

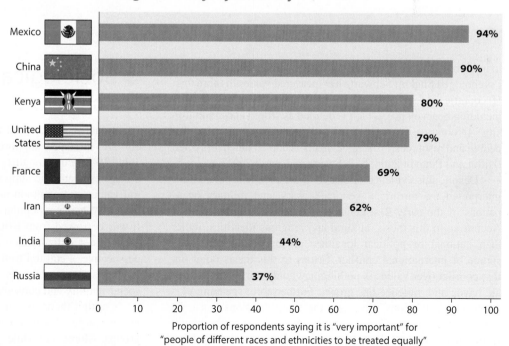

Proportion of respondents saying it is "very important" for "people of different races and ethnicities to be treated equally"

Source: Council on Foreign Relations 2009.

A Culture of Cheating?

A Harvard teaching assistant noticed something strange while grading students' take-home exams. Several students had cited the same obscure event in 1912. Curiously, all had responded to another question using the same wording. The assistant looked more closely. Eventually, Harvard launched a formal investigation of 125 students suspected of plagiarism and illicit collaboration. At the same time, in New York City more than 70 students at a high school for high achievers were caught sharing test information using their cell phones.

Now that students can use personal computers to surf the Internet, most do their research online. Apparently, the temptation to cut and paste passages from website postings and pass them off as one's own is irresistible to many. In 2012, 51 percent of high school students admitted cheating on a test, and 75 percent of them copied homework.

Research suggests that the proportion of students who cheat is even higher among college students. The Center for Academic Integrity estimates that at most colleges and universities, more than 75 percent of the students engage in some form of cheating. Students not only cut passages from the Internet and paste them into their papers without citing the

source; they share questions and answers on exams, collaborate on assignments they

> The Center for Academic Integrity estimates that at most colleges and universities, more than 75 percent of the students engage in some form of cheating.

are supposed to do independently, and even falsify the results of their laboratory experiments.

To address what they consider an alarming trend, many colleges are rewriting or adopting new academic honor codes. Observers contend that the increase in student cheating reflects widely publicized instances of cheating in public life, which have served to create an alternative set of values in which the end justifies the means. When young people see sports heroes, authors, entertainers, and corporate executives exposed for cheating in one form or another, the message seems to be "Cheating is okay, as long as you don't get caught."

LET'S DISCUSS

1. Do you know anyone who has engaged in Internet plagiarism? What about cheating on tests or falsifying laboratory results? If so, how did the person justify these forms of dishonesty?

2. Even if cheaters aren't caught, what negative effects does their academic dishonesty have on them? What effects does it have on students who are honest? Could an entire college or university suffer from students' dishonesty?

Sources: Argetsinger and Krim 2002; Bartlett 2009; Center for Academic Integrity 2006; Sarah Glazer 2013; R. Thomas 2003; Toppo 2011; Zernike 2002.

---

in interpreting value concepts in a similar manner across cultures. Psychologist Shalom Schwartz has measured values in more than 60 countries. Around the world, certain values are widely shared, including benevolence, which is defined as "forgiveness and loyalty." In contrast, power, defined as "control or dominance over people and resources," is a value that is endorsed much less often (Hitlin and Piliavin 2004; S. Schwartz and Bardi 2001).

Despite this evidence of shared values, some scholars have interpreted the terrorism, genocide, wars, and military occupations of the early 21st century as a "clash of civilizations." According to this thesis, cultural and religious identities, rather than national or political loyalties, are becoming the prime source of international conflict. Critics of this thesis point out that conflict over values is nothing new; only our ability to create havoc and violence has grown. Furthermore, speaking of a clash of "civilizations" disguises the sharp divisions that exist within large groups. Christianity, for example, runs the gamut from Quaker-style pacifism to certain elements of the Ku Klux Klan's ideology (Berman 2003; Huntington 1993; Said 2001).

Sociological Perspectives on Culture

Functionalist and conflict theorists agree that culture and society are mutually supportive, but for different reasons (see Table 10-2). Functionalists maintain that social stability requires a consensus and the support of society's members; strong central values and common norms provide that support. This view of culture became popular in sociology beginning in the 1950s. It was borrowed from British anthropologists who saw cultural traits as a stabilizing element in a culture. From a functionalist perspective, a cultural trait or practice will persist if it performs functions that society seems to need or contributes to overall social stability and consensus.

Conflict theorists agree that a common culture may exist, but they argue that it serves to maintain the privileges of certain groups. Moreover, while protecting their self-interest, powerful groups may keep others in a subservient position. The term

TABLE **10-2** SOCIOLOGICAL PERSPECTIVES
ON CULTURE

Tracking Sociological Perspectives

	Functionalist Perspective	Conflict Perspective	Feminist Perspective	Interactionist Perspective
Norms	Reinforce societal standards	Reinforce patterns of dominance	Reinforce roles of men and women	Are maintained through face-to-face interaction
Values	Are collective conceptions of what is good	May perpetuate social inequality	May perpetuate men's dominance	Are defined and redefined through social interaction
Culture and Society	Culture reflects a society's strong central values	Culture reflects a society's dominant ideology	Culture reflects society's view of men and women	A society's core culture is perpetuated through daily social interactions
Cultural Variation	Subcultures serve the interests of subgroups	Countercultures question the dominant social order; ethnocentrism devalues groups	Cultural relativism respects variations in the way men and women are viewed in different societies	Customs and traditions are transmitted through intergroup contact and through the media

dominant ideology describes the set of cultural beliefs and practices that helps to maintain powerful social, economic, and political interests. This concept was first used by Hungarian Marxist Georg Lukacs (1923) and Italian Marxist Antonio Gramsci (1929), but it did not gain an audience in the United States until the early 1970s. In Karl Marx's view, a capitalist society has a dominant ideology that serves the interests of the ruling class.

From a conflict perspective, the dominant ideology has major social significance. Not only do a society's most powerful groups and institutions control wealth and property; even more important, they control the means of producing beliefs about reality through religion, education, and the media. Feminists would also argue that if all a society's most important institutions tell women they should be subservient to men, that dominant ideology will help to control women and keep them in a subordinate position.

A growing number of social scientists believe that it is not easy to identify a core culture in the United States. For support, they point to the lack of consensus on national values, the diffusion of cultural traits, the diversity within our culture, and the changing views of young people (look again at Figure 10-1). Instead, they suggest that the core culture provides the tools that people of all persuasions need to develop strategies for social change. Still, there is no denying that certain expressions of values have greater influence than others, even in as complex a society as the United States (Swidler 1986).

MODULE 10 | Recap and Review

Summary

This module discusses the major elements that all cultures share: **language, norms,** and **values.**

1. **Language** includes speech, written characters, numerals, and **symbols,** as well as gestures and other forms of nonverbal communication. Language both describes culture and shapes it.
2. Sociologists distinguish between **norms** in two ways, classifying them as **formal** or **informal** and as **mores** or **folkways.**
3. The formal norms of a culture will carry the heaviest **sanctions;** informal norms will carry light sanctions.
4. The **dominant ideology** of a culture is the set of cultural beliefs and practices that help to maintain powerful social, economic, and political interests.

Thinking Critically

1. In the United States, is the norm of heterosexuality a formal norm or an informal norm? Would you categorize it with mores or folkways? Explain your reasoning.
2. Do you believe that the world is experiencing a clash of civilizations rather than of nations, as some scholars assert? Why or why not?
3. Look around your campus. Do the people you see suggest that the United States has a core culture with a dominant ideology, or a diverse culture with differing values and ideologies? What about the city or town where your college or university is located—does it suggest the same conclusion?

MODULE 11 | Development of Culture around the World

Today, despite the preference most of us have for our own way of life, powerful forces link us to others around the world. Thus, students in the United States may study the novels of Leo Tolstoy, the art of Pablo Picasso, or the films of Ang Lee. They may listen to pop music from Nigeria or South Korea, or follow the progress of social movements in Iran, Egypt, or Syria via satellite TV and social media. In this section we will examine two of the social processes that make these global links possible: innovation and the diffusion of culture through globalization and technology.

Innovation

The process of introducing a new idea or object to a culture is known as **innovation.** Innovation interests sociologists because of the social consequences of introducing something new. There are two forms of innovation: discovery and invention. **Discovery** involves making known or sharing the existence of an aspect of reality. The finding of the structure of the DNA molecule and the identification of a new moon of Saturn are both acts of discovery. A significant factor in the process of discovery is the sharing of newfound knowledge with others. In contrast, an **invention** results when existing cultural items are combined into a form that did not exist before. The bow and arrow, the automobile, and the television are all examples of inventions, as are Protestantism and democracy.

 use your **sociological imagination**

If you grew up in your parents' generation—without computers, e-mail, MP3 players, and cell phones—how would your daily life differ from the one you lead today?

Globalization, Diffusion, and Technology

The recent emergence of Starbucks, the worldwide chain of coffeehouses, is just one illustration of the rapidly escalating trend toward globalization (see Module 4). While people in Asia are

beginning to enjoy coffee, people in North America are discovering sushi. Some have become familiar with the *bento box,* a small lunchbox that is often used to serve sushi. A trademark Japanese cuisine, sushi has evolved from a once-exotic dish in the United States to a mainstream food commonly found in supermarket refrigerators. Yet its move across the Pacific has changed the delicacy. Americans tend to treat sushi as a take-out or menu item. The authentic way to eat sushi is to sit at a bar and engage the chef in conversation about the day's catch.

More and more cultural expressions and practices are crossing national borders and affecting the traditions and customs of the societies exposed to them. Sociologists use the term **diffusion** to refer to the process by which a cultural item spreads from group to group or society to society. Diffusion can occur through a variety of means, among them exploration, military conquest, missionary work, and the influence of the mass media, tourism, the Internet (Box 11-1), and the fast-food restaurant.

Sociologist George Ritzer coined the term *McDonaldization of society* to describe how the principles of fast-food restaurants, developed in the United States, have come to dominate more and more sectors of societies throughout the world. For example, hair salons and medical clinics now take walk-ins. In Hong Kong, sex selection clinics offer a menu of items, from fertility enhancement to methods of increasing the likelihood of having a child of the desired sex. And religious groups—from evangelical preachers on local stations or websites to priests at the Vatican Television Center—use marketing techniques similar to those that are used to sell Happy Meals.

McDonaldization is associated with the melding of cultures, through which we see more and more similarities in cultural expression. In Japan, for example, African entrepreneurs have found a thriving market for hip-hop fashions popularized by teens in the United States. Similarly, the familiar Golden Arches of McDonald's can be seen around the world. Yet corporations like McDonald's have had to make some adjustments of their own. Until 2001, McDonald's ran its *overseas* operations from corporate headquarters in suburban Chicago. After a few false starts, executives recognized the need to develop the restaurant's menus and marketing strategies overseas, relying on advice from local people. Now, at over 3,700 restaurants in Japan, customers can enjoy the Mega Tamago Burger—beef, bacon, and fried egg with special sauces. In India, patrons who don't eat beef can order a vegetarian McAloo Tikki potato burger. Because some strict vegetarians in India refuse to eat among nonvegetarians,

Life in the Global Village

Imagine a "borderless world" in which culture, trade, commerce, money, and even people move freely from one place to another. Popular culture is widely shared, whether it be Japanese sushi or U.S. running shoes, and the English speaker who answers questions over the telephone about your credit card account is as likely to be in India or Ireland as in the United States. In this world, even the sovereignty of nations is at risk, challenged by political movements and ideologies that span nations.

What caused this great wave of cultural diffusion? First, sociologists take note of advances in communications technology. Satellite TV, cell phones, the Internet, and the like allow information to flow freely across the world, linking global markets. In 2008, this process reached the point where consumers could view videos on handheld devices and surf the Internet on their wireless cell phones, shopping online at Amazon.com, eBay, and other commercial websites from cars, airports, and cafeterias. Second, corporations in the industrial nations have become multinational, with both factories and markets in developing countries. Business leaders welcome the opportunity to sell consumer goods in populous countries such as China. Third, these multinational firms have cooperated with global financial institutions, organizations, and governments to promote free trade—unrestricted or

lightly restricted commerce across national borders.

Globalization is not universally welcomed. Many critics see the dominance of "businesses without borders" as benefiting the rich, particularly the very wealthy in industrial countries, at the expense of the poor in less developed nations. They consider globalization to be a successor to the imperialism and colonialism that oppressed Third World nations for centuries.

> Even *Pirates of the Caribbean* movies and Lady Gaga may be seen as threats to native cultures.

Another criticism of globalization comes from people who feel overwhelmed by global culture. Embedded in the concept of globalization is the notion of the cultural domination of developing nations by more affluent nations. Simply put, people lose their traditional values and begin to identify with the culture of dominant nations. They may discard or neglect their native languages and dress as they attempt to copy the icons of mass-market entertainment and fashion.

Even *Pirates of the Caribbean* movies and Lady Gaga may be seen as threats to native cultures, if they dominate the media at the expense of local art forms. As Sembene Ousmane, one of Africa's most prominent writers and filmmakers, noted, "[Today] we are more familiar with European fairy tales than with our own traditional stories" (World Development Forum 1990:4).

Globalization has its positive side, too. Many developing nations are taking their place in the world of commerce and bringing in much needed income. The communications revolution helps people to stay connected and gives them access to knowledge that can improve living standards and even save lives.

LET'S DISCUSS

1. How are you affected by globalization? Which aspects of globalization do you find advantageous and which objectionable?

2. How would you feel if the customs and traditions you grew up with were replaced by the culture or values of another country? How might you try to protect your culture?

Sources: Dodds 2000; Giddens 1991; Hirst and Thompson 1996; D. Martin et al. 2006; Ritzer 2007; Sernau 2001; Tedeschi 2006.

Members of Big Toe Crew, a Vietnamese hip-hop group, rehearse for a performance. Through tourism and the mass media, music and dance spread from one culture to another in a process called diffusion.

in 2013 McDonald's began opening vegetarian-only restaurants there (Gasparro and Jargon 2012; Ritzer 2010, 2013).

Technology in its many forms has increased the speed of cultural diffusion and broadened the distribution of cultural elements. Sociologist Gerhard Lenski has defined **technology** as "cultural information about the ways in which the material resources of the environment may be used to satisfy human needs and desires" (Nolan and Lenski 2009:357). Today's technological developments no longer await publication in journals with limited circulation. Press conferences, often carried simultaneously on the Internet, trumpet the new developments.

Technology not only accelerates the diffusion of scientific innovations but also transmits culture. The English language and North American culture dominate the Internet and World Wide Web. Such control, or at least dominance, of technology influences the direction of cultural diffusion. For example, websites cover even the most superficial aspects of U.S. culture but offer little information about the pressing issues faced by citizens of other nations. People all over the world find it easier to visit electronic chat rooms about the latest reality TV shows than to learn about their own governments' policies on day care or infant nutrition.

Sociologist William F. Ogburn (1922) made a useful distinction between the elements of *material* and *nonmaterial culture.* **Material culture** refers to the physical or technological aspects of our daily lives, including food, houses, factories, and raw materials. **Nonmaterial culture** refers to ways of using material objects, as well as to customs, beliefs, philosophies, governments, and patterns of communication. Generally, the nonmaterial culture is more resistant to change than the material culture. Consequently, Ogburn introduced the term **culture lag** to refer to the period of maladjustment when the nonmaterial culture is still struggling to adapt to new material conditions. For example, in 2010, manufacturers introduced electronic cigarettes, battery-powered tubes that turn nicotine-laced liquid into a vapor mist. The innovation soon had officials at airlines (which ban smoking) and the Food and Drug Administration scrambling to respond to the latest technology (Kesmodel and Yadron 2010; Swidler 1986).

Resistance to technological change can lead not only to culture lag, but to some real questions of cultural survival (Box 11-2).

When a society's nonmaterial culture (its values and laws) does not keep pace with rapid changes in its material culture, people experience an awkward period of maladjustment called culture lag. The transition to nuclear power generation that began in the second half of the 20th century brought widespread protests against the new technology, as well as serious accidents that government officials were poorly prepared to deal with. Tensions over the controversial technology have not run as high in some countries as in others, however. France, where this nuclear power plant is situated, generates 78 percent of all its electricity through nuclear power. The technology is not as controversial there as in the United States and Canada, which generate less than 20 percent of their electricity through nuclear reaction.

Sociology in the Global Community

BOX 11-2

Cultural Survival in Brazil

When the first Portuguese ships landed on the coast of what we now know as Brazil, more than 2 million people inhabited the vast, mineral-rich land. The natives lived in small, isolated settlements, spoke a variety of languages, and embraced many different cultural traditions.

Today, over five centuries later, Brazil's population has grown to more than 192 million, only about 650,000 of whom are indigenous peoples descended from the original inhabitants. Over 200 different indigenous groups have survived, living a life tied closely to the land and the rivers, just as their ancestors did. But over the past two generations, their numbers have dwindled as booms in mining, logging, oil drilling, and agriculture have encroached on their land and their settlements.

Many indigenous groups were once nomads, moving around from one hunting or fishing ground to another. Now they are hemmed in on the reservations the government confined them to, surrounded by huge farms or ranches whose owners deny their right to live off the land. State officials may insist that laws restrict the development of indigenous lands, but indigenous peoples tell a different story. In Mato Grosso, a heavily forested state near the Amazon River, loggers have been clear-cutting the land at a rate that alarms the Bororo, an indigenous group that has lived in the area for centuries. According to one elder, the Bororo are now confined to six small reservations of about 500 square miles—much less than the area officially granted them in the 19th century.

In the face of dwindling resources, indigenous groups like the Bororo struggle to maintain their culture. Though the tribe still observes the traditional initiation rites for adolescent boys, members are finding it difficult to continue their hunting and fishing rituals, given the scarcity of game and fish in the area. Pesticides in the runoff from nearby farms have poisoned the water they fish and bathe in, threatening both their health and their culture's survival.

> In Mato Grosso, a heavily forested state near the Amazon River, loggers have been clear-cutting the land at a rate that alarms the Bororo.

LET'S DISCUSS

1. Compare the frontier in Brazil today to the American West in the 1800s. What similarities do you see?

2. What does society lose when indigenous cultures die?

Sources: Brazier and Hamed 2007; H. Chu 2005; Survival international 2012.

Summary

In this module we examine the ways in which culture changes and spreads.

1. Human culture is constantly expanding through the process of **innovation,** which includes both **discovery** and **invention.**

2. **Diffusion**—the spread of cultural items from one place to another—has fostered globalization. Still, people resist ideas that seem too foreign, as well as those they perceive as threatening to their own values and beliefs.

Thinking Critically

1. Name one culturally significant discovery and one culturally significant invention that occurred in your lifetime. Explain how these innovations have changed your culture.

2. Describe one positive example and one negative of McDonaldization that you have experienced.

Key Terms

Culture lag

Diffusion

Discovery

Innovation

Invention

Material culture

Nonmaterial culture

Technology

MODULE 12 | Cultural Variation

Despite the presence of cultural universals such as courtship and religion, great diversity exists among the world's many cultures. Inuit tribes in northern Canada, dressed in fur for the hunt, share little with farmers in southeast Asia, who dress lightly for work in their hot, humid rice paddies. Cultures adapt to meet specific circumstances, such as climate, level of technology, population, and geography.

Even *within* a single nation, certain segments of the populace develop cultural patterns that differ from the patterns of the dominant society—thus the difficulty of identifying a core culture in the United States, where regional differences fuel culture wars between conservatives and liberals. Moreover, in every region, specific communities tend to band together to form their own culture within a culture, called a *subculture.*

Subcultures

Rodeo riders, residents of a retirement community, workers on an offshore oil rig—all are examples of what sociologists refer to as *subcultures.* A **subculture** is a segment of society that shares a distinctive pattern of customs, rules, and traditions that differs from the pattern of the larger society.

The existence of many subcultures is characteristic of complex societies such as the United States.

Members of a subculture participate in the dominant culture while engaging in unique and distinctive forms of behavior. Frequently, a subculture will develop an **argot,** or specialized language that distinguishes it from the wider society. Athletes who play *parkour,* an extreme sport that combines forward running with fence

Employees of an international call center in India socialize after their shift has ended. Call center employees, whose odd working hours isolate them from others, tend to form tight-knit subcultures.

leaping and the vaulting of walls, water barriers, and even moving cars, speak an argot they devised especially to describe their feats. Parkour runners talk about doing *King Kong vaults*—diving arms first over a wall or grocery cart and landing in a standing position. They may follow this maneuver with a *tic tac*—kicking off a wall to overcome some kind of obstacle (Kidder 2012).

Such argot allows insiders—the members of the subculture—to understand words with special meanings. It also establishes patterns of communication that outsiders can't understand. Sociologists associated with the interactionist perspective emphasize that language and symbols offer a powerful way for a subculture to feel cohesive and maintain its identity.

In India, a new subculture has developed among employees at the international call centers established by multinational corporations. To serve customers in the United States and Europe, the young men and women who work there must be fluent speakers of English. But the corporations that employ them demand more than proficiency in a foreign language; they expect their Indian employees to adopt Western values and work habits, including the grueling pace U.S. workers take for granted.

In effect, workers at these call centers live in a state of virtual migration—not quite in India, but not in the United States, either. Significantly, call centers allow employees to take the day off only on U.S. holidays, like Labor Day and Thanksgiving—not on Indian holidays like Diwali, the Hindu festival of lights. While most Indian families are home celebrating, call center employees see only each other; when they have the day off, no one else is free to socialize with them. As a result, these employees have formed a tight-knit subculture based on hard work and a taste for Western luxury goods and leisure-time pursuits (Rowe et al. 2013).

Another shared characteristic among some employees at Indian call centers is their contempt for the callers they serve. In performing their monotonous, repetitive job day after day,

hundreds of thousands of these workers have come to see the faceless Americans they deal with as slow, often rude customers. Such shared understandings underpin this emerging subculture (Bhagat 2007; Gentleman 2006; Patel 2010).

Functionalist and conflict theorists agree that variation exists within cultures. Functionalists view subcultures as variations of particular social environments and as evidence that differences can exist within a common culture. However, conflict theorists suggest that variations often reflect the inequality of social arrangements within a society. A conflict theorist would view the challenges to dominant social norms by African American activists, the feminist movement, and the gay rights movement as reflections of inequity based on race, gender, and sexual orientation. Conflict theorists also argue that subcultures sometimes emerge when the dominant society unsuccessfully tries to suppress a practice, such as the use of illegal drugs.

Countercultures

By the end of the 1960s, an extensive subculture had emerged in the United States, composed of young people turned off by a society they believed was too materialistic and technological. The group included primarily political radicals and hippies who had dropped out of mainstream social institutions. These young men and women rejected the pressure to accumulate cars, homes, and an endless array of material goods. Instead, they expressed a desire to live in a culture based on more humanistic values, such as sharing, love, and coexistence with the environment. As a political force, this subculture opposed the United States' involvement in the war in Vietnam and encouraged draft resistance (Flacks 1971; Roszak 1969).

When a subculture conspicuously and deliberately opposes certain aspects of the larger culture, it is known as a **counterculture.** Countercultures typically thrive among the young, who have the least investment in the existing culture. In most cases, a 20-year-old can adjust to new cultural standards more easily than someone who has spent 60 years following the patterns of the dominant culture (Zellner 1995).

In the last decade, counterterrorism experts have become concerned about the growth of ultraconservative militia groups in the United States. Secretive and well armed, members of these countercultural groups tend to be antigovernment, and they often tolerate racism in their midst. Watchdogs estimate that 334 militias are operating in the United States today (Southern Poverty Law Center 2013).

Members of the militia group Ohio Defense Force engage in paramilitary exercises, imagining they are destroying a threatening Muslim stronghold in the United States. Ultraconservative militia groups are a form of counterculture.

Culture Shock

Ever stepped out the door on your first day in a foreign country and felt weak in the knees? Anyone who feels disoriented, uncertain, out of place, or even fearful when immersed in an unfamiliar culture may be experiencing **culture shock.** This unsettling experience may even be mutual—the visitor's cultural habits may shock members of the host culture. Imagine, for example, that you are traveling in Japan. You know that you should remove your shoes and leave them at the door when you visit someone's home. However, there are many more customs that you are unfamiliar with. During a visit with one family, as you enter the bathroom, you see several pairs of identical slippers. Thinking they are for guests, you put on a pair and rejoin your host, who reacts with horror. Unwittingly, you have worn a pair of toilet slippers into the living room (McLane 2013).

All of us, to some extent, take for granted the cultural practices of our society. As a result, it can be surprising and even disturbing to realize that other cultures do not follow our way of life. The fact is, customs that seem strange to us may be considered normal and proper in other cultures, which may see our social practices as odd.

 use your **sociological imagination**

You arrive in a developing African country as a Peace Corps volunteer. What aspects of a very different culture do you think would be the hardest to adjust to? Explain. What might the citizens of that country find shocking about your culture?

social

policy and Culture | Bilingualism

Looking at the Issue

The staff in the emergency room is unprepared. Although the issue is not a medical one, the doctors and nurses do not understand the patient's complaints, nor can they communicate effectively with her companion. This type of incident, which occurs frequently, can have serious consequences. According to a study of two large pediatric emergency departments in Massachusetts, even when the second language is a common one like Spanish, interpreting errors can lead to clinically significant mistakes in 22 percent of such cases. In other words, language errors put patients at risk (Flores et al. 2012).

How can we learn to work and live effectively when Americans speak so many different languages? Throughout the world, not just emergency rooms but schools and other institutions must deal with people who speak many languages. **Bilingualism** refers to the use of two languages in a particular setting, such as the workplace or schoolroom, treating each language as equally legitimate. Thus, a teacher of bilingual education may instruct children in their native language while gradually introducing them to the language of the host society. If the curriculum is also bicultural, children will learn about the mores and folkways of both the dominant culture and the subculture.

To what degree should schools in the United States present the curriculum in a language other than English? This issue has prompted a great deal of debate among educators and policymakers. According to the Bureau of the Census, 61 million U.S. residents over age five—that's about 21 percent of the population—spoke a language other than English as their primary language at home in 2011 (Figure 12-1). Indeed, 29 other languages are each spoken by at least 200,000 U.S. residents (C. Ryan 2013).

This segment of the population is expected to increase modestly by 2020. For example, the proportion of older Hispanics who speak Spanish is expected to hold steady or increase slightly. However, younger Hispanics—those under 45—will be less likely than their elders to speak Spanish. A similar trend is expected for speakers of European and Asian languages: many elders will continue to speak a second language, while the younger generation will tend to favor English.

This trend toward linguistic diversity is expected to continue into the foreseeable future. Even as the children and grandchildren of immigrants adopt English as their first language, a significant proportion of the U.S. population will continue to speak a language other than English (Ortman and Shin 2011).

Do bilingual programs help the children of these families to learn English? It is difficult to reach firm conclusions, because bilingual programs in general vary so widely in their quality and approach. They differ in the length of the transition to English and in how long they allow students to remain in bilingual classrooms. Moreover, results have been mixed. In the years since California effectively dismantled its bilingual education program, reading and math scores of students with limited English proficiency rose dramatically, especially in the lower grades. Yet a major overview of 17 studies, done at Johns Hopkins University, found that students who are offered lessons in both English and their home languages make better progress than similar students who are taught only in English (R. Slavin and Cheung 2003).

Applying Sociology

For a long time, people in the United States demanded conformity to a single language. This demand coincided with the functionalist view that language serves to unify members of

—Continued

MAPPING LIFE NATIONWIDE

FIGURE 12-1 **Percentage of People Who Speak a Language Other Than English at Home, by State**

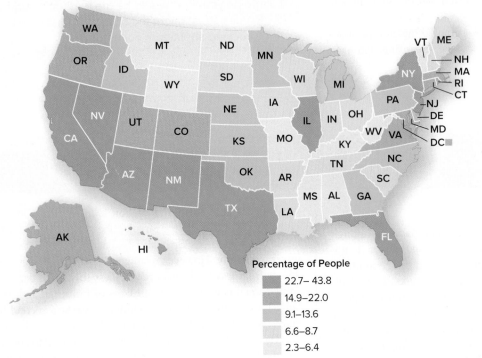

Percentage of People

	22.7– 43.8
	14.9–22.0
	9.1–13.6
	6.6–8.7
	2.3–6.4

Note: Data drawn from the 2011 American Community Survey of people five years and over. National average was 20.8 percent.
Source: C. Ryan 2013.

not take into account that success in bilingual education may actually have beneficial results, such as decreasing the number of high school dropouts and increasing the number of Hispanics in colleges and universities.

Initiating Policy

Bilingualism has policy implications largely in two areas: efforts to maintain language purity and programs to enhance bilingual education. Nations vary dramatically in their tolerance for a variety of languages. China continues to tighten its cultural control over Tibet by extending instruction of Mandarin, a Chinese dialect, from high school into the elementary schools there, which will now be bilingual along with Tibetan. In contrast, nearby Singapore establishes English as the medium of instruction but allows students to take their mother tongue as a second language, be it Chinese, Malay, or Tamil.

a society. Little respect was granted to immigrants' cultural traditions; a young person would often be teased about his or her "funny" name, accent, or style of dress.

Recent decades have seen challenges to this pattern of forced obedience to the dominant ideology. Beginning in the 1960s, active movements for Black pride and ethnic pride insisted that people regard the traditions of all racial and ethnic subcultures as legitimate and important. Conflict theorists explain this development as a case of subordinated language minorities seeking opportunities for self-expression. Partly as a result of these challenges, people began to view bilingualism as an asset. It seemed to provide a sensitive way of assisting millions of non-English-speaking people in the United States to *learn* English in order to function more effectively within the society.

The perspective of conflict theory also helps us to understand some of the attacks on bilingual programs. Many of them stem from an ethnocentric point of view, which holds that any deviation from the majority is bad. This attitude tends to be expressed by those who wish to stamp out foreign influence wherever it occurs, especially in our schools. It does

One bilingual hot spot is Québec, the French-speaking province of Canada. The Québécois, as they are known, represent 83 percent of the province's population, but only 25 percent of Canada's total population. A law implemented in 1978 mandated education in French for all Québec's children except those whose parents or siblings had learned English elsewhere in Canada. While special laws like this one have advanced French in the province, dissatisfied Québécois have tried to form their own separate country. In 1995, the people of Québec indicated their preference of remaining united with Canada by only the narrowest of margins (50.5 percent). Language and language-related cultural areas both unify and divide this nation of 33 million people (*The Economist* 2005b; R. Schaefer 2014).

Policymakers in the United States have been somewhat ambivalent in dealing with the issue of bilingualism. In 1965, the Elementary and Secondary Education Act (ESEA) provided for bilingual, bicultural education. In the 1970s, the federal government took an active role in establishing the proper form for bilingual programs. However, more recently, federal policy has been less supportive of bilingualism, and local school districts have been forced to provide an increased share of funding for their bilingual programs. Yet bilingual programs are an expense that many communities and states are unwilling to pay for and are quick to cut back. In 1998, voters in California approved a proposition that all but eliminated bilingual education: it requires instruction in English for 1.4 million children who are not fluent in the language.

In the United States, repeated efforts have been made to introduce a constitutional amendment declaring English as the nation's official language. As of 2014, 31 states had declared English their official language—an action that is now more symbolic than legislative in its significance.

Public concern over a potential decline in the use of English appears to be overblown. In reality, most immigrants and their offspring quickly become fluent in English and abandon their mother tongue. Nevertheless, many people are impatient with those immigrants who continue to use their mother tongue. The release in 2006 of *"Nuestro Himno,"* the Spanish-language version of the "Star-Spangled Banner," produced a strong public reaction: 69 percent of those who were surveyed on the topic said the anthem should be sung only in English. In reaction against the Spanish version, at least one congressman defiantly sang the national anthem in English—with incorrect lyrics. And the proprietor of a restaurant in Philadelphia posted signs advising patrons that he would accept orders for his famous steak sandwiches only in English. Throughout the year, passions ran high as policymakers debated how much support to afford people who speak other languages (J. Carroll 2006; U.S. English 2012).

In the end, the immigrant's experience is not only about learning a new language. It is about learning a whole new culture—a new totality of socially transmitted customs, knowledge, material objects, and behavior (Viramontes 2007).

TAKE THE ISSUE WITH YOU

1. Have you attended a school with students for whom English is a second language? If so, can you identify the presence of different cultures or subcultures?

2. The ultimate goal of both English-only and bilingual programs is for foreign-born students to become proficient in English. In what ways is this goal functional? Analyze the goal of such programs from the conflict and interactionist perspectives.

3. Besides bilingualism, can you think of another issue that has become controversial recently because of a clash of cultures? If so, analyze the issue from a sociological point of view.

MODULE 12 | **Recap and Review**

Summary

Each human culture has unique characteristics that evolve to meet specific circumstances of climate, geography, technological development, and population.

1. A **subculture** is a small culture that exists within a larger, dominant culture. **Countercultures** are subcultures that deliberately oppose aspects of the larger culture.

2. A person who becomes immersed in an unfamiliar culture may experience **culture shock.**

3. The social policy of **bilingualism** calls for the use of two or more languages, treating each as equally legitimate. It is supported by those who want to ease the transition of non-native-language speakers into a host society, but opposed by those who adhere to a single cultural tradition and language.

Thinking Critically

1. To what subcultures do you belong? How do they function in relation to the larger society?

2. Why do people experience culture shock? What does this phenomenon reveal about the role of culture and of everyday customs?

Key Terms

Argot

Bilingualism

Counterculture

Culture shock

Subculture

taking sociology with you

1 Locate ethnocentrism. For two days, bearing in mind what sociologists mean by *ethnocentrism,* systematically record the places where you see or hear evidence of it.

2 Study popular culture. For two days, record whatever evidence of the dominant culture you

see on the Internet or in literature, music, movies, theater, television programs, and sporting events.

3 Document a subculture. For two days, record the norms, values, sanctions, and argot evident in a subculture you are familiar with.

key terms

Argot Specialized language used by members of a group or subculture.

Bilingualism The use of two languages in a particular setting, such as the workplace or schoolroom, treating each language as equally legitimate.

Counterculture A subculture that deliberately opposes certain aspects of the larger culture.

Cultural relativism The viewing of people's behavior from the perspective of their own culture.

Cultural universal A common practice or belief found in every culture.

Culture The totality of learned, socially transmitted customs, knowledge, material objects, and behavior.

Culture industry The worldwide media industry that standardizes the goods and services demanded by consumers.

Culture lag A period of maladjustment when the nonmaterial culture is still struggling to adapt to new material conditions.

Culture shock The feeling of surprise and disorientation that people experience when they encounter cultural practices that are different from their own.

Culture war The polarization of society over controversial cultural elements.

Diffusion The process by which a cultural item spreads from group to group or society to society.

Discovery The process of making known or sharing the existence of an aspect of reality.

Dominant ideology A set of cultural beliefs and practices that helps to maintain powerful social, economic, and political interests.

Ethnocentrism The tendency to assume that one's own culture and way of life represent the norm or are superior to all others.

Folkway A norm governing everyday behavior whose violation raises comparatively little concern.

Formal norm A norm that has been written down and that specifies strict punishments for violators.

Informal norm A norm that is generally understood but not precisely recorded.

Innovation The process of introducing a new idea or object to a culture through discovery or invention.

Invention The combination of existing cultural items into a form that did not exist before.

Language An abstract system of word meanings and symbols for all aspects of culture; includes gestures and other nonverbal communication.

Law Governmental social control.

Material culture The physical or technological aspects of our daily lives.

Mores Norms deemed highly necessary to the welfare of a society.

Nonmaterial culture Ways of using material objects, as well as customs, beliefs, philosophies, governments, and patterns of communication.

Norm An established standard of behavior maintained by a society.

Sanction A penalty or reward for conduct concerning a social norm.

Sapir-Whorf hypothesis A hypothesis concerning the role of language in shaping our interpretation of reality. It holds that language is culturally determined.

Society A fairly large number of people who live in the same territory, are relatively independent of people outside their area, and participate in a common culture.

Sociobiology The systematic study of how biology affects human social behavior.

Subculture A segment of society that shares a distinctive pattern of customs, rules, and traditions that differs from the pattern of the larger society.

Symbol A gesture, object, or word that forms the basis of human communication.

Technology Cultural information about the ways in which the material resources of the environment may be used to satisfy human needs and desires.

Value A collective conception of what is considered good, desirable, and proper—or bad, undesirable, and improper—in a culture.

Read each question carefully and then select the best answer.

1. Which of the following is an aspect of culture?
   a. a comic book
   b. patriotic attachment to the flag of the United States
   c. slang words
   d. all of the above

2. People's adaptations to meet the needs for food, shelter, and clothing are examples of what George Murdock referred to as
   a. norms.
   b. folkways.
   c. cultural universals.
   d. cultural practices.

3. What term do sociologists use to refer to the process by which a cultural item spreads from group to group or society to society?
   a. diffusion
   b. globalization
   c. innovation
   d. cultural relativism

4. The appearance of Starbucks coffeehouses in China is a sign of what aspect of culture?
   a. innovation
   b. globalization
   c. diffusion
   d. cultural relativism

5. Which of the following statements is true according to the Sapir-Whorf hypothesis?
   a. Language simply describes reality.
   b. Language does not transmit stereotypes related to race.
   c. Language precedes thought.
   d. Language is not an example of a cultural universal.

6. Which of the following statements about norms is correct?
   a. People do not follow norms in all situations. In some cases, they evade a norm because they know it is weakly enforced.
   b. In some instances, behavior that appears to violate society's norms may actually represent adherence to the norms of a particular group.
   c. Norms are violated in some instances because one norm conflicts with another.
   d. all of the above

7. Which of the following statements about values is correct?
   a. Values never change.
   b. The values of a culture may change, but most remain relatively stable during any one person's lifetime.
   c. Values are constantly changing; sociologists view them as being very unstable.
   d. all of the above

8. Which of the following terms describes the set of cultural beliefs and practices that help to maintain powerful social, economic, and political interests?
   a. mores
   b. dominant ideology
   c. consensus
   d. values

9. Terrorist groups are examples of
   a. cultural universals.
   b. subcultures.
   c. countercultures.
   d. dominant ideologies.

10. What is the term used when one places a priority on understanding other cultures, rather than dismissing them as "strange" or "exotic"?
    a. ethnocentrism
    b. culture shock
    c. cultural relativism
    d. cultural value

11. _____ are gestures, objects, and/or words that form the basis of human communication.

12. _____ is the process of introducing a new idea or object to a culture.

13. The bow and arrow, the automobile, and the television are all examples of _____ .

14. Sociologists associated with the _____ perspective emphasize that language and symbols offer a powerful way for a subculture to maintain its identity.

15. "Put on some clean clothes for dinner" and "Thou shalt not kill" are both examples of _____ found in U.S. culture.

16. The United States has strong _____ against murder, treason, and other forms of abuse that have been institutionalized into formal norms.

17. From a(n) _____ perspective, the dominant ideology has major social significance. Not only do a society's most powerful groups and institutions control wealth and property; more important, they control the means of production.

18. Countercultures (for example, hippies) are typically popular among the _____, who have the least investment in the existing culture.

19. A person experiences _____ _____ when he or she feels disoriented, uncertain, out of place, even fearful when immersed in an unfamiliar culture.

20. From the _____ perspective, subcultures are evidence that differences can exist within a common culture.

Answers

1 (d); 2 (c); 3 (a); 4 (b); 5 (c); 6 (d); 7 (b); 8 (b); 9 (c); 10 (c); 11 Symbols; 12 Innovation; 13 inventions; 14 interactionist; 15 norms; 16 mores; 17 conflict; 18 young; 19 culture shock; 20 functionalist

4

Socialization and the Life Course

A father teaches his daughter to ride a bike. Around the world, the family is the most important agent of socialization.

Have you ever wondered what military basic training might be like? Ever gone through it?

Military journalist Jim Garamone went to Parris Island, South Carolina, to watch young Marine recruits go through basic training.

" PARRIS ISLAND, S.C.—Make basic training tougher. This is the challenge for the military services.

But what does "tough" mean? Is it just physical toughness or does mental toughness also come into play? What about military skills and the ability to operate in a tough, unforgiving combat environment? At what point in basic training do recruits finally prove they are tough, that they are ready, that they belong?

For the . . . Marines, the essence of this passage from one world to another comes into razor-sharp focus in a final gut check field exercise that each of their recruits must face and overcome. The Marines call this last challenge, the "Crucible" . . . In military terms, these trials of toughness are simply referred to as culminating events.

The Crucible emphasizes trainee teamwork under stress. "Recruits get eight hours of sleep during the entire 54-hour exercise," said Sgt. Roger Summers, a Delta Company drill instructor in the 1st Recruit Training Battalion at Parris Island. "They get two-and-a-half MREs [field rations] and they are responsible for rationing out the food to themselves. Then we put them through tough physical activities like road marches and night infiltration courses. They march about 40 miles in those 54 hours."

It isn't long before the recruits are tired and hungry, Summers said, but as they keep going they realize they can call on reserves they never knew they had.

"Some of these recruits do things they never thought they could do," he said. "Some of them come from middle-class homes where everything has been handed to them. Others come from poorer homes where nothing was ever expected of them. If they finish the Crucible, they have accomplished something."

One recruit put it best. "I am going to finish this," he said. "And when I do, it will be the most positive thing I have done in my life."

"You see the team learn as they go along," he continued. "At the beginning, they just charge ahead without a plan and without asking if anyone has an idea. By the end of the Crucible you see them working together better, getting advice from all team members, and solving more of the problems."

"They . . . realize after the first day they have to work together to finish. No one gets through the Crucible alone."

One warrior station, for example, is built around an enemy-mined rope bridge that the recruits must cross with their gear and ammunition boxes. They have only a couple of short ropes and their personal gear to solve the problem. At another event, recruits run into firing positions and engage pop-up targets with 10 rounds in two magazines. Recruit teams battle each other with pugil sticks [long, padded training poles] in yet another event.

The recruits grab food and water when they can. After the first two events comes a five-mile night march. "The night march was the toughest thing we've done here," said 18-year-old Pfc. Josh Lunceford of Charleston, W.Va. "The whole company went on it and whoever led it set a real fast pace. You couldn't see very well and people were tripping over stuff, and everyone was tired."

The recruits hit the rack for four hours of sleep, then begin another day and finish the final two events. "On the second day they are tired and hungry and it really starts to show," said Capt. John H. Rochford, Delta Company commander. "They start getting short with one another, but they realize after the first day they have to work together to finish. No one gets through the Crucible alone."

At the end of the second day, the recruits go through a night infiltration course and then hit the rack for another four hours. When they get up, they face a nine-mile march and the end of the Crucible.

As the sun rises, the recruits cross [a bridge]. Once across, the drill instructors start Jody calls and the recruits join in. As they get closer to the main base, the Jody calls get louder until they reach the Parade Deck. The recruits form up around a half-size replica of the Marine Corps Memorial—also known as the Iwo Jima Memorial. There, a significant transformation takes place.

"We're not just giving them basic training, we're turning them into Marines," Rochford said. "There's more to being a Marine than knowing how to fire a weapon. There's a whole tradition behind it, and we want these recruits to measure up to the men and women who went before them."

A color guard raises the flag on the memorial. The chaplain reads a prayer specifically written for the finish of the Crucible, and the company first sergeant addresses the recruits. Then the drill instructors present each of their recruits with the Marine Corps insignia—the eagle, globe, and anchor. He shakes their hands and calls them "Marine" for the first time. Many accept the honor with tears streaming down their faces. "

(Garamone 1999)

n this excerpt from "The Challenge," Jim Garamone describes the final, life-changing trial young Marine recruits face. Basic training develops raw recruits into Marines through tests of both physical endurance and team building. This transformative period, which lasts 8 to 12 weeks, ends with a *rite of passage*, or ritual that marks the symbolic transition from one social position to another. Such ceremonies dramatize and celebrate changes in a person's status throughout the life span. Rites of passage can mark a separation, as at a graduation, or an incorporation, as at an initiation. Baptisms, weddings, bar and bat mitzvahs, funerals—all are rites of passage (Van Gennep [1909] 1960). Because they help prepare individuals to assume new social roles as they move through the life course, rites of passage are important cultural elements of socialization.

How much of a person's personality is shaped by culture, as opposed to inborn traits? In what ways does socialization continue throughout the life course? Who are the most powerful agents of socialization? In these modules we will examine the role of socialization in human development. We will begin by analyzing the interaction of heredity with environmental factors. Then we will explore how people develop perceptions, feelings, and beliefs about themselves. We will pay particular attention to important agents of socialization, including the family, schools, peers, the media and technology, the workplace, and religion. As we will see, socialization is a process that spans the entire life course. In the Social Policy section that closes the chapter, we will focus on the socialization experience of group child care for young children.

MODULE 13 | The Role of Socialization

Sociologists, in general, are interested in the patterns of behavior and attitudes that emerge *throughout* the life course, from infancy to old age. These patterns are part of the lifelong process of **socialization,** in which people learn the attitudes, values, and behaviors appropriate for members of a particular culture. Socialization occurs through human interactions that begin in infancy and continue through retirement. We learn a great deal from those people most important in our lives—immediate family members, best friends, and teachers. But we also learn from people we see on the street, on television, on the Internet, and in films and magazines. From a microsociological perspective, socialization helps us to discover how to behave "properly" and what to expect from others if we follow (or challenge) society's norms and values. From a macrosociological perspective, socialization provides for the transmission of a culture from one generation to the next, to ensure the long-term continuity of a society.

Socialization also shapes our self-images. For example, in the United States, a person who is viewed as "too heavy" or "too short" does not conform to the ideal cultural standard of physical attractiveness. This kind of unfavorable evaluation can significantly influence the person's self-esteem. In this sense, socialization experiences can help to shape our personalities. In everyday speech, the term **personality** is used to refer to a person's typical patterns of attitudes, needs, characteristics, and behavior.

What makes us who we are? Is it the genes we are born with, or the environment in which we grow up? Researchers have traditionally clashed over the relative importance of biological inheritance and environmental factors in human development—a conflict called the *nature versus nurture* (or *heredity versus environment*) debate. Today, most social scientists have moved beyond this debate, acknowledging instead the *interaction* of these variables in shaping human development. However, we can better appreciate how heredity and environmental factors interact and influence the socialization process if we first examine situations in which one factor operates almost entirely without the other (Homans 1979).

Social Environment: The Impact of Isolation

In the 1994 movie *Nell,* Jodie Foster played a young woman hidden from birth by her mother in a backwoods cabin. Raised without normal human contact, Nell crouches like an animal, screams wildly, and speaks or sings in a language all her own. This movie was drawn from the actual account of an emaciated 16-year-old boy who appeared mysteriously in 1828 in the town square of Nuremberg, Germany (Lipson 1994).

Some viewers may have found the story of Nell difficult to believe, but social scientists have encountered similar cases. The two cases that follow describe the documented effects of extreme social isolation and neglect.

Extreme Isolation: Isabelle

The dramatic story of a child called Isabelle was all too real. For the first six years of her life, Isabelle lived in almost total seclusion in a darkened room. She had little contact with other people, with the exception of her mother, who could neither speak nor hear. Isabelle's mother's parents had been so deeply ashamed of Isabelle's illegitimate birth that they kept her hidden away from the world. Ohio authorities finally discovered the child in 1938, when Isabelle's mother escaped from her parents' home, taking her daughter with her.

When she was discovered at age six, Isabelle could not speak; she could merely make various croaking sounds. Her only communications with her mother were simple gestures. Isabelle had been largely deprived of the typical interactions and socialization experiences of childhood. Since she had seen few people, she showed a strong fear of strangers and reacted almost like a wild animal when confronted with an unfamiliar person. As she became accustomed to seeing certain individuals, her reaction changed to one of extreme apathy. At first, observers believed that Isabelle was deaf, but she soon began to react to nearby sounds. On tests of maturity, she scored at the level of an infant rather than a six-year-old.

Specialists developed a systematic training program to help Isabelle adapt to human relationships and socialization. After a few days of training, she made her first attempt to verbalize. Although she started slowly, Isabelle quickly passed through six years of development. In a little over two months she was speaking in complete sentences. Nine months later she could identify both words and sentences. Before Isabelle reached age nine, she was ready to attend school with other children. By age 14 she was in sixth grade, doing well in school, and emotionally well adjusted.

Yet without an opportunity to experience socialization in her first six years, Isabelle had been hardly human in the social sense when she was first discovered. Her inability to communicate at the time of her discovery—despite her physical and cognitive potential to learn—and her remarkable progress over the next few years underscore the impact of socialization on human development (K. Davis 1947:435–437).

The scientists involved with Isabelle's case concluded that all children need socialization in the form of love, care, and affection. Absent that kind of attention, humans cannot learn to speak and interact with others as expected. This need for positive social interaction does not end with childhood; it continues throughout the life span.

Unfortunately, other children who have been locked away or severely neglected have not fared so well as Isabelle. In many instances, the consequences of their social isolation have proved much more damaging.

Extreme Neglect: Romanian Orphans

Isabelle's experience is important to researchers because there are only a few cases of children who were reared in total isolation. However, there are many cases of children raised in extremely neglectful social circumstances. In the 1990s, public attention focused on infants and young children who grew up in orphanages in the formerly communist countries of Eastern Europe. In Romanian orphanages, babies once lay in their cribs for 18 to 20 hours a day, curled against their feeding bottles, receiving little care from adults. This minimal attention continued for the first five years of their lives. Many of them grew up fearful of human contact, and prone to unpredictable antisocial behavior. As recently as 2004, some 32,000 Romanian children were institutionalized in this manner.

This situation came to light as families in North America and Europe began to adopt thousands of the orphans. For about 20 percent of those adopted, adjustment problems were so dramatic that the adopting families suffered guilty fears of being ill-fit parents. Many of them have asked for assistance in dealing with the children. Slowly, efforts are being made to introduce the deprived youngsters to feelings of attachment and socialization that they have never experienced before (Groza et al. 1999; Craig Smith 2006).

In 2001, Romania bowed to pressure and placed a moratorium on international adoptions. The state took steps to reunite orphans with their birth families, place them with adoptive families in Romania, or settle them in small group homes. With supervision from attentive caregivers and specialists, the once-abandoned children have made remarkable progress. UNICEF is now using the program as a model for other nations that are dealing with such children. Worldwide, an estimated 2 million

In Romania, special programs emphasizing social interaction have helped orphans to overcome years of social isolation.

children are living in institutional care (Aslanian 2006; *The Economist* 2013a; Ironside 2011; UNICEF 2009).

As with Isabelle, the Romanian orphans underscored the significance of the social environment in a child's development. Increasingly, researchers are emphasizing the importance of the earliest socialization experiences for all children, including those who grow up in more normal environments. We know now that it is not enough to care for an infant's physical needs; parents must also concern themselves with their children's social development. If, for example, children are discouraged from having friends even as toddlers, they will miss out on experiences with peers that are critical to their socialization and emotional growth.

Primate Studies

Studies of animals raised in isolation also support the importance of socialization in development. Harry Harlow (1971), a researcher at the primate laboratory of the University of Wisconsin, conducted tests with rhesus monkeys that had been raised away from their mothers and away from contact with other monkeys. As was the case with Isabelle, the rhesus monkeys raised in isolation were fearful and easily frightened. They did not mate, and the females who were artificially inseminated became abusive mothers. Apparently, isolation had had a damaging effect on the monkeys.

A creative aspect of Harlow's experimentation was his use of "artificial mothers." In one such experiment, Harlow presented monkeys raised in isolation with two substitute mothers—one cloth-covered replica and one covered with wire that had the ability to offer milk. Monkey after monkey went to the wire mother for the life-giving milk, yet spent much more time clinging to the more motherlike cloth model. It appears that the infant monkeys developed greater social attachments from their need for warmth, comfort, and intimacy than from their need for milk.

While these studies may seem to suggest that heredity can be dismissed as a factor in the social development of humans and animals, studies of twins reveal a fascinating interplay between heredity and environment.

use your sociological imagination

What events in your life have had a strong influence on who you are?

Despite the striking physical resemblance between these identical twins, there are undoubtedly many differences between them. Research points to some behavioral similarities between twins, but little beyond the likenesses found among nontwin siblings.

The Influence of Heredity

Identical twins Oskar Stohr and Jack Yufe were separated soon after their birth and raised on different continents, in very different cultural settings. Oskar was reared as a strict Catholic by his maternal grandmother in the Sudetenland of Czechoslovakia. As a member of the Hitler Youth movement in Nazi Germany, he learned to hate Jews. In contrast, his brother Jack was reared in Trinidad by the twins' Jewish father. Jack joined an Israeli kibbutz (a collective settlement) at age 17 and later served in the Israeli army. When the twins were reunited in middle age, however, some startling similarities emerged: They both wore wire-rimmed glasses and mustaches. They both liked spicy foods and sweet liqueurs, were absentminded, flushed the toilet before using it, stored rubber bands on their wrists, and dipped buttered toast in their coffee (Holden 1980).

The twins also differed in many important respects: Jack was a workaholic; Oskar enjoyed leisure-time activities. Oskar was a traditionalist who was domineering toward women; Jack was a political liberal who was much more accepting of feminism. Finally, Jack was extremely proud of being Jewish, whereas Oskar never mentioned his Jewish heritage (Holden 1987).

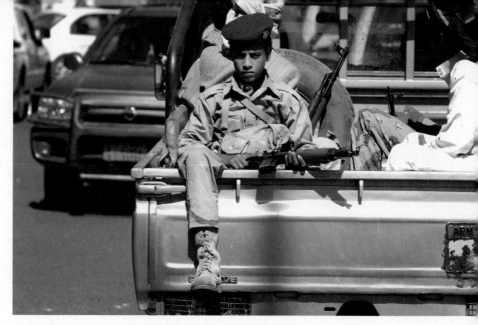

Oskar and Jack are prime examples of the interplay of heredity and environment. For a number of years, the Minnesota Twin Family Study has been following 137 sets of identical twins reared apart to determine what similarities, if any, they show in personality traits, behavior, and intelligence. Preliminary results from the available twin studies indicate that *both* genetic factors *and* socialization experiences are influential in human development. Certain characteristics, such as temperaments, voice patterns, and nervous habits, appear to be strikingly similar even in twins reared apart, suggesting that these qualities may be linked to hereditary causes. However, identical twins reared apart differ far more in their attitudes, values, chosen mates, and even drinking habits; these qualities, it would seem, are influenced by environmental factors. In examining clusters of personality traits among such twins, researchers have found marked similarities in their tendency toward leadership or dominance, but significant differences in their need for intimacy, comfort, and assistance.

Researchers have also been impressed with the similar scores on intelligence tests of twins reared apart in *roughly similar* social settings. Most of the identical twins register scores even closer than those that would be expected if the same person took a test twice. At the same time, however, identical twins brought up in *dramatically different* social environments score quite differently on intelligence tests—a finding that supports the impact of socialization on human development (Segal 2012).

We need to be cautious in reviewing studies of twin pairs and other relevant research. Widely broadcast findings have often been based on preliminary analysis of extremely small samples.

Socialization can be negative as well as positive. When the very young come to view harmful behaviors like smoking or illegal drug use as "normal," socialization is negative. In Yemen, this child soldier has learned to use an automatic weapon.

For example, one study (not involving twin pairs) was frequently cited as confirming genetic links with behavior. Yet the researchers had to retract their conclusions after they increased the sample and reclassified two of the original cases. After those changes, the initial findings were no longer valid.

Critics add that studies of twin pairs have not provided satisfactory information concerning the extent to which separated identical twins may have had contact with each other, even though they were raised apart. Such interactions—especially if they were extensive—could call into question the validity of the twin studies. As this debate continues, we can certainly anticipate numerous efforts to replicate the research and clarify the interplay between heredity and environmental factors in human development (Horgan 1993; Plomin 1989).

MODULE 13 | **Recap and Review**

Summary

Socialization is the process through which people learn the attitudes, values, and actions appropriate for members of a particular culture.

1. Socialization affects the overall cultural practices of a society; it also shapes the images we hold of ourselves.

2. Heredity and environmental factors interact in influencing the socialization process.

Thinking Critically

1. What might be some ethical concerns regarding research on the influences of heredity and environment?

2. What are some social policy implications of research on the effects of early socialization experiences?

Key Terms

Personality

Socialization

We all have various perceptions, feelings, and beliefs about who we are and what we are like. How do we come to develop them? Do they change as we age?

We were not born with these understandings. Building on the work of George Herbert Mead (1964b), sociologists recognize that our concept of who we are, the *self,* emerges as we interact with others. The **self** is a distinct identity that sets us apart from others. It is not a static phenomenon, but continues to develop and change throughout our lives.

Sociologists and psychologists alike have expressed interest in how the individual develops and modifies the sense of self as a result of social interaction. The work of sociologists Charles Horton Cooley and George Herbert Mead, pioneers of the interactionist approach, has been especially useful in furthering our understanding of these important issues.

◼ Sociological Approaches to the Self

Cooley: Looking-Glass Self

In the early 1900s, Charles Horton Cooley advanced the belief that we learn who we are by interacting with others. Our view of ourselves, then, comes not only from direct contemplation of our personal qualities but also from our impressions of how others perceive us. Cooley used the phrase **looking-glass self** to emphasize that the self is the product of our social interactions.

The process of developing a self-identity or self-concept has three phases. First, we imagine how we present ourselves to others—to relatives, friends, even strangers on the street. Then we imagine how others evaluate us (attractive, intelligent, shy, or strange). Finally, we develop some sort of feeling about ourselves, such as respect or shame, as a result of these impressions (Cooley 1902; Michael C. Howard 1989).

A subtle but critical aspect of Cooley's looking-glass self is that the self results from an individual's "imagination" of how others view him or her. As a result, we can develop self-identities based on *incorrect* perceptions of how others see us. A student may react strongly to a teacher's criticism and decide (wrongly) that the instructor views the student as stupid. This misperception may be converted into a negative self-identity through the following process: (1) the teacher criticized me, (2) the teacher must think that I'm stupid, (3) I *am* stupid. Yet self-identities are also subject to change. If the student receives an A at the end of the course, he or she will probably no longer feel stupid.

Mead: Stages of the Self

George Herbert Mead continued Cooley's exploration of interactionist theory. Mead (1934, 1964a) developed a useful model of the process by which the self emerges, defined by three distinct stages: the preparatory stage, the play stage, and the game stage.

The Preparatory Stage   During the *preparatory stage,* children merely imitate the people around them, especially family members with whom they continually interact. Thus, a small child will bang on a piece of wood while a parent is engaged in carpentry work, or will try to throw a ball if an older sibling is doing so nearby.

As they grow older, children become more adept at using symbols, including the gestures and words that form the basis of human communication. By interacting with relatives and friends, as well as by watching cartoons on television and looking at picture books, children in the preparatory stage begin to understand symbols. They will continue to use this form of communication throughout their lives.

The Play Stage   Mead was among the first to analyze the relationship of symbols to socialization. As children develop skill in communicating through symbols, they gradually become more aware of social relationships. As a result, during the *play stage,* they begin to pretend to be other people. Just as an actor "becomes" a character, a child becomes a doctor, parent, superhero, or ship captain.

Mead, in fact, noted that an important aspect of the play stage is role-playing. **Role taking** is the process of mentally assuming the perspective of another and responding from that imagined viewpoint. For example, through this process a young child will gradually learn when it is best to ask a parent for favors. If the parent usually comes home from work in a bad mood, the child will wait until after dinner, when the parent is more relaxed and approachable.

The Game Stage   In Mead's third stage, the *game stage,* the child of about age eight or nine no longer just plays roles but begins to consider several tasks and relationships simultaneously. At this point in development, children grasp not only their own social positions but also those of others around them—just as in a football game the players must understand their own and everyone else's positions. Consider a girl or boy who is part of a Scout troop out on a weekend hike in the mountains. The child must understand what he or she is expected to do but must also recognize the responsibilities of other Scouts as well as the leaders. This is the final stage of development under Mead's model; the child can now respond to numerous members of the social environment.

Mead uses the term **generalized other** to refer to the attitudes, viewpoints, and expectations of society as a whole that a child takes into account in his or her behavior. Simply put, this concept suggests that when an individual acts, he or she takes into account an entire group of people. For example, a child will not act courteously merely to please a particular parent. Rather, the child comes to understand that courtesy is a widespread social value endorsed by parents, teachers, and religious leaders.

TABLE **14-1** MEAD'S STAGES OF THE SELF

Stage	Self Present?	Definition	Example
Preparation	No	Child imitates the actions of others.	When adults laugh and smile, child laughs and smiles.
Play	Developing	Child takes the role of a single other, as if he or she were the other.	Child first takes the role of doctor, then the role of patient.
Game	Yes	Child considers the roles of two or more others simultaneously.	In game of hide-and-seek, child takes into account the roles of both hider and seeker.

Table 14-1 summarizes the three stages of the self outlined by George Herbert Mead.

Mead: Theory of the Self

Mead is best known for his theory of the self. According to Mead (1964b), the self begins at a privileged, central position in a person's world. Young children picture themselves as the focus of everything around them and find it difficult to consider the perspectives of others. For example, when shown a mountain scene and asked to describe what an observer on the opposite side of the mountain might see (such as a lake or hikers), young children describe only objects visible from their vantage point. This childhood tendency to place ourselves at the center of events never entirely disappears. Many people with a fear of flying automatically assume that if any plane goes down, it will be the one they are on. And who reads the horoscope section in the paper without looking at their own horoscope first? Why else do we buy lottery tickets, if we do not imagine ourselves winning?

Nonetheless, as people mature, the self changes and begins to reflect greater concern about the reactions of others. Parents, friends, co-workers, coaches, and teachers are often among those who play a major role in shaping a person's self. The term **significant others** is used to refer to those individuals who are most important in the development of the self. Many young people, for example, find themselves drawn to the same kind of work their parents engage in (H. Sullivan [1953] 1968).

 use your **sociological imagination**

How do you view yourself as you interact with others around you? How do you think you formed this view of yourself?

Goffman: Presentation of the Self

How do we manage our "self"? How do we display to others who we are? Erving Goffman, a sociologist associated with the interactionist perspective, suggested that many of our daily activities involve attempts to convey impressions of who we are. His observations help us to understand the sometimes subtle yet critical ways in which we learn to present ourselves

socially. They also offer concrete examples of this aspect of socialization.

Early in life, the individual learns to slant his or her presentation of the self in order to create distinctive appearances and satisfy particular audiences. Goffman (1959) referred to this altering of the presentation of the self as **impression management.** Box 14-1 describes an everyday example of this concept—the way students behave after receiving their exam grades.

In analyzing such everyday social interactions, Goffman makes so many explicit parallels to the theater that his view has been termed the **dramaturgical approach.** According to this perspective, people resemble performers in action. For example, a clerk may try to appear busier than he or she actually is if a supervisor happens to be watching. A customer in a singles' bar may try to look as if he or she is waiting for a particular person to arrive.

Goffman (1959) also drew attention to another aspect of the self, **face-work.** How often do you initiate some kind of face-saving behavior when you feel embarrassed or rejected? In response to a rejection at the singles' bar, a person may engage in face-work by saying, "There really isn't an interesting person in this entire crowd." We feel the need to maintain a proper image of the self if we are to continue social interaction.

Face-work is a necessity for those who are unemployed. In an economic downturn like the recent recession, unemployment affects people of all social classes, many of whom are unaccustomed to being jobless. A recent ethnographic study found the newly unemployed redefining what it means to be out of work. They were focusing more than in the past on what they were accomplishing, and had begun to value volunteer work more since they had become volunteers themselves. Participants in this study engaged in both impression management and face-work (Garrett-Peters 2009).

Goffman's work on the self represents a logical progression of sociological studies begun by Cooley and Mead on how personality is acquired through socialization and how we manage the presentation of the self to others. Cooley stressed the process by which we create a self; Mead focused on how the self develops as we learn to interact with others; Goffman emphasized the ways in which we consciously create images of ourselves for others.

Impression Management by Students

When you and fellow classmates get an exam back, you probably react differently depending on the grades that you and they earned. This distinction is part of *impression management*. Researchers have found that students' reactions differ depending on the grades that others received, compared to their own. These encounters can be divided into three categories: those in which all students earned high grades (Ace–Ace encounters); those between Aces and students who received low or failing grades (Ace–Bomber encounters); and those between students who all got low grades (Bomber–Bomber encounters).

Ace–Ace encounters occur in a rather open atmosphere, because there is comfort in sharing a high mark with another high achiever. It is even acceptable to violate the norm of modesty and brag when among other Aces, since as one student admitted, "It's much easier to admit a high mark to someone who has done better than you, or at least as well."

Ace–Bomber encounters are often sensitive. Bombers generally attempt to avoid such exchanges, because "you . . . emerge

looking like the dumb one" or "feel like you are lazy or unreliable." When forced into interactions with Aces, Bombers work to appear gracious and congratulatory. For their part, Aces offer sympathy and support to the dissatisfied Bombers and even rationalize their own "lucky" high scores. To help Bombers save face, Aces may empha-

> When forced into interactions with Aces, Bombers work to appear gracious and congratulatory.

size the difficulty and unfairness of the examination.

Bomber–Bomber encounters tend to be closed, reflecting the group effort to wall off the feared disdain of others. Yet within the safety of these encounters, Bombers openly share their disappointment and engage in expressions of mutual self-pity that they

themselves call "pity parties." They devise face-saving excuses for their poor performance, such as "I wasn't feeling well all week" or "I had four exams and two papers due that week."

Of course, grade comparisons are not the only occasion when students engage in impression management. Another study has shown that students' perceptions of how often fellow students work out can also influence their social encounters. In athletic terms, a bomber would be someone who doesn't work out; an ace would be someone who works hard at physical fitness.

LET'S DISCUSS

1. How do you react to those who have received higher or lower grades than you? Do you engage in impression management? How would you like others to react to your grade?

2. What social norms govern students' impression management strategies?

Sources: Albas and Albas 1988, 1996; Austin 2009; M. Mack 2003.

People judge us by our appearance, attire, body language, demeanor, and mannerisms. Knowing that they do, most of us alter the way we present ourselves to others, a strategy that Goffman called impression management.

Psychological Approaches to the Self

Psychologists have shared the interest of Cooley, Mead, and other sociologists in the development of the self. Early work in psychology, such as that of Sigmund Freud (1856–1939),

stressed the role of inborn drives—among them the drive for sexual gratification—in channeling human behavior. More recently, psychologists such as Jean Piaget have emphasized the stages through which human development progresses.

Like Charles Horton Cooley and George Herbert Mead, Freud believed that the self is a social product, and that aspects of one's personality are influenced by other people (especially one's parents). However, unlike Cooley and Mead, he suggested that the self has components that work in opposition to each other. According to Freud, our natural impulsive instincts are in constant conflict with societal constraints. Part of us seeks limitless pleasure, while another part favors rational behavior. By interacting with others, we learn the expectations of society and then select behavior most appropriate to our culture. (Of course, as Freud was well aware, we sometimes distort reality and behave irrationally.)

Research on newborn babies by the Swiss child psychologist Jean Piaget (1896–1980) has underscored the importance of social interactions in developing a sense of self. Piaget found that newborns have no self in the sense of a looking-glass image. Ironically, though, they are quite self-centered; they demand that all attention be directed toward them. Newborns have not yet separated themselves from the universe of which they are a part. For these babies, the phrase "you and me" has no meaning; they understand only "me." However, as they mature, children are

TABLE **14-2** THEORETICAL APPROACHES TO
DEVELOPMENT OF THE SELF

Tracking Sociological Perspectives

Scholar	Key Concepts and Contributions	Major Points of Theory
Charles Horton Cooley 1864–1929 sociologist (USA)	Looking-glass self	Stages of development not distinct; feelings toward ourselves developed through interaction with others
George Herbert Mead 1863–1931 sociologist (USA)	The self Generalized other	Three distinct stages of development; self develops as children grasp the roles of others in their lives
Erving Goffman 1922–1982 sociologist (USA)	Impression management Dramaturgical approach Face-work	Self developed through the impressions we convey to others and to groups
Sigmund Freud 1856–1939 psychotherapist (Austria)	Psychoanalysis	Self influenced by parents and by inborn drives, such as the drive for sexual gratification
Jean Piaget 1896–1980 child psychologist (Switzerland)	Cognitive theory of development	Four stages of cognitive development

gradually socialized into social relationships, even within their rather self-centered world.

In his well-known **cognitive theory of development,** Piaget (1954) identified four stages in the development of children's thought processes. In the first, or *sensorimotor,* stage, young children use their senses to make discoveries. For example, through touching they discover that their hands are actually a part of themselves. During the second, or *preoperational,* stage, children begin to use words and symbols to distinguish objects and ideas. The milestone in the third, or *concrete operational,* stage is that children engage in more logical thinking. They learn that even when a formless lump of clay is shaped into a snake, it is still the same clay. In the fourth, or *formal operational,* stage, adolescents become capable of sophisticated abstract thought and can deal logically with ideas and values.

According to Piaget, social interaction is the key to development. As children grow older, they pay increasing attention to how other people think and why they act in particular ways. In order to develop a distinct personality, each of us needs opportunities to interact with others. As we saw earlier, Isabelle was deprived of the chance for normal social interactions, and the consequences were severe (Kitchener 1991).

We have seen that a number of thinkers considered social interaction the key to the development of an individual's sense of self. As is generally true, we can best understand this topic by drawing on a variety of theory and research. Table 14-2 summarizes the rich literature, both sociological and psychological, on the development of the self.

Socialization throughout the Life Course

The Life Course

Among the Kota people of the Congo in Africa, adolescents paint themselves blue. Mexican American girls go on a daylong religious retreat before dancing the night away.

Egyptian mothers step over their newborn infants seven times, and graduating students at the Naval Academy throw their hats in the air. These are all ways of celebrating **rites of passage,** a means of dramatizing and validating changes in a person's status. Rites of passage mark a separation, as in a graduation ceremony, or an incorporation, as in the opening excerpt about the Marine Corps (Van Gennep [1909] 1960).

Rites of passage are a worldwide social phenomenon. The Kota rite marks the passage to adulthood. The color blue, viewed as the color of death, symbolizes the death of childhood. Hispanic girls celebrate reaching womanhood with a *quinceañera* ceremony at age 15. In the Cuban American community of Miami, the popularity of the *quinceañera* supports a network of party planners, caterers, dress designers, and the Miss Quinceañera Latina pageant. For thousands of years, Egyptian mothers have welcomed their newborns to the world in

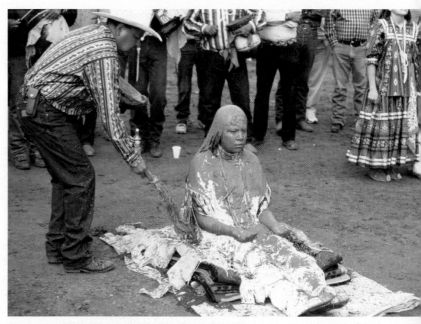

A young Apache woman undergoes a mudding ceremony traditionally used in rites of passage, such as puberty and in some cases weddings.

the Soboa ceremony by stepping over the seven-day-old infant seven times.

These specific ceremonies mark stages of development in the life course. They indicate that the process of socialization continues through all stages of the life cycle. In fact, some researchers have chosen to concentrate on socialization as a lifelong process. Sociologists and other social scientists who take such a **life course approach** look closely at the social factors that influence people throughout their lives, from birth to death, including gender and income. They recognize that biological changes mold but do not dictate human behavior.

Several life events mark the passage to adulthood, including marriage and the birth of a first child. Of course, these turning points vary from one society or even one generation to the next. In the United States, the key event seems to be the completion of formal schooling. However, educational completion is not as clearly defined today as it was a generation or two ago. More and more people are taking full-time jobs while finishing their schooling, or returning to school to obtain a professional certificate or advanced degree. Similarly, the milestones associated with leaving home, finding a stable job, and establishing a long-term personal relationship do not now occur at specific ages (Silva 2012; T. Smith 2003).

One result of these overlapping steps to independence is that in the United States, unlike some other societies, there is no clear dividing line between adolescence and adulthood. Nowadays, few young people finish school, get married, and leave home at about the same age, clearly establishing their transition to adulthood. The terms *youthhood, emerging adulthood,* and *not quite adult* have been coined to describe the prolonged ambiguous status that young people in their 20s experience (Côté 2000; Settersten and Ray 2011; Christian Smith 2007).

 use your **sociological imagination**

Why do you think the end of formal schooling is the most important milestone of adulthood today? What about marriage, full-time employment, or financial independence from parents or guardians? Which milestone do you think is the most important?

Anticipatory Socialization and Resocialization

The development of a social self is literally a lifelong transformation that begins in the crib and continues as one prepares for death. Two types of socialization occur at many points throughout the life course: anticipatory socialization and resocialization.

Anticipatory socialization refers to processes of socialization in which a person rehearses for future positions, occupations, and social relationships. A culture can function more efficiently and smoothly if members become acquainted with the norms, values, and behavior associated with a social position before actually assuming that status. Preparation for many aspects of adult life begins with anticipatory socialization during childhood and adolescence, and continues throughout our lives as we prepare for new responsibilities.

You can see the process of anticipatory socialization take place when high school students start to consider what colleges they may attend. Traditionally, this task meant looking at publications received in the mail or making campus visits. However, with new technology, more and more students are using the web to begin their college experience. Colleges are investing more time and money in developing attractive websites through which students can take virtual campus tours and hear audio clips of everything from the college anthem to a sample zoology lecture.

Occasionally, assuming a new social or occupational position requires us to *unlearn* an established orientation. **Resocialization** refers to the process of discarding former behavior patterns and accepting new ones as part of a transition in one's life. Often resocialization occurs during an explicit effort to transform an individual, as happens in reform schools, therapy groups, prisons, religious conversion settings, and political indoctrination camps. The process of resocialization typically involves considerable stress for the individual—much more so than socialization in general, or even anticipatory socialization (Gecas 2004).

Resocialization is particularly effective when it occurs within a total institution. Erving Goffman (1961) coined the term **total institution** to refer to an institution that regulates all aspects of a person's life under a single authority, such as a prison, the military, a mental hospital, or a convent. Because the total institution is generally cut off from the rest of society, it provides for all the needs of its members. Quite literally, the crew of a merchant vessel at sea becomes part of a total institution. So elaborate are its requirements, so all-encompassing its activities, a total institution often represents a miniature society.

Goffman (1961) identified four common traits of total institutions:

- All aspects of life are conducted in the same place under the control of a single authority.

- Any activities within the institution are conducted in the company of others in the same circumstances—for example, army recruits or novices in a convent.

- The authorities devise rules and schedule activities without consulting the participants.

- All aspects of life within a total institution are designed to fulfill the purpose of the organization. Thus, all activities in a monastery might be centered on prayer and communion with God (Davies 1989; P. Rose et al. 1979).

People often lose their individuality within total institutions. For example, a person entering prison may experience the humiliation of a **degradation ceremony** as he or she is stripped of clothing, jewelry, and other personal possessions. From this point on, scheduled daily routines allow for little or no personal initiative. The individual becomes secondary and rather invisible in the overbearing social environment (Garfinkel 1956).

Summary

This module examines sociological and psychological views of the development of the **self.**

1. In the early 1900s, Charles Horton Cooley advanced the belief that we learn who we are by interacting with others, a phenomenon he called the **looking-glass self.**

2. George Herbert Mead, best known for his theory of the self, proposed that as people mature, their selves begin to reflect their concern about reactions from others, both **generalized others** and **significant others.**

3. Erving Goffman has shown that in many of our daily activities, we try to convey distinct impressions of who we are, a process he called **impression management.**

4. According to Jean Piaget's **cognitive theory of development,** social interaction is the key to psychological development.

5. Socialization proceeds throughout the life course. Some societies mark stages of development with formal **rites of passage.** In the culture of the United States, significant events such as marriage and parenthood serve to change a person's status.

Thinking Critically

1. Use Erving Goffman's dramaturgical approach to describe impression management among members of one of the following groups: athletes, college instructors, parents, physicians, or politicians.

2. What are some similarities between Mead's stages of the self and Piaget's cognitive development stages? What are some differences?

Key Terms

Anticipatory socialization

Cognitive theory of development

Degradation ceremony

Dramaturgical approach

Face-work

Generalized other

Impression management

Life course approach

Looking-glass self

Resocialization

Rites of passage

Role taking

Self

Significant other

Total institution

MODULE 15 | **Agents of Socialization**

As we have seen, the culture of the United States is defined by rather gradual movements from one stage of socialization to the next. The continuing and lifelong socialization process involves many different social forces that influence our lives and alter our self-images.

The family is the most important agent of socialization in the United States, especially for children. In this module, we'll also discuss six other agents of socialization: the school, the peer group, the mass media and technology, the workplace, religion, and the state.

Family

The lifelong process of learning begins shortly after birth. Since newborns can hear, see, smell, taste, and feel heat, cold, and pain, they are constantly orienting themselves to the surrounding world. Human beings, especially family members, constitute an important part of their social environment. People minister to the baby's needs by feeding, cleaning, carrying, and comforting the baby.

All families engage in socialization, but the way that Amish families encourage their children to accept their community's subculture is particularly striking. Box 15-1 describes their tolerance for the period of rebellion known as *rum springa,* during which Amish children flirt with the adolescent subculture of mainstream American society.

In the United States, social development also includes exposure to cultural assumptions regarding gender and race. Black parents, for example, have learned that children as young as age two can absorb negative messages about Blacks in children's books, toys, and television shows—all of which are designed primarily for White consumers. At the same time, Black children are exposed more often than others to the inner-city youth gang culture. Because most Blacks, even those who are middle class, live near very poor neighborhoods, their children are susceptible to these influences, despite their parents' strong family values (Linn and Poussaint 1999; Pattillo-McCoy 1999).

The term **gender role** refers to expectations regarding the proper behavior, attitudes, and activities of males and females. For

A daughter learns how to weave fabric from her mother in Guatemala. The family is the most important agent of socialization.

example, we traditionally think of "toughness" as masculine—and desirable only in men—while we view "tenderness" as feminine. Other cultures do not necessarily assign these qualities to each gender in the way that our culture does. The existence of gender roles does not imply that inevitably, males and females will assume certain roles, nor does it imply that those roles are quite distinct from one another. Rather, gender roles emphasize the fact that males and females are not genetically predetermined to occupy certain roles.

As the primary agents of childhood socialization, parents play a critical role in guiding children into those gender roles deemed appropriate in a society. Other adults, older siblings, the mass media, and religious and educational institutions also have a noticeable impact on a child's socialization into feminine and masculine norms. A culture or subculture may require that one sex or the other take primary responsibility for the socialization of children, economic support of the family, or religious or intellectual leadership. In some societies, girls are socialized mainly by their mothers and boys by their fathers—an arrangement that may prevent girls from learning critical survival skills. In South Asia, fathers teach their sons to swim to prepare them for a life as fishermen; girls typically do not learn to swim. When a deadly tsunami hit the coast of South Asia in 2004, many more men survived than women.

School

Like the family, schools have an explicit mandate to socialize people in the United States—especially children—into the norms and values of our culture.

As conflict theorists Samuel Bowles and Herbert Gintis (1976) have observed, schools in this country foster competition through built-in systems of reward and punishment, such as grades and evaluations by teachers. Consequently, a child who is experiencing difficulty trying to learn a new skill can sometimes come to feel stupid and unsuccessful. However, as the self matures, children become capable of increasingly realistic assessments of their intellectual, physical, and social abilities.

Functionalists point out that schools, as agents of socialization, fulfill the function of teaching children the values and customs of the larger society. Conflict theorists agree, but add that schools can reinforce the divisive aspects of society, especially those of social class. For example, higher education in the United States is costly despite the existence of financial aid programs. Students from affluent backgrounds therefore have an advantage in gaining access to universities and professional training. At the same time, less affluent young people may never receive the preparation that would qualify them for the best-paying and most prestigious jobs.

Peer Group

As a child grows older, the family becomes somewhat less important in social development. Instead, peer groups increasingly assume the role of Mead's significant others. Within the peer group, young people associate with others who are approximately their age, and who often enjoy a similar social status (Giordano 2003).

We can see how important peer groups are to young people when their social lives are strained by war or disaster. In Baghdad, the overthrow of Saddam Hussein has profoundly changed teenagers' worlds, casting doubt on their future. Some young people have lost relatives or friends; others have become involved with fundamentalist groups or fled with their families to safer countries. Those youths who are left behind can suffer intense loneliness and boredom. Confined to their homes by crime and terrorism, those fortunate enough to have computers turn to Internet chat rooms or immerse themselves in their studies. Through e-mail, they struggle to maintain old friendships interrupted by wartime dislocation (Sanders 2004).

Gender differences are noteworthy among adolescents. Boys and girls are socialized by their parents, peers, and the media to identify many of the same paths to popularity, but to different degrees. Table 15-1 compares male and female college students' reports of how girls and boys they knew became popular in high school. The two groups named many of the same paths to popularity but gave them a different order of importance. While neither men nor women named sexual activity, drug use, or alcohol

BOX 15-1

Research Today

Rum Springa: Raising Children Amish Style

All families face challenges raising their children, but what if your parents expected you not to dance, listen to music, watch television, or access the Internet? This is the challenge faced by Amish teens and their parents, who embrace a lifestyle of the mid-1800s. Amish youths—boys in particular—often rebel against their parents' strict morals by getting drunk, behaving disrespectfully, and indulging in "worldly" activities, such as buying a car. At times even the girls may become involved, to their families' dismay. As one scholar puts it, "The rowdiness of Amish youth is an embarrassment to church leaders and a stigma in the larger community" (Kraybill 2001:138).

Yet the strong pull of mainstream American culture has led Amish parents to routinize, almost to accept, some of their

> All families face challenges raising their children, but what if your parents expected you not to dance, listen to music, watch television, or access the Internet?

children's worldly activities. They expect adolescents to test their subculture's boundaries during a period of discovery called *rum springa,* a German term meaning "running around." A common occurrence during which

young people attend barn dances and break social norms that forbid drinking, smoking, and driving cars, *rum springa* is definitely not supported by the Amish religion.

Parents often react to these escapades by looking the other way, sometimes literally. If they hear radio music coming from the barn, or a motorcycle driving onto their property in the middle of the night, they don't retaliate by punishing their offspring. Instead, they

pretend not to notice, secure in the knowledge that Amish children almost always return to the community's traditional values. Indeed, despite the flirtation with popular culture and modern technology that is common during the *rum springa,* the vast majority of Amish youths do return to the Amish community and become baptized. Scholars report that 85 to 90 percent of Amish children accept the faith as young adults.

To mainstream Americans, this little known and understood subculture became a source of entertainment when in 2004, UPN aired a 10-week reality program called *Amish in the City.* In the series, five Amish youths allegedly on *rum springa* moved in with six worldly wise young adults in Los Angeles. On behalf of the Amish community, some critics called the series exploitative, a sign of how vulnerable the Amish are. No similar series would be developed on the rebellion of Muslim or Orthodox Jewish youths, they charged.

LET'S DISCUSS

1. Do you or anyone you know come from a subculture that rejects mainstream American culture? If so, describe the community's norms and values. How do they resemble and how do they differ from Amish norms and values?

2. Why do you think so many Amish youths return to their families' way of life after rebelling against it?

Sources: Kraybill 2001; R. Schaefer and Zellner 2011; Shachtman 2006; Stevick 2007; Weinraub 2004.

TABLE 15-1 HIGH SCHOOL POPULARITY

What makes high school girls popular?		What makes high school boys popular?	
According to college men:	**According to college women:**	**According to college men:**	**According to college women:**
1. Physical attractiveness	1. Grades/intelligence	1. Participation in sports	1. Participation in sports
2. Grades/intelligence	2. Participation in sports	2. Grades/intelligence	2. Grades/intelligence
3. Participation in sports	3. General sociability	3. Popularity with girls	3. General sociability
4. General sociability	4. Physical attractiveness	4. General sociability	4. Physical attractiveness
5. Popularity with boys	5. Clothes	5. Car	5. School clubs/government

Note: Students at the following universities were asked in which ways adolescents in their high schools had gained prestige with their peers: Cornell University, Louisiana State University, Southeastern Louisiana University, State University of New York at Albany, State University of New York at Stony Brook, University of Georgia, and University of New Hampshire.

Source: Suitor et al. 2001:445.

use as one of the top five paths, college men were much more likely than women to mention those behaviors as a means to becoming popular, for both boys and girls.

Mass Media and Technology

In the past century, media innovations—radio, motion pictures, recorded music, television, and the Internet—have become important agents of socialization. The question is no longer whether young people are plugged in, but how they use these resources. Today, 95 percent of those aged 12 to 17 are on the Internet. No surprise there, but 91 percent of them post photos identifying themselves by name. Ninety-two percent use their real names, and 82 percent post their birth dates on social media. Increasingly, then, socialization occurs online. The age at which young people go online has also been dropping, prompting concern about the potential for media abuse at an earlier and earlier age. Over the last decade, the American Academy of Pediatrics began by publishing concerns about teen use of the Internet. Recently, the organization published guidelines for the 90 percent of *infants* who use the Internet—via their parents, of course (American Academy of Pediatrics 2011, 2013; Madden et al. 2013).

The media, however, are not always a negative socializing influence. Television programs and even commercials can introduce young people to unfamiliar lifestyles and cultures. Not only do children in the United States learn about life in "faraway lands," but inner-city children learn about the lives of farm children, and vice versa. The same thing happens in other countries.

Sociologists and other social scientists have begun to consider the impact of technology on socialization. They are

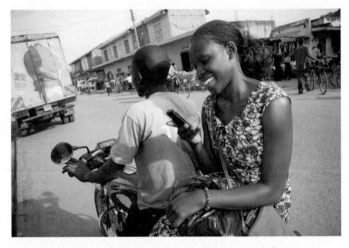

In Soroti, Uganda, a woman makes a quick telephone call. Cell phones play a critical role in communications and commerce in developing countries, where other ways of connecting are less available or more expensive.

particularly interested in the online friendship networks, like Facebook and Twitter. To assess the importance of social media in our daily lives, they typically begin by studying how we use them. In a novel approach, some researchers have asked what would happen if we stopped using social media: see Box 15-2.

Not just in industrial nations, but in Africa and other developing areas, people have been socialized into relying on new communications technologies. Not long ago, if Zadhe Iyombe wanted to talk to his mother, he had to make an eight-day trip from the capital city of Kinshasa up the Congo River by boat to the rural town where he was born. Now both he and his mother

BOX 15-2

Sociology on Campus

Unplugging the Media: What Happens?

What happens when a college campus goes media-free for a whole day? Beginning in 2010, researchers at the University of Maryland and in Salzburg, Austria, challenged students to abstain from all media for 24 hours. By the end of 2013, almost 1,000 students from a dozen colleges on five continents had accepted the challenge. After their media-free day was over, students were asked to report their successes and failures in going without social media. Together, they wrote almost half a million words.

As the accompanying figure shows, there were some differences among countries in how students felt about their day without media. "Alienation" and "distress" were common responses across the 10 participating nations. Although students had volunteered for the project and understood that their abstinence was only temporary, they found the experience extremely difficult. To give up media even for 24 hours, they said, was virtually impossible.

"For people in the modern society," said one student in China, "communication [media] is as important as breath." Without media, said another student from Slovakia, "I felt as though everything I knew was taken away from me and that I was being tortured." A student in Mexico moaned, "I feel that not even the sun can warm me." Others reported that they felt unbearably constrained, almost "paralyzed." "What really bothered me and made me feel 'tied down' was the inability to do what I wanted when I wanted it," said a student in Lebanon.

> Although students had volunteered for the project and understood that their abstinence was only temporary, they found the experience extremely difficult.

Not all responses were negative; a minority of students (from a low of 16 percent in Argentina to a high of 36 percent in Uganda) mentioned some benefits. As one Chinese student observed, "I invited my fellows to play badminton and enjoy the sunshine in our beautiful campus, chatting, laughing, eating, drinking, wandering, etc." And a British student concluded, "I have legs, which I now believe are underestimated as a social tool, as they allowed me to go and see people and communicate with them wirelessly." In effect, the unplugged students undertook more face-to-face socialization than usual.

Researchers concluded that going without media for a day made students more aware of the media, both the benefits and limitations. Students discovered that they were unable to go about their daily lives without the media. The "addiction" that many reported prompted some to confess a need to curb their media use—although most doubted they would have much success doing so.

LET'S DISCUSS

1. Could you go without media for a day? Get together with a group of friends or classmates and try going media-free for 24 hours; then share your reactions.

2. How well did students in the United States react to a media-free day compared to those in other countries? What might explain the differences?

Sources: Moeller et al. 2012; World Unplugged 2013. World Unplugged 2013 is the source of all student quotations.

Responses to a Day without Media

Country	"Addiction"	Failure	Boredom	Confusion	Distress	Isolation	Benefits of unplugging
Argentina	12%	23%	3%	11%	14%	21%	16%
Chile	19%	14%	5%	5%	17%	18%	21%
China-Mainland	22%	7%	6%	9%	23%	7%	25%
China-Hong Kong	22%	10%	6%	14%	22%	10%	16%
Great Britain	20%	11%	5%	11%	19%	11%	21%
Lebanon	19%	4%	9%	12%	27%	5%	25%
Mexico	20%	13%	5%	15%	21%	7%	20%
Slovakia	15%	13%	5%	11%	21%	8%	27%
Uganda	14%	0%	14%	0%	21%	14%	36%
United States	23%	12%	6%	8%	21%	8%	22%

have access to a cell phone, and they send text messages to each other daily. Iyombe and his mother are not atypical. Although cell phones aren't cheap, 1.4 billion owners in developing countries have come to consider them a necessity. Today, there are more cell phones in developing nations than in industrial nations—the first time in history that developing nations have outpaced the developed world in the adoption of a telecommunications technology (K. Sullivan 2006).

That said, not all new communications technologies are widely available in developing nations. For example, many people in these countries cannot afford broadband Internet service. In terms of their relative income, broadband service is 40 times more expensive to people in developing countries than it is to the typical person in an industrialized nation (International Telecommunication Union 2012).

■ Workplace

Learning to behave appropriately in an occupation is a fundamental aspect of human socialization. It used to be that going to work began with the end of our formal schooling, but that is no longer the case, at least not in the United States. More and more young people work today, and not just for a parent or relative. Adolescents generally seek jobs in order to make spending money; 80 percent of high school seniors say that little or none of what they earn goes to family expenses. These teens rarely look on their employment as a means of exploring vocational interests or getting on-the-job training.

Some observers feel that the increasing number of teenagers who are working earlier in life and for longer hours are finding the workplace almost as important an agent of socialization as school. In fact, a number of educators complain that student time at work is adversely affecting schoolwork. The level of teenage employment in the United States is the highest among industrial countries, which may provide one explanation for why U.S. high school students lag behind those in other countries on international achievement tests.

Socialization in the workplace changes when it involves a more permanent shift from an after-school job to full-time employment. Occupational socialization can be most intense during the transition from school to job, but it continues throughout one's work history. Technological advances may alter the requirements of the position and necessitate some degree of resocialization. Today, men and women change occupations, employers, or places of work many times during their adult years. For example, the typical worker spends about four years with an employer. Occupational socialization continues, then, throughout a person's years in the labor market (Bialik 2010).

College students today recognize that occupational socialization is not socialization into one lifetime occupation. They anticipate going through a number of jobs. The Bureau of Labor Statistics (2010) has found that from ages 18 to 42, the typical person has held 11 jobs. This high rate of turnover in employment applies to both men and women, and to those with a college degree as well as those with a high school diploma.

■ Religion and the State

Increasingly, social scientists are recognizing the importance of both religion and government ("the state") as agents of socialization, because of their impact on the life course. Traditionally, family members have served as the primary caregivers in our culture, but in the 20th century, the family's protective function was steadily transferred to outside agencies such as hospitals, mental health clinics, and child care centers. Many of these agencies are run by groups affiliated with certain religions or by the state.

Both organized religion and government have impacted the life course by reinstituting some of the rites of passage once observed in agricultural communities and early industrial societies. For example, religious organizations stipulate certain traditional rites that may bring together all the members of an extended family, even if they never meet for any other reason. And government regulations stipulate the ages at which a person may drive a car, drink alcohol, vote in elections, marry without parental permission, work overtime, and retire. These regulations do not constitute strict rites of passage: most 18-year-olds choose not to vote, and most people choose their age of retirement without reference to government dictates.

In the Social Policy section at the end of this chapter, we will see that government is under pressure to become a provider of child care, which would give it a new and direct role in the socialization of infants and young children.

social policy and Socialization |
Child Care around the World

Child care programs are not just babysitting services; they have an enormous influence on the development of young children—an influence that has been growing with the movement of more and more women into the paid labor force. The rise in single-parent families, increased job opportunities for women, and the need for additional family income have all propelled mothers of young children into the working world. Who should care for the children of working mothers during working hours?

Looking at the Issue

Preschoolers typically are not cared for by their parents. Seventy-three percent of employed mothers depend on others to care for their children, and 30 percent of mothers who aren't employed have regular care arrangements. In fact, children under age five are more likely to be cared for on a daily basis by their grandparents than by their parents. Over a third of them are cared for by nonrelatives in nursery schools, Head Start programs, day care centers, family day care, and other arrangements (Bureau of the Census 2008c).

Researchers have found that high-quality child care centers do not adversely affect the socialization of children; in fact, good day care benefits children. The value of preschool programs was documented in a series of studies conducted in the United States. Researchers found no significant differences in infants who had received extensive nonmaternal care compared with those who had been cared for solely by their mothers. They also reported that more and more infants in the United States are being placed in child care outside the home, and that overall, the quality of those arrangements is better than has been found in previous studies. It is difficult, however, to generalize about child care, since there is so much variability among day care providers, and even among government policies from one state to another (Loeb et al. 2004; Ludwig and Sawhill 2007; NICHD 2007).

Few people in the United States or elsewhere can afford the luxury of having a parent stay at home, or of paying for high-quality live-in child care. For millions of mothers and fathers, finding the right kind of child care is a challenge both to parenting and to the pocketbook. At present, the federal government supports child care through subsidized programs, which target low-income families, and income tax credits, which benefit families with moderate incomes. The annual expenditure to assist low-income parents is about $12 billion; the expenditure to support parents with moderate incomes is $58 billion (Cushing-Daniels and Zedlewski 2008).

Applying Sociology

Studies that assess the quality of child care outside the home reflect the micro level of analysis and the interest of interactionists in the impact of face-to-face interaction. These studies also explore macro-level implications for the functioning of social institutions like the family. Some of the issues surrounding day care have also been of interest to those who take the conflict perspective.

In the United States, high-quality day care is not equally available to all families. Parents in affluent communities have an easier time finding day care than those in poor or working-class communities. Finding *affordable* child care is also a problem. Viewed from a conflict perspective, child care costs are an especially serious burden for lower-class families. The poorest families spend 25 percent of their income for preschool child care, whereas families who are *not* poor pay only 6 percent or less of their income. Despite these problems, subsidized child care has steadily declined over the last decade.

Feminist theorists echo the concern of conflict theorists that high-quality child care receives little government support because it is regarded as "merely a way to let women work." Nearly all child care workers (97 percent) are women; many find themselves in low-status, minimum-wage jobs. Typically, food servers, messengers, and gas station attendants make more money than the 23 million child care workers in the United States, whose average annual salary of $19,605 puts them right at the poverty level for a family of three (Barnett et al. 2013; Bureau of the Census 2011a; Ruiz 2010).

Initiating Policy

Policies regarding child care outside the home vary throughout the world. Most developing nations do not have the economic base to provide subsidized child care. Thus, working mothers rely largely on relatives or take their children to work. In the comparatively wealthy industrialized

Children play at the Communicare day care center in Perth, Australia. The Australian government subsidizes children's attendance at day care and afterschool programs from birth to age 12.

countries of western Europe, government provides child care as a basic service, at little or no expense to parents. But even those countries with tax-subsidized programs occasionally fall short of the need for high-quality child care.

When policymakers decide that child care is desirable, they must determine the degree to which taxpayers should subsidize it. In Sweden and Denmark, one-half to two-thirds of preschoolers were in government-subsidized child care full-time in 2003. In the United States, annual fees for full-time child care of a four-year-old range from an average of $3,900 in Mississippi to an average of $11,678 in Massachusetts (Immervoll and Barber 2005; NACCRRA 2010).

Japan is facing a special dilemma. Traditionally, married women and certainly married mothers did not remain in the labor force. Although this social pattern is slowly changing, the availability of day care has not kept pace. Many Japanese policymakers have difficulty recognizing the need for day care. "Is your work so important that you must put your baby in child-care?" they ask. "Why are you being so self-centered?" Little wonder that a single private day care center in Japan recently had a waiting list of 25,000 children (Tabuchi 2013:A9).

We have a long way to go in making high-quality child care more affordable and accessible, not just in the United States but throughout the world as well. In an attempt to reduce government spending, France is considering cutting back the budgets of subsidized nurseries, even though waiting lists exist and the French public heartily disapproves of cutbacks. In Germany, reunification has reduced the options previously open to East German mothers, who had become accustomed to government-supported child care. Experts in child development view such reports as a vivid reminder of the need for greater government and private-sector support for child care. From a public policy point of view, the case for expanded child care is especially persuasive. According to recent research, reductions in public assistance, together with increased tax revenue from parents' earnings, would outweigh the cost of government subsidies to child care programs (Domeij and Klein 2013; L. King 1998).

TAKE THE ISSUE WITH YOU

1. Were you ever in a day care program? If so, do you recall the experience as good or bad? In general, do you think it is desirable to expose young children to the socializing influence of day care?

2. In the view of conflict theorists, child care receives little government support because it is "merely a way to let women work." Can you think of other explanations?

3. Should the costs of day care programs be paid by government, by the private sector, or entirely by parents?

MODULE 15 | Recap and Review

Summary

Important agents of socialization include the family, schools, peer groups, the mass media, the workplace, religious institutions, and the state.

1. As the primary agents of socialization, parents play a critical role in guiding children into those **gender roles** deemed appropriate in a society.

2. Like the family, schools in the United States have an explicit mandate to socialize people—especially children—into the norms and values of our culture.

3. Peer groups and the mass media, especially television and the Internet, are important agents of socialization for adolescents.

4. Socialization in the workplace begins with part-time employment while we are in school and continues as we work full-time and change jobs throughout our lives.

5. Religion and the state shape the socialization process by regulating the life course and influencing our views of appropriate behaviors at particular ages.

6. As more and more mothers of young children have entered the labor market, the demand for child care has increased dramatically, posing policy questions for many nations around the world.

Thinking Critically

1. How would functionalist and conflict theorists differ in their analysis of socialization by the mass media?

2. What sanctions limit participation in social networking? Describe the rules you have observed that limit the way people access and use online social networks. What are the purposes of such sanctions?

Key Terms

Gender role

Mastering This Chapter

taking sociology with you

1 Examine your looking-glass self. What was it like in high school? How did it change when you entered college, and who were the people who caused you to see yourself differently?

2 For two days, keep a record of your use of the mass media—television, the Internet, and so on—including what you watched, read, or communicated and your reasons for doing so. Then take the role of a sociologist and ask how you might have been socialized by the media you used. What norms and values were you exposed to, and how did they affect you?

3 Interview a person who has recently changed jobs. Ask about the process of resocialization required by the new job. Was the job change voluntary or involuntary, and how did it affect the person's adjustment? Which of the concepts you learned in this chapter seem relevant to the experience?

key terms

Anticipatory socialization Processes of socialization in which a person rehearses for future positions, occupations, and social relationships.

Cognitive theory of development The theory that children's thought progresses through four stages of development.

Degradation ceremony An aspect of the socialization process within some total institutions, in which people are subjected to humiliating rituals.

Dramaturgical approach A view of social interaction in which people are seen as theatrical performers.

Face-work The efforts people make to maintain the proper image and avoid public embarrassment.

Gender role Expectations regarding the proper behavior, attitudes, and activities of males and females.

Generalized other The attitudes, viewpoints, and expectations of society as a whole that a child takes into account in his or her behavior.

Impression management The altering of the presentation of the self in order to create distinctive appearances and satisfy particular audiences.

Life course approach A research orientation in which sociologists and other social scientists look closely at the social factors that influence people throughout their lives, from birth to death.

Looking-glass self A concept that emphasizes the self as the product of our social interactions.

Personality A person's typical patterns of attitudes, needs, characteristics, and behavior.

Resocialization The process of discarding former behavior patterns and accepting new ones as part of a transition in one's life.

Rites of passage Rituals marking the symbolic transition from one social position to another.

Role taking The process of mentally assuming the perspective of another and responding from that imagined viewpoint.

Self A distinct identity that sets us apart from others.

Significant other An individual who is most important in the development of the self, such as a parent, friend, or teacher.

Socialization The lifelong process in which people learn the attitudes, values, and behaviors appropriate for members of a particular culture.

Total institution An institution that regulates all aspects of a person's life under a single authority, such as a prison, the military, a mental hospital, or a convent.

self-quiz

Read each question carefully and then select the best answer.

1. Which of the following social scientists used the phrase *looking-glass self* to emphasize that the self is the product of our social interactions with other people?
   a. George Herbert Mead
   b. Charles Horton Cooley
   c. Erving Goffman
   d. Jean Piaget

2. In what he called the *play stage* of socialization, George Herbert Mead asserted that people mentally assume the perspectives of others, thereby enabling them to respond from that imagined viewpoint. This process is referred to as
   a. role taking.
   b. the generalized other.
   c. the significant other.
   d. impression management.

3. George Herbert Mead is best known for his theory of what?
   a. presentation of the self
   b. cognitive development
   c. the self
   d. impression management

4. Suppose a clerk tries to appear busier than he or she actually is when a supervisor happens to be watching. Erving Goffman would study this behavior from what approach?
   a. functionalist
   b. conflict
   c. psychological
   d. interactionist

5. According to child psychologist Jean Piaget's cognitive theory of development, children begin to use words and symbols to distinguish objects and ideas during which stage in the development of the thought process?
   a. the sensorimotor stage
   b. the preoperational stage
   c. the concrete operational stage
   d. the formal operational stage

6. On the first day of basic training in the army, a recruit has his civilian clothes replaced by army "greens," has his hair shaved off, loses his privacy, and finds that he must use a communal bathroom. All these humiliating activities are part of
   a. becoming a significant other.
   b. impression management.
   c. a degradation ceremony.
   d. face-work.

7. Which social institution is considered to be the most important agent of socialization in the United States, especially for children?
   a. the family
   b. the school
   c. the peer group
   d. the mass media

8. The term *gender role* refers to
   a. the biological fact that we are male or female.
   b. a role that is given to us by a teacher.
   c. a role that is given to us in a play.
   d. expectations regarding the proper behavior, attitudes, and activities of males and females.

9. Which sociological perspective emphasizes that schools in the United States foster competition through built-in systems of reward and punishment?
   a. the functionalist perspective
   b. the conflict perspective
   c. the interactionist perspective
   d. the psychological perspective

10. Which of the following statements about teenagers in Baghdad is true?
    a. They have lost much of their peer group due to death and relocation.
    b. They have lost peers who have joined fundamentalist groups.
    c. If they own a computer, they use it in an attempt to stay in contact with their pre-war peer group.
    d. all of the above

11. _____ is the term used by sociologists in referring to the lifelong process whereby people learn the attitudes, values, and behaviors appropriate for members of a particular culture.

12. In everyday speech, the term _____ is used to refer to a person's typical patterns of attitudes, needs, characteristics, and behavior.

13. Studies of twins raised apart suggest that both _____ and _____ influence human development.

14. A _____ _____ is an individual such as a parent, friend, or teacher who is most important in the development of the self.

15. Early work in _____, such as that by Sigmund Freud, stressed the role of inborn drives—among them the drive for sexual gratification—in channeling human behavior.

16. The Swiss psychologist Jean Piaget developed the _____ theory of development.

17. Preparation for many aspects of adult life begins with _____ socialization during childhood and adolescence and continues throughout our lives as we prepare for new responsibilities.

18. Resocialization is particularly effective when it occurs within a(n) _____ institution.

19. The _____ perspective emphasizes the role of schools in teaching the values and customs of the larger society.

20. As children grow older, the family becomes less important in social development, while _____ groups become more important.

5 Social Interaction, Social Structure, and Groups

Groups help individuals to navigate through the larger social world, including complex social organizations.

If you were a prison guard, would you mistreat the inmates?

To find the answer to this question, social psychologist Philip Zimbardo created a mock prison and enlisted college students to serve as the inmates and guards.

" The quiet of a summer Sunday morning in Palo Alto, California, was shattered by a screeching squad car siren as police swept through the city picking up college students in a surprise mass arrest. Each suspect was charged with a felony; warned of his constitutional rights; spread-eagled against the car; searched, handcuffed, and carted off in the back seat of the squad car to the police station for booking.

After being fingerprinted and having identification forms prepared for his "jacket" (central information file), each prisoner was left isolated in a detention cell to wonder what he had done to get himself into this mess. After a while, he was blindfolded and transported to the "Stanford County Prison." Here he began the induction process of becoming a prisoner—stripped naked, skin searched, deloused, and issued a uniform, bedding, soap, and towel.

The quiet of a summer Sunday morning in Palo Alto, California, was shattered by a screeching squad car siren as police swept through the city picking up college students in a surprise mass arrest.

By late afternoon when nine such arrests had been completed, these youthful "first offenders" sat in dazed silence on the cots in their barren cells. These men were part of a very unusual kind of prison, an experimental or mock prison, created by social psychologists for the purpose of intensively studying the effects of imprisonment upon volunteer research subjects. When we planned our two-week-long simulation of prison life, we were primarily concerned about understanding the process by which people adapt to the novel and alien environment in which those called "prisoners" lose their liberty, civil rights, independence, and privacy, while those called "guards" gain social power by accepting the responsibility for controlling and managing the lives of their dependent charges. . . .

Our final sample of participants (10 prisoners and 11 guards) were selected from over 75 volunteers recruited through ads in the city and campus newspapers. . . . Half were randomly assigned to role-play being guards, the others to be prisoners. Thus, there were no measurable differences between the guards and the prisoners at the start of this experiment. . . .

At the end of only six days we had to close down our mock prison because what we saw was frightening. It was no longer apparent to most of the subjects (or to us) where reality ended and their roles began. The majority had indeed become prisoners or guards, no longer able to clearly differentiate between role-playing and self. There were dramatic changes in virtually every aspect of their behavior, thinking, and feeling. In less than a week the experience of imprisonment undid (temporarily) a lifetime of learning: human values were suspended; self-concepts were challenged; and the ugliest, most base, pathological side of human nature surfaced. We were horrified because we saw some boys (guards) treat others as if they were despicable animals, taking pleasure in cruelty, while other boys (prisoners) became servile, dehumanized robots who thought only of escape, of their own individual survival, and of their mounting hatred for the guards. "

(Zimbardo 1972:4; Zimbardo et al. 1974:61, 62, 63)

In this study, directed and described by author Philip Zimbardo, college students adopted the patterns of social interaction expected of guards and prisoners when they were placed in a mock prison. Sociologists use the term *social interaction* to refer to the ways in which people respond to one another, whether face-to-face or over the telephone or on the computer. In the mock prison, social interactions between guards and prisoners were highly impersonal. The guards addressed the prisoners by number rather than name, and they wore reflective sunglasses that made eye contact impossible.

As in many real-life prisons, the simulated prison at Stanford University had a social structure in which guards held virtually total control over prisoners. The term *social structure* refers to the way in which a society is organized into predictable relationships. The social structure of Zimbardo's mock prison influenced how the guards and prisoners interacted. Zimbardo and his colleagues (2009:516) note that it was a real prison "in the minds of the jailers and their captives." His simulated prison experiment, first conducted more than 30 years ago, has subsequently been repeated (with similar findings) both in the United States and in other countries.

In these modules we will study social structure and its effect on our social interactions. What determines a person's status in society? How do our social roles affect our social interactions? What is the place of social institutions such as the family, religion, and government in our social structure? How can we better understand and manage large organizations such as multinational corporations? We'll begin by considering how social interactions shape the way we view the world around us. Next, we'll focus on the five basic elements of social structure: statuses, social roles, groups, social networks, and social institutions such as the family, religion, government, and the mass media. We'll see that functionalists, conflict theorists, and interactionists approach social institutions quite differently. Finally, we'll compare our modern social structure with simpler forms, using typologies developed by Émile Durkheim, Ferdinand Tönnies, and Gerhard Lenski. The Social Policy section at the end of the chapter focuses on the changing role of labor unions.

MODULE 16 | Social Interaction and Social Structure

The prison experiment described in the opening excerpt took on new relevance in 2004, in the wake of shocking revelations of prisoner abuse at the U.S.-run Abu Ghraib military facility in Iraq. Graphic "trophy photos" showed U.S. soldiers humiliating naked Iraqi prisoners and threatening to attack them with police dogs. The structure of the wartime prison, coupled with intense pressure on military intelligence officers to secure information regarding terrorist plots, contributed to the breakdown in the guards' behavior. But Zimbardo himself noted that the guards' depraved conduct could have been predicted simply on the basis of his research. So strong was public reaction to the Abu Ghraib scandal that in 2009, during his first week in office, President Barack Obama declared that henceforth interrogators will use only noncoercive methods for questioning suspected terrorists (Ratnesar 2011).

The two concepts of social interaction and social structure are central to sociological study. They are closely related to socialization, the process through which people learn the attitudes, values, and behaviors appropriate to their culture. When the students in Zimbardo's experiment entered the mock prison, they began a process of resocialization. In that process, they adjusted to a new social structure and learned new rules for social interaction.

Social Interaction and Reality

When someone in a crowd shoves you, do you automatically push back? Or do you consider the circumstances of the incident and the attitude of the instigator before you react? Chances are you do the latter. According to sociologist Herbert Blumer (1969:79), the distinctive characteristic of **social interaction** among people is that "human beings interpret or 'define' each other's actions instead of merely reacting to each other's actions." In other words, our response to someone's behavior is based on the *meaning* we attach to his or her actions. Reality is shaped by our perceptions, evaluations, and definitions.

These meanings typically reflect the norms and values of the dominant culture and our socialization experiences within that culture. As interactionists emphasize, the meanings that we attach to people's behavior are shaped by our interactions with them and with the larger society. Social reality is literally constructed from our social interactions (Berger and Luckmann 1966).

How do we define our social reality? Consider something as simple as how we regard tattoos. At one time, most of us in the United States considered tattoos weird or kooky. We associated them with fringe countercultural groups, such as punk rockers, biker gangs, and skinheads. Among many people, a tattoo elicited an automatic negative response. Now, however, so many people have tattoos—including society's trendsetters and major sports figures—and the ritual of getting a tattoo has become so legitimized, that mainstream culture regards tattoos differently. At this point, as a result of increased social interaction with tattooed people, tattoos look perfectly at home to us in a number of settings.

The nature of social interaction and what constitutes reality varies across cultures. In Western societies, with their emphasis on romantic love, couples see marriage as a relationship as well as a social status. From Valentine's Day flowers to more informal, everyday gestures, professions of love are an expected part of marriage. In Japan, however, marriage is considered more a social status than a relationship. Although many or most Japanese couples undoubtedly do love each other, saying "I love you" does not come easily to them, especially not to husbands. Nor do most husbands call their wives by name (they prefer "Mother") or look them in the eyes. In 2006, in an effort to change these restrictive customs, some Japanese men formed the Devoted Husband Organization, which has been sponsoring a new holiday, Beloved Wives Day. In 2008, this group organized an event called Shout Your Love from the Middle of a Cabbage Patch Day. Dozens of men stood in a cabbage patch north of Tokyo and shouted, "I love you!" to their wives, some of whom had never heard their husbands say those words. In another rare gesture, husbands pledged to be home by 8 p.m. that day (Japan Aisaika Organization 2012; Kambayashi 2008).

The ability to define social reality reflects a group's power within a society. In fact, one of the most crucial aspects of the relationship between dominant and subordinate groups is the ability of the dominant or majority group to define a society's values. Sociologist William I. Thomas (1923), an early critic of theories of racial and gender differences, recognized that the "definition of the situation" could mold the thinking and personality of the individual. Writing from an interactionist perspective, Thomas observed that people respond not only to the objective features of a person or situation but also to the *meaning* that person or situation has for them. For example, in Philip Zimbardo's mock prison experiment, student "guards" and "prisoners" accepted the definition of the situation (including the traditional roles and behavior associated with being a guard or prisoner) and acted accordingly.

As we have seen throughout the past 60 years—first in the civil rights movement of the 1950s and 1960s and since then among such groups as women, the elderly, gays and lesbians, and people with disabilities—an important aspect of the process of social change involves redefining or reconstructing social reality. Members of subordinate groups challenge traditional definitions and begin to perceive and experience reality in a new way.

Elements of Social Structure

All social interaction takes place within a **social structure,** including those interactions that redefine social reality. For purposes of study, we can break down any social structure into five elements: statuses, social roles, groups, social networks, and social institutions. These elements make up social structure just as a foundation, walls, and ceilings make up a building's structure.

Statuses

We normally think of a person's *status* as having to do with influence, wealth, and fame. However, sociologists use the term **status** to refer to any of the full range of socially defined positions within a large group or society, from the lowest to the highest. Within our society, a person can occupy the status of president of the United States, fruit picker, son or daughter, violinist, teenager, resident of Minneapolis, dental technician, or neighbor. A person can hold a number of statuses at the same time.

Ascribed and Achieved Status
Sociologists view some statuses as *ascribed* and others as *achieved* (Figure 16-1). An **ascribed status** is assigned to a person by society without regard for the person's unique talents or characteristics. Generally, the assignment takes place at birth; thus, a person's racial background, gender, and age are all considered ascribed statuses. Though these characteristics are biological in origin, they are significant mainly because of the *social* meanings they have in our culture. Conflict theorists are especially interested in ascribed statuses, since they often confer privileges or reflect a person's membership in a subordinate group.

In most cases, we can do little to change an ascribed status, but we can attempt to change the traditional constraints associated with it. For example, the Gray Panthers—an activist political group founded in 1971 to work for the rights of older people—have tried to modify society's negative and confining

stereotypes of the elderly. As a result of their work and that of other groups supporting older citizens, the ascribed status of "senior citizen" is no longer as difficult for millions of older people.

An ascribed status does not necessarily have the same social meaning in every society. In a cross-cultural study, sociologist Gary Huang (1988) confirmed the long-held view that respect for the elderly is an important cultural norm in China. In many cases, the prefix "old" is used respectfully: calling someone "old teacher" or "old person" is like calling a judge in the United States "your honor." Huang points out that positive age-seniority language distinctions are uncommon in the United States; consequently, we view the term *old man* as more of an insult than a celebration of seniority and wisdom.

Unlike ascribed statuses, an **achieved status** comes to us largely through our own efforts. Both "computer programmer" and "prison guard" are achieved statuses, as are "lawyer," "pianist," "sorority member," "convict," and "social worker." We must do something to acquire an achieved status—go to school, learn a skill, establish a friendship, invent a new product. But as we will see in the next section, our ascribed status heavily influences our achieved status. Being male, for example, would decrease the likelihood that we would consider child care as a career.

FIGURE 16-1 Social Statuses

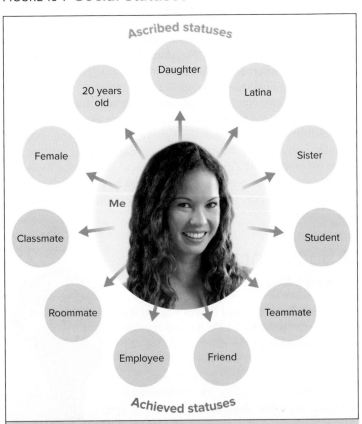

Think about It The young woman in this figure—"me"—occupies many positions in society, each of which involves distinct statuses. How would you define your statuses? Which have the most influence in your life?

Source: Developed by author.

Master Status Each person holds many different and sometimes conflicting statuses; some may connote higher social position and some, lower position. How, then, do others view one's overall social position? According to sociologist Everett Hughes (1945), societies deal with inconsistencies by agreeing that certain statuses are more important than others. A **master status** is a status that dominates others and thereby determines a person's general position in society. For example, Arthur Ashe, who died of AIDS in 1993, had a remarkable career as a tennis star, but at the end of his life, his status as a well-known personality with AIDS may have outweighed his statuses as a retired athlete, author, and political activist. Throughout the world, many people with disabilities find that their status as disabled receives undue weight, overshadowing their actual ability to perform successfully in meaningful employment (Box 16-1).

Our society gives such importance to race and gender that they often dominate our lives. These ascribed statuses frequently influence our achieved status. The Black activist Malcolm X (1925–1965), an eloquent and controversial advocate of Black power and Black pride during the early 1960s, recalled that his feelings and perspectives changed dramatically in middle school. Elected class president and finishing near the top of his class academically, he had developed a positive outlook. However, his teachers, all of them White, discouraged him from taking more challenging courses, which they felt were not appropriate for Black students. When his eighth-grade English teacher, a White man, advised him that his goal of becoming a lawyer was not realistic, and encouraged him instead to become a carpenter, Malcolm X concluded that his being a Black man (ascribed status) was an obstacle to his dream of becoming a lawyer (achieved status). In the United States, the ascribed statuses of race and gender can function as master statuses that have an important impact on one's potential to achieve a desired professional and social status (Malcolm X [1964] 1999:37; Marable 2011:36–38).

Social Roles

What Are Social Roles? Throughout our lives, we acquire what sociologists call social roles. A **social role** is a set of expectations for people who occupy a given social position or status. Thus, in the United States, we expect that cab drivers will know how to get around a city, that receptionists will be reliable in handling phone messages, and that police officers will take action if they see a citizen being threatened. With each distinctive social status—whether ascribed or achieved—come particular role expectations. However, actual performance varies from individual to individual. One secretary may assume extensive administrative responsibilities, while another may focus on clerical duties. Similarly, in Philip Zimbardo's mock prison experiment, some students were brutal and sadistic guards; others were not.

Roles are a significant component of social structure. Viewed from a functionalist perspective, roles contribute to a society's stability by enabling members to anticipate the behavior of

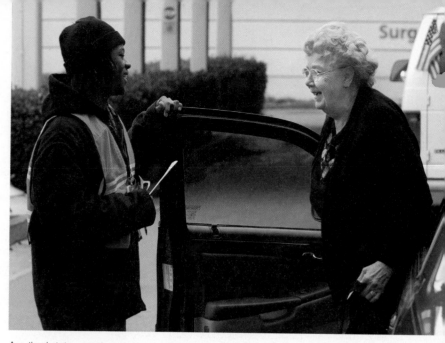

Ascribed status may intersect with a person's achieved status. This man's achieved status as a low-income worker, combined with his minority ethnic status, contrast sharply with the high status of his customer.

others and to pattern their actions accordingly. Yet social roles can also be dysfunctional if they restrict people's interactions and relationships. If we view a person *only* as a "police officer" or "supervisor," it will be difficult to relate to him or her as a friend or neighbor.

Role Conflict Imagine the delicate situation of a woman who has worked for a decade on an assembly line in an electrical plant, and has recently been named supervisor of her unit. How is this woman expected to relate to her longtime friends and co-workers? Should she still go out to lunch with them, as she has done almost daily for years? Is it her responsibility to recommend the firing of an old friend who cannot keep up with the demands of the assembly line?

Role conflict occurs when incompatible expectations arise from two or more social positions held by the same person. Fulfillment of the roles associated with one status may directly violate the roles linked to a second status. In the example just given, the newly promoted supervisor will most likely experience a sharp conflict between her social and occupational roles. Such role conflicts call for important ethical choices. The new supervisor will have to make a difficult decision about how much allegiance she owes her friend and how much she owes her employers, who have given her supervisory responsibilities.

Another type of role conflict occurs when individuals move into occupations that are not common among people with their ascribed status. Male preschool teachers and female police officers experience this type of role conflict. In the latter case, female officers must strive to reconcile their workplace role in law enforcement with the societal view of a woman's role, which does not embrace many skills needed in police work. And while female police officers encounter sexual harassment, as women do throughout the labor force, they must also deal with the "code of silence," an informal norm that precludes their implicating fellow officers in wrongdoing (Fletcher 1995; S. Martin 1994).

Disability as a Master Status

Throughout history and around the world, people with disabilities have been subjected to cruel and inhuman treatment. For example, in the 20th century, the disabled were frequently viewed as subhuman creatures who were a menace to society. In Japan more than 16,000 women with disabilities were involuntarily sterilized with government approval from 1945 to 1995. Sweden apologized for the same action taken against 62,000 of its citizens in the 1970s.

Such blatantly hostile treatment of people with disabilities has given way to a *medical model,* in which the disabled are viewed as chronic patients. Increasingly, however, people concerned with the rights of the disabled have criticized this model as well. In their view, it is the unnecessary and discriminatory barriers present in the environment—both physical and attitudinal—that stand in the way of people with disabilities, more than any biological limitations. Applying a *civil rights model,* activists emphasize that those with disabilities face widespread prejudice, discrimination, and segregation. For example, most voting places are inaccessible to wheelchair users and fail to provide ballots that can be used by those unable to read print.

Drawing on the earlier work of Erving Goffman, contemporary sociologists have suggested that society attaches a stigma to many forms of disability, a stigma that leads to prejudicial treatment. People with disabilities frequently observe that the nondisabled see them only as blind, wheelchair users, and so forth, rather than as complex human

> In Japan more than 16,000 women with disabilities were involuntarily sterilized with government approval from 1945 to 1995.

beings with individual strengths and weaknesses, whose blindness or use of a wheelchair is merely one aspect of their lives.

Although discrimination against the disabled occurs around the world, attitudes are changing. The African nation of Botswana has plans to assist its disabled, most of whom live in rural areas and need special services for mobility and economic development. In many countries, disability rights activists are targeting issues essential to overcoming this master status and becoming a full citizen, including employment, housing, education, and access to public buildings.

LET'S DISCUSS

1. Does your campus present barriers to disabled students? If so, what kinds of barriers—physical, attitudinal, or both? Describe some of them.

2. Why do you think nondisabled people see disability as the most important characteristic of a disabled person? What can be done to help people see beyond the wheelchair and the Seeing Eye dog?

Sources: Albrecht 2004; Goffman 1963; Murphy 1997; *Newsday* 1997; R. Schaefer 2012; J. Shapiro 1993.

---

 use your **sociological imagination**

If you were a male nurse, what aspects of role conflict might you experience? Now imagine you are a professional boxer and a woman. What conflicting role expectations might that involve? In both cases, how well do you think you would handle role conflict?

Role Strain Role conflict describes the situation of a person dealing with the challenge of occupying two social positions simultaneously. However, even a single position can cause problems. Sociologists use the term **role strain** to describe the difficulty that arises when the same social position imposes conflicting demands and expectations.

People who belong to minority cultures may experience role strain while working in the mainstream culture. Criminologist Larry Gould (2002) interviewed officers of the Navajo Nation Police Department about their relations with conventional law enforcement officials, such as sheriffs and FBI agents. Besides enforcing the law, Navajo Nation officers practice an alternative form of justice known as Peacemaking, in which they seek reconciliation between the parties to a crime. The officers expressed great confidence in Peacemaking, but worried that if they did not make arrests, other law enforcement officials would think they were too soft, or "just taking care of their own." Regardless of the strength of their ties to traditional Navajo ways, all felt the strain of being considered "too Navajo" or "not Navajo enough."

Role Exit Often, when we think of assuming a social role, we focus on the preparation and anticipatory socialization a person undergoes for that role. Such is true if a person is about to become an attorney, a chef, a spouse, or a parent. Yet until recently, social scientists have given little attention to the adjustments involved in *leaving* social roles.

Sociologist Helen Rose Fuchs Ebaugh (1988) developed the term **role exit** to describe the process of disengagement from a role that is central to one's self-identity in order to establish a new role and identity. Drawing on interviews with 185 people—among them ex-convicts, divorced men and women, recovering alcoholics, ex-nuns, former doctors, retirees, and transsexuals—Ebaugh (herself an ex-nun) studied the process of voluntarily exiting from significant social roles.

Sarah Levy, *Owner, S. Levy Foods*

Sarah Levy didn't know anything about sociology when she entered Northwestern University, but she knew that someday she wanted to start a bakery. After graduating from Northwestern with a major in sociology, she enrolled in Chicago's French Pastry School and spent some time interning at local bakeries and restaurants. A year later she started her own bakery in her mother's kitchen. Today Sarah owns and manages S. Levy Foods, which operates food concessions at airports in New York, Sacramento, Phoenix, and San Diego.

Like many small-business owners, Sarah does anything and everything in a typical work-week, from consulting to blogging ("Simply Sweet") and serving as brand ambassador for Callebut chocolate, Karo, and Fleischmann's yeast. She is also the dining editor for *Today's Chicago Woman* magazine. A gifted publicist, Sarah once participated in a Food Network challenge that involved baking a three-foot animated dinosaur cake. Through Sarah's Pastries & Candies, a bricks-and-mortar store she once owned in downtown Chicago, she contributed to several charities, including Meals on Wheels, Common Threads, and For the Love of Chocolate Foundation.

Sarah saw the connection between business and sociology in her introductory sociology course, in which she used this textbook. Learning about how people interact, she says, has broadened her horizons and taught her how to step back and analyze a situation from a sociological perspective. "In my job, I am constantly interacting with people—employees, customers, vendors," she explains. "I think one of my greatest strengths is my ability to get along with people from all sorts of backgrounds, and make everyone get along with each other and work together towards the same goal."

LET'S DISCUSS

1. Have you ever thought of starting your own business? If so, what do you think the key to your success might be?

2. Would business have been a more practical major for Sarah? Why or why not?

According to sociologist Helen Rose Fuchs Ebaugh, role exit is a four-stage process. Is this transgendered person in the first or the fourth stage of changing genders?

Ebaugh has offered a four-stage model of role exit. The first stage begins with *doubt.* The person experiences frustration, burnout, or simply unhappiness with an accustomed status and the roles associated with the social position. The second stage involves a *search for alternatives.* A person who is unhappy with his or her career may take a leave of absence; an unhappily married couple may begin what they see as a temporary separation.

The third stage of role exit is the *action stage* or *departure.* Ebaugh found that the vast majority of her respondents could identify a clear turning point that made them feel it was essential to take final action and leave their jobs, end their marriages, or engage in another type of role exit. Twenty percent of respondents saw their role exit as a gradual, evolutionary process that had no single turning point.

The fourth stage of role exit involves the *creation of a new identity.* Many of you participated in a role exit when you made the transition from high school to college. You left behind the role of offspring living at home and took on the role of a somewhat independent college student living with peers in a dorm. Sociologist Ira Silver (1996) has studied the central role that material objects play in this transition. The objects students choose to leave at home (like stuffed animals and dolls) are associated with their prior identities. They may remain deeply attached to those objects, but do not want them to be seen as part of their new identities at college. The objects they bring with them symbolize how they now see themselves and how they wish to be perceived. iPods and wall posters, for example, are calculated to say, "This is me."

Groups

In sociological terms, a **group** is any number of people with similar norms, values, and expectations who interact with one another on a regular basis. The members of a women's basketball team, a hospital's business office, a synagogue, or a symphony orchestra constitute a group. However, the residents of a suburb would not be considered a group, since they rarely interact with one another at one time.

Groups play a vital part in a society's social structure. Much of our social interaction takes place within groups and is influenced by their norms and sanctions. Being a teenager or a retired person takes on special meanings when we interact within groups designed for people with that particular status. The expectations associated with many social roles, including those accompanying the statuses of brother, sister, and student, become more clearly defined in the context of a group.

Social Networks

Groups do not merely serve to define other elements of the social structure, such as roles and statuses; they also link the individual with the larger society. We all belong to a number of different groups, and through our acquaintances make connections with people in different social circles. These connections are known as a **social network**—a series of social relationships that links a person directly to others, and through them indirectly to still more people. Social networks are one of the five basic elements of social structure.

Broadly speaking, social networks encompass all the routine social interaction we have with other individuals. Traditionally, researchers have limited their network studies to face-to-face contacts and phone conversations, although recently they have begun to study interaction through all types of new media. We should be careful, however, not to equate social media like Facebook and Twitter with social networks, which include a much broader spectrum of social interaction.

Social networks can center on virtually any activity, from sharing job information to exchanging news and gossip, or even sharing sex. In the mid-1990s, sociologists studied romantic relationships at a high school with about 1,000 students. They found that about 61 percent of the girls had been sexually active over the past 18 months. Among the sexually active respondents, the researchers counted only 63 steady couples, or pairs with no other partners. A much larger group of 288 students—almost a third of the sample—was involved in a free-flowing network of relationships (Bearman et al. 2004).

This research on high schoolers' sexual activity, an example of applied sociology, has clear implications for public health. Box 16-2 describes a similar but longer-term study in which public health officials used network analysis to curb obesity.

Involvement in social networks—commonly known as *networking*—is especially valuable in finding employment. Albert Einstein was successful in finding a job only when a classmate's father put him in touch with his future employer. These kinds of contacts—even those that are weak and distant—can be crucial in establishing social networks and facilitating the transmission of information.

During the recent economic downturn, electronic social networks have served a new purpose, encouraging the jobless. Websites and chat rooms that cannot locate jobs for those who have been thrown out of work concentrate instead on helping them to stick together, support one another, and maintain a positive attitude. For the unemployed, online conversations with friends or even strangers in the same predicament can be an invaluable morale booster (R. Scherer 2010b).

Research indicates, however, that both in person and online, not everyone participates equally in social networks. Women and racial and ethnic minorities are at a disadvantage when seeking new and better job opportunities or social contacts (Trimble and Kmec 2011).

Social Institutions

The mass media, the government, the economy, the family, and the health care system are all examples of social institutions found in our society. **Social institutions** are organized patterns of beliefs and behavior centered on basic social needs, such as replacing personnel (the family) and preserving order (the government).

A close look at social institutions gives sociologists insight into the structure of a society. Consider religion, for example. The institution of religion adapts to the segment of society that it serves. Church work has very different meanings for ministers who serve a skid row area and those who serve a suburban middle-class community. Religious leaders assigned to a skid row mission will focus on tending to the ill and providing food and shelter. In contrast, clergy in affluent suburbs will be occupied with counseling those considering marriage and divorce, arranging youth activities, and overseeing cultural events.

Functionalist Perspective One way to understand social institutions is to see how they fulfill essential functions. Anthropologists and sociologists have identified five major tasks, or functional prerequisites, that a society or relatively permanent group must accomplish if it is to survive:

1. *Replacing personnel.* Any group or society must replace personnel when they die, leave, or become incapacitated. This task is accomplished through such means as immigration, annexation of neighboring groups, acquisition of slaves, or sexual reproduction. The Shakers, a religious sect that came to the United States in 1774, are a conspicuous example of a group that has *failed* to replace personnel. Their religious beliefs commit the Shakers to celibacy; to survive, the group must recruit new members. At first, the Shakers proved quite successful in attracting members, reaching a peak of about 6,000 members in the United States during the 1840s. As of 2011, however, the only Shaker community left in this country was a farm in Maine with three members—one man and two women (R. Schaefer and Zellner 2011).

2. *Teaching new recruits.* No group or society can survive if many of its members reject the group's established behavior and responsibilities. Thus, finding or producing new members is not sufficient; the group or society must also encourage recruits to learn and accept its values and customs. Such learning can take place formally, within schools (where learning is a manifest function), or informally, through interaction in peer groups (where learning is a latent function).

Social Networks and Obesity

Over the past two generations, obesity has become a public health problem in the United States. To explain the trend toward excess weight, researchers have focused on Americans' nutritional practices, as well as on their genetic tendencies. Another variable that contributes to obesity, less obvious than diet and heredity, is social networking.

The people we network with have a powerful effect on our behavior, for better or worse, and that effect includes our health. Researchers identified networking as a factor in the course of a long-term heart health survey, during which they tracked the weight of 12,067 respondents. At the same time, they mapped the social networks that respondents belonged to. Over the three decades since the survey began, they have noted that weight gain in one person is often associated with weight gain in his or her friends, siblings, spouse, and neighbors. In fact, a person's chances of becoming obese increased by 57 percent if a friend became

overweight during the same period. This association, they found, was attributable solely to selectivity in the choice of friends—that is, to people of a certain weight seeking out others of roughly the same weight.

This study shows that social networks do influence the way people behave. More

> Weight gain in one person is often associated with weight gain in his or her friends, siblings, spouse, and neighbors.

important, the results suggest that networking could be exploited to spread positive health behaviors—for example, by recruiting friends to participate in a person's weight-loss plan. Other possibilities include

persuading friends to wear pedometers and share data on the distance they walk, or to compete with one another in active video games, like Nintendo Wii Fit or Microsoft Kinect. Through a similar approach, health practitioners could include social networking in efforts to control smoking, drinking, and drug abuse.

LET'S DISCUSS

1. Have you ever tried to lose weight, and if so, did your cluster of friends and family help or hinder you? In your experience, do people who are overweight tend to cluster in separate groups from those of normal weight?

2. Besides public health campaigns, what applications can you think of for research on social networking?

Sources: Christakis and Fowler 2007, 2009; Haas et al. 2010; Harmon 2011; Li et al. 2013.

---

3. *Producing and distributing goods and services.* Any relatively permanent group or society must provide and distribute desired goods and services to its members. Each society establishes a set of rules for the allocation of financial and other resources. The group must satisfy the needs of most members to some extent, or it will risk the possibility of discontent and ultimately disorder.

4. *Preserving order.* Throughout the world, indigenous and aboriginal peoples have struggled to protect themselves from outside invaders, with varying degrees of success. Failure to preserve order and defend against conquest leads to the death not only of a people, but of a culture as well.

5. *Providing and maintaining a sense of purpose.* In order to fulfill the first four requirements, people must feel motivated to continue as members of a group or society. Patriotism, tribal identities, religious values, or personal moral codes can help people to develop and maintain such a sense of purpose. Whatever the motivator, in any society there remains one common and critical reality: if an individual does not have a sense of purpose, he or she has little reason to contribute to a society's survival.

This list of functional prerequisites does not specify *how* a society and its corresponding social institutions will perform each task. For example, one society may protect itself from external attack by amassing a frightening arsenal of weaponry, while another may make determined efforts to remain neutral in world politics and to promote cooperative relationships with its neighbors. No matter what its particular strategy, any society

or relatively permanent group must attempt to satisfy all these functional prerequisites for survival. If it fails on even one condition, the society runs the risk of extinction (Aberle et al. 1950; R. Mack and Bradford 1979).

Conflict Perspective Conflict theorists do not agree with the functionalist approach to social institutions. Although proponents of both perspectives agree that social institutions are organized to meet basic social needs, conflict theorists object to the idea that the outcome is necessarily efficient and desirable.

From a conflict perspective, the present organization of social institutions is no accident. Major institutions, such as education, help to maintain the privileges of the most powerful individuals and groups within a society, while contributing to the powerlessness of others. To give one example, public schools in the United States are financed largely through property taxes. This arrangement allows more affluent areas to provide their children with better-equipped schools and better-paid teachers than low-income areas can afford. As a result, children from prosperous communities are better prepared to compete academically than children from impoverished communities. The structure of the nation's educational system permits and even promotes such unequal treatment of schoolchildren.

Conflict theorists argue that social institutions such as education have an inherently conservative nature. Without question, it has been difficult to implement educational reforms that promote equal opportunity—whether bilingual education, school desegregation, or mainstreaming of students with disabilities. From a functionalist perspective, social change can be dysfunctional, since it often leads

TABLE 16-1 SOCIOLOGICAL PERSPECTIVES ON SOCIAL INSTITUTIONS

Tracking Sociological Perspectives

Perspective	Role of Social Institutions	Focus
Functionalist	Meeting basic social needs	Essential functions
Conflict	Meeting basic social needs	Maintenance of privileges and inequality
Interactionist	Fostering everyday behavior	Influence of the roles and statuses we accept

to instability. However, from a conflict view, why should we preserve the existing social structure if it is unfair and discriminatory?

Social institutions also operate in gendered and racist environments, as conflict theorists, as well as feminists and interactionists, have pointed out. In schools, offices, and government institutions, assumptions about what people can do reflect the sexism and racism of the larger society. For instance, many people assume that women cannot make tough decisions—even those in the top echelons of corporate management. Others assume that all Black students at elite colleges represent affirmative action admissions. Inequality based on gender, economic status, race, and ethnicity thrives in such an environment—to which we might add discrimination based on age, physical disability, and sexual orientation. The truth of this assertion can be seen in routine decisions by employers on how to advertise jobs, as well as whether to provide fringe benefits such as child care and parental leave.

Interactionist Perspective Social institutions affect our everyday behavior, whether we are driving down the street or waiting in a long shopping line. Sociologist Mitchell Duneier (1994a, 1994b) studied the social behavior of the word processors, all women, who work in the service center of a large Chicago law firm. Duneier was interested in the informal social norms that emerged in this work environment and the rich social network these female employees created.

The Network Center, as it is called, is a single, windowless room in a large office building where the law firm occupies seven floors. The center is staffed by two shifts of word processors, who work either from 4:00 p.m. to midnight or from midnight to 8:00 a.m. Each word processor works in a cubicle with just enough room for her keyboard, terminal, printer, and telephone. Work assignments for the word processors are placed in a central basket and then completed according to precise procedures.

At first glance, we might think that these women labor with little social contact, apart from limited breaks and occasional conversations with their supervisor. However, drawing on the interactionist perspective, Duneier learned that despite working in a large office, these women find private moments to talk (often in the halls or outside the washroom) and share a critical view of the law firm's attorneys and day-shift secretaries. Indeed, the word processors routinely suggest that their assignments represent work that the "lazy" secretaries should have completed during the normal workday. Duneier (1994b) tells of one word processor who resented the lawyers' superior attitude and pointedly refused to recognize or speak with any attorney who would not address her by name.

Interactionist theorists emphasize that our social behavior is conditioned by the roles and statuses we accept, the groups to which we belong, and the institutions within which we function. For example, the social roles associated with being a judge occur within the larger context of the criminal justice system. The status of judge stands in relation to other statuses, such as attorney, plaintiff, defendant, and witness, as well as to the social institution of government. Although courts and jails have great symbolic importance, the judicial system derives its continued significance from the roles people carry out in social interactions (Berger and Luckmann 1966).

Table 16-1 summarizes the three major sociological perspectives on social institutions.

MODULE 16 | **Recap and Review**

Summary

Social interaction refers to the ways in which people respond to one another. **Social structure** refers to the way in which a society is organized into predictable relationships. This module examines the five basic elements of social structure: **statuses, social roles, groups, social networks,** and **social institutions.**

1. People shape their social reality based on what they learn through **social interactions.** Social change comes from redefining or reconstructing social reality.

2. An **ascribed status** is generally assigned to a person at birth, whereas an **achieved status** is attained largely through one's own effort. Some ascribed statuses, such as race and gender, can function as **master statuses** that affect one's potential to achieve a certain professional or social status.

3. With each distinctive status—whether ascribed or achieved—comes a particular **social role,** the set of expectations for people who occupy that status.

4. Much of our social behavior takes place in **groups.**

5. **Social institutions** fulfill essential functions, such as replacing personnel, training new recruits, and preserving order. The mass media, the government, the economy, the family, and the health care system are all examples of social institutions.

6. **Social networks** form linkages between individuals and groups and can center on virtually any activity.

Thinking Critically

1. Think back over the events of the past few days. Identify two occasions on which different people defined the same social reality differently.

2. Describe a specific master status and explain how it was established. Is it a negative status? If so, how would a person overcome it?

Key Terms

Achieved status

Ascribed status

Group

Master status

Role conflict

Role exit

Role strain

Social institution

Social interaction

Social network

Social role

Social structure

Status

MODULE 17 | Social Structure in Global Perspective

Modern societies are complex, especially compared to earlier social arrangements. Sociologists Émile Durkheim, Ferdinand Tönnies, and Gerhard Lenski developed ways to contrast modern societies with simpler forms of social structure.

Durkheim's Mechanical and Organic Solidarity

In his *Division of Labor* ([1893] 1933), Durkheim argued that social structure depends on the division of labor in a society—in other words, on the manner in which tasks are performed. Thus, a task such as providing food can be carried out almost totally by one individual, or it can be divided among many people. The latter pattern is typical of modern societies, in which the cultivation, processing, distribution, and retailing of a single food item are performed by literally hundreds of people.

In societies in which there is minimal division of labor, a collective consciousness develops that emphasizes group solidarity. Durkheim termed this collective frame of mind **mechanical solidarity,** implying that all individuals perform the same tasks. In this type of society, no one needs to ask, "What do your parents do?" since all are engaged in similar work. Each person prepares food, hunts, makes clothing, builds homes, and so forth. Because people have few options regarding what to do with their lives, there is little concern for individual needs. Instead, the group is the dominating force in society. Both social interaction and negotiation are based on close, intimate, face-to-face social contacts. Since there is little specialization, there are few social roles.

As societies become more advanced technologically, they rely on greater division of labor, so that no individual can go it alone. Dependence on others becomes essential for group survival. In Durkheim's terms, mechanical solidarity is replaced by **organic solidarity,** a collective consciousness resting on the need a society's members have for one another. Durkheim chose the term *organic solidarity* because in his view, individuals become interdependent in much the same way as organs of the human body.

Tönnies's *Gemeinschaft* and *Gesellschaft*

Ferdinand Tönnies (1855–1936) was appalled by the rise of an industrial city in his native Germany during the late 1800s. In his view, the city marked a dramatic change from the ideal of a close-knit community, which Tönnies termed a *Gemeinschaft,* to that of an impersonal mass society, known as a *Gesellschaft* (Tönnies [1887] 1988).

The *Gemeinschaft* (pronounced guh-mine-shoft) is typical of rural life. It is a small community in which people have similar backgrounds and life experiences. Virtually everyone knows one another, and social interactions are intimate and familiar, almost as among kinfolk. In this community there is a commitment to the larger social group and a sense of togetherness among members. People relate to others in a personal way, not just as "clerk" or "manager." With this personal interaction comes little privacy, however: we know too much about everyone.

Social control in the *Gemeinschaft* is maintained through informal means such as moral persuasion, gossip, and even gestures. These techniques work effectively because people genuinely care how others feel about them. Social change is relatively limited in the *Gemeinschaft;* the lives of members of one generation may be quite similar to those of their grandparents.

In contrast, the *Gesellschaft* (pronounced guh-zell-shoft) is an ideal community that is characteristic of modern urban life. In

"I'd like to think of you as a person, David, but it's my job to think of you as personnel."

In a *Gesellschaft,* people are likely to relate to one another in terms of their roles rather than their relationships.

this community most people are strangers who feel little in common with other residents. Relationships are governed by social roles that grow out of immediate tasks, such as purchasing a product or arranging a business meeting. Self-interest dominates, and there is little consensus concerning values or commitment to the group. As a result, social control must rest on more formal techniques, such as laws and legally defined punishments. Social change is an important aspect of life in the *Gesellschaft;* it can be strikingly evident even within a single generation.

Table 17-1 summarizes the differences between the *Gemeinschaft* and the *Gesellschaft.* Sociologists have used these terms to compare social structures that stress close relationships with those that emphasize less personal ties. It is easy to view the *Gemeinschaft* with nostalgia, as a far better way of life than the rat race of contemporary existence. However, the more intimate relationships of the *Gemeinschaft* come at a price. The prejudice

and discrimination found there can be quite confining; ascribed statuses such as family background often outweigh a person's unique talents and achievements. In addition, the *Gemeinschaft* tends to distrust individuals who seek to be creative or just to be different.

● Lenski's Sociocultural Evolution Approach

Sociologist Gerhard Lenski takes a very different view of society and social structure. Rather than distinguishing between two opposite types of society, as Tönnies did, Lenski sees human societies as undergoing a process of change characterized by a dominant pattern known as **sociocultural evolution.** This term refers to long-term social trends resulting from the interplay of continuity, innovation, and selection (Nolan and Lenski 2009:361).

In Lenski's view, a society's level of technology is critical to the way it is organized. Lenski defines **technology** as "cultural information about the ways in which the material resources of the environment may be used to satisfy human needs and desires" (Nolan and Lenski 2009:357). The available technology does not completely define the form that a particular society and its social structure take. Nevertheless, a low level of technology may limit the degree to which a society can depend on such things as irrigation or complex machinery. As technology advances, Lenski writes, a community evolves from a preindustrial to an industrial and finally a postindustrial society.

Preindustrial Societies

How does a preindustrial society organize its economy? If we know that, we can categorize the society. The first type of preindustrial society to emerge in human history was the **hunting-and-gathering**

TABLE **17-1** COMPARISON OF THE *GEMEINSCHAFT* AND *GESELLSCHAFT*

Summing Up

Gemeinschaft	Gesellschaft
Rural life typifies this form.	Urban life typifies this form.
People share a feeling of community that results from their similar backgrounds and life experiences.	People have little sense of commonality. Their differences appear more striking than their similarities.
Social interactions are intimate and familiar.	Social interactions are likely to be impersonal and task-specific.
People maintain a spirit of cooperation and unity of will.	Self-interest dominates.
Tasks and personal relationships cannot be separated.	The task being performed is paramount; relationships are subordinate.
People place little emphasis on individual privacy.	Privacy is valued.
Informal social control predominates.	Formal social control is evident.
People are not very tolerant of deviance.	People are more tolerant of deviance.
Emphasis is on ascribed statuses.	Emphasis is on achieved statuses.
Social change is relatively limited.	Social change is very evident, even within a generation.

Think about It How would you classify the communities with which you are familiar? Are they more *Gemeinschaft* or *Gesellschaft*?

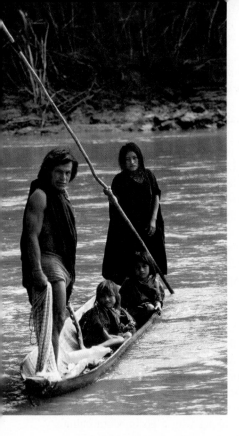

Preindustrial societies still exist in some remote areas. These indigenous people are from the Envira region of the Amazon rain forest, in Brazil.

society, in which people simply rely on whatever foods and fibers are readily available. Technology in such societies is minimal. Organized into groups, people move constantly in search of food. There is little division of labor into specialized tasks.

Hunting-and-gathering societies are composed of small, widely dispersed groups. Each group consists almost entirely of people who are related to one another. As a result, kinship ties are the source of authority and influence, and the social institution of the family takes on a particularly important role. Tönnies would certainly view such societies as examples of the *Gemeinschaft.*

Social differentiation within the hunting-and-gathering society is based on ascribed statuses such as gender, age, and family background. Since resources are scarce, there is relatively little inequality in terms of material goods. By the close of the 20th century, hunting-and-gathering societies had virtually disappeared (Nolan and Lenski 2009).

Horticultural societies, in which people plant seeds and crops rather than merely subsist on available foods, emerged about 12,000 years ago. Members of horticultural societies are much less nomadic than hunters and gatherers. They place greater emphasis on the production of tools and household objects. Yet technology remains rather limited in these societies, whose members cultivate crops with the aid of digging sticks or hoes (Wilford 1997).

The last stage of preindustrial development is the **agrarian society,** which emerged about 5,000 years ago. As in horticultural societies, members of agrarian societies engage primarily in the production of food. However, technological innovations such as the plow allow farmers to dramatically increase their crop yields. They can cultivate the same fields over generations, allowing the emergence of larger settlements.

The agrarian society continues to rely on the physical power of humans and animals (as opposed to mechanical power). Nevertheless, its social structure has more carefully defined roles than that of horticultural societies. Individuals focus on specialized tasks, such as the repair of fishing nets or blacksmithing. As human settlements become more established and stable, social institutions become more elaborate and property rights more important. The comparative permanence and greater surpluses of an agrarian society allow members to create artifacts such as statues, public monuments, and art objects and to pass them on from one generation to the next.

Table 17-2 summarizes Lenski's three stages of sociocultural evolution, as well as the stages that follow, described next.

Industrial Societies

Although the Industrial Revolution did not topple monarchs, it produced changes every bit as significant as those resulting from political revolutions. The Industrial Revolution, which took place largely in England during the period 1760 to 1830, was a scientific revolution focused on the application of nonanimal (mechanical) sources of power to labor tasks. An **industrial society** is a society that depends on mechanization to produce its goods and services. Industrial societies rely on new inventions that facilitate agricultural and industrial production, and on new sources of energy, such as steam.

As the Industrial Revolution proceeded, a new form of social structure emerged. Many societies underwent an irrevocable shift from an agrarian-oriented economy to an industrial base. No longer did an individual or a family typically make an entire product. Instead, specialization of tasks and manufacturing of goods became increasingly common. Workers, generally men but also women and even children, left their family homesteads to work in central locations such as factories.

TABLE 17-2 STAGES OF SOCIOCULTURAL EVOLUTION

Summing Up

Societal Type	First Appearance	Characteristics
Hunting-and-gathering	Beginning of human life	Nomadic; reliance on readily available food and fibers
Horticultural	About 12,000 years ago	More settled; development of agriculture and limited technology
Agrarian	About 5,000 years ago	Larger, more stable settlements; improved technology and increased crop yields
Industrial	1760–1850	Reliance on mechanical power and new sources of energy; centralized workplaces; economic interdependence; formal education
Postindustrial	1960s	Reliance on services, especially the processing and control of information; expanded middle class
Postmodern	Latter 1970s	High technology; mass consumption of consumer goods and media images; cross-cultural integration

Postindustrial and Postmodern Societies

When Lenski first proposed the sociocultural evolutionary approach in the 1960s, he paid relatively little attention to how maturing industrialized societies may change with the emergence of even more advanced forms of technology. More recently, he and other sociologists have studied the significant changes in the occupational structure of industrial societies as they shift from manufacturing to service economies. In the 1970s, sociologist Daniel Bell wrote about the technologically advanced **postindustrial society,** whose economic system is engaged primarily in the processing and control of information. The main output of a postindustrial society is services rather than manufactured goods. Large numbers of people become involved in occupations devoted to the teaching, generation, or dissemination of ideas. Jobs in fields such as advertising, public relations, human resources, and computer information systems would be typical of a postindustrial society (D. Bell [1973] 1999).

Bell views the transition from industrial to postindustrial society as a positive development. He sees a general decline in organized working-class groups and a rise in interest groups concerned with national issues such as health, education, and the environment. Bell's outlook is functionalist, because he portrays the postindustrial society as basically consensual. As organizations and interest groups engage in an open and competitive process of decision making, Bell believes, the level of conflict between diverse groups will diminish, strengthening social stability.

Conflict theorists take issue with Bell's functionalist analysis of the postindustrial society. For example, Michael Harrington (1980), who alerted the nation to the problems of the poor in his book *The Other America,* questioned the significance that Bell attached to the growing class of white-collar workers. Harrington conceded that scientists, engineers, and economists are involved in important political and economic decisions, but he disagreed with Bell's claim that they have a free hand in decision making, independent of the interests of the rich. Harrington followed in the tradition of Marx by arguing that conflict between social classes will continue in the postindustrial society.

Sociologists have gone beyond discussion of the postindustrial society to the ideal of the postmodern society. A **postmodern society** is a technologically sophisticated society that is preoccupied with consumer goods and media images (Brannigan 1992). Such societies consume goods and information on a mass scale. Postmodern theorists take a global perspective, noting the ways that culture crosses national boundaries. For example, residents of the United States may listen to reggae music from Jamaica, eat sushi and other Japanese foods, and wear clogs from Sweden. And online social networks know no national boundaries. Box 17-1 describes one of the fixtures of the postmodern society, the theme park.

The emphasis of postmodern theorists is on observing and describing newly emerging cultural forms and patterns of social interaction. Within sociology, the postmodern view offers support for integrating the insights of various theoretical perspectives—functionalism, conflict theory, feminist theory, and interactionism—while incorporating other contemporary approaches. Feminist sociologists argue optimistically that with its indifference to hierarchies and distinctions, the postmodern society will discard traditional values of male dominance in favor of gender equality. Yet others contend that despite new technologies, postindustrial and postmodern societies can be expected to display the same problems of inequality that plague industrial societies (Denzin 2004; Smart 1990; B. Turner 1990; van Vucht Tijssen 1990).

Durkheim, Tönnies, and Lenski present three visions of society's social structure. While they differ, each is useful, and this textbook will draw on all three. The sociocultural evolutionary approach emphasizes a historical perspective. It does not picture different types of social structure coexisting within the same society. Consequently, one would not expect a single society to include hunters and gatherers along with a postmodern culture. In contrast, Durkheim's and Tönnies's theories allow for the existence of different types of community—such as a *Gemeinschaft* and a *Gesellschaft*—in the same society. Thus, a rural New Hampshire community located 100 miles from Boston can be linked to the city by modern information technology. The main difference between these two theories is a matter of emphasis. While Tönnies emphasized the overriding concern in each type of community—one's own self-interest or the well-being of the larger society—Durkheim emphasized the division (or lack of division) of labor.

The work of these three thinkers reminds us that a major focus of sociology has been to identify changes in social structure and the consequences for human behavior. At the macro level, we see society shifting to more advanced forms of technology. The social structure becomes increasingly complex, and new social institutions emerge to assume some functions that once were performed by the family. On the micro level, these changes affect the nature of social interactions. Each individual takes on multiple social roles, and people come to rely more on social networks and less on kinship ties. As the social structure becomes more complex, people's relationships become more impersonal, transient, and fragmented.

Sociology in the Global Community

BOX 17-1

Disney World: A Postmodern Theme Park

In the late 1970s, scholars began writing about the postmodern society and its preoccupation with consumer goods and media images. Walt Disney World is a living example of this type of society. Over 120 million people visit a Disney theme park each year. In fact, Disney operates the eight most visited amusement parks in the world. On three different continents, the Magic Kingdom funnels newly arrived visitors through a quaint-looking Main Street, where Cinderella's Castle beckons to children of all ages.

—Continued

—*Continued*

Behind the Main Street façade, one finds endless opportunities to shop. In heavily air-conditioned stores, visitors can indulge in buying sprees that typify the postmodern preoccupation with consumer goods. Later, at the exits from popular attractions, visitors encounter more shopping opportunities, tailored to what they have just seen. This practice of piggy-backing shops on exhibits is now duplicated in prestigious museums throughout the world, where shops are located just outside special exhibitions of real art and authentic treasures.

The French sociologist Jean Baudrillard (1929–2007) coined the term **hyperconsumerism** to refer to the practice of buying more than we need or want, and often more than we can afford, under such circumstances. Of course, one need not walk down Main Street in Orlando to engage in hyperconsumerism. Advertising permeates the modern world, whether we are on foot or online, tempting us to engage in unnecessary purchases out of a desire that approaches greed. Consumption is so important in the postmodern world that it has become a means of self-identification. Today, conversations are more likely to start with "Where did you get that stroller?" or "Who are you wearing?" than with any reference to the social issues that plague the postmodern world.

Another essential element of postmodernism, *globalism,* is on display at Disney World, where cultural elements have been stripped of any foreign trappings. Here, Cinderella and Snow White are not figures

In the postmodern world, time-space is often compressed. Clutching a toy version of a fictional bear from the 1920s (Winnie-the-Pooh), a young visitor to Disney World reserves a ticket for a trip to New Orleans in the 1850s (the Pirates of the Caribbean attraction). In the meantime, she will travel through the 1930s in one continuous boat ride on the Congo, Zambezi, Amazon, and Irrawaddy rivers (the Jungle Cruise attraction).

> Behind the Main Street façade, one finds endless opportunities to shop.

taken from German folklore, but "Disney characters." Similarly, Belle from *Beauty and the Beast* has largely lost her 18th-century

French roots, and Pinocchio is no longer recognizable as an Italian.

Nearby, Epcot's World Showcase takes the opposite approach, offering museum-like re-creations of specific cultures. Here one finds no evidence of cultural diffusion or globalization—no Starbucks in Epcot's China, no Dunkin' Donuts in Great Britain, no hip-hop in Japan. Instead, a representation of a Mayan temple is flanked by a replica of a medieval Norwegian wooden-stave church and a re-creation of the Temple of Heaven in Beijing. Visitors stroll through a managed reality that is both an ideal and a simplified rendering of 10 different cultures, compressed in time-space.

Postmodernism is on display everywhere, not just in the theme park. It can be seen in the information-driven, consumer-oriented global society we all inhabit. Whether we like it or not, new technologies and the digital transmission of culture are constantly disengaging us from a particular time or place, facilitating our hyperconsumerism.

LET'S DISCUSS

1. In just the last 24 hours, what evidence of hyperconsumerism have you witnessed?

2. How often do you find yourself moving seamlessly across time or space, in one way or another?

Sources: Baudrillard [1970] 1998; Boje 1995; Brannigan 1992; Bryman 1995; Fjellman 1992; L. Klein 1994; Kratz and Karp 1993; Scoville 2010; Themed Entertainment Association 2012.

MODULE 17 | **Recap and Review**

Summary

Sociologists have developed classification systems that help us contrast complex modern societies with simpler forms of social structure.

1. Émile Durkheim thought that social structure depends on the division of labor in a society. According to Durkheim, societies with minimal division of labor have a collective consciousness called **mechanical solidarity.** Those with greater division of labor show an interdependence called **organic solidarity.**

2. Ferdinand Tönnies distinguished the close-knit community of *Gemeinschaft* from the impersonal mass society known as *Gesellschaft.*

3. Gerhard Lenski thinks that a society's social structure changes as its culture and technology become more sophisticated, a process he calls **sociocultural evolution.**

Thinking Critically

1. According to Lenski, technology is the key to sociocultural evolution. What social factors are most likely to influence whether a society's culture evolves to a new stage of sociocultural evolution?

2. How are Durkheim's and Tönnies's classifications similar? How are they different?

3. Describe any personal experiences you have had with a nonindustrial, or developing, society. If you have not had that kind of experience, how do you think you would prepare for it?

Key Terms

Agrarian society
Gemeinschaft
Gesellschaft
Horticultural society

Hunting-and-gathering society
Hyperconsumerism
Industrial society
Mechanical solidarity
Organic solidarity
Postindustrial society
Postmodern society
Sociocultural evolution
Technology

MODULE 18 | **Understanding Groups**

Most of us use the term *group* loosely to describe any collection of individuals, whether three strangers sharing an elevator or hundreds attending a rock concert. However, in sociological terms a **group** is any number of people with similar norms, values, and expectations who interact with one another on a regular basis. A college sorority or fraternity, a dance company, a tenant association, and a chess club are each considered a group. The important point is that members of a group share some sense of belonging. This characteristic distinguishes groups from mere *aggregates* of people, such as passengers who happen to be together on an airplane flight, or from *categories* of people, such as those who share a common feature (such as being retired) but otherwise do not act together.

Consider the case of a college singing group. It has agreed-on values and social norms. All members want to improve their singing skills and schedule lots of performances. In addition, like many groups, the singing ensemble has both a formal and an informal structure. The members meet regularly to rehearse; they choose leaders to run the rehearsals and manage their affairs. At the same time, some group members may take on unofficial leadership roles by coaching new members in singing techniques and performing skills.

The groups we interact with also play an important role in our daily lives, sometimes in unexpected ways. Émile Durkheim ([1893] 1933) noted how a heinous crime can shock us, eliciting a communal response that serves to protect us in the future. In April 2007, a senior at Virginia Tech fired nearly 300 rounds of ammunition at two locations on campus, killing 32 people and wounding 17 others. Sociologists James Hawdon and John Ryan (2011) of Virginia Tech conducted three web-based surveys of the students and faculty, the first of them nine days after the shooting and the last of them 10 months later. They found that people who joined in with established, ongoing group activities that were specific to the tragedy did not necessarily find relief or a sense of solidarity with other members of the community. More critical to people's recovery was continued participation in clubs and friendship groups in the weeks following the tragedy. Group solidarity does make a difference.

Types of Groups

Sociologists have made a number of useful distinctions between types of groups—primary and secondary groups, in-groups and out-groups, reference groups, and coalitions.

Primary and Secondary Groups

Charles Horton Cooley (1902) coined the term **primary group** to refer to a small group characterized by intimate, face-to-face association and cooperation. The members of a street gang constitute a primary group; so do members of a family living in the same household, as do a group of "sisters" in a college sorority.

Primary groups play a pivotal role both in the socialization process and in the development of roles and statuses. Indeed, primary groups can be instrumental in a person's day-to-day existence. When we find ourselves identifying closely with a group, it is probably a primary group.

We also participate in many groups that are not characterized by close bonds of friendship, such as large college classes and business associations. The term **secondary group** refers to a formal, impersonal group in which there is little social intimacy or mutual understanding (Table 18-1). Secondary groups often

Summing Up

TABLE **18-1** COMPARISON OF PRIMARY AND SECONDARY GROUPS

Primary Group	Secondary Group
Generally small	Usually large
Relatively long period of interaction	Relatively short duration, often temporary
Intimate, face-to-face association	Little social intimacy or mutual understanding
Some emotional depth to relationships	Relationships generally superficial
Cooperative, friendly	More formal and impersonal

emerge in the workplace among those who share special understandings about their occupation. The distinction between primary and secondary groups is not always clear-cut, however. Some social clubs may become so large and impersonal that they no longer function as primary groups.

In-Groups and Out-Groups

A group can hold special meaning for members because of its relationship to other groups. For example, people in one group sometimes feel antagonistic toward or threatened by another group, especially if that group is perceived as being different, either culturally or racially. To identify these "we" and "they" feelings, sociologists use two terms first employed by William Graham Sumner (1906): *in-group* and *out-group*.

An **in-group** can be defined as any group or category to which people feel they belong. Simply put, it comprises everyone who is regarded as "we" or "us." The in-group may be as narrow as a teenage clique or as broad as an entire society. The very existence of an in-group implies that there is an out-group that is viewed as "they" or "them." An **out-group** is a group or category to which people feel they do *not* belong.

In-group members typically feel distinct and superior, seeing themselves as better than people in the out-group. Proper

At a powwow, a drum circle breathes spirit into an ancient tribal tradition. These accomplished ceremonial musicians may serve as a reference group for onlookers who want to know more about drumming.

behavior for the in-group is simultaneously viewed as unacceptable behavior for the out-group. This double standard enhances the sense of superiority. Sociologist Robert Merton (1968) described this process as the conversion of "in-group virtues" into "out-group vices." We can see this differential standard operating in worldwide discussions of terrorism. When a group or a nation takes aggressive actions, it usually justifies them as necessary, even if civilians are hurt or killed. Opponents are quick to label such actions with the emotion-laden term of *terrorist* and appeal to the world community for condemnation. Yet these same people may themselves retaliate with actions that hurt civilians, which the first group will then condemn.

 use your **sociological imagination**

Try putting yourself in the shoes of an out-group member. What does your in-group look like from that perspective?

Conflict between in-groups and out-groups can turn violent on a personal as well as a political level. In 1999 two disaffected students at Columbine High School in Littleton, Colorado, launched an attack on the school that left 15 students and teachers dead, including themselves. The gunmen, members of an out-group that other students referred to as the Trenchcoat Mafia, apparently resented taunting by an in-group referred to as the Jocks. Similar episodes have occurred in schools across the nation, where rejected adolescents, overwhelmed by personal and family problems, peer group pressure, academic responsibilities, or media images of violence, have struck out against more popular classmates.

A pizza delivery crew is an example of a *secondary group*—a formal, impersonal group in which there is little social intimacy or mutual understanding. While waiting for the next delivery, members of this crew in Surrey, England, will become well enough acquainted to distinguish those who see the job as temporary from those who view it as permanent. They will learn who looks forward to deliveries in perceived high-risk areas and who does not. They may even spend time together after work, joking or boasting about their exploits on the job, but their friendships typically will not develop beyond that point.

Reference Groups

Both primary groups and in-groups can dramatically influence the way an individual thinks and behaves. Sociologists call any group that individuals use as a standard for evaluating themselves and their own behavior a **reference group.** For example, a high school student who aspires to join a social circle of hip-hop music devotees will pattern his or her behavior after that of the group. The student will begin dressing like these peers, listening to the same downloads and DVDs, and hanging out at the same stores and clubs.

Reference groups have two basic purposes. They serve a normative function by setting and enforcing standards of conduct and belief. The high school student who wants the approval of the hip-hop crowd will have to follow the group's dictates, at least to some extent. Reference groups also perform a comparison function by serving as a standard against which people can measure themselves and others. An actor will evaluate himself or herself against a reference group composed of others in the acting profession (Merton and Kitt 1950).

Reference groups may help the process of anticipatory socialization. For example, a college student majoring in finance may read the *Wall Street Journal,* study the annual reports of corporations, and listen to midday stock market news on the radio. Such a student is using financial experts as a reference group to which he or she aspires.

Often, two or more reference groups influence us at the same time. Our family members, neighbors, and co-workers all shape different aspects of our self-evaluation. In addition, reference group attachments change during the life cycle. A corporate executive who quits the rat race at age 45 to become a social worker will find new reference groups to use as standards for evaluation. We shift reference groups as we take on different statuses during our lives.

Coalitions

As groups grow larger, coalitions begin to develop. A **coalition** is a temporary or permanent alliance geared toward a common goal. Coalitions can be broad-based or narrow and can take on many different objectives. Sociologist William Julius Wilson (1999) has described community-based organizations in Texas that include Whites and Latinos, working class and affluent, who have banded together to work for improved sidewalks, better drainage systems, and comprehensive street paving. Out of

Can you outwit, outplay, outlast your competition? Maybe a coalition can help. In *Survivor: Blood vs. Water,* filmed on Palaui Island in the Philippines, coalition building continued to be a key to success in the long-running television series, now in its 29th season.

this type of coalition building, Wilson hopes, will emerge better interracial understanding.

Some coalitions are intentionally short-lived. For example, short-term coalition building is a key to success in popular TV programs like *Survivor.* In the program's first season, *Survivor: Borneo,* broadcast in 2000, the four members of the "Tagi alliance" banded together to vote fellow castaways off the island. The political world is also the scene of many temporary coalitions. For example, in 1997 big tobacco companies joined with antismoking groups to draw up a settlement for reimbursing states for tobacco-related medical costs. Soon after the settlement was announced, the coalition members returned to their decades-long fight against each other (Pear 1997).

 use your **sociological imagination**

Describe an experience you have had with coalition building, or one that you have read about—perhaps in politics. Was the coalition effective? What problems did the members need to overcome?

MODULE 18 | **Recap and Review**

Summary

Much of our social behavior takes place in **groups.**

1. When we find ourselves identifying closely with a group, it is probably a **primary group.** A **secondary group** is more formal and impersonal.

2. People tend to see the world in terms of **in-groups** and **out-groups,** a perception often fostered by the very groups to which they belong.

3. **Reference groups** set and enforce standards of conduct and serve as a source of comparison for people's evaluations of themselves and others.

4. Interactionist researchers have noted that groups allow **coalitions** to form and serve as links to social networks and their vast resources.

Thinking Critically

1. Describe an example of coalition building you have experienced or read about (perhaps in the political realm). Was the coalition effective? What problems had to be overcome?

2. Think of a primary and a secondary group to which you belong. Under what circumstances might the primary group become a secondary group, or the secondary group become a primary group?

Key Terms

Coalition

Group

In-group

Out-group

Primary group

Reference group

Secondary group

MODULE 19 | Understanding Organizations

Formal Organizations and Bureaucracies

As contemporary societies have shifted to more advanced forms of technology and their social structures have become more complex, our lives have become increasingly dominated by large secondary groups referred to as *formal organizations*. A **formal organization** is a group designed for a special purpose and structured for maximum efficiency. The U.S. Postal Service, McDonald's, and the Boston Pops orchestra are examples of formal organizations. Though organizations vary in their size, specificity of goals, and degree of efficiency, they are all structured to facilitate the management of large-scale operations. They also have a bureaucratic form of organization, described in the next section.

In our society, formal organizations fulfill an enormous variety of personal and societal needs, shaping the lives of every one of us. In fact, formal organizations have become such a dominant force that we must create organizations to supervise other organizations, such as the Securities and Exchange Commission (SEC) to regulate brokerage companies. Although it sounds more exciting to say that we live in the "computer age" than to say that we live in the "age of formal organization," the latter is probably a more accurate description (Azumi and Hage 1972; Etzioni 1964).

Ascribed statuses such as gender, race, and ethnicity can influence how we see ourselves within formal organizations. For example, a study of female lawyers in the nation's largest law firms found significant differences in the women's self-images, depending on the relative presence or absence of women in positions of power. In firms in which less than 15 percent of partners were women, the female lawyers were likely to believe that "feminine" traits were strongly devalued and that "masculine" traits were equated with success. As one female attorney put it, "Let's face it: this is a man's environment, and it's sort of Jock City, especially at my firm." Women in firms where female lawyers were better represented in positions of power had a stronger desire for and higher expectations of promotion (Ely 1995:619).

Characteristics of a Bureaucracy

A **bureaucracy** is a component of formal organization that uses rules and hierarchical ranking to achieve efficiency. Rows of desks staffed by seemingly faceless people, endless lines and forms, impossibly complex language, and frustrating encounters with red tape—all these unpleasant images have combined to make *bureaucracy* a dirty word and an easy target in political campaigns. As a result, few people want to identify their occupation as "bureaucrat," despite the fact that all of us perform various bureaucratic tasks. In an industrial society, elements of bureaucracy enter into almost every occupation.

Max Weber ([1913–1922] 1947) first directed researchers to the significance of bureaucratic structure. In an important sociological advance, Weber emphasized the basic similarity of structure and process found in the otherwise dissimilar enterprises of religion, government, education, and business. Weber saw bureaucracy as a form of organization quite different from the family-run business. For analytical purposes, he developed an ideal type of bureaucracy that would reflect the most characteristic aspects of all human organizations. By **ideal type** Weber meant a construct or model for evaluating specific cases. In actuality, perfect bureaucracies do not exist; no real-world organization corresponds exactly to Weber's ideal type.

Weber proposed that whether the purpose is to run a church, a corporation, or an army, the ideal bureaucracy displays five basic characteristics. A discussion of those characteristics, as well as the dysfunctions of a bureaucracy, follows.

1. **Division of labor.** Specialized experts perform specific tasks. In your college bureaucracy, the admissions officer does not do the job of registrar; the guidance counselor does not see to the maintenance of buildings. By working at a specific task, people are more likely to become highly skilled and carry out a job with

maximum efficiency. This emphasis on specialization is so basic a part of our lives that we may not realize it is a fairly recent development in Western culture.

The downside of division of labor is that the fragmentation of work into smaller and smaller tasks can divide workers and remove any connection they might feel to the overall objective of the bureaucracy. In *The Communist Manifesto* (written in 1848), Karl Marx and Friedrich Engels charged that the capitalist system reduces workers to a mere "appendage of the machine" (Tucker 1978). Such a work arrangement, they wrote, produces extreme **alienation**—a condition of estrangement or dissociation from the surrounding society. According to both Marx and conflict theorists, restricting workers to very small tasks also weakens their job security, since new employees can easily be trained to replace them.

Although division of labor has certainly enhanced the performance of many complex bureaucracies, in some cases it can lead to **trained incapacity;** that is, workers become so specialized that they develop blind spots and fail to notice obvious problems. Even worse, they may not care about what is happening in the next department. Some observers believe that such developments have caused workers in the United States to become less productive on the job.

In some cases, the bureaucratic division of labor can have tragic results. In the wake of the coordinated attacks on the World Trade Center and the Pentagon on September 11, 2001, Americans wondered aloud how the FBI and CIA could have failed to detect the terrorists' elaborately planned operation. The problem, in part, turned out to be the division of labor between the FBI, which focuses on domestic matters, and the CIA, which operates overseas. Officials at these intelligence-gathering organizations, both of which are huge bureaucracies, are well known for jealously guarding information from one another. Subsequent investigations revealed that they knew about Osama bin Laden and his Al-Qaeda

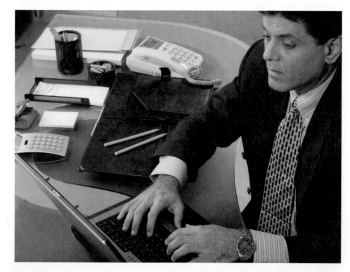

Being an accountant in a large corporation may be a relatively high-paying occupation. In Marxist terms, however, accountants are vulnerable to alienation, since they are far removed from the product or service that the corporation creates.

terrorist network in the early 1990s. Unfortunately, five federal agencies—the CIA, FBI, National Security Agency, Defense Intelligence Agency, and National Reconnaissance Office—failed to share their leads on the network. Although the hijacking of the four commercial airliners used in the massive attacks may not have been preventable, the bureaucratic division of labor definitely hindered efforts to defend against terrorism, undermining U.S. national security.

2. **Hierarchy of authority.** Bureaucracies follow the principle of hierarchy; that is, each position is under the supervision of a higher authority. A president heads a college bureaucracy; he or she selects members of the administration, who in turn hire their own staff. In the Roman Catholic Church, the pope is the supreme authority; under him are cardinals, bishops, and so forth.

3. **Written rules and regulations.** What if your sociology professor gave your classmate an A for having such a friendly smile? You might think that wasn't fair, that it was against the rules. Through written rules and regulations, bureaucracies generally offer employees clear standards for an adequate (or exceptional) performance. In addition, procedures provide a valuable sense of continuity in a bureaucracy. Individual workers will come and go, but the structure and past records of the organization give it a life of its own that outlives the services of any one bureaucrat.

Of course, rules and regulations can overshadow the larger goals of an organization to the point that they become dysfunctional. What if a domestic abuse counselor failed to listen to an injured woman because she had no valid proof of U.S. citizenship? If blindly applied, rules no longer serve as a means to achieving an objective, but instead become important (and perhaps too important) in their own right. Robert Merton (1968) used the term **goal displacement** to refer to overzealous conformity to official regulations.

4. **Impersonality.** Max Weber wrote that in a bureaucracy, work is carried out *sine ira et studio,* "without hatred or passion." Bureaucratic norms dictate that officials perform their duties without giving personal consideration to people as individuals. Although this norm is intended to guarantee equal treatment for each person, it also contributes to the often cold and uncaring feeling associated with modern organizations. We typically think of big government and big business when we think of impersonal bureaucracies. In some cases, the impersonality that is associated with a bureaucracy can have tragic results. More frequently, bureaucratic impersonality produces frustration and disaffection. Today, even small firms filter callers with electronic menus.

5. **Employment based on technical qualifications.** Within the ideal bureaucracy, hiring is based on technical qualifications rather than on favoritism, and performance is measured against specific standards. Written personnel policies dictate who gets promoted, and people often have a right to appeal if they believe that particular rules have been violated. Such procedures protect bureaucrats against arbitrary dismissal, provide a measure of security, and encourage loyalty to the organization.

Although ideally, any bureaucracy will value technical and professional competence, personnel decisions do not always follow that ideal pattern. Dysfunctions within bureaucracy have become well publicized, particularly because of the work of Laurence J. Peter. According to the **Peter principle,** every employee within a hierarchy tends to rise to his or her level of incompetence (Peter and Hull 1969). This hypothesis, which has not been directly or systematically tested, reflects a possible dysfunctional outcome of advancement on the basis of merit. Talented people receive promotion after promotion, until sadly, some of them finally achieve positions that they cannot handle with their usual competence.

Table 19-1 summarizes the five characteristics of bureaucracy. These characteristics, developed by Max Weber a century ago, describe an ideal type rather than an actual bureaucracy. Not every formal organization will possess all five of Weber's characteristics. In fact, wide variation exists among actual bureaucratic organizations.

Bureaucracy pervades modern life; through McDonaldization, it has reached new heights. As Box 19-1 shows, the McDonald's organization provides an excellent illustration of Weber's concept of bureaucracy (Ritzer 2013).

use your sociological imagination

Your school or workplace suddenly ceases to exhibit one of the five characteristics of bureaucracy. Which characteristic is it, and what are the consequences?

Bureaucratization as a Process

Have you ever had to speak to 10 or 12 individuals in a corporation or government agency just to find out which official has jurisdiction over a particular problem? Ever been transferred from one department to another until you finally hung up in disgust? Sociologists have used the term **bureaucratization** to refer to the process by which a group, organization, or social movement becomes increasingly bureaucratic.

Normally, we think of bureaucratization in terms of large organizations. But bureaucratization also takes place within small-group settings. Sociologist Jennifer Bickman Mendez (1998) studied domestic houseworkers employed in central California by

a nationwide franchise. She found that housekeeping tasks were minutely defined, to the point that employees had to follow 22 written steps for cleaning a bathroom. Complaints and special requests went not to the workers, but to an office-based manager.

Bureaucratization is not limited to Western industrial societies. In 2012, Xi Jinping became general secretary of China's Communist Party, the nation's highest office. In his first public address, Jinping pledged to end the party's "undue emphasis on formalities and bureaucracy" in order to deliver a "better life" for the Chinese people (I. Johnson 2012:A19; Malcolm Moore 2012).

Oligarchy: Rule by a Few

Conflict theorists have examined the bureaucratization of social movements. The German sociologist Robert Michels (1915) studied socialist parties and labor unions in Europe before World War I and found that such organizations were becoming increasingly bureaucratic. The emerging leaders of the organizations— even some of the most radical—had a vested interest in clinging to power. If they lost their leadership posts, they would have to return to full-time work as manual laborers.

Through his research, Michels originated the idea of the **iron law of oligarchy,** which describes how even a democratic organization will eventually develop into a bureaucracy ruled by a few, called an oligarchy. Why do oligarchies emerge? People who achieve leadership roles usually have the skills, knowledge, or charismatic appeal (as Weber noted) to direct, if not control, others. Michels argued that the rank and file of a movement or organization look to leaders for direction and thereby reinforce the process of rule by a few. In addition, members of an oligarchy are strongly motivated to maintain their leadership roles, privileges, and power.

Bureaucracy and Organizational Culture

How does bureaucratization affect the average individual who works in an organization? The early theorists of formal organizations tended to neglect this question. Max Weber, for example, focused

TABLE **19-1** CHARACTERISTICS OF A BUREAUCRACY

Summing Up

		Negative Consequence	
	Positive Consequence	For the Individual	For the Organization
Division of labor	Produces efficiency in a large-scale corporation	Produces trained incapacity	Produces a narrow perspective
Hierarchy of authority	Clarifies who is in command	Deprives employees of a voice in decision making	Permits concealment of mistakes
Written rules and regulations	Let workers know what is expected of them	Stifle initiative and imagination	Lead to goal displacement
Impersonality	Reduces bias	Contributes to feelings of alienation	Discourages loyalty to company
Employment based on technical qualifications	Discourages favoritism and reduces petty rivalries	Discourages ambition to improve oneself elsewhere	Fosters Peter principle

Sociology in the Global Community

BOX 19-1

McDonald's and the Worldwide Bureaucratization of Society

In his book *The McDonaldization of Society*, sociologist George Ritzer notes the enormous influence of a well-known fast-food organization on modern-day culture and social life.

Not surprisingly, Max Weber's five characteristics of bureaucracy are apparent in McDonald's restaurants, as well as in the global corporation behind them. Food preparation and order-taking reflect a painstaking *division of labor*, implemented by a *hierarchy of authority* that stretches from the food workers up to the store operator, and ultimately to the corporate board of directors. Store operators learn McDonald's *written rules and regulations*, which govern even the amount of ketchup or mustard placed on a hamburger, at McDonald's Hamburger University. Little bonding occurs between servers and customers, creating a pervasive sense of *impersonality*. The emphasis on efficiency is partly to blame for this characteristic. Because McDonald's French fry machines lift the fries out of the hot oil automatically, for example, employees cannot meet a customer request for "crispy" fries. Finally, employees are expected to have specific *technical qualifications*, although most of the skills they need to perform routine tasks can be learned in a brief training period.

McDonaldization is the process by which the principles of bureaucratization have increasingly shaped organizations worldwide. Its real significance is that it is not confined to the food-service industry or to coffee shops like Starbucks. Worldwide, McDonald's brand of predictability, efficiency, and dependence on nonhuman technology have become customary in a number of services, ranging from medical care to wedding planning to education.

Even sporting events reflect the influence of bureaucratization. Around the world, stadiums are becoming increasingly similar, both physically and in the way they present the sport to spectators. All seats offer spectators an unrestricted view, and a big screen guarantees them access to instant replays, which fans have become accustomed to seeing at home and in sports bars. Scores, player

The worldwide success of highly efficient fast-food operations has led to the bureaucratization of many other services, including eye care and other forms of medical treatment.

statistics, and attendance figures are updated automatically by computer and displayed on an automated scoreboard or fed to people's smartphones. Spectator enthusiasm is manufactured through digital displays urging applause or rhythmic chanting. And of course, the merchandising of teams' and even players' names and images is highly controlled.

McDonald's reliance on the five characteristics of bureaucracy is not revolutionary. What is new is the bureaucratization of services and life events that once were highly individualized, at times even spontaneous. More and more, society itself is undergoing McDonaldization.

> Worldwide, McDonald's brand of predictability, efficiency, and dependence on nonhuman technology have become customary in a number of services, ranging from medical care to wedding planning to education.

LET'S DISCUSS

1. What features of fast-food restaurants do you appreciate? Do you have any complaints about them?
2. Analyze life at your college using Weber's model of bureaucracy. What elements of McDonaldization do you see? Do you wish life were less McDonaldized?

Sources: Ormond 2005; Ritzer 2013.

---

on the management personnel in bureaucracies, but had little to say about workers in industry or clerks in government agencies.

According to the **classical theory** of formal organizations, or **scientific management approach,** workers are motivated almost entirely by economic rewards. This theory stresses that only the physical constraints on workers limit their productivity. Therefore, workers may be treated as a resource, much like the machines that began to replace them in the 20th century. Under the scientific management approach, management attempts to achieve maximum work efficiency through scientific planning, established performance standards, and careful supervision of workers and production. Planning involves efficiency studies but not studies of workers' attitudes or job satisfaction.

Not until workers organized unions—and forced management to recognize that they were not objects—did theorists of formal organizations begin to revise the classical approach. Social scientists

118 ■ Social Interaction, Social Structure, and Groups

became aware that along with management and administrators, informal groups of workers have an important impact on organizations. An alternative way of considering bureaucratic dynamics, the **human relations approach,** emphasizes the role of people, communication, and participation in a bureaucracy. This type of analysis reflects the interest of interactionist theorists in small-group behavior. Unlike planning under the scientific management approach, planning based on the human relations approach focuses on workers' feelings, frustrations, and emotional need for job satisfaction.

The gradual move away from a sole focus on the physical aspects of getting the job done—and toward the concerns and needs of workers—led advocates of the human relations approach to stress the less formal aspects of bureaucratic structure. Informal groups and social networks within organizations develop partly as a result of people's ability to create more direct forms of communication than under the formal structure. Charles Page (1946) used the term *bureaucracy's other face* to refer to the unofficial activities and interactions that are such a basic part of daily organizational life.

Today, research on formal organizations is following new avenues. Among them are

- the recent arrival of a small number of women and minority group members in high-level management;
- in large corporations, the decision-making role of groups that lie outside the top ranks of leadership;
- the loss of fixed boundaries in organizations that have outsourced key functions; and
- the role of the Internet in influencing business and consumer preferences.

Though research on organizations still embraces Max Weber's insights, then, it has gone well beyond them (Hamm 2007; Kleiner 2003; W. Scott and Davis 2007).

social policy and Organizations | The State of the Unions Worldwide

How many people do you know who belong to a labor union? Chances are you can name a lot fewer people than someone could 50 years ago. In 1954 unions represented 39 percent of workers in the private sector of the U.S. economy; in 2012 they represented only 11.3 percent—the lowest share in more than 70 years. As Figure 19-1 shows, the decline in unionization is common to virtually all industrial nations. What has happened to diminish the importance of organized labor? Can workers be represented adequately without strong unions?

Looking at the Issue

Labor unions consist of organized workers who share either the same skill (as in electronics) or the same employer (as in the case of postal employees). Unions began to emerge during the Industrial Revolution in England, in the 1700s. Groups of workers banded together to extract concessions from employers (for example, safer working conditions, a shorter workweek) and to protect their positions.

Historically, labor unions have engaged in restrictive practices that are regarded today as discriminatory. They frequently tried to protect their jobs by limiting entry to their occupation based on gender, race, ethnicity, citizenship, age, and sometimes rather arbitrary measures of skill levels. Today we see less of this protection of special interests. In selected industries, unions now play a vital role in keeping Blacks' wages competitive with those of Whites (Rosenfeld and Klegkamp 2012).

The power of labor unions varies widely from country to country. In some countries, such as Britain and Mexico, unions play a key role in the foundation of governments. In others, such as Japan and Korea, their role in politics is very limited, and their ability to influence even the private sector is relatively weak. In the United States, unions can sometimes

—Continued

FIGURE 19-1 Labor Union Membership Worldwide

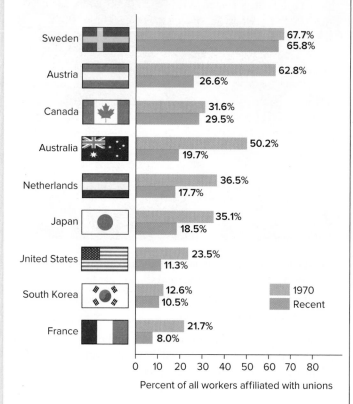

Percent of all workers affiliated with unions

■ 1970
■ Recent

Note: Recent data from 2008–2010, except for Sweden and the United States (2012) and the Netherlands (2007).
Sources: New Unionism Network 2011; Trottman and Maher 2013; Visser 2006:45.

have a significant influence on employers and elected officials, but their effect varies dramatically by type of industry and even region of the country (S. Zimmerman 2008b).

Few people today would dispute the fact that union membership is declining. Among the reasons for the decline are the following:

1. **Changes in the type of industry.** Manufacturing jobs, the traditional heart of the labor union, have declined, giving way to postindustrial service jobs.

2. **Growth in part-time jobs.** Between 1982 and 1998 the number of temporary jobs in the United States rose 577 percent, while total employment increased only 41 percent. Only in 2000 did laws governing collective bargaining allow temporary workers to join a union.

3. **The legal system.** The United States has not made it particularly easy for unions to organize and bargain, and some government measures have made it more difficult. A dramatic example was President Ronald Reagan's firing of 11,000 air traffic controllers in 1981, when their union threatened they would walk off the job while seeking a new contract.

4. **Globalization.** The threat of jobs leaving the country has undercut the ability of union leaders to organize workers at home. Some say that labor union demands for wage increases and additional benefits have themselves spurred the exodus of jobs to developing nations, where wages are significantly lower and unions are virtually nonexistent.

5. **Employer offensives.** Increasingly hostile employers have taken court action to block unions' efforts to represent their members.

Around the world, the economic downturn that began in 2008 has had special consequences for labor unions. Like nonunion workers, many union members lost their jobs in the recession; others saw their contracts renegotiated. As part of the $17.4 billion auto bailout legislation passed by the U.S. Congress in 2008, the United Auto Workers (UAW) accepted a nearly 20 percent pay cut. This and other rollbacks of benefits were largely accepted by U.S. unions, but in Europe, thousands of workers turned out in protest. Although some union leaders in the United States expect the hardship caused by the economic slowdown to raise union membership, how well unions will be able to represent their members through tough times remains to be seen (S. Greenhouse 2008a, 2009).

Applying Sociology

Both Marxists and functionalists would view unions as a logical response to the emergence of impersonal, large-scale, formal, and often alienating organizations. This view certainly characterized the growth of unions in major manufacturing industries with a sharp division of labor. However, as manufacturing has declined, unions have had to look elsewhere for growth.

Worldwide, today's labor unions bear little resemblance to those early unions organized spontaneously by exploited workers. In line with Robert Michels's iron law of oligarchy, unions have become increasingly bureaucratized under a sometimes self-serving leadership. Conflict theorists would point out that the longer union leaders are in office, the less responsive they are to the needs and demands of the rank and file, and the more concerned with maintaining their own positions and power. Yet research shows that under certain circumstances, union leadership can change significantly. Smaller unions are vulnerable to changes in leadership, as are unions whose membership shifts in composition from predominantly White to African American or Latino.

Sociologists have linked the recent decline in private-sector union membership to a widening gap between hourly workers' wages and managerial and executive compensation. As union membership declined—and with it the unions' bargaining power—employers began to offer union workers less attractive pay packages. Eventually, the trend spread to non-unionized companies in the same industries, which typically strive to match union compensation in order to be competitive.

In these businesses, employers no longer feel a need to raise wages to attract employees (Western and Rosenfeld 2011).

Initiating Policy

U.S. law grants workers the right to self-organize via unions. However, the United States is unique among industrial democracies in allowing employers to actively oppose their employees' decision to organize. The recent economic recession has compounded employers' opposition to unions and is even threatening workers' rights in established unions. Today, state and local governments across the United States are facing significant budget deficits. In an effort to cut costs, many elected officials are moving to shrink the pensions that government workers gained through collective bargaining. In some states, officials want not only to reduce retirees' benefits, but also to curtail union workers' collective bargaining rights.

In Europe, labor unions tend to play a major role in political elections. The ruling party in Great Britain, in fact, is called the Labour Party. Unions play a lesser role in U.S. politics, although they have recently been attacked for their large financial contributions to political campaigns. In addition to the role of unions in national politics, international trade unions sometimes speak out on common issues. In 2009 one of them condemned "corporate grand theft"—a reference to corporate executives who

spend lavishly on themselves while laying off workers. Despite efforts dating back to Karl Marx and Friedrich Engels's call for the workers of all countries to unite (1847), no global union has emerged (International Trade Union Confederation 2009).

Though unions are a global force, their form and substance varies from country to country. In China, where there is only one political party, the government ordered Walmart's 31,000 workers to unionize, over the corporation's objections. Chinese unions are controlled by the Communist Party, whose membership has declined as the party's pervasive control has weakened. Nevertheless, these unions are more likely to listen to the government than independent unions, which listen to the workers who are their members (E. Wang 2013; Zhang 2009).

TAKE THE ISSUE WITH YOU

1. What unions are represented on your college campus? Have you been aware of union activity? Has there been any opposition to the unions on the part of the administration?

2. Why should employees who provide essential public services, such as nurses, teachers, and police officers, be allowed to organize into a union? What impact does union membership have on their representation if they cannot strike?

3. Should state and local officials be allowed to reduce government workers' retirement benefits and take away their right to collective bargaining?

MODULE 19 | Recap and Review

Summary

As societies become larger and more complex, daily life is increasingly dominated by large **formal organizations.**

1. Max Weber argued that in its ideal form, a **bureaucracy** has five basic characteristics: division of labor, hierarchical authority, written rules and regulations, impersonality, and employment based on technical qualifications. Carefully constructed bureaucratic policies can be either undermined or redefined by an organization's informal structure.

2. The **scientific management approach** to management considers workers to be economic resources. In contrast, the **human relations approach** emphasizes the role of people, communications, and participation.

Thinking Critically

1. What are some of the benefits and drawbacks of large formal organizations?

2. Recall a job that you once held. First, analyze the workplace using classical theory (the scientific

management approach). Then analyze it using the human relations approach. Which approach do you find more useful in understanding that workplace?

Key Terms

Alienation
Bureaucracy
Bureaucratization
Classical theory
Formal organization
Goal displacement
Human relations approach
Ideal type
Iron law of oligarchy
Labor union
McDonaldization
Peter principle
Scientific management approach
Trained incapacity

Mastering This Chapter

taking sociology with you

1 Interview a professional in a field of your choice. What role conflicts does a professional in that field commonly experience? What guidance does the profession's code of conduct offer regarding such conflicts?

2 Talk with two or three business students or businesspeople about the bureaucratization of business. On balance, do they see

bureaucratization as a positive or negative trend? What bureaucratic dysfunctions are common in business, and how do managers attempt to counteract them?

3 Speak with some members of a labor union. What work issues are important to them? What changes have they seen in unions and in the workplace since they began working?

key terms

Achieved status A social position that a person attains largely through his or her own efforts.

Agrarian society The most technologically advanced form of preindustrial society. Members engage primarily in the production of food, but increase their crop yields through technological innovations such as the plow.

Alienation A condition of estrangement or dissociation from the surrounding society.

Ascribed status A social position assigned to a person by society without regard for the person's unique talents or characteristics.

Bureaucracy A component of formal organization that uses rules and hierarchical ranking to achieve efficiency.

Bureaucratization The process by which a group, organization, or social movement becomes increasingly bureaucratic.

Classical theory An approach to the study of formal organizations that views workers as being motivated almost entirely by economic rewards.

Coalition A temporary or permanent alliance geared toward a common goal.

Formal organization A group designed for a special purpose and structured for maximum efficiency.

Gemeinschaft A close-knit community, often found in rural areas, in which strong personal bonds unite members.

Gesellschaft A community, often urban, that is large and impersonal, with little commitment to the group or consensus on values.

Goal displacement Overzealous conformity to official regulations of a bureaucracy.

Group Any number of people with similar norms, values, and expectations who interact with one another on a regular basis.

Horticultural society A preindustrial society in which people plant seeds and crops rather than merely subsist on available foods.

Human relations approach An approach to the study of formal organizations that emphasizes the role of people, communication,

and participation in a bureaucracy and tends to focus on the informal structure of the organization.

Hunting-and-gathering society A preindustrial society in which people rely on whatever foods and fibers are readily available in order to survive.

Hyperconsumerism The practice of buying more than we need or want, and often more than we can afford; a preoccupation of postmodern consumers.

Ideal type A construct or model for evaluating specific cases.

Industrial society A society that depends on mechanization to produce its goods and services.

In-group Any group or category to which people feel they belong.

Iron law of oligarchy A principle of organizational life under which even a democratic organization will eventually develop into a bureaucracy ruled by a few individuals.

Labor union Organized workers who share either the same skill or the same employer.

Master status A status that dominates others and thereby determines a person's general position in society.

McDonaldization The process by which the principles of bureaucratization have increasingly shaped organizations worldwide.

Mechanical solidarity A collective consciousness that emphasizes group solidarity, characteristic of societies with minimal division of labor.

Organic solidarity A collective consciousness that rests on mutual interdependence, characteristic of societies with a complex division of labor.

Out-group A group or category to which people feel they do not belong.

Peter principle A principle of organizational life according to which every employee within a hierarchy tends to rise to his or her level of incompetence.

Postindustrial society A society whose economic system is engaged primarily in the processing and control of information.

Postmodern society A technologically sophisticated society that is preoccupied with consumer goods and media images.

Primary group A small group characterized by intimate, face-to-face association and cooperation.

Reference group Any group that individuals use as a standard for evaluating themselves and their own behavior.

Role conflict The situation that occurs when incompatible expectations arise from two or more social positions held by the same person.

Role exit The process of disengagement from a role that is central to one's self-identity in order to establish a new role and identity.

Role strain The difficulty that arises when the same social position imposes conflicting demands and expectations.

Scientific management approach Another name for the classical theory of formal organizations.

Secondary group A formal, impersonal group in which there is little social intimacy or mutual understanding.

Social institution An organized pattern of beliefs and behavior centered on basic social needs.

Social interaction The ways in which people respond to one another.

Social network A series of social relationships that links a person directly to others, and through them indirectly to still more people.

Social role A set of expectations for people who occupy a given social position or status.

Social structure The way in which a society is organized into predictable relationships.

Sociocultural evolution Long-term social trends resulting from the interplay of continuity, innovation, and selection.

Status A term used by sociologists to refer to any of the full range of socially defined positions within a large group or society.

Technology Cultural information about the ways in which the material resources of the environment may be used to satisfy human needs and desires.

Trained incapacity The tendency of workers in a bureaucracy to become so specialized that they develop blind spots and fail to notice obvious problems.

self-quiz

Read each question carefully and then select the best answer.

1. In the United States, we expect that cab drivers will know how to get around a city. This expectation is an example of which of the following?
   a. role conflict
   b. role strain
   c. social role
   d. master status

2. What occurs when incompatible expectations arise from two or more social positions held by the same person?
   a. role conflict
   b. role strain
   c. role exit
   d. both a and b

3. In sociological terms, what do we call any number of people with similar norms, values, and expectations who interact with one another on a regular basis?
   a. a category
   b. a group
   c. an aggregate
   d. a society

4. The Shakers, a religious sect that came to the United States in 1774, has seen their group's membership diminish significantly due to their inability to
   a. teach new recruits.
   b. preserve order.
   c. replace personnel.
   d. provide and maintain a sense of purpose.

5. Which sociological perspective argues that the present organization of social institutions is no accident?
   a. the functionalist perspective
   b. the conflict perspective
   c. the interactionist perspective
   d. the global perspective

6. The U.S. Postal Service, the Boston Pops orchestra, and the college or university in which you are currently enrolled as a student are all examples of
   a. primary groups.
   b. reference groups.
   c. formal organizations.
   d. triads.

7. One positive consequence of bureaucracy is that it reduces bias. Reduction of bias results from which characteristic of a bureaucracy?
   a. impersonality
   b. hierarchy of authority
   c. written rules and regulations
   d. employment based on technical qualifications

8. According to the Peter principle,
   a. all bureaucracies are notoriously inefficient.
   b. if something *can* go wrong, it *will*.
   c. every employee within a hierarchy tends to rise to his or her level of incompetence.
   d. all line workers get burned in the end.

9. Social control in what Ferdinand Tönnies termed a *Gemeinschaft* community is maintained through all but which of the following means?
   a. moral persuasion
   b. gossip
   c. legally defined punishment
   d. gestures

10. Sociologist Daniel Bell uses which of the following terms to refer to a society whose economic system is engaged primarily in the processing and control of information?
    a. postmodern
    b. horticultural
    c. industrial
    d. postindustrial

11. The term _____ _____ refers to the way in which a society is organized into predictable relationships.

12. The African American activist Malcolm X wrote in his autobiography that his position as a Black man, a(n) _____ status, was an obstacle to his dream of becoming a lawyer, a(n) _____ status.

13. Sociologist Helen Rose Fuchs Ebaugh developed the term _____ _____ to describe the process of disengagement from a role that is central to one's self-identity in order to establish a new role and identity.

14. _____ groups often emerge in the workplace among those who share special understandings about their occupation.

15. In many cases, people model their behavior after groups to which they may not belong. These groups are called _____ groups.

16. In studying the social behavior of word processors in a Chicago law firm, sociologist Mitchell Duneier drew on the _____ perspective.

17. Max Weber developed a(n) _____ _____ of bureaucracy, which reflects the most characteristic aspects of all human organizations.

18. According to Émile Durkheim, societies with a minimal division of labor are characterized by _____ solidarity, while societies with a complex division of labor are characterized by _____ solidarity.

19. In Gerhard Lenski's theory of sociocultural evolution, a society's level of _____ is critical to the way it is organized.

20. A(n) _____ society is a technologically sophisticated society that is preoccupied with consumer goods and media images.

Answers

1 (c); 2 (a); 3 (b); 4 (c); 5 (b); 6 (c); 7 (a); 8 (c); 9 (c); 10 (d); 11 social structure; 12 ascribed, achieved; 13 role exit; 14 Secondary; 15 reference; 16 interactionist; 17 ideal type; 18 mechanical, organic; 19 technology; 20 postmodern

6 The Mass Media

World's First 3D VideoWall

World's Largest 3D VideoWa

Innovations in mass media seem to have no limits. This three-dimensional video wall was featured at the Consumer Electronics Show in Las Vegas. As they say, "Coming soon to stores near you."

Think about the media you use today. How many of those media existed five years ago?

Lynne Gross is amazed by the rapid change that is occurring in the mass media.

" You would be hard-pressed in modern American society to find someone who does not interact with electronic media on a daily basis—someone who does not surf the Internet, watch TV, listen to the radio, download music to an iPod, go to a movie, play a video game, send an email, or talk on a smartphone. In fact, many people in this age of multitasking interact with several media at the same time. They watch a movie downloaded from the Internet while playing a video game and texting a friend.

In addition, everyone has opinions that relate to media. Our opinions decide whether a movie or a TV series is a hit or a dud. We vote for our favorite *American Idol* singer. We argue about the media's coverage of political candidates. We talk about the tactics used in the commercials and the sex and violence seen on TV and heard in radio song lyrics. We worry about the predators on the Internet and whether or not our cell phones will cause cancer.

The media are constantly changing. Not very long ago there was no Internet, no iPad, no Twitter. Within the past few decades, a number of technologies that were highly touted have gone by the wayside—subscription TV, VCRs,

Now anyone can be a producer, distributing to those who click on their site or download their information.

teletext. The way people used electronic media and how they perceived the media were quite different 10 years ago from what they are today.

Here are some things that were not available at the beginning of the 21st century: iPod, iTunes, iPhone, iPad, Xbox, hotspots, YouTube, Hulu, Skype, Facebook, and Twitter. The technological innovation that has occurred since 2000 has been a blur. Each month seems to bring faster computer speeds and greater storage capacities that expand capabilities of the Internet, portable platforms, and video games. Traditional media such as radio, television, and movies were separate for many years. But these new inventions now incorporate material from all of them—as well as from newspapers, magazines, the record business, the telephone industry, and many other media entities.

The interactive capabilities of the Internet, portable platforms, and video games have taken media in a new direction. Previous media forms were basically one way—producers of content distributed to the public, most of whom simply listened to or watched the material passively. Now anyone can be a producer, distributing to those who click on their site or download their information. When people interact with Internet-based media, whether for shopping, texting, emailing, or any of many other activities, they are in an active stage that involves thinking and doing. The Internet did not start out that way, however. It had humble beginnings and then took hold in ways no one had originally envisioned. "

(L. Gross 2013:2–3, 27–28)

n this excerpt from her book *Electronic Media,* Gross sketches the rapid transition from old-fashioned technologies to the new interactive technologies. That transition has profoundly changed the ways people use media. Once the only media available to us—radio, television, the Internet—were a one-way experience, from the producer to the audience. Today, anyone can become a producer and distribute content to others.

And that's not all; the lines between various media are blurring. Today we use the telephone not just to talk with others, but to watch television and movies. Both television and the Internet are examples of the *mass media,* which embrace print and electronic means of communication that carry messages to widespread audiences. Print media include newspapers, magazines, and books; electronic media include radio, satellite radio, television, motion pictures, and the Internet.

Advertising, which falls into both categories, is also a form of mass media.

The social impact of the mass media is obvious. Consider a few examples. TV dinners were invented to accommodate the millions of couch potatoes who can't bear to miss their favorite television programs. Today, screen time has gone well beyond television viewing to include time spent on smartphones. Candidates for political office rely on their media consultants to project a winning image both in print and in the electronic media. World leaders use all forms of media for political advantage, whether to gain territory or to bid on hosting the Olympics. And in parts of Africa and Asia, AIDS education projects owe much of their success to media campaigns.

Why are the media so influential? Who benefits from media influence and why? How do we maintain cultural and ethical standards in the face of negative media images? In these modules we will consider the ways sociology helps us to answer these questions. First we will look at how proponents of the various sociological perspectives view the media. Then we will examine who makes up the media's audience, not just at home but around the world. The chapter closes with a Social Policy section on the right to privacy in a digital age.

MODULE 20

Sociological Perspectives on the Media

Few aspects of society are as central as the **mass media,** a term that refers to print and electronic means of communication that carry messages to widespread audiences. Through the media we expand our understanding of people and events beyond what we experience in person. The media inform us about different cultures and lifestyles and about the latest forms of technology. For sociologists, the key questions are how the mass media affect our social institutions and how they influence our social behavior.

The social impact of the mass media has become so huge, in fact, that scholars have begun to speak of *cultural convergence.* The term **cultural convergence** refers to the flow of content across multiple media, and the accompanying migration of media audiences. As you watch a television program, for example, you wonder what the star of the show is doing at the moment, and turn to the Internet. Later, while texting your best friend, you tell her what you learned, accompanied by a Google Earth map showing the celebrity's location. Using Photoshop, you may even include the star's image next to your own, post the photo on your Facebook page, and then Tweet your friends (send them a mini-blog) to create a caption. Media convergence is not orchestrated by the media, sophisticated though they may be. You initiate it, using techniques you likely learned by interacting with others, either face-to-face or through the media (Jenkins 2006).

Over the past decade, new technologies have made new forms of mass media available to U.S. households. These new technologies have changed people's viewing and listening habits. People spend a lot of time with the media, more and more of it on the Internet. Media consumers have moved away from television and toward digital images downloaded to their computers and portable devices. Increasingly, they learn not just about the famous but about ordinary people by viewing their Facebook or MySpace pages or by keeping in touch with their friends via Twitter.

How do people's viewing and listening habits affect their social behavior? In the following sections we'll use the four major sociological perspectives to examine the impact of the mass media and changes in their usage patterns (Nelson 2004).

Functionalist Perspective

One obvious function of the mass media is to entertain. Except for clearly identified news or educational programming, we often think the explicit purpose of the mass media is to occupy our leisure time—from newspaper comics and crossword puzzles to the latest music releases on the Internet. While that is true, the media have other important functions. They also socialize us, enforce social norms, confer status, and promote consumption. An important dysfunction of the mass media is that they may act as a narcotic, desensitizing us to distressing events (Lazarsfeld and Merton 1948; C. Wright 1986).

Agent of Socialization

The media increase social cohesion by presenting a common, more or less standardized view of culture through mass communication. Sociologist Robert Park (1922) studied how newspapers helped immigrants to the United States adjust to their environment by changing their customary habits and teaching them the opinions of people in their new home country. Unquestionably, the mass media play a significant role in providing a collective experience for members of society. Think about how the mass media bring together members of a community or even a nation by broadcasting important events and ceremonies (such

Time to Tweet! In 2012, after struggling briefly with an iPad touch screen, Pope Benedict XVI dispatched his first Twitter message, which read in part, "I bless all you from my heart." Using the handle @Pontifex, the pope posts in eight of the many languages used by members of the worldwide Roman Catholic community (Donadio 2012:A8).

as inaugurations, press conferences, parades, state funerals, and the Olympics) and by covering disasters.

Which media outlets did people turn to in the aftermath of the September 11, 2001, tragedy? Television, radio, and the telephone were the primary means by which people in the United States bonded. But the Internet also played a prominent role. About half of all Internet users—more than 5 million people—received some kind of news about the attacks online (D. Miller and Darlington 2002).

Today, the news media have moved further online. Afghans of all political persuasions now connect with the Muslim community overseas to gain both social and financial support. In the realm of popular culture, a spontaneous global sharing of reactions to Michael Jackson's sudden death in 2009 crashed the websites for Google, the *Los Angeles Times,* TMZ celebrity news, Perez Hilton's blog, and Twitter (Rawlinson and Hunt 2009; Shane 2010).

Some are concerned about the media's socialization function, however. For instance, many people worry about the effect of using television as a babysitter and the impact of violent programming on viewer behavior. Some people adopt a blame-the-media mentality, holding the media accountable for anything that goes wrong, especially with young people. Yet the media also have positive effects on young people. For young and even not-so-young adults, for example, a new sort of tribalism is emerging online, in which communities develop around common interests or shared identities (Tyrene Adams and Smith 2008).

Enforcer of Social Norms

The media often reaffirm proper behavior by showing what happens to people who act in a way that violates societal expectations. These messages are conveyed when the bad guy gets clobbered in cartoons or is thrown in jail on *CSI.* Yet the media also sometimes glorify disapproved behavior, whether it is physical violence, disrespect to a teacher, or drug use.

The media also play a critical role in human sexuality. For example, programs have been created to persuade teens not to send nude images of themselves to selected friends. Such images often go viral (that is, spread across the Internet) and may be used to harass teens and their parents. To define normative behavior regarding these images, one organization has launched a "That's not cool" campaign, complete with stalker messages that can be e-mailed to those who misuse such images. The widespread dissemination of compromising images that were meant to be shared only among close friends is just one aspect of the social phenomenon called *cyberbullying* (Chan 2009; Clifford 2009a; Gentile 2009).

Conferral of Status

The mass media confer status on people, organizations, and public issues. Whether it is an issue like the homeless or a celebrity like Kim Kardashian, they single out one from thousands of other similarly placed issues or people to become significant. Table 20-1 shows how often certain public figures are prominently featured on magazine covers and the online source for celebrity information, IMDb. Obviously, *People* magazine alone was not responsible for making Princess Diana into a worldwide figure, but collectively, all the media outlets created a notoriety that Princess Victoria of Sweden, for one, did not enjoy.

Another way the media confer celebrity status on individuals is by publishing information about the frequency of Internet searches. Some newspapers and websites carry regularly updated lists of the most heavily researched individuals and topics of the week. The means may have changed since the first issue of *Time* magazine hit the stands in 1923, but the media still confer status—often electronically.

 use your **sociological imagination**

You are browsing through media outlets. Are you more likely than not to go to an outlet based on the person being featured? What kind of image would attract you?

Promotion of Consumption

Postmodern societies are characterized by **hyperconsumerism,** a term coined by the French sociologist Jean Baudrillard (1929–2007) to refer to the practice of buying more than we need or want, and often more than we can afford. The media certainly promote this

Product placement ("brand casting") is an increasingly important source of revenue for motion picture studios. The movie *Men in Black 3* (2012) featured many brands, including Cadillac, Cracker Jack, Dunkin' Donuts, John Deere, Rolaids, and Viagra (Brandchannel.com 2013).

TABLE 20-1 STATUS CONFERRED BY THE MEDIA

Time Rank/Person/Times on Cover	People Rank/Person/Times on Cover	Ebony Rank/Person/Times on Cover	Rolling Stone Rank/Person/Times on Cover	IMDb Rank/Person
1. Richard Nixon (55)	1. Princess Diana (54)	1. Janet Jackson (18)	1. Paul McCartney (28)	1. Johnny Depp
2. Ronald Reagan (38)	2. Jennifer Aniston (41)	2. Halle Berry (17)	2. John Lennon (26)	2. Brad Pitt
3. Bill Clinton (35)	3. Julia Roberts (35)	2. Michael Jackson (17)	3. Bono (22)	3. Angelina Jolie
4. Barack Obama (31)	4. Brad Pitt (33)	4. Muhammad Ali (16)	3. Bob Dylan (22)	4. Tom Cruise
4. Hillary Clinton (31)	5. Prince William (24)	4. Whitney Houston (16)	5. Mick Jagger (21)	5. Natalie Portman
4. George W. Bush (31)	5. Demi Moore (24)	6. Denzel Washington (11)	5. Bruce Springsteen (21)	6. Christian Bale
7. George H. W. Bush (25)	7. Angelina Jolie (21)	6. Diahann Carroll (11)	7. Madonna (19)	7. Scarlett Johansson
8. Dwight Eisenhower (22)	8. Britney Spears (18)	6. Lena Horne (11)	8. Jimi Hendrix (18)	8. Jennifer Aniston
8. Lyndon Johnson (22)	9. Michael Jackson (17)	6. Sidney Poitier (11)	8. Keith Richards (18)	9. Keira Knightley
8. Gerald Ford (22)	9. Elizabeth Taylor (17)	10. Beyoncé (10)	10. George Harrison (17)	10. Emma Watson
		10. Vanessa Williams (10)		
		10. Bill Cosby (10)		

Think about It How do these media outlets differ in the types of people they feature? Which type do you think enjoys the most status? Why?

Source: Author's content analysis of primary cover subject for full run of the periodicals beginning with *Time*, March 3, 1923; *People*, March 4, 1974; *Ebony*, November 1945; and *Rolling Stone*, September 1967 through September 1, 2013. When a periodical runs multiple covers, each version is counted. In case of ties, the more recent cover person is listed first. IMDb rank based on cumulative 2003–2012 page views by the more than 110 million unique viewers per month at IMDb.com.

behavior pattern. Twenty thousand commercials a year—that is the number the average child in the United States watches on television alone, not to mention other media platforms.

Young people cannot escape commercial messages. They show up on high school scoreboards, at rock concerts, and as banners on web pages. They also surface in the form of *product placement*—for example, the Coca-Cola glasses that sit in front of the judges on *American Idol*. Product placement is nothing new. In 1951 *The African Queen* prominently displayed Gordon's Gin aboard the boat carrying Katharine Hepburn and Humphrey Bogart. However, commercial promotion has become far more common today: *American Idol* alone features over 4,600 product appearances each season. Moreover, advertisers are attempting to develop brand or logo loyalty at younger and younger ages (Buckingham 2007; Rodman 2011:395).

Using advertising to develop a brand name with global appeal is an especially powerful way to encourage consumption. U.S. corporations have been particularly successful in creating global brands. An analysis of the 100 most successful brands worldwide, each of which derives at least a third of its earnings outside the home country, shows that 55 of them originated in the United States; 45 others come from 13 different countries (Figure 20-1).

Media advertising has several clear functions: it supports the economy, provides information about products, and underwrites the cost of media. In some cases, advertising becomes part of the entertainment. A national survey showed that 51 percent of viewers watch the Super Bowl primarily for the commercials, and one-third of online conversations about the Super Bowl the day of and the day after the event are driven by Super Bowl advertising. Yet advertising's functions are related to dysfunctions. Media advertising contributes to a consumer culture that creates needs and raises unrealistic expectations of what is required to be happy or satisfied. Moreover, because the media depend heavily on advertising revenue, advertisers can influence media content (Carey and Gelles 2010; Nielsen Company 2010).

 use your **sociological imagination**

You are a news junkie. Where do you gather your facts or information—from newspapers, tabloids, magazines, TV newscasts, blogs, or the Internet? Why did you choose that medium?

FIGURE 20-1 Branding the Globe

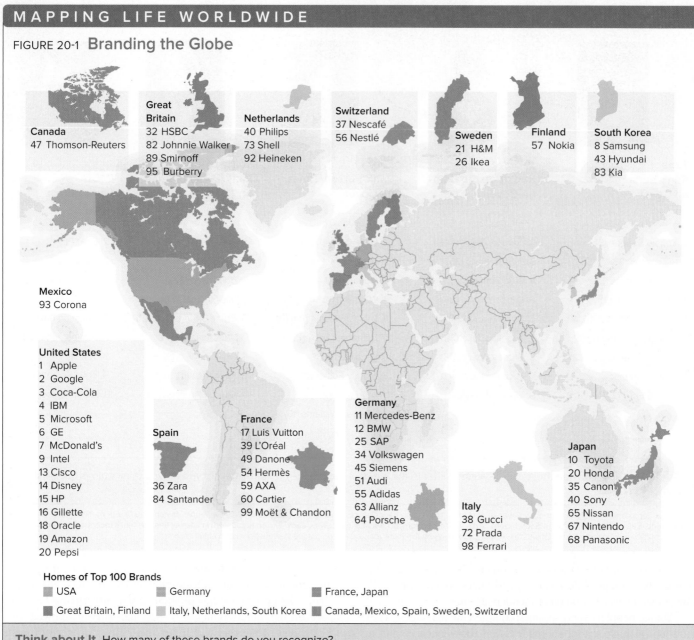

Canada
47 Thomson-Reuters

Great Britain
32 HSBC
82 Johnnie Walker
89 Smirnoff
95 Burberry

Netherlands
40 Philips
73 Shell
92 Heineken

Switzerland
37 Nescafé
56 Nestlé

Sweden
21 H&M
26 Ikea

Finland
57 Nokia

South Korea
8 Samsung
43 Hyundai
83 Kia

Mexico
93 Corona

United States
1 Apple
2 Google
3 Coca-Cola
4 IBM
5 Microsoft
6 GE
7 McDonald's
9 Intel
13 Cisco
14 Disney
15 HP
16 Gillette
18 Oracle
19 Amazon
20 Pepsi

Spain
36 Zara
84 Santander

France
17 Luis Vuitton
39 L'Oréal
49 Danone
54 Hermès
59 AXA
60 Cartier
99 Moët & Chandon

Germany
11 Mercedes-Benz
12 BMW
25 SAP
34 Volkswagen
45 Siemens
51 Audi
55 Adidas
63 Allianz
64 Porsche

Italy
38 Gucci
72 Prada
98 Ferrari

Japan
10 Toyota
20 Honda
35 Canon
40 Sony
65 Nissan
67 Nintendo
68 Panasonic

Homes of Top 100 Brands

- USA
- Germany
- France, Japan
- Great Britain, Finland
- Italy, Netherlands, South Korea
- Canada, Mexico, Spain, Sweden, Switzerland

Think about It How many of these brands do you recognize?

Note: Map shows the top 100 brands in the world in 2013 by country of ownership, except for the United States, for which only brands in the top 20 are shown. The United States has a total of 55 of the 100 leading brands.

Source: Based on Interbrand 2013.

Based on revenue and name recognition, these are the brands that dominate the global marketplace. Just 14 nations account for all the top 100 brands.

Dysfunction: The Narcotizing Effect

In addition to the functions just noted, the media perform a *dysfunction*. Sociologists Paul Lazarsfeld and Robert Merton (1948) created the term **narcotizing dysfunction** to refer to the phenomenon in which the media provide such massive amounts of coverage that the audience becomes numb and fails to act on the information, regardless of how compelling the issue. Interested citizens may take in the information but make no decision or take no action.

Consider how often the media initiate a great outpouring of philanthropic support in response to natural disasters or family crises. But then what happens? Research shows that as time passes, viewer fatigue sets in. The mass media audience becomes numb, desensitized to the suffering, and may even conclude that a solution to the crisis has been found (S. Moeller 1999).

The media's narcotizing dysfunction was identified 70 years ago, when just a few homes had television—well before the advent of electronic media. At that time, the dysfunction went largely unnoticed, but today commentators often point out the ill effects of addiction to television or the Internet, especially among young people. Street crime, explicit sex, war, and HIV/AIDS apparently are such overwhelming topics that some in the audience may feel they have acted—or at the very least learned all they need to know—simply by watching the news.

● Conflict Perspective

Conflict theorists emphasize that the media reflect and even exacerbate many of the divisions in our society and world, including those based on gender, race, ethnicity, and social class. They point in particular to the media's ability to decide what is transmitted, through a process called *gatekeeping*. Conflict theorists also stress the way interest groups monitor media content; the way powerful groups transmit society's dominant ideology through the mass media; and the technological gap between the haves and have-nots, which limits people's access to the Internet.

Gatekeeping

What story pops up when you check your favorite news outlet? What motion picture plays on three screens rather than one at the local cineplex? What picture isn't released at all? Behind these decisions are powerful figures—publishers, editors, and other media moguls.

The mass media constitute a form of big business in which profits are generally more important than the quality of the programming. Within the mass media, a relatively small number of people control what eventually reaches the audience through **gatekeeping.** This term describes how material must travel through a series of gates (or checkpoints) before reaching the public. Thus, a select few decide what images to bring to a broad audience. In many countries the government plays a gatekeeping role. Even the champions of Internet freedom, who pride themselves on allowing people to pass freely through the gate, may quickly channel them in certain directions (see Box 20-1).

Gatekeeping, which prevails in all kinds of media, is not a new concept. The term was coined by a journalism scholar in the 1940s to refer to the way that small-town newspaper editors control which events receive public attention. As sociologist C. Wright Mills ([1956] 2000b) observed, the real power of the media is that they can control what is being presented. In the recording industry, gatekeepers may reject a popular local band because it competes with a group already on their label. Even if the band is recorded, radio programmers may reject the music because it does not fit the station's sound. Television programmers may keep a pilot for a new TV series off the air because they believe it does not appeal to the target audience (which is sometimes determined by advertising sponsors). Similar decisions are made by gatekeepers in the publishing industry.

Gatekeeping is not as dominant in at least one form of mass media, the Internet. You can send virtually any message to an electronic bulletin board, and create a web page or web log (blog) to advance any argument, including one that insists the earth is flat. The Internet is a means of quickly disseminating information (or misinformation) without going through any significant gatekeeping process.

Nevertheless, the Internet is not totally without restrictions. In many nations, laws regulate content on issues such as gambling, pornography, and even politics. And popular Internet service providers will terminate accounts for offensive behavior. After the terrorist attacks in 2001, eBay did not allow people to sell parts of the World Trade Center via its online auction. Despite such interference, growing numbers of people are actively involved in online communities.

Today, many countries try to control political dissent by restricting citizens' access to online comments unfavorable to the government. Beginning in 2011, online criticism fueled dissent in Arab countries like Egypt, Tunisia, Libya, Bahrain, and Syria. Using social media, activists in these countries encouraged their followers to demonstrate against the government at predetermined locales. To further encourage citizen engagement, activists posted cell phone videos of the protests on the Internet. In China, however, government officials marshaled the state's vast resources to mobilize an army of cyber-police, software developers, web monitors, and paid online propagandists. These cyber-soldiers watch, filter, censor, and guide Chinese Internet users in an effort to minimize online dissent (Castells 2012; *The Economist* 2013b; Preston and Stelter 2011).

Media Monitoring

The term *media monitoring* is used most often to refer to interest groups' monitoring of media content. The public reaction to the shootings at Virginia Tech in April 2007 provides one example. People did not need to be constant news monitors to learn of the rampage. Ever since the mass shootings at Columbine High School near Littleton, Colorado, in 1999, news outlets of every type have descended on the sites of such school shootings, offering insight into the perpetrators and their families, covering the mass expressions of grief, and following the communities' efforts to recover. Once again, though media outlets provided valuable information and quickly reassured viewers, listeners, and readers that the shooters posed no further danger, many people criticized the reality that they constructed through their coverage.

The term *media monitoring* can also be applied to government monitoring of individuals' phone calls without their knowledge. For example, the federal government has been criticized for authorizing wiretaps of U.S. citizens' telephone conversations without judicial approval. Government officials argue that the wiretaps were undertaken in the interest of national security, to monitor contacts between U.S. citizens and known terrorist groups following the terrorist attacks of September 11, 2001. But critics who take the conflict perspective, among others, are concerned by the apparent invasion of people's privacy (Gertner 2005). We will examine the right to privacy in greater detail in the Social Policy section at the end of this chapter.

What are the practical and ethical limits of media monitoring? In daily life, parents often oversee their children's online

Inside the Bubble: Internet Search Filters

Through Facebook, Classmates, and LinkedIn, the Internet allows us to reach out to those who are different from ourselves—or does it? Today, the search engines we use to navigate the Internet are personalized. Google, for example, uses as many as 57 sources of information, including a person's location and past searches, to make calculated guesses about the sites a person might like to visit. Its searches have been personalized in this way since 2009. In 2012 Google carried the process one step further by collecting information from the websites that people "friend" through social media, and then using it to direct their web searches. Google sees this personalization of its searches as a service, one that helps people to cut through irrelevant information and quickly find what they are looking for.

Although Google's approach may at first sound convenient, critics charge that it can trap users in their own worlds, by routing them ever more narrowly in the same direction. In his book *The Filter Bubble*, online political activist Eli Pariser complains that when a search engine filters our searches, it encloses us in a kind of invisible bubble that limits what we see to what we are already familiar with. Thus, we are not likely to discover people, places, and ideas that are outside our comfort zone. Secure in our online bubble, which we may not even realize is there, we visit only safe, predictable sites.

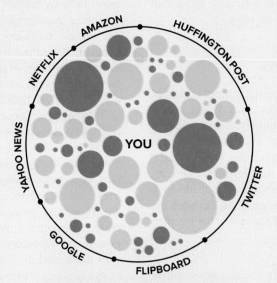

> When a search engine filters our searches, it encloses us in a kind of invisible bubble that limits what we see to what we are already familiar with.

What is wrong with that result? Given a choice, most of us go only to restaurants whose food we enjoy, read and listen to only those books and radio programs we know we like. Yet wasn't the Internet supposed to open new vistas to us? And if we are investigating a major news event, shouldn't we all see the same information when we search for it? Pariser describes what happened when two friends searched for the term "BP" in the spring of 2010, during the Deepwater Horizon oil rig's accidental discharge of crude oil into the Gulf of Mexico. Using the same browser, the two friends got very different results. One saw links to information about the oil spill; the other saw links to information about BP's CEO, intended for investors.

To remedy this perceived difficulty, researchers at MIT and Yahoo Labs are developing ways to include contrasting or opposing views in online searches. Although their work is just beginning, the hope is that someday, despite the technological challenges, the Internet will become less isolating and more open to different perspectives.

LET'S DISCUSS

1. Have you ever been frustrated by the results of an Internet search? Describe what happened, or what didn't happen.

2. Choose a topic of interest to you and do an Internet search on it; ask several friends or classmates to do the same. Do your results differ? In what way?

Sources: Basulto 2011; Elgan 2011; Graells-Garrido et al. 2013; Pariser 2011a, 2011b; Stray 2012; Swartz 2012.

---

activities and scan the blogs they read—which are, of course, available for anyone to see. Most parents see such monitoring of children's media use and communications as an appropriate part of adult supervision. Yet their snooping sets an example for their children, who may use the technique for their own ends. Some media analysts have noted a growing trend among adolescents: the use of new media to learn not-so-public information about their parents (Delaney 2005).

One unanticipated benefit of government monitoring of private communications has been expedited disaster relief. As in the aftermath of Hurricane Katrina in 2005, the U.S. government turned to media monitoring following the 2010 earthquake in Haiti. At the Department of Homeland Security, employees at the National Operations Center monitored 31 social media sites for information regarding the disaster. The intelligence they gathered helped responders to locate people in need of rescue and identify areas outside Port-au-Prince where relief was necessary (Department of Homeland Security 2010).

Dominant Ideology: Constructing Reality

Conflict theorists argue that the mass media maintain the privileges of certain groups. Moreover, powerful groups may limit the media's representation of others to protect their own interests. The term **dominant ideology** describes a set of cultural beliefs and practices that helps to maintain powerful social, economic, and political interests. The media transmit messages that essentially define what we regard as the real world, even though those images frequently vary from the ones that the larger society experiences.

Despite the popularity of Hollywood entertainment, media that are produced abroad for local consumption also do well. The animated series *Freej* features Muslim grandmothers who stumble on a cursed book while tackling their culture's wedding traditions. Produced in Dubai, the United Arab Emirates, for adult viewers, the series was launched in 2006.

Mass media decision makers are overwhelmingly White, male, and wealthy. It may come as no surprise, then, that the media tend to ignore the lives and ambitions of subordinate groups, among them working-class people, African Americans, Hispanics, gays and lesbians, people with disabilities, overweight people, and older people. Worse yet, media content may create false images or stereotypes of these groups that then become accepted as accurate portrayals of reality. **Stereotypes** are unreliable generalizations about all members of a group that do not recognize individual differences within the group. Some broadcasters use stereotypes deliberately in a desperate bid for attention, with the winking approval of media executives.

Queer theorists have long studied the way the media present homosexuality. They have analyzed the frequent invisibility of homosexual characters, as well as the problematic ways in which they are made visible. From the perspective of queer theorists, significant strides have been made in the portrayal of nonheterosexuality as a normal and possible alternative to heterosexuality. Still, stigmatization of gays and lesbians persists, in the media as well as in society (Sloop 2009).

Television offers many examples of this tendency to ignore reality. How many overweight TV characters can you name? Even though in real life 1 out of every 4 women is obese (30 or more pounds over a healthy body weight), only 3 out of 100 TV characters are portrayed as obese. Heavyset television characters have fewer romances, talk less about sex, eat more often, and are more often the object of ridicule than their thin counterparts (Hellmich 2001).

On the other hand, television news and other media outlets do alert people to the health implications of obesity. As with constructions of reality, whether some of this coverage is truly educational is debatable. Increasingly, the media have framed the problem not merely as an individual or personal one, but as a broad structural problem involving, for example, the manner in which food is processed and sold (Saguy and Almeling 2008).

Similarly, about 45 percent of all youths in the United States are children of color, yet few of the faces they see on television reflect their race or cultural heritage. Using content analysis, sociologists have found that only 2 of the nearly 60 prime-time series aired in recent years—*Ugly Betty* and *George Lopez*—focused on minority performers. What is more, programs that are shown earlier in the evening, when young people are most likely to watch television, are the least diverse (Grazian 2010:129; NAACP 2008; Wyatt 2009).

Another concern about the media, from the conflict perspective, is that television distorts the political process. Until the U.S. campaign finance system is truly reformed, the candidates with the most money (often backed by powerful lobbying groups) will be able to buy exposure to voters and saturate the air with commercials attacking their opponents.

Dominant Ideology: Whose Culture?

CSI: Crime Scene Investigation (Les Experts) is a big hit in France, despite that nation's pride in its *"exception culturelle,"* which protects French film, television, and music producers from foreign competition. In Japan, *Glee* is must-watch TV, and *Columbo* reruns still garner viewers. Those are only the legally viewed hit shows. In Latin America, where illicit downloading of TV programs is common, the most popular shows include *The X-Factor, Breaking Bad, Homeland,* and *Modern Family.* In North Korea, *Desperate Housewives* is a cult hit. Although government officials and cultural purists may decry these shows' popularity, U.S. media are still widely watched and imitated. As sociologist Todd Gitlin puts it, American popular culture is something that "people love, and love to hate" (2002:177; Agence France-Presse 2013).

We risk being ethnocentric if we overstress U.S. dominance, however. For example, *Survivor, Who Wants to Be a Millionaire, Big Brother,* and *Iron Chef*—immensely popular TV programs in the United States—came from Sweden, Britain, the Netherlands, and Japan, respectively. Even *American Idol* originated in Britain as *Pop Idol,* featuring Simon Cowell. And the steamy telenovelas of Mexico and other Spanish-speaking countries owe very little of their origin to the soap operas on U.S. television. Unlike motion pictures, television is gradually moving away from U.S. domination and is now more likely to be locally produced (Bielby and Harrington 2008; Colucci 2008).

Lindsey Wallem, *Social Media Consultant*

Lindsey Wallem graduated from DePaul University with a major in sociology. She chose sociology because she wanted to help people, perhaps as a social worker for a nonprofit organization. Then, in her junior year, when her political science professor offered extra credit for work on a political campaign, Wallem's life took an unexpected turn. "I showed up at the Obama headquarters just as they were moving in to their downtown Chicago office," Wallem remembers. "I was assigned to the New Media department, using Facebook and MySpace to reach out to voters." At the time, the use of social media tools in a political campaign was groundbreaking. "It was an exciting place to be," she recalls. "I stayed on as a volunteer in New Media through the end of the campaign. When I graduated in 2008, I used that experience to pitch my social media services to nonprofits."

Today, Wallem is a social media manager for several nonprofit organizations in the Chicago area. She enjoys using her expertise in online organizing to help these worthy organizations grow. Wallem's work with a nonprofit that fights homelessness has been particularly satisfying to her. In 2010–11, her client joined a coalition of organizations dedicated to creating more affordable housing in the city. "My role was to attend city council meetings and 'live-Tweet' the proceedings for supporters who couldn't be in the room," she explains. "On the day when a version of our legislation was passed, it was an exciting task indeed!"

Wallem also teaches an online course in social media to high school students, through the Gifted LearningLinks program at Northwestern University. In the first few weeks of the course, she draws from her old textbooks to give students a brief lesson in sociological theory. Then she asks them to apply the theory to Facebook and Twitter. "For the next generation, the Internet is the new frontier," she muses. "It's pretty amazing to see the perspectives of these 'digital natives' at work."

Wallem finds that her background in sociology is quite relevant to her career. "I spend much of my workweek interacting with communities on Facebook and Twitter, building a content schedule, and looking for content to share with my audience," she explains. To measure and track the success of her social media campaigns—a necessity in online organizing—Wallem relies on her training in statistics. "Metrics in social media is more than just counting the number of 'Likes' you have," she notes. "You need to look at the data and determine what kind of story it is telling you, what your audience is like and what they need from you." Wallem also applies what she learned in her senior capstone course, Visual Sociology, which taught her to use photography or video to tell a story about a sociological trend. "I use this tactic every day on Facebook and YouTube—visuals are what grab attention and add weight to the message you are trying to convey," she says.

LET'S DISCUSS

1. Have you ever used social media to participate in an online campaign? If so, how did you participate—by donating money, for example, or attending a fundraising event?

2. How might you use social media in your own career?

A related trend, the most novel one to date in this century, is the growth of **hyper-local media,** which refers to reporting that is highly local. What has been going on in that vacant lot down the street? Which Chinese takeout food is popular in your neighborhood? Why did all those police cars converge on Main Street the night before last? Hyper-local media answer these questions. The term was coined in 1991, to refer to the inclusion of local news on 24-hour cable news channels.

Today, with the development of online websites and blogs, hyper-local media have become even more localized and oriented toward special interests. As a result, cultural values and media profiles are no longer defined only by nation, but by community and even by neighborhood. During the Arab Spring, for example, residents of Cairo, armed with cell phones and personal computers, provided hyper-local media coverage of street incidents in their neighborhoods—incidents that had national and international implications (Pavlik 2013).

Nations that feel a loss of identity may try to defend against the cultural invasion from foreign countries, especially the economically dominant United States. Yet as sociologists know, audiences are not necessarily passive recipients of foreign cultural messages, either in developing nations or in industrial nations. Thus, research on consumers of cultural products like television, music, and film must be placed in social context. Although people may watch and even enjoy media content, that does not mean that they will accept values that are alien to their own (Bielby and Harrington 2008).

Many developing nations have long argued for a greatly improved two-way flow of news and information between industrial nations and developing nations. They complain that news from the Third World is scant, and what news there is reflects unfavorably on the developing nations. For example, what do you know about South America? Most people in the United States will mention the two topics that dominate the news from countries south of the border: revolution and drugs. Most know little else about the continent.

To remedy this imbalance, a resolution to monitor the news and content that cross the borders of developing nations was passed by the United Nations Educational, Scientific, and Cultural Organization (UNESCO) in the 1980s. The United States disagreed with the proposal, which became one factor in the U.S. decision to withdraw from UNESCO in the mid-1980s. In 2005, the United States opposed another UNESCO plan, meant to reduce the diminishment of cultural differences. Hailed as an important step toward protecting threatened cultures, particularly the media markets in developing nations, the measure passed the UN's General Assembly by a vote of 148–2. The United States, one of the two dissenters, objected officially to the measure's vague wording, but the

Sociology in the Global Community

BOX 20-2

The Global Disconnect

Bogdan Ghirda, a Romanian, is paid 50 cents an hour to participate in multiplayer Internet games like City of Heroes and Star Wars. He is sitting in for someone in an industrialized country who does not want to spend days ascending to the highest levels of competition in order to compete with players who are already "well armed." This arrangement is not unusual. U.S.-based services can earn hundreds of dollars for recruiting someone in a less developed country, like Ghirda, to represent a single player in an affluent industrial country.

Meanwhile, in Africa, the resource-poor nation of Rwanda is developing its economy by encouraging investments in information and communications technologies. In 2011, through a combination of public investment and private competition among telecommunications companies, mobile phone and data transmission service in the country reached 96 percent. The challenges Rwanda faces remain immense: energy needs that are expensive to meet, a shortage of skilled computer specialists, and weak finances, to name a few. However, this nation of 11 million, with a per capita income of just $605 a year, may be able to create a stable economy based on new telecommunications technologies.

These two situations illustrate the technological disconnect between the developing and industrial nations. Around the world, developing nations lag far behind industrial nations in their access to and use of new technologies. The World Economic Forum's Networked Readiness Index (NRI), a ranking of 144 nations, shows the relative preparedness of individuals, businesses, and governments to benefit from information technologies. As the accompanying table shows, the haves of the world—countries like Singapore, Switzerland, and the United States—are network ready; the have-nots—countries like Swaziland, Yemen, and Haiti—are not.

> For developing nations, the consequences of the global disconnect are far more serious than an inability to surf the Net.

For developing nations, the consequences of the global disconnect are far more serious than an inability to surf the Net. Thanks to the Internet, multinational organizations can now function as a single global unit, responding instantly in real time, 24 hours a day. This new capability has fostered the emergence of what sociologist Manuel Castells calls a "global economy." But if large numbers of people—indeed, entire nations—are disconnected from the new global economy, their economic growth will remain slow and the well-being of their people will remain retarded. Those citizens who are educated and skilled will immigrate to other labor markets, deepening the impoverishment of nations on the periphery.

NETWORKED READINESS INDEX

Top 10 Countries	Bottom 10 Countries
1. Finland	135. Mauritania
2. Singapore	136. Swaziland
3. Sweden	137. Madagascar
4. Netherlands	138. Lesotho
5. Norway	139. Yemen
6. Switzerland	140. Guinea
7. Great Britain	141. Haiti
8. Denmark	142. Chad
9. United States	143. Sierra Leone
10. Taiwan	144. Burundi

LET'S DISCUSS

1. For nations on the periphery, what might be some specific social and economic consequences of the global disconnect?

2. What factors might complicate efforts to remedy the global disconnect in developing nations?

Sources: Anatale et al. 2013; Bilbao-Osorio et al. 2013; Castells 2010a; T. Thompson 2005.

---

real concern was clearly the measure's potential impact on a major U.S. export (Dominick 2009; Riding 2005).

 use your **sociological imagination**

How do your favorite media reflect U.S. culture? How do they reflect the cultures of the rest of the world?

The Digital Divide

Finally, as numerous studies have shown, advances in communications technology are not evenly distributed. Worldwide, low-income groups, racial and ethnic minorities, rural residents, and the citizens of developing countries have far less access than others to the latest technologies—a gap that is called the **digital divide.** People in low-income households, rural areas, and developing countries, for example, are less likely than others to have Internet access. When marginalized people do gain Internet access, they are still likely to trail the privileged. They may have dial-up service instead of broadband, or broadband instead of wireless Internet. The issue is not merely access to the Internet, but the cost and availability of broadband service. High-speed Internet connections are becoming increasingly essential for everything from completing school assignments to consulting with medical personnel and conducting business through routine financial transactions.

The digital divide is most evident in developing countries. In Africa, 4 percent of the population has Internet access. These fortunate few typically pay the highest rates in the world—$250 to $300 a month—for the slowest connection speeds. Box 20-2 examines the global disconnect between the haves and have-nots of the information age (Robinson and Crenshaw 2010; P. Schaefer 2008).

Feminist Perspective

Feminists share the view of conflict theorists that the mass media stereotype and misrepresent social reality. According to this view, the media powerfully influence how we look at men and women, communicating unrealistic, stereotypical, and limiting images of the sexes.

Educators and social scientists have long noted the stereotypical portrayal of women and men in the mass media. Women are often shown as being shallow and obsessed with beauty. They are more likely than men to be presented unclothed, in danger, or even physically victimized. When women achieve newsworthy feats in fields traditionally dominated by men, such as professional sports, the media are often slow to recognize their accomplishments.

Even when they are covered by the press, female athletes are not treated equally by television commentators. Communications researchers conducted a content analysis of over 200 hours of nationally televised coverage of professional golf events. The study showed that when female golfers are successful, they are more likely than male golfers to be called strong and intelligent. When they are not successful, they are more likely than men to be described as lacking in athletic ability. In contrast, male golfers receive more comments on their concentration and commitment. These findings suggest a subtle sexism, with women being portrayed as innately talented and men being portrayed as superior in mental or emotional makeup (T. Jacobs 2009).

Another aim of feminist research is to determine whether the media have a different impact on women than on men. Recently, researchers found that adolescent boys are almost three times as likely as adolescent girls to participate in online gaming. Young females who do participate are more likely than boy gamers to get into serious fights and report obesity. Clearly, this topic deserves further study (Desai et al. 2010).

A continuing, troubling issue for feminists and society as a whole is pornography. Feminists tend to be very supportive of freedom of expression and self-determination, rights that are denied to women more often than to men. Yet pornography presents women as sex objects and seems to make viewing women that way acceptable. Nor are concerns about pornography limited to this type of objectification and imagery, as well as their implicit endorsement of violence against women. The industry that creates risqué adult images for videos, DVDs, and the Internet is largely unregulated, even putting its performers at risk.

Feminist scholars are cautiously optimistic about new media. Although women are represented among bloggers, by some measures they are responsible for only about 10 percent of the most popular blogs. Still, in conservative cultures like Saudi Arabia, online media offer women the opportunity to explore lifestyles that traditional media outlets largely ignore (Jesella 2008; Worth 2008).

As in other areas of sociology, feminist researchers caution against assuming that what holds true for men's media use is true for everyone. Researchers, for example, have studied the different ways that women and men approach the Internet. Though men are only slightly more likely than women ever to have used the Internet, they are much more likely to use it daily. Yet according to a 2009 study, more women than men use the Internet. Not surprisingly, men account for 91 percent of the players in online sports fantasy leagues. Perhaps more socially significant, however, is the finding that women are more likely than men to maintain friendship networks through e-mail (Boase et al. 2006; Fallows 2006; Pew Internet Project 2009; Rainie 2005).

Interactionist Perspective

Interactionists are especially interested in shared understandings of everyday behavior. These scholars examine the media on the micro level to see how they shape day-to-day social behavior. Increasingly, researchers talk about mass media in the context of *social capital,* as described by sociologist Pierre Bourdieu. **Social capital** is the collective benefit of social networks, which are built on reciprocal trust. The Internet generally, and social media in particular, offer us almost constant connectivity with others. These media increase our contact with family members, friends, and acquaintances, both those who live nearby and those who are far away. They also facilitate the development of new ties and new social networks (Bourdieu and Passerson 1990; Neves 2013).

Online social networks, in fact, have become a new way of promoting consumption. As Figure 20-2 shows, advertisers have

FIGURE 20-2 Marketing Online through Social Networks

Traditional forms of advertising (left) allow only one-way communication, from the advertiser to the consumer. Online social networks (right) offer two-way communication, allowing advertisers to develop a relationship with consumers.

BOX 20-3

Our Wired World

Charity Begins Online

Increasingly, technology plays a part in the contributions people make to the causes and organizations they support. Research shows that in the United States, 20 percent of adults have contributed to charities online. Ten percent have done so from their cell phones, using text messaging. The new trend was especially noticeable in 2010, after the massive earthquake in Haiti, when cell phone owners used text messaging to contribute an estimated $43 million to relief efforts. The story of the disaster, which displaced millions of people, dominated the news and social media for weeks afterward.

For charities, mobile giving opened up a new way to reach donors. Most of those who made text donations to Haiti—almost 9 out of 10—responded quickly to television news reports, without stopping to investigate the charities. About half of them donated immediately; another quarter did so later in the day.

Mobile giving has also created a friend network that can spread news of natural disasters almost instantaneously. Unlike traditional contributors, many of these donors shared their decisions through their electronic friend networks. In a survey, 43 percent of respondents who had made text donations to Haiti said they had encouraged friends or relatives to do the same. Of that group, 76 percent said that their friends or family had

complied. Young and non-White donors were particularly active in spreading the word.

Online charity is not a panacea, however. Unfortunately, text donors' interest in the island nation's fate seemed to evaporate just as quickly as it had developed. Less than half of them have stayed informed on the charities' reconstruction efforts, and 15 percent have lost all interest. For the charities, the new donors' fickleness spells uncertainty about

the success of future fund-raising efforts. Traditional donors—those who research charities online before donating, and follow up on their effectiveness over the years—are more likely to stay involved and to support charities over the long term, regardless of what is or is not in the news.

Yet another innovation that lends itself to mobile giving is **crowdsourcing,** also called *crowdfunding.* Crowdsourcing is the use of the Internet to seek assistance from the general public in the form of financing, services, or even ideas. Generally, these appeals are for small donations to support relatively small improvement projects, such as a single well or classroom. Yet the small sums they bring in add up. Nonprofits raised an estimated $5 billion through crowdsourcing in 2013.

> For charities, mobile giving opened up a new way to reach donors.

LET'S DISCUSS

1. Have you ever texted a donation to a charity and then shared your concern with friends and family? If so, did you or anyone you know follow up on the charity's efforts? If not, why not?

2. If you worked for a charity, how would you deal with the here-today, gone-tomorrow nature of text donations?

Sources: Choney 2010; Hall 2013; Pickett 2012; A. Smith 2012.

---

traditionally marketed products and services through one-way spot ads, mass mailings, or billboards, whether they are promoting flat-screen televisions or public service messages like "Don't drink and drive." Now, using social networks, they can find consumers online and attempt to develop a two-way relationship with them there. Through Facebook, for example, Burger King awarded a free Whopper to anyone who would delete 10 friends. Facebook's staff was not happy with Burger King's promotion, which notified 239,906 Facebook users that they had been dropped for a burger—an action that violated the network's policy. Nevertheless, Burger King created a vast network of consumers who enjoy Whoppers.

Similarly, Kraft Foods encouraged people to post images of the Wiener-mobile on the photo site Flickr (Bacon Lovers' Talk 2009; Burger King 2009; Gaudin 2009).

Relationship marketing is not the only new use for online social networks. As Box 20-3 shows, in 2010, texting became a new source of philanthropy in the aftermath of the massive earthquake in Haiti.

Interactionists note, too, that friendship networks can emerge from shared viewing habits or from recollection of a cherished television series from the past. Family members and friends often gather for parties centered on the broadcasting of popular events such as the Super Bowl or the Academy Awards. And as we've seen, television often serves as a babysitter or playmate for children and even infants.

The rise of the Internet has also facilitated new forms of communication and social interaction. Grandparents can now keep up with their grandchildren via e-mail, or even watch them on their laptops via Skype. Gay and lesbian teens have online resources for support and information. People can even find their lifetime partners through computer dating services.

Some troubling issues have been raised about day-to-day life on the Internet, however. What, if anything, should be done about terrorists and other extremist groups who use the Internet to exchange messages of hatred and even bomb-making recipes? What, if anything, should be done about the issue of sexual expression on the Internet? How can children be protected from it? Should "hot chat" and X-rated film clips be censored? Or should expression be completely free?

Though the Internet has created a new platform for extremists, hate groups, and pornographers, it has also given people greater control over what they see and hear. That is, the Internet allows people to manage their media exposure so as to avoid sounds, images, and ideas they do not enjoy or approve of. The legal scholar Cass Sunstein (2002) has referred to this personalized approach to news information gathering as *egocasting.* One social consequence of this trend may be a less tolerant society. If we read, see, and hear only what we know and

FIGURE 20-3 **Who's on the Internet**

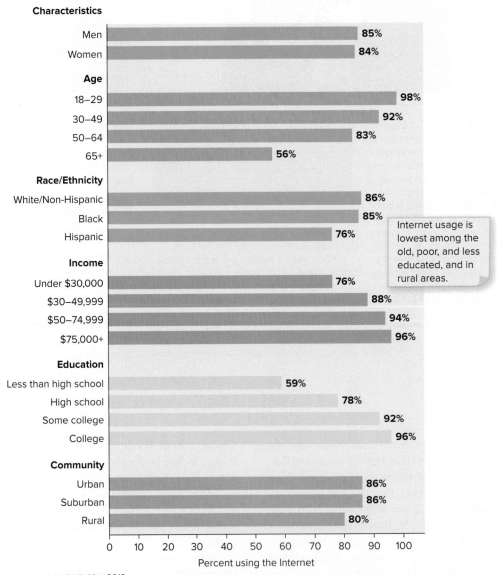

Characteristics

| Men | 85% |
| Women | 84% |

Age

18–29	98%
30–49	92%
50–64	83%
65+	56%

Race/Ethnicity

White/Non-Hispanic	86%
Black	85%
Hispanic	76%

> Internet usage is lowest among the old, poor, and less educated, and in rural areas.

Income

Under $30,000	76%
$30–49,999	88%
$50–74,999	94%
$75,000+	96%

Education

Less than high school	59%
High school	78%
Some college	92%
College	96%

Community

Urban	86%
Suburban	86%
Rural	80%

Percent using the Internet

Note: Based on a national survey taken April–May 2013.

Source: Pew Internet and American Life Project 2013.

agree with, we may be much less prepared to meet people from different backgrounds or converse with those who express new viewpoints.

Furthermore, while many people in the United States embrace the Internet, we should note that information is not evenly distributed throughout the population. The same people, by and large, who experience poor health and have few job opportunities have been left off the information highway. Figure 20-3 breaks down Internet usage by gender, age, race, income, education, and community type. Note the large disparities in usage between those with high and low incomes, and between those with more and less education. The data also show a significant racial disparity. Though educators and politicians have touted the potential benefits to the disadvantaged, Internet usage may be reinforcing existing social-class and racial barriers.

The interactionist perspective helps us to understand one important aspect of the entire mass media system—the audience. How do we actively participate in media events? How do we construct with others the meaning of media messages? We will explore these questions in the section that follows. (Table 20-2 summarizes the various sociological perspectives on the media.)

Tracking Sociological Perspectives

TABLE **20-2** SOCIOLOGICAL PERSPECTIVES ON THE MASS MEDIA

Theoretical Perspective	Emphasis
Functionalist	Socialization
	Enforcement of social norms
	Conferral of status
	Promotion of consumption
	Narcotizing effect (dysfunction)
Conflict	Gatekeeping
	Media monitoring
	Construction of reality
	Digital divide
Feminist	Misrepresentation of women
	Differential impact on women
Interactionist	Impact on social behavior
	Source of friendship networks
	Social capital

MODULE 20 | **Recap and Review**

Summary

The **mass media** are print and electronic instruments of communication that carry messages to often widespread audiences. They pervade all social institutions, from entertainment to education to politics.

1. From the functionalist perspective, the media entertain, socialize, enforce social norms, confer status, and promote consumption. They can be dysfunctional to the extent that they desensitize us to serious events and issues (the **narcotizing dysfunction**).

2. Conflict theorists think the media reflect and even deepen the division in society through **gatekeeping**, or control over which material reaches the public; media monitoring, the covert observation of people's media usage and choices; and support of the **dominant ideology**, which defines reality, overwhelming local cultures.

3. Feminist theorists point out that media images of the sexes communicate unrealistic, stereotypical, limiting, and sometimes violent perceptions of women.

4. Interactionists examine the media on the micro level to see how they shape day-to-day social behavior.

Interactionists have studied shared TV viewing and staged public appearances intended to convey self-serving definitions of reality.

Thinking Critically

1. What do you think is the most important function of the mass media in our society? Why?

2. Which of the problems associated with the media troubles you most, and why?

3. Americans now get their news from many different cable news networks rather than from just three national networks. What is the effect of this trend on the media's tendency to promulgate a dominant ideology?

Key Terms

Crowdsourcing

Cultural convergence

Digital divide

Dominant ideology

Gatekeeping	Narcotizing dysfunction
Hyperconsumerism	Social capital
Hyper-local media	Stereotype
Mass media	

MODULE 21 | The Audience

Ever feel like text-messaging everyone you know, to encourage them to vote for your favorite performer on a certain reality program? Ever looked over someone's shoulder as he watched last week's episode of *American Idol* on his iPhone—and been tempted to reveal the ending to him? Ever come across an old CD and tried to remember the last time you or a friend listened to one, or heard the songs in the order in which they were recorded? In this and many other ways, we are reminded that we are all part of a larger audience.

Typically we think of an audience as a large gathering of people attending the same performance, but sociologists recognize that audience can take many forms. Indeed, an entire field of research called *visual sociology* has developed to view media representations as a way to inform us about society and social behavior. In Box 21-1 we see how sociologists use visual media to study society.

Who Is in the Audience?

The mass media are distinguished from other social institutions by the necessary presence of an audience. It can be an identifiable, finite group, such as an audience at a jazz club or a Broadway musical, or a much larger and undefined group, such as *Dancing with the Stars* viewers or readers of the same issue of *USA Today*. The audience may be a secondary group gathered in a large auditorium or a primary group, such as a family watching the latest Disney video at home.

We can look at the audience from the level of both *microsociology* and *macrosociology*. At the micro level, we might consider how audience members, interacting among themselves, respond to the media, or in the case of live performances, actually influence the performers. At the macro level, we might examine broader societal consequences of the media, such as the early childhood education delivered through programming like *Sesame Street*.

Even if an audience is spread out over a wide geographic area and members don't know one another, it is still distinctive in terms of age, gender, income, political party, formal schooling, race, and ethnicity. The audience for a ballet, for example, would likely differ substantially from the audience for alternative music.

The Segmented Audience

Increasingly, the media are marketing themselves to a *particular* audience. Once a media outlet, such as a radio station or a magazine, has identified its audience, it targets that group. To some degree, this specialization is driven by advertising. Media specialists have sharpened their ability, through survey research, to identify particular target audiences. Thus, during the midterm elections in 2010, the two major political parties placed TV advertisements in markets where surveys indicated they would find support. For example, the Republican Party placed ads on college football games and *America's Funniest Home Videos*. The Democratic Party bought time on *Dr. Phil* (Parker 2010).

The specialized targeting of audiences has led some scholars to question the "mass" in mass media. For example, the British social psychologist Sonia Livingstone (2004) has written that the media have become so segmented, they have taken on the appearance almost of individualization. Are viewing audiences so segmented that large collective audiences are a thing of the past? That is not yet clear. Even though we seem to be living in an age of *personal* computers, large formal organizations still do transmit public messages that reach a sizable, heterogeneous, and scattered audience.

 use your **sociological imagination**

Think about the last time you were part of an audience. Describe the performance. How similar to or different from yourself were the other audience members? What might account for whatever similarities or differences you noticed?

Audience Behavior

Sociologists have long researched how audiences interact with one another and how they share information after a media event. The role of audience members as opinion leaders particularly intrigues social researchers. An **opinion leader** is someone who influences the opinions and decisions of others through day-to-day personal contact and communication. For example, a movie or theater critic functions as an opinion leader. Sociologist Paul Lazarsfeld and his colleagues (1948) pioneered the study of opinion leaders in their research on voting behavior in the 1940s. They found that opinion leaders encourage their relatives, friends, and co-workers to think positively about a particular candidate, perhaps pushing them to listen to the politician's speeches or read the campaign literature.

Despite the role of opinion leaders, members of an audience do not all interpret media in the same way. Often their response is influenced by their social characteristics, such as occupation, race, education, and income. Take the example of the televised

BOX 21-1

Research Today

Visual Sociology

As a discipline, sociology relies on the scientific observation of human behavior, whether directly or through data gathered in surveys, experiments, and existing sources. Increasingly, however, sociologists are also recognizing visual documents as a significant research tool. **Visual sociology** is the use of photographs, film, and video to study society. Howard Becker, known for his contributions to labeling theory, drew attention to the importance of images in his influential essay "Photography and Sociology." For over three decades the International Visual Sociology Association has encouraged scholarship in visual sociology, not only by sociologists but by anthropologists, communications scholars, and psychologists as well.

Although the term *visual sociology* is relatively new, the roots of visual research methods go much deeper. As Becker (1974:3) reminds us, "Photography and sociology have approximately the same birth date," in the 1830s. Early sociological works made use of photographs and other visuals, such as maps, not merely as illustrations but as the basis of research. The hardships of the Civil War, conflicts between American Indians and the U.S. Cavalry, and the Crimean War were all analyzed using early photographs. In the 20th century, scholars assessed the toll of the Depression in the United States by looking at photographs assembled by the Farm Security Administration. At the time, however, such studies did not receive much acceptance by sociologists. Until recently, the only data deemed appropriate for study were numerical data.

Today, the value of visuals in comprehending social behavior is easy to understand. For generations, music was shared and promoted through the radio. Then music videos transformed popular music. MTV launched its cable television broadcasts in 1981 with the Buggles video "Video Killed the Radio Star," followed by Pat Benatar's "You Better Run," which suggested the changes that were about to occur in the music industry. Now, scholars study these videos online, as extensively as they do the melodies and lyrics of pop music.

Visual sociology includes the conscious creation of a visual record through documentary films or photography. Sociologist Charles Suchar studied gentrification by photographing commercial and residential areas over time and then analyzing the record to note how neighborhoods had changed. The photographs became the basis for interviews with residents and merchants about the details they revealed and the concerns they suggested, such as the desire for privacy and the need for security. Photographic records can also be useful in comparative studies. Imagine what sociologists might learn by contrasting images of a suburban barbecue with those of an Amish community raising a barn. In both those cases, images would be treated as data, not merely as instructional aids.

Another path-breaking contribution was Erving Goffman's *Gender Advertisements,* a penetrating examination of how differently men and women are represented in television advertisements and mass-circulation magazines. Unlike Suchar, Goffman analyzed existing materials (rather than creating his own record) using a technique known as *content analysis.* **Content analysis** may be defined as the systematic coding and objective recording of data, guided by some rationale.

Today, visual sociology is proving useful in *applied sociology.* **Applied sociology** is the use of the discipline of sociology with the specific intent of yielding practical applications for human behavior and organizations. In England, public health researchers photographed neighborhoods where illegal drug use was common. The images they took, which showed addicts injecting themselves in parks and public toilets, helped to identify unsafe areas where discarded needles and syringes littered the ground. Although the visuals were not necessary to the research, they proved invaluable in the researchers' effort to convince social services and law enforcement agencies that intervention was needed.

In short, the uses of visual sociology are as wide as the discipline of sociology itself. Technological innovations such as the Internet, social media, and even 3D copiers will only expand this field further.

Photographs and other visual images improve our understanding of events that affect social behavior. This scene from a Civil War battlefield suggests the utter devastation visited on society by that war.

Asking residents to describe photographs helps to call attention to details that are often overlooked, such as an emphasis on security.

LET'S DISCUSS

1. Choose an image or series of images from reality TV or social media and discuss it from a sociological perspective. What can you learn from it? What sociological concepts can you relate to it?

2. Might some images be misinterpreted by researchers? Give an example. How might scholars guard against such misinterpretation?

Sources: Becker 1974; Goffman 1979; J. Grady 2007; Harper 1988; Parker and Comber 2009; Stryker and Wood 1973 [1935–43]; Suchar 1997; Visual Sociology Association 2013.

news coverage of the riots in Los Angeles in 1992. The riots were an angry response to the acquittal of two White police officers accused of severely beating a Black motorist. Sociologist Darnell Hunt (1997) wondered how the social composition of audience members would affect the way they interpreted the news coverage. Hunt gathered 15 groups from the Los Angeles area, whose members were equally divided among Whites, Blacks, and Latinos. He showed each group a 17-minute clip from the televised coverage of the riots and asked members to discuss how they would describe what they had just seen to a 12-year-old. In analyzing the discussions, Hunt found that although gender and class did not cause respondents to vary their answers much, race did.

Hunt went beyond noting simple racial differences in perceptions; he analyzed how the differences were manifested. For example, Black viewers were much more likely than Latinos or Whites to refer to the events in terms of "us" versus "them." Another difference was that Black and Latino viewers were more animated and critical than White viewers as they watched the film clip. White viewers tended to sit quietly, still and unquestioning, suggesting that they were more comfortable with the news coverage than the Blacks or Latinos.

MODULE 21 | Recap and Review

Summary

The need for an audience distinguishes the mass media from other social institutions.

1. An audience may be small and well defined or large and amorphous. With increasing numbers of media outlets has come more and more targeting of segmented (or specialized) audiences.

2. Social researchers have studied the role of **opinion leaders** in influencing audiences.

Thinking Critically

1. What kind of audience is targeted by the producers of televised professional wrestling? By the creators of an animated film? By a rap group? What factors determine who makes up a particular audience?

2. Who do you consider to be your opinion leaders? Why are those individuals influential to you? Would your parents, friends, or teachers select the same opinion leaders?

Key Terms

Applied sociology

Content analysis

Opinion leader

Visual sociology

MODULE 22 | The Media's Global Reach

Has the rise of the electronic media created a *global village?* Canadian media theorist Marshall McLuhan predicted it would nearly 50 years ago. Today, physical distance is no longer a barrier, and instant messaging is possible across the world. The mass media have indeed created a global village. Not all countries are equally connected, as Figure 22-1 shows, but the progress has been staggering, considering that voice transmission was just beginning 100 years ago (McLuhan 1964, 1967).

Sociologist Todd Gitlin considers *global torrent* a more apt metaphor for the media's reach than *global village*. The media permeate all aspects of everyday life. Take advertising, for example. Consumer goods are marketed vigorously worldwide, from advertisements on airport baggage carriers to imprints on sandy beaches. Little wonder that people around the world develop loyalty to a brand and are as likely to sport a Nike, Coca-Cola, or Harley-Davidson logo as they are their favorite soccer or baseball insignia (Gitlin 2002; Klein 1999).

The Internet has facilitated all forms of communication. Reference materials and data banks can now be made accessible across national boundaries. Information related to international finance, marketing, trade, and manufacturing is literally just a keystroke away. We have seen the emergence of true world news outlets and the promotion of a world music that is not clearly identifiable with any single culture. Even the most future-oriented thinker would find the growth in the reach of the mass media in postindustrial and postmodern societies remarkable (Castells 2001, 2010b; Croteau and Hoynes 2006, 2014).

FIGURE 22-1 Media Penetration in Selected Countries

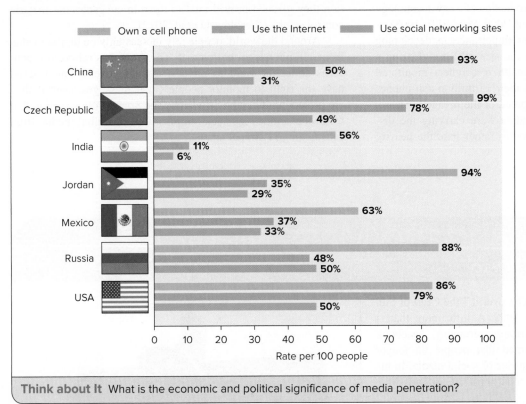

Legend:
- Own a cell phone
- Use the Internet
- Use social networking sites

Country	Own a cell phone	Use the Internet	Use social networking sites
China	93%	50%	31%
Czech Republic	99%	78%	49%
India	56%	11%	6%
Jordan	94%	35%	29%
Mexico	63%	37%	33%
Russia	88%	48%	50%
USA	86%	79%	50%

Rate per 100 people (0–100)

Think about It What is the economic and political significance of media penetration?

Note: Data from multinational interviews of 26,210 adults, March–April 2012.
Source: Pew Research Center Global Attitudes Project 2012:1, 5.

Cell phone ownership is high around the world, but in some countries outside the United States, texting is more common than calling.

Although in the United States we may take television for granted, even thinking of it as an old-fashioned medium, worldwide that is not necessarily the case. In India, half of all households do not have television; in Nigeria and Bangladesh, more than 70 percent of households go without. Two technological advances are likely to change this pattern, however. First, advances in battery power now allow viewers to watch television even in areas where there is no electricity. Second, digital signal transmission permits television reception via cable or satellite.

In some developing countries, people manage to watch television even though they don't own one. Consider the town of Gurupá, in the remote Amazon area of Brazil. In 1982, the wealthiest three households in this community bought televisions. To please the rest of the town, they agreed to place their TVs near the window so that their neighbors could watch them as well. As the TV owners

In 2012 "Sexy and I Know It," by the LMFAO duo of SkyBlu and Redfoo, was the most frequently downloaded cell phone ringtone. Because today's media provide multiple services, music fans can use the Internet to access recorded music and listen to it on their cell phones (Billboard 2012).

New technologies can create new social norms. In Gurupá, Brazil, television watching became a community social activity when three new TV owners agreed to share their sets with the community of 3,000.

proudly displayed their new status symbol, TV watching became a community social activity. The introduction of a new technology had created a new social norm (Kenny 2009; Pace 1993, 1998).

Media use can take on added importance in developing nations. Consider Kenya, a nation the size of Texas. During a recent malaria outbreak, public health researchers monitored the text messages Kenyans sent on their 15 million cell phones and used the content to map the spread of the dreaded disease. Surprisingly, they found that travelers were carrying the disease along less-traveled regional routes rather than the heavily traveled roads to and from the capital city, Nairobi. The information they gleaned proved vital to them in concentrating malaria control efforts (Wesolowski et al. 2012).

Around the world, people rely increasingly on digital media, from cell phones to the Internet. This trend has raised new concerns about the right to privacy. Should government officials have the right to monitor people's text messages, even if they are protecting the public's health? The Social Policy section that follows examines the social implications of digital media, from censorship to criminal activity.

social policy and the Mass Media

The Right to Privacy

"You have no privacy anyway. Get over it," the CEO of Sun Microsystems stated bluntly in 1999. A little more than a decade later, speaking at an awards ceremony, Facebook founder Mark Zuckerberg claimed that people no longer expect to have privacy, given the rise of social media. In his view, privacy is no longer a "social norm" (Carr 2010:W2; Bobbie Johnson 2010).

If there was any doubt about the effect of the new mass media on people's privacy, it disappeared in 2013 when Edward Snowden, an IT specialist working as a contractor to the U.S. government, began leaking information about the National Security Agency's data-gathering activities. The NSA is charged with gathering intelligence on foreign security threats, both within the United States and abroad. However, Snowden revealed that in an operation code-named PRISM, agency sleuths had been secretly gathering huge amounts of information on ordinary citizens by infiltrating their accounts at some of the nation's largest technology companies—Google, Apple, Microsoft, Facebook, AOL, YouTube, and Yahoo. In light of such revelations, we might ask whether any of us can expect to keep our private information private in the postmodern digital age.

Looking at the Issue

This sweeping challenge to privacy comes from **big data,** a term coined by sociologist Charles Tilly (1980) to refer to the rapid collection and analysis of enormous amounts of information by supercomputers. The accumulation of digital data has made it increasingly easy for business firms, government agencies, and even criminals to retrieve and store information about private individuals. In public places, at work, and on the Internet, surveillance devices track our every move, whether it is a keystroke or an ATM withdrawal. The information they accumulate includes everything from our buying habits to our websurfing patterns.

A Google Street View car drives through an English town, photographing it for use with Google's online map service. Even though Google's activities occur largely on public property, people have objected to them as an invasion of privacy. Some of the images Google captures include bystanders who happen to be in the area, as well as people's backyards and even the interior of their homes, as seen through open windows and doors.

—Continued

As these technologies increase the power to monitor our behavior, they raise fears of their misuse for criminal or even undemocratic purposes. In short, they threaten not just our privacy, but our freedom from crime and censorship as well. Some obvious violations of privacy, such as identity theft—the misuse of credit card and Social Security numbers to masquerade as another person—have been well documented. Other violations involve online surveillance of dissident political groups by authoritarian regimes and the unauthorized release of classified government documents. In 2010, WikiLeaks released thousands of classified U.S. foreign policy documents on its website, causing some people to condemn the action as treasonous and others to praise it as a blow against government censorship (O'Harrow Jr. 2005).

Other privacy violations are subtler, and not strictly illegal. For example, many commercial websites use "cookies" and tracking technology to monitor visitors' websurfing. Using that information, marketers can estimate a visitor's age, gender, and zip code, and from that data, the person's income. They can then select advertisements that will appeal specifically to that person. So depending on who we are, or at least appear to be, one of us might see ads about weight-loss products and another, ads about travel to exotic locations.

Is this approach to online marketing just effective advertising, or is it an invasion of privacy? Because the information that marketers gather in this way can be tied to other devices a person uses, such as a cell phone or computer, some critics see online tracking as a form of fingerprinting (Angwin 2010; Angwin and Valentino-DeVries 2010a).

Applying Sociology

From a sociological point of view, the complex issues of privacy and censorship can be considered illustrations of **culture lag,** a period of maladjustment when the nonmaterial culture is still struggling to adapt to new material conditions. As usual, the material culture (technology) is changing faster than the nonmaterial culture (norms for controlling the use of technology). Too often, the result is an anything-goes approach to the use of new technologies.

Sociologists' views on the use and abuse of new technologies differ depending on their theoretical perspective. Functionalists take a generally positive view of the Internet, pointing to its manifest function of facilitating communication. From their perspective, the Internet performs the latent function of empowering people with few resources—from hate groups to special-interest organizations—to communicate with the masses.

Functionalists also note that digital surveillance can assist law enforcement agencies in preventing or detecting crimes in progress. For example, facial recognition technology can be used to identify stalkers, find lost children, or even track terrorists. Yet they admit that warrantless surveillance of people who lead mostly normal lives is dysfunctional.

In contrast, conflict theorists stress the danger that the most powerful groups in a society will use technology to violate the privacy of the less powerful.

Interactionists observe that making our web profiles and other information about ourselves publicly available may affect our future social interactions, and not necessarily for the good. One out of four college and university admissions officers reports Googling or checking out applicants' social media pages. Over a third of those gatekeepers have found something online that can hurt applicants (Belkin and Porter 2012).

Initiating Policy

Legislation regarding the surveillance of electronic communications has not always upheld citizens' right to privacy. In 1986, the federal government passed the Electronic Communications Privacy Act, which outlawed the surveillance of telephone calls except with the permission of both the U.S. attorney general and a federal judge. Telegrams, faxes, and e-mails did not receive the same degree of protection, however. In 2001, one month after the terrorist attacks of September 11, Congress passed the Patriot Act, which relaxed existing legal checks on surveillance by law enforcement officers. Federal agencies are now freer to gather data electronically, including people's credit card receipts and banking records (Gertner 2005).

Today, most other types of online monitoring have yet to be tested in court, including the use of tracking technologies and the compilation and sale of personal profiles to merchandisers. Consistent with the concept of culture lag, privacy advocates complain that the 1986 law, which was enacted before the Internet as we know it even existed, has not kept pace with advancing technology. For example, in 2011 federal and state courts approved a total of 2,732 wiretaps using Supreme Court–approved methods that date back to 1928. However, in the same year government agencies made well over a million requests of mobile-phone companies for information on cell phone users—requests that require only a subpoena, not court approval. Many of those requests included "tower dumps," which reveal the whereabouts of everyone in the area with a cell phone, suspects or not. Such sweeps resemble the NSA's PRISM operation in their indiscriminate nature. To date, proposed legislation has focused mainly on the consumer side of privacy. For example, in 2012 the Federal Trade Commission issued a strong call for legislation

—*Continued*

that would require companies like Google to respect Internet users' privacy by adding a "Do Not Track" button to their browsers (Angwin 2012; *The Economist* 2013c).

If anything, however, people seem to be less vigilant about maintaining their privacy today than they were before the information age. Young people who have grown up browsing the Internet seem to accept the existence of the "cookies" and "spyware" they may pick up while surfing. They have become accustomed to adult surveillance of their conversation in electronic chat rooms. And many see no risk in providing personal information about themselves to strangers they meet online. Little wonder that college professors find their students do not appreciate the political significance of their right to privacy (Turkle 2004, 2011).

The need for online privacy seems only to be increasing, however. In a new practice called *weblining*, data-gathering companies are monitoring people's online activities not so much for merchandising purposes, but to collect negative personal information. Based on this information, collected from the websites people search or the products and people they friend, a person may be denied a job opportunity or assigned a low credit rating. Data-gathering companies also offer information on searches having to do with mental issues like bipolar disorder and anxiety, which can make it difficult for a person to secure affordable health insurance. Although weblining has not yet drawn policymakers' attention, it is sure to do so in the future (Andrews 2012).

In the near future, new technological innovations will again redefine the limits of surveillance. Sensors are being installed in more and more objects, from appliances to electronic readers, to facilitate their use. It is only a matter of time before manufacturers begin compiling big data on how we use our refrigerators and microwaves, on what we read or scan down to the sentence level. Some corporations are installing sensors on security badges, to record employees' movements and conversations.

To many people, there is a fine line between this use of big data and Big Brother, a fictional character in George Orwell's *Nineteen Eighty-Four*. Published in 1949, the novel describes a future in which the government, directed by the quasi-divine leader Big Brother, secretly scrutinizes people's every move, then manipulates their view of society and even themselves. Little wonder that in 2013, sales of *Nineteen*

George Orwell's novel *Nineteen Eighty-Four* describes a future in which all citizens suffer intensive surveillance by the government ("Big Brother"). In this poster for the 1956 motion picture version, Big Brother hovers over editor Winston Smith, played by Edmund O'Brien.

Eighty-Four increased 7,000 percent within a week of news about Edward Snowden's leaks (Orwell 1949; Price 2013; Silverman 2013).

TAKE THE ISSUE WITH YOU

1. How would you react if you discovered that the government was monitoring your use of the mass media?
2. If your safety were in jeopardy, would you be willing to sacrifice your privacy?
3. Which do you consider the greatest threat to society: government censorship, cybercrime, or Internet surveillance? Explain.

Summary

The media have a global reach thanks to new communications technologies, especially the Internet.

1. Some people are concerned that the media's global reach will spread unhealthy influences to other cultures.

2. The media industry is becoming more and more concentrated, creating media conglomerates. This raises concerns about how innovative and independent the media can be. In some countries, governments own and control the media.

3. The Internet is the one significant exception to the trend toward media concentration, allowing millions of people to produce their own media content.

Thinking Critically

1. Use the functionalist, conflict, and interactionist perspectives to assess the effects of global TV programming on developing countries.

2. Give one example of how individualization of the media, through the Internet, and media concentration, through journalism, films, TV, and radio, have affected your life.

Key Terms

Big data

Culture lag

Mastering This Chapter

World's Largest 3D VideoWall

taking sociology with you

1 For one day, categorize every media message you receive in terms of its function: Does it socialize, enforce a social norm, confer status, or promote consumption? Keep a record and tally the results. Which function was the most common? What can you conclude from the results?

2 Pick a specific audience—residents of your dorm, for example—and track their media preferences over the next day or two. Which mass media are they watching, reading, or listening to? Which media are the most popular and which the least popular? How segmented is this particular mass media audience?

3 Pick a foreign film, television program, or Internet site and study it from the point of view of a sociologist. What does it tell you about the culture that produced it?

key terms

Applied sociology The use of the discipline of sociology with the specific intent of yielding practical applications for human behavior and organizations.

Big data The rapid collection and analysis of enormous amounts of information by supercomputers.

Content analysis The systematic coding and objective recording of data, guided by some rationale.

Crowdsourcing Use of the Internet to seek assistance from the general public in the form of financing, services, or even ideas.

Cultural convergence The flow of content across multiple media, and the accompanying migration of media audiences.

Culture lag A period of maladjustment when the nonmaterial culture is still struggling to adapt to new material conditions.

Digital divide The relative lack of access to the latest technologies among low-income groups, racial and ethnic minorities, rural residents, and the citizens of developing countries.

Dominant ideology A set of cultural beliefs and practices that helps to maintain powerful social, economic, and political interests.

Gatekeeping The process by which a relatively small number of people in the media industry control what material eventually reaches the audience.

Hyperconsumerism The practice of buying more than we need or want, and often more than we can afford; a preoccupation of postmodern consumers.

Hyper-local media Reporting that is highly local and typically Internet-based.

Mass media Print and electronic means of communication that carry messages to widespread audiences.

Narcotizing dysfunction The phenomenon in which the media provide such massive amounts of coverage that the audience

becomes numb and fails to act on the information, regardless of how compelling the issue.

Opinion leader Someone who influences the opinions and decisions of others through day-to-day personal contact and communication.

Social capital The collective benefit of social networks, which are built on reciprocal trust.

Stereotype An unreliable generalization about all members of a group that does not recognize individual differences within the group.

Visual sociology The use of photographs, film, and video to study society.

self-quiz

Read each question carefully and then select the best answer.

1. From the functionalist perspective, the media can be dysfunctional in what way?
   a. They enforce social norms.
   b. They confer status.
   c. They desensitize us to events.
   d. They are agents of socialization.

2. Sociologist Robert Park studied how newspapers helped immigrants to the United States adjust to their environment by changing their customary habits and by teaching them the opinions held by people in their new home country. His study was conducted from which sociological perspective?
   a. the functionalist perspective
   b. the conflict perspective
   c. the interactionist perspective
   d. the dramaturgical perspective

3. There are problems inherent in the socialization function of the mass media. For example, many people worry about
   a. the effect of using the television as a babysitter.
   b. the impact of violent programming on viewer behavior.
   c. the unequal ability of all individuals to purchase televisions.
   d. both a and b.

4. Media advertising has several clear functions, but it also has dysfunctions. Sociologists are concerned that
   a. it creates unrealistic expectations of what is required to be happy.
   b. it creates new consumer needs.
   c. advertisers are able to influence media content.
   d. all of the above

5. Gatekeeping, the process by which a relatively small number of people control what material reaches an audience, is largely dominant in all but which of the following media?
   a. television
   b. the Internet
   c. publishing
   d. music

6. Which sociological perspective is especially concerned with the media's ability to decide what gets transmitted through gatekeeping?
   a. the functionalist perspective
   b. the conflict perspective
   c. the interactionist perspective
   d. the dramaturgical perspective

7. Which of the following is not a problem feminist theorists see with media coverage?
   a. Women are underrepresented, suggesting that men are the cultural standard and that women are insignificant.
   b. Men and women are portrayed in ways that reflect and perpetuate stereotypical views of gender.
   c. Female athletes are treated differently from male athletes in television commentary.
   d. The increasing frequency of single moms in the media is providing a negative role model for women.

8. Which of the following is not true concerning how men and women use the Internet?
   a. Men are more likely to use the Internet daily.
   b. Women are more likely to use e-mail to maintain friendships.
   c. Men account for 100 percent of players in online sports fantasy leagues.
   d. Men are slightly more likely to have ever used the Internet than women are.

9. Sociologist Paul Lazarsfeld and his colleagues pioneered the study of
   a. the audience.
   b. opinion leaders.
   c. the media's global reach.
   d. media violence.

10. In his study of how the social composition of audience members affected how they interpreted the news coverage of riots in Los Angeles in 1992, sociologist Darnell Hunt found what kind of differences in perception?
   a. racial
   b. gender
   c. class
   d. religious

11. The mass media increase social cohesion by presenting a more or less standardized, common view of culture through mass communication. This statement reflects the _____ perspective.

12. Paul Lazarsfeld and Robert Merton created the term _____ _____ to refer to the phenomenon in which the media provide such massive amounts of information that the audience becomes numb and generally fails to act on the information, regardless of how compelling the issue.

13. _____ _____ is the term used to describe the set of cultural beliefs and practices that helps to maintain powerful social, economic, and political interests.

14. Sociologists blame the mass media for the creation and perpetuation of _____, or generalizations about all members of a group that do not recognize individual differences within the group.

15. The _____ perspective contends that television distorts the political process.

16. We risk being _____ if we overstress U.S. dominance and assume that other nations do not play a role in media cultural exports.

17. Both _____ and _____ theorists are troubled that the victims depicted in violent imagery are often those who are given less respect in real life: women, children, the poor, racial minorities, citizens of foreign countries, and even the physically disabled.

18. The _____ perspective examines the media on the micro level to see how they shape day-to-day social behavior.

19. From a sociological point of view, the current controversy over privacy and media censorship illustrates the concept of _____ _____.

20. Nearly 50 years ago, Canadian media theorist _____ _____ predicted that the rise of the electronic media would create a "global village."

7

Deviance, Crime, and Social Control

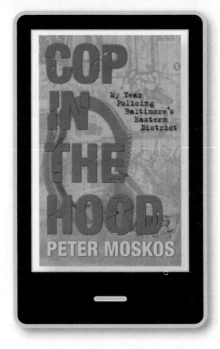

What do you think (or know) life is like in a high-crime area?

To learn about crime firsthand, sociologist Peter Moskos became a Baltimore police officer.

66 Living in Baltimore City, I was required to carry my gun both on and off duty. I never fired a shot outside of training. Only rarely was my service weapon—a charged semi-automatic nine-millimeter Glock-17 with no safety and a seventeen-round clip—pointed at somebody. But in my police duties, my gun was very routinely removed from its holster, probably every other shift. I did occasionally chase people down alleys and wrestled a few suspects. I maced one person, but did not hit anybody. As a police officer, I tried to speak softly and carry a big stick. The department issued a twenty-nine-inch straight wooden baton just for this purpose. I brought it along to all my calls.

In any account of police work, inevitably the noncriminal public, the routine, and the working folks all get short shrift. Police don't deal with a random cross-section of society, even within the areas they work. And this book reflects that. The ghetto transcends stereotypes. Families try to make it against the odds. Old women sweep the streets. People rise before dawn to go to work. On Sundays, ladies go to church wearing beautiful hats and preachers preach to the choir. But if you're looking for stereotypes, they're there. Between the vacant and abandoned buildings you'll find liquor stores, fast food, Korean corner stores, and a Jewish pawn shop. Living conditions are worse than third-world shanty towns:

children in filthy apartments without plumbing or electricity, entire homes put out on eviction day, forty-five-year-old great-grand parents, junkies not raising their kids, drug dealers, and everywhere signs of violence and despair.

As a middle-class white man policing the ghetto, I should address the charge of "exoticism," that I use poor residents for my own advantage. I plead no-contest. If you're not from the ghetto, and though it may not be politically correct to say so, the ghetto *is* exotic. One field-training officer accused me of being "*fascinated* by the ghetto." I am. There are very few aspects of urban life that don't fascinate me. But it is not my intent to sensationalize the ghetto. This is a book about police.

If you want to read about the ghetto, good books are out there. Ghettos are diverse and encompass many cultures and classes. Some object to the very term ghetto. I use the word because it is the vernacular of police officers and many (though by no means all) of the residents. If you really want to learn about the ghetto, go there. There's probably one near you. Visit a church; walk down the street; buy something from the corner store; have a beer; eat. But most importantly, talk to people. That's how you learn. When the subject turns to drugs and crime, you'll hear a common refrain: "It just don't make sense."

Twenty months in Baltimore wasn't very long, but it was long enough to see five police officers killed in the line of duty.

Twenty months in Baltimore wasn't very long, but it was long enough to see five police officers killed in the line of duty. And there were other cops, friends of mine, who were hurt, shot, and lucky to live. A year after I quit the force, my friend and academy classmate became the first Baltimore police woman killed in the line of duty, dying in a car crash on the way to back up another police officer. 99

(Moskos 2008:15–17)

Peter Moskos's route to becoming a sworn police officer was a bit unusual, considering that becoming one was never his goal. None of his friends were on the force, nor did he come from a family of police officers: his father was a well-known and respected sociologist. During his graduate studies, however, Moskos decided that he wanted to learn more about law enforcement. So he persuaded Baltimore's police commissioner to let him attend the police academy, as both a student and a sociologist.

On the second day of class, the commissioner was suddenly and unexpectedly ousted from office, to be replaced by a new commissioner who questioned Moskos's motives. "Why don't you want to be a cop for real?" he challenged Moskos. That was the beginning of Moskos's 20-month tour of duty with the Baltimore Police Department, during which he responded to crimes that included disorderly conduct, domestic abuse, and a 12-person shooting.

In this excerpt from his book *Cop in the Hood: My Year Policing Baltimore's Eastern District*, Moskos describes his beat as seen through the eyes of a sociologist doing an ethnographic study. Looking beyond the stereotypes, he found a diverse and vibrant community, one he would get to know by mingling with its residents. Moskos took the same approach in his study of police work, taking sociology with him to the academy, the station house, and the street.

Moskos notes that the residents he served simply could not fathom the crime that plagued their inner-city neighborhood. What does explain it? Although drug dealing, prostitution, and the sale of stolen goods are illegal activities, they provide a certain level of stability to those who live on the edge, including the homeless, drug addicts, and frightened, neglected youths. Only a thin line separates their *deviant behavior*—behavior that violates social norms, such as dropping out of school or sleeping on the street—from their illegal activities. Crime is functional in their subculture, even if it is socially unacceptable to the rest of the neighborhood.

Another example of a behavior that can be seen as either socially acceptable or socially unacceptable depending on your reference group is binge drinking. On the one hand, we can view binge drinking as *deviant,* as violating a school's standards of conduct and endangering a person's health. On the other hand, we can see it as *conforming,* or complying with peer culture. In the United States, people are socialized to have mixed feelings about both conforming and nonconforming behavior. The term *conformity* can conjure up images of mindless imitation of a peer group—whether a circle of teenagers wearing "phat pants" or a group of business executives all dressed in gray suits. Yet the same term can also suggest that an individual is cooperative, or a "team player." What about those who do not conform? They may be respected as individualists, leaders, or creative thinkers who break new ground. Or they may be labeled as "troublemakers" and "weirdos."

This chapter examines the relationships among deviance and conformity, crime and social control. What is deviance, and what are its consequences? What causes crime? How does society control people's behavior, convincing us to conform to both unwritten rules and formal laws? We will begin by distinguishing between conformity and deviance, and we will examine a surprising experiment on obedience to authority. Next, we will analyze the formal and informal mechanisms societies use to encourage conformity and discourage deviance; we will also focus on theoretical explanations for deviance. The final module focuses on crime, a specific type of deviant behavior subject to official, written norms. Crime has been a special concern of both policymakers and the public in general. We will look at various types of crime found in the United States, the ways crime is measured, and international crime rates. Finally, the Social Policy section considers the controversial topic of gun control.

MODULE 23 | Social Control

As we saw in Module 12, each culture, subculture, and group has distinctive norms governing appropriate behavior. Laws, dress codes, organizational bylaws, course requirements, and the rules of sports and games all express social norms.

How does a society bring about acceptance of basic norms? The term **social control** refers to the techniques and strategies for preventing deviant human behavior in any society. Social control occurs on all levels of society. In the family, we are socialized to obey our parents simply because they are our parents. Peer groups introduce us to informal norms, such as dress codes, that govern the behavior of their members. Colleges establish standards they expect of students. In bureaucratic organizations,

In Finland (left), a young man relaxes in his prison cell, which resembles a college dorm room. In the United States (right), prisoners at a super-maximum-security prison watch television in cages that prevent them from making physical contact with guards or other prisoners. The rate of imprisonment in Finland is less than one-half that of England and one-fourth that of the United States.

workers encounter a formal system of rules and regulations. Finally, the government of every society legislates and enforces social norms.

Most of us respect and accept basic social norms and assume that others will do the same. Even without thinking, we obey the instructions of police officers, follow the day-to-day rules at our jobs, and move to the rear of elevators when people enter. Such behavior reflects an effective process of socialization to the dominant standards of a culture. At the same time, we are well aware that individuals, groups, and institutions *expect* us to act "properly." This expectation carries with it **sanctions,** or penalties and rewards for conduct concerning a social norm. If we fail to live up to the norm, we may face punishment through informal sanctions such as fear and ridicule or formal sanctions such as jail sentences or fines.

The challenge to effective social control is that people often receive competing messages about how to behave. While the state or government may clearly define acceptable behavior, friends or fellow employees may encourage quite different behavior patterns. Historically, legal measures aimed at blocking discrimination based on race, religion, gender, age, and sexual orientation have been difficult to implement, because many people tacitly encourage the violation of such measures.

Functionalists maintain that people must respect social norms if any group or society is to survive. In their view, societies literally could not function if massive numbers of people defied standards of appropriate conduct. In contrast, conflict theorists contend that the successful functioning of a society will consistently benefit the powerful and work to the disadvantage of other groups. They point out that in the United States, widespread resistance to social norms was necessary to win our independence from Great Britain, to overturn the institution of slavery, to allow women to vote, to secure civil rights, and to force an end to the war in Vietnam.

● Conformity and Obedience

Techniques for social control operate on both the group level and the societal level. People we think of as peers or equals influence us to act in particular ways; the same is true of people who hold authority over us or occupy awe-inspiring positions. Social psychologist Stanley Milgram (1975) made a useful distinction between these two levels of social control.

The Milgram Experiment

Milgram used the term **conformity** to mean going along with peers—individuals of our own status who have no special right to direct our behavior. In contrast, **obedience** is compliance with higher authorities in a hierarchical structure. Thus, a recruit entering military service will typically *conform* to the habits and language of other recruits and *obey* the orders of superior officers. Students will *conform* to the drinking behavior of their peers and *obey* the requests of campus security officers.

If ordered to do so, would you comply with an experimenter's instruction to administer increasingly painful electric shocks to a subject? Most people would say no; yet Milgram's research

(1963, 1975) suggests that most of us *would* obey such orders. In his words (1975:xi), "Behavior that is unthinkable in an individual . . . acting on his own may be executed without hesitation when carried out under orders."

Milgram placed advertisements in New Haven, Connecticut, newspapers to recruit subjects for a learning experiment at Yale University. Participants included postal clerks, engineers, high school teachers, and laborers. They were told that the purpose of the research was to investigate the effects of punishment on learning. The experimenter, dressed in a gray technician's coat, explained that in each test, one subject would be randomly selected as the "learner," while another would function as the "teacher." However, the experiment was rigged so that the real subject would always be the teacher, while an associate of Milgram's served as the learner.

At this point, the learner's hand was strapped to an electric apparatus. The teacher was taken to an electronic "shock generator" with 30 levered switches labeled from 15 to 450 volts. Before beginning the experiment, all subjects received sample shocks of 45 volts, to convince them of the authenticity of the experiment. The experimenter then instructed the teacher to apply shocks of increasing voltage each time the learner gave an incorrect answer on a memory test. Teachers were told that "although the shocks can be extremely painful, they cause no permanent tissue damage." In reality, the learner did not receive any shocks.

In a prearranged script, the learner deliberately gave incorrect answers and expressed pain when "shocked." For example, at 150 volts, the learner would cry out, "Get me out of here!" At 270 volts, the learner would scream in agony. When the shock reached 350 volts, the learner would fall silent. If the teacher wanted to stop the experiment, the experimenter would insist that the teacher continue, using such statements as "The experiment requires that you continue" and "You have no other choice; you *must* go on" (Milgram 1975:19–23).

Reflecting on the Milgram Experiment

The results of this unusual experiment stunned and dismayed Milgram and other social scientists. A sample of psychiatrists had predicted that virtually all subjects would refuse to shock innocent victims. In their view, only a "pathological fringe" of less than 2 percent would continue administering shocks up to the maximum level. Yet almost *two-thirds* of participants fell into the category of "obedient subjects."

Why did these subjects obey? Why were they willing to inflict seemingly painful shocks on innocent victims who had never done them any harm? There is no evidence that these subjects were unusually sadistic; few seemed to enjoy administering the shocks. Instead, in Milgram's view, the key to obedience was the experimenter's social role as a "scientist" and "seeker of knowledge."

Milgram pointed out that in the modern industrial world, we are accustomed to submitting to impersonal authority figures whose status is indicated by a title (professor, lieutenant, doctor) or by a uniform (the technician's coat). Because we view the authority as larger and more important than the individual, we shift responsibility for our behavior to the authority figure.

In one of Stanley Milgram's experiments, the learner supposedly received an electric shock from a shock plate when he answered a question incorrectly. At the 150-volt level, the learner would demand to be released and would refuse to place his hand on the shock plate. The experimenter would then order the actual subject, the teacher, to force the hand onto the plate, as shown in the photo. Though 40 percent of the true subjects stopped complying with Milgram at this point, 30 percent did force the learner's hand onto the shock plate, despite his pretended agony.

Milgram's subjects frequently stated, "If it were up to me, I would not have administered shocks." They saw themselves as merely doing their duty (Milgram 1975).

From a conflict perspective, our obedience may be affected by the value we place on those whom our behavior affects. While Milgram's experiment shows that in general, people are willing to obey authority figures, other studies show that they are even more willing to obey if they feel the "victim" is deserving of punishment. Sociologist Gary Schulman (1974) re-created Milgram's experiment and found that White students were significantly more likely to shock Black learners than White learners. By a margin of 70 percent to 48 percent, they imposed more shocks on the Black learners than on the White learners.

From an interactionist perspective, one important aspect of Milgram's findings is the fact that subjects in follow-up studies were less likely to inflict the supposed shocks as they were moved physically closer to their victims. Moreover, interactionists emphasize the effect of *incrementally* administering additional dosages of 15 volts. In effect, the experimenter negotiated with the teacher and convinced the teacher to continue inflicting higher levels of punishment. It is doubtful that anywhere near the two-thirds rate of obedience would have been reached had the experimenter told the teachers to administer 450 volts immediately (Allen 1978; Katovich 1987).

Milgram launched his experimental study of obedience to better understand the involvement of Germans in the annihilation of 6 million Jews and millions of other people during World War II. In an interview conducted long after the publication of his study, he suggested that "if a system of death camps were set up in the United States of the sort we had seen in Nazi Germany, one would be able to find sufficient personnel for those camps in any medium-sized American town." Though many people questioned his remark, the revealing photos taken at Iraq's Abu Ghraib prison in 2004, showing U.S. military guards humiliating if not torturing Iraqi prisoners, recalled the experiment Milgram had done two generations earlier. Under conducive circumstances, otherwise normal people can and often do treat one another inhumanely (CBS News 1979:7–8; Hayden 2004; Zimbardo 2007a).

How willing would participants in this experiment be to shock learners today? Although many people may be skeptical of the high levels of conformity Milgram found, recent replications of his experiment confirm his findings. In 2006, using additional safeguards to protect participants' welfare, psychologist Jerry Burger (2009) repeated part of Milgram's experiment with college undergraduates. To avoid biasing the participants, Burger was careful to screen out students who had heard of Milgram's study. The results of the replication were startlingly similar to Milgram's: participants showed a high level of willingness to shock the learner, just as the participants in Milgram's experiment had almost half a century earlier. At the most comparable point in the two studies, Burger measured a rate of 70 percent full obedience—lower, but not significantly so, than the rate of 82.5 percent measured two generations earlier.

 use your **sociological imagination**

If you were a participant in Milgram's research on conformity, how far do you think you would go in carrying out orders? Do you see any ethical problem with the experimenter's manipulation of the subjects? Explain your answer.

Informal and Formal Social Control

The sanctions that are used to encourage conformity and obedience—and to discourage violation of social norms—are carried out through both informal and formal social control. As the term implies, people use **informal social control** casually to enforce norms. Examples include smiles, laughter, a raised eyebrow, and ridicule.

In the United States and many other cultures, adults often view spanking, slapping, or kicking children as a proper and necessary means of informal social control. Child development specialists counter that such corporal punishment is inappropriate because it teaches children to solve problems through violence. They warn that slapping and spanking can escalate into more serious forms of abuse. Yet, despite a policy statement by the American Academy of Pediatrics that corporal punishment is not effective and can indeed be harmful, 59 percent of pediatricians support the use of corporal punishment, at least in certain situations. Our culture widely accepts this form of informal social control (Chung et al. 2009).

Binge Drinking

About 1,700 college students die each year of unintentional alcohol-related injuries. According to a study published by the Harvard School of Public Health, 44 percent of college students indulge in binge drinking (defined as at least five drinks in a row for men and four in a row for women). These numbers represent an increase from 1990s data, despite efforts on many campuses across the nation to educate students about the risks of binge drinking.

The problem is not confined to the United States—Britain, Russia, and South Africa all report regular "drink till you drop" alcoholic consumption among young people. According to a study that compared data from 22 countries, however, college students in the United States have the highest rate of drinking and driving. Nor does binge drinking begin in college. A national study found that over a 30-day period, 29 percent of high school students engaged in binge drinking.

Binge drinking on campus presents a difficult social problem. On the one hand, it can be regarded as *deviant,* violating the standards of conduct expected of those in an academic setting. In fact, Harvard researchers consider binge drinking the most serious public health hazard facing colleges. On the other hand, binge drinking represents *conformity* to the peer culture, especially in fraternities and sororities, which serve as social centers on many campuses. Most students seem to take an "everybody does it—no big deal" attitude toward the behavior.

Some colleges and universities are taking steps to make binge drinking a bit less "normal" by means of *social control*—banning kegs, closing fraternities and sororities, encouraging liquor retailers not to sell in

Forty-four percent of college students indulge in binge drinking.

high volume to students, and expelling students after three alcohol-related infractions. Despite privacy laws, many schools are notifying parents whenever their underage children are caught drinking. Even with these measures, however, curbing underage drinking is a challenge.

LET'S DISCUSS

1. Why do you think most college students regard binge drinking as a normal rather than a deviant behavior?

2. Which do you think would be more effective in stopping binge drinking on your campus, informal or formal social control?

Sources: Bernstein 2007; Centers for Disease Control and Prevention 2010, 2012a; J. Miller et al. 2007; National Center on Addiction and Substance Abuse at Columbia University 2007; Outside the Classroom 2009; Parker-Pope 2012; Wechsler et al. 2002, 2004.

Formal social control is carried out by authorized agents, such as police officers, judges, school administrators, employers, military officers, and managers of movie theaters. It can serve as a last resort when socialization and informal sanctions do not bring about desired behavior. Sometimes, informal social control can actually undermine formal social control, encouraging people to violate social norms. Box 23-1 examines binge drinking among college students, who receive conflicting messages about the acceptability of the behavior from sources of social control.

Historically, the death penalty has served as a significant form

of social control. The threat of execution was meant as much to discourage others from committing capital crimes as it was to punish those who did. However, researchers have been unable to establish what if any deterrence effect executions may have, leading many people to question the effectiveness of the death penalty. As Figure 23-1 shows, the death penalty is still on the books in 35 states, where it is used to a greater or lesser extent.

In 2007, in the wake of the mass shootings at Virginia Tech, many college officials reviewed security measures on their campuses. Administrators were reluctant to end or even limit the relative freedom of movement students on their campuses enjoyed. Instead, they concentrated on improving emergency communications between campus police and students, faculty, and staff. Reflecting a reliance on technology to maintain social control, college leaders called for replacement of the "old" technology

FIGURE 23-1 **Executions by State Since 1976**

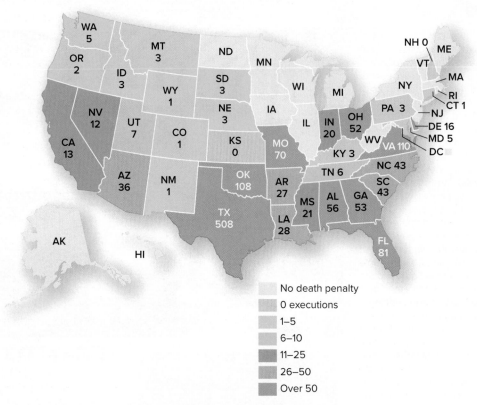

No death penalty
0 executions
1–5
6–10
11–25
26–50
Over 50

Note: Number of executions carried out from January 17, 1977, to December 18, 2013, not including three federal executions. Illinois carried out 12 executions before abolishing the death penalty. Maryland and New Mexico, which still have people on death row, have abolished the death penalty for future cases.
Source: Death Penalty Information Center 2014.

of e-mail with instant alerts that could be sent to people's cell phones via instant messaging.

In the aftermath of September 11, 2001, new measures of social control became the norm in the United States. Some of them, such as stepped-up security and surveillance at airports and high-rise buildings, were highly visible to the public. The federal government has also publicly urged citizens to engage in informal social control by watching for and reporting people whose actions seem suspicious (Monahan 2011).

Many people think this kind of social control goes too far. Civil rights advocates worry that the government's request for information on suspicious activities may encourage negative stereotyping of Muslims and Arab Americans. Clearly, there is a trade-off between the benefits of surveillance and the right to privacy.

■ Law and Society

Some norms are so important to a society that they are formalized into laws regarding people's behavior. **Law** may be defined as governmental social control (Black 1995). Some laws, such as the prohibition against murder, are directed at all members of society. Others, such as fishing and hunting regulations, affect

particular categories of people. Still others govern the behavior of social institutions (for instance, corporate law and laws regarding the taxing of nonprofit enterprises).

Sociologists see the creation of laws as a social process. Because laws are passed in response to a perceived need for formal social control, sociologists have sought to explain how and why such a perception arises. In their view, law is not merely a static body of rules handed down from generation to generation. Rather, it reflects continually changing standards of what is right and wrong, of how violations are to be determined, and of what sanctions are to be applied (Schur 1968).

Sociologists representing varying theoretical perspectives agree that the legal order reflects the values of those in a position to exercise authority. Therefore, the creation of civil and criminal law can be a most controversial matter. Should it be against the law to employ illegal immigrants, to have an abortion, to allow prayer in public schools, or to smoke on an airplane? Such issues have been bitterly debated, because they require a choice among competing values. Not surprisingly, laws that are unpopular— such as the one-time prohibition of alcohol under the Eighteenth Amendment and the widespread establishment of a 55-mile-per-hour speed limit on highways—become difficult to enforce when there is no consensus supporting the norms.

FIGURE 23-2 The Status of Medical Marijuana

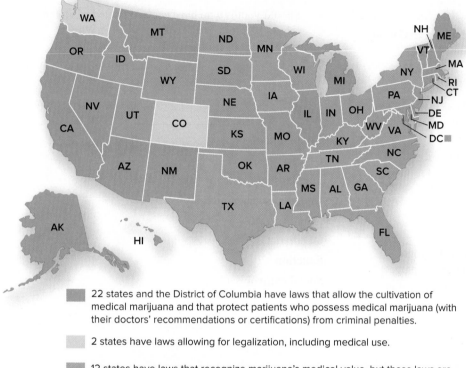

22 states and the District of Columbia have laws that allow the cultivation of medical marijuana and that protect patients who possess medical marijuana (with their doctors' recommendations or certifications) from criminal penalties.

2 states have laws allowing for legalization, including medical use.

12 states have laws that recognize marijuana's medical value, but these laws are ineffective because they rely on federal cooperation.

18 states have no provisions for medical marijuana.

Source: NORML 2014.

The actions some states have taken to legalize marijuana are largely symbolic. Federal law still prohibits doctors from writing prescriptions for marijuana, and pharmacies from distributing the substance. Although patients can still be prosecuted by the federal government for possessing or using marijuana, the Obama administration has decided not to prosecute medical marijuana users who comply with state laws.

In Singapore, a custodian removes a bit of litter from an otherwise spotless floor. Strict social controls prevail in the city-state, where the careless disposal of a cigarette butt or candy wrapper carries a $200 fine.

One current and controversial debate over laws governing behavior is whether people should be allowed to use marijuana legally, for medical purposes. Although the majority of adults polled in national surveys support such a use, the federal government continues to regard all uses of marijuana as illegal. In 2005 the Supreme Court upheld the federal government's position. Nevertheless, 22 states and the District of Columbia have granted citizens the right to use marijuana for medical purposes—even if that privilege rests on dubious legal grounds (Figure 23-2).

Socialization is the primary source of conforming and obedient behavior, including obedience to law. Generally, it is not external pressure from a peer group or authority figure that makes us go along with social norms. Rather, we have internalized such norms as valid and desirable and are committed to observing them. In a profound sense, we want to see ourselves (and to be seen) as loyal, cooperative, responsible, and respectful of others. In the United States and other societies around the world, people are socialized both to want to belong and to fear being viewed as different or deviant.

Control theory suggests that our connection to members of society leads us to systematically conform to society's norms. According to sociologist Travis Hirschi and other control theorists, our bonds to family members, friends, and peers induce us to follow the mores and folkways of our society. We give little conscious thought to whether we will be sanctioned if we fail to conform. Socialization develops our self-control so well that we don't need further pressure to obey social norms. Although control theory does not effectively explain the rationale for every conforming act, it nevertheless reminds us that while the media may focus on crime and disorder, most members of most societies conform to and obey basic norms (Brewis et al. 2011; Gottfredson and Hirschi 1990; Hirschi 1969).

Summary

This module examines the relationship between conformity and mechanisms of **social control.**

1. A society uses **social control** to encourage the acceptance of basic norms.

2. Stanley Milgram defined **conformity** as going along with one's peers; **obedience** is compliance with higher authorities in a hierarchical structure.

3. Some norms are so important to a society that they are formalized into **laws.** Socialization is a primary source of conforming and obedient behavior, including obedience to laws.

Thinking Critically

1. Think about a job you once held. How did your employer exercise social control over the employees? How did you, as an employee, use social control in relating to those around you?

2. Should youths who have been convicted of violent crimes be subject to the death penalty? Why or why not?

3. Should some illegal drugs be decriminalized? Why or why not?

Key Terms

Conformity

Control theory

Formal social control

Informal social control

Law

Obedience

Sanction

Social control

MODULE 24 | **What Is Deviance?**

For sociologists, the term *deviance* does not mean perversion or depravity. **Deviance** is behavior that violates the standards of conduct or expectations of a group or society. In the United States, alcoholics, compulsive gamblers, and people with mental illness would all be classified as deviants. Being late for class is categorized as a deviant act; the same is true of wearing jeans to a formal wedding. On the basis of the sociological definition, we are all deviant from time to time. Each of us violates common social norms in certain situations (Best 2004).

Is being overweight an example of deviance? In the United States and many other cultures, unrealistic standards of appearance and body image place a huge strain on people—especially women and girls—based on how they look. Journalist Naomi Wolf (1992) has used the term *beauty myth* to refer to an exaggerated ideal of beauty, beyond the reach of all but a few females, which has unfortunate consequences. In order to shed their "deviant" image and conform to unrealistic societal norms, many women and girls become consumed with adjusting their appearances. Yet what is deviant in one culture may be celebrated in another.

Deviance involves the violation of group norms, which may or may not be formalized into law. It is a comprehensive concept that includes not only criminal behavior but also many actions that are not subject to prosecution. The public official who takes a bribe has defied social norms, but so has the high school student who refuses to sit in an assigned seat or cuts class. Of course, deviation from norms is not always negative, let alone criminal. A member of an exclusive social club who speaks out against a traditional policy of not admitting women, Blacks, and Jews is deviating from the club's norms. So is a police officer who blows the whistle on corruption or brutality within the department.

From a sociological perspective, deviance is hardly objective or set in stone. Rather, it is subject to social definition within a particular society and at a particular time. For that reason, what is considered deviant can shift from one social era to another. In most instances, those individuals and groups with the greatest status and power define

In 2009, baseball fans were shocked by the revelation that like several other baseball greats, superstar Alex Rodriguez had used banned substances and lied about it. In 2013, he was suspended for 211 games, including the entire 2014 season.

Think about It If your friends or teammates violate a social norm, is their behavior deviant?

Deviant or normal? Television personality and recording artist Heidi Montag shocked fans in 2010 by revealing that she had undergone 10 plastic surgery procedures in a single day. Montag had already undergone breast augmentation, collagen lip injections, and rhinoplasty. Would you consider her behavior deviant?

what is acceptable and what is deviant. For example, despite serious medical warnings against the dangers of tobacco, made since 1964, cigarette smoking continued to be accepted for decades—in good part because of the power of tobacco farmers and cigarette manufacturers. Only after a long campaign led by public health and anticancer activists did cigarette smoking become more of a deviant activity. Today, many state and local laws limit where people can smoke.

Deviance and Social Stigma

A person can acquire a deviant identity in many ways. Because of physical or behavioral characteristics, some people are unwillingly cast in negative social roles. Once assigned a deviant role, they have trouble presenting a positive image to others and may even experience lowered self-esteem. Whole groups of people—for instance, "short people" or "redheads"—may be labeled in this way. The interactionist Erving Goffman coined the term **stigma** to describe the labels society uses to devalue members of certain social groups (Goffman 1963; Heckert and Best 1997).

In the aftermath of the 2012 school shooting in Newtown, Connecticut, the issue of mental illness surfaced almost immediately, amid rumors that the shooter suffered from an untreated mental disorder. In many people's eyes, such assumptions stigmatize all people with mental illness, whatever the definition of

the term, as potentially violent criminals. Overwhelming evidence shows that the opposite is true, however: the vast majority of people with psychiatric disorders do *not* commit violent acts. Only 4 percent of violent crimes in the United States can be attributed to people with mental illness. Gun violence is discussed further in the Social Policy section at the end of this chapter, on gun control (R. Friedman 2012; Nocera 2012).

Stigmatization also affects people who look different from others in the eyes of their peers. Prevailing expectations about beauty and body shape may prevent people who are regarded as ugly or obese from advancing as rapidly as their abilities permit. Both overweight and anorexic people are assumed to be weak in character, slaves to their appetites or to media images. Because they do not conform to the beauty myth, they may be viewed as "disfigured" or "strange" in appearance, bearers of what Goffman calls a "spoiled identity." However, what constitutes disfigurement is a matter of interpretation. Of the 17 million cosmetic procedures done every year in the United States alone, many are performed on women who would be defined objectively as having a normal appearance. And while feminist sociologists have accurately noted that the beauty myth makes many women feel uncomfortable with themselves, men too lack confidence in their appearance. The number of males who choose to undergo cosmetic procedures has risen sharply in recent years (American Academy of Cosmetic Surgery 2010).

Often people are stigmatized for deviant behaviors they may no longer engage in. The labels "compulsive gambler," "ex-convict," "recovering alcoholic," and "ex–mental patient" can stick to a person for life. Goffman draws a useful distinction between a prestige symbol that draws attention to a positive aspect of one's identity, such as a wedding band or a badge, and a stigma symbol that discredits or debases one's identity, such as a conviction for child molestation. While stigma symbols may not always be obvious, they can become a matter of public knowledge. Starting in 1994, many states required convicted sex offenders to register with local police departments. Some communities publish the names and addresses, and in some instances even the pictures, of convicted sex offenders on the web.

While some types of deviance will stigmatize a person, other types do not carry a significant penalty. Examples of socially tolerated forms of deviance can be found in the world of high technology.

Deviance and Technology

Technological innovations such as pagers and voice mail can redefine social interactions and the standards of behavior related to them. When the Internet was first made available to the general public, no norms or regulations governed its use. Because online communication offers a high degree of anonymity, uncivil behavior—speaking harshly of others or monopolizing chat room space—quickly became common. Online bulletin boards designed to carry items of community interest became littered with commercial advertisements. Such deviant acts are beginning to provoke calls for the establishment of formal rules for online behavior. For example, policymakers have debated whether to regulate the content of websites featuring hate speech and pornography.

Some deviant uses of technology are criminal, though not all participants see it that way. On the street, the for-profit pirating of software, motion pictures, and music has become a big business. On the Internet, the downloading of music by individual listeners, which is typically forbidden by copyright, is widely accepted. The music and motion picture industries have waged much publicized campaigns to stop these illegal uses of their products, yet among many people, no social stigma attaches to them. Deviance, then, is a complex concept. Sometimes it is trivial, sometimes profoundly harmful. Sometimes it is accepted by society and sometimes soundly rejected.

Sociological Perspectives on Deviance

Why do people violate social norms? We have seen that deviant acts are subject to both informal and formal social control. The nonconforming or disobedient person may face disapproval, loss of friends, fines, or even imprisonment. Why, then, does deviance occur?

Early explanations for behavior that deviated from societal expectations blamed supernatural causes or genetic factors (such as "bad blood" or evolutionary throwbacks to primitive ancestors). By the 1800s, substantial research efforts were being made to identify biological factors that lead to deviance, and especially to criminal activity. Though such research was discredited in the 20th century, contemporary studies, primarily by biochemists, have sought to isolate genetic factors that suggest a likelihood of certain personality traits. Although criminality (much less deviance) is hardly a personality characteristic, researchers have focused on traits that might lead to crime, such as aggression. Of course, aggression can also lead to success in the corporate world, in professional sports, or in other walks of life.

The contemporary study of the possible biological roots of criminality is but one aspect of the larger debate over sociobiology. In general, sociologists have been critical of any emphasis on the genetic roots of crime and deviance. The limitations of current knowledge about the link between genetics and antisocial behavior have led them to draw largely on other approaches to explain deviance (Walsh 2000).

Functionalist Perspective

According to functionalists, deviance is a common part of human existence, with positive as well as negative consequences for social stability. Deviance helps to define the limits of proper behavior. Children who see one parent scold the other for belching at the dinner table learn about approved conduct. The same is true of the driver who receives a speeding ticket, the department store cashier who is fired for yelling at a customer, and the college student who is penalized for handing in papers weeks overdue.

Durkheim's Legacy Émile Durkheim ([1895] 1964) focused his sociological investigations mainly on criminal acts, yet his conclusions have implications for all types of deviant behavior. In Durkheim's view, the punishments established within a culture (including both formal and informal mechanisms of social control) help to define acceptable behavior and thus contribute to stability. If improper acts were not sanctioned, people might stretch their standards of what constitutes appropriate conduct.

Sociologist Kai Erikson (1966) illustrated the boundary-maintenance function of deviance in his study of the Puritans of 17th-century New England. By today's standards, the Puritans placed tremendous emphasis on conventional morals. Their persecution and execution of women as witches represented a continuing attempt to define and redefine the boundaries of their community. In effect, their changing social norms created crime waves, as people whose behavior was previously acceptable suddenly faced punishment for being deviant (R. Schaefer and Zellner 2011).

Durkheim ([1897] 1951) introduced the term **anomie** into sociological literature to describe the loss of direction felt in a society when social control of individual behavior has become ineffective. Anomie is a state of normlessness that typically occurs during a period of profound social change and disorder, such as a time of economic collapse. People become more aggressive or depressed, which results in higher rates of violent crime and suicide. Since there is much less agreement on what constitutes proper behavior during times of revolution, sudden prosperity, or economic depression, conformity and obedience become less significant as social forces. It also becomes much more difficult to state exactly what constitutes deviance.

Merton's Theory of Deviance What do a mugger and a teacher have in common? Each is "working" to obtain money that can then be exchanged for desired goods. As this example illustrates, behavior that violates accepted norms (such as mugging) may be based on the same basic objectives as the behavior of people who pursue more conventional lifestyles.

On the basis of this kind of analysis, sociologist Robert Merton (1968) adapted Durkheim's notion of anomie to explain why people accept or reject the goals of a society, the socially approved means of fulfilling their aspirations, or both. Merton maintained that one important cultural goal in the United States is success, measured largely in terms of money. In addition to providing this goal for people, our society offers specific instructions on how to pursue success—go to school, work hard, do not quit, take advantage of opportunities, and so forth.

What happens to individuals in a society with a heavy emphasis on wealth as a basic symbol of success? Merton reasoned that people adapt in certain ways, either by conforming to or by deviating from such cultural expectations. His **anomie theory of deviance** posits five types of behavior or basic forms of adaptation (Table 24-1).

Conformity to social norms, the most common adaptation in Merton's typology, is the opposite of deviance. It involves acceptance of both the overall societal goal ("acquisition of wealth") and the approved means ("hard work"). In Merton's view, there must be some consensus regarding accepted cultural goals and the legitimate means for attaining them. Without such a consensus, societies could exist only as collectives of people rather than as unified cultures, and might experience continual chaos.

The other four types of behavior represented in Table 24-1 all involve some departure from conformity. The *retreatist* has basically retreated (or withdrawn) from both the goals and the means of society. In the United States, drug addicts and vagrants are typically portrayed as retreatists. Concern has been growing that adolescents who are addicted to alcohol will become retreatists at an early age.

In Merton's typology, the *innovator* accepts the goals of society but pursues them with means that are regarded as improper. For instance, a safecracker may steal money to buy consumer goods and expensive vacations.

TABLE **24-1** MERTON'S DEVIANCE THEORY

Summing Up

Does the individual accept:	Type of Behavior				
	Nondeviant	*Deviant*			
	Conformity	Retreatism	Innovation	Ritualism	Rebellion
the goals of society, such as acquisition of wealth?	👍	👎	👍	👎	👎 👍
the use of acceptable means, such as hard work?	👍	👎	👎	👍	👎 👍

Source: Adapted by author, Richard Schaefer, from Chapter VI, "Social Structure and Anomie," in Merton 1968.

The *ritualist* has abandoned the goal of material success and become compulsively committed to the institutional means. Work becomes simply a way of life rather than a means to the goal of success. An example would be the bureaucratic official who blindly applies rules and regulations without remembering the larger goals of the organization. Certainly that would be true of a welfare caseworker who refuses to assist a homeless family because their last apartment was in another district.

The final type of behavior or adaptation identified by Merton reflects people's attempts to create a *new* social structure. The *rebel* feels alienated from the dominant means and goals and may seek a dramatically different social order. Members of a revolutionary political organization, such as a militia group, can be categorized as rebels according to Merton's model.

Merton made a key contribution to the sociological understanding of deviance by pointing out that deviants such as innovators and ritualists share a great deal with conforming people. The convicted felon may hold many of the same aspirations as people with no criminal background. The theory helps us to understand deviance as a socially created behavior rather than as the result of momentary pathological impulses. However, this theory of deviance has not been applied systematically to real-world crime. Box 24-1 examines scholars' efforts to confirm the theory's validity.

Interactionist Perspective

The functionalist approach to deviance explains why rule violations continue to happen despite pressure to conform and obey. However, functionalists do not indicate how a given person comes to commit a deviant act or why on some occasions crimes do or do not occur. The emphasis on everyday behavior that is the focus of the interactionist perspective offers such an explanation: cultural transmission theory.

Cultural Transmission   In the course of studying graffiti writing by gangs in Los Angeles, sociologist Susan A. Phillips (1999) discovered that the writers learned from one another. In fact, Phillips was surprised by how stable their focus was over time. She also noted how other ethnic groups built on the models of the African American and Chicano gangs, superimposing Cambodian, Chinese, or Vietnamese symbols.

Humans *learn* how to behave in social situations, whether properly or improperly. There is no natural, innate manner in which people interact with one another. These simple ideas are not disputed today, but such was not the case when sociologist Edwin Sutherland (1883–1950) first advanced the idea that an individual undergoes the same basic socialization process in learning conforming and deviant acts.

Sutherland's ideas have been the dominating force in criminology. He drew on the **cultural transmission** school, which emphasizes that one learns criminal behavior by interacting with others. Such learning includes not only the techniques of lawbreaking (for example, how to break into a car quickly and quietly) but also the motives, drives, and rationalizations of the criminal. The cultural transmission approach can also be used to explain the behavior of those who habitually abuse alcohol or drugs.

Sutherland maintained that through interactions with a primary group and significant others, people acquire definitions of proper and improper behavior. He used the term **differential association** to describe the process through which exposure to attitudes *favorable* to criminal acts leads to the violation of rules.

Does Crime Pay?

A driver violates the speed limit to get to a job interview on time. A financially strapped parent shoplifts goods that her family needs. These people may feel justified in violating the law because they do so to meet a reasonable objective. In Robert Merton's terms, they are *innovators*—people who violate social norms to achieve a commonly shared societal goal. Although their actions are criminal and potentially hurtful to others, from their own short-term perspective, their actions are functional.

Carried to its logical conclusion, innovation can and does become a career for some people. Yet from a purely economic point of view, even considering the fact that crime may pay is controversial, because doing so may seem to tolerate or encourage rule violation. Nothing is more controversial than the suggestion that gang-run drug deals are profitable and produce "good jobs." Although some people may see drug dealers as a cross between MBA-educated professionals and streetwise entrepreneurs, society in general does not admire these innovators.

Sociologist Sudhir Venkatesh collected detailed data on the illegal drug trade during his observation research on a Chicago street gang. Working with economist Steven Levitt, coauthor of the best seller

Freakonomics, to analyze the business of selling crack cocaine, he found that less than 5 percent of even the gang leaders earned $100,000 per year. The rest of the leaders and virtually all the rank and file earned less than the minimum wage. In fact, most were unpaid workers seeking to move up in the gang hierarchy. (Thus the title of a chapter in Levitt's book, "Why Do Drug Dealers Still Live with Their Moms?") As Levitt notes, the drug gang is like most corporations: the top 2 percent of workers take home most of the money.

> Less than 5 percent of even the gang leaders earned $100,000 per year. The rest of the leaders and virtually all the rank and file earned less than the minimum wage.

Why, from a sociological *and* an economic perspective, do these nonprofitable practices persist, especially considering that one in every four members of drug-oriented street

gangs is eventually killed? One reason, of course, is the public's almost insatiable demand for illegal drugs. And from the drug peddler's perspective, few legitimate jobs are available to young adults in poverty-stricken areas, urban or rural. Functionally, these youths are contributing to their household incomes by dealing drugs.

Scholars see a need for further research on Merton's concept of innovation. Why, for example, do some disadvantaged groups have lower rates of reported crime than others? Why do many people who are caught in adverse circumstances reject criminal activity as a viable alternative? Merton's theory of deviance does not easily answer such questions.

LET'S DISCUSS

1. Do you know anyone who has stolen out of need? If so, did the person feel justified in stealing, or did he or she feel guilty? How long did the theft continue?

2. Economically, profit is the difference between revenues and costs. What are the costs of the illegal drug trade, both economic and social? Is this economic activity profitable for society?

Sources: Clinard and Miller 1998; Kingsbury 2008; S. Levitt and Dubner 2006; S. Levitt and Venkatesh 2000; Rosen and Venkatesh 2008; Venkatesh 2008.

Research suggests that this view of differential association also applies to noncriminal deviant acts, such as smoking, truancy, and early sexual behavior.

Sutherland offers the example of a boy who is sociable, outgoing, and athletic and who lives in an area with a high rate of delinquency. The youth is very likely to come into contact with peers who commit acts of vandalism, fail to attend school, and so forth, and may come to adopt such behavior. However, an introverted boy who lives in the same neighborhood may stay away from his peers and avoid delinquency. In another community, an outgoing and athletic boy may join a Little League baseball team or a scout troop because of his interactions with peers. Thus, Sutherland views improper behavior as the result of the types of groups to which one belongs and the kinds of friendships one has.

According to critics, the cultural transmission approach may explain the deviant behavior of juvenile delinquents or graffiti artists, but it fails to explain the conduct of the first-time impulsive shoplifter or the impoverished person who steals out of necessity. While it is not a precise statement of the process through which one becomes a criminal, differential association theory does direct our attention to the paramount role of social

interaction in increasing a person's motivation to engage in deviant behavior (Loughran et al. 2013; Sutherland et al. 1992).

Social Disorganization Theory The social relationships that exist in a community or neighborhood affect people's behavior. Philip Zimbardo (2007a:24–25), author of the mock prison experiment described in Chapter 5, once did an experiment that demonstrated the power of communal relationships. He abandoned a car in each of two different neighborhoods, leaving its hood up and removing its hub caps. In one neighborhood, people started to strip the car for parts before Zimbardo had finished setting up a remote video camera to record their behavior. In the other neighborhood, weeks passed without the car being touched, except for a pedestrian who stopped to close the hood during a rainstorm.

What accounts for the strikingly different outcomes of Zimbardo's experiment in the two communities? According to **social disorganization theory,** increases in crime and deviance can be attributed to the absence or breakdown of communal relationships and social institutions, such as the family, school, church, and local government. This theory was developed at the University of Chicago in the early 1900s to describe the apparent disorganization

According to social disorganization theory, strong communal bonds can enhance neighborhood ties, reducing the likelihood of criminal behavior.

that occurred as cities expanded with rapid immigration and migration from rural areas. Using the latest survey techniques, Clifford Shaw and Henry McKay literally mapped the distribution of social problems in Chicago. They found high rates of social problems in neighborhoods where buildings had deteriorated and the population had declined. Interestingly, the patterns persisted over time, despite changes in the neighborhoods' ethnic and racial composition.

This theory is not without its critics. To some, social disorganization theory seems to "blame the victim," leaving larger societal forces, such as the lack of jobs or high-quality schools, unaccountable. Critics also argue that even troubled neighborhoods have viable, healthy organizations, which persist despite the problems that surround them.

More recently, social disorganization theorists have taken to emphasizing the effect of social networks on communal bonds. These researchers acknowledge that communities are not isolated islands. Residents' bonds may be enhanced or weakened by their ties to groups outside the immediate community (Jensen 2005; Sampson and Graves 1989; Shaw and McKay 1942).

Labeling Perspective

The Saints and the Roughnecks were groups of high school males who were continually engaged in excessive drinking, reckless driving, truancy, petty theft, and vandalism. There the similarity ended. None of the Saints was ever arrested, but every Roughneck was frequently in trouble with police and townspeople. Why the disparity in their treatment? On the basis of observation research in their high school, sociologist William Chambliss (1973) concluded that social class played an important role in the varying fortunes of the two groups.

The Saints hid behind a facade of respectability. They came from "good families," were active in school organizations, planned on attending college, and received good grades. People generally viewed their delinquent acts as a few isolated cases of sowing wild oats. The Roughnecks had no such aura of respectability. They drove around town in beat-up cars, were generally unsuccessful in school, and aroused suspicion no matter what they did.

We can understand such discrepancies by using an approach to deviance known as **labeling theory.** Unlike Sutherland's work, labeling theory does not focus on why some individuals come to commit deviant acts. Instead, it attempts to explain why certain people (such as the Roughnecks) are *viewed* as deviants, delinquents, bad kids, losers, and criminals, whereas others whose behavior is similar (such as the Saints) are not seen in such harsh terms. Reflecting the contribution of interactionist theorists, labeling theory emphasizes how a person comes to be labeled as deviant or to accept that label. Sociologist Howard Becker (1963:9; 1964), who popularized this approach, summed it up with this statement: "Deviant behavior is behavior that people so label."

Labeling theory is also called the **societal-reaction approach,** reminding us that it is the *response* to an act, not the behavior itself, that determines deviance. For example, studies have shown that some school personnel and therapists expand educational programs designed for learning-disabled students to include those with behavioral problems. Consequently, a "troublemaker" can be improperly labeled as "learning-disabled," and vice versa (Grattet 2011).

Labeling and Agents of Social Control Traditionally, research on deviance has focused on people who violate social norms. In contrast, labeling theory focuses on police, probation officers, psychiatrists, judges, teachers, employers, school officials, and other regulators of social control. These agents, it is argued, play a significant role in creating the deviant identity by designating certain people (and not others) as deviant. An important aspect of labeling theory is the recognition that some individuals or groups have the power to *define* labels and *apply* them to others. This view ties into the conflict perspective's emphasis on the social significance of power.

In recent years the practice of *racial profiling,* in which people are identified as criminal suspects purely on the basis of their race, has come under public scrutiny. Studies confirm the public's suspicions that in some jurisdictions, police officers are much more likely to stop Black males than White males for routine traffic violations, in the expectation of finding drugs or guns in their cars. Civil rights activists refer to these cases sarcastically as DWB (Driving While Black) violations. Beginning in 2001, profiling took a new turn as people who appeared to be Arab or Muslim came under special scrutiny. (Racial profiling will be examined in more detail in Module 32.)

The popularity of labeling theory is reflected in the emergence of a related perspective, called social constructionism. According to the **social constructionist perspective,** deviance is the product of the culture we live in. Social constructionists focus specifically on the decision-making process that creates the deviant identity. They point out that "child abductors," "deadbeat dads," "spree killers," and "date rapists" have always been with us, but at times have become *the* major social concern of policymakers because of intensive media coverage (Liska and Messner 1999; E. R. Wright et al. 2000).

How do certain behaviors come to be viewed as a problem? Cigarette smoking, which was once regarded as a polite, gentlemanly activity, is now considered a serious health hazard, not only to the smoker but also to others nearby who don't smoke. Recently, people have become concerned about the danger, especially to children, posed by *thirdhand smoke*—smoke-related chemicals that cling to clothes and linger in rooms, cars, even elevators (Winickoff et al. 2009).

use your **sociological imagination**

You are a teacher. What labels, freely used in education, might you attach to your students?

Conflict Perspective

Conflict theorists point out that people with power protect their interests and define deviance to suit their needs. Sociologist Richard Quinney (1974, 1979, 1980) was a leading exponent of the view that the criminal justice system serves the interests of the powerful. Crime, according to Quinney (1970), is a definition of conduct created by authorized agents of social control—such as legislators and law enforcement officers—in a politically organized society. He and other conflict theorists argue that lawmaking is often an attempt by the powerful to coerce others into their morality (see also Spitzer 1975).

This theory helps to explain why our society has laws against gambling, drug use, and prostitution, many of which are violated on a massive scale. (We will examine these "victimless crimes" in Module 25.) According to conflict theorists, criminal law does not represent a consistent application of societal values, but instead reflects competing values and interests. Thus,

In the 1930s, the Federal Bureau of Narcotics launched a campaign to portray marijuana as a dangerous drug rather than a pleasure-inducing substance. From a conflict perspective, those in power often use such tactics to coerce others into adopting a different point of view.

the U.S. criminal code outlaws marijuana because of its alleged harm to users, yet cigarettes and alcohol—both of which can be harmful to users—are sold legally almost everywhere.

In fact, conflict theorists contend that the entire criminal justice system in the United States treats suspects differently based on their racial, ethnic, or social-class background. In many cases, officials in the system use their own discretion to make biased decisions about whether to press charges or drop them, whether to set bail and how much, whether to offer parole or deny it. Researchers have found that this kind of **differential justice**—differences in the way social control is exercised over different groups—puts African Americans and Latinos at a disadvantage in the justice system, both as juveniles and as adults. On average, White offenders receive shorter sentences than comparable Latino and African American offenders, even when prior arrest records and the relative severity of the crime are taken into consideration (Brewer and Heitzeg 2008; Sandefur 2008; Schlesinger 2011).

The perspective advanced by conflict and labeling theorists forms quite a contrast to the functionalist approach to deviance. Functionalists see standards of deviant behavior as merely reflecting cultural norms; conflict and labeling theorists point out that the most powerful groups in a society can shape laws and standards and determine who is (or is not) prosecuted as a criminal. These groups would be unlikely to apply the label "deviant" to the corporate executive whose decisions lead to large-scale environmental pollution. In the opinion of conflict theorists, agents of social control and other powerful groups can impose their own self-serving definitions of deviance on the general public.

Feminist Perspective

Feminist criminologists such as Freda Adler and Meda Chesney-Lind have suggested that many of the existing approaches to deviance and crime were developed with only men in mind. For example, in the United States, for many years any husband who forced his wife to have sexual intercourse—without her consent and against her will—was not legally considered to have committed rape. The law defined rape as pertaining only to sexual relations between people who were not married to each other, reflecting the overwhelmingly male composition of state legislatures at the time.

It took repeated protests by feminist organizations to get changes in the criminal law defining rape. Beginning in 1993, husbands in all 50 states could be prosecuted under most circumstances for the rape of their wives. There remain alarming exceptions in no fewer than 30 states, however. For example, the husband is exempt when he does not need to use force because his wife is asleep, unconscious, or mentally or physically impaired. These interpretations still rest on the notion that the marriage contract entitles a husband to sex (Bergen 2006).

In the future, feminist scholarship can be expected to grow dramatically. Particularly on topics such as white-collar crime, drinking behavior, drug abuse, and differential sentencing rates between the genders, as well as on the fundamental question of how to define deviance, feminist scholars will have much to say.

We have seen that over the past century, sociologists have taken many different approaches in studying deviance, arousing some controversy in the process. Table 24-2 summarizes the various theoretical approaches to this topic.

TABLE **24-2** SOCIOLOGICAL PERSPECTIVES
ON DEVIANCE

Tracking Sociological Perspectives

Approach	Theoretical Perspective	Proponents	Emphasis
Anomie	Functionalist	Émile Durkheim	Adaptation to societal norms
		Robert Merton	
Cultural transmission/ Differential association	Interactionist	Edwin Sutherland	Patterns learned through others
Social disorganization	Interactionist	Clifford Shaw	Communal relationships
		Henry McKay	
Labeling/Social constructionist	Interactionist	Howard Becker	Societal response to acts
		William Chambliss	
Conflict	Conflict	Richard Quinney	Dominance by authorized agents
			Discretionary justice
Feminist	Conflict/Feminist	Freda Adler	Role of gender
		Meda Chesney-Lind	Women as victims and perpetrators

MODULE 24 | **Recap and Review**

Summary

Deviant behavior is behavior that violates social norms. A
wide range of behavior may be classified as deviant, and
everyone violates social norms in some situations.

1. Some forms of **deviance** carry a negative social **stigma,**
   while other forms are more or less accepted.

2. From a functionalist point of view, deviance and its
   consequences help to define the limits of proper behavior.

3. Some interactionists maintain that people learn
   criminal behavior by interacting with others (**cultural
   transmission**). To them, deviance results from
   exposure to attitudes that are favorable to criminal acts
   (**differential association**).

4. Other interactionists attribute increases in crime and
   deviance to the absence or breakdown of communal
   relationships and social institutions, such as the
   family, school, church, and local government (**social
   disorganization theory**).

5. An important aspect of **labeling theory** is the
   recognition that some people are viewed as deviant,
   while others who engage in the same behavior are not.

6. From the conflict perspective, laws and punishments are
   a reflection of the interests of the powerful.

7. The feminist perspective emphasizes cultural attitudes
   and differential economic relationships to help explain
   gender differences in deviance and crime.

Thinking Critically

1. Research a culture you are unfamiliar with. Do any of
   the customs seem deviant to you? Which of your own
   customs might seem deviant to members of that culture?

2. Using examples drawn from work or college life,
   illustrate each of Merton's five modes of individual
   adaptation.

3. Explain the presence of both criminals and law-abiding
   citizens in an inner-city neighborhood in terms of the
   interactionist perspective.

Key Terms

Anomie

Anomie theory of deviance

Cultural transmission

Deviance

Differential association

Differential justice

Labeling theory

Social constructionist perspective

Social disorganization theory

Societal-reaction approach

Stigma

Crime is on everyone's mind. Until recently, college campuses were viewed as havens from crime. But as Box 25-1 shows, at today's colleges and universities, crime goes well beyond cheating and senior class pranks.

Crime is a violation of criminal law for which some governmental authority applies formal penalties. It represents a deviation from formal social norms administered by the state. Laws divide crimes into various categories, depending on the severity of the offense, the age of the offender, the potential punishment, and the court that holds jurisdiction over the case.

Types of Crime

Rather than relying solely on legal categories, however, sociologists classify crimes in terms of how they are committed and how society views the offenses. In this module we will examine six types of crime differentiated by sociologists: victimless crimes, professional crime, organized crime, white-collar and technology-based crime, hate crimes, and transnational crime.

Victimless Crimes

When we think of crime, we tend to think of acts that endanger people's economic or personal well-being against their will (or without their direct knowledge). In contrast, sociologists use the term **victimless crime** to describe the willing exchange among adults of widely desired but illegal goods and services, such as prostitution (Schur 1965, 1985).

Some activists are working to decriminalize many of these illegal practices. Supporters of decriminalization are troubled by the attempt to legislate a moral code for adults. In their view, prostitution, drug abuse, gambling, and other victimless crimes are impossible to prevent. The already overburdened criminal justice system should instead devote its resources to street crimes and other offenses with obvious victims.

Sociology on Campus

BOX 25-1

Campus Crime

According to a national survey released in 2008, 72 percent of college students consider campus safety "very important" in selecting a college. A generation earlier, would campus crime have been uppermost in the minds of prospective students?

Research on crime in college has focused on interpersonal violence ("date rape," as it is sometimes trivialized) and the way in which colleges handle such incidents. In 2007, two very different events brought campus crime to national attention. First, there was the April 16, 2007, rampage at Virginia Tech. In its aftermath, observers questioned whether campus officials should have notified students and employees of the first shootings, at a dormitory, during the two hours that passed before the gunman's second attack in a classroom building. The federal law known as the Clery Act, passed in 1990, requires timely warnings of campus crime, but how they should be delivered and how specific they should be (for example, whether the

names of alleged assailants should be revealed) is unclear.

The second incident, the death of a girl in her dormitory room at Eastern Michigan University, led to the resignation of the university's president. For two months, officials had assured her parents that she died a natural death. Later, her family learned that she had been raped and murdered, and that her body had been missing for three days.

These and other less publicized incidents have prompted colleges to become more forthcoming about campus crime and to provide better security. However, the growing trend toward living (and partying) off campus poses a challenge to their efforts. Student safety at internship sites and study-abroad programs is even more difficult to ensure.

Making judgments about campus crime based on the reports mandated by the Clery Act is difficult. Because these documents include only reported incidents, they may or may not be accurate. The 2012 data from UCLA, which has over 27,000 students, for example, show that the total number of forcible sex offenses was 14.

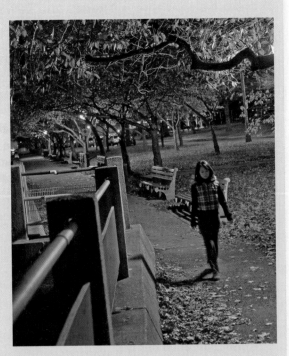

> The federal law known as the Clery Act, passed in 1990, requires timely warnings of campus crime, but how they should be delivered and how specific they should be is unclear.

LET'S DISCUSS

1. Do some research on campus crime. What is the crime rate on your college campus, and how does it compare to crime rates at other schools? Relate what you have learned to sociological theory.

2. What have officials at your college done to discourage campus crime?

Sources: Department of Justice 2013:Table 9; Interface Group Report (Virginia Tech) 2007; Lipka 2009; National Institute of Justice 2005; *New York Times* 2007, 2008; Security on Campus 2008.

Despite widespread use of the term *victimless crime,* however, many people object to the notion that there is no victim other than the offender in such crimes. Excessive drinking, compulsive gambling, and illegal drug use contribute to an enormous amount of personal and property damage. A person with a drinking problem may become abusive to a spouse or children; a compulsive gambler or drug user may steal to pursue his or her obsession. And feminist sociologists contend that prostitution, as well as the more disturbing aspects of pornography, reinforce the misconception that women are "toys" who can be treated as objects rather than people. According to critics of decriminalization, society must not give tacit approval to conduct that has such harmful consequences (Melissa Farley and Malarek 2008).

The controversy over decriminalization reminds us of the important insights of labeling that conflict theorists presented earlier. Underlying this debate are two questions: Who has the power to label gambling, prostitution, and public drunkenness as "crimes"? and Who has the power to label such behaviors as "victimless"? The answer is generally the state legislatures, and in some cases, the police and the courts.

Professional Crime

Although the adage "Crime doesn't pay" is familiar, many people do make a career of illegal activities. A **professional criminal,** or *career criminal,* is a person who pursues crime as a day-to-day occupation, developing skilled techniques and enjoying a certain degree of status among other criminals. Some professional criminals specialize in burglary, safecracking, hijacking of cargo, pickpocketing, and shoplifting. Such people have acquired skills that reduce the likelihood of arrest, conviction, and imprisonment. As a result, they may have long careers in their chosen professions.

Edwin Sutherland (1937) offered pioneering insights into the behavior of professional criminals by publishing an annotated account written by a professional thief. Unlike the person who engages in crime only once or twice, professional thieves make a business of stealing. They devote their entire working time to planning and executing crimes, and sometimes travel across the nation to pursue their "professional duties." Like people in regular occupations, professional thieves consult with their colleagues concerning the demands of work, becoming part of a subculture of similarly occupied individuals. They exchange information on places to burglarize, on outlets for unloading stolen goods, and on ways of securing bail bonds if arrested.

Organized Crime

A 1976 government report devotes three pages to defining the term *organized crime.* For our purposes, we will consider **organized crime** to be the work of a group that regulates relations among criminal enterprises involved in illegal activities, including prostitution, gambling, and the smuggling and sale of illegal drugs. Organized crime dominates the world of illegal business just as large corporations dominate the conventional business world. It allocates territory, sets prices for goods and services, and acts as an arbitrator in internal disputes. A secret, conspiratorial activity, it generally evades law enforcement. It takes over legitimate businesses, gains influence over labor unions, corrupts public officials, intimidates witnesses in criminal trials, and even "taxes" merchants in exchange for "protection" (National Advisory Commission on Criminal Justice 1976).

Organized crime serves as a means of upward mobility for groups of people struggling to escape poverty. Sociologist Daniel Bell (1953) used the term *ethnic succession* to describe the sequential passage of leadership from Irish Americans in the early part of the 20th century to Jewish Americans in the 1920s and then to Italian Americans in the early 1930s. Ethnic succession has become more complex, reflecting the diversity of the nation's latest immigrants. Colombian, Mexican, Russian, Chinese, Pakistani, and Nigerian immigrants are among those who have begun to play a significant role in organized crime activities (Chin 1996; Kleinknecht 1996).

White-Collar and Technology-Based Crime

Income tax evasion, stock manipulation, consumer fraud, bribery and extraction of kickbacks, embezzlement, and misrepresentation in advertising—these are all examples of **white-collar crime,** illegal acts committed in the course of business activities, often by affluent, "respectable" people. In his 1939 presidential address to the American Sociological Association, Edwin Sutherland (1949, 1983) likened these crimes to organized crime because they are often perpetrated through occupational roles.

"KICKBACKS, EMBEZZLEMENT, PRICE-FIXING, BRIBERY... THIS IS AN EXTREMELY HIGH-CRIME AREA."

A new type of white-collar crime has emerged in recent decades: computer crime. The use of high technology allows criminals to carry out embezzlement or electronic fraud, often leaving few traces, or to gain access to a company's inventory without leaving home. According to a study by the FBI and the National White Collar Crime Center, over 300,000 Internet crimes are reported every year, ranging from scams on online auction sites to identity theft (Internet Crime Complaint Center 2012).

When Charles Horton Cooley spoke of the self and Erving Goffman of impression management, surely neither scholar could have envisioned the insidious crime of identity theft. Each year about 14 percent of all adults find that their personal information has been misused for criminal purposes. Unfortunately, with our society's growing reliance on electronic financial transactions, assuming someone else's identity has become increasingly easy (Vamosi et al. 2010).

Identity theft does not necessarily require technology. A criminal can obtain someone's personal information by pickpocketing or by intercepting mail. However, the widespread exchange of information online has allowed criminals to access large amounts of personal information. Public awareness of the potential harm from identity theft took a giant leap in the aftermath of September 11, 2001, when investigations revealed that several hijackers had used fraudulent IDs to open bank accounts, rent apartments, and board planes. A law enacted in 2004 makes identity theft punishable by a mandatory prison sentence if it is linked to other crimes. Still, unauthorized disclosures of information, even if accidental, persist (Brubaker 2008).

Sutherland (1940) coined the term *white-collar crime* in 1939 to refer to acts by individuals, but the term has been broadened more recently to include offenses by businesses and corporations as well. *Corporate crime,* or any act by a corporation that is punishable by the government, takes many forms and includes individuals, organizations, and institutions among its victims. Corporations may engage in anticompetitive behavior, environmental pollution, medical fraud, tax fraud, stock fraud and manipulation, accounting fraud, the production of unsafe goods, bribery and corruption, and health and safety violations (J. Coleman 2006).

For many years, corporate wrongdoers got off lightly in court by documenting their long history of charitable contributions and agreeing to help law enforcement officials find other white-collar criminals. Unfortunately, that is still the case. The highly visible jailing of multimedia personality Martha Stewart in 2004, as well as recent disclosures of "Wall Street greed," may lead the casual observer to think that government is cracking down on white-collar crime. However, an independent analysis found that from 2000 through 2009, the number of white-collar crimes that were prosecuted increased only modestly (Transactional Records Access Clearinghouse 2009).

The leniency shown to white-collar criminals is not limited to the United States. Japan did not level a fine for insider trading on a major financial corporation until 2012. The profit from the crime was about $119,000; the penalty was $600 (Fukase and Inagaki 2012).

Even when a person is convicted of corporate crime, the verdict generally does not harm his or her reputation and career

aspirations nearly so much as conviction for street crime would. Apparently, the label "white-collar criminal" does not carry the stigma of the label "felon convicted of a violent crime." Conflict theorists don't find such differential treatment surprising. They argue that the criminal justice system largely disregards the crimes of the affluent, focusing on crimes committed by the poor. Generally, if an offender holds a position of status and influence, his or her crime is treated as less serious, and the sanction is much more lenient (Simpson 2013).

Hate Crimes

In contrast to other crimes, hate crimes are defined not only by the perpetrators' actions, but by the purpose of their conduct as well. The government considers an ordinary crime to be a **hate crime** when the offender is motivated to choose a victim based on race, religion, ethnic group, national origin, or sexual orientation, and when evidence shows that hatred prompted the offender to commit the crime. Hate crimes are sometimes referred to as *bias crimes* (Department of Justice 2008).

In 1990, Congress passed the Hate Crime Statistics Act, which created a national mandate to identify crimes based on race, religion, ethnic group, and national origin. (Before that time, only 12 states had monitored such crimes.) Since then the act has been broadened to include disabilities, both physical and mental, and sexual orientation. In addition, some jurisdictions impose harsher sanctions (jail time or fines) for hate crimes than for other crimes. For example, if the penalty for assault is a year in jail, the penalty for an assault identified as a hate crime might be two years.

In 2013, law enforcement agencies submitted data on hate crimes to the federal government. The statistics included official reports of almost 7,200 hate crimes and bias-motivated offenses. As Figure 25-1 shows, race was the apparent motivation in approximately 48 percent of the reports. Although vandalism and intimidation were the most common crimes, 40 percent of the incidents involved assault, rape, or murder.

The vast majority of hate crimes, although not all of them, are committed by members of the dominant group against those who are relatively powerless. One in every six racially based hate crimes is an anti-White incident. Except for the most horrific hate crimes, these offenses receive little media attention; anti-White incidents probably receive even less. Clearly, hostility based on race knows no boundaries.

FIGURE 25-1 **Categorization of Reported Hate Crimes**

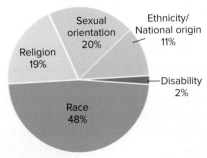

Source: Incidents reported for 2012 in 2013. Federal Bureau of Investigation 2013.

Transnational Crime

More and more, scholars and police officials are turning their attention to **transnational crime,** or crime that occurs across multiple national borders. In the past, international crime was often limited to the clandestine shipment of goods across the border between two countries. But increasingly, crime is no more restricted by such borders than is legal commerce. Rather than concentrating on specific countries, international crime now spans the globe.

Historically, probably the most dreadful example of transnational crime has been slavery. At first, governments did not regard slavery as a crime, but merely regulated it as they would the trade in goods. In the 20th century, transnational crime grew to embrace trafficking in endangered species, drugs, and stolen art and antiquities.

Transnational crime is not exclusive of some of the other types of crime we have discussed. For example, organized criminal networks are increasingly global. Technology definitely facilitates their illegal activities, such as trafficking in child pornography. Beginning in the 1990s, the United Nations began to categorize transnational crimes; Table 25-1 lists some of the more common types.

Bilateral cooperation in the pursuit of border criminals such as smugglers has been common for many years. The first global effort to control international crime was the International Criminal Police Organization (Interpol), a cooperative network of European police forces founded to stem the movement of political revolutionaries across borders. While such efforts to fight transnational crime may seem lofty—an activity with which any government should cooperate—they are complicated by sensitive legal and security issues. Most nations that have signed protocols issued by the United Nations, including the United States, have expressed concern over potential encroachments on their national judicial systems, as well as concern over their national security. Thus, they have been reluctant to share certain types of intelligence data. The terrorist attacks of September 11, 2001, increased both the interest in combating transnational crime and sensitivity to the risks of sharing intelligence data (Deflem 2005; Felson and Kalaitzidis 2005).

use your **sociological imagination**

As the editor of an online news service, how might you treat stories on corporate or white-collar crime differently from those on violent crime?

Crime Statistics

Crime statistics are not as accurate as social scientists would like, especially since they deal with an issue of grave concern to the people of the United States. Unfortunately, they are frequently cited as if they were completely reliable. Such data do serve as an indicator of police activity, as well as an approximate indication of the level of certain crimes. Yet it would be a mistake to interpret these data as an exact representation of the incidence of crime.

Index Crimes and Victimization Surveys

Typically, the crime data reported in the United States are based on **index crimes,** or the eight types of crime tabulated each year by the Federal Bureau of Investigation (FBI). This category of criminal behavior generally consists of those serious offenses that people think of when they express concern about the nation's crime problem. Index crimes include murder, rape, robbery, and assault—all of which are violent crimes committed against people—as well as the property crimes of burglary, larceny-theft, motor vehicle theft, and arson (Table 25-2). The crime index is published annually by the FBI as part of the *Uniform Crime Reports.*

Obviously, many serious offenses, such as white-collar crimes, are not included in this index (although they are recorded elsewhere). In addition, the crime index is disproportionately devoted to property crimes, whereas most citizens are more worried about violent crimes. Thus, a significant decrease in the number of rapes and robberies could be overshadowed by a slightly larger increase in the number of automobiles stolen, leading to the mistaken impression that *personal* safety is more at risk than before.

The most serious limitation of official crime statistics is that they include only those crimes actually *reported* to law enforcement agencies. Because members of racial and ethnic minority groups often distrust law enforcement agencies, they may not contact the police. Feminist sociologists and others have noted that many women do not report rape or spousal abuse out of fear they will be blamed for the crime.

TABLE **25-1** TYPES OF TRANSNATIONAL CRIME

Bankruptcy and insurance fraud

Computer crime (treating computers as both a tool and a target of crime)

Corruption and bribery of public officials

Environmental crime

Hijacking of airplanes (skyjacking)

Illegal drug trade

Illegal money transfers (money laundering)

Illegal sales of firearms and ammunition

Infiltration of legal businesses

Intellectual property crime

Networking of criminal organizations

Sea piracy

Terrorism

Theft of art and cultural objects

Trafficking in body parts (includes illegal organ transplants)

Trafficking in human beings (includes sex trade)

Source: Compiled and updated by the author based on Mueller 2001 and United Nations Office on Drugs and Crime 2010.

TABLE 25-2 NATIONAL CRIME RATES AND PERCENTAGE CHANGE

Crime Index Offenses in 2012	Number Reported	Rate per 100,000 Inhabitants	Percentage Change in Rate Since 2003
Violent crime			
Murder	14,827	5	−17
Forcible rape	84,376	27	−17
Robbery	354,520	113	−21
Aggravated assault	760,739	242	−18
Total	1,214,462	387	−19
Property crime			
Burglary	2,103,787	670	−10
Larceny-theft	6,150,598	1,959	−19
Motor vehicle theft	721,053	230	−47
Total	8,975,438	2,859	−20

Notes: Arson was designated an index offense beginning in 1979; data on arson were still incomplete as of 2012. Because of rounding, the offenses may not add to totals.
Source: Department of Justice 2013: Tables 1, 1a.

Partly because of these deficiencies in official statistics, the National Crime Victimization Survey was initiated in 1972. The Bureau of Justice Statistics, in compiling this annual report, seeks information from law enforcement agencies, but also interviews households across the nation and asks if they were victims of a specific set of crimes during the preceding year. In general, those who administer **victimization surveys** question ordinary people, not police officers, to determine whether they have been victims of crime.

Unfortunately, like other crime data, victimization surveys have particular limitations. They require that victims understand what has happened to them and are willing to disclose such information to interviewers. Fraud, income tax evasion, and blackmail are examples of crimes that are unlikely to be reported in victimization studies.

Crime Trends

Crime fills the news reports on television, over the Internet, and in the newspaper. As a result, the public regards crime as a major social problem. Yet there has been a significant decline in violent crime in the United States in recent years, after many years of increases.

How much has crime declined? Consider this: the rate of crime being reported in 2012 was comparable to what it was back when gasoline cost 29 cents a gallon and the average person earned less than $6,000 a year. That was 1963.

Dramatic declines have occurred within the last decade. As Table 25-2 shows, both violent crime and property crime dropped about 20 percent in the last 10 years. Although a tragic 14,827 people were murdered in 2012, in 1991 that number was a staggering 24,700. Declines have also been registered in victimization surveys (Figure 25-2).

FIGURE 25-2 Victimization Rates, 1993–2012

Today's victimization rate has dropped to less than half the 1993 rate.

Source: Truman et al. 2013.

What explains these declines in both index crimes and victimization rates? Possible explanations include the following:

- Community-oriented policing and crime prevention programs
- New gun control laws
- A massive increase in the prison population, which at least prevents inmates from committing crimes outside prison
- New surveillance technologies
- Better residential and business security
- The decline of the crack cocaine epidemic, which soared in the late 1980s
- The aging of the population, as the number of people in their 50s increased and the number in their 20s decreased

No single explanation could account for such a marked change in crime rates. Taken together, however, these changes in public policy, public health, technology, and demographics may well explain it (Florida 2011; Uggen 2012; James Q. Wilson 2011; Wood 2012).

Feminist scholars draw our attention to one significant countertrend: the proportion of major crimes committed by women has increased. However, violent crimes committed by women, which have never been common, have declined. Despite the "mean girls" headlines in the tabloid magazines, every reliable measure shows that among women, fights, weapons possession, assaults, and violent injuries have plunged over the last decade (Males and Lind 2010).

International Crime Rates

If developing reliable crime data is difficult in the United States, making useful cross-national comparisons is even more difficult. Nevertheless, with some care, we can offer preliminary conclusions about how crime rates differ around the world.

During the 1980s and 1990s, violent crimes were much more common in the United States than in western Europe. Murders, rapes, and robberies were reported to the police at much higher rates in the United States. Yet the incidence of certain other types of crime appears to be higher elsewhere. For example, England, Ireland, Denmark, and New Zealand all have higher rates of car theft than the United States. Developing nations have significant rates of reported homicide due to civil unrest and political conflict among civilians (van Dijk et al. 2007).

A particularly worrisome development has been the rapid escalation in homicide rates in developing countries that supply drugs to industrialized countries, especially the United States. The huge profits generated by cocaine exports to North America and Europe have allowed drug gangs to arm themselves to the point of becoming illegal armies. Homicide rates in Mexico are now about twice as high as those in the United States. Honduras, Guatemala, Venezuela, and El Salvador's homicide rates are three to five times those of Mexico (*The Economist* 2010c).

Why are rates of violent crime generally so much higher in the United States than in western Europe? Sociologist Elliott Currie (1985, 1998) has suggested that our society places greater emphasis on individual economic achievement than other societies. At the same time, many observers have noted that the culture of the United States has long tolerated, if not condoned, many forms of violence. Coupled with sharp disparities between poor and affluent citizens, significant unemployment, and substantial alcohol and drug abuse, these factors combine to produce a climate conducive to crime.

Another contributor to violent crime in the United States is the prevalence of guns in our society. Although gun rights activists claim that access to guns does not contribute to violent behavior, the United States has a far higher rate of gun violence than other countries where gun ownership is more tightly controlled. In the Social Policy section that follows, we'll consider the pros and cons in the heated debate over gun control.

Taking Sociology to Work

Stephanie Vezzani, Special Agent, U.S. Secret Service

Stephanie Vezzani wasn't sure what she wanted to major in when she entered the University of Akron, but she did know what she wanted to do with her life: she wanted a career as a crime fighter. Vezzani began as an accounting major, but switched to sociology when she discovered the department offered a special concentration in law enforcement.

Vezzani is now an agent with the U.S. Secret Service, whose twofold mission is to protect high-ranking officials and their families and to investigate financial crimes, including counterfeiting, identity theft, and computer-based attacks on the financial, banking, and telecommunications industries.

She has tackled both aspects of the job. For her, a typical week would include working on a criminal investigation in a field office or traveling around the country with a government official in need of protection.

Vezzani finds that travel is one of the most exciting aspects of her job. Over the past six years she has visited Russia, Turkey, Jordan, Vietnam, and South Korea. She also attended the 2002 Winter Olympics in Salt Lake City, where she provided protection for the athletes living in the Olympic Village. Vezzani relishes meeting people from different cultures, and of course she loves the sights she gets to see. "The architecture in St. Petersburg, Russia, was amazing," she says.

Vezzani uses her training in sociology on a daily basis, as she interviews suspects, witnesses, and victims of crime. "It is critical in the field of law enforcement to have an understanding of people's relationships and the beliefs and value systems that contribute to their decision making," she explains. "Sociology has provided me the knowledge to speak to and listen to people with different values and cultures in order to complete my job at the highest level possible."

LET'S DISCUSS

1. Besides an awareness of different beliefs, values, and cultures, what else might sociology offer to those who serve in law enforcement?

2. Law enforcement is a relatively new career option for women. What special strengths do you think a woman might bring to police work?

About 20 minutes into the midnight screening of *The Dark Knight Rises,* James Holmes, a disturbed young man armed with a handgun, a shotgun, and a semiautomatic rifle, burst into the Century 16 movie theater in Aurora, Colorado, and began firing indiscriminately. When the attack was over, 12 people lay dead and 58 others were injured. On that day in July 2012, journalists noted that the crime marked the 125th fatal mass shooting since the 1999 attack on Columbine High, also in Colorado.

Before the year's end, another mass shooting took place in Newtown, Connecticut. Twenty-six people, most of them children, were killed at the Sandy Hook Elementary School. Unlike other mass killings, the event in Newtown galvanized the public, raising calls for stricter gun controls. Yet as gun ownership advocates were quick to point out, Connecticut already had the fifth most restrictive gun laws of any state in the nation (Brady Campaign 2013; Hopper and Ortiz 2012).

Looking at the Issue

Guns and ammunition are big business in the United States, where the Second Amendment to the Constitution guarantees the "right of the people to keep and bear arms." Currently, about 35 percent of U.S. households have some type of firearm on the premises. Informal gun clubs of both a primary- and secondary-group nature flourish across the country. On a national basis, powerful formal organizations promote gun ownership. Clearly, owning a gun is not a deviant act in our society (Federal Bureau of Investigation 2012).

Those U.S. households that own guns possess a lot of them. To put the statistics into perspective, the United States has more guns per person than any other country in the world—89 firearms per 100 people. Yemen holds second place with 55 firearms per 100 people; Switzerland has 46 and Finland, 45 guns per 100 residents (Zakaria 2012).

Over the last two decades, the demand for stricter gun controls has declined rather than grown. At its highest point of support, 66 percent of Americans felt that controlling gun ownership was more important than protecting the right to own a gun. By 2012, even in the aftermath of the shootings in Newtown, that measure had dropped to 49 percent. During this time, the National Rifle Association (NRA) used its impressive power to block or dilute gun control efforts.

Although reported crime has declined in recent years, the role of firearms in crime has remained fairly consistent. Over the past five years, two-thirds of all murders were committed with firearms. Although gun owners frequently insist that they need to own firearms to protect themselves and their loved ones from violent criminals, high-profile assassinations of public figures such as President John F. Kennedy, Senator

Robert Kennedy, Dr. Martin Luther King Jr., and Beatle John Lennon have forced legislators to consider stricter gun control measures.

Gun control legislation began with the Brady Handgun Violence Prevention Act, named after White House press secretary Jim Brady, who was seriously wounded in the 1981 assassination attempt against President Ronald Reagan. John Hinckley, the would-be assassin, had given false information about himself at the pawnshop where he bought the gun that he used to shoot Reagan and Brady. The Brady Act, which took effect in 1994, mandates that firearms dealers must run criminal history background checks on people who wish to purchase guns. About 2 percent of all gun purchases are denied as a result of such background checks. Denials are most commonly made because the prospective purchaser is a convicted felon or has had a restraining order filed against him because of domestic violence (Federal Bureau of Investigation 2012; Frandsen et al. 2013).

Not satisfied with the restrictions in the Brady Act, gun control advocates claim that even stricter legislation is needed. Opponents respond that the Brady Act hampers only honest people; those with criminal intent can turn to other sources for guns. Instead of passing further legislation, they suggest strengthening and enforcing existing penalties for the illegal use of guns.

In 2008, in the landmark case *District of Columbia v. Heller,* the Supreme Court struck down a near-total ban on firearms in the nation's capital by a 5-4 ruling. Two years later, by a 5-4 vote in *McDonald v. City of Chicago,* the Court overturned a firearms ban that had stood in Chicago for 28 years. The two verdicts were lauded by those who favor gun rights, but denounced by

A gun owner engages in target practice with her bolt-action rifle. Many gun enthusiasts enjoy competing in marksmanship contests.

—Continued

advocates of gun control. Gun rights groups continue to test the constitutionality of other restrictions on gun ownership, even as gun control advocates work to craft legislation that will be acceptable to the justices (Pilkington 2010; Winkler 2009).

Applying Sociology

As we have noted before, sociologists and other researchers often have difficulty securing funding for research on controversial issues (see the Social Policy section in Chapter 2, on human sexual behavior). In 1993, a study commissioned by the Centers for Disease Control (CDC) concluded that statistically, a firearm that is kept in the home is far more likely to be involved in the death of a family member than to be used in self-defense. In response, gun supporters charged that the CDC's study was politically motivated. Three years later, under pressure from lobbyists, Congress prohibited all federal agencies from collecting data and from funding or conducting research on firearms ownership and gun violence. The ban has stood since 1996. Although privately funded research continues, donors' willingness and financial ability to support it varies over time (Kellerman et al. 1993; S. Lee 2013).

Particularly alarming to sociologists has been the virtual cutoff of federal funding for research into the causes of gun violence. Studies of the links between video games, media images, and gun violence have effectively been blocked by those who suspect that such research would support gun controls. Lobbyists have even blocked funds that would help the CDC to better understand how and when the use of firearms results in violent death (Hillsman 2013).

Conflict theorists contend that powerful groups like the NRA can dominate the legislative process in this way because of their ability to mobilize resources in opposition to the will of the majority. Founded in 1871, the NRA has over 4 million members; state rifle associations, with 4 to 5 million members, support many of the NRA's goals. In contrast, the Brady Campaign to Prevent Gun Violence, a key organization in the gun control battle, has only 400,000 members. Compared to the NRA's formidable war chest, the Brady Campaign's resources are limited.

Interactionists note that both opponents and proponents of gun control use symbols to their advantage. Opponents typically point to the Constitution and the tradition of gun ownership. Proponents point to spectacular episodes of violence, such as spree shootings on college campuses, as proof of the need to restrict firearms sales. Yet gun rights supporters see the same events as proof that students need guns to defend themselves (Lio et al. 2008).

Interactionists have also studied how gun rights organizations like the NRA present their argument to their own members. Among sympathizers, they frame the issue not so much as one of safety or crime, but of civil rights. Gun rights advocates see the Constitution as the basis for their campaign to facilitate gun ownership (Gregory 2007).

Initiating Policy

Advocates for stricter gun control laws recommend a series of measures that they would like to see enacted:

- Strengthen the tools that law enforcement officers need to crack down on corrupt gun dealers and curb illegal gun trafficking.
- Extend Brady background checks to all gun sales.
- Seek to regulate assault weapons and large-capacity ammunition magazines.
- Stop large-volume gun sales that supply gun traffickers.

Towns, states, and the federal government all have the authority to regulate the possession and sale of firearms, and gun control advocates have attempted to pass these measures at all levels of government.

These proposed legal restrictions on gun ownership have met strong opposition from both the NRA and firearms manufacturers. The NRA—which spent $20 million in the 2012 election cycle alone—has been particularly successful in defeating political candidates who favor stricter gun controls, and in backing those who seek to weaken such restrictions. Except in a handful of states, office seekers rarely risk taking an antigun position. Alarmed by the NRA's rhetoric, many voters fear that gun controls will restrict their ability to protect themselves, independent of law enforcement. Thus, in the year after the Newtown shootings, state legislatures enacted 109 new gun laws, 70 of which *loosened* firearms restrictions (M. Scherer 2013; Yourish and Buchanan 2013).

Public health advocates have weighed in on the issue, noting the 30,000 people in the United States who die every year through gun violence, whether by suicide, homicide, or accidental discharge. This group advocates making guns safer—for example, by adding an indicator that the gun is loaded and/or a latch that prevents a magazine from being removed with a bullet still in the firing chamber. A more sophisticated approach to increasing safety would be to "personalize" firearms by requiring the owner/user to activate a code before the gun can be used. Public safety officials have also weighed in, observing that in 10 states firearms deaths exceed motor vehicle deaths (G. Brown 2008a, 2008b; Violence Policy Center 2012).

TAKE THE ISSUE WITH YOU

1. Do you see guns more as weapons that could jeopardize your safety or as a protection against those who would harm you?

2. What are the statistics on crimes committed with a firearm in your state? How many people die or are injured by guns every year? How strict are restrictions on gun ownership?

3. Does the government have a right to limit the types of weapons that manufacturers can sell? Why or why not?

Summary

Crime is deviation from formal social norms administered by the state.

1. Sociologists differentiate among **victimless crimes** (such as drug use and prostitution), crime committed by **professional criminals, organized crime, white-collar crime,** and **international crime.**

2. Crime statistics are among the least reliable social data, partly because so many crimes are not reported to law enforcement agencies. Rates of violent crime are higher in the United States than in other Western societies, although they have been dropping.

3. Gun violence has become a major problem not just in the United States, but around the world. Yet gun control legislation is extremely controversial, opposed by powerful interest groups whose members see it as an abridgment of their constitutional right to bear arms.

Thinking Critically

1. Why is it useful to sociologists to have victimization surveys in addition to reported crime data?

2. Apply at least two of the theories discussed in Module 24 to the problem of professional crime. Which theory seems to provide the best explanation?

Key Terms

Crime

Hate crime

Index crimes

Organized crime

Professional criminal

Transnational crime

Victimization survey

Victimless crime

White-collar crime

Mastering This Chapter

taking sociology with you

1 Describe the mechanisms of social control, both formal and informal, on your campus. Which is more effective, formal or informal control?

2 Explain the presence of both criminals and law-abiding citizens in an inner-city neighborhood in terms of the functionalist perspective.

3 Pay a visit to your local courthouse and observe a trial by jury from the point of view of a sociologist. Then describe what you saw and heard using sociological concepts.

Anomie Durkheim's term for the loss of direction felt in a society when social control of individual behavior has become ineffective.

Anomie theory of deviance Robert Merton's theory of deviance as an adaptation of socially prescribed goals or of the means governing their attainment, or both.

Conformity Going along with peers—individuals of our own status who have no special right to direct our behavior.

Control theory A view of conformity and deviance that suggests that our connection to members of society leads us to systematically conform to society's norms.

Crime A violation of criminal law for which some governmental authority applies formal penalties.

Cultural transmission A school of criminology that argues that criminal behavior is learned through social interactions.

Deviance Behavior that violates the standards of conduct or expectations of a group or society.

Differential association A theory of deviance that holds that violation of rules results from exposure to attitudes favorable to criminal acts.

Differential justice Differences in the way social control is exercised over different groups.

Formal social control Social control that is carried out by authorized agents, such as police officers, judges, school administrators, and employers.

Hate crime A criminal offense committed because of the offender's bias against a race, religion, ethnic group, national origin, or sexual orientation. Also referred to as *bias crime*.

Index crimes The eight types of crime tabulated each year by the FBI in the *Uniform Crime Reports:* murder, rape, robbery, assault, burglary, theft, motor vehicle theft, and arson.

Informal social control Social control that is carried out casually by ordinary people through such means as laughter, smiles, and ridicule.

Labeling theory An approach to deviance that attempts to explain why certain people are viewed as deviants while others engaged in the same behavior are not.

Law Governmental social control.

Obedience Compliance with higher authorities in a hierarchical structure.

Organized crime The work of a group that regulates relations among criminal enterprises involved in illegal activities, including prostitution, gambling, and the smuggling and sale of illegal drugs.

Professional criminal A person who pursues crime as a day-to-day occupation, developing skilled techniques and enjoying a certain degree of status among other criminals.

Sanction A penalty or reward for conduct concerning a social norm.

Social constructionist perspective An approach to deviance that emphasizes the role of culture in the creation of the deviant identity.

Social control The techniques and strategies for preventing deviant human behavior in any society.

Social disorganization theory The theory that crime and deviance are caused by the absence or breakdown of communal relationships and social institutions.

Societal-reaction approach Another name for *labeling theory*.

Stigma A label used to devalue members of certain social groups.

Transnational crime Crime that occurs across multiple national borders.

Victimization survey A questionnaire or interview given to a sample of the population to determine whether people have been victims of crime.

Victimless crime A term used by sociologists to describe the willing exchange among adults of widely desired but illegal goods and services.

White-collar crime Illegal acts committed by affluent, "respectable" individuals in the course of business activities.

Read each question carefully and then select the best answer.

1. Society brings about acceptance of basic norms through techniques and strategies for preventing deviant human behavior. This process is termed
   a. stigmatization.
   b. labeling.
   c. law.
   d. social control.

2. Which sociological perspective argues that people must respect social norms if any group or society is to survive?
   a. the conflict perspective
   b. the interactionist perspective
   c. the functionalist perspective
   d. the feminist perspective

3. Stanley Milgram used the word *conformity* to mean
   a. going along with peers.
   b. compliance with higher authorities in a hierarchical structure.
   c. techniques and strategies for preventing deviant human behavior in any society.
   d. penalties and rewards for conduct concerning a social norm.

4. Which sociological theory suggests that our connection to members of society leads us to conform systematically to society's norms?
   a. feminist theory
   b. control theory
   c. interactionist theory
   d. functionalist theory

5. Which of the following statements is true of deviance?
   a. Deviance is always criminal behavior.
   b. Deviance is behavior that violates the standards of conduct or expectations of a group or society.
   c. Deviance is perverse behavior.
   d. Deviance is inappropriate behavior that cuts across all cultures and social orders.

6. Which sociologist illustrated the boundary-maintenance function of deviance in his study of Puritans in 17th-century New England?
   a. Kai Erikson
   b. Émile Durkheim
   c. Robert Merton
   d. Edwin Sutherland

7. Which of the following is an example of innovation as defined in Robert Merton's anomie theory of deviance?
   a. An advocate for a new form of government initiates a blog.
   b. A bureaucrat demands higher wages.
   c. A prison guard agitates for a labor union.
   d. Rather than writing an original essay, a student copies his submission from the Internet.

8. Which sociologist first advanced the idea that an individual undergoes the same basic socialization process whether learning conforming or deviant acts?
   a. Robert Merton
   b. Edwin Sutherland
   c. Travis Hirschi
   d. William Chambliss

9. Which of the following theories contends that criminal victimization increases when communal relationships and social institutions break down?
   a. labeling theory
   b. conflict theory
   c. social disorganization theory
   d. differential association theory

10. Which of the following conducted observation research on two groups of high school males (the Saints and the Roughnecks) and concluded that social class played an important role in the varying fortunes of the two groups?
   a. Richard Quinney
   b. Edwin Sutherland
   c. Émile Durkheim
   d. William Chambliss

11. If we fail to respect and obey social norms, we may face punishment through informal or formal _____ .

12. Police officers, judges, administrators, employers, military officers, and managers of movie theaters are all instruments of _____ social control.

13. Some norms are considered so important by a society that they are formalized into _____ controlling people's behavior.

14. It is important to underscore the fact that _____ is the primary source of conformity and obedience, including obedience to law.

15. _____ is a state of normlessness that typically occurs during a period of profound social change and disorder, such as a time of economic collapse.

16. Labeling theory is also called the _____ _____ approach.

17. _____ theorists view standards of deviant behavior as merely reflecting cultural norms, whereas _____ and _____ theorists point out that the most powerful groups in a society can shape laws and standards and determine who is (or is not) prosecuted as a criminal.

18. Feminists contend that prostitution and some forms of pornography are not _____ crimes.

19. Daniel Bell used the term _____ _____ to describe the process during which leadership of organized crime was transferred from Irish Americans to Jewish Americans and later to Italian Americans and others.

20. Consumer fraud, bribery, and income tax evasion are considered _____ _____ crimes.

8

Stratification and Social Mobility in the United States

Pedestrians pass by a homeless man panhandling for change in New York City. The United States is a society of contrasts between great wealth, modest means, and deep poverty.

How much do you think it costs to house a homeless person?

The National Alliance to End Homelessness has calculated the cost, including emergency medical treatment and police intervention, and it is staggering.

"Homelessness can be surprisingly costly for taxpayers. Fortunately, socially-responsible, cost-effective solutions exist.

For many city officials, community leaders, and even direct service providers, it often seems that placing homeless people in shelters is the most inexpensive way to meet the basic needs of people experiencing homelessness; some may even believe that shelters are an ideal solution. Research, however, has shown something surprisingly different.

The cost of homelessness can be quite high. Hospitalization, medical treatment, incarceration, police intervention, and emergency shelter expenses can add up quickly, making homelessness surprisingly expensive for municipalities and taxpayers.

People experiencing homelessness are more likely to access the most costly health care services.

According to a report in the *New England Journal of Medicine,* homeless people spent an average of four days longer per hospital visit than comparable non-homeless people. This extra cost, approximately $2,414 per hospitalization, is attributable to homelessness. . . .

Homelessness both causes and results from serious health care issues, including addiction, psychological disorders, HIV/AIDS, and a host of other ailments that require long-term, consistent care. Homelessness inhibits this care, as housing instability often detracts from regular medical attention, access to treatment, and recuperation. This inability to treat medical problems can aggravate these problems, making them both more dangerous and more costly.

As an example, physician and health care expert Michael Siegel found that the average cost to cure an alcohol-related illness is approximately $10,660. Another study found that the average cost to California hospitals of treating a substance abuser is about $8,360 for those in treatment, and $14,740 for those who are not.

People who are homeless spend more time in jail or prison, which is tremendously costly to the state and locality.

According to a University of Texas two-year survey of homeless individuals, each person cost the taxpayers $14,480 per year, primarily for overnight jail.

Often, time served is a result of laws specifically targeting the homeless population, including regulations against loitering, sleeping in cars, and begging.

According to a University of Texas two-year survey of homeless individuals, each person cost the taxpayers $14,480 per year, primarily for overnight jail.

A typical cost of a prison bed in a state or federal prison is $20,000 per year.

Emergency shelter is a costly alternative to permanent housing. While it is sometimes necessary for short-term crises, too often it serves as long-term housing. The cost of an emergency shelter bed funded by HUD's Emergency Shelter Grants program is approximately $8,067 more than the average annual cost of a federal housing subsidy (Section 8 Housing Certificate). A recent HUD study found that the cost of providing emergency shelter to families is generally as much or more than the cost of placing them in transitional or permanent housing.

Studies have shown that—in practice, and not just in theory—providing people experiencing chronic homelessness with permanent supportive housing saves taxpayers money. Permanent supportive housing refers to permanent housing coupled with supportive services. . . .

A cost study of rural homelessness from Portland, ME, found significant cost reductions when providing permanent supportive housing as opposed to serving the people while they remain homeless. The study specifically noted a 57 percent reduction in the cost of mental health services over a six-month period, partly due to a 79 percent drop in the cost of psychiatric hospitalization.

A study from Los Angeles, CA—home to 10 percent of the entire homeless population—found that placing four chronically homeless people into permanent supportive housing saved the city more than $80,000 per year. . . .

While seemingly counterintuitive, these examples clearly demonstrate that a housing-based approach to homelessness is not only more cost-effective than a shelter-based approach, but more effective in the long term. By focusing our resources on ending homelessness, we can make real progress toward eradicating the social problem while helping the country's most vulnerable residents."

(National Alliance to End Homelessness 2014)

eing down and out is a miserable experience; being homeless is worse. Yet recently, public patience with the homeless has begun to wear thin. In this excerpt from "Cost of Homelessness," the National Alliance to End Homelessness notes that in many places, homelessness is not just a deviant social status, but a criminal offense that could land you in jail. Paradoxically, just as those who can no longer pay the rent or the mortgage are swelling the ranks of the homeless, cities have been taking steps to remove them from view, to ban them from public places.

What explains this paradox? Conflict between people of different social classes is largely to blame. In a period when real estate values have declined precipitously, the presence of homeless people on city streets sends much the same signal as boarded-up, foreclosed properties. These signs of decay are deeply disturbing to the middle class and to those who inhabit newly gentrified neighborhoods.

Is social inequality an inescapable part of society? How does government policy affect the life chances of the working poor? Is this country still a place where a hardworking person can move up the social ladder? This chapter focuses on the unequal distribution of socially valued rewards and its consequences. We will begin by examining four general systems of stratification, including the one most familiar to us, the social class system. We will examine three sociological perspectives on stratification, paying particular attention to the theories of Karl Marx and Max Weber. We'll also ask whether stratification is universal and see what sociologists, including functionalist and conflict theorists, have to say about that question.

We will see too how sociologists define social class, and examine the consequences of stratification for people's wealth and income, safety, and educational opportunities. Then we will take a close look at poverty, particularly the question of who belongs to the underclass and why. And we will confront the question of social mobility, both upward and downward. Finally, in the Social Policy section, we will examine the issue of minimum wage laws.

Ever since people first began to speculate about the nature of human society, their attention has been drawn to the differences between individuals and groups within society. The term **social inequality,** which has been much in the headlines recently, describes a condition in which members of society have differing amounts of wealth, prestige, or power. Some degree of social inequality characterizes every society.

When a system of social inequality is based on a hierarchy of groups, sociologists refer to it as **stratification:** a structured ranking of entire groups of people that perpetuates unequal economic rewards and power in a society. These unequal rewards are evident not only in the distribution of wealth and income, but even in the distressing mortality rates of impoverished communities. Stratification involves the ways in which one generation passes on social inequalities to the next, producing groups of people arranged in rank order, from low to high.

Stratification is a crucial subject of sociological investigation because of its pervasive influence on human interactions and institutions. It results inevitably in social inequality, because certain groups of people stand higher in social rankings, control scarce resources, wield power, and receive special treatment. As we will see in Module 27, the consequences of stratification are evident in the unequal distribution of both income and wealth in industrial societies. The term **income** refers to salaries and wages. In contrast, **wealth** is an inclusive term encompassing all a person's material assets, including land, stocks, and other types of property.

Sociologists consider stratification on many levels, ranging from its impact on the individual to worldwide patterns of inequality. No matter where we look, however, disparities in wealth and income are substantial. Take income and poverty patterns in the United States, for example. As the top part of Figure 26-1 shows, in some states the median household income is 25 percent higher than that in other states. And as the bottom part of the figure shows, the poverty rate in many states is 200 percent that of other states. In Module 28, we will address the meaning of such statistics. We'll begin our discussion here with an overview of the four basic systems of stratification. Then we'll see what sociologists have had to say on the subject of social inequality.

Look at the four general systems of stratification examined here—slavery, castes, estates, and social classes—as ideal types useful for purposes of analysis. Any stratification system may include elements of more than one type. For example, prior to the Civil War, you could find in the southern states of the United States both social classes dividing Whites from Whites and the institutionalized enslavement of Blacks.

To understand these systems better, it may be helpful to review the distinction between *achieved status* and *ascribed status,* explained in Chapter 5. **Ascribed status** is a social position assigned to a person by society without regard for the person's unique talents or characteristics. In contrast, **achieved status** is a social position that a person attains largely through his or her own efforts. The two are closely linked. The nation's most affluent families generally inherit wealth and status, while many members of racial and ethnic minorities inherit disadvantaged status. Age and gender, as well, are ascribed statuses that influence a person's wealth and social position.

Four Forms of Stratification

Slavery

The most extreme form of legalized social inequality for both individuals and groups is **slavery.** What distinguishes this oppressive system of stratification is that enslaved individuals are *owned* by other people, who treat these human beings as property, just as if they were household pets or appliances.

FIGURE 26-1 The 50 States: Contrasts in Income and Poverty Levels

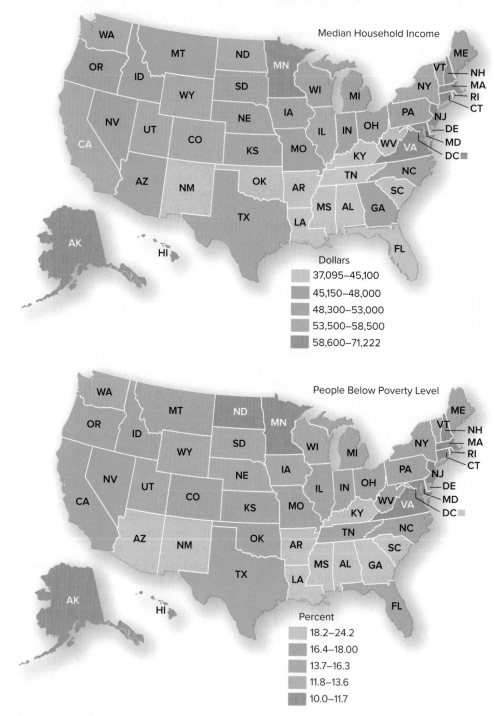

Median Household Income

Dollars
- 37,095–45,100
- 45,150–48,000
- 48,300–53,000
- 53,500–58,500
- 58,600–71,222

People Below Poverty Level

Percent
- 18.2–24.2
- 16.4–18.00
- 13.7–16.3
- 11.8–13.6
- 10.0–11.7

Note: National median household income was $51,371; national poverty rate, 15.9 percent.
Source: 2012 census data presented in Bureau of the Census 2013a: Tables R1701, R1901.

Slavery has varied in the way it has been practiced. In ancient Greece, the main source of slaves was piracy and captives of war. Although succeeding generations could inherit slave status, it was not necessarily permanent. A person's status might change, depending on which city-state happened to triumph in a military conflict. In effect, all citizens had the potential to become slaves or receive freedom, depending on the circumstances of history. In contrast, in the United States and Latin America, where slavery was an ascribed status, racial and legal barriers prevented the freeing of slaves.

Today, the Universal Declaration of Human Rights, which is binding on all members of the United Nations, prohibits slavery in all its forms. Yet more people are enslaved today than at

TABLE 26-1 HUMAN TRAFFICKING REPORT

Tier 1 Full Compliance	Tier 2 Significant Effort	Tier 2 Watch List Some Effort, But Trafficking Remains a Concern	Tier 3 Noncompliant, No Effort
Australia	Bolivia	Afghanistan	China
Canada	Brazil	Burma	Congo (Dem. Rep.)
Colombia	Chile	Haiti	Cuba
Denmark	Greece	Iraq	Iran
France	India	Kenya	Kuwait
Germany	Japan	Lebanon	North Korea
Great Britain	Mexico	Malaysia	Russia
Norway	Philippines	Panama	Saudi Arabia
Poland	South Africa	Thailand	Sudan
South Korea	Turkey	Ukraine	Syria
Spain	Vietnam	Venezuela	Zimbabwe

Note: Each tier lists only a sample of all nations classified. Since the *Human Trafficking Report* is created by the State Department, in the report the level of compliance by the United States is considered to be "full compliance."

Source: Department of State 2013.

any point in world history. In many developing countries, bonded laborers are imprisoned in virtual lifetime employment; in some countries, human beings are owned outright. But a form of slavery also exists in Europe and the United States, where guest workers and illegal immigrants have been forced to labor for years under terrible conditions, either to pay off debts or to avoid being turned over to immigration authorities.

Both these situations are likely to involve the transnational crime of trafficking in humans. Each year an estimated 600,000 to 800,000 men, women, and children are transported across international borders for slavery or sexual exploitation. In 2000, the U.S. Congress passed the Trafficking Victims Protection Act, which established minimum standards for the elimination of human trafficking. The act requires the State Department to monitor other countries' efforts to vigorously investigate, prosecute, and convict individuals who participate in trafficking—including government officials. Each year, the department reports its findings, some of which are shown in Table 26-1. Tier 1 and Tier 2 countries are thought to be largely in compliance with the act. Tier 2 Watch countries are making efforts to comply, though trafficking remains a significant concern. Tier 3 countries are not compliant and are not making significant efforts to comply.

Castes

Castes are hereditary ranks that are usually religiously dictated and that tend to be fixed and immobile. Caste membership is an ascribed status (at birth, children automatically assume the same position as their parents). Each caste is quite sharply defined, and members are expected to marry within that caste.

The caste system is generally associated with Hinduism in India and other countries. In India there are four major castes, called *varnas*. A fifth category of outcastes, referred to as the *untouchables*, represents 16 percent of the population; its members are considered so lowly and unclean as to have no place within this stratification system. In an effort to avoid perpetuating the historical stigma these people bear, the government now refers to the untouchables as *scheduled castes*. The untouchables themselves prefer *Dalit* ("the repressed"), a term that communicates their desire to overcome their disadvantaged status.

In 1950, after gaining independence from Great Britain, India adopted a new constitution that formally outlawed the caste system. Over the past decade or two, however, urbanization and technological advances have brought more change to India's caste system than the government or politics has in more than half a century. The anonymity of city life tends to blur caste boundaries, allowing the *Dalit* to pass unrecognized in temples, schools, and places of employment. And the globalization of high technology has opened up India's social order, bringing new opportunities to those who possess the skills and ability to capitalize on them.

The term *caste* can also be applied in recent historical contexts outside India. For example, the system of stratification that characterized the southern United States from the end of the Civil War through the 1960s resembled a caste system. So did the rigid system of segregation that prevailed in the Republic of South Africa under apartheid, from 1948 through the 1990s. In both cases, race was the defining factor that placed a person in the social hierarchy.

Estates

A third type of stratification system, called *estates*, was associated with feudal societies during the Middle Ages. The **estate system,** or *feudalism*, required peasants to work land leased to them by nobles in exchange for military protection and other

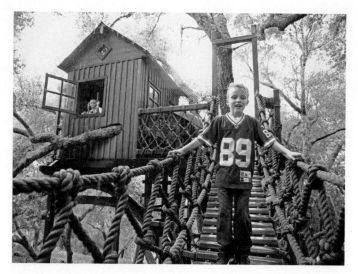

Worried about home foreclosures? Not the wealthy. The rich now spend $50,000 to $250,000 on their children's playhouses and tree houses.

services. The basis for the system was the nobles' ownership of land, which was critical to their superior and privileged status. As in systems based on slavery and caste, inheritance of one's position largely defined the estate system. The nobles inherited their titles and property; the peasants were born into a subservient position within an agrarian society.

As the estate system developed, it became more differentiated. Nobles began to achieve varying degrees of authority. By the 12th century, a priesthood had emerged in most of Europe, along with classes of merchants and artisans. For the first time there were groups of people whose wealth did not depend on land ownership or agriculture. This economic change had profound social consequences as the estate system ended and a class system of stratification came into existence.

Social Classes

A **class system** is a social ranking based primarily on economic position in which achieved characteristics can influence social mobility. In contrast to slavery and caste systems, the boundaries between classes are imprecisely defined, and one can move from one stratum, or level, of society to another. Even so, class systems maintain stable stratification hierarchies and patterns of class division, and they, too, are marked by unequal distribution of wealth and power. Class standing, although it is achieved, is heavily dependent on family and ascribed factors, such as race and ethnicity.

Sociologist Daniel Rossides (1997) uses a five-class model to describe the class system of the United States: the upper class, the upper-middle class, the lower-middle class, the working class, and the lower class. Although the lines separating social classes in his model are not so sharp as the divisions between castes, members of the five classes differ significantly in ways other than just income level.

Upper and Lower Classes Rossides characterizes about 1 to 2 percent of the people of the United States as *upper class*. This group is limited to the very wealthy, who associate in exclusive clubs and social circles. In contrast, the *lower class,* consisting of approximately 20 to 25 percent of the population, disproportionately consists of Blacks, Hispanics, single mothers with dependent children, and people who cannot find regular work or must make do with low-paying work. This class lacks both wealth and income and is too weak politically to exercise significant power.

Both these classes, at opposite ends of the nation's social hierarchy, reflect the importance of ascribed status and achieved status. Ascribed statuses such as race and disability clearly influence a person's wealth and social position. People with disabilities are particularly vulnerable to unemployment, are often poorly paid, and tend to occupy the lower rungs of the occupational ladder. Regardless of their actual performance on the job, the disabled are stigmatized as not earning their keep. Such are the effects of ascribed status. We will look again at the plight of the lower class when we consider poverty and welfare policies.

The economist John Kenneth Galbraith (1977:44) observed that "of all classes the rich are the most noticed and the least studied." The poor receive a good deal of attention from reporters, social activists, and policymakers seeking to alleviate their poverty, but the very affluent, who live apart from the rest of the population, are largely a mystery. Since Galbraith's comment, moreover, the residential separation of the rich has grown. The newspaper's society page may give us a peek at members of this class, but we know very little about their everyday lives. Statistically, over 2 million households in the United States are worth more than $10 million each. Less than 10 percent of these people inherited their money, and very few of them are celebrities (Massey 2007).

Middle Class Sandwiched between the upper and lower classes in this model are the upper-middle class, the lower-middle class, and the working class. The *upper-middle class,* about 10 to 15 percent

Today, the once broadly based middle class is on the defensive and is slowly being squeezed by two growing groups, the rich and the poor.

Source: Steve Greenberg/Rights available from Cartoonstock.com. Reproduced by permission.

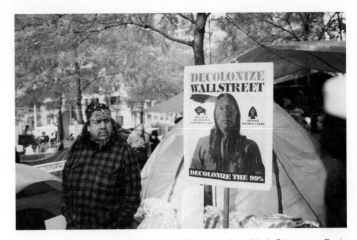

Reactions to the Occupy Wall Street movement varied with people's socioeconomic status. "How about you occupy a job?" former New York City mayor Rudy Giuliani (left) retorted. At the other extreme, Native American leaders observed that their lands have been occupied for five centuries.

of the population, includes professionals such as doctors, lawyers, and architects. They participate extensively in politics and take leadership roles in voluntary associations. The *lower-middle class,* about 30 to 35 percent of the population, includes less affluent professionals (such as elementary school teachers and nurses), owners of small businesses, and a sizable number of clerical workers. While not all members of the middle class hold degrees from a college, they share the goal of sending their children there.

The middle class is currently under a great deal of economic pressure. Close analysis indicates that of those who lost their middle-class standing during the latter 20th century, about half rose to a higher ranking in the social class system, while half dropped to a lower position. These data mean that the United States is moving toward a "bipolar income distribution." That is, a broadly based middle class is slowly being replaced by two growing groups of rich and poor.

Sociologists and other scholars have identified several factors that have contributed to the shrinking size of the middle class:

- *Disappearing opportunities for those with little education.* Today, most jobs require formal schooling, yet less than a third of adults between ages 35 and 44 have prepared themselves with a college degree.

- *Global competition and rapid advances in technology.* These two trends, which began several decades ago, mean that workers are more easily replaced now than they were in the past. Increasingly, globalization and technological advances are affecting the more complex jobs that were once the bread and butter of middle-class workers.

- *Growing dependence on the temporary workforce.* For those workers who have no other job, temporary positions are tenuous at best, because they rarely offer health care coverage or retirement benefits.

- *The rise of new growth industries and nonunion workplaces, like fast-food restaurants.* Industries may have added employment opportunities, but they are at the lower end of the wage scale.

Middle-class families want comfortable homes, college degrees for their children, occasional family vacations, affordable health care—the cost of which has been growing faster than inflation—and retirement security. The answer, for many people, is either to go without or to work longer hours at multiple jobs (Blank 2010, 2011; Khan 2013; Massey 2007; Thurow 1984).

Working Class   Rossides describes the *working class*—about 40 to 45 percent of the population—as people who hold regular manual or blue-collar jobs. Certain members of this class, such as electricians, may have higher incomes than people in the lower-middle class. Yet even if they have achieved some degree of economic security, they tend to identify with manual workers and their long history of involvement in the labor movement of the United States.

Of the five classes, the working class is declining noticeably in size. In the economy of the United States, service and technical jobs are replacing those involved in the actual manufacturing or transportation of goods.

Class Warfare   On September 17, 2011, two thousand protesters assembled in New York City, claiming to represent the vast majority of Americans. In their own words, these members of what soon became known as the Occupy Wall Street movement were "the 99 percent"—those Americans who had suffered as the wealthiest 1 percent flourished. In the next few weeks the movement, which had begun in Canada, spread across the United States to Honolulu and then throughout the world (Peralta 2011; M. Scherer 2011).

With Occupy Wall Street in the headlines, political leaders began to speak of class conflict. To some, the Occupy movement's call for a reduction in social inequality seemed a reply to the federal government's favorable tax treatment of the affluent. Before the recession began, the Bush administration had lowered the income tax rate paid by high-income filers. In 2009, the Tea Party pushed Congress to maintain that tax cut, despite a growing deficit. Others insisted that the affluent actually paid less in taxes than the average citizen, given the many loopholes—offshore bank accounts, and so on—available to them. In Congress, the suggestion that the rich should pay the same effective tax rate as other citizens was met with an angry charge of class warfare.

As we will see shortly, by any statistical measure, the gulf between the rich and everyone else in the United States has grown over the last decade—indeed, over the last 50 years. Yet people do not tend to identify with or see themselves as members of a specific social class. Still, as the rhetoric heated up during the 2012 presidential campaign, and the Occupy Wall Street movement remained visible, a growing share of the population thought they saw evidence of class conflict. In December 2011, 66 percent of the public (compared to 47 percent in 2009) said they perceived "strong" conflict between the rich and the poor. Younger adults, women, and African Americans were most likely to hold this view. Interestingly, personal income had little to do with such perceptions: the rich were just as likely as the poor to agree with the existence of class conflict (Archer and Orr 2011; Morin and Motel 2013; Skocpol and Williamson 2012).

Indeed, the growing perception that the rich have been flourishing at the expense of everyone else is supported by the facts. Between 2002 and 2012, family incomes of the top hundredth of 1 percent of Americans increased 76 percent, to an average of $21.6 million a year. That figure does not include income from stocks, bonds, and real estate holdings, which was considerable. During the same period, family incomes of the bottom 90 percent of Americans *dropped* 11 percent, to $34,000 a year (Saez 2013).

◼ Sociological Perspectives on Stratification

Sociologists have hotly debated stratification and social inequality and have reached varying conclusions. No theorist stressed the significance of class for society—and for social change—more strongly than Karl Marx. Marx viewed class differentiation

A miner peers into the dark at Peabody Energy's Gateway Mine near Coulterville, Illinois. Karl Marx would identify coal miners as members of the proletariat, or working class. Even today, miners are poorly compensated for the considerable dangers they face. Such exploitation of the working class is a core principle of Marxist theory.

as the crucial determinant of social, economic, and political inequality. In contrast, Max Weber questioned Marx's emphasis on the overriding importance of the economic sector, arguing that stratification should be viewed as having many dimensions.

Karl Marx's View of Class Differentiation

Karl Marx was concerned with stratification in all types of human society, beginning with primitive agricultural tribes and continuing into feudalism. However, his main focus was on the effects of economic inequality on all aspects of 19th-century Europe. The plight of the working class made him feel that it was imperative to strive for changes in the class structure of society.

In Marx's view, social relations during any period of history depend on who controls the primary mode of economic production, such as land or factories. Differential access to scarce resources shapes the relationship between groups. Thus, under the feudal estate system, most production was agricultural, and the land was owned by the nobility. Peasants had little choice but to work according to terms dictated by those who owned the land.

Using this type of analysis, Marx examined social relations within **capitalism**—an economic system in which the means of production are held largely in private hands and the main incentive for economic activity is the accumulation of profits. Marx focused on the two classes that began to emerge as the feudal estate system declined, the bourgeoisie and the proletariat. The **bourgeoisie,** or capitalist class, owns the means of production, such as factories and machinery; the **proletariat** is the working class. In capitalist societies, the members of the bourgeoisie maximize profit in competition with other firms. In the process, they exploit workers, who must exchange their labor for subsistence wages. In Marx's view, members of each class share a distinctive culture. Marx was most interested in the culture of the proletariat, but he also examined the ideology of the bourgeoisie, through which that class justifies its dominance over workers.

According to Marx, exploitation of the proletariat will inevitably lead to the destruction of the capitalist system, because the workers will revolt. But first, the working class must develop **class consciousness**—a subjective awareness of common vested interests and the need for collective political action to bring about social change. Often, workers must overcome what Marx termed **false consciousness,** or an attitude held by members of a class that does not accurately reflect their objective position. A worker with false consciousness may adopt an individualistic viewpoint toward capitalist exploitation ("*I* am being exploited by *my* boss"). In contrast, the class-conscious worker realizes that all workers are being exploited by the bourgeoisie and have a common stake in revolution.

For Marx, class consciousness was part of a collective process in which the proletariat comes to identify the bourgeoisie as the source of its oppression. Revolutionary leaders will guide the working class in its struggle. Ultimately, the proletariat will overthrow the rule of both the bourgeoisie and the government (which Marx saw as representing the interests of capitalists) and will eliminate private ownership of the means of production. In Marx's rather utopian view, classes and oppression will cease to exist in the postrevolutionary workers' state.

How accurate were Marx's predictions? He failed to anticipate the emergence of labor unions, whose power in collective bargaining weakens the stranglehold that capitalists maintain over workers. Moreover, as contemporary conflict theorists note, he did not foresee the extent to which political liberties and relative prosperity could contribute to false consciousness. Many workers came to view themselves as individuals striving for improvement within free societies that offer substantial mobility, rather than as downtrodden members of a social class who face a collective fate. Even today, "class warfare" seems to refer more to diminished individual expectations than to a collective identity. Finally, Marx did not predict that Communist Party rule would be established and later overthrown in the former Soviet Union and throughout Eastern Europe. Still, the Marxist approach to the study of class is useful in stressing the importance of stratification as a determinant of social behavior and the fundamental separation in many societies between two distinct groups, the rich and the poor.

 use your **sociological imagination**

Have you ever been unaware of your true position in society—that is, have you experienced false consciousness? Explain.

Max Weber's View of Stratification

Unlike Karl Marx, Max Weber ([1913–1922] 1947) insisted that no single characteristic (such as class) totally defines a person's position within the stratification system. Instead, writing in 1916, he identified three distinct components of stratification: class, status, and power.

Weber used the term **class** to refer to a group of people who have a similar level of wealth and income. For example, certain workers in the United States try to support their families through minimum-wage jobs. According to Weber's definition, these wage earners constitute a class because they share the same economic position and fate. Although Weber agreed with Marx on the importance of this economic dimension of stratification, he argued that the actions of individuals and groups cannot be understood *solely* in economic terms.

Weber used the term **status group** to refer to people who have the same prestige or lifestyle. An individual gains status through membership in a desirable group, such as the medical profession. But status is not the same as economic class standing. In our culture, a successful pickpocket may belong to the same income class as a college professor. Yet the thief is widely regarded as holding low status, whereas the professor holds high status.

For Weber, the third major component of stratification has a political dimension. **Power** is the ability to exercise one's will over others. In the United States, power stems from membership in particularly influential groups, such as corporate boards of directors, government bodies, and interest groups. Conflict theorists generally agree that two major sources of power—big business and government—are closely interrelated. For instance, many of the heads of major corporations also hold powerful positions in the government or military.

To summarize, in Weber's view, each of us has not one rank in society but three. Our position in a stratification system reflects some combination of class, status, and power. Each factor influences the other two, and in fact the rankings on these three dimensions often tend to coincide. John F. Kennedy came from an extremely wealthy family, attended exclusive preparatory schools, graduated from Harvard University, and went on to become president of the United States. Like Kennedy, many people from affluent backgrounds achieve impressive status and power.

Interactionist Perspective

Both Karl Marx and Max Weber looked at inequality primarily from a macrosociological perspective, considering the entire society or even the global economy. Marx did suggest the importance of a more microsociological analysis, however, when he stressed the ways in which individuals develop a true class consciousness.

Interactionists, as well as economists, have long been interested in the importance of social class in shaping a person's lifestyle. The theorist Thorstein Veblen (1857–1929) noted that those at the top of the social hierarchy typically convert part of

With Mt. Everest in the background, a wealthy golfer plays a shot in a remote location, which he reached by helicopter. Traveling to exotic places to indulge in sports that most people play at home is an example of Thorstein Veblen's concept of conspicuous consumption, a spending pattern common to those at the very top of the social ladder.

their wealth into **conspicuous consumption**—that is, they purchase goods not to survive but to flaunt their superior wealth and social standing. For example, they may purchase more automobiles than they can reasonably use, or build homes with more rooms than they can possibly occupy. In an element of conspicuous consumption called *conspicuous leisure,* they may jet to a remote destination, staying just long enough to have dinner or view a sunset over some historic locale (Veblen [1899] 1964).

Today, conspicuous consumption has found a new outlet in the cyberworld. Users of social media can now see their friends' vacations and snazzy new cars online—an experience that can provoke what researchers call *Facebook envy.* Studies done in the United States and Germany show that even otherwise happy people can suffer envy and distress over this kind of digitally shared conspicuous consumption (Shea 2013).

At the other end of the spectrum, behavior that is judged to be typical of the lower class is subject not only to ridicule but even to legal action. Communities have, from time to time, banned trailers from people's front yards and sofas from their front porches. In some communities, it is illegal to leave a pickup truck in front of the house overnight. In others, street vendors who sell fruit, flowers, and water face restrictions meant not to serve the general public, but to protect their storefront competitors (Campo-Flores 2013).

● Is Stratification Universal?

Must some members of society receive greater rewards than others? Do people need to feel socially and economically superior to others? Can social life be organized without structured inequality? These questions have been debated for centuries, especially among political activists. Utopian socialists, religious minorities, and members of recent countercultures have all attempted to establish communities that to some extent or other would abolish inequality in social relationships.

Social scientists have found that inequality exists in all societies—even the simplest. For example, when anthropologist Gunnar Landtman ([1938] 1968) studied the Kiwai Papuans of New Guinea, at first he noticed little differentiation among them. Every man in the village did the same work and lived in similar housing. However, on closer inspection, Landtman observed that certain Papuans—men who were warriors, harpooners, and sorcerers—were described as "a little more high" than others. In contrast, villagers who were female, unemployed, or unmarried were considered "down a little bit" and were barred from owning land.

Stratification is universal in that all societies maintain some form of social inequality among members. Depending on its values, a society may assign people to distinctive ranks based on their religious knowledge, skill in hunting, physical attractiveness, trading expertise, or ability to provide health care. But why has such inequality developed in human societies? And how much differentiation among people, if any, is actually essential?

Functionalist and conflict theorists offer contrasting explanations for the existence and necessity of social stratification. Functionalists maintain that a differential system of rewards and punishments is necessary for the efficient operation of society. Conflict theorists argue that competition for scarce resources results in significant political, economic, and social inequality.

Functionalist Perspective

Would people go to school for many years to become physicians if they could make as much money and gain as much respect working as street cleaners? Functionalists say no, which is partly why they believe that a stratified society is universal.

In the view of Kingsley Davis and Wilbert Moore (1945), society must distribute its members among a variety of social positions. It must not only make sure that these positions are filled but also see that they are filled by people with the appropriate talents and abilities. Rewards, including money and prestige, are based on the importance of a position and the relative scarcity of qualified personnel. Yet this assessment often devalues work performed by certain segments of society, such as women's work in the home or in occupations traditionally filled by women, or low-status work in fast-food outlets.

Davis and Moore argue that stratification is universal and that social inequality is necessary so that people will be motivated to fill functionally important positions. But critics say that unequal rewards are not the only means of encouraging people to fill critical positions and occupations. Personal pleasure, intrinsic satisfaction, and value orientations also motivate people to enter particular careers. Functionalists agree, but they note that society must use some type of reward to motivate people to enter unpleasant or dangerous jobs and professions that require a long training period. This response does not address stratification systems in which status is largely inherited, such as slave or caste societies. Moreover, even if stratification is inevitable, the functionalist explanation for differential rewards does not explain the wide disparity between the rich and the poor (R. Collins 1975; Kerbo 2012).

Conflict Perspective

The writings of Karl Marx lie at the heart of conflict theory. Marx viewed history as a continuous struggle between the oppressors and the oppressed, which ultimately would culminate in an egalitarian, classless society. In terms of stratification, he argued that under capitalism, the dominant class—the bourgeoisie—manipulates the economic and political systems in order to maintain control over the exploited proletariat. Marx did not believe that stratification was inevitable, but he did see inequality and oppression as inherent in capitalism (E. O. Wright et al. 1982; E. O. Wright 2011).

Like Marx, contemporary conflict theorists believe that human beings are prone to conflict over scarce resources such as wealth, status, and power. However, Marx focused primarily on class conflict; more recent theorists have extended the analysis to include conflicts based on gender, race, age, and other dimensions. British sociologist Ralf Dahrendorf (1929–2009) is one of the most influential contributors to the conflict approach.

Dahrendorf (1959) has modified Marx's analysis of capitalist society to apply to modern capitalist societies. For Dahrendorf, social classes are groups of people who share common interests resulting from their authority relationships. In identifying the most powerful groups in society, he includes not only the bourgeoisie—the owners of the means of production—but also the managers of industry, legislators, the judiciary, heads of the government bureaucracy, and others. In that respect, Dahrendorf has merged Marx's emphasis on class conflict with Weber's recognition that power is an important element of stratification (Cuff et al. 1990).

As the reality television series *Ice Road Truckers,* now in its eighth season, suggests, long-haul truck drivers take pride in their low-prestige job. According to the conflict perspective, the cultural beliefs that form a society's dominant ideology, such as the popular image of the truck driver as hero, help the wealthy to maintain their power and control at the expense of the lower classes.

dominant ideology describes a set of cultural beliefs and practices that helps to maintain powerful social, economic, and political interests. For Marx, the dominant ideology in a capitalist society served the interests of the ruling class. From a conflict perspective, the social significance of the dominant ideology is that not only do a society's most powerful groups and institutions control wealth and property; even more important, they control the means of producing beliefs about reality through religion, education, and the media (Abercrombie et al. 1980, 1990; Robertson 1988).

The powerful, such as leaders of government, also use limited social reforms to buy off the oppressed and reduce the danger of challenges to their dominance. For example, minimum-wage laws and unemployment compensation unquestionably give some valuable assistance to needy men and women. Yet these reforms also serve to pacify those who might otherwise rebel. Of course, in the view of conflict theorists, such maneuvers can never entirely eliminate conflict, since workers will continue to demand equality, and the powerful will not give up their control of society.

Conflict theorists see stratification as a major source of societal tension and conflict. They do not agree with Davis and Moore that stratification is functional for a society or that it serves as a source of stability. Rather, conflict sociologists argue that stratification will inevitably lead to instability and social change (R. Collins 1975; L. Coser 1977).

Table 26-2 summarizes and compares the three major perspectives on social stratification.

Lenski's Viewpoint

Let's return to the question posed earlier—Is stratification universal?—and consider the sociological response. Some form of differentiation is found in every culture, from the most primitive to the most advanced industrial societies of our time. Sociologist Gerhard Lenski, in his sociocultural evolution approach, described how economic systems change as their level of technology becomes more complex, beginning with hunting and gathering and culminating eventually with industrial society.

In subsistence-based hunting-and-gathering societies, people focus on survival. While some inequality and differentiation are evident, a stratification system based on social class does not emerge because there is no real wealth to be claimed. As a society advances technologically, it becomes capable of producing a considerable surplus of goods. The emergence of surplus resources greatly expands the possibilities for inequality in status, influence, and power, allowing a well-defined, rigid social class system to develop. To minimize strikes, slowdowns, and industrial sabotage, the elites

Conflict theorists, including Dahrendorf, contend that the powerful of today, like the bourgeoisie of Marx's time, want society to run smoothly so that they can enjoy their privileged positions. Because the status quo suits those with wealth, status, and power, they have a clear interest in preventing, minimizing, or controlling societal conflict.

One way for the powerful to maintain the status quo is to define and disseminate the society's dominant ideology. The term

TABLE **26-2** SOCIOLOGICAL PERSPECTIVES ON SOCIAL STRATIFICATION

Tracking Sociological Perspectives

	Functionalist	Conflict	Interactionist
Purpose of social stratification	Facilitates filling of social positions	Facilitates exploitation	Influences people's lifestyles
Attitude toward social inequality	Necessary to some extent	Excessive and growing	Influences intergroup relations
Analysis of the wealthy	Talented and skilled, creating opportunities for others	Use the dominant ideology to further their own interests	Exhibit conspicuous consumption and conspicuous leisure

may share a portion of the economic surplus with the lower classes, but not enough to reduce their own power and privilege.

As Lenski argued, the allocation of surplus goods and services controlled by those with wealth, status, and power reinforces the social inequality that accompanies stratification systems. While this reward system may once have served the overall purposes of society, as functionalists contend, the same cannot be said for the large disparities separating the haves from the have-nots in current societies. In contemporary industrial society, the degree of social and economic inequality far exceeds what is needed to provide for goods and services (Lenski 1966; Nolan 2004; Nolan and Lenski 2009).

MODULE 26 | Recap and Review

Summary

Stratification is the structured ranking of entire groups of people that perpetuates unequal economic rewards and **power** in a society.

1. Some degree of **social inequality** characterizes all cultures.

2. Systems of social stratification include **slavery, castes,** the **estate system,** and social classes.

3. Karl Marx saw that differences in access to the means of production created social, economic, and political inequality, as well as two distinct classes, owners and laborers.

4. Max Weber identified three analytically distinct components of stratification: **class, status group,** and **power.**

5. Functionalists argue that stratification is necessary to motivate people to fill society's important positions. Conflict theorists see stratification as a major source of societal tension and conflict. Interactionists stress the importance of social class in determining a person's lifestyle.

Thinking Critically

1. What are the differences between slavery and caste systems? What are the similarities?

2. Give some examples of conspicuous consumption among your fellow college students. Which are obvious and which more subtle?

3. In your view, is the extent of social inequality in the United States helpful or harmful to society as a whole? Explain.

Key Terms

Achieved status

Ascribed status

Bourgeoisie

Capitalism

Caste

Class

Class consciousness

Class system

Conspicuous consumption

Dominant ideology

Estate system

False consciousness

Income

Power

Proletariat

Slavery

Social inequality

Status group

Stratification

Wealth

MODULE 27 | Stratification by Social Class

We continually assess how wealthy people are by looking at the cars they drive, the houses they live in, the clothes they wear, and so on. Yet it is not so easy to locate an individual within our social hierarchies as it would be in slavery or caste systems of stratification. To determine someone's class position, sociologists generally rely on the objective method.

⬤ Objective Method of Measuring Social Class

In the **objective method** of measuring social class, class is viewed largely as a statistical category. Researchers assign individuals to social classes on the basis of criteria such as occupation, education, income, and place of residence. The key to the objective method is that the *researcher,* rather than the person being classified, identifies an individual's class position.

The first step in using this method is to decide what indicators or causal factors will be measured objectively, whether wealth, income, education, or occupation. The prestige ranking of occupations has proved to be a useful indicator of a person's class position. For one thing, it is much easier to determine accurately than income or wealth. The term **prestige** refers to the respect and admiration that an occupation holds in a society. "My daughter, the physicist" connotes something very different from "my daughter, the waitress." Prestige is independent of the particular individual who occupies a job, a characteristic that distinguishes it from esteem. **Esteem** refers to the reputation that a specific person has earned within an occupation. Therefore, one can say that the position of president of the United States has high prestige, even though it has been occupied by people with varying degrees of esteem. A hairdresser may have the esteem of his clients, but he lacks the prestige of a corporate executive.

Table 27-1 ranks the prestige of a number of well-known occupations. In a series of national surveys, sociologists assigned prestige rankings to about 500 occupations, ranging from surgeon to panhandler. The highest possible prestige score was 100; the lowest was 0. Surgeon, physician, lawyer, dentist, and college professor were the most highly regarded occupations. Sociologists have used such data to assign prestige rankings to virtually all jobs and have found a stability in rankings from 1925 to the present. Similar studies in other countries have also developed useful prestige rankings of occupations (Nakao and Treas 1994).

Gender and Occupational Prestige

For many years, studies of social class tended to neglect the occupations and incomes of *women* as determinants of social rank. With more than half of all married women now working outside the home, this approach seems outmoded. How should we judge class or status in dual-career families—by the occupation regarded as having greater prestige, the average, or some other combination of the two? Sociologists—in

TABLE 27-1 PRESTIGE RANKINGS OF OCCUPATIONS

Occupation	Score	Occupation	Score
Physician	86	Bank teller	50
College professor	78	Electrician	49
Lawyer	76	Farm manager	48
Dentist	74	Insurance agent	47
Banker	72	Secretary	46
Architect	71	Mail carrier	42
Airline pilot	70	Farmer	41
Clergy	69	Correctional officer	40
Registered nurse	66	Carpenter	40
High school teacher	63	Barber	38
Legislator	61	Child care worker	36
Pharmacist	61	Hotel clerk	32
Elementary school teacher	60	Bus driver	32
Veterinarian	60	Truck driver	30
Police officer or detective	60	Salesworker (shoes)	28
Prekindergarten teacher	60	Waiter and waitress	28
Accountant	57	Cook (short-order)	28
Librarian	55	Bartender	25
Firefighter	53	Garbage collector	17
Funeral director	52	Janitor	16
Social worker	52	Newspaper vendor	15

Think about It Can you name what you think are two more high-prestige occupations? Two more low-prestige occupations? Explain why you consider those jobs to be of high or low prestige.

Note: 100 is the highest and 0 the lowest possible prestige score.
Source: General Social Survey 2012.

particular, feminist sociologists in Great Britain—are drawing on new approaches to assess women's social class standing. One approach is to focus on the individual (rather than the family or household) as the basis for categorizing a woman's class position. Thus, a woman would be classified according to her own occupational status rather than that of her spouse (O'Donnell 1992).

Another feminist effort to measure the contribution of women to the economy reflects a more clearly political agenda. International Women Count Network, a global grassroots feminist organization, has sought to give a monetary value to women's unpaid work. Besides providing symbolic recognition of women's role in labor, this value would also be used to calculate pension and other benefits, which are usually based on wages received. The United Nations has placed an $11 trillion price tag on unpaid labor by women, largely in child care, housework, and agriculture. Whatever the figure, the continued undercounting of many workers' contributions to a family and to an entire economy means that virtually all measures of stratification are in need of reform (United Nations Development Programme 1995; United Nations Economic and Social Council 2010; Wages for Housework Campaign 1999).

Multiple Measures

Another complication in measuring social class is that advances in statistical methods and computer technology have multiplied the factors used to define class under the objective method. No longer are sociologists limited to annual income and education in evaluating a person's class position. Today, studies use as criteria the value of homes, sources of income, assets, years in present occupations, neighborhoods, and considerations regarding dual careers. Adding these variables will not necessarily paint a different picture of class differentiation in the United States, but it does allow sociologists to measure class in a more complex and multidimensional way. When researchers use multiple measures, they typically speak of **socioeconomic status (SES),** a measure of social class that is based on income, education, and occupation. To determine the socioeconomic status of a young person, such as a college student under age 25, they use *parental* income, education, and occupation.

Whatever the technique used to measure class, the sociologist is interested in real and often dramatic differences in power, privilege, and opportunity in a society. The study of stratification is a study of inequality. Nowhere is the truth of that statement more evident than in the distribution of income and wealth.

● Income and Wealth

By all measures, income in the United States is distributed unevenly. Nobel Prize–winning economist Paul Samuelson has described the situation in the following words: "If we made an income pyramid out of building blocks, with each layer portraying $500 of income, the peak would be far higher than Mount Everest, but most people would be within a few feet of the ground" (Samuelson and Nordhaus 2010:324).

Recent data support Samuelson's analogy. In 2012, the median household income in the United States was $51,017. In other words, half of all households had higher incomes that year and half had lower incomes. However, this fact does not fully convey the income disparities in our society. We can get some sense of income inequality by contrasting this median (middle) income with the mean arithmetic average, which in 2012 was $71,274. The mean is so much higher than the median because some people make a lot more money than others, which draws the mean up. Thus, the mean is a less useful statistic than the median for describing the average, or typical, income (DeNavas-Walt et al. 2013:33).

We can gain additional insight into income inequality in the United States by looking at the relative placement of households

FIGURE 27-1 Mean Household Income by Quintile

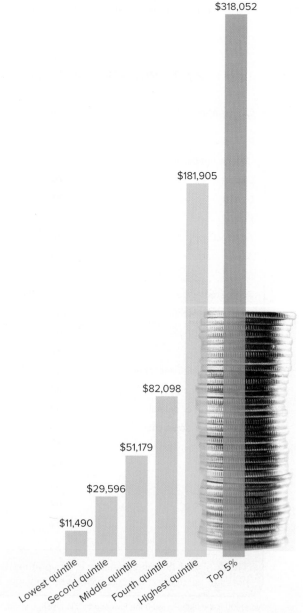

$318,052

$181,905

$82,098

$51,179

$29,596

$11,490

Lowest quintile Second quintile Middle quintile Fourth quintile Highest quintile Top 5%

Source: Data for 2012 in DeNavas-Walt et al. 2013:40; Bureau of the Census 2011d: Table H-3.

within the income distribution. One of the most common ways of doing so is to line up all income-earning households from low to high and then break them into quintiles, or fifths. Because there are approximately 122 million households in the United States, each quintile includes an equal number of about 24 million households. This method gives us a sense of the average income within each quintile, along with the percentage of the nation's total income earned in each quintile.

As Figure 27-1 shows, looking at the population in this way reveals a significant degree of income inequality. The mean income for households in the lowest quintile is $11,490; in the highest quintile, it is $181,905. If we were to move up to the highest end of the income distribution, we would find that the top 0.01 percent of taxpayers—about 15,000 households—make incomes of at least $11.5 million a year. Collectively, they control 6 percent of the nation's total income (DeNavas-Walt et al. 2013:41; Sloan 2009:27).

There has been a modest redistribution of income in the United States over the past 80 years, but not always to the benefit of the poor or even the middle class. From 1929 through 1970, the government's economic and tax policies shifted some income to the poor. However, in the past four decades—especially in the 1980s and in the decade from 2001 through 2010—federal tax policies favored the affluent. Moreover, while the salaries of highly skilled workers and professionals have continued to rise, the wages of less skilled workers have *decreased* when controlled for inflation.

Careful economic analysis has shown that over the past 30 years, federal and state tax policies have tended to accentuate this trend toward income inequality. During one 25-year period, the top 1 percent of income earners *after taxes* saw their incomes rise 228 percent, compared to only 21 percent for households in the middle quintile. Little wonder that the middle class is shrinking (Billitteri 2009; A. Sherman 2007).

Globalization is often blamed for this growing inequality, because it has forced less skilled workers to compete with lower-paid foreign-born workers. While that is true, research suggests that the number of displaced workers who are reemployed at similarly paid or even higher-paid jobs roughly equals the number of workers whose earnings drop (S. Zimmerman 2008a). The growing inequality in income is mirrored in increasing inequality in wealth. Consider the years between 1980 and 2010. During this period of less than a generation, the real net worth of middle-income earners rose only 2 percent, while that of low-income families dropped 7 percent. Yet for upper-income families, net worth climbed 87 percent. The pattern is clear: the biggest winners have been the affluent (Pew Research Center 2012b:92).

Indeed, wealth is distributed much more unevenly than income in the United States. A 2009 Federal Reserve Bank study showed that half the population controls 2.5 percent of the nation's wealth; the other half controls over 97 percent (Figure 27-2). Put another way, the wealth of the top 1 percent exceeds the collective wealth of the bottom 90 percent.

Researchers have also found a dramatic disparity in the wealth of African Americans and Hispanics compared to that of Whites. The median wealth of White households is now 18 times the median wealth of Latino households and 20 times that of Blacks. Furthermore, evidence suggests that the gap is widening (Pew Social and Demographic Trends 2011; T. Shapiro et al. 2010).

FIGURE 27-2 **Distribution of Wealth in the United States**

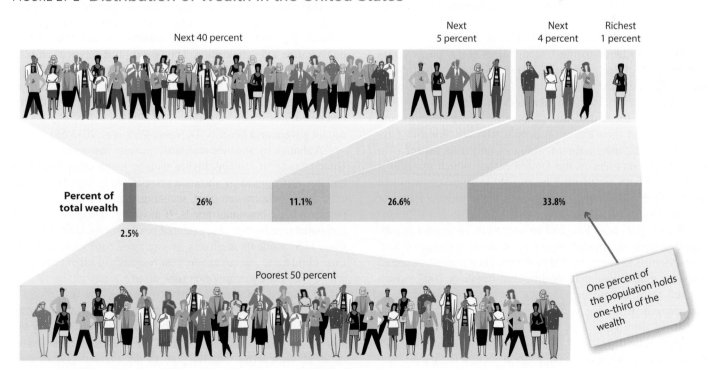

Source: Data for 2007, as reported in a 2009 Federal Reserve Bank study. See Kennickell 2009:35.

Summary

One consequence of social class in the United States is that both **income** and **wealth** are distributed unevenly.

1. Sociologists use the **objective method** of measuring social class, which uses criteria such as occupation, education, and income. **Socioeconomic status (SES)** is an objective measure based on these criteria.

2. Regardless of the measure used, income inequality rose from the late 1960s to the end of the 20th century.

Thinking Critically

1. To what degree are students motivated by the prestige of their future occupations?

2. What does the pattern of income distribution in the United States tell you about your own future income? How much can you expect it to grow over the years?

Key Terms

Esteem

Objective method

Prestige

Socioeconomic status (SES)

About 15 percent of the people in the United States live below the poverty line established by the federal government. In 2012, no fewer than 46.5 million people were living in poverty. The economic boom of the 1990s passed these people by. A Bureau of the Census report shows that one in five households has trouble meeting basic needs, from paying the utility bills to buying dinner (Bauman 1999; DeNavas-Walt et al. 2013).

One contributor to the United States' high poverty rate has been the large number of workers employed at minimum wage. At current minimum wage rates, which are quite low, most workers cannot make ends meet. The Social Policy section at the end of this chapter will examine minimum wage laws and their effect on people who are living in poverty. However, the minimum wage is only one aspect of a much larger problem in the United States, which includes a shortage of both well-paid jobs and skilled workers who can do those jobs. Typically, workers earn the minimum wage for unskilled work.

Sociologists have long had an interest in the impact of substandard work on society, beginning with the writings of Karl Marx, Émile Durkheim, and Max Weber. Their interest increased with the global economic decline that began in 2008, which trapped many people in jobs they did not want or left them unemployed. Box 28-1 considers recent sociological work on *precarious work.*

In this module, we'll consider just how social scientists define *poverty.* We'll also take a closer look at the people who fall into that category—including the working poor.

Studying Poverty

The efforts of sociologists and other social scientists to better understand poverty are complicated by the difficulty of defining it. This problem is evident even in government programs that conceive of poverty in either absolute or relative terms. **Absolute poverty** refers to a minimum level of subsistence that no family should be expected to live below.

One commonly used measure of absolute poverty is the federal government's *poverty line,* a money income figure that is adjusted annually to reflect the consumption requirements of families based on their size and composition. The poverty line serves as an official definition of which people are poor. In 2012, for example, any family of four (two adults and two children) with a combined income of $23,283 or less fell below the poverty line. This definition determines which individuals and families will be eligible for certain government benefits (DeNavas-Walt et al. 2013:59).

Although by absolute standards, poverty has declined in the United States, it remains higher than in many other industrial nations. As Figure 28-1 shows, a comparatively high proportion of U.S. households are poor, meaning that they are unable to purchase basic consumer goods. If anything, this cross-national comparison understates the extent of poverty in the United States, since U.S. residents are likely to pay more for housing, health care, child care, and education than residents of other countries, where such expenses are often subsidized.

In contrast, **relative poverty** is a floating standard of deprivation by which people at the bottom of a society, whatever their lifestyles, are judged to be disadvantaged *in comparison with the nation as a whole.* Therefore, even if the poor of 2014 are better off in absolute terms than the poor of the 1930s or 1960s, they are still seen as deserving of special assistance.

BOX 28-1

Research Today

Precarious Work

In 2008 Jim Marshall, age 39, lost his job in Detroit's faltering auto industry. Figuring that job prospects had to be better elsewhere, he moved to Florida. But by May 2009 Jim was homeless, living in a tent city just north of St. Petersburg. "My parents always taught me to work hard in school, graduate high school, go to college, get a degree and you'll do fine. You'll do better than your parents' generation," Marshall says. "I did all those things. . . . For a while, I did have that good life, but nowadays that's not the reality" (Bazar 2009:A2).

Jim's story is all too common. He is one of the millions of Americans who have been reduced to doing **precarious work**—employment that is poorly paid, and from the worker's perspective, insecure and unprotected. People who engage in precarious work often cannot support a household, and they are vulnerable to falling into poverty.

Even before economists recognized the economic downturn in 2009, there was ample statistical evidence that precarious work was increasing, despite the fact that the unemployment rate remained steady. In his presidential address to the ASA, Arne L. Kalleberg offered the following five social indicators:

1. *A decline in the average length of time workers remain with an employer.* This trend has been especially noticeable among older White men, who in the past were protected by employers.

2. *An increase in long-term unemployment.* The proportion of workers who remained unemployed after six months rose in the 2000s, when the number of manufacturing jobs shrank and fewer new jobs were created.

3. *A decrease in job security.* Given the increase in long-term unemployment and the decrease in average time spent with an employer, workers

To meet cyclical fluctuations in supply and demand, employers have turned more and more to nontraditional labor sources. Today, virtually any job can be outsourced, including accounting, legal, and military services.

became increasingly insecure about their ability to replace a lost job.

4. *An increase in outsourcing and temporary work.* To meet cyclical fluctuations in supply and demand, employers have turned more and more to nontraditional labor sources. Today, virtually any job can be outsourced, including accounting, legal, and military services.

5. *A shift in risk from employers to employees.* Few companies offer traditional pensions anymore. Employees are being asked to shoulder at least part of the cost and risk not only of their retirement investments, but of their health insurance plans as well.

Precarious workers are seeking political recognition by using social media, as well as other forms of communication, to draw attention to their plight. The Occupy Wall Street movement, which included some precarious workers, relied on social media. In Italy, clothing workers mounted a satirical runway show to underscore the precariousness of work in their industry. Their stunt created a flash of coverage, bringing attention to precarious work across all media and outlets, from the printed press to web applications and from mainstream to alternative media.

What can be done to revitalize labor markets so that fewer workers end up doing substandard work—or at least, so that those who do will suffer less from it? Denmark is one country that has tried to deal with the problem. Although the government there cannot make jobs more secure, it does provide significant assistance to the unemployed. Help finding a job, significant income compensation (90 percent of a worker's previous wage for one year, without conditions), and subsidized education and training are all available to Danish workers who have lost their jobs.

LET'S DISCUSS

1. Has the trend toward increasing reliance on precarious work touched your family or friends? Has anyone you know been unemployed longer than six months?

2. Looking forward to your own career, can you think of a strategy for avoiding precarious work, frequent job loss, and long-term unemployment?

Sources: European Metalworkers' Federation 2010; Fudge and Owens 2006; Kalleberg 2009, 2012; Mattoni 2012; Purser 2013; Somavia 2008; Westergaard-Nielsen 2008.

Debate has been growing over the accuracy of the federal government's measure of poverty, which has remained largely unchanged since 1963. If noncash benefits such as Medicare, Medicaid, tax credits, food stamps (the Supplemental Nutrition Assistance Program, or SNAP), public housing, and health care and other employer-provided fringe benefits were included, the reported poverty rate would be lower. On the other hand, if out-of-pocket medical expenses and mandatory work expenses for transportation and child care were included, the poverty rate would be higher. Furthermore, although the current poverty measure does consider family size, it does not consider a household's location, whether in a relatively expensive city like New York or in a less expensive rural area. Nor does it consider whether a householder pays rent or a mortgage installment, lives at home or with someone else.

To address some of these shortcomings, in 2010 the federal government launched a second statistic called the Supplemental Poverty Measure (SPM), which will be used to estimate economic hardship. The SPM is a relative poverty measure that is based on a broad range of changing household resources and

FIGURE 28-1 Poverty in Selected Countries

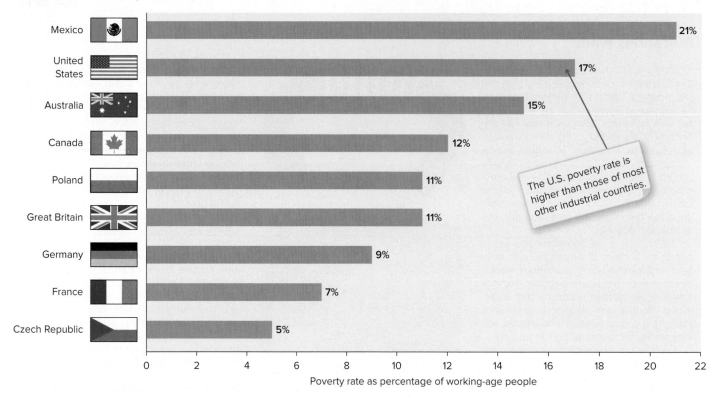

Poverty rate as percentage of working-age people

The U.S. poverty rate is higher than those of most other industrial countries.

Note: Data are averages for late 2000s, as reported in 2013. Poverty threshold is 50 percent of a nation's median household income.
Source: Organisation for Economic Co-Operation and Development 2013a.

expenses. It was calculated beginning in late 2011, but will not replace the poverty line in determining a household's eligibility for benefits (Blank 2011; Short 2012).

TABLE **28-1** WHO ARE THE POOR IN THE UNITED STATES?

Group	Percentage of the Population of the United States	Percentage of the Poor of the United States
Age		
Under 18 years old	24%	35%
18 to 64 years old	63	57
65 years and older	13	8
Race-Ethnicity		
Whites (non-Hispanic)	63	41
Blacks	13	23
Hispanics	17	29
Asians and Pacific Islanders	5	4
Family Composition		
Couples with male householders	73	39
Female householders	19	50
People with Disabilities	8	16

Note: People with disabilities includes ages 18–64.
Source: Data for 2012 in DeNavas-Walt et al. 2013:14, 17.

Who Are the Poor?

Not only does the category of the poor defy any simple definition; it counters the common stereotypes about "poor people." For example, many people in the United States believe that the poor are able to work but will not. Yet 40 percent of poor adults *do* work outside the home—27 percent of them full time—compared to 65 percent of all adults. Such stereotypes lead to the criminalization of the poor, described by the National Alliance to End Homelessness in the opening excerpt for this chapter (DeNavas-Walt et al. 2013:14).

Though many of the poor live in urban slums, a majority live outside those poverty-stricken areas. Poverty is no stranger in rural areas, from Appalachia to hard-hit farming regions to Native American reservations. Table 28-1 provides additional statistical information regarding low-income people in the United States.

Feminization of Poverty

Since World War II, an increasing proportion of the poor people of the United States have been women, many of whom are divorced or never-married mothers. In 1959, female householders accounted for 26 percent of the nation's poor; by 2012, that figure had risen to 50 percent (see Table 28-1). This alarming trend, known as the **feminization of poverty,** is evident not just in the United States but around the world.

About half of all women living in poverty in the United States are in transition, coping with an economic crisis caused by the departure, disability, or death of a husband. The other half tend to be economically dependent either on the welfare system or on friends and relatives living nearby. A major factor in the feminization of poverty has been the increase in families with women as single heads of the household. Conflict theorists and other observers trace the higher rates of poverty among women to three distinct factors: the difficulty in finding affordable child care, sexual harassment, and sex discrimination in the labor market (Burns 2010).

The Underclass

In 2012, 43 percent of poor people in the United States were living in central cities. These highly visible urban residents are the focus of most government efforts to alleviate poverty. Yet according to many observers, the plight of the urban poor is growing worse, owing to the devastating interplay of inadequate education and limited employment prospects. Traditional employment opportunities in the industrial sector are largely closed to the unskilled poor. Past and present discrimination heightens these problems for those low-income urban residents who are Black or Hispanic.

Along with other social scientists, sociologist William Julius Wilson (1996, 2012a, 2012b) and his colleagues (2004) have used the term **underclass** to describe the long-term poor who lack training and skills. According to an analysis of census data, 10.3 million people live in extremely impoverished areas. Although not all of them are poor, living in such disadvantaged neighborhoods means limited educational opportunities, greater exposure to crime and health risks, reduced access to private investment, and higher prices for goods and services. About 38 percent of the population in these neighborhoods is Black, 30 percent Hispanic, and 26 percent White non-Hispanic (Bishaw 2011).

Those statistics may sound high, but they could climb higher. Some scholars are predicting that the recent economic downturn may swell the ranks of the underclass, increasing the proportion of the U.S. population that they represent. Indeed, the recession seems to have accelerated the demise of less efficient, less profitable firms. When the downturn is over, jobs will not return to declining industries.

Analyses of the poor in general reveal that they are not a static social class. The overall composition of the poor changes continually, because some individuals and families near the top edge of poverty move above the poverty level after a year or two, while others slip below it. Still, hundreds of thousands of people remain in poverty for many years at a time. Blacks and Latinos are more likely than Whites to be persistently poor. Both Latinos and Blacks are less likely than Whites to leave the welfare rolls as a result of welfare reform (Jäntti 2009; Sampson 2011).

Even if this single parent works her way up the ladder, supporting her family will still be difficult.

Explaining Poverty

Why is it that poverty pervades a nation of such vast wealth? In 2013, poverty levels matched those of 50 years earlier. Sociologist Herbert Gans (1995), who has applied functionalist analysis to the existence of poverty, argues that various segments of society actually *benefit* from the existence of the poor. Gans has identified a number of social, economic, and political functions that the poor perform for society (Porter 2013):

- The presence of poor people means that society's dirty work—physically dirty or dangerous, dead-end and underpaid, undignified and menial jobs—will be performed at low cost.

- Poverty creates jobs for occupations and professions that serve the poor. It creates both legal employment (public health experts, welfare caseworkers) and illegal jobs (drug dealers, numbers runners).

- The identification and punishment of the poor as deviants upholds the legitimacy of conventional social norms and mainstream values regarding hard work, thrift, and honesty.

- Within a relatively hierarchical society, the existence of poor people guarantees the higher status of the rich. As psychologist William Ryan (1976) noted, affluent people may justify inequality (and gain a measure of satisfaction) by *blaming the victims* of poverty for their disadvantaged condition.

- Because of their lack of political power, the poor often absorb the costs of social change. Under the policy of deinstitutionalization, mental patients released from long-term hospitals have been transferred primarily to low-income communities and neighborhoods. Similarly, halfway houses for rehabilitated drug abusers, rejected by more affluent communities, often end up in poorer neighborhoods.

In Gans's view, then, poverty and the poor actually satisfy positive functions for many nonpoor groups in the United States.

Life Chances

Max Weber saw class as being closely related to people's **life chances**—that is, their opportunities to provide themselves with material goods, positive living conditions, and favorable life experiences (Gerth and Mills 1958). Life chances are reflected in measures such as housing, education, and health. Occupying a higher social class in a society improves your life chances and brings greater access to social rewards. In contrast, people in the lower social classes are forced to devote a larger proportion of their limited resources to the necessities of life. In some cases, life chances are a matter of life and death. According to a medical study published in 2011, in the United States, approximately

133,000 deaths a year can be attributed to individual poverty, and another 119,000 to income inequality. That is over a quarter million deaths per year caused by severely limited resources (Galea et al. 2011).

In times of danger, the affluent and powerful have a better chance of surviving than people of ordinary means. When the supposedly unsinkable British ocean liner *Titanic* hit an iceberg in 1912, it was not carrying enough lifeboats to accommodate all passengers. Plans had been made to evacuate only first- and second-class passengers. About 62 percent of the first-class passengers survived the disaster. Despite a rule that women and children would go first, about a third of those passengers were male. In contrast, only 25 percent of the third-class passengers survived. The first attempt to alert them to the need to abandon ship came well after other passengers had been notified. In an ironic demonstration of continuing social inequality, a luxury travel organization called Bluefish recently charged passengers $60,000 each to view the underwater remains of the *Titanic* from a deep-sea submersible (Butler 1998; Crouse 1999; Dickler 2011; Riding 1998).

Class position also affects people's vulnerability to natural disasters. When Hurricane Katrina hit the Gulf Coast of the United States in 2005, affluent and poor people alike became its victims. However, poor people who did not own automobiles (100,000 of them in New Orleans alone) were less able than others to evacuate in advance of the storm. The poor who survived its fury had no nest egg to draw on, and thus were more likely than others to accept relocation wherever social service agencies could place them—sometimes hundreds or thousands of miles from home. Those who were able to return are still dealing with the toxic debris left behind (Bullard and Wright 2009).

Wealth, status, and power may not ensure happiness, but they certainly provide additional ways of coping with problems and disappointments. For this reason, the opportunity for advancement—for social mobility—is of special significance to those on the bottom of society. Most people want the rewards and privileges that are granted to high-ranking members of a

Class position affects people's vulnerability to disasters. When the ill-fated *Titanic* sank in 1912, many more first-class passengers than third-class passengers survived. This photograph, taken recently on the ocean floor, shows the remains of a first-class cabin on the luxury liner.

culture. What can society do to increase their social mobility? One strategy is to offer financial aid to college students from low-income families, on the theory that education lifts people out of poverty. Yet such programs are not having as great an effect as their authors once hoped (Box 28-2).

use your **sociological imagination**

Imagine a society in which there are no social classes—no differences in people's wealth, income, and life chances. What would such a society be like? Would it be stable, or would its social structure change over time?

Social Mobility

In the movie *Maid in Manhattan,* Jennifer Lopez plays the lead in a modern-day Cinderella story, rising from the lowly status of chambermaid in a big-city hotel to a company supervisor and the girlfriend of a well-to-do politician. The ascent of a person from a poor background to a position of prestige, power, or financial reward is an example of social mobility. Formally defined, the term **social mobility** refers to the movement of individuals or groups from one position in a society's stratification system to another. But how significant—how frequent, how dramatic—is mobility in a class society such as the United States?

Open versus Closed Stratification Systems

Sociologists use the terms *open stratification system* and *closed stratification system* to indicate the degree of social mobility in a society. An **open system** implies that the position of each individual is influenced by his or her *achieved* status. Such a system encourages competition among members of society. The United States is moving toward this ideal type as the government attempts to reduce the barriers faced by women, racial and ethnic minorities, and people born in lower social classes. Even in the midst of the economic downturn of 2008–2009, nearly 80 percent of people in the United States felt they could get ahead (Economic Mobility Project 2009).

At the other extreme of social mobility is the **closed system,** which allows little or no possibility of individual social mobility. The slavery and caste systems of stratification are examples of closed systems. In such societies, social placement is based on *ascribed* statuses, such as race or family background, which cannot be changed.

Types of Social Mobility

An elementary school teacher who becomes a police officer moves from one social position to another of the same rank. Each occupation has the same prestige ranking: 60 on a scale ranging from a low of 0 to a high of 100 (see Table 27-1). Sociologists call this kind of movement **horizontal mobility.** However, if the teacher were to become a lawyer (prestige ranking of 76), he or she would experience **vertical mobility,** the movement of an individual from one social position to another of a different rank. Vertical mobility can also involve moving *downward* in a society's stratification system, as would be the case if the teacher became a bank teller (ranking of 50). Pitirim Sorokin ([1927] 1959) was the first sociologist to distinguish between horizontal and vertical mobility. Most sociological analysis, however, focuses on vertical rather than horizontal mobility.

One way of examining vertical social mobility is to contrast its two types, intergenerational and intragenerational mobility. **Intergenerational mobility** involves changes in the social position of children relative to their parents. Thus, a plumber whose father was a physician provides an example of downward intergenerational mobility. The celebrated movie star Leonardo DiCaprio, who was raised by a single mother in a neighborhood frequented by drug dealers and prostitutes, illustrates upward intergenerational mobility. Because education contributes significantly to upward mobility, any barrier to the pursuit of advanced degrees can definitely limit intergenerational mobility (see Box 28-2).

Figure 28-2 shows intergenerational mobility based on income. In 1978–1980, a national survey looked at the family income of 6,000 young people. Two decades later, in 1997–2003, researchers followed up on those young adults and their income. The results showed a strong stickiness in both the bottom and top quintiles, or fifths, of the income distribution. Just over 33 percent

Sociology on Campus

BOX 28-2

Social Class and Financial Aid

Today's young people have been dubbed Millennials, but a more appropriate name for them might be Generation Debt. In 2011, young people graduating from college with student loans left school carrying an average of $27,200 in debt, up 12 percent in just two years.

Every year, millions of prospective college students and their parents struggle through the intricate and time-consuming process of applying for financial aid. Originally, financial aid programs were intended to level the playing field—to allow qualified students from all walks of life to attend college, regardless of the cost. But have those programs fulfilled their promise?

> Statistics that show the educational level in the United States rising overall obscure the widening gap between the advantaged and the less advantaged.

In 2004, 40 percent of first-year students at major state universities came from families with incomes of more than $100,000 a year. In other words, close to half of all students came from high-income families. For students from families with the lowest incomes, however, the cost can be prohibitive. Only 11 percent of children from the poorest families in the United States have earned college degrees, compared to 53 percent of children from families in the top fifth of the population.

Despite all the talk about assisting the most needy, then, those students appear to be getting the least help. The pattern persists after students leave school. Among young adults, those who come from low-income backgrounds are most likely to be burdened with debt. Students from high-income families carry relatively little debt from student loans.

Community colleges, with their low tuition, are often regarded as a hedge against the high costs of higher education. Although these two-year commuter colleges may be cheaper than four-year residential schools, they are not inexpensive. In the academic year 2012–2013, the annual cost of attending a public in-state community college was about $11,000. For students at these schools, a greater proportion of their expenses goes to transportation and child care than for students who live on campus at four-year schools.

Besides the spiraling cost of an education, the widespread difficulty in paying for college stems from three trends. First, over the past few decades, colleges and universities have been moving away from making outright grants, such as scholarships, to deserving students, and toward low-interest student loans. Second, much of the assistance schools offer in the form of loans is not based strictly on need. Third, interest rates on federally guaranteed loans have risen steadily, increasing the burden of repayment.

These trends in financial aid for higher education are closely tied to trends in social inequality. As noted earlier in this chapter, over the past half century, rather than declining, inequality in income and

wealth has actually increased. In a variation on the truism that the rich tend to get richer while the poor get poorer, the rich are getting better educations and the poor are getting poorer educations. Statistics that show the educational level in the United States rising overall obscure the widening gap between the advantaged and the less advantaged.

LET'S DISCUSS

1. How important are student loans to you and your friends? Without them, would you be able to cover your college expenses?

2. Aside from a reduction in individual social mobility, what might be the long-term effects of the shortage of need-based financial aid? Relate your answer to the trend toward globalization.

Sources: Boushey 2005; Campbell et al. 2005; College Board Advocacy and Policy Center 2012; Houle 2013; Isaacs et al. 2008; Kamenetz 2006; Leonhardt 2004; Lewin 2011; Michals 2003; Trumbull 2006.

FIGURE 28-2 Intergenerational Income Mobility

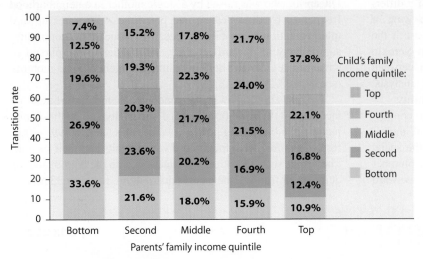

Source: Mazumder 2008:11.

Over a 25-year period, adult children often end up in the same income bracket as their parents. For example, as the first column shows, only 7 percent of those who begin in the bottom quintile reach the top quintile as adults; their story is one of rags to riches. By comparison, a third of the people in their quintile (33 percent) stay at the bottom, where they began.

of those whose parents were in the bottom quintile and 37 percent of those who were in the top quintile remained in the same quintile as adults. Yet the study also showed mobility: almost 66 percent of those in the bottom quintile moved up, and over 60 percent of those at the top experienced downward mobility.

Among men born in the 1960s, this consistent intergenerational mobility resulted largely from economic growth. On average, these men earned more than their fathers did at the same age; their family incomes improved as well. However, the trend has not continued into the next generation. Currently, young men are earning less than their fathers did at the same age—about 12 percent less. Family incomes are slightly higher than in the last generation, but only because women have moved into the paid labor force to supplement their husbands' earnings. With so few women left to join the labor force, most families will need to increase their wages to raise their incomes further (Sawhill and Haskins 2009).

Intragenerational mobility involves changes in social position within a person's adult life. A woman who begins work as a teacher's aide and eventually becomes superintendent of the school district experiences upward intragenerational mobility. A man who becomes a taxicab driver after his accounting firm goes bankrupt undergoes downward intragenerational mobility.

Social Mobility in the United States

The belief in upward mobility is an important value in our society. Does that mean that the United States is indeed the land of opportunity? Not unless such ascriptive characteristics as race, gender, and family background have ceased to be significant in determining one's future prospects. We can see the impact of these factors in the occupational structure.

Occupational Mobility   Two sociological studies conducted a decade apart offer insight into the degree of mobility in the

nation's occupational structure (Blau and Duncan 1967; Featherman and Hauser 1978). Taken together, these investigations lead to several noteworthy conclusions. First, occupational mobility (both intergenerational and intragenerational) has been common among males. Approximately 60 to 70 percent of sons are employed in higher-ranked occupations than their fathers.

Second, although there is a great deal of mobility in the United States, much of it is minor. That is, people who reach an occupational level above or below that of their parents usually advance or fall back only one or two out of a possible eight occupational levels. Thus, the child of a laborer may become an artisan or a technician, but he or she is less likely to become a manager or professional. The odds against reaching the top are extremely high unless one begins from a relatively privileged position.

The Impact of Education   Another conclusion of both studies is that education plays a critical role in social mobility. The impact of formal schooling on adult status is even greater than that of family background (although as we have seen, family background influences the likelihood that one will receive higher education). Furthermore, education represents an important means of intergenerational mobility. A person who was born into a poor family but who graduates from college has a one in five chance of entering the top fifth of all income earners as an adult (Isaacs et al. 2008).

The impact of education on mobility has diminished somewhat in the past decade, however. An undergraduate degree—a BA or a BS—serves less as a guarantee of upward mobility now than it did in the past, simply because more and more entrants into the job market hold such a degree. Moreover, intergenerational mobility is declining, since there is no longer such a stark difference between generations. In earlier decades, many high school–educated parents successfully sent their children to college, but today's college students are increasingly likely to have college-educated parents (Sawhill and Morton 2007).

The Impact of Race and Ethnicity   Sociologists have long documented the fact that the class system is more rigid for African Americans than it is for members of other racial groups. African American men who have good jobs, for example, are less likely than White men to see their adult children attain the same status. The cumulative disadvantage of discrimination plays a significant role in the disparity between the two groups' experiences. Compared to White households, the relatively modest wealth of African American households means that adult African American children are less likely than adult White children to receive financial support from their parents. Indeed, young African American couples are much more likely than young White couples to be assisting their parents—a sacrifice that hampers their social mobility.

Not surprisingly, African Americans are more likely than Whites to experience downward intergenerational mobility, and less likely to move up the social ladder. A study of people born

If this lawyer were the daughter of a car mechanic, her rise to the upper-middle class would illustrate intergenerational mobility. If she had begun as a paralegal and worked her way up the occupational ladder, her career would illustrate intragenerational mobility.

in the 1980s and 1990s found that based on their projected adult incomes, 68 percent of Whites should reach the middle class or better by age 40, compared to 34 percent of African Americans. If we focus on the ability of Blacks to climb out of poverty compared to Whites, the differences become even more marked.

The African American middle class has grown over the past few decades, due to economic expansion and the benefits of the civil rights movement of the 1960s. Yet many of these middle-class households have little savings, a fact that puts them in danger during times of crisis. We noted earlier that recession hits Black and Latino households harder than White households. Studies have consistently shown that downward mobility is significantly higher for Blacks than it is for Whites (Conley 2010; Oliver and Shapiro 2006; Sawhill et al. 2012; Sernau 2001; Wessel 2012; W. Wilson 1996).

The Latino population is not doing much better. According to one analysis, the median wealth of White non-Hispanic households is 18 times that of Hispanic households. This lopsided wealth ratio is the largest since the government first published the data in the 1980s. Continuing immigration accounts for part of the disparity: most of the new arrivals are destitute. But even the wealthiest 10 percent of Latino households have only a third as much net worth as the top 5 percent of White households (Kochhar et al. 2011).

The Impact of Gender   Studies of mobility, even more than those of class, have traditionally ignored the significance of gender, but some research findings are now available that explore the relationship between gender and mobility.

Women's employment opportunities are much more limited than men's. Moreover, according to recent research, women whose skills far exceed the jobs offered them are more likely than men to withdraw entirely from the paid labor force. Their withdrawal violates an assumption common to traditional mobility studies: that most people will aspire to upward mobility and seek to make the most of their opportunities.

In contrast to men, women have a rather large range of clerical occupations open to them. But the modest salary ranges and few prospects for advancement in many of these positions limit the possibility of upward mobility. Self-employment as shopkeepers, entrepreneurs, independent professionals, and the like—an important road to upward mobility for men—is more difficult for women, who find it harder to secure the necessary financing. Although sons commonly follow in the footsteps of their fathers, women are unlikely to move into their fathers' positions. Consequently, gender remains an important factor in shaping social mobility. Women in the United States (and in other parts of the world) are especially likely to be trapped in poverty, unable to rise out of their low-income status (Beller 2009; Heilman 2001).

On the positive side, though today's women lag behind men in employment, their earnings have increased faster than their mothers' did at a comparable age, so that their incomes are substantially higher. The one glaring exception to this trend is the daughters of low-income parents. Because these women typically care for children—many as single parents—and sometimes for other relatives as well, their mobility is severely restricted (Isaacs 2007b).

Mary Barra, CEO of General Motors, began her career in 1980 as a plant engineer. In 2014 she reached the top of the corporate ladder. Despite equal opportunity laws, occupational barriers still limit women's climb to the top. As of January 2014, women ran just 25 of the Fortune 500 companies; men ran the other 475.

Who works for the minimum wage? A generation ago, many of those who earned the minimum wage were teens who worked after school and on weekends. Today, only 12 percent of minimum wage workers are under age 20. A third of them are over 40.

Morris Cornley, 57, works as a delivery driver at Jimmy Johns in Kansas City, Missouri. Cornley, who makes $7.35 an hour, takes home about $370 after taxes every two weeks. His wages are supplemented by $1,000 a month in military disability pay plus $46 a month in food stamps. Cornley's rent is $475 a month. "I struggle to pay all the bills at one time," he says. "I'm not really living—I'm surviving" (P. Davidson 2013:7; Dube 2013a).

Looking at the Issue

Cornley's case is typical: by itself, the minimum wage simply is not high enough to support workers. This shortfall in income has severe consequences. In the United States, the large number of workers who are employed at minimum wage contributes to our high poverty rate and to the presence of an underclass.

Not only is the minimum wage too low; it also tends to shrink in value. Although the federal government has repeatedly raised the minimum—from 75 cents an hour in 1950 to $7.25 in 2009—in terms of its real value after inflation, the minimum wage often has not kept pace with the cost of living. Since the current minimum wage was enacted, it has lost 6 percent of its spending power; in real terms, it is now below its level in 1968 (*The Economist* 2013d).

The federal minimum wage does not apply to certain jobs, such as those for which employees receive tips. Waitpersons, nail salon workers, and parking attendants receive a minimum wage of $2.13. It also does not apply in states and cities that require employers to pay a higher minimum wage. Table 28-2 summarizes the current minimum wage rates in those states.

Applying Sociology

Conflict theorists argue that low-wage workers are vulnerable in other ways beyond the struggle to pay their bills. Although the minimum wage is the law, it is not always enforced. Many low-wage earners, especially those who are engaged in precarious work, may fear that they could lose their jobs if they complain to authorities that they are receiving less than the minimum wage.

Low-wage workers are also vulnerable to *wage theft*—the deliberate withholding of wages they have earned. Employers may shortchange workers of their rightful income by asking them to work "off the clock" (without pay), by failing to pay them time and half for overtime, by stealing their tips, by misclassifying

TABLE 28-2   MINIMUM WAGE RATES BY STATE

Hourly	Minimum Wage
$7.25	*Federal minimum wage*
7.40	Michigan
7.50	Maine, Missouri, New Mexico
7.75	Alaska
7.79	Florida
7.90	Arizona, Montana
7.95	Ohio
8.00	California, Colorado, Massachusetts, New York, Rhode Island
8.25	District of Columbia, Illinois, Nevada, New Jersey
8.70	Connecticut
8.73	Vermont
9.10	Oregon
9.32	Washington

Note: Minimum wage rates as of July 1, 2014. In states with rates that are lower than the federal minimum (Arkansas, Georgia, Minnesota, and Wyoming), employers must pay the federal minimum wage.

Sources: Bureau of the Census 2011a: Table 653; Department of Labor 2013a; Loecke 2014.

them as independent contractors, or by taking illegal deductions from their paychecks. Employers may also limit workers' wages by pressuring them not to file for workers' compensation after on-the-job injuries. According to a survey of people in various low-wage occupations, workers lose about 15 percent of their pay through such wage violations (Bernhardt et al. 2009).

Interactionists note that wages are only one kind of reward for work; the social contact that workers have on the job can also be beneficial. Depending on the workplace, the impact of the minimum wage on employees' lives can vary. Studies have shown that some low-wage workplaces offer a positive environment. Especially for younger workers, who see their wages as "spending money," work is a place to socialize with friends, away from their parents' watchful eyes. However, other studies have found high levels of alienation among minimum wage workers. Although well-paid workers can also feel alienated, at least they have the comfort of earning a livable wage (Bessen-Cassino 2013).

Initiating Policy

Few people would argue that low-wage workers should not be paid more. Instead, they disagree about the implications of such pay raises. Will a higher minimum wage result in

—Continued

higher prices for consumers? Will the extra pay that workers have to spend stimulate the economy? Will employers hire fewer workers or cut back on the number of hours they offer to minimum wage workers? Would other measures, such as the earned-income tax credit, better address the needs of the working poor? These concerns arise every time an increase in the minimum wage is debated, whether the increase is $3 an hour, $6 an hour, or $10 an hour (Neumark 2009).

Research shows that the effects of a change in the minimum wage are exceedingly complex. To predict the effects of a new increase in the minimum wage, economists have studied the impact of past increases. They have also examined the impact of changes in state minimum wage rates, both within the state and in neighboring states. The results of these studies have been far from conclusive, however.

Even if the minimum wage does have an economic impact, many other economic and social variables must be taken into account, including economic conditions in general. Moreover, economists do not necessarily agree on the effects of these other variables. For example, some studies note that certain wage hikes coincided with an economic slowdown; others note that the slowdowns affected primarily manufacturing—a sector that employs few minimum wage workers. No such slowdown has been observed in retail services or accommodation and food services, which together hire nearly two-thirds of all minimum wage workers. According to a recent Federal Reserve study, increasing the minimum wage to $9.25 would both increase spending by low-wage workers and decrease spending by consumers facing higher prices. Overall, it would increase consumer spending by $48 billion a year (Aaronson and French 2013; Dube 2013b).

In his 2013 State of the Union message, President Obama proposed raising the minimum wage to $9 an hour by 2015—a change that would affect an estimated 15 million workers. Critics of the proposal argue that it would raise labor costs for businesses, which would then hire fewer workers. Public opinion seems to support the president's proposal, however. A recent national survey found that although 25 percent of respondents oppose raising the federal minimum wage, 33 percent favor raising it to $9, and 36 percent favor raising it to $10.10.

Women, people with lower incomes, and those under age 30 are more likely than others to favor these changes (S. Greenhouse 2013:34; Peterson 2013; White House 2013).

In the United States, changes in the minimum wage require legislative action, which often lags the need for a wage hike by years. Some labor specialists suggest that the United States should adopt a different model, like those used in Great Britain and some other nations. Such a model would either tie the minimum wage to an economic indicator like inflation or create an independent board of economists to set its level (*The Economist* 2013d).

Many people argue that raising the minimum wage is not all that should be done for low-wage workers. These people advocate for a **living wage,** or a wage that meets workers' basic needs, allowing them to maintain a safe, decent standard of living within their community. Because community needs differ significantly from place to place, a living wage must vary in response to regional differences. For a single adult in Lincoln, Nebraska, a living wage might be $8.08; in Gainesville, Florida, it might be $9.27; in Los Angeles, it might be $11.37; and in New York City, $12.75. If the single adult is supporting a child, the living wage would more than double (National Employment Law Project 2013).

Workers and supporters of a living wage have mounted a public campaign on behalf of the idea. In 2013, from August through the holiday shopping season, they protested outside fast-food restaurants and big-box stores, calling for a minimum wage of $15 an hour. Industry spokespersons claimed that such a steep jump in the wage would increase the cost of a $3 hamburger by 60 cents; others countered with an estimate closer to 30 cents (Dewan 2013; Dube 2013a).

—*Continued*

—Continued

While politicians debated the policy, critics expressed concern over the potential loss of jobs, and employers cut back their hiring just as the economy was beginning to improve. Meanwhile, McDonald's advised workers to take a second job to make ends meet, but failed to consider workers' child care expenses and the cost of their health insurance. About the same time, managers of a Walmart store in Ohio launched a food drive to ensure that employees would have enough food to eat (P. Davidson 2013).

TAKE THE ISSUE WITH YOU

1. Have you ever worked for the minimum wage? If so, where were you living, and who paid for your basic living expenses? Could you have survived if the minimum wage had been your only source of support?

2. Relate the changes in the minimum wage over the past half century to changes in the U.S. social structure during that time. How have those changes affected you and your family?

3. What might be the macro effects of a living wage on U.S. society?

MODULE 28 | **Recap and Review**

Summary

Poverty is difficult to explain or define, although its effects are obvious and pervasive.

1. Many of those who live in poverty are full-time workers who struggle to support their families at minimum-wage jobs. The long-term poor—those who lack the training and skills to lift themselves out of poverty—form an **underclass.**

2. Functionalists find that the poor satisfy positive functions for many of the nonpoor in the United States.

3. One's **life chances**—opportunities for obtaining material goods, positive living conditions, and favorable life experiences—are related to one's social class. Occupying a high social position improves a person's life chances.

4. **Social mobility** is more likely to be found in an **open system** that emphasizes achieved status than in a **closed system** that emphasizes ascribed status. Race, gender, and family background are important factors in social mobility.

5. The large number of workers who are employed at minimum wage contributes to the high poverty rate in the United States, and to the presence of an underclass. Because the minimum wage often does not keep pace with the cost of living, some people have begun to advocate for a living wage that will meet workers' basic needs, allowing them to maintain a safe, decent standard of living within their community.

Thinking Critically

1. How do you identify areas of poverty in your own community or one nearby? Do you consider residents' achieved or ascribed characteristics?

2. How do people's life chances affect society as a whole?

3. Which factor—occupation, education, race and ethnicity, or gender—do you expect will have the greatest impact on your own social mobility? Explain.

Key Terms

Absolute poverty

Closed system

Feminization of poverty

Horizontal mobility

Intergenerational mobility

Intragenerational mobility

Life chances

Living wage

Open system

Precarious work

Relative poverty

Social mobility

Underclass

Vertical mobility

Mastering This Chapter

taking sociology with you

1 Do some research on the educational and occupational levels in the city or town where you live. Based on what you have learned, describe the social-class stratification of your community.

2 Use census data to create a map showing the median income levels and/or property values in the

geographic areas surrounding your home. What patterns does it show?

3 Talk with a parent or grandparent about your family's history. What can you learn about your forebears' life chances? About their social mobility? How do you hope to fit into the story?

key terms

Absolute poverty A minimum level of subsistence that no family should be expected to live below.

Achieved status A social position that a person attains largely through his or her own efforts.

Ascribed status A social position assigned to a person by society without regard for the person's unique talents or characteristics.

Bourgeoisie Karl Marx's term for the capitalist class, comprising the owners of the means of production.

Capitalism An economic system in which the means of production are held largely in private hands and the main incentive for economic activity is the accumulation of profits.

Caste A hereditary rank, usually religiously dictated, that tends to be fixed and immobile.

Class A group of people who have a similar level of wealth and income.

Class consciousness In Karl Marx's view, a subjective awareness held by members of a class regarding their common vested interests and the need for collective political action to bring about social change.

Class system A social ranking based primarily on economic position in which achieved characteristics can influence social mobility.

Closed system A social system in which there is little or no possibility of individual social mobility.

Conspicuous consumption Purchasing goods not to survive but to flaunt one's superior wealth and social standing.

Dominant ideology A set of cultural beliefs and practices that helps to maintain powerful social, economic, and political interests.

Estate system A system of stratification under which peasants were required to work land leased to them by nobles in exchange for military protection and other services. Also known as *feudalism*.

Esteem The reputation that a specific person has earned within an occupation.

False consciousness A term used by Karl Marx to describe an attitude held by members of a class that does not accurately reflect their objective position.

Feminization of poverty A trend in which women constitute an increasing proportion of the poor people of both the United States and the world.

Horizontal mobility The movement of an individual from one social position to another of the same rank.

Income Salaries and wages.

Intergenerational mobility Changes in the social position of children relative to their parents.

Intragenerational mobility Changes in social position within a person's adult life.

Life chances The opportunities people have to provide themselves with material goods, positive living conditions, and favorable life experiences.

Living wage A wage that meets workers' basic needs, allowing them to maintain a safe, decent standard of living within their community.

Objective method A technique for measuring social class that assigns individuals to classes on the basis of criteria such as occupation, education, income, and place of residence.

Open system A social system in which the position of each individual is influenced by his or her achieved status.

Power The ability to exercise one's will over others.

Precarious work Employment that is poorly paid, and from the worker's perspective, insecure and unprotected.

Prestige The respect and admiration that an occupation holds in a society.

Proletariat Karl Marx's term for the working class in a capitalist society.

Relative poverty A floating standard of deprivation by which people at the bottom of a society, whatever their lifestyles, are judged to be disadvantaged *in comparison with the nation as a whole.*

Slavery A system of enforced servitude in which some people are owned by other people.

Social inequality A condition in which members of society have differing amounts of wealth, prestige, or power.

Social mobility Movement of individuals or groups from one position in a society's stratification system to another.

Socioeconomic status (SES) A measure of social class that is based on income, education, and occupation.

Status group People who have the same prestige or lifestyle, independent of their class positions.

Stratification A structured ranking of entire groups of people that perpetuates unequal economic rewards and power in a society.

Underclass The long-term poor who lack training and skills.

Vertical mobility The movement of an individual from one social position to another of a different rank.

Wealth An inclusive term encompassing all a person's material assets, including land, stocks, and other types of property.

Read each question carefully and then select the best answer.

1. Which of the following describes a condition in which members of a society have different amounts of wealth, prestige, or power?
   a. stratification
   b. status inconsistency
   c. slavery
   d. social inequality

2. In Karl Marx's view, the destruction of the capitalist system will occur only if the working class first develops
   a. bourgeois consciousness.
   b. false consciousness.
   c. class consciousness.
   d. caste consciousness.

3. Which of the following were viewed by Max Weber as analytically distinct components of stratification?
   a. conformity, deviance, and social control
   b. class, status, and power
   c. class, caste, and age
   d. class, prestige, and esteem

4. Which sociological perspective argues that stratification is universal and that social inequality is necessary so that people will be motivated to fill socially important positions?
   a. the functionalist perspective
   b. the conflict perspective
   c. the interactionist perspective
   d. the labeling perspective

5. British sociologist Ralf Dahrendorf viewed social classes as groups of people who share common interests resulting from their authority relationships. Dahrendorf's ideology aligns best with which theoretical perspective?
   a. the functionalist perspective
   b. the conflict perspective

   c. the interactionist perspective
   d. sociocultural evolution

6. The respect or admiration that an occupation holds in a society is referred to as
   a. status.
   b. esteem.
   c. prestige.
   d. ranking.

7. Approximately how many people in the United States live below the poverty line established by the federal government?
   a. 5 percent
   b. 10 percent
   c. 15 percent
   d. 25 percent

8. Which sociologist has applied functionalist analysis to the existence of poverty and argues that various segments of society actually benefit from the existence of the poor?
   a. Émile Durkheim
   b. Max Weber
   c. Karl Marx
   d. Herbert Gans

9. A measure of social class that is based on income, education, and occupation is known as
   a. the objective method.
   b. stratification.
   c. socioeconomic status.
   d. the open system.

10. A plumber whose father was a physician is an example of
    a. downward intergenerational mobility.
    b. upward intergenerational mobility.
    c. downward intragenerational mobility.
    d. upward intragenerational mobility.

11. _____ is the most extreme form of legalized social inequality for individuals or groups.

12. In the _____ system of stratification, or feudalism, peasants were required to work land leased to them by nobles in exchange for military protection and other services.

13. Karl Marx viewed _____ differentiation as the crucial determinant of social, economic, and political inequality.

14. _____ _____ is the term Thorstein Veblen used to describe the extravagant spending patterns of those at the top of the class hierarchy.

15. _____ poverty is the minimum level of subsistence that no family should be expected to live below.

16. _____ poverty is a floating standard of deprivation by which people at the bottom of a society, whatever their lifestyles, are judged to be disadvantaged in comparison with the nation as a whole.

17. Sociologist William Julius Wilson and other social scientists have used the term _____ to describe the long-term poor who lack training and skills.

18. Max Weber used the term _____ _____ to refer to people's opportunities to provide themselves with material goods, positive living conditions, and favorable life experiences.

19. An open class system implies that the position of each individual is influenced by the person's _____ status.

20. _____ mobility involves changes in social position within a person's adult life.

Answers

1 (d); 2 (c); 3 (b); 4 (a); 5 (b); 6 (c); 7 (c); 8 (d); 9 (c); 10 (a); 11 Slavery; 12 estate; 13 class; 14 Conspicuous consumption; 15 Absolute; 16 Relative; 17 underclass; 18 life chances; 19 achieved; 20 Intragenerational

9 Global Inequality

Poorly built shanties lie in the shadow of the high-rise homes of the affluent in Singapore.

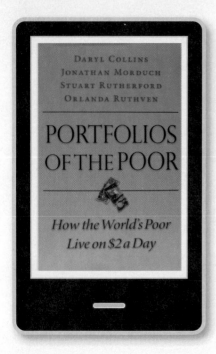

Could you live on less than $2 a day, including your rent or campus housing?

When a team of researchers asked poor people in developing countries how they spent their meager incomes, the results were surprising.

❝ To get a first sense of what the financial diaries [of the poor] reveal, consider Hamid and Khadeja. The couple married in a poor coastal village of Bangladesh where there was very little work for a poorly educated and unskilled young man like Hamid. Soon after their first child was born they gave up rural life and moved, as so many hundreds of thousands had done before them, to the capital city, Dhaka, where they settled in a slum. After spells as a cycle-rickshaw driver and construction laborer and many days of unemployment, Hamid, whose health was not good, finally got taken on as a reserve driver of a motorized rickshaw. That's what he was doing when we first met Hamid and Khadeja in late 1999, while Khadeja stayed home to run the household, raise their child, and earn a little from taking in sewing work. Home was one of a strip of small rooms with cement block walls and a tin roof, built by their landlord on illegally occupied land, with a toilet and kitchen space shared by the eight families that lived there.

In an average month they lived on the equivalent of $70, almost all of it earned by Hamid, whose income arrived in unpredictable daily amounts that varied according to whether he got work that day (he was only the reserve driver) and, if he did get work, how much business he attracted, how many hours he was allowed to keep his vehicle, and how often it broke down. A fifth of the $70 was spent on rent (not always paid on time), and much of the rest went toward the most basic necessities of life—food and the means to prepare it. By the couple's own reckoning, which our evidence agrees with, their income put them among the poor of Bangladesh, though not among the very poorest. By global standards they would fall into the bottom two-fifths of the world's income distribution tables.

An unremarkable poor household: a partly educated couple trying to stay alive, bring up a child, run a one-room home, and keep Hamid's health in shape—on an uncertain $0.78 per person per day. You wouldn't expect them to have much of a financial life. Yet the diversity of instruments in their year-end household balance sheet shows that Hamid and Khadeja, as part of their struggle to survive within their slim means, were active money managers.

Far from living hand-to-mouth, consuming every taka as soon as it arrived, Hamid and Khadeja had built up reserves in six different instruments, ranging from $2 kept at home for minor day-to-day shortfalls to $30 sent for safe-keeping to his parents, $40 lent out to a relative, and $76 in a life insurance savings policy. In addition, Hamid always made sure he had $2 in his pocket to deal with anything that might befall him on the road.

In addition to saving, borrowing, and repaying *money*, Hamid and Khadeja, like nearly all poor and some not-so-poor households, also saved, borrowed, and repaid in kind. Khadeja, sharing a crude kitchen with seven other wives, would often swap small amounts of rice or lentils or salt with her neighbors. She would keep a note of the quantities in her head, and so would her partners in these exchanges, to ensure that their transactions were fair over the long haul. Virtually all of the rural Bangladeshi households followed the well-established tradition of *musti chaul*—of keeping back one fistful of dry rice each time a meal was cooked, to hold against lean times, to have ready when a beggar called, or to donate to the mosque or temple when called on to do so. For rural respondents in India and Bangladesh, the intermediation of goods and services rather than cash was common, and included borrowing grain to be repaid after the harvest, repaying a loan with one's labor, or using labor to buy farm inputs. We recorded much of this activity. **❞**

> *An unremarkable poor household: a partly educated couple trying to stay alive, bring up a child, run a one-room home, and keep Hamid's health in shape—on an uncertain $0.78 per person per day. You wouldn't expect them to have much of a financial life.*

(D. Collins et al. 2009:7–8, 10–11)

Well over 2.5 billion people live on less than $2 a day—the widely recognized definition of poverty in the developing world. Incredibly, over 50 percent of them live on less than the extreme poverty level of $1.25 a day (World Bank 2012a). To find out how these poor households survive, four researchers conducted an intensive study of 250 families in Bangladesh, India, and South Africa. Daryl Collins, Jonathan Morduch, Stuart Rutherford, and Orlanda Ruthven wanted to know how best to use *microfinance*—small lending—to assist poor families in the developing world. As explained in the book *Portfolios of the Poor: How the World's Poor Live on $2 a Day,* rather than simply interviewing the families, Collins and his colleagues asked them to maintain financial diaries for a year. Through the diaries, the research team discovered that the families were quite adept at managing their income. Financial management, although not necessarily in currency, was a fundamental part of their lives, a skill they used every day of the year. Because the stakes were high—there is no room for error on $1 or $2 a day—these mostly uneducated people had developed surprisingly sophisticated methods for managing their resources.

In developing countries like Bangladesh, where Hamid and Khadeja live, most but not all the people are poor. Even in the poorest countries, the poor rub shoulders with the very wealthy. Inequality, then, exists within all countries, not just within the United States. On a global scale, inequality also exists *between* developing and developed nations, which is why a living allowance of $2 a day is so difficult for those of us in the developed world to comprehend. In this chapter we will consider social inequality both within developing nations and between the developing and developed worlds.

What economic and political conditions explain the divide between rich nations and poor? Within developing nations, how are wealth and income distributed, and how much opportunity does the average worker have to move up the social ladder? How do race and gender affect social mobility in these countries? In this chapter we will focus on global inequality, beginning with the global divide. We will consider the impact of colonialism and neocolonialism, globalization, the rise of multinational corporations, and the trend toward modernization. Then we will focus on stratification within nations, in terms of the distribution of wealth and income as well as social mobility. Module 30 closes with a Social Policy section on welfare reform in Europe and North America.

MODULE 29 | Stratification in the World System

● The Global Divide

In some parts of the world, the people who have dedicated their lives to fighting starvation refer to what they call "coping mechanisms"—ways in which the desperately poor attempt to control their hunger. Eritrean women will strap flat stones to their stomachs to lessen their hunger pangs. In Mozambique, people eat the grasshoppers that have destroyed the crops, calling them "flying shrimp." Though dirt eating is considered a pathological condition (called *pica*) among the well-fed, the world's poor eat dirt to add minerals to their diet. And in many countries, mothers have been known to boil stones in water, to convince their hungry children that supper is almost ready. As they hover over the pot, these women hope that their malnourished children will fall asleep (McNeil 2004).

Around the world, inequality is a significant determinant of human behavior, opening doors of opportunity to some and closing them to others. Indeed, disparities in life chances are so extreme that in some places, the poorest of the poor may not be aware of them. Western media images may have circled the globe, but in extremely depressed rural areas, those at the bottom of society are not likely to see them.

A few centuries ago, such vast divides in global wealth did not exist. Except for a very few rulers and landowners, everyone in the world was poor. In much of Europe, life was as difficult as it was in Asia or South America. This was true until the Industrial Revolution and rising agricultural productivity produced explosive economic growth. The resulting rise in living standards was not evenly distributed across the world.

Although the divide between industrialized and developing nations is sharp, sociologists recognize a continuum of nations, from the richest of the rich to the poorest of the poor. For example, in 2008, the average value of goods and services produced per citizen (or per capita gross national income) in the industrialized countries of the United States, the Netherlands, Switzerland, France, and Norway was more than $47,000. In at least 39 poorer countries, the value was just $1,000 or less. However, most countries fell somewhere between those extremes, as Figure 29-1 shows.

To reduce global poverty, wealthy industrialized countries must address the problem consistently, on a long-term basis.

Source: Steve Greenberg/Cartoon Movement. Reproduced by permission.

MAPPING LIFE WORLDWIDE

FIGURE 29-1 Gross National Income Per Capita

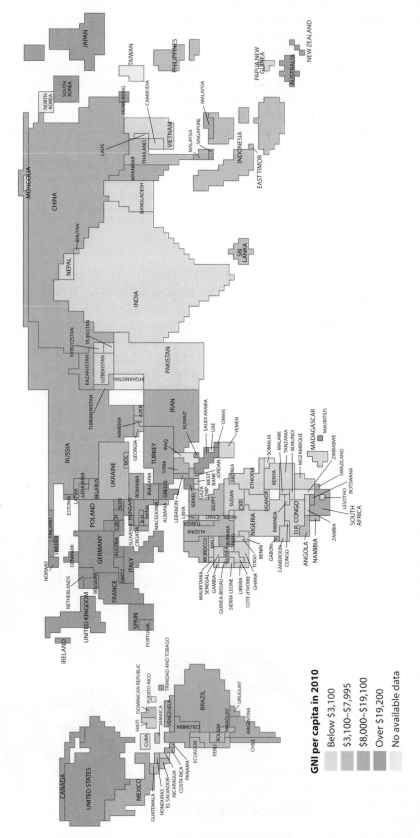

GNI per capita in 2010

Below $3,100
$3,100–$7,995
$8,000–$19,100
Over $19,200
No available data

Note: Country sizes and incomes based on 2010 estimates. Includes only those countries with 3 million or more people.

Sources: Haub 2010; Weeks 2012.

This stylized map reflects the relative population sizes of the world's nations. The color for each country shows the gross national income (the total value of goods and services produced by the nation in a given year) per capita.

What do we stand in line for? People's needs and desires differ dramatically depending on where they live. On the left, eager customers line up outside a store in Beijing to purchase the newly released iPhone 5s. On the right, residents of Ethiopia line up to receive water.

Still, the contrasts are stark. Four forces discussed here are particularly responsible for the domination of the world marketplace by a few nations: the legacy of colonialism, poverty worldwide which is particularly overwhelming in selected nations, the advent of multinational corporations, and modernization.

The Legacy of Colonialism

Colonialism occurs when a foreign power maintains political, social, economic, and cultural domination over a people for an extended period. In simple terms, it is rule by outsiders. The long reign of the British Empire over much of North America, parts of Africa, and India was an example of colonial domination. The same can be said of French rule over Algeria, Tunisia, and other parts of North Africa. Relations between the colonial nation and colonized people are similar to those between the dominant capitalist class and the proletariat, as described by Karl Marx.

By the 1980s, colonialism had largely disappeared. Most of the nations that were colonies before World War I had achieved political independence and established their own governments. However, for many of those countries, the transition to genuine self-rule was not yet complete. Colonial domination had established patterns of economic exploitation that continued even after nationhood was achieved—in part because former colonies were unable to develop their own industry and technology. Their dependence on more industrialized nations, including their former colonial masters, for managerial and technical expertise, investment capital, and manufactured goods kept former colonies in a subservient position. Such continuing dependence and foreign domination are referred to as **neocolonialism.**

The economic and political consequences of colonialism and neocolonialism are readily apparent. Drawing on the conflict perspective, sociologist Immanuel Wallerstein (1974, 1979a, 2000, 2012) views the global economic system as being divided between nations that control wealth and nations from which resources are taken. Through his **world systems analysis,** Wallerstein has described an interdependent global economy resting on unequal economic and political relationships. Critical

to his analysis is the understanding that by themselves, nations do not, nor have they ever, constituted whole systems. Instead, they exist within a larger, global social context.

In Wallerstein's view, certain industrialized nations (among them the United States, Japan, and Germany) and their global corporations dominate the *core* of this system (Figure 29-2). At the *semiperiphery* of the system are countries with marginal economic status, such as Israel, Ireland, and South Korea. Wallerstein suggests that the poor developing countries of Asia, Africa, and Latin America are on the *periphery* of the world economic system. The key to Wallerstein's macro-level analysis is the exploitative relationship of *core* nations toward *noncore* nations. Core nations and their corporations control and exploit noncore nations' economies. Unlike other nations, they are relatively independent of outside control (Chase-Dunn and Grimes 1995).

FIGURE 29-2 **World Systems Analysis**

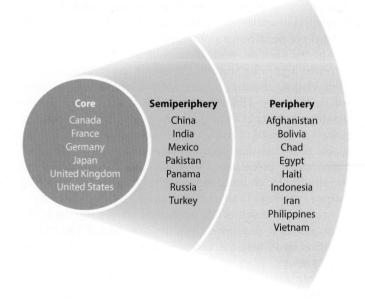

Core	Semiperiphery	Periphery
Canada	China	Afghanistan
France	India	Bolivia
Germany	Mexico	Chad
Japan	Pakistan	Egypt
United Kingdom	Panama	Haiti
United States	Russia	Indonesia
	Turkey	Iran
		Philippines
		Vietnam

Note: Figure shows only a partial listing of countries, selected by the author.

Chinese workers assemble toys for export to the United States. Globalization impacts both foreign and domestic workers, limiting employment opportunities at home and worsening working conditions abroad.

The division between core and periphery nations is significant and remarkably stable. A study by the International Monetary Fund (2000) found little change over the course of the *past 100 years* for the 42 economies that were studied. The only changes were Japan's movement up into the group of core nations and China's movement down toward the margins of the semiperiphery nations. Yet Immanuel Wallerstein (2012:9) speculates that the world system as we currently understand it may soon undergo unpredictable changes. The world is becoming increasingly urbanized, a trend that is gradually eliminating the large pools of low-cost workers in rural areas. In the future, core nations will have to find other ways to reduce their labor costs. Exhaustion of land and water resources through clear-cutting and pollution is also driving up the costs of production.

Wallerstein's world systems analysis is the most widely used version of **dependency theory.** According to this macro-level theory, even as developing countries make economic advances, they remain weak and subservient to core nations and corporations in an increasingly intertwined global economy. This interdependency allows industrialized nations to continue to exploit developing countries. In a sense, dependency theory applies the conflict perspective on a global scale.

In the view of world systems analysts and dependency theorists, a growing share of the human and natural resources of developing countries is being redistributed to the core industrialized nations. This redistribution happens in part because developing countries owe huge sums of money to industrialized nations as a result of foreign aid, loans, and trade deficits. The global debt crisis has intensified the Third World dependency begun under colonialism, neocolonialism, and multinational investment. International financial institutions are pressuring indebted countries to take severe measures to meet their interest payments. The result is that developing nations may be forced to devalue their currencies, freeze workers' wages, increase the privatization of industry, and reduce government services and employment.

Closely related to these problems is **globalization,** the worldwide integration of government policies, cultures, social movements, and financial markets through trade and the exchange of ideas. Because world financial markets transcend governance by conventional nation-states, international organizations such as the World Bank and the International Monetary Fund have emerged as major players in the global economy. The function of these institutions, which are heavily funded and influenced by core nations, is to encourage economic trade and development and to ensure the smooth operation of international financial markets. As such, they are seen as promoters of globalization and defenders primarily of the interests of core nations.

Critics call attention to a variety of issues, including violations of workers' rights, the destruction of the environment, the loss of cultural identity, and discrimination against minority groups in periphery nations. The impact of globalization appears to be most problematic for developing countries in Latin America and Africa. In Asia, developing nations seem to do better. Foreign investment there involves the high-tech sector, which produces more sustainable economic growth. Even there, however, globalization definitely has not reduced income disparities, either between nations or within countries (Kerbo 2006).

Some observers see globalization and its effects as the natural result of advances in communications technology, particularly the Internet and worldwide transmission of the mass media. Others view it more critically, as a process that allows multinational corporations to expand unchecked, as we will see shortly (Chase-Dunn et al. 2000).

 use your **sociological imagination**

You are traveling through a developing country. What evidence do you see of neocolonialism and globalization?

Poverty Worldwide

In developing countries, any deterioration of the economic well-being of those who are least well off threatens their very survival. By U.S. standards, even those who are well-off in the developing world are poor. Those who are poor in developing countries are truly destitute.

What would a map of the world look like if we drew it to a scale that reflects the number of *poor* people in each country instead of the number of people, as in Figure 29-1? As Figure 29-3 shows, when we focus on the poverty level rather than the population, the world looks quite different. Note the huge areas of poverty in Africa and Asia, and the comparatively small areas of affluence in industrialized North America and Europe. Poverty is a worldwide problem that blights the lives of billions of people.

How do social scientists measure global poverty? There is significant disagreement over where to draw the poverty line in the United States; adding the rest of the world to the equation further complicates the task. Individually, many developing nations define poverty based on the minimum income a person needs to survive—an amount that typically ranges from a low of

FIGURE 29-3 Poverty Worldwide

Population poor at US$1/day

= 50 million people
= 25 million people
= 10 million people
= 5 million people
= 1 million people

Legend:
- Across-the-board chronically deprived
- Partially chronically deprived
- Across-the-board other
- Partial consistent improver
- Across-the-board consistent improver
- OECD country
- Insufficient data

Think about It To what degree does this map minimize those countries you have studied or might want to visit? To what degree does it emphasize parts of the world about which you know very little?

Source: Chronic Poverty Research Centre 2009.

The scale of this map is based on the number of people in each region who are chronically poor. The colors represent the income levels of those who are poorest. In OECD countries—those that belong to the Organisation for Economic Co-Operation and Development (white)—chronic poverty is not a nationwide issue.

$1 a day to a high of $2 a day. Zambia defines poverty in terms of the inability to afford specific foods in a subsistence diet (Oxford Poverty and Human Development Initiative 2012).

In 2000 the United Nations launched the Millennium Project, whose objective is to halve extreme poverty worldwide by the year 2015. Although 15 years may seem a long time, the challenge was great. To reach the project's goal, planners estimated that industrialized nations must set aside 0.51 percent of their *gross national income*—that is, the total value of a nation's goods and services (GNP), plus or minus income received from and sent to other nations—to aid developing countries.

At the time the Millennium Project was launched, only five countries were giving at that target rate: Denmark, Luxembourg, the Netherlands, Norway, and Sweden. Although in dollar terms the U.S. government delivers far more aid to foreign countries and multinational organizations than any other nation, the

amount is not impressive considering the nation's tremendous wealth compared to other countries. In terms of the percentage of gross national income, the United States' contribution is among the lowest of the 23 most advanced industrialized countries, on a par with Japan's (Figure 29-4).

Despite the shortfall in recommended contributions, the Millennium Project reached its goal of halving poverty early, in 2013. Declines have been significant worldwide, especially in China, which ironically did not participate in the program. However, most of the project's other goals, including significant reductions in deaths among women in childbirth and among infants in their first year, will not be met in the near future (J. Moore 2013; Sachs 2005; United Nations 2005).

Another global concern is malnourishment, which prevents young children from receiving necessary nutrients during their first three years of life. The condition can lead to developmental problems that affect a child's quality of life through adulthood, and can even prevent a person from contributing to economic growth. Conflict theorists see malnourishment and its developmental effects as yet another result of inequality. However, functionalists point out that for developing societies—indeed, for any society—malnourishment is not only dysfunctional; it contributes to the growth of inequality over time (Warrell 2013).

Privileged people in industrialized nations tend to assume that the world's poor lack significant assets. Yet again and again, observers from these countries have been startled to discover how far even a small amount of capital can go. Numerous microfinance programs, which involve relatively small grants or loans, have encouraged marginalized people to invest not in livestock, which may die, or jewelry, which may be stolen, but in technological improvements such as small stoves. Box 29-1 describes another low-cost approach to delivering aid to developing countries, the direct-selling network.

● Multinational Corporations

We have seen that globalization has not necessarily improved the lives of the poor in the developing world. Another trend that does not always serve developing countries well has been the rise of

Open displays of social inequality are apparent in every nation. In Mumbai, India, billionaire Mukesh Ambani built this 27-story home for his wife and three children, complete with three helicopter pads and a 160-vehicle garage. To run the building, Ambani employs a staff of 600.

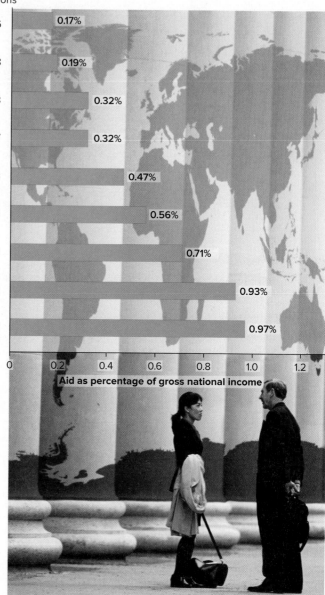

FIGURE 29-4 Foreign Aid Per Capita in Nine Countries

Country	Total aid in $ millions	Aid as percentage of gross national income
Japan	10.6	0.17%
USA	30.8	0.19%
Australia	3.8	0.32%
Canada	5.7	0.32%
Ireland	.8	0.47%
Great Britain	13.9	0.56%
Netherlands	5.5	0.71%
Norway	4.8	0.93%
Sweden	5.2	0.97%

Note: Actual net development assistance in 2012.
Source: Organisation for Economic Co-Operation and Development 2013b:Table 1.

multinational corporations. Worldwide, corporate giants play a key role in neocolonialism. The term **multinational corporation** refers to commercial organizations that are headquartered in one country but do business throughout the world. Such private trade and lending relationships are not new; merchants have conducted business abroad for hundreds of years, trading gems, spices, garments, and other goods. However, today's multinational giants are not merely buying and selling overseas; they are also *producing* goods all over the world (Wallerstein 1974).

Moreover, today's "global factories" (factories throughout the developing world that are run by multinational corporations) may soon have the "global office" sitting alongside them. Multinationals based in core countries are beginning to establish reservation services and centers for processing data and insurance

BOX 29-1

Sociology in the Global Community

Walking the Last Mile in Uganda: The Avon Approach

Avon, the cosmetics house that promotes itself as "the company for women," was founded in the United States in 1886. The company was born when a traveling book salesman noticed that female customers were more interested in the free perfume samples he offered along with the books than they were in the books themselves. Soon he had developed a network of female sales representatives who sold cosmetics both at home and door to door. In the 1960s, Avon began expanding into Italy, the Philippines, and then around the world through a global direct-selling network and investments in local retailing. By 2013, the company was marketing its beauty, fashion, and home products in over a hundred countries, through more than 6 million active sales representatives.

Today, the direct-selling model that Avon pioneered is being used to empower the poor in developing countries. In Africa, distribution is often the missing link between an aid project and its impact. To address that issue, in 2007 an organization called Living Goods established a network of 850 female representatives to sell health-oriented products in Uganda, along with the more traditional cosmetics. As with Avon representatives, these women sell to other women, many of whom they know as friends or neighbors. Along with lipsticks and perfumes, they offer iodized salt, condoms for preventing exposure to AIDS, kits for the sanitary delivery of babies, and bed nets to reduce the risk of malaria.

Just as Avon representatives do, Living Goods representatives communicate with their organization via cell phones and text messaging. Unlike direct sellers in developed countries, however, Living Goods agents walk what poverty workers refer to as "the last mile" to reach remote areas that are inaccessible to conventional aid organizations. In

a country where 6 out of 100 babies die in their first year, and half of all women do not have even an elementary education, their visits can make a marked difference in women's and children's health.

Living Goods representatives undergo two weeks of training that emphasizes health promotion more than salesmanship. The health-oriented products they offer, which are subsidized by outside agencies and donors, can be sold for a tenth the cost of similar products carried in West African retail outlets. Yet new customers are often more interested in soap than in de-worming pills, which they may not have seen before. The sales agent's job is to develop a market for the health products.

> Living Goods agents walk what poverty workers refer to as "the last mile" to reach remote areas that are inaccessible to conventional aid organizations.

Living Goods agents benefit from their work as much as their customers do. Like Avon representatives, they receive a starter kit of sample goods, such as body lotion and laundry detergent, and then must purchase additional supplies at a discount as

they sell the goods. Through their profits they typically become self-supporting, serving as models to other women who want to become economically self-sufficient.

Like any good entrepreneurial organization, Living Goods is always experimenting with ways to expand its outreach. In 2012 the company tried hiring male representatives in a pilot project designed to test whether men could perform as well as women as direct sellers.

LET'S DISCUSS

1. Do you know anyone who is a representative for Avon, Amway, or some other direct seller? How would you compare the challenge of direct selling in a developed country to direct selling in a developing country?

2. Why don't aid organizations establish their own direct-selling networks to offer only health-related products?

Sources: Avon 2013; *The Economist* 2012u; Living Goods 2013; T. Rosenberg 2012; Slaughter 2011; World Bank 2013.

---

claims in periphery nations. As service industries become a more important part of the international marketplace, many companies are concluding that the low costs of overseas operations more than offset the expense of transmitting information around the world.

Do not underestimate the size of these global corporations. As Figure 29-5 shows, the total revenues of multinational businesses are on a par with the total value of goods and services exchanged in *entire nations*. Foreign sales represent an important source of profit for multinational corporations,

which are constantly seeking to expand into other countries (in many cases, developing nations). The economy of the United States depends heavily on foreign commerce, much of which is conducted by multinationals. Over 12 percent of all goods and services produced in the United States relates to the export of goods to foreign countries, which supports an estimated 10.3 million jobs (Office of the United States Trade Representative 2012).

Functionalist and conflict theorists differ on the social and economic effects of multinational corporations, as we will see next.

FIGURE 29-5 **Multinational Corporations Compared to Nations**

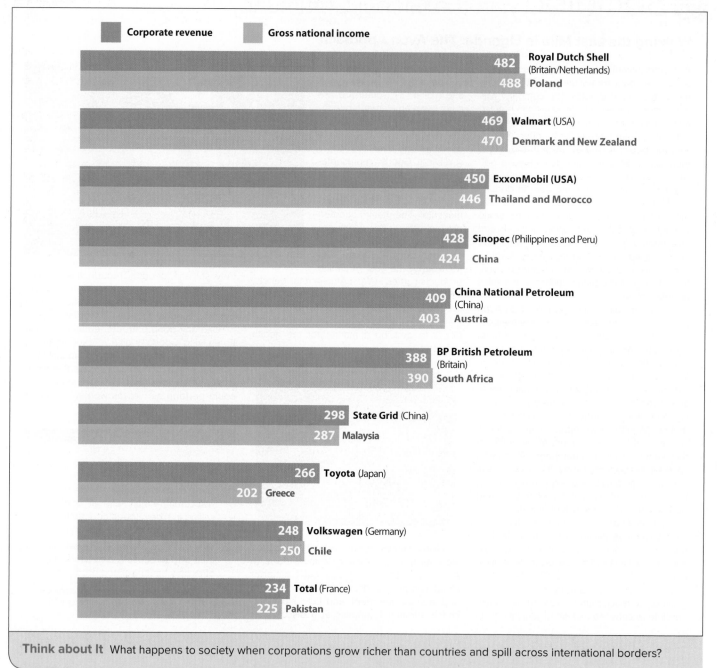

Corporate revenue ■   Gross national income ■

	Corporate revenue	Gross national income
Royal Dutch Shell (Britain/Netherlands)	482	
Poland		488
Walmart (USA)	469	
Denmark and New Zealand		470
ExxonMobil (USA)	450	
Thailand and Morocco		446
Sinopec (Philippines and Peru)	428	
China		424
China National Petroleum (China)	409	
Austria		403
BP British Petroleum (Britain)	388	
South Africa		390
State Grid (China)	298	
Malaysia		287
Toyota (Japan)	266	
Greece		202
Volkswagen (Germany)	248	
Chile		250
Total (France)	234	
Pakistan		225

Think about It What happens to society when corporations grow richer than countries and spill across international borders?

Sources: Ranking prepared by author. Revenue from corporate quarterly report statements for 2012. GNI from World Bank 2013:Table 1.1.

Functionalist Perspective

Functionalists believe that multinational corporations can actually help the developing nations of the world. They bring jobs and industry to areas where subsistence agriculture once served as the only means of survival. Multinationals also promote rapid development through the diffusion of inventions and innovations from industrialized nations. Viewed from a functionalist perspective, the combination of skilled technology and management provided by multinationals and the relatively cheap labor available in developing nations is ideal for a global enterprise. Multinationals can take maximum advantage of technology while reducing costs and boosting profits.

Through their international ties, multinational corporations also make the nations of the world more interdependent. These ties may prevent certain disputes from reaching the point of serious conflict. A country cannot afford to sever diplomatic relations or engage in warfare with a nation that is the headquarters for its main business suppliers or a key outlet for its exports.

Conflict Perspective

Conflict theorists challenge this favorable evaluation of the impact of multinational corporations. They emphasize that multinationals exploit local workers to maximize profits. Starbucks—the international coffee retailer based in Seattle—gets some of its coffee from farms in Guatemala. But to earn enough money to buy a pound of Starbucks coffee, a Guatemalan farmworker would have to pick 500 pounds of beans, representing five days of work; see Box 4-1, (Entine and Nichols 1996).

The pool of cheap labor in the developing world prompts multinationals to move factories out of core countries. An added bonus for the multinationals is that the developing world discourages strong trade unions. In industrialized countries, organized labor insists on decent wages and humane working conditions, but governments seeking to attract or keep multinationals may develop a "climate for investment" that includes repressive antilabor laws which restrict union activity and collective bargaining. If labor's demands become too threatening, the multinational firm will simply move its plant elsewhere, leaving a trail of unemployment behind. Nike, for example, moved its factories from the United States to Korea to Indonesia to Vietnam in search of the lowest labor costs. Conflict theorists conclude that on the whole, multinational corporations have a negative social impact on workers in *both* industrialized and developing nations.

Several sociologists who have surveyed the effects of foreign investment by multinationals conclude that although it may at first contribute to a host nation's wealth, it eventually increases economic inequality within developing nations. This conclusion holds true for both income and land ownership. The upper and middle classes benefit most from economic expansion; the lower classes benefit least. As conflict theorists point out, multinationals invest in limited economic sectors and restricted regions of a nation. Although certain sectors of the host nation's economy expand, such as hotels and expensive restaurants, their very expansion appears to retard growth in agriculture and other economic sectors. Moreover, multinational corporations often buy out or force out local entrepreneurs and companies, thereby increasing economic and cultural dependence (Chase-Dunn and Grimes 1995; Kerbo 2012; Wallerstein 1979b).

 use your **sociological imagination**

Think of something you bought recently that was made by a multinational corporation. How do you know the maker was a multinational?

Modernization

Globalization and the rise of multinational corporations have affected developing countries not just economically, but culturally. Around the world, millions of people are witnessing a revolutionary transformation of their day-to-day life. Contemporary social scientists use the term **modernization** to describe the far-reaching process through which periphery nations move from traditional or less developed institutions to those characteristic of more developed societies.

Sociologist Wendell Bell (1981), whose definition of modernization we are using, notes that modern societies tend to be urban, literate, and industrial. These societies have sophisticated transportation and media systems. Their families tend to be organized within the nuclear family model rather than the

extended-family model. Thus, members of societies that undergo modernization must shift their allegiance from traditional authorities, such as parents and priests, to newer authorities, such as government officials.

Many sociologists are quick to note that terms such as *modernization* and even *development* contain an ethnocentric bias. The unstated assumption behind these terms is that "they" (people living in developing nations) are struggling to become more like "us" (people in core industrialized nations). Viewed from a conflict perspective, these terms perpetuate the dominant ideology of capitalist societies.

The term *modernization* also suggests positive change. Yet change, if it comes, often comes slowly, and when it does it tends to serve the affluent segments of industrialized nations. This truism seems to apply to the spread of the latest electronic technologies to the developing world.

A similar criticism has been made of **modernization theory,** a functionalist approach that proposes that modernization and development will gradually improve the lives of people in developing nations. According to this theory, even though nations develop at uneven rates, the development of peripheral nations will be assisted by innovations transferred from the industrialized world. Critics of modernization theory, including dependency theorists, counter that any such technology transfer only increases the dominance of core nations over developing nations and facilitates further exploitation.

When we see all the Coca-Cola and IBM signs going up in developing nations, it is easy to assume that globalization and economic change are effecting cultural change. But that is not always the case, researchers note. Distinctive cultural traditions, such as a particular religious orientation or a nationalistic identity, often persist and can soften the impact of modernization on a developing nation. Some contemporary sociologists emphasize that both industrialized and developing countries are "modern." Increasingly, researchers gauge modernization using

Where am I wearing? This UNICEF poster reminds affluent Western consumers that the brand-name jeans they wear may be produced by exploited workers in developing countries. In sweatshops throughout the developing world, nonunion garment workers—some of them children—labor long hours for what we would consider extremely low wages—even if for the workers in those semiperiphery countries, wages are relatively high.

a series of social indicators—among them degree of urbanization, energy use, literacy, political democracy, and use of birth control. Clearly, some of these are subjective indicators; even in industrialized nations, not everyone would agree that wider use of birth control is an example of progress (Armer and Katsillis 1992; Hedley 1992; Inglehart and Baker 2000).

Current modernization studies generally take a convergence perspective. Using the indicators just noted, researchers focus on how societies are moving closer together, despite traditional differences. From a conflict perspective, the modernization of developing nations often perpetuates their dependence on and continued exploitation by industrialized nations. Conflict theorists view such continuing dependence on foreign powers as an example of contemporary neocolonialism.

Table 29-1 summarizes the three major approaches to global inequality.

Tracking Sociological Perspectives

TABLE **29-1** SOCIOLOGICAL PERSPECTIVES ON GLOBAL INEQUALITY

Approach	Sociological Perspective	Explanation
World systems analysis	Functionalist and conflict	Unequal economic and political relationships maintain sharp divisions between nations.
Dependency theory	Conflict	Industrialized nations exploit developing nations through colonialism and multinational corporations.
Modernization theory	Functionalist	Developing nations move away from traditional cultures and toward the cultures of industrialized nations.

MODULE **29** | **Recap and Review**

Summary

Worldwide, stratification can be seen both in the gap between rich and poor nations and in the inequality within countries. This module examines the global divide and stratification within nations as well as the impact of **globalization, modernization,** and **multinational corporations** on developing countries.

1. Developing nations account for most of the world's population and most of its births, but they also bear the burden of most of its poverty, disease, and childhood deaths.

2. Former colonized nations are kept in a subservient position, subject to foreign domination, through the process of **neocolonialism.**

3. Drawing on the conflict perspective, Immanuel Wallerstein's **world systems analysis** views the global economic system as divided between nations that control wealth (core nations) and those from which capital is taken (periphery nations).

4. According to **dependency theory,** even as developing countries make economic advances, they remain weak and subservient to core nations and corporations in an increasingly integrated global economy.

5. **Globalization,** the worldwide integration of government policies, cultures, social movements, and financial markets through trade and the exchange of ideas, is a controversial trend that critics blame for contributing to the cultural domination of periphery nations by core nations.

6. **Multinational corporations** bring jobs and industry to developing nations, but they also tend to exploit workers in order to maximize profits.

7. Sociologists note that terms such as **modernization** and even *development* carry an ethnocentric bias. **Modernization theory** suggests that the development of periphery countries will be assisted by innovations transferred from the industrialized world.

Thinking Critically

1. Relate Durkheim's, Tönnies's, and Lenski's theories of social structure to the global divide that exists today. Could sociocultural evolution have something to do with the global divide?

2. Relate modernization theory to dependency theory. Do you agree with critics that modernization will increase the dominance of core nations? Why or why not?

Key Terms

Colonialism

Dependency theory

Globalization

Modernization

Modernization theory

Multinational corporation

Neocolonialism

World systems analysis

MODULE 30 | Stratification within Nations: A Comparative Perspective

At the same time that the gap between rich and poor nations is widening, so too is the gap between rich and poor citizens *within* nations. As discussed earlier, stratification in developing nations is closely related to their relatively weak and dependent position in the global economy. Local elites work hand in hand with multinational corporations and prosper from such alliances. At the same time, the economic system creates and perpetuates the exploitation of industrial and agricultural workers. That is why foreign investment in developing countries tends to increase economic inequality. As Box 30-1 makes clear, inequality within a society is evident in Latin America's most populous nation, Brazil.

Distribution of Wealth and Income

Global inequality is staggering. Worldwide, the richest 2 percent of adults own more than 50 percent of the world's household wealth. In at least 22 nations around the world, the most affluent 10 percent of the population receives at least 40 percent of all income. The list includes the African nation of Namibia (the leader, at 65 percent of all income), as well as Nicaragua, Thailand, and South Africa. Figure 30-1 compares the distribution of income in selected industrialized and developing nations (World Bank 2011:68–70).

use your **sociological imagination**

Imagine that the United States borders a country with a much higher standard of living. In this neighboring country, the salaries of workers with a college degree start at $120,000 a year. What is life in the United States like?

Social Mobility

Mobility in Industrialized Nations

Studies of intergenerational mobility in industrialized nations have found the following patterns:

1. Substantial similarities exist in the ways that parents' positions in the stratification system are transmitted to their children.

2. As in the United States, mobility opportunities in other nations have been influenced by structural factors, such as labor market changes that lead to the rise or decline of an occupational group within the social hierarchy.

3. Immigration continues to be a significant factor in shaping a society's level of intergenerational mobility.

Cross-cultural studies suggest that intergenerational mobility has been increasing over the past 50 years in most but not all countries. In particular, researchers have noted a common pattern of movement away from agriculture-based occupations. However, they are quick to point out that growth in mobility does not necessarily bring growth in equality. Indeed, despite the evidence of steady upward mobility, their studies show that the gap between the rich and the poor has grown. Over the past 20 years, poverty levels in the 30 largest industrial economies have remained relatively constant (Organisation for Economic Co-operation and Development 2008).

Mobility in Developing Nations

Mobility patterns in industrialized countries are usually associated with both intergenerational and intragenerational mobility. However, in developing nations, macro-level social and economic changes often overshadow micro-level movement from one occupation to another. For example, there is typically a substantial wage differential between rural and urban areas, which leads to high levels of migration to the cities. Yet the urban industrial sectors of developing countries generally cannot provide sufficient employment for all those seeking work.

In large developing nations, the most socially significant mobility is the movement out of poverty. This type of mobility is difficult to measure and confirm, however, because economic trends can differ from one area of a country to another. As noted earlier in this chapter, in China, large numbers of people have moved out of poverty. However, income has not grown as rapidly in the rural areas of China as in the cities, or in some regions compared to others. In China, people who live in rural areas are basically shut out of the economic gains enjoyed by residents who live in centers of skilled labor and technology. Similarly, in India during the 1990s, poverty declined in urban areas but may have remained static at best in rural areas. Around the world, downward social mobility is also dramatically influenced by catastrophes such as crop failure and warfare.

Despite the continuing struggles of massive numbers of people, the global economic situation is not entirely bleak. Although economists have documented the persistence of poverty around the world despite some gains, they have also noted some growth in the number of people who enjoy a middle-class lifestyle. At the beginning of the 21st century, millions of people entered the middle class in the populous nations of China, India, Russia, Brazil, and Mexico. Entrepreneurship, microfinancing, merchandising, and in some countries, a growing, relatively well-paid government sector have fostered this increase in upward social mobility (Beddoes 2012).

Gender Differences in Mobility

Women in developing countries find life especially difficult. Karuna Chanana Ahmed, an anthropologist from India who has studied women in developing nations, calls women the most exploited of oppressed people. Beginning at birth women face sex discrimination. They are commonly fed less than male children, are denied educational opportunities, and are often hospitalized only when they are critically ill. Inside or outside the

Stratification in Brazil

Brazil conjures up exotic images: dazzling beaches, tropical foliage, colorful *Carnival* in Rio de Janeiro. Deep, grinding poverty and persistent inequality may not spring to mind, yet they are as much a part of South America's largest nation and economy as the expensive tourist resorts. Brazil has been described as three nations in one: a rich country with a population the size of Canada's; a poor country with a population equal to Mexico's; and a third nation of indigents—totally impoverished people with no income at all—whose population equals Argentina's.

Not until 1988 did Brazil's

> As in the United States, Brazil's social inequality is compounded by racial distinctions that originated in slavery.

government begin to consider a redistribution of wealth or land to remedy these inequities. The resulting program did not get under way until 2003. Since then, the gap between rich and poor has narrowed only a bit.

As in the United States, Brazil's social inequality is compounded by racial distinctions that originated in slavery. However, race is not socially constructed as it is in the United States. In Brazil, unlike the United States, dark skin color has never been a measure of innate inferiority.

Still, Brazil is no racial paradise. Rather, it is a multitiered racist society, one whose government has acknowledged the existence of racism. A

country that once prided itself on its freedom from racial intolerance, Brazil has now outlawed discrimination against people of color. Opinion is divided over the effectiveness of the legislation.

Today, the Brazilian economy shows a significant degree of racially related income disparity. As the accompanying figure shows, people of color are clustered disproportionately on the lowest levels of the income pyramid. To remedy this entrenched inequality, Brazil's government has instituted a quota-based affirmative action program that ensures access to higher education for people of color. Because of the lack of clear-cut racial categories in Brazil—Brazilians recognize many different color gradients—charges of reverse racism and complaints about inexplicable classifications have been common. As in the United States, finding solutions to the twin problems of racism and inequality is a challenge.

LET'S DISCUSS

1. Look at the bottom of each of the accompanying graphs. Which income distribution, Brazil's or the United States', appears to be more unequal? Now look at the top of each graph. Which income distribution appears to be more unequal? What aspect of these graphs do you find most striking?

2. Race-based college admissions quotas have been the subject of hot debate in the United States. Why do you think they have been accepted as law in Brazilian society?

Sources: Ash 2007; Daniel 2006; Dzidzienyo 1987; Fiola 2008; Margolis 2009; Santos 2006; SustainAbility 2006; Telles 2004.

Income by Race, Brazil and the United States

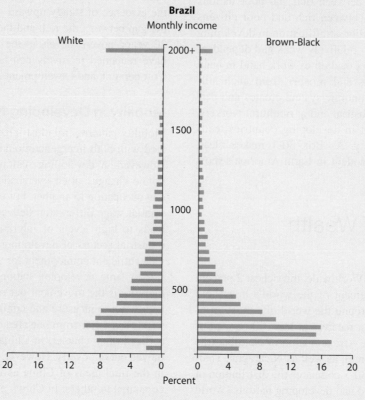

Brazil
Monthly income

White / Brown-Black

United States
Monthly income

White / Black

Source: Government agencies, as reported in Telles 2004:108.

FIGURE 30-1 Distribution of Income in Nine Nations

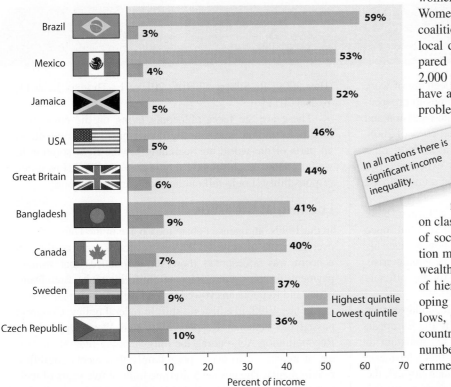

Brazil — 59% / 3%
Mexico — 53% / 4%
Jamaica — 52% / 5%
USA — 46% / 5%
Great Britain — 44% / 6%
Bangladesh — 41% / 9%
Canada — 40% / 7%
Sweden — 37% / 9%
Czech Republic — 36% / 10%

In all nations there is significant income inequality.

Highest quintile
Lowest quintile

Percent of income

Note: Data are considered comparable although based on statistics covering 1996 to 2010.
Source: World Bank 2013:Table 2-19.

United Nations Partners in Development Programme, women volunteers established the Pan-Cordillera Women's Network for Peace and Development, a coalition of women's groups dedicated to resolving local disputes. The women mapped boundaries, prepared development plans, and negotiated more than 2,000 peace pacts among community members. They have also run in elections, campaigned against social problems, and organized residents to work together for the common good (United Nations Development Programme 2000:87).

Studies of the distribution of wealth and income within various countries, together with cross-cultural research on mobility, consistently reveal stratification based on class, gender, and other factors within a wide range of societies. Clearly, a worldwide view of stratification must include not only the sharp contrast *between* wealthy and impoverished nations but also the layers of hierarchy *within* industrialized nations and developing nations. In the Social Policy section that follows, we will see that even in the relatively wealthy countries of Europe and North America, significant numbers of families require assistance from the government to meet their basic needs.

home, women's work is devalued. When economies fail, as they did in Asian countries in the late 1990s, women are the first to be laid off from work (J. Anderson and Moore 1993; Kristof 1998).

Surveys show a significant degree of *female infanticide* (the killing of baby girls) in China and rural areas of India. Only one-third of Pakistan's sexually segregated schools are for women, and one-third of those schools have no buildings. In Kenya and Tanzania, it is illegal for a woman to own a house. In Saudi Arabia, women are prohibited from driving, walking alone in public, and socializing with men outside their families.

Only recently have researchers begun to investigate the impact of gender on the mobility patterns of developing nations. Many aspects of the development process—especially modernization in rural areas and the rural-to-urban migration just described—may result in the modification or abandonment of traditional cultural practices and even marital systems. The effects on women's social standing and mobility are not necessarily positive. As a country develops and modernizes, women's vital role in food production deteriorates, jeopardizing both their autonomy and their material well-being. Moreover, the movement of families to the cities weakens women's ties to relatives who can provide food, financial assistance, and social support (Lawson 2008).

In the Philippines, however, women have moved to the forefront of the indigenous peoples' struggle to protect their ancestral land from exploitation by outsiders. Having established their right to its rich minerals and forests, members of indigenous groups had begun to feud among themselves over the way in which the land's resources should be developed. Aided by the

In developing countries, people who hope to rise out of poverty often move from the country to the city, where employment prospects are better. The jobs available in industrialized urban areas offer perhaps the best means of upward mobility. This woman works in an electronics factory in Kuala Lumpur, Malaysia.

In Pasadena, Denise Sims-Bowles, who has been out of work for more than three years, has sent 273 résumés to prospective employers. A victim of the deep economic recession and jobless recovery that followed the stock market crash of 2008, she has more than two decades of experience as a white-collar worker, yet she cannot find an opening. Her experience is a common one. About 45 percent of the nation's unemployed have been out of work for half a year or more.

In Barcelona, Spain, Paco Gonzalez, a former bank cashier, worries about the future. The 70-year-old once dreamed of a quiet retirement near the beach; now he fears his pension may not outlive him. The European economic crisis has pushed Spain's government to the brink, forcing officials to make difficult budget cuts (Somaskanda 2012).

In Athens, Greece, where the economic collapse was so bad that the nation had to be bailed out by the European Union, the story is even worse. Anargyros D., reluctant to give his last name, has lost everything—his father's business, his home, his personal possessions. Among men his age, the unemployment rate has more than doubled since 2008. His father is supporting him now, on a government pension that has been cut by a third. Looking broken, Anargyros says he has entertained thoughts of suicide. He is not alone. Calls to a local suicide help line have doubled in the last two years (Hay 2009; R. Scherer 2010a, 2010c; L. Thomas Jr. 2011; Wessel 2011).

These are the faces of people living on the edge. In a time of economic stress and growing need, governments in all parts of the world are searching for the right solution to welfare: How much subsidy should they provide? How much responsibility should fall on the shoulders of the poor?

Looking at the Issue

In the 1990s, an intense debate took place in the United States over the issue of welfare. Welfare programs were costly, and concern was widespread (however unfounded) that welfare payments discouraged recipients from seeking jobs. Both Democrats and Republicans vowed to "end welfare as we know it."

In late 1996, in a historic shift in federal policy, Congress passed the Personal Responsibility and Work Opportunity Reconciliation Act, ending the long-standing federal guarantee of assistance to every poor family that meets eligibility requirements. The law set a lifetime limit of five years of welfare benefits, and required all able-bodied adults to work after receiving two years of benefits (although hardship exceptions were allowed). The federal government would give block grants to the states to use as they wished in assisting poor and needy residents, and it would permit states to experiment with ways to move people off welfare (Seccombe 2011).

In the United States, the government safety net now falls far short of that in Europe, even after recent cutbacks there. Available data indicate that in Great Britain, 83 percent of health expenditures are paid for by the government; in Sweden, 81 percent; in Canada, 70 percent; but in the United States, only 50 percent. In fact, most industrialized nations devote higher proportions of their expenditures to housing, social security, welfare, health care, and unemployment compensation than the United States does. As U.S. economist Dean Baker declared recently, "The increase in social spending is still relatively modest given the severity of the downturn. We're not France" (Cauchon 2009; World Bank 2012a:100–102).

In northern and western Europe, following the deep worldwide recession that began in 2008, countries with strong social safety nets were forced to cut back benefits. These civil servants in Granada, Spain, are protesting salary cutbacks.

—Continued

Applying Sociology

Many sociologists tend to view the debate over welfare reform in industrialized nations from a conflict perspective: the "haves" in positions of policymaking listen to the interests of other "haves," while the cries of the "have-nots" are drowned out. Critics of welfare reform believe that the nation's economic problems are unfairly blamed on welfare spending and the poor. From a conflict perspective, this backlash against welfare recipients reflects deep fears and hostility toward the nation's urban, predominantly African American and Hispanic underclass.

Those who are critical of the backlash note that "welfare scapegoating" conveniently ignores the lucrative federal handouts that go to *affluent* individuals and families. For example, while federal housing aid to the poor was cut drastically in the 1980s, tax deductions for mortgage interest and property taxes more than doubled.

Conflict theorists have noted an oft-ignored aspect of the welfare system, administrative sanctions. The law allows administrators to end welfare payments if clients fail to complete job-readiness classes, community work, or job searches. A great deal of discretion is used in applying sanctions. According to one study, Black clients are more likely to be sanctioned than White clients (Schram et al. 2009).

Those who take a conflict perspective also urge policymakers and the general public to look closely at **corporate welfare**—the tax breaks, bailouts, direct payments, and grants that the government gives to corporations—rather than looking closely at the comparatively small allowances being given to mothers and their children. Yet any suggestion to curtail such corporate welfare brings a strong response from special-interest groups that are much more powerful than any coalition on behalf of the poor. One example of corporate welfare is the huge federal bailouts given to distressed financial institutions in fall 2008 and to bankrupt automobile companies in 2009. Although the outlay of hundreds of billions of dollars was vital to the nation's economic recovery, the measure received relatively little scrutiny from Congress. Just a few months later, however, when legislation was proposed to extend the safety net for laid-off workers—unemployment compensation, food stamps, subsidized child care, assistance to the homeless, disability support, and infant nutrition—it met with loud demands for the monitoring of expenditures (DeParle 2009; Piven and Cloward 1996).

Initiating Policy

The government likes to highlight welfare-reform success stories. Though many people who once depended on tax dollars are now working and paying taxes themselves, it is much too soon to see if "workfare" will be successful. The new jobs that were generated by the booming economy of the late 1990s were an unrealistic test of the system. Prospects have faded for the hard-core jobless—people who are difficult to train or are encumbered by drug or alcohol abuse, physical disabilities, or child care needs—since that boom passed.

True, fewer people remain on the rolls since welfare reform was enacted in August 1996. By September 2013 just under 1.6 million families were still on the rolls, down 65 percent from a high of 5.1 million in 1994. But while those families that have left the rolls are modestly better off now, most of their breadwinners continue to hold low-paying, unskilled jobs. For them, the economic downturn that was well in place by 2009 made finding work tougher than ever. Of those adults who remain on welfare, nearly 70 percent are not in school or in welfare-to-work programs, as the law requires them to be. This group tends to face the greatest challenges—substance abuse, mental illness, or a criminal record (Bitler and Hoynes 2010; Danziger 2010; Department of Health and Human Services 2013).

European governments have encountered many of the same citizen demands as in North America: keep our taxes low, even if it means reducing services to the poor. However, nations in eastern and central Europe have faced a special challenge since the end of communism. Though governments in those nations traditionally provided an impressive array of social services, they differed from capitalist systems in several important respects. First, the communist system was premised on full employment, so there was no need to provide unemployment insurance; social services focused on the old and the disabled. Second, subsidies for housing and even utilities played an important role. With new competition from the West and tight budgets, some of these countries are beginning to realize that universal coverage is no longer affordable and must be replaced with targeted programs.

The reduction in state assistance to the unemployed is not limited to the former Soviet bloc. Even Denmark, despite its long history of social welfare programs, is feeling the pinch. Student stipends are being reduced, early retirement plans have been reduced, and the maximum time for receiving unemployment benefits has been cut in half (although it is still a generous *two years*). Yet by any standard, the European safety net is still significantly stronger than that of the United States (Daley 2013; Petrášová 2006).

This decline in public assistance has not escaped public attention. Erik O. Wright, 2012 president of the American Sociological Society, has observed that the Occupy Wall Street movement "is not a uniquely American event . . . it is part of a global wave of protests." Wright senses rising concern that "harsh inequalities" are becoming "increasingly illegitimate. It would appear the present trends in welfare policy are doing little to address these concerns" (E. O. Wright 2011).

—Continued

MODULE 30 | Recap and Review

Summary

This module examines the effects of stratification within nations.

1. The global economic system creates and perpetuates the gap between the rich and poor in developing nations.

2. Intergenerational mobility has been increasing over the past 50 years in most but not all countries. In large developing nations, the most socially significant mobility is the movement out of poverty.

3. Gender differences in mobility exist in both developed and developing societies. Women tend to have more difficulties moving up the economic ladder at all phases of the life course.

Thinking Critically

1. Contrast social mobility in developing and industrialized nations. Do you think the differences will eventually disappear? Why or why not?

2. What social structural factors contribute to making women "the most exploited of oppressed people"?

Key Terms

Corporate welfare

Mastering This Chapter

taking sociology with you

1 Pick a multinational corporation whose products you are familiar with and look up its financial statements. In which countries does the corporation produce products and in which does it sell products? In which country does the corporation pay taxes? To which country do its profits flow? Why should the answers to these questions matter to you?

2 Choose a foreign country that you are interested in and do some research on social stratification in that country. How equally or unequally are wealth and income distributed there, in comparison to the United States? How extensive is social mobility? Explain the reasons for any differences in stratification.

3 Choose a European country and a developing country and do some research on their welfare systems. How do the two systems differ? How does each reflect the culture and society it serves?

Colonialism The maintenance of political, social, economic, and cultural domination over a people by a foreign power for an extended period.

Corporate welfare Tax breaks, bailouts, direct payments, and grants that the government gives to corporations.

Dependency theory An approach that contends that industrialized nations continue to exploit developing countries for their own gain.

Globalization The worldwide integration of government policies, cultures, social movements, and financial markets through trade and the exchange of ideas.

Modernization The far-reaching process through which periphery nations move from traditional or less developed institutions to those characteristic of more developed societies.

Modernization theory A functionalist approach that proposes that modernization and development will gradually improve the lives of people in developing nations.

Multinational corporation A commercial organization that is headquartered in one country but does business throughout the world.

Neocolonialism Continuing dependence of former colonies on foreign countries.

World systems analysis The global economy as an interdependent system of economically and politically unequal nations.

self-quiz

Read each question carefully and then select the best answer.

1. The maintenance of political, social, economic, and cultural domination over a people by a foreign power for an extended period is referred to as
   a. neocolonialism.
   b. government-imposed stratification.
   c. colonialism.
   d. dependency.

2. In viewing the global economic system as divided between nations that control wealth and those that are controlled and exploited, sociologist Immanuel Wallerstein draws on the
   a. functionalist perspective.
   b. conflict perspective.
   c. interactionist perspective.
   d. dramaturgical approach.

3. Which of the following nations would Immanuel Wallerstein classify as a *core* country within the world economic system?
   a. Germany
   b. South Korea
   c. Ireland
   d. Mexico

4. Which of the following goals of the Millennium Project has already been reached?
   a. convince industrialized nations to set aside 0.51 percent of their gross national income to aid developing countries
   b. halve extreme poverty worldwide
   c. significantly reduce deaths to women in childbirth
   d. significantly reduce deaths to infants in their first year

5. Which of the following approaches to the delivery of aid to developing countries has been successful in Uganda?
   a. the Millennium Project
   b. microfinancing
   c. direct selling
   d. none of the above

6. Which sociological perspective argues that multinational corporations can actually help the developing nations of the world?
   a. the interactionist perspective
   b. the feminist perspective
   c. the functionalist perspective
   d. the conflict perspective

7. Which of the following terms is used by contemporary social scientists to describe the far-reaching process by which peripheral nations move from traditional or less developed institutions to those characteristic of more developed societies?
   a. dependency
   b. globalization
   c. industrialization
   d. modernization

8. Which of the following statements about the division of income in Brazil is *not* true?
   a. Income is distributed more evenly across the population in Brazil than in the United States.
   b. In Brazil there is a noticeable difference between the races in the top income bracket.
   c. In Brazil there is a noticeable difference between the races in the bottom income brackets.
   d. Both b and c are true.

9. In at least 22 nations around the world, the most affluent 10 percent receives at least what percentage of all income?
   a. 20 percent
   b. 30 percent
   c. 40 percent
   d. 50 percent

10. Karuna Chanana Ahmed, an anthropologist from India who has studied developing nations, calls which group the most exploited of oppressed people?
    a. children
    b. women
    c. the elderly
    d. the poor

11. Colonial domination established patterns of economic exploitation leading to former colonies remaining dependent on more industrialized nations. Such continuing dependence and foreign domination are referred to as _____.

12. According to Immanuel Wallerstein's analysis, the United States is at the _____ while neighboring Mexico is on the _____ of the world economic system.

13. Wallerstein's world systems analysis is the most widely used version of _____ theory.

14. In many developing nations, _____ is defined as the minimum income a person needs to survive, typically $1 to $2 a day.

15. _____ factories are factories found throughout the developing world that are run by multinational corporations.

16. As _____ industries become a more important part of the international marketplace, many companies have concluded that the low costs of overseas operations more than offset the expense of transmitting information around the world.

17. Viewed from a(n) _____ perspective, the combination of skilled technology and management provided by multinationals and the relatively cheap labor available in developing nations is ideal for a global enterprise.

18. Modernization theory reflects the_____ perspective.

19. In large developing nations, the most significant form of social mobility is the movement out of _____.

20. Tax breaks, bailouts, direct payments, and grants are all forms of _____ _____.

10 Racial and Ethnic Inequality

U.S. society is becoming increasingly diverse as immigrants from around the world bring their skills, languages, and cultures with them to their new home.

MODULE 31 Minority, Racial, and Ethnic Groups

MODULE 32 Sociological Perspectives on Race and Ethnicity

MODULE 33 Race and Ethnicity in the United States

Have you ever been torn between fitting in and being true to who you are?

Charles Trimble has been rethinking that trade-off.

❝ I am an Iyeska, a mixed-blood—Oglala Lakota and bits of European nationalities, mostly Irish and English. Over the years we were called half-breeds, breeds, as well as various other names from both sides of our ancestry, many of them unprintable.

Iyeska in Lakota translates as "speaks white," but through the years has taken on the generic term for "mixed blood." What I write here comes from my own experiences as an Iyeska, and from what I have observed among Iyeskas I have known.

Whether or not we admit it, most of the mixed blood kids that I knew in the Indian boarding school I attended and in my home village on the Pine Ridge Reservation through the 1940s and 50s wished sometimes that we were not Indian at all. That came perhaps from seeing movies and reading books in which the white guys always won, had all the money, nice cars and girls. Indians were always the bad guys, killing innocent settlers who only wanted us dead and our land theirs. And in most towns on the reservation, the stores and other businesses were owned by whites. In reservation border towns, we often faced discrimination. In short, our futures sometimes didn't look all that promising as Indians.

So we bought into what was being pushed on us anyway: assimilation; and we acted out what was expected of us to get jobs and fit into the larger society. . . .

We need to take pride in our Indianness, no matter how thin our tribal blood quantum; but we also need to give some credit to our white or Latino or black forebears.

In the schools, there was often a sense of superiority among Iyeskas over the full-bloods, and sometimes there was tension between them. "Buck" was a common term used to describe a person who the Iyeska considered backward—mainly full-bloods. But an Iyeska didn't say it too loudly, because many of the best athletes and the toughest boys were full-bloods.

It seems to me that during our growing-up years, we used our white characteristics to our advantage in getting scholarships and employment opportunities, and now that there are more opportunities for Indians—especially from casino earnings—we want to take back our Indianness, at least in our fantasies.

Admittedly, what I have written above could be seen as cynical or even mean. I admit that the scenario applies to me to a greater or lesser degree, or I would not have written it. It is true that most Iyeskas who stayed on the reservation are very comfortable in their status, and their relations in their communities. And many Iyeskas are very serious in their search to find their roots and a culture they may feel to have been deprived of. For whatever reason they may have "returned to the blanket," some are happy in finding that special goodness and peace that can be found in traditional life.

But for many of us Iyeskas, I think that perhaps it's time to quit trying to impress white people and younger generations of Indians with fantasy stories of another life, or blaming someone else for having given up a culture that was largely peripheral to our lives anyway. We need to take pride in our Indianness, no matter how thin our tribal blood quantum; but we also need to give some credit to our White or Latino or black forebears. The inner peace of living a real life, with a true life story, is worth it. **❞**

(Trimble 2008:5)

I n this excerpt from "Iyeska: Notes from Mixed-Blood Country," Charles Trimble, scholar, journalist, and former executive director of the National Congress for American Indians, recalls his childhood as a mixed-blood Indian from the Pine Ridge Reservation in South Dakota. A member of the Oglala Lakota Sioux, Trimble attended a boarding school where Native American youths were pressed to renounce their tribal heritage and adopt White culture instead. Although he went on to succeed in mainstream American society, later in life he began to question the choice he had made as a youth. "Who am I, really?" Trimble seems to ask himself in these notes.

What sense are we to make of the issues of race, ethnicity, and immigration in the 21st century? Today, members of racial and ethnic minorities still struggle with the question of whether to assimilate. As they age, many look back with regret. Too often, those who do assimilate face continued prejudice and discrimination. Like class, race and ethnicity still affect people's place and status in a stratification system, not only in this country, but throughout the world. High incomes, a good command of English, and hard-earned professional credentials do not always override racial and ethnic stereotypes or protect those who fit them from the sting of racism.

What is prejudice, and how is it institutionalized in the form of discrimination? In what ways have race and ethnicity affected the experience of immigrants from other countries? What are the fastest-growing minority groups in the United States today? In this chapter we will focus on the meaning of race and ethnicity. We will begin by identifying the basic characteristics of a minority group and distinguishing between racial and ethnic groups. Then we will examine the dynamics of prejudice and discrimination. After considering four sociological perspectives on race and ethnicity, we'll take a look at common patterns of intergroup relations. In Module 33, we will describe the major racial and ethnic groups in the United States, and in the Social Policy section we explore the issue of global immigration.

MODULE 31 | **Minority, Racial, and Ethnic Groups**

Sociologists frequently distinguish between racial and ethnic groups. The term **racial group** describes a group that is set apart from others because of physical differences that have taken on social significance. Whites, African Americans, and Asian Americans are all considered racial groups in the United States. While race does turn on physical differences, it is the culture of a particular society that constructs and attaches social significance to those differences, as we will see later. Unlike racial groups, an **ethnic group** is set apart from others primarily because of its national origin or distinctive cultural patterns. In the United States, Puerto Ricans, Jews, and Polish Americans are all categorized as ethnic groups (Table 31-1).

Minority Groups

A numerical minority is any group that makes up less than half of some larger population. The population of the United States includes thousands of numerical minorities, including television actors, green-eyed people, tax lawyers, and descendants of the Pilgrims who arrived on the *Mayflower*. However, these numerical minorities are not considered to be minorities in the sociological sense; in fact, the number of people in a group does not necessarily determine its status as a social minority (or a dominant group). When sociologists define a minority group, they are concerned primarily with the economic and political power, or powerlessness, of that group. A **minority group** is a subordinate group whose members have significantly less control or power over their own lives than the members of a dominant or majority group have over theirs.

Sociologists have identified five basic properties of a minority group: unequal treatment, physical or cultural traits, ascribed status, solidarity, and in-group marriage (Wagley and Harris 1958):

1. Members of a minority group experience unequal treatment compared to members of a dominant group. For example, the management of an apartment complex may refuse to rent to African Americans, Hispanics, or Jews. Social inequality may be created or maintained by prejudice, discrimination, segregation, or even extermination.

2. Members of a minority group share physical or cultural characteristics that distinguish them from the dominant group. Each society arbitrarily decides which characteristics are most important in defining groups.

3. Membership in a minority (or dominant) group is not voluntary; people are born into the group. Thus, race and ethnicity are considered *ascribed* statuses.

4. Minority group members have a strong sense of group solidarity. William Graham Sumner, writing in 1906, noted that people make distinctions between members of their own group (the *in-group*) and everyone else (the *out-group*). When a group is the object of long-term prejudice and discrimination, the feeling of "us versus them" can and often does become extremely intense.

5. Members of a minority group generally marry others from the same group. A member of a dominant group is often unwilling to marry into a supposedly inferior minority group. In addition, the minority group's sense of solidarity encourages marriage within the group and discourages marriage to outsiders.

Race

Many people think of race as a series of biological classifications. However, research shows that is not a meaningful way of differentiating people. Genetically, there are no systematic differences between the races that affect people's social behavior and abilities. Instead, sociologists use the term *racial group* to refer to those minorities (and the corresponding dominant groups) who are set apart from others by obvious physical differences. But what is an "obvious" physical difference? Each society labels those differences that people consider important, while ignoring other characteristics that could serve as a basis for social differentiation.

Social Construction of Race

Because race is a social construction, the process of defining races typically benefits those who have more power and privilege than others. In the United States, we see differences in both skin color and hair color. Yet people learn informally that differences in skin color have a dramatic social and political meaning, whereas differences in hair color do not.

When observing skin color, many people in the United States tend to lump others rather casually into the traditional categories of "Black," "White," and "Asian." Subtle differences in skin color often go unnoticed. In many nations of Central America and South America, in contrast, people recognize color gradients on a continuum from light to dark skin color. Brazil has approximately 40 color groupings, while in other countries people may be described as "Mestizo Hondurans," "Mulatto Colombians," or "African Panamanians." What we see as "obvious" differences, then, are subject to each society's social definitions.

TABLE 31-1 RACIAL AND ETHNIC GROUPS IN THE UNITED STATES, 2010

Classification	Number in Thousands	Percentage of Total Population
Racial Groups		
Whites (non-Hispanic)	195,371	60.3
Blacks/African Americans	37,686	12.2
Native Americans, Alaskan Natives	2,247	0.7
Asian Americans	15,553	5.0
Chinese	3,347	1.1
Asian Indians	2,843	0.9
Filipinos	2,556	0.8
Vietnamese	1,548	0.5
Koreans	1,424	0.5
Japanese	763	0.2
Pacific Islanders, Native Hawaiians	1,847	0.6
Other Asian Americans	1,225	0.5
Arab Americans	1,517	0.5
Two or more races	9,009	2.9
Ethnic Groups		
White ancestry		
Germans	49,341	16.0
Irish	35,664	11.6
English	26,873	8.7
Italians	17,486	5.7
Poles	9,757	3.2
French	9,159	3.0
Scottish and Scots-Irish	9,122	3.0
Jews	6,452	2.1
Hispanics (or Latinos)	50,478	16.4
Mexican Americans	31,798	10.3
Puerto Ricans	4,624	1.5
Cubans	1,785	0.6
Salvadorans	1,648	0.5
Dominicans	1,415	0.5
Guatemalans	1,044	0.3
Other Hispanics	8,164	2.7
TOTAL (all groups)	**308,746**	

Note: Arab American population excluded from White total. All data are for 2010. Percentages do not total 100 percent, and when subcategories are added they do not match totals in major categories because of overlap between groups (e.g., Polish American Jews or people of mixed ancestry such as Irish and Italian).

Sources: American Community Survey 2011:Table C04006; Asi and Beaulieu 2013; DellaPergola 2012; Ennis et al. 2011; Hixson et al. 2012; Hoeffel et al. 2012; Humes et al. 2011; T. Norris et al. 2012.

The largest racial minorities in the United States are African Americans (or Blacks), Native Americans (or American Indians), and Asian Americans (Japanese Americans, Chinese Americans, and other Asian peoples). Figure 31-1 provides information about the population of racial and ethnic groups in the United States over the past five centuries, projected through 2060.

Given current population patterns, it is clear that the nation's diversity will continue to increase. In 2011, for the first time ever, census data revealed that the majority of all children ages three and under are now either Hispanic or non-White. This turning point marks the beginning of a pattern in which the nation's minority population will slowly become the majority. By 2050, if not sooner, the majority of all school-age children in the United States will belong to racial or ethnic minority groups (Frey 2011).

Racial definitions are crystallized through what Michael Omi and Howard Winant (1994) have called **racial formation,** a sociohistorical process in which racial categories are created, inhabited, transformed, and destroyed. In this process, those who have power define groups of people according to a racist social structure. The creation of a reservation system for Native Americans in the late 1800s, which later influenced Charles Trimble's life and work, is one example of racial formation. Federal officials combined what were distinctive tribes into a single racial group, which we refer to today as Native Americans. The extent and frequency with which peoples are subject to racial formation is such that no one escapes it.

Another example of racial formation from the 1800s was known as the "one-drop rule." If a person had even a single drop of "Black blood," that person was defined and viewed as Black, even if he or she *appeared* to be White. Clearly, race had social significance, enough so that White legislators established official standards about who was "Black" and who was "White."

The one-drop rule was a vivid example of the *social construction of race*—the process by which people come to define a group as a race based in part on physical characteristics, but also on historical, cultural, and economic factors. For example, in the 1800s, immigrant groups such as Italian and Irish Americans were not at first seen as being "White," but as foreigners who were not necessarily trustworthy. The social construction of race is an ongoing process that is subject to debate, especially in a diverse society such as the United States, where each year increasing numbers of children are born to parents of different racial backgrounds.

Recognition of Multiple Identities

In 1900, in an address to the Anti-Slavery Union in London, scholar W. E. B. DuBois predicted that "the color line" would become the foremost problem of the 20th century. DuBois, born a free Black man in 1868, had witnessed prejudice and discrimination throughout the United States. His comment was prophetic. Today, over a century later, race and ethnicity still carry enormous weight in the United States (DuBois [1900] 1969).

The color line has blurred significantly since 1900, however. Interracial marriage is no longer forbidden by law and custom. Thus, Geetha Lakshmi-narayanan, a native of Ann Arbor, Michigan, is both White and Asian Indian. Often mistaken for a Filipina or Latina, she has grown accustomed to the blunt question "What are you?" (Navarro 2005).

In the late 20th century, with immigration from Latin America rising, the fluid nature of racial formation became evident. Suddenly, people were speaking about the "Latin Americanization" of the United States, or about a biracial, Black/White society being replaced by a triracial one. In the 2010 Census, over 9 million people in the United States (or about 2.9 percent of the population) reported that they were of two or more races. Half the people classified as multiracial were under age 18, suggesting that this segment of the population will grow in the years to come. People who claimed both White and American Indian ancestry, like Charles Trimble (see the chapter-opening excerpt), were the largest group of multiracial residents (Bonilla-Silva 2004; Humes et al. 2011).

This statistical finding of millions of multiracial people obscures how individuals are often asked to handle their identity. For example, the enrollment forms for government programs typically include only a few broad racial-ethnic categories. This approach to racial categorization is part of a long history that dictates single-race identities. Still, many individuals, especially young adults, struggle against social pressure to choose a single identity, and instead openly embrace multiple heritages. Public figures, rather than hide their mixed ancestry, now flaunt it. Singer Mariah Carey celebrates her Irish American background, and President Barack Obama speaks of being born in Hawaii to a Kenyan father and a White mother from Kansas. Tiger Woods, the world's best-known professional golfer, considers himself both Asian and African American.

 use your **sociological imagination**

Using a TV remote control, how quickly do you think you could find a television show in which all the characters share your racial or ethnic background? What about a show in which all the characters share a different background from yours—how quickly could you find one?

Ethnicity

An ethnic group, unlike a racial group, is set apart from others because of its national origin or distinctive cultural patterns. Among the ethnic groups in the United States are peoples with a Spanish-speaking background, referred to collectively as *Latinos* or *Hispanics,* such as Puerto Ricans, Mexican Americans, Cuban Americans, and other Latin Americans. Other ethnic groups in this country include Jewish, Irish, Italian, and Norwegian Americans. Although these groupings are convenient, they serve to obscure differences *within* ethnic categories (as in the case of Hispanics), as well as to overlook the mixed ancestry of so many people in the United States.

The distinction between racial and ethnic minorities is not always clear-cut. Some members of racial minorities, such as Asian Americans, may have significant cultural differences from other racial groups. At the same time, certain ethnic minorities, such as Latinos, may have obvious physical differences that set them apart from other ethnic groups in the United States.

Despite categorization problems, sociologists continue to feel that the distinction between racial groups and ethnic groups is socially significant. In most societies, including the United States,

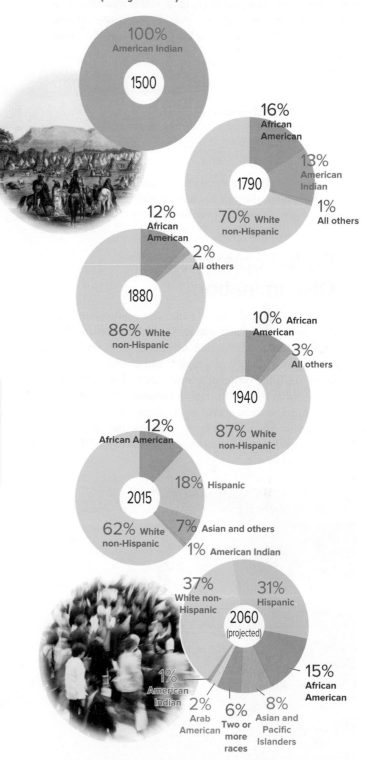

FIGURE 31-1 **Racial and Ethnic Groups in the United States, 1500–2060 (Projected)**

Note: Data for 2010 and 2060, African American and others, are for non-Hispanics.
Sources: Author's estimate; Bureau of the Census 2004a, 2012e:Table 4, 2013b; Humes et al. 2011.
The racial and ethnic composition of what is today the United States has been undergoing change not just for the past 50 years, but for the past 500. Five centuries ago the land was populated only by indigenous Native Americans.

socially constructed physical differences tend to be more visible than ethnic differences. Partly as a result of this fact, stratification along racial lines is more resistant to change than stratification along ethnic lines. Over time, members of an ethnic minority can sometimes become indistinguishable from the majority—although the process may take generations and may never include all members

Today, some children of mixed-race families identify themselves as biracial or multiracial, rejecting efforts to place them in a single racial category.

of the group. In contrast, members of a racial minority find it much more difficult to blend in with the larger society and gain acceptance from the majority.

Prejudice and Discrimination

Looking at the United States in the 21st century, some people wonder aloud if race and ethnicity are still relevant to social stratification. After all, African Americans have served as secretary of state, secretary of defense, and chairman of the Joint Chiefs of Staff; the office of attorney general has been held by both an African American and a Hispanic. Most notably, an African American now serves as president. As historic as these leaders' achievements have been, however, in every case their elevation meant that they left behind a virtually all-White government department or assembly.

The inauguration of President Barack Obama in 2009 was clearly historic. To put its significance in perspective, however, Obama's Senate seat was the only one held by a Black man when he left it to become president. Four years later, more than half of White voters in the 2012 presidential election—59 percent—cast their ballots for candidates other than Obama.

At the same time, college campuses across the United States have been the scene of bias-related incidents. Student-run newspapers and radio stations have ridiculed racial and ethnic minorities; threatening literature has been stuffed under the doors of minority students; graffiti endorsing the views of White supremacist organizations such as the Ku Klux Klan have been scrawled on university walls. In some cases, there have even been violent clashes between groups of White and Black students (Southern Poverty Law Center 2010). What causes such ugly incidents?

Prejudice

Prejudice is a negative attitude toward an entire category of people, often an ethnic or racial minority. If you resent your roommate because he or she is sloppy, you are not necessarily guilty of prejudice. However, if you immediately stereotype your roommate on the basis of such characteristics as race, ethnicity, or religion, that is a form of prejudice. Prejudice tends to perpetuate false definitions of individuals and groups.

Sometimes prejudice results from **ethnocentrism**—the tendency to assume that one's own culture and way of life represent the norm or are superior to all others. Ethnocentric people judge other cultures by the standards of their group, which leads quite easily to prejudice against cultures they view as inferior.

One important and widespread ideology that reinforces prejudice is **racism,** the belief that one race is supreme and all others are innately inferior. When racism prevails in a society, members of subordinate groups generally experience prejudice, discrimination, and exploitation. In 1990, as concern mounted about racist attacks in the United States, Congress passed the Hate Crime Statistics Act. As a result, hate crimes are now beginning to be reported and investigated in much the same way as conventional crimes against property and people.

Prejudice is also rooted in racial and ethnic **stereotypes**—unreliable generalizations about all members of a group that do not recognize individual differences within the group. The dominant or majority group creates these stereotypes through the process of racial formation. As the interactionist William I. Thomas (1923) noted, the dominant group's "definition of the situation" is often so powerful, it can mold the individual personality. That is, people respond not only to the objective features of a situation or person, but to the *social meaning* that situation or person carries. Thus, the false images or stereotypes created by the dominant group can become real in their consequences.

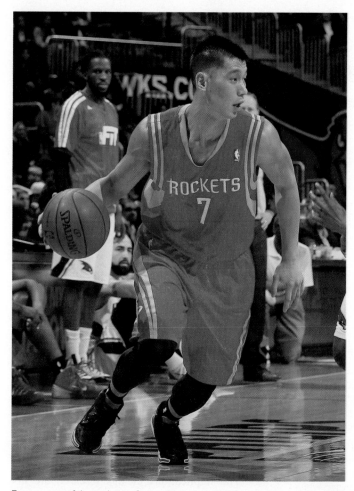

Even successful members of minority groups, like Jeremy Lin, point guard for the Houston Rockets, are subjected to ethnic slurs. "Chink in the Armor" proclaimed a headline on ESPN's website in 2012 after Lin, who had spearheaded a multigame winning streak, had a bad night. The network later apologized for the remark.

Color-Blind Racism

Over the past three generations, nationwide surveys have consistently shown growing support among Whites for integration, interracial dating, and the election of minority group members to public office—including the presidency of the United States. How can this trend be explained, given the persistence of residential segregation and the commission of thousands of hate crimes every year? The answer, to some extent, is that prejudice and discriminatory attitudes are no longer expressed as freely as they once were. Often, they are couched in terms of equal opportunity.

Color-blind racism is the use of the principle of race neutrality to defend a racially unequal status quo. Proponents of race neutrality claim they believe that everyone should be treated equally. However, the way they apply the principle to government policy is anything but neutral. Proponents

of this approach oppose affirmative action, public welfare assistance, and to a large extent, government-funded health insurance, all of which they see largely as favors to minority groups. Yet they do not object to practices that privilege Whites, such as college admissions criteria that give preference to the relatives of alumni. Nor do they oppose tax breaks for homeowners, most of whom are White, or government financial aid to college students, who are also disproportionately White. Though race neutrality is not based on theories of racial superiority or inferiority, then, the idea that society should be color-blind only perpetuates racial inequality.

Color-blind racism has also been referred to as "covert racism." Although its proponents rarely speak of racism, other indicators of social status, such as social class or citizenship, tend to become proxies for race. Thus, many White people can convince themselves that they are not racist—nor do they know anyone who is—and yet remain prejudiced against "welfare mothers" and "immigrants." They can conclude, mistakenly, that racial tolerance, or even racial and ethnic equality, has been achieved.

Researchers who have surveyed White attitudes toward African Americans over the past several decades have reached two inescapable conclusions. First, people's attitudes do change. In periods of social upheaval, dramatic attitudinal shifts can occur within a single generation. Second, less racial progress was made in the late 20th and early 21st centuries than in the relatively brief period of the 1950s and 1960s. Today, economically disadvantaged groups such as African Americans and Latinos have become so closely associated with urban decay, homelessness, welfare, and crime that those problems are now viewed as racial issues, even if they are not labeled as such. The tendency to *blame the victims* of these social ills complicates their resolution, especially at a time when government's ability to address

People in need of help crowd a government public assistance office. Those who oppose government welfare programs but support other forms of government assistance, such as financial aid to college students, may be exhibiting color-blind racism.

FIGURE 31-2 U.S. Median Income by Race, Ethnicity, and Gender

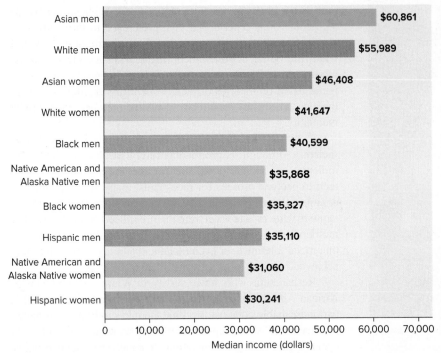

	Median income (dollars)
Asian men	$60,861
White men	$55,989
Asian women	$46,408
White women	$41,647
Black men	$40,599
Native American and Alaska Native men	$35,868
Black women	$35,327
Hispanic men	$35,110
Native American and Alaska Native women	$31,060
Hispanic women	$30,241

Note: Data released in 2013 for income earned in 2012. Median income is from all sources and is limited to year-round, full-time workers at least 25 years old (American Indian data for 16 years or older). Data for White men and women are for non-Hispanics.

Sources: American Community Survey 2013a:Table B20017C; DeNavas-Walt et al. 2013:PINC-03.

Even at the highest levels of schooling, the income gap remains between Whites and Blacks. Education also has little apparent effect on the income gap between male and female workers. Even a brief analysis reveals striking differences in earning power between White men and women, especially African American, Native American, and Hispanic women.

social problems is limited by recession, antitax initiatives, and concern over terrorism. In short, the color line is still in place, even if more and more people refuse to acknowledge its existence (Ansell 2008; Bonilla-Silva 2006; Coates 2008; M. King 2007; Quillian 2006; Winant 1994).

Discriminatory Behavior

Prejudice often leads to **discrimination,** the denial of opportunities and equal rights to individuals and groups because of prejudice or other arbitrary reasons. Say that a White corporate president with a prejudice against Asian Americans has to fill an executive position. The most qualified candidate for the job is a Vietnamese American. If the president refuses to hire this candidate and instead selects an inferior White candidate, he or she is engaging in an act of racial discrimination.

Prejudiced *attitudes* should not be equated with discriminatory *behavior.* Although the two are generally related, they are not identical; either condition can be present without the other. A prejudiced person does not always act on his or her biases. The White corporate president, for example, might choose—despite his or her stereotypes—to hire the Vietnamese American. That would be prejudice without discrimination. On the other hand, a White corporate president with a completely respectful view of Vietnamese Americans might refuse to hire them for executive posts out of fear that biased clients would

take their business elsewhere. In that case, the president's action would constitute discrimination without prejudice.

A field experiment by sociologist Devah Pager, then a doctoral candidate at the University of Wisconsin–Madison, documented racial discrimination in hiring. Pager sent four polite, well-dressed young men out to look for an entry-level job in Milwaukee, Wisconsin. All were 23-year-old college students, but they presented themselves as high school graduates with similar job histories. Two of the men were Black and two were White. One Black applicant and one White applicant claimed to have served 18 months in jail for a felony conviction—possession of cocaine with intent to distribute.

As one might expect, the four men's experiences with 350 potential employers were vastly different. Predictably, the White applicant with a purported prison record received only half as many callbacks as the other White applicant—17 percent compared to 34 percent. But as dramatic as the effect of his criminal record was, the effect of his race was more significant. Despite his prison record, he received slightly more callbacks than the Black applicant *with no criminal record* (17 percent compared to 14 percent). Race, it seems, was more of a concern to potential employers than a criminal background.

The implications of this research are not limited to any one city, such as Milwaukee. Similar studies have confirmed discriminatory handling of job applications in Chicago; New York City; Long Island, New York; San Diego; and Washington, D.C. Over time, the cumulative effect of such differential behavior by employers contributes to significant differences in income. Figure 31-2 vividly illustrates the income inequality between White men and almost everyone else (Pager 2007; Pager et al. 2009).

If race serves as a barrier, why do Asian American men earn slightly more income than White men (see Figure 31-2)? Not all Asian American men earn high incomes; indeed, some Asian American groups, such as Laotians and Vietnamese, have high levels of poverty. Nevertheless, a significant number of Asian Americans have advanced degrees that qualify them for highly paid jobs, and which raise the median income for the group as a whole. Although these highly educated Asian Americans earn a lot of money, they do not earn quite as much as their White counterparts, however. With a doctorate holder in the family, the typical Asian American family earns an estimated $124,000, compared to $140,000 for a White family (DeNavas-Walt et al. 2013:FINC-01).

Sometimes racial and ethnic discrimination is overt. Internet forums like Craigslist.org or Roommate.com feature classified ads that state "African Americans and Arabians tend to clash with me" or "Clean, Godly Christian men only." While anti-discrimination laws prevent such notices from being published in the newspapers, existing law has not caught up with online bigotry in hiring and renting (Liptak 2006).

Discrimination persists even for the most educated and qualified minority group members from the best family backgrounds. Despite their talents and experiences, they sometimes encounter attitudinal or organizational bias that prevents them from reaching their full potential. The term **glass ceiling** refers to an invisible barrier that blocks the promotion of a qualified individual in a work environment because of the individual's gender, race, or ethnicity (R. Schaefer 2014).

In early 1995, the federal Glass Ceiling Commission issued the first comprehensive study of barriers to promotion in the United States. The commission found that glass ceilings continue to block women and minority group men from top management positions in the nation's industries.

 use your sociological imagination

How might online social networking maintain prejudice and discrimination?

The Privileges of the Dominant

One aspect of discrimination that is often overlooked is the privileges that dominant groups enjoy at the expense of others. For instance, we tend to focus more on the difficulty women have getting ahead at work and getting a hand at home than on the ease with which men manage to make their way in the world and avoid household chores. Similarly, we concentrate more on discrimination against racial and ethnic minorities than on the advantages members of the White majority enjoy. Indeed, most White people rarely think about their "Whiteness," taking their status for granted.

Sociologists and other social scientists are becoming increasingly interested in what it means to be "White," for White privilege is the other side of the proverbial coin of racial discrimination. In this context, **White privilege** refers to rights or immunities granted to people as a particular benefit or favor simply because they are White (Ferber and Kimmel 2008). This view of whiteness as a privilege echoes an observation by W. E. B. DuBois, that rather than wanting fair working conditions for all laborers, White workers had accepted the "public and psychological wage" of whiteness ([1935] 1962:700).

The feminist scholar Peggy McIntosh (1988) became interested in White privilege after noticing that most men would not acknowledge that there were privileges attached to being male—even if they would agree that being female had its disadvantages. Did White people suffer from a similar blind spot regarding their racial privilege? she wondered. Intrigued, McIntosh began to list all the ways in which she benefited from her Whiteness. She soon realized that the list of unspoken advantages was long and significant.

McIntosh found that as a White person, she rarely needed to step out of her comfort zone, no matter where she went. If she wished to, she could spend most of her time with people of her race. She could find a good place to live in a pleasant neighborhood, buy the foods she liked to eat from almost any grocery store, and get her hair styled in almost any salon. She could attend a public meeting without feeling that she did not belong, that she was different from everyone else.

McIntosh discovered, too, that her skin color opened doors for her. She could cash checks and use credit cards without suspicion, browse through stores without being shadowed by security guards. She could be seated without difficulty in a restaurant. If she asked to see the manager, she could assume he or she would be of her race. If she needed help from a doctor or a lawyer, she could get it.

McIntosh also realized that her Whiteness made the job of parenting easier. She did not need to worry about protecting her children from people who didn't like them. She could be sure that their schoolbooks would show pictures of people who looked like them, and that their history texts would describe White people's achievements. She knew that the television programs they watched would include White characters.

Finally, McIntosh had to admit that others did not constantly evaluate her in racial terms. When she appeared in public, she didn't need to worry that her clothing or behavior might reflect poorly on White people. If she was recognized for an achievement, it was seen as her achievement, not that of an entire race. And no one ever assumed that the personal opinions she voiced should be those of all White people. Because McIntosh blended in with the people around her, she wasn't always onstage.

These are not all the privileges White people take for granted as a result of their membership in the dominant racial group in the United States. As Devah Pager's study showed, White job seekers enjoy a tremendous advantage over equally well-qualified—even

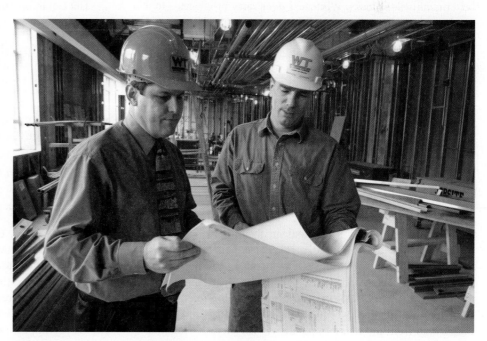

White people are accustomed to seeing other White people in professional positions and jobs with authority and prestige. Whiteness *does* have its privileges.

Prudence Hannis is a First Nations (Native American) woman who belongs to the Abenaki tribe. As associate director of the First Nations Post-Secondary Institution, which opened in 2011, she is helping to establish a school "built for and by First Nations." Hannis sees the new institution as a significant step toward self-determination among First Nations peoples. Historically, graduation rates have been very low among Québec's First Nations, for political, cultural, social, and economic reasons. The First Nations Post-Secondary Institution was conceived to provide the kind of support that mainstream educational institutions don't offer First Nations students, including everything from day care services to academic support.

The school also offers social-emotional support to students who may not be comfortable in an academic environment. In the social sciences, students participate in weekly sharing circles, where they learn about the root causes of high dropout rates and are encouraged to become agents of change. In deciding to "step out of victimization," students exert a positive influence on the school, on their own future and that of generations to come, and on their peoples' relationship with mainstream society. Hannis is proud to report that in 2011, all the incoming students finished the first term (the dropout rate was zero). The next term, 19 additional students enrolled.

Before taking her current position, Hannis was a liaison officer at the National Institute of Science Research at the University of Québec, where she advised scholars wishing to do research on First Nations communities. She has also worked on women's health issues, first at the Centre of Excellence on Women's Health, Consortium Université de Montréal, and later as a researcher and community activist with Québec Native Women. Her job with Québec Native Women, she explains, was "to defend First Nations women's concerns, to be their spokesperson when needed, to analyze critical situations for our sisters, and mostly, to determine ways in which women can empower themselves, their families, and their communities."

Hannis received her BA in sociology from the University of Québec at Montréal in 2000. "I have made good use of what I have learned concerning gender inequality, social class, racial and ethnic inequality (tensions, conflict, and struggles), domination, oppression, and social exclusion," she says. "These concepts allow for a better analysis of social problems First Nations are facing (high rates of unemployment, low graduation rates, greater health risks, ghettoization)." Hannis finds her studies have also helped in her work with government agencies, allowing her to raise public awareness of issues such as violence against native women and to identify possible solutions. "I have never been hired as a 'sociologist' per se," she explains, "but the work I was given always involved sociological analysis of issues relevant to First Nations."

LET'S DISCUSS

1. What is the dropout rate at your school? What political, cultural, social, and economic conditions might contribute to that dropout rate?

2. In speaking of empowering First Nations women, what sociological perspective do you think Hannis is drawing on?

---

better-qualified—Blacks. Whiteness *does* carry privileges—to a much greater extent than most White people realize (Fitzgerald 2008; Picca and Feagin 2007).

 use your **sociological imagination**

How often do you think people are privileged because of their race or ethnicity? How about yourself—how often are you privileged?

Institutional Discrimination

Discrimination is practiced not only by individuals in one-to-one encounters but also by institutions in their daily operations. Social scientists are particularly concerned with the ways in which structural factors such as employment, housing, health care, and government operations maintain the social significance of race and ethnicity. **Institutional discrimination** refers to the denial of opportunities and equal rights to individuals and groups that results from the normal operations of a society. This kind of discrimination consistently affects certain racial and ethnic groups more than others.

The Commission on Civil Rights (1981:9–10) has identified various forms of institutional discrimination:

- Rules requiring that only English be spoken at a place of work, even when it is not a business necessity to restrict the use of other languages.

- Preferences shown by law and medical schools in the admission of children of wealthy and influential alumni, nearly all of whom are White.

- Restrictive employment-leave policies, coupled with prohibitions on part-time work, that make it difficult for the heads of single-parent families (most of whom are women) to obtain and keep jobs.

In some cases, even seemingly neutral institutional standards can have discriminatory effects. African American students at a midwestern state university protested a policy under which fraternities and sororities that wished to use campus facilities for a dance were required to pay a $150 security deposit to cover possible damages. They complained that the policy had a discriminatory impact on minority student organizations. Campus police countered that the university's policy applied to all student groups interested in using the facilities. However, since the

BOX 31-1

Research Today

Institutional Discrimination in the Voting Booth

Eddie Lee Holloway Jr. has been voting since he was 18. Now, decades later, he is having trouble not only casting his ballot but receiving disability benefits. Because of a clerical error that was made when he was born—Eddie's birth certificate names him Eddie Junior Holloway—the state of Wisconsin will not allow him to vote. Eddie's Social Security card shows his correct name, as does an expired Illinois photo ID. His father's name, Eddie Lee Holloway, appears on his birth certificate. Still, the state government will not recognize him as a U.S. citizen. Like a lot of non-White Americans, Eddie has lost his birthright to institutional discrimination.

How should government establish the authenticity of a person's right to vote? Today, many states have begun to require a government-issued ID bearing a photograph, presumably to prevent voter fraud. Other states will accept any photo ID (see the figure). In the past, voters usually did not need to show any kind of identification at the polls; their identity was established at the time they registered to vote.

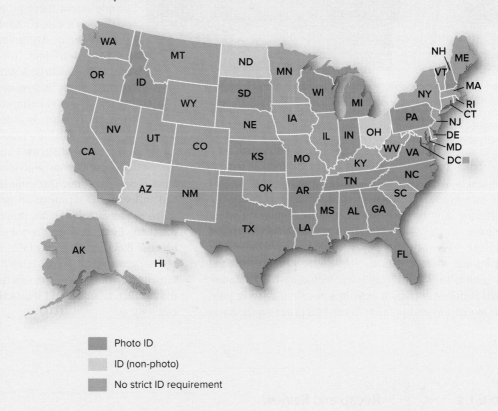

MAPPING LIFE NATIONWIDE

Voter Id Requirements

- Photo ID
- ID (non-photo)
- No strict ID requirement

Source: National Conference of State Legislatures 2013.

Courts have been reluctant to uphold the new voter ID laws, for not all eligible voters can easily obtain these credentials. Such laws disproportionately disenfranchise the elderly and members of minority groups, simply because they do not have a driver's license. According to national surveys, 25 percent of African American citizens and 16 percent of Latino citizens do not have a valid government-issued photo ID, compared to 8 percent of White citizens. These findings fit the definition of institutional discrimination, in that *through the normal operations of society*—in this case, the holding of elections—people of color are more likely than others to be denied their rights. Indeed, research into who can and cannot vote suggests the existence of institutional discrimination in our national elections.

Why the sudden emphasis on establishing voters' identity? There is little evidence to suggest that people have been

impersonating eligible voters at the polls. Yet surveys show that most Americans prefer strict voter ID enforcement, whether or

> Such laws disproportionately disenfranchise the elderly and members of minority groups, simply because they do not have a driver's license.

not such tactics constitute institutional discrimination. In 2013 a national telephone survey found that 70 percent of likely U.S. voters believe that all voters should be required to prove their identity before being

allowed to vote. Only 25 percent opposed such a requirement.

These findings are one more example of the painful underlying context of American intergroup relations. Institutional discrimination consistently imposes more hindrances on, and awards fewer benefits to, certain racial and ethnic groups compared to others.

LET'S DISCUSS

1. Are you a registered voter? If so, how does your local polling place verify voters' identity? Have you ever had difficulty establishing your identity on election day?

2. Why are citizens and state legislators suddenly so concerned about requiring voters to establish their identity?

Sources: ACLU 2013; Brennan Center 2006, 2013; Dade 2012; Rasmussen Reports 2013.

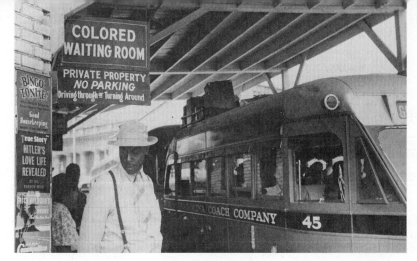

Before passage of the Civil Rights Act (1964), segregation of public accommodations was the norm throughout the South. Whites used the most up-to-date bathrooms, waiting rooms, and even drinking fountains, while Blacks ("Colored") were directed to older facilities in inferior condition. Such separate but unequal arrangements are a blatant example of institutional discrimination.

of race, color, creed, national origin, and gender). Yet today, voting rights are still an issue in some states (Box 31-1).

For more than 40 years, affirmative action programs have been instituted to overcome past discrimination. **Affirmative action** refers to positive efforts to recruit minority group members or women for jobs, promotions, and educational opportunities. Many people resent these programs, arguing that advancing one group's cause merely shifts the discrimination to another group. By giving priority to African Americans in admissions, for example, schools may overlook more qualified White candidates. In many parts of the country and many sectors of the economy, affirmative action is being rolled back, even though it was never fully implemented.

Discriminatory practices continue to pervade nearly all areas of life in the United States today. In part, that is because various individuals and groups actually *benefit* from racial and ethnic discrimination in terms of money, status, and influence. Discrimination permits members of the majority to enhance their wealth, power, and prestige at the expense of others. Less qualified people get jobs and promotions simply because they are members of the dominant group. Such individuals and groups will not surrender these advantages easily. We'll turn now to a closer look at this functionalist analysis, as well as the conflict, labeling, and interactionist perspectives on race and ethnicity.

overwhelmingly White fraternities and sororities at the school had their own houses, which they used for dances, the policy indeed affected only the African American and other minority organizations.

Attempts have been made to eradicate or compensate for institutional discrimination. The 1960s saw the passage of many pioneering civil rights laws, including the landmark 1964 Civil Rights Act (which prohibits discrimination in public accommodations and publicly owned facilities on the basis

MODULE 31 | Recap and Review

Summary

The social dimensions of race and ethnicity are important factors in shaping people's lives.

1. A **racial group** is set apart from others by physical differences; an **ethnic group** is set apart primarily by national origin or cultural patterns.

2. When sociologists define a **minority group,** they are concerned primarily with the economic and political power, or powerlessness, of the group.

3. The meaning people attach to the physical differences between races gives social significance to race, producing **stereotypes.**

4. **Prejudice** often but not always leads to **discrimination.** Sometimes, through **color-blind racism,** prejudiced people try to use the principle of racial neutrality to defend a racially unequal status quo.

5. **Institutional discrimination** results from the normal operations of a society.

Thinking Critically

1. Why does the social construction of race defy the traditional notion of race as a biological category?

2. Which would be more socially significant, the elimination of prejudice or the elimination of discrimination?

Key Terms

Affirmative action	**Minority group**
Color-blind racism	**Prejudice**
Discrimination	**Racial formation**
Ethnic group	**Racial group**
Ethnocentrism	**Racism**
Glass ceiling	**Stereotype**
Institutional discrimination	**White privilege**

MODULE 32 | Sociological Perspectives on Race and Ethnicity

Relations among racial and ethnic groups lend themselves to analysis from four major sociological perspectives. Viewing race from the macro level, functionalists observe that racial prejudice and discrimination serve positive functions for dominant groups. Conflict theorists see the economic structure as a central factor in the exploitation of minorities. Labeling theorists note the way in which minorities are singled out for differential treatment by law enforcement officers. On the micro level, interactionist researchers stress the manner in which everyday contact between people from different racial and ethnic backgrounds contributes to tolerance or hostility.

Functionalist Perspective

What possible use could racial bigotry have? Functionalist theorists, while agreeing that racial hostility is hardly to be admired, point out that it serves positive functions for those who practice discrimination.

Anthropologist Manning Nash (1962) has identified three functions of racially prejudiced beliefs for the dominant group:

1. Racist views provide a moral justification for maintaining an unequal society that routinely deprives a minority group of its rights and privileges. Southern Whites justified slavery by believing that Africans were physically and spiritually subhuman and devoid of souls.

2. Racist beliefs discourage the subordinate minority from attempting to question its lowly status, which would be to question the very foundations of society.

3. Racial myths suggest that any major societal change (such as an end to discrimination) would only bring greater poverty to the minority and lower the majority's standard of living. As a result, racial prejudice grows when a society's value system (one underlying a colonial empire or slavery, for example) is threatened.

Although racial prejudice and discrimination may serve the powerful, such unequal treatment can also be dysfunctional for a society, and even for the dominant group. Sociologist Arnold Rose (1951) has outlined four dysfunctions that are associated with racism:

1. A society that practices discrimination fails to use the resources of all individuals. Discrimination limits the search for talent and leadership to the dominant group.

2. Discrimination aggravates social problems such as poverty, delinquency, and crime, and places the financial burden of alleviating those problems on the dominant group.

3. Society must invest a good deal of time and money to defend its barriers to the full participation of all members.

4. Racial prejudice and discrimination often undercut goodwill and friendly diplomatic relations between nations.

Conflict Perspective

Conflict theorists would certainly agree with Arnold Rose that racial prejudice and discrimination have many harmful consequences for society. Sociologists such as Oliver Cox (1948), Robert Blauner (1972), and Herbert M. Hunter (2000) have used the **exploitation theory** (or *Marxist class theory*) to explain the basis of racial subordination in the United States. Karl Marx viewed the exploitation of the lower class as a basic part of the capitalist economic system. From a Marxist point of view, racism keeps minorities in low-paying jobs, thereby supplying the capitalist ruling class with a pool of cheap labor. Moreover, by forcing racial minorities to accept low wages, capitalists can restrict the wages of *all* members of the proletariat. Workers from the dominant group who demand higher wages can always be replaced by minorities who have no choice but to accept low-paying jobs.

The conflict view of race relations seems persuasive in a number of instances. Japanese Americans were the object of little prejudice until they began to enter jobs that brought them into competition with Whites. The movement to keep Chinese immigrants out of the United States became most fervent during the latter half of the 19th century, when Chinese and Whites fought over dwindling work opportunities. Both the enslavement of Blacks and the extermination and removal westward of Native Americans were economically motivated.

However, the exploitation theory is too limited to explain prejudice in its many forms. Not all minority groups have been exploited to the same extent. In addition, many groups (such as the Quakers and the Mormons) have been victimized by prejudice for other than economic reasons. Still, as Gordon Allport (1979:210) concludes, the exploitation theory correctly "points a sure finger at one of the factors involved in prejudice, . . . rationalized self-interest of the upper classes."

Labeling Perspective

One practice that fits both the conflict perspective and labeling theory is racial profiling. **Racial profiling** is any arbitrary action initiated by an authority based on race, ethnicity, or national origin rather than on a person's behavior. Generally, racial profiling occurs when law enforcement officers, including customs officials, airport security, and police, assume that people who fit a certain description are likely to be engaged in illegal activities. Beginning in the 1980s with the emergence of the crack cocaine market, skin color became a key characteristic in racial profiling. This practice is often based on very explicit stereotypes. For example, one federal antidrug initiative encouraged officers to look specifically for people with dreadlocks and for Latino men traveling together.

Today, authorities continue to rely on racial profiling, despite overwhelming evidence that it is misleading. A recent study showed that Blacks are still more likely than Whites to be frisked and handled with force when they are stopped. Yet Whites are more likely than Blacks to possess weapons, illegal drugs, or stolen property (Farrell and McDevitt 2010).

In U.S. retail stores, Black customers have different experiences from White customers. They are more likely than Whites to have their checks or credit cards refused and more likely to be profiled by security personnel.

Research on the ineffectiveness of racial profiling, coupled with calls by minority communities to end the stigmatization, has led to growing demands to end the practice. But these efforts came to an abrupt halt after the September 11, 2001, terrorist attacks on the United States, when suspicions arose about Muslim and Arab immigrants. Foreign students from Arab countries were summoned for special questioning by authorities. Legal immigrants who were identified as Arab or Muslim were scrutinized for possible illegal activity and prosecuted for violations that authorities routinely ignored among immigrants of other ethnicities and faiths. National surveys have found little change since 2001 in public support for profiling of Arab Americans at airports. In 2010, 53 percent of Americans favored "ethnic and religious profiling" of air travelers—even those who are U.S. citizens—together with more intensive security checks of passengers who fit certain profiles (Zogby 2010).

Interactionist Perspective

A Hispanic woman is transferred from a job on an assembly line to a similar position working next to a White man. At first, the White man is patronizing, assuming that she must be incompetent. She is cold and resentful; even when she needs assistance, she refuses to admit it. After a week, the growing tension between the two leads to a bitter quarrel. Yet over time, each slowly comes to appreciate the other's strengths and talents. A year after they begin working together, these two workers become respectful friends. This story is an example of what interactionists call the *contact hypothesis* in action.

The **contact hypothesis** states that in cooperative circumstances, interracial contact between people of equal status will cause them to become less prejudiced and to abandon old

stereotypes. People begin to see one another as individuals and discard the broad generalizations characteristic of stereotyping. Note the phrases *equal status* and *cooperative circumstances*. In the story just told, if the two workers had been competing for one vacancy as a supervisor, the racial hostility between them might have worsened (Allport 1979; Fine 2008).

As Latinos and other minorities slowly gain access to better-paying and more responsible jobs, the contact hypothesis may take on even greater significance. The trend in our society is toward increasing contact between individuals from dominant and subordinate groups. That may be one way of eliminating—or at least reducing—racial and ethnic stereotyping and prejudice. Another may be the establishment of interracial coalitions, an idea suggested by sociologist William Julius Wilson (1999). To work, such coalitions would obviously need to be built on an equal role for all members.

Table 32-1 summarizes the four major sociological perspectives on race. No matter what the explanation for racial and ethnic distinctions—functionalist, conflict, labeling, or interactionist—these socially constructed inequalities can have powerful consequences in the form of prejudice and discrimination. In the next section, we will see how inequality based on the ascribed characteristics of race and ethnicity can poison people's interpersonal relations, depriving whole groups of opportunities others take for granted.

Spectrum of Intergroup Relations

Racial and ethnic groups can relate to one another in a wide variety of ways, ranging from friendships and intermarriages to hostility, from behaviors that require mutual approval to behaviors imposed by the dominant group.

One devastating pattern of intergroup relations is **genocide**—the deliberate, systematic killing of an entire people

Tracking Sociological Perspectives

TABLE **32-1** SOCIOLOGICAL PERSPECTIVES ON RACE AND ETHNICITY

Perspective	Emphasis
Functionalist	The dominant majority benefits from the subordination of racial minorities.
Conflict	Vested interests perpetuate racial inequality through economic exploitation.
Labeling	People are profiled and stereotyped based on their racial and ethnic identity.
Interactionist	Cooperative interracial contacts can reduce hostility.

French police remove a member of the Roma minority who is resisting deportation to his home country. The expulsion of certain racial or ethnic groups is an extreme result of prejudice.

EU. In 2011, the EU withdrew the threat of legal action when the French government modified its policy to apply only to those Roma who lived in "illegal camps." However, many observers saw the concession as a thinly veiled attempt to circumvent the EU's long-standing human rights policies.

In a variation of expulsion, called *secession,* failure to resolve an ethnic or racial conflict results in the drawing of formal boundaries between the groups. In 1947, India was partitioned into two separate countries in an attempt to end violent conflict between Hindus and Muslims. The predominantly Muslim areas in the north became the new country of Pakistan; the rest of India became predominantly Hindu.

Secession, expulsion, and genocide are extreme behaviors, clustered on the negative end of what is called the Spectrum of Intergroup Relations (Figure 32-1). More typical intergroup relations follow four identifiable patterns: (1) segregation, (2) amalgamation, (3) assimilation, and (4) pluralism. Each pattern defines the dominant group's actions and the minority group's responses. Intergroup relations are rarely restricted to only one of the four patterns, although invariably one does tend to dominate. Think of these patterns primarily as ideal types.

Segregation

Separate schools, separate seating on buses and in restaurants, separate washrooms, even separate drinking fountains—these were all part of the lives of African Americans in the South when segregation ruled early in the 20th century. **Segregation** refers to the physical separation of two groups of people in terms of residence, workplace, and social events. Generally, a dominant group imposes this pattern on a minority group. Segregation is rarely complete, however. Intergroup contact inevitably occurs, even in the most segregated societies.

From 1948 (when it received its independence) to 1990, the Republic of South Africa severely restricted the movement of Blacks and other non-Whites by means of a wide-ranging system of segregation known as **apartheid.** Apartheid even included the creation of separate homelands where Blacks were expected to live. However, decades of local resistance to apartheid, combined with international pressure, led to marked political changes in the 1990s. In 1994, a prominent Black activist,

or nation. This term describes the killing of 1 million Armenians by Turkey beginning in 1915. It is most commonly applied to Nazi Germany's extermination of 6 million European Jews, as well as gays, lesbians, and the Roma ("Gypsies"), during World War II. The term *genocide* is also appropriate in describing the United States' policies toward Native Americans in the 19th century. In 1800, the Native American (or American Indian) population of the United States was about 600,000; by 1850, it had been reduced to 250,000 through warfare with the U.S. cavalry, disease, and forced relocation to inhospitable environments.

The *expulsion* of a people is another extreme means of acting out racial or ethnic prejudice. In 1979, for example, the government of Vietnam expelled nearly 1 million ethnic Chinese from the country. The action resulted partly from centuries of hostility between Vietnam and neighboring China.

More recently (beginning in 2009), France expelled over 10,000 ethnic Roma (or Gypsies) who had immigrated from their home countries of Bulgaria and Romania. The action appeared to violate the European Union's ban against targeting ethnic groups, as well as its policy of "freedom of movement" throughout the

FIGURE 32-1 **Spectrum of Intergroup Relations**

EXPULSION	SEGREGATION		ASSIMILATION
INCREASINGLY UNACCEPTABLE ⇐ ⇐ ⇒ ⇒			MORE TOLERABLE
EXTERMINATION or genocide	SECESSION or partitioning	FUSION or amalgamation or melting pot	PLURALISM or multiculturalism

Source: Prepared by author, Richard T. Schaefer.

Nelson Mandela, was elected South Africa's president in the first election in which Blacks (the majority of the nation's population) were allowed to vote. Mandela had spent almost 28 years in South African prisons for his anti-apartheid activities. His election was widely viewed as the final blow to South Africa's oppressive policy of segregation.

In contrast to the enforced segregation in South Africa, the United States exemplifies an unmandated but nevertheless persistent separation of the races. In their book *American Apartheid*, sociologists Douglas Massey and Nancy Denton (1993) described segregation in U.S. cities using 1990 census data. As the book's title suggests, the racial makeup of U.S. neighborhoods resembles the rigid government-imposed segregation that prevailed for so long in South Africa.

Analysis of recent census data shows continuing segregation despite the nation's racial and ethnic diversity. To measure the degree of separation between groups, scholars use a segregation index that ranges from 0 (complete integration) to 100 (complete segregation). The index value indicates the percentage of the minority group that needs to move for the minority group to be distributed exactly as Whites. For example, a segregation index of 60 for Blacks–Whites would mean that 60 percent of all African Americans need to move to achieve the same racial distribution as Whites.

Table 32-2 shows the eight most segregated metropolitan areas in the United States; all have large African American, Latino, and Asian American populations. Blacks and Whites are most separated from each other in Detroit; Whites and Latinos, in the Los Angeles/Long Beach metropolitan area. Asians and Whites are most segregated in the New Brunswick, New Jersey area. Roughly half to three quarters of the population in these areas would need to move in order to even the distribution of racial/ethnic groups throughout the city and surrounding suburbs.

Over the last 40 years, Black–White segregation has declined only modestly. Hispanic–White and Asian–White segregation, although they are lower, have not changed significantly in the last 30 years. Even when we consider social class, the pattern of minority group segregation persists, despite the occasional multiracial neighborhood (Bureau of the Census 2010b; Frey 2011; Krysan et al. 2008; Wilkes and Iceland 2004).

Amalgamation

Amalgamation happens when a majority group and a minority group combine to form a new group. Through intermarriage over several generations, various groups in society combine to form a new group. This pattern can be expressed as A + B + C → D, where A, B, and C represent different groups in a society, and D signifies the end result, a unique cultural-racial group unlike any of the initial groups (W. Newman 1973).

The belief in the United States as a "melting pot" became compelling in the first part of the 20th century, particularly since that image suggested that the nation had an almost divine mission to amalgamate

various groups into one people. However, in actuality, many residents were not willing to include Native Americans, Jews, African Americans, Asian Americans, and Irish Roman Catholics in the melting pot. Therefore, this pattern does not adequately describe dominant–subordinate relations in the United States. There *has* been a significant increase in interracial marriage among Whites, Blacks, Asians, and Hispanics in recent years—a trend we will examine in Chapter 13.

Assimilation

In India, many Hindus complain about Indian citizens who copy the traditions and customs of the British. In France, people of Arab and African origin, many of them Muslim, complain they are treated as second-class citizens—a charge that provoked riots in 2005 and again in 2012. And in the United States, some Italian Americans, Polish Americans, Hispanics, and Jews have changed their ethnic-sounding family names to names that are typically found among White Protestant families.

Assimilation is the process through which a person forsakes his or her cultural tradition to become part of a different culture. Generally, it is practiced by a minority group member who wants to conform to the standards of the dominant group. Assimilation can be described as a pattern in which A + B + C → A. The majority, A, dominates in such a way that members of minorities B and C imitate it and attempt to become indistinguishable from it (W. Newman 1973).

 use your **sociological imagination**

You have immigrated to another country with a very different culture. What steps might you take to assimilate?

A recent comparison study of immigrant groups in the United States, Canada, and Europe found that for the most part, assimilation has progressed further in the United States than in Europe, although more slowly than in Canada. In the United States, the rate of assimilation has generally been constant across groups. However, the recent recession has hampered new groups' ability to move into a broad range of jobs (Myers and Pitkin 2011; Vigdor 2011).

Pluralism

In a pluralistic society, a subordinate group does not have to forsake its lifestyle and traditions to avoid prejudice or discrimination. **Pluralism** is based on mutual respect for one another's cultures among the various groups in a society. This pattern allows a minority group to express its own culture and still participate without prejudice in the larger society. Earlier, we described amalgamation as A + B + C → D, and assimilation as A + B + C → A. Using this same approach,

TABLE 32-2 SEGREGATED METROPOLITAN AMERICA

Black–White	Hispanic–White	Asian–White
1. Detroit 79.6	1. Los Angeles/Long Beach 63.4	1. Edison/New Brunswick, NJ 53.7
2. Milwaukee 79.6	2. New York/White Plains 63.1	2. New York/White Plains 49.5
3. New York/White Plains 79.1	3. Newark 62.6	3. Houston 48.7
4. Newark 78.0	4. Boston 62.0	4. Los Angeles/Long Beach 47.6
5. Chicago/Naperville 75.9	5. Salinas, CA 60.0	5. Boston 47.4
6. Philadelphia 73.7	6. Philadelphia 58.8	6. Sacramento, CA 46.8
7. Miami/Miami Beach 73.0	7. Chicago/Naperville 57.0	7. San Francisco 46.7
8. Cleveland 72.6	8. Oxford/Ventura, CA 54.5	8. Warren/Farmington Hills, MI 46.3

Note: The higher the value, the more segregated the metropolitan area.
Source: Logan and Stults 2011.

we can conceive of pluralism as A + B + C → A + B + C. All the groups coexist in the same society (W. Newman 1973).

In the United States, pluralism is more of an ideal than a reality. There are distinct instances of pluralism—the ethnic neighborhoods in major cities, such as Koreatown, Little Tokyo, Andersonville (Swedish Americans), and Spanish Harlem—yet there are also limits to cultural freedom. To survive, a society must promote a certain consensus among its members regarding basic ideals, values, and beliefs. Thus, if a Hungarian immigrant to the United States wants to move up the occupational ladder, he or she cannot avoid learning the English language.

Switzerland exemplifies the modern pluralistic state. There, the absence of both a national language and a dominant religious faith leads to a tolerance for cultural diversity. In addition, various political devices safeguard the interests of ethnic groups in a way that has no parallel in the United States. In contrast, Great Britain has had difficulty achieving cultural pluralism in a multiracial society. East Indians, Pakistanis, and Blacks from the Caribbean and Africa experience prejudice and discrimination within the dominant White society there. Some British advocate cutting off all Asian and Black immigration, and a few even call for expulsion of those non-Whites currently living in Britain.

MODULE 32 | Recap and Review

Summary

Four major theoretical perspectives—functionalism, conflict theory, labeling theory, and interactionism—are useful for analyzing relations among racial and ethnic groups.

1. Functionalists point out that discrimination is both functional and dysfunctional for society.

2. Conflict theorists explain racial subordination through **exploitation theory.**

3. **Racial profiling** is any arbitrary action initiated by an authority based on race, ethnicity, or national origin rather than on a person's behavior. Based on false stereotypes of certain racial and ethnic groups, the practice is not an effective way to fight crime.

4. Interactionists pose the **contact hypothesis** as a means of reducing prejudice and discrimination.

5. Four patterns describe typical intergroup relations in North America and elsewhere: **amalgamation, assimilation, segregation,** and **pluralism.** Pluralism remains more of an ideal than a reality.

Thinking Critically

1. Describe an example of labeling that you are personally familiar with.

2. Give examples of amalgamation, assimilation, segregation, and pluralism that you have seen on your campus or in your workplace.

Key Terms

Amalgamation

Apartheid

Assimilation

Contact hypothesis

Exploitation theory

Genocide

Pluralism

Racial profiling

Segregation

Few societies have a more diverse population than the United States; the nation is truly a multiracial, multiethnic society. Of course, that has not always been the case. The population of what is now the United States has changed dramatically since the arrival of European settlers in the 1600s, as Figure 31-1 shows. Immigration, colonialism, and in the case of Blacks, slavery determined the racial and ethnic makeup of our present-day society.

Today, the largest racial minorities in the United States are African Americans, Native Americans, and Asian Americans. The largest ethnic groups are Latinos, Jews, and the various White ethnic groups. Figure 33-1 shows where the major racial and ethnic minorities are concentrated.

African Americans

"I am an invisible man," wrote Black author Ralph Ellison in his novel *Invisible Man* (1952:3). "I am a man of substance, of flesh and bone, fiber and liquids—and I might even be said to possess a mind. I am invisible, understand, simply because people refuse to see me."

Over five decades later, many African Americans still feel invisible. Despite their large numbers, they have long been treated as second-class citizens. Currently, by the standards of the federal government, more than 1 out of every 4 African Americans—as opposed to 1 out of every 11 White non-Hispanics—is poor (DeNavas-Walt et al. 2011:15).

Contemporary institutional discrimination and individual prejudice against African Americans are rooted in the history of slavery in the United States. Many other subordinate groups had little wealth and income, but as sociologist W. E. B. DuBois ([1909] 1970) and others have noted, enslaved African Americans were in an even more oppressive situation, because by law they could not own property and could not pass on the benefits of their labor to their children. Today, increasing numbers of African Americans and sympathetic Whites are calling for *slave reparations* to compensate for the injustices of forced servitude. Reparations could include official expressions of apology from governments such as the United States, ambitious programs to improve African Americans' economic status, or even direct payments to descendants of slaves (D. Williams and Collins 2004).

The end of the Civil War did not bring genuine freedom and equality for Blacks. The Southern states passed Jim Crow laws to enforce official segregation, and the Supreme Court upheld them as constitutional in 1896. In addition, Blacks faced the danger of lynching campaigns, often led by the Ku Klux Klan, during the late 1800s and early 1900s. From a conflict perspective, Whites maintained their dominance formally through legalized segregation and informally by means of vigilante terror and violence (Franklin and Higginbotham 2011).

During the 1960s, a vast civil rights movement emerged, with many competing factions and strategies for change. The Southern Christian Leadership Conference (SCLC), founded by Dr. Martin Luther King Jr., used nonviolent civil disobedience to oppose segregation. The National Association for the Advancement of Colored

MAPPING LIFE NATIONWIDE

FIGURE 33-1 Minority Population by County

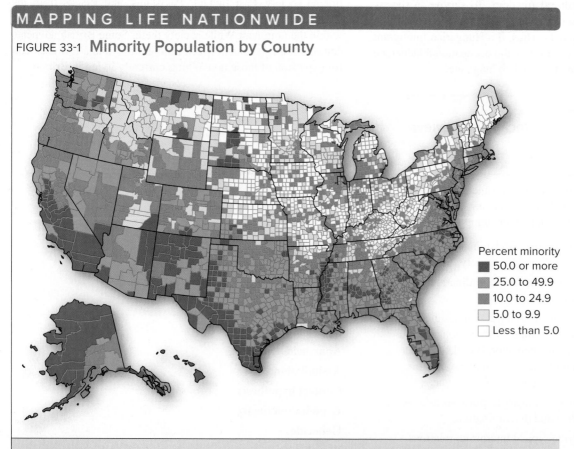

Percent minority
- 50.0 or more
- 25.0 to 49.9
- 10.0 to 24.9
- 5.0 to 9.9
- Less than 5.0

Think about It The United States is a diverse nation. Why, in many parts of the country, can't people see that diversity in their towns?

Source: Jones-Puthoff 2013:slide 5.

In four states (California, Hawaii, New Mexico, and Texas) and the District of Columbia, as well as in about one out of every nine counties, minorities constitute the numerical majority.

People (NAACP) favored use of the courts to press for equality for African Americans. But many younger Black leaders, most notably Malcolm X, turned toward an ideology of Black power. Proponents of **Black power** rejected the goal of assimilation into White middle-class society. They defended the beauty and dignity of Black and African cultures and supported the creation of Black-controlled political and economic institutions (Ture and Hamilton 1992).

Despite numerous courageous actions to achieve Black civil rights, Black and White citizens are still separate, still unequal. From birth to death, Blacks suffer in terms of their life chances. Life remains difficult for millions of poor Blacks, who must attempt to survive in ghetto areas shattered by high unemployment and abandoned housing. Today the median household income of Blacks is still 60 percent that of Whites, and the unemployment rate among Blacks is more than twice that of Whites.

Some African Americans—especially middle-class men and women—have made economic gains over the past 50 years. For example, data show that the number of African Americans in management increased nationally from 2.4 percent of the total in 1958 to 6.4 percent in 2010. Yet Blacks still represent only 7 percent or less of all physicians, engineers, scientists, lawyers, judges, and marketing managers (Bureau of Labor Statistics 2013:Table 11).

● Native Americans

Today, about 2.2 million Native Americans represent a diverse array of cultures distinguishable by language, family organization, religion, and livelihood. The outsiders who came to the United States—European settlers—and their descendants came to know these native peoples' forefathers as "American Indians." By the time the Bureau of Indian Affairs (BIA) was organized as part of the War Department in 1824, Indian–White relations had already included more than two centuries of hostile actions that had led to the virtual elimination of native peoples (see Figure 31-1). During the 19th century, many bloody wars wiped out a significant part of the Indian population. By the end of the century, schools for Indians—operated by the BIA or by church missions—prohibited the practice of Native American cultures. Yet at the same time, such schools did little to make the children effective members of White society.

Today, life remains difficult for members of the 554 tribal groups in the United States, whether they live in cities or on reservations. For example, one Native American teenager in six has attempted suicide—a rate four times higher than the rate for other teenagers. Traditionally, some Native Americans have chosen to assimilate and abandon all vestiges of their tribal cultures to escape certain forms of prejudice. However,

by the 1990s, an increasing number of people in the United States were openly claiming a Native American identity. Since 1960, the federal government's count of Native Americans has tripled.

Native Americans have made some progress in redressing their past mistreatment. In 2009, the federal government settled a 13-year-old lawsuit for the recovery of lease payments due on tribal lands used by the government for oil and gas exploration and grazing. Although the $3.4 billion settlement was large, it was long overdue—some of the government's debts dated back to 1887—and from the perspective of tribal leaders, it was too little, too late. The United States is not the only country that has tried to redress the government's past actions toward indigenous peoples (see Box 33-1).

The introduction of gambling on Indian reservations has transformed the lives of some Native Americans. Native Americans got into the gaming industry in 1988, when Congress passed the Indian Gambling Regulatory Act. The law stipulates that states must negotiate agreements with tribes interested in commercial gaming; they cannot prevent tribes from engaging in gambling operations, even if state law prohibits such ventures. The income from these lucrative operations is not evenly distributed, however. About two-thirds of recognized Indian tribes are not involved in gambling ventures. Those tribes that earn substantial revenues from gambling constitute a small fraction of Native Americans (Conner and Taggart 2009).

Like Native Americans, many native peoples living in the United States have successfully established their autonomy, gaining control over their resources and business enterprises.

💡 use your **sociological imagination**

You are a Native American whose tribe is about to open a reservation-based casino. Will the casino further the assimilation of your people into mainstream society or encourage pluralism? Explain your reasoning.

Asian Americans

Asian Americans are a diverse group, one of the fastest-growing segments of the U.S. population (up 43 percent between 2000 and 2010). Among the many groups of Americans of Asian descent are Vietnamese Americans, Chinese Americans, Japanese Americans, and Korean Americans (Figure 33-2).

Native American artists often break new ground to represent their life experiences. Dunne-Za member Brian Jungen used Nike shoes to make this three-dimensional piece, which suggests both his Pacific Northwest culture and his family's practice of stretching their modest means by reusing everything.

BOX 33-1

Sociology in the Global Community

The Aboriginal People of Australia

The indigenous, or Aboriginal, people of Australia have inhabited their home continent continuously for at least 50,000 years. Today they make up about 2.4 percent of Australia's total population. Although their numbers are small, they are highly visible in Australian society.

The cultural practices of the Aboriginal people are quite diverse, given their many clans, language groups, and communities. Except for occasional connections between kin or trading partners, these groups have little social contact. When Europeans first arrived in Australia, the diversity of Aborigines was even greater: an estimated 600 to 700 different groups spoke 200 to 250 languages as distinct from each other as French is from German. The existence of many dialects, or variants of languages that were more or less understandable to others, increased the complexity.

Like the American Indians, Australia's Aboriginal population declined dramatically following European settlement. New diseases, some of which were not life-threatening to Europeans, had a devastating effect on Aboriginal communities, which lacked immunity to them. Mistreatment under the British colonial regime, dispossession of their land, and the disruption and disintegration of their culture also overwhelmed the Aboriginal people. Decades of protests and legal efforts regarding their land rights have brought little change.

Historically, the Aboriginal people received little legal recognition from Europeans. Only in 1967 did the government of Australia extend citizenship and voting rights to the Aboriginals, along with access to welfare and unemployment benefits. Yet it would be misleading to view the Aboriginal people as passive victims, either in colonial days or in more recent times. They have worked actively to secure their rights.

As in the United States, Whites' low regard for the Aboriginal people became the basis for an effort to stamp out their culture. From 1910 to 1970, thousands of Aboriginal children were forcibly removed from their families so they could be raised by Whites and impressed into the dominant culture. Between 10 and 30 percent of all Aboriginal children were affected by this program. Not until 2008 did the

improve the Aboriginal people's living conditions and their prospects for the future.

> From 1910 to 1970, thousands of Aboriginal children were forcibly removed from their families so they could be raised by Whites and impressed into the dominant culture.

Australian government finally apologize to Aboriginals for "the Stolen Generations." The government has expressed its intention to

LET'S DISCUSS

1. Try to think of a situation in your culture in which the government might forcibly remove a child from his or her family. Do you know anyone who has had such an experience? If so, what were the repercussions?

2. What kind of reasoning do you think lay behind the Australian government's forced removal of Aboriginal children from their families? In sociological terms, what actually happened?

Sources: W. Anderson 2003; Attwood 2003; Australia 1997, 2008; R. Schaefer 2012.

Asian Americans are also economically diverse. There are rich and poor Japanese Americans, rich and poor Filipino Americans, and so forth. In fact, Southeast Asians living in the United States have the highest rate of welfare dependency of any racial or ethnic group. According to a study published in 2011, poverty rates are particularly high among the adult children of Cambodian, Hmong, and Thai immigrants to the United States. Though Asian Americans have substantially more schooling than other ethnic groups, their median income is only slightly higher than Whites' income, and their poverty rate is higher. In 2012, for every Asian American household with an annual income of $150,000 or more, there was another earning less than $20,000 a year (DeNavas-Walt et al. 2013; Takei and Sakamoto 2011).

The fact that as a group, Asian Americans work in the same occupations as Whites suggests that they have been successful—and many have. However, there are some differences between the two groups. Asian immigrants, like other minorities and immigrants before them, are found disproportionately in low-paying service occupations. At the same time, better-educated Asian Americans are concentrated near the top in professional and managerial positions, although they rarely reach the pinnacle. Instead, they hit the glass ceiling, or try to "climb a broken ladder," as some put it.

Ironically, Asian Americans are often held up as an unqualified success story. According to popular belief, they have succeeded in adapting to mainstream U.S. culture despite past prejudice and discrimination, and without resorting to confrontations with Whites. Box 33-2 compares this common conception with Asian Americans' actual experience.

Chinese Americans

Unlike African slaves and Native Americans, the Chinese were initially encouraged to immigrate to the United States. From 1850 to 1880, thousands of Chinese immigrated to this country, lured by job opportunities created by the discovery of gold. However, as employment possibilities decreased and competition for mining jobs grew, the Chinese became the target of a bitter campaign to limit their numbers and restrict their rights. Chinese laborers were exploited, then discarded.

FIGURE 33-2 Asian American and Pacific Islander Population by Origin

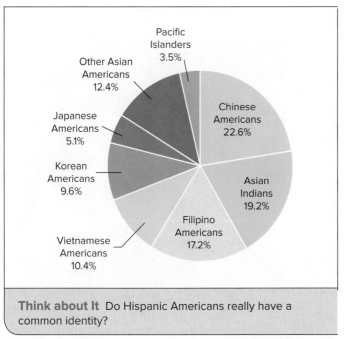

Pacific Islanders 3.5%

Other Asian Americans 12.4%

Japanese Americans 5.1%

Korean Americans 9.6%

Vietnamese Americans 10.4%

Filipino Americans 17.2%

Chinese Americans 22.6%

Asian Indians 19.2%

Think about It Do Hispanic Americans really have a common identity?

Sources: Census 2010 data in Hixson et al. 2012:Table 2.5; Hoeffel et al. 2012:Tables 2, 3.

In 1882, Congress enacted the Chinese Exclusion Act, which prevented Chinese immigration and even forbade Chinese in the United States to send for their families. As a result, the Chinese population declined steadily until after World War II. More recently, the descendants of the 19th-century immigrants have been joined by a new influx from Hong Kong and Taiwan. These groups may contrast sharply in their degree of assimilation, desire to live in Chinatowns, and feelings about this country's relations with the People's Republic of China.

Currently, over 3 million Chinese Americans live in the United States. Some Chinese Americans have entered lucrative occupations, yet many immigrants struggle to survive under living and working conditions that belie the model-minority stereotype. New York City's Chinatown district is filled with illegal sweatshops in which recent immigrants—many of them Chinese women—work for minimal wages. Outside of Chinatown, 23 percent of Asian Americans fall into the low-income category. At the other end of the income distribution, barely 5 percent of Chinatown's residents earn more than $100,000 a year, compared to 25 percent of Asian Americans who live elsewhere in New York City (Logan et al. 2002; Wong 2006).

Asian Indians

After Chinese Americans, the second-largest Asian American group, immigrants from India and their descendants, numbers over 2.8 million. It is difficult to generalize about Asian Indian Americans because Asian Indians are such a diverse population. India, a country of more than 1.2 billion people that is fast becoming the most populous nation in the world, is multiethnic. Perhaps because Asian Indian immigrants feel threatened by mainstream U.S. culture, religious orthodoxy is often stronger among first-generation immigrants to the United States than it is in India. New immigrants try to practice their religion just as they did in India rather than join congregations already established by other immigrant groups.

Maintaining family traditions is a major challenge for Asian Indian immigrants to the United States. Family ties remain strong despite their immigration—so much so that many Asian Indians feel more connected to their relatives in India than Americans do to relatives nearby. These *Desi* (pronounced day-see, colloquial for people who trace their ancestry to South Asia, especially India) are particularly concerned about the erosion of traditional family authority. Indian American children dress like their peers, go to fast-food restaurants, and even eat hamburgers, rejecting the vegetarian diet typical of both Hindus and many Asian Indian Muslims. Sons do not feel the extent of responsibility to the family that tradition dictates. Daughters, whose occupations and marriage partners the family could control in India, assert their right to choose their careers, and even their husbands (Rangaswamy 2005).

Filipino Americans

Filipinos are the third-largest Asian American group in the United States, with nearly 2.6 million people. For geographic reasons, social scientists consider them to be of Asian extraction, but physically and culturally this group also reflects centuries of Spanish and U.S. colonial rule, as well as the more recent U.S. military occupation.

Filipinos began immigrating to the United States as American nationals when the U.S. government gained possession of the Philippine Islands at the end of the Spanish–American War (1899). When the Philippines gained their independence in 1948, Filipinos lost their unrestricted immigration rights, although farmworkers were welcome to work in Hawai'i's pineapple

Asian Americans rarely head the casts of motion pictures, unless those films feature the martial arts. Two exceptions to the rule are John Cho (left) and Kal Penn, who co-star in the successful Harold & Kumar movies. Penn is the stage name used by Kalpen Modi, the son of Asian Indian immigrants to the United States. In 2009, President Obama appointed Modi associate director of the Office of Public Engagement, where he served as a liaison to the Asian American and Pacific Islander communities.

Research Today

BOX 33-2

Asian Americans: A Model Minority?

Many people suppose that Asian Americans constitute a **model,** or **ideal, minority** group. According to this belief, Asian Americans have succeeded economically, socially, and educationally despite past prejudice and discrimination, and without resorting to political and violent confrontations with Whites. Proponents of this view add that because Asian Americans have achieved success, they are no longer disadvantaged. This portrayal of Asian Americans as a model minority ignores their economic diversity. Moreover, even those Asian Americans who are clustered at the high end of the social scale face some barriers to advancement.

The dramatic success of Asian Americans in the U.S. educational system has undoubtedly contributed to the model minority stereotype. Compared with their numbers in the population as a whole, Asian Americans are greatly overrepresented in the student bodies of the most prestigious universities, public and private. Their upward mobility in schooling can be attributed in part to a strong cultural belief in the value of education, to family pressure to succeed, and to the desire to escape discrimination through academic achievement.

The resulting perception of Asian Americans as academic stars does not always work to their advantage. Asian American students who do not excel in school may face criticism from parents or teachers for their failure to conform to the "whiz kid" image. In fact, the high school dropout rate among Asian Americans is increasing rapidly. In

California's special program for low-income, academically disadvantaged students, Asian Americans make up 30 percent of the students, and their proportion of all students in the program is rising.

Some observers see Asian Americans' supposed success as a reaffirmation of the cherished belief that with talent and hard work, anyone can get ahead in the United States. This view of Asian Americans as a successful minority carries an implicit critique of Blacks, Hispanics, and other groups who have not fared as well as the model minority. The tacit assumption is that

Viewed from a conflict perspective, this flip side to the Asian American stereotype is yet another instance of "blaming the victim."

> This view of Asian Americans as a successful minority carries an implicit critique of Blacks, Hispanics, and other groups who have not fared as well as the model minority.

minorities who have been less successful than Asian Americans are completely responsible for their failure to get ahead.

LET'S DISCUSS

1. Are Asian Americans seen as "whiz kids" at your school? If so, how close to reality do you think that stereotype is?

2. Talk with some Asian American students about their grades and their study habits. Do they all have the same work ethic? How does your own work ethic compare to theirs?

Sources: Ryan 1976; Tachibana 1990; Takei and Sakamoto 2011; Teranishi 2010.

groves. Aside from this exception, immigration was restricted to 50 to 100 Filipinos a year until 1965, when the Immigration Act lifted the strict quotas.

Today, a significant percentage of Filipino immigrants are well-educated professionals who work in the field of health care. Although they are a valuable human resource in the United States, their immigration has long drained the medical establishment in the Philippines. When the U.S. Immigration and Naturalization Service stopped giving preference to physicians, Filipino doctors began entering the country as nurses—a dramatic illustration of the incredible income differences between the two countries. Like other immigrant groups, Filipino Americans save much of their income and send a significant amount of money, called **remittances,** back to their extended families.

For several reasons, Filipino Americans have not coalesced in a single formal social organization, despite their numbers. Their strong loyalty to the family (*sa pamilya*) and to the church—particularly Roman Catholicism—reduces their need

for a separate organization. Moreover, their diversity complicates the task of uniting the Filipino American community, which reflects the same regional, religious, and linguistic distinctions that divide their homeland. Thus, the many groups that Filipino Americans have organized tend to be club-like or fraternal in nature. Because those groups do not represent the general population of Filipino Americans, they remain largely invisible to Anglos. Although Filipinos remain interested in events in their homeland, they also seek to become involved in broader, non-Filipino organizations and to avoid exclusive activities (Bonus 2000; Kang 1996; Lau 2006; Padilla 2008).

Vietnamese Americans

Vietnamese Americans came to the United States primarily during and after the Vietnam War—especially after U.S. withdrawal from the conflict in 1975. Refugees from the communist government in Vietnam, assisted by local agencies, settled throughout the United States, tens of thousands of them in small towns.

Over time, however, Vietnamese Americans have gravitated toward the larger urban areas, establishing Vietnamese restaurants and grocery stores in their ethnic enclaves there.

In 1995, the United States resumed normal diplomatic relations with Vietnam. Gradually, the *Viet Kieu,* or Vietnamese living abroad, began to return to their old country to visit, but usually not to take up permanent residence. Today, more than 35 years after the end of the Vietnam War, sharp differences of opinion remain among Vietnamese Americans, especially the older ones, concerning the war and the present government of Vietnam (Pfeifer 2008).

Korean Americans

At over 1.4 million, the population of Korean Americans now exceeds that of Japanese Americans. Yet Korean Americans are often overshadowed by other groups from Asia.

Today's Korean American community is the result of three waves of immigration. The initial wave arrived between 1903 and 1910, when Korean laborers migrated to Hawai'i. The second wave followed the end of the Korean War in 1953; most of those immigrants were wives of U.S. servicemen and war orphans. The third wave, continuing to the present, has reflected the admissions priorities set up in the 1965 Immigration Act. These well-educated immigrants arrive in the United States with professional skills. Yet because of language difficulties and discrimination, many must settle at least initially for positions of lower responsibility than those they held in Korea and must suffer through a period of disenchantment. Stress, loneliness, and family strife may accompany the pain of adjustment.

In the early 1990s, the apparent friction between Korean Americans and another subordinate racial group, African Americans, attracted nationwide attention. Conflict between the two groups was dramatized in Spike Lee's 1989 movie *Do the Right Thing.* The situation stemmed from Korean Americans' position as the latest immigrant group to cater to the needs of inner-city populations abandoned by those who have moved up the economic ladder. This type of friction is not new; generations of Jewish, Italian, and Arab merchants have encountered similar hostility from what to outsiders seems an unlikely source—another oppressed minority (K. Kim 1999).

Japanese Americans

Approximately 763,000 Japanese Americans live in the United States. As a people, they are relatively recent arrivals. In 1880, only 148 Japanese lived in the United States, but by 1920 there were more than 110,000. Japanese immigrants—called the *Issei* (pronounced ee-say), or first generation—were usually males seeking employment opportunities. Many Whites saw them (along with Chinese immigrants) as a "yellow peril" and subjected them to prejudice and discrimination.

In 1941, the attack on Hawai'i's Pearl Harbor by Japan had severe repercussions for Japanese Americans. The federal government decreed that all Japanese Americans on the West Coast must leave their homes and report to "evacuation camps." In effect, Japanese Americans became scapegoats for the anger that other people in the United States felt concerning Japan's role in World War II. By August 1943, in an unprecedented application of guilt by virtue of ancestry, 113,000 Japanese Americans had been forced into hastily built camps. In striking contrast, only a few German Americans and Italian Americans were sent to evacuation camps (Hosokawa 1969).

In 1983, a federal commission recommended government payments to all surviving Japanese Americans who had been held in detention camps. The commission reported that the detention was motivated by "race prejudice, war hysteria, and a failure of political leadership." It added that "no documented acts of espionage, sabotage, or fifth-column activity were shown to have been committed" by Japanese Americans. In 1988, President Ronald Reagan signed the Civil Liberties Act, which required the federal government to issue individual apologies for all violations of Japanese Americans' constitutional rights, and established a $1.25 billion trust fund to pay reparations to the approximately 77,500 surviving Japanese Americans who had been interned (Department of Justice 2000).

● Arab Americans

Arab Americans are immigrants, and their descendants, from the 22 nations of the Arab world. As defined by the League of Arab States, these are the nations of North Africa and what is popularly known as the Middle East, including Lebanon, Syria, Palestine, Morocco, Iraq, Saudi Arabia, and Somalia. Not all residents of

In Chicago, a young Muslim woman sports an "I Love New York" T-shirt. Across the United States, racial and ethnic diversity has increased dramatically.

those countries are Arab; for example, the Kurds, who live in northern Iraq, are not Arab. And some Arab Americans may have immigrated to the United States from non-Arab countries such as Great Britain or France, where their families have lived for generations.

The Arabic language is the single most unifying force among Arabs, although not all Arabs, and certainly not all Arab Americans, can read and speak Arabic. Moreover, the language has evolved over the centuries so that people in different parts of the Arab world speak different dialects. Still, the fact that the Koran (or Qur'an) was originally written in Arabic gives the language special importance to Muslims, just as the Torah's compilation in Hebrew gives that language special significance to Jews.

Estimates of the size of the Arab American community differ widely. Nearly 4 million people of Arab ancestry reside in the United States. Among those who identify themselves as Arab Americans, the most common country of origin is Lebanon, followed by Syria, Egypt, and Palestine. In 2000, these four countries of origin accounted for two-thirds of all Arab Americans. Their rising numbers have led to the development of Arab retail centers in several cities, including Dearborn and Detroit, Michigan; Los Angeles; Chicago; New York City; and Washington, D.C.

As a group, Arab Americans are extremely diverse. Many families have lived in the United States for several generations; others are foreign born. Their points of origin range from the metropolis of Cairo, Egypt, to the rural villages of Morocco. Despite the stereotype, most Arab Americans are *not* Muslim (Figure 33-3). Nor can Arab Americans be characterized as having a specific family type, gender role, or occupational pattern (David 2004, 2008).

In spite of this great diversity, profiling of potential terrorists at airports has put Arab and Muslim Americans under special surveillance. For years, a number of airlines and law enforcement authorities have used appearance and ethnic-sounding names to identify and take aside Arab Americans and search their belongings. After the terrorist attacks of September 2001, criticism of this practice declined as concern for the public's safety mounted.

FIGURE 33-3 **Arab American Religious Affiliations**

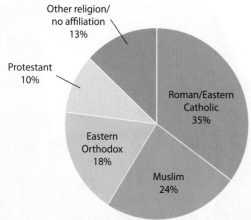

Notes: Roman/Eastern Catholic includes Roman Catholic, Maronite, and Melkite (Greek Catholic); Eastern Orthodox includes Antiochian, Syrian, Greek, and Coptic; Muslim includes Sunni, Shi'a, and Druze.
Source: Arab American Institute 2010, based on 2002 Zogby International Survey.

Unlike Arabs in other parts of the world, most Arab Americans are Christian.

FIGURE 33-4 **Hispanic Population by Origin**

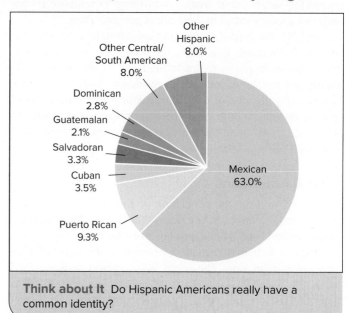

Think about It Do Hispanic Americans really have a common identity?

Note: "Other Hispanic" includes Spanish Americans and Latinos identified as mixed ancestry as well as other Central and South Americans not otherwise indicated by specific country.
Source: 2010 census data in Ennis et al. 2011:33. All nationalities with more than 1 million are represented.

Latinos

Together, the various groups included under the general category *Latinos* represent the largest minority in the United States. There are more than 50 million Hispanics in this country, including 32 million Mexican Americans, more than 4 million Puerto Ricans, and smaller numbers of Cuban Americans and people of Central and South American origin (Figure 33-4). The latter group represents the fastest-growing and most diverse segment of the Hispanic community.

According to Census Bureau data, the Latino population now outnumbers the African American population in 6 of the 10 largest metropolitan areas of the United States: New York City, Los Angeles, Chicago, Dallas–Fort Worth, Houston, and Miami–Fort Lauderdale. The rise of the Hispanic population of the United States—fueled by comparatively high birthrates and immigration levels—has Latinos beginning to flex their muscles as voters. In the 2012 presidential election, Latinos accounted for more than 10 percent of eligible voters. As Hispanics age and immigrants become citizens, their presence in the voting booth will be felt even more strongly (Bureau of the Census 2011a:Table 23 on page 31; Lopez 2011).

The various Latino groups share a heritage of Spanish language and culture, which can cause serious problems in their assimilation. An intelligent student whose first language is Spanish may be presumed slow or even unruly by English-speaking schoolchildren, and frequently by English-speaking teachers as well. The labeling of Latino children as underachievers, as learning disabled, or as emotionally disturbed can act as a self-fulfilling prophecy for some children. Bilingual education aims at easing the educational difficulties experienced by Hispanic children and others whose first language is not English.

The educational difficulties of Latino students certainly contribute to Hispanics' generally low economic status. In 2012, about 17 percent of all Hispanic households earned less than $15,000, compared to 11 percent of White non-Hispanic households; the poverty rate was 25.6 percent for Hispanics, compared to 9.7 percent for White non-Hispanics. Although Latinos are not as affluent as White non-Hispanics, a middle class is beginning to emerge (DeNavas-Walt et al. 2013:14, 34, 38).

Mexican Americans

The largest Latino population is Mexican Americans, who can be further subdivided into those descended from residents of the territories annexed after the Mexican American War of 1848 and those who have immigrated from Mexico to the United States. The opportunity for a Mexican to earn in one hour what it would take an entire day to earn in Mexico has pushed millions of legal and illegal immigrants north.

Many people view Mexican Americans as primarily an immigrant group. Since at least 2000, however, the number of Mexican Americans who were born in the United States has far exceeded those who immigrated here. Overall, Mexican Americans accounted for 42 percent of the nation's population growth in the decade 2000–2010. Two-thirds of them were born here; the other third were new arrivals (Bureau of the Census 2011a:8; Pew Hispanic Center 2011).

Puerto Ricans

The second-largest segment of Latinos in the United States is Puerto Ricans. Since 1917, residents of Puerto Rico have held the status of American citizens; many have migrated to New York and other eastern cities. Unfortunately, Puerto Ricans have experienced serious poverty both in the United States and on the island. Those who live in the continental United States earn barely half the family income of Whites. As a result, a reverse migration began in the 1970s, when more Puerto Ricans were leaving for the island than were coming to the mainland (Torres 2008).

Politically, Puerto Ricans in the United States have not been as successful as Mexican Americans in organizing for their rights. For many mainland Puerto Ricans—as for many residents of the island—the paramount political issue is the destiny of Puerto Rico itself: should it continue in its present commonwealth status, petition for admission to the United States as the 51st state, or attempt to become an independent nation? This question has divided Puerto Rico for decades and remains a central issue in Puerto Rican elections. In a 1998 referendum, voters supported a "none of the above" option, effectively favoring continuation of the commonwealth status over statehood or independence.

Cuban Americans

Cuban immigration to the United States dates back as far as 1831, but it began in earnest following Fidel Castro's assumption of power in the Cuban revolution (1959). The first wave of 200,000 Cubans included many professionals with relatively high levels of schooling; these men and women were largely welcomed as refugees from communist tyranny. However, more recent waves of immigrants have aroused growing concern, partly because they were less likely to be skilled professionals. Throughout these waves of immigration, Cuban Americans have been encouraged to locate around the United States. Nevertheless, many continue to settle in (or return to) metropolitan Miami, Florida, with its warm climate and proximity to Cuba.

The Cuban experience in the United States has been mixed. Some detractors worry about the vehement anticommunism of Cuban Americans and the apparent growth of an organized crime syndicate that engages in the drug trade and ganglike violence. Recently, Cuban Americans in Miami have expressed concern over what they view as the indifference of the city's Roman

Sonia Sotomayor was born in the Bronx, New York, of Puerto Rican parents. In 2009 she became the first Hispanic, and one of only 4 women, ever to be appointed to the U.S. Supreme Court. Of the other 108 justices, 2 have been African American men and 106 have been White men.

Catholic hierarchy. Like other Hispanics, Cuban Americans are underrepresented in leadership positions within the church. Also—despite many individual success stories—as a group, Cuban Americans in Miami remain behind Whites in income, rate of employment, and proportion of professionals (Masud-Piloto 2008).

Central and South Americans

Immigrants from Central and South America are a diverse population that has not been closely studied. Indeed, most government statistics treat members of this group collectively as "other," rarely differentiating among them by nationality. Yet people from Chile and Costa Rica have little in common other than their hemisphere of origin and the Spanish language—if that. The fact is, not all Central and South Americans speak Spanish. Immigrants from Brazil, for example, speak Portuguese; immigrants from French Guyana speak French; and immigrants from Suriname speak Dutch.

Racially, many of the nations of Central and South America follow a complex classification system that recognizes a multitude of color gradients. Experience with this multiracial system does not prepare immigrants to the United States for the stark Black–White racial divide that characterizes U.S. society. Beyond their diversity in color and language, immigrants from Central and South America are differentiated by social class distinctions, religious differences, urban or rural upbringings, and dialects. Some of them may come from indigenous populations, especially in Guatemala and Belize. If so, their social identity would be separate from any national allegiance.

In short, social relations among Central and South Americans, who collectively number nearly 7 million people, defy generalization. The same can be said about their relations with other Latinos and with non-Latinos. Central and South Americans do not form, nor should they be expected to form, a cohesive group.

For practicing Jews, the Hebrew language is an important part of religious instruction. This young pupil learns the Hebrew alphabet with a Jewish teacher.

Nor do they easily form coalitions with Cuban Americans, Mexican Americans, or Puerto Ricans.

Jewish Americans

Jews constitute about 2 percent of the population of the United States. They play a prominent role in the worldwide Jewish community, because the United States has the world's largest concentration of Jews. Like the Japanese, many Jewish immigrants came to this country and became white-collar professionals in spite of prejudice and discrimination.

Anti-Semitism—anti-Jewish prejudice—has often been vicious in the United States, although rarely so widespread and never so formalized as in Europe. In many cases, Jews have been used as scapegoats for other people's failures. Not surprisingly, Jews have not achieved equality in the United States. Despite high levels of education and professional training, they are still conspicuously absent from the top management of large corporations (except for the few firms founded by Jews). Nonetheless, a national survey in 2009 showed that one out of four people in the United States blames "the Jews" for the financial crisis. In addition, private social clubs and fraternal groups frequently continue to limit membership to Gentiles (non-Jews), a practice upheld by the Supreme Court in the 1964 case *Bell v. Maryland* (Malhotra and Margalit 2009).

The Anti-Defamation League (ADL) of B'nai B'rith coordinates an annual tally of reported anti-Semitic incidents. Although the number has fluctuated, in 2012 the tabulation of the total reported incidents of harassment, threats, vandalism, and assaults came to 927. Some incidents were inspired and carried out by neo-Nazi skinheads—groups of young people who champion racist and anti-Semitic ideologies. Such threatening behavior only intensifies the fears of many Jewish Americans, who remember the Holocaust—the extermination of 6 million Jews by the Nazi Third Reich during World War II (Anti-Defamation League 2013).

As is true for other minorities discussed in this chapter, Jewish Americans face the choice of maintaining ties to their long religious and cultural heritage or becoming as indistinguishable as possible from Gentiles. Many Jews have tended to assimilate, as is evident from the rise in marriages between Jews and Christians. In marriages that occurred in the 1970s, more than 70 percent of Jews married Jews or people who converted to Judaism. In marriages since 1996, that proportion has dropped to 53 percent. This trend means that today, American Jews are almost as likely to marry a Gentile as a Jew. For many, religion is a nonissue—neither parent practices religious rituals. Two-thirds of the children of these Jewish–Gentile marriages are not raised as Jews. Finally, in 2005, two-thirds of Jews felt that the biggest threat to Jewish life was anti-Semitism; only one-third named intermarriage as the biggest threat (American Jewish Committee 2005; Sanua 2007).

● White Ethnics

A significant segment of the population of the United States is made up of White ethnics whose ancestors arrived from Europe within the last century and a half. The nation's White ethnic population includes about 49 million people who claim at least partial German ancestry, 36 million Irish Americans, 17 million Italian Americans, and 10 million Polish Americans, as well as immigrants from other European nations. Some of these people continue to live in close-knit ethnic neighborhoods, whereas others have largely assimilated and left the "old ways" behind.

Many White ethnics today identify only sporadically with their heritage. **Symbolic ethnicity** refers to an emphasis on concerns such as ethnic food or political issues rather than on deeper ties to one's ethnic heritage. It is reflected in the occasional family trip to an ethnic bakery, the celebration of a ceremonial event such as St. Joseph's Day among Italian Americans, or concern about the future of Northern Ireland among Irish Americans. Such practices are another example of the social construction of race and ethnicity. Except in cases in which new immigration reinforces old traditions, symbolic ethnicity tends to decline with each passing generation (Alba 1990; Winter 2008).

Although the White ethnic identity may be a point of pride to those who share it, they do not necessarily celebrate it at the expense of disadvantaged minorities. It is all too easy to assume that race relations are a zero-sum game in which one group gains at the expense of the other. Rather, the histories of several White ethnic groups, such as the Irish and the Italians, show that once marginalized people can rise to positions of prestige and influence (Alba 2009).

That is not to say that White ethnics and racial minorities have not been antagonistic toward one another because of economic competition—an interpretation that agrees with the

White Americans often express their ethnicity with special celebrations, such as this Scandinavian Festival parade in Junction City, Oregon. Participants proudly display the flag of Denmark.

conflict approach to sociology. As Blacks, Latinos, and Native Americans emerge from the lower class, they must compete with working-class Whites for jobs, housing, and educational opportunities. In times of high unemployment or inflation, any such competition can easily generate intense intergroup conflict.

In many respects, the plight of White ethnics raises the same basic issues as that of other subordinate people in the United States. How ethnic can people be—how much can they deviate from an essentially White, Anglo-Saxon, Protestant norm—before society punishes them for their willingness to be different? Our society does seem to reward people for assimilating, yet as we have seen, assimilation is no easy process. In the years to come, more and more people will face the challenge of fitting in, not only in the United States but around the world, as the flow of immigrants from one country to another continues to increase. In the Social Policy section that follows, we focus on global immigration and its implications for the future.

social policy and Racial and Ethnic Inequality | Global Immigration

Worldwide, immigration is at an all-time high. Each year, about 191 million people move from one country to another—a number that is roughly the equivalent of the total populations of Russia and Italy. A million of these immigrants enter the United States legally, to join the 13 percent of the U.S. population who are foreign born. Perhaps more significantly, one-fourth of the U.S. labor force is foreign born—the largest proportion in at least 120 years (Motel and Patten 2012).

Globally, these mass migrations have had a tremendous social impact. The constantly increasing numbers of immigrants and the pressure they put on job opportunities and welfare capabilities in the countries they enter raise troubling

questions for many of the world's economic powers. Who should be allowed in? At what point should immigration be curtailed (United Nations 2009)?

Looking at the Issue

The migration of people is not uniform across time or space. At certain times, war or famine may precipitate large movements of people, either temporarily or permanently. Temporary dislocations occur when people wait until it is safe to return to their home areas. However, more and more migrants who cannot make an adequate living in their home nations are making permanent moves to developed nations. The major migration

—*Continued*

FIGURE 33-5 Legal Migration to the United States, 1820–2010

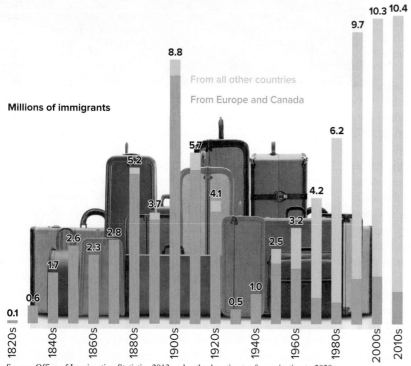

Millions of immigrants

From all other countries
From Europe and Canada

0.1 (1820s)
0.6 1.7 (1840s)
2.6 2.3 (1860s)
2.8 (1880s)
5.2 3.7 (1900s) 8.8
5.7 4.1 (1920s)
0.5 1.0 (1940s) 2.5
3.2 4.2 (1960s)
6.2 (1980s)
9.7 (2000s) 10.3 10.4 (2010s)

1820s · 1840s · 1860s · 1880s · 1900s · 1920s · 1940s · 1960s · 1980s · 2000s · 2010s

Source: Office of Immigration Statistics 2013 and author's estimates for projection to 2020.

For the past four decades, the majority of immigrants to the United States have come from outside Europe and Canada.

streams flow into North America, the oil-rich areas of the Middle East, and the industrial economies of western Europe and Asia. Currently, seven of the world's wealthiest nations (including Germany, France, the United Kingdom, and the United States) shelter about one-third of the world's migrant population, but less than one-fifth of the world's total population. As long as disparities in job opportunities exist among countries, there is little reason to expect this international trend to reverse.

One consequence of global immigration is the emergence of **transnationals**—immigrants who sustain multiple social relationships that link their societies of origin with the society of settlement. The industrial tycoons of the early 20th century, whose power outmatched that of many nation-states, were among the world's first transnationals. Today, millions of people, many of very modest means, move back and forth between countries much as commuters do between city and suburbs. More and more of these people have dual citizenship. Rather than being shaped by allegiance to one country, their identity is rooted in their struggle to survive—and in some instances prosper—by transcending international borders (Croucher 2004; Sassen 2005).

Countries that have long been a destination for immigrants, such as the United States, usually have policies regarding who has preference to enter. Often, clear racial and ethnic biases are built into these policies. In the 1920s, U.S. policy gave preference to people from western Europe, while making it difficult for residents of southern and eastern Europe, Asia, and Africa to enter the country. During the late 1930s and early 1940s, the federal government refused to lift or loosen restrictive immigration quotas in order to allow Jewish refugees to escape the terror of the Nazi regime. In line with this policy, the SS *St. Louis,* with more than 900 Jewish refugees on board, was denied permission to land in the United States in 1939. The ship was forced to sail back to Europe, where it is estimated that at least a few hundred of its passengers later died at the hands of the Nazis (Morse 1967; G. Thomas and Witts 1974).

Since the 1960s, U.S. policy has encouraged the immigration of relatives of U.S. residents as well as of people who have desirable skills. This change has significantly altered the pattern of sending nations. Previously, Europeans dominated, but for the past 50 years, immigrants have come primarily from Latin America and Asia. Thus, an ever-growing proportion of the U.S. population will be Asian or Hispanic (Figure 33-5). To a large degree, fear and resentment of growing racial and ethnic diversity is a key factor in opposition to immigration. In many nations, people are concerned that the new arrivals do not reflect their own cultural and racial heritage.

Applying Sociology

Research suggests that immigrants adapt well to life in the United States, becoming an asset to the nation's economy. In some areas, heavy immigration may drain a local community's resources, but in other areas it revitalizes the local economy.

Despite people's fears, immigration performs many valuable functions. For the receiving society, it alleviates labor shortages, as it does in health care and technology in the United States. For the sending nation, migration can relieve an economy unable to support large numbers of people. Often overlooked is the large amount of money (*remittances*) that immigrants send *back* to their home nations.

Immigration can be dysfunctional as well. Although studies generally show that it has a positive impact on the receiving nation's economy, areas that accept high concentrations

—Continued

of immigrants may find it difficult to meet short-term social service needs. And when migrants with skills or educational potential leave developing countries, their departure can be dysfunctional for those nations. No amount of payments sent back home can make up for the loss of valuable human resources from poor nations (Borjas et al. 2006; Kochhar 2006; Sum et al. 2006).

Conflict theorists note how much of the debate over immigration is phrased in economic terms. The debate intensifies when the arrivals are of a different racial or ethnic background from the host population. For example, Europeans often refer to "foreigners," but the term does not necessarily mean one of foreign birth. In Germany, "foreigners" refers to people of non-German ancestry, even if they were *born* in Germany; it does not refer to people of German ancestry born in another country, who may choose to return to their mother country. Fear and dislike of "new" ethnic groups divides countries throughout the world.

The feminist perspective pays special attention to the role that women play in global immigration. Immigrant women face all the challenges that immigrant men do, and some additional ones. Typically, they bear the responsibility for obtaining services for their families, particularly their children. Because the men are likely to be consumed with work, the women are left to navigate through the bureaucratic tangle of schools, city services, and medical facilities, as well as the unfamiliar stores and markets they must visit to feed their families. Women who need special medical services or are victims of domestic violence are often reluctant to seek outside help. Yet they are more likely than the men to serve as the liaison between their households and community and religious associations. Also, because many new immigrants view the United States as a dangerous place to raise a family, women must be especially watchful over their children's lives (Hondagneu-Sotelo 2003).

Initiating Policy

The long border with Mexico provides ample opportunity for illegal immigration into the United States. Throughout the 1980s, the public perception that the United States had lost control of its borders grew. Feeling pressure for immigration control, Congress ended a decade of debate by approving the Immigration Reform and Control Act of 1986. The act marked a historic change in the nation's immigration policy. For the first time, the hiring of illegal aliens was outlawed, and employers caught violating the law became subject to fines and even prison sentences. Just as significant a change was the extension of amnesty and legal status to many illegal immigrants already living in the United States. More than 20 years later, however, the act appears to have had mixed results. Substantial numbers of illegal immigrants continue

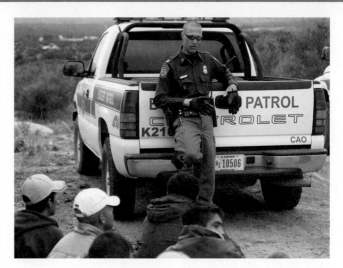

Despite a decline in illegal immigration to the United States since the economic downturn that began in 2007, the number of people deported has increased due to greater pressure to identify illegal immigrants. These suspected illegal immigrants are being detained in California.

to enter the country each year, with an estimated 11 million or more present at any given time—a marked increase since 2000, when their number was estimated at close to 8 million (Passel et al. 2013).

In 2010, frustrated by the continuing flow of illegal immigrants across the Mexican border, Arizona enacted a law empowering police to detain without authorization people whom they reasonably suspect of being illegal immigrants and to verify their immigration status. Immediately, opponents charged that the new law would lead to racial profiling. In 2012 the Supreme Court upheld the right of police to check the immigration status of anyone they stop or detain if they have a "reasonable suspicion" that the person has entered the country illegally. The debate continues between those seeking to tighten border controls and those advocating reform of the nation's immigration laws. Legal experts question whether state enforcement of immigration law is constitutional. Although implementation of the law has been problematic, it has highlighted the resolve of those seeking to tighten control of the nation's borders. It has also galvanized those seeking to reform the nation's immigration law.

In recent years Latinos have staged massive marches to pressure Congress to speed up the naturalization process and allow illegal immigrants to gain legal residency. Despite this political pressure, little action has been taken or even debated. The presidential election of 2012 saw the Democrats' strength among Hispanic voters grow at Republicans' expense, further encouraging the two parties to agree on immigration reform. Any new policy is likely to be linked to additional steps to strengthen the U.S.–Mexican border, while still facilitating the entry of workers needed in U.S. industries.

—*Continued*

The entire world feels the overwhelming impact of globalization on immigration patterns. The European Union agreement of 1997 gave the governing commission authority to propose a Europe-wide policy on immigration. An EU policy that allows residents of one EU country to live and work in another EU country is expected to complicate efforts by sending nations, such as Turkey, to become members of the EU. Immigrants from Turkey's predominantly Muslim population are not welcome in many EU countries (Denny 2004).

In the wake of the attacks of September 11, 2001, on the World Trade Center and the Pentagon, immigration procedures were complicated by the need to detect potential terrorists. Illegal immigrants especially, but even legal immigrants, have felt increased scrutiny by government officials around the world. For would-be immigrants to many nations, the wait to receive the right to enter a country—even to join relatives—has increased substantially, as immigration officials scrutinize more closely what were once routine applications.

The intense debate over immigration reflects deep value conflicts in the cultures of many nations. One strand of our culture, for example, has traditionally emphasized egalitarian principles and a desire to help people in time of need. At the same time, hostility to potential immigrants and refugees—whether the Chinese in the 1880s, European Jews in the 1930s and 1940s, or Mexicans, Haitians, and Arabs today—reflects not only racial, ethnic, and religious prejudice, but a desire to maintain the dominant culture of the in-group by keeping out those viewed as outsiders.

TAKE THE ISSUE WITH YOU

1. Did you or your parents or grandparents immigrate to the United States from another nation? If so, when and where did your family come from, and why?

2. On balance, do the functions of immigration to the United States outweigh the dysfunctions?

3. Do you live, work, or study with recent immigrants to the United States? If so, are they well accepted in your community, or do they face prejudice and discrimination?

MODULE 33 | **Recap and Review**

Summary

The U.S. population is highly diverse, both racially and ethnically.

1. Contemporary prejudice and discrimination against African Americans are rooted in the history of slavery in the United States.

2. Asian Americans are commonly viewed as a **model,** or **ideal minority,** a false stereotype that is not necessarily beneficial to members of that group.

3. The various groups included under the general term *Latinos* represent the largest ethnic minority in the United States.

4. Worldwide, immigration is at an all-time high, fueling controversy not only in the United States but also in the European Union. A new kind of immigrant, the **transnational,** moves back and forth across international borders in search of a better job or education.

Thinking Critically

1. Mexican culture seems alive in many Mexican American communities. Native Americans routinely display their tribal identities. Why do White ethnic identities seem more elusive?

2. To what extent has U.S. society achieved pluralism? Give examples from your own experience to support your viewpoint.

Key Terms

Anti-Semitism

Black power

Model, or ideal, minority

Remittances

Symbolic ethnicity

Transnational

Mastering This Chapter

taking sociology with you

1 Consider one or more jobs you have had, or an occupation you aspire to. How diverse is the staff you worked or would work with? What about your clients or customers? Do you expect racial and ethnic diversity to play an important role in your future career?

2 Talk with an older relative about your family's past. Did your ancestors experience prejudice or discrimination because of their race or ethnicity, and if so, in what way? Did they ever use racial or ethnic slurs to refer to people of other races or ethnicities? Have your family's attitudes toward members of other groups changed over the years, and if so, why?

3 Look up the census statistics on the racial and ethnic composition of your community. What are the predominant racial and ethnic groups? How many other groups are represented? How many members of your community are immigrants, and where do they come from?

key terms

Affirmative action Positive efforts to recruit minority group members or women for jobs, promotions, and educational opportunities.

Amalgamation The process through which a majority group and a minority group combine to form a new group.

Anti-Semitism Anti-Jewish prejudice.

Apartheid A former policy of the South African government, designed to maintain the separation of Blacks and other non-Whites from the dominant Whites.

Assimilation The process through which a person forsakes his or her cultural tradition to become part of a different culture.

Black power A political philosophy, promoted by many younger Blacks in the 1960s, that supported the creation of Black-controlled political and economic institutions.

Color-blind racism The use of the principle of race neutrality to defend a racially unequal status quo.

Contact hypothesis An interactionist perspective which states that in cooperative circumstances, interracial contact between people of equal status will reduce prejudice.

Discrimination The denial of opportunities and equal rights to individuals and groups because of prejudice or other arbitrary reasons.

Ethnic group A group that is set apart from others primarily because of its national origin or distinctive cultural patterns.

Ethnocentrism The tendency to assume that one's own culture and way of life represent the norm or are superior to all others.

Exploitation theory A Marxist theory that views racial subordination in the United States as a manifestation of the class system inherent in capitalism.

Genocide The deliberate, systematic killing of an entire people or nation.

Glass ceiling An invisible barrier that blocks the promotion of a qualified individual in a work environment because of the individual's gender, race, or ethnicity.

Institutional discrimination The denial of opportunities and equal rights to individuals and groups that results from the normal operations of a society.

Minority group A subordinate group whose members have significantly less control or power over their own lives than the members of a dominant or majority group have over theirs.

Model, or ideal, minority A subordinate group whose members supposedly have succeeded economically, socially, and educationally despite past prejudice and discrimination, and without resorting to political and violent confrontations with Whites.

Pluralism Mutual respect for one another's cultures among the various groups in a society, which allows minorities to express their cultures without experiencing prejudice.

Prejudice A negative attitude toward an entire category of people, often an ethnic or racial minority.

Racial formation A sociohistorical process in which racial categories are created, inhabited, transformed, and destroyed.

Racial group A group that is set apart from others because of physical differences that have taken on social significance.

Racial profiling Any arbitrary action initiated by an authority based on race, ethnicity, or national origin rather than on a person's behavior.

Racism The belief that one race is supreme and all others are innately inferior.

Remittances The monies that immigrants return to their families of origin. Also called *migradollars*.

Segregation The physical separation of two groups of people in terms of residence, workplace, and social events; often imposed on a minority group by a dominant group.

Stereotype An unreliable generalization about all members of a group that does not recognize individual differences within the group.

Symbolic ethnicity An ethnic identity that emphasizes concerns such as ethnic food or political issues rather than deeper ties to one's ethnic heritage.

Transnational An immigrant who sustains multiple social relationships that link his or her society of origin with the society of settlement.

White privilege Rights or immunities granted to people as a particular benefit or favor simply because they are White.

Read each question carefully and then select the best answer.

1. Sociologists have identified five basic properties of a minority group. Which of the following is *not* one of those properties?
   a. unequal treatment
   b. physical traits
   c. ascribed status
   d. cultural bias

2. The largest racial minority group in the United States is
   a. Asian Americans.
   b. African Americans.
   c. Native Americans.
   d. Jewish Americans.

3. Racism is a form of which of the following?
   a. ethnocentrism
   b. discrimination
   c. prejudice
   d. both b and c

4. Suppose that a White employer refuses to hire a qualified Vietnamese American but hires an inferior White applicant. This decision is an act of
   a. prejudice.
   b. ethnocentrism.
   c. discrimination.
   d. stigmatization.

5. Suppose that a workplace requires that only English be spoken, even when it is not a business necessity to restrict the use of other languages. This requirement would be an example of
   a. prejudice.
   b. scapegoating.
   c. a self-fulfilling prophecy.
   d. institutional discrimination.

6. Working together as computer programmers for an electronics firm, a Hispanic woman and a Jewish man overcome their initial prejudices and come to appreciate each other's strengths and talents. This scenario is an example of
   a. the contact hypothesis.
   b. a self-fulfilling prophecy.
   c. amalgamation.
   d. reverse discrimination.

7. Intermarriage over several generations, resulting in various groups combining to form a new group, would be an example of
   a. amalgamation.
   b. assimilation.
   c. segregation.
   d. pluralism.

8. Alphonso D'Abruzzo changed his name to Alan Alda. His action is an example of
   a. amalgamation.
   b. assimilation.
   c. segregation.
   d. pluralism.

9. In which of the following racial or ethnic groups has one teenager in every six attempted suicide?
   a. African Americans
   b. Asian Americans
   c. Native Americans
   d. Latinos

10. Advocates of *Marxist class theory* argue that the basis for racial subordination in the United States lies within the capitalist economic system. Another representation of this point of view is reflected in which of the following theories?
    a. exploitation
    b. functionalist
    c. interactionist
    d. contact

11. Sociologists consider race and ethnicity to be _____ statuses, since people are born into racial and ethnic groups.

12. The one-drop rule was a vivid example of the social _____ of race—the process by which people come to define a group as a race based in part on physical characteristics, but also on historical, cultural, and economic factors.

13. _____ are unreliable generalizations about all members of a group that do not recognize individual differences within the group.

14. Sociologists use the term _____ to refer to a negative attitude toward an entire category of people, often an ethnic or racial minority.

15. When White Americans can use credit cards without suspicion and browse through stores without being shadowed by security guards, they are enjoying _____ _____.

16. _____ _____ refers to positive efforts to recruit minority group members or women for jobs, promotions, and educational opportunities.

17. After the Civil War, the Southern states passed "_____ _____" laws to enforce official segregation, and the Supreme Court upheld them as constitutional in 1896.

18. In the 1960s, proponents of _____ _____ rejected the goal of assimilation into White, middle-class society. They defended the beauty and dignity of Black and African cultures and supported the creation of Black-controlled political and economic institutions.

19. Asian Americans are held up as a(n) _____ or _____ minority group, supposedly because despite past suffering from prejudice and discrimination, they have succeeded economically, socially, and educationally without resorting to political and violent confrontations with Whites.

20. Together, the various groups included under the general category _____ represent the largest minority group in the United States.

11

Stratification by Gender

Gender stratification exists in all societies. Around the world, most occupations are dominated by either men or women.

What would it be like to live in a society that restricts women's freedom, simply because they are women?

Azadeh Moaveni found that in Iran, women took every opportunity to push against government social controls.

❝ Young people sought Elvis's café [in Tehran, Iran] as refuge from the relentless ugliness that pervaded most public gathering places. Even in the rainy winter, people would crowd outside in the drizzle for an hour, smoking soggy cigarettes and waiting for a table. It was the only café in Tehran designed with innovative elegance and attracted young people starved for aesthetic beauty—the artists, writers, and musicians whose sensibilities suffered acutely in a city draped with grim billboards of war martyrs.

Elvis's coffeehouse inspired imitations all over the neighborhood and then the city. In early 2000, when Celine and I first began to haunt the tiny, modern nook, it was one of a kind. By the following summer of 2001, dozens of tastefully decorated cafés dotted the city, but Elvis's remained the original. In the Gandhi shopping complex, where it was located, at least six others sprang up, and the area became center stage in a café scene of shocking permissiveness. By that time, the dress code was so relaxed that everyone buzzed with tales of "You'll never believe what I saw this girl wearing!"; the fashion spring was likened to a silent coup.

Girls dressed in every color imaginable—veils of bright emerald, violet, buttercup—and in short, coat-like tunics called *manteaus* (also known by the Farsi word *roopoosh*) that hugged their curves, Capri pants that exposed long

Often, once we finished discussing work, men, and the new styles of head scarf we coveted, Celine and I would sit and people-watch. The throng of students and young professionals flirted brazenly, and the coquettish slipping of veils produced nothing less than social theater.

stretches of calf, pedicured toes in delicate sandals. They sat at the tables outside, in mixed groups, alone with boyfriends, laughing and talking into the late evening, past eleven. For a few weeks, Tehran actually had something like nightlife in public, not just sequestered parties inside people's houses. . . .

Often, once we finished discussing work, men, and the new styles of head scarf we coveted, Celine and I would sit and people-watch. The throng of students and young professionals flirted brazenly, and the coquettish slipping of veils produced nothing less than social theater. The Tehran of the revolution was one of the most sexualized milieus I had ever encountered. Even the chat rooms, Celine informed me, were rife with erotic discussion. People really, really wanted to talk about sex.

. . . Made neurotic by the innate oppressiveness of restriction, Iranians were preoccupied with sex in the manner of dieters constantly thinking about food. The subject meant to be *unmentionable*—to which end women were forced to wear veils, sit in the back of the bus, and order hamburgers from the special "women's line" at fast food joints—had somehow become the most mentioned of all. The constant exposure to covered flesh—whether it was covered hideously, artfully, or plainly—brought to mind, well, flesh.

The relaxing of the dress code encouraged this tendency, by breathing sexuality back into public space. Women walked down the street with their elbows, necks, and feet exposed, their figures outlined in form-fitting tunics. After two decades in exile, skin was finally back. And so imaginations flared, everyone eagerly thought about and talked about sex a lot, as though they were afraid if they didn't exploit the new permissiveness in dress and mood, they might wake up to find it had disappeared. ❞

(Moaveni 2005a:69–70, 71)

Azadeh Moaveni, the author of *Lipstick Jihad*, was born in California after her parents, both Iranian, fled the political turbulence of the Iranian revolution. In 1979, Islamic religious leaders overthrew the U.S.-backed monarchy that had ruled the country for decades. Almost overnight, the country was transformed from a relatively secular, Western-oriented society into a conservative Muslim state. Women who had been accustomed to

dressing much as American women did were suddenly expected to cover themselves in dark robes. Young women, who had been required to attend school and serve in the armed forces under the old regime, were now forbidden even to appear in public without a male escort.

Though Moaveni grew up in the United States, she was conversant with her Persian cultural heritage, albeit from a distance. After graduating from college, she lived in Iran for two years, where she covered the country's affairs as a news correspondent. There she found a different society from the one her parents had fled a generation before. The lipstick jihad she refers to in the title of her book is an allusion to the recent relaxation of the strict standards for women's dress and behavior—a change that Iranian women effected by personally defying government sanctions. (*Jihad* is the Arabic term for one's inner struggle against the forces of ungodliness [Moaveni 2005b].)

In her role as the *Guardian*'s contributor on the Middle East, Moaveni (2007, 2009) continues to observe women's lives inside the Islamic Republic of Iran. She has noted a new trend in the formerly austere capital—an appetite for high-priced designer-label fashion accessories, particularly among the young. Today, *nouveau riche* Iranians are indulging in Western-style conspicuous consumption—something their parents would never have done. Iranian housewives can be seen driving through the city in BMW SUVs, Burberry scarves showing beneath their full-length black *chadors* (coats).

How do gender roles differ from one culture to another? Are women in the United States still oppressed because of their gender? Have men's and women's positions in society changed? In these modules we will study these and other questions by looking first at how various cultures, including our own, assign women and men to particular social roles. Then we will consider sociological explanations for gender stratification. We will see that around the world, women constitute an oppressed majority of the population. We'll learn that women have developed a collective consciousness of their oppression and the way in which their gender combines with other factors to create social inequality. Finally, we will close with a Social Policy section on the controversy over a woman's right to abortion.

MODULE 34 | Social Construction of Gender

How many airline passengers do you think are startled on hearing a female captain's voice from the cockpit? What do we make of a father who announces that he will be late for work because his son has a routine medical checkup? Consciously or unconsciously, we are likely to assume that flying a commercial plane is a *man's* job and that most parental duties are, in fact, a *woman's*. Gender is such a routine part of our everyday activities that we typically take notice only when someone deviates from conventional behavior and expectations.

Although a few people begin life with an unclear sexual identity, the overwhelming majority begin with a definite sex and quickly receive societal messages about how to behave. In fact, virtually all societies have established social distinctions between females and males that do not inevitably result from biological differences between the sexes (such as women's reproductive capabilities).

In studying gender, sociologists are interested in the gender-role socialization that leads females and males to behave differently. In Module 15, **gender roles** were defined as expectations regarding the proper behavior, attitudes, and activities of males and females. The application of dominant gender roles leads to many forms of differentiation between women and men. Both sexes are capable of learning to cook and sew, yet most Western societies determine that women should perform those tasks. Both men and women are capable of learning to weld and to fly airplanes, but those functions are generally assigned to men.

As we will see throughout these modules, however, social behavior does not mirror the mutual exclusivity suggested by these gender roles. Nor are gender roles independent: in real life, the way men behave influences women's behavior, and the way women behave affects men's behavior. Thus, most people do not display strictly "masculine" or "feminine" qualities all the time. Indeed, such standards can be ambiguous. For instance, though men are supposed to be unemotional, they are allowed to become emotional when their favorite athletic team wins or loses a critical game. Yet our society still focuses on "masculine" and "feminine" qualities as if men and women must be evaluated in those terms. Despite recent inroads by women into male-dominated occupations, our construction of gender continues to define significantly different expectations for females and males.

Gender roles are evident not only in our work and behavior but also in how we react to others. We are constantly "doing gender" without realizing it. If the father mentioned earlier sits in the doctor's office with his son in the middle of a workday, he will probably receive approving glances from the receptionist and from other patients. "Isn't he a wonderful father?" runs through their minds. But if the boy's mother leaves *her* job and sits with the son in the doctor's office, she will not receive such silent applause.

We socially construct our behavior so as to create or exaggerate male/female differences. For example, men and women come in a variety of heights, sizes, and ages. Yet traditional norms regarding marriage and even casual dating tell us that in heterosexual couples, the man should be older, taller, and wiser than the woman. As we will see throughout these modules, such social norms help to reinforce and legitimize patterns of male dominance.

Gender Roles in the United States

Gender-Role Socialization

Male babies get blue blankets; females get pink ones. Boys are expected to play with trucks, blocks, and toy soldiers; girls receive dolls and kitchen goods. Boys must be masculine—active, aggressive, tough, daring, and dominant—but girls must be feminine—soft, emotional, sweet, and submissive. These traditional gender-role patterns have been influential in the socialization of children in the United States.

An important element in traditional views of proper "masculine" and "feminine" behavior is **homophobia,** fear of and

TABLE 34-1 AN EXPERIMENT IN GENDER NORM VIOLATION BY COLLEGE STUDENTS

Norm If by Women	Norm If by Men
Send men flowers	Wear fingernail polish
Spit in public	Do needlepoint in public
Use men's bathroom	Throw Tupperware party
Buy jock strap	Cry in public
Buy/chew tobacco	Have pedicure
Talk knowledgeably about cars	Apply to babysit
Open doors for men	Shave body hair

Source: Nielsen et al. 2000:287.

In an experiment testing gender-role stereotypes, sociology students were asked to behave in ways that might be regarded as violations of gender norms, and to keep notes on how others reacted. This is a sample of their choices of behavior over a seven-year period. Do you agree that these actions test the boundaries of conventional gender behavior?

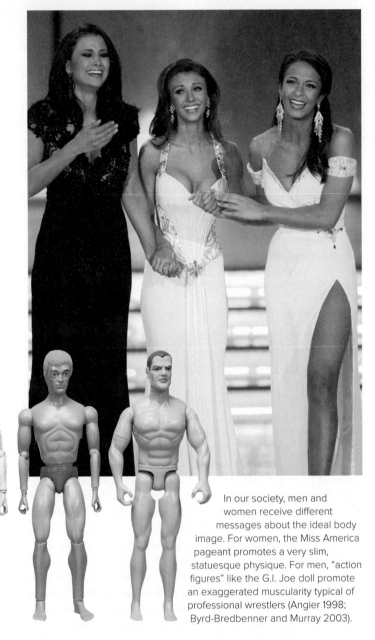

In our society, men and women receive different messages about the ideal body image. For women, the Miss America pageant promotes a very slim, statuesque physique. For men, "action figures" like the G.I. Joe doll promote an exaggerated muscularity typical of professional wrestlers (Angier 1998; Byrd-Bredbenner and Murray 2003).

prejudice against homosexuality. Homophobia contributes significantly to rigid gender-role socialization, since many people stereotypically associate male homosexuality with femininity and lesbianism with masculinity. Consequently, men and women who deviate from traditional expectations about gender roles are often presumed to be gay. Despite the advances made by the gay liberation movement, the continuing stigma attached to homosexuality in our culture places pressure on all males (whether gay or not) to exhibit only narrow masculine behavior and on all females (whether lesbian or not) to exhibit only narrow feminine behavior (Seidman 1994).

It is *adults,* of course, who play a critical role in guiding children into those gender roles deemed appropriate in a society. Parents are normally the first and most crucial agents of socialization. But other adults, older siblings, the mass media, and religious and educational institutions also exert an important influence on gender-role socialization, in the United States and elsewhere.

It is not hard to test how rigid gender-role socialization can be. Just try transgressing some gender norm—say, by smoking a cigar in public if you are female, or by carrying a purse if you are male. That was exactly the assignment given to sociology students at the University of Colorado and Luther College in Iowa. Professors asked students to behave in ways that they thought violated the norms of how a man or woman should act. The students had no trouble coming up with gender-norm transgressions (Table 34-1), and they kept careful notes on others' reactions to their behavior, ranging from amusement to disgust (Nielsen et al. 2000).

Women's Gender Roles

How does a girl come to develop a feminine self-image, while a boy develops one that is masculine? In part, they do so by identifying with females and males in their families and neighborhoods and in the media. If a young girl regularly sees female television characters of all ages and body types, she is likely to grow up with a normal body image. And it will not hurt if the women she knows—her mother, sister, parents' friends, and neighbors—are comfortable with their body types, rather than constantly obsessed with their weight. In contrast, if this young girl sees only wafer-thin actresses and models on television, her self-image will be quite different. Even if she grows up to become a well-educated professional, she may secretly regret falling short of the media stereotype—a thin, sexy young woman in a bathing suit.

Television is far from alone in stereotyping women. Studies of children's books published in the United States in the 1940s,

1950s, and 1960s found that females were significantly underrepresented in central roles and illustrations. Virtually all female characters were portrayed as helpless, passive, incompetent, and in need of a strong male caretaker. Studies of picture books published from the 1970s through the present have found some improvement, but males still dominate the central roles. While males are portrayed as a variety of characters, females tend to be shown mostly in traditional roles, such as mother, grandmother, or volunteer, even if they also hold nontraditional roles, such as working professional (Etaugh 2003).

Traditional gender roles have restricted females more severely than males. These modules show how women have been confined to subordinate roles in the political and economic institutions of the United States. Yet it is also true that gender roles have restricted males.

Men's Gender Roles

Stay-at-home fathers? Until recent decades such an idea was unthinkable. Yet in a 2012 nationwide survey, 22 percent of men said they preferred to stay at home and take care of the house and family. That lifestyle preference is much more common among women, however; 44 percent of women said they preferred to stay at home. But while people's conceptions of gender roles are obviously changing, the fact is that men who stay home to care for their children are still an unusual phenomenon. For every stay-at-home dad there are 38 stay-at-home moms (Fields 2004:11–12; Saad 2012).

While attitudes toward parenting may be changing, studies show little change in the traditional male gender role. Men's roles are socially constructed in much the same way as women's are. Family, peers, and the media all influence how a boy or man comes to view his appropriate role in society. The male gender role, besides being antifeminine (no "sissy stuff"), includes proving one's masculinity at work and sports—often by using force in dealing with others—as well as initiating and controlling all sexual relations (Coontz 2012).

Males who do not conform to the socially constructed gender role face constant criticism and even humiliation, both from children when they are boys and from adults as men. It can be agonizing to be treated as a "chicken" or a "sissy" as a youth—particularly if such remarks come from one's father or brothers. And grown men who pursue nontraditional occupations, such as preschool teaching or nursing, must constantly deal with others' misgivings and strange looks. In one study, interviewers found that such men frequently had to alter their behavior in order to minimize others' negative reactions. One 35-year-old nurse reported that he had to claim he was "a carpenter or something like that" when he "went clubbing," because women weren't interested in getting to know a male nurse. The subjects made similar accommodations in casual exchanges with other men (Cross and Bagilhole 2002:215).

At the same time, boys who successfully adapt to cultural standards of masculinity may grow up to be inexpressive men who cannot share their feelings with others. They remain forceful and tough, but as a result they are also closed and isolated. In fact, a small but growing body of scholarship suggests that for men as well as women, traditional gender roles may be disadvantageous. In many communities across the nation, girls seem to outdo boys in high school, grabbing a disproportionate share of the leadership positions, from valedictorian to class president to yearbook editor—everything, in short, except captain of the boys' athletic teams. Their advantage continues after high school. In the 1980s, girls in the United States became more likely than boys to go to college. Since then, women have consistently accounted for 54 to 55 percent of first-year students at community colleges and four-year colleges. This trend is projected to continue through at least 2021 (Hussar and Bailey 2013:Table 30).

Aside from these disadvantages, many men find that traditional masculinity does not serve them well in the job market. The growth of a service economy over the past two generations has created a demand for skills, attitudes, and behaviors that are the antithesis of traditional masculinity. Increasingly, this sector is the place where low-skilled men must look for jobs. As a British study showed, many out-of-work men are reluctant to engage in the kind of sensitive, deferential behavior required by service sector jobs (Nixon 2009).

In the past 40 years, inspired in good part by the contemporary feminist movement (examined in Module 35), increasing numbers of men in the United States have criticized the restrictive aspects of the traditional male gender role. Some men have taken strong public positions in support of women's struggle for full equality and have even organized voluntary

Gender roles serve to discourage men from entering certain low-paying female-dominated occupations, such as child care. Only 5 percent of day care workers are male.

Sociology in the Global Community

BOX 34-1

Women in Combat Worldwide

In 2012 an estimated 250,000 women, or about 16 percent of the nation's armed forces, served in the U.S. military. Yet these women had never been allowed to fight alongside men—at least, not officially.

For some time now, women in uniform have been serving—and dying—in supportive roles on the warfront. In 2004 Tammy Duckworth, an Army reservist, was serving as a co-pilot in Iraq when a rocket-propelled grenade took down her Black Hawk helicopter. Duckworth, who was severely injured in the attack, received the Purple Heart. She now serves as a U.S. congresswoman from Illinois.

Although the Army does recognize women for their distinguished service—Duckworth was promoted to major soon after the attack—historically, the official prohibition against women serving in combat has prevented them from receiving full credit for their service. In the U.S. Army, the most desirable jobs and career paths require combat experience. Because women officially could not serve in combat positions until 2013, they have been shut out of many types of duty that might interest them. Little wonder that today, the top brass at the Pentagon is almost exclusively male.

Conflict theorists call this obstacle to women's advancement in the Army (their official exclusion from combat) the **brass ceiling.** They note that for women, second-class service in dangerous jobs is nothing new. Historically, both women and racial minorities have often served under hazardous conditions without full recognition.

In 2013, recognizing the injustice of the situation, the Army finally lifted the ban on women serving directly in ground combat. From a sociological point of view, the decision can be related to past directives regarding other minority groups. Functionalists would note that historically, African Americans, Asian Americans, and gays and lesbians were excluded from combat based in part on the fear that their presence would prove dysfunctional. That is, prejudice against those groups would cause conflict in military units, which would undermine their effectiveness on the battlefield. When experience with those minority groups proved that such fears were unfounded, the Army dropped its exclusionary policies. Among women, opposition to full service can also be related to the fixed gender roles women and men have traditionally played, which reflect stereotypical images of masculinity and femininity.

Interactionists find that women feel empowered by the experience of combat.

Despite their full-fledged service, however, these women are often pushed into roles based on traditional gender expectations. In Israel, sociologist Orlee Hauser (2011) interviewed female soldiers aged 18 to 31. She found that like women in the civilian workforce, many female soldiers became the targets of sexual harassment. In active war zones, these women were more likely than men to be assigned educational or training duties, or to perform what was essentially social work. Off the battlefield, women reported being asked to choose a new carpet or bake a cake.

In a national opinion poll taken immediately after the Army's announcement that women would be allowed in combat, an overwhelming 75 percent of U.S. voters supported the decision. There was little difference between men and women on the subject. On the question of whether the change would increase the military's effectiveness, however, the poll showed a sizable gender difference. Among women, 46 percent thought that it would enhance the military's effectiveness; only 36 percent of men held that opinion. All in all, women were less likely than men to see the decision as a concern for the armed forces.

In 2004 Army reservist Tammy Duckworth, now a member of Congress, was co-piloting a Black Hawk helicopter in Iraq when a rocket-propelled grenade hit the aircraft and severely wounded her; she lost both legs. At the time, although women in uniform often served in dangerous roles, they were officially banned from combat operations.

> Historically, both women and racial minorities have often served under hazardous conditions without official recognition.

Nevertheless, the argument over who gets to participate in the military, or indeed any organization, is directly related to its effectiveness. In response to such concerns, the Army is expected to review the training requirements for all recruits, male and female. Some physical standards may be rethought, and lowered if they are found to be unnecessarily high. Psychological and intellectual standards may be strengthened.

The United States is hardly a trailblazer in deciding to allow women in combat. Women have served in combat positions not just in Israel, but also in many other countries. Soviet women did so in World War II, although they are not allowed in combat today in Russia. Israel has assigned women to combat regularly since the late 1990s. Australia,

Canada, China, Denmark, France, Germany, the Netherlands, and North Korea have also opened up combat to women. Although it would be incorrect to assume that the transition has been smooth—indeed, in Canada and Israel, it happened under court order—the new gender-integrated combat units are proving to be capable and effective on the battlefield.

As in other countries that have opened up combat to women, the new policy in the United States will go through a long period of implementation. At the time of the announcement, Pentagon officials stressed that the standards for combat positions would be "gender-neutral." Strength tests, such as the ability to repeatedly load 55-pound tank shells, might limit women's access to certain positions. Similarly, women would face the same qualifications as men for admission to elite units like the Navy SEALs or the Army Rangers and Green Berets.

LET'S DISCUSS

1. Have you or a woman you know experienced combat? If so, describe the challenges and opportunities women faced on or near the battlefield. Do you agree that women should be allowed to serve in combat without restrictions? Explain your reasoning.

2. What do you think will be the military effect of women's presence in combat roles? Will the Army be stronger or weaker as a result of the new policy? Justify your position.

Sources: Bowman 2013; Domi 2013; Hauser 2011; Llana and Eulich 2013; Mulrine 2012; Myre 2013; Quinnipiac University 2013.

associations for the purpose. However, their actions have been countered by other men who feel they are unfairly penalized by laws related to alimony, child support and custody, family violence, and affirmative action (Kimmel 2008; National Organization for Men Against Sexism 2012).

Research on gender roles has shown that in fact there is no single, simple characterization of the male gender role. Australian sociologist R. W. Connell (1987, 2002, 2005) has spoken of **multiple masculinities,** meaning that men play a variety of gender roles, including a nurturing-caring role and an effeminate-gay role, in addition to their traditional gender role of dominating women. Nevertheless, society reinforces their traditional, dominating role more than any other role (McCormack 2010).

Few aspects of contemporary life dramatize contemporary gender roles more than modern warfare. Box 34-1 looks at women's roles in today's military.

Gender and Human Sexuality

How do gender roles affect a person's sexuality? Separating sex from gender is of course impossible. Yet it would be incorrect simply to equate males with stereotypically masculine expressions of sexuality, or females with stereotypically feminine expressions of sexuality.

Over time, social norms regarding sexual behavior have changed as gender roles have changed, becoming more ambiguous. Today, popularly coined words like *metrosexual* and *bromance* suggest that men should feel comfortable embracing traditionally feminine tastes or developing deep friendships with other men. Similarly, society is beginning to accept not only same-sex couples, but individuals whose gender and identity do not fit a simple either/or pattern, such as bisexuals and transgendered people.

As we saw in Chapter 7, society uses labels such as "good kids" and "delinquents" to condone or sanction certain behaviors by certain groups of people. The same is true of sexual behaviors. In Chapter 13, on the family, we will see how society uses labels to brand specific sexual behaviors as deviant. Traditionally, those labels have derived from gender-role distinctions.

 use your **sociological imagination**

What evidence can you see of women's changing roles over the past few generations?

Cross-Cultural Perspective

To what extent do actual biological differences between the sexes contribute to the cultural differences associated with gender? This question brings us back to the debate over "nature versus nurture." In assessing the alleged and real differences between men and women, it is useful to examine cross-cultural data.

Around the world, anthropologists have documented highly diverse constructions of gender that do not always conform to our ideals of masculinity and femininity. Beginning with the path-breaking work of Margaret Mead ([1935] 2001) and continuing through contemporary fieldwork, these scholars have shown that gender roles can vary greatly from one physical environment, economy, and political system to the next.

In any society, gender stratification requires not only individual socialization into traditional gender roles within the family, but also the promotion and support of those traditional roles by other social institutions, such as religion and education. Moreover, even with all major institutions socializing the young into conventional gender roles, every society has women and men who resist and successfully oppose the stereotypes: strong women who become leaders or professionals, gentle men who care for children, and so forth. It seems clear that differences between the sexes are not dictated by biology. Indeed, the maintenance of traditional gender roles requires constant social controls—and those controls are not always effective.

We can see the social construction of gender roles in process in societies strained by war and social upheaval. U.S. troops were sent to Afghanistan primarily to quell terrorist operations, but also to improve women's rights in a country where social protections and the rule of law have broken down. In this patriarchal society wracked by poverty and war, Afghani women have never been secure; their appearance in public is especially dangerous. Not only is violence against women common in

Being harassed or groped on public transit is a problem for women all over the world. In Tokyo, separate subway cars are reserved for women to protect them from sex offenses.

emphasis on tasks, a focus on more distant goals, and a concern for the external relationship between one's family and other social institutions. According to this theory, women's interest in expressive goals frees men for instrumental tasks, and vice versa. Women become anchored in the family as wives, mothers, and household managers; men become anchored in the occupational world outside the home. Of course, Parsons and Bales offered this framework in the 1950s, when many more women were full-time homemakers than is true today. These theorists did not explicitly endorse traditional gender roles, but they implied that dividing tasks between spouses was functional for the family as a unit.

Given the typical socialization of women and men in the United States, the functionalist view is initially persuasive. However, it would lead us to expect girls and women who have no interest in children to become babysitters and mothers. Similarly, males who love spending time with children might be programmed into careers in the business world. Such differentiation might harm the individual who does not fit into prescribed roles, as well as deprive society of the contributions of many talented people who feel confined by gender stereotyping. Moreover, the functionalist approach does not convincingly explain why men should be assigned categorically to the instrumental role and women to the expressive role.

Afghanistan; it is seldom investigated or prosecuted, even in the most severe cases. Victims of violence risk being charged with adultery if they report the crime to authorities. Thanks to UN intervention on women's behalf, however, Afghanis are beginning to recognize that violence against women is a social problem (Organisation for Economic Co-Operation and Development 2012b).

Sociological Perspectives on Gender

Cross-cultural studies indicate that societies dominated by men are much more common than those in which women play the decisive role. Sociologists have turned to all the major theoretical perspectives to understand how and why these social distinctions are established. Each approach focuses on culture rather than biology as the primary determinant of gender differences. Yet in other respects, advocates of these sociological perspectives disagree widely.

Functionalist Perspective

Functionalists maintain that gender differentiation has contributed to overall social stability. Sociologists Talcott Parsons and Robert Bales (1955) argued that to function most effectively, the family requires adults who specialize in particular roles. They viewed the traditional gender roles as arising out of the need to establish a division of labor between marital partners.

Parsons and Bales contended that women take the expressive, emotionally supportive role and men the instrumental, practical role, with the two complementing each other. **Expressiveness** denotes concern for the maintenance of harmony and the internal emotional affairs of the family. **Instrumentality** refers to an

Conflict Perspective

Viewed from a conflict perspective, the functionalist approach masks the underlying power relations between men and women. Parsons and Bales never explicitly presented the

Conflict theorists emphasize that men's work is uniformly valued, whereas women's work (whether unpaid labor in the home or wage labor) is devalued. This woman is removing pencils from a conveyor belt at General Pencil Co.'s factory in Jersey City, New Jersey.

expressive and instrumental roles as being of unequal value to society, yet their inequality is quite evident. Although social institutions may pay lip service to women's expressive skills, men's instrumental skills are more highly rewarded, whether in terms of money or prestige. Consequently, according to feminists and conflict theorists, any division of labor by gender into instrumental and expressive tasks is far from neutral in its impact on women.

Conflict theorists contend that the relationship between females and males has traditionally been one of unequal power, with men in a dominant position over women. Men may originally have become powerful in preindustrial times because their size, physical strength, and freedom from childbearing duties allowed them to dominate women physically. In contemporary societies, such considerations are not so important, yet cultural beliefs about the sexes are long established, as anthropologist Margaret Mead and feminist sociologist Helen Mayer Hacker (1951, 1974) both stressed. Such beliefs support a social structure that places males in controlling positions.

Conflict theorists, then, see gender differences as a reflection of the subjugation of one group (women) by another group (men). If we use an analogy to Marx's analysis of class conflict, we can say that males are like the bourgeoisie, or capitalists; they control most of the society's wealth, prestige, and power. Females are like the proletariat, or workers; they can acquire valuable resources only by following the dictates of their bosses. Men's work is uniformly valued; women's work (whether unpaid labor in the home or wage labor) is devalued.

Feminist Perspective

A significant component of the conflict approach to gender stratification draws on feminist theory. Although use of the term *feminist theory* is comparatively recent, the critique of women's position in society and culture goes back to some of the earliest works that have influenced sociology. Among the most important are Mary Wollstonecraft's *A Vindication of the Rights of Women* (originally published in 1792), John Stuart Mill's *The Subjection of Women* (originally published in 1869), and Friedrich Engels's *The Origin of the Family, Private Property, and the State* (originally published in 1884).

Engels, a close associate of Karl Marx, argued that women's subjugation coincided with the rise of private property during industrialization. Only when people moved beyond an agrarian economy could males enjoy the luxury of leisure and withhold rewards and privileges from women. Drawing on the work of Marx and Engels, many contemporary feminist theorists view women's subordination as part of the overall exploitation and injustice that they see as inherent in capitalist societies. Some radical feminist theorists, however, view the oppression of women as inevitable in *all* male-dominated societies, whether they are labeled capitalist, socialist, or communist (Feuer 1989; Tuchman 1992; Tucker 1978:734–759).

Feminist sociologists would find little to disagree with in the conflict

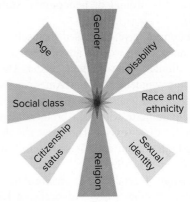

FIGURE 34-1 **Matrix of Domination**

Source: Developed by author.

The matrix of domination illustrates how several social factors, including gender, social class, and race and ethnicity, can converge to create a cumulative impact on a person's social standing.

theorists' perspective, but are more likely to embrace a political agenda. Rather than be caught up in discussing progress toward gender equality over the last generation, they would draw attention to the need for greater progress. Feminists would also argue that until the 1970s, the very discussion of women and society, however well meant, was distorted by the exclusion of women from academic thought, including sociology. Despite the many accomplishments of Jane Addams and Ida Wells-Barnett, they generally worked outside the discipline, focusing on what we would now call applied sociology and social work. At the time, their efforts, while valued as humanitarian, were seen as unrelated to the research and conclusions being reached in academic circles, which of course were male academic circles (Andersen 2007; J. Howard 1999; Ridgeway 2011).

Intersections with Race, Class, and Other Social Factors

Contemporary feminists recognize the differential treatment of some women not only because of their gender, but also because of the intersection of their race, ethnicity, and socioeconomic status. Simply put, Whites dominate these poor, non-White women because they are non-White; men dominate them because they are women; and the affluent dominate them because they are poor. The African American feminist theorist Patricia Hill Collins (2000) has termed the convergence of social forces that contributes to the subordinate status of these low-status women the **matrix of domination** (Figure 34-1).

Gender, race, and social class are not the only sources of oppression in the United States, though they profoundly affect women and people of color. Other forms of categorization and stigmatization that might be included in the matrix are sexual orientation, religion, disability, and age. If we apply the matrix to the world as a whole, we might add citizenship status or perceived colonial or neocolonial status to the list (Winant 2006).

Though feminists have addressed themselves to the needs of minority women, these women are oppressed much more by their race and ethnicity than by their gender. The question for Latinas (Hispanic women), African American women, Asian American women, and Native American women appears to be whether they should unite with their brothers against racism or challenge them for their sexism. The answer is that our society must eradicate both sexism and racism (Beisel and Kay 2004; Breines 2007; C. Epstein 1999).

The discussion of gender roles among African Americans has always provoked controversy. Advocates of Black nationalism contend that feminism only distracts women from participating fully in the African American struggle. The existence of feminist groups among Blacks, in their view, simply divides the Black community, thereby serving the dominant White majority. In contrast, Black feminists such as bell hooks (1994) argue that little is to be gained by accepting the gender-role divisions of the dominant society, which place women in a separate, subservient position. Though the media commonly portray Black women in a negative light—as illiterates, welfare queens, or prostitutes—Black feminists emphasize that it is not solely Whites and the White-dominated media who focus on such negative images. Black men (most recently, Black male rap artists) have also portrayed Black women in a negative way (Threadcraft 2008; Wilkins 2012).

Historically, Native Americans stand out as an exception to the patriarchal tradition in North America. At the time of the European settlers' arrival, Native American gender roles varied greatly from tribe to tribe. Southern tribes, for reasons unclear to today's scholars, were usually matriarchal and traced their descent through the mother. European missionaries, who sought to make the native peoples more like Europeans, set out to transform this arrangement, which was not entirely universal. Like members of other groups, some Native American women have resisted gender stereotypes (Marubbio 2006).

Latinas are usually considered as part of either the Hispanic or feminist movements, and their distinctive experience ignored. In the past, they have been excluded from decision making in the two social institutions that most affect their daily lives: the family and the church. Particularly in the lower class, the Hispanic family suffers from the pervasive tradition of male domination. And the Catholic Church relegates women to supportive roles, while reserving the leadership positions for men (Browne 2001; De Anda 2004).

Prior to this chapter, much of our discussion has focused on the social effects of race and ethnicity, coupled with poverty, low incomes, and meager wealth. The matrix of domination highlights the confluence of these factors with gender discrimination, which we must include to fully understand the plight of women of color.

 use your **sociological imagination**

Which elements of the matrix of domination privilege you? Which place you at a disadvantage?

Interactionist Perspective

While functionalists and conflict theorists who study gender stratification typically focus on macro-level social forces and institutions, interactionist researchers tend to examine gender stratification on the micro level of everyday behavior. The key to this approach is the way gender is socially constructed in everyday interactions. We "do gender" by reinforcing traditionally masculine and feminine actions. For example, a man "does masculinity" by opening a door for his girlfriend; she "does femininity" by consenting to his assistance. Obviously, the social construction of gender goes beyond these relatively trivial rituals. Interactionists recognize, too, that people can challenge traditional gender roles. A female golfer who uses the men's tees and a man who actively arranges a birthday luncheon at work are redoing gender (Deutsch 2007; West and Zimmerman 1987).

One continuing subject of investigation is the role of gender in cross-sex conversations (sometimes referred to as "crosstalk"), specifically the idea that men interrupt women more than women interrupt men. Interestingly, empirical research does not clearly support this assertion. True, people in positions of authority or status—who are much more likely to be male than female—dominate interpersonal conversations. That does not necessarily mean that women per se cannot be heard, however. Future research results may deemphasize the clichéd advice that women must speak up and focus instead on the situational structures that cast men in dominant positions (Cameron 2007; Hyde 2005; Tannen 1990).

Table 34-2 summarizes the major sociological perspectives on gender.

Tracking Sociological Perspectives

TABLE **34-2** SOCIOLOGICAL PERSPECTIVES ON GENDER

Theoretical Perspective	Emphasis
Functionalist	Gender differentiation contributes to social stability
Conflict	Gender inequality is rooted in the female–male power relationship
Feminist	Women's subjugation is integral to society and social structure
Interactionist	Gender distinctions and "doing gender" are reflected in people's everyday behavior

MODULE 34 | Recap and Review

Summary

Gender is an ascribed status that provides a basis for social differentiation. This module examines the social construction of gender and theories of stratification by gender.

1. In the United States, the social construction of gender continues to define significantly different expectations for females and males.

2. **Gender roles** show up in our work and behavior and in how we react to others. Throughout history, these roles have constricted women much more than they have men.

3. Though men may exhibit a variety of different gender roles, or **multiple masculinities,** society reinforces their traditional role of dominating women.

4. Anthropological research points to the importance of cultural conditioning in defining the social roles of males and females.

5. Functionalists maintain that sex differentiation contributes to overall social stability, but conflict theorists charge that the relationship between females and males is one of unequal power, with men dominating women. This dominance shows up in people's everyday interactions.

6. Many women experience differential treatment, not only because of their gender but because of their race, ethnicity, and social class. This convergence of social forces is called the **matrix of domination.**

7. As an example of their micro-level approach to the study of gender stratification, interactionists have analyzed men's verbal dominance over women through conversational interruption.

Thinking Critically

1. Compare the social construction of gender with the social construction of race.

2. Which aspects of the functionalist and conflict perspectives on gender make the most sense to you? Explain.

Key Terms

Brass ceiling

Expressiveness

Gender role

Homophobia

Instrumentality

Matrix of domination

Multiple masculinities

MODULE 35 | Women: The Oppressed Majority

Many people, both male and female, find it difficult to conceive of women as a subordinate and oppressed group. Yet take a look at the political structure of the United States: women remain noticeably underrepresented. Following the 2012 elections, for example, only 5 of the nation's 50 states had a female governor (Arizona, New Hampshire, New Mexico, Oklahoma, and South Carolina).

Women have made slow but steady progress in certain political arenas. In 1981, out of 535 members of Congress, there were only 21 women: 19 in the House of Representatives and 2 in the Senate. In contrast, the Congress that held office following the 2012 elections had 98 women: 78 in the House and 20 in the Senate. Yet the membership and leadership of Congress remain overwhelmingly male.

In October 1981, Sandra Day O'Connor was sworn in as the nation's first female Supreme Court justice. Still, no woman has ever served as president of the United States, vice president, or chief justice of the Supreme Court.

● Sexism and Sex Discrimination

Just as African Americans are victimized by racism, women in our society are victimized by sexism. **Sexism** is the ideology that one sex is superior to the other. The term is generally used to refer to male prejudice and discrimination against women. In Chapter 10, we noted that Blacks can suffer from both individual acts of racism and institutional discrimination. **Institutional discrimination** was defined as the denial of opportunities and equal rights to individuals and groups that results from the normal operations of a society. In the same sense, women suffer from both individual acts of sexism (such as sexist remarks and acts of violence) and institutional sexism.

It is not simply that particular men in the United States are biased in their treatment of women. All the major institutions of our society—including the government, armed forces, large corporations, the media, universities, and the medical establishment—are controlled by men. These institutions, in their normal, day-to-day operations, often discriminate against women and perpetuate sexism. For example, if the central office of a nationwide bank sets a policy that single women are a bad risk for loans—regardless of their incomes and investments—that bank will discriminate against women in state after state. It will do

The Head Scarf and the Veil: Complex Symbols

The wearing of a veil or head scarf by women is common to many but not all Middle Eastern societies. All Muslims, men and women alike, are expected to cover themselves and avoid revealing clothes designed to accentuate the body's contours or emphasize its physical beauty. The Koran does permit Muslims to wear revealing garments in private, with their families or with members of the same sex.

The Prophet Muhammad recommended that women cover all of their bodies except for the face, hands, and feet. The Koran adds that a woman's headcovering should fall over the neck and upper chest. A variety of women's outergarments comply with these guidelines for modest attire; collectively, they are referred to as the *hijab*. Face veils are dictated by cultural tradition, however—not by Islam.

In effect, the veil represents a rejection of the beauty myth (see Chapter 7), which is so prevalent in Western societies. By covering themselves almost completely, Muslim women assure themselves and their families that their physical appearance will not play a role in their contacts outside the family. Rather, these women will be known only for their faith, their intellect, and their personalities.

The veil was politicized by modernization movements that pitted Western cultural values against traditional Islamic values. In Turkey, for instance, in the early 20th century, government officials attempted to subordinate traditional ethnic and religious influences to their nationalistic goals. Though women weren't forbidden to wear the veil, they were not allowed to veil themselves in public places like schools. Many Muslims resented these forced social changes.

In the United States today, Muslim women select from an array of traditional garments, including a long, loose tailored coat and a loose black overgarment that is worn with a scarf or perhaps a face veil. However, they are just as apt to wear an overblouse and a long skirt or loose pants, which they can buy at local clothing stores.

In some non-Muslim countries, notably France, officials have come under fire for

> In effect, the veil represents a rejection of the beauty myth, which is so prevalent in Western societies.

banning the hijab, or the head scarf, in public schools, as well as a full-body, face-covering robe anywhere in public. The custom of covering generally has not been an issue in the United States, though one 11-year-old had to go to federal court to establish her right to wear a head scarf at school in Muskogee, Oklahoma. Interestingly, the U.S. Department of Justice supported her lawsuit.

The head scarf—an expression of modesty, a woman's right as an individual, or a sign of oppression?

LET'S DISCUSS

1. Consider life in a society in which women wear veils. Can you see any advantages, from the woman's point of view? From the man's?

2. Do you find the Western emphasis on physical beauty oppressive? If so, in what ways?

Sources: Charrad 2011; Chrisafis 2013; Gurbuz and Gurbuz-Kucuksari 2009; Killian 2003; Selod 2008b.

---

so even at branches where loan officers hold no personal biases toward women, but are merely "following orders."

Our society is run by male-dominated institutions, yet with the power that flows to men come responsibility and stress. Men have higher reported rates of certain types of mental illness than women, and a greater likelihood of death due to heart attack or stroke. The pressure on men to succeed, and then to remain on top in the competitive world of work, can be especially intense. That is not to suggest that gender stratification is as damaging to men as it is to women. But it is clear that the power and privilege men enjoy are no guarantee of personal well-being.

 use your **sociological imagination**

Think of organizations or institutions you belong to whose leadership positions are customarily held by men. What would those organizations be like if they were led by women?

The Status of Women Worldwide

According to a detailed overview of the status of the world's women, issued by the World Bank in 2012, the lives of girls and women have changed dramatically over the past quarter century. Progress has been limited in some respects, however. In many parts of the world, women still lag far behind men in their earnings and in their ability to speak out politically (World Bank 2012b).

This critique applies to Western as well as non-Western countries. Although Westerners tend to view some societies—for example, Muslim countries—as being particularly harsh toward women, that perception is actually an overgeneralization. Muslim countries are exceedingly varied and complex and do not often fit the stereotypes created by the Western media. For a detailed discussion of the status of Muslim women today, see Box 35-1.

Regardless of culture, however, women everywhere suffer from second-class status. It is estimated that women grow half the world's food, but they rarely own land. They constitute one-third of the world's paid labor force, but are generally found in the lowest-paying jobs. Single-parent households headed by women, which appear to be on the rise in many nations, are typically found in the poorest sections of the population. The feminization of poverty has become a global phenomenon. As in the United States, women around the world are underrepresented politically.

Despite these challenges, women are not responding passively. They are mobilizing, individually and collectively. Given the significant underrepresentation of women in government offices and national legislatures, however, the task is difficult.

Not surprisingly, there is a link between the wealth of industrialized nations and the poverty of women in developing countries. Viewed from a conflict perspective or through the lens of Immanuel Wallerstein's world systems analysis, the economies of developing nations are controlled and exploited by industrialized countries and multinational corporations based in those countries. Much of the exploited labor in developing nations, especially in the nonindustrial sector, is performed by women. Women workers typically toil long hours for low pay, but contribute significantly to their families' incomes (Chubb et al. 2008).

In industrialized countries, women's unequal status can be seen in the division of housework, as well as in the jobs they hold and the pay they earn. Sociologist Jan Paul Heisig analyzed gender inequality among the rich (the top decile in income) and the poor (the bottom decile) in 33 industrialized countries. Typically, poor men did more housework than rich men, but as Figure 35-1 shows, rich or poor, men did much less housework than women. The recent economic recession accentuated this unequal division of housework. Obviously, being unemployed leaves both men and women with more time for household chores. However, unemployed women do double the amount of extra housework as unemployed men (Gough and Killewald 2011).

● Women in the Workforce of the United States

Nearly 40 years ago, the U.S. Commission on Civil Rights (1976:1) concluded that the passage in the Declaration of Independence proclaiming that "all men are created equal" has been taken too literally for too long—especially with respect to women's opportunities for employment. In this section we will see how gender bias has limited women's opportunities for employment outside the home, at the same time that it forces them to carry a disproportionate burden inside the home.

FIGURE 35-1 Gender Inequality in Housework

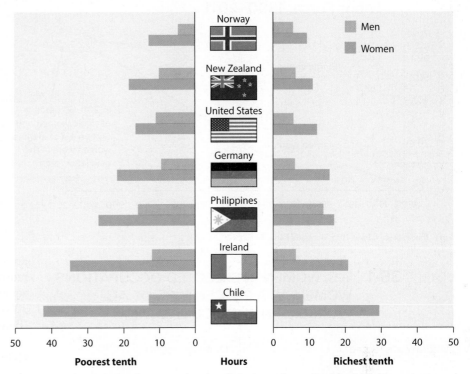

Note: Housework includes laundry, grocery shopping, dinner preparation, and care for sick family members.
Source: Adapted from Heisig 2011:84.

Around the world, rich or poor, women do much more housework than men.

Labor Force Participation

Women's participation in the paid labor force of the United States increased steadily throughout the 20th century and into the 21st century (Figure 35-2). Today, millions of women—married or single, with or without children, pregnant or recently having given birth—are in the labor force.

Overall, 58 percent of adult women in the United States were in the labor force in 2011, compared to 41 percent in 1970. For men, the data were 71 percent in 2011, compared to 76 percent in 1970 (Bureau of Labor Statistics 2013a:Table 4).

Still, women entering the job market find their options restricted in important ways. Women are *underrepresented* in occupations historically defined as "men's jobs," which often carry much greater financial rewards and prestige than women's jobs. For example, in 2011, women accounted for approximately 47 percent of the paid labor force of the United States, yet they constituted only 14 percent of civil engineers, 31 percent of computer systems analysts, and 34 percent of physicians (Table 35-1).

Such occupational segregation is not unique to the United States but typical of industrial countries. In Great Britain, for example, only 6 percent of engineers are women, while 71 percent of cashiers and 88 percent of nurses are women (Office for National Statistics 2013).

Women from all groups and men from minority groups sometimes encounter attitudinal or organizational bias that prevents them from reaching their full potential. As we saw in Module 31, the term **glass ceiling** refers to an invisible barrier that blocks the promotion of a qualified individual in a work environment because

FIGURE 35-2 Trends in U.S. Women'S Participation in the Paid Labor Force, 1890–2011

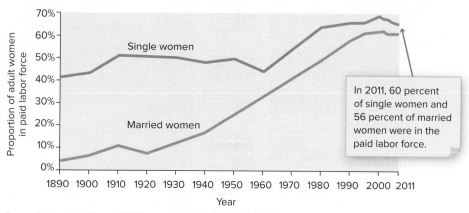

In 2011, 60 percent of single women and 56 percent of married women were in the paid labor force.

Source: Bureau of the Census 1975; Bureau of Labor Statistics 2013a:Table 4.

TABLE 35-1 U.S. WOMEN IN SELECTED OCCUPATIONS: WOMEN AS A PERCENTAGE OF ALL WORKERS IN THE OCCUPATION

Underrepresented		Overrepresented	
Firefighters	3%	High school teachers	57%
Aircraft pilots and engineers	4	Cashiers	72
Police officers	13	Social workers	81
Civil engineers	14	Elementary teachers	81
Clergy	21	File clerks	81
Chefs and head cooks	22	Librarians	87
Dentists	24	Tellers	87
Computer systems analysts	31	Word processors and typists	89
Lawyers	31	Registered nurses	91
Physicians	34	Receptionists	92
Athletes, coaches, and umpires	37	Child care workers	95
Postal mail carriers	38	Dental hygienists	99

Note: Women constitute 47 percent of the entire labor force.
Source: Data for 2012 reported in Bureau of Labor Statistics 2013b: Table 11.

of the individual's gender, race, or ethnicity. Furthermore, women and minority men confront not only a glass ceiling that limits their upward mobility, but glass walls that reduce their ability to move horizontally into fast-track jobs that lead directly up to the highest rungs on the corporate ladder. A study of the *Fortune* 500 largest corporations in the United States showed that in 2013, barely 16 percent of the seats on their boards of directors were held by women (Alliance for Board Diversity 2013).

When women do gain entry to corporate boards of directors, the response in the financial world is not entirely positive. Despite objective tests that show strong financial performance under gender-diverse leadership, some investors tend to balk. Research by Frank Dobbin and Jiwook Jung (2010) shows that small investors often sell their shares when women become corporate leaders, apparently falling for the stereotype that associates males with success. This sell pattern is not characteristic of larger investors, who have long argued that gender-diverse leadership is good for business.

This type of inequality is not unique to the United States. Worldwide, women hold less than 1 percent of corporate managerial positions. In recognition of the underrepresentation of women on boards of directors, the Norwegian legislature established minimum quotas for the number of female board members. As the architects of the plan put it, "instead of assuming what people *can't* do at work, provide opportunities for employees to prove what they can do." The goal was not complete equity for women, but 40 percent representation by 2008. By 2012 the percentage stood at 18 percent (European PWN 2012).

Compensation

He works. She works. Both are physicians—a high-status occupation with considerable financial rewards. He makes $140,000. She makes $88,000.

These median annual earnings for physicians in the United States were released by the Census Bureau. They are typical of the results of the bureau's detailed study of occupations and income. Take air traffic controllers. He makes $67,000; she makes $56,000. Or housekeepers: he makes $19,000; she makes $15,000. What about teachers' assistants? He makes $20,000; she makes $15,000. Statisticians at the bureau looked at the median annual earnings for no fewer than 821 occupations ranging from dishwasher to chief executive. After adjusting for workers' ages, education, and work experience, they came to an unmistakable conclusion: across the board, there is a substantial gender gap in the median earnings of full-time workers.

Men do not always earn more than women for doing the same work. Researchers at the Census Bureau found 2 occupations out of 821 in which women typically earn about 1 percent more income than men: hazardous materials recovery and telecommunications line installation. These two occupations employed less than 1 out of every 1,000 workers the bureau studied. Forecasting analyses show no convincing evidence that the wage gap is narrowing.

What accounts for these yawning wage gaps between men and women in the same occupation? Scholars at the Census Bureau studied the following characteristics of men and women in the same occupation:

- Age and degree of formal education
- Marital status and the presence of children at home

Give Me a Male Boss, Please

As women increased their presence in the managerial ranks from 19.7 percent in 1972 to 51.5 percent in 2012, the desirability of having a male supervisor became a topic of casual conversation. Numerous studies suggest that compared to all the other social factors present in the workplace, the boss's gender has little effect on the nature and quality of the manager–employee relationship. However, that fact does not prevent potential workers—male or female—from preferring a male boss. National opinion polls consistently show that in general—that is, without reference to particular people—workers prefer to take orders from a man by a two-to-one margin. If anything, women are more likely than men to prefer a male supervisor.

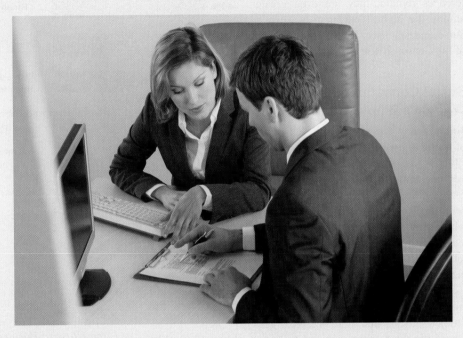

> National opinion polls consistently show that in general, workers prefer to take orders from a man by a two-to-one margin.

This preference is so strong that many people are willing to accept less pay to get a male boss. Researchers at the University of Chicago's business school asked college students who were about to graduate to consider hypothetical job opportunities at consulting firms. The positions varied in terms of their starting salary, location, paid holidays, and the boss's sex. The results showed that students' choices matched their stated preferences for salary, location, and holidays. Surprisingly, the boss's sex turned out to be a far more important variable than the other three, whether students were male or female. In a variety of scenarios describing both salary and the boss's characteristics, students chose to take a 22 percent reduction in starting salary to get a male boss.

LET'S DISCUSS

1. Have you ever worked for a female boss? If so, were you comfortable taking orders from her? Did you notice any differences in the way your boss was treated, compared to men on her level?

2. What might explain the strong preference for a male boss? Do you expect this preference to remain stable or disappear over time? Explain.

Sources: Bureau of Labor Statistics 2013b; Bureau of Labor Statistics 2003; Caruso et al. 2009; Gibbs 2009:31; G. Powell 2010; Whittaker 2006.

- Specialization within the occupation (for example, family practice versus surgical practice)
- Years of work experience
- Hours worked per year

Taking all these factors into consideration reduced the pay gap between men and women by only 3 cents. Women still earned 80 cents for every dollar earned by men. In sum, the disparity in pay between men and women cannot be explained by pointing to women's career choices (Government Accountability Office 2003; Weinberg 2004, 2007).

Legally, sex discrimination in wage payments is difficult to prove. Witness the case of former Goodyear worker Lilly Ledbetter, who learned 19 years after she was hired that she was being paid less than men doing the same job. Ledbetter sued and was awarded damages, only to have the Supreme Court overturn the decision on the grounds that she made her claim more than six months after the first discriminatory paycheck was issued. Congress relaxed this restriction in 2009 (Pear 2009).

Not all the obstacles women face in the workplace originate with management. Unfortunately, many workers, both male and female, would prefer not to work for a woman (Box 35-2).

What happens to men who enter traditionally women's occupations? Research shows that the glass ceiling that women face does not appear to hamper them. Instead, men who enter traditionally female occupations are more likely than women to rise to the top. Male elementary teachers become principals; male nurses become supervisors. The term **glass escalator** refers to this advantage men experience in occupations dominated by women. Whereas women who enter traditionally male occupations may be seen as tokens, men who move out of sex-typical jobs are likely to be advantaged.

This difference between the sexes is associated with a pay differential. A national study released in 2013 found that among full-time, year-round registered nurses, females earn 7 percent less on average than their male counterparts. Even when specializations are considered, pay differences remain; they are even greater among the highest paid nurses, such as nurse anaesthetists (Budig 2002; Bureau of the Census 2013c).

Social Consequences of Women's Employment

Today, many women face the challenge of trying to juggle work and family. Their situation has many social consequences. For one thing, it puts pressure on child care facilities, public financing of day care, and even the fast-food industry, which provides many of the meals women used to prepare themselves. For another, it raises questions about what responsibility male wage earners have in the household.

Who does the housework when women become productive wage earners? Studies indicate that there is a clear gender gap in the performance of housework, although it has been narrowing (see Figure 35-1). Women do more housework and spend more time on child care than men do, whether on a workday or a nonworkday. Taken together, then, a woman's workday on and off the job is much longer than a man's (Sayer et al. 2004).

Sociologist Arlie Hochschild (1990, 2005, 2012) has used the phrase **second shift** to describe the double burden—work outside the home followed by child care and housework—that many women face and few men share equitably. Unfortunately, today's workplace is becoming a 24/7 virtual office thanks to the advent of mobile information technologies. As these devices take over what little personal time employees have left, the physical toll on women becomes even more burdensome.

What is life like for these women? On the basis of interviews with and observations of 52 couples over an eight-year period, Hochschild reports that the wives (and not their husbands) drive home from the office while planning domestic schedules and play dates for children—and then begin their second shift. Drawing on national studies, she concludes that women spend 15 fewer hours each week in leisure activities than their husbands. In a year, these women work an extra month of 24-hour days because of the second shift; over a dozen years, they work an extra year of 24-hour days. Hochschild found that the married couples she studied were fraying at the edges, and so were their careers and their marriages. With such reports in mind, many feminists have advocated greater governmental and corporate support for child care, more flexible family leave policies, and other reforms designed to ease the burden on the nation's families (Eby et al. 2010).

The greater amounts of time women put into caring for their children, and to a lesser degree into housework, take a special toll on women who are pursuing careers. In a survey published in

FIGURE 35-3 Why Leave Work?

Women / Five Top Reasons for Leaving / Men

Reason	Women	Men
Family time	44%	12%
Change in career	16%	29%
Earn a degree, other training	23%	25%
Work not enjoyable, satisfying	17%	24%
Not interested in field	*	18%
Moved away	17%	*

* Not one of top 5 reasons

Note: Based on a representative Harris Interactive survey of "highly qualified" workers, defined as those with a graduate degree, a professional degree, or a high honors undergraduate degree.
Source: Adapted by author, Richard Schaefer, based on data in Hewlett and Luce 2005.

the *Harvard Business Review*, about 40 percent of women indicated that they had voluntarily left work for months or years, compared to only 24 percent of men. As Figure 35-3 shows, women were much more likely than men to take time off for family reasons. Even women in the most prestigious professions have difficulty balancing home and work responsibilities.

● Emergence of a Collective Consciousness

Feminism is an ideology that favors equal rights for women. The feminist movement of the United States was born in upstate New York, in a town called Seneca Falls, in the summer of 1848. On July 19, the first women's rights convention began, attended by Elizabeth Cady Stanton, Lucretia Mott, and other pioneers in the struggle for women's rights. This first wave of *feminists,* as they are currently known, battled ridicule and scorn as they fought for legal and political equality for women. They were not afraid to risk controversy on behalf of their cause; in 1872, Susan B. Anthony was arrested for attempting to vote in that year's presidential election.

Ultimately, the early feminists won many victories, among them the passage and ratification of the Nineteenth Amendment to the Constitution, which granted women the right to vote in national elections beginning in 1920. But suffrage did not lead to other reforms in women's social and economic position, and in the early and middle 20th century the women's movement became a much less powerful force for social change.

The second wave of feminism in the United States emerged in the 1960s and came into full force in the 1970s. In part, the movement was inspired by three pioneering books arguing for women's rights: Simone de Beauvoir's *The Second Sex,* Betty Friedan's *The Feminine Mystique,* and Kate Millett's *Sexual Politics.* In addition, the general political activism of the 1960s led women—many of whom were working for Black civil rights or against the war in Vietnam—to reexamine their own powerlessness. The sexism often found within even allegedly progressive and radical political circles convinced many women that they needed to establish a movement for women's liberation (Stansell 2011).

As more and more women became aware of sexist attitudes and practices, including attitudes they themselves had accepted through socialization into traditional gender roles, they began to challenge male dominance. A sense of sisterhood, much like the class consciousness that Marx hoped would emerge in the proletariat, became evident. Individual women identified their interests with those of the collectivity *women.* No longer were women happy in submissive, subordinate roles ("false consciousness" in Marxist terms).

By the 1980s, however, the movement's influence was beginning to wane. In 1998, in a provocative cover illustration, the editors of *Time* magazine asked "Is Feminism Dead?" Young women, they wrote, seemed to take women's improved status for granted, to see their mothers' struggles for equal rights as irrelevant to their own lives. Fewer women, they noted, were identifying themselves as feminists.

How do today's women perceive the movement? According to a national survey done in 2013, about 23 percent of women (and 12 percent of men) call themselves feminists. There is little reason to believe that younger women are less willing to accept the label than older women. Perhaps more telling is the fact that 32 percent of women and 42 percent of men think the term *feminist* has negative connotations.

Is feminism dead? Many feminists resent that question, because it seems to imply that all their concerns have been resolved. Today's feminists argue that they have moved beyond early criticism that the movement was too obsessed with the concerns of White middle-class women, that it marginalized African American feminists and others. Indeed, current polling shows that African American and Latino women are more likely than others to call themselves feminists. Recognizing the legal and economic victories they have made over the last 40 years, feminists are now working to improve women's lives in nonindustrial countries, where they focus on eliminating malnutrition, starvation, extreme poverty, and violence (Breines 2007; Schnittker et al. 2003; Swanson 2013).

social policy and Gender Stratification|

The Battle over Abortion from a Global Perspective

Few issues seem to stir as much intense conflict as abortion. A critical victory in the struggle for legalized abortion in the United States came in 1973, when the Supreme Court granted women the right to terminate pregnancies. This ruling, known as *Roe v. Wade,* was based on a woman's right to privacy. The Court's decision was generally applauded by pro-choice groups, which believe women should have the right to make their own decisions about their bodies and should have access to safe and legal abortions. It was bitterly condemned by those opposed to abortion. For these pro-life groups, abortion is a moral and often a religious issue. In their view, human life begins at the moment of conception, so that its termination through abortion is essentially an act of murder.

Looking at the Issue

The debate that has followed *Roe v. Wade* revolves around prohibiting abortion altogether, or at the very least, limiting it. In 1979, for example, Missouri required parental consent for minors wishing to obtain an abortion, and the Supreme Court upheld the law. Parental notification and consent have become especially sensitive issues in the debate. Pro-life activists argue that the parents of teenagers should have the right to be notified about—and to permit or prohibit—abortions. In their view, parental authority deserves full support at a time when the traditional nuclear family is embattled. However, pro-choice activists counter that many pregnant teenagers come from troubled families where they have been abused. These young women may have good reason to avoid discussing such explosive issues with their parents.

In the United States, people support a woman's right to a legal abortion, but with reservations. According to a 2012 national survey, 52 percent say that abortion should be legal in any case; 28 percent, legal only under certain circumstances; and 18 percent, illegal in all cases. There is no gender difference in opinion on this issue: women and men hold similar views on the legality of abortion (Saad 2013).

The United States is not alone in debating abortion. Latin American countries typically have the strictest measures against the practice, but occasionally changes occur. In 2007, Mexico loosened decade-old restrictions to permit legal abortions during the first three months of a pregnancy, for any reason (M. Davis 2010).

Applying Sociology

Sociologists see gender and social class as the defining issues surrounding abortion. That is, the intense conflict over abortion reflects broader differences over women's position in

—Continued

society. Feminists involved in defending abortion rights typically believe that men and women are essentially similar. They support women's full participation in work outside the home and oppose all forms of sex discrimination. Feminists also claim that pregnancy and childbirth have been socially constructed by male-centered health care systems and patriarchal religious traditions. In contrast, most antiabortion activists believe that men and women are fundamentally different. In their view, men are best suited to the public world of work, while women are best suited to the demanding and

MAPPING LIFE NATIONWIDE

FIGURE 35-4 **State Abortion-Related Policies, 2000–2014**

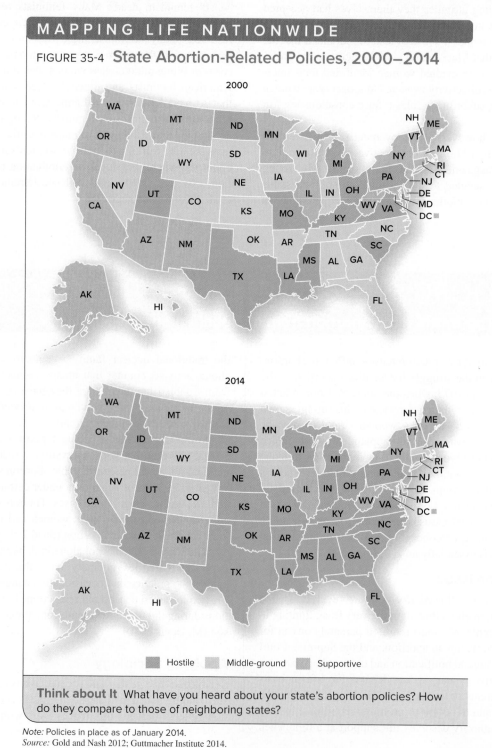

Think about It What have you heard about your state's abortion policies? How do they compare to those of neighboring states?

Note: Policies in place as of January 2014.
Source: Gold and Nash 2012; Guttmacher Institute 2014.

—*Continued*

crucial task of rearing children. These activists are troubled by women's growing participation in work outside the home, which they view as destructive to the family, and ultimately to society (Lorber 2005).

Another obstacle facing the poor is access to abortion providers. In the face of vocal pro-life sentiment, fewer and fewer hospitals throughout the world are allowing physicians to perform abortions, except in extreme cases. Moreover, some doctors who work in clinics, intimidated by death threats and murders, have stopped performing abortions. For poor people in rural areas, this reduction in service makes it more difficult to locate and travel to a facility that will accommodate their wishes. Viewed from a conflict perspective, this is one more financial burden that falls especially heavily on low-income women.

These obstacles are compounded by state and local policies that further hamper the doctors and clinics that provide abortions: building requirements and bans on public funding; restrictions or outright bans on public health insurance, such as Medicaid and Obamacare. Other policies, such as long waiting periods and required ultrasound tests, are meant to discourage women from seeking abortions. These requirements have become more onerous since 2000. By 2014, the 15 states labeled "supportive" in Figure 35-4 had no more than one such requirement on the books; the 27 states labeled "hostile" had adopted most if not all of them. About 56 percent of the country's population lives in those 27 states. People who take a right-to-life position see these states' restrictions as part of an effort "to create and sustain a culture of life" (Guttmacher Institute 2014; Paulson 2013).

Initiating Policy

In 1973 the Supreme Court supported the general right to terminate a pregnancy by a narrow 5–4 majority. Although pro-life activists continue to hope for an overruling of *Roe v. Wade*, they have focused in the interim on weakening the decision through tactics such as limiting the use of fetal tissue in

MAPPING LIFE WORLDWIDE

FIGURE 35-5 **The Global Divide on Abortion**

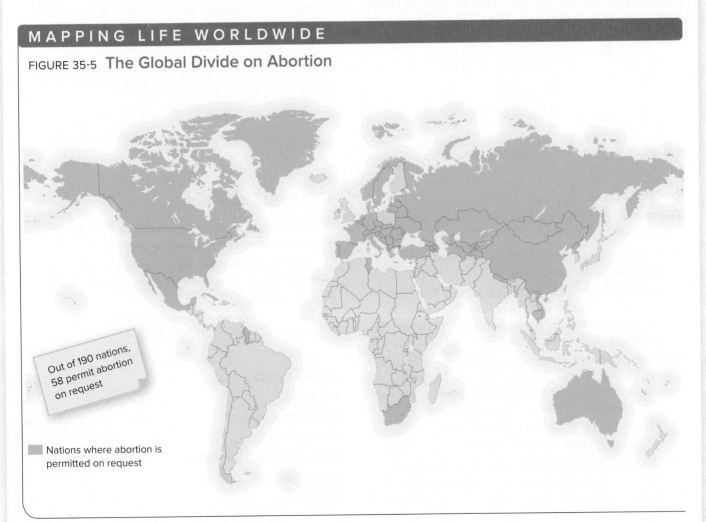

Out of 190 nations, 58 permit abortion on request

Nations where abortion is permitted on request

Note: Data current as of March 2013.
Source: Developed by the author, Richard Schaefer, based on United Nations Population Division 2013.

—*Continued*

medical experiments and prohibiting certain late-term abortions, which they term "partial-birth" abortions. The Supreme Court continues to hear cases involving such restrictions.

What is the policy in other countries? As in the United States, many European nations responded to public opinion and liberalized abortion laws beginning in the 1970s. However, many of those nations limit the procedure to the first 12 weeks of a pregnancy. (The United States, in contrast, allows abortions up to about the 24th week and beyond.) Inspired by the strong antiabortion movement in the United States, antiabortion activists in Europe have become more outspoken, especially in Great Britain, France, Portugal, Spain, Italy, and Germany.

The policies of the United States are intertwined with those of developing nations. From the 1980s through January 2009, members of Congress who opposed abortion successfully blocked foreign aid to countries that might use the funds to encourage abortion. Yet developing nations generally have the most restrictive abortion laws. As Figure 35-5 shows, it is primarily in Africa, Latin America, and

parts of Asia that women are not allowed to terminate a pregnancy on request. As might be expected, illegal abortions are most common in those nations. An estimated quarter of the world's women live in countries where abortion is illegal or is permitted only if a woman's life is in jeopardy. Indeed, the rate of abortions in countries with legal restrictions on the procedure matches the rate in countries that permit it. Hence, 40 percent of abortions worldwide—about 16 million procedures each year—are performed illegally (P. Baker 2009; Guttmacher Institute 2008).

TAKE THE ISSUE WITH YOU

1. How easy do you think it is for a young adult woman to obtain an abortion? What do you think should be the first step she takes in considering one?

2. Do you think teenage girls should be required to get their parents' consent before having an abortion? Why or why not?

3. Under what circumstances should abortions be allowed? Explain your reasoning.

MODULE 35 | Recap and Review

Summary

This module examines the status of women as an oppressed minority in the United States and around the world.

1. Women around the world suffer from **sexism** and **institutional discrimination.**

2. In the United States today, almost as many women as men participate in the paid labor force, but women are underrepresented in managerial positions and underpaid compared to men with the same jobs.

3. As women have taken on more and more hours of paid employment outside the home, they have been only partially successful in getting their husbands to take on more homemaking duties, including child care.

4. Many women agree with the positions of the feminist movement but reject the label *feminist.*

5. The issue of abortion has bitterly divided the United States (as well as other nations), pitting pro-choice activists against pro-life activists.

Thinking Critically

1. What are the challenges to comparing the status of women across different nations?

2. How would you argue that women have come either very far or not far enough in their labor force participation?

3. Today, is feminism more likely to produce social change or respond to social change? Explain.

Key Terms

Feminism

Glass ceiling

Glass escalator

Institutional discrimination

Second shift

Sexism

taking sociology with you

1 For a day or two, watch for examples of people "doing gender" on your campus. Record your sightings in a journal and compare them with those of your classmates.

2 Find out what percentage of the faculty members at your college are women. What percentage of the women has tenure, compared to the men? What percentage holds full professorships? Do the percentages vary much from one department to another, and if so, why?

3 Use your school's alumni network to get in touch with graduates who have entered the workforce. Are mothers of young children having difficulty balancing work and parenting? Do both men and women feel they have a chance to get ahead? Are both men and women well compensated?

key terms

Brass ceiling An invisible barrier that blocks the promotion of a woman in the military because of her official (not necessarily actual) exclusion from combat.

Expressiveness Concern for the maintenance of harmony and the internal emotional affairs of the family.

Feminism An ideology that favors equal rights for women.

Gender role Expectations regarding the proper behavior, attitudes, and activities of males and females.

Glass ceiling An invisible barrier that blocks the promotion of a qualified individual in a work environment because of the individual's gender, race, or ethnicity.

Glass escalator The advantage men experience in occupations dominated by women.

Homophobia Fear of and prejudice against homosexuality.

Institutional discrimination The denial of opportunities and equal rights to individuals and groups that results from the normal operations of a society.

Instrumentality An emphasis on tasks, a focus on more distant goals, and a concern for the external relationship between one's family and other social institutions.

Matrix of domination The cumulative impact of oppression because of race and ethnicity, gender, and social class, as well as religion, sexual orientation, disability, age, and citizenship status.

Multiple masculinities A variety of male gender roles, including nurturing-caring and effeminate-gay roles, that men may play along with their more pervasive traditional role of dominating women.

Second shift The double burden—work outside the home followed by child care and housework—that many women face and few men share equitably.

Sexism The ideology that one sex is superior to the other.

self-quiz

Read each question carefully and then select the best answer.

1. Both males and females are physically capable of learning to cook and sew, yet most Western societies determine that women should perform these tasks. This illustrates the operation of
   a. gender roles.
   b. sociobiology.
   c. homophobia.
   d. comparable worth.

2. An important element in traditional views of proper "masculine" and "feminine" behavior is fear of homosexuality. This fear, along with accompanying prejudice, is referred to as
   a. lesbianism.
   b. femme fatalism.
   c. homophobia.
   d. claustrophobia.

3. The most crucial agents of socialization in teaching gender roles in the United States are
   a. peers.
   b. teachers.
   c. media personalities.
   d. parents.

4. Research by anthropologist Margaret Mead has shown that
   a. biology is the most important factor in determining the social roles of males and females.
   b. cultural conditioning is the most important factor in determining the social roles of males and females.
   c. biology and cultural conditioning have an equal impact in determining the social roles of males and females.
   d. biology and cultural conditioning have a negligible impact in determining the social roles of males and females.

5. Which sociological perspective would acknowledge that it is not possible to change gender roles drastically without dramatic revisions in a culture's social structure?
   a. functionalist perspective
   b. conflict perspective
   c. interactionist perspective
   d. both a and b

6. The term *sexism* is generally used to refer to
   a. female prejudice and discrimination against men.
   b. male prejudice and discrimination against women.
   c. female discrimination against men and male discrimination against women equally.
   d. discrimination between members of the same sex.

7. Which of these statements is true?
   a. More boys than girls take AP exams.
   b. Women in the United States are more likely than men to attend college.
   c. Women in the United States are less likely than men to obtain doctoral degrees.
   d. all of the above

8. Which sociological perspective distinguishes between instrumental and expressive roles?
   a. functionalist perspective
   b. conflict perspective

c. interactionist perspective
d. labeling theory

9. Contemporary feminists recognize the differential treatment of some women not only because of their gender, but also because of their
   a. race.
   b. ethnicity.
   c. socioeconomic status.
   d. all of the above

10. The sense of sisterhood that became evident during the rise of the contemporary feminist movement resembled the Marxist concept of
    a. alienation.
    b. dialectics.
    c. class consciousness.
    d. false consciousness.

11. Talcott Parsons and Robert Bales contend that women take the _____, emotionally supportive role in the family and that men take the _____, practical role, with the two complementing each other.

12. A significant component of the _____ approach to gender stratification draws on feminist theory.

13. It is not simply that particular men in the United States are biased in their treatment of women. All the major institutions of our society—including the government, the armed forces, large corporations, the media, universities, and the medical establishment—are controlled by men. This situation is symptomatic of institutional _____.

14. Women from all groups and men from minority groups sometimes encounter attitudinal or organizational bias that prevents them from reaching their full potential. This is known as the _____ _____.

15. Sociologist Arlie Hochschild has used the phrase _____ _____ to describe the double burden that many women face and few men share equitably: work outside the home followed by child care and housework.

16. Within the general framework of their theory, _____ sociologists maintain that gender differentiation has contributed to overall social stability.

17. Through the rise of contemporary _____, women are developing a greater sense of group solidarity.

18. _____ _____ contributes significantly to rigid gender-role socialization, since many people stereotypically associate male homosexuality with femininity and lesbianism with masculinity.

19. The term _____ _____ _____ was coined by feminist theorist Patricia Hill Collins to describe the convergence of social forces that contributes to the subordinate status of poor, non-White women.

20. The author of the pioneering argument for women's rights, *The Feminine Mystique*, was _____ _____.

12 Stratification by Age

MODULE 36 | Aging and Society

MODULE 37 | Aging Worldwide

MODULE 38 | Age Stratification in the United States

Individuals from several generations enjoy an outdoor pool. Age serves as a basis for social stratification, sometimes separating the old from the young more than is necessary or desirable. To a great extent, older people's quality of life, including their livelihoods, their social relationships, and their leisure pursuits, depend on society's view of aging.

279

How do different cultures regard elderly people?

Sociologist Jill Quadagno investigated the many ways in which culture determines what it means to be elderly.

❝ On January 15, 2009, Captain Chesley Sullenberger, known as Sully, became a national hero when he landed an engineless plane in the Hudson River, saving the lives of 154 passengers. It was the first time in 45 years that a major aircraft crash-landed in the water without fatalities. Sullenberger had decades of experience flying everything from a glider to a jumbo jet.

After both engines blew, Sullenberger reportedly told his 150 passengers to brace for impact because they were going down before maneuvering over a bridge and between skyscrapers to land the plane safely on the river. He walked the length of the sinking jet twice to verify that all his passengers had got off safely before exiting himself. Sully was nearing his 60th birthday at the time of the crash. If he had not been flying that day, the outcome might well have been different. Yet as late as 2007, airline pilots were required to retire at age 60. The presumption was that older pilots are less alert and less able to act decisively than younger pilots. In this instance, however, experience clearly trumped age.

In non-western traditional cultures, the elderly are often accorded great respect and esteem. Among the Kirghiz, for example, a small community of 2,000 people who live in the high valleys of Afghanistan, the household head, called *oey bashi,* is the most senior male, or, in the absence of a male, the most senior female. The *oey bashi* exercises complete authority over the household and represents its social relations with the community.

As late as 2007, airline pilots were required to retire at age 60. . . . In this instance, however, experience clearly trumped age.

Traditional Chinese culture also places a high value on old age. The veneration of the old is linked to Confucian values emphasizing that the parent should treat the child with *zi,* or nurturance, and the child should treat the parent with *xiao,* meaning filial piety or absolute obedience. *Xiao* means showing one's parents with respect at all times, performing acts of ancestor worship after they die, and generating grandsons to carry on the family name.

Xiao extends beyond respect for one's own parents to include deference to all elderly people. It is accompanied by many symbolic and conventional gestures, such as speaking politely, deferring in conversation to those older than oneself, and never ridiculing or insulting the aged. It would be a shameful breach of *xiao* to neglect the needs of the elderly or to put them in a nursing home. Although women always have lower status than men, the position of a woman in Chinese culture improves as she ages, and a few old women become genuinely powerful. . . .

Singer Dean Martin was a superstar in his heyday. He was comedian Jerry Lewis's sidekick and a member of Frank Sinatra's rat pack. His Las Vegas shows were sold out months in advance. In his later years, however, he became a recluse, sitting in his mansion in Los Angeles watching old cowboy movies and refusing all interviews.

Then there's "Banana" George Blair (known for his neon-yellow wetsuit), who water skis barefoot at 40 miles per hour. At age 71, George won a place in the *Guinness Book of World Records* as the first person to water ski barefoot on all seven continents. Which lifestyle represents normal aging? ❞

(*Source: Quadagno 2014:47, 60, 147. Also see Amoss and Harrell 1981; Henderson 1971; Shahrani 1981.*)

A s sociologist Jill Quadagno demonstrates in her work on social gerontology, not all old people are frail and dependent, in need of support. Many are healthy, energetic, and engaged. Unfortunately, younger people tend to stereotype the aged. Like race or gender, age is socially constructed, an ascribed status that dominates people's perceptions of others, obscuring individual differences. Rather than suggesting that a particular elderly person is no longer competent to drive, for instance, we may condemn the entire age group: "These old codgers shouldn't be allowed on the road!

How do people's roles change as they age? What are the social implications of the growing number of elderly in the United States? In these modules we will look at the process of aging throughout the life course and around the world. After exploring various theories of the impact of aging, we will discuss the role transitions typical of the major stages in the life course. We will consider the challenges facing the "sandwich generation," middle-aged people who care for both their children and their aging parents. We will pay particular attention to the effects of prejudice and discrimination on older people, and to the rise of a political consciousness among the elderly. Finally, in the Social Policy section we will discuss the controversial issue of the right to die.

The Sherpas—a Tibetan-speaking Buddhist people in Nepal—live in a culture that idealizes old age. Almost all elderly members of the Sherpa culture own their homes, and most are in relatively good physical condition. Typically, older Sherpas value their independence and prefer not to live with their children. Among the Fulani of Africa, however, older men and women move to the edge of the family homestead. Since that is where people are buried, the elderly sleep over their own graves, for they are viewed socially as already dead. Like gender stratification, age stratification varies from culture to culture. One society may treat older people with great reverence, while another sees them as unproductive and "difficult" (M. Goldstein and Beall 1981; Stenning 1958; Tonkinson 1978).

Age Stratification

It is understandable that all societies have some system of age stratification that associates certain social roles with distinct periods in life. Some of this age differentiation seems inevitable; it would make little sense to send young children off to war, or to expect most older citizens to handle physically demanding tasks, such as loading freight at shipyards. However, as is the case with stratification by gender, in the United States age stratification goes far beyond the physical constraints on human beings at different ages.

"Being old" is a master status that commonly overshadows all others in the United States. Thus, the insights of labeling theory can help us in analyzing the consequences of aging. Once people have been labeled "old," the designation has a major impact on how others perceive them, and even on how they view themselves. Negative stereotypes of the elderly contribute to their position as a minority group subject to discrimination, as we will see later in the chapter.

The model of five basic properties of a minority or subordinate group (introduced in Module 31) can be applied to older people in the United States to clarify their subordinate status:

1. Older people experience unequal treatment in employment and may face prejudice and discrimination.

2. Older people share physical characteristics that distinguish them from younger people. In addition, their cultural preferences and leisure-time activities often differ from those of the rest of society.

3. Membership in this disadvantaged group is involuntary.

4. Older people have a strong sense of group solidarity, as is reflected in the growth of senior citizens' centers, retirement communities, and advocacy organizations.

5. Older people generally are married to others of comparable age.

There is one crucial difference between older people and other subordinate groups, such as racial and ethnic minorities or women: *all* of us who live long enough will eventually assume the ascribed status of an older person (Barron 1953; Levin and Levin 1980; Wagley and Harris 1958).

Sociological Perspectives on Aging

Aging is one important aspect of socialization—the lifelong process through which an individual learns the cultural norms and values of a particular society. There are no clear-cut definitions for different periods of the aging cycle in the United States. *Old age* has typically been regarded as beginning at 65, which corresponds to the retirement age for many workers, but not everyone in the United States accepts that definition. With the increase in life expectancy, writers are beginning to refer to people in their 60s as the "young old," to distinguish them from those in their 80s and beyond (the "old old").

The particular problems of the elderly have become the focus of a specialized field of research and inquiry known as gerontology. **Gerontology** is the scientific study of the sociological and psychological aspects of aging and the problems of the aged. It originated in the 1930s, as an increasing number of social scientists became aware of the plight of the elderly.

Extended family arrangements are important to Americans, especially Latinos. Thirty-one percent of Hispanic women age 65 and older live with their relatives, compared to 13 percent of White non-Hispanic women. Among men of the same age, the rate is 15 percent for Hispanics, compared to 6 percent for White non-Hispanics (Jacobsen et al. 2011).

Gerontologists rely heavily on sociological principles and theories to explain the impact of aging on the individual and society. They also draw on psychology, anthropology, physical education, counseling, and medicine in their study of the aging process. Two influential views of aging—disengagement theory and activity theory—can best be understood in terms of the sociological perspectives of functionalism and interactionism, respectively. The conflict perspective also contributes to our sociological understanding of aging.

 use your **sociological imagination**

Time has passed, and you are now in your 70s or 80s. How does old age in your generation compare with your parents' or grandparents' experience of old age?

Functionalist Perspective: Disengagement Theory

After studying elderly people in good health and relatively comfortable economic circumstances, Elaine Cumming and William Henry (1961) introduced their **disengagement theory**, which implicitly suggests that society and the aging individual mutually sever many of their relationships. In keeping with the functionalist perspective, disengagement theory emphasizes that passing social roles on from one generation to another ensures social stability.

According to this theory, the approach of death forces people to drop most of their social roles—including those of worker, volunteer, spouse, hobby enthusiast, and even reader. Younger members of society then take on these functions. The aging person, it is held, withdraws into an increasing state of inactivity while preparing for death.

Since it was first outlined five decades ago, disengagement theory has generated considerable controversy. Today, gerontologists and sociologists are more likely to see the elderly in terms of social connectedness, postretirement employment, and volunteerism. For their part, producers and retailers of electronic products are likely to see the older set as e-savvy consumers. Since 2008, they note, growth in computer and digital camera sales has been greatest in that market segment. And retirement homes have had to make room for residents who want to bowl or play tennis on Nintendo's Wii system (Cornwell et al. 2008; NPD Group 2008).

Interactionist Perspective: Activity Theory

How important is it for older people to stay actively involved, whether at a job or in other pursuits? A tragic disaster in Chicago in 1995 showed that it can be a matter of life and death. An intense heat wave lasting more than a week—with a heat index exceeding 115 degrees on two consecutive days—resulted in 733 heat-related deaths. About three-fourths of the deceased were 65 and older. Subsequent analysis showed that older people who lived alone had the highest risk of dying, suggesting that support networks for the elderly literally help to save lives. Older Hispanics and Asian Americans had lower death rates from the heat wave than other racial and ethnic groups. Their stronger social networks probably resulted in more regular contact with family members and friends (Klinenberg 2002; R. Schaefer 1998).

Often seen as an opposing approach to disengagement theory, **activity theory** suggests that those elderly people who remain active and socially involved will be best adjusted. Proponents of this perspective acknowledge that a person age 70 may not have the ability or desire to perform various social roles that he or she had at age 40. Yet they contend that old people have essentially the same need for social interaction as any other group.

The improved health of older people—sometimes overlooked by social scientists—has strengthened the arguments of activity theorists. Illness and chronic disease are no longer quite the scourge of the elderly that they once were. The recent emphasis on fitness, the availability of better medical care, greater control of infectious diseases, and the reduction of fatal strokes and heart attacks have combined to mitigate the traumas of growing old. As we saw at the beginning of the chapter, Captain Sully Sullenberger is certainly both physically and mentally fit.

Accumulating medical research also points to the importance of remaining socially involved. Among those who decline in their mental capacities later in life, deterioration is most rapid in those who withdraw from social relationships and activities. Fortunately, older people are finding new ways to remain socially engaged, as evidenced by their increasing use of the Internet, especially to keep in touch with family and friends (Clifford 2009b).

Admittedly, many activities open to older adults involve unpaid labor, for which younger adults may receive salaries.

These "silver surfers" in California still enjoy life to the fullest, just as they did when they were young. According to activity theory, staying active and involved is healthy for the older population.

Unpaid elderly workers include hospital volunteers (versus aides and orderlies), drivers for charities such as the Red Cross (versus chauffeurs), tutors (as opposed to teachers), and craftspeople for charity bazaars (as opposed to carpenters and dressmakers). However, some companies have recently begun programs to hire retirees for full-time or part-time work.

Though disengagement theory suggested that older people find satisfaction in withdrawal from society, conveniently receding into the background and allowing the next generation to take over, proponents of activity theory view such withdrawal as harmful to both the elderly and society. Activity theorists focus on the potential contributions of older people to the maintenance of society. In their opinion, aging citizens will feel satisfied only when they can be useful and productive in society's terms—primarily by working for wages (Charles and Carstensen 2009; Quadagno 2014).

Labeling Perspective

Just who are "the elderly"? Labeling theorists, who study the way reality is constructed through our culture and social interactions, have noted that recently, our society has begun to reconsider what makes a person old.

As early as 1975, social scientists were suggesting that old age should be defined not in terms of how old one is, but in terms of how long one can be expected to live. As life expectancy lengthens, then, the age at which one is labeled old rises. Some have suggested that the threshold of old age should begin in the last 10 or 15 years of a person's expected life. Using that definition, old age would begin at about age 70 or 75, at least for those of us who live in the United States.

Is this new definition of old age likely to be accepted? From the labeling perspective, it all depends on who you are. Understandably, many people would prefer to be considered old later rather than sooner. Those who advocate for the elderly would prefer a broader definition. For example, the AARP offers membership to anyone age 50 or older. It argues that people should begin planning for old age in their 50s, but clearly, encouraging the "young old" to join gives them strength in numbers.

The labeling of old age also differs from one culture to the next, due in part to differences in physical health and life opportunities. In relatively prosperous cultures like the United States, 70 is the new 60. But in countries whose health and social support systems have been significantly weakened over the past 20 years—Russia, for example—50 is the new 60 (Sanderson and Scherbov 2008).

Conflict Perspective

Conflict theorists have criticized both disengagement theorists and activity theorists for failing to consider the impact of social structure on aging patterns. Neither approach, they say, questions why social interaction must change or decrease in old age. In addition, they often ignore the impact of social class on the lives of elderly people.

The privileged upper class generally enjoys better health and vigor and less likelihood of dependency in old age. Affluence cannot forestall aging indefinitely, but it can soften the economic hardships people face in later years. Although pension plans, retirement

TABLE **36-1** SOCIOLOGICAL PERSPECTIVES ON AGING

Sociological Perspective	View of Aging	Social Roles	Portrayal of Elderly
Functionalist	Disengagement	Reduced	Socially isolated
Interactionist	Activity	Changed	Involved in new networks
Labeling	Socially constructed	Changing	Varies by audience
Conflict	Competition	Relatively unchanged	Victimized, organized to confront their victimization

packages, and insurance benefits may be developed to assist older people, those whose wealth allows them access to investment funds can generate the greatest income for their later years.

In contrast, the working class often faces greater health hazards and a greater risk of disability; aging is particularly difficult for those who suffer job-related injuries or illnesses. Working-class people also depend more heavily on Social Security benefits and private pension programs. During inflationary times, their relatively fixed incomes from these sources barely keep pace with the escalating costs of food, housing, utilities, and other necessities (Atchley and Barusch 2004).

According to the conflict approach, the treatment of older people in the United States reflects the many divisions in our society. The low status of older people is seen in prejudice and discrimination against them, in age segregation, and in unfair job practices—none of which are directly addressed by either disengagement or activity theory.

Conflict theorists have noted, too, that in the developing world, the transition from agricultural economies to industrialization and capitalism has not always been beneficial to the elderly. As a society's production methods change, the traditionally valued role of older people tends to erode. Their wisdom is no longer relevant in the new economy.

In sum, the four perspectives considered here take different views of the elderly. Functionalists portray older people as socially isolated, with reduced social roles; interactionists see them as involved in new networks and changing social roles. Labeling theorists see old age as a life stage that is defined by society. Conflict theorists see it as a time when people are victimized and their social roles devalued. Table 36-1 summarizes these perspectives.

 use your **sociological imagination**

Have you noticed signs of second-class treatment of older people? If so, in what ways?

MODULE 36 | Recap and Review

Summary

Age, like gender and race, is an ascribed status that forms the basis for social differentiation.

1. Like other forms of stratification, age stratification varies from culture to culture.

2. In the United States, being old is a master status that seems to overshadow all others.

3. The particular problems of the aged have become the focus of a specialized area of research and inquiry known as **gerontology.**

4. **Disengagement theory** implies that society should help older people withdraw from their accustomed social roles. In contrast, **activity theory** suggests that the elderly person who remains active and socially involved will be better adjusted.

5. Labeling theorists note that people of the same age are labeled differently in different societies, based largely on difference in physical health, life opportunities, and life expectancy.

6. From a conflict perspective, the low status of older people is reflected in prejudice and discrimination against them and in unfair job practices.

Thinking Critically

1. Why is disengagement theory an example of functionalism?

2. Is labeling the same as stereotyping? Why or why not?

Key Terms

Activity theory

Disengagement theory

Gerontology

MODULE 37 | Aging Worldwide

Today the world's population is evenly divided between those people who are under age 28 and those who are over age 28. By the middle of the 21st century, the median age will have risen to 40. Even though the United Nations held the first world assembly on aging in 1982, few people gave much thought to this prospect of whole populations—that is, nations—growing older until the 1990s. By 2013, the world had more than 570 million people age 65 and over. Together they constituted about 8 percent of the world's population. By 2045, nearly twice that proportion, or 15.2 percent of the world's people, will be over 65.

In an important sense, this trend toward the aging of the world's population represents a major success story, one that unfolded during the latter years of the 20th century. Through the efforts of national governments and international agencies, many societies have drastically reduced their incidence of disease, and with it their rate of death. As a result, these nations—particularly the industrialized countries of Europe and North America—have a high and steadily rising proportion of older members (Figure 37-1) (Fishman 2010a, 2010b; Haub and Kaneda 2013).

Overall, Europe's population is older than that of any other continent. Though many European countries have long prided themselves on their generous pension programs, as the proportion of older people continues to rise, government officials have reluctantly begun to reduce pension benefits and raise the age at which workers can receive them. Japan, too, has a relatively old population; the Japanese enjoy a life expectancy of 83 years, compared to 79 in the United States. But though four more years of life may sound like a bonus, it presents a real and growing challenge to Japanese society (see Box 37-1).

In most developing countries, people over 60 are likely to be in poorer health than their counterparts in industrialized nations. Yet few of those countries are in a position to offer extensive financial support to the elderly. Ironically, though the modernization of the developing world has brought many social and economic advances, it has undercut the traditionally high status of the elderly. In many cultures, the earning power of younger adults now exceeds that of their older relatives (Beck 2009).

Role Transitions throughout the Life Course

Socialization is a lifelong process. We simply do not experience things the same way at different points in the life course. For example, one study found that even falling in love differs according to where we are in the life course. Young unmarried adults tend to treat love as a noncommittal game or an obsession characterized by possessiveness and dependency. People over age 50 are much more likely to see love as involving commitment, and they tend to take a practical approach to finding a partner who meets a set of rational criteria. That does not mean that romance is dead among the older generation, however. Among those age 65 and over, 39 percent are "head over heels in love," compared to only 25 percent of those ages 18 to 34. The life course, then, affects the manner in which we relate to one another (G. Anderson 2009; Montgomery and Sorell 1997).

FIGURE 37-1 World's "Oldest" Countries versus the United States

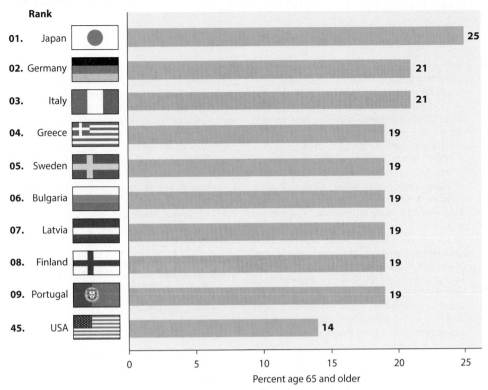

Rank		Percent age 65 and older
01.	Japan	25
02.	Germany	21
03.	Italy	21
04.	Greece	19
05.	Sweden	19
06.	Bulgaria	19
07.	Latvia	19
08.	Finland	19
09.	Portugal	19
45.	USA	14

Source: Developed by Richard Schaefer from Haub and Kaneda 2013.

challenge faced by a growing number of middle-aged adults: caring for two generations at once.

The Sandwich Generation

During the late 1990s social scientists focused on the **sandwich generation**—adults who simultaneously try to meet the competing needs of their parents and their children. That is, caregiving goes in two directions: (1) to children, who even as young adults may still require significant direction, and (2) to aging parents, whose health and economic problems may demand intervention by their adult children. By 2010, 13 million Americans were caring for both their children *and* their parents.

Like the role of caring for children, the role of caring for aging parents falls disproportionately on women. Overall, women provide 66 percent of the care their parents receive, and even more as the demands of the role grow more intense and time-consuming. Increasingly, middle-aged women and younger women are finding themselves on the "daughter track," as their time and attention are diverted by the needs of their aging mothers and fathers. (National Alliance for Caregiving 2009).

How we move through the life course varies dramatically, depending on our personal preferences and circumstances. Some of us marry early, others late; some have children and some don't. These individual patterns are influenced by social factors such as class, race, and gender. Only in the most general terms, then, can we speak of stages or periods in the life course.

One transitional stage, identified by psychologist Daniel Levinson, begins at the time at which an individual gradually enters the adult world, perhaps by moving out of the parental home, beginning a career, or entering a marriage. The next transitional period, the midlife transition, typically begins at about age 40. Men and women often experience a stressful period of self-evaluation, commonly known as the **midlife crisis,** in which they realize that they have not achieved basic goals and ambitions and have little time left to do so. Thus, Levinson (1978, 1996) found that most adults surveyed experienced tumultuous midlife conflicts within the self and with the external world.

Not all the challenges at this time of life come from career or one's partner. In the next section we will examine a special

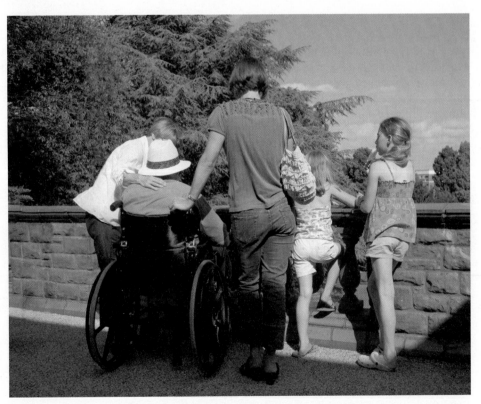

This sandwich-generation mom cares for both her aging parent and her children. Increasingly, members of the baby boom generation find themselves caring for two generations at once.

Aging, Japanese Style

An electric water kettle is wired so that people in another location can determine whether it has been used in the previous 24 hours. This arrangement may seem a zany use of modern technology, but it symbolizes a change that is taking place around the globe: the growing needs of an aging population. The Japanese Welfare Network Ikebukuro Honcho installed these wired hotpots so that volunteers can monitor whether the elderly have prepared morning tea. An unused pot initiates contacts to see whether that person needs help. This technological monitoring system indicates not just the tremendous growth in Japan's elderly population, but the increasing numbers of elderly people who live alone.

Indeed, Japan is struggling to confront the challenges posed by the world's most rapidly aging population. For generations, Japanese families have lived with and cared for their aging parents and grandparents. But this tradition of living under the same roof with one's elders is fading as more and more couples and even single adults strike out on their own. Hence the need for the wired hotpots.

Compared to the United States and Canada, Japan is less well equipped to deal with this social phenomenon. Assisted living, in-home services, and nursing homes are all much less common in Japan than they are in North America.

As in the United States, research documents that the more elders connect with others and with the larger community, the more their health and quality of life improve.

One challenge many aging couples face is the "retired-husband syndrome." In their working days, most older Japanese men labored long hours in workplaces where women traditionally did not hold supervisory positions. When these men retire and begin to stay home full-time, some of them tend to treat their wives as subservient laborers. Moreover, many of them were so "married" to their jobs that they failed to develop hobbies or outside interests that might occupy them in retirement. Their wives, who have had free rein around the house all their lives, often find sharing the home with their dictatorial husbands a real challenge. Though Japanese gender roles are changing as record numbers of women enter positions of real responsibility, the senior generation is still hampered by yesterday's stereotypes.

The aging of Japan's workforce has forced government officials to reexamine the nation's policy toward immigrant workers. Although work opportunities dried up during the global economic downturn, the government does not want to lose this small group of immigrants, given Japan's looming labor shortage. So policymakers are devising programs that will allow immigrant workers to stay and will encourage their countrymen to join them when Japan's economy rebounds. Little wonder that a 21-nation study conducted in 2014 found the highest proportion of people (87 percent) in Japan agreeing that "aging is a major problem for the country" (Kochinar 2014:1).

LET'S DISCUSS

1. What do you think caused the change in housing patterns that has resulted in so many elderly Japanese living alone? Could the change in housing patterns be related to the change in life expectancy? How?

2. How might living alone contribute to the retired-husband syndrome noted among aging Japanese couples?

Sources: Crump 2006; Faiola 2005, 2006; Hani 1998; Harden 2009; Inoue et al., 2013; Kochinar 2014.

The last major transition identified by Levinson occurs after age 60—sometimes well after that age, given advances in health care, greater longevity, and gradual acceptance within society of older people. Nonetheless, there is a point at which people transition to a different lifestyle. As we will see, this is a time of dramatic changes in people's everyday lives.

Adjusting to Retirement

Retirement is a rite of passage that marks a critical transition from one phase of a person's life to another. Typically, symbolic events are associated with this rite of passage, such as retirement gifts, a retirement party, and special moments on the last day on the job. The preretirement period itself can be emotionally charged, especially if the retiree is expected to train his or her successor (Atchley 1976).

Today, the retirement stage is complicated by economic deterioration. From 1950 to 1990, the average age at retirement in the United States declined; since then, however, it has risen. In 1990, 11.8 percent of those over age 64 were in the labor force. By 2010, the proportion had increased to 17.4 percent, and is projected to hit 22.6 percent by 2020. In that year, the proportion of people still working in their upper 70s will match the proportion of those who were working in their upper 60s in 1990. Indeed, as recently as 2011, 5 percent of women and 10 percent of men over age 75 were still working.

A variety of factors explains this reversal in the trend toward earlier retirement. Changes in Social Security benefits, the recent economic recession, and workers' concern about maintaining

"Have you given much thought to what kind of job you want after you retire?"

their health insurance and pension benefits have all contributed. At the same time, life expectancy has increased and the quality of people's health has improved (Toossi 2012).

Phases of Retirement Gerontologist Robert Atchley (1976) has identified several phases of the retirement experience:

- *Preretirement,* a period of anticipatory socialization as the person prepares for retirement
- *The near phase,* when the person establishes a specific departure date from his or her job
- *The honeymoon phase,* an often euphoric period in which the person pursues activities that he or she never had time for before
- *The disenchantment phase,* in which retirees feel a sense of letdown or even depression as they cope with their new lives, which may include illness or poverty
- *The reorientation phase,* which involves the development of a more realistic view of retirement alternatives
- *The stability phase,* a period in which the person has learned to deal with life after retirement in a reasonable and comfortable fashion
- *The termination phase,* which begins when the person can no longer engage in basic, day-to-day activities such as self-care and housework

Retirement is not a single transition, then, but rather a series of adjustments that varies from one person to another. The length and timing of each phase will differ for each individual, depending on such factors as financial status and health. A particular person will not necessarily go through all the phases identified by Atchley (Reitzes and Mutran 2006).

Some factors, such as being forced into retirement or being burdened with financial difficulties, can further complicate the retirement process. People who enter retirement involuntarily or without the necessary means may never experience the honeymoon phase. In the United States, many retirees continue in the paid labor force, often taking part-time jobs to supplement their pensions. It remains to be seen what the impact of the prolonged economic downturn, which began in 2008, will have on retirement plans. From a 2011 survey of baby boomers (age 46–65), there is a larger group whose outlook is negative, but overall most see little or positive change (Figure 37-2).

Like other aspects of life in the United States, the experience of retirement varies according to gender, race, and ethnicity. White males are most likely to benefit from retirement wages, as well as to have participated in a formal retirement preparation program. As a result, anticipatory socialization for retirement is most complete for White men. In contrast, members

FIGURE 37-2 Baby Boomers Eyeing Retirement

2003

Changed for the better 46%
No change 40%
Changed for the worse 14%

2011

Changed for the better 31%
No change 43%
Changed for the worse 26%

Source: AARP 2011.

of racial and ethnic minority groups—especially African Americans—are more likely to exit the paid labor force through disability than through retirement. Because of their comparatively lower incomes and smaller savings, men and women from racial and ethnic minority groups work intermittently after retirement more often than older Whites (National Institute on Aging 1999; Quadagno 2014).

Naturally Occurring Retirement Communities (NORCs)
With recent improvements in health care, older Americans have gained new choices in where to live. Today, rather than residing in nursing homes or planned retirement communities, many of them congregate in areas that have gradually become informal centers for senior citizens. Social scientists have dubbed such areas **naturally occurring retirement communities (NORCs).**

use your **sociological imagination**

How have people close to you, such as relatives, personally handled their retirement from the labor force?

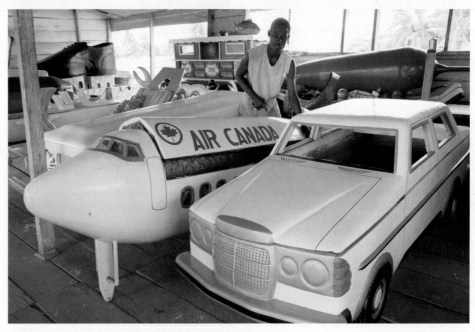

Did you guess that this is the shop of an expert woodcarver working with an undertaker? Coffins in Ghana sometimes are quite elaborate to try to reflect status or the way the dead lived their lives.

Using observation research, census data, and interviews, sociologists have developed some interesting conclusions about NORCs in the United States, which numbered approximately 300 in 2009. These communities can be as small as a single apartment building or as large as a neighborhood in a big city. Often, they emerge as singles and young couples move out and older people move in. Sometimes couples simply remain where they are; as they grow older, the community becomes noticeably grayer. In time, business establishments that cater to the elderly—pharmacies, medical supply outlets, small restaurants—relocate to NORCs, making them even more attractive to older citizens.

Unfortunately, residents of some of these communities are threatened by gentrification, or the takeover of low-income neighborhoods by higher-income residents. In Chicago, a high-rise building known as Ontario Place is converting to a condominium, at prices that current residents cannot afford. About half the building's occupants are Russian immigrants; most of the others are elderly or disabled people living on fixed incomes. These people are distressed not just because they will need to move, but because their community is being destroyed (Gregor 2013; Piturro 2012; Sheehan 2005).

Q Research Today

BOX 37-2

Native Americans and Death

The native peoples of North America include hundreds of distinctive cultures, as different from one another as English culture is from Turkish culture. Their practices with respect to death and dying reflect this cultural diversity. Sociologist Gerry Cox conducted ethnographic fieldwork and interviews with tribal peoples on 42 reservations throughout the United States and Canada. He found that among the Creek and some other tribes, those closest to the deceased accompany the body in the days before the burial. In other tribes, such as the Navajo, Apache, and Hopi, relatives spend little time with the body.

> Family members smudge the body with ashes immediately after death, then go with it to a funeral home for embalming.

Among the Navajo, the taboo against speaking of death is so strong that health care providers can only approach the subject of end-of-live care with patients and family members indirectly through a poem. Written in both Navajo and English, the poem about death allows elderly patients and family members to begin a discussion about end-of-life issues.

In many cases, these practices evolved after contact with European Americans. Religious proselytizing, intermarriage, and the enforcement of colonial regulations all had an impact on cultural traditions. Among the first to experience Hispanic contact in the 16th century were the Zuni and other Pueblo peoples of present-day Arizona and New Mexico. In those cultures, burials that had once been done quickly, with little ceremony, moved onto church grounds or to graveyards consecrated by Christian ritual. At the same time,

Native Americans continued their traditional burial practices, in secret when necessary.

Among the Flathead of Montana, who converted to Roman Catholicism a century ago, traditional practices persist. Family members smudge the body with ashes immediately after death, then go with it to a funeral home for embalming. Before the body is placed in a coffin, they wash it in rose water. The Catholic funeral mass that precedes the burial includes native songs and ceremonial drums.

Today, Native Americans have won some concessions from hospitals that care for the dying. Lakota patients are allowed to have more relatives in the room than other patients. They may ask to use smoke for ceremonial purposes, even though smoking is strictly forbidden. Apaches, in contrast, prefer to die alone. Navajos may want to hold a "sing."

Native American rituals demonstrate reverence and respect for life as well as death. Despite the great diversity in their values,

beliefs, and normative behavior regarding death, one broad belief unites Native Americans: death is a natural and accepted part of the life cycle. Native Americans also share the belief that their dear ones continue to love, care for, and protect families and friends after death.

LET'S DISCUSS

1. Does your own family observe traditional cultural practices regarding death and dying, independent of formal religious ritual? If so, explain their meaning and importance to your family.

2. Apply the concepts you learned in Chapter 3 to Native American burial practices. Which of them do you find most useful in understanding these practices?

Sources: G. Cox 2010; Daitz 2011; Sharon Kaufman and Morgan 2005; A. Walker and Balk 2007.

Death and Dying

Among the role transitions that typically (but not always) come later in life is death. Until recently, death was viewed as a taboo topic in the United States. However, psychologist Elisabeth Kübler-Ross (1969), through her pioneering book *On Death and Dying,* greatly encouraged open discussion of the process of dying. Drawing on her work with 200 cancer patients, Kübler-Ross identified five stages of the experience: denial, anger, bargaining, depression, and finally acceptance.

Despite its popular appeal, the five-stage theory of dying has been challenged. Observers often cannot substantiate these stages. With medical advances, dying now tends to be a much longer process than it was when Kübler-Ross did her research a half-century ago. Moreover, research suggests that each person declines in his or her own way. Thus, one should not expect—much less counsel—a person to approach death in any particular way. Cross-culturally, the variation in approaches is even more marked. Box 37-2 describes some of the ways in which different Native American tribes acknowledge death (Okun and Nowinski 2011).

Functionalist analysis brings to mind the cherished yet controversial concept of a "good death." One researcher described a good death among the Kaliai, a people of the South Pacific. In that culture, the dying person calls together all his relatives, settles his debts, disposes of his possessions, and then announces that it is time for him to die (Counts and Counts 2004).

The Kaliai concept of a good death has a parallel in Western societies, where people may speak of a "natural death," an "appropriate death," or "death with dignity." The practice of **hospice care,** introduced in London, England, in 1967, is founded on this concept. Hospice workers seek to improve the quality of a dying person's last days by offering comfort and by helping the person to remain at home, or in a homelike setting at a hospital or other special facility, until the end. Currently, more than 3,400 hospice programs serve over 1 million people a year in the United States through federal programs such as Medicare and Medicaid (Hospice Association of America 2010).

Although the Western ideal of the good death makes the experience of dying as positive as possible, some critics fear that acceptance of the concept of a good death may direct both individual efforts and social resources away from attempts to extend life. Still others argue that fatally ill older people should not just passively accept death, but should forgo further treatment in order to reduce public health care expenditures. Such issues are at the heart of current debates over the right to die and physician-assisted suicide.

Today, in many varied ways, people have broken through the historic taboos about death and are attempting to arrange certain aspects of the idealized good death. For example, bereavement practices—once highly structured—are becoming increasingly varied and therapeutic. More and more people are actively addressing the inevitability of death by making wills, leaving "living wills" (health care proxies that explain their feelings about the use of life-support equipment), donating organs, and providing instructions for family members about funerals, cremations, and burials. Given medical and technological advances and a breakthrough in open discussion and negotiation regarding death and dying, it is possible that good deaths may become a social norm in the United States.

MODULE 37 | **Recap and Review**

Summary

The industrialized nations of Europe, North America, and Asia have high and steadily rising proportions of older citizens.

1. People move through the life course in highly individual ways that vary with culture and individual circumstance. The **midlife crisis** is a stressful period of self-evaluation that many individuals experience at around age 40.

2. Adults who simultaneously care for their children and their parents belong to the **sandwich generation.**

3. Retirement is not a single transition but is rather a series of stages in itself. The experience of retirement varies because of individual factors but also because of factors related to race, gender, and ethnicity.

4. Dying is increasingly seen as the last stage of life, as people attempt to break through traditional taboos regarding death in order to achieve a good death.

Thinking Critically

1. Today, many young adults continue to live with their parents after finishing their schooling. Contrast their situation with that of the elderly who live with their children. Does society treat dependent adult children in the same way as dependent parents? Why or why not?

2. How might interactionists consider a NORC?

Key Terms

Hospice care

Midlife crisis

Naturally occurring retirement community (NORC)

Sandwich generation

MODULE 38 | Age Stratification in the United States

● The "Graying of America"

When Lenore Schaefer, a ballroom dancer, tried to get on the *Tonight Show,* she was told she was "too young": she was in her early 90s. When she turned 101, she made it. But even at that age, Lenore is no longer unusual in our society. Today, people over 100 constitute, proportionately, the country's fastest-growing age group. They are part of the increasing proportion of the population of the United States that is composed of older people (Himes 2001; Rimer 1998).

As Figure 38-1 shows, in the future, an increasing proportion of the U.S. population will be composed of older people. This trend is expected to continue well into the 21st century, as the mortality rate declines and members of the postwar baby boom age. At the same time, the "oldest old"—that is, the segment of the population representing those who are age 85 or older—will grow at an even faster rate.

Compared with the rest of the population, the elderly are more likely to be female than male. Men tend to have higher death rates than women at every age. By old age, women outnumber men by a ratio of 3 to 2. The gap widens with advancing age, so that among the oldest old, the ratio is 5 to 2.

The elderly are also more likely than others to be White: about 80 percent of the elderly are White and non-Hispanic. Although this segment of the population is becoming more racially and ethnically diverse, the higher death rates of racial and ethnic minorities, together with the continuing immigration of younger Latinos and Asians, is likely to keep it more White than the nation as a whole. Yet the overall pattern of an increasingly diversified population will show up among older

Americans. As the projections in Figure 38-2 show, as the 21st century advances, non-Whites and Latinos will make up an increasing proportion of those who are 65 and over.

Finally, the elderly are more likely than the rest of the population to live in certain states. The highest proportions of older people are found in Florida, Pennsylvania, Rhode Island, Iowa, West Virginia, and Arkansas. However, that will soon change. In 2010, Florida was the state most populated by the elderly, with 17.4 percent of the population over age 65. Yet as Figure 38-3 shows, in less than 20 years, more than half the states will have an even greater proportion of elderly people than Florida does now.

The graying of the United States is a phenomenon that can no longer be ignored, either by social scientists or by government policymakers. Advocates for the elderly have spoken out on a wide range of issues. Politicians court the votes of older people, since they are the age group most likely to register and vote. In fact, in the 2010 general election, people over 65 made up 24 percent of those who voted, compared to 6 percent for those under 25 (Bureau of the Census 2012c: Table A-1).

Wealth and Income

There is significant variation in wealth and poverty among the nation's older people. Some individuals and couples find themselves poor in part because of fixed pensions and skyrocketing health care costs (see Chapter 17). Nevertheless, as a group, older people in the United States are neither homogeneous nor poor. The typical elderly person enjoys a standard of living that is much higher now than at any point in the nation's past. Class differences among the elderly remain evident, but tend to narrow somewhat: those older people who enjoyed middle-class incomes while younger tend to remain better off after retirement, but less so than before (Denise Smith and Tillipman 2000).

To some extent, older people owe their overall improved standard of living to a greater accumulation of wealth—in the form of home ownership, private pensions, and other financial assets. Indeed, the median net worth of the elderly has increased by 42 percent over the past 25 years. But much of the

FIGURE 38-1 **Percentage of U.S. Population in Selected Age Groups, 1970–2050**

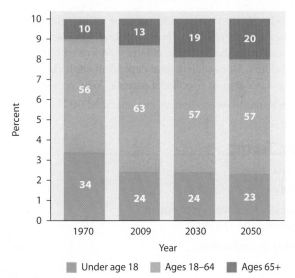

Source: Population Reference Bureau analysis of Bureau of the Census data, in Jacobsen et al. 2011:3.

FIGURE 38-2 **Minority Population Age 65 and Older, 2012–2050**

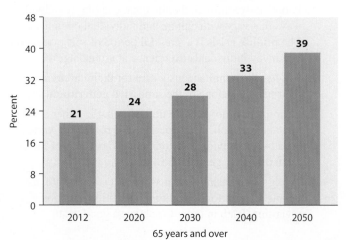

Source: Bureau of the Census in Ortman et al. 2014:11.

FIGURE 38-3 **Twenty-Eight Floridas by 2030**

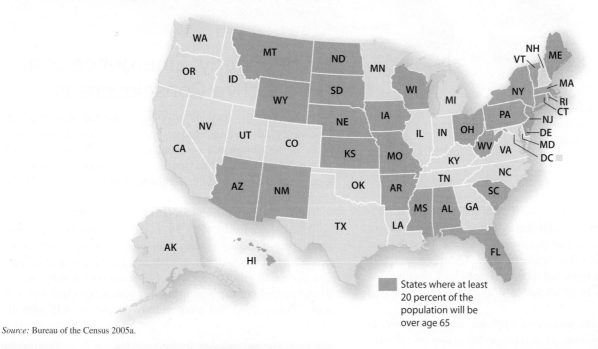

States where at least 20 percent of the population will be over age 65

Source: Bureau of the Census 2005a.

improvement is due to more generous Social Security benefits. While modest when compared with other countries' pension programs, Social Security nevertheless provides 39 percent of all income received by older people in the United States. Still, about 9 percent of the nation's elderly population lives below the federal government's poverty line. At the extremes of poverty are those groups who were more likely to be poor at earlier points in the life cycle: female-headed households and racial and ethnic minorities (Richard Fry et al. 2011; He et al. 2005).

Viewed from a conflict perspective, it is not surprising that older women experience a double burden; the same is true of elderly members of racial and ethnic minorities. For example, in 2012 the proportion of older Latinos with incomes below the poverty level (20.8 percent) was almost three times as large as the proportion of older White non-Hispanics (6.8 percent). Moreover, 18.3 percent of older African Americans fell below the federal government's poverty line (DeNavas-Walt et al. 2012: Table B-2).

Ageism

Physician Robert Butler (1990) became concerned 49 years ago when he learned that a housing development near his home in metropolitan Washington, D.C., barred the elderly. Butler coined the term **ageism** to refer to prejudice and discrimination based on a person's age. Research shows that in the United States, a large majority of people over age 60—84 percent—have experienced ageism, from insulting jokes to outright disrespect (Roscigno 2010:7).

Ageism is especially difficult for the old, because at least youthful recipients of prejudice know that in time they will be "old enough." For many, old age

symbolizes disease. While physical condition does weaken with age, today's older people are in much better shape than their counterparts even one generation ago. In any event, most jobs today require little brawn. Studies also indicate that older workers are better at jobs that require personnel skills, which comprise a growing proportion of the jobs available. In what has been termed the *silver collar economy,* more companies are hiring people 65 and older because they believe these workers are reliable and productive (*The Economist* 2011d; Trumbull 2006).

Competition in the Labor Force

Although paid employment is not typical after age 65, it is becoming increasingly common (see Figure 38-4). Concerned over their pension benefits, more and more people who are healthy enough to continue working have decided to postpone their retirement. Their decision has further eroded job opportunities for younger workers, already handicapped by the highest unemployment rates in a generation. Unfortunately, some people view older workers as "job stealers"—a biased judgment similar to that directed against illegal immigrants—instead of as experienced contributors to the labor force. Moreover, unemployed workers in their 50s find that potential employers rarely give them serious consideration. These difficulties not only intensify age conflict but lead to age discrimination as well (Jacobsen et al. 2011).

From the 1940s through the early 1990s, the proportion of people over age 65 who were working declined steadily, and the rate dropped faster for men than for women. Since the 1990s this pattern has reversed for both men and women. In little more than a decade, the percentage of older people who are working doubled.

FIGURE 38-4 Labor Force by Age, 2000—2050

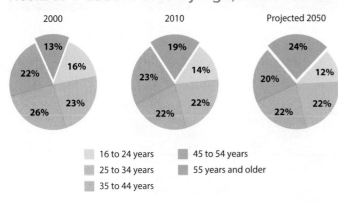

2000	2010	Projected 2050

16 to 24 years   45 to 54 years
25 to 34 years   55 years and older
35 to 44 years

Source: Toossi 2012: 11.

Even more remarkable is the shift of older workers to full-time employment. In 2002, for the first time, more older people were working full-time than part-time. This trend has continued through the recession that began in 2008. Older workers face high unemployment rates, but more and more have continued to seek work, perhaps to offset losses to their retirement savings (see Figure 38-4).

As the baby boom generation ages, the share of workers in the 55-years-and-older age group is expected to increase dramatically, at least through 2018. Despite this trend, the participation rates of older workers are not expected to reach the working levels of those in their 40s (Bureau of Labor Statistics 2008b, 2010; Toossi 2012).

The federal Age Discrimination in Employment Act (ADEA), which went into effect in 1968, was passed to protect workers who are age 40 and older from being fired because of their age and replaced with younger workers, who would presumably receive lower salaries. The Supreme Court strengthened federal protection against age discrimination in 1996, ruling unanimously that such lawsuits can be successful even if an older worker is replaced by someone who is older than 40. Consequently, firing a 65-year-old employee to make way for a 45-year-old can be construed as age discrimination.

While firing people simply because they are old violates federal law, courts have upheld the right to lay off older workers for economic reasons. Critics contend that later, the same firms hire young, cheaper workers to replace experienced older workers. When economic growth began to slow in 2008 and companies cut back on their workforces, complaints of age bias grew sharply as older workers began to suspect they were bearing a disproportionate share of the layoffs. Little wonder, then, in the wake of a bad economy, that workers are approaching their retirement warily. A national survey showed that only 14 percent of workers are confident of living comfortably in retirement, compared with 27 percent in 2007, before the recent recession (Ruth Helman et al. 2012:7; Roscigno 2010).

Given recent legislative and legal advances, has the climate changed significantly for older workers? Box 38-1 presents several studies that have attempted to assess the extent of ageism, both in everyday life and in hiring.

use your sociological imagination

How likely are you to watch a television show that is based on older characters who spend a lot of time together? Explain.

The Elderly: Emergence of a Collective Consciousness

During the 1960s, students at colleges and universities across the country, advocating "student power," collectively demanded a role in the governance of educational institutions. In the following decade, many older people became aware that *they* were being treated as second-class citizens and turned to collective action.

The largest organization representing the nation's elderly is the AARP, founded in 1958 by a retired school principal who was having difficulty getting insurance because of age prejudice. Many of the AARP's services involve discounts and insurance for its 40 million members (43 percent of Americans age 50 and older), but the organization is also a powerful lobbying group. Recognizing that many elderly people are still gainfully

The AARP is a major voice for the elderly. By featuring Bruce Springsteen (born in 1949) on the cover of its widely distributed magazine, the organization is signaling a desire to represent the younger members of the older generation, as well as to portray the active lives many older people lead.

BOX 38-1

Research Today

Elderspeak and Other Signs of Ageism

"Who did you used to be?" This comment reveals an unflattering assumption about what happens to people when they grow old. Unfortunately, such remarks are far too frequent. In fact, condescending language is so often directed at elderly people that gerontologists have come to call it *elderspeak*.

According to scholars who have done observation research in nursing homes and retirement facilities, staff in these institutions tend to relate to the elderly residents in a manner befitting infants, calling them "dear," "good girl," and "sweetie." Medical professionals may patronize elderly patients, asking "Did you understand what I said?" or cajole them with "You don't want to upset your family, do you?" Although the people who make these remarks do not regard them as derogatory, older people find the unintended insults demoralizing.

Many older people experience ageism long before they retire. They may find that past a certain age, they will not be hired or even interviewed for a job. Yet research has shown that older workers can be an asset to employers. In response to such findings, some U.S. corporations, including Home Depot, are actively recruiting retired people.

Still, many older people have difficulty finding work, often as the result of ageism. Economist Johanna Lahey sent similar résumés for fictitious women of different ages to employers in Boston and St. Petersburg, Florida. The results were striking. In Boston,

a younger worker was 42 percent more likely than an older worker to be offered an interview for an entry-level job, such as a clerical position. In St. Petersburg, the difference was 46 percent.

To determine why the older applicants had more difficulty getting an interview, Lahey tried making them look more desirable. To prevent a 62-year-old applicant from being seen as inflexible, undependable, or out of touch, she added a certificate of completion of a recent computer course to the person's application, along with an indication of health insurance coverage. However, these "extras" had no effect on the call-back rate.

> Many older people experience ageism long before they retire. They may find that past a certain age, they will not be hired or even interviewed for a job.

This study mirrored the results of one done two decades earlier, which showed that younger applicants are significantly more welcome in the job market than older applicants. Although further research might be done, the pattern seems clear: ageism is entrenched in our society.

About 30 percent of older workers choose to remain on the job past the usual retirement age. Research shows they can be retrained in new technologies and are more dependable than younger workers.

LET'S DISCUSS

1. Have you ever worked alongside an older person? If so, did that person's age affect the way he or she did the job? In what ways?

2. Are older people the only ones who experience ageism? What signs of ageism might those who are not old experience?

Sources: Bendick et al. 1993; Charness and Villeval 2009; Freudenheim 2005; Lahey 2006; Leland 2008; Lohr 2008; Roscigno 2010; K. Williams et al. 2009.

---

employed, it has dropped its full name, American Association of *Retired* Persons (Donnelly 2007; Eggen 2009).

The potential power of the AARP is enormous. It is the third-largest voluntary association in the United States (behind only the Roman Catholic Church and the American Automobile Association), representing one out of every four registered voters in the United States. The AARP has endorsed voter registration campaigns, nursing home reforms, and pension reforms. In acknowledgment of its difficulties recruiting members of racial and ethnic minority groups, the AARP recently began a Minority Affairs Initiative. The spokeswoman for the initiative, Margaret Dixon, became the AARP's first African American president in 1996 (Birnbaum 2005).

People grow old in many different ways. Not all elderly people face the same challenges or enjoy the same resources. While the AARP lobbies to protect the elderly in general, other groups work in more specific ways. For example, the National Committee to Preserve Social Security and Medicare, founded in 1982, has successfully lobbied Congress to keep Medicare benefits for the ailing poor elderly. Other large special-interest groups represent retired federal employees, retired teachers, and retired union workers (Quadagno 2014).

Still another manifestation of the new awareness of older people is the formation of organizations for elderly homosexuals. One such group, Services and Advocacy for GLBT Elders (SAGE), was established in New York City in 1977 and now oversees a nationwide network of community groups, as well as affiliates in Canada and Germany. Like traditional senior citizens' groups, SAGE sponsors workshops, classes, dances, and food deliveries to the homebound. Throughout the United States, retirement homes are self-identifying themselves as seeking older lesbian, gay, bisexual and transgender couples. Some of these facilities are gay owned, but that is not necessarily true (Chris Lehman 2012; SAGE 2012).

The elderly in the United States are better off today both financially and physically than ever before. Many of them have strong financial assets and medical care packages that will meet almost any health need. But as we have seen, a significant segment is impoverished, faced with the prospect of declining health and mounting medical bills. And some older people must now add being aged to a lifetime of disadvantage. Like people in all other stages of the life course, the aged constitute a diverse group in the United States and around the world.

On August 4, 1993, Dr. Jack Kevorkian, a retired pathologist, helped a 30-year-old Michigan man with Lou Gehrig's disease to commit suicide in a van. The patient died after inhaling carbon monoxide through a mask designed by Dr. Kevorkian; in doing so, he became the 17th person to commit suicide with Kevorkian's assistance. Kevorkian was openly challenging a Michigan law (aimed at him) that makes it a felony—punishable by up to four years in jail—to assist in a suicide. Since then Kevorkian has assisted in numerous other suicides, but not until he did it on television in 1998 did the charges brought against him result in his imprisonment for second-degree murder. Kevorkian completed his sentence in 2007 and died of circulatory problems in 2011.

Looking at the Issue

The issue of physician-assisted suicide is but one aspect of the larger debate in the United States and other countries over the ethics of suicide and euthanasia. The term **euthanasia** has been defined as the "act of bringing about the death of a hopelessly ill and suffering person in a relatively quick and painless way for reasons of mercy" (Council on Ethical and Judicial Affairs, American Medical Association 1992:229). This type of mercy killing reminds us of the ideal of the "good death" discussed in Module 37. The debate over euthanasia and assisted suicide often focuses on cases involving older people, although it can involve younger adults with terminal and degenerative diseases, or even children.

National surveys show that public opinion on this controversial practice is divided. In 2010, 70 percent of respondents said that a physician should be legally permitted to end a patient's life if both the patient and the patient's family make such a request (Angus Reid Public Opinion, 2010).

Currently, public policy in the United States does not permit *active euthanasia* (such as a deliberate injection of lethal drugs into a terminally ill patient) or physician-assisted suicide. Although suicide itself is no longer a crime, assisting suicide is illegal in at least 29 states. There is greater legal tolerance for *passive euthanasia* (such as disconnecting life-support equipment from a comatose patient).

Applying Sociology

Many societies are known to have practiced *senilicide*—"killing of the aged"—because of extreme difficulties in providing basic necessities such as food and shelter. In a study of the treatment of elderly people in 41 nonindustrialized societies, Anthony Glascock (1990) found some form of "death-hastening" behavior in 21 of them. Killing of elderly people was evident in 14 of the societies; abandoning them was evident in 8. Typically, death hastening occurs when older people become decrepit and are viewed as already dead. In these nonindustrialized cultures it is open and socially approved. Family members generally make the decisions, often after open consultation with those who are about to die.

Although formal norms against euthanasia are still strict, informal norms seem to permit mercy killings. According to an estimate by the American Hospital Association, as many as 70 percent of all deaths in the United States are quietly negotiated, with patients, family members, and physicians agreeing not to use life-support technology. In an informal poll of internists, one in five reported that he or she had assisted or helped cause the death of a patient. In a period in which AIDS-related deaths are common, an AIDS underground is known to share information and assistance regarding suicide (N. Gibbs 1993; Martinez 1993).

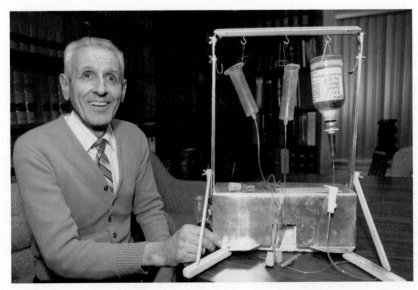

Dr. Jack Kevorkian with the apparatus that administered a lethal injection to those who wanted assistance in committing suicide.

—Continued

Conflict theorists ask questions about the values raised by such decisions. By endorsing physician-assisted suicide, are we devaluing the disabled through an acceptance of their premature death? Critics note that we are all only temporarily able-bodied; disease or a speeding automobile can place any one of us among the disabled. By establishing a precedent for ending the lives of selected disabled people, we may unwittingly contribute to negative social views and labeling of all disabled people. Further reflecting the conflict perspective, gerontologist Elizabeth Markson (1992:6) argues that the "powerless, poor or undesirable are at special risk of being 'encouraged' to choose assisted death."

Despite these concerns, research to date shows little bias. In studies of physician-assisted suicide in Oregon and the Netherlands, researchers looked at how implementation of the controversial policy might affect people who were vulnerable because of their disability, age, mental health, or race and ethnicity. People with AIDS proved to be the only vulnerable group with a heightened use of physician-assisted suicide. Overall, those people who died with a doctor's help were more likely to be socially, economically, and educationally privileged than to be particularly vulnerable (Battin et al. 2007).

Initiating Policy

In the industrialized world, euthanasia is legal and widely accepted in only three countries: the Netherlands, Belgium, and Switzerland. Unlike the Netherlands and Belgium, Switzerland allows foreigners to be euthanized. While physician-assisted suicide is accepted by the public in all three countries, the "suicide tourism" that occurs in Switzerland is controversial (Wesley Smith 2011).

In the United States, the first state to allow assisted suicide was Oregon, where the Death with Dignity Act became law in 1997. Through 2012, nearly 700 terminally ill Oregonians had taken their lives with the assistance of a physician. President George W. Bush's administration had made an unsuccessful attempt to stop the prescription of lethal drugs to terminally ill patients in Oregon. In 2006, the Supreme Court ruled 6–3 that the federal government had overstepped its authority in punishing doctors in Oregon who had helped terminally ill patients to end their lives. Subsequently, assisted suicide became legal in Montana, Vermont, and Washington State. Some local courts and state legislatures are also moving to legalize the practice, despite strong opposition (Bendavid 2013).

Advances in technology now allow us to prolong life in ways that were unimaginable decades ago. But should people be forced or expected to prolong lives that are unbearably painful, or that are in effect "lifeless"? Unfortunately, medical and technological advances cannot provide answers to these complex ethical, legal, and political questions.

TAKE THE ISSUE WITH YOU

1. Why do you think "death-hastening" behavior is common in nonindustrialized countries?
2. In what ways are conflict theory and disengagement theory relevant to the debate over the "right to die"?
3. Do you think someone should be allowed to choose to die? Why or why not?

MODULE 38 | Recap and Review

Summary

An increasing proportion of the population of the United States is composed of older people.

1. **Ageism** reflects a deep uneasiness about growing old on the part of younger people.
2. The AARP is a powerful lobbying group that backs legislation to benefit senior citizens.
3. The "right to die" often entails physician-assisted suicide, a controversial issue worldwide.

Thinking Critically

1. Discuss ageism from a conflict perspective.
2. What social, economic, and political changes are likely to result from the aging of the U.S. population?

Key Terms

Ageism

Euthanasia

Mastering This Chapter

taking sociology with you

1 Think about your grandparents: Would you describe them as active or disengaged? Do you think their social class has had an impact on the way they have aged? Explain. How well have they adjusted to retirement?

2 What public agency or organization—the senior center, council on aging—is responsible for serving seniors in your community? Visit the site and learn about the programs offered there. Then relate your findings to what you learned in this chapter.

3 Find out the percentage of people age 65 and over who live in your community. How does that percentage compare to your state or to the United States as a whole? If you can, determine whether residents in this age bracket are clustered in particular areas. Are you aware of any naturally occurring retirement communities (NORCs) where you live?

key terms

Activity theory An interactionist theory of aging that suggests that those elderly people who remain active and socially involved will be best adjusted.

Ageism Prejudice and discrimination based on a person's age.

Disengagement theory A functionalist theory of aging that suggests that society and the aging individual mutually sever many of their relationships.

Euthanasia The act of bringing about the death of a hopelessly ill and suffering person in a relatively quick and painless way for reasons of mercy.

Gerontology The scientific study of the sociological and psychological aspects of aging and the problems of the aged.

Hospice care Treatment of the terminally ill in their own homes, or in special hospital units or other facilities, with the goal of helping them to die easily, without pain.

Midlife crisis A stressful period of self-evaluation that begins at about age 40.

Naturally occurring retirement community (NORC) An area that has gradually become an informal center for senior citizens.

Sandwich generation The generation of adults who simultaneously try to meet the competing needs of their parents and their children.

self-quiz

Read each question carefully and then select the best answer.

1. Activity theory is associated with the
   a. functionalist perspective.
   b. conflict perspective.
   c. interactionist perspective.
   d. labeling perspective.

2. What is the one crucial difference between older people and other subordinate groups, such as racial and ethnic minorities or women?
   a. Older people do not experience unequal treatment in employment.
   b. Older people have a strong sense of group solidarity and other groups do not.
   c. All of us who live long enough will eventually assume the ascribed status of being an older person.
   d. Older people are generally married to others of comparable age and other minorities do not marry within their group.

3. Which field of study was originally developed in the 1930s as an increasing number of social scientists became aware of the plight of the elderly?
   a. sociology
   b. gerontology
   c. gerontocracy
   d. senilicide

4. Which sociological perspective is most likely to emphasize the important role of social networks in providing life satisfaction for elderly people?
   a. functionalist perspective
   b. conflict perspective
   c. interactionist perspective
   d. labeling theory

5. Elaine Cumming and William Henry introduced an explanation of the impact of aging known as
   a. disengagement theory.
   b. activity theory.
   c. labeling theory.
   d. the contact hypothesis.

6. According to psychologist Elisabeth Kübler-Ross, the first stage of the experience of dying that a person may undergo is
   a. denial.
   b. anger.
   c. depression.
   d. bargaining.

7. Which of the following statements about the elderly is correct?
   a. Being old is a master status.

b. Once people are labeled as "old," the designation has a major impact on how others perceive them, and even on how they view themselves.

c. Negative stereotypes of the elderly contribute to their position as a minority group subject to discrimination.

d. all of the above

8. The text points out that the model of five basic properties of a minority or subordinate group can be applied to older people in the United States. Which of the following is *not* one of those basic properties?

a. Older people experience unequal treatment in employment and may face prejudice and discrimination.

b. Statistically, the elderly represent a majority.

c. Membership in this group is involuntary.

d. Older people have a strong sense of group solidarity.

9. Which of the following theories argues that elderly people have essentially the same need for social interaction as any other group and that those who remain active and socially involved will be best adjusted?

a. conflict theory

b. functionalist theory

c. activity theory

d. disengagement theory

10. According to your text, which of the following statements is true?

a. Functionalists portray the elderly as being socially isolated, with reduced social roles.

b. Interactionists see older people as being involved in new networks of people and in changing social roles.

c. Conflict theorists regard older people as being victimized by social structure, with their social roles relatively unchanged but devalued.

d. all of the above

11. The elderly are _____ regarded in the traditional Sherpa (Tibet) culture.

12. In keeping with the _____ perspective of sociology, disengagement theory emphasizes that a society's stability is ensured when social roles are passed on from one generation to another.

13. The final phase of retirement, according to Robert Atchley, is the _____ phase, which begins when the person can no longer engage in basic, day-to-day activities such as self-care and housework.

14. _____ theorists argue that both the disengagement and the activity perspectives often ignore the impact of social class in the lives of elderly people.

15. The fastest-growing age group in the United States is people over age _____.

16. _____ is the scientific study of the sociological and psychological aspects of aging and the problems of the aged. It originated in the 1930s as an increasing number of social scientists became aware of the plight of elderly people.

17. Based on a study of elderly people in good health and relatively comfortable economic circumstances, _____ theory suggests that society and the aging individual mutually sever many of their relationships.

18. During the late 1990s, social scientists focused on the _____ _____—adults who simultaneously try to meet the competing needs of their parents and their children.

19. In 2010, _____ was the state most populated by the elderly, with 17.4 percent of the population over age 65.

20. Physician Robert Butler coined the term _____ to refer to prejudice and discrimination based on a person's age.

13

The Family and Human Sexuality

In Ann Arbor, Michigan, several generations of Dulins celebrate their 18th family reunion. Despite marital strains and geographical separation, countless families come together every year to reaffirm the importance of this social institution.

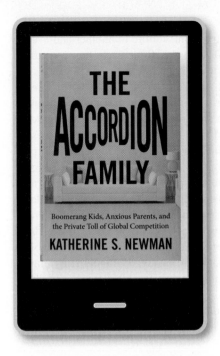

Do you know adult children in their 20s and 30s who continue to live at home or have returned to their parents' home? Are you one of them?

Some people call these families "accordion families" because they expand and contract as the adult children come and go.

" William Rollo and his wife arrived in Newton [Massachusetts] in 1989 after having lived in Seattle, Philadelphia, and Summit, New Jersey. A Brooklyn native, William married Janet at the age of twenty-two and set about completing a residency in podiatry. Their eldest son, John, grew up in Newton and did well enough in high school to attend the liberal arts college Williams, one of the nation's most selective. Even so, he beat it home after graduating and has lived with his parents for several years while preparing to apply to graduate school. "A lot of my friends are living at home to save money," he explains.

Tight finances are not all that is driving John's living arrangements. The young man had choices and decided he could opt for more of the ones he wanted if he sheltered under his parents' roof. John is saving money from his job in an arts foundation for a three-week trip to Africa, where he hopes to work on a mobile health-care project in a rural region. It's a strategic choice designed to increase his chances to be accepted into Harvard University's competitive graduate program in public health.

John needs to build up his credentials if he wants to enter a school like that. To get from here to there, he needs more experience working with patients in clinics or out in the field. It takes big bucks to travel to exotic locations, and a master's degree will cost him dearly, too. In order to make good on his aspirations, John needs his parents to cover him for the short run. On his own, John could pay the rent on an apartment, especially if he had roommates. What he

On his own, John could pay the rent on an apartment, especially if he had roommates. What he can't afford is to pay for both privacy and travel, to support himself and save for his hoped-for future.

can't afford is to pay for both privacy *and* travel, to support himself *and* save for his hoped-for future. Autonomy turns out to be the lesser priority, so he has returned to the bedroom he had before he left for college, and there he stays.

John sees few drawbacks to this arrangement. His parents don't nag him or curtail his freedom. Janet wonders if they should ask him to pay rent, to bring him down to earth a bit and teach him some life skills, like budgeting. William is not so sure. He enjoys his son's company and was happy when he moved back into his old bedroom. Having a son around to talk to is a joy, particularly since John's younger brother is out of the house now, studying at the University of Vermont. That empty nest has refilled, and thank goodness, says William, rather quietly.

If John had no goals, no sense of direction, William would not be at ease with this "boomerang arrangement." Hiding in the basement playing video games would not do. Happily, that is not on John's agenda. William is glad to help his son realize his ambitions. He approves of John's career plans and doesn't really care if they don't involve making a handsome living. What really matters is that the work *means* something. It will help to remake the world, something William has not felt he could contribute to very directly in his work. Having a son who can reach a bit higher—if not financially, then morally—is an ambition worth paying for.

And it will cost this family, big time. William and Janet have invested nearly two hundred thousand dollars in John's education already. They will need to do more if John is going to become a public health specialist. They are easily looking at another fifty thousand dollars, even if John attends a local graduate program and continues to live with them. Fortunately, there are excellent options—some of the nation's finest—close by. Whatever it costs, they reason, the sacrifice is worth it. "

(*Newman 2012: xv–xvii*)

I n this excerpt from *The Accordion Family: Boomerang Kids, Anxious Parents, and the Private Toll of Global Competition*, sociologist Katherine S. Newman describes one of the major trends in family life today. In the United States as well as in many other countries, parenthood is being extended as single adult children remain at home, or return home after college or a brief foray into the job market. In the United States in 2012, 14 percent of men and women between the ages of 25 and 34

lived with their parents. Some of those adult children were still pursuing an education, but in many cases financial difficulties underlay their living arrangements. For younger job seekers, employment is often short term or low paying—not secure enough to support a separate household. And with many marriages now ending in divorce—most commonly in the first seven years—divorced sons and daughters often return to their parents, sometimes with their own children in tow (Vespa et al. 2013).

Whether we refer to such combined households as "accordion families," as Newman does, or to the returning adult children as "boomerang kids," this trend is an example of the increasing complexity of family life. The family of today is not what it was a century ago, or even a generation ago. New roles, new gender distinctions, new child-rearing patterns have all combined to create new forms of family life. Today, for example, more and more women are taking the breadwinner's role, whether married or as a single parent. Blended families—the result of divorce and remarriage—are almost the norm. And many people are seeking intimate relationships without being married, whether in gay partnerships or in cohabiting arrangements (Cherlin 2009, 2011). The word *family* is inadequate to describe some of these arrangements, including cohabiting partners, same-sex marriages, and single-parent households. In 2011, the nation crossed a major threshold: the majority of births to women under age 30 occurred outside of marriage (Cherlin 2011; Wildsmith et al. 2011).

These modules address family and human sexuality in the United States as well as other parts of the world. As we will see, family patterns differ from one culture to another and even within the same culture. Despite the differences, however, the family is universal—found in every culture.

What are families in different parts of the world like? How do people select their mates? When a marriage fails, how does the divorce affect the children? What are the alternatives to the nuclear family, and how prevalent are they? In these modules we will look at the family and intimate relationships from the functionalist, conflict, interactionist, and feminist points of view. We'll examine variations in marital patterns and family life, including child rearing, paying particular attention to the increasing numbers of people in dual-income and single-parent families. We'll examine divorce in the United States and consider diverse lifestyles such as cohabitation and marriage without children. We'll conclude by considering the complexity of human sexual behavior, and the growing acceptance of lesbian and gay relationships. Finally, in the Social Policy section we'll confront the controversial issue of gay marriage.

MODULE 39 | **Global View of the Family**

Among Tibetans, a woman may be married simultaneously to more than one man, usually brothers. This system allows sons to share the limited amount of good land. Among the Betsileo of Madagascar, a man has multiple wives, each one living in a different village where he cultivates rice. Wherever he has the best rice field, that wife is considered his first or senior wife. Among the Yanomami of Brazil and Venezuela, it is considered proper to have sexual relations with your opposite-sex cousins if they are the children of your mother's brother or your father's sister. But if your opposite-sex cousins are the children of your mother's sister or your father's brother, the same practice is considered to be incest (Haviland et al. 2008; Kottak 2011).

Universal Principles

As these examples illustrate, there are many variations in the family from culture to culture. Yet the family as a social institution exists in all cultures. A **family** can be defined as a set of people related by blood, marriage, some other agreed-on relationship, or adoption, who share the primary responsibility for reproduction and caring for members of society. Moreover, certain general principles concerning its composition, kinship patterns, and authority patterns are universal.

Composition: What Is the Family?

If we were to take our information on what a family is from what we see on television, we might come up with some strange scenarios. The media do not always present a realistic view of the family. Moreover, many people still think of the family in very narrow terms—as a married couple and their unmarried children living together, like the family in the old *Cosby Show*. However,

this is but one type of family, what sociologists refer to as a **nuclear family.** The term *nuclear family* is well chosen, since this type of family serves as the nucleus, or core, on which larger family groups are built.

Most people in the United States see the nuclear family as the preferred family arrangement. Yet by 2000, only about a third of the nation's family households fit this model. The proportion of households in the United States that is composed of married couples with children at home has decreased steadily over the past 40 years and is expected to continue shrinking. At the same time, the number of single-parent households has increased (Figure 39-1).

A family in which relatives—such as grandparents, aunts, or uncles—live in the same home as parents and their children is known as an **extended family.** Although not common, such living arrangements do exist in the United States. The structure of the extended family offers certain advantages over that of the nuclear family. Crises such as death, divorce, and illness put less strain on family members, since more people can provide assistance and emotional support. In addition, the extended family constitutes a larger economic unit than the nuclear family. If the family is engaged in a common enterprise—a farm or a small business—the additional family members may represent the difference between prosperity and failure.

In considering these different family types, we have limited ourselves to the form of marriage that is characteristic of the United States—monogamy. The term **monogamy** describes a form of marriage in which an individual has only one partner. Until recently, the societal expectation was that the couple would be a man and a woman. Increasingly, however, same-sex couples are entering legal marriages. Regardless, observers, noting the high rate of divorce in the United States, have suggested that "serial monogamy" is a more accurate description of the form marriage takes in this country. In **serial monogamy,** a person may have several spouses in a lifetime, but only one spouse at a time.

Some cultures allow an individual to have several husbands or wives simultaneously. This form of marriage is known as

FIGURE 39-1 U.S. Households by Family Type, 1970–2012

1970

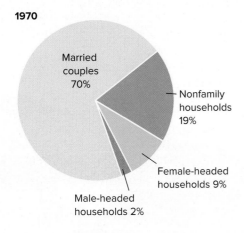

Married couples 70%

Nonfamily households 19%

Female-headed households 9%

Male-headed households 2%

2012

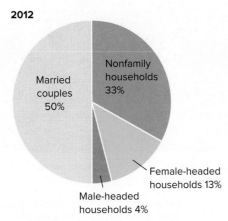

Married couples 50%

Nonfamily households 33%

Female-headed households 13%

Male-headed households 4%

Note: Nonfamily households include women and men living alone or exclusively with people to whom they are not related, as in a college dormitory, homeless shelter, or military base.
Sources: Bureau of the Census 1981:2; Vespa et al. 2013:5, also Table HH1.

polygamy. In fact, most societies throughout the world, past and present, have preferred polygamy to monogamy. According to a mid-20th century analysis of 565 societies, polygamy was preferred in more than 80 percent. While polygamy declined steadily through most of the 20th century, in at least five countries in Africa 20 percent of men still have polygamous marriages (Murdock 1949, 1957; Population Reference Bureau 1996).

There are two basic types of polygamy. According to Murdock, the most common—endorsed by the majority of cultures he sampled—is *polygyny*. **Polygyny** refers to the marriage of a man to more than one woman at the same time. The wives are often sisters, who are expected to hold similar values and have already had experience sharing a household. In polygynous societies, relatively few men actually have multiple spouses. Most individuals live in monogamous families; having multiple wives is viewed as a mark of status.

The other principal variation of polygamy is **polyandry,** in which a woman may have more than one husband at the same time. Such is the case in the culture of the Nyinba, described in Box 39-1. Polyandry, however, is exceedingly rare today, though it is accepted in some extremely poor societies. Like many other societies, polyandrous cultures devalue the social worth of women (Zeitzen 2008).

By the end of the 20th century, polygamy had been relegated to the margins of U.S. society, and to discussion of other cultures. Recently, however, it has resurfaced. As the concept of marriage is redefined to include same-sex marriage, Mormon fundamentalists and Muslims who practice polygamy have asked why it should not also embrace polygamy. Some support this perspective; others suspect that the issue is being raised by those who oppose same-sex marriage. This is certainly not the first time that family cultural practices have collided with social norms (Keenan 2013).

Kinship Patterns: To Whom Are We Related?

Many of us can trace our roots by looking at a family tree or by listening to elderly family members talk about their lives—and about the lives of ancestors who died long before we were born. Yet a person's lineage is more than simply a personal history; it also reflects societal patterns that govern descent. In every culture, children encounter relatives to whom they are expected to show an emotional attachment. The state of being related to others is called **kinship.** Kinship is culturally learned, however, and is not totally determined by biological or marital ties. For example, adoption creates a kinship tie that is legally acknowledged and socially accepted.

The family and the kin group are not necessarily one and the same. Whereas the family is a household unit, kin do not always live together or function as a collective body on a daily basis. Kin groups include aunts, uncles, cousins, in-laws, and so forth. In a society such as the United States, the kinship group may come together only rarely, for a wedding or funeral. However, kinship ties frequently create obligations and responsibilities. We may feel compelled to assist our kin, and we may feel free to call on them for many types of aid, including loans and babysitting.

How do we identify kinship groups? The principle of descent assigns people to kinship groups according to their relationship to a mother or father. There are three primary ways of determining descent. The United States follows the system of **bilateral descent,** which means that both sides of a person's family are regarded as equally important. For example, no higher value is given to the brothers of one's father than to the brothers of one's mother.

Most societies—according to George Murdock, 64 percent—give preference to one side of the family or the other in tracing descent. In **patrilineal** (from the Latin *pater,* "father") **descent,** only the father's relatives are significant in terms of property, inheritance, and emotional ties. Conversely, in societies that favor **matrilineal** (from the Latin *mater,* "mother") **descent,** only the mother's relatives are significant.

New forms of reproductive technology will necessitate a new way of looking at kinship. Today, a combination of biological and social processes can "create" a family member, requiring that more distinctions be made about who is related to whom.

 use your **sociological imagination**

In your family, which relatives do you have a significant relationship with? Which do you hardly ever see? Explain the reasons for the difference in relationships.

One Wife, Many Husbands: The Nyinba

The Nyinba culture of Nepal and Tibet is an agrarian society located in the remote valleys of the Himalaya Mountains, more than 9,000 feet above sea level. Despite the Nyinba's isolation, they have been closely studied. Scholars from around the world have traveled to the Himalayas to observe this people, one of the few remaining cultures on earth to practice polyandry.

In the physically challenging environment of the Himalayas, polyandry seems to work well. Because the land and climate make it

> Favoritism toward a particular husband is frowned on by the Nyinba. Thus, it is the wife's responsibility to see that each husband shares time with her in a rotational fashion.

A Nyinba family threshing buckwheat in the field. At left is the wife; in the center, one of her five husbands (with raised mallet); at right, her mother-in-law.

difficult to sustain crops, farming is labor-intensive: many Nyinba laborers must work the fields to support a single family. Thus, a typical marriage involving three brothers and one wife provides the necessary adult male laborers, yet minimizes the number of offspring—a necessity in a place where the food supply is limited.

While an outsider might suppose that Nyinba women dominate their families, in fact authority and inheritance rest on the husband or son. The birth of a son is celebrated; the birth of a daughter, regardless of who might be the father, brings disappointment. Paternity appears to be a nonissue in this culture, since households are shared by brothers from the same family. The literal head of the household is the oldest brother,

who typically chooses a wife from outside his extended family.

Favoritism toward a particular husband is frowned on by the Nyinba. Thus, it is the wife's responsibility to see that each husband shares time with her in a rotational fashion. Often, over the morning meal, she will indicate which husband will sleep with her that night. To avoid any confusion, the chosen husband will place his shoes outside her bedroom door.

As in any society (for example, the United States), not all Nyinba households conform to the social norm. If a family has only one son, he must of necessity marry monogamously—an unfortunate outcome in

this society. If a wife is unable to have children, a second wife, typically her sister or cousin, may be welcomed into the marriage.

LET'S DISCUSS

1. Why would a monogamous marriage be considered an unfortunate one in the Nyinba culture?

2. What might be some other ways for a society to handle the physical constraints of life in a mountainous terrain?

Sources: Kelly 2012; N. Levine 1988; Stockard 2002; Zeitzen 2008.

Authority Patterns: Who Rules?

Imagine that you have recently married and must begin to make decisions about the future of your new family. You and your spouse face many questions. Where will you live? How will you furnish your home? Who will do the cooking, the shopping, the cleaning? Whose friends will be invited to dinner? Each time a decision must be made, an issue is raised: Who has the power to make the decision? In simple terms, who rules the family? Conflict theorists examine these questions in the context of traditional gender stratification, under which men have held a dominant position over women.

Societies vary in the way power is distributed within the family. A society that expects males to dominate in all family decision making is termed a **patriarchy.** In patriarchal societies, such as Iran, the eldest male often wields the greatest power, although wives are expected to be treated with respect and kindness. An Iranian woman's status is typically defined by her relationship to a male relative, usually as a wife or daughter. In many patriarchal societies, women find it more difficult to obtain a divorce than a man does. In contrast, in a **matriarchy,** women have greater authority than men. Matriarchies, which are very uncommon, emerged among Native American tribal societies and in nations

Although spouses in an egalitarian family may not share all their decisions, they regard themselves as equals. This pattern of authority is becoming more common in the United States.

in which men were absent for long periods because of warfare or food-gathering expeditions (Farr 1999).

In a third type of authority pattern, the **egalitarian family,** spouses are regarded as equals. That does not mean, however, that all decisions are shared in such families. Wives may hold authority in some spheres, husbands in others. Many sociologists believe the egalitarian family has begun to replace the patriarchal family as the social norm in the United States.

● Sociological Perspectives on the Family

Do we really need the family? Over a century ago, Friedrich Engels ([1884] 1959), a colleague of Karl Marx, described the family as the ultimate source of social inequality because of its role in the transfer of power, property, and privilege. More recently, conflict theorists have argued that the family contributes to societal injustice, denies women opportunities that are extended to men, and limits freedom in sexual expression and

mate selection. In contrast, the functionalist view focuses on the ways in which the family gratifies the needs of its members and contributes to social stability. The interactionist view considers the intimate, face-to-face relationships that occur in the family. And the feminist approach examines the role of the wife and mother, especially in the absence of an adult male.

Functionalist Perspective

The family performs six paramount functions, first outlined 80 years ago by sociologist William F. Ogburn (Ogburn and Tibbits 1934):

1. **Reproduction.** For a society to maintain itself, it must replace dying members. In this sense, the family contributes to human survival through its function of reproduction.

2. **Protection.** In all cultures, the family assumes the ultimate responsibility for the protection and upbringing of children.

3. **Socialization.** Parents and other kin monitor a child's behavior and transmit the norms, values, and language of their culture to the child.

4. **Regulation of sexual behavior.** Sexual norms are subject to change both over time (for instance, in the customs for dating) and across cultures (compare strict Saudi Arabia to the more permissive Denmark). However, whatever the time period or cultural values of a society, standards of sexual behavior are most clearly defined within the family circle.

5. **Affection and companionship.** Ideally, the family provides members with warm and intimate relationships, helping them to feel satisfied and secure. Of course, a family member may find such rewards outside the family—from peers, in school, at work—and may even perceive the home as an unpleasant or abusive setting. Nevertheless, we expect our relatives to understand us, to care for us, and to be there for us when we need them.

6. **Provision of social status.** We inherit a social position because of the family background and reputation of our parents and siblings. The family presents the newborn child with an ascribed status based on race and ethnicity that helps to determine his or her place within society's stratification system. Moreover, family resources affect children's ability to pursue certain opportunities, such as higher education.

Traditionally, the family has fulfilled a number of other functions, such as providing religious training, education, and recreational outlets. But Ogburn argued that other social institutions have gradually assumed many of those functions. Education once took place at the family fireside; now it is the responsibility of professionals working in schools and colleges. Even the family's traditional recreational function has often been transferred to outside groups such as soccer leagues, athletic clubs, and Twitter.

Conflict Perspective

Conflict theorists view the family not as a contributor to social stability, but as a reflection of the inequality in wealth and power that is found within the larger society. Feminist and conflict theorists note that the family has traditionally legitimized and perpetuated male dominance. Throughout most of human history—and in a wide range of societies—husbands have exercised overwhelming power and authority within the family. Not until the first wave of contemporary feminism in the United States, in the mid-1800s, was there a substantial challenge to the historic status of wives and children as the legal property of husbands.

While the egalitarian family has become a more common pattern in the United States in recent decades—owing in good part to the activism of feminists beginning in the late 1960s and early 1970s—male dominance over the family has hardly disappeared. Sociologists have found that while married men are increasing their involvement in child care, their wives still perform a disproportionate amount of it. Furthermore, for every stay-at-home dad there are 38 stay-at-home moms. And unfortunately, many husbands reinforce their power and control over wives and children through acts of domestic violence (Fields 2004:11–12; Garcia-Moreno et al. 2005; Sayer et al. 2004).

Conflict theorists also view the family as an economic unit that contributes to societal injustice. The family is the basis for transferring power, property, and privilege from one generation to the next. Although the United States is widely viewed as a land of opportunity, social mobility is restricted in important ways. Children inherit the privileged or less-than-privileged social and economic status of their parents (and in some cases, of earlier generations). The social class of parents significantly influences children's socialization experiences and the degree of protection they receive. Thus, the socioeconomic status of a child's family will have a marked influence on his or her nutrition, health care, housing, educational opportunities, and in many respects, life chances as an adult. For this reason, conflict theorists argue that the family helps to maintain inequality.

Interactionist Perspective

Interactionists focus on the micro level of family and other intimate relationships. They are interested in how individuals interact with one another, whether they are cohabiting partners or longtime married couples. For example, in a study of both Black and White two-parent households, researchers found that when fathers are more involved with their children (reading to them, helping them with homework, or restricting their television viewing), the children have fewer behavior problems, get along better with others, and are more responsible (Mosley and Thomson 1995).

Another interactionist study might examine the role of the stepparent. The increased number of single parents who remarry has sparked an interest in those who are helping to raise other people's children. Studies have found that stepmothers are more likely than stepfathers to accept the blame for bad relations with their stepchildren. Interactionists theorize that stepfathers (like

Interactionists are particularly interested in the ways in which parents relate to each other and to their children. The close and loving relationship illustrated here is one of the foundations of a strong family.

most fathers) may simply be unaccustomed to interacting directly with children when the mother isn't there (Bray and Kelly 1999; F. Furstenberg and Cherlin 1991).

Feminist Perspective

Because "women's work" has traditionally focused on family life, feminist sociologists have taken a strong interest in the family as a social institution. Research on gender roles in child care and household chores has been extensive. Sociologists have looked particularly closely at how women's work outside the home impacts their child care and housework—duties Arlie Hochschild (1990, 2005, 2012) has referred to as the "second shift." Today, researchers recognize that for many women, the second shift includes the care of aging parents as well.

Feminist theorists have urged social scientists and social agencies to rethink the notion that families in which no adult male is present are automatically a cause for concern, or even dysfunctional. They have also contributed to research on single women, single-parent households, and lesbian couples. In the case of single mothers, researchers have focused on the resiliency of many such households, despite economic stress. According to Velma McBride Murray and her colleagues (2001) at the University of Georgia, such studies show that among African Americans, single mothers draw heavily on kinfolk for material resources, parenting advice, and social support. Considering feminist research on the family as a whole, one researcher concluded that the family is the "source of women's strength" (V. Taylor et al. 2009).

Finally, feminists who take the interactionist perspective stress the need to investigate neglected topics in family studies. For instance, in a growing number of dual-income households, the wife earns a higher income than the husband.

In 2005, a study of 58 married couples revealed that 26 percent of the wives earned more than their husbands. In 1981, the proportion was just 16 percent. Yet beyond individual case studies, little research has been done on how these families may differ from those in which the husband is the major breadwinner (Wills and Risman 2006).

Table 39-1 summarizes the four major theoretical perspectives on the family.

Tracking Sociological Perspectives

TABLE **39-1** SOCIOLOGICAL PERSPECTIVES ON THE FAMILY

Theoretical Perspective	Emphasis
Functionalist	The family as a contributor to social stability Roles of family members
Conflict	The family as a perpetuator of inequality Transmission of poverty or wealth across generations
Interactionist	Relationships among family members
Feminist	The family as a perpetuator of gender roles Female-headed households

MODULE **39** | **Recap and Review**

Summary

The family, in its many forms, is present in all human cultures.

1. Families vary from culture to culture and even within the same culture.

2. The structure of the **extended family** can offer certain advantages over that of the **nuclear family.**

3. Societies determine **kinship** by descent from both parents **(bilateral descent),** from the father only **(patrilineal descent),** or from the mother only **(matrilineal descent).**

4. Sociologists do not agree on whether the **egalitarian family** has replaced the patriarchal family in the United States.

5. William F. Ogburn outlined six basic functions of the family: reproduction, protection, socialization, regulation of sexual behavior, companionship, and the provision of social status.

6. Conflict theorists argue that male dominance of the family contributes to societal injustice and denies women opportunities. Interactionists focus on how individuals interact within the family and other intimate relationships. Feminists stress the need to broaden research on the family. Like conflict theorists, they see the family's role in socializing children as the primary source of sexism.

Thinking Critically

1. From a woman's point of view, what are the economic advantages and disadvantages of monogamous, polygamous, and polyandrous families? What are the advantages and disadvantages of each of these family situations for men?

2. How would functionalist, conflict, interactionist, and feminist theorists explain a polygamous family structure?

Key Terms

Bilateral descent

Egalitarian family

Extended family

Family

Kinship

Matriarchy

Matrilineal descent

Monogamy

Nuclear family

Patriarchy

Patrilineal descent

Polyandry

Polygamy

Polygyny

Serial monogamy

Currently, over 95 percent of all men and women in the United States marry at least once during their lifetimes. Historically, the most consistent aspect of family life in this country has been the high rate of marriage. In fact, despite the high rate of divorce, there are some indications of a miniboom in marriages of late.

In this module, we will examine various aspects of love, marriage, and parenthood in the United States and contrast them with cross-cultural examples. Though we're used to thinking of romance and mate selection as strictly a matter of individual preference, sociological analysis tells us that social institutions and distinctive cultural norms and values also play an important role.

Courtship and Mate Selection

In the past, most couples met their partners through family or friends in their neighborhood or workplace. Today, however, many couples meet on the Internet, through online dating services. Box 40-1 takes a look at this new meeting place.

Internet romance is only the latest courtship practice. In the central Asian nation of Uzbekistan and many other traditional cultures, courtship is defined largely through the interaction of two sets of parents, who arrange marriages for their children. Typically, a young Uzbekistani woman will be socialized to eagerly anticipate her marriage to a man whom she has met only once, when he is presented to her family at the time of the final inspection of her dowry. In the United States, in contrast, courtship is conducted primarily by individuals who have a romantic interest in each other. In our culture, courtship often requires these individuals to rely heavily on intricate games, gestures, and signals. Despite such differences, courtship—whether in the United States, Uzbekistan, or elsewhere—is influenced by the norms and values of the larger society (C. Williams 1995).

One unmistakable trend in mate selection is that the process appears to be taking longer today than in the past. A variety of factors, including concerns about financial security and personal independence, has contributed to this delay in marriage. Back in 1966, men were typically under age 23 and women under 21 when they were first married. In 2013, the average age was 29 for men and close to 27 years for women (Bureau of the Census 2013b). Most people are now well into their 20s before they marry, both in the United States and in most other countries (Figure 40-1).

Aspects of Mate Selection

Many societies have explicit or unstated rules that define potential mates as acceptable or unacceptable. These norms can be distinguished in terms of endogamy and exogamy. **Endogamy** (from the Greek *endon,* "within") specifies the groups within which a spouse must be found and prohibits marriage with others. For example, in the United States, many people are expected to marry within their racial, ethnic, or religious group, and are strongly discouraged or even prohibited from marrying outside the group. Endogamy is intended to reinforce the cohesiveness of the group by suggesting to the young that they should marry someone "of their own kind."

Even in the United States, interracial and interethnic marriages are still the exception. According to a report released in 2012, among newly married White couples, about 9 percent marry someone of a different race or ethnicity. Among African American couples the proportion is 17 percent; among Latinos, 26 percent; and among Asian Americans, 28 percent (W. Wang 2012).

In contrast, **exogamy** (from the Greek *exo,* "outside") requires mate selection outside certain groups, usually one's family or certain kinfolk. The **incest taboo,** a social norm common to virtually all societies, prohibits sexual relationships between certain culturally specified relatives. For those of us in the United States, this taboo means that we must marry outside the nuclear family. We cannot marry our siblings, and in most states we cannot marry our first cousins.

Although most interracial couples are not as visible as Robert De Niro and Grace Hightower, such unions are becoming increasingly common and accepted. They are also blurring the definitions of race. Will the children of these couples be considered Black or White? Why do you think so?

BOX 40-1

Our Wired World

Love Is in the Air and on the Web

"What sort of work do you do?" "What are your favorite movies?" "Your favorite websites?" "What do you enjoy doing most?" "What are your favorite songs?" These questions could come up on a first date, but they are drawn from a questionnaire that a popular website uses to match people who may be compatible with one another.

According to a 2013 national survey, 1 in 10 people has used an online dating site or mobile dating app. Among online daters, 66 percent have gone out with someone they met through an online dating site; 23 percent have met a spouse or long-term partner that way. As a source of romantic partners, the Internet is second only to friends—ahead of family, workplace, and neighborhood.

Significantly, online networking is just as important to mate-seekers in their 40s and 50s as it is to those under 30. It is especially important to gays and lesbians: 61 percent of same-sex couples meet online, compared to 23 percent of heterosexual couples. Sociologists have observed that members of groups with a thin or limited market for romantic partners, such as middle-aged people or gays and lesbians, are more likely than others to see the advantage of online dating services.

The Internet dating site eHarmony claims to be the first to use a "scientific approach" to matching people, one that is based on a variety of abilities and interests. This approach is based on a concept called *homogamy*. Sharing interests is so important to prospective mates that certain online dating services target specific segments of the population, such as pet lovers, fans of a particular sport, or members of a certain religion, nationality, or immigrant group. As in real life, online searchers typically do not seek out people of a different race. According to one study of Yahoo daters, over 71

> Among online daters, 66 percent have gone out with someone they met through an online dating site; 23 percent have met a spouse or long-term partner that way.

percent of women and 53 percent of men indicate their racial preferences explicitly.

As we might suspect, **impression management**—the altering of the presentation of the self in order to create distinctive appearances and satisfy particular audiences—is common in online dating. That is, prospective mates make a conscious attempt to present themselves in a favorable light. Compared to real-world dating, online dating services offer users more opportunity to manage their self-presentations, based on the way they answer questions about themselves. Do you want to come across as serious, athletic, or fun-loving? Then compose your answers accordingly. And why stop there? Although not much research has been done on the topic, studies show that the majority of those who participate in online dating think that others often lie about their age, marital status, and appearance. In response, some people have gone online to check public records and search for discrepancies in the way others answer questions.

Online dating and mate selection, then, is not the same as meeting people face-to-face. Through an online dating service, a person can now meet and date complete strangers. Studies show that online daters are more apprehensive about meeting online prospects in person than they are about meeting people they don't know in the real world. At some point the two approaches may converge, however. Phone apps now allow singles to identify other singles who happen to be sitting, standing, or walking near them.

LET'S DISCUSS

1. Have you ever gone out with a person you met online? If so, did the person resemble his or her online presentation? In what ways?

2. Which method of locating other singles do you think would be more useful, going to an online dating site or using an app to locate singles near you? Explain.

Sources: Cali et al. 2013; N. Ellison et al. 2006; J. Gibbs et al. 2011; Jayson 2013; Ortulay 2013; Paul 2014; Robnett and Feliciano 2011; J. Rosenfeld 2010; M. Rosenfeld and Thomas 2012; A. Smith and Duggan 2013.

Another factor that influences the selection of a marriage partner is **homogamy,** the conscious or unconscious tendency to select a mate with personal characteristics similar to one's own. The "like marries like" rule can be seen in couples with similar personalities and cultural interests. However, mate selection is unpredictable. Though some people may follow the homogamous pattern, others observe the "opposites attract" rule: one person is dependent and submissive—almost childishly so—while the other is dominant and controlling.

The Love Relationship

Today's generation of college students seems more likely to hook up or cruise in large packs than to engage in the romantic dating relationships of their parents' and grandparents' generations. Still, at some point in their adult lives, the great majority of today's students will meet someone they love and enter into a long-term relationship that focuses on creating a family.

Parents in the United States tend to value love highly as a rationale for marriage, so they encourage their children to develop intimate relationships based on love and affection. Songs, films, books, magazines, television shows, and even cartoons and comic books reinforce the theme of love. At the same time, our society expects parents and peers to help a person confine his or her search for a mate to "socially acceptable" members of the opposite sex.

Though most people in the United States take the importance of falling in love for granted, the coupling of love and marriage is by no means a cultural universal. Many of the world's cultures give priority in mate selection to factors other than romantic feelings. In societies with *arranged marriages* engineered by parents or religious authorities, economic considerations play a significant role. The newly married couple is expected to develop a feeling of love *after* the legal union is formalized, if at all (J. Lee 2013).

FIGURE 40-1 Median Age at First Marriage in Eight Countries

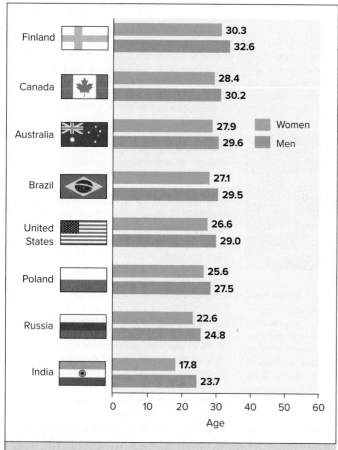

Country	Women	Men
Finland	30.3	32.6
Canada	28.4	30.2
Australia	27.9	29.6
Brazil	27.1	29.5
United States	26.6	29.0
Poland	25.6	27.5
Russia	22.6	24.8
India	17.8	23.7

Think about It Why do people marry earlier in India than in Finland?

Source: United Nations Statistics Division 2013; Bureau of the Census 2013b.

 use your **sociological imagination**

Your parents and/or a matchmaker are going to arrange a marriage for you. What kind of mate will they select? Will your chances of having a successful marriage be better or worse than if you selected your own mate?

Variations in Family Life and Intimate Relationships

Within the United States, social class, race, and ethnicity create variations in family life. Studying these variations will give us a more sophisticated understanding of contemporary family styles in our country.

Social Class Differences

Various studies have documented the differences in family organization among social classes in the United States. In the upper class, the emphasis is on lineage and maintenance of family position. If you are in the upper class, you are not simply a member of a nuclear family, but rather a member of a larger family tradition (think of the Rockefellers or the Kennedys). As a result, upper-class families are quite concerned about what they see as proper training for children.

Lower-class families do not often have the luxury of worrying about the "family name"; they must first struggle to pay their bills and survive the crises often associated with a life of poverty. Such families are more likely to have only one parent at home, which creates special challenges in child care and financial management. Children from lower-class families typically assume adult responsibilities—including marriage and parenthood—at an earlier age than children from affluent homes. In part, that is because they may lack the money needed to remain in school.

Social class differences in family life are less striking today than they once were. In the past, family specialists agreed that the contrasts in child-rearing practices were pronounced. Lower-class families were found to be more authoritarian in rearing children and more inclined to use physical punishment. Middle-class families were more permissive and more restrained in punishing their children. And compared to lower-class families, middle-class families tended to schedule more of their children's time, or even to overstructure it. However, these differences may have narrowed as more and more families from all social classes turned to the same books, magazines, and even television talk shows for advice on rearing children (Kronstadt and Favreault 2008; Luster et al. 1989; J. Sherman and Harris 2012).

Among the poor, women often play a significant role in the economic support of the family. Men may earn low wages, may be unemployed, or may be entirely absent from the family. In 2012, 31 percent of all families headed by women with no husband present fell below the federal government's poverty line. In comparison, the poverty rate for married couples was only 6.2 percent. The disproportionate representation of female-headed households among the poor is a persistent and growing trend, referred to by sociologists as the *feminization of poverty* (DeNavas-Walt et al. 2013:17).

Finally, in her book *The Accordion Family* (see the opening excerpt), Katherine S. Newman (2012) noted that the accordion or boomerang family differs by social class. An upper-middle-class family like the one described in the opening excerpt can afford to provide space to an adult child who is working toward an advanced degree. Less privileged families tend to hang on to their adult children for the labor or income they can contribute to the family's welfare.

Many racial and ethnic groups appear to have distinctive family characteristics. However, racial and class factors are often closely related. In examining family life among racial and ethnic minorities, keep in mind that certain patterns may result from class as well as cultural factors.

Racial and Ethnic Differences

The subordinate status of racial and ethnic minorities in the United States profoundly affects their family lives. For example, the lower incomes of African Americans, Native Americans, most Hispanic groups, and selected Asian American groups make creating and maintaining successful marital unions a difficult task. The economic restructuring of the past 60 years, described by sociologist William Julius Wilson (1996, 2009) and others, has especially affected people living in inner cities and desolate rural areas, such as reservations. Furthermore, the immigration policy of the United States has complicated the successful relocation of intact families from Asia and Latin America.

The African American family suffers from many negative and inaccurate stereotypes. It is true that in a significantly higher proportion of Black than White families, no husband is present in the home (Figure 40-2). Yet Black single mothers often belong to stable, functioning kin networks, which mitigate the pressures of sexism and racism. Members of these networks—predominantly female kin such as mothers, grandmothers, and aunts—ease financial strains by sharing goods and services. In addition to these strong kinship bonds, Black family life has emphasized deep religious commitment and high aspirations for achievement (DuBois [1909] 1970; F. Furstenberg 2007).

Like African Americans, Native Americans draw on family ties to cushion many of the hardships they face. On the Navajo reservation, for example, teenage parenthood is not regarded as the crisis that it is elsewhere in the United States. The Navajo trace their descent matrilineally. Traditionally, couples reside with the wife's family after marriage, allowing the grandparents to help with the child rearing. While the Navajo do not approve of teenage parenthood, the deep emotional commitment of their extended families provides a warm home environment for children, even when no father is present or involved (Dalla and Gamble 2001; John 2012).

Sociologists also have taken note of differences in family patterns among other racial and ethnic groups. For example, Mexican American men have been described as exhibiting a sense of virility, personal worth, and pride in their maleness that is called **machismo.** Mexican Americans are also described as being more familistic than many other subcultures. **Familism** (or *familismo*) refers to pride in the extended family, expressed through the maintenance of close ties and strong obligations to kinfolk outside the immediate family. Traditionally, Mexican Americans have placed proximity to their extended families above other needs and desires.

Although familism is often seen as a positive cultural attribute, it may also have negative consequences. Sociologists who

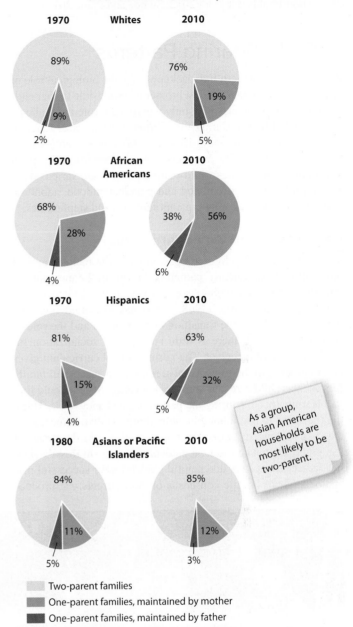

FIGURE 40-2 Rise of Single-Parent Families in the United States, 1970–2010

Two-parent families

One-parent families, maintained by mother

One-parent families, maintained by father

As a group, Asian American households are most likely to be two-parent.

Note: Families are groups with children under 18. Early data for Asian Americans are for 1980. Hispanics can be of any race. Not included are unrelated people living together with no children present. All data exclude the 11 percent of children in nonparental households.
Sources: Bureau of the Census 2008a:56, 2010c:Table FG10.

have studied the relatively low college application rates of Hispanic students have found they have a strong desire to stay at home. Even the children of college-educated parents express this preference, which diminishes the likelihood of their getting a four-year degree and dramatically reduces the possibility that they will apply to a selective college.

These family patterns are changing, however, in response to changes in Latinos' social class standing, educational achievements, and occupations. Like other Americans, career-oriented Latinos in search of a mate but short on spare time are turning to Internet sites. As Latinos and other groups assimilate into the dominant culture of the United States, their family lives take on both the positive and negative characteristics associated with White households (Negroni 2012; Suárez and Perez 2012).

Child-Rearing Patterns

The Nayars of southern India acknowledge the biological role of fathers, but the mother's eldest brother is responsible for her children. In contrast, uncles play only a peripheral role in child care in the United States. Caring for children is a universal function of the family, yet the ways in which different societies assign this function to family members can vary significantly. Even within the United States, child-rearing patterns are varied. We'll take a look here at parenthood and grandparenthood, adoption, dual-income families, single-parent families, and stepfamilies.

Parenthood and Grandparenthood

The socialization of children is essential to the maintenance of any culture. Consequently, parenthood is one of the most important (and most demanding) social roles in the United States. Sociologist Alice Rossi (1968, 1984) has identified four factors that complicate the transition to parenthood and the role of socialization. First, there is little anticipatory socialization for the social role of caregiver. The normal school curriculum gives scant attention to the subjects most relevant to successful family life, such as child care and home maintenance. Second, only limited learning occurs during the period of pregnancy itself. Third, the transition to parenthood is quite abrupt. Unlike adolescence, it is not prolonged; unlike the transition to work, the duties of caregiving cannot be taken on gradually. Finally, in Rossi's view, our society lacks clear and helpful guidelines for successful parenthood. There is little consensus on how parents can produce

happy and well-adjusted offspring—or even on what it means to be well adjusted. For these reasons, socialization for parenthood involves difficult challenges for most men and women in the United States.

In some homes, the full nest holds grandchildren. By 2009, 9 percent of White children, 17 percent of Black children, and 14 percent of Hispanic children lived with at least one grandparent. In about a third of these homes, no parent was present to assume responsibility for the youngsters. Special difficulties are inherent in such relationships, including legal custodial concerns, financial issues, and emotional problems for adults and youths alike. It is not surprising that support groups such as Grandparents as Parents have emerged to provide assistance (Kreider and Ellis 2011).

Adoption

In a legal sense, **adoption** is the transfer of the legal rights, responsibilities, and privileges of parenthood to a new legal parent or parents. In many cases, these rights are transferred from a biological parent or parents (often called birth parents) to an adoptive parent or parents. Every year, about 135,000 children are adopted (Child Welfare Information 2011).

Viewed from a functionalist perspective, government has a strong interest in encouraging adoption. Policymakers, in fact, have both a humanitarian and a financial stake in the process. In theory, adoption offers a stable family environment for children who otherwise might not receive satisfactory care. Moreover, government data show that unwed mothers who keep their babies tend to be of lower socioeconomic status and often require public assistance to support their children. The government can lower its social welfare expenses, then, if children are transferred to economically self-sufficient families. From an interactionist perspective, however, adoption may require a child to adjust to a very different family environment and parental approach to child rearing.

There are two legal methods of adopting an unrelated person: the adoption may be arranged through a licensed agency, or in some states it may be arranged through a private agreement sanctioned by the courts. Adopted children may come from the United States or from abroad. In 2012, over 8,600 children entered the United States as the adopted children of U.S. citizens (Bureau of Consular Affairs 2013).

Having a new child is a major adjustment for everyone in the family; adopting a child is an even bigger adjustment. If the adopted child comes from another culture and is racially or ethnically different from the adopting family, the challenge is that much greater. Box 40-2 describes research on the adjustment that occurs when a U.S. family adopts a child from South Korea.

The 2010 earthquake in Haiti drew attention to the foreign perspective on international adoptions, which is not

When nine-year-old Blake Brunson shows up for a basketball game, so do his *eight* grandparents—the result of his parents' remarriages. Blended families can be very supportive to children, but what message do they send to them on the permanency of marriage?

Transracial Adoption: The Experience of Children from Korea

Caleb Littell was born in South Korea and adopted by a White couple in the United States as an infant. He joined a loving family in the predominantly White suburb of Renton, Washington, just outside Seattle. Now in his 30s, Caleb always knew that he was loved and fiercely wanted by his parents. Still, he struggled with his identity. Why did he look different from his parents? Why was he adopted? What did it mean to be Korean? These questions didn't trouble him at home, but at school and in the wider community, where he was often teased for being "Oriental" or "Asian." His White parents, whom he identified with, didn't see him as different from themselves, he reasoned, yet people outside the family did—why? Caleb wasn't just hurt; he was confused.

This story, recounted by educator Mia Tuan and sociologist Jiannbin Lee Shiao, is all too familiar to children who have experienced **transracial adoption,** the adoption of a non-White child by White parents or a Hispanic child by non-Hispanics. According to a 2011 estimate, there are about 300,000 such children under age 16 in the United States today. Although this type of adoption has occurred for generations, it became more common in the 1990s with the increase in international adoptions. About 85 percent of international adoptions are transracial.

Although no single case is typical, the lifelong socialization of the transracially adopted child does present some special challenges. A child's relationship to his or her parents is an ascribed status, as is ethnicity or race. Korean children who were adopted by White families find that when they move outside their protective nuclear families, their ascribed identities are immediately questioned. Sociologists and other researchers point out that their experience

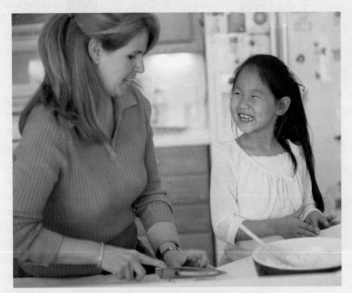

> Now in his 30s, Caleb always knew that he was loved and fiercely wanted by his parents. Still, he struggled with his identity.

reflects contemporary racial and ethnic relations in the United States. That is to say, these children find acceptance and opportunity as well as intolerance and conflict in their new home country.

Assessing the long-term success of transracial adoption is difficult, since the outcomes of raising children in general are complex. The researcher must separate normal parenting problems from transracial parenting problems. One common transracial parenting problem is that White parents may lack the individual experiences, and at first the resources, to transmit positive identity messages to their adopted children. For advice, parents often turn to support groups and online chat rooms. Some send their

children to heritage camps, which have emerged over the last 30 years to immerse children in cultural experiences reflective of their cultural background, be it African, Asian, or Hispanic. Besides offering language instruction, such camps allow children to socialize with others who were transracially adopted. The degree and quality of support from other relatives and from the surrounding community is also important to the children's adjustment.

In terms of the children's adult identity, there is no single outcome. Adult Korean American adoptees may describe themselves as "Korean American," "Caucasian, except when looking in the mirror, " or "Amerasian trying to be White." Research indicates that their identification with Korea is weak, although it has strengthened a bit among more recent adoptees, as support structures have improved. Few of them really learn to speak the Korean language or to truly enjoy Korean food.

LET'S DISCUSS

1. As a child, did you know anyone who may have been transracially adopted? If so, did the child fit in well with his or her peers? Relate your answer to the community you grew up in.

2. Compare the experience of transracial adoption to the experience of entering a blended family. From the child's point of view, what might be the advantages and disadvantages of each? From the parents' point of view, what might be the challenges of each?

Sources: Freundlich and Lieberthal 2000; Kreider 2011; Randolph and Holtzman 2010; Tuan and Shiao 2011; Woon 2005.

always positive. When well-meaning people from the United States arrived in Haiti to rescue alleged orphans and arrange for their adoption in other countries, government officials objected. Some of the children, it turned out, were not orphans; their parents were simply too poor to care for them. For the governments of overstressed developing nations, adoption can be both a solution and a problem.

Adoption is controversial not only abroad but at home as well. In some cases, those who adopt children are not married.

In 1995, an important court decision in New York held that a couple does not need to be married to adopt a child. Under this ruling, unmarried heterosexual couples, lesbian couples, and gay couples can all adopt children in New York. Today, most states permit gay and lesbian couples to adopt. Significant restrictions or outright prohibitions exist in Mississippi, Nebraska, and Utah (ACLU 2014).

For every child who is adopted, many more remain the wards of state-sponsored child protective services. At any given

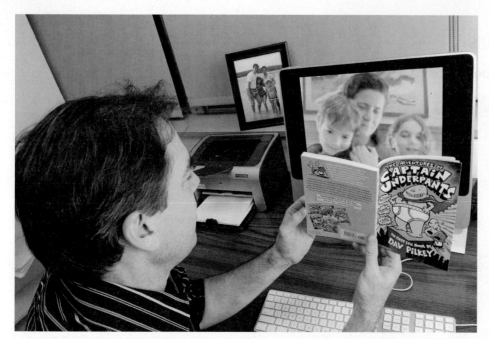

Miles Harvey reads to his children via Skype. Harvey, who is happily married, lives 900 miles from his family in Chicago. He accepted a job in New Orleans for economic reasons.

time, around half a million children in the United States are living in foster care. Every year, about 52,000 of them are adopted; another 101,000 are eligible and waiting to be adopted (Department of Health and Human Services 2013).

Dual-Income Families

The idea of a family consisting of a wage-earning husband and a wife who stays at home has largely given way to the dual-income household. Among married people between ages 25 and 64, 96 percent of the men and 69 percent of the women were in the labor force in 2010 (Bureau of the Census 2011a:Table 597).

Why has there been such a rise in the number of dual-income couples? A major factor is economic need, coupled with a desire by both men *and* women to pursue their careers. Evidence of this trend can be found in the rise in the number of married couples living apart for reasons other than marital discord. The 3.6 million couples who now live apart represent 1 out of every 33 marriages. More than half of them live farther than 100 miles apart, and half of those live 1,000 or more miles apart. Of course, couples living apart are nothing new; men have worked at transient jobs for generations as soldiers, truck drivers, or traveling salesmen. Now, however, the woman's job is often the one that creates the separation. The existence of such household arrangements reflects an acceptance of the egalitarian family type (Higgins et al. 2010; Holmes 2009; Silverman 2009).

Single-Parent Families

The 2004 *American Idol* winner Fantasia Barrino's song "Baby Mama" offers a tribute to young single mothers—a subject she knows about. Barrino was 17 when she became pregnant with her daughter. Though critics charged that the song sends the wrong message to teenage girls, Barrino says it is not about encouraging teens to have sex. Rather, she sees the song as an anthem

for young mothers courageously trying to raise their children alone (Cherlin 2006).

In recent decades, the stigma attached to unwed mothers and other single parents has significantly diminished. **Single-parent families,** in which only one parent is present to care for the children, can hardly be viewed as a rarity in the United States. In 2010, a single parent headed about 24 percent of White families with children under 18, 37 percent of Hispanic families with children, and 62 percent of African American families with children (see Figure 40-2).

The lives of single parents and their children are not inevitably more difficult than life in a traditional nuclear family. It is as inaccurate to assume that a single-parent family is necessarily deprived as it is to assume that a two-parent family is always secure and happy. Nevertheless, life in a single-parent family can be extremely stressful, in both economic and emotional terms. A family headed by a single mother faces especially difficult problems when the mother is a teenager.

Why might low-income teenage women wish to have children and face the obvious financial difficulties of motherhood? Viewed from an interactionist perspective, these women tend to have low self-esteem and limited options; a child may provide a sense of motivation and purpose for a teenager whose economic worth in our society is limited at best. Given the barriers that many young women face because of their gender, race, ethnicity, and class, many teenagers may believe they have little to lose and much to gain by having a child.

According to a widely held stereotype, "unwed mothers" and "babies having babies" in the United States are predominantly African American. However, this view is not entirely accurate. African Americans account for a disproportionate share of births to unmarried women and teenagers, but the majority of all babies born to unmarried teenage mothers are born to White adolescents. Moreover, since 1980, birthrates among Black teenagers have generally declined (J. Martin et al. 2009).

Although 84 percent of single parents in the United States are mothers, the number of households headed by single fathers more than quadrupled from 1980 to 2013. Though single mothers often develop social networks, single fathers are typically more isolated. In addition, they must deal with schools and social service agencies that are more accustomed to women as custodial parents (Bureau of the Census 1981, 2013d).

 use your **sociological imagination**

What personal experience do you have with child rearing by grandparents, dual-income families, or single-parent families? Describe what you observed using sociological concepts.

Stepfamilies

Approximately 45 percent of all people in the United States will marry, divorce, and then remarry. The rising rates of divorce and remarriage have led to a noticeable increase in stepfamily relationships.

The exact nature of blended families has social significance for adults and children alike. Certainly resocialization is required when an adult becomes a stepparent or a child becomes a stepchild and stepsibling. Moreover, an important distinction must be made between first-time stepfamilies and households where there have been repeated divorces, breakups, or changes in custodial arrangements.

In evaluating the rise of stepfamilies, some observers have assumed that children would benefit from remarriage because they would be gaining a second custodial parent, and would potentially enjoy greater economic security. However, after reviewing many studies of stepfamilies, sociologist Andrew J. Cherlin (2010) concluded that children whose parents have remarried do not have higher levels of well-being than children in divorced single-parent families.

Stepparents can play valuable and unique roles in their stepchildren's lives, but their involvement does not guarantee an improvement in family life. In fact, standards may decline. Studies suggest that children raised in families with stepmothers are likely to have less health care, education, and money spent on their food than children raised by biological mothers. The measures are also negative for children raised by stepfathers, but only half as negative as in the case of stepmothers. These results don't

Most households in the United States do not consist of two parents living with their unmarried children.

mean that stepmothers are "evil"—it may be that the stepmother holds back out of concern for seeming too intrusive, or relies mistakenly on the biological father to carry out parental duties (Schmeeckle 2007; Schmeeckle et al. 2006).

 use your **sociological imagination**

What special challenges might stepfamilies face? What advantages might they enjoy? Explain using sociological concepts.

MODULE 40 | **Recap and Review**

Summary

People select mates in a variety of ways: in some societies, marriages are arranged, while in others, people select their own mates.

1. Some societies require mates to be chosen within a certain group (**endogamy**) or outside certain groups (**exogamy**). Consciously or unconsciously, many people look for a mate with similar personal characteristics (**homogamy**).

2. In the United States, family life varies with social class, race, and ethnicity.

3. Currently, in the majority of all married couples in the United States, both husband and wife work outside the home.

4. **Single-parent families** account for an increasing proportion of U.S. families.

Thinking Critically

1. How do both cultural and socioeconomic factors contribute to the following trends: later age of first marriage, the increasing number of extended-family households, and the boomerang generation?

2. Explain mate selection from the functionalist and interactionist perspectives.

Key Terms

Adoption	**Impression management**
Endogamy	**Incest taboo**
Exogamy	**Machismo**
Familism (*Familismo*)	**Single-parent family**
Homogamy	**Transracial adoption**

Divorce

In the United States, the pattern of family life includes commitments both to marriage and to self-expression and personal growth. Needless to say, the tension between those competing commitments can undermine a marriage, working against the establishment of a lasting relationship. This approach to family life is distinctive to the United States. In some nations, such as Italy, the culture strongly supports marriage and discourages divorce. In others, such as Sweden, people treat marriage the same way as cohabitation, and both arrangements are just as lasting (Cherlin 2009).

Statistical Trends in Divorce

Just how common is divorce? Surprisingly, this is not a simple question; divorce statistics are difficult to interpret. The media frequently report that one out of every two marriages ends in divorce, but that figure is misleading. It is based on a comparison of all divorces that occur in a single year (regardless of when the couples were married) with the number of new marriages in the same year.

In many countries, divorce began to increase in the late 1960s but then leveled off; since the late 1980s, it has declined by 30 percent. (Figure 41-1 shows the pattern in the United States.) This trend is due partly to the aging of the baby boomer population and the corresponding decline in the proportion of people of marriageable age. But it also indicates an increase in marital stability in recent years (Coontz 2006).

Getting divorced obviously does not sour people on marriage. About 63 percent of all divorced people in the United States have remarried. Women are less likely than men to remarry because many retain custody of their children after a divorce, which complicates a new adult relationship (Bianchi and Spain 1996; Saad 2004).

Some people regard the nation's high rate of remarriage as an endorsement of the institution of marriage, but it does lead to the new challenges of a kin network composed of both current and prior marital relationships. Such networks can be particularly complex if children are involved or if an ex-spouse remarries.

Factors Associated with Divorce

Perhaps the most important factor in the increase in divorce over the past hundred years has been the greater social *acceptance* of divorce. It is no longer considered necessary to endure an unhappy marriage. More important, various religious denominations have relaxed their negative attitudes toward divorce, so that most religious leaders no longer treat it as a sin.

The growing acceptance of divorce is a worldwide phenomenon. A decade ago, Sunoo, South Korea's foremost matchmaking service, had no divorced clients. Few Koreans divorced; those who did felt social pressure to resign themselves to the single life. But in one recent seven-year period, South Korea's divorce rate doubled. Today, 15 percent of Sunoo's membership are divorced (Onishi 2003; United Nations Statistics Division 2009:Table 23).

In the United States, several factors have contributed to the growing social acceptance of divorce:

- Most states have adopted more liberal divorce laws in the past three decades. No-fault divorce laws, which allow a couple to end their marriage without fault on either side (by specifying adultery, for instance), accounted for an initial surge in the divorce rate after they were introduced in the 1970s, but appear to have had little effect beyond that.

- Divorce has become a more practical option in newly formed families, since families tend to have fewer children now than in the past.

- A general increase in family incomes, coupled with the availability of free legal aid to some poor people, has meant that more couples can afford costly divorce proceedings.

- As society provides greater opportunities for women, more and more wives are becoming less dependent on their husbands, both economically and emotionally. They may feel more able to leave a marriage if it seems hopeless.

Impact of Divorce on Children

Divorce is traumatic for all involved, but it has special meaning for the more than 1 million children whose parents divorce each year. Of course, for some of these children, divorce signals the welcome end to a very dysfunctional relationship. Perhaps that is why a national study that tracked 6,332 children both before and after their parents' divorce found that their behavior did not suffer from the marital breakups. Other studies have shown greater unhappiness among children who live amid parental conflict than among children whose parents are divorced. Still, it would be simplistic to assume that children are automatically better off following the breakup of their parents' marriage. The interests of the parents do not necessarily serve children well (H. Kim 2011; Zi 2007).

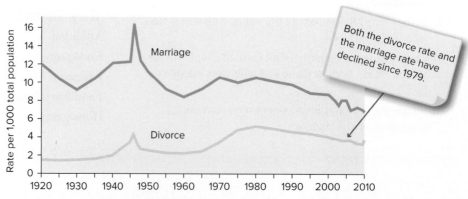

FIGURE 41-1 **Trends in Marriage and Divorce in the United States, 1920–2010**

Both the divorce rate and the marriage rate have declined since 1979.

Sources: Bureau of the Census 1975:64; Centers for Disease Control and Prevention 2012b.

Diverse Lifestyles

Marriage is no longer the presumed route from adolescence to adulthood. Instead, it is treated as just one of several paths to maturity. As a result, the marriage ceremony has lost much of its social significance as a rite of passage. The nation's marriage rate has declined since 1960 because people are postponing marriage until later in life, and because more couples, including same-sex couples, are deciding to form partnerships without marriage (Haq 2011).

Cohabitation

In the United States, testing the marital waters by living together before making a commitment is a common practice among marriage-wary 20- and 30-somethings. The tremendous increase in the number of male–female couples who choose to live together without marrying, a practice called **cohabitation,** is one of the most dramatic trends of recent years.

About half of all *currently* married couples in the United States say that they lived together before marriage. This percentage is likely to increase. The number of households in the United States that are headed by unmarried opposite-sex couples has been rising steadily; in 2012 it was 7.8 million. About 40 percent of cohabiting couples' households included children under age 18—nearly the same proportion as married couples' households (Jacobsen et al. 2012; Kreider 2010; Vespa et al. 2013:22).

In much of Europe, cohabitation is so common that the general sentiment seems to be "Love, yes; marriage, maybe." In Iceland, 62 percent of all children are born to single mothers; in France, Great Britain, and Norway, about 40 percent. Government policies in these countries make few legal distinctions between married and unmarried couples or households. Perhaps as a result, partnerships between cohabiting adults are not necessarily brief or lacking in commitment. Children born to a cohabiting couple in Sweden, for example, are less likely than children born to a cohabiting couple in the United States to see their parents break up (Cherlin 2009; Lyall 2002; M. Moore 2006).

People tend to associate cohabitation with younger, childless couples. Although that stereotype may have been accurate a generation or more ago, it is not now. Since 1970, the number of unmarried couples with children has increased 12-fold.

Periodically, legislators attempt to bolster the desirability of a lifelong commitment to marriage. In 2002, President George W. Bush backed funding for an initiative to promote marriage among those who receive public assistance. Under the Healthy Marriage Initiative, the federal government created a resource center that promoted marriage-related programs. Critics charged that the effort was underfunded or an inappropriate mission for the federal government. The Obama administration has indicated a desire to continue the initiative, renaming it the Healthy Marriage and Responsible Fatherhood Initiative. As the name implies, the initiative extends grants to programs that strengthen fathers' ties with their children and partners. It has also established pilot projects to serve formerly incarcerated parents and their families, designed to provide activities that strengthen their marriages and encourage responsible parenting and economic stability (Jayson 2009; Office of Family Assistance 2014).

Remaining Single

Looking at TV programs today, you would be justified in thinking that most households are composed of singles. Although that is not the case, it is true that more and more people in the United States are postponing entry into a first marriage. Over one out of three households with children in the United States is a single-parent household. Even so, less than 4 percent of women and men in the United States are likely to remain single throughout their lives (Bureau of the Census 2011c).

The trend toward maintaining a single lifestyle for a longer period is related to the growing economic independence of young people. This trend is especially significant for women. Freed from financial needs, women don't necessarily need to marry to enjoy a satisfying life. Divorce, late marriage, and longevity also figure into this trend.

There are many reasons why a person may choose not to marry. Some singles do not want to limit their sexual intimacy to one lifetime partner. Some men and women do not want to become highly dependent on any one person—and do not want anyone depending heavily on them. In a society that values individuality and self-fulfillment, the single lifestyle can offer certain freedoms that married couples may not enjoy. Even divorced parents may not feel the need to remarry. Andrew J. Cherlin (2009) contends that a single parent who connects with other adults, such as grandparents, to form a solid, supportive relationship for child rearing should not feel compelled to re-partner.

Nevertheless, remaining single represents a clear departure from societal expectations; indeed, it has been likened to "being single on Noah's Ark." A single adult must confront the inaccurate view that he or she is always lonely, is a workaholic, or is immature. These stereotypes help to support the traditional assumption in the United States and most other societies that to be truly happy and fulfilled, a person must get married and raise a family. To counter these societal expectations, singles have formed numerous support groups (Hertz 2006; Klinenberg 2012; Lundquist 2006).

Marriage without Children

There has been a modest increase in childlessness in the United States. According to census data, about 16 to 17 percent of women will now complete their childbearing years without having borne any children, compared to 10 percent in 1980. As many as 20 percent of women in their 30s expect to remain childless (Biddlecom and Martin 2006).

Childlessness within marriage has generally been viewed as a problem that can be solved through such means as adoption and artificial insemination. More and more couples today, however, choose not to have children and regard themselves as child-free rather than childless. They do not believe that having children automatically follows from marriage, nor do they feel that reproduction is the duty of all married couples. Childless couples have formed support groups (with names like No Kidding) and set up websites.

Economic considerations have contributed to this shift in attitudes; having children has become quite expensive. According to a government estimate made for 2012, the average middle-class family will spend $241,080 to feed, clothe, and shelter a child from birth to age 18. If the child attends college, that amount could double, depending on the college chosen. In 1960, parents spent only 2 percent of their income on child care and education; now they spend 16 percent, reflecting the rising dependence on non-family child care. Aware of the financial pressures, some couples are weighing the advantages of a child-free marriage (Lino 2013).

Childless couples are beginning to question current practices in the workplace. While applauding employers' efforts to provide child care and flexible work schedules, some nevertheless express concern about tolerance of employees who leave early to take children to doctors, ball games, or after-school classes. As more dual-career couples enter the paid labor force and struggle to balance career and familial responsibilities, conflicts with employees who have no children may increase (Biddlecom and Martin 2006).

 use your **sociological imagination**

What would happen to our society if many more married couples suddenly decided not to have children? How would society change if cohabitation and/or singlehood became the norm?

MODULE 41 | **Recap and Review**

Summary

Divorce and alternatives to traditional marriage such as cohabitation now represent common choices of family style.

1. Among the factors that contribute to the rising divorce rate in the United States are greater social acceptance of divorce and the liberalization of divorce laws in many states.

2. More and more people are living together without marrying, a practice known as **cohabitation.**

3. People are staying single longer, and some married couples are deciding not to have children.

Thinking Critically

1. Do you think it is correct to say that marriage has lost much of its social significance as a rite of passage? Explain your response. What are the major rites of passage into adulthood in today's society?

2. In a society that maximizes the welfare of all family members, how easy should it be for couples to divorce? How easy should it be to get married?

Key Terms

Cohabitation

MODULE 42 | **Human Sexuality**

Human sexuality spans a broad range of behaviors, including some that are not condoned by particular societies. From the sociologist's perspective, however, sexuality is not limited to physical behaviors, but includes the beliefs, values, and social norms that collectively govern its expression. For example, most societies seek to restrict sexual expression to marriage because of its effect on the family, particularly the welfare of women and children (C. Schneider 2008).

Although human sexuality is expressed in all societies, the way it is sanctioned differs widely, both geographically and historically. In South Africa, following the end of apartheid in 1990, legislators removed barriers to interracial cohabitation and marriage. Then in 1998 they passed the Recognition of Customary Marriages Act, which legalized polygamy among some African tribal groups, but not among Muslims and other religious groups. Finally, under the Civil Union Act of 2006, they granted gay and lesbian couples the same rights and responsibilities as opposite-sex couples (Stacey 2011).

Clearly, sexual attitudes and practices change over time. The publication of Alfred Kinsey's first study of human sexuality in 1948 profoundly shocked Americans. Today, online sites routinely solicit descriptions of almost any kind of human sexuality. Besides the new cultural openness about sex, medical advances have encouraged what many refer to as a sexual revolution. For example, the development of oral contraceptives ("the pill") in 1965 and of remedies for erectile dysfunction (Viagra and other such drugs) in 1998 reduced the risk and increased the likelihood of frequent sexual activity. Today, young people engage in sexual practices that few people in earlier generations would have dared to participate in (see Box 42-1, which describes an interactionist study of the sexual networks in one American high school).

BOX 42-1

Q Research Today

Adolescent Sexual Networks

If you drew a chart of the sexual network at a typical American high school, what would it look like? In the mid-1990s, sociologists Peter Bearman, James Moody, and Katherine Stovel asked themselves that question. While studying romantic relationships at a high school with 1,000 students, they found that about 61 percent of the boys and 55 percent of the girls had been sexually active over the past 18 months. Those percentages did not differ much from the results of similar studies done during the period. What surprised the research team was what they saw when they began to chart the students' relationships.

To obtain their data, Bearman and his colleagues conducted in-home interviews with the respondents. Instead of asking students for a face-to-face interview—a technique that might have embarrassed them or distorted their answers—the researchers gave them an audio recording of the questions, a pair of earphones, and a laptop computer on which to record their answers. The research team also asked respondents to look at a list of all the students at the high school and identify those with whom they had had romantic or sexual relationships.

The results showed that 573 of the 832 students surveyed had had at least one sexual relationship over the past 18 months. Among those respondents, the sociologists found only 63 steady couples, or pairs with no other partners. A much larger group of 288 students—almost a third of the sample—

> A particularly significant implication of this study is the risk of sexually transmitted diseases (STDs) to those who participate in such a network.

was involved in a free-flowing network of relationships. Another 90 students were involved in relationships outside the school.

A particularly significant implication of this study is the risk of sexually transmitted diseases (STDs) to those who participate in such a network. Through the complicated chain of relationships, even students who have only one or two sexual partners are exposing themselves to a relatively high degree of risk. But while parents and even students may be alarmed by the data, public health officials are encouraged. Experts at the Centers for Disease Control and Prevention who have reviewed the network charts from this and other studies see them as blueprints for change. If experts can alter participants' behavior anywhere along these chains—by counseling abstinence, condom use, or treatment of STDs—they can significantly reduce transmission of the diseases.

LET'S DISCUSS

1. Do the results of the study surprise you? How does the sexual network described in this study compare to the network where you went to high school?

2. Do you see any problems with the research method used in this study? Can you think of anything that might have compromised the validity of the data?

Sources: Bearman et al. 2004; C. F. Turner et al. 1998; Wallis 2005.

● Labeling and Human Sexuality

We have seen how society singles out certain groups of people by labeling them in positive or negative ways—as "good kids" or "delinquents," for example. Labeling theorists have also studied how labels are used to sanction certain sexual behaviors as "deviant."

The definition of deviant sexual behavior has varied significantly over time and from one culture to another. Until 1973, the American Psychiatric Association considered homosexuality a "sociopathic personality disorder," which in effect meant that homosexuals should seek therapy. Two years later, however, the association removed homosexuality from its list of mental illnesses. Today, the organization publicly proclaims that "being gay is just as healthy as being straight." To use Goffman's term, mental health professionals have removed the *stigma* from this form of sexual expression. As a result, in the United States and many other countries, consensual sex between same-sex adults is no longer a crime (American Psychological Association 2008; International Gay and Lesbian Human Rights Commission 2010).

Despite the change in health professionals' attitudes, however, the social stigma of homosexuality lingers. As a result, many people prefer the more positive terms *gay* and *lesbian.* Others, in defiance of the stigma, have proudly adopted the pejorative term *queer* in a deliberate reaction to the ridicule they have borne because of their sexual identity. Still others maintain that constructing one's sexual identity as either homosexual or heterosexual is too limiting. Indeed, such labels ignore those

Lady Gaga's 2011 hit single "Born This Way" was written as an anthem to diversity and acceptance of all people, including gays and lesbians.

who are *bisexual,* or sexually attracted to both sexes.

Another group whose sexual identity does not fit into the usual categories is *transgendered persons,* or those people whose current gender identity does not match their physical identity at birth. Some transgendered persons see themselves as both male and female. Others, called *transsexuals,* may take hormones or undergo surgery in an effort to draw physically closer to their chosen gender identity. Transgendered persons are sometimes confused with *transvestites,* or cross-dressers who wear the clothing of the opposite sex. Transvestites are typically men, either gay or heterosexual, who choose to wear women's clothing.

The use of these terms even in a positive or nonjudgmental way is problematic, since they imply that human sexuality can be confined in neat, mutually exclusive categories. Moreover, the destigmatization of these labels tends to reflect the influence of the socially privileged—that is, the affluent—who have the resources to overcome the stigma. In contrast, the traditional Native American concept of the *two spirit,* a personality that blends the masculine and the feminine, has been largely ridiculed or ignored (Gilley 2006; Wentling et al. 2008).

What does constitute sexual deviance, then? The answer to this question seems to change with each generation. Today, U.S. laws allow married women to accuse their husbands of rape, when a generation ago such an offense was not recognized. Similarly, *pedophilia*—an adult having sex with a minor—is generally regarded with disgust today, even when it is consensual. Yet in many countries, fringe groups now speak positively of "intergenerational sex," arguing that "childhood" is not a biological given (Hendershott 2002).

Though pedophilia and some other aspects of sexual expression are still against the law, the meaning of the labels is beginning to blur. Although child pornography is both illegal and abhorrent to most people, many fashion advertisements in mainstream magazines seem to verge on it. And while sex work and sex trafficking seem wrong to most of us, society tolerates and even regulates many aspects of those activities (Barton 2006).

use your **sociological imagination**

Do your friends react differently to some expressions of human sexuality? If so, in what way?

MAPPING LIFE NATIONWIDE

FIGURE 42-1 **Same-Sex Couple Households as Percent of All Households**

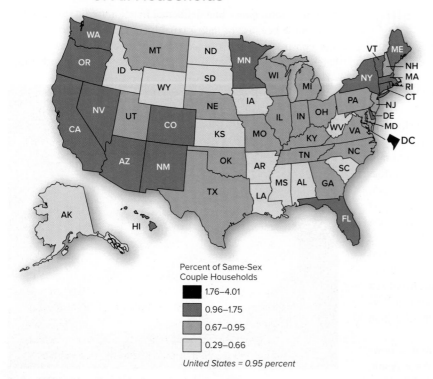

Percent of Same-Sex Couple Households

- 1.76–4.01
- 0.96–1.75
- 0.67–0.95
- 0.29–0.66

United States = 0.95 percent

Source: 2010 American Community Survey data in Lofquist 2011:4.

About 600,000 same-sex couples lived in the United States in 2010.

Lesbian and Gay Relationships

Twenty-one-year-old Parke, a junior in college, grew up in a stable, loving family. A self-described fiscal conservative, he credits his parents with instilling in him a strong work ethic. Sound like an average child of an average family? The only break with traditional expectations in this case is that Parke is the son of a lesbian couple (P. Brown 2004).

The lifestyles of lesbians and gay men are varied. Some live in long-term, monogamous relationships; others live alone or with roommates. Some remain in "empty-shell" heterosexual marriages and do not publicly acknowledge their homosexuality. Others live with children from a former marriage or with adopted children. Based on election exit polls, researchers for the National Health and Social Life Survey and the Voter News Service estimate that 2 to 5 percent of the adult population identify themselves as either gay or lesbian. An analysis of the 2010 Census shows about 600,000 gay households, and a gay and lesbian adult population approaching 10 million (Figure 42-1) (Laumann et al. 1994b:293; Lofquist 2011).

The last few years have seen dramatic changes in legal discrimination against lesbian, gay, bisexual, and transgender (LGBT) people. Although significant barriers remain, especially in family law and in publicly expressed prejudicial attitudes, progress has been made in other areas. Increasingly, businesses are seeing the benefit of hiring LGBT people. In 2012 the CIA began active recruitment in the LGBT community—a sharp departure from the past, when the CIA and other federal agencies routinely denied security clearances to gay men and women. As a result, a 2012 survey showed that 91 percent of gay men and lesbians in the United States are experiencing greater acceptance of their lifestyle (G. Allen 2012; S. Page 2012).

One remaining and highly publicized issue is prohibitions against gay marriage. The inability to marry denies gay people many rights that married couples take for granted, from the ability to make decisions for an incapacitated partner to the right to receive government benefits to dependents, such as Social Security payments. Though gay couples consider themselves families just like the straight couples who live down the street, they are often treated as if they are not.

Precisely because of such inequities, many gay and lesbian couples are now demanding the right to marry with increasing success. In the Social Policy section that follows, we will examine the highly controversial issue of gay marriage.

social policy and the Family | Gay Marriage

In the United States, attitudes toward marriage are complex. As always, society and popular culture suggest that a young man or woman should find the perfect mate, settle down and marry, have children, and live happily ever after. But young people are also bombarded by messages implying the frequency of adultery and the acceptability of divorce. In this atmosphere, the idea of same-sex marriage strikes some people as only the latest of many attacks on traditional marriage. To others, it seems an overdue acknowledgment of the formal relationships that faithful, monogamous gay couples have long maintained.

Looking at the Issue

What has made gay marriage the focus of national attention? Events in two states brought the issue to the forefront. In 1999, Vermont gave gay couples the legal benefits of marriage through civil union, but stopped short of calling the arrangement a marriage. Then, in 2003, the Massachusetts Supreme Court ruled 4–3 that under the state's constitution, gay couples have the right to marry—a ruling the U.S. Supreme Court has refused to review. Almost immediately, gay couples began crossing state lines to get married in Massachusetts. As of 2013, an estimated 124,000 gay and lesbian couples in the United States are married and raising more than 30,000 children. Now that some of them have been legally married 10 years or more, scholars are beginning to study their family experiences compared to those of opposite-sex couples (Rodriquez and Gatlin 2014).

In a 2014 national survey, 55 percent of respondents said marriage between same-sex couples should be recognized by law. Another 42 percent said such arrangements should not be recognized (McCarthy 2014).

Applying Sociology

Functionalists have traditionally seen marriage as a social institution that is closely tied to human reproduction. Same-sex marriage would at first appear not to fit that arrangement. However, many same-sex couples are entrusted with the socialization of young children, whether or not their relationship is recognized by the state. Functionalists also wonder whether religious views toward marriage can be ignored. The courts have focused on civil marriage, but religious views are hardly irrelevant, even

—Continued

in a country like the United States, which observes a separation between religion and the state. Indeed, religious teachings have led even some staunch supporters of gay rights to oppose same-sex marriage on spiritual grounds.

Conflict theorists have charged that denial of the right to marry reinforces the second-class status of gays and lesbians. Some have compared the ban on gay marriage to past policies that until 1967 banned interracial marriage in 32 states.

Interactionists generally avoid the policy question and focus instead on the nature of same-sex households. They ask many of the same questions about gay partner relations and child rearing that they ask about conventional couples. Of course, much less research has been done on same-sex households than on other families, but the studies published to date raise the same issues as those that apply to conventional married couples, plus a few more. For gay couples, the support or opposition of family, co-workers, and friends looms large (Dundas and Kaufman 2000; Dunne 2000; B. Powell et al. 2010).

MAPPING LIFE NATIONWIDE

FIGURE 42-2 **Gay Marriage Recognition by State**

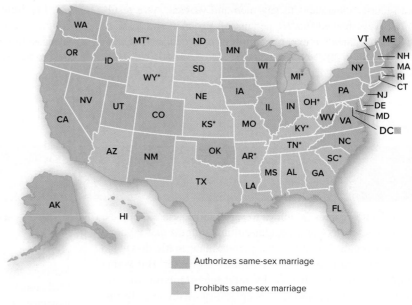

Authorizes same-sex marriage

Prohibits same-sex marriage

*Legal-challenges underway and gay marriage likely to be recognized.

Note: Recognition has been instituted state-by-state by state legislative action, statewide referendum, state supreme courts, or federal appeals court. Also recognized by 10 American Indian tribes.

Sources: As of October 12, 2014; Human Rights Campaign 2014 and various news reports during October 2014.

Queer theorists see these issues as significant, arguing that they are often understudied by researchers (although that is beginning to change). In particular, queer theorists point to the relative lack of high-quality research on LGBT households and their relationship to the larger society, not to mention non-LGBT relatives. As the campaign for same-sex marriage gains momentum, some scholars see a need to focus on gay men and lesbians who do not fit the new "gay norm," who reject the desire to create a nuclear family household. Continuing to focus on the margins of society, queer theorists argue for more attention to people of color, the working class, the poor, and immigrants in the LGBT community (Mignon Moore and Stambolis-Ruhstorfer 2013).

Initiating Policy

The United States is not the first nation to consider this issue. In 2001, the Netherlands became the first nation to legalize same-sex marriage. In less than 14 years, 15 other nations followed: Argentina, Belgium, Brazil, Canada, Denmark, France, Great Britain, Iceland, New Zealand, Norway, Portugal, South Africa, Spain, Sweden, and Uruguay. Typically, same-sex couples account for 2 to 3 percent of all marriages in these nations (R. Taylor 2013).

In the United States, marriage has traditionally been under the jurisdiction of state lawmakers. However, in 1996, responding to conservatives, Congress enacted the Defense of

Marriage Act (DOMA). The act defined marriage as a union between one man and one woman and allowed states and the federal government to deny legal recognition of same-sex marriages. Despite criticism from the gay community and those who support the recognition of same-sex marriage, the measure proved popular with the public.

Then in 2013, by a 5–4 vote in *United States v. Windsor,* the Supreme Court struck down a key section of DOMA, in effect declaring that the federal government must recognize gay marriage in the 12 states where it was legal at the time. As of October 2014, 31 states and the District of Columbia were issuing marriage licenses to same-sex couples (Figure 42-2). In states that have yet to recognize gay marriage, the ruling in *United States v. Windsor* has kept the movement toward legalization going.

At the local level, opponents to gay marriage are finding new ways to declare their views. There is growing evidence that some photographers, wedding cake bakers, and florists are refusing to provide their services at same-sex wedding and civil union ceremonies. Their discriminatory rejection of customers based on sexual identification raises complex legal questions that must await future court decisions (Dimrock et al. 2013; Koppel and Jones 2013).

Not everyone in the LGBT community sees the legalization of same-sex marriage as necessarily the central issue. Assimilation—the process through which individuals forsake

—Continued

—Continued

their own heritage to become a part of a different culture—has emerged as a hot issue in the gay community. Some argue that in promoting marriage equality, LGBT people are merely trying to assimilate, to become like the oppressor and adopt the oppressor's social conventions. Many fear that such efforts will detract from efforts to help more marginalized gays and lesbians, such as people of color, transgender people, and those who prefer forms of intimacy other than marriage (Bernstein and Taylor 2013).

MODULE 42 | Recap and Review

Summary

Human sexuality spans a wide range of behaviors, and different societies condone different behaviors.

1. From the sociological perspective, sexuality is not limited to physical behaviors, but includes the beliefs, values, and social norms that collectively govern its expression.

2. Because homosexuality has traditionally been labeled as a deviant behavior, gay and lesbian couples face significant discrimination, including the denial of their right to marry.

3. The gay marriage movement, which would confer equal rights on gay and lesbian couples and their dependents, is strongly opposed by conservative religious and political groups.

Thinking Critically

1. What do you believe constitutes sexual deviance today? How might this change over the next decade or two?

2. How is cohabitation similar to marriage? How is it different? Could gay and lesbian couples achieve all the benefits of marriage without actually marrying?

Mastering This Chapter

taking sociology with you

1 Go online and try tracing your family roots using one of the genealogical search sites. How far back can you go? Why might certain ancestral paths be more difficult to trace than others?

2 Do some research on the divorce law in your state. Has the law changed much over the past few decades, and if so, how? From a sociological perspective, why would the law change? Explain.

3 Talk to a marriage and family counselor or a professor of family law about the benefits of marriage versus cohabitation, or read what practical advice you can find on the Internet or in the library. What advantages does marriage offer that cohabitation does not? How important do those advantages seem to you?

Adoption In a legal sense, the transfer of the legal rights, responsibilities, and privileges of parenthood to a new legal parent or parents.

Bilateral descent A kinship system in which both sides of a person's family are regarded as equally important.

Cohabitation The practice of living together as a male–female couple without marrying.

Egalitarian family An authority pattern in which spouses are regarded as equals.

Endogamy The restriction of mate selection to people within the same group.

Exogamy The requirement that people select a mate outside certain groups.

Extended family A family in which relatives—such as grandparents, aunts, or uncles—live in the same home as parents and their children.

Familism (*Familismo*) Pride in the extended family, expressed through the maintenance of close ties and strong obligations to kinfolk outside the immediate family.

Family A set of people related by blood, marriage or some other agreed-on relationship, or adoption, who share the primary responsibility for reproduction and caring for members of society.

Homogamy The conscious or unconscious tendency to select a mate with personal characteristics similar to one's own.

Impression management The altering of the presentation of the self in order to create distinctive appearances and satisfy particular audiences.

Incest taboo The prohibition of sexual relationships between certain culturally specified relatives.

Kinship The state of being related to others.

Machismo A sense of virility, personal worth, and pride in one's maleness.

Matriarchy A society in which women dominate in family decision making.

Matrilineal descent A kinship system in which only the mother's relatives are significant.

Monogamy A form of marriage in which an individual has only one partner.

Nuclear family A married couple and their unmarried children living together.

Patriarchy A society in which men dominate in family decision making.

Patrilineal descent A kinship system in which only the father's relatives are significant.

Polyandry A form of polygamy in which a woman may have more than one husband at the same time.

Polygamy A form of marriage in which an individual may have several husbands or wives simultaneously.

Polygyny A form of polygamy in which a man may have more than one wife at the same time.

Serial monogamy A form of marriage in which a person may have several spouses in his or her lifetime, but only one spouse at a time.

Single-parent family A family in which only one parent is present to care for the children.

Transracial adoption The adoption of a non-White child by White parents or a Hispanic child by non-Hispanics.

self-quiz

Read each question carefully and then select the best answer.

1. Alice, age seven, lives in a private home with her parents, her grandmother, and her aunt. Alice's family is an example of a(n)
   a. nuclear family.
   b. dysfunctional family.
   c. extended family.
   d. polygynous family.

2. In which form of marriage may a person have several spouses in his or her lifetime, but only one spouse at a time?
   a. serial monogamy
   b. monogamy
   c. polygamy
   d. polyandry

3. The marriage of a woman to more than one man at the same time is referred to as
   a. polygyny.
   b. monogamy.
   c. serial monogamy.
   d. polyandry.

4. Which system of descent is followed in the United States?
   a. matrilineal
   b. patrilineal
   c. bilateral
   d. unilateral

5. According to the functionalist perspective, which of the following is *not* one of the paramount functions performed by the family?
   a. mediation
   b. reproduction
   c. regulation of sexual behavior
   d. affection and companionship

6. Which norm requires mate selection outside certain groups, usually one's own family or certain kinfolk?
   a. exogamy
   b. endogamy
   c. matriarchy
   d. patriarchy

7. According to the discussion of social class differences in family life and intimate relationships, which of the following statements is true?
   a. Social class differences in family life are more striking than they once were.
   b. The upper class emphasizes lineage and maintenance of family position.
   c. Among the poor, women usually play an insignificant role in the economic support of the family.
   d. In examining family life among racial and ethnic minorities, most patterns result from cultural, but *not* class, factors.

8. One recent development in family life in the United States has been the extension of parenthood as adult children continue to live at home or return home after college. The reason for this is
   a. the rising divorce rate.
   b. high rents.
   c. financial difficulties.
   d. all of the above

9. In the United States, the *majority* of all babies born to unmarried teenage mothers are born to whom?
   a. African American adolescents
   b. White adolescents
   c. Latina adolescents
   d. Asian American adolescents

10. Which of the following factors is associated with the high divorce rate in the United States?
    a. the liberalization of divorce laws
    b. the fact that contemporary families have fewer children than earlier families did
    c. the general increase in family incomes
    d. all of the above

11. The principle of _____ assigns people to kinship groups according to their relationship to an individual's mother or father.

12. _____ emerged among Native American tribal societies, and in nations in which men were absent for long periods because of warfare or food-gathering expeditions.

13. In the view of many sociologists, the _____ family has begun to replace the patriarchal family as the social norm in the United States.

14. As _____ theorists point out, the social class of couples and their children significantly influences the socialization experiences to which the children are exposed and the protection they receive.

15. _____ focus on the micro level of family and other intimate relationships; for example, they are interested in whether people are cohabiting partners or are longtime married couples.

16. The rule of _____ specifies the groups within which a spouse must be found and prohibits marriage with others.

17. Social class differences in family life are less striking today than they once were; however, in the past, _____ -class families were found to be more authoritarian in rearing children and more inclined to use physical punishment.

18. Caring for children is a(n) _____ function of the family, yet the ways in which different societies assign this function to family members can vary significantly.

19. Viewed from the _____ perspective, the government has a strong interest in encouraging adoption.

20. The rising rates of divorce and remarriage have led to a noticeable increase in _____ relationships.

14

Education

"The library is on the right." Prospective students and their parents tour the campus of the University of Texas–Austin. From informal learning in the family to formal study at institutions of higher learning, education is a cultural universal.

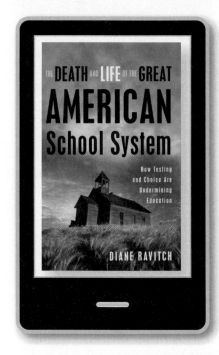

After a long career, Diane Ravitch lost faith in the educational reforms she had once championed as a way to rescue failing schools. Searching for a better answer, she looked back on her own experience in high school, to her favorite English teacher.

" My favorite teacher was Mrs. Ruby Ratliff. She is the teacher I remember best, the one who influenced me most, who taught me to love literature and to write with careful attention to grammar and syntax. More than fifty years ago, she was my homeroom teacher at San Jacinto High School in Houston, and I was lucky enough to get into her English class as a senior.

Mrs. Ratliff was gruff and demanding. She did not tolerate foolishness or disruptions. She had a great reputation among students. . . . What I remember most about her was what she taught us. We studied the greatest writers of the English language. . . . We read Shakespeare, Keats, Shelley, Wordsworth, Milton, and other major English writers. Now, many years later, in times of stress or sadness, I still turn to poems that I first read in Mrs. Ratliff's class. Mrs. Ratliff did nothing for our self-esteem. She challenged us to meet her exacting standards. I think she imagined herself bringing enlightenment to the barbarians (that was us). When you wrote something for her class, which happened with frequency, you paid close attention to proper English. Accuracy mattered. She had a red pen and she used it freely. Still, she was always sure to make a comment that encouraged us to do a better job. Clearly she had multiple goals for her students, beyond teaching literature and grammar. She was also teaching about character and personal responsibility. These are not the sorts of things that appear on any standardized test.

She loved her subject, and she enjoyed the respect the students showed her, especially since this was a large high school where students did not easily give respect to their teachers. Despite the passage of years, I still recall a

Clearly she had multiple goals for her students, beyond teaching literature and grammar. She was also teaching about character and personal responsibility. These are not the sorts of things that appear on any standardized test.

class discussion of Shelley's "Ozymandias," and the close attention that thirty usually rowdy adolescents paid to a poem about a time and a place we could barely imagine. I wonder if Mrs. Ratliff has her counterparts today, teachers who love literature and love to teach it, or whether schools favor teachers who have been trained to elicit mechanical responses from their students about "text-to-self connections," "inferencing," "visualizing," and the other formalistic behaviors so beloved by au courant pedagogues. If Mrs. Ratliff were planning to teach these days, I expect that her education professors and supervisors would warn her to get rid of that red pen, to abandon her insistence on accuracy, and to stop being so judgmental. And they would surely demand that she replace those dated poems and essays with young adult literature that teaches adolescents about the lives of other adolescents just like themselves. . . .

I think of Mrs. Ratliff when I hear the latest proposals to improve the teaching force. Almost every day, I come across a statement by a journalist, superintendent, or economist who says we could solve all our problems in American education if we could just recruit a sufficient number of "great" teachers. I believe Mrs. Ratliff was a great teacher, but I don't think she would have been considered "great" if she had been judged by the kind of hard data that is used now. The policy experts who insist that teachers should be judged by their students' scores on standardized tests would have been frustrated by Mrs. Ratliff. Her classes never produced hard data. They didn't even produce test scores. How would the experts have measured what we learned? We never took a multiple-choice test. We wrote essays and took written tests, in which we had to explain our answers, not check a box or fill in a bubble. If she had been evaluated by the grades she gave, she would have been in deep trouble, because she did not award many A grades. An observer might have concluded that she was a very ineffective teacher who had no measurable gains to show for her work. "

(Ravitch 2010:169, 170, 171)

I n her book *The Death and Life of the Great American School System,* education historian Diane Ravitch laments our failure in improving the quality of education in the United States. In recalling her favorite teacher, Ravitch questions what she sees as our current tendency to reduce the art of teaching to test cramming and relying solely on standardized tests as measures of students' performance. She is really asking the same questions that sociologists ask about education: What are its goals, and what is it supposed to accomplish, for individuals and for society as a whole? After considering how sociologists answer these questions, we will return to the issue of measuring school performance in the Social Policy section.

As we saw in Module 15, socialization can occur in the classroom or at home, through interactions with parents, teachers, friends, and even strangers. These modules focus in particular on the formal systems of education that characterize modern industrial societies. Do public schools offer everyone a way up the socioeconomic ladder, or do they reinforce existing divisions among social classes? What is the "hidden curriculum" in U.S. schools? And what have sociologists learned about the latest trends in education,

such as competency testing? We will begin with discussion of four theoretical perspectives on education, and will then examine schools as formal organizations—as bureaucracies and subcultures of teachers and students. One contemporary educational trend, homeschooling, merits special mention. We close with a Social Policy section on the controversial charter-schools movement.

Besides being a major industry in the United States, **education** is the social institution that formally socializes members of our society. In the past few decades, increasing proportions of people have obtained high school diplomas, college degrees, and advanced professional degrees. Figure 43-1 shows the proportion of the college-educated population in selected countries.

Throughout the world, education has become a vast and complex social institution that prepares citizens for the roles demanded by other social institutions, such as the family, government, and the economy. The functionalist, conflict, feminist, and interactionist perspectives offer distinctive views of education as a social institution.

Functionalist Perspective

Like other social institutions, education has both manifest (open, stated) and latent (hidden) functions. The most basic *manifest* function of education is the transmission of knowledge. Schools teach students how to read, speak foreign languages, and repair automobiles. Another important manifest function is the

bestowal of status. Because many believe this function is performed inequitably, we will consider it later, in the section on the conflict view of education.

In addition to these manifest functions, schools perform a number of *latent* functions: transmitting culture, promoting social and political integration, maintaining social control, and serving as an agent of change.

Transmitting Culture

As a social institution, education performs a rather conservative function—transmitting the dominant culture. Schooling exposes each generation of young people to the existing beliefs, norms, and values of their culture. In our society, we learn respect for social control and reverence for established institutions, such as religion, the family, and the presidency. Of course, this statement is true of many other cultures as well. While schoolchildren in the United States are hearing about the accomplishments of George Washington and Abraham Lincoln, British children are hearing about the distinctive contributions of Queen Elizabeth I and Winston Churchill.

Sometimes nations reassess the ways in which they transmit culture to students. In the last decade, the Chinese government revised the nation's history curriculum. Students are now taught that the Chinese Communist Party, not the United States, played a central role in defeating Japan in World War II. No mention is made of the estimated 30 million Chinese who died

FIGURE 43-1 **Current Higher Education Graduation Rates (BA/BS), Selected Countries**

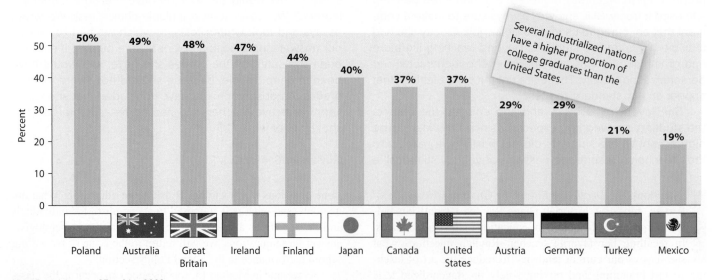

Note: For adults ages 25 to 64 in 2009.
Source: Organisation for Economic Co-Operation and Development 2012c:Table A3.

from famine because of party founder Mao Zedong's disastrous Great Leap Forward (1958–1962), a failed effort to transform China's agrarian economy into an industrial powerhouse. In the urban, Western-oriented areas of Shanghai, textbooks acknowledge the technological advances made in Western industrialized countries but avoid any criticism of past policies of the Chinese government (French 2004; J. Kahn 2006).

Culture has been transmitted to students in schools, through books and the spoken word, for centuries. Today, however, the Internet offers a new and potentially revolutionary way of transmitting culture. Box 43-1 discusses the educational impact of Google and other search engines.

Promoting Social and Political Integration

Many institutions require students in their first year or two of college to live on campus, to foster a sense of community among diverse groups. Education serves the latent function of promoting social and political integration by transforming a population composed of diverse racial, ethnic, and religious groups into a society whose members share—to some extent—a common identity. Historically, schools in the United States have played

Although the school Harry Potter attends in the film *Harry Potter and the Deathly Hallows: Part 2* is fictitious, like real schools, it transmits a socially sanctioned culture to students.

Sociology on Campus

BOX 43-1

Google University

From comic books, television, and fast-paced video games to educational films and online college courses, technological innovations in communication have been seen as both a threat to culture and a boon to education. Like these new media, the search engine called Google has been greeted with both praise and scorn. Founded by two students at Stanford University in 1998, Google handled some 65 percent of all Internet searches in the United States in early 2011. Its familiar multicolored logo stands for one of the most trusted brands in the world (see Figure 20-1).

Using Google or some other search engine, a researcher can now retrieve facts, viewpoints, images, and sounds within minutes. Just a few years ago, that task would have taken days. As Nicholas Carr (2008b:56), former editor of the *Harvard Business Review*, notes, "Once I was a scuba diver in the sea of words. Now I zip along the surface like a guy on a Jet Ski." Yet some critics of search engines charge that placing more and more of the world's knowledge just a mouse click away has made students lazy. Quick access to information, they point out, does not necessarily encourage

> Like the invention of the printing press, Google's advent is changing not just the university, but the universe of learning.

concentration, let alone contemplation. The availability of information online may also be changing the way people read. Educators worry that habitual skimming of the computer screen may carry over to students' print reading. Some have found that younger readers, faced with anything of length online, such as a short PDF file, simply ignore it. In response, researchers have begun to study whether those who read online in preference to books and other printed media still read sentence by sentence, as they were taught to do in school.

Other scholars are not disturbed by potential changes in what and how people read. They note that true literacy is not merely the ability to read to the end of an article or book, but to find the information you need amid a flood of sources—not all of them trustworthy—and use it correctly and responsibly. In other words, literacy includes critical thinking. Ultimately, education is more than just collecting, organizing, and comprehending

information. Accessing information and arguments regarding political and social issues is a form of civic engagement. Thus, the search feature on a web page becomes a portal to a virtual town square. Perhaps that is why today's students are not only spending more time online than yesterday's students, but also doing more volunteer work. Well before the advent of the Internet, much less Google, sociologist Daniel Bell (1973) wrote that *intellectual technologies* tend to institutionalize new approaches to the gathering and dissemination of information. Like the invention of the printing press, Google's advent is changing not just the university, but the universe of learning.

LET'S DISCUSS

1. Do you prefer to do your reading online or in a magazine, newspaper, or book? Has the availability of online information changed the way that you read the written word?

2. Have you participated in any social or political causes or volunteered your time while on campus? If so, did you use the Internet to organize or disseminate information about your activities?

Sources: Mark Bauerlein 2008; Brabazon 2007; Carr 2008a, 2008b; Maestretti 2009; Search Engine Watch 2011; Vaidhyanathan 2008.

Google™

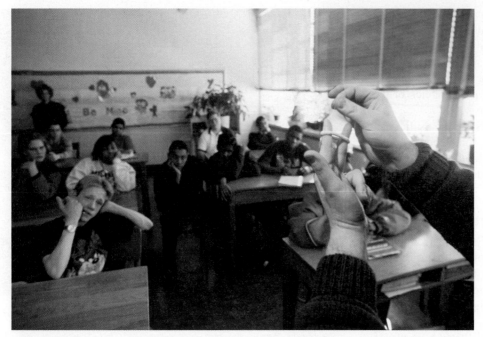

In response to a high pregnancy rate among adolescent girls, many schools now offer sex education courses that promote abstinence as well as safe sex. When schools attempt to remedy negative social trends, they are serving as an agent of social change.

an important role in socializing the children of immigrants into the norms, values, and beliefs of the dominant culture. From a functionalist perspective, the common identity and social integration fostered by education contribute to societal stability and consensus (Touraine 1974).

In the past, the integrative function of education was most obvious in its emphasis on promoting a common language. Immigrant children were expected to learn English. In some instances, they were even forbidden to speak their native language on school grounds. More recently, bilingualism has been defended both for its educational value and as a means of encouraging cultural diversity. However, critics argue that bilingualism undermines the social and political integration that education has traditionally promoted.

Maintaining Social Control

In performing the manifest function of transmitting knowledge, schools go far beyond teaching skills like reading, writing, and mathematics. Like other social institutions, such as the family and religion, education prepares young people to lead productive and orderly lives as adults by introducing them to the norms, values, and sanctions of the larger society.

Through the exercise of social control, schools teach students various skills and values essential to their future positions in the labor force. They learn punctuality, discipline, scheduling, and responsible work habits, as well as how to negotiate the complexities of a bureaucratic organization. As a social institution, education reflects the interests of both the family and another social institution, the economy. Students are trained for what is ahead, whether it be the assembly line or a physician's office. In effect, then, schools serve as a transitional agent of social control, bridging the gap between parents and employers in the life

cycle of most individuals (Bowles and Gintis 1976; Cole 1988).

Schools direct and even restrict students' aspirations in a manner that reflects societal values and prejudices. School administrators may allocate ample funds for athletic programs but give much less support to music, art, and dance. Teachers and guidance counselors may encourage male students to pursue careers in the sciences but steer female students into careers as early childhood teachers. Such socialization into traditional gender roles can be viewed as a form of social control.

Serving as an Agent of Change

So far, we have focused on the conservative functions of education—on its role in transmitting the existing culture, promoting social and political integration, and maintaining social control. Yet education can also stimulate or bring about desired social change. Sex education classes were introduced to public schools in response to the soaring pregnancy rate among teenagers. Affirmative action in admissions—giving priority to females or minorities—has been endorsed as a means of countering racial and sexual discrimination. And Project Head Start, an early childhood program that serves more than 904,000 children annually, has sought to compensate for the disadvantages in school readiness experienced by children from low-income families (Bureau of the Census 2011a:Table 574).

These educational programs can and have transformed people's lives. For example, continued formal education has had a positive effect on the income people earn; median earnings rise significantly with each step up the educational ladder. Consider the significance of those increased earnings when they stretch over an entire lifetime. Obviously, racial, ethnic, and gender differences in income are also significant. Yet as significant as those inequalities are, the best indicator of a person's lifetime earnings is still the number of years of formal schooling that person has received (see Figure 43-2) (Julian and Kominski 2011; Wessel and Banchero 2012).

Numerous sociological studies have revealed that additional years of formal schooling are also associated with openness to new ideas and liberal social and political viewpoints. Sociologist Robin Williams points out that better-educated people tend to have greater access to factual information, to hold more diverse opinions, and to possess the ability to make subtle distinctions in analysis. Formal education stresses both the importance of qualifying statements (in place of broad generalizations) and the need at least to question (rather than simply accept) established truths and practices. The scientific method, which relies on *testing* hypotheses, reflects the questioning spirit that characterizes modern education (R. Williams et al. 1964).

FIGURE 43-2 Lifetime Earnings by Race, Gender, and Degree Level

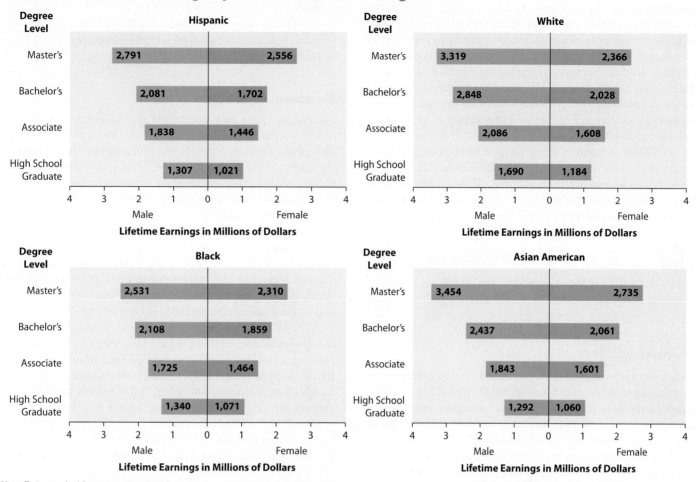

Note: Estimates for lifetime earnings for full-time, year-round workers ages 25 to 64 based on the American Community Survey for 2006–2008. Data are for Hispanics, non-Hispanic Whites, Blacks, and Asian Americans. Data points shown in thousands of dollars.
Source: Julian and Kominski 2011:6.

● Conflict Perspective

The functionalist perspective portrays contemporary education as a basically benign institution. For example, it argues that schools rationally sort and select students for future high-status positions, thereby meeting society's need for talented and expert personnel. In contrast, the conflict perspective views education as an instrument of elite domination. Conflict theorists point out the sharp inequalities that exist in the educational opportunities available to different racial and ethnic groups. In 2014, the nation marked the 60th anniversary of the Supreme Court's landmark decision *Brown v. Board of Education,* which declared unconstitutional the segregation of public schools. Yet today, our schools are still characterized by racial isolation. For example, although White students account for just over half the nation's school enrollment, the typical White student attends a school where three-quarters of his or her peers are White. Fully 15 percent of Black students and 14 percent of Latino students attend what have been termed "apartheid schools," where Whites make up less than 1 percent of the enrollment. And despite the dramatic suburbanization of African American and Hispanic families in recent decades, across the nation, 80 percent of Latino

students and 74 percent of Black students still attend majority non-White schools—that is, schools that are 50 to 100 percent minority (Orfield et al. 2012).

Conflict theorists also argue that the educational system socializes students into values dictated by the powerful, that schools stifle individualism and creativity in the name of maintaining order, and that the level of change they promote is relatively insignificant. From a conflict perspective, the inhibiting effects of education are particularly apparent in the "hidden curriculum" and the differential way in which status is bestowed.

The Hidden Curriculum

Schools are highly bureaucratic organizations, as we will see later. To maintain order, many teachers rely on rules and regulations. Unfortunately, the need for control and discipline can take precedence over the learning process. Teachers may focus on obedience to the rules as an end in itself, in which case students and teachers alike become victims of what Philip Jackson (1968) has called the *hidden curriculum.*

The term **hidden curriculum** refers to standards of behavior that are deemed proper by society and are taught subtly in schools. According to this curriculum, children must not speak until the teacher calls on them and must regulate their activities according to the clock or bells. In addition, they are expected to concentrate on their own work rather than to assist other students who learn more slowly. A hidden curriculum is evident in schools around the world. For example, Japanese schools offer guidance sessions that seek to improve the classroom experience and develop healthy living skills. In effect, these sessions instill values and encourage behavior that is useful in the Japanese business world, such as self-discipline and openness to group problem solving and decision making (Okano and Tsuchiya 1999).

In a classroom that is overly focused on obedience, value is placed on pleasing the teacher and remaining quiet rather than on creative thought and academic learning. Habitual obedience to authority may result in the type of distressing behavior documented by Stanley Milgram in his classic obedience studies.

 use your **sociological imagination**

In what ways did the high school you attended convey the hidden curriculum of education?

Credentialism

Sixty years ago, a high school diploma was the minimum requirement for entry into the paid labor force of the United States. Today, a college diploma is virtually the bare minimum. This change reflects the process of **credentialism**—a term used to describe an increase in the lowest level of education needed to enter a field.

In recent decades, the number of occupations that are viewed as professions has risen. Credentialism is one symptom of this trend. Employers and occupational associations typically contend that such changes are a logical response to the increasing complexity of many jobs. However, in many cases, employers raise the degree requirements for a position simply because all applicants have achieved the existing minimum credential (David K. Brown 2001; Hurn 1985).

Conflict theorists observe that credentialism may reinforce social inequality. Applicants from poor and minority backgrounds are especially likely to suffer from the escalation of qualifications, since they lack the financial resources needed to obtain degree after degree. In addition, upgrading of credentials serves the self-interest of the two groups most responsible for this trend. Educational institutions profit from prolonging the investment of time and money that people make by staying in school. Moreover, as C. J. Hurn (1985) has suggested, current jobholders have a stake in raising occupational requirements, since credentialism can increase the status of an occupation and lead to demands for higher pay. Max Weber anticipated this possibility as early as 1916, concluding that the "universal clamor for the creation of educational certificates in all fields makes for the formation of a privileged stratum in businesses and in offices" (Gerth and Mills 1958:240–241).

 use your **sociological imagination**

How would you react if the job you have or plan to pursue suddenly required a higher-level degree? If suddenly the requirements were lowered?

Bestowal of Status

Sociologists have long recognized that schooling is central to social stratification. Both functionalist and conflict theorists agree that education performs the important function of bestowing status. According to Kingsley Davis and Wilbert E. Moore (1945), society must distribute its members among a variety of social positions. Education can contribute to this process by sorting people into appropriate levels and courses of study that will prepare them for positions in the labor force.

As noted earlier, an increasing proportion of people in the United States are obtaining high school diplomas, college degrees, and advanced professional degrees. From a functionalist perspective, this widening bestowal of status is beneficial not only to particular recipients but to society as a whole.

Conflict theorists are far more critical of the *differential* way in which education bestows status. They stress that schools sort pupils according to their social class backgrounds. Although the educational system helps certain poor children to move into middle-class professional positions, it denies most disadvantaged children the same educational opportunities afforded to children of the affluent. In this way, schools tend to preserve social class inequalities in each new generation. Higher education in particular acts more like a sieve that sorts people out of the educated classes than a social ladder that helps all with ambition to rise (Alon 2009; Giroux 1988; Sacks 2007).

The status that comes with advanced training is not cheap and has been getting progressively more expensive for several decades. Over the past 30 years, average tuition and fees at community colleges have risen at a relatively modest pace that matches the inflation rate (Figure 43-3). The increases have been greater at four-year institutions. At the same time as tuition has been increasing, financial aid has become more difficult to obtain (see Box 28-2).

Even a single school can reinforce class differences by putting students in tracks. The term **tracking** refers to the practice of placing students in specific curriculum groups on the basis of their test scores and other criteria. Tracking begins very early, often in reading groups during first grade. The practice can reinforce the disadvantages that children from less affluent families may face if they haven't been exposed to reading materials, computers, and other forms of educational stimulation during their early childhood years. To ignore this connection between tracking and students' race and social class is to fundamentally misunderstand how schools perpetuate the existing social structure.

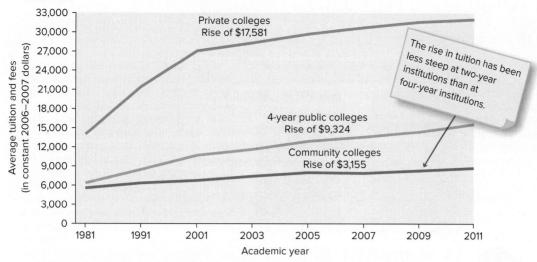

FIGURE 43-3 **Tuition Costs, 1981–2011**

Y-axis: Average tuition and fees (in constant 2006–2007 dollars)

Private colleges
Rise of $17,581

4-year public colleges
Rise of $9,324

Community colleges
Rise of $3,155

The rise in tuition has been less steep at two-year institutions than at four-year institutions.

*X-axis:* Academic year (1981, 1991, 2001, 2003, 2005, 2007, 2009, 2011)

Source: National Center for Education Statistics 2013.

Not surprisingly, most recent research on tracking raises questions about its effectiveness, especially for low-ability students. In one study of low-income schools in California, researchers discovered a staggering difference between students who were tracked and those who were not. At one school, all interested students were allowed to enroll in advanced placement (AP) courses, not just those who were selected by the administration. Half the open enrollment students scored high enough to qualify for college credit—a much higher proportion than in selective programs, in which only 17 percent of students qualified for college credit. Tracking programs do not necessarily identify those students with the potential to succeed (B. Ellison 2008; Sacks 2007).

Conflict theorists hold that the educational inequalities produced by tracking are designed to meet the needs of modern capitalist societies. Samuel Bowles and Herbert Gintis (1976) have argued that capitalism requires a skilled, disciplined labor force, and that the educational system of the United States is structured with that objective in mind. Citing numerous studies, they offer support for what they call the **correspondence principle.** According to this approach, schools promote the values expected of individuals in each social class and perpetuate social class divisions from one generation to the next. Thus, working-class children, assumed to be destined for subordinate positions, are likely to be placed in high school vocational and general tracks, which emphasize close supervision and compliance with authority. In contrast, young people from more affluent families are likely to be directed to college preparatory tracks, which stress leadership and decision making—the skills they are expected to need as adults (McLanahan and Percheski 2008).

Feminist Perspective

The educational system of the United States, like many other social institutions, has long been characterized by discriminatory treatment of women. In 1833, Oberlin College became the first institution of higher learning to admit female students—some 200 years after the first men's college was established. But Oberlin believed that women should aspire to become wives and mothers, not lawyers and intellectuals. In addition to attending classes, female students washed men's clothing, cared for their rooms, and served them at meals. In the 1840s, Lucy Stone, then an Oberlin undergraduate and later one of the nation's most outspoken feminist leaders, refused to write a commencement address because it would have been read to the audience by a male student.

In the 20th century, sexism in education showed up in many ways—in textbooks with negative stereotypes of women, counselors' pressure on female students to prepare for "women's work," and unequal funding for women's and men's athletic programs. But perhaps nowhere was educational discrimination more evident than in the employment of teachers. The positions of university professor and college administrator, which hold relatively high status in the United States, were generally filled by men. Public school teachers, who earn much lower salaries, were largely female.

Women have made great strides in one area: the proportion of women who continue their schooling. As recently as 1969, twice as many men as women received college degrees; today, women outnumber men at college commencements. Moreover, women's access to graduate education and to medical, dental, and law schools has increased dramatically in the past few decades as a result of the Education Act of 1972. Box 43-2 examines the far-reaching effects of Title IX, the part of the act that concerns discrimination against women in education.

Much has been made of the superior academic achievement of girls and women. Today, researchers are beginning to examine the reasons for their comparatively strong performance in school—or to put it another way, for men's lackluster performance. Some studies suggest that men's aggressiveness, together with the fact that they do better in the workplace than women, even with less schooling, predisposes them to undervalue higher education. While the "absence of men" on many college campuses has captured headlines, it has also created a false crisis in public discourse. Few students realize their potential exclusively through formal education; other factors, such as ambition and personal talent, contribute to their success. And many students, including low-income and immigrant children, face much greater challenges than the so-called gender gap in education (Buchmann et al. 2008; Corbett et al. 2008; Kimmel 2006).

The Debate over Title IX

Few federal policies have had such a visible effect on education as Title IX, which mandates gender equity in education in federally funded schools. Congressional amendments to the Education Act of 1972 have brought significant changes for both men and women at all levels of schooling. Title IX eliminated sex-segregated classes, prohibited sex discrimination in admissions and financial aid, and mandated that girls receive more opportunities to play sports, in proportion to their enrollment and interest.

Under this landmark legislation, to receive federal funds, a school or college must pass one of three tests. First, the numbers of male and female athletes must be proportional to the numbers of men and women enrolled at the school. Second, lacking that, the school must show a continuing history of expanding opportunities for female athletes. Or third, the school must demonstrate that the level of female participation in sports meets female students' level of interest or ability.

Today, Title IX is still one of the more controversial attempts ever made by the federal government to promote equality for all citizens. Its consequences for the funding of college athletics programs are hotly debated, while its real and lasting effects on college admissions and employment are often

> Critics charge that men's teams have suffered from proportional funding of women's teams and athletic scholarships.

forgotten. Critics charge that men's teams have suffered from proportional funding of women's teams and athletic scholarships, since schools with tight athletic budgets can expand women's sports only at the expense of men's sports. Yet from 1972, when Title IX was passed, to 2013, the number of girls participating in high school athletics jumped from 300,000 to over 3.2 million.

From the women's point of view, however, the increased funding for women's sports has benefited men in some ways. In terms of coaching and administration, men have increasingly replaced women as directors of women's sports since Title IX was passed. Today only 19 percent of collegiate women's athletic administrators are women, compared to over 90 percent in the early 1970s. No national data exists for high school sports leadership, but an analysis of Minnesota youth soccer found that only 15 percent of head coaches were women.

Sociologists caution that the social effects of sports on college campuses are not all positive. Michael A. Messner, professor of sociology at the University of Southern California, points to some troubling results of a survey by the Women's Sports Foundation. The study shows that teenage girls who play sports simply for fun have more positive body images than girls who don't play sports. But those who are "highly involved" in sports are more likely than other girls to take steroids and to become risk takers. "Everyone has tacitly agreed, it seems, to view men's sports as the standard to which women should strive to have equal access," Messner writes. He is skeptical of a system that propels a lucky few college athletes to stardom each year while leaving the majority, many of them African American, without a career or an education. Certainly that was not the kind of equal opportunity legislators envisioned when they wrote Title IX.

LET'S DISCUSS

1. Has Title IX had an effect on you personally? If so, explain. On balance, do you think the increase in women's participation in sports has been good for society as a whole?

2. How might Title IX affect the way students and the public view gender roles?

Sources: Brady 2010; Cooky and LaVoi 2012; *The Economist* 2013e; Messner 2002; Pennington 2008; Spencer 2008; Tigay 2011; Women's Sports Foundation 2011.

In cultures in which traditional gender roles remain the social norm, women's education suffers appreciably. Since September 11, 2001, the growing awareness of the Taliban's repression of Afghan women has dramatized the gender disparities in education in developing nations. Research has demonstrated that women are critical to economic development and good governance, and that education is instrumental in preparing them for those roles. Educating women, especially young girls, yields high social returns by lowering birthrates and improving agricultural productivity through better management (I. Coleman 2004).

Interactionist Perspective

High school students know who they are—the kids who qualify for a free lunch. So stigmatized are they that in some schools, these students will buy a bit of food in the cash line or simply go without eating to avoid being labeled a "poor kid." School officials in San Francisco are so concerned about their plight that they are moving to cashless cafeterias, in which everyone, rich or poor, uses a debit card (Pogash 2008).

The labeling approach suggests that if we treat people in particular ways, they may fulfill our expectations. Children who are labeled as "troublemakers" may come to view themselves as delinquents. Similarly, a dominant group's stereotyping of racial minorities may limit their opportunities to break away from expected roles.

Can the labeling process operate in the classroom? Because interactionist researchers focus on micro-level classroom dynamics, they have been particularly interested in this question. Sociologist Howard S. Becker (1952) studied public schools in low-income and affluent areas of Chicago. He noticed that administrators expected less of students from poor neighborhoods, and wondered if teachers accepted their view. A decade later, in *Pygmalion in the Classroom,* psychologist Robert Rosenthal and school principal Lenore Jacobson (1968, 1992) documented what

In Tokyo, parents escort their daughter to an admissions interview at a highly competitive private school. Some Japanese families enroll children as young as 2 years of age in cram schools. Like parents in the United States, Japanese parents know that higher education bestows status.

TABLE **43-1** SOCIOLOGICAL PERSPECTIVES ON EDUCATION

Theoretical Perspective	Emphasis
Functionalist	Transmission of the dominant culture Integration of society Promotion of social norms, values, and sanctions Promotion of desirable social change
Conflict	Domination by the elite through unequal access to schooling Hidden curriculum Credentialism Bestowal of status
Interactionist	Teacher-expectancy effect
Feminist	Treatment of female students Role of women's education in economic development

they referred to as a **teacher-expectancy effect**—the impact that a teacher's expectations about a student's performance may have on the student's actual achievements. This effect is especially evident in the lower grades (through Grade 3).

Studies in the United States have revealed that teachers wait longer for an answer from a student they believe to be a high achiever and are more likely to give such children a second chance. In one experiment, teachers' expectations were even shown to have an impact on students' athletic achievements. Teachers obtained better athletic performance—as measured in the number of sit-ups or push-ups performed—from those students of whom they *expected* higher numbers. Despite the controversial nature of these findings, researchers continue to document the existence of the teacher-expectancy effect. Interactionists emphasize that ability alone may be less predictive of academic success than one might think (Babad and Taylor 1992; Brint 1998; Rosenthal and Jacobson 1992:247–262).

Table 43-1 summarizes the four major theoretical perspectives on education.

MODULE 43 | **Recap and Review**

Summary

Education is a cultural universal found in varied forms throughout the world.

1. The transmission of knowledge and bestowal of status are manifest functions of education. Among the latent functions are transmitting culture, promoting social and political integration, maintaining social control, and serving as an agent of social change.

2. In the view of conflict theorists, education serves as an instrument of elite domination by creating standards for entry into occupations, bestowing status unequally, and subordinating the role of women.

3. Although U.S. women attain higher levels of education than do men, their performance in the workplace continues to lag. In cultures that maintain traditional gender roles, education of women is critical to economic and social development.

4. Teacher expectations about a student's performance can sometimes affect the student's actual achievement.

Thinking Critically

1. How do the functions of integration and social control reinforce each other? How do they work against each other?

2. What are the functions and dysfunctions of tracking in schools? In what ways might tracking have a positive impact on the self-concepts of various students? In what ways might it have a negative impact?

Key Terms

Correspondence principle

Credentialism

Education

Hidden curriculum

Teacher-expectancy effect

Tracking

Nineteenth-century educators would be amazed at the scale of schools in the United States in the 21st century. The nation has about 15 million high school students today, compared to 10 million in 1961 and 5 million in 1931 (Bureau of the Census 2012c:Table H S-20; 2011a:Table 246).

In many respects, today's schools, when viewed as an example of a formal organization, are similar to factories, hospitals, and business firms. Like those organizations, schools do not operate autonomously; they are influenced by the market of potential students. This statement is especially true of private schools, but could have broader impact if acceptance of voucher plans and other school choice programs increases. The parallels between schools and other types of formal organizations will become more apparent as we examine the bureaucratic nature of schools, teaching as an occupation, and the student subculture (Dougherty and Hammack 1992).

Bureaucratization of Schools

It simply is not possible for a single teacher to transmit culture and skills to children of varying ages who will enter many diverse occupations. The growing number of students being served by school systems and the greater degree of specialization required within a technologically complex society have combined to bureaucratize schools.

Max Weber noted five basic characteristics of bureaucracy, all of which are evident in the vast majority of schools, whether at the elementary, secondary, or even college level:

1. **Division of labor.** Specialized experts teach particular age levels and specific subjects. Public elementary and secondary schools now employ instructors whose sole responsibility is to work with children with learning disabilities or physical impairments.

2. **Hierarchy of authority.** Each employee of a school system is responsible to a higher authority. Teachers must report to principals and assistant principals and may also be supervised by department heads. Principals are answerable to a superintendent of schools, and the superintendent is hired and fired by a board of education.

3. **Written rules and regulations.** Teachers and administrators must conform to numerous rules and regulations in the performance of their duties. This bureaucratic trait can become dysfunctional; the time invested in completing required forms could instead be spent in preparing lessons or conferring with students.

4. **Impersonality.** As class sizes have swelled at schools and universities, it has become more difficult for teachers to give personal attention to each student. In fact, bureaucratic norms may actually encourage teachers to treat all students in the same way, despite the fact that students have distinctive personalities and learning needs.

5. **Employment based on technical qualifications.** At least in theory, the hiring of instructors is based on professional competence and expertise. Promotions are normally dictated by written personnel policies; people who excel may be granted lifelong job security through tenure.

Functionalists take a generally positive view of the bureaucratization of education. Teachers can master the skills needed to work with a specialized clientele, since they no longer are expected to cover a broad range of instruction. The chain of command within schools is clear. Students are presumably treated in an unbiased fashion because of uniformly applied rules. Finally, security of position protects teachers from unjustified dismissal. In general, then, functionalists stress that the bureaucratization of education increases the likelihood that students, teachers, and administrators will be dealt with fairly—that is, on the basis of rational and equitable criteria.

In contrast, conflict theorists argue that the trend toward more centralized education has harmful consequences for disadvantaged people. The standardization of educational curricula, including textbooks, will generally reflect the values, interests, and lifestyles of the most powerful groups in our society, and may ignore those of racial and ethnic minorities. In addition, the disadvantaged, more so than the affluent, will find it difficult to sort through complex educational bureaucracies and to organize effective lobbying groups. Therefore, in the view of conflict theorists, low-income and minority parents will have even less influence over citywide and statewide educational administrators than they have over local school officials (Bowles and Gintis 1976; Katz 1971).

Sometimes schools can seem overwhelmingly bureaucratic, with the effect of stifling rather than nourishing intellectual curiosity in students. This concern has led many parents and policymakers to push for school choice programs—allowing parents to

Despite efforts to establish positive relationships among students and between teachers and students, many young people view their schools as impersonal institutions.

Taking Sociology to Work

Diane Belcher Gray, *Assistant Director of Volunteer Services, New River Community College*

Not until Diane Belcher Gray enrolled at New River Community College in Dublin, Virginia, did she realize that social work had always been part of her daily life. To this mother of two teenagers, helping people in need was something she just did, without even thinking about it.

Today, as assistant director of Volunteer Services at New River, Belcher Gray assists Partners for Success, a mentoring program that matches struggling students with people in the community who have the time and energy to help them. With the director, she recruits and trains a "talent bank" of mentors, matches the mentors with student partners, and develops support programs for students experiencing problems with child care, transportation, and other necessities. The program's goal is to develop confident and successful learners who can take charge of their own studies.

Before she moved to Volunteer Services, Belcher Gray was an administrative assistant in Workforce Development at New River, where she helped youths who lack direction and workers laid off from local factories to develop more marketable skills. In that job, she facilitated new students' transition to college, helping them to register and apply for financial aid and connecting them with professors in their fields of interest. Belcher Gray also worked directly with the administration to develop a special fast-track program for laid-off workers.

As in all human services jobs, people skills, particularly sensitivity and compassion, are of paramount importance in Belcher Gray's work. An understanding of the social and economic forces that affect the larger society is also essential. Belcher Gray credits her sociology courses with helping her to "engage where needed." "Sociology exposed me to other people's situations and the role of society in creating them," she explains. "It helped me look beyond the individual level to understand societal impacts and solutions."

Asked to advise current sociology majors, Belcher Gray says, "Drink it up, try and take it all in, relate it to the real world. Take notice of current cultural and economic conditions, understanding that when you attempt to 'fix' one part of society you must also be aware of how that will affect other parts of society."

LET'S DISCUSS

1. Have you, like Diane Belcher Gray, realized through education that something you were doing without thinking about it has helped to prepare you for employment? Explain.

2. Do some research on Dublin, Virginia, and the surrounding area. What kind of economy does this community have? Relate the layoffs the community has been experiencing to larger societal forces.

choose the school that suits their children's needs, and forcing schools to compete for their "customers."

In the United States, another significant countertrend to the bureaucratization of schools is the availability of education over the Internet. Increasingly, colleges and universities are reaching out via the web, offering entire courses and even majors to students in the comfort of their homes. Online curricula provide flexibility for working students and others who may have difficulty attending conventional classes because of distance or disability. Research on this type of learning is just beginning, so the question of whether teacher–student contact can thrive online remains to be settled. Computer-mediated instruction may also have an impact on instructors' status as employees, which we will discuss next, as well as on alternative forms of education like homeschooling.

use your **sociological imagination**

How would you make your school less bureaucratic? What would it be like?

Teachers: Employees and Instructors

Whether they serve as instructors of preschoolers or of graduate students, teachers are employees of formal organizations with bureaucratic structures. There is an inherent conflict in serving

as a professional in a bureaucracy. The organization follows the principles of hierarchy and expects adherence to its rules, but professionalism demands the individual responsibility of the practitioner. This conflict is very real for teachers, who experience all the positive and negative consequences of working in bureaucracies.

A teacher undergoes many perplexing stresses every day. While teachers' academic assignments have become more specialized, the demands on their time remain diverse and contradictory. Conflicts arise from serving as an instructor, a disciplinarian, and an employee of a school district at the same time. In too many schools, discipline means dealing with

From preschool through high school, teachers face a variety of challenges, including preparing students for standardized tests.

Violence in the Schools

Littleton, Colorado; Red Lake, Minnesota; Jonesboro, Arkansas; West Paducah, Kentucky; Newtown, Connecticut; Edinboro, Pennsylvania; Springfield, Oregon—these are now more than just the names of small towns and medium-size cities. They resonate with the sound of gunshots, or kids killing kids on school grounds. As a result, people no longer perceive schools to be safe havens. But how accurate is that impression?

Studies of school violence put the recent spate of school killings in perspective:

- 17 homicides of children ages 5 to 18 occurred at school during the 2009–2010 year.
- Less than 2 percent of youth homicides occur at school.
- About 7 percent of teachers report being threatened with injury or physically attacked by a student from their school.

Schools, then, are safer than neighborhoods, but people are still unnerved by the perception of an alarming rise in school violence generated by heavy media coverage of recent incidents. Some conflict theorists object to the huge outcry about recent violence in schools. After all, they note, violence in and around inner-city schools has a long history. It seems that only when middle-class White children are the victims does

school violence become a plank on the national policy agenda. When violence hits the middle class, the problem is viewed not as an extension of delinquency but a structural issue in need of legislative remedies such as gun control (see the Social Policy section in Chapter 7).

Feminists observe that virtually all the offenders in these incidents are male, and in some instances, such as the case in Jonesboro, the victims are disproportionately female. The precipitating factor in the violence is often a broken-off dating relationship—yet another example of the violence of men against women (or in this case, boys against girls).

Increasingly, efforts to prevent school violence are focusing on the ways in which the socialization of young people contributes to violence. For example, the American Medical Association has invested in a violence-prevention curriculum for elementary school students that teaches social skills related to anger management, impulse control, and empathy.

> A child has a less than one in a million chance of being killed at school.

Some people believe that a key ingredient in the prevention of violence, in and out of school, is greater parental supervision of and responsibility for their children. In her book *A Tribe Apart,* Patricia Hersch documents the lives of eight teens growing up in a Virginia suburb over a three-year period. Her conclusion: children need meaningful adult relationships in their lives. Former Secretary of Education Richard Riley cites studies showing that youths who feel connected to their parents and schools are less likely than others to engage in high-risk behaviors.

LET'S DISCUSS

1. Has a shooting or other violent episode ever occurred at your school? If so, how did students react? Do you feel safer at school than at home, as experts say you are?

2. What steps have administrators at your school taken to prevent violence? Have they been effective, or should other steps be taken?

Sources: Centers for Disease Control and Prevention 2008b, 2013; Department of Education 1999, 2004; Donohue et al., 1998; Hersch 1998; National Center for Education Statistics 2002.

---

violence (see Box 44-1). Burnout is one result of these stresses: between a quarter and a third of new teachers quit within their first three years, and as many as half leave poor urban schools in their first five years (Wallis 2008).

Given these difficulties, does teaching remain an attractive profession in the United States? In 2012, 3.2 percent of male first-year college students and 8.2 percent of women indicated that they were interested in becoming either elementary or high school teachers. These figures are dramatically lower than the 11 percent of first-year male students and 37 percent of first-year female students who held those occupational aspirations in 1966 (Pryor et al. 2007:122, 76; 2013).

Undoubtedly, economic considerations enter into students' feelings about the attractiveness of teaching. In 2012, the average salary for all public elementary and secondary school teachers in the United States was reported at $55,418, placing teachers somewhere near the average of all the nation's wage earners. In most other industrialized countries, teachers' salaries are higher in relation to the general standard of living. Of course, teachers' salaries vary considerably from state to state (Figure 44-1), and even more from one school district to another. Nevertheless, the economic reward for teaching is miniscule compared to some

career options: the CEO of a major corporation makes more money in a day than the average teacher makes in a year.

The status of any job reflects several factors, including the level of education required, financial compensation, and the respect given the occupation by society. The teaching profession (see Table 27-1) is feeling pressure in all three of these areas. First, the level of formal schooling required for teaching remains high, and the public has begun to call for new competency examinations. Second, the statistics just cited demonstrate that teachers' salaries are significantly lower than those of many professionals and skilled workers. Third, the overall prestige of the teaching profession has declined in the past decade. Many teachers have become disappointed and frustrated and have left the educational world for careers in other professions.

Student Subcultures

An important latent function of education relates directly to student life: schools provide for students' social and recreational needs. Education helps toddlers and young children to develop interpersonal skills that are essential during adolescence and adulthood. In their high school and college years, students may

FIGURE 44-1 **Average Salary for Teachers**

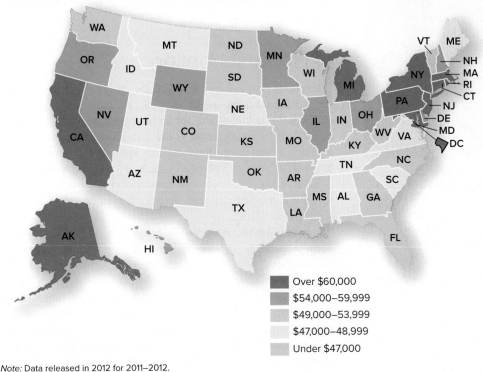

- Over $60,000
- $54,000–59,999
- $49,000–53,999
- $47,000–48,999
- Under $47,000

Note: Data released in 2012 for 2011–2012.
Source: National Education Association 2012.

State averages for teacher salaries range from a low of $38,804 in South Dakota to a high of $73,998 in New York.

Teachers and administrators are becoming more sensitized to these issues. Perhaps more important, some schools are creating gay–straight alliances (GSAs), school-sponsored support groups that bring gay teens together with sympathetic straight peers. Begun in Los Angeles in 1984, these programs numbered nearly 3,000 nationwide in 2005; most were founded after the murder of Matthew Shepard, a gay college student, in 1998. In some districts parents have objected to these organizations, but the same court rulings that protect the right of conservative Bible groups to meet on school grounds also protect GSAs. In 2003, the gay–straight movement reached a milestone when the New York City public schools moved an in-school program for gays, bisexuals, and transgendered students to a separate school. The Harvey Milk High School was named in memory of San Francisco's first openly gay city supervisor, who was assassinated in 1978 (Gay, Lesbian and Straight Education Network 2012).

We can find a similar diversity of student groups at the college level. Burton Clark and Martin Trow (1966) and, more recently, Helen Lefkowitz Horowitz (1987) have identified four distinctive subcultures among college students:

1. The *collegiate* subculture focuses on having fun and socializing. These students define what constitutes a "reasonable" amount of academic work (and what amount of work is "excessive" and leads to being labeled a "grind"). Members of the collegiate subculture have little commitment to academic pursuits. Athletes often fit into this subculture.

2. The *academic* subculture identifies with the intellectual concerns of the faculty and values knowledge for its own sake.

3. The *vocational* subculture is interested primarily in career prospects and views college as a means of obtaining degrees that are essential for advancement.

4. Finally, the *nonconformist* subculture is hostile to the college environment and seeks ideas that may or may not relate to academic studies. This group may find outlets through campus publications or issue-oriented groups.

Each college student is eventually exposed to these competing subcultures and must determine which (if any) seems most in line with his or her feelings and interests.

The typology used by the researchers reminds us that school is a complex social organization—almost like a community with

meet future husbands and wives and establish lifelong friendships. It is important to remember that these informal aspects of schools, community colleges, and universities do not exist independently of schools' explicit educational functions. Furthermore, informal social systems can be as important as the academic system in determining students' positive and negative outcomes (Crosnoe 2011).

When people observe high schools, community colleges, or universities from the outside, students appear to constitute a cohesive, uniform group. However, the student subculture is actually quite complex and diverse. High school cliques and social groups may crop up according to race, social class, physical attractiveness, placement in courses, athletic ability, and leadership roles in the school and community. In his classic community study of "Elmtown," August B. Hollingshead (1975) found some 259 distinct cliques in a single high school. The cliques, whose average size was five, were centered on the school itself, on recreational activities, and on religious and community groups.

Amid these close-knit and often rigidly segregated cliques, gay and lesbian students are particularly vulnerable. Peer group pressure to conform is intense at this age. Although coming to terms with one's sexuality is difficult for all adolescents, it can be downright dangerous for those whose sexual orientation does not conform to societal expectations.

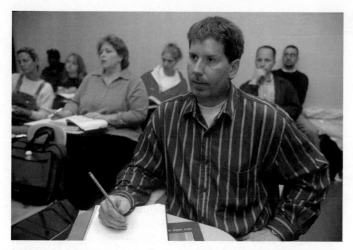

Student subcultures are more diverse today than in the past. Many adults are returning to college to obtain further education, advance their careers, or change their line of work.

use your sociological imagination

What distinctive subcultures can you identify at your college?

different neighborhoods. Of course, these four subcultures are not the only ones evident on college campuses in the United States. For example, one might find subcultures of Vietnam veterans or former full-time homemakers at community colleges and four-year commuter institutions. And as more and more students from minority groups decide to continue their formal education beyond high school, subcultures based on race and ethnicity will become more evident. As Figure 44-2 shows, college campuses are becoming increasingly diverse.

Sociologist Joe R. Feagin has studied a distinctive collegiate subculture: Black students at predominantly White universities. These students must function academically and socially within universities where there are few Black faculty members or administrators, where harassment of Blacks by campus police is common, and where curricula place little emphasis on Black contributions. Feagin (1989:11) suggests that "for minority students life at a predominantly White college or university means long-term encounters with pervasive whiteness." In Feagin's view, Black students at such institutions experience both blatant and subtle racial discrimination, which has a cumulative impact that can seriously damage the students' confidence (see also Feagin et al. 1996).

Homeschooling

When most people think of school, they think of bricks and mortar and the teachers, administrators, and other employees who staff school buildings. But for an increasing number of students in the United States, home is the classroom and the teacher is a parent. About 1.5 million students are now being educated at home. That is about 3 percent of the K–12 school population. For these students, the issues of bureaucratization and social structure are less significant than they are for public school students (Grady et al. 2010).

In the 1800s, after the establishment of public schools, families that taught their children at home lived in isolated environments or held strict religious views that were at odds with the secular environment of public schools. But today, homeschooling is attracting a broader range of families not necessarily tied to organized religion. Poor academic quality, peer pressure, and school violence are motivating many parents to teach their children at home. In addition, some immigrants choose homeschooling as a way to ease their children's transition to a new society. For example, the growing Arab American population recently joined the movement toward homeschooling (MacFarquhar 2008; National Center for Education Statistics 2009).

While supporters of homeschooling believe children can do just as well or better in homeschools as in public schools, critics counter that because homeschooled children are isolated from the larger community, they lose an important chance to improve their socialization skills. But proponents of homeschooling claim their children benefit from contact with others besides their own age group. They also see homeschools as a good alternative for children who suffer from attention-deficit/

FIGURE 44-2 **College Campuses by Race and Ethnicity: Then, Now, and in the Future**

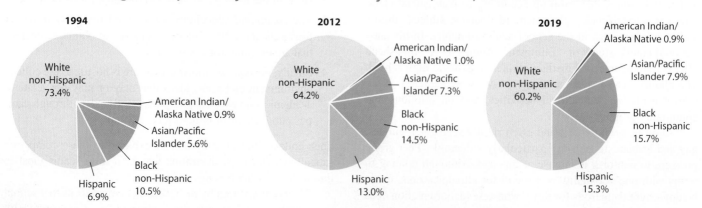

Note: Percentages do not add to 100 due to rounding error. Nonresident aliens whose race/ethnicity is unknown excluded.
Source: Hussar and Bailey 2011:Table 29.

hyperactivity disorder (ADHD) and learning disorders (LDs). Such children often do better in smaller classes, which present fewer distractions to disturb their concentration.

Quality control is an issue in homeschooling. While homeschooling is legal in all 50 states, 10 states require no notification that a child will be homeschooled, and another 14 require notification only. Other states may require parents to submit their children's curricula or test scores for professional evaluation. Despite the lack of uniform standards, a research review by the Home School Legal Defense Association (2005) reports that homeschooled students score higher than others on standardized tests, in every subject and every grade.

Who are the people who are running homeschools? In general, they tend to have higher-than-average incomes and educational levels. Most are two-parent families, and their children watch less television than average—both factors that are likely to support superior educational performance. The same students, with the same support from their parents, would probably do just as well in the public schools. As research has repeatedly shown, small classes are better than big classes, and strong parental and community involvement is key (R. Cox 2003:28).

Whatever the controversy over homeschooling in the United States, it is much less serious than in some other nations. In 2010, the U.S. Immigration and Naturalization Service began granting political asylum to German families who homeschool their children, in violation of their country's constitution. German parents can be fined and imprisoned for homeschooling their children (Francis 2010).

Charter schools are another area of controversy in the educational system. In the Social Policy section that follows we consider the significance of these schools and whether parents should be able to enroll their children in them

social policy and Education | Charter Schools

Discontent with public schools stretches back for decades. In the 1970s, "classrooms without walls" were supposed to open up the curriculum to students' creativity. In 2002, the No Child Left Behind initiative was supposed to guarantee that all students would learn the basics. Although test scores inched up a bit in response, critics complained that schools were becoming too test-oriented, and scores on interactive science and math tests sank compared to those in other nations (K. Clark 2010). Meanwhile, the charter school movement had been gathering strength. **Charter schools** are experimental schools that are developed and managed by individuals, groups of parents, or an educational management organization. Although these schools are typically considered to be public schools, they are administered outside the official public school system. Their charters (legal contracts) permit them to establish their own rules, curricula, and admissions and professional standards. Within their communities, however, charter schools must still abide by prevailing standards for health, public safety, and equal opportunity (Renzulli and Roscigno 2007).

Looking at the Issue

Charter schools first opened in Minnesota in 1992; by 2014, about 2.6 million children were enrolled in them in 42 different states (Figure 44-3). Advocates of charter schools claim that they offer parents accountability for their children's education. In effect, charter schools compete with public schools, offering an alternative that was once

MAPPING LIFE NATIONWIDE

FIGURE 44-3 **Charter Schools**

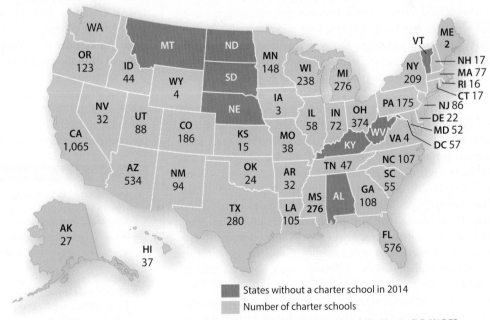

States without a charter school in 2014

Number of charter schools

Sources: National Alliance for Public Charter Schools, 2012. The Public Charter Schools Dashboard, Washington, DC: NAPCS.

—Continued

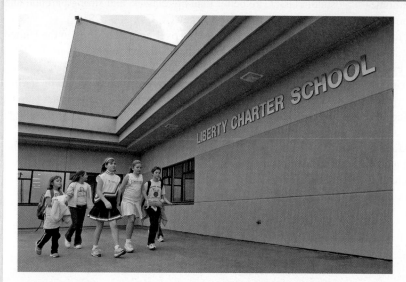

Charter Schools such as this one in Nampa, Idaho, are the latest answer to efforts to improve the quality of education.

available only to the wealthy (National Alliance for Public Charter Schools 2014).

Applying Sociology

Functionalists argue that charter schools meet society's need for education while serving a diverse student body. Despite criticism that charter schools are elitist institutions that serve the children of privileged White families, data show that 55 percent of the students enrolled in these schools are African American or Latino. More than a third of them qualify for free or reduced price lunches (Gabriel 2010).

Although charter schools are publicly financed, most are not unionized. From a conflict perspective, charter schools do not represent teachers' interests well and are contributing to the decline of labor unions. Partly in response to this concern, public school districts in Denver, Detroit, Milwaukee, Boston, and Minnesota have empowered teachers to create their own charter schools (Dillon 2008; Hu 2010).

Because the charter school movement is a comparatively recent one, we do not have much research on the long-term impact of charter versus noncharter schools. Of course, there is great variation among both within the same city much less the same state. News stories about individual charter schools and high-profile advocates like the Bill and Melinda Gates Foundation suggest that these schools' outcomes are quite positive. However, the diversity in purpose, funding, organization, and curriculum that characterizes charter schools makes generalizing from one school or community to another very difficult.

As an example of the different conclusions that can be reached, many top school lists disproportionately identify charter schools as outperforming noncharter schools. Yet research released in 2012 shows that at least a third of

charter schools do *worse* than the public schools they replaced. However, research done at Stanford University on charter schools in 26 states shows that charter school students had an equivalent of eight extra days of learning each year beyond their peers in traditional schools (Bankston et al. 2013; Lubienski and Weitzel 2012; Paulson 2013; E. Thomas and Wingert 2010).

Initiating Policy

In the United States, unlike virtually all other industrial nations, school policy is driven at the local level. Although the federal government may encourage certain policies through public funding, and may dictate certain standards like nondiscrimination, school policy is created largely at the community level following statewide standards. Thus, in 2010, when the Department of Education began to expend $4.3 billion as part of a general educational stimulus program, it left the structure and organization of schools to local communities. Programs such as Race to the Top stressed only improvements in academic achievement (K. Clark 2010).

Today, the charter school movement is not the only approach to educational reform; other school choice programs are available to families. Homeschooling, described earlier in this module, could be viewed as the most complete alternative to public schools. In addition, some cities offer parents vouchers that allow them, in effect, to send their children to any local school, public, private, or religious, at taxpayers' expense. Yet as Karl Alexander (1997:17) eloquently noted in his presidential address to the Southern Sociological Society, "The charter school movement, with its 'let 1,000 flowers bloom' philosophy, is certain to yield an occasional prize-winning rose. But is . . . [this approach to school choice] likely to prove a reliable guide for broadbased, systematic reform—the kind of reform that will carry the great mass of our children closer to where we want them to be? I hardly think so." Indeed, with such diversity in learning environments found among thousands of charter schools, the jury is still out on their effectiveness. As with most educational institutions, one cannot assume quality just based on a certain structure, size, affiliation, or funding source.

TAKE THE ISSUE WITH YOU

1. Do you have any experience with educational reform, either as a student yourself or as a parent? If so, describe the changes that you witnessed. Were they successful in improving educational outcomes?

2. Which type of school choice program, if any, would you favor—homeschooling, charter schools, or school vouchers? Explain your choice.

3. Are you concerned about educational standards in the United States? If so, do you think schools should be reformed at the local level? Should the federal government become more involved in school reform?

Summary

Most schools in the United States are organized like formal organizations such as factories and hospitals.

1. Weber's five basic characteristics of bureaucracies are all evident in schools.

2. Teachers are professionals who serve as part of a bureaucracy. There is an inherent conflict in combining those two different roles.

3. Schools provide for students' social and emotional needs as well as their educational needs. Student subcultures within high schools and colleges are complex and varied.

4. Homeschooling has become a viable alternative to traditional public and private schools. In some countries homeschooling is illegal.

5. **Charter schools**—experimental schools that are developed and managed by individuals, groups of parents, or an educational management organization—are one of

several recent attempts to reform the public school system in the United States. Although charter schools are popular with parents, research shows that about a third of them do worse than the public schools they replaced.

Thinking Critically

1. Select two functions of education and suggest how they could be fulfilled through homeschooling.

2. What student subcultures can you identify on your campus? Which have the highest and lowest social status? How would functionalists, conflict theorists, and interactionists view the existence of student subcultures on a college campus?

Key Terms

Charter school

Mastering This Chapter

taking sociology with you

1 Attend a meeting of a local Parent Teacher Association (PTA). What issues are parents talking about? Describe their concerns using one or more sociological perspectives.

2 Make a list of the student subcultures on your campus, then describe them using the concepts you learned in Module 12. Do any of

these subcultures serve as outgroups for other subcultures?

3 Does your school have a gay–straight alliance? If so, speak with one of the officers. What are members doing to reduce prejudice and foster better relations among gay and straight students? Explain their approach using sociological theory.

Charter school An experimental school that is developed and managed by individuals, groups of parents, or educational management organizations.

Correspondence principle The tendency of schools to promote the values expected of individuals in each social class and to perpetuate social class divisions from one generation to the next.

Credentialism An increase in the lowest level of education needed to enter a field.

Education A formal process of learning in which some people consciously teach, while others adopt the social role of learner.

Hidden curriculum Standards of behavior that are deemed proper by society and are taught subtly in schools.

Teacher-expectancy effect The impact that a teacher's expectations about a student's performance may have on the student's actual achievements.

Tracking The practice of placing students in specific curriculum groups on the basis of their test scores and other criteria.

self-quiz

Read each question carefully and then select the best answer.

1. Which sociological perspective emphasizes that the common identity and social integration fostered by education contribute to overall societal stability and consensus?
   a. the functionalist perspective
   b. the conflict perspective
   c. the interactionist perspective
   d. labeling theory

2. Which one of the following was introduced into school systems to promote social change?
   a. sex education classes
   b. affirmative action programs
   c. Project Head Start
   d. all of the above

3. The correspondence principle was developed by
   a. Max Weber.
   b. Karl Marx and Friedrich Engels.
   c. Samuel Bowles and Herbert Gintis.
   d. James Thurber.

4. The student subculture that is hostile to the college environment and seeks out ideas that may or may not relate to studies is called the
   a. collegiate subculture.
   b. academic subculture.
   c. vocational subculture.
   d. nonconformist subculture.

5. Most recent research on ability grouping raises questions about its
   a. effectiveness, especially for lower-achieving students.
   b. failure to improve the prospects of higher-achieving students.
   c. ability to improve the prospects of lower- and higher-achieving students.
   d. both a and b

6. The most basic *manifest* function of education is
   a. transmitting knowledge.
   b. transmitting culture.

   c. maintaining social control.
   d. serving as an agent of change.

7. Sixty years ago, a high school diploma was the minimum requirement for entry into the paid labor force of the United States. Today, a college diploma is virtually the bare minimum. This change reflects the process of
   a. tracking.
   b. credentialism.
   c. the hidden curriculum.
   d. the correspondence principle.

8. Samuel Bowles and Herbert Gintis have argued that capitalism requires a skilled, disciplined labor force and that the educational system of the United States is structured with that objective in mind. Citing numerous studies, they offer support for what they call
   a. tracking.
   b. credentialism.
   c. the correspondence principle.
   d. the teacher-expectancy effect.

9. The teacher-expectancy effect is most closely associated with
   a. the functionalist perspective.
   b. the conflict perspective.
   c. the interactionist perspective.
   d. anomie theory.

10. Sociologist Max Weber noted five basic characteristics of bureaucracy, all of which are evident in the vast majority of schools, whether at the elementary, secondary, or even college level. Which of the following is *not* one of them?
    a. division of labor
    b. written rules and regulations
    c. impersonality
    d. shared decision making

11. The _____ perspective stresses the importance of education in transmitting culture, maintaining social control, and promoting social change.

12. In the past, the integrative function of education was most obvious through its emphasis on promoting a common _____.

13. The _____ subculture identifies with the intellectual concerns of the faculty and values knowledge for its own sake.

14. A _____ _____ is an experimental school that is developed and managed outside the public school system.

15. Women's education tends to suffer in those cultures with traditional _____ _____.

16. Schools perform a variety of _____ functions, such as transmitting culture, promoting social and political integration, and maintaining social control.

17. Sociologist _____ _____ points out that better-educated people tend to have greater access to information, to hold more diverse opinions, and to possess the ability to make subtle distinctions in analysis.

18. The term _____ _____ refers to standards of behavior that are deemed proper by society and are taught subtly in schools. For example, children must not speak until the teacher calls on them and must regulate their activities according to the clock or the bell.

19. _____ is the practice of placing students in specific curriculum groups on the basis of their test scores and other criteria.

20. Of the four distinctive subcultures among college students discussed in the text, the _____ subculture is interested primarily in career prospects, and views college as a means of obtaining degrees that are essential for advancement.

Answers

1 (a); 2 (d); 3 (c); 4 (d); 5 (a); 6 (a); 7 (b); 8 (b); 9 (c); 10 (d); 11 functionalist; 12 language; 13 academic; 14 charter school; 15 gender roles; 16 latent; 17 Robin Williams; 18 hidden curriculum; 19 Tracking; 20 vocational

15 Religion

Religion is expressed in a variety of social settings. At the Pagoda Yangon in Myanmar (Burma), devotees pour water and make offerings to a Buddha image to pray for well-being.

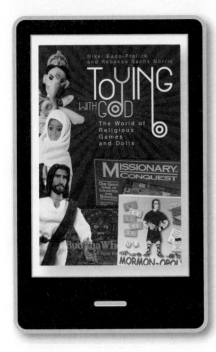

Did you have religious toys when you were young? If so, how did you play with them, and what did you learn?

Nikki Bado-Fralick and Rebecca Sachs Norris have spent years studying religious toys and their sociological meaning.

❝ There are many types of religious toys: stuffed torahs; Moses, David, and Jesus and the Tomb action figures; Noah's ark collections; and Resurrection Eggs, which supplement a young child's Easter book. "Lead your kids on a fun, faith-filled Easter egg hunt this year— one that teaches them about Jesus' death and resurrection! Each egg carton is filled with a dozen colorful plastic eggs. Pop them open and find miniature symbols of the Easter story inside." One of the dozen plastic eggs contains a crown of thorns, another is empty, representing the disappearance of the body of Jesus from the tomb, and pointing to his resurrection. Muslim toys include a mosque building set, mosque jewelry cases, and a prayer practice chart. Jewish toys include dreidels, wooden Shabbat sets, toy *sukkahs,* and a Plush Plagues Bag that includes "all 10 Plagues!"

Religious dolls are part of this wonderland of sacred fun. There are plush and plastic talking Bible dolls, pumped-up Christian action figures, dolls designed to support a Jewish girl's religious identity and conform to religious requirements, Goddess dolls designed for affluent young feminists, talking Muslim dolls that teach Arabic phrases, and "anti-Barbies"— Muslim dolls deliberately designed to compete with Barbie for the hearts and minds of young girls. There are plush Buddha and Siva dolls, and cuddly Jesus and Esther dolls as well.

Contemporary religious games have their roots in ancient practices, but their flavor—their style and substance—as well as their commercial focus reveal a specifically twenty-first century American form of religiosity.

Numerous card games and puzzles teach a variety of languages, including Hebrew, Arabic, and Punjabi. The Christian Book Distributors Web site not only offers religiously themed educational materials, they also offer nonreligious toys that appeal to parents with religious consciences who may be looking for nonviolent toys, such as a food groups toy with hand-painted pieces in four wooden crates, a pizza party game with different toppings, and a car towing game.

Not all religious toys are meant for the edification of the young. Many religious games and toys are satirical or simply products meant to be amusing enough to sell in an era where we are oversatiated with things, and any cultural phenomenon is fair game for marketing purposes. These items amuse or appall us, depending on how clever or offensive the item is, and for whom it is intended. . . .

Games and toys not only transmit cultural values but reflect them as well. . . . Games and religion have a long and complex history—they were used for divination and gambling, for this-worldly satire, and in the afterlife. Games were objects and methods used to interpret divine powers and influence supernatural forces. These religious and magical functions reflect the presence and movement of the sacred in the material world, indicators of a complex whole rather than a dualism where sacred and ordinary occupy separate realms.

Contemporary religious games have their roots in ancient practices, but their flavor—their style and substance—as well as their commercial focus reveal a specifically twenty-first century American form of religiosity. ❞

(*Bado-Fralick and Norris 2010:7–8, 29–30*)

I n this excerpt from *Toying with God: The World of Religious Games and Dolls,* Bado-Fralick and Norris consider how religiously themed toys and games reflect both popular and religious culture. Depending on their purpose and design, the authors note, as well as on the social context in which they are used, these dolls and board games can either reinforce or undermine organized religion. Their impact on the children who play with them parallels the broader influence of religion on society. Despite the much-publicized decline of organized religion over the past century, even a casual observer can see that religion still permeates our social environment. As a result, nonbelievers are influenced by believers, whether they want to be or not. Similarly, believers are influenced by nonbelievers and by those of different faiths, despite any attempts they may make to screen out other points of view.

Indeed, religion plays a major role in people's lives, and religious practices of some sort are evident in every society. That makes religion a cultural universal, along with other common practices or beliefs found in every culture, such as dancing, food preparation, the family, and personal names. At present, an estimated 4 billion people belong to the world's many religious faiths.

What social purposes does religion serve? Does religion help to hold society together or foster social change? Do public schools offer everyone a way up the socioeconomic ladder, or do they reinforce divisions among social classes? We will begin this chapter with a discussion of the sociological perspective on religion, followed by an overview of the world's major religions. We'll explore religion's role in social integration, social support, social change, and social control. Then we'll examine three important components of religious behavior—belief, ritual, and experience—as well as the basic forms of religious organization, including new religious movements. Finally, in the Social Policy section we'll return to the subject of religion with a discussion of religion in the schools.

Durkheim and the Importance of Religion

If a group believes that it is being directed by a "vision from God," sociologists do not attempt to prove or disprove the revelation. Instead, they assess the effects of the religious experience on the group. What sociologists are interested in is the social impact of religion on individuals and institutions.

Émile Durkheim was perhaps the first sociologist to recognize the critical importance of religion in human societies. He saw its appeal for the individual, but more important, he stressed the *social* impact of religion. In Durkheim's view, religion is a collective act that includes many forms of behavior in which people interact with others. As in his work on suicide, Durkheim was not so interested in the personalities of religious believers as he was in understanding religious behavior within a social context.

Durkheim defined **religion** as a "unified system of beliefs and practices relative to sacred things." In his view, religion involves a set of beliefs and practices that are uniquely the property of religion, as opposed to other social institutions and ways of thinking. Durkheim ([1893] 1933; [1912] 2001) argued that religious faiths distinguish between certain transcending events and the everyday world. He referred to those realms as the *sacred* and the *profane*.

The **sacred** encompasses elements beyond everyday life that inspire awe, respect, and even fear. People become part of the sacred realm only by completing some ritual, such as prayer or sacrifice. Because believers have faith in the sacred, they accept what they cannot understand. In contrast, the **profane** includes the ordinary and commonplace. This concept can be confusing, however, because the same object can be either sacred or profane, depending on how it is viewed. A normal dining room table is profane, but it becomes sacred to some Christians if it bears the elements of a communion. A candelabra becomes sacred to Jews if it is a menorah. For Confucians and Taoists, incense sticks are not mere decorative items, but highly valued offerings to the gods in religious ceremonies that mark the new and full moons.

When religion's influence on other social institutions in a society diminishes, the process of **secularization** is said to be under way. During this process, religion will survive in the private sphere of individual and family life (as in the case of many Native American families); it may even thrive on a personal level. But at the same time, other social institutions—such as the economy, politics, and education—maintain their own sets of norms, independent of religious guidance. Even so, religion is enormously resilient. Although specific faiths or organizations may change, their transformation does not signal the demise of religious faith. Rather, it contributes to the diversity of religious expression and organization (Christian Smith 2008; Stark 2004).

Following the direction established by Durkheim a century ago, contemporary sociologists view religion in two different ways. First, they study the norms and values of religious faiths by examining their substantive beliefs. For example, it is possible to compare the degree to which Christian faiths interpret the Bible literally, or Muslim groups follow the Qur'an (or Koran), the sacred book of Islam. At the same time, sociologists examine religion in terms of the social functions it fulfills, such as providing social support or reinforcing social norms. By exploring both the beliefs and the functions of religion, we can better understand its impact on the individual, on groups, and on society as a whole.

Sociological Perspectives on Religion

Since religion is a cultural universal, it is not surprising that it plays a basic role in human societies. In sociological terms, it performs both manifest and latent functions. Among its *manifest* (open and stated) functions, religion defines the spiritual world and gives meaning to the divine. It provides an explanation for events that seem difficult to understand, such as what lies beyond the grave. The *latent* functions of religion are unintended, covert, or hidden. Even though the manifest function of a church service is to offer a forum for religious worship, it might at the same time fulfill a latent social function as a meeting ground for unmarried members.

Functionalists and conflict theorists both evaluate religion's impact on human societies. We'll consider a functionalist view of religion's role in integrating society, providing social support, and promoting social change, and then look at religion from the conflict and feminist perspectives, as a means of social control. Note that for the most part, religion's impact is best understood from a macro-level viewpoint that is oriented toward the larger society. Its social support function is an exception: it is best understood on the micro, or individual, level.

The Integrative Function of Religion

Émile Durkheim viewed religion as an integrative force in human society—a perspective that is reflected in functionalist thought today. Durkheim sought to answer a perplexing question: "How

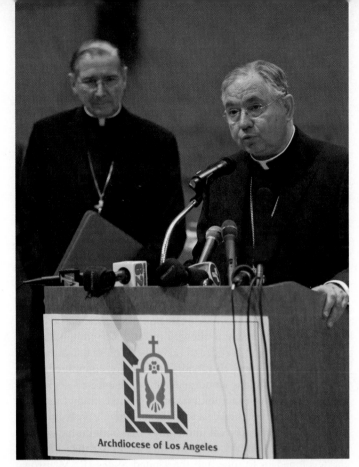

In 2010 José H. Gomez (at the podium) became archbishop of Los Angeles, the largest Roman Catholic archdiocese in the United States. Born in Mexico, Gomez became a U.S. citizen while serving as a priest in Texas. His elevation reflects the growth of the Hispanic faithful among Roman Catholics in the United States.

can human societies be held together when they are generally composed of individuals and social groups with diverse interests and aspirations?" In his view, religious bonds often transcend these personal and divisive forces. Durkheim acknowledged that religion is not the only integrative force; nationalism or patriotism may serve the same end.

How does religion provide this "societal glue"? Religion, whether it be Buddhism, Islam, Christianity, or Judaism, gives meaning and purpose to people's lives. It offers certain ultimate values and ends to hold in common. Although they are subjective and not always fully accepted, these values and ends help society to function as an integrated social system. For example, funerals, weddings, bar and bat mitzvahs, and confirmations serve to integrate people into larger communities by providing shared beliefs and values about the ultimate questions of life.

The integrative power of religion can be seen, too, in the role that churches, synagogues, and mosques have traditionally played and continue to play for immigrant groups in the United States. For example, Roman Catholic immigrants may settle near a parish church that offers services in their native language, such as Polish or Spanish. Similarly, Korean immigrants may join a Presbyterian church that has many Korean American members and follows religious practices like those of churches in Korea. Like other religious organizations, these Roman Catholic and Presbyterian churches help to integrate immigrants into their new homeland.

In recent years, the most talked about immigrant religious group has been Muslims. Throughout the world, including the United States, Muslims are divided into a variety of sects, including Sunni and Shia (or Shiite). However, inside and outside these sects, people express their Islamic faith in many different ways. To speak of Muslims as being either Sunni or Shia would be like speaking of Christians as either Roman Catholic or Baptist.

Depending on the circumstances, Islam in the United States can be integrative by faith, ethnicity, or both. The great majority of Muslims in the United States are Sunni Muslims—literally, those who follow the *Sunnah,* or way of the Prophet. Compared to other Muslims, Sunnis tend to be more moderate in their religious orthodoxy. The Shia, who come primarily from Iraq and Iran, are the second-largest group. Shia Muslims are more attentive to guidance from accepted Islamic scholars than are Sunnis. In sufficient numbers, these two Muslim groups will choose to worship separately, even if they must cross ethnic or linguistic lines to do so. Whatever group Muslims belong to, however, there has been a remarkable increase in the number of Islamic places of worship in the United States. Between 2000 and 2010, the number of mosques rose 74 percent (Bagby 2012: Selod 2008a).

In some instances, religious loyalties are *dysfunctional;* that is, they contribute to tension and even conflict between groups or nations. During the Second World War, the German Nazis attempted to exterminate the Jewish people; approximately 6 million European Jews were killed. In modern times, nations such as Lebanon (Muslims versus Christians), Israel (Jews versus Muslims, as well as Orthodox versus secular Jews), Northern Ireland (Roman Catholics versus Protestants), and India (Hindus versus Muslims, and more recently, Sikhs) have been torn by clashes that are in large part based on religion.

Religion and Social Support

Most of us find it difficult to accept the stressful events of life—the death of a loved one, serious injury, bankruptcy, divorce, and so forth—especially when something "senseless" happens. How can family and friends come to terms with the death of a talented college student, not even 20 years old?

Through its emphasis on the divine and the supernatural, religion allows us to "do something" about the calamities we face. In some faiths, adherents can offer sacrifices or pray to a deity in the belief that such acts will change their earthly condition. On a more basic level, religion encourages us to view our personal misfortunes as relatively unimportant in the broader perspective of human history—or even as part of an undisclosed divine purpose. Friends and relatives of the deceased college student may see his death as being "God's will," or as having some ultimate benefit that we cannot understand now. This perspective may be much more comforting than the terrifying feeling that any of us can die senselessly at any moment—and that there is no divine answer to why one person lives a long and full life, while another dies tragically at a relatively early age.

The religious function of social support is also apparent in people's use of social media. Overall, 31 percent of Facebook users in the United States and 24 percent of them outside the United States identify their religion in their profiles. Tens of millions indicate that they are fans or "friends" of a religious figure or category. Consequently, religious organizations are turning to Twitter and Facebook to strengthen their connections with these followers and provide them with 24/7 social support (Preston 2011).

Religion and Social Change

The Weberian Thesis   When someone seems driven to work and succeed, we often attribute the Protestant work ethic to that person. The term comes from the writings of Max Weber, who carefully examined the connection between religious allegiance and capitalist development. Weber's findings appeared in his pioneering work *The Protestant Ethic and the Spirit of Capitalism* ([1904] 2011).

Weber noted that in European nations with both Protestant and Catholic citizens, an overwhelming number of business leaders, owners of capital, and skilled workers were Protestant. In his view, this fact was no mere coincidence. Weber pointed out that the followers of John Calvin (1509–1564), a leader of the Protestant Reformation, emphasized a disciplined work ethic, this-worldly concerns, and a rational orientation to life that have become known as the **Protestant ethic.** One by-product of the Protestant ethic was a drive to accumulate savings that could be used for future investment. This "spirit of capitalism," to use Weber's phrase, contrasted with the moderate work hours, leisurely work habits, and lack of ambition that Weber saw as typical of the times.

Few books on the sociology of religion have aroused as much commentary and criticism as Weber's work. It has been hailed as one of the most important theoretical works in the field and an excellent example of macro-level analysis. Like Durkheim, Weber demonstrated that religion is not solely a matter of intimate personal beliefs. He stressed that the collective nature of religion has consequences for society as a whole. Indeed, a recent analysis of historical economic data shows that the Protestant ethic was an important factor in the growth of capitalism from 1500 through 1870 (Sanderson et al. 2011).

Weber provided a convincing description of the origins of European capitalism. However, this economic system has now been adopted by non-Calvinists in many parts of the world. Studies done in the United States today show little or no difference in achievement orientation between Roman Catholics and Protestants. Apparently, the "spirit of capitalism" has emerged as a generalized cultural trait rather than a specific religious tenet (Greeley 1989).

Conflict theorists caution that Weber's theory—even if it is accepted—should not be regarded as an analysis of mature capitalism, as reflected in the rise of multinational corporations. Marxists would disagree with Weber not on the origins of capitalism, but on its future. Unlike Marx, Weber believed that capitalism could endure indefinitely as an economic system. He added, however, that the decline of religion as an overriding force in society opened the way for workers to express their discontent more vocally (R. Collins 1980).

Liberation Theology   Sometimes the clergy can be found in the forefront of social change. Many religious activists, especially in the Roman Catholic Church in Latin America, support **liberation theology**—the use of a church in a political effort to eliminate poverty, discrimination, and other forms of injustice from a secular society. Advocates of this religious movement sometimes sympathize with Marxism. Many believe that radical change, rather than economic development in itself, is the only acceptable solution to the desperation of the masses in impoverished developing countries. Activists associated with liberation theology believe that organized religion has a moral responsibility to take a strong public stand against the oppression of the poor, racial and ethnic minorities, and women (Christian Smith 1991).

The term *liberation theology* dates back to the publication in 1973 of the English translation of *A Theology of Liberation.* The book was written by a Peruvian priest, Gustavo Gutiérrez, who lived in a slum area of Lima during the early 1960s. After years of exposure to the vast poverty around him, Gutiérrez concluded that "in order to serve the poor, one had to move into political action." Eventually, politically committed Latin American theologians came under the influence of social scientists who viewed the domination of capitalism and multinational corporations as central to the hemisphere's problems. One result was a new approach to theology that built on the cultural and religious traditions of Latin America rather than on models developed in Europe and the United States (R. M. Brown 1980:23; Gutiérrez 1990).

Liberation theology may be dysfunctional, however. Some Roman Catholic worshippers have come to believe that by

Television scripts often poke fun at organized religion, while presenting characters who are atheists as enlightened people. A notable exception is the character Booth (left) in *Bones,* who does not hide his Roman Catholicism. Like many others who are both thoughtful and religious, Booth receives social support from his faith.

A Protestant congregation worships at Sunday service. Although Weber traced the "spirit of capitalism" to Protestant teachings, in the United States today Protestants and Catholics share the same work ethic.

focusing on political and governmental injustice, the clergy are no longer addressing their personal and spiritual needs. Partly as a result of such disenchantment, some Catholics in Latin America are converting to mainstream Protestant faiths or to Mormonism.

 use your **sociological imagination**

The social support that religious groups provide is suddenly withdrawn from your community. How will your life or the lives of others change? What will happen if religious groups stop pushing for social change?

Religion and Social Control: A Conflict Perspective

Liberation theology is a relatively recent phenomenon that marks a break with the traditional role of churches. It was this traditional role that Karl Marx ([1844] 1964) opposed. In his view, religion *impeded* social change by encouraging oppressed people to focus on otherworldly concerns rather than on their immediate poverty or exploitation. Marx described religion as an opiate that was particularly harmful to oppressed peoples. He felt that religion often drugged the masses into submission by offering a consolation for their harsh lives on earth: the hope of salvation in an ideal afterlife. For example, during the period of slavery in the United States, White masters forbade Blacks to practice native African religions, while encouraging them to adopt Christianity, which taught them that obedience would lead to salvation and eternal happiness in the hereafter. Viewed from a conflict perspective, Christianity may have pacified certain slaves and blunted the rage that often fuels rebellion.

Today, however, people around the world see religion more as a source of support through adversity than a source of oppression. In a combination of public opinion polls taken across 114 nations, 95 percent of those living in the poorest nations felt that religion was important in daily life, compared to only 47 percent of those in the wealthiest countries (Crabtree 2010).

Religion does play an important role in propping up the existing social structure. The values of religion, as already noted, tend to reinforce other social institutions and the social order as a whole. From Marx's perspective, however, religion's promotion of social stability only helps to perpetuate patterns of social inequality. According to Marx, the dominant religion reinforces the interests of those in power.

For example, contemporary Christianity reinforces traditional patterns of behavior that call for the subordination of the less powerful. The role of women in the church is an example of this uneven distribution of power. Assumptions about gender roles leave women in a subservient position both within Christian churches and at home. In fact, women find it as difficult to achieve leadership positions in many churches as they do in large corporations. A "stained glass ceiling" tends to stunt clergywomen's career development, even in the most liberal denominations.

Like Marx, conflict theorists argue that to whatever extent religion actually does influence social behavior, it reinforces existing patterns of dominance and inequality. From a Marxist perspective, religion keeps people from seeing their lives and societal conditions in political terms—for example, by obscuring the overriding significance of conflicting economic interests. Marxists suggest that by inducing a "false consciousness" among the disadvantaged, religion lessens the possibility of collective political action that could end capitalist oppression and transform society.

Feminist Perspective

Drawing on the feminist approach, researchers and theorists have stressed the fundamental role women play in religious socialization. Most people develop their allegiance to a particular faith in their childhood, with their mothers playing a critical role in the

Although the number of women clergy has increased, only about one in six spiritual leaders is a woman, and in many faiths women are still banned from serving.

TABLE 45-1 SOCIOLOGICAL PERSPECTIVES ON RELIGION

Tracking Sociological Perspectives

Theoretical Perspective	Emphasis
Functionalist	Religion as a source of social integration and unification
	Religion as a source of social support for individuals
Conflict	Religion as a potential obstacle to structural social change
	Religion as a potential source of structural social change (through liberation theology)
Feminist	Religion as an instrument of women's subordination, except for their role in religious socialization
Interactionist	Individual religious expression through belief, ritual, and experience

process. Significantly, nonworshipping mothers tend to influence their children to be highly skeptical of organized religion.

However, women generally take a subordinate role in religious governance. Indeed, most faiths have a long tradition of exclusively male spiritual leadership. Furthermore, because most religions are patriarchal, they tend to reinforce men's dominance in secular as well as spiritual matters. Women do play a vital role as volunteers, staff, and religious educators, but even today, religious decision making and leadership typically fall to the men. Exceptions to this rule, such as the Shakers and Christian Scientists, as well as Hinduism with its long goddess heritage, are rare (R. Schaefer and Zellner 2011).

In the United States, women are much more likely than men to be affiliated with religion, to pray, to believe in God, to claim that religion is important in their lives, and to attend weekly worship services. Yet organized religion typically does not give them leadership roles. Nationally, women compose 21 percent of U.S. clergy, though they account for 34 percent of students enrolled in theological institutions. Women clerics typically have shorter careers than men, often in related fields that do not involve congregational leadership, such as counseling. In faiths that restrict leadership positions to men, women serve unofficially. For example, about 4 percent of Roman Catholic congregations are led by women who hold nonordained pastoral positions—a necessity in a church facing a shortage of male priests (Association of Theological Schools 2013; Bureau of Labor Statistics 2013b).

Table 45-1 summarizes the four major sociological perspectives on religion.

MODULE 45 | Recap and Review

Summary

Religion is a cultural universal found throughout the world in various forms.

1. Émile Durkheim stressed the social impact of religion in attempting to understand individual religious behavior within the context of the larger society.

2. Religion helps to integrate a diverse society and provides social support in time of need.

3. Max Weber saw a connection between religious allegiance and capitalistic behavior in a religious orientation he termed the **Protestant ethic.**

4. In **liberation theology,** the teachings of Christianity become the basis for political efforts to alleviate poverty and social injustice.

5. From a Marxist point of view, religion serves to reinforce the social control of those in power. It discourages collective political action, which could end capitalist oppression and transform society.

Thinking Critically

1. What objects that you regard as profane might others consider to be sacred?

2. Explain how the Weberian thesis and liberation theology promote social change.

Key Terms

Liberation theology

Profane

Protestant ethic

Religion

Sacred

Secularization

Worldwide, tremendous diversity exists in religious beliefs and practices. Overall, about 89 percent of the world's population adheres to some religion; thus, only about 10 percent is nonreligious. This level of adherence changes over time and also varies by country and age group. In the United States today, those who are nonreligious account for about 16 percent of the population; in 1900, they accounted for a mere 1.3 percent of all Americans. And in 2012, 24 percent of incoming U.S. college students had no religious preference, compared to 12 percent of their mothers (Newport 2010b; Pryor et al. 2013:30–31).

Christianity is the largest single faith in the world; the second largest is Islam (Table 46-1). Although global news events often suggest an inherent conflict between Christians and Muslims, the two faiths are similar in many ways. Both are monotheistic (based on a single deity); both include a belief in prophets, an afterlife, and a judgment day. In fact, Islam recognizes Jesus as a prophet, though not as the son of God. Both faiths impose a moral code on believers, which varies from fairly rigid proscriptions for fundamentalists to relatively relaxed guidelines for liberals.

The followers of Islam, called *Muslims,* believe that Islam's holy scriptures were received from Allah (God) by the prophet Muhammad nearly 1,400 years ago. They see Muhammad as the last in a long line of prophets, preceded by Adam, Abraham, Moses, and Jesus. Islam is more communal in its expression than Christianity, particularly the more individualistic Protestant denominations. Consequently, in countries that are predominantly Muslim, the separation of religion and the state is not considered necessary or even desirable. In fact, Muslim governments often reinforce Islamic practices through their laws. Muslims do vary sharply in their interpretation of several traditions, some of which—such as the wearing of veils by women—are more cultural than religious in origin.

Like Christianity and Islam, Judaism is monotheistic. Jews believe that God's true nature is revealed in the Torah, which

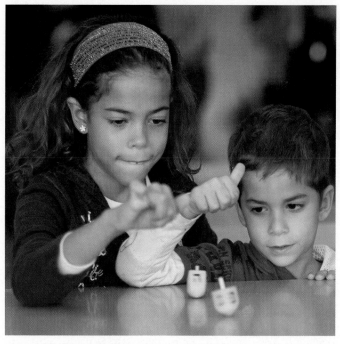

Most of the world's religions seek to give children an appreciation of their faith. Jewish youths who spin the dreidel, a four-sided top, during the Hanukkah holiday are recalling a tradition born before Christianity, when the children of Greek Jews who studied the Torah secretly in caves played with the tops to pass the time.

Christians know as the first five books of the Old Testament. According to these scriptures, God formed a covenant, or pact, with Abraham and Sarah, the ancestors of the tribes of Israel. Even today, Jews believe, this covenant holds them accountable to God's will. If they follow both the letter and spirit of the Torah, a long-awaited Messiah will one day bring paradise to earth. Although Judaism has a relatively small following compared to other major faiths, it forms the historical foundation for both Christianity and Islam. That is why Jews revere many of the same sacred Middle Eastern sites as Christians and Muslims.

TABLE 46-1 MAJOR WORLD RELIGIONS

Summing Up

Faith	Current Following, in Millions (and Percentage of World Population)	Primary Location of Followers Today	Founder (and Approximate Birth Date)	Important Texts (and Holy Sites)
Buddhism	463 (6.7%)	Southeast Asia, Mongolia, Tibet	Gautama Siddhartha (563 B.C.)	Triptaka (areas in Nepal)
Christianity	2,281 (33.0%)	Europe, North America, South America	Jesus (6 B.C.)	Bible (Jerusalem, Rome)
Hinduism	935 (13.7%)	India, Indian communities overseas	No specific founder (1500 B.C.)	Sruti and Smrti texts (seven sacred cities, including Vavansi)
Islam	1,553 (22.5%)	Middle East, Central Asia, North Africa, Indonesia	Muhammad (A.D. 570)	Qur'an, or Koran (Mecca, Medina, Jerusalem)
Judaism	15 (0.2%)	Israel, United States, France, Russia	Abraham (2000 B.C.)	Torah, Talmud (Jerusalem)

Sources: Author, based on Britannica Online 2011; Swatos 1998.

Two other major faiths developed in a different part of the world, India. The earliest, Hinduism, originated around 1500 B.C. Hinduism differs from Judaism, Christianity, and Islam in that it embraces a number of gods and minor gods, although most worshippers are devoted primarily to a single deity, such as Shiva or Vishnu. Hinduism is also distinguished by a belief in reincarnation, or the perpetual rebirth of the soul after death. Unlike Judaism, Christianity, and Islam, which are based largely on sacred texts, Hindu beliefs have been preserved mostly through oral tradition.

A second religion, Buddhism, developed in the sixth century B.C. as a reaction against Hinduism. This faith is founded on the teachings of Siddhartha (later called Buddha, or "the enlightened one"). Through meditation, followers of Buddhism strive to overcome selfish cravings for physical or material pleasures, with the goal of reaching a state of enlightenment, or nirvana. Buddhists created the first monastic orders, which are thought to be the models for monastic orders in other religions, including Christianity. Though Buddhism emerged in India, its followers were eventually driven out of that country by the Hindus. It is now found primarily in other parts of Asia. (Contemporary adherents of Buddhism in India are relatively recent converts.)

Although the differences among religions are striking, they are exceeded by variations within faiths. Consider the variations within Christianity, from relatively liberal denominations such as Presbyterians or the United Church of Christ to the more conservative Mormons and Greek Orthodox Catholics. Similar variations exist within Hinduism, Islam, and other world religions (Barrett et al. 2008; Swatos 1998).

use your **sociological imagination**

What evidence do you see of different religions in the area surrounding your college or university? What about on campus?

Components of Religion

All religions have certain elements in common, yet those elements are expressed in the distinctive manner of each faith. These patterns of religious behavior, like other patterns of social behavior, are of great interest to sociologists—especially interactionists—because they underscore the relationship between religion and society.

Religious beliefs, religious rituals, and religious experience all help to define what is sacred and to differentiate the sacred from the profane. Let's examine these three components of religion, as seen through the eyes of interactionists.

Belief

Some people believe in life after death, in supreme beings with unlimited powers, or in supernatural forces. **Religious beliefs**

are statements to which members of a particular religion adhere. These views can vary dramatically from religion to religion.

In the late 1960s, something rather remarkable took place in the expression of religious beliefs in the United States. Denominations that held to relatively liberal interpretations of religious scripture (such as the Presbyterians, Methodists, and Lutherans) declined in membership, while those that held to more conservative interpretations grew in numbers. Furthermore, in most faiths, those members who held strict views of scripture became more outspoken, questioning those who remained open to a variety of newer interpretations.

This trend toward *fundamentalism* ran counter to the secularization that was evident in the wider society. **Fundamentalism** may be defined as an emphasis on doctrinal conformity and the literal interpretation of sacred texts. The phrase "religious fundamentalism" was first applied to Protestant believers in the United States who took a literal interpretation of the Bible, but fundamentalism is found worldwide among all major religious groups, including Roman Catholicism, Islam, and Judaism. Even in relatively new faiths, some adherents contend that too much has changed. For followers of many religions, fundamentalists can be as challenging to accommodate as secularists.

Fundamentalists vary immensely in their behavior. Some stress the need to be strict in their own personal faith but take little interest in broad social issues. Others are watchful of societal actions, such as government policies, that they see as conflicting with fundamentalist doctrine.

The Adam and Eve account of creation found in Genesis, the first book of the Old Testament, is an example of a religious belief. Many people in the United States strongly adhere to this biblical explanation of creation and even insist that it be taught in public schools. These people, known as *creationists,* are worried by the secularization of society, and oppose teaching that directly or indirectly questions biblical scripture.

In general, spirituality is not as strong in industrialized nations as in developing nations. The United States is an

Pilgrims on *hajj* to the Grand Mosque in Mecca, Saudi Arabia. Islam requires all Muslims who are able to undertake this religious ritual at least once in a lifetime.

exception to the trend toward secularization, in part because the government encourages religious expression (without explicitly supporting it) by allowing religious groups to claim charitable status, and even to receive federal aid for activities such as educational services. And although belief in God is relatively weak in formerly communist states such as Russia, surveys show a growth in spirituality in those countries over the past 10 years (Norris and Inglehart 2004). Religious views are also changing in the United States.

Ritual

Religious rituals are practices required or expected of members of a faith. Rituals usually honor the divine power (or powers) worshipped by believers; they also remind adherents of their religious duties and responsibilities. Rituals and beliefs can be interdependent; rituals generally affirm beliefs, as in a public or private statement confessing a sin. Like any social institution, religion develops distinctive norms to structure people's behavior. Moreover, sanctions are attached to religious rituals, whether rewards (bar mitzvah gifts) or penalties (expulsion from a religious institution for violation of norms).

In the United States, rituals may be quite simple, such as saying grace at a meal or observing a moment of silence to commemorate someone's death. Yet certain rituals, such as the process of canonizing a saint, are quite elaborate. Most religious rituals in our culture focus on services conducted at houses of worship. Attendance at a service, silent and spoken prayers, communion, and singing of spiritual hymns and chants are common forms of ritual behavior that generally take place in group settings. From an interactionist perspective, these rituals serve as important face-to-face encounters in which people reinforce their religious beliefs and their commitment to their faith.

For Muslims, a very important ritual is the *hajj*, a pilgrimage to the Grand Mosque in Mecca, Saudi Arabia. Every Muslim who is physically and financially able is expected to make this trip at least once. Each year 3 million pilgrims go to Mecca during the one-week period indicated by the Islamic lunar calendar. Muslims from all over the world make the *hajj*, including those in the United States, where many tours are arranged to facilitate the trip.

In recent decades, participation in religious rituals has tended to hold steady or decline in most countries. Figure 46-1 shows religious participation in selected countries.

Experience

In the sociological study of religion, the term **religious experience** refers to the feeling or perception of being in direct contact with the ultimate reality, such as a divine being, or of being overcome with religious emotion. A religious experience may be rather slight, such as the feeling of exaltation a person receives from hearing a choir sing Handel's "Hallelujah Chorus." But many religious experiences are more profound, such as a Muslim's experience on a *hajj*. In his autobiography, the late African American activist Malcolm X ([1964] 1999:338) wrote of his *hajj* and how deeply moved he was by the way that Muslims in Mecca came together across race and color lines. For Malcolm X, the color blindness of the Muslim world "proved to me the power of the One God."

Another profound religious experience, for many Christians, is being *born again*—that is, at a turning point in one's

FIGURE 46-1 **Religious Participation in Selected Countries**

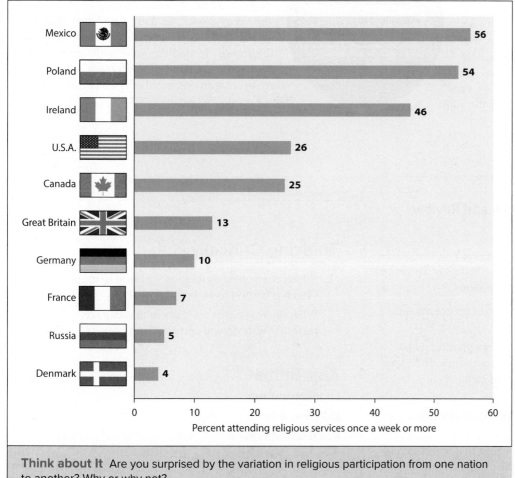

Think about It Are you surprised by the variation in religious participation from one nation to another? Why or why not?

Note: Data are for 2006, except for Canada and Mexico, which are for 2004.
Source: Tom W. Smith 2009:28, 60, 72.

life, making a personal commitment to Jesus. According to a 2010 national survey, 42 percent of people in the United States claim they have had a born-again Christian experience at some time in their lives. An earlier survey found that Southern Baptists (75 percent) were the most likely to report such experiences; in contrast, only 21 percent of Catholics and 24 percent of Episcopalians stated that they had been born again. The collective nature of religion, as emphasized by Durkheim, is evident in these statistics. The beliefs and rituals of a particular faith can create an atmosphere either friendly or indifferent to this type of religious experience. Thus, a Baptist would be encouraged to come forward and share such experiences with others, whereas an Episcopalian who claims to have been born again would receive much less interest (Gallup 2011a; Gallup Opinion Index 1978).

Table 46-2 summarizes the three components of religion.

None of the Above: The Nonreligious

Many people noted and were dismayed by a statement in President Obama's 2009 inaugural address: "We are a nation of Christians and Muslims, Jews and Hindus, and nonbelievers." Yet the president was merely acknowledging a long-noted pattern, the gradual growth in the proportion of U.S. residents who indicate they have no religion.

National surveys reveal that between 1990 and 2008, the number of Americans who identify themselves as having no religion doubled. Moreover, the proportion of people who give no answer to questions about religion suggests that currently, about 20 percent of the adult

population—well over 60 million people—has no overt religious identity.

The growth of the "none of the above" category does not mean that those respondents do not believe in God, however. A third of them say that they pray weekly or daily, and fewer than 1 percent call themselves atheists. Nevertheless, while the phrase "In God We Trust" still seems to apply, more and more people are choosing not to affiliate themselves with organized religion (Baker and Smith 2009; Kosmin and Keysar 2009).

Summing Up

TABLE **46-2** COMPONENTS OF RELIGION

Element	Definition	Examples
Belief	Statement to which members of a particular religion adhere	Creation account Sacred characters or people
Ritual	Practice required or expected of members of a faith	Worship Prayer Singing or chanting
Experience	Feeling or perception of being in direct contact with the ultimate reality (such as a divine being) or of being overcome with religious emotion	Born-again experience Communion with holy spirit

---

MODULE 46 | **Recap and Review**

Summary

Tremendous diversity exists in religious beliefs and practices, although all religions share basic components.

1. Of the world's population, 85 percent adheres to some form of religion.

2. Religious behavior is expressed through three major components: beliefs, rituals, and experience. **Religious beliefs** are statements to which all members of a faith adhere.

3. **Religious rituals** vary from the very simple to the highly complex.

4. **Religious experience,** or the feeling that one is having a direct encounter with the divine, is part of all major religions.

Thinking Critically

1. Which component of religion is easiest to measure? Which is hardest to measure? Explain.

2. What rituals—either religious or nonreligious—do you perform? Why do you perform them?

Key Terms

Fundamentalism

Religious belief

Religious experience

Religious ritual

The collective nature of religion has led to many forms of religious association. In modern societies, religion has become increasingly formalized. Specific structures such as churches and synagogues have been constructed for religious worship; individuals have been trained for occupational roles within various fields. These developments make it possible to distinguish clearly between the sacred and secular parts of one's life—a distinction that could not be made easily in earlier times, when religion was largely a family activity carried out in the home.

Four Basic Forms of Organization

Sociologists find it useful to distinguish between four basic forms of organization: the ecclesia, the denomination, the sect, and the new religious movement, or cult. We can see differences among these four forms of organization in their size, power, degree of commitment that is expected from members, and historical ties to other faiths.

Ecclesiae

An **ecclesia** (plural, *ecclesiae*) is a religious organization that claims to include most or all members of a society and is recognized as the national or official religion. Since virtually everyone belongs to the faith, membership is by birth rather than conscious decision. Examples of ecclesiae include Islam in Saudi Arabia and Buddhism in Thailand. However, significant differences exist within this category. In Saudi Arabia's Islamic regime, leaders of the ecclesia hold vast power over actions of the state. In contrast, the Lutheran Church in contemporary Sweden holds no such power over the Riksdag (parliament) or the prime minister.

Generally, ecclesiae are conservative, in that they do not challenge the leaders of a secular government. In a society with an ecclesia, the political and religious institutions often act in harmony and reinforce each other's power in their relative spheres of influence. In the modern world, ecclesiae are declining in power.

Denominations

A **denomination** is a large, organized religion that is not officially linked to the state or government. Like an ecclesia, it tends to have an explicit set of beliefs, a defined system of authority, and a generally respected position in society. Denominations claim as members large segments of a population. Generally, children accept the denomination of their parents and give little thought to membership in other faiths. Denominations also resemble ecclesiae in that they make few demands on members. However, there is a critical difference between these two forms of religious organization. Although the denomination is considered respectable and is not viewed as a challenge to the secular government, it lacks the official recognition and power held by an ecclesia (Doress and Porter 1977).

The United States is home to a large number of denominations. In good measure, this diversity is a result of our nation's immigrant heritage. Many settlers brought with them the religious commitments native to their homelands. Some Christian denominations in the United States, such as the Roman Catholics, Episcopalians, and Lutherans, are the outgrowth of ecclesiae established in Europe. New Christian denominations also emerged, including the Mormons and Christian Scientists. Within the past generation, immigrants have increased the number of Muslims, Hindus, and Buddhists living in the United States.

Although by far the largest denomination in the United States is Roman Catholicism, at least 24 other Christian faiths have 1 million or more members. Protestants collectively accounted for about 45 percent of the nation's adult population in 2010, compared to 21 percent for Roman Catholics and 2 percent for Jews. Mormons make up close to 2 percent, with about 6 million members in the United States. There are also 5 million Muslims in the United States, and large numbers of people adhere to Eastern faiths such as Buddhism (3 million) and Hinduism (1 million) (Britannica Online 2011; Gallup 2011a; Lindner 2012).

Box 47-1 examines Mormonism, one of the most controversial denominations in the United States.

Sects

A **sect** can be defined as a relatively small religious group that has broken away from some other religious organization to renew what it considers the original vision of the faith. Many sects, such as that led by Martin Luther during the Reformation, claim to be the "true church," because they seek to cleanse the established faith of what they regard as extraneous beliefs and rituals (Stark and Bainbridge 1985). Max Weber ([1916] 1958:114) termed the sect a "believer's church," because affiliation is based on conscious acceptance of a specific religious dogma.

Sects are fundamentally at odds with society and do not seek to become established national religions. Unlike ecclesiae and denominations, they require intensive commitments and demonstrations of belief by members. Partly owing to their outsider status, sects frequently exhibit a higher degree of religious fervor and loyalty than more established religious groups. Recruitment focuses mainly on adults, and acceptance comes through conversion.

Sects are often short-lived. Those that survive may become less antagonistic to society over time and begin to resemble denominations. In a few instances, sects have endured over several generations while remaining fairly separate from society. Sociologist J. Milton Yinger (1970:226–273) uses the term **established sect** to describe a religious group that is the outgrowth of a sect, yet remains isolated from society. Hutterites, Jehovah's Witnesses, Seventh-Day Adventists, and Amish are contemporary examples of established sects in the United States.

 use your **sociological imagination**

Choose a religious tradition other than your own. How would your religious beliefs, rituals, and experience differ if you had been raised in that tradition?

Mormons: A Controversial Denomination

In a 2008 public opinion poll, one-third of Americans stated that they would not vote for Mitt Romney, then a candidate in the Republican presidential primary, because he was a Mormon. Romney lost the primary. Just four years later, having captured the Republican nomination, he received 47 percent of the popular vote in the general election. At the same time, the Tony Award–winning musical *The Book of Mormon,* written by the irreverent creators of *South Park,* played to sold-out audiences on Broadway.

What is Mormonism? The faith originated in upstate New York in the early 19th century, led by a young man named Joseph Smith. Born into a family that questioned many of the accepted faiths of the time, Smith had his first religious experience at age 15, when he entered the woods to ask God which church he should join. There in 1820, he wrote, he was visited by both God the Father and His son Jesus Christ, who advised him not to join any existing sect, for "they were all wrong." Three years later, Smith claimed, an angel named Moroni revealed to him the location of a box of buried gold plates inscribed in an ancient tongue. The plates, which Smith said he translated through revelations from God, became the basis for the Book of Mormon.

From the beginning, Smith faced considerable doubt and opposition, not just because of his youth and his rejection of established religion, but because of the teachings contained in the Book of Mormon. The mammoth, fairly intricate work begins in 600 B.C. with a Jewish prophet and a small band of followers traveling to the west coast of America with God's guidance. The prophet's descendants, who first become Christian but later lose touch with the faith, eventually become the forebears of today's Native Americans. Shortly after His resurrection, Jesus Christ reappears to these native peoples.

Despite opposition from established religions and a turbulent history, Mormonism survived. Persecuted by mainstream groups, Smith's followers moved from place to place in search of a home where they could worship in peace. In 1844, Smith was killed by a mob in Illinois. Undeterred, Brigham Young assumed leadership of the largest group of Mormons, officially called the Church of Jesus Christ of Latter Day Saints (LDS), and moved the faithful to Utah. Other Mormon groups formed at the same time, some of which have a substantial following today.

The Church of Latter Day Saints has grown over the last 180 years, despite strong opposition. Mormons still face criticism for their early practice of *polygamy,* a form of marriage in which an individual may have several husbands or wives simultaneously. To secure statehood for Utah in 1890, church leaders agreed to denounce the practice. Today, in rural areas of the United States and Canada, some splinter sects still practice this form of marriage. However, the church condemns those sects and does not regard their members as Mormons.

The church has also faced charges of racism and sexism. In 1852, drawing on the Bible story of the curse of Cain, Brigham Young banned Black men from becoming lay priests, stating that God had marked Cain's descendants with black skin so they would be persecuted forever. In several places, the Book of Mormon implies that white skin is pure and black skin is vile. Although Mormons welcomed Black men and women into church membership, it took a revelation from God—reported by church president Spencer W. Kimball in 1978—to overturn the ban on their priesthood. Women, regardless of their color, play no leadership role in the church, but are praised for their efforts to maintain the family and for their volunteer activities. So rare is their participation in official LDS events that when a woman was allowed to lead a prayer at the church's annual convention in 2012, Mormons working to include women more fully in the church hailed the move as a major step forward.

> Culturally, the Mormon values of hard work, thrift, and the importance of the family are embraced by all Americans.

Two centuries after Smith's revelations, the decidedly American faith of Mormonism has become a *denomination*—a large, organized religion that is not officially linked to the state or government. Culturally, the Mormon values of hard work, thrift, and the importance of the family are embraced by all Americans. But the church's past history, the continued suppression of women as church leaders, and the secretive aspects of church rituals—only Mormons in good standing can enter the temple—are clearly off-putting to some. Significantly, although Mormons see themselves as Christians, only a bare majority of the general public, 52 percent, agrees.

Today, the Church of Latter Day Saints has more than 14 million members, the majority of whom live outside the United States and Canada. Some of the aspects of Mormonism that most Americans find baffling, including the account of Jesus in the Americas and the gold plates, have proven appealing to other cultures. Foreign converts are attracted to a faith in which divine revelation occurred not in the distant past but in the recent past, and in which the flow of messages from God continues. At death, they look forward not only to eternal life, but to an eternity shared with their spouses. And in Muslim cultures, the LDS teaching that the covenant began with Abraham, but that Jesus' message was distorted by the Christian church, strikes a familiar chord.

Although practitioners of other world religions, such as Roman Catholicism and Islam, often include local customs in their religious rituals, for the most part the Church of Jesus Christ of Latter Day Saints does not allow such adaptations. For example, Mormons have had great success in Nigeria, but they worship there as they would in Utah, even though they could easily accommodate local dancing and drum music in their services. Mormons do encourage members from other cultures to express a culturally traditional concern for their ancestors, however. In reverence for their ancestors, these believers may choose to baptize their forebears into Mormonism, with the church's blessing.

LET'S DISCUSS

1. Mormons are not supposed to drink alcohol, soft drinks, coffee, or tea. What aspects of your own religious faith are sometimes observable to others?

2. Do you have any reservations about a Mormon becoming president of the United States? If so, on what grounds?

Sources: Fowler 2013; Jordan 2007; Ostling and Ostling 2000; Pew Research Center 2010; R. Schaefer and Zellner 2011; Stark 2005.

New Religious Movements or Cults

In 1997, 38 members of the Heaven's Gate cult were found dead in Southern California after a mass suicide timed to occur with the appearance of the Hale-Bopp comet. They believed the comet hid a spaceship on which they could catch a ride once they had broken free of their "bodily containers."

Partly as a result of the notoriety generated by such groups, the popular media have stigmatized the word *cult,* associating it with the occult and the use of intense and forceful conversion techniques. The stereotyping of cults as uniformly bizarre and unethical has led sociologists to abandon the term and refer instead to a *new religious movement (NRM).* While some NRMs exhibit strange behavior, many do not. They attract new members just like any other religion, and often follow teachings similar to those of established Christian denominations, though with less ritual.

Sects are difficult to distinguish from cults. A **new religious movement (NRM)** or **cult** is generally a small, secretive religious group that represents either a new religion or a major innovation of an existing faith. NRMs are similar to sects in that they tend to be small and are often viewed as less respectable than more established faiths. Unlike sects, however, NRMs normally do not result from schisms or breaks with established ecclesiae or denominations. Some cults, such as those focused on UFO sightings, may be totally unrelated to existing faiths. Even when a cult does accept certain fundamental tenets of a dominant faith—such as a belief in Jesus as divine or in Muhammad as a messenger of God—it will offer new revelations or insights to justify its claim to being a more advanced religion (Stark and Bainbridge 1979, 1985).

Like sects, NRMs may be transformed over time into other types of religious organization. An example is the Christian Science Church, which began as a new religious movement under the leadership of Mary Baker Eddy. Today, this church exhibits the characteristics of a denomination. In fact, most major religions, including Christianity, began as cults. NRMs may be in the early stages of developing into a denomination or new religion, or they may just as easily fade away through the loss of members or weak leadership (R. Schaefer and Zellner 2011).

Comparing Forms of Religious Organization

How can we determine whether a particular religious group falls into the sociological category of ecclesia, denomination, sect, or NRM? As we have seen, these types of religious organization have somewhat different relationships to society. Ecclesiae are recognized as national churches; denominations, although not officially approved by the state, are generally widely respected. In contrast, sects and NRMs are much more likely to be at odds with the larger culture.

Still, ecclesiae, denominations, and sects are best viewed as types along a continuum rather than as mutually exclusive categories. Table 47-1 summarizes some of the primary characteristics of the ideal types. Since the United States has no ecclesiae, sociologists studying this country's religions have focused on the denomination and the sect. These religious forms have been pictured on either end of a continuum, with denominations accommodating to the secular world and sects protesting against established religions. Although NRMs also are included in the table, they lie outside the continuum, because they generally define themselves in terms of a new view of life rather than in terms of existing religious faiths. In fact, one of the most controversial NRMs, Wicca, may not fully qualify as a religion (Box 47-2).

Sociologists look at religion from an organizational perspective, which tends to stress the stability of religious adherence, but there are other ways to view religion. From an individual perspective, religion and spirituality are remarkably fluid. People often change their places of worship or move from one denomination to another. In many countries, including the United States, churches, temples, and mosques operate in a highly competitive market (Pew Forum on Religion and Public Life 2008; Wolfe 2008).

One sign of this fluidity is the rapid rise of still another form of religious organization, the electronic church. Facilitated by cable television and satellite transmission, *televangelists* (as they

TABLE 47-1 CHARACTERISTICS OF ECCLESIAE, DENOMINATIONS, SECTS, AND NEW RELIGIOUS MOVEMENTS

Summing Up

Characteristic	Ecclesia	Denomination	Sect	New Religious Movement (or Cult)
Size	Very large	Large	Small	Small
Wealth	Extensive	Extensive	Limited	Variable
Religious services	Formal, little participation	Formal, little participation	Informal, emotional	Variable
Doctrines	Specific, but interpretation may be tolerated	Specific, but interpretation may be tolerated	Specific, purity of doctrine emphasized	Innovative, pathbreaking
Clergy	Well-trained, full-time	Well-trained, full-time	Trained to some degree	Unspecialized
Membership	By virtue of being a member of society	By acceptance of doctrine	By acceptance of doctrine	By an emotional commitment
Relationship to the state	Recognized, closely aligned	Tolerated	Not encouraged	Ignored or challenged

Sources: Adapted from Vernon 1962; see also Chalfant et al. 1994.

Wicca: Religion or Quasi-Religion?

"I'm not a Witch," Christine O'Donnell famously declared in her 2010 campaign for the U.S. Senate. Eleven years earlier, she admitted, she had dabbled in Witchcraft. To most voters, the idea was beyond the pale. Yet today, thousands of people, both men and women, do view themselves as Witches; they practice a little-known religion called Wicca (which should not be confused with Satanism—there is no place in the Craft for devil worship).

Wicca (Anglo-Saxon for *witch* and *wizard*) is a modern form of Witchcraft, practiced for the last hundred years. The Englishman Gerald Gardner, born in 1884, drew on past rituals to found the Craft. Gardner stressed the importance of worshipping *skyclad,* or "clothed by the sky"—that is, naked. Being skyclad, he believed, helped a person to gain insight.

Not all Wiccans follow in Gardner's tradition. Today, Wiccan ritual takes on a dizzying variety of forms, ranging from the elementary to the highly detailed and sophisticated. A Wiccan circle or meeting can include a single heartfelt prayer or a highly complex and time-consuming ritual. Like members of more accepted religions, Wiccans observe several rituals associated with the life cycle. Parents name their children at a *Wiccaning,* which includes a dedication to the Goddess and the God. Contemporary Wiccans also celebrate a wedding-like ceremony called a *handfasting,* which is typically performed by a High Priest and/or Priestess.

Just as Wiccans' worship varies, so does their organization. Some Witches practice alone, as a *solitaire;* others practice in a group

of similarly minded Witches, called a *coven.* A coven may include just 3 or 4 Witches, male and/or female, or as many as 30; members tend to come and go just as they do in a church, temple, or mosque. In a mixed coven, the assembly is often governed by a High Priest or Priestess, or by both.

Revealing one's membership in any non-traditional group is always difficult, but perhaps especially so for Wiccans, who refer to the experience as "coming out of the broom closet." Many Wiccans are young, and so must come out to their parents. Parental reactions range from cutting off contact with the Witch to wanting to learn more about the Craft. Many parents treat the religion as a "phase" in their child's spiritual journey.

Most scholars treat Wicca as a **quasi-religion,** a category that includes organizations that may see themselves as religious, but are seen by others as "sort of religious." National surveys that allow respondents to self-identify showed 8,000 Wiccans in 1990; 134,000 in 2001; and 342,000 in 2008, the latest year for which reliable national data are available. These estimates suggest

either an increase in willingness to identify as Wiccan or an absolute growth in the faithful—probably both.

> Some Witches practice alone, as a *solitaire;* others practice in a group of similarly minded Witches, called a *coven.*

LET'S DISCUSS

1. Do you know anyone who practices Wicca? If so, describe the person's practices.

2. Do you think that Wicca should be considered a religion? Why or why not?

Sources: Chase 2010; M. Howard 2009; Kosmin and Keysar 2009; Rabinovitch and Lewis 2004; R. Schaefer and Zellner 2011:347–377.

---

are called) direct their messages to more people—especially in the United States—than are served by all but the largest denominations. While some televangelists are affiliated with religious denominations, most give viewers the impression that they are dissociated from established faiths.

At the close of the 1990s, the electronic church began to take on another dimension: the Internet. Today, rather than going to a service in person, many people shop online for a church or faith. Surfers can go to GodTube.com, a video-sharing and social-networking website, for spiritually oriented content.

social policy and Religion | Religion in the Schools

Should public schools be allowed to sponsor organized prayer in the classroom? How about Bible reading, or just a collective moment of silence? Can athletes at public schools offer up a group prayer in a team huddle? Should students be able to initiate voluntary prayers at school events? Each of these situations has been an object of great dissension among those

who see a role for prayer in the schools and those who want to maintain strict separation of church and state.

Another controversy concerns the teaching of theories about the origin of humans and the universe. Mainstream scientific thinking holds that humans evolved over billions of years from one-celled organisms, and that the universe came

—*Continued*

into being 15 billion years ago as a result of a huge cosmic explosion (the big bang theory). These theories are challenged by people who hold to the biblical account of the creation of humans and the universe some 10,000 years ago—a viewpoint known as **creationism.** Creationists, many of whom are Christian fundamentalists, want their belief taught in the schools as the only one—or at the very least, as an alternative to the theory of evolution.

Looking at the Issue

The issues just described go to the heart of the First Amendment's provisions regarding religious freedom. On the one hand, the government must protect the right to practice one's religion; on the other, it cannot take any measures that would seem to establish one religion over another (separation of church and state).

In the key case of *Engle v. Vitale,* the Supreme Court ruled in 1962 that the use of nondenominational prayer in New York schools was "wholly inconsistent" with the First Amendment's prohibition against government establishment of religion. In finding that organized school prayer violated the Constitution—even when no student was required to participate—the Court argued, in effect, that promoting religious observance was not a legitimate function of government or education. Subsequent Court decisions have allowed *voluntary* school prayer by students, but forbid school officials to *sponsor* any prayer or religious observance at school events. Despite these rulings, many public schools still regularly lead their students in prayer recitations or Bible readings. Public schools and even states have mandated a moment of silence at the start of the school day, in what critics contend is a transparent attempt to get around *Engle v. Vitale* and similar legal precedents. Although legislators clearly intended to set aside time for prayer or religious thoughts when they created these "moments," to date the courts have recognized such policies as constitutional, treating them as secular rather than sacred. In 2013 Arkansas became the latest state to mandate an opening moment of silence (ABC Television 2013; Yemma 2013).

As with school prayer, the teaching of creationism has significant support among the general public. Unlike Europeans, many people in the United States seem highly skeptical of evolutionary theory, which is taught as a matter of course in science classes. In 2012, a national survey showed that 46 percent of adults believe that God created humans in their present form. Almost as many believe that humans developed their present form with divine guidance (Newport 2012a).

The controversy over whether the biblical account of creation should be presented in school curricula recalls the famous "monkey trial" of 1925. In that trial, high school biology teacher John T. Scopes was convicted of violating a Tennessee law making it a crime to teach the scientific theory

People on both sides of the debate between science and creationism invoke the name of Albert Einstein. Evolutionists emphasize the need for verifiable scientific data, like that which confirmed Einstein's groundbreaking scientific theories. Advocates of intelligent design quote the Nobel Prize–winning physicist's assertion that religion and science should coexist.

of evolution in public schools. Today, creationists have gone beyond espousing fundamentalist religious doctrine; they are attempting to reinforce their position regarding the origins of humanity and the universe with quasi-scientific data.

In 1987, the Supreme Court ruled that states could not compel the teaching of creationism in public schools if the primary purpose was to promote a religious viewpoint. In response, those who believe in the divine origin of life have recently advanced a concept called **intelligent design (ID),** the idea that life is so complex that it could only have been created by intelligent design. Though this concept is not based explicitly on the biblical account of creation, fundamentalists feel comfortable with it. Supporters of intelligent design consider it a more accurate account of the origin of life than Darwinism and hold that at the very least, ID should be taught as an alternative to the theory of evolution. But in 2005, in *Kitzmiller v. Dove Area School District,* a federal judge ended a Pennsylvania school district's plans to require teachers to present the concept in class. In essence, the judge found ID to be "a religious belief," a subtler but similar approach to creationism in that both find God's fingerprints in nature. The issue continues to be hotly debated and is expected to be the subject of future court cases (Clemmitt 2005; Tierney and Holley 2008).

Applying Sociology

Supporters of school prayer and of creationism feel that strict Court rulings have forced too great a separation between what Émile Durkheim called the *sacred* and the *profane.* They

—*Continued*

insist that the use of nondenominational prayer can in no way lead to the establishment of an ecclesia in the United States. Moreover, they believe that school prayer—and the teaching of creationism—can provide the spiritual guidance and socialization that many children today do not receive from parents or regular church attendance. Many communities also believe that schools should transmit the dominant culture of the United States by encouraging prayer.

Opponents of school prayer and creationism argue that a religious majority in a community might impose viewpoints specific to its faith at the expense of religious minorities. These critics question whether school prayer can remain truly voluntary. Drawing on the interactionist perspective and small-group research, they suggest that children will face enormous social pressure to conform to the beliefs and practices of the majority.

Initiating Policy

Public school education is fundamentally a local issue, so most initiatives and lobbying have taken place at the local or state level. Federal courts have taken a hard line on religion in the schools. In a decision that the Supreme Court reversed

in 2004, a federal appeals court ruled that reciting the phrase "under God" during the Pledge of Allegiance that opens each school day violates the U.S. Constitution (Religion News Service 2003).

Religion–school debates show no sign of ending. The activism of religious fundamentalists in the public school system raises the question "Whose ideas and values deserve a hearing in classrooms?" Critics see this campaign as one step toward sectarian religious control of public education. They worry that at some point in the future, teachers may not be able to use books or make statements that conflict with fundamentalist interpretations of the Bible. For advocates of a liberal education and of intellectual (and religious) diversity, this is a genuinely frightening prospect (Wilgoren 2005).

TAKE THE ISSUE WITH YOU

1. Was there organized prayer in any school you attended? Was creationism part of the curriculum?
2. Do you think that promoting religious observance is a legitimate function of education?
3. How might a conflict theorist view the issue of organized school prayer?

MODULE 47 | Recap and Review

Summary

Religious organizations grow and evolve over time and in reaction to social changes.

1. Four basic types of religious organizations are the **ecclesia,** the **denomination,** the **sect,** and the **new religious movement,** or **cult.**

2. Advances in communication have led to a new type of church organization, the electronic church. Televangelists now preach to more people than belong to many denominations, and every day millions of people use the Internet for religious purposes.

3. India is a secular state that is dominated by a religious majority, the Hindus. The creation of a separate nation, Pakistan, for the Muslim minority following India's independence in 1947 did not end the centuries-old strife between the two groups, which has worsened with political polarization.

4. Today, the question of how much religion, if any, should be permitted in U.S. public schools is a matter of intense debate.

Thinking Critically

1. What do you think attracts people to new religious movements?
2. What is the difference between a new religious movement and a quasi-religion?

Key Terms

Creationism

Denomination

Ecclesia

Established sect

Intelligent design (ID)

New religious movement (NRM) or cult

Quasi-religion

Sect

Mastering This Chapter

taking sociology with you

1 Find out how many different religious groups there are at your school or in your community. How many belong to mainstream denominations? How many are fundamentalist? Are there any sects or new religious movements?

2 If your school or community has an interfaith organization, attend a meeting. What issues are the members currently dealing with? What sociological concepts are relevant to those issues?

3 Make a list of the student subcultures on your campus, then describe them using the concepts you learned in Chapter 3. Do any of these subcultures serve as out-groups for other subcultures?

key terms

Creationism A literal interpretation of the Bible regarding the creation of humanity and the universe, used to argue that evolution should not be presented as established scientific fact.

Denomination A large, organized religion that is not officially linked to the state or government.

Ecclesia A religious organization that claims to include most or all members of a society and is recognized as the national or official religion.

Established sect A religious group that is the outgrowth of a sect, yet remains isolated from society.

Fundamentalism An emphasis on doctrinal conformity and the literal interpretation of sacred texts.

Intelligent design (ID) The idea that life is so complex it could only have been created by intelligent design.

Liberation theology Use of a church, primarily Roman Catholic, in a political effort to eliminate poverty, discrimination, and other forms of injustice from a secular society.

New religious movement (NRM) or **cult** A small, secretive religious group that represents either a new religion or a major innovation of an existing faith.

Profane The ordinary and commonplace elements of life, as distinguished from the sacred.

Protestant ethic Max Weber's term for the disciplined work ethic, this-worldly concerns, and rational orientation to life emphasized by John Calvin and his followers.

Quasi-religion A scholarly category that includes organizations that may see themselves as religious but may be seen by others as "sort of religious."

Religion A unified system of beliefs and practices relative to sacred things.

Religious belief A statement to which members of a particular religion adhere.

Religious experience The feeling or perception of being in direct contact with the ultimate reality, such as a divine being, or of being overcome with religious emotion.

Religious ritual A practice required or expected of members of a faith.

Sacred Elements beyond everyday life that inspire awe, respect, and even fear.

Sect A relatively small religious group that has broken away from some other religious organization to renew what it considers the original vision of the faith.

Secularization The process through which religion's influence on other social institutions diminishes.

self-quiz

Read each question carefully and then select the best answer.

1. Which of the following sociologists stressed the social impact of religion and was perhaps the first to recognize the critical importance of religion in human societies?
   a. Max Weber
   b. Karl Marx
   c. Émile Durkheim
   d. Talcott Parsons

2. A Roman Catholic parish church offers services in the native language of an immigrant community. This is an example of
   a. the integrative function of religion.
   b. the social support function of religion.
   c. the social control function of religion.
   d. none of the above.

3. Sociologist Max Weber pointed out that the followers of John Calvin emphasized a disciplined work ethic, this-worldly concerns, and a rational orientation to life. Collectively, this point of view has been referred to as
   a. capitalism.
   b. the Protestant ethic.
   c. the sacred.
   d. the profane.

4. The use of a church, primarily Roman Catholic, in a political effort to eliminate poverty, discrimination, and other forms of injustice evident in a secular society is referred to as
   a. creationism.
   b. ritualism.
   c. religious experience.
   d. liberation theology.

5. Many people in the United States strongly adhere to the biblical explanation of the beginning of the universe. Adherents of this point of view are known as
   a. liberationists.
   b. creationists.
   c. ritualists.
   d. experimentalists.

6. The Adam and Eve account of creation found in Genesis, the first book of the Old Testament, is an example of a religious
   a. ritual.
   b. experience.
   c. custom.
   d. belief.

7. Which of the following is *not* an example of an ecclesia?
   a. the Lutheran church in Sweden
   b. Islam in Saudi Arabia
   c. Buddhism in Thailand
   d. the Episcopal church in the United States

8. Religion defines the spiritual world and gives meaning to the divine. These are _____ functions of religion.
   a. manifest
   b. latent
   c. positive
   d. negative

9. Which sociological perspective emphasizes the integrative power of religion in human society?
   a. functionalist perspective
   b. conflict perspective
   c. interactionist perspective
   d. all of the above

10. John Calvin, a leader of the Protestant Reformation, emphasized
    a. disciplined work ethic.
    b. this-worldly concerns.
    c. a rational orientation to life.
    d. all of the above.

11. The _____ encompasses elements beyond everyday life that inspire awe, respect, and even fear, as compared to the _____, which includes the ordinary and the commonplace.

12. Wicca is an example of a(n) _____.

13. _____ is the largest single faith in the world; the second largest is _____.

14. _____ _____ are statements to which members of a particular religion adhere.

15. A(n) _____ is a religious organization that claims to include most or all members of a society and is recognized as the national or official religion.

16. Because they are _____, most religions tend to reinforce men's dominance in secular as well as spiritual matters.

17. The single largest denomination in the United States is _____ _____.

18. The big bang theory is challenged by _____, who hold to the biblical account of creation of humans and the universe.

19. Unlike ecclesiae and denominations, _____ require intensive commitments and demonstrations of belief by members.

20. A possible dysfunction of _____ _____ would be the belief that when Roman Catholics focus on political and governmental injustice, the clergy are no longer addressing people's personal and spiritual needs.

Answers

1 (c); 2 (a); 3 (b); 4 (d); 5 (b); 6 (d); 7 (d); 8 (a); 9 (a); 10 (d); 11 sacred; profane; 12 quasi-religion; 13 Christianity; Islam; 14 Religious beliefs; 15 ecclesia; 16 patriarchal; 17 Roman Catholicism; 18 creationists; 19 sects; 20 liberation theology

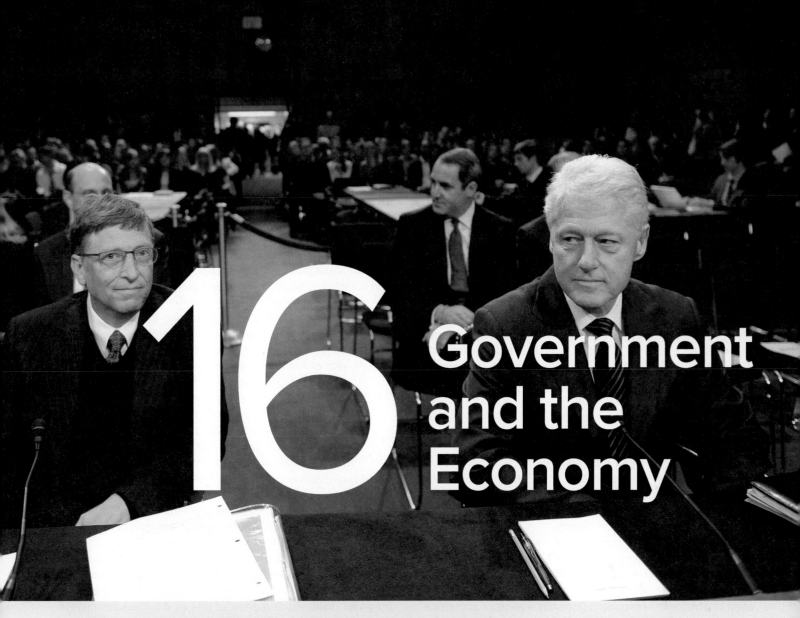

16 Government and the Economy

Government affects society at all levels. In 2010, Microsoft founder Bill Gates and former president Bill Clinton testified before the U.S. Senate's Foreign Relations Committee on approaches to global health problems.

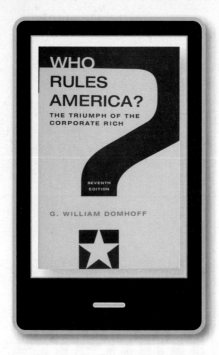

How much power do you think you have over the U.S. economy? Over the economic policies of the U.S. government?

According to sociologist G. William Domhoff, unless you belong to the corporate elite, you have no real power.

" How can the owners and managers of highly competitive corporations develop the policy unity to shape government policies? And how can large corporations have such great power in a democratic country? The step-by-step argument and evidence presented in previous chapters provide the foundation for a theory that can explain these paradoxes—a *class-domination* theory of power in the United States.

Domination means that the commands of a group or class are carried out with relatively little resistance, which is possible because that group or class has been able to establish the organizations, rules, and customs through which everyday life is conducted. Domination, in other words, is the institutionalized outcome of great distributive power ("power over"). The corporate rich are a dominant class in terms of this definition because the cumulative effect of their various distributive powers leads to a situation in which most Americans generally accept (or acquiesce in) its policies. Even when there are highly vocal complaints, the routinized ways of acting in the United States follow from the rules and regulations needed by the corporate community to continue to grow and make profits.

The overall distributive power of the dominant class is first of all based in its structural power, which falls to it by virtue of being owners and high-level executives in corporations that sell goods and services for a profit in a market economy that is fashioned in good part to benefit the sellers of goods and services, not employees or consumers. The power to invest or not invest and to hire and fire employees leads to a political context in which most elected officials try to do as much as they can to create a favorable investment climate in order to avoid being voted out of office in the event of an economic downturn. This structural power is augmented by the ability to create new policies through the policy-planning network, which it was possible for the corporate rich to develop gradually over many decades because their common economic interests and social cohesion give them enough unity to sustain such an endeavor.

But even these powers might not have been enough to generate a system of extreme class domination if the bargains

Despite their lack of power, many Americans feel a sense of empowerment because they have religious freedom, freedom of expression, the right to vote, and the hope that they can make more money or rise in the class structure if they try hard enough.

and compromises embodied in the Constitution had not led unexpectedly to a two-party system in which one party was controlled by the Northern rich and the other by the Southern rich. This in turn reinforced a personality-oriented candidate-selection process that is heavily dependent on large campaign donations—now and in the nineteenth century as well. The system of party primaries is the one adaptation to this constrictive two-party system that has provided some openings for insurgent liberals and trade unionists on one side and social conservatives and libertarians on the other.

Structural power, policies generated in the policy-planning network, and control of the two parties resulted in a polity in which there is little or no organized public opinion on specific legislative issues that is independent of the limits, doubts, and obfuscations generated by the opinion-shaping network. In addition, the fragmented and constrained system of government crafted by the Founding Fathers led to a relatively small federal government that is easily entered and influenced by wealthy and well-organized private citizens, whether through Congress, the separate departments of the executive branch, or a myriad of regulatory agencies.

Despite their lack of power, many Americans feel a sense of empowerment because they have religious freedom, freedom of expression, the right to vote, and the hope that they can make more money or rise in the class structure if they try hard enough. Those with educational credentials and/or secure employment experience a degree of dignity and respect that allows them to hold their heads high and maintain their sense of self-regard, because elite arrogance and condescension toward average people is rarely expressed publicly. Then, too, liberals and leftists retain hope because they had success in helping to expand individual rights and freedom—for people of color, for women, and for gays and lesbians.

But individual rights and freedoms do not necessarily add up to distributive power. In the same time period between 1965 and 2000 in which individual rights and freedoms expanded, corporate power also became greater because industrial unions were decimated, the civil rights movement dissipated, and the liberal-labor alliance splintered as part of the resistance to the integration of job sites, neighborhoods, and schools. Thus, class domination actually increasd in recent decades in spite of increases in individual freedom. It is therefore possible to have class domination in a society based on individualistic liberal values, as many decisions by the Supreme Court also demonstrate. "

(Domhoff 2014:192–194)

n this excerpt from his book *Who Rules America? The Triumph of the Corporate Rich*, Domhoff explains how large corporations increased their power in recent decades. The general public seems to share Domhoff's assertion about who rules America: two-thirds or more of Americans think that banks, financial institutions, and major corporations have too much power. In comparison, only a third or less of those surveyed think that the courts, local government, organized religion, or the military are too powerful (Saad 2011).

The unequal distribution of power in the United States, where a small group of corporate elites wields more power than the entire citizenry, is compounded by inequality of income and wealth. The same is true of the world as a whole. Shortly after *Who Rules America?* was published, the human rights organization Oxfam announced that 85 of the world's richest people own the same amount of wealth as half the world's population.

The inequality both within the United States and between the United States and other nations—between the big industrial powers and the developing world—underscores the importance of understanding our economic and political institutions. To many observers, the massive concentration of economic resources in the hands of just a few threatens our founding fathers' vision of an inclusive political and economic system. Instead of moving forward together, Americans seem increasingly split by inequality in economic and political power—a trend that will inevitably heighten social tensions (Fuentes-Nieva and Galasso 2014).

This chapter will present a combined analysis of the economy and government. It is hard to imagine two social institutions more intertwined. Besides serving as the largest employer in the nation, government at all levels regulates commerce and entry into many occupations. At the same time, the economy generates the revenue to support government services.

We begin with a general discussion of power and authority, and specific descriptions of four major types of government in which that power and authority operates. We'll also briefly touch on war, peace, and terrorism. Next we'll see how politics works, and we'll look at two models of power in the United States. We'll then turn to a macro-level analysis of capitalism and socialism. We'll examine how the U.S. economy is changing in response to globalization. Finally, in the Social Policy section, we'll explore the effects of a financial innovation called *microfinancing* on the lives of poor people in developing countries.

MODULE 48 | Government, Power, and Authority

Power and Authority

In any society, someone or some group—whether it be a tribal chief, a dictator, or a parliament—makes important decisions about how to use resources and how to allocate goods. One cultural universal, then, is the exercise of power and authority. Inevitably, the struggle for power and authority involves **politics,** which political scientist Harold Lasswell (1936) tersely defined as "who gets what, when, and how." In their study of politics and government, sociologists are concerned with social interactions among individuals and groups and their impact on the larger political and economic order.

The social institution that is responsible for implementing and achieving society's goals is the **political system.** Each country has a unique political system that is founded on a recognized set of procedures. The political system interacts closely with the **economic system,** the social institution through which goods and services are produced, distributed, and consumed. As we will see throughout the next four modules, the political and economic systems are inextricably intertwined, and together they regulate power and authority within society.

Power

Power lies at the heart of a political system. According to Max Weber, **power** is the ability to exercise one's will over others. To put it another way, whoever can overcome the resistance of others and control their behavior is exercising power. Power relations can involve large organizations, small groups, or even people in an intimate association.

Because Weber developed his conceptualization of power in the early 1900s, he focused primarily on the nation-state and its sphere of influence. Today scholars recognize that the trend toward globalization has brought new opportunities, and with them new concentrations of power. Power is now exercised on a global as well as a national stage, as countries and multinational corporations vie to control access to resources and manage the distribution of capital (R. Schaefer 2008b; Sernau 2001).

There are three basic sources of power within any political system: force, influence, and authority. **Force** is the actual or threatened use of coercion to impose one's will on others. When leaders imprison or even execute political dissidents, they are applying force; so, too, are terrorists when they seize or bomb an embassy or assassinate a political leader.

Influence, on the other hand, refers to the exercise of power through a process of persuasion. A citizen may change his or her view of a Supreme Court nominee because of a newspaper editorial, the expert testimony of a law school dean before the Senate Judiciary Committee, or a stirring speech by a political activist at a rally. In each case, sociologists would view such efforts to persuade people as examples of influence. Now let's take a look at the third source of power, *authority*.

Types of Authority

The term **authority** refers to institutionalized power that is recognized by the people over whom it is exercised. Sociologists commonly use the term in connection with those who hold legitimate power through elected or publicly acknowledged positions. A person's authority is often limited. Thus, a referee has the authority to decide whether a penalty should be called during a football game, but has no authority over the price of tickets to the game.

Max Weber ([1913–1922] 1947) developed a classification system for authority that has become one of the most useful and frequently cited contributions of early sociology. He identified three ideal types of authority: traditional, rational-legal, and charismatic. Weber did not insist that only one type applies to a given society or organization. All can be present, but their relative importance will vary. Sociologists have found Weber's typology valuable in understanding different manifestations of legitimate power within a society.

Traditional Authority

Until the middle of the past century, Japan was ruled by a revered emperor whose absolute power was passed down from generation to generation. In a political system based on **traditional authority,** legitimate power is conferred by custom and accepted practice. A king or queen is accepted as ruler of a nation simply by virtue of inheriting the crown; a tribal chief rules because that is the accepted practice. The ruler may be loved or hated, competent or destructive; in terms of legitimacy, that does not matter. For the traditional leader, authority rests in custom, not in personal characteristics, technical competence, or even written law. People accept the ruler's authority because that is how things have always been done. Traditional authority is absolute when the ruler has the ability to determine laws and policies.

Rational-Legal Authority

The U.S. Constitution gives Congress and our president the authority to make and enforce laws and policies. Power made legitimate by law is known as **rational-legal authority.** Leaders derive their rational-legal authority from the written rules and regulations of political systems, such as a constitution. Generally, in societies based on rational-legal authority, leaders are thought to have specific areas of competence and authority but are not thought to be endowed with divine inspiration, as in certain societies with traditional forms of authority.

Steve Jobs, visionary co-founder of Apple, was a charismatic figure not only to Apple employees but to Apple users as well. Max Weber would have agreed with Jobs's admirers; Weber considered any kind of leader with exceptional personal appeal to be charismatic.

Charismatic Authority

Joan of Arc was a simple peasant girl in medieval France, yet she was able to rally the French people and lead them into major battles against English invaders. How was this possible? As Weber observed, power can be legitimized by the *charisma* of an individual. The term **charismatic authority** refers to power made legitimate by a leader's exceptional personal or emotional appeal to his or her followers.

Charisma lets a person lead or inspire without relying on set rules or traditions. In fact, charismatic authority is derived more from the beliefs of followers than from the actual qualities of leaders. So long as people perceive a charismatic leader such as Jesus, Joan of Arc, Gandhi, Malcolm X, or Martin Luther King Jr. as having qualities that set him or her apart from ordinary citizens, that leader's authority will remain secure and often unquestioned.

Observing charismatic authority from an interactionist perspective, sociologist Carl Couch (1996) points out that the growth of the electronic media has facilitated the development of charismatic authority. During the 1930s and 1940s, the heads of state of the United States, Great Britain, and Germany all used radio to issue direct appeals to citizens. Now, television and the Internet allow leaders to "visit" people's homes and communicate with them. In both Taiwan and South Korea in 1996, troubled political leaders facing reelection campaigns spoke frequently to national audiences and exaggerated military threats from neighboring China and North Korea, respectively.

As we noted earlier, Weber used traditional, rational-legal, and charismatic authority as ideal types. In reality, particular leaders and political systems combine elements of two or more of these forms. Presidents Franklin D. Roosevelt, John F. Kennedy, and Ronald Reagan wielded power largely through the rational-legal basis of their authority. At the same time, they were unusually charismatic leaders who commanded the personal loyalty of large numbers of citizens.

● Types of Government

Each society establishes a political system through which it is governed. In modern industrialized nations, these formal systems of government make a significant number of critical political decisions. We will survey five basic types of government here: monarchy, oligarchy, dictatorship, totalitarianism, and democracy.

Monarchy

A **monarchy** is a form of government headed by a single member of a royal family, usually a king, queen, or some other hereditary ruler. In earlier times, many monarchs claimed that God had granted them a divine right to rule. Typically, they governed on the basis of traditional forms of authority, sometimes accompanied by the use of force. By the beginning of the 21st century, however, monarchs held genuine governmental power in only a few nations, such as Monaco. Most monarchs now have little practical power; they serve primarily ceremonial purposes.

Oligarchy

An **oligarchy** is a form of government in which a few individuals rule. A rather old method of governing that flourished in ancient Greece and Egypt, oligarchy now often takes the form of military rule. In developing nations in Africa, Asia, and Latin America, small factions of military officers will forcibly seize power, either from legally elected regimes or from other military cliques.

Strictly speaking, the term *oligarchy* is reserved for governments that are run by a few selected individuals. However, the People's Republic of China can be classified as an oligarchy if we stretch the meaning of the term. In China, power rests in the hands of a large but exclusive ruling *group,* the Communist Party. In a similar vein, drawing on conflict theory, one might argue that many industrialized nations of the West should be considered oligarchies (rather than democracies), since only a powerful few—leaders of big business, government, and the military—actually rule. In Module 49, we will examine the *elite model* of the U.S. political system in greater detail.

Dictatorship and Totalitarianism

A **dictatorship** is a government in which one person has nearly total power to make and enforce laws. Dictators rule primarily through the use of coercion, which often includes torture and executions. Typically, they *seize* power rather than being freely elected (as in a democracy) or inheriting power (as in a monarchy). Some dictators are quite charismatic and manage to achieve a certain popularity, though their supporters' enthusiasm is almost certainly tinged with fear. Other dictators are bitterly hated by the people over whom they rule.

Frequently, dictators develop such overwhelming control over people's lives that their governments are called *totalitarian.* (Monarchies and oligarchies may also achieve this type of dominance.) **Totalitarianism** involves virtually complete government control and surveillance over all aspects of a society's social and political life. Germany during Hitler's reign, the Soviet Union in the 1930s, and North Korea today are classified as totalitarian states.

Democracy

In a literal sense, **democracy** means government by the people. The word *democracy* originated in two Greek roots—*demos,* meaning "the populace" or "the common people," and *kratia,* meaning "rule." Of course, in large, populous nations such as the United States, government by the people is impractical at the national level.

North Korea has a totalitarian government whose leadership attempts to control all aspects of people's lives. This old billboard, a blatant example of government propaganda, portrayed the country's ruthless leader as a benevolent father figure.

Americans cannot vote on every important issue that comes before Congress. Consequently, popular rule is generally maintained through **representative democracy,** a form of government in which certain individuals are selected to speak for the people.

The United States is commonly classified as a representative democracy, since the elected members of Congress and state legislatures make our laws. However, critics have questioned whether our democracy really is representative. Even today, not everyone in the United States feels included. Conspicuous among those who view themselves as excluded are Native Hawaiians (Box 48-1).

Do Congress and the state legislatures genuinely represent the masses, including minorities? Are the people of the United States legitimately self-governing, or has our government become a forum for powerful elites? We will explore these issues in Module 49.

Sovereignty in the Aloha State

The people of Hawai'i are definitely multiracial. Twenty-three percent of the population is White; 38 percent, Asian American; 9 percent, Hawaiian or other Pacific Islander; 9 percent, Hispanic; and 2 percent, African American. Another 19 percent of the population, including Hawai'i-born Barack Obama, declare themselves to be of two or more races. Yet Hawai'i is not a racial paradise: certain occupations and even social classes tend to be dominated by Whites, Chinese, or Japanese Americans. Nor is Hawai'i immune to intolerance, although compared to the mainland and much of the rest of the world, race relations there are more harmonious than discordant.

For one group in particular, Native Hawaiians, access to any kind of power has been severely limited for generations. Now, through the **sovereignty movement,** the indigenous people of Hawai'i are hoping to win self-government, as well as restoration of—or compensation for—1.2 million acres of ancestral lands they have lost over the last century. Their movement is comparable to efforts made by American Indian tribes in the continental United States, both in its roots and in its significance.

The sovereignty movement began in 1996, when Native Hawaiians held a referendum on the question "Shall the Hawaiian people elect delegates to propose a Native Hawaiian government?" The results indicated that 73 percent of those who voted favored such an effort. Since then, the state Office of Hawaiian Affairs has sought to create a registry of the estimated 200,000 people of significant Hawaiian descent on the islands. Officials are about halfway to reaching their goal of convincing all Native Hawaiians to come forward and register.

In Washington, D.C., Hawai'i's congressional delegation is seeking passage of the Native Hawaiian Government Reorganization Act, also referred to as the Akaka Bill, after U.S. Senator Daniel Akaka. The act would give people of Hawaiian ancestry more say over the use of local resources, including land and fresh water; provide them with affordable housing; take steps to preserve their culture; and create ways for them to better express their grievances. If the act passes, Native Hawaiians will become the last remaining indigenous group in the United States to be allowed to establish their own government—a right already extended to Alaskan Natives and 564 Native American tribes. As of early 2014, the measure had passed the U.S. House of Representatives, but had not yet been discussed on the floor of the Senate.

Meanwhile, Native Hawaiians do what they can to create political pressure for their

cause. On occasion, they form alliances with environmental groups that want to halt commercial development on the islands. In 2008 and again in 2011, a Native Hawaiian independence group seized the royal palace in

> If the act passes, Native Hawaiians will become the last remaining indigenous group in the United States to be allowed to establish their own government.

Honolulu to protest the U.S.-backed overthrow of the Hawaiian monarchy in 1893. Although these occupations lasted barely a day, the political discontent they revealed persists. Little wonder that in 2009, the 50th anniversary of Hawai'i's statehood passed without a single government-sponsored celebration. Instead, Native Hawaiians concentrated their attention on Washington, D.C., and pushed for passage of the Akaka Bill.

LET'S DISCUSS

1. From a mainstream point of view, what might be the advantages and disadvantages of extending sovereignty to an indigenous group? Discuss using sociological concepts.
2. Do some research on the legal basis for tribal sovereignty. How did American Indian tribes gain the status of separate nations?

Sources: Halualani 2002; Kelleher 2011; Niesse 2008, 2011; Staton 2004; Toensing 2009; Welch 2011.

War and Peace

Conflict is a central aspect of social relations. Too often it becomes ongoing and violent, engulfing innocent bystanders as well as intentional participants. Sociologists Theodore Caplow and Louis Hicks (2002:3) have defined **war** as conflict between organizations that possess trained combat forces equipped with deadly weapons. This meaning is broader than the legal definition, which typically requires a formal declaration of hostilities.

War

Sociologists approach war in three different ways. Those who take a *global view* study how and why two or more nations become engaged in military conflict. Those who take a *nation-state view* stress the interaction of internal political, socioeconomic, and cultural forces. And those who take a *micro view* focus on the social impact of war on individuals and the groups they belong to (Kiser 1992).

From the nation-state perspective, there is little to be said for the supposed socioeconomic benefits of war. Although armed conflicts increase government expenditures on troops and weapons, which tend to stimulate the economy, they also divert workers from civilian health and medical services. Thus, they have a negative effect on civilians' life chances, causing higher levels of civilian mortality. It is exceedingly difficult for a society to engage in armed conflict while maintaining citizens' well-being at home (Carlton-Ford 2010).

Although the decision to go to war is made by government leaders, public opinion plays a significant role in its execution. By 1971, the number of U.S. soldiers killed in Vietnam had surpassed 50,000, and antiwar sentiment was strong. Surveys done at that time showed the public was split roughly equally on the question of whether war was an appropriate way to settle differences between nations.

A major change in the composition of the U.S. military is the growing presence of women. Over 206,000 women, or about 14 percent of active U.S. military forces, are now in uniform, serving not just as support personnel but as an integral part of combat units. The first casualty of the war in Iraq, in fact, was Private First Class Lori Piestewa, a member of the Hopi tribe and a descendant of Mexican settlers in the Southwest (Bureau of the Census 2011a:Table 510).

From a micro view, war can bring out the worst as well as the best in people. In 2004, graphic images of the abuse of Iraqi prisoners by U.S. soldiers at Iraq's Abu Ghraib prison shocked the world. For social scientists, the deterioration of the guards' behavior brought to mind Philip Zimbardo's mock prison experiment, done in 1971. Although the results of the experiment, highlighted in Chapter 5, have been applied primarily to civilian correctional facilities, Zimbardo's study was actually funded by the Office of Naval Research. In July 2004, the U.S. military began using a documentary film about the experiment to train military interrogators to avoid mistreatment of prisoners (Zarembo 2004a; Zimbardo 2004).

Peace

Sociologists have considered **peace** both as the absence of war and as a proactive effort to develop cooperative relations among nations. While we will focus here on international relations, we should note that in the 1990s, 90 percent of the world's armed conflicts occurred *within* rather than between states. Often, outside powers became involved in these internal conflicts, either as supporters of particular factions or in an attempt to broker a peace accord. In at least 28 countries where such conflicts occurred—none of which would be considered core nations in world systems analysis—at least 10,000 people died (Kriesberg 1992; D. Smith 1999).

Another way of picturing the relative peacefulness of nations around the world is the Global Peace Index (Figure 48-1). This index is based on 24 indicators, including organized internal conflict, violent crime, political instability, the potential for terrorist acts, and a nation's level of military expenditures compared to its neighbors'. Currently, Iceland and Denmark are at the top of the index (very peaceful); Syria, Somalia, and Afghanistan are at the bottom (great civil unrest). The United States ranks 99 on this list of 162 nations, between Papua New Guinea and China.

Sociologists and other social scientists who draw on sociological theory and research have tried to identify conditions that deter war. One of their findings is that international trade may act as a deterrent to armed conflict. As countries exchange

Taking Sociology to Work

Joseph W. Drummond, *Management Analyst, U.S. Army Space and Missile Defense Command*

When Joseph Drummond entered Morehouse College, he was planning to major in political science. But after taking an introductory sociology course, he felt that sociology gave him a clearer picture of the complexity and interconnectedness of society. "The career track that I had in mind was to enter the field of sociology as a researcher/policy maker," he explains. However, he soon ran into "a disconnect between academia and policy making," and an apparent lack of representation of sociologists at the policymaking level.

Drummond credits one of his sociology professors for steering him toward quantitative courses. "If you ever plan on having a job," the professor suggested, "make sure you have a lot of classes with quantitative analysis—for example, statistics and data analysis. These classes tell whatever company you want to work for that you have practical skills." Later, when Drummond asked his current employer why he had gotten the job he now holds, he was told that his data analysis and social statistics courses had made him competitive.

Today, Drummond works at the U.S. Army's Space and Missile Defense Command (SMDC), near Huntsville, Alabama. He began there as an intern, after responding to an e-mail from Morehouse College's career office. Drummond is now a junior analyst with a team that formulates and develops doctrine, organization, and material requirements for Army units assigned to space and missile defense. In a typical workweek, he reviews military force structure—units, battalions, and so on—and helps to implement directives from Department of the Army headquarters. "A lot of what we do is attempting to translate very high-level guidance to something that's practical," he explains.

Drummond values the support and professional development he has received from the Army, including classes on program management, data analysis, national security, and force management. An Army-sponsored Technology and Government in Your Future event emphasized the need for interns to pursue graduate studies in math and science to land the best jobs. Drummond says the real-world experience he got as an intern at SMDC not only brought classroom theory to life; it also made him more attractive to future employers.

Asked how he uses sociology in his work, Drummond replies that his academic training has helped him to look critically at problems and to think about the second- and third-order effects of a decision. Seeing society from a macro-level view is also invaluable to him. "When U.S. leadership began to realize that a 'hearts and minds' campaign means that we need to understand the social-historical context of the people whose country we're occupying, that changed the way that we did business and also impacted the way U.S. military force structure was managed," he explains. "A lot of people had problems making the connection." Finally, sociology has taught Drummond not to take things at face value. "Most problems/issues that we come across very seldom have easy fixes," he notes. "Sociology taught me that thorough analysis means leaving no stone unturned."

LET'S DISCUSS

1. Have you ever considered a career in national defense? Do you know anyone with a college degree who works in the field?

2. Why do you think quantitative analysis is such an important skill to employers? How might you use it in your career?

FIGURE 48-1 Global Peace Index

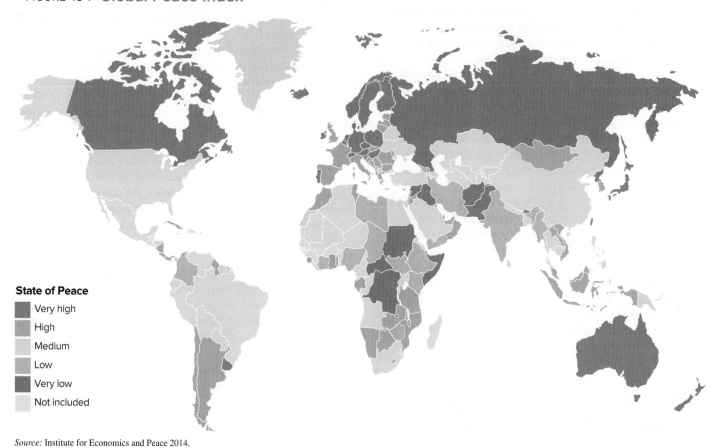

State of Peace

- Very high
- High
- Medium
- Low
- Very low
- Not included

Source: Institute for Economics and Peace 2014.

goods, people, and then cultures, they become more integrated and less likely to threaten each other's security. Viewed from this perspective, not just trade but immigration and foreign exchange programs have a beneficial effect on international relations.

Another means of fostering peace is the activity of international charities and activist groups called nongovernmental organizations (NGOs). The Red Cross and Red Crescent, Doctors Without Borders, and Amnesty International donate their services wherever they are needed, without regard to nationality. In the past decade or more, these global organizations have been expanding in number, size, and scope. By sharing news of local conditions and clarifying local issues, they often prevent conflicts from escalating into violence and war. Some NGOs have initiated cease-fires, reached settlements, and even ended warfare between former adversaries.

Finally, many analysts stress that nations cannot maintain their security by threatening violence. Peace, they contend, can best be maintained by developing strong mutual security agreements between potential adversaries (Etzioni 1965; Shostak 2002).

In recent years, the United States has begun to recognize that its security can be threatened not just by nation-states, but by political groups that operate outside the bounds of legitimate authority. Indeed, terrorism is now considered the foremost threat to U.S. security—one the U.S. military is unaccustomed to fighting.

💡 use your **sociological imagination**

Do you hear much discussion of how to promote worldwide peace, or do the conversations you hear focus more on ending a particular conflict? Which approach would more likely result in a positive outcome? Why?

Terrorism

Acts of terror, whether perpetrated by a few or by many people, can be a powerful political force. Formally defined, **terrorism** is the use or threat of violence against random or symbolic targets in pursuit of political aims. For terrorists, the end justifies the means. They believe the status quo is oppressive and that desperate measures are essential to end the suffering of the deprived. Convinced that working through the formal political process will not effect the desired political change, terrorists insist that illegal actions—often directed against innocent people—are needed. Ultimately, they hope to intimidate society and thereby bring about a new political order.

An essential aspect of contemporary terrorism involves use of the media. Terrorists may wish to keep secret their individual identities, but they want their political messages and goals to receive as much publicity as possible. Drawing on Erving Goffman's dramaturgical approach, sociologist Alfred McClung Lee has likened terrorism to the theater, where certain scenes are played out in predictable fashion. Whether through calls to the media, anonymous manifestos, or other means, terrorists typically admit responsibility for and defend their violent acts.

Sociologists and others have studied the role of different factors in the development of terrorism. They find that both democratic and repressive regimes can facilitate terrorism, although in different ways. The likelihood of violence is higher in youthful populations and among alienated groups, especially expatriate (overseas) communities (P. Davis and Cragin 2009).

Since September 11, 2001, governments worldwide have renewed their efforts to fight terrorism. Although the public generally regards increased surveillance and social control as a necessary evil, these measures have nonetheless raised governance issues. For example, some citizens in the United States and elsewhere have questioned whether measures such as the USA Patriot Act of 2001 threaten civil liberties. Citizens have also complained about the heightened anxiety created by the vague alerts issued by the federal government from time to time. Worldwide, immigration and the processing of refugees have slowed to a crawl, separating families and preventing employers from filling job openings. As these efforts to combat political violence illustrate, the term *terrorism* is an apt one (R. Howard and Sawyer 2003; A. Lee 1983; R. Miller 1988).

At the 2014 Winter Olympics in Sochi, members of the Russian military guard against disruptions. Around the world, major international events have become targets of terrorism.

Increasingly, governments are becoming concerned about another form of political violence, the potential for malicious cyberattacks. In an age in which computer viruses can spread worldwide through the Internet, this kind of attack could render a nation's computer systems useless, or even shut down its power plants. A few years ago, such a scenario would have been considered pulp fiction, but it is now the subject of contingency planning throughout the world (Clayton 2011).

MODULE 48 | **Recap and Review**

Summary

Every society must have a **political system** to allocate valued resources.

1. There are three basic sources of **power** within any political system: **force, influence,** and **authority.**

2. Max Weber identified three ideal types of authority: **traditional, rational-legal,** and **charismatic.**

3. There are four basic types of government: **monarchy, oligarchy, dictatorship,** and **democracy.**

4. **War** may be defined as conflict between organizations that possess trained combat forces equipped with deadly weapons—a definition that includes conflict with terrorist organizations.

Thinking Critically

1. On your campus, what are some examples of the three types of authority?

2. Contrast the use of power in a dictatorship with its use in a democracy, as defined by Max Weber.

3. What is the greatest threat to world peace, and how would you counter it?

Key Terms

Authority	**Political system**
Charismatic authority	**Politics**
Democracy	**Power**
Dictatorship	**Rational-legal authority**
Economic system	**Representative democracy**
Force	**Sovereignty movement**
Influence	**Terrorism**
Monarchy	**Totalitarianism**
Oligarchy	**Traditional authority**
Peace	**War**

Citizens of the United States take for granted many aspects of their political system. They are accustomed to living in a nation with a Bill of Rights, two major political parties, voting by secret ballot, an elected president, state and local governments distinct from the national government, and so forth. Yet each society has its own ways of governing itself and making decisions. U.S. residents expect Democratic and Republican candidates to compete for public office; residents of Cuba and the People's Republic of China are accustomed to one-party rule by the Communist Party. In this module, we will examine several aspects of political behavior within the United States.

Participation and Apathy

In theory, a representative democracy will function most effectively and fairly if an informed and active electorate communicates its views to government leaders. Unfortunately, that is hardly the case in the United States. Virtually all citizens are familiar with the basics of the political process, and a small majority tend to identify to some extent with a political party. In 2012, about 29 percent of registered voters in the United States saw themselves as Democrats and 27 percent as Republicans; an impressive 43 percent were independent. However, only a small minority of citizens, often members of the higher social classes, actually participate in political organizations on a local or national level. Studies reveal that only 8 percent of Americans belong to a political club or organization. Not more than 20 percent have ever contacted an official of national, state, or local government about a political issue or problem (Gallup 2012; Orum and Dale 2009).

By the 1980s, it had become clear that many people in the United States were beginning to be turned off by political parties, politicians, and big government. The most dramatic indication of this growing alienation came from voting statistics. Today, voters of all ages and races appear to be less enthusiastic than ever about elections, even presidential contests. For example, in the presidential election of 1896, almost 80 percent of eligible voters in the United States went to the polls. Yet by the 2008 election, despite its drama and historic nature, turnout was only 63.6 percent of citizens—well below the levels of the 1960s. Four years later, in the 2012 general election, turnout fell slightly to 61.8 percent, lower than in most other nations (Figure 49-1).

Despite poor voter turnout, participation in politics may be increasing, especially on the Internet. In terms of both antigovernment activities and financial contributions to political parties, online participation rivals the political rallies and doorbell-ringing efforts of yesteryear. Fifty-five percent of the entire adult population of the United States went online in 2008 to get news and information about the presidential election. One in every five of those online participants went so far as to post comments for others to read (A. Smith 2009).

FIGURE 49-1 Voter Turnout Worldwide

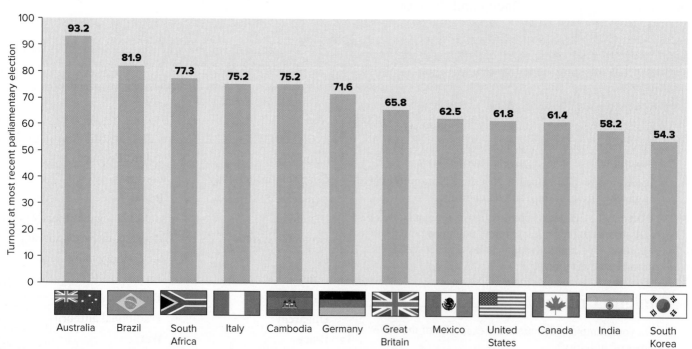

Note: Based on turnout in recent elections for seats in national congress or parliament. Data are for 2010 except for Cambodia (2008); South Africa and India (2009); Canada (2011); Mexico and South Korea (2012); and Australia, Germany, and Italy (2013). USA 2012 Bureau of the Census data in File 2013.
Source: International Institute for Democracy and Electoral Assistance 2014.

In the end, political participation makes government accountable to the voters. If participation declines, government operates with less of a sense of accountability to society. This issue is most serious for the least powerful individuals and groups in the United States. Historically, voter turnout has been particularly low among members of racial and ethnic minorities. However, in postelection surveys following the 2012 presidential election, a higher proportion of African Americans than Whites reported that they actually voted.

Many more potential voters fail to register to vote. The poor—whose focus understandably is on survival—are traditionally underrepresented among voters as well. The low turnout found among these groups is explained at least in part by their common feeling of powerlessness. Yet these low statistics encourage political power brokers to continue to ignore the interests of the less affluent and the nation's minorities. The segment of the voting population that has shown the most voter apathy is the young, as discussed in Box 49-1 (File 2013).

 use your **sociological imagination**

Were you brought up to consider political involvement an important civic duty? If so, do you take that duty seriously by informing yourself about the issues and voting? Why or why not?

Race and Gender in Politics

Because politics is synonymous with power and authority, we should not be surprised that political strength is lacking in marginalized groups, such as women and racial and ethnic minorities. Nationally, women did not get the vote until 1920. Most Chinese Americans were turned away from the polls until 1926. And African Americans were disenfranchised until 1965, when national voting rights legislation was passed. Predictably, it has taken these groups some time to develop their political power and begin to exercise it effectively.

Progress toward the inclusion of minority groups in government has been slow. As of early 2014, 20 out of 100 U.S. senators were women (including one Asian American); 2 were Latinos and 2 were African Americans, leaving 76 White non-Hispanic men. Among the 435 members of the U.S. House of Representatives, 297 were White non-Hispanic men; 80 were women, 40 were African Americans (including 13 women), 33 were Latinos (including 7 Latinas), 9 were Asian Americans (including 6 women), and 2 were American Indians. In sum, 24 percent of the Senate and 32 percent of the House membership is comprised of women or minority men. These numbers, although relatively low, represent a high-water mark for most of these groups.

Today, with record-high numbers of Blacks and Latinos holding elective office, many critics still decry what has been termed *fiesta politics*. White power brokers tend to visit racial and ethnic minority communities only when they need electoral support, making a quick appearance on a national or

Minnesota Democrat Keith Ellison created quite a stir in 2007 when he became the first person to take the congressional oath of office on a Qur'an. The newly elected member of the House of Representatives, who is Muslim, thought the Qur'an would make his oath more meaningful than a Bible. Speaker of the House Nancy Pelosi (left) borrowed Thomas Jefferson's two-volume Qur'an for the occasion—a reminder that acknowledging diversity is nothing new in U.S. politics.

ethnic holiday to get their pictures taken and then vanishing. When the election is over, they too often forget to consult the residents who supported them about community needs and concerns.

Female politicians may be enjoying more electoral success now than in the past, but there is some evidence that the media cover them differently from male politicians. A content analysis of newspaper coverage of recent gubernatorial races showed that reporters wrote more often about a female candidate's personal life, appearance, or personality than a male candidate's, and less often about her political positions and voting record. Furthermore, when political issues were raised in newspaper articles, reporters were more likely to illustrate them with statements made by male candidates than by female candidates (Devitt 1999; Jost 2008).

Figure 49-2 shows the representation of women in selected national legislatures. While the proportion of women in national legislatures has increased in the United States and many other nations, in all but one country women still do not account for half the members of the national legislature. The African Republic of Rwanda, the exception, ranks the highest, with 63.8 percent of its legislative seats held by women. Overall, the United States ranked 95th among 187 nations in the proportion of women serving as national legislators at the end of 2013.

To remedy this situation, many countries have adopted quotas for female representatives. In some, the government sets aside a certain percentage of seats for women, usually from 14 to 30 percent. In others, political parties have decided that 20 to 40 percent of their candidates should be women. Thirty-two countries now have some kind of female quota system (Rubin and Dagher 2009; Vasagar 2005).

Why Don't More Young People Vote?

All through the 1960s, young people in the United States participated actively in a range of political issues, from pushing civil rights to protesting the Vietnam War. They were especially disturbed by the fact that young men were barred from voting but were being drafted to serve in the military and were dying for their country. In response to these concerns, the Twenty-Sixth Amendment to the Constitution was ratified in 1971, lowering the voting age from 21 to 18.

Now, more than 40 years later, we can consider the available research and see what happened. Frankly, what is remarkable is what did *not* happen. First, young voters have not united in any particular political sentiment. We can see in the way the young vote the same divisions of race, ethnicity, and gender that are apparent among older age groups.

Second, while the momentum for lowering the voting age came from college campuses, the majority of young voters are not students. Third, and particularly troubling, is their relatively low turnout. The 2012 presidential election, held against the background of President Obama's reelection bid and continuing global economic decline, did not pique the interest of voters ages 18 to 24. Only 41.2 percent of them voted, compared to 71.9 percent of those age 65 and older.

What lies behind voter apathy among the young? The popular explanation is that people—especially young people—are alienated from the political system, turned off by the shallowness and negativity of candidates and campaigns. However, young people do vote as they age.

> While the momentum for lowering the voting age came from college campuses, the majority of young voters are not students.

Other explanations for the lower turnout among the young seem more plausible.

First, the United States is virtually alone in requiring citizens to vote twice, in effect. They must first register to vote, often at a time when issues are not on the front burner and candidates haven't even declared. Second, though citizens in the United States tend to be more active in politics at the community level than those in other countries, young people often feel unmoved by local issues such as public school financing.

LET'S DISCUSS

1. How often do you vote? If you do not vote, what accounts for your apathy? Are you too busy to register? Are community issues uninteresting to you?

2. Do you think voter apathy is a serious social problem? What might be done to increase voter participation in your age group and community?

Sources: Alwin 2002; Clymer 2000; File 2013; Niemi and Hanmer 2010; Patterson 2005; Wattenberg 2008.

Reasons for Not Voting, 18- to 24-Year-Olds

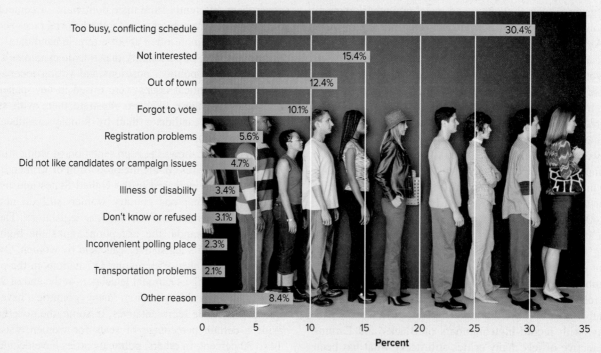

- Too busy, conflicting schedule — 30.4%
- Not interested — 15.4%
- Out of town — 12.4%
- Forgot to vote — 10.1%
- Registration problems — 5.6%
- Did not like candidates or campaign issues — 4.7%
- Illness or disability — 3.4%
- Don't know or refused — 3.1%
- Inconvenient polling place — 2.3%
- Transportation problems — 2.1%
- Other reason — 8.4%

Percent (0 to 35)

Source: Bureau of the Census 2011e:Table 10.

FIGURE 49-2 **Women in National Legislatures, Selected Countries**

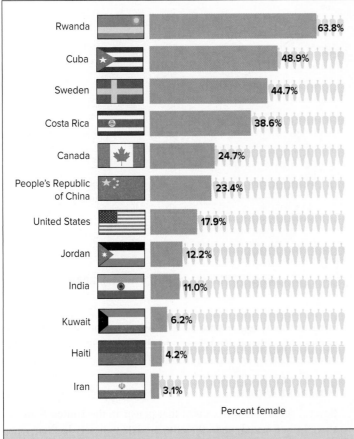

	Percent female
Rwanda	63.8%
Cuba	48.9%
Sweden	44.7%
Costa Rica	38.6%
Canada	24.7%
People's Republic of China	23.4%
United States	17.9%
Jordan	12.2%
India	11.0%
Kuwait	6.2%
Haiti	4.2%
Iran	3.1%

Percent female

Think about It Why do you think being elected to Congress is so difficult for women?

Notes: Data are for lower legislative houses only, as of November 1, 2013; data on upper houses, such as the U.S. Senate, are not included.
Source: Inter-Parliamentary Union 2014.

● Models of Power Structure in the United States

Who really holds power in the United States? Do "we the people" genuinely run the country through our elected representatives? Or is it true that behind the scenes, a small elite controls both the government and the economic system? It is difficult to determine the location of power in a society as complex as the United States. In exploring this critical question, social scientists have developed two basic views of our nation's power structure: the power elite and the pluralist models.

Power Elite Models

Karl Marx believed that 19th-century representative democracy was essentially a sham. He argued that industrialized societies were dominated by relatively small numbers of people who owned factories and controlled natural resources. In Marx's view, government officials and military leaders were essentially servants of this capitalist class and followed their wishes. Therefore, any key

decisions made by politicians inevitably reflected the interests of the dominant bourgeoisie. Like others who share an **elite model** of power relations, Marx believed that society is ruled by a small group of individuals who share a common set of political and economic interests.

Mills's Model Sociologist C. Wright Mills took this model a step further in his pioneering work *The Power Elite* ([1956] 2000b). Mills described a small group of military, industrial, and government leaders who controlled the fate of the United States—the **power elite.** Power rested in the hands of a few, both inside and outside government.

A pyramid illustrates the power structure of the United States in Mills's model (Figure 49-3a). At the top are the corporate rich, leaders of the executive branch of government, and heads of the military (whom Mills called the "warlords"). Directly below are local opinion leaders, members of the legislative branch of government, and leaders of special-interest groups. Mills contended that these individuals and groups would basically follow the wishes of the dominant power elite. At the bottom of the pyramid are the unorganized, exploited masses.

The power elite model is in many respects similar to the work of Karl Marx. The most striking difference is that Mills believed that the economically powerful coordinate their maneuvers with the military and political establishments to serve their common interests. He rejected Marx's belief that by itself, the economic structure of capitalism could create a ruling class. Still, the powerless masses at the bottom of Mills's power elite model certainly bring to mind Marx's portrait of the oppressed workers of the world, who have "nothing to lose but their chains."

A fundamental element in Mills's thesis is that the power elite not only includes relatively few members but also operates as a self-conscious, cohesive unit. Although not necessarily diabolical or ruthless, the elite comprises similar types of people who interact regularly with one another and have essentially the same political and economic interests. Mills's power elite is not a conspiracy, but rather a community of interest and sentiment among a small number of influential people (A. Hacker 1964).

Admittedly, Mills failed to clarify when the elite opposes protests and when it tolerates them; he also failed to provide detailed case studies that would substantiate the interrelationships among members of the power elite. Nevertheless, his challenging theories forced scholars to look more critically at the democratic political system of the United States.

In commenting on the scandals that have rocked major corporations such as Enron and AIG over the past 15 years, observers have noted that members of the business elite *are* closely interrelated. In a study of the members of the boards of directors of *Fortune* 1000 corporations, researchers found that each director can reach *every* other board of directors in just 3.7 steps. That is, by consulting acquaintances of acquaintances, each director can quickly reach someone who sits on each of the other 999 boards. Furthermore, the face-to-face contact directors regularly have in their board meetings makes them a highly

FIGURE 49-3 Power Elite Models

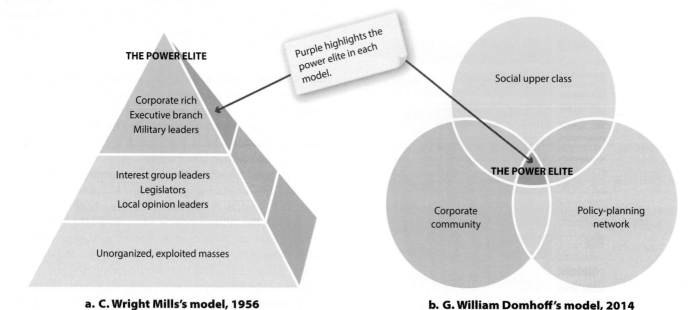

THE POWER ELITE

Corporate rich
Executive branch
Military leaders

Interest group leaders
Legislators
Local opinion leaders

Unorganized, exploited masses

a. C. Wright Mills's model, 1956

Purple highlights the power elite in each model.

Social upper class

THE POWER ELITE

Corporate community

Policy-planning network

b. G. William Domhoff's model, 2014

Sources: Left, author based on Mills [1956] 2000b; right, Domhoff 2014:116.

cohesive elite. Finally, the corporate elite is not only wealthy, powerful, and cohesive; it is also overwhelmingly White and male (G. Davis 2003, 2004; Kentor and Jang 2004; Mizruchi 1996; R. Schaefer 2008b).

One outgrowth of Mills's power elite model is current research on the presence of a *global* power elite—that is, those business, political, and former military leaders who exercise influence across national borders. Because this avenue of scholarship is relatively new, there is some disagreement on the definition of the term. Must the members of the global power elite demonstrate as much consensus as the members of Mills's power elite? Or can the global power elite include such diverse voices as publisher Rupert Murdoch, illegal arms dealer Viktor Bout, and former president Bill Clinton, in his role as head of the Clinton Global Initiative (L. Miller 2008; Rothkopf 2008)?

Domhoff's Model Over the past three decades, sociologist G. William Domhoff (2014), author of the chapter-opening excerpt, has agreed with Mills that a powerful elite runs the United States. He finds that it is still largely older, White, male, and upper class. However, Domhoff stresses the role played both by elites of the corporate community and by leaders of organizations in the policy-planning network, such as chambers of commerce and labor unions. Many of the people in both groups are also members of the social upper class. And he notes the presence of a small number of women and minority men in key positions—groups that were excluded from Mills's top echelon and are still underrepresented today.

Though the three groups in Domhoff's power elite model overlap, as Figure 49-3b shows, they do not necessarily agree on specific policies. Domhoff notes that in the electoral arena, two coalitions have exercised influence. A *corporate-conservative coalition* has played a large role in both political parties, generating support for particular candidates through direct-mail appeals. A *liberal-labor coalition* is based in unions, local

environmental organizations, a segment of the minority group community, liberal churches, and the university and arts communities (Zweigenhaft and Domhoff 2006).

Pluralist Model

Several social scientists insist that power in the United States is shared more widely than the elite models indicate. In their view, a pluralist model more accurately describes the nation's political system. According to the **pluralist model,** many competing groups within the community have access to government, so that no single group is dominant.

Pluralism can be seen in action in the activity of lobbying groups attempting to influence public policy. The highly publicized battle over stem cell research is one example; it has pitted conservative religious groups against health advocacy groups, dividing political leaders in the process. Legislation to support the research technique had the backing of several prominent Republican lawmakers, including Senator Orrin Hatch (R-Utah), shown here with actor and activist Michael J. Fox. Nevertheless, in 2001 President George W. Bush banned federal funding of stem cell research. Eight years later President Obama lifted the restrictions.

Politicking Online

Until recently, citizens could exercise their political rights by voting, supporting candidates for office with their time or money, and writing an occasional letter to the local newspaper. Public rallies or protests, though not for everyone, were another way to display support for a particular politician or social issue. Then came the Internet, and the possibilities for politicking broadened dramatically.

Today, social media are playing a growing part in Americans' political and civic engagement. In the middle of the 2012 presidential campaign, over a third of people who visited social networking sites took the opportunity to "like" or promote political candidates or social issues. A similar proportion posted their own thoughts or comments about politics and urged others to take action.

Although online politicking is more common among younger people, the differences between age groups are not great. For example, 44 percent of those under age 30 "like" or promote political material, compared to 24 percent of those 65 and older. The age differences narrow when poll takers ask about encouraging others to act: 36 percent of younger adults are inclined to do so, compared to 27 percent of those 65 and older. Racial and ethnic differences in online politicking are not significant, but gender differences are: women are much more likely than men to go online because of politics.

Research is just beginning on the effectiveness of online civic engagement. What impact, if any, does online social networking have on people's politics or political views? According to a 2012 study, it definitely does have an impact. One out of four social media users say they "have become more active in a political issue" after discussing it or reading online posts about it. One out of six report they have "changed their views about a political issue" after discussing it online or reading posts about it.

> One out of four social media users say they "have become more active in a political issue" after discussing it or reading online posts about it.

Another question of interest is the effect of social media on campaign contributions. In 2012, the Federal Election Commission allowed political campaigns to accept contributions via text messages. At that point, 10 percent of all donors were already using the new method to back their candidates.

Given the tendency of the Internet and social media to encourage political activity, governments have tried to suppress them. Nations frequently clamp down on online activity that opposes the central government or asserts human rights, such as the right to freedom of expression or to minority or religious views. In 2006, when a military coup overthrew the democratically elected government of Thailand, citizens lost access to websites critical of the takeover. Such actions give new meaning to the use of force as a source of power, for censorship of online content is just as much a use of force as closing down a newspaper or arresting dissidents.

Like citizens, governments also use the Internet to reach well beyond national borders. In what has been described as "public diplomacy," the U.S. State Department has taken to using Twitter abroad. In 2012, within minutes of violent attacks on U.S. embassies and consulates in the Middle East, the U.S. embassy in Cairo tweeted an emergency number to American citizens, and thanked fellow tweeters for their condolences on the murder of the ambassador to Libya.

LET'S DISCUSS

1. Do you use the Internet or social media for political purposes? If so, do those in your social network affect your political views or participation?
2. What might be some drawbacks of online political activity?

Sources: Deibert et al. 2008; Duggan 2012; *The Economist* 2012; Pew Internet and American Life Project 2012; A. Smith and Duggan 2012; Zittrain and Palfrey 2008.

The pluralist model suggests that a variety of groups play a significant role in decision making. Typically, pluralists make use of intensive case studies or community studies based on observation research. One of the most famous—an investigation of decision making in New Haven, Connecticut—was reported by Robert Dahl (1961). Dahl found that although the number of people involved in any important decision was rather small, community power was nonetheless diffuse. Few political actors exercised decision-making power on all issues. One individual or group might be influential in a battle over urban renewal, but have little impact on educational policy.

The pluralist model, however, has not escaped serious questioning. Domhoff (1978, 2014) reexamined Dahl's study of decision making in New Haven and argued that Dahl and other pluralists had failed to trace how local elites who were prominent in decision making belonged to a larger national ruling class. In addition, studies of community power, such as Dahl's work in New Haven, can examine decision making only on issues that become part of the political agenda. They fail to address the potential power of elites to keep certain matters entirely out of the realm of government debate.

Dianne Pinderhughes (1987) has criticized the pluralist model for failing to account for the exclusion of African Americans from the political process. Drawing on her studies of Chicago politics, Pinderhughes points out that the residential and occupational segregation of Blacks and their long political disenfranchisement violates the logic of pluralism—which would hold that such a substantial minority should always have been influential in community decision making. This critique applies to many cities across the United States, where other large racial and ethnic minorities, among them Asian Americans, Puerto Ricans, and Mexican Americans, are relatively powerless.

Historically, pluralists have stressed ways in which large numbers of people can participate in or influence governmental decision making. New communications technologies like the Internet are increasing the opportunity to be heard, not just in countries such as the United States, but in developing countries the world over. One common point of the elite and pluralist perspectives stands out, however: in the political system of the United States, power is unequally distributed. All citizens may be equal in theory, yet those who are high in the nation's power structure are "more equal." New communications technology may or may not change that distribution of power (McFarland 2007).

Regardless of the form of government, the Internet and people's ability to access it has transformed political life, as Box 49-2 illustrates.

Perhaps the ultimate test of power, no matter what a nation's power structure, is the decision to go to war. Because the rank and file of any army is generally drawn from the lower classes—the least powerful groups in society—such a decision has life-and-death consequences for people far removed from the center of power. In the long run, if the general population is not convinced that war is necessary, military action is unlikely to succeed. Thus, war is a risky way in which to address conflict between nations. In Module 48 we contrasted war and peace as ways of addressing societal conflict, and more recently, the threat of terrorism.

MODULE 49 | Recap and Review

Summary

Political participation makes government accountable to citizens.

1. Both in the United States and in other countries, voters display a good deal of apathy toward the political system.

2. Women are still underrepresented in politics but are becoming more successful at winning election to public office.

3. Advocates of the **elite model** of the U.S. power structure see the nation as being ruled by a small group of individuals who share common political and economic interests (a **power elite**). Advocates of a **pluralist model** believe that power is shared more widely among conflicting groups.

Thinking Critically

1. In the United States, which plays a more significant role in political behavior, gender or race? Explain.

2. Which is a better model of the power structure in the United States, the power elite model or the pluralist model? Justify your answer.

Key Terms

Elite model

Pluralist model

Power elite

MODULE 50 | Economic Systems

The sociocultural evolution approach developed by Gerhard Lenski categorizes preindustrial society according to the way in which the economy is organized. The principal types of preindustrial society, as you recall, are hunting-and-gathering societies, horticultural societies, and agrarian societies.

The *Industrial Revolution*—which took place largely in England during the period 1760 to 1830—brought about changes in the social organization of the workplace. People left their homesteads and began working in central locations such as factories. As the Industrial Revolution proceeded, a new form of social structure emerged: the **industrial society,** a society that depends on mechanization to produce its goods and services.

The scope of these large economies is massive, as Figure 50-1 shows. Over the last three centuries, industrialization has greatly increased the wealth of nations. Since 1990 China, which only began to mechanize its rural areas in the second half of the 20th century, has grown from eleventh largest economy in the world to second largest.

Two basic types of economic system distinguish contemporary industrial societies: capitalism and socialism. As described in this module, capitalism and socialism serve as ideal types of economic system. No nation precisely fits either model. Instead, the economy of each individual state represents a mixture of capitalism and socialism, although one type or the other is generally more useful in describing a society's economic structure.

Capitalism

In preindustrial societies, land functioned as the source of virtually all wealth. The Industrial Revolution changed all that. It required that certain individuals and institutions be willing to take substantial risks in order to finance new inventions, machinery, and business enterprises. Eventually, bankers, industrialists, and other holders of large sums of money replaced landowners as the most powerful economic force. These people invested their funds in the hope of realizing even greater profits, and thereby became owners of property and business firms.

The transition to private ownership of business was accompanied by the emergence of the capitalist economic system. **Capitalism** is an economic system in which the means of production are held largely in private hands and the main incentive for economic activity is the accumulation of profits. In practice, capitalist systems vary in the degree to which the government regulates private ownership and economic activity (D. Rosenberg 1991).

FIGURE 50-1 **World's Largest Economies**

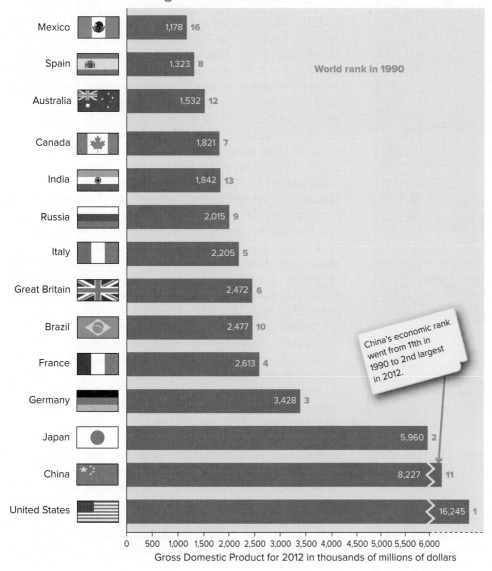

World rank in 1990

Mexico	1,178	16
Spain	1,323	8
Australia	1,532	12
Canada	1,821	7
India	1,842	13
Russia	2,015	9
Italy	2,205	5
Great Britain	2,472	6
Brazil	2,477	10
France	2,613	4
Germany	3,428	3
Japan	5,960	2
China	8,227	11
United States	16,245	1

China's economic rank went from 11th in 1990 to 2nd largest in 2012.

0   500 1,000 1,500 2,000 2,500 3,000 3,500 4,000 4,500 5,000 5,500 6,000

Gross Domestic Product for 2012 in thousands of millions of dollars

Note: Forecasted GDP for 2012–2013.
Sources: World Bank 2013:Table 2-19.

Immediately following the Industrial Revolution, the prevailing form of capitalism was what is termed **laissez-faire** ("let them do"). Under the principle of laissez-faire, as expounded and endorsed by British economist Adam Smith (1723–1790), people could compete freely, with minimal government intervention in the economy. Business retained the right to regulate itself and operated essentially without fear of government interference (Smelser 1963).

Two centuries later, capitalism has taken on a somewhat different form. Private ownership and maximization of profits still remain the most significant characteristics of capitalist economic systems. However, in contrast to the era of laissez-faire, capitalism today features government regulation of economic relations. Without restrictions, business firms can mislead consumers, endanger workers' safety, and even defraud the companies' investors—all in the pursuit of greater profits. That is why the government of a capitalist nation often monitors prices, sets safety and environmental standards for industries, protects the rights of consumers, and regulates collective bargaining between labor unions and management. Yet under capitalism as an ideal type, government rarely takes over ownership of an entire industry.

Contemporary capitalism also differs from laissez-faire in another important respect: capitalism tolerates monopolistic practices. A **monopoly** exists when a single business firm controls the market. Domination of an industry allows the firm to effectively control a commodity by dictating pricing, quality standards, and availability. Buyers have little choice but to yield to the firm's decisions; there is no other place to purchase the product or service. Monopolistic practices violate the ideal of free competition cherished by Adam Smith and other supporters of laissez-faire capitalism.

Some capitalistic nations, such as the United States, outlaw monopolies through antitrust legislation. Such laws prevent any business from taking over so much of the competition in an industry that it controls the market. The U.S. federal government allows monopolies to exist only in certain exceptional cases, such as the utility and transportation industries. Even then, regulatory agencies scrutinize these officially approved monopolies to protect the public. The protracted legal battle between the Justice Department and Microsoft, owner of the dominant operating system for personal computers, illustrates the uneasy relationship between government and private monopolies in capitalistic countries.

Conflict theorists point out that although *pure* monopolies are not a basic element of the economy of the United States, competition is still much more restricted than one might expect in what is called a *free enterprise system.* In numerous industries, a few companies largely dominate the field and keep new enterprises from entering the marketplace.

During the severe economic downturn that began in 2008, the United States moved even farther away from the laissez-faire ideal. To keep major financial institutions from going under, the federal government invested hundreds of billions of dollars in distressed banking, investment, and insurance companies. Then in 2009, the government bailed out the failing automobile industry, taking a 60 percent interest in General Motors. The Canadian government took another 12 percent.

As we have seen in earlier chapters, globalization and the rise of multinational corporations have spread the capitalistic pursuit of profits around the world. Especially in developing countries, governments are not always prepared to deal with the sudden influx of

For more than a century, the board game of Monopoly has entertained millions of people around the world. In the game, players strive to dominate the fictitious economy, gleefully bankrupting other players. Ironically, Monopoly was actually developed to demonstrate the weaknesses of capitalist economies, such as excessive rents and the tendency for money to accumulate in the hands of a few.

foreign capital and its effects on their economies. One particularly striking example of how unfettered capitalism can harm developing nations is found in the Democratic Republic of Congo (formerly Zaire). The Congo has significant deposits of the metal columbite-tantalite—coltan, for short—which is used in the production of electronic circuit boards. Until the market for cell phones, pagers, and laptop computers heated up recently, U.S. manufacturers got most of their coltan from Australia. But at the height of consumer demand, they turned to miners in the Congo to increase their supply.

Predictably, the escalating price of the metal—as much as $600 a kilogram at one point, or more than three times the average Congolese worker's yearly wages—attracted undesirable attention. Soon the neighboring countries of Rwanda, Uganda, and Burundi, at war with one another and desperate for resources to finance the conflict, were raiding the Congo's national parks, slashing and burning to expose the coltan beneath the forest floor. Indirectly, the sudden increase in the demand for coltan was financing war and the rape of the environment. U.S. manufacturers have since cut off their sources in the Congo in an effort to avoid abetting the destruction. But their action has only penalized legitimate miners in the impoverished country (*The Economist* 2011c; Friends of the Congo 2011).

 use your **sociological imagination**

Which aspects of capitalism do you personally appreciate? Which do you find worrisome? Explain.

Socialism

Socialist theory was refined in the writings of Karl Marx and Friedrich Engels. These European radicals were disturbed by the exploitation of the working class that emerged during the Industrial Revolution. In their view, capitalism forced large numbers of people to exchange their labor for low wages. The owners of an industry profit from the labor of workers primarily because they pay workers less than the value of the goods produced.

As an ideal type, a socialist economic system attempts to eliminate such economic exploitation. Under **socialism,** the means of production and distribution in a society are collectively rather than privately owned. The basic objective of the economic system is to meet people's needs rather than to maximize profits. Socialists reject the laissez-faire philosophy that free competition benefits the general public. Instead, they believe that the central government, acting as the representative of the people, should make basic economic decisions. Therefore, government ownership of all major industries—including steel production, automobile manufacturing, and agriculture—is a primary feature of socialism as an ideal type.

In practice, socialist economic systems vary in the extent to which they tolerate private ownership. For example, in Great Britain, a nation with some aspects of both a socialist and a capitalist economy, passenger airline service was once concentrated in the government-owned corporation British Airways. Even before the airline was privatized in 1987, however, private airlines were allowed to compete with it.

Socialist nations differ from capitalist nations in their commitment to social service programs. For example, the U.S. government provides health care and health insurance to the elderly and poor through the Medicare and Medicaid programs. But socialist countries typically offer government-financed medical care to *all* citizens. In theory, the wealth of the people as a collectivity is used to provide health care, housing, education, and other key services to each individual and family.

Workers mine for coltan with sweat and shovels. The sudden increase in demand for the metal by U.S. computer manufacturers caused incursions into the Congo by neighboring countries hungry for capital to finance a war. Too often, globalization can have unintended consequences for a nation's economy and social welfare.

Marx believed that socialist societies would eventually "wither away" and evolve into *communist* societies. As an ideal type, **communism** refers to an economic system under which all property is communally owned and no social distinctions are made on the basis of people's ability to produce. In recent decades, the Soviet Union, the People's Republic of China, Vietnam, Cuba, and nations in Eastern Europe were popularly thought of as examples of communist economic systems. However, this usage represents an incorrect application of a term with sensitive political connotations. All nations known as communist in the 20th century actually fell far short of the ideal type (Walder and Nguyen 2008).

By the early 1990s, Communist parties were no longer ruling the nations of Eastern Europe. Just two decades later, in 2012, Moscow had no fewer than 78 billionaires—more than New York (58) and London (39). That year, only China, Cuba, Laos, North Korea, and Vietnam remained socialist societies ruled by Communist parties. Yet even in those countries, capitalism had begun to make inroads. In Vietnam, for example, the Ho Chi Minh City Stock Exchange opened in 1990; the market now trades 600 stocks representing almost 40 percent of Vietnam's gross domestic product (GDP). Even in Cuba, a socialist stalwart, the government has begun to expand citizens' ability to own their own businesses and hire employees. By mid-2011, over 325,000 owners had received licenses for a range of businesses, including hairstyling, carpentry, shoemaking, and restaurant establishments (K. Chu 2010; Forbes 2012; Wilkinson 2011).

As we have seen, capitalism and socialism serve as ideal types of economic system. In reality, the economy of each industrial society—including the United States, the European Union, and Japan—includes certain elements of both capitalism and socialism (Table 50-1). Whatever the differences—whether a society more closely fits the ideal type of capitalism or socialism—all industrial societies rely chiefly on mechanization in the production of goods and services.

The Informal Economy

In many countries, one aspect of the economy defies description as either capitalist or socialist. In the **informal economy,** transfers of money, goods, or services take place but are not reported to the government. Examples of the informal economy include trading services with someone—say, a haircut for a computer lesson; selling goods on the street; and engaging in illegal transactions, such as gambling or drug deals. The informal economy also includes off-the-books work in landscaping, child care, and housecleaning. Participants in this type of economy avoid taxes and government regulations.

In the United States, the informal economy accounts for about 8 percent of total economic activity. In other industrialized nations it varies, from 11 percent in Great Britain to 20 percent in Spain and Portugal and 25 percent in Greece. In developing nations, the informal economy represents a much larger (40 to 60 percent) and often unmeasured part of total economic activity. Yet because this sector of the economy depends to a large

TABLE **50-1** CHARACTERISTICS OF THE THREE MAJOR ECONOMIC SYSTEMS

Economic System	Characteristics	Contemporary Examples
Capitalism	Private ownership of the means of production	Canada
		Mexico
	Accumulation of profits the main incentive	United States
Socialism	Collective ownership of the means of production	Russia
		Sweden
	Meeting people's needs the basic objective	
Communism	Communal ownership of all property	Cuba
		North Korea
	No social distinctions made on basis of people's ability to produce	Vietnam

Note: Countries listed in column 3 are typical of one of the three economic systems, but not perfectly so. In practice, the economies of most countries include a mix of elements from the three major systems.

extent on the labor of women, work in the informal economy is undervalued or even unrecognized the world over (T. Barnes 2009; F. Schneider 2010).

Functionalists contend that bureaucratic regulations sometimes contribute to the rise of an informal, or underground, economy. In the developing world, governments often set up burdensome business regulations that overworked bureaucrats must administer. When requests for licenses and permits pile up, delaying business projects, legitimate entrepreneurs find they need to go underground to get anything done. Despite its apparent efficiency, this type of informal economy is dysfunctional for a country's overall political and economic well-being. Since informal firms typically operate in remote locations to avoid detection, they cannot easily expand when they become profitable. And given the limited protection for their property and contractual rights, participants in the informal economy are less likely than others to save and invest their income.

Whatever the functions an informal economy may serve, it is in some respects dysfunctional for workers. Working conditions in these illegal businesses are often unsafe or dangerous, and the jobs rarely provide any benefits to those who become ill or cannot continue to work. Perhaps more significant, the longer a worker remains in the informal economy, the less likely that person is to make the transition to the formal economy. No matter how efficient or productive a worker, employers expect to see experience in the formal economy on a job application. Experience as a successful street vendor or self-employed cleaning person does not carry much weight with interviewers (Venkatesh 2006).

Summary

A society's **economic system** has an important influence on social behavior and on other social institutions.

1. With the Industrial Revolution, a new form of social structure emerged: the **industrial society.**

2. Systems of **capitalism** vary in the degree to which the government regulates private ownership and economic activity, but all emphasize the profit motive.

3. The basic objective of **socialism** is to eliminate economic exploitation and meet people's needs. Marx believed that **communism** would evolve naturally out of socialism.

4. In developing nations, the **informal** economy represents a significant part of total economic activity. Yet because this sector depends largely on women's work, it is undervalued.

Thinking Critically

1. In the United States, what factors might encourage the growth of the informal economy? Are those factors related to the country's economic system?

2. Why have so-called communist countries failed to achieve communist systems according to Marx's definition?

Key Terms

Capitalism

Communism

Industrial society

Informal economy

Laissez-faire

Monopoly

Socialism

MODULE 51 | **Changing Economies**

As advocates of the power elite model point out, the trend in capitalist societies has been toward concentration of ownership by giant corporations, especially multinational ones. In this module we will examine four outgrowths of this trend in the United States: the changing face of the workforce, deindustrialization, the temporary workforce, and offshoring. As these trends show, any change in the economy has social and political implications.

◼ The Changing Face of the Workforce

The workforce in the United States is constantly changing. During World War II, when men were mobilized to fight abroad, women entered the workforce in large numbers. And with the rise of the civil rights movement in the 1960s, minorities found numerous job opportunities opening to them. Box 51-1 takes a closer look at the active recruitment of women and minorities into the workplace, known as *affirmative action.*

Although predictions are not always reliable, sociologists and labor specialists foresee a workforce increasingly composed of women and racial and ethnic minorities. In 1960 there were twice as many men in the labor force as women. From 1988 to 2018, however, 52 percent of new workers are expected to be women. The dynamics for minority group workers are even more dramatic, as the number of Black, Latino, and Asian American workers continues to increase at a faster rate than the number of White workers (Toossi 2009).

More and more, then, the workforce reflects the diversity of the population, as ethnic minorities enter the labor force and immigrants and their children move from marginal jobs or employment in the informal economy to positions of greater visibility and responsibility. The impact of this changing labor force is not merely statistical. A more diverse workforce means that relationships between workers are more likely to cross gender, racial, and ethnic lines. Interactionists note that people will soon find themselves supervising and being supervised by people very different from themselves.

Deindustrialization

What happens when a company decides it is more profitable to move its operations out of a long-established community to another part of the country, or out of the country altogether? People lose jobs; stores lose customers; the local government's tax base declines and it cuts services. This devastating process has occurred again and again in the past decade or so.

The term **deindustrialization** refers to the systematic, widespread withdrawal of investment in basic aspects of productivity, such as factories and plants. Giant corporations that deindustrialize are not necessarily refusing to invest in new economic opportunities. Rather, the targets and locations of investment change, and the need for labor decreases as advances in technology continue to automate production. First, companies may move their plants from the nation's central cities to the suburbs. The next

Research Today

BOX 51-1

Affirmative Action

The term *affirmative action* first appeared in an executive order issued by President John F. Kennedy in 1961. That order called for contractors to "take affirmative action to ensure that applicants are employed, and that employees are treated during employment, without regard to their race, creed, color, or national origin." In 1967, the order was amended by President Lyndon Johnson to prohibit discrimination on the basis of sex as well, but affirmative action remained a vague concept. Currently, affirmative action refers to positive efforts to recruit minority group members or women for jobs, promotions, and educational opportunities.

Sociologists—especially conflict and feminist theorists—view **affirmative action** as a legislative attempt to reduce the inequality

> Critics warn against hiring and admissions quotas, complaining that they constitute a kind of "reverse discrimination" against White males.

embedded in the social structure by increasing opportunities for groups who were deprived in the past, such as women and African Americans. Despite the clear disparity in earnings between White males and other groups, however, many people doubt that everything done in the name of affirmative action is desirable. Critics warn against hiring and admissions quotas, complaining that they constitute a kind of "reverse discrimination" against White males.

Affirmative action became a prominent issue in state and national political campaigns in 1996, when California's voters approved by a 54 to 46 percent margin the California Civil Rights Initiative. Better known as Proposition 209, this measure amends the state constitution to prohibit any program that gives preference to women and minorities in college admissions, hiring, promotion, or government contracts. In other words, it aims to abolish affirmative action programs. The courts have since upheld the measure. In 1998, voters in Washington State passed a similar anti–affirmative action measure.

Colleges and universities responded with new policies designed to broaden opportunities for traditionally underrepresented minority students. However, opponents of affirmative action continue to argue in court that such actions unconstitutionally disadvantage White applicants. And colleges continue to reexamine their policies in light of the latest legal rulings.

Increasingly, critics of affirmative action are calling for color-blind policies that would end affirmative action. Presumably, such policies would allow all applicants to be judged fairly. However, opponents warn against the danger of **color-blind racism**—the use of the principle of race neutrality to defend a racially unequal status quo. Will "color-blind" policies put an end to institutional practices that now favor Whites, they ask? According to the latest data, for example, Harvard University admits 40 percent of those applicants who are children of alumni—almost all

The Supreme Court's many decisions on the constitutionality of affirmative action programs have made it difficult for organizations to encourage diversity without transgressing the law.

of whom are White—compared to 11 percent of nonalumni children. Ironically, studies show that children of alumni are far more likely than either minority students or athletes to run into trouble academically.

LET'S DISCUSS

1. Is affirmative action part of the admissions policy at the college or university you attend? If so, do you think the policy has helped to level the playing field? Might it have excluded some qualified White applicants?

2. Take a poll of your classmates. What percentage of the class supports affirmative action in hiring and college admissions? How does that group break down in terms of gender, race, and ethnicity?

Sources: Massey and Mooney 2007; Pincus 2003, 2008; University of Michigan 2003.

---

step may be relocation from suburban areas of the Northeast and Midwest to the South, where labor laws place more restrictions on unions. Finally, a corporation may simply relocate *outside* the United States to a country with a lower rate of prevailing wages. General Motors, for example, decided to build a multi-billion-dollar plant in China rather than in Kansas City or even in Mexico (Lynn 2003).

Although deindustrialization often involves relocation, in some instances it takes the form of corporate restructuring, as companies seek to reduce costs in the face of growing world-wide competition. When such restructuring occurs, the impact on the bureaucratic hierarchy of formal organizations can be

significant. A large corporation may choose to sell off or entirely abandon less productive divisions and to eliminate layers of management viewed as unnecessary. Wages and salaries may be frozen and benefits cut—all in the name of restructuring. Increasing reliance on automation also spells the end of work as we have known it.

The term **downsizing** was introduced in 1987 to refer to reductions taken in a company's workforce as part of deindustrialization. Viewed from a conflict perspective, the unprecedented attention given to downsizing in the mid-1990s reflected the continuing importance of social class in the United States. Conflict theorists note that job loss has long been a feature of deindustrialization among blue-collar workers. But when large numbers of middle-class managers and other white-collar employees with substantial incomes began to be laid off, suddenly the media began expressing great concern over downsizing.

The extended economic downturn that began in 2008 accelerated the processes of deindustrialization and downsizing. As the recession deepened, many plants shut down either temporarily or permanently, leaving more and more workers without jobs. With those jobs and shuttered plants went the hope of restoring or expanding heavy industry, including automobile manufacturing. The bankruptcy of Chrysler and General Motors hit the midwestern states particularly hard.

The social costs of deindustrialization and downsizing cannot be overemphasized. Plant closings lead to substantial unemployment in a community, which has a devastating impact on both the micro and macro levels. On the micro level, the unemployed person and his or her family must adjust to a loss of spending power. Painting or re-siding the house, buying health insurance or saving for retirement, even thinking about having another child must be put aside. Both marital happiness and family cohesion may suffer as a result. Although many dismissed workers eventually reenter the paid labor force, they must often accept less desirable positions with lower salaries and fewer benefits. Unemployment and underemployment are tied to many of the social problems discussed throughout this textbook, among them the need for child care and the controversy over welfare.

The Temporary Workforce

Over the last four decades, U.S. employers have been relying more and more on the part-time workforce. The recent economic downturn and the slow recovery that followed only accelerated the trend, which began in 1970. In 2013, about 26 million of the 143 million people employed in the United States were working part time, many of them at more than one job (Bureau of Labor Statistics 2013; Chris Tilly 1991).

This pattern of expanding part-time work is slowly reshaping the U.S. workforce. Traditionally, businesses employed workers through good times and bad, protecting them from economic ups and downs. In numerous industries, however, that is no longer the case. Today, many part-time employees—those who work 1 to 34 hours a week—are actually temporary or seasonal employees, who work part time for part of the year. These workers typically do not enjoy benefits like health insurance, paid sick-leave, or even unemployment compensation.

Certainly some workers seek out part-time jobs, welcoming the flexibility they offer. For example, students taking college classes may prefer part-time work. For most workers, however, part-time employment is not a first choice. In response to the trend away from traditional full-time jobs, more and more workers are adopting a "free agent mentality," actively seeking work wherever and whenever they can find it instead of expecting to be hired full time. This change in attitude is related to an increase in what has been termed **precarious work**—employment that is poorly paid, and from the worker's perspective, insecure and unprotected (P. Davidson 2012).

As Figure 51-1 shows, the spread of part-time employment is not unique to the United States. Indeed, in many nations, part-timers account for an even larger proportion of the workforce than they do in the United States. Around the world, women are much more likely than men to be employed less than full time.

Offshoring

U.S. firms have been outsourcing certain types of work for generations. For example, moderate-sized businesses such as furniture stores and commercial laundries have long relied on outside trucking firms to make deliveries to their customers. The new trend toward **offshoring** carries this practice one step further, by transferring other types of work to foreign contractors. Now, even large companies are turning to overseas firms, many of them located in developing countries. Offshoring has become the latest tactic in the time-worn business strategy of raising profits by reducing costs.

Significantly, the transfer of work from one country to another is no longer limited to manufacturing. Office and professional

Gutted factories like this one in Boston, Massachusetts, contrast with the glamorous corporate campus of Google Corporation in Mountain View, California. Deindustrialization and the rise of high technology have shifted the U.S. labor market, displacing many workers in the process.

jobs are being exported, too, thanks to advanced telecommunications. Table 51-1 lists those occupations most likely to be offshored.

In 2012, complaints about working conditions in Apple's factories in China called attention to the fact that the company's financial success had been built on outsourced labor. At one time, Apple manufactured its computers in the United States. Today the company still employs about 43,000 full-time workers in the United States, and another 20,000 full-time workers abroad. However, Apple contracts on a short-term basis with an additional 700,000 workers who both engineer and build its products overseas. As complaints grew about Apple's offshoring, economists released estimates that in the next four years, another 375,000 well-paid jobs in information technology, human resources, and finance and merchandising would be lost to overseas competition (Duhigg and Bradsher 2012; P. Davidson 2012).

Offshoring is not completely inevitable. In a recent countertrend called *reshoring,* widely reported in the media, some U.S. companies have been bringing manufacturing jobs and service centers back to the United States. General Electric, Ford, and Whirlpool are among the 200 or more companies that have already made the move. Typically, quality concerns or rising wages—notably in China—make developing countries less competitive than the home country for these companies,

FIGURE 51-1 Temporary Workforce in Six Countries, by Gender

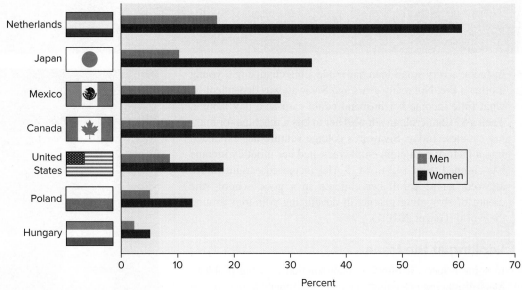

Source: Bureau of Labor Statistics 2012c:21.

In all the countries surveyed, the proportion of women who worked part time was greater than the proportion of men.

especially when shipping costs are factored in (*The Economist* 2013f; Northam 2014).

Because offshoring, like outsourcing in general, tends to improve the efficiency of business operations, it can be viewed as functional to society. Offshoring also increases economic interdependence in the production of goods and services, both in enterprises located just across town and in those located around the globe. Still, conflict theorists charge that this aspect of globalization furthers social inequality. Although moving high-tech work to developing countries does help to lower a company's costs, the impact on technical and service workers at home is clearly devastating. Certainly middle-class workers are alarmed by the trend. Because offshoring increases efficiency, economists oppose efforts to block the practice and instead recommend assistance to displaced workers.

There is a downside to offshoring for foreigners, as well. Although outsourcing is a significant source of employment for the upper-middle class in developing countries, hundreds of millions of other foreign workers have seen little to no positive impact from the trend. Thus the long-term impact of offshoring on developing nations is difficult to predict. Another practice, *microfinancing,* is having a more positive impact on the lower classes in developing nations: see the Social Policy section that follows (Goering 2008b; Waldman 2004a, 2004b, 2004c).

TABLE **51-1** OCCUPATIONS MOST VULNERABLE TO OFFSHORING

Rank	Occupation
1	Computer programming
2	Data entry
3	Electrical and electronics drafting
4	Mechanical drafting
5	Computer and information science, research
6	Actuarial science
7	Mathematics
8	Statistics
9	Mathematical science (all other)
10	Film and video editing

Sources: Bureau of Labor Statistics data cited in Hira 2008; Moncarz et al. 2008.

 use your **sociological imagination**

Do you know anyone whose job has been transferred to a foreign country? If so, was the person able to find a comparable job in the same town, or did he or she have to relocate? How long was the person unemployed?

In India, a very small loan has made a big change in a young mother's life. Not many years ago Siyawati was dependent on what little income her husband could earn as a day laborer. Then a $212 microloan allowed her to buy a machine for making candles. Today, Siyawati's cottage venture has expanded into a factory with eight employees, and her monthly income has climbed from $42 to $425. Her increased earnings have allowed her to enroll her children in a good school—the dream of struggling parents in developing countries around the world (Glazer 2010:1).

Looking at the Issue

In some respects it offers a small solution to a big problem. **Microfinancing** is lending small sums of money to the poor so they can work their way out of poverty. Borrowers use the money to start small businesses in the informal economy—to buy yarn to weave into cloth, cows to produce milk, or tools, equipment, and bamboo to make stools. The products they produce are then sold in the local shops. Typically, microloans are less than $600, often as little as $20. The recipients are people who ordinarily would not be able to qualify for banking services.

Sometimes referred to as "banking the unbanked," microfinancing was the brainchild of Bangladeshi economist Muhammad Yunus (pronounced Iunus). In 1976, in the midst of a devastating famine in Bangladesh, Yunus founded the Grameen (meaning "Village") Bank, which he headed until 2011. The idea came to him when he reached into his pocket to lend money to a group of villagers who had asked him for help. Working through local halls or meeting places, the Grameen Bank has now extended credit to nearly 7 million people. The idea has spread, and has even been underwritten by over a thousand for-profit banks and multinational organizations. According to the most recent estimates, microfinancing is now reaching 190 million families in 100 countries (Ledgerwood 2013; Microfinance Information Exchange 2014; Yunus 2010).

Although microfinancing has benefited many families, critics charge that some lenders are taking advantage of the poor. Especially in India, the extension of microloans to financially questionable projects with little chance for success has left some borrowers in debt. At the other extreme, some lenders have reaped extraordinary profits, both for themselves and for the investment banks they have created. Proponents of microfinancing acknowledge that improvements can be made.

The microfinance movement is not a failure, however. It has evolved to offer borrowers scholarships, low-cost health care, and even solar power. Research supports the conclusion that the poorest of the poor can and do become entrepreneurs when they can obtain credit at acceptable interest rates (Dickson 2013; Ledgerwood 2013).

In 2006 Muhammad Yunus, founder of the Grameen Bank, was awarded the Nobel Peace Prize for his work in championing the concept of microfinancing. The small loans his bank makes to the poor, many of them women, have improved the quality of life of countless families.

Applying Sociology

Researchers who draw on the interactionist approach have shown that there is more to microfinancing than money. A study done by microfinance expert Daryl Collins and his colleagues (2009), described in the opening excerpt to Chapter 9, shows how even with modest assistance, poor people can significantly improve their circumstances through mutual support. Collins asked villagers and slum dwellers in Bangladesh, India, and South Africa to keep diaries of how they spent every penny they earned. He and his team found that most of the poor households they studied did not live hand to

—Continued

mouth, spending everything they earned as soon as they got it. Instead, they used financial tools that were linked to their extended families and informal social networks. They saved money, squeezed it out of creditors whenever possible, ran sophisticated savings clubs, and took advantage of microfinancing whenever it was available. Their tactics suggested new methods of fighting poverty and encouraged the development of broader microfinance programs.

Because an estimated 90 percent of the recipients of microcredit are women, feminist theorists are especially interested in the growth of microfinancing. Women's economic status has been found to be critical to the well-being of their children, and the key to a healthy household environment. In developing countries, where women often are not treated as well as men, being entrusted with credit is particularly empowering to them. Research indicates that women recipients are more likely than men to participate in networks and collective action groups, perhaps because they must overcome resistance to women as economic decision makers (Dickson 2013).

Drawing on world systems analysis, sociologist Marina Karides (2010) contrasts microfinancing with the Western model of economic development, in which multinational corporations based in core countries take advantage of the low wages and natural resources in periphery and semi-periphery countries. The low-wage workers employed by the multinationals rarely escape subsistence living, while the vast majority of people in core nations enjoy a comparatively high standard of living. Microfinanciers hope that in contrast, the cottage industries they help to establish will contribute to the local economies in developing countries, and ultimately to the well-being of those societies, rather than merely serve the economic interests of core nations.

Some critics complain that the creation of small home-based industries reduces the demand for formal employment opportunities. Supporters of microenterprise counter that much time has passed without a significant change in job growth. Microfinancing, they claim, is the best way to create sustainable market opportunities for the poor in developing nations, even if those opportunities are much less attractive than those available in core nations.

Initiating Policy

Even supporters of microfinancing acknowledge the need to reduce overlending and monitor the success of small loans in helping borrowers to escape poverty. Some indicators suggest that many borrowers do not achieve self-sufficiency. If that

At a workshop in Mumbai, India, Sharda Bhandare cuts the pieces for a pair of gloves from a towel. Microloans make such small businesses possible, and help them to become self-sustaining.

is true, lenders should increase their oversight and attempt to identify best practices—that is, those types of assistance that are most effective in helping the poor. Less than a decade ago, microfinancing was hailed as the single best solution to world poverty. With modifications, it should continue to reduce hardship and suffering among the poor (Bajaj 2011a, 2011b; Glazer 2010).

Lenders also need to work with political leaders, and vice versa, to ensure that they do not regard one another as competitors for political support from the poor. Some government leaders have gone so far as to charge lenders with profiteering at the expense of the poor, and to take extraordinary measures for the protection of borrowers. In 2010, officials of one state in India required all loans to be approved by the government, and their eventual repayment to be made in person before a public official. To the degree that profiteering is truly a problem, some type of remedy, whether through legislation or self-monitoring, may need to be introduced. Given the cultural, political, and legal differences among nations where microfinanciers operate, the development of this type of government policy will be a major undertaking.

TAKING SOCIOLOGY WITH YOU

1. Do you think microfinancing might be useful in the United States? If so, how and under what conditions?

2. Using sociological concepts, explain why some politicians might resent microfinancing programs.

3. What obstacles might prevent poor people, either in the United States or elsewhere, from improving their lives through microfinancing? Might the government have a role to play in removing those obstacles?

Summary

Any change in the economy has both social and political implications.

1. In the United States, workers are coping with **deindustrialization** and **offshoring** and employers are training an increasingly diverse workforce.

2. **Affirmative action** is intended to remedy the effects of discrimination against minority groups and women. The concept is controversial, however, because some people see it as reverse discrimination against majority groups.

3. In developing countries, **microfinancing** is improving the lives of millions of poor people.

Thinking Critically

1. What are the implications of trends such as deindustrialization and offshoring on social institutions such as the family, education, and government in the United States?

2. What evidence of deindustrialization or downsizing do you see, specifically, in your own community? What broad economic shifts brought about those changes?

Key Terms

Affirmative action

Color-blind racism

Deindustrialization

Downsizing

Microfinancing

Offshoring

Precarious work

Mastering This Chapter

taking sociology with you

1 Pick a nongovernmental organization with worldwide recognition, such as the Red Cross, Doctors Without Borders, or Amnesty International. Go online and find out how the organization works on behalf of peace. What specifically has this NGO done to prevent or stop war?

2 If you aren't already familiar with it, visit your local community college and stop by the administration office. Ask what programs the college has to offer in workforce development.

What skills is the college currently developing for tomorrow's workforce? What will those skills mean, not just for students, but for the community as a whole?

3 If your college has a club for young Republicans or Democrats, attend one of their meetings. What issues are members interested in, and why? How are they planning to put their beliefs into action? Are they concerned about voter apathy among young people?

Affirmative action Positive efforts to recruit minority group members or women for jobs, promotions, and educational opportunities.

Authority Institutionalized power that is recognized by the people over whom it is exercised.

Capitalism An economic system in which the means of production are held largely in private hands and the main incentive for economic activity is the accumulation of profits.

Charismatic authority Power made legitimate by a leader's exceptional personal or emotional appeal to his or her followers.

Color-blind racism The use of the principle of race neutrality to defend a racially unequal status quo.

Communism As an ideal type, an economic system under which all property is communally owned and no social distinctions are made on the basis of people's ability to produce.

Deindustrialization The systematic, widespread withdrawal of investment in basic aspects of productivity, such as factories and plants.

Democracy In a literal sense, government by the people.

Dictatorship A government in which one person has nearly total power to make and enforce laws.

Downsizing Reductions taken in a company's workforce as part of deindustrialization.

Economic system The social institution through which goods and services are produced, distributed, and consumed.

Elite model A view of society as being ruled by a small group of individuals who share a common set of political and economic interests.

Force The actual or threatened use of coercion to impose one's will on others.

Industrial society A society that depends on mechanization to produce its goods and services.

Influence The exercise of power through a process of persuasion.

Informal economy Transfers of money, goods, or services that are not reported to the government.

Laissez-faire A form of capitalism under which people compete freely, with minimal government intervention in the economy.

Microfinancing Lending small sums of money to the poor so they can work their way out of poverty.

Monarchy A form of government headed by a single member of a royal family, usually a king, queen, or some other hereditary ruler.

Monopoly Control of a market by a single business firm.

Offshoring The transfer of work to foreign contractors.

Oligarchy A form of government in which a few individuals rule.

Peace The absence of war, or more broadly, a proactive effort to develop cooperative relations among nations.

Pluralist model A view of society in which many competing groups within the community have access to government, so that no single group is dominant.

Political system The social institution that is founded on a recognized set of procedures for implementing and achieving society's goals.

Politics In Harold Lasswell's words, "who gets what, when, and how."

Power The ability to exercise one's will over others.

Power elite A small group of military, industrial, and government leaders who control the fate of the United States.

Precarious work Employment that is poorly paid, and from the worker's perspective, insecure and unprotected.

Rational-legal authority Power made legitimate by law.

Representative democracy A form of government in which certain individuals are selected to speak for the people.

Socialism An economic system under which the means of production and distribution are collectively owned.

Sovereignty movement The effort by the indigenous people of Hawai'i to win self-government, as well as the restoration of—or compensation for—their ancestral lands.

Terrorism The use or threat of violence against random or symbolic targets in pursuit of political aims.

Totalitarianism Virtually complete government control and surveillance over all aspects of a society's social and political life.

Traditional authority Legitimate power conferred by custom and accepted practice.

War Conflict between organizations that possess trained combat forces equipped with deadly weapons.

Read each question carefully and then select the best answer.

1. Which two basic types of economic system distinguish contemporary industrial societies?
   a. capitalism and communism
   b. capitalism and socialism
   c. socialism and communism
   d. capitalism and dictatorship

2. According to the discussion of capitalism in the text, which of the following statements is true?
   a. The means of production are held largely in private hands.
   b. The main incentive for economic activity is the accumulation of profits.
   c. The degree to which the government regulates private ownership and economic activity will vary.
   d. all of the above

3. G. William Domhoff's model is an example of a(n)
   a. elite theory of power.
   b. pluralist theory of power.

   c. functionalist theory of power.
   d. interactionist theory of power.

4. In terms of voter turnout, the United States typically ranks
   a. highest among all countries.
   b. highest among industrialized nations.
   c. lowest among industrialized nations.
   d. lowest among all countries.

5. What are the three basic sources of power within any political system?
   a. force, influence, and authority
   b. force, influence, and democracy
   c. force, legitimacy, and charisma
   d. influence, charisma, and bureaucracy

6. Which of the following is *not* part of the classification system of authority developed by Max Weber?
   a. traditional authority
   b. pluralist authority
   c. rational-legal authority
   d. charismatic authority

7. According to C. Wright Mills, power rests in the hands of the
   a. people.
   b. representative democracy.
   c. aristocracy.
   d. power elite.

8. The systematic, widespread withdrawal of investment in basic aspects of productivity such as factories and plants is called
   a. deindustrialization.
   b. downsizing.
   c. postindustrialization.
   d. gentrification.

9. Sociologists and labor specialists foresee a workforce increasingly composed of
   a. women.
   b. racial minorities.
   c. ethnic minorities.
   d. all of the above

10. Currently, _____ _____ refers to positive efforts to recruit minority group members or women for jobs, promotions, and educational opportunities.
    a. equal rights
    b. affirmative action
    c. work programs
    d. equal action

11. The principle of _____, as expounded and endorsed by the British economist Adam Smith, was the prevailing form of capitalism immediately following the Industrial Revolution.

12. Under _____, the means of production and distribution in a society are collectively rather than privately owned, and the basic objective of the economic system is to meet people's needs rather than to maximize profits.

13. _____ is an economic system under which all property is communally owned and no social distinctions are made based on people's ability to produce.

14. _____ theorists point out that while pure monopolies are not a basic element of the economy of the United States, competition is much more restricted than one might expect in what is called a free enterprise system.

15. Some capitalist nations, such as the United States, outlaw _____ through antitrust legislation.

16. The elite model of political power implies that the United States has a(n) _____ as its form of government.

17. Sexism has been the most serious barrier to women interested in holding public office. To remedy this situation, many countries have adopted _____ for female representatives.

18. _____ is the exercise of power through a process of persuasion.

19. The United States is commonly classified as a(n) _____ _____, because the elected members of Congress and state legislatures make our laws.

20. Advocates of the _____ model suggest that competing groups within the community have access to government, so that no single group is dominant.

The answers are printed upside down.

Answers

1 (b); 2 (d); 3 (a); 4 (c); 5 (a); 6 (b); 7 (d); 8 (a); 9 (d); 10 (b); 11 laissez-faire; 12 socialism; 13 Communism; 14 Conflict; 15 monopolies; 16 oligarchy; 17 quotas; 18 Influence; 19 representative democracy; 20 pluralist

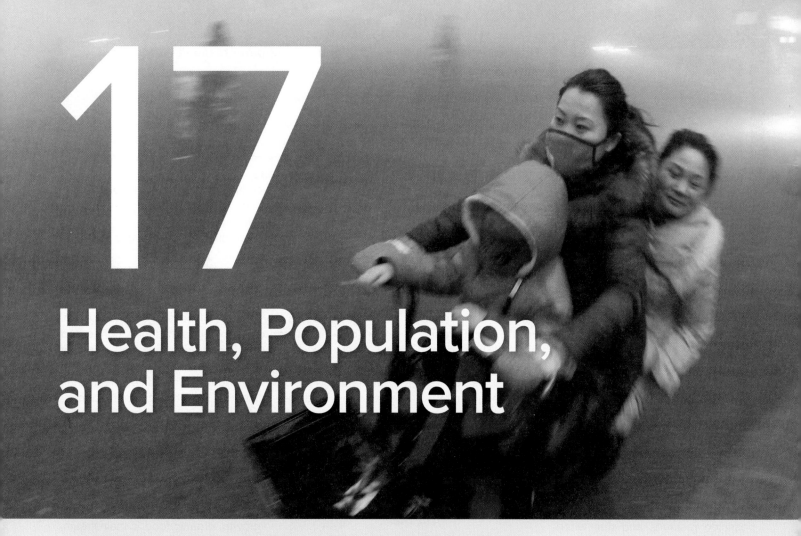

17

Health, Population, and Environment

In Beijing, one of the 15 largest cities in the world, commuters travel through a street shrouded in dense smog. So dangerous is the pollution to residents that the government closes schools and factories when smog descends on the city.

Do you remember a time when you or your parents didn't worry about the food you ate and the water you drank?

Andrew Szasz does. It was a time before the environmental movement.

❝ Not that long ago, hardly a generation back, people did not worry about the food they ate. They did not worry about the water they drank or the air they breathed. It never occurred to them that eating, drinking water, satisfying basic, mundane bodily needs, might be dangerous things to do. Parents thought it was good for their kids to go outside, get some sun.

That is all changed now. People see danger everywhere. Food, water, air, sun. We cannot do without them. Sadly, we now also fear them. We suspect that the water that flows from the tap is contaminated with chemicals that can make us ill. We have learned that conventionally grown fruits and vegetables have pesticide residues and that when we eat meat from conventionally raised animals, we are probably getting a dose of antibiotics and hormones, too. Contaminants can be colorless, tasteless, and odorless, invisible to the senses, and that fact increases the feeling of vulnerability.

According to the Environmental Protection Agency (EPA), indoor air is more toxic than outdoor air. That is because many household cleaning products and many contemporary home furnishings—carpets, drapes, the fabrics that cover sofas and easy chairs, furniture made of particle board—outgas toxic volatile organic chemicals. OK, we will go outside . . . only to inhale diesel exhaust, particulates suspended in the air, molecules of toxic chemicals wafting from factory smokestacks.

Even sunshine is now considered by many a hazard. Expose yourself to too much sun and your skin will age

People see danger everywhere. Food, water, air, sun. We cannot do without them. Sadly, we now also fear them.

prematurely. You risk getting skin cancer. The ozone layer has thinned, making exposure to sunlight even more dangerous. The incidence of melanoma, the deadliest form of skin cancer, is on the rise.

The response has been swift. Everywhere one looks, Americans are buying consumer products that promise to reduce their exposure to harmful substances.

In 1975, Americans were drinking, on average, one gallon of bottled water per person per year. By 2005, the latest year for which we have data, consumption had grown to twenty-six gallons per person per year, over seven and a half billion gallons of bottled water. Bottled water used to account for only a tiny fraction of beverage consumption, inconsequential when compared to soft drinks, coffee and tea, beer, milk, and juice. Today, after enjoying years of "enviable, unending growth," bottled water has become the "superstar [of] the beverage industry." In addition, nearly half of all households use some kind of water filter in the home.

A couple of decades back, organic foods had only a tiny share of the overall food market. Organically grown foods were sold, typically, in small "health food" stores. They were hard to find, even if you wanted them. Few people did. But now, after years of 20 percent annual growth, organic food is mainstream. There are not only organic fruits and vegetables but organic breads and cereals, organic meat, fish, and dairy, organic beer, organic snack food. One can find organic foods in large, attractive, upscale chain stores, such as Whole Foods, and also increasingly in mainstream supermarkets. Safeway and Wal-Mart both sell organic foods.

Those who can afford it buy "organic" or "natural" personal hygiene products, shampoo, soap, makeup; "nontoxic" home cleaning products; clothing made of natural fibers; furniture made of real wood; and rugs made of natural fiber. There is a new ritual in America (at least in middle-class America): applying 30 SPF sunscreen to our children's exposed skin every morning before they go to school, to summer camp, or to the beach. ❞

(A. Szasz 2007:1–2)

In this excerpt from *Shopping Our Way to Safety: How We Changed from Protecting the Environment to Protecting Ourselves*, sociologist Andrew Szasz links the environmental consciousness that arose from the environmental movement to a new category of products and services. Today, he notes, many people fear the everyday environmental hazards present in their immediate environment, from the tap water to the air.

Rather than work for the health of the environment as a whole, some try to quarantine themselves from these perceived threats by shopping for supposedly pure, uncontaminated food, clothing, furniture, and cleaning products.

There is little question that some people do try to shop their way to safety. However, as Szasz notes, unless their largely individual responses go beyond self-protection, they won't improve society's health. What are the many people who cannot afford to drink bottled water or move to a healthier environment supposed to do? Won't the environment eventually reach a state that will threaten everyone, no matter how much organic food they consume?

What defines a healthy environment? How is the environment connected to our health as a society? How do health and health care vary from one social class to another and from one nation to another? In these modules, we present a sociological overview of health, illness, health care, and medicine as a social institution. We begin by examining how functionalists, conflict theorists, interactionists, and labeling theorists look at health-related issues. Then we study the distribution of diseases in a society by social class, race and ethnicity, gender, and age.

We'll look too at the evolution of the U.S. health care system. Sociologists are interested in the roles people play in the health care system and the organizations that deal with issues of health and sickness. Therefore, we will analyze the interactions among physicians, nurses, and patients; alternatives to traditional health care; the role of government in providing health care services to the needy; and the issues people with mental illness face.

Later in the chapter, we examine the way in which population trends affect both health and the environment. Then we turn to the environmental problems facing the world in the 21st century, and we draw on the functionalist and conflict perspectives to better understand environmental issues. We'll see that it is important not to oversimplify the relationship between health and the environment. Finally, in the Social Policy section we explore the recently renewed interest in environmentalism.

MODULE 52 — Sociological Perspectives on Health and Illness

How can we define health? Imagine a continuum with health on one end and death on the other. In the preamble to its 1946 constitution, the World Health Organization defined **health** as a "state of complete physical, mental, and social well-being, and not merely the absence of disease and infirmity" (Leavell and Clark 1965:14). In this definition, the "healthy" end of the continuum represents an ideal rather than a precise condition.

Along the continuum, individuals define themselves as healthy or sick on the basis of criteria established by themselves and relatives, friends, co-workers, and medical practitioners. Health and illness, in other words, are socially constructed. They are rooted in culture and are defined by claims makers—people who describe themselves as healthy or ill—as well as by a broad range of interested parties, including health care providers, pharmaceutical firms, and even food providers (Conrad and Barker 2010).

Because health is socially constructed, we can consider how it varies in different situations or cultures. Why is it that you may consider yourself sick or well when others do not agree? Who controls definitions of health and illness in our society, and for what ends? What are the consequences of viewing yourself (or of being viewed) as ill or disabled? By drawing on four sociological perspectives—functionalism, conflict theory, interactionism, and labeling theory—we can gain greater insight into the social context that shapes definitions of health and the treatment of illness.

Functionalist Perspective

Illness entails breaks in our social interactions, both at work and at home. From a functionalist perspective, being sick must therefore be controlled, so that not too many people are released from their societal responsibilities at any one time. Functionalists contend that an overly broad definition of illness would disrupt the workings of a society.

Health practices vary from one country to another. Unlike people in most other societies, the Japanese often wear surgical masks in public, to protect themselves from disease or pollution. The practice began in 1919, when the worldwide Spanish flu epidemic became a public health menace. Today mask-wearing persists even when there is no public health threat.

Sickness requires that one take on a social role, if only temporarily. The **sick role** refers to societal expectations about the attitudes and behavior of a person viewed as being ill. Sociologist Talcott Parsons (1951, 1975), well known for his contributions to functionalist theory, outlined the behavior required of people who are considered sick. They are exempted from their normal, day-to-day responsibilities and generally do not suffer blame for their condition. Yet they are obligated to try to get well, which includes seeking competent professional care. This obligation arises from the common view that illness is dysfunctional, because it can undermine social stability. Attempting to get well is particularly important in the world's developing countries. Modern automated industrial societies can absorb a greater degree of illness or disability than horticultural or agrarian societies, in which the availability of workers is far more critical (Conrad and Leiter 2013).

According to Parsons's theory, physicians function as *gatekeepers* for the sick role. They verify a patient's condition either as "illness" or as "recovered." The ill person becomes dependent on the physician, because the latter can control valued rewards (not only treatment of illness, but also excused absences from work and school). Parsons suggests that the physician–patient relationship is somewhat like that between parent and child. Like a parent, the physician helps the patient to enter society as a full and functioning adult (Weitz 2009).

The concept of the sick role is not without criticism. First, patients' judgments regarding their own state of health may be related to their gender, age, social class, and ethnic group. For example, younger people may fail to detect warning signs of a dangerous illness, while elderly people may focus too much on the slightest physical malady. Second, the sick role may be more applicable to people who are experiencing short-term illnesses than to those with recurring, long-term illnesses. Finally, even simple factors, such as whether a person is employed, seem to affect one's willingness to assume the sick role—as does the impact of socialization into a particular occupation or activity. For example, beginning in childhood, athletes learn to define certain ailments as "sports injuries" and therefore do not regard themselves as "sick." Nonetheless, sociologists continue to rely on Parsons's model for functionalist analysis of the relationship between illness and societal expectations of the sick (Curry 1993).

 use your **sociological imagination**

Describe some situations you have witnessed that illustrate different definitions of the "sick role."

Conflict Perspective

Conflict theorists observe that the medical profession has assumed a preeminence that extends well beyond whether to excuse a student from school or an employee from work. Sociologist Eliot Freidson (1970:5) has likened the position of medicine today to that of state religions yesterday—it has an officially approved monopoly of the right to define health and illness and to treat illness. Conflict theorists use the term *medicalization of society* to refer to the growing role of medicine as a major institution of social control (Conrad 2009; McKinlay and McKinlay 1977; Zola 1972, 1983).

The Medicalization of Society

Social control involves techniques and strategies for regulating behavior in order to enforce the distinctive norms and values of a culture. Typically, we think of informal social control as occurring within families and peer groups, and formal social control as being carried out by authorized agents such as police officers, judges, school administrators, and employers. Viewed

from a conflict perspective, however, medicine is not simply a "healing profession"; it is a regulating mechanism.

How does medicine manifest its social control? First, medicine has greatly expanded its domain of expertise in recent decades. Physicians now examine a wide range of issues, among them sexuality, old age, anxiety, obesity, child development, alcoholism, and drug addiction. We tolerate this expansion of the boundaries of medicine because we hope that these experts can bring new "miracle cures" to complex human problems, as they have to the control of certain infectious diseases.

In defining these new conditions, physicians determine and control the course of treatment, and even affect patients' views of themselves. Once a problem is viewed using this **medical model**, it becomes more difficult for common people to join the discussion and exert influence on decision making. It also becomes more difficult to view these issues as being shaped by social, cultural, or psychological factors, rather than simply by physical or medical factors (Caplan 1989; Conrad 2009).

Second, medicine serves as an agent of social control by retaining absolute jurisdiction over many health care procedures. It has even attempted to guard its jurisdiction by placing health care professionals such as chiropractors and nurse-midwives outside the realm of acceptable medicine. Despite the fact that midwives first brought professionalism to child delivery, they have been portrayed as having invaded the "legitimate" field of obstetrics, in both the United States and Mexico. Nurse-midwives have sought licensing as a way to achieve professional respectability, but physicians continue to exert power to ensure that midwifery remains a subordinate occupation (Scharnberg 2007).

Inequities in Health Care

The medicalization of society is but one concern of conflict theorists as they assess the workings of health care institutions. As

The growing concern about obesity among the young has focused attention on their eating habits and their need for exercise. Concern about obesity is a sign of the medicalization of society.

we have seen throughout this textbook, in analyzing any issue, conflict theorists seek to determine who benefits, who suffers, and who dominates at the expense of others. Viewed from a conflict perspective, glaring inequities exist in health care delivery in the United States. For example, poor areas tend to be underserved because medical services concentrate where people are wealthy.

Similarly, from a global perspective, obvious inequities exist in health care delivery. Today, the United States has about 24 physicians per 10,000 people, while African nations have fewer than 1 per 10,000. This situation is only worsened by the **brain drain**—the immigration to the United States and other industrialized nations of skilled workers, professionals, and technicians who are desperately needed in their home countries. As part of this brain drain, physicians, nurses, and other health care professionals have come to the United States from developing countries such as India, Pakistan, and various African states. Conflict theorists view their emigration out of the Third World as yet another way in which the world's core industrialized nations enhance their quality of life at the expense of developing countries. One way the developing countries suffer is in lower life expectancy. In Africa and much of Latin America and Asia, life expectancy is far lower than in industrialized nations (World Bank 2013).

Conflict theorists emphasize that inequities in health care have clear life-and-death consequences. From a conflict perspective, the dramatic differences in *infant mortality rates* around the world (Figure 52-1) reflect, at least in part, unequal distribution of health care resources based on the wealth or poverty of various nations. The **infant mortality rate** is the number of deaths of infants under 1 year old per 1,000 live births in a given year. This measure is an important indicator of a society's level of health care; it reflects prenatal nutrition, delivery procedures, and infant screening measures. Still, despite the wealth of the United States, at least 48 nations have *lower* infant mortality rates. Conflict theorists point out that unlike the United States, these countries offer some form of government-supported health care for all citizens, which typically leads to greater availability and use of prenatal care.

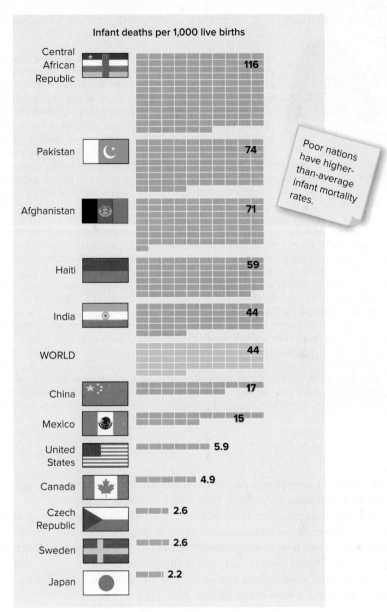

FIGURE 52-1 Infant Mortality Rates in Selected Countries

Infant deaths per 1,000 live births

Country	Rate
Central African Republic	116
Pakistan	74
Afghanistan	71
Haiti	59
India	44
WORLD	44
China	17
Mexico	15
United States	5.9
Canada	4.9
Czech Republic	2.6
Sweden	2.6
Japan	2.2

Poor nations have higher-than-average infant mortality rates.

Source: Haub and Kaneda 2013.

use your **sociological imagination**

From a sociological point of view, what might be the greatest challenge to reducing inequities in health care?

Interactionist Perspective

From an interactionist point of view, patients are not passive; often, they actively seek the services of a health care practitioner. In examining health, illness, and medicine as a social institution, then, interactionists engage in micro-level study of the roles played by health care professionals and patients. Interactionists are particularly interested in how physicians learn to play their occupational role. For example, in one of his earliest works, sociologist Howard Becker took the perspective that medical education socialized students into the role of doctor as much as it transferred medical knowledge to them (H. Becker et al. 1961).

Following this approach, Brenda Beagan (2001) found that the technical language students learn in medical school becomes the basis for the script they follow as novice physicians. The familiar white coat is their costume—one that helps them to appear confident and professional at the same time that it identifies them as doctors to patients and other staff members. Beagan found that many medical students struggle to project the appearance of competence that they think their role demands. More recently, she has considered how medical personnel interact with patients

Taking Sociology to Work

Lola Adedokun, *Independent Consultant, Health Care Research*

When Lola Adedokun entered Dartmouth College, she was thinking of concentrating in biology and premedical studies. But after taking a sociology course on racial disparities, she realized that sociology was the only subject that offered courses on topics she was passionate about. Eventually, she settled on sociology, along with a special social science major in health policy that she created herself.

Today, Adedokun is a consultant on a number of health-related research projects. One, funded by the National Institutes of Health (NIH), is a follow-up study of an international training program for researchers and clinicians working on HIV/AIDS. Another, funded by the Centers for Disease Control and Prevention (CDC), focuses on the sexual behaviors of heterosexuals at high risk of contracting HIV. "Understanding human behavior and human sexual behavior as well as the cultural and social issues that drive this behavior is essential," she explains. Adedokun is also a graduate

research assistant at the National Center for Children in Poverty, where she conducts and analyzes interviews with families, children, and mental health professionals.

Each week is different for this self-employed researcher. Often she works from home, conducting interviews over the phone and analyzing data on her own computer. At other times she works at her clients' offices, using their proprietary software. Adedokun also trains teams of interviewers and serves as a liaison between agencies. "I have a lot of face-to-face contact interviewing clients and researching people from high-risk communities," she says. "The nature of the work is much like the field of sociology—it is vast and broad, and I'm thinking about it all the time. In that way, my work does not feel like work."

Travel has been one of the high points in Adedokun's career. "The most amazing opportunity I have had in the last few years was traveling to Asia, Africa, and Latin America to conduct interviews with some of the world's leading HIV/AIDS researchers," she says. "I was able to truly get a sense of the challenges and the achievements that these researchers have encountered."

Asked what advice she would give to current students of sociology, Adedokun replies, "One piece of advice is that you would be doing yourself a disservice to distance yourself from this important material. It is the fundamentals of sociology that will be most relevant to any area that you choose to pursue in your future," she continues, "so ask questions, debate, discuss, and argue, as the knowledge that you will pull from that will prove to be the greatest academic lessons you may ever learn."

LET'S DISCUSS

1. What social issue or problem do you feel passionate about, and how can sociology help to address it?

2. Adedokun is a self-starter who created her own major and is now pursuing a career on her own. Have you ever considered creating your own career path, rather than relying on large institutions to map your future? What might be the benefits of such an approach? The drawbacks?

---

undergoing sex-change procedures and hormonal therapy to conform their bodies to their deeply held sexual identities. Because most health care providers receive little or no prior formal education in this complex undertaking, they learn from experienced colleagues. More than in most clinical situations, they may also be "educated" by the patients themselves (Beagan et al. 2013).

Sometimes patients play an active role in health care by *failing* to follow a physician's advice. For example, some patients stop taking medications long before they should. Some take an incorrect dosage on purpose, and others never even fill their prescriptions. Such noncompliance results in part from the prevalence of self-medication in our society; many people are accustomed to self-diagnosis and self-treatment. On the other hand, patients' active involvement in their health care can sometimes have very *positive* consequences. Some patients read books about preventive health care techniques, attempt to maintain a healthful and nutritious diet, carefully monitor any side effects of medication, and adjust the dosage based on perceived side effects.

Labeling Perspective

Labeling theory helps us to understand why certain people are *viewed* as deviants, "bad kids," or criminals, whereas others whose behavior is similar are not. Labeling theorists also suggest that the designation "healthy" or "ill" generally involves social definition by others. Just as police officers, judges, and other regulators of social control have the power to define certain people as criminals, health care professionals (especially physicians) have the power to define certain people as sick. Moreover, like labels that suggest nonconformity or criminality, labels that are associated with illness commonly reshape how others treat us and how we see ourselves. Our society attaches serious consequences to labels that suggest less-than-perfect physical or mental health (H. Becker 1963; C. Clark 1983; H. Schwartz 1994).

A historical example illustrates perhaps the ultimate extreme in labeling social behavior as a sickness. As enslavement of Africans in the United States came under increasing attack in the 19th century, medical authorities provided new rationalizations for the oppressive practice. Noted

TABLE 52-1 SOCIOLOGICAL PERSPECTIVES ON HEALTH AND ILLNESS

Tracking Sociological Perspectives

	Functionalist	Conflict	Interactionist	Labeling
Major emphasis	Control of the number of people who are considered sick	Overmedicalization Gross inequities in health care	Doctor–patient relationship Interaction of medical staff	Definition of illness and health
Controlling factors	Physician as gatekeeper	Medical profession Social inequities	Medical profession	Medical profession
Proponents	Talcott Parsons	Thomas Szasz Irving Zola	Howard Becker	Thomas Szasz

physicians published articles stating that the skin color of Africans deviated from "healthy" white skin coloring because Africans suffered from congenital leprosy. Moreover, the continuing efforts of enslaved Africans to escape from their White masters were classified as an example of the "disease" of drapetomania (or "crazy runaways"). The prestigious *New Orleans Medical and Surgical Journal* suggested that the remedy for this "disease" was to treat slaves kindly, as one might treat children. Apparently, these medical authorities would not entertain the view that it was healthy and sane to flee slavery or join in a slave revolt (T. Szasz 2010).

Similarly, labeling theorists suggest that other behaviors viewed today as mental illnesses may not really be illnesses. Instead, the individual's problems arise from living in society, not from physical maladies. From this perspective, a variety of life experiences treated as illnesses today may not be illnesses at all. Premenstrual syndrome, post-traumatic stress disorders, and hyperactivity are examples of medically recognized disorders that labeling theorists would consider questionable.

Probably the most noteworthy medical example of labeling is the case of homosexuality. For years, psychiatrists classified being gay or lesbian not as a lifestyle but as a mental disorder subject to treatment. This official sanction became an early target of the growing gay and lesbian rights movement in the United States. In 1974, members of the American Psychiatric Association voted to drop homosexuality from the standard manual on mental disorders (Conrad 2009).

Table 52-1 summarizes four major sociological perspectives on health and illness. Although they may seem quite different, two common themes unite them. First, any person's health or illness is more than an organic condition, since it is subject to the interpretation of others. The impact of culture, family and friends, and the medical profession means that health and illness are not purely biological occurrences, but sociological occurrences as well. Second, since members of a society (especially industrial societies) share the same health care delivery system, health is a group and societal concern. Although health may be defined as the complete well-being of an individual, it is also the result of one's social environment, as Module 53 will show (Cockerham 2012).

MODULE **52** | **Recap and Review**

Summary

The concept of **health** is shaped by social definitions of behavior.

1. According to Talcott Parsons's functionalist perspective, physicians function as "gatekeepers" for the **sick role,** either verifying a person's condition as "ill" or designating the person as "recovered."

2. Conflict theorists use the term *medicalization of society* to refer to medicine's growing role as a major institution of social control.

3. Labeling theorists suggest that the designation of a person as "healthy" or "ill" generally involves social definitions by others. These definitions affect how others see us and how we view ourselves.

Thinking Critically

1. Define the term "health" from the functionalist, conflict, interactionist, and labeling perspectives.

2. Describe an occasion on which people you know disagreed about a socially applied medical label. What was the label, and why did people disagree?

Key Terms

Brain drain

Health

Infant mortality rate

Labeling theory

Medical model

Sick role

Social Epidemiology and Health

Social epidemiology is the study of the distribution of disease, impairment, and general health status across a population. Initially, epidemiologists concentrated on the scientific study of epidemics, focusing on how they started and spread. Contemporary social epidemiology is much broader in scope, concerned not only with epidemics but also with nonepidemic diseases, injuries, drug addiction and alcoholism, suicide, and mental illness. Epidemiologists have taken on the new role of tracking bioterrorism. In 2001, they mobilized to trace the anthrax outbreak and prepare for any terrorist use of smallpox or other lethal microbes. Epidemiologists draw on the work of a wide variety of scientists and researchers, among them physicians, sociologists, public health officials, biologists, veterinarians, demographers, anthropologists, psychologists, and meteorologists.

Epidemiologists have found that worldwide, an estimated 35 million people were infected with HIV at the end of 2013. Women account for a growing proportion of new cases of HIV/AIDS, especially among racial and ethnic minorities. Although the spread of AIDS is stabilizing, with fewer new cases reported, the disease is not evenly distributed. Those areas that are least equipped to deal with it—the developing nations of sub-Saharan Africa—face the greatest challenge (Figure 53-1).

When disease data are presented as rates, or as the number of reports per 100,000 people, they are called **morbidity rates.** (The term **mortality rate** refers to the rate of *death* in a given population.) Sociologists find morbidity rates useful because they reveal that a specific disease occurs more frequently in one segment of a population than another. As we shall see, social class, race, ethnicity, gender, and age can all affect a population's morbidity rates.

FIGURE 53-1 AIDS by the Numbers Worldwide

	New infections (children)	New HIV infections (millions)	AIDS related deaths (millions)	People accessing treatment (millions)
2001	550 000	3.4		
2002	560 000	3.3		
2003	560 000	3.1		
2004	550 000	3.0	2.3	
2005	540 000	2.9	2.3	1.3
2006	520 000	2.8	2.3	2.0
2007	480 000	2.7	2.2	2.9
2008	450 000	2.6	2.1	4.1
2009	400 000	2.6	2.0	5.3
2010	360 000	2.5	1.9	6.6
2011	310 000	2.5	1.8	8.1
2012	260 000	2.3	1.6	9.7

Source: UNAIDS 2013.

Social Class

Social class is clearly associated with differences in morbidity and mortality rates. Studies in the United States and other countries have consistently shown that people in the lower classes have higher rates of mortality and disability than others.

Why is class linked to health? Crowded living conditions, substandard housing, poor diet, and stress all contribute to the ill health of many low-income people in the United States. In certain instances, poor education may lead to a lack of awareness of measures necessary to maintain good health. Financial strains are certainly a major factor in the health problems of less affluent people.

What is particularly troubling about social class differences is that they appear to be cumulative. Little or no health care in childhood or young adulthood is likely to mean more illness later in life. The longer that low income presents a barrier to adequate health care, the more chronic and difficult to treat illness becomes (Pampel et al. 2010; Phelan et al. 2010).

Another reason for the link between social class and health is that the poor—many of whom belong to racial and ethnic minorities—are less able than others to afford quality medical care. The affluent are more likely than others to have health insurance, either because they can afford it or because they have jobs that provide it. Pharmacists report that people purchase only those medications they "need the most," or buy in small quantities, such as four pills at a time. Even for children, many of whom are eligible for government-subsidized health insurance, coverage varies widely, ranging from 96.2 percent in Massachusetts and Maine to 83.5 percent in Alaska (Figure 53-2).

 use your **sociological imagination**

In what ways do the costs of health care affect the way you receive medical services?

FIGURE 53-2 **Percentage of Children without Health Insurance**

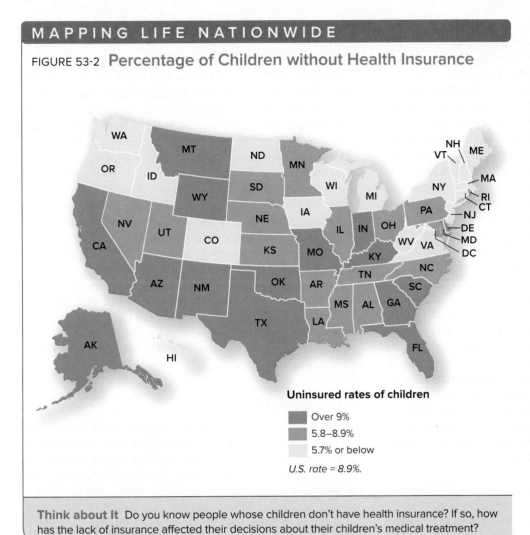

Uninsured rates of children

- ■ Over 9%
- ■ 5.8–8.9%
- ☐ 5.7% or below

U.S. rate = 8.9%.

Think about It Do you know people whose children don't have health insurance? If so, how has the lack of insurance affected their decisions about their children's medical treatment?

Note: In 2012, children under 18 years without private or government health insurance, not covered by Medicaid, Medicare, or military health care.

Source: DeNavas-Walt et al. 2013:Table HI05.

Race and Ethnicity

The health profiles of many racial and ethnic minorities reflect the social inequality evident in the United States. The poor economic and environmental conditions of groups such as African Americans, Hispanics, and Native Americans are manifested in high morbidity and mortality rates for those groups. It is true that some diseases, such as sickle-cell anemia among Blacks, have a clear genetic basis. But in most instances, environmental factors contribute to the differential rates of disease and death.

As noted in Module 52, infant mortality is regarded as a primary indicator of health care. There is a significant gap in the United States between the infant mortality rates of African Americans and Whites. Generally, the rate of infant death is more than twice as high among Blacks (MacDorman and Mathews 2009).

The medical establishment is not exempt from racism. Unfortunately, the media often focus on obvious forms of racism, such as hate crimes, while overlooking more insidious forms in social institutions like the medical establishment. Minorities receive inferior medical care even when they are insured. Despite having access to care, Blacks, Latinos, and Native Americans are treated unequally as a result of racial prejudice and differences in the quality of various health care plans. Furthermore, national clinical studies have shown that even allowing for differences in income and insurance coverage, racial and ethnic minorities are less likely than other groups to receive both standard health care and life-saving treatment for conditions such as HIV infection (Centers for Disease Control and Prevention 2011b; Long and Masi 2009).

Drawing on the conflict perspective, sociologist Howard Waitzkin (1986) suggests that racial tensions also contribute to the medical problems of Blacks. In his view, the stress that results from racial prejudice and discrimination helps to explain the higher rates of hypertension found among African Americans (and Hispanics) compared to Whites. Hypertension—twice as common in Blacks as in Whites— is believed to be a critical factor in Blacks' high mortality rates from heart disease, kidney disease, and stroke (Centers for Disease Control and Prevention 2011b).

Some Mexican Americans and many other Latinos adhere to cultural beliefs that make them less likely than others to use the established medical system. They may interpret their illnesses according to *curanderismo,* or traditional Latino folk medicine—a form of holistic health care and healing. *Curanderismo* influences how one approaches health care and even how one defines illness. Most Hispanics probably use *curanderos,* or folk healers, infrequently, but perhaps 20 percent rely on home remedies. Some define such illnesses as *susto* (fright sickness) and *atague* (fighting attack) according to folk beliefs. Because these complaints often have biological bases, sensitive medical practitioners need to deal with them carefully in order to diagnose and treat illnesses accurately. Moreover, it would be a mistake to blame the poor health care that Latinos receive on cultural differences. Latinos are much more likely to seek treatment for pressing medical problems at clinics and emergency rooms than they are to receive regular preventive care through a family physician (Centers for Disease Control and Prevention 2011b; Durden and Hummer 2006; Trotter and Chavira 1997).

Gender

A large body of research indicates that compared with men, women experience a higher occurrence of many illnesses, although they tend to live longer. There are some variations—for example, men are more likely to have parasitic diseases, whereas women are more likely to become diabetic—but as a group, women appear to be in poorer health than men.

The apparent inconsistency between the ill health of women and their greater longevity deserves an explanation, and researchers have advanced a theory. Women's lower rate of cigarette smoking (reducing their risk of heart disease, lung cancer, and emphysema), lower consumption of alcohol (reducing the risk of auto accidents and cirrhosis of the liver), and lower rate of employment in dangerous occupations explain about one-third of their greater longevity than men. Moreover, some clinical studies suggest that the differences in morbidity may actually be less pronounced than the data show. Researchers argue that women are much more likely than men to seek treatment, to be diagnosed as having a disease, and thus to have their illnesses reflected in the data examined by epidemiologists.

From a conflict perspective, women have been particularly vulnerable to the medicalization of society, with everything from birth to beauty being treated in an increasingly medical context. Such medicalization may contribute to women's higher morbidity rates compared to those of men. Ironically, even though women have been especially affected by medicalization, medical researchers have often excluded them from clinical studies. Female physicians and researchers charge that sexism lies at the heart of such research practices, and insist there is a desperate need for studies of female subjects (Centers for Disease Control and Prevention 2011b; Rieker and Bird 2000).

Age

Health is the overriding concern of the elderly. Most older people in the United States report having at least one chronic illness, but only some of those conditions are potentially life threatening or require medical care. At the same time, health problems can affect the quality of life of older people in important ways. Almost half of older people in the United States are troubled by arthritis, and many have visual or hearing impairments that can interfere with the performance of everyday tasks.

Older people are also especially vulnerable to certain mental health problems. Alzheimer's disease, the leading cause of dementia in the United States, afflicts an estimated 5.4 million people age 65 or over—that is, 13 percent of that segment of the population. While some individuals with Alzheimer's exhibit only mild symptoms, the risk of severe problems resulting from the disease rises substantially with age (Alzheimer's Association 2012).

Not surprisingly, older people in the United States (age 75 and older) are five times more likely to use health services than younger people (ages 15–24). The disproportionate use of the U.S. health care system by older people is a critical factor in all discussions about the cost of health care and possible reforms of the health care system (Bureau of the Census 2011a).

In sum, to achieve greater access and reduce health disparities, federal health officials must overcome inequities that are rooted not just in age, but in social class, race and ethnicity, and gender. If that were not enough, they must also deal with a geographical disparity in health care resources.

● Health Care in the United States

As the entire nation is well aware, the costs of health care have skyrocketed. In 1997, total expenditures for health care in the United States crossed the trillion-dollar threshold—more than four times the 1980 total (Figure 53-3). In 2000, the amount spent on health care equaled that spent on education, defense, prisons, farm subsidies, food stamps, and foreign aid combined. By the year 2020, total expenditures for health care in the United States are expected to exceed $4.6 trillion. The rising costs of medical care are especially burdensome in the event of catastrophic illnesses or confinement to a nursing home. Bills of tens of thousands of dollars are not unusual in the treatment of cancer, Alzheimer's disease, and other chronic illnesses requiring custodial care.

The health care system of the United States has moved far beyond the days when general practitioners living in a neighborhood or community typically made house calls and charged modest fees for their services. How did health care become a big business involving nationwide hospital chains and marketing campaigns? How have these changes reshaped the interactions between doctors, nurses, and patients? We will address these questions next.

A Historical View

Today, state licensing and medical degrees confer an authority on medical professionals that is maintained from one generation to the next. However, health care in the United States has not always followed this model. The "popular health movement" of the 1830s and 1840s emphasized preventive care and what is termed "self-help." Strong criticism was voiced of "doctoring" as a paid occupation. New medical philosophies or sects established their own medical schools and challenged the authority and methods of more traditional doctors. By the 1840s, most states had repealed medical licensing laws.

In response, through the leadership of the American Medical Association (AMA), founded in 1848, "regular" doctors attacked lay practitioners, sectarian doctors, and female physicians in general. Once they had institutionalized their authority through standardized programs of education and licensing, they conferred it on all who successfully completed their programs. The authority of the physician no longer depended on lay attitudes or on the person occupying the sick role; increasingly, it was built into the structure of the medical profession and the health care system. As the institutionalization of health care proceeded, the medical profession gained control over both the market for its services and the various organizational hierarchies that govern medical practice, financing, and policymaking. By the 1920s, physicians controlled hospital technology, the division of labor of health personnel, and indirectly, other professional practices such as nursing and pharmacy (R. Coser 1984).

Patients have traditionally relied on medical personnel to inform them of health care issues, but increasingly they are turning to the media for health care information. Recognizing this change, pharmaceutical firms are advertising their prescription drugs directly to potential customers through television and magazines. The Internet is another growing source for patient

FIGURE 53-3 Total Health Care Expenditures in the United States, 1970–2020 (Projected)

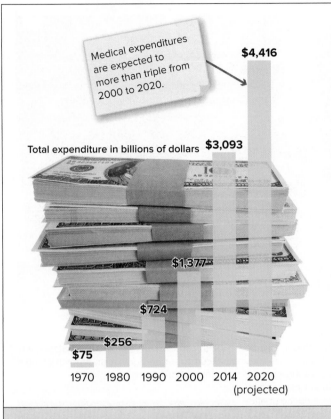

Medical expenditures are expected to more than triple from 2000 to 2020.

$4,416

Total expenditure in billions of dollars $3,093

$1,377

$724

$256

$75

| 1970 | 1980 | 1990 | 2000 | 2014 | 2020 (projected) |

Think about It What social changes in the United States might account for the rise in health care costs from $75 billion in 1970 to almost $3.1 trillion in 2014?

Sources: Centers for Medicare and Medicaid Services 2013a, 2013b:Table 1.

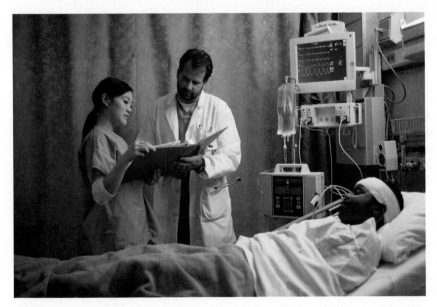

As if the status differences between nurses and physicians were not clear to all, the more colorful uniform of nurses and the formal white doctor's coat reinforce the distinction.

information. Medical professionals are understandably suspicious of these new sources of information.

Today, consumers get more than their health care information in new ways. Over the past decade, they have discovered a new way to access traditional medicine: going to the store (Box 53-1).

 use your **sociological imagination**

If you were a patient, would you put yourself entirely in the physician's hands, or would you do some research on your own? If you were a doctor, would you want your patient checking medical information on the Internet? Explain your positions.

Physicians, Nurses, and Patients

Traditionally, physicians have held a position of dominance in their dealings with both patients and nurses. The functionalist and interactionist perspectives offer a framework for understanding the professional socialization of physicians as it relates to patient care. Functionalists suggest that established physicians and medical school professors serve as mentors or role models who transmit knowledge, skills, and values to the passive learner—the medical student. Interactionists emphasize that students are molded by the medical school environment as they interact with their classmates.

Both approaches argue that the typical training of physicians in the United States leads to rather dehumanizing physician–patient encounters. As Dr. Lori Arviso Alvord, a Navajo physician, writes in *The Scalpel and the Silver Bear,* "I had been trained by a group of physicians who placed much more emphasis on their technical abilities and clinical skills than on their abilities to be caring and sensitive" (Alvord and Van Pelt 1999:13). Despite many efforts to formally introduce a humanistic approach to patient care into the medical school curriculum, patient overload and cost-cutting by hospitals have tended to undercut positive relations. Moreover, widespread publicity about malpractice suits and high medical costs has further strained the physician–patient relationship. Interactionists have closely examined compliance and negotiation between physician and patient. They concur with Talcott Parsons's view that the relationship is generally asymmetrical, with doctors holding a position of dominance and controlling rewards.

Just as physicians have maintained dominance in their interactions with patients, they have controlled interactions with nurses. Despite their training and professional status, nurses commonly take orders from physicians. Traditionally, the relationship between doctors and nurses has paralleled the male dominance of the United States: most physicians have been male, while virtually all nurses have been female.

Health Care, Retail Style

Greeting cards are in aisle 7; vaccinations, in aisle 4. Today, over 1,200 health clinics are located in retail stores throughout the United States, including Walgreens, CVS, and Walmart. Staffed by nurse-practitioners and nurses with advanced degrees, these in-store clinics treat a limited menu of complaints, including sore throats, ear infections, pinkeye, and noncomplicated respiratory conditions. And the nurses do write prescriptions.

What are the implications of these new clinics for traditional health care? Having a regular physician is becoming less and less common in the United States, given the many people who lack health insurance, as well as the frequent changes in corporate health plans. Like it or not, the physician you see this year simply may not be available to you next year. Under these circumstances, retail medical care may not pose much of a challenge to traditional medical practices.

> For three acute conditions—sore throat, middle ear infection, and urinary tract infection—retail clinics delivered the same or better-quality care than traditional medical settings.

What about the quality of care offered at in-store clinics? Recently, researchers compared the care delivered in retail clinics to the care available in doctors' offices, urgent care departments, and emergency rooms. For three acute conditions—sore throat, middle ear infection, and urinary tract infection—they found that retail clinics delivered the same or better-quality care than traditional medical settings, including preventive care during or after the first visit. Costs were much lower, especially compared to those in emergency rooms.

In-store clinics are another example of **McDonaldization,** the process by which the principles of bureaucratization have increasingly shaped organizations worldwide. McDonaldization offers the benefit of clearly stated services and prices, but the drawback of impersonality. Family doctors note that 40 percent of clinic patients have a family physician. Yet given the shortcomings of health care delivery in the United States, it is difficult to argue against an innovative new method of providing health care.

LET'S DISCUSS

1. Have you ever been treated at an in-store clinic? If so, were you satisfied with the care you received? What about the price you paid—was it reasonable?

2. Evaluate the emergence of clinics from a functionalist and then a conflict perspective. On balance, do you think these clinics are a benefit to society?

Sources: Pickert 2009; RAND 2010; Ritzer 2013:63–64.

Like other women in subordinate roles, nurses have been expected to perform their duties without challenging the authority of men. Psychiatrist Leonard Stein (1967) refers to this process as the *doctor–nurse game.* According to the rules of this "game," the nurse must never openly disagree with the physician. When she has recommendations concerning a patient's care, she must communicate them indirectly, in a deferential tone. For example, if asked by a hospital's medical resident, "What sleeping medication has been helpful to Mrs. Brown in the past?" (an indirect request for a recommendation), the nurse will respond with a disguised recommendation, such as "Pentobarbital 100 mg was quite effective night before last." Her careful response allows the physician to authoritatively restate the same prescription as if it were *his* idea.

Like nurses, female physicians have traditionally found themselves in a subordinate position because of their gender, but that is slowly changing as their numbers increase. Box 53-2 considers the social impact of the growing number of female physicians and surgeons on the medical field.

Alternatives to Traditional Health Care

In traditional forms of health care, people rely on physicians and hospitals for the treatment of illness. Yet at least one out of every three adults in the United States attempts to maintain good health or respond to illness through the use of alternative health care techniques. For example, in recent decades interest has been growing in *holistic* (also spelled *wholistic*)

BOX 53-2

Research Today

Women as Physicians and Surgeons

When Perri Klass told her four-year-old son she would be taking him to the pediatrician, he replied, "Is she a nice doctor?" Klass, a professor of pediatrics, was struck by his innocent assumption that like his mother, all pediatricians were female. "Boys can be doctors, too," she told him.

Not long ago, there would have been little potential for confusion on her son's part. Klass probably would not have been admitted to medical school, no less appointed a professor of medicine. Today, women represent nearly half of all medical students in the United States, where they account for one-third of all physicians and two-thirds of physician assistants. Yet female doctors make less income than men, even within the same specialty and even in the first years of their careers.

What has been the impact of this increase in the number of women in medicine? For one thing, female physicians may have improved physician–patient communication. Female primary care physicians spend an extra two minutes talking with patients—10 percent more time than male primary care physicians. They also engage in more patient-centered communication, listening more, asking questions about patients' personal well-being, and counseling patients about the concerns they bring to the doctor's office. Perhaps more important, female physicians tend to see their relationship with patients as an active partnership, one in which they discuss several treatment options rather than recommending a single course of treatment. From an interactionist perspective, these differences

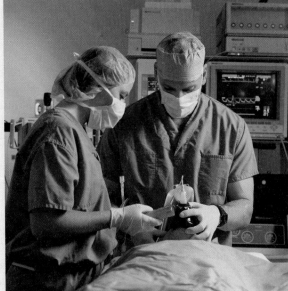

between female and male physicians correspond to typical gender differences in communication.

> Female physicians tend to see their relationship with patients as an active partnership, one in which they discuss several treatment options rather than recommending a single course of treatment.

Women physicians may also have made medicine a more family-friendly profession. Nowadays, physicians who wish to, both male and female, can develop practices that allow them to spend more time at home. Despite this change in the medical field, female doctors still seem to experience more frustration than male doctors. A national study of nearly 8,000 surgeons found that 62 percent of women complained of a work–home conflict, compared to 49 percent of the men. Female surgeons were also three times as likely as male surgeons to believe that child rearing would slow their career advancement. That complaint may disappear over time, however. Ultimately, the growing participation of women in this traditionally male-dominated field has the potential to completely reshape the health profession.

LET'S DISCUSS

1. In your own experience, have you noted a gender difference in the way doctors communicate with patients? Explain.

2. Why is the quality of a doctor's communication with patients important? What might be the benefit of female physicians' superior communication style?

Sources: Tracey Adams 2010; Buddeberg-Fischer et al. 2012; Bureau of the Census 2011a:Table 616; Dyrbye et al. 2011; Klass 2003:319; Lo Sasso et al. 2011; Roter et al. 2002.

---

medical principles, first developed in China. **Holistic medicine** refers to therapies in which the health care practitioner considers the person's physical, mental, emotional, and spiritual characteristics. The individual is regarded as a totality rather than a collection of interrelated organ systems. Treatment methods include massage, chiropractic medicine, acupuncture (which involves the insertion of fine needles into surface points), respiratory exercises, and the use of herbs as remedies. Nutrition, exercise, and visualization may also be used to treat ailments that are generally treated through medication or hospitalization (Sharma and Bodeker 1998).

Practitioners of holistic medicine do not necessarily function totally outside the traditional health care system. Some have medical degrees and rely on X-rays and EKG machines for diagnostic assistance. Others who staff holistic clinics, often referred to as *wellness clinics,* reject the use of medical technology. The recent resurgence of holistic medicine comes amid widespread recognition of the value of nutrition and the dangers of overreliance on prescription drugs (especially those used to reduce stress, such as Valium).

The medical establishment—professional organizations, research hospitals, and medical schools—has generally served as a stern protector of traditionally accepted health care techniques. However, a major breakthrough occurred in 1992 when the federal government's National Institutes of Health—the nation's major funding source for biomedical research—opened the National Center for Complementary and Alternative Medicine, empowered to accept grant requests. NIH-sponsored national surveys found that one in four adults in the United States had used some form of "complementary and alternative medicine" during the previous month or year. Examples included acupuncture, folk medicine, meditation, yoga, homeopathic treatments, megavitamin therapy, and chiropractic treatment. When prayer was included as an alternative or complementary form of medicine, the proportion of adults who used alternative medicine rose to over 62 percent (Figure 53-4).

On the international level, the World Health Organization (WHO) has begun to monitor the use of alternative medicine around the world. According to WHO, 80 percent of people who live in the poorest countries in the world use some form of alternative medicine, from herbal treatments to the services of a faith healer. In most countries, these treatments are largely unregulated, even though some of them can be fatal. For example, kava kava, an herbal tea used in the Pacific Islands to relieve anxiety, can be toxic to the liver in concentrated form. However, other alternative treatments have been found to be effective in the treatment of serious diseases, such as malaria and sickle-cell anemia. WHO's goal is to compile a list of such practices, as well as to encourage the development of universal training programs and ethical standards for practitioners of alternative

medicine. To date, the organization has published findings on about 100 of the 5,000 plants believed to be used as herbal remedies (McNeil 2002).

The Role of Government

Not until the 20th century did health care receive federal aid. The first significant involvement was the 1946 Hill-Burton Act, which provided subsidies for building and improving hospitals, especially in rural areas. A far more important change came with the enactment in 1965 of two wide-ranging government assistance programs: Medicare, which is essentially a compulsory health insurance plan for the elderly, and Medicaid, which is a noncontributory federal and state insurance plan for the poor. These programs greatly expanded federal involvement in health care financing for needy men, women, and children.

Given the high rates of illness and disability among elderly people, Medicare has had a huge impact on the health care system. Initially, Medicare simply reimbursed health care providers such as physicians and hospitals for the billed costs of their services. However, in 1983, as the overall costs of Medicare increased dramatically, the federal government introduced a price-control system. Under this system, private hospitals often transfer patients whose treatment may be unprofitable to public facilities. In fact, many private hospitals have begun to conduct "wallet biopsies"—that is, to investigate the financial status of

FIGURE 53-4 **Use of Complementary and Alternative Medicine**

Diets	3.6 %
Yoga	6.1 %
Massage	8.3%
Chiropractic	8.6%
Meditation	9.4%
Prayer group	9.6%
Deep breathing	12.7%
Natural products	17.1%
Prayer/others	24.4%
Prayer/self	43.0%

Note: Data from 2007 survey, except for prayer data from 2002 survey.
Source: P. Barnes et al. 2004, 2008.

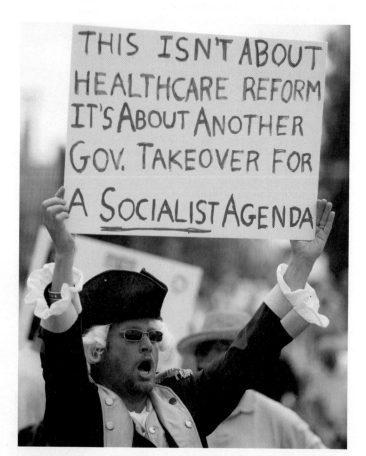

Tensions ran high as the Supreme Court heard arguments on the constitutionality of controversial new federal health care legislation. These citizens are indicating their opposition to the 2010 Affordable Care Act.

potential patients. Those judged undesirable are then refused admission or dumped. Although a federal law passed in 1987 made it illegal for any hospital receiving Medicare funds to dump patients, the practice continues (E. Gould 2007; Light 2004).

The 2010 Affordable Care Act improved health insurance coverage for people of all ages, especially young adults, who were allowed to remain longer on their parents' policies. President Obama's administration had pushed for the act in response to several problems, including high out-of-pocket costs for the uninsured and the inability of people with preexisting conditions to get insurance. In 2012 the Supreme Court upheld the federal government's authority to implement the law's provisions. Opponents of the legislation, which they dubbed "Obamacare," complain that the act is too expensive for taxpayers, and unnecessarily—perhaps even unconstitutionally—dictates citizens' health care decisions.

MODULE 53 | Recap and Review

Summary

Social epidemiology is concerned both with epidemic and with nonepidemic diseases, injuries, drug addiction and alcoholism, suicide, and mental illness. The health care system in the United States is a complex and expensive social institution that has evolved from relatively simple roots.

1. Studies consistently show that people from lower socioeconomic groups have higher rates of mortality and disability than others.

2. Racial and ethnic minorities have higher rates of morbidity and mortality than Whites.

3. Women tend to be in poorer health than men, but nevertheless they live longer.

4. Older people are especially vulnerable to mental health problems such as Alzheimer's disease, as well as to physical ailments.

5. The preeminent role of physicians in the U.S. health care system gives them a position of dominance in their dealings with nurses and patients.

6. Many people use alternative health care techniques such as **holistic medicine** and self-help groups.

Thinking Critically

1. Which is a more important factor in the adequate delivery of health care, race or gender?

2. In the United States, a nation with a world-renowned medical system, why do so many people seek alternative forms of health care?

Key Terms

Curanderismo

Holistic medicine

McDonaldization

Morbidity rate

Mortality rate

Social epidemiology

MODULE 54 | What Is Mental Illness?

Like other illnesses, mental disorders affect not just individuals and their families, but society as a whole. In industrial economies, mental disorders are a significant cause of disability. Thus, as a British medical journal declared in connection with the Global Mental Health Summit, there can be "no health without mental health" (Prince et al. 2007).

Sadly, the words *mental illness* and *insanity* evoke dramatic and often inaccurate images of emotional problems. Though the media routinely emphasize the most violent behavior of those with emotional disturbances, mental health and mental illness can more appropriately be viewed as a continuum of behavior that we ourselves move along. Using this definition, we can consider a person to have a mental disorder "if he or she is so disturbed that coping with routine, everyday life is difficult or impossible." The term **mental illness** should be reserved for a disorder of the brain that disrupts a person's thinking, feeling, and ability to interact with others (J. Coleman and Cressey 1980:315; National Alliance on Mental Illness 2008).

Traditionally, people in the United States have maintained a negative and suspicious view of those with mental disorders. Holding the status of "mental patient" or even "former mental patient" can have unfortunate and undeserved consequences. Voting rights are denied in some instances, acceptance for jury duty is problematic, and past emotional problems are an issue in divorce and custody cases. Moreover, content analysis of network television programs and films shows that mentally ill characters are uniformly portrayed in a demeaning and derogatory fashion; many are labeled as "criminally insane," "wackos," or "psychos." From an interactionist perspective, a key social institution is shaping social behavior by manipulating symbols and intensifying people's fears about the mentally ill (Diefenbach and West 2007).

In 2012, a tragic mass shooting at an elementary school in Newtown, Connecticut, led to renewed scrutiny of the role of mental illness in incidents of gun violence. The shooter was said to have had a mental illness, for which he apparently went untreated. As a result, some people argued that to curb gun violence, legislators should focus on mental health rather than on gun control. Unfortunately, such public debates tend to perpetuate the false assumption that people with mental illness are dangerous, furthering the *stigma* associated with their illness. The term **stigma,** coined by the interactionist Erving Goffman (1963), describes the labels society uses to devalue members of certain social groups.

A review of the available survey data shows that over time, the general public has become more sophisticated about mental illness, and perhaps a bit more open to disclosure, recognition, and response to mental health problems. Yet since 1950, people

In 2011, actress Catherine Zeta-Jones announced that she was being treated for bipolar disorder, a condition she shares with an estimated 2 percent of the U.S. population. The stigma of mental illness is slowly diminishing as celebrities come forward to reveal they are being treated for various mental disorders.

have become much more likely to associate "violence" with "mental illness," despite overwhelming evidence to the contrary. In fact, the vast majority of people with psychiatric disorders *do not* commit violent acts. Only 4 percent of violent crimes in the United States can be attributed to people with mental illness (R. Friedman 2012; Nocera 2012; Pescosolido 2013).

Certainly many in the mental health community would welcome expanded services for those with mental illness, especially given the billions of dollars that were cut from mental health programs during the recession. However, members of this community have questioned hastily drawn-up proposals that would lower the threshold for involuntary commitment or broaden the requirements for reporting potentially dangerous patients to the authorities. Their concerns may not receive a fair hearing, though, because the mental health community is far less powerful politically than the advocacy groups representing gun owners and sellers (E. Goode and Healy 2013).

Despite the stigmatization of mental illness, more people are seeking care and professional assistance than in the past. In the military services, the depression and post-traumatic stress that many veterans experience is receiving growing attention. And increasingly, legislators are recognizing the need to provide services for all who suffer from mental illness (Kessler et al. 2006; Tanielian 2009).

● Theoretical Models of Mental Disorders

In studying mental illness, we can draw on both the medical model and a more sociological approach derived from labeling theory. Each model rests on distinctive assumptions regarding treatment of people with mental disorders.

According to the medical model, mental illness is rooted in biological causes that can be treated through medical intervention. Problems in brain structure or in the biochemical balance in the brain, sometimes due to injury and sometimes due to genetic inheritance, are thought to be at the bottom of these disorders. The U.S. Surgeon General (1999) released an exhaustive report on mental health in which he declared that the accumulated weight of scientific evidence leaves no doubt about the physical origins of mental illness.

That is not to say that social factors do not contribute to mental illness. Just as culture affects the occurrence of illness and its treatment, so too it can affect mental illness. In fact, the very definition of mental illness differs from one culture to the next. Mainstream U.S. culture, for instance, considers hallucinations highly abnormal. However, many traditional cultures view them as evidence of divine favor and confer a special status on those who experience them. As we have noted throughout this textbook, a given behavior may be viewed as normal in one society, disapproved of but tolerated in a second, and labeled as sick and heavily sanctioned in a third.

A major focus of the controversy over the medical model is the *Diagnostic and Statistical Manual of Mental Disorders (DSM),* which came out in its fifth edition in 2013 (*DSM-5*). The *DSM,* which was introduced in 1952 by the American Psychiatric

Association (APA), is intended to establish standard criteria for diagnosing mental disorders. Over time, however, the classification of various conditions has changed, seeming to undercut the notion that mental disorders are fixed medical conditions. A 1987 revision, for example, dropped the diagnosis "sexual orientation disturbance," ending the treatment of homosexuality as a curable disorder. In *DSM-5,* binge eating and some forms of hoarding have been added to the list of disorders, and bereavement has been removed as a symptom of depression.

Importantly, the *DSM* is more than an academic volume. The categories it sets forth become the basis for insurance coverage, special educational and behavioral services, and medical prescriptions, and may qualify those with a diagnosis for disability benefits. Although supporters of the *DSM* acknowledge its limitations, they stress the need for practitioners to reach a consensus on the definition and treatment of mental disorders (American Psychiatric Association 2013; Satel 2013; Scheid 2013).

In contrast to the medical model, labeling theory suggests that some behaviors that are viewed as mental illnesses may not really be illnesses. For example, the U.S. Surgeon General's report (1999:5) notes that "bereavement symptoms" of less than two months' duration do not qualify as a mental disorder, but beyond that they may be redefined. Sociologists would see this approach to bereavement as labeling by those with the power to affix labels rather than as an acknowledgment of a biological condition.

Psychiatrist Thomas Szasz ("Sahz"), in his book *The Myth of Mental Illness* (2010), advanced the view that numerous personality disorders are not diseases, but simply patterns of conduct labeled as disorders by significant others. The response to Szasz's challenging thesis was sharp: the commissioner of the New York State Department of Hygiene demanded his dismissal from his university position because Szasz did not "believe" in mental illness. But many sociologists embraced his model as a logical extension of examining individual behavior in a social context.

For generations, many thousands of people with mental illness were effectively removed from society and placed in residential facilities. The now-abandoned Harlem Valley Psychiatric Center in Dover, New York, which operated from 1924 to 1993, included 80 buildings; at its peak it housed 5,000 patients.

In sum, the medical model is persuasive because it pinpoints the causes of mental illness and offers treatment for disorders. Yet proponents of the labeling perspective maintain that mental illness is a distinctively social process, whatever other processes are involved. From a sociological perspective, the ideal approach to mental illness integrates the insights of labeling theory with those of the medical approach (Horwitz 2002; Scheid 2013).

Patterns of Care

For most of human history, those who suffered from mental disorders were deemed the responsibility of their families. Yet mental illness has been a matter of governmental concern much longer than physical illness has. That is because severe emotional disorders threaten stable social relationships and entail prolonged incapacitation. As early as the 1600s, European cities began to confine the insane in public facilities along with the poor and criminals. Prisoners, indignant at being forced to live with "lunatics," resisted this approach. The isolation of people with mental illness from others in the same facility and from the larger society soon made physicians the central and ultimate authority over their welfare.

A major policy development in caring for those with mental disorders came with the passage of the Community Mental Health Centers Act (1963). The CMHC program, as it is known, not only increased the federal government's involvement in the treatment of people with mental illness. It also established community-based mental health centers to treat clients on an *outpatient* basis, thereby allowing them to continue working and living at home. The program showed that outpatient treatment could be more effective than the institutionalized programs of state and county mental hospitals.

Expansion of the federally funded CMHC program decreased inpatient care. By the 1980s, community-based mental health care had replaced hospitalization as the typical form of treatment. Across the United States, deinstitutionalization of the mentally ill reached dramatic proportions. Deinstitutionalization had been conceived as a social reform that would effectively reintegrate the mentally ill into the outside world. However, the authentic humanitarian concern behind the approach proved to be a convenient front for politicians whose goal was simply to cut costs. In 1950, 339 people per 100,000 population resided in state psychiatric hospitals. By 2010 the number had declined to 14 per 100,000 (Kelly 2009; Szabo 2013; Torrey 2013).

In a marked shift from public policy over the past three decades, several states have recently made it easier to commit mental patients to hospitals involuntarily. These changes have come in part because community groups and individual residents have voiced increasing fear and anger about the growing number of people with mental illness who are homeless and living in their midst, many of them on the streets. All too often, the severely mentally ill end up in jail or prison after committing crimes that lead to their prosecution. Ironically, family members of these men and women with mental illness complain that they cannot get adequate treatment for their loved ones *until* they have committed violent acts. Nevertheless, civil liberties advocates and voluntary associations of people with mental illness worry about the risks of denying people their constitutional rights, and cite horror stories about the abuses people have experienced during institutionalization (Marquis and Morain 1999; Shogren 1994).

The Mental Health Parity and Addiction Equity Act of 2008, which took effect in 2010, requires insurers to extend comparable benefits for mental and physical health care. This congressional effort to ensure equal treatment for mental health patients is not the first or only such effort. Although the act has helped to dispel the stigma associated with mental illness, most mental health providers agree that true parity in financial benefits for those with mental disorders has not been achieved. For example, the act exempts group health insurance plans if providing comparable mental health benefits would increase premiums by 1 percent or more. Higher co-pays, deductibles, and out-of-pocket maximums also have undercut the legislation's effectiveness (Health Cost Institute 2013; Hernandez and Uggen 2012).

Finally, although mental health care is often considered to be qualitatively different from other types of health care, many of the observations that apply to traditional medicine also apply to mental health care. For example, African Americans, Latinos, and American Indians have higher rates for several mental disorders, but are much less likely than Whites to receive treatment. Documented prejudice by practitioners contributes to the disparity, along with inadequate insurance and geographic isolation. In both rural and inner-city areas, mental health care is difficult to access and often poor in quality, especially for members of minority groups (McGuire and Miranda 2008).

 use your **sociological imagination**

How are your views of mental illness different from or similar to your views of physical illness?

MODULE 54 | **Recap and Review**

Summary

Mental illness is a disorder of the brain that disrupts a person's thinking, feeling, and ability to interact with others.

1. Mental illness should be seen within a continuum of behavior that ranges from mental health to mental illness.

2. People with mental illness bear a **stigma** that devalues members of their social group. The false assumption that people who suffer from mental illness are violent contributes to that stigma.

3. Mental disorders may be viewed from two different perspectives, the **medical model** and the sociological model, which is based on labeling theory. In the United States, society has traditionally taken a negative, suspicious attitude toward people with mental disorders.

Thinking Critically

1. What factors perpetuate the social stigma associated with mental illness? How could that stigma be eliminated?

2. Why did the policy of deinstitutionalization result in negative outcomes for people with mental illness? How can the shortcomings of the policy be eliminated?

Key Terms

Mental illness

Stigma

MODULE 55 | **Population**

Demography: The Study of Population

The study of population issues engages the attention of both natural and social scientists. The biologist explores the nature of reproduction and casts light on factors that affect **fertility,** the

level of reproduction in a society. The medical pathologist examines and analyzes trends in the causes of death. Geographers, historians, and psychologists also have distinctive contributions to make to our understanding of population. Sociologists, more than these other researchers, focus on the *social* factors that influence population rates and trends.

In their study of population issues, sociologists are aware that the norms, values, and social patterns of a society profoundly affect various elements of population, such as fertility, *mortality* (the death rate), and migration. Fertility is influenced by people's age of entry into sexual unions and by their use of

An immigration officer checks the passports of passengers arriving at Palermo Airport, on the Italian island of Sicily. Population growth is a dynamic process that is affected not just by birth and death rates, but by the migration of people from one place or country to another.

contraception—both of which, in turn, reflect the social and religious values that guide a particular culture. Mortality is shaped by a nation's level of nutrition, acceptance of immunization, and provisions for sanitation, as well as its general commitment to health care and health education. Migration from one country to another can depend on marital and kinship ties, the relative degree of racial and religious tolerance in various societies, and people's evaluation of their employment opportunities.

Demography is the scientific study of population. It draws on several components of population, including size, composition, and territorial distribution, to understand the social consequences of population change. Demographers study geographical variations and historical trends in their effort to develop population forecasts. They also analyze the structure of a population—the age, gender, race, and ethnicity of its members. A key figure in this analysis was Thomas Malthus.

Malthus's Thesis and Marx's Response

The Reverend Thomas Robert Malthus (1766–1834), who was educated at Cambridge University, spent his life teaching history and political economy. He strongly criticized two major institutions of his time—the church and slavery—yet his most significant legacy to contemporary scholars is his still-controversial *Essays on the Principle of Population,* published in 1798.

Essentially, Malthus held that the world's population was growing more rapidly than the available food supply. He argued that food supply increases in arithmetic progression (1, 2, 3, 4, and so on), whereas population expands by geometric progression (1, 2, 4, 8, and so on). According to his analysis, the gap between food supply and population will continue to grow over time. Even though the food supply will increase, it will not increase nearly enough to meet the needs of an expanding world population.

Malthus advocated population control to close the gap between rising population and the food supply, yet he explicitly denounced artificial means of birth control because they were not sanctioned by religion. For Malthus, one appropriate way to control population was to postpone marriage. He argued that couples must take responsibility for the number of children they choose to bear; without such restraint, the world would face widespread hunger, poverty, and misery (Malthus et al. [1824] 1960; W. Petersen 1979).

Karl Marx strongly criticized Malthus's views on population. Marx pointed to the nature of economic relations in Europe's industrial societies as the central problem. He could not accept the Malthusian notion that rising world population, rather than capitalism, was the cause of social ills. In Marx's opinion, there was no special relationship between world population and the supply of resources (including food). If society were well ordered, increases in population would lead to greater wealth, not to hunger and misery.

Of course, Marx did not believe that capitalism operated under these ideal conditions. He maintained that capitalism devoted resources to the financing of buildings and tools rather than to the equitable distribution of food, housing, and other necessities of life. Marx's work is important to the study of population because he linked overpopulation to the unequal distribution of resources. His concern with the writings of Malthus also testifies to the importance of population in political and economic affairs.

The insights of Malthus and Marx regarding population issues have come together in what is termed the *neo-Malthusian view,* best exemplified by the work of Paul Ehrlich (1968; Ehrlich and Ehrlich 1990), author of *The Population Bomb.* Neo-Malthusians agree with Malthus that population growth is outstretching the world's natural resources. However, in contrast to the British theorist, they insist that birth control measures are needed to regulate population increases. Showing a Marxist bent, neo-Malthusians condemn the developed nations, which despite their low birthrates consume a disproportionately large share of world resources. While rather pessimistic about the future, these theorists stress that birth control and sensible use of resources are essential responses to rising world population (J. Tierney 1990; Weeks 2012).

In this cartoon, Manny Francisco, based in the heavily populated Philippine Islands, takes a grim Malthusian view of world hunger.

Cartoon by Manny Francisco © 2008 www.PoliticalCartoons.com. Reproduced by permission.

Studying Population Today

The relative balance of births and deaths is no less important today than it was during the lifetime of Malthus and Marx. The suffering that Malthus spoke of is certainly a reality for many people of the world. Malnutrition remains the largest contributing factor to illness and death among children in developing countries. Almost 18 percent of these children will die before age five—a rate over 11 times higher than in developed nations. Warfare and large-scale migration intensify problems of population and food supply. For example, recent strife in Afghanistan, the Congo, and Iraq has caused maldistribution of food supplies, leading to regional health concerns. Combating world hunger may require reducing human births, dramatically increasing the world's food supply, or perhaps both. The study of population-related issues, then, seems to be essential.

In the United States and most other countries, the census is the primary mechanism for collecting population information. A **census** is an enumeration, or counting, of a population. The Constitution of the United States requires that a census be held every 10 years to determine congressional representation. This periodic investigation is supplemented by **vital statistics,** or records of births, deaths, marriages, and divorces that are gathered through a registration system maintained by governmental units. In addition, other government surveys provide up-to-date information on commercial developments, educational trends, industrial expansion, agricultural practices, and the status of groups such as children, the elderly, racial minorities, and single parents.

In administering a nationwide census and conducting other types of research, demographers employ many skills and techniques, including questionnaires, interviews, and sampling. The precision of population projections depends on the accuracy of a series of estimates demographers must make. First, they must determine past population trends and establish a current base population. Next, birthrates and death rates must be determined, along with estimates of future fluctuations. In projecting a nation's population trends for the future, demographers must consider migration as well, since a significant number of individuals may enter and leave a country.

Elements of Demography

Demographers communicate population facts with a language derived from the basic elements of human life—birth and death. The **birthrate** (or more specifically, the *crude birthrate*) is the number of live births per 1,000 population in a given year. In 2012, for example, there were 13 live births per 1,000 people in the United States. The birthrate provides information on the reproductive patterns of a society.

One way demographers can project future growth in a society is to make use of the **total fertility rate (TFR).** The TFR is the average number of children born alive to any woman, assuming that she conforms to current fertility rates. The TFR reported for the United States in 2013 was 1.9 live births per woman, compared to nearly 8 births per woman in a developing country such as Niger.

Mortality, like fertility, is measured in several different ways. The **death rate** (also known as the *crude death rate*) is the number of deaths per 1,000 population in a given year. In 2013, the United States had a death rate of 8.0 per 1,000 population. The infant mortality rate serves as an important indicator of a society's level of health care; it reflects prenatal nutrition, delivery procedures, and infant screening measures. The infant mortality rate also functions as a useful indicator of future population growth, since those infants who survive to adulthood will contribute to further population increases.

A general measure of health used by demographers is **life expectancy,** the median number of years a person can be expected to live under current mortality conditions. Usually the figure is reported as life expectancy *at birth*. At present, Japan reports a life expectancy at birth of 83 years—slightly higher than the United States' figure of 79 years. In contrast, life

Taking Sociology to Work

Kelsie Lenor Wilson-Dorsett, *Deputy Director, Department of Statistics, Government of Bahamas*

Kelsie Wilson-Dorsett was born in the Bahamas, where she received her primary and secondary education. She graduated from McMaster University in Hamilton, Ontario, with a combined honors degree in sociology and political science. In studying for her master's degree in sociology at the University of Western Ontario in London, she specialized in demography.

Currently, Wilson-Dorsett holds the positions of Deputy Director, Department of Statistics and Head of the Social Statistics Division, Government of Bahamas, where she oversees the country's census, vital statistics, and other surveys. In this position, she is responsible for the execution of the Bahamas' first Living Conditions Survey (BLCS), which when completed will enable the government to establish a poverty line and to measure the incidence and extent of poverty in that country.

Wilson-Dorsett's study of sociology is directly related to her current job. She states, "The study of sociology has enabled me to put meaning to the figures which come into my office and has provided me with avenues to interpret these figures and determine the direction of future data collection. The analysis of census data, for instance, allows me to see where my country was several years ago, where it is now, and where it is likely to be in the years ahead."

LET'S DISCUSS

1. What challenges do you think Wilson-Dorsett might encounter as she oversees a national census in a country like the Bahamas?

2. What other areas of specialization in sociology would be helpful to someone interpreting the results of a project such as the Living Conditions Survey (BLCS)?

FIGURE 55-1 **Population Growth Rate in Selected Countries**

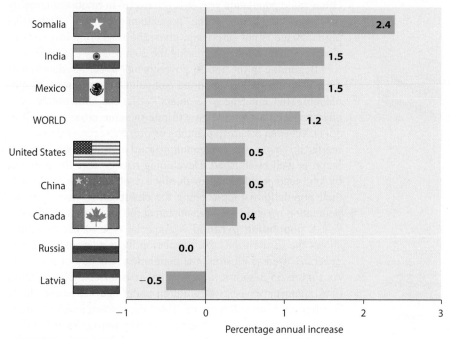

Source: Haub and Kaneta 2013.

in the late 1700s—and continuing until the mid-1900s—death rates in northern and western Europe gradually decreased. People were beginning to live longer because of advances in food production, sanitation, nutrition, and public health care. But while death rates fell, birthrates remained high; as a result, this period of European history brought unprecedented population growth. By the late 1800s, however, the birthrates of many European countries had begun to decline, and the rate of population growth had also decreased.

The changes in birthrates and death rates that occurred in 19th-century Europe serve as an example of *demographic transition*. Demographers use the term **demographic transition** to describe changes in birthrates and death rates that occur during a nation's development, resulting in new patterns of vital statistics. In many nations today, we are seeing a demographic transition from high birthrates and death rates to low birthrates and death rates. As Figure 55-2 shows, this process typically takes place in three stages:

1. Pretransition stage: high birthrates and death rates with little population growth.

2. Transition stage: declining death rates—primarily the result of reductions in infant deaths—along with high to medium fertility, resulting in significant population growth.

3. Posttransition stage: low birthrates and death rates with little population growth.

The demographic transition should be regarded not as a "law of population growth," but rather as a generalization of the population history of industrial nations. This concept helps us to understand

expectancy at birth is as low as 45 in the African nation of Sierra Leone (Haub and Kaneta 2013).

The **growth rate** of a society is the difference between births and deaths, plus the difference between *immigrants* (those who enter a country to establish permanent residence) and *emigrants* (those who leave a country permanently) per 1,000 population. For the world as a whole, the growth rate is simply the difference between births and deaths per 1,000 population, since worldwide immigration and emigration must of necessity be equal. In 2012, the United States had a growth rate of 0.5 percent, compared to an estimated 1.2 percent for the entire world (Figure 55-1).

● World Population Patterns

One important aspect of demographic work involves a study of the history of population. But how is that possible? After all, official national censuses were relatively rare before 1850. Researchers interested in early population must turn to archaeological remains, burial sites, baptismal and tax records, and oral history sources. In the next section we will see what such detective work has told us about changes in population over time.

Demographic Transition

On October 13, 1999, in a maternity clinic in Sarajevo, Bosnia-Herzegovina, Helac Fatina gave birth to a son who has been designated the 6 billionth person on this planet. Until modern times, relatively few humans lived in the world. One estimate places the global population of a million years ago at only 125,000 people. As Table 55-1 indicates, in the past 200 years the world's population has exploded (World Health Organization 2000:3).

The phenomenal growth of population in recent times can be accounted for by changing patterns in births and deaths. Beginning

TABLE **55-1** ESTIMATED TIME FOR EACH SUCCESSIVE INCREASE OF 1 BILLION PEOPLE IN WORLD POPULATION

Population Level	Time Taken to Reach New Population Level	Year of Attainment
First billion	Human history before 1800	1804
Second billion	123 years	1927
Third billion	32 years	1959
Fourth billion	15 years	1974
Fifth billion	13 years	1987
Sixth billion	12 years	1999
Seventh billion	12 years	2011
Eighth billion	15 years	2026
Ninth billion	16 years	2042

Sources: Bureau of the Census 2013b; Kunzig 2011:40.

FIGURE 55-2 Demographic Transition

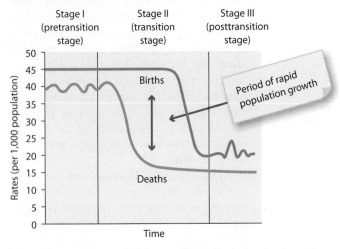

Stage I (pretransition stage)   Stage II (transition stage)   Stage III (posttransition stage)

Births

Period of rapid population growth

Deaths

Rates (per 1,000 population)

Time

Demographers use the concept of *demographic transition* to describe changes in birthrates and death rates that occur during a nation's development. This graph shows the pattern that took place in presently developed nations. In the first stage, both birthrates and death rates were high, so that there was little population growth. In the second stage, the birthrate remained high while the death rate declined sharply, which led to rapid population growth. By the last stage, which many developing countries have yet to enter, the birthrate had declined as well, reducing population growth.

world population problems better. About two-thirds of the world's nations have yet to pass fully through the second stage of the demographic transition. Even if such nations make dramatic advances in fertility control, their populations will nevertheless increase greatly because of the large base of people already at prime childbearing age.

The pattern of demographic transition varies from nation to nation. One particularly useful distinction is the contrast between the rapid transition now occurring in developing nations—which include about two-thirds of the world's population—and that which occurred over the course of almost a century in more industrialized countries. In developing nations, the demographic transition has involved a rapid decline in death rates, with adjustments in birthrates in some nations but not in others.

Specifically, in the post–World War II period, the death rates of developing nations began a sharp decline. This revolution in "death control" was triggered by antibiotics, immunization, insecticides (such as DDT, used to strike at malaria-bearing mosquitoes), and largely successful campaigns against such fatal diseases as smallpox. Substantial medical and public health technology was imported almost overnight from more developed nations. As a result, the drop in death rates that had taken a century in Europe was telescoped into two decades in many developing countries.

Birthrates had little time to adjust. Cultural beliefs about the proper size of families could not possibly change as quickly as the falling death rates. For centuries, couples had given birth to as many as eight or more children, knowing that perhaps only two or three would survive to adulthood. Families were more willing to accept technological advances that prolonged life than to abandon fertility patterns that reflected time-honored tradition and religious training. The result was an astronomical population explosion that was well under way by the middle 1900s. By the middle 1970s, however, demographers had observed a slight decline in the growth rate of some developing nations, as family-planning efforts began to take hold (Haub 2013; R. Lee and Reher 2011).

The Population Explosion

Often, rapid population growth is referred to in emotional terms as the "population bomb" or the "population explosion." Such striking language is not surprising, given the staggering increases in world population recorded during the 20th century (Table 55-1).

Beginning in the 1960s, governments in certain developing nations sponsored or supported campaigns to encourage family planning. In China, the government's strict one-child policy actually produced a negative growth rate in some urban areas (Box 55-1). Yet even if family-planning efforts are successful in reducing fertility rates, the momentum toward a growing world population is well established. Developing nations face the prospect of continued population growth, since a substantial proportion of their population is approaching the childbearing years (see the population pyramid for Afghanistan at the top of Figure 55-3).

A **population pyramid** is a special type of bar chart that shows the distribution of a population by gender and age; it is generally used to illustrate the population structure of a society. As Figure 55-3 shows, a substantial portion of the population of Afghanistan consists of children under age 15, whose childbearing years are still to come. Thus, the built-in momentum for population growth is much greater in Afghanistan (and in many other developing countries in other parts of the world) than in the United States and especially in many European nations (see the population pyramid for Italy in the middle of Figure 55-3).

Consider the population data for India, which in 2000 surpassed 1 billion residents. Sometime around 2025, India's population will exceed China's. The substantial momentum for growth that is built into India's age structure means that the nation will face a staggering increase in population in the coming decades, even if its birthrate declines sharply (Bureau of the Census 2013b).

Population growth is not a problem in all nations. Today, a handful of countries are even adopting policies that encourage growth. One such country is Japan, where the total fertility rate has fallen sharply. Nevertheless, a global perspective underscores the serious consequences that could result from continued population growth overall.

 use your **sociological imagination**

You are living in a country that is so heavily populated, basic resources such as food, water, and living space are running short. What will you do? How will you respond to the crisis if you are a government social planner? A politician?

Fertility Patterns in the United States

Over the past six decades, the United States and other industrial nations have passed through two different patterns of population growth—the first marked by high fertility and rapid growth (stage II in the theory of demographic transition), the second marked by

FIGURE 55-3 Population Structure of Afghanistan, Italy, and the United States, 2014

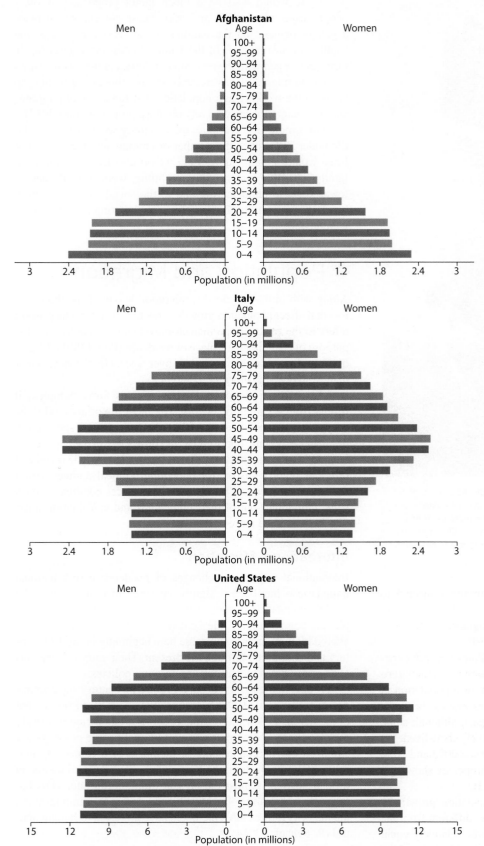

Source: Projections updated as of December 2010. Bureau of the Census 2011b.

declining fertility and little growth (stage III). Sociologists are keenly aware of the social impact of these fertility patterns.

The Baby Boom

The most recent period of high fertility in the United States has often been referred to as the *baby boom*. During World War II, large numbers of military personnel were separated from their spouses. When they returned, the annual number of births began to rise dramatically. Still, the baby boom was not a return to the large families common in the 1800s. In fact, there was only a slight increase in the proportion of couples having three or more children. Instead, the boom was the result of a striking decrease in the number of childless marriages and one-child families. Although a peak was reached in 1957, the nation maintained a relatively high birthrate of over 20 live births per 1,000 population until 1964. By 2013 the birthrate had fallen to 13 live births per 1,000 population (Bureau of the Census 1975; Haub and Kaneta 2013).

It would be a mistake to attribute the baby boom solely to the return home of large numbers of soldiers. High wages and general prosperity during the postwar period encouraged many married couples to purchase homes and have children. In addition, several sociologists—as well as feminist author Betty Friedan (1963)—have noted the strong societal pressure on women during the 1950s to marry and become mothers and homemakers (Bouvier 1980).

Stable Population Growth

Although the total fertility rate of the United States has remained low over the past three decades, the nation continues to grow in size because of two factors: the momentum built into our age structure by the postwar population boom and continued high rates of immigration. First, because of the upsurge of births beginning in the 1950s, there are now many more people in their childbearing years than in older age groups (in which most deaths occur). This growth of the childbearing population represents a "demographic echo" of the baby boom generation. Consequently, the number of people born each year in the United States continues to exceed the number who die.

Second, the nation allows a large number of immigrants to enter each year.

Population ■ **413**

Throughout the world, population patterns vary widely. As this scene in Warsaw, the capital of Poland, suggests, Eastern Europe has been losing population as the birthrate falls and young people emigrate to other countries. In Africa, in contrast, the population is growing. Over the next four decades, the country of Somalia is expected to double in population.

2010). As a result, the population pyramid of the United States (as shown in Figure 55-3) would look more like a rectangle.

There would also be a much larger proportion of older people, especially age 75 and over. These citizens would place a greater demand on the nation's social service programs and health care institutions. In the United States today, the drop in births that began with the recession of 2008, coupled with a slowdown in immigration, has created concerns about the growing gap between the working-age population that funds social programs and the senior citizens who rely on those programs (Last 2013).

On a more positive note, the economy would be less volatile under ZPG, since the number of entrants into the paid labor force would remain stable. ZPG would also lead to changes in family life. With fertility rates declining, women would devote fewer years to child rearing and to the social roles of motherhood; the proportion of married women entering the labor force would continue to rise.

Population and Migration

Along with births and deaths, migration is one of the three factors that affect population growth or decline. The term **migration** refers to the relatively permanent movement of people, with the purpose of changing their place of residence (Prehn 1991). Migration usually describes movement over a sizable distance, rather than from one side of a city to another.

As a social phenomenon, migration is fairly complex; it results from a variety of factors. The most important tend to be economic—financial failure in the "old country" and a perception of greater economic opportunity and prosperity in the new homeland. Other factors that contribute to migration include racial and religious bigotry, dislike for prevailing political regimes, and a desire to reunite one's family. All these forces combine to *push* some individuals out of their homelands and *pull* them to areas they believe to be more attractive.

International Migration

International migration—changes of residence across national boundaries—has been a significant force in redistributing the world's population during certain periods of history. For example, the composition of the United States has been significantly altered by immigrants who came here beginning in the 19th century and continuing through the present. Their entry was encouraged or restricted by various immigration policies.

Today, in the second decade of the 21st century, legal immigrants to the United States account for about 50 to 60 percent of the nation's growth. To some observers, this nation is already overpopulated. Recognizing that additional people place greater strain on our natural resources, members of a respected environmental organization, the Sierra Club, have debated taking an official position against the present immigration rate. Thus far, rather than enter the politically charged debate over immigration, the majority of the club's members have preferred to remain neutral (R. Schaefer 2014).

In the past decade, immigration has become a controversial issue throughout much of Europe. Western Europe in particular

Immigration, both legal and illegal, is currently projected to account for nearly 50 percent of the nation's growth from 2005 to 2050. The children and grandchildren of immigrants are projected to account for another 35 percent (Kotkin 2010).

Many countries other than the United States will not experience population growth but rather are expected to reach **zero population growth (ZPG).** ZPG is the state of a population in which the number of births plus immigrants equals the number of deaths plus emigrants. In the recent past, although some nations have achieved ZPG, it has been relatively short-lived. Yet today, projections of population change between 2013 and 2050 indicate that 40 countries, including 25 in Europe, are showing a *decline* in population (Haub and Kaneta 2013).

What would a society with stable population growth be like? In demographic terms, it would be quite different from the United States of around 2015. There would be relatively equal numbers of people in each age group, and the median age of the population might perhaps be as high as 45 (compared to 37.2 in

Population Policy in China

In a residential district in Shanghai, a member of the local family-planning committee knocks on the door of a childless couple. Why, she inquires, have they not started a family? Such a question would have been unthinkable in 1979, when family-planning officials, in an attempt to avoid a looming population explosion, began resorting to sterilization to enforce the government rule of one child per family.

Since then, the government has granted some limited exceptions to the one-child policy. In certain small ethnic minorities, couples are allowed to have two children; so are rural couples whose first child is a girl. Major events have created other exceptions. For example, in 2008 officials allowed parents who had lost a child in an earthquake to have another child.

In other cases, however, having two or three children has turned families into fugitives and forced them into hiding. Social class differences have allowed the few elite to escape such harsh consequences. Some merely pay fines for breaking the one-child rule; others avoid prosecution entirely. Zhang Yimou, the celebrated film director and arranger of the 2008 Summer Olympics, has fathered seven children by four different women with no apparent penalties.

Chinese families are beset, too, by the unforeseen results of their attempts to circumvent the one-child policy. In the past, in an effort to ensure that their one child would be a male capable of perpetuating the family line, many couples chose to abort female fetuses, or quietly allowed female infants to die of neglect. As a result, in 2013, among children ages one to four, China's sex ratio (the ratio of males to females) was about 118 to 100—well above the normal rate at birth of 105 to 100.

As a result of the high sex ratio, Chinese officials have begun to worry about a future with too few women. In about 20 to 25 years, they expect, almost one-fifth of the baby boys now being born will be unable to find brides. In an attempt to reverse the situation, the government is paying the parents of daughters to speak with other parents and persuade them to raise girls.

Another legacy of the one-child policy is a shortage of caretakers for the elderly.

This billboard, photographed in China, promotes the government's policy of allowing only one child per family. For several decades, the People's Republic of China has been struggling with a population explosion that threatens to outstrip the nation's ability to provide for all its citizens.

> As a result of the high sex ratio, Chinese officials have begun to worry about a future with too few women.

Coupled with improvements in longevity, the generation-long decline in births has greatly increased the ratio of dependent elders to able-bodied children. The migration of young adults to other parts of China has further compromised the care of the elderly. To compound the crisis, barely one in four of China's elders receives any pension at all. No other country in the world faces the prospect of caring for such a large population of seniors with so little social support.

In spite of the difficulties created by the one-child policy, reforming the system may be easier said than done. A possible obstacle to reform, according to some observers, is the central government's dependency on fines from violations of the policy. One estimate places the total income from those fines to date at over $326 billion—a significant source of government revenue.

LET'S DISCUSS

1. Does any government, no matter how overpopulated a country is, have a right to sterilize people who do not voluntarily limit the size of their families? Why or why not?

2. What do you think has been the most dramatic consequence of the one-child policy?

Sources: The Economist 2011b, 2013; Greenhalgh 2008; J. Page 2011; F. Wang 2011; F. Wang and Yong 2011.

---

has become a desirable destination for individuals and families from former colonies or former communist-bloc countries who are fleeing the poverty, persecution, and warfare of their native lands. The number of immigrants and refugees has been increasing at a time of widespread unemployment and housing shortages, provoking a striking rise in antiforeign (and often openly racist) sentiment in Germany, France, the Netherlands, and other countries.

Developing countries in Asia and Africa are also encountering difficulties as thousands of displaced people seek assistance and asylum. At the end of 2009, an estimated 10.4 million people worldwide were refugees or asylum seekers. Needless to say, the political and economic problems of developing nations are only intensified by such massive migration, begun under desperate conditions (UNHCR 2010).

Refugees at this camp in Turkey are fleeing the violent conflict in Syria which began in 2011. Catastrophic conflicts such as war and terrorism often trigger massive international migrations.

Internal Migration

Migratory movements within societies can vary in important ways. In traditional societies, migration often represents a way of life, as people move to accommodate the changing availability of fertile soil and wild game. In industrial societies, people may relocate because of job transfers or because they believe that a particular region offers better employment opportunities or a more desirable climate.

Although nations typically have laws and policies governing movement across their borders, the same is not true of internal movement. Generally, the residents of a country are legally free to move from one locality to another. Of course, that is not the case in all nations; historically, the Republic of South Africa restricted the movement of Blacks and other non-Whites through the system of segregation known as *apartheid*.

 use your **sociological imagination**

What would happen if present patterns of migration, both internal and international, reversed themselves? How would your hometown change? What would be the effect on the nation's economy? Would your own life change?

MODULE 55 | **Recap and Review**

Summary

This module explains how population trends affect the world's communities. It covers the size, composition, and distribution of the population, as well as the means of measuring population.

1. Thomas Malthus suggested that the world's population was growing more rapidly than the available food supply, and that the gap would increase over time. Karl Marx saw capitalism, not rising population, as the real cause of social ills.

2. The primary mechanism for obtaining population information in the United States and most other countries is the **census.**

3. Roughly two-thirds of the world's nations have yet to pass fully through the second stage of **demographic transition.** Thus they continue to experience significant population growth.

4. Developing nations face the prospect of continued population growth because a substantial portion of their population is approaching childbearing age. Some developed nations have begun to stabilize their population growth.

5. The most important factors in **migration** tend to be economic—financial failure in the "old country" and a perception of greater economic opportunity elsewhere.

Thinking Critically

1. Choose a developing country and look up its population statistics. Based on those statistics, in what stage of the demographic transition would you put that country? Explain.

2. Select a social policy issue that particularly interests you. How would the size, composition, and distribution of the population influence that issue?

Key Terms

Birthrate

Census

Death rate

Demographic transition

Demography

Fertility

Growth rate

Life expectancy

Migration

Population pyramid

Total fertility rate (TFR)

Vital statistics

Zero population growth (ZPG)

MODULE 56 | Sociological Perspectives on the Environment

We have seen that the environment people live in has a noticeable effect on their health. Those who live in stressful, overcrowded places suffer more from disease than those who do not. Likewise, people have a noticeable effect on their environment. Around the world, increases in population, together with the economic development that accompanies them, have had serious environmental consequences. We can see signs of despoliation almost everywhere: our air, our water, and our land are being polluted, whether we live in St. Louis, Mexico City, or Lagos, Nigeria.

Though environmental problems may be easy to identify, devising socially and politically acceptable solutions to them is much more difficult. In this section we will see what sociologists have to say about the trade-off between economic growth and development and its effects on the environment. In the section that follows we will look more closely at specific environmental issues.

Human Ecology

Human ecology is an area of study that is concerned with the interrelationships between people and their environment. As the environmentalist Barry Commoner (1971:39) put it, "Everything is connected to everything else." Human ecologists focus on how the physical environment shapes people's lives and on how people influence the surrounding environment.

There is no shortage of illustrations of the interconnectedness of people and their environment. For example, scientific research has linked pollutants in the physical environment to people's health and behavior. The increasing occurrences of asthma, lead poisoning, and cancer have all been tied to human alterations to the environment. Similarly, the rise in melanoma (skin cancer) diagnoses has been linked to global warming. Ecological changes in our food and diet have been related to early obesity and diabetes. And finally, global population growth has had a huge impact on the environment (Table 55-1).

With its view that "everything is connected to everything else," human ecology stresses the trade-offs inherent in every decision that alters the environment. In facing the environmental challenges of the 21st century, government policymakers and environmentalists must determine how they can fulfill humans' pressing needs for food, clothing, and shelter while preserving the environment.

Conflict Perspective

World systems analysis shows how a growing share of the human and natural resources of developing countries is being redistributed to the core industrialized nations. This process only intensifies the destruction of natural resources in poorer regions of the world. From a conflict perspective, less affluent nations are being forced to exploit their mineral deposits, forests, and fisheries in order to meet their debt obligations. The poor turn to the only means of survival available to them: they plow mountain slopes, burn plots in tropical forests, and overgraze grasslands (Pellow and Brehm 2013).

Brazil exemplifies this interplay between economic troubles and environmental destruction. Each year more than 5.7 million acres of forest are cleared for crops and livestock. The elimination of the rain forest affects worldwide weather patterns, heightening the gradual warming of the earth. These socioeconomic patterns, with their harmful environmental consequences, are evident not only in Latin America but in many regions of Africa and Asia.

Conflict theorists are well aware of the environmental implications of land use policies in the Third World, but they contend that focusing on the developing countries is ethnocentric. First, throughout most of history, developed countries have been the major source of greenhouse gas emissions. As Figure 56-1 shows, only recently have developing nations begun to emit greenhouse gases in the same quantities as developed nations. (Greenhouse gas emissions will be discussed in more detail later.)

Second, the industrialized nations of North America and Europe account for only 12 percent of the world's population but are responsible for 60 percent of worldwide consumption. Who, these theorists ask, is more to blame for environmental deterioration: the poverty-stricken and "food-hungry" populations of the world or the "energy-hungry" industrialized

Can you identify these slowly sinking replicas of world-famous landmarks? Greenpeace staged the publicity stunt to draw attention to global warming during climate talks in Cancún, Mexico, in 2010.

FIGURE 56-1 Projected Greenhouse Gas Emissions

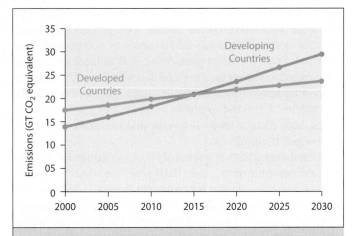

Developing Countries

Developed Countries

Think about It Why do you think the contemporary debate about greenhouse gas emissions focuses on developing nations, when for decades industrial nations have been the main culprits?

Source: Environmental Protection Agency 2012.

By 2015, total greenhouse gas emissions from developing countries are expected to exceed those from developed countries.

nations? The money that residents of developed countries spend on ocean cruises each year could provide clean drinking water for everyone on the planet. Ice cream expenditures in Europe alone could be used to immunize every child in the world. Thus, conflict theorists charge, the most serious threat to the environment comes from the global consumer class (Pellow and Brehm 2013).

Allan Schnaiberg (1994) further refined this analysis by shifting the focus from affluent consumers to the capitalist system as the cause of environmental troubles. In his view, a capitalist system creates a "treadmill of production" because of its inherent need to build ever-expanding profits. This treadmill necessitates the creation of increasing demand for products, the purchase of natural resources at minimal cost, and the manufacturing of products as quickly and cheaply as possible—no matter what the long-term environmental consequences. Indeed, over a century ago, Max Weber predicted that rampant industrialism would continue until "the last ton of fossil fuel has burnt to ashes" ([1904] 2011:157).

Ecological Modernization

Critics of the human ecological and conflict models argue that they are too rooted in the past. People who take these approaches, they charge, have become bogged down in addressing existing practices. Instead, proponents of **ecological modernization,** an approach that emerged in the 1980s, focus on the alignment of environmentally favorable practices with economic self-interest through constant adaptation and restructuring (Mol 2010; Mol and Sonnenfeld 2000; Mol et al. 2009).

Ecological modernization can occur on both the macro and micro levels. On a macro level, adaptation and restructuring can mean reintegrating industrial waste back into the production process. On a micro level, it can mean reshaping individual lifestyles, including the consumption patterns described at the start of this chapter. In a sense, those who practice ecological modernization seek to refute the oft-expressed notion that being environmentally conscious means "going back to nature" or "living off the grid." Even modest changes in production and consumption patterns, they believe, can increase environmental sustainability (York et al. 2010).

Environmental Justice

In autumn 1982, nearly 500 African Americans participated in a six-week protest against a hazardous waste landfill in North Carolina. Their protests and legal actions against the dangerous cancer-causing chemicals continued until 2002, when decontamination of the site finally began. This 20-year battle could be seen as yet another "not in my backyard" (NIMBY) event. But today, the Warren County struggle is viewed as a transformative moment in contemporary environmentalism: the beginning of the *environmental justice* movement (Bullard 1993; McGurty 2000; North Carolina Department of Environmental and Natural Resources 2008).

Environmental justice is a legal strategy based on claims that racial minorities are subjected disproportionately to environmental hazards. Some observers have heralded environmental justice as the "new civil rights of the 21st century" (Kokmen 2008:42). Since the start of the environmental justice movement, activists and scholars have discovered other environmental disparities that break along racial and social class lines. In general, poor people and people of color are much more likely than others to be victimized by the everyday consequences of our built environment, including the air pollution from expressways and incinerators.

Sociologists Paul Mohai and Robin Saha (2007) examined over 600 identified hazardous waste treatment, storage, and disposal facilities in the United States. They found that non-Whites and Latinos make up 43 percent of the people who live within one mile of these dangerous sites. Skeptics often argue that minorities move near such sites because of low housing prices. However, two recent longitudinal (long-term) research studies, done over 30- and 50-year periods, found that toxic facilities tend to be located in minority communities (Mohai et al. 2009:413).

The environmental justice movement has become globalized, for several reasons. In many nations, activists have noticed similar patterns in the location of hazardous waste sites. These groups have begun to network across international borders, to share their tactics and remedies. Their unified approach is wise, because the offending corporations are often multinational entities; influencing their actions, much less prosecuting them, is difficult. As we have noted before, the global warming debate often focuses criticism on developing nations like China and India, rather than on established industrial giants with a long history of greenhouse gas emissions (Pellow and Brehm 2013).

Sociologists, then, have emphasized both the interconnectedness of humans and the environment and the divisiveness of race and social class in their work on humans and their alteration of the environment. Scientists, too, have taken different approaches, disagreeing sharply on the likely outcomes of environmental change. When these disagreements threaten to affect government policy and economic regulations, they become highly politicized.

Environmental Issues

Around the world, people are recognizing the need to address challenges to the environment. Yet in the United States, survey respondents do not see environmental issues as the most pressing of concerns, and they often balk at proposed solutions. Unfortunately, framing environmental issues as "problems" may prevent people from seeing environmental deterioration as the by-product of both institutional practices and their own behavior. Thus, in

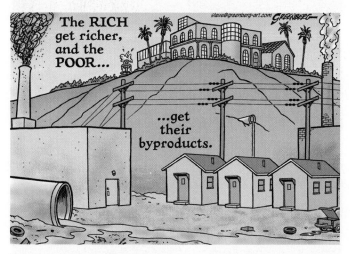

Environmental justice draws attention to the fact that the poor, along with racial and ethnic minorities, are more likely than the rich to live near refineries, waste dumps, and other environmental hazards.

a 2013 national survey, 41 percent of respondents thought the seriousness of global warming was generally exaggerated (Saad 2013b).

We will discuss the enormous challenge of global warming in this section, along with three broad areas of environmental concern. Two of them, air and water pollution, are thought to be contributors to global warming.

Air Pollution

Worldwide, more than 1 billion people are exposed to potentially health-damaging levels of air pollution. Unfortunately, in cities around the world, residents have come to accept smog and polluted air as normal. Urban air pollution is caused primarily by emissions from automobiles and secondarily by emissions from electric power plants and heavy industries. Smog not only limits visibility; it also can lead to health problems as uncomfortable as eye irritation and as deadly as lung cancer. Such problems are especially severe in developing countries.

Although people are capable of changing their behavior, they are unwilling to make such changes permanent. During the 1984 Olympics in Los Angeles, residents were asked to carpool and stagger their work hours to relieve traffic congestion and improve the quality of the air athletes would breathe. These changes resulted in a remarkable 12 percent drop in ozone levels. But when the Olympians left, people reverted to their normal behavior and the ozone levels climbed back up. Similarly, in the 2008 Olympics, China took drastic action to ensure that Beijing's high levels of air pollution did not mar the games. Construction work in the city ceased, polluting factories and power plants closed down, and roads were swept and sprayed with water several times a day. This temporary solution hardly solved China's ongoing problem, however (A. Jacobs 2010).

On an everyday basis—that is, when cities are not holding down their emissions because of global sports events—air pollution remains a serious issue. Today, half of all people live in countries where they are exposed to dangerously high levels of air pollution, either short-term or year-round. Solutions range from community efforts to clean up power plants and enforce or strengthen air quality standards to individual actions, like driving less often or using less electricity (American Lung Association 2011).

Water Pollution

Throughout the United States, dumping of waste materials by industries and local governments has polluted streams, rivers, and lakes. Consequently, many bodies of water have become unsafe for drinking, fishing, and swimming. Around the world, pollution of the oceans is an issue of growing concern. Such pollution results regularly from waste dumping and is made worse by fuel leaks from shipping and occasional oil spills. When the oil tanker Exxon *Valdez* ran aground in Prince William Sound, Alaska, in 1989, its cargo of more than 11 million gallons of crude oil spilled into the sound and washed onto the shore, contaminating 1,285 miles of shoreline. All together, about 11,000 people joined in a massive cleanup effort that cost over $2 billion. Globally, oil tanker spills occur regularly. The oil spilled from BP's Deepwater Horizon oil platform in 2010 is estimated at *sixteen times* or more that of the Exxon *Valdez* (ITOPF 2006; Shapley 2010).

Less dramatic than large-scale accidents or disasters, but more common in many parts of the world, are problems with the basic water supply. The situation is worsened by heavy, widespread pollution of surface and groundwater by towns, industries, agriculture, and mining operations. In Egypt, a typical example, agricultural and industrial waste pours into the Nile. Every year about 17,000 Egyptian children die from diarrhea and dehydration after contact with the river's polluted water. Although water conditions in North America are not as deadly, from 2000 through 2014 the western United States and Canada experienced moderate to exceptional drought and an escalating demand for water (Hengeveld 2012; National Oceanic and Atmospheric Administration 2014).

Climate Change

Climate change is an observable alteration of the global atmosphere that affects natural weather patterns over several decades or longer. Periods of climate change occurred well before humans walked the earth. Recently, climate change has included rapid *global warming.*

The term **global warming** refers to the significant rise in the earth's surface temperatures that occurs when industrial gases like carbon dioxide turn the planet's atmosphere into a virtual greenhouse. These *greenhouse gas emissions,* which also include methane, nitrous oxide, and ozone, trap heat in the lower atmosphere. Even one additional degree of warmth in the globe's average surface temperature can increase the likelihood of wildfires, shrinkage of rivers and lakes, expansion of deserts, and torrential downpours, including typhoons and hurricanes. Greenhouse gas emissions are highest per capita in industrialized nations like the United States, Russia, and Japan, where energy consumption in the form of coal and oil is high. Because of their

large populations and their reliance on these fossil fuels, just three nations—China, the United States, and India—account for half of all greenhouse gas emissions (Myers and Kulish 2013).

"The End of Snow?" asked a newspaper headline during the 2014 Winter Olympics. Although snow will not disappear from the earth, climatologists predict that finding suitable sites for the snow-dependent international competition will become increasingly difficult. Of the 19 cities that have hosted the Winter Olympics in the past, as few as 10 might be cold enough to do so in 2050, and just 6 in 2100. For people digging out from the record snowfalls of 2013–2014, that prediction might have seemed laughable, but the global trend is toward reduced snowfall. Decline in the snowpack is now jeopardizing half of all ski resorts in the northeastern United States; if it continues, they may not be viable 30 years from now. Similar trends are threatening ski resorts in the western United States. More important, snowpack is not just for skiers; the spring runoff from melting snow is critical to maintaining water supplies (Fox 2014).

Although scientific concern over global warming has heated up, climate change remains low on policymakers' list of concerns. The problem seems abstract, and in many countries, officials think that the real impact of any action they may take depends on decisive action by other nations. The Kyoto Protocol (1997) was intended to reduce global emissions of heat-trapped gases, which can contribute to global warming and climate change. To date, 191 countries are party to the accord; the United States and Canada are the only major nations that have failed to ratify it. Opponents of the protocol argue that doing so would place the nation at

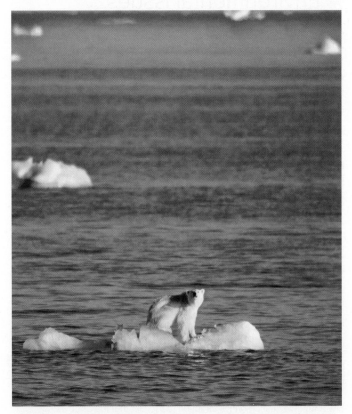

Images like this one have been combined with scientific data to draw attention to global warming.

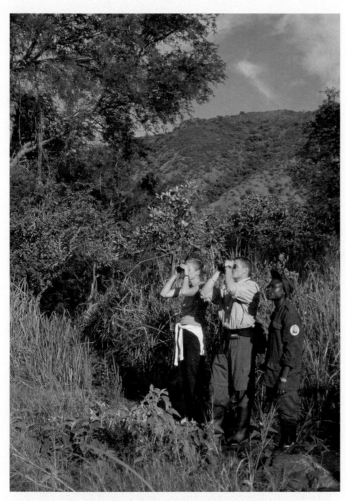

Vacation in an unspoiled paradise! Increasingly, people from developed countries are turning to ecotourism as an environmentally friendly way to see the world. The new trend bridges the interests of environmentalists and businesspeople, especially in developing countries. These birdwatchers, accompanied by a local guide, are vacationing in Uganda.

nations, which have contributed disproportionately to the problem. We want our hamburgers, but we decry the destruction of the rain forests to create grazing land for cattle. We want inexpensive clothes and toys, but we condemn developing countries for depending on coal-fired power plants. Coal-fired power generation is expected to increase from 2 to 4 percent a year for decades to come, tripling between 2010 and 2050 and surpassing oil as the world's primary energy source (L. Smith 2011).

What are the causes of this global environmental crisis? Some observers, such as Paul Ehrlich and Anne Ehrlich, see the pressure of world population growth as the central factor in environmental deterioration. They argue that population control is essential in preventing widespread starvation and environmental decay.

Barry Commoner, a biologist, counters that the primary cause of environmental ills is the increasing use of technological innovations that are destructive to the environment—among them plastics, detergents, synthetic fibers, pesticides, herbicides, and chemical fertilizers. Conflict theorists see the despoliation of the environment through the lens of world systems analysis. And interactionists stress efforts by informed individuals and groups to reduce their carbon footprint—that is, their daily or even lifetime production of greenhouse gases—through careful selection of the goods they consume (Carbon Trust 2012; Commoner 1990, 2007; Ehrlich and Ellison 2002).

 use your **sociological imagination**

As you think about all the issues facing our society, how often do you consider global warming? If often, identify your concerns and outline some possible solutions. If not often, which issues strike you as more important than others? Explain your ranking.

The Impact of Globalization

Globalization can be both good and bad for the environment. On the negative side, it can create a race to the bottom, as polluting companies relocate to countries with less stringent environmental standards. Similarly, globalization allows multinationals to reap the resources of developing countries for short-term profit. From Mexico to China, the industrialization that often accompanies globalization has increased pollution of all types.

Yet globalization can have a positive impact, as well. As barriers to the international movement of goods, services, and people fall, multinational corporations have an incentive to carefully consider the cost of natural resources. Overusing or wasting resources makes little sense, especially when they are in danger of depletion (Gallagher 2009; Kwong 2005).

One reflection of the interplay between globalization and the environment is the emergence of **environmental refugees,** people who have been displaced by rising seas, destructive storms, expanding deserts, water shortages, and high levels of toxic pollutants. Europe in particular is beginning to see an influx of such immigrants from developing nations. Viewed through the lens of world systems analysis, periphery countries may become

a disadvantage in the global marketplace. The United States has attempted to address global warming and climate change in other ways, including bilateral agreements with China to reduce the two nations' emissions. However, these efforts regularly bog down amidst conflict over other political and economic issues.

In writing about the global environment, activists often assert, "We're all in this together." Though we are all in this together, the reality is that globally, the most vulnerable countries tend to be the poorest. Developing nations are more likely than others to have economies that are built on limited resources or on a small number of crops that are vulnerable to drought, flood, and fluctuations in worldwide demand (Nordhaus and Shellenberger 2007; Revkin 2007).

We can view global warming from the point of view of world systems analysis. Historically, core nations have been the major emitters of greenhouse gases. Today, however, manufacturing has moved to semi-periphery and periphery nations, where greenhouse gas emissions are escalating. Ironically, many of the forces that are now calling for a reduction in the human activity that contributes to global warming are located in core overburdened by environmental problems, precipitating either migrations to industrial nations or conflicts that cause mass displacements of their populations. Even within the United States, environmental change prompts migrations. In the western United States, drought has displaced people whose livelihood once centered on freshwater fishing and irrigated crops. And in Alaska, rising waters caused by ice melt are displacing many of the Native peoples who live in coastal regions and along waterways (Susan F. Martin 2013; National Public Radio 2013).

Against these potentially negative effects of globalization we must note the potential for new jobs in what are called green industries. Installing solar panels, weatherizing homes, brewing biofuels, building hybrid cars, growing organic foods, manufacturing organic garments, and erecting giant wind turbines are all classified as *green-collar jobs.* However, skeptics question how many such jobs will be created, and to what degree they will offset job losses in pollution-prone industries like oil, gas, and coal mining (S. Greenhouse 2008b; R. Pinderhughes 2008).

social policy and the Environment |
Environmentalism

On April 22, 1970, in a dramatic manifestation of growing grassroots concern over preservation of the environment, an estimated 25 million people turned out to observe the nation's first Earth Day. Two thousand communities held planned celebrations, and more than 2,000 colleges and 10,000 schools hosted environmental teach-ins. In many parts of the United States, citizens marched on behalf of specific environmental causes. That same year, the activism of these early environmentalists convinced Congress to establish the Environmental Protection Agency. The Clean Air, Clean Water, and Endangered Species acts soon followed (Brulle and Jenkins 2008).

Looking at the Issue

Sociologist Manuel Castells (2010a:72) has declared environmentalism "the most comprehensive, influential movement of our time." Several social trends helped to mobilize the environmental movement. First, the activist subculture of the 1960s and early 1970s encouraged people, especially young people, to engage in direct action regarding social issues. Second, the dissemination of scientific knowledge about serious environmental problems like oil spills and air pollution alarmed many Americans. And third, the growing popularity of outdoor recreation increased the number of people who were concerned about the environment. In this climate of broad-based interest in environmental issues, many organizations that had once focused narrowly on the conservation of natural resources evolved into full-fledged environmental groups (Dunlap and Mertig 1991).

Today, Earth Day has been enshrined on the calendars of city councils, zoos, and museums worldwide. Environmental issues have also moved up the agenda of mainstream political parties. Increasingly, efforts to publicize environmental concerns and create support for action have moved to the Internet. Although times have changed, two beliefs continue to galvanize environmentalists: the environment is in dire need of protection, and the government must take strong action in response. Although environmentalists recognize that they

must "think locally" and monitor their own carbon footprints, they also see preservation of the environment as a global challenge. They note that while significant progress has been made toward environmental protection, government regulation of the environment has been curtailed in some ways (Brulle and Jenkins 2008; Rootes 2007; Sieber et al. 2006).

The general public has a mixed reaction to environmental issues. On the one hand, many people question the scientific arguments behind the theory of climate change. On the other, many recognize that there is a trade-off between cheap energy and preserving the environment (Figure 56-2). The public seems evenly divided on the issue.

In times of economic stress, people tend to put off or ignore environmental concerns. Thus, there seems to be little public enthusiasm for the positive, forward-looking approach of ecological modernization. Not surprisingly, the political debate over the environmental movement grew more partisan between 2000 and 2012: Democrats became more sympathetic and Republicans more antagonistic (Dunlap 2010).

Today's college students show less interest in the environment than students of past decades. In 2012, 26.5 percent of first-year college students in the United States wanted to clean up the environment—down from 45.9 percent in 1972. And as Figure 56-3 shows, U.S. high school students' interest in the issue does not compare favorably with that of teens in other major countries. In a 30-nation comparative study, 15-year-olds in the United States tied those in another country for 22nd place in their knowledge of environmental issues (Pryor et al. 2007, 2013).

Applying Sociology

Even those who support environmentalists' goals are troubled by the fact that nationwide, the most powerful environmental organizations are predominantly White, male-dominated, and affluent. One study notes that while women are overrepresented in the environmental movement (particularly in grassroots

—Continued

FIGURE 56-2 The Environment versus Energy Production

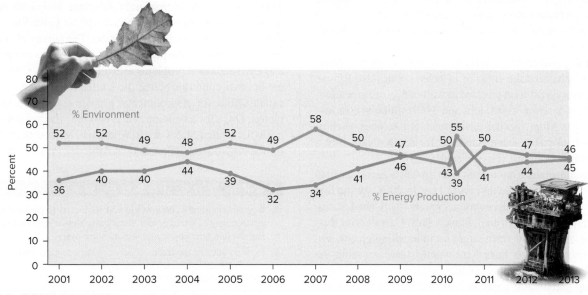

Source: Gallup Poll 2013; J. Jones 2013.

FIGURE 56-3 Are U.S. Teens Green Enough?

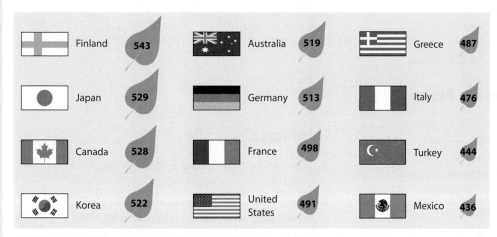

Finland	543	Australia	519	Greece	487
Japan	529	Germany	513	Italy	476
Canada	528	France	498	Turkey	444
Korea	522	United States	491	Mexico	436

Note: Mean score for 15-year-old students' knowledge of environmental issues such as climate change and biodiversity. Mean score was 543.
Source: Organisation for Economic Co-Operation and Development 2009b.

found that an average Black household with an income of $50,000 to $60,000 a year coped with higher levels of pollution than an average White household with an income of less than $10,000 a year.

Viewed from a conflict perspective, this disproportionate exposure of the poor and minorities to environmental pollutants can act as a disincentive for others to take action. As Andrew Szasz (2007) noted in his book *Shopping Our Way to Safety* (see the chapter-opening excerpt), more affluent households can try to avoid exposing themselves and their children to health hazards by drinking bottled spring water, installing water and air filters in their homes, and buying organic food. Unfortunately, these individual actions have the unintended consequence of weakening collective environmental efforts.

environmental groups), men continue to hold most of the high-profile upper-management positions in mainstream national organizations. The perceived middle-class orientation of the movement is especially relevant given the class, racial, and ethnic factors associated with environmental hazards. As we saw earlier in the context of environmental justice, low-income communities and areas with significant minority populations are more likely than affluent White communities to be located near waste sites. Sociologists Liam Downey and Brian Hawkins (2008)

Another concern, from the conflict perspective, is the fact that many environmental movements either do not include the poor and minorities or do not address their concerns. Although environmental justice issues have been well publicized, environmentalists do not always consider the implications of their demands for excluded groups (Rudel et al. 2011).

—*Continued*

Initiating Policy

The global economic downturn that began in 2008 has been a mixed blessing for environmentalists. Currently, public opinion in the United States favors economic growth over environmental protection. Yet at the same time, the recent recession has sharply reduced the use of fossil fuels such as coal and oil. Moreover, the federal government's efforts to stimulate economic activity have emphasized the creation of green-collar jobs. By one estimate, every $1 billion invested in well-conceived green programs generates over 30,000 jobs and $450 million in cost savings per year. More specific environmental measures, such as raising federal gas mileage standards for automobiles, face a tough battle in Congress (Houser et al. 2009).

Environmentalism has moved onto a much bigger stage than the one it occupied on the first Earth Day. In 2008, for the first time, the leaders of the G8 economic powers (the United States, Japan, Germany, Great Britain, France, Italy, Canada, and Russia) set an explicit long-term target for eliminating greenhouse gases, which scientists have long warned were warming the planet. "Long-term" may be an understatement: their target date for cutting greenhouse gases in half is 2050. Environmentalists sharply criticized the G8's failure to set specific goals for the nearer term. The challenge is significant, given the fact that G8 emissions *increased* 35 percent over the preceding 15 years (Longhofer and Schofer 2010; Stolberg 2008).

Conventional wisdom holds that concern for environmental quality is limited to wealthy industrialized nations. However, the results of a 47-nation survey show that around the world, people are increasingly reluctant to ignore environmental issues. Concern has risen sharply in Latin America and Europe, as well as in Japan and India. The survey also noted a general increase in the percentage of people who cite pollution and environmental problems as a top global threat. Many people in other countries blame the United States, and to a lesser extent China, for environmental problems, and look to Washington, D.C., for a solution. Time will tell whether policymakers in the United States or elsewhere will address their concern for the environment (Pew Global Attitudes Project 2007).

TAKE THE ISSUE WITH YOU

1. In your community, how would you act locally to preserve the environment? Describe your community's environmental problems and explain how you would seek to solve them.

2. How do you see the trade-off between the economy and the environment? Which is more important? Is it possible to improve both at the same time? Explain.

3. Thinking globally about the environment, list what you consider the most pressing priorities. How important are world hunger and economic justice compared to global warming, clean air and water, and economic development? Are some of your priorities related? In what way?

MODULE 56 | Recap and Review

Summary

The **human ecology** perspective suggests that the environment serves three basic functions: it provides essential resources, serves as a waste repository, and houses our species.

1. Conflict theorists charge that the most serious threat to the environment comes from Western industrialized nations.

2. **Environmental justice** addresses the disproportionate subjection of minorities to environmental hazards.

3. Four broad areas of environmental concern include air and water pollution, global warming, and globalization. Although globalization can contribute to environmental woes, it can also have beneficial effects.

4. Environmentalism is a social movement that is dominated by wealthy White people from industrialized countries. Increasingly, however, people of all races, ethnicities, social classes, and nationalities are becoming concerned about global warming and the threat it poses to our planet's health.

Thinking Critically

1. How are the physical and human environments connected in your neighborhood or community?

2. Which issue is more significant in your local community, air or water pollution? Why?

Key Terms

Climate change

Ecological modernization

Environmental justice

Environmental refugee

Global warming

Human ecology

Mastering This Chapter

taking sociology with you

1 Do some research on HIV/AIDS in your city or state. Now look up the corresponding morbidity and mortality rates. How do those rates compare to the rates in other cities or states? What might account for any differences in the rates from one place to another?

2 Visit the emergency room of your local hospital and observe what is going on in the waiting room. How crowded is the waiting room? How many people in the room appear to be severely ill or injured? How many do not seem to have an emergency? What else can you observe about the people who are gathered there, and how might that help to explain their presence?

3 Do an Internet search to locate the hazardous waste sites nearest your school or home. How many of them have been cleaned up, and at what cost? Who paid that cost? How many of these sites are still a problem?

key terms

Birthrate The number of live births per 1,000 population in a given year. Also known as the *crude birthrate*.

Brain drain The immigration to the United States and other industrialized nations of skilled workers, professionals, and technicians who are desperately needed in their home countries.

Census An enumeration, or counting, of a population.

Climate change An observable alteration of the global atmosphere that affects natural weather patterns over several decades or longer.

Curanderismo Latino folk medicine, a form of holistic health care and healing.

Death rate The number of deaths per 1,000 population in a given year. Also known as the *crude death rate*.

Demographic transition A term used to describe the change from high birthrates and death rates to low birthrates and death rates.

Demography The scientific study of population.

Ecological modernization The alignment of environmentally favorable practices with economic self-interest through constant adaptation and restructuring.

Environmental justice A legal strategy based on claims that racial minorities are subjected disproportionately to environmental hazards.

Environmental refugee A person who has been displaced by rising seas, destructive storms, expanding deserts, water shortages, or high levels of toxic pollutants.

Fertility The level of reproduction in a society.

Global warming A significant rise in the earth's surface temperatures that occurs when industrial gases like carbon dioxide turn the planet's atmosphere into a virtual greenhouse.

Growth rate The difference between births and deaths, plus the difference between immigrants and emigrants, per 1,000 population.

Health As defined by the World Health Organization, a state of complete physical, mental, and social well-being, and not merely the absence of disease and infirmity.

Holistic medicine Therapies in which the health care practitioner considers the person's physical, mental, emotional, and spiritual characteristics.

Human ecology An area of study that is concerned with the interrelationships between people and their environment.

Infant mortality rate The number of deaths of infants under 1 year old per 1,000 live births in a given year.

Labeling theory An approach to deviance that attempts to explain why certain people are viewed as deviants while others engaged in the same behavior are not.

Life expectancy The median number of years a person can be expected to live under current mortality conditions.

McDonaldization The process by which the principles of bureaucratization have increasingly shaped organizations worldwide.

Medical model An approach in which medical experts define illness or disease, determine and control the course of treatment, and even affect patients' view of themselves.

Mental illness A disorder of the brain that disrupts a person's thinking, feeling, and ability to interact with others.

Migration The relatively permanent movement of people, with the purpose of changing their place of residence.

Morbidity rate The rate of disease in a given population.

Mortality rate The rate of death in a given population.

Population pyramid A special type of bar chart that shows the distribution of a population by gender and age.

Sick role Societal expectations about the attitudes and behavior of a person viewed as being ill.

Social epidemiology The study of the distribution of disease, impairment, and general health status across a population.

Stigma A label used to devalue members of certain social groups.

Total fertility rate (TFR) The average number of children born alive to any woman, assuming that she conforms to current fertility rates.

Vital statistics Records of births, deaths, marriages, and divorces gathered through a registration system maintained by governmental units.

Zero population growth (ZPG) The state of a population in which the number of births plus immigrants equals the number of deaths plus emigrants.

Read each question carefully and then select the best answer.

1. Which sociologist developed the concept of the sick role?
   a. Émile Durkheim
   b. Talcott Parsons
   c. C. Wright Mills
   d. Erving Goffman

2. Regarding health care inequities, the conflict perspective would note that
   a. physicians serve as gatekeepers for the sick role, either verifying a patient's condition as "illness" or designating the patient as "recovered."
   b. patients play an active role in health care by failing to follow a physician's advice.
   c. emigration out of the Third World by physicians is yet another way that the world's core industrialized nations enhance their quality of life at the expense of developing countries.
   d. the designation "healthy" or "ill" generally involves social definition by others.

3. Which one of the following nations has the lowest infant mortality rate?
   a. the United States
   b. Mozambique
   c. Canada
   d. Japan

4. Compared with Whites, Blacks have higher death rates from
   a. heart disease.
   b. diabetes.
   c. cancer.
   d. all of the above.

5. Which theorist notes that capitalist societies, such as the United States, care more about maximizing profits than they do about the health and safety of industrial workers?
   a. Thomas Szasz
   b. Talcott Parsons
   c. Erving Goffman
   d. Karl Marx

6. Which program is essentially a compulsory health insurance plan for the elderly?
   a. Medicare
   b. Medicaid
   c. Blue Cross
   d. Healthpac

7. Which of the following is a criticism of the sick role?
   a. Patients' judgments regarding their own state of health may be related to their gender, age, social class, and ethnic group.
   b. The sick role may be more applicable to people experiencing short-term illnesses than to those with recurring long-term illnesses.
   c. Even such simple factors as whether a person is employed or not seem to affect the person's willingness to assume the sick role.
   d. all of the above

8. The final stage in demographic transition is marked by
   a. high birthrates and high death rates.
   b. high birthrates and low death rates.
   c. low birthrates and high death rates.
   d. low birthrates and low death rates.

9. The most recent period of high fertility in the United States, which began after the end of World War II, has often been referred to as the
   a. baby bust.
   b. baby boom.
   c. population bomb.
   d. age of Aquarius.

10. Conflict theorists would contend that blaming developing countries for the world's environmental deterioration contains an element of
    a. ethnocentrism.
    b. xenocentrism.
    c. separatism.
    d. goal displacement.

11. A _____ _____ studies the effects of social class, race and ethnicity, gender, and age on the distribution of disease, impairment, and general health across a population.

12. From a(n) _____ perspective, "being sick" must be controlled so as to ensure that not too many people are released from their societal responsibilities at any one time.

13. The immigration to the United States and other industrialized nations of skilled workers, professionals, and technicians who are desperately needed by their home countries is known as the _____ _____.

14. Traditionally, the relationship between doctors and nurses has paralleled _____ dominance of the larger society.

15. Sociologists find it useful to consider _____ rates because they reveal that a specific disease occurs more frequently among one segment of a population compared with another.

16. Drawing on several components, including size, composition, and territorial distribution, _____ is the scientific study of population.

17. _____ _____ are records of births, deaths, marriages, and divorces that are gathered through a registration system maintained by governmental units.

18. The biologist _____ _____ blames environmental degradation primarily on technological innovations such as plastics and pesticides.

19. Regarding environmental problems, four broad areas of concern stand out: _____ pollution, _____ pollution, _____ _____, and _____.

20. _____ _____ is a legal strategy based on claims that racial minorities are subjected disproportionately to environmental hazards.

18

Social Movements and Social Change in the Global Community

Social change is global, its effects both obvious and subtle. In Fang, Thailand, novice Buddhist monks amuse themselves by playing computer games. Computers and the Internet also promote the Dharma—the Buddha's teachings—in ways unimaginable just a decade ago.

DIGITAL SHOCK

Has the pace of change, whether social or technological, ever made you feel anxious?

Karl Albrecht thinks that technology is changing so rapidly, we may not be able to control its social effects.

66 Big revolutions usually start with big hopes, big dreams, big visions, and big promises. Of all the biggest revolutions in our history—from agriculture and industrialization to the automobile and television—the Internet and all things digital have raised heart rates and hormone levels more than perhaps any other.

The "third wave," as futurist Alvin Toffler (1980) christened it, became a tidal wave with the arrival of the microchip and digital information technology. . . . Today, about twenty years into the revolution, perhaps we need to waken from our infatuated trance with the electronic experience and see what the revolution has done for, with, and to us. . . .

Looking back, . . . it seems that some of the grandest fantasies promoted by the early self-nominated philosophers of the digital age have not really caught fire, or have misfired, or even backfired. We didn't get some of what we were promised, and some of what we got we hadn't expected. . . .

The Internet Will Create a "New Economy"

In the red-hot Nineties, that phrase became the defining mantra of the Internet priesthood. A wider, flatter, democratized marketplace would mean that every entrepreneur with a dream and a computer might strike it rich. Old-economy companies would go the way of the dinosaur. It was "e-business or out of business."

Sober Reality: More fortunes have been lost on the Internet than made.

Probably 70% or more of the Internet content has been built out by unpaid volunteer labor. The vast online marketplace is now controlled by just a handful of large monopoly firms: Google, Amazon, Facebook, eBay, Twitter, Yahoo, YouTube, LinkedIn, Skype, and a few others. Add a dozen or so secondary players, some rising and some declining,

The human impact of digital information technologies—both costs and benefits—is likely to become one of the dominant themes in social and political discourse over the next decade.

and you have about 80% of the online information structure concentrated in the hands of a few mega-firms. That's a far greater degree of monopolization than has ever existed in "real space." With mergers and acquisitions, plus occasional extinctions, the "new economy" of the Internet is looking increasingly like the "old economy," only more so. . . .

Updated Prediction: Entrepreneurs with ideas and energy will still get their turns at bat, but the days of "garage to global" are mostly over. Small businesses will increasingly benefit from cheap and accessible cloud-based software services. . . .

Toffler (1970) gave us the term *future shock,* referring to the sense of anxiety that people are feeling with the pace of change, the increasing impermanence of their environments, and the loss of familiar social and psychological landmarks. Now, we would update his terminology to *digital shock.*

Those whom I'd characterize as digital zealots, who can't or won't recognize a dark side to the revolution, will probably view this discussion as unfairly critical, pessimistic, or ungrateful. Those who are concerned about long-term effects, such as the impact of social media on child development and maturity, might feel that their concerns are validated.

The larger purpose for this discussion, however, is to advocate an open-minded and balanced view of digital information technology. I believe we can value and appreciate the many benefits it has brought, and will bring, while also understanding its side effects, unanticipated consequences, and potentially destructive impacts. Neither zealots nor Luddites can give us a balanced perspective. That will take thoughtful analysis and informed conversations about its many implications. . . .

The human impact of digital information technologies—both costs and benefits—is likely to become one of the dominant themes in social and political discourse over the next decade. By the time we fully realize what the pervasive use of these technologies has done to us, it will be too late to change their course. Either we'll be living with a default future, one that simply arrives one day at a time, or we'll have confronted the major issues and questions head-on and shaped the technological future we want. 99

(K. Albrecht 2014:22–23, 28)

In this excerpt from "The Information Revolution's Broken Promises," futurist Albrecht takes a critical look at the effects of the much-trumpeted digital revolution. He finds that the Internet has not created the new economy that many people predicted it would. It has not leveled the playing field for new entrepreneurs, democratizing the marketplace in the process. In fact, as his article makes clear, the digital revolution has failed to deliver many of the benefits we were told to expect from it. Instead, it has created unforeseen social change, not all of it good. We have grappled with some of that change elsewhere in this book.

Social change often follows the introduction of a new technology, in this case the computer. *Social change* has been defined as significant alteration over time in behavior patterns and culture (W. Moore 1967). But what constitutes a "significant" alteration? Certainly the dramatic rise in formal education in the last century represents a change that has had profound social consequences. Other social changes that have had long-term and important consequences include the emergence of slavery as a system of stratification, the Industrial Revolution, and the increased participation of women in the paid labor forces of the United States and Europe.

How does social change happen? Is the process unpredictable, or can we make certain generalizations about it? Has globalization contributed to social change? In these modules we examine the process of social change, with special emphasis on the impact of globalization. We begin with collective behavior, from rumors, fads, and fashions to social movements behavior that can bring about genuine social change. We will see that recent advances in communications technology have allowed some social movements to circle the world. Next, we examine three theories of social change: the evolutionary, functionalist, and conflict perspectives. Then we discuss vested interests, which often attempt to block changes they see as threatening. And we recognize the influence of globalization in spreading social change around the world, noting the rapid social change that has occurred over a matter of decades in the Middle Eastern city-state of Dubai. Finally, we turn to the unanticipated social change that occurs when innovations such as new technologies sweep through society. We close with a Social Policy section on a controversial aspect of global social change, the creation of *transnationals*—immigrants with an allegiance to more than one nation.

MODULE 57 | Collective Behavior

Practically all behavior can be thought of as *collective behavior*. For sociologists, however, the term has a more distinct meaning. According to Neil Smelser (1981:431), a sociologist who specializes in this field of study, **collective behavior** is the "relatively spontaneous and unstructured behavior of a group of people who are reacting to a common influence in an ambiguous situation." Rumors are a form of collective behavior, as is public opinion—people's reactions to shared events such as wars and elections. In this module we will examine three sociological theories of collective behavior, as well as 10 different forms of collective behavior, from fads and fashions to social movements.

Theories of Collective Behavior

In 1979, 11 rock fans died of suffocation after a crowd outside Cincinnati's Riverfront Stadium pushed to gain entrance to a concert by The Who. In 2003, 100 people died after a pyrotechnics display by Great White ignited a fire at a nightclub in West Warwick, Rhode Island. Many had watched excitedly as flames engulfed the bandstand, thinking they were part of the act. And in 2008, a healthy 34-year-old security guard was crushed to death—still standing but unable to breathe—as excited shoppers at a Walmart store in Long Island, New York, surged through the doors in quest of Black Friday bargains.

Like these incidents, collective behavior is usually unstructured and spontaneous. Its fluidity makes it more difficult for sociologists to generalize about people's behavior in such situations. Nevertheless, sociologists have developed various theoretical perspectives that can help us to study—and deal with in a constructive manner—crowds, riots, fads, and other types of collective behavior.

Emergent-Norm Perspective

Early writings on collective behavior implied that crowds are basically ungovernable. However, that is not always the case. In many situations, crowds are effectively governed by norms and procedures, including queuing, or waiting in line. We routinely

Because collective behavior is often unstructured and spontaneous, it can prove deadly. So strong was the surge of shoppers when this Walmart store opened on the day after Thanksgiving, a security guard was asphyxiated.

encounter queues when we await service in a fast-food restaurant or bank, or when we enter or exit a movie theater or football stadium. Normally, physical barriers, such as guardrails and checkout counters, help to regulate queuing. When massive crowds are involved, ushers or security personnel may be present to assist in the orderly movement of the crowd. Nevertheless, there are times when such measures prove inadequate, as the examples just given and the one that follows demonstrate.

In December 1991, more than 5,000 people showed up early for a heavily promoted celebrity basketball game at the City College gymnasium in New York City. Seeing the size of the crowd, many of them must have realized that they could not all fit into the gym, which would accommodate only 2,730 people. As frustrated patrons waited to see which of them would be allowed in, restlessness and discontent swept through the crowd, and sporadic fights broke out.

When the doors to the gym finally opened, only 50 people at a time were allowed to enter. They then had to descend two flights of stairs and enter the gym through a single unlocked entrance—a maddeningly slow process in the overcrowded passageway. Finally, well past the game's starting time and with the arena more than full, the doors to the gym were closed. As rumors spread outside the building that the game was beginning, more than 1,000 additional fans poured through the building's entrance and headed for the stairs. Trapped between the locked gymnasium doors and those pushing down the stairs behind them, 9 young men and women died and 29 were injured through the sheer pressure of bodies pressing against walls and doors (Mollen 1992).

Sociologists Ralph Turner and Lewis Killian (1987) have offered a view of collective behavior that is helpful in assessing a tragic event like this. It begins with the assumption that a large crowd, such as a group of rock or soccer fans, is governed by expectations of proper behavior just as much as four people playing doubles tennis. But during an episode of collective behavior, a definition of what behavior is appropriate or not emerges from the crowd. Turner and Killian call this view the **emergent-norm perspective.** Like other social norms, the emergent norm reflects shared convictions held by members of the group and is enforced through sanctions. The new norm of proper behavior may arise in what seems at first to be an ambiguous situation. There is latitude for a wide range of acts within a general framework established by the emergent norm (for a critique of this perspective, see McPhail 1991).

Using the emergent-norm perspective, we can see that fans outside the charity basketball game at City College found themselves in an ambiguous situation. Normal procedures of crowd control, such as orderly queues, were rapidly dissolving. Simultaneously, a new norm was emerging: it is acceptable to push forward, even if the people in front protest. Some members of the crowd—especially those with valid tickets—may have felt that their push forward was justified as a way of ensuring that they would get to see the game. Others pushed forward simply to relieve the physical pressure of those pushing behind them. Even individuals who rejected the emergent norm may have felt afraid to oppose it, fearing ridicule or injury. Thus, conforming behavior, which we usually associate with highly structured situations, was evident in this rather chaotic crowd, as it had been at the concerts by The Who and Great White and at Walmart's Black Friday sale. However, it would be misleading to assume that these fans acted simply as a united, collective unit in creating a dangerous situation.

Value-Added Perspective

Neil Smelser (1962) proposed a different sociological explanation for collective behavior. He used the **value-added model** to explain how broad social conditions are transformed in a definite pattern into some form of collective behavior. This model outlines six important determinants of collective behavior: structural conduciveness, structural strain, a generalized belief, a precipitating factor, mobilization for action, and the exercise of social control.

In Smelser's view, certain elements must be present for an incident of collective behavior to take place. He used the term *structural conduciveness* to indicate that the organization of society can facilitate the emergence of conflicting interests. Structural conduciveness was evident in the former East Germany in 1989, just a year before the collapse of the ruling Communist Party and the reunification of Germany. The government of East Germany was extremely unpopular, and there was growing freedom to publicly express and be exposed to new and challenging viewpoints. Such structural conduciveness makes collective behavior possible, though not inevitable.

The second determinant of collective behavior, *structural strain*, occurs when the conduciveness of the social structure to potential conflict gives way to a perception that conflicting interests do, in fact, exist. The intense desire of many East Germans to travel to or emigrate to western European countries placed great strain on the social control exercised by the Communist Party. Such structural strain contributes to what Smelser calls a *generalized belief*—a shared view of reality that redefines social action and serves to guide behavior. The overthrow of communist rule in East Germany and other Soviet-bloc nations occurred in part as a result of a generalized belief that the communist regimes were oppressive and that popular resistance *could* lead to social change.

Smelser suggests that a specific event or incident, known as a *precipitating factor,* triggers collective behavior. The event may grow out of the social structure, but whatever its origins, it contributes to the strains and beliefs shared by a group or community. For example, studies of race riots have found that interracial fights or arrests and searches of minority individuals by police officers often precede disturbances. The 1992 riots in South Central Los Angeles, which claimed 58 lives, were sparked by the acquittal of four White police officers charged after the videotaped beating of Rodney King, a Black construction worker.

According to Smelser, the four determinants just identified are necessary for collective behavior to occur. In addition to these factors, the group must be *mobilized for action.* An extended thundershower or severe snowstorm may preclude such mobilization. People are more likely to come together on weekends than on weekdays, and in the evening rather than during the day.

The *manner in which social control is exercised*—both formally and informally—can be significant in determining whether the preceding factors will end in collective behavior. Stated simply, social control may prevent, delay, or interrupt a collective outburst. In some instances, those using social control may be guilty of misjudgments that intensify the severity of an outbreak. Many observers believe that the Los Angeles police did not respond fast enough when the rioting began in 1992, which allowed the level of violence to escalate.

Sociologists have questioned the validity of both the emergent-norm and value-added perspectives because of their imprecise definitions and the difficulty of testing them empirically. Some have criticized the emergent-norm perspective for being too vague in defining what constitutes a norm; others have challenged the value-added model for lack of specificity in defining generalized belief and structural strain. Of the two theories, the emergent-norm perspective appears to offer a more useful explanation of society-wide episodes of collective behavior, such as crazes, than the value-added approach (M. Brown and Goldin 1973; Quarantelli and Hundley 1975; K. Tierney 1980).

Smelser's value-added model, however, represents an advance over earlier theories that treated crowd behavior as being dominated by irrational, extreme impulses. The value-added approach firmly relates episodes of collective behavior to the overall social structure of a society (G. Marx 2012; for a critique, see McPhail 1991, 1994).

Assembling Perspective

A series of football victory celebrations at the University of Texas that had spilled over into the main streets of Austin came under the scrutiny of sociologists (Snow et al. 1981). Some participants had actively tried to recruit passersby for the celebrations by thrusting out open palms "to get five," or by yelling at drivers to honk their horns. In fact, encouraging further assembling became a preoccupation of the celebrators. Whenever passersby were absent, participants were relatively quiet. As we have seen, a key determinant of collective behavior is mobilization for action. How do people come together to undertake collective action?

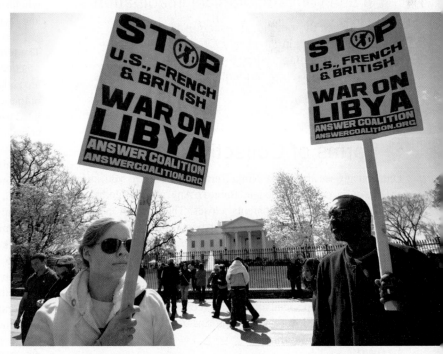

Antiwar protesters rally against their nation's participation in the military intervention in Libya in 2011. According to the assembling perspective, nonperiodic assemblies like this one are relatively spontaneous, loosely organized reactions to galvanizing events.

Clark McPhail, perhaps the most prolific researcher of collective behavior in the past four decades, sees people and organizations consciously responding to one another's actions. Building on the interactionist approach, McPhail and Miller (1973) introduced the concept of the assembling process. In their **assembling perspective,** they sought to examine how and why people move from different points in space to a common location. Before the advent of new technologies, the process of assembling for collective action was slower and more deliberate than it is today, but McPhail's approach still applies.

A basic distinction has been made between two types of assemblies. **Periodic assemblies** include recurring, relatively routine gatherings of people such as work groups, college classes, and season-ticket holders in an athletic series. These assemblies are characterized by advance scheduling and recurring attendance of the majority of participants. For example, members of an introductory sociology class may gather for lectures every Monday, Wednesday, and Friday morning at 10 a.m. In contrast, **nonperiodic assemblies** include demonstrations, parades, and gatherings at the scene of fires, accidents, and arrests. Such assemblies, which often result from word-of-mouth information, are generally less formal than periodic assemblies. One example would be an organized rally held at Gallaudet University in 1988 to back a deaf person for president of the school for deaf students (McPhail 2006, 2008; D. L. Miller 2014).

These three approaches to collective behavior give us deeper insight into relatively spontaneous and unstructured situations. Although episodes of collective behavior may seem irrational to outsiders, norms emerge among the participants, and organized efforts are made to assemble at a certain time and place.

 use your **sociological imagination**

Think about the practice of assembling to attend class or to study in the library. On a daily basis, how is this practice affected by the direct or indirect actions of your fellow students, co-workers, relatives, or teammates?

Forms of Collective Behavior

Did you go see the latest Ninja Turtles movie? Do you know anyone who collected Beanie Babies? Any grunge clothes or tube tops lurking in your parents' closet? These are all fads and fashions that depend on collective behavior. Using the emergent-norm, value-added, and assembling perspectives along with other aspects of sociological study, sociologists have investigated many forms of collective behavior—not only fads and fashions but also crowds, disaster behavior, panics and crazes, rumors, public opinion, and social movements (covered in Module 58). In this section we will study all these forms of collective behavior.

Crowds

A **crowd** is a temporary gathering of people in close proximity who share a common focus or interest. Spectators at a baseball game, participants at a pep rally, and rioters are all examples of a crowd. Sociologists have been interested in the characteristics that are common to crowds. Of course, it can be difficult to generalize, since the nature of crowds varies dramatically. Think about how hostages on a hijacked airplane might feel, as opposed to participants in a religious revival.

Like other forms of collective behavior, crowds are not totally lacking in structure. Even during riots, participants are governed by identifiable social norms and exhibit definite patterns of behavior. In fact, crowds are no more emotional, suggestible, or destructive than any other social gathering. Sociologists Richard Berk and Howard Aldrich (1972) analyzed patterns of vandalism in 15 cities in the United States during the riots of the 1960s. They found that the stores of merchants who were perceived as exploitative were more likely to be attacked, while private homes and public agencies with positive reputations were more likely to be spared. Apparently, looters had reached a collective agreement as to what constituted a "proper" or "improper" target for destruction. Today, this type of information can be shared instantly via social media.

The emergent-norm perspective suggests that during urban rioting, a new social norm that basically condones looting is accepted, at least temporarily. The norms of respect for private property—as well as norms involving obedience to the law—are replaced by a concept of all goods being community property. All desirable items, including those behind locked doors, can be used for the "general welfare." In effect, the emergent norm allows looters to take what they regard as properly theirs—a scenario that was played out in Baghdad after the collapse of Saddam Hussein's regime in 2003. Yet not everyone participates in the free-for-all. Typically, most community residents reject the new norm, and either stand by passively or attempt to stop the wholesale theft (Couch 1968; Koerth-Baker 2012; Quarantelli and Dynes 1970; see also McPhail 1991, 2006, 2008).

Crowds have taken on new meaning in the Internet age. The term *crowdsourcing* has been coined to describe the online practice of asking Internet surfers for ideas or participation in an activity or movement. The compilation of Wikipedia, an online encyclopedia that is written and edited entirely by unrelated users, is the best-known example of crowdsourcing. Online crowds have also helped astronomers to map the galaxy, political activists to track politicians' travels, and marketers to spread the word about a new product (*The Economist* 2008b:10).

Another new use for crowds in the Internet era is the **flash mob:** a group of people organized by social media to assemble suddenly in a public space, perform some collective activity, and then quickly disperse. The activity can range from inane behaviors, like jumping up and down 10 times near an intersection, to artistic expressions, such as singing in unison at a shopping mall, or even more elaborately staged events. It can also be political in nature, such as demonstrations of approval or disapproval of an organization or elected official. In 2001, in one of the first flash mobs, residents of Manila gathered to demonstrate against the president of the Philippines after receiving the text message "Go 2EDSA, Wear blck." Over a period of four days, more than a million of them converged on Eifano de los Santos Avenue ("EDSA") clothed in black. Within a few days, the military dropped their support of the president, who was facing impeachment, and allowed a new president to be named.

Flash mobs are often recorded on smartphones by passersby, who upload their video clips to YouTube, where they can be viewed by millions. In 2009 a "historic" flash mob performed "Do Re Mi" in a train station in Antwerp, Belgium, and the Internet video of the event went viral. To capitalize on the popularity of such online videos, especially among young people, some corporations have hired actors to stage flash mobs in an effort to spread their advertising messages through social media. Indeed, the supposedly spontaneous rendering of "Do Re Mi" in Antwerp was orchestrated to promote a talent search for the lead performer in a stage revival of *The Sound of Music*. More recently, Nike paid an amateur dance troop in San Francisco to stage a flash mob at the product launch for a new golf shoe.

 use your **sociological imagination**

Have you ever witnessed a flash mob in person or participated in one? How organized did it seem to be? Did some participants seem to give directions or cues to others?

In a deviant application of flash mobs, gangs have used social media to assemble members at a specific time and location to commit a crime, such as shoplifting, and then disperse. This type of action has become so common that law enforcement officials routinely refer to it as a *flash gang*. To anticipate such events, detectives have begun to monitor social media. In sum, like many elements of collective action, crowds and mobs can vary significantly in both their structure and their purpose (Freund 2013; Rheingold 2003; Carter Smith et al. 2012; YouTube [2009] 2013).

Disaster Behavior

Newspapers, television reports, and even rumors bring word of many disasters around the world. The term **disaster** refers to a sudden or disruptive event or set of events that overtaxes a community's resources, so that outside aid is necessary. Traditionally, disasters have been catastrophes related to nature, such as earthquakes, floods, and fires. Yet in an industrial age, natural disasters have been joined by such "technological disasters" as airplane crashes, industrial explosions, nuclear power plant meltdowns, and massive chemical poisonings. However, there is no real distinction between the two types of disaster. As environmentalists have observed, human practices either contribute to or trigger natural disasters. Building in floodplains, engineering natural waterways, clear-cutting forests, and erecting rigid structures in earthquake zones all create the potential for disaster (Marshall and Picou 2008).

Disaster Research Sociologists have made enormous strides in disaster research, despite the problems inherent in this type of investigation. The work of the Disaster Research Center at the University of Delaware has been especially important. The

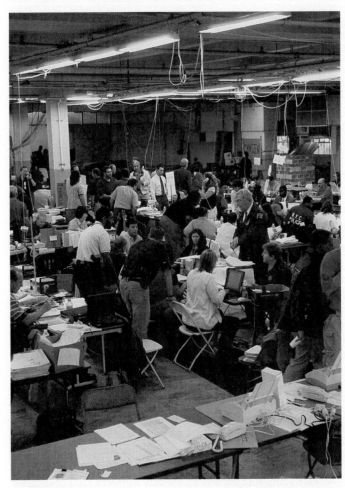

When a terrorist attack destroyed New York City's emergency command center, officials quickly set up a new one to direct the search and recovery effort. Even in times of unimaginable disaster, people respond in predictable ways.

center has teams of trained researchers prepared to leave for the site of any disaster on four hours' notice. Their field kits include identification material, recording equipment, and interview guidelines for use in various types of disasters. En route to the scene, these researchers try to become informed about the conditions they may encounter. On arrival, they establish a communication post to coordinate fieldwork and maintain contact with the center's headquarters.

Since its founding in 1963, the Disaster Research Center has conducted more than 695 field studies of natural and technological disasters in the United States and other nations. Its research has been used to develop effective planning in the delivery of emergency health care, the establishment and operation of rumor-control centers, the coordination of mental health services after disasters, and the implementation of disaster-preparedness and emergency-response programs. The center has also provided training and field research for graduate students, who maintain a professional commitment to disaster research and often go on to work for disaster service organizations such as the Red Cross and civil defense agencies (Disaster Research Center 2013; K. Tierney 2007).

Case Studies: Collapse of the World Trade Center and Hurricane Katrina

Two devastating but very different disasters have provided fascinating case studies for researchers to examine. One was the collapse of the World Trade Center following the terrorist attack of September 11, 2001, which caused nearly three thousand deaths and billions of dollars worth of property damage. The other was the unprecedented destruction caused by Hurricane Katrina in August 2005, which left hundreds of thousands of people homeless. Sociologists who have studied such disasters have found that they are often followed by the creation of an emergency operations group, which coordinates both public services and some private-sector services, such as food distribution. Decision making becomes more centralized during these periods than it is in normal times.

Such was the case on September 11, 2001. New York City's well-designed Emergency Management Center, located in the World Trade Center, was destroyed when the building collapsed and all power at nearby City Hall was cut off. Yet within hours, both an incident command post and a new emergency operations center had been established to direct the search and recovery effort at the 16-acre site. Shortly thereafter came a victims' center, information kiosks, and an office for issuing death certificates, staffed around the clock by counselors, as well as facilities for serving meals to rescue workers. To identify potential hazards to rescuers and survey what had become a gigantic crime scene, police and public safety officials turned to computer maps and aerial photographs. They also designated places where victims could be identified, human resource functions relocated, and charitable contributions collected (Wachtendorf 2002).

Hurricane Katrina was an entirely different kind of disaster. Although unlike September 11, the storm's arrival was expected, its path of destruction was much greater, covering 90,000 square miles—an enormous area compared to the World Trade Center. In the four years since September 11, 2001, all levels of government in the United States had worked to improve their response to disasters, whatever the origin. Yet while the destruction of low-lying coastal areas in the Southeast by a catastrophic hurricane could have been anticipated, days passed before authorities managed to mount a full-scale rescue effort in response to Katrina. With streets flooded and communications knocked out, stranded residents waited on their rooftops for food, water, or a helicopter lift, wondering where the rescue teams were.

What went wrong? A monumental lack of coordination stymied government authorities. Confusion reigned among the numerous agencies involved in the effort, including the Federal Emergency Management Agency (FEMA), which had been reorganized under the authority of the Department of Homeland Security less than two years earlier; the National Guard, with a different command structure in each state; the active-duty military; and literally thousands of city, county, and state governments, each with its own sphere of authority. Amidst all this confusion, the biggest challenge facing FEMA was that in revising the nation's emergency response plan following September 11, federal officials had decided to rely on local government to manage in the first few days after a disaster. However, Katrina overwhelmed both local police and National Guard units stationed near the Gulf. In this case, the centralization of decision

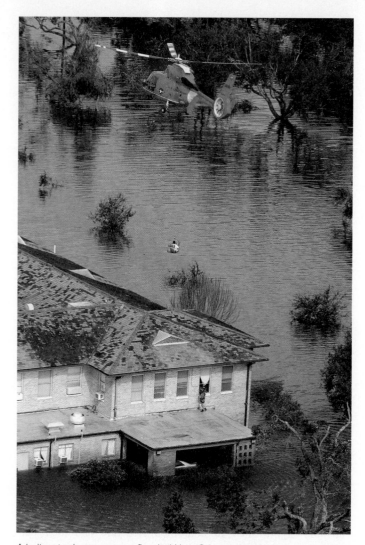

A helicopter hovers over a flooded New Orleans neighborhood, searching for survivors on the rooftops. In the days that followed the storm, federal, state, and local authorities struggled to coordinate their rescue efforts, as thousands of stranded residents went without food or water.

making that typically follows a disaster occurred over a period of days, not hours. In reviewing what happened, federal officials revised their emergency-response plan and reexamined laws governing change-of-command authority to expedite federal and military aid when necessary.

The long-term recovery from Katrina was even more complicated than the rescue operation. In contrast to the World Trade Center's collapse, Hurricane Katrina had a disproportionately large effect on the poor, who possessed few if any resources to draw on in the emergency. Lacking a nest egg, these families had little choice in where to relocate, and they faced much more difficulty than others in finding permanent shelter and employment.

Disaster research has shown that in the wake of calamity, maintaining and restoring communications is vital not just to directing relief efforts, but to reducing survivors' anxiety. On September 11, most cell phones in Manhattan were rendered useless by the destruction of communications towers and relay stations. To contact loved ones or to plan their escape from a city clogged with emergency vehicles, people stood in line at pay phones. In the days to follow, families seeking information about their loved ones posted fliers at makeshift information centers. Following Hurricane Katrina, survivors who had been dispersed to shelters across the nation—often without knowing whether family members were alive or dead—turned to special websites to find their kin, business associates, teachers, and even pets. In the aftermath of unimaginable disaster, people and organizations responded in predictable ways (Dreifus 2003, 2004; Hall 2005; P. Light 2005).

Fads and Fashions

An almost endless list of objects and behavior patterns seems temporarily to catch the fancy of adults and children. Think about Silly Putty, Hula Hoops, the Rubik's Cube, break dancing, Mentos and Coke, speed dating, Sudoku puzzles, Nintendo video, and mosh pits. Fads and fashions are sudden movements toward the acceptance of some lifestyle or particular taste in clothing, music, or recreation (Aguirre et al. 1988; R. Johnson 1985).

Fads are temporary patterns of behavior involving large numbers of people; they spring up independently of preceding trends and do not give rise to successors. In contrast, **fashions** are pleasurable mass involvements that feature a certain amount of acceptance by society and have a line of historical continuity. Thus, punk haircuts would be considered a fashion, part of the constantly changing standards of hair length and style, whereas dancing the Macarena would be considered a fad of the mid-1990s (J. Lofland 1981, 1985).

Typically, when people think of *fashions,* they think of clothing, particularly women's clothing. In reality, fads and fashions enter every aspect of life in which choices are not dictated by sheer necessity—vehicles, sports, music, drama, beverages, art, and even the selection of pets. Any area of our lives that is subject to continuing change is open to fads and fashions. There is a clear commercial motive behind these norms of collective behavior. For example, in about seven months of 1955, retailers sold over $100 million of Davy Crockett items (worth over $846 million in 2012 dollars), including coonskin caps, toy rifles, knives, camping gear, cameras, and jigsaw puzzles. In 1999 Nintendo took in $5 billion from sales of Pokémon paraphernalia, ranging from virtual pets to compact discs (S. King 1999).

Fads and fashions allow people to identify with something different from the dominant institutions and symbols of a culture. Members of a subculture can break with tradition while remaining in with a significant reference group of peers. Fads are generally short-lived and tend to be viewed with amusement or lack of interest by most nonparticipants. Fashions, in contrast, often have wider implications, because they can reflect (or give the impression of) wealth and status.

 use your **sociological imagination**

List some current fads and fashions. Now think back to when you were in elementary school. Can you name at least two fads from that time that seem to have faded away?

Panics and Crazes

Panics and crazes both represent responses to some generalized belief. A **craze** is an exciting mass involvement that lasts for a relatively long period. For example, in late 1973, a press release from a Wisconsin congressman described how the federal bureaucracy had failed to contract for enough toilet paper for government buildings. Then, on December 19, as part of his nightly monologue, *Tonight Show* host Johnny Carson suggested that it would not be strange if the entire nation experienced a shortage of toilet paper. Millions of people took his humorous comment seriously and immediately began stockpiling the item out of fear that it would soon be unavailable. Shortly thereafter, as a consequence of this craze, a shortage of toilet paper actually did occur. Its effects were felt into 1974 (J. Lofland 1981, 1985; Malcolm 1974; *Money* 1987).

In contrast, a **panic** is a fearful arousal or collective flight based on a generalized belief that may or may not be accurate. In a panic, people commonly think there is insufficient time or inadequate means to avoid injury. Panics often occur on battlefields, in overcrowded burning buildings, or during stock market crashes. The key distinction between panics and crazes is that panics are flights *from* something, whereas crazes are movements *toward* something.

One of the most famous cases of panic in the United States was touched off by a media event: the 1938 Halloween eve radio dramatization of H. G. Wells's science fiction novel *The War of the Worlds.* This broadcast told realistically of an invasion from Mars, with interplanetary visitors landing in northern New Jersey and taking over New York City 15 minutes later. The announcer

In the fad called *planking,* facilitated by the Internet, people pretend they are wooden planks and rest rigid—often precariously—on trees, police cars, basketball hoops, or just about anything else. Often, someone photographs the stunt and shares the image through social media. This photograph was taken in York, England.

"Did you hear that?" Rumors are a common type of social interaction that underscores shared understandings—even if the information they convey is incorrect. Today more and more rumors, many of them personal and highly inflammatory, are spread through the Internet.

indicated at the beginning of the broadcast that the account was fictional, but about 80 percent of the listeners tuned in late. Many became frightened by what they assumed to be a news report.

Some accounts have exaggerated the extent of people's reactions to *The War of the Worlds*. One report concluded that "people all over the United States were praying, crying, fleeing frantically to escape death from the Martians." In contrast, a CBS national survey of listeners found that only 20 percent were genuinely scared by the broadcast. Although perhaps a million people *reacted* to the program, many reacted by switching to other stations to see if the "news" was being carried elsewhere. This "invasion from outer space" set off a limited panic rather than mass hysteria (Roger Brown 1954; Cantril 1940; Houseman 1972).

It is often believed that people who are engaged in panics or crazes are unaware of their actions, but that is certainly not the case. As the emergent-norm perspective suggests, people take cues from one another about how to act during such forms of collective behavior. Even in the midst of an escape from a life-threatening situation, such as a fire in a crowded theater, people do not tend to run in a headlong stampede. Rather, they adjust their behavior on the basis of the perceived circumstances and the conduct of others who are assembling in a given location. To outside observers studying the events, people's decisions may seem foolish (pushing against a locked door) or suicidal (jumping from a balcony). Yet for that individual at that moment, the action may genuinely seem appropriate—or the only desperate choice available (L. Clarke 2002; Quarantelli 1957).

Rumors

Slender Man might cause nightmares, but he seems like an unlikely basis for homicide. He is a fictitious figure that emerged on a website where people create short horror stories. Created in 2009 with computer graphic techniques and a bit of a storyline alongside other fictional characters including vampires, zombies, and aliens, Slender Man was usually portrayed as a disproportionately tall, skinny man dressed in a dark suit who silently stalked his victims.

Slender Man's fan base grew, even though most people, certainly most adults, had never heard of him. In 2014, Slender Man became very real for two 12-year-old girls in Wisconsin. They believed that he haunted a nearby woods and in a macabre effort to appease him, they brutally stabbed another girl to near death in the woods. Slender Man, a figure that exists only on the Internet, has indeed taken a victim—in a way the legendary Sasquatch, or Yeti, or Loch Ness monster could never have imagined.

None of us is immune to hearing or starting such rumors. A **rumor** is a piece of information gathered informally that is used to interpret an ambiguous situation. Rumors serve a function by providing a group with a shared belief. As a group strives for consensus, members eliminate those rumors that are least useful or credible. Research reveals that in the workplace, rumors about what is or may be happening are usually highly accurate. Therefore, rumors can serve as a means of adapting to change. If a business is about to be taken over by another firm, rumors will usually abound as to the significance the move will have for personnel. Gradually, such rumors are either verified or discarded, but the very exchange of rumors allows people to cope with changes over which they have little control. Scary rumors probably spread the fastest, because fear induces stress and stress is reduced by sharing the fear with others. Moreover, some people enjoy provoking fear in others (D. E. Miller 2006; Rooks et al. 2011; Shibutani 1966).

The attack on the Pentagon and the World Trade Center produced a flurry of rumors. According to one false account, a police officer "surfed" a steel beam down 86 floors as one of the towers collapsed. Given the role of the media in covering the event, many rumors centered on them. For example, one rumor suggested that a CNN film of Palestinians dancing in the streets after the attack was actually file footage photographed during the Gulf War. In Pakistan, rumors spread that the vivid photos of the hijacked planes crashing into the World Trade Center had actually been staged. Like these examples, rumors often reinforce people's ideologies and their suspicion of the mass media (Fine and Ellis 2011; Slackman 2008).

Publics and Public Opinion

The least organized and most individualized form of collective behavior is the public. The term **public** refers to a dispersed group of people, not necessarily in contact with one another, who share an interest in an issue. As the term is used in the study of collective behavior, the public does not include everyone. Rather, it is a collective of people who focus on some issue, engage in discussion, agree or disagree, and sometimes dissolve when the issue has been decided (Blumer 1955, 1969; R. Turner and Killian 1987).

The term **public opinion** refers to expressions of attitudes on matters of public policy that are communicated to decision makers. The last part of this definition is particularly important. Theorists of collective behavior see no public opinion without both a public and a decision maker. In studying public opinion, we are not concerned with the formation of an *individual's* attitudes on social and political issues. Instead, we focus on the ways in which a public's attitudes are communicated to decision makers, and on the ultimate outcome of the public's attempts to influence policymaking (R. Turner and Killian 1987).

TABLE 57-1 FORMS OF COLLECTIVE BEHAVIOR

Form	Definition	Example
Crowd	Temporary gathering of people in close proximity who share a common focus or interest	Political or team rally
Disaster	Sudden or disruptive event or set of events that overtaxes a community's resources, so that outside aid is necessary	Response to a tornado, hurricane, or refinery fire
Fad	Temporary pattern of behavior that involves large numbers of people and is independent of preceding trends	Backpack zipper pulls (charms, cartoon characters, superheroes)
Fashion	Pleasurable mass involvement that has a line of historical continuity	Designer purses
Panic	Fearful arousal or collective flight based on a generalized belief that may or may not be accurate	Travel cancellations during an epidemic
Craze	Exciting mass involvement that lasts for a relatively long period	Traveling fans of a music group or sports team
Rumor	Piece of information gathered informally that is used to interpret an ambiguous situation	Fabrication of U.S. moon landings using special effects
Public	Dispersed group of people, not necessarily in contact with one another, who share an interest in an issue	Environmentalists
Public opinion	Expressions of attitudes on matters of public policy that are communicated to decision makers	Views on global warming
Social movement	Organized collective activity to bring about or resist fundamental change in an existing group or society	Gay rights movement

Polls and surveys play a major role in assessing public opinion. Using the techniques for developing reliable questionnaire and interview schedules, survey specialists conduct studies of public opinion for business firms (market analyses), the government, the mass media (program ratings), and of course, politicians. Survey data have become extremely influential not only in preselecting the products we buy but in determining which political candidates are likely to win an election and even which potential Supreme Court nominees should be selected (Manza and Brooks 2012).

Today's political polls are well-constructed surveys based on representative sampling techniques. As a result, their projections of presidential elections often fall within a few percentage points of the actual vote. In marked contrast to these polls, some surveys are downright misleading, such as those in which people are asked to text a certain number to register an opinion.

 use your **sociological imagination**

Can you recall a time when you changed your view on some issue after hearing or reading about prevailing public opinion on that issue?

In sum, sociologists study collective behavior because it incorporates activities that we all engage in on a regular basis. Moreover, they acknowledge the crucial role that social movements can play in mobilizing discontented members of a society and initiating social change. Table 57-1 summarizes the 10 forms of collective behavior that sociologists study.

MODULE 57 | **Recap and Review**

Summary

Collective behavior is the relatively spontaneous and unstructured behavior of a group that is reacting to a common influence in an ambiguous situation.

1. The **emergent-norm perspective** suggests that new forms of behavior may emerge during an episode of collective behavior. The **value-added model** outlines six determinants of collective behavior: structural conduciveness, structural strain, generalized belief, a precipitating factor, mobilization of participants for action, and the operation of social control. The **assembling perspective** examines how and why people move from different points in space to a common location.

2. In **crowds,** people are in relatively close contact and interaction for a period and are focused on something of common interest.

3. Researchers are interested in how groups interact in times of **disaster.**

4. **Fads** are temporary patterns of behavior involving large numbers of people; **fashions** have more historical continuity than fads.

5. A **panic** is a flight *from* something, whereas a **craze** is a mass movement *toward* something.

6. A **rumor** is a piece of information that is used to interpret an ambiguous situation and provide a group with a shared belief.

7. **Publics** represent the most individualized and least organized form of collective behavior. **Public opinion** is the expression of individuals' attitudes on public policy to decision makers.

Thinking Critically

1. Describe the emergency response that followed the Boston Marathon bombings of 2013. Did the collective response to the attack illustrate the findings of disaster research? In what ways?

2. What other forms of collective behavior were evident on that day? Describe their role.

Key Terms

Assembling perspective

Collective behavior

Craze

Crowd

Disaster

Emergent-norm perspective

Fad

Fashion

Flash mob

Nonperiodic assembly

Panic

Periodic assembly

Public

Public opinion

Rumor

Value-added model

MODULE 58 | Social Movements

Although such factors as the physical environment, population, technology, and social inequality serve as sources of change, it is the *collective* effort of individuals organized into social movements that ultimately leads to change. Sociologists use the term **social movement** to refer to an organized collective activity to bring about or resist fundamental change in an existing group or society (Benford 1992). Herbert Blumer (1955:19) recognized the special importance of social movements when he defined them as "collective enterprises to establish a new order of life."

In many nations, including the United States, social movements have had a dramatic impact on the course of history and the evolution of the social structure. Consider the actions of abolitionists, suffragists, civil rights workers, activists opposed to the war in Vietnam, and Occupy Wall Street protesters. Members of each social movement stepped outside traditional channels for bringing about social change, yet each had a noticeable influence on public policy. In Eastern Europe, equally dramatic collective efforts helped to topple communist regimes in a largely peaceful manner, in nations that many observers had thought were "immune" to such social change (Ramet 1991).

Though social movements imply the existence of conflict, we can also analyze their activities from a functionalist perspective. Even when they are unsuccessful, social movements contribute to the formation of public opinion. Initially, people thought the ideas of Margaret Sanger and other early advocates of birth control were radical, yet contraceptives are now widely available in the United States.

Because social movements know no borders, even nationalistic movements are deeply influenced by global events. Increasingly, social movements are taking on an international dimension from the start. Global enterprises, in particular, lend themselves to targeting through international mobilization, whether they are corporations like McDonald's or governmental bodies like the World Trade Organization. Global activism is not new, however; it began with the writing of Karl Marx, who sought to mobilize oppressed peoples in other industrialized countries. Today, activist networking is facilitated by the Internet. Participation in transnational activism is much more widespread now than in the past, and passions are quicker to ignite.

The Emergence of Social Movements

How and why do social movements emerge? Obviously, people are often discontented with the way things are. What causes them to organize at a particular moment in a collective effort to effect change? Sociologists rely on two explanations for why people mobilize: the relative deprivation and resource mobilization approaches.

 use your **sociological imagination**

What social movements are most visible on your campus? In the community where you live? What do you think these groups need to do to be effective?

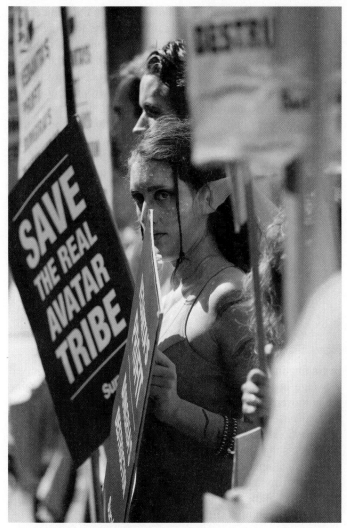

In 2010, protesters in London disguised themselves as characters in the movie *Avatar* to draw attention to the plight of an indigenous tribe in India. The Dongria Kondh people's way of life, the protesters charged, was threatened by a multinational corporation's plan to construct a mine on their land. The Indian government blocked the project, agreeing with protesters that it would have violated the tribe's rights.

Relative Deprivation Approach

Those members of a society who feel most frustrated and disgruntled by social and economic conditions are not necessarily the worst off in an objective sense. Social scientists have long recognized that what is more significant is the way in which people *perceive* their situation. As Karl Marx pointed out, although the misery of the workers was important to their perception of their oppressed state, so was their position *in relation to* the capitalist ruling class (Marx and Engels [1847] 1955).

The term **relative deprivation** is defined as the conscious feeling of a negative discrepancy between legitimate expectations and present actualities (J. Wilson 1973). In other words, things aren't as good as you hoped they would be. Such a state may be characterized by scarcity rather than a complete lack of necessities (as we saw in the distinction between absolute and relative poverty in Chapter 8). A relatively deprived person is dissatisfied because he or she feels downtrodden relative to some

appropriate reference group. Thus, blue-collar workers who live in two-family houses on small plots of land—though hardly at the bottom of the economic ladder—may nevertheless feel deprived in comparison to corporate managers and professionals who live in lavish homes in exclusive suburbs.

In addition to the feeling of relative deprivation, two other elements must be present before discontent will be channeled into a social movement. People must feel that they have a *right* to their goals, that they deserve better than what they have. At the same time, the disadvantaged group must perceive that its goals cannot be attained through conventional means. This belief may or may not be correct. Whichever is the case, the group will not mobilize into a social movement unless there is a shared perception that members can end their relative deprivation only through collective action (D. Morrison 1971).

Critics of this approach have noted that people don't need to feel deprived to be moved to act. In addition, this approach fails to explain why certain feelings of deprivation are transformed into social movements, whereas in similar situations, no collective effort is made to reshape society. Consequently, in recent years, sociologists have paid increasing attention to the forces needed to bring about the emergence of social movements (Alain 1985; Finkel and Rule 1987; Orum and Dale 2009).

 use your **sociological imagination**

Why might well-off people feel deprived?

Resource Mobilization Approach

It takes more than desire to start a social movement. It helps to have money, political influence, access to the media, and personnel. The term **resource mobilization** refers to the ways in which a social movement utilizes such resources. Indeed, the success of a movement for change will depend in good part on what resources it has and how effectively it mobilizes them. In other words, recruiting adherents and marshalling resources is critical to the growth and success of social movements (D. Miller 2014; Tilly 1964, 2003; Walder 2009).

Leadership is a central factor in the mobilization of the discontented into social movements. Often, a movement will be led by a charismatic figure, such as Dr. Martin Luther King Jr. As Max Weber described it in 1904, *charisma* is that quality of an individual that sets him or her apart from ordinary people. Of course, charisma can fade abruptly, which helps to account for the fragility of certain social movements (Morris 2000).

Many social movements are mobilized by institutional insiders. During the nationwide debate of the Obama administration's plan for health care reform in 2009, for example, health insurance companies encouraged their employees to attend the forums arranged by the White House. Managers distributed "Town Hall Tips" that included a list of concerns employees could raise and suggestions on how to make their comments as personal as possible, by talking about their own health issues (E. Walker 2010).

Why do certain individuals join a social movement while others who are in similar situations do not? Some of them are recruited to join. Karl Marx recognized the importance of recruitment when he called on workers to become *aware* of their oppressed status and to develop a class consciousness. Like theorists of the resource mobilization approach, Marx held that a social movement (specifically, the revolt of the proletariat) would require leaders to sharpen the awareness of the oppressed. They would need to help workers to overcome feelings of **false consciousness,** or attitudes that did not reflect workers' objective position, in order to organize a revolutionary movement. Similarly, one of the challenges faced by women's liberation activists of the late 1960s and early 1970s was to convince women that they were being deprived of their rights and of socially valued resources.

Gender and Social Movements

Sociologists point out that gender is an important element in understanding social movements. In our male-dominated society, women find it more difficult than men to assume leadership positions in social movement organizations. Though women often serve disproportionately as volunteers in these movements, their work is not always recognized, nor are their voices as easily heard as men's. Gender bias causes the real extent of their influence to be overlooked. Indeed, traditional examination of the sociopolitical system tends to focus on such male-dominated corridors of power as legislatures and corporate boardrooms, to the neglect of more female-dominated domains such as households, community-based groups, and faith-based networks. However, efforts to influence family values, child rearing, relationships between parents and schools, and spiritual values are clearly significant to a culture and society (Ferree and Merrill 2000; Noonan 1995).

Scholars of social movements now realize that gender can affect even the way we view organized efforts to bring about or resist change. For example, an emphasis on using rationality and cold logic to achieve goals helps to obscure the importance of passion and emotion in successful social movements. It would be difficult to find any movement—from labor battles to voting rights to animal rights—in which passion was not part of the consensus-building force. Yet calls for a more serious study of the role of emotion are frequently seen as applying only to the women's movement, because emotion is traditionally thought of as being feminine (Ferree and Merrill 2000; V. Taylor 1999, 2004).

 use your **sociological imagination**

Try to imagine a society without any social movements. Under what conditions could such a society exist? Would you want to live in it?

New Social Movements

Beginning in the late 1960s, European social scientists observed a change in both the composition and the targets of emerging social movements. Previously, traditional social movements had focused on economic issues, often led by labor unions or by people who shared the same occupation. However, many social movements that have become active in recent decades—including the contemporary women's movement, the peace movement, and the environmental movement—do not have the social class roots typical of the labor protests in the United States and Europe over the past century (Tilly 1993, 2004).

Gallaudet University in Washington, D.C., is the only four-year liberal arts college for deaf students in the United States. A leaflet (left) was distributed in 1988 as part of a successful effort by students, faculty, and alumni to force the appointment of the university's first deaf president. In 2007, after that president's retirement, students protested once again over the election process (right). The mobilization of resources, including leaflets, is one key to the success of a social movement.

Sociology in the Global Community

BOX 58-1

Women's Social Movements in South Korea and India

Women have long played a significant role in social movements. Scholars have taken two different approaches to studying these movements: a macro-level, national approach and a more local approach to new social movements.

The macro-level approach has proved useful in studying the women's movement in South Korea. In 1987, a nationwide movement that included a variety of women's organizations toppled the country's long-time authoritarian ruler. In the democratic environment that followed his overthrow, women joined together in Korean Women's Association United (KWAU) to seek a voice on issues involving families, the environment, education, and sexuality, including sexual harassment and assault. The KWAU staged public demonstrations, held hearings, and presented petitions. Recognizing the women's right to be heard, the national government created special commissions to focus specifically on women's issues.

Eventually, the women's movement in South Korea became an institutionalized collaborator with the central government, even receiving government grants. Progress on women's issues has not been steady, however, as some administrations have been less friendly than others to the KWAU. To gain traction, the KWAU reached out to the United Nations in its efforts to further women's social equality, and to other international bodies, such as those seeking to curb human trafficking.

In the last 10 years, groups of younger women, often based on college campuses, have questioned the KWAU's ability to speak for them. These women charge that the KWAU has in effect become part of the state, and by extension, "part of the problem."

Disabled women and lesbians, for example, feel unrepresented by the KWAU. And an organization of prostitutes has argued for the decriminalization of sex work—a position clearly at odds with the KWAU's stance against human trafficking.

In India, the women's social movement tends to be locally based, often in farming communities, where about 71 percent of the nation's 1.2 billion people live. As in other parts of the developing world, rural families in India are quite poor. For decades, villagers have been moving to the cities in

> From workers' rights to the voting booth, from education to freedom from sexual violence, women's issues are an increasingly common feature of politics in both India and South Korea.

hopes of earning a better income, only to be exploited in sweatshops and multinational factories. In the mid-1980s, 5,000 striking textile workers returned to their rural villages to mobilize support for their movement. As the strike wore on, some of those women remained in the villages and sought work on government drought-relief projects. However, there weren't enough jobs for the villagers, much less for the striking textile workers.

This experience inspired a new social movement in rural India. With unemployment threatening an expanded population in rural villages, activists formed what came to be called the Shoshit, Shetkari, Kashtakari, Kamgar, Mukti Sangharsh (SSKKMS), which means "exploited peasants, toilers, workers liberation struggle." The movement's initial goal was to provide drought relief for farmers, but the deeper goal was to empower rural residents.

Indian women have also worked to improve their families' lot through microfinance programs. They have marched on government offices to demand that at least a third of the seats in Parliament and the state assemblies be reserved for them. Clearly, Indian women's traditional role of maintaining their households' health and nutrition is critical to their families' survival. Thus, their leadership in seeking improved living conditions is winning them new respect in India's patriarchal society.

From workers' rights to the voting booth, from education to freedom from sexual violence, women's issues are an increasingly common feature of politics in both India and South Korea.

LET'S DISCUSS

1. What do you think might explain the differences between women's social movements and issues in South Korea and in India?

2. What would happen if "powerless" people in the United States formed a social movement of their own? Would it succeed? Why or why not?

Sources: Hur 2011; Korean Women's Association United 2010; Sengupta 2009; Subramaniam 2006; Suh 2011; Working Women's Forum 2012.

The term **new social movement** refers to an organized collective activity that addresses values and social identities, as well as improvements in the quality of life. These movements may be involved in developing collective identities. Many have complex agendas that go beyond a single issue, and even cross national boundaries. Educated, middle-class people are significantly represented in some of these new social movements, such as the women's movement and the movement for lesbian and gay rights. Box 58-1 describes the women's movements in South Korea and India.

New social movements generally do not view government as their ally in the struggle for a better society. While they typically do not seek to overthrow the government, they may criticize, protest, or harass public officials. Researchers have found that members of new social movements show little inclination to accept established authority, even scientific or technical authority. This characteristic is especially evident in the environmental and anti–nuclear power movements, whose activists present their own experts to counter those of government or big business (Garner 1996; Polletta and Jasper 2001; A. Scott 1990).

The environmental movement is one of many new movements with a worldwide focus (see the Social Policy section in Chapter 17). In their efforts to reduce air and water pollution, curtail global warming, and protect endangered animal species, environmental activists have realized that strong regulatory measures within a single country are not sufficient. Similarly, labor union leaders and human rights advocates cannot adequately address exploitative sweatshop conditions in a developing country if multinational corporations can simply move their factories to another country, where workers earn even less. Whereas traditional views

Social Movements • 441

TABLE **58-1** CONTRIBUTIONS TO SOCIAL MOVEMENT THEORY

Approach	Emphasis
Relative deprivation	Social movements are especially likely to arise when expectations are frustrated.
Resource mobilization	The success of social movements depends on which resources are available and how effectively they are used.
New social movement	Social movements arise when people are motivated by value issues and social identity questions.

of social movements tended to emphasize resource mobilization on a local level, new social movement theory offers a broader, global perspective on social and political activism.

Table 58-1 summarizes the sociological approaches that have contributed to social movement theory. Each has added to our understanding of the development of social movements.

Communications and the Globalization of Social Movements

Today, through global text-messaging and the Internet, social activists can reach a large number of people around the world almost instantaneously, with relatively little effort and expense.

Rural residents of Mongolia pose outside their home with their satellite dish. In the 21st century, technology links people in even the remotest areas. In 2008 protesters rocked Mongolia's capital in anger over election fraud. Two years later, they gathered to demand more equitable distribution of the nation's mining wealth. In both cases, people from rural areas organized for action on the Internet.

The Internet's listservs and chat rooms—a form of social networking—allow organizers of social movements to enlist like-minded people without face-to-face contact, or even simultaneous interaction (Calhoun 1998; Kavada 2005).

Moreover, television and the Internet, as contrasted with books and newspapers, often convey a false sense of intimacy reinforced by immediacy. We seem to be personally affected by the latest celebrity news. Therefore, the latest technology brings us together to act and react in an electronic global village (Della Porta and Tarrow 2005; Garner 1999).

This sense of online togetherness extends to social movements, which more and more are being mounted on the web. Through the instantaneous communication that is possible over the Internet, Mexican Zapatistas and other groups of indigenous peoples can transform their cause into an international lobbying effort, and Greenpeace organizers can link environmental activists throughout the world via video recorded on members' cell phones.

Sociologists have begun to refer to such electronic enhancement of established social movements as **computer-mediated communication** (CMC). Computer-mediated communication may be defined as communicative interaction through two or more networked devices, such as a computer or cell phone. The term applies to a variety of text-based or video interactions, including e-mails, chat rooms, and text messages, some of which may be supported by social media. This kind of electronic communication strengthens a group's solidarity, allowing fledgling social movements to grow and develop faster than they might otherwise. Thus the face-to-face contact that once was critical to a social movement is no longer necessary. As Box 58-2 suggests, however, the legitimacy of such online movements is a matter of opinion (Castells 2010b; Niezen 2005).

The new global communications technology also helps to create enclaves of similarly minded people. Alex Steffen (2008), editor of the book *World Changing,* notes that the Internet is changing the way people relate to one another across vast distances, allowing small, focused audiences to become part of a global conversation. In doing so, they may find a common purpose. These social connections happen because of the Internet's technological structure. Websites are not autonomous and independent; they are connected by a global electronic network. One website generally lists a variety of other sites that serve as links. For example, seeking information on domestic partnerships may lead you to an electronic enclave that is supportive of cohabitation between men and women or to an enclave that is supportive of gay and lesbian couples. New developments in communications technology have clearly broadened the way we interact with one another (Calhoun 1998).

Organizing for Controversy via Computer-Mediated Communication

With the Arab Spring, which began in Tunisia in 2011, and the Occupy Wall Street movement, which sprang up later that year, computer-mediated communication became a social necessity. In a remarkably short period, the two tech-savvy social movements overthrew dictators and mounted mass protests in cities across the United States. What gave their new form of communication such power? Unlike more traditional forms of communication, social media can be used almost anywhere by almost anyone with a cause, from street protesters to people trying to launch a petition from home.

The widespread use of computer-mediated communication in social movements is not lost on those in authority, who monitor and sometimes seek to control citizens' access to networked communications. Around the world, government leaders worry about people using the Internet and social media to incite terrorist acts. And they have good reason. Islamic extremist websites, many of which are technologically advanced and written in English, have been garnering support for Islamic causes outside the Middle East. Ku Klux Klan websites have also been growing in number,

> On the street or on the Internet, social movements may be seen either as promoting desirable social change or as supporting negative behaviors that many people find objectionable.

complete with online "news shows" and streaming video.

Yet drawing the line between criminal activity and legitimate activity is not

necessarily easy. A troubling example of what can happen when authorities gain unbridled control of computer-mediated communication occurred in Maryland, where a public school teacher could not figure out why she was unable to send or receive e-mails. The woman, whose first name happened to be Gay, finally learned that the school system had banned all homosexual-bisexual-transgendered content. The site's filters had automatically blocked all messages bearing her name. They did, however, allow users to access anti-LGBT information.

Just as disturbing to many people are sites that promote what they see as

destructive or self-destructive behavior. The Internet allows people who engage in odd forms of vandalism, such as collecting parking meters, to network and become a virtual group. More troubling to many doctors and parents are the slick websites that encourage self-injury (see the opening to Chapter 2) or anorexia and bulimia (disorders characterized by little or no eating or by overeating and purging). Internet chat rooms for those who engage in these life-threatening behaviors are flourishing. Screen displays urge participants to "go public" by sending in for a beaded bracelet that supports their behavior.

To counteract these sites, members of the medical community have established websites to promote recovery and safe behavior. Their actions illustrate the double-edged nature of free expression. On the street or on the Internet, social movements may be seen either as promoting desirable social change or as supporting negative behaviors that many people find objectionable.

LET'S DISCUSS

1. Have you ever been involved in a social or political movement whose legitimacy some people considered questionable? If so, what was the movement, and what were the objections to it? Did you consider the objections to be legitimate?

2. Can any social movement ever be totally free from controversy? Would you want to live in a society in which controversy is not tolerated?

Sources: Teaching Tolerance 2012; Thomasrobb.com 2007; Tibbles 2007; Whitlock 2005.

MODULE 58 | **Recap and Review**

Summary

Social movements are more structured than other forms of collective behavior and persist over longer periods.

1. A group will not mobilize into a social movement without a shared perception that its **relative deprivation** can be ended only through collective action.

2. The success of a social movement depends in good part on effective **resource mobilization.**

3. **New social movements** tend to focus on more than just economic issues and often cross national boundaries.

4. Advances in communications technology—especially the Internet—have had a major impact on social movements.

Thinking Critically

1. What might be some drawbacks of global communications technology?

2. What aspects of traditional gender roles explain the roles that women and men typically play in social movements?

Key Terms

Computer-mediated communication

False consciousness

New social movement

Relative deprivation

Resource mobilization

Social movement

MODULE 59 | Social Change

Theories of Social Change

A new millennium provides the occasion to offer explanations of **social change,** which we have defined as significant alteration over time in behavior patterns and culture. Social change can occur so slowly as to be almost undetectable to those it affects, but it can also happen with breathtaking rapidity. As Table 59-1 shows, some changes that have occurred in U.S. society over the past century and a half have been relatively slow or slight; others have been rapid or striking in magnitude.

Explanations of social change are clearly a challenge in the diverse and complex world we inhabit today. Nevertheless, theorists from several disciplines have sought to analyze social change. In some instances, they have examined historical events to arrive at a better understanding of contemporary changes. We will review three theoretical approaches to change—evolutionary, functionalist, and conflict—and then take a look at resistance to social change.

Evolutionary Theory

The pioneering work of Charles Darwin (1809–1882) in biological evolution contributed to 19th-century theories of social change. Darwin's approach stresses a continuing progression of successive life-forms. For example, human beings came at a later stage of evolution than reptiles and represent a more complex form of life. Social theorists seeking an analogy to this biological model originated **evolutionary theory,** in which society is viewed as moving in a definite direction. Early evolutionary theorists generally agreed that society was progressing inevitably toward a higher state. As might be expected, they concluded in ethnocentric fashion that their behavior and culture were more advanced than those of earlier civilizations.

Auguste Comte (1798–1857), a founder of sociology, was an evolutionary theorist of change. He saw human societies as moving forward in their thinking, from mythology to the scientific method. Similarly, Émile Durkheim ([1893] 1933) maintained that society progressed from simple to more complex forms of social organization.

Today, evolutionary theory influences sociologists in a variety of ways. For example, it has encouraged sociobiologists to investigate the behavioral links between humans and other animals. It has also influenced human ecology, the study of the interaction between communities and their environment (Maryanski 2004).

Functionalist Perspective

Because functionalist sociologists focus on what *maintains* a system, not on what changes it, they might seem to offer little to the study of social change. Yet as the work of sociologist Talcott Parsons demonstrates, functionalists have made a distinctive contribution to this area of sociological investigation.

Parsons (1902–1979), a leading proponent of the functionalist perspective, viewed society as being in a natural state of equilibrium. By "equilibrium," he meant that society tends toward a state of stability or balance. Parsons would view even prolonged labor strikes or civilian riots as temporary disruptions in the status quo rather than as significant alterations in social structure. Therefore, according to his **equilibrium model,** as changes occur in one part of society, adjustments must be made in other parts. If not, society's equilibrium will be threatened and strains will occur.

Reflecting the evolutionary approach, Parsons (1966) maintained that four processes of social change are inevitable. *Differentiation* refers to the increasing complexity of social organization. The transition from medicine man to physician, nurse, and pharmacist is an illustration of differentiation in the field of health. This process is accompanied by *adaptive upgrading,* in which social institutions become more specialized in their purposes. The division of physicians into obstetricians, internists, surgeons, and so forth is an example of adaptive upgrading.

The next process Parsons identified is the *inclusion* of groups that were previously excluded because of their gender, race, ethnicity, or social class. Medical schools have practiced inclusion by admitting increasing numbers of women and African Americans. Finally, Parsons contends that societies experience *value generalization,* the development of new values that tolerate and legitimate a greater range of activities. The acceptance of preventive and alternative medicine is an example of value generalization: society has broadened its view of health care. All four processes identified by Parsons stress consensus—societal agreement on the nature of social organization and values (B. Johnson 1975; Wallace and Wolf 1980).

Although Parsons's approach explicitly incorporates the evolutionary notion of continuing progress, the dominant theme in his model is stability. Society may change, but it remains stable through new forms of integration. For example, in place of the kinship ties

TABLE 59-1 THE UNITED STATES: A CHANGING NATION

Population	1850	1940	1960	2012
Total in millions	23.2	132.1	180.7	308.8
Percentage under age 15	41%	25%	31%	20%
Education	**1850**	**1940**	**1960**	**2012**
Percentage not completing high school or equivalent	88%	18%	13%	7%
Percentage ages 19–24 enrolled in higher education	Under 1%	8%	40%	41%
Labor Force Participation	**1850**	**1940**	**1960**	**2011**
Men in their 20s	94%	88%	86%	81%
Women in their 20s	22%	39%	74%	76%
Health	**1850**	**1940**	**1960**	**2010**
Physicians per 100,000 population	176	133	150	272
Life expectancy at birth, in years	38	63	70	78.7
Technology	**1870**	**1940**	**1960**	**2011**
Copyrights issued	5,600	176,997	243,926	670,000
Patents issued	12,127	42,238	47,170	253,155
Family	**1890**	**1940**	**1960**	**2013**
Median age at first marriage				
Men	26	24	23	29
Women	22	22	20	28.6
Number of children born per family	3.25	2.7	3.65	1.9

Think about It Which of the social changes shown in this table surprises you the most? Which category do you think will change the most in the next 20 years? Explain your answers.

Note: Data are comparable, although definitions vary. Definition of the United States changes between 1850 and 1940 and between 1940 and 1960. Earliest date for children born per family is 1905.

Sources: Author, based on federal data collected in Bureau of the Census 2011a, 2012f, 2013b; Bureau of Labor Statistics 2013a; National Center for Education Statistics 2013; National Center for Health Statistics 2013:Tables 10, 18; Sutch and Carter 2006; United States Copyright Office 2012; United States Patent and Trademark Office 2012; World Bank 2013.

that provided social cohesion in the past, people develop laws, judicial processes, and new values and belief systems.

Conflict Perspective

The functionalist perspective minimizes the importance of change. It emphasizes the persistence of social life and sees change as a means of maintaining society's equilibrium (or balance). In contrast, conflict theorists contend that social institutions and practices persist because powerful groups have the ability to maintain the status quo. Change has crucial significance, since it is needed to correct social injustices and inequalities.

Karl Marx accepted the evolutionary argument that societies develop along a particular path. However, unlike Comte and Spencer, he did not view each successive stage as an inevitable improvement over the previous one. History, according to Marx, proceeds through a series of stages, each of which exploits a

class of people. Ancient society exploited slaves; the estate system of feudalism exploited serfs; modern capitalist society exploits the working class. Ultimately, through a socialist revolution led by the proletariat, human society will move toward the final stage of development: a classless communist society, or "community of free individuals," as Marx described it in 1867 in *Das Kapital* (see Bottomore and Rubel 1956:250).

As we have seen, Marx had an important influence on the development of sociology. His thinking offered insights into such institutions as the economy, the family, religion, and government. The Marxist view of social change is appealing because it does not restrict people to a passive role in responding to inevitable cycles or changes in material culture. Rather, Marxist theory offers a tool for those who wish to seize control of the historical process and gain their freedom from injustice. In contrast to functionalists' emphasis on stability, Marx argues that conflict is a normal and desirable aspect of social change. In fact, change must be encouraged as a means of eliminating social inequality (Lauer 1982).

One conflict theorist, Ralf Dahrendorf (1958), has noted that the contrast between the functionalist perspective's emphasis on stability and the conflict perspective's focus on change reflects the contradictory nature of society. Human societies are stable and long-lasting, yet they also experience serious conflict. Dahrendorf found that the functionalist and conflict perspectives were ultimately compatible, despite their many points of disagreement. Indeed, Parsons spoke of new functions that result from social change, and Marx recognized the need for change so that societies could function more equitably.

Table 59-2 summarizes the differences between the three major perspectives on social change.

Tracking Sociological Perspectives

TABLE 59-2 SOCIOLOGICAL PERSPECTIVES ON SOCIAL CHANGE

Evolutionary	Social change moves society in a definite direction, frequently from simple to more complex.
Functionalist	Social change must contribute to society's stability.
	Modest adjustments must be made to accommodate social change.
Conflict	Social change can correct social injustices and inequalities.

On the outskirts of Buenos Aires, Argentina, a squatter settlement forms a stark contrast to the gleaming skyscrapers in the wealthy downtown area. Marxists and conflict theorists see social change as a way of overcoming the kind of social inequality evident in this photograph.

Resistance to Social Change

Efforts to promote social change are likely to meet with resistance. In the midst of rapid scientific and technological innovations, many people are frightened by the demands of an ever-changing society. Moreover, certain individuals and groups have a stake in maintaining the existing state of affairs.

Social economist Thorstein Veblen (1857–1929) coined the term **vested interests** to refer to those people or groups who will suffer in the event of social change. For example, in 2010 President Obama proposed scuttling NASA's Constellation project, whose primary goal was to return humans to the moon. Although many people expressed disappointment with the decision to abandon manned space flights, key opposition came from just 27 members of Congress. All represented districts in Alabama and Texas that were home to large suppliers to the project. Ironically, many of those representatives had gone on record as opponents of large federal spending projects. In general, those with a disproportionate share of society's wealth, status, and power, such as members of Congress and representatives of big business, have a vested interest in preserving the status quo (Friedman 2010; Veblen 1919).

Economic and Cultural Factors

Economic factors play an important role in resistance to social change. For example, it can be expensive for manufacturers to meet high standards for the safety of products and workers, and for the protection of the environment. Conflict theorists argue that in a capitalist economic system, many firms are not willing to pay the price of meeting strict safety and environmental standards. They may resist social change by cutting corners or by pressuring the government to ease regulations.

Communities, too, protect their vested interests, often in the name of "protecting property values." The abbreviation *NIMBY* stands for "not in my backyard," a cry often heard when people protest landfills, prisons, nuclear power facilities, and even bike trails and group homes for people with developmental disabilities. The targeted community may not challenge the need for the facility, but may simply insist that it be located elsewhere. The "not in my backyard" attitude has become so common that it is almost impossible for policymakers to find acceptable locations for facilities such as hazardous-waste dumps (Jasper 1997).

On the world stage, what amounts to a "not on planet Earth" campaign has emerged. Members of this movement stress many issues, from profiteering to nuclear proliferation, from labor rights to the eradication of poverty and disease. Essentially an antiglobalization movement, it manifests itself at international meetings of trade ministers and heads of state.

Like economic factors, cultural factors frequently shape resistance to change. William F. Ogburn (1922) distinguished between material and nonmaterial aspects of culture. *Material culture* includes inventions, artifacts, and technology; *nonmaterial culture* encompasses ideas, norms, communications, and social organization. Ogburn pointed out that one cannot devise methods for controlling and using new technology before the introduction of a technique. Thus, nonmaterial culture typically must respond to changes in material culture. Ogburn introduced the term **culture lag** to refer to the period of maladjustment when the nonmaterial culture is still struggling to adapt to new material conditions. One example is the Internet. Its rapid, uncontrolled growth raises questions about whether to regulate it, and if so, how much.

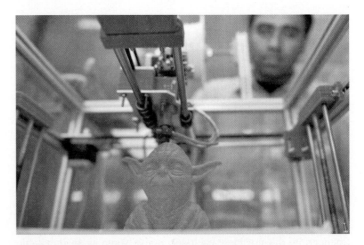

3D printers are now widely available, although still expensive, and are used increasingly to transmit both designs and objects. This bust of a *Star Wars* film character was constructed by a 3D printer in Bangalore, India, in 2014.

In certain cases, changes in material culture can strain the relationships between social institutions. For example, new means of birth control have been developed in recent decades. Large families are no longer economically necessary, nor are they commonly endorsed by social norms. However, certain religious faiths, among them Roman Catholicism, continue to extol large families and to disapprove methods of limiting family size, such as contraception and abortion. This issue represents a lag between aspects of material culture (technology) and nonmaterial culture (religious beliefs). Conflicts may also emerge between religion and other social institutions, such as government and the educational system, over the dissemination of birth control and family-planning information (Riley et al. 1994a, 1994b).

 use your **sociological imagination**

What kind of change do you find the hardest to accept? The easiest?

Resistance to Technology

Technology is cultural information about the ways in which the material resources of the environment may be used to satisfy human needs and desires. Technological innovations are examples of changes in material culture that often provoke resistance. The *Industrial Revolution*, which took place largely in England during the period 1760 to 1830, was a scientific revolution focused on the application of nonanimal sources of power to labor tasks. As this revolution proceeded, societies came to rely on new inventions that facilitated agricultural and industrial production and on new sources of energy, such as steam. In some industries, the introduction of power-driven machinery reduced the need for factory workers and made it easier for factory owners to cut wages.

Strong resistance to the Industrial Revolution emerged in some countries. In England, beginning in 1811, masked craft workers took extreme measures: they mounted nighttime raids on factories and destroyed some of the new machinery. The government hunted these rebels, known as **Luddites,** and ultimately banished or hung them. In a similar effort in France, angry workers threw their *sabots* (wooden shoes) into factory machinery to destroy it, giving rise to the term *sabotage*. While the resistance of the Luddites and the French workers was short-lived and unsuccessful, they have come to symbolize resistance to technology.

Are we now in the midst of a second industrial revolution, with a contemporary group of Luddites engaged in resisting? Many sociologists believe that we are living in a *postindustrial society*. It is difficult to pinpoint exactly when this era began. Generally, it is viewed as having begun in the 1950s, when for the first time the majority of workers in industrial societies became involved in services rather than in the actual manufacture of goods.

Just as the Luddites resisted the Industrial Revolution, people in many countries have resisted postindustrial technological changes. The term *neo-Luddites* refers to those who are wary of technological innovations and who question the incessant expansion of industrialization, the increasing destruction of the natural and agrarian world, and the "throw-it-away" mentality of contemporary capitalism, with its resulting pollution of the environment (Volti 2010).

A new slang term, *urban amish,* refers specifically to those who resist technological devices that have become part of our daily lives, such as cell phones. Such people insist that whatever the presumed benefits of industrial and postindustrial technology, such technology has distinctive social costs and may represent a danger to both the future of the human species and our planet (Bauerlein 1996; Rifkin 1995; Sale 1996; Slack and Wise 2007; Snyder 1996; Urban Dictionary 2012).

Other people will resist a new technology simply because they find it difficult to use or because they suspect that it will complicate their lives. Both these objections are especially true of new information and media technologies. Whether it is TiVo, the iPhone, or even the latest digital camera, many consumers are leery of these so-called must-have items.

MODULE 59 | **Recap and Review**

Summary

Social change is significant alteration over time in behavior patterns and culture, including mores and values.

1. Early advocates of the **evolutionary theory** of social change believed that society was progressing inevitably toward a higher state.

2. Talcott Parsons, a leading advocate of functionalist theory, viewed society as being in a natural state of equilibrium or balance.

3. Conflict theorists see change as having crucial significance, since it is needed to correct social injustices and inequalities.

4. In general, those with a disproportionate share of society's wealth, status, and power have a **vested interest** in preserving the status quo and will resist change.

5. The period of maladjustment when a nonmaterial culture is still struggling to adapt to new material conditions is known as **culture lag.**

MODULE 60 | Global Social Change

The recent past has been a truly dramatic time in history to consider global social change. Maureen Hallinan (1997), in her presidential address to the American Sociological Association, asked those present to consider just a few of the recent events: the collapse of communism; terrorism in various parts of the world, including the United States; major regime changes and severe economic disruptions in Africa, the Middle East, and Eastern Europe; the spread of AIDS; and the computer revolution. Just a few months after her remarks came the first verification of the cloning of a complex animal, Dolly the sheep.

● Anticipating Change

In this era of massive social, political, and economic change, global in scale, is it possible to predict change? Some technological changes seem obvious, but the collapse of communist governments in the former Soviet Union and Eastern Europe in the early 1990s took people by surprise. Yet prior to the Soviet collapse, sociologist Randall Collins (1986, 1995), a conflict theorist, had observed a crucial sequence of events that most observers had missed.

In seminars as far back as 1980, and in a book published in 1986, Collins had argued that Soviet expansionism had resulted in an overextension of resources, including disproportionate spending on military forces. Such an overextension will strain a regime's stability. Moreover, geopolitical theory suggests that nations in the middle of a geographic region, such as the Soviet Union, tend to fragment into smaller units over time. Collins predicted that the coincidence of social crises on several frontiers would precipitate the collapse of the Soviet Union.

And that is just what happened. In 1979, the success of the Iranian revolution had led to an upsurge of Islamic fundamentalism in nearby Afghanistan, as well as in Soviet republics with substantial Muslim populations. At the same time, resistance to communist rule was growing both throughout Eastern Europe and within the Soviet Union itself. Collins had predicted that the rise of a dissident form of communism within the Soviet Union might facilitate the breakdown of the regime. Beginning in the late 1980s, Soviet leader Mikhail Gorbachev chose not to use military power and other types of repression to crush dissidents in Eastern Europe. Instead, he offered plans for democratization and social reform of Soviet society, and seemed willing to reshape the Soviet Union into a loose federation of somewhat autonomous states. But in 1991, six republics on the western periphery declared their independence, and within months the entire Soviet Union had formally disintegrated into Russia and a number of other independent nations.

In her presidential address, Maureen Hallinan (1997) cautioned that we need to move beyond the restrictive models of social change—the linear view of evolutionary theory and the assumptions about equilibrium in the functionalist perspective. Hallinan noted that upheavals and major shifts do occur, and that sociologists must learn to predict their occurrence, as Collins did with the Soviet Union. Imagine, for example, the dramatic nonlinear social change that accompanies the transformation of a small, undeveloped principality into a major financial and communications hub called Dubai.

● Social Change in Dubai

The story of Dubai, a Middle Eastern principality the size of Rhode Island, is a tale of two cities. When the Maktoum family took control of Dubai (pronounced Doo-Bye) in 1883, it was a pearl-fishing village on the Persian Gulf. But in 1966, the discovery of oil changed everything. When the state's oil reserves proved too limited to fund significant economic and social change, Dubai reinvented itself as a free-trade oasis. By 2000 it had become a tax-free information-technology hub. In less than a single generation—barely a decade—Dubai had transformed itself into what *Forbes* magazine calls the richest city in the world. This is a place that in the late 1950s had no electricity and no paved roads.

Wide-eyed journalists have described Dubai's air-conditioned indoor ski run, open year-round in a country where the daytime temperature averages 92 degrees. Then there is the 160-story Burj Khalifa, which opened in 2010; at a half-mile high, it is by far the world's tallest building. At one point, so much of the city was under construction that 10 percent of the world's construction cranes were located there.

A constitutional monarchy, Dubai is no democratic utopia—there are no contested elections, and there is little public

From 1990 to 2008, the area surrounding the Emirates Golf Club in Dubai changed dramatically.

opposition to the government. Socially, however, Dubai is relatively progressive for an Arab state. Women are encouraged to work, and there is little separation of the sexes, as is common in neighboring states. Alcohol is freely available, speech is relatively free, and the media are largely uncensored.

The citizens of Dubai share its affluence: they receive cheap electricity, free land and water, free health care and education (including graduate study abroad), as well as an average subsidy of $55,000 per year. They pay no income or property taxes. Ironically, the government handouts that citizens enjoy mean that most have little interest in competitive work, so high-skilled positions tend to go to foreigners. The social consequences of Dubai's wealth have been less than benign, however. Environmentally, the cost of its lavish lifestyle is exorbitant. Dubai ranks at the top of the list in terms of its greenhouse gas emissions, at twice the level of the United States and triple the global average.

Another significant social problem, hidden from the investment bankers and tourists who visit Dubai, is the treatment of immigrant laborers. About 95 percent of Dubaians are foreigners from India, Pakistan, the Philippines, Sri Lanka, North Korea, Bangladesh, China, and Yemen. A million of them—seven times the number of Dubai nationals—come from India alone. These migrant laborers sold everything they owned to come to Dubai and take jobs stacking bricks, watering lawns, and cleaning floors. The pay is good relative to their home countries—$275 a month for a skilled electrician—but very poor compared to what the lowest-paid citizen of Dubai earns. At best, an immigrant must work two years just to break even.

There is little government oversight of working or living conditions in Dubai, both of which are poor. For foreign workers seeking to escape the slums in distant deserts, one-bedroom apartments rent for $1,400 per month. In 2008, fire investigators found 500 laborers living in a house built for a single family. Little wonder that late in 2009, when Dubai's economic expansion ground to a halt, foreign workers were heading home at an estimated rate of 5,000 a day.

The global economic downturn that began in 2008 has been particularly savage to Dubai. Having borrowed heavily and invested not always wisely, both the government and major companies are groaning under a debt load that is heavier than even the United States' or Europe's. By 2010, however, Dubai's economy was back on the move, although a bit moderated. The state's story is hardly finished. At the beginning of the second decade of the 21st century, the well-to-do are still flying lobster in for extravagant parties. Overworked foreign laborers, although many fewer of them remain, are still earning wages well above those available in their home countries. Political analysts note that Dubai is the most stable country in the Arab world, with a measured tolerance for outside cultural influences and an intolerance for corruption (Alderman 2010; Ali 2010; Gill 2011; Gorney 2014; Harman 2009; Krane 2009, 2010; McGirk 2009; Rogan 2009; Tatchell 2009).

● Technology and the Future

Technological advances—the airplane, the automobile, the television, the atomic bomb, and more recently, the computer, digital media, and the cell phone—have brought striking changes to our cultures, our patterns of socialization, our social institutions, and our day-to-day social interactions. Technological innovations are, in fact, emerging and being accepted with remarkable speed (see the chapter-opening excerpt).

In the past generation alone, industrial countries have seen a major shift in consumer technologies. No longer do we buy electronic devices to last for even 10 years. Increasingly, we buy them with the expectation that within as little as 3 years, we will need to upgrade to an entirely new technology, whether it be a handheld device or a home computer. Of course, there are those people who either reject the latest gadgets or become frustrated trying to adapt to them. And then there are the "tech-no's"— people who resist the worldwide movement toward electronic networking. Those who become tech-no's are finding that it is a life choice that sets them apart from their peers, much like deciding to be "child free" (Darlin 2006; Kornblum 2007).

In the following sections, we examine various aspects of our technological future and consider their impact on social change, including the social strain they will cause. We focus in particular on recent developments in computer technology, electronic censorship, and biotechnology.

Meet your new teacher! A humanoid robot interacts with school pupils. "Saya" can call the rolls, display six basic expressions—surprise, fear, disgust, anger, happiness, and sadness—and speak basic phrases. Some people think robots provide a solution to the shortage of skilled laborers, but others question their ability to care for people.

Computer Technology

The past decade witnessed an explosion of computer technology in the United States and around the world. Its effects were particularly noteworthy with regard to the Internet, the world's largest computer network. In 2012 the Internet reached 2.3 billion users, compared to just 50 million in 1996. Box 60-1 sketches the worldwide access to and use of the Internet.

The Internet evolved from a computer system built in 1962 by the U.S. Defense Department to enable scholars and military researchers to continue their government work even if part of the nation's communications system were destroyed by a nuclear attack. Until a generation ago, it was difficult to gain access to the Internet without holding a position at a university or a government research laboratory. Today, however, virtually anyone can reach the Internet with a phone line, a computer, and a modem. People buy and sell cars, trade stocks, auction off items, research new medical remedies, vote, and track down long-lost friends online—to mention just a few of the thousands of possibilities.

Unfortunately, not everyone can get onto the information highway, especially not the less affluent. Moreover, this pattern of inequality is global. The core nations that Immanuel Wallerstein described in his world systems analysis have a virtual monopoly on information technology; the peripheral nations of Asia, Africa, and Latin America depend on the core nations both for technology and for the information it provides. For example, North America, Europe, and a few industrialized nations in other regions possess almost all the world's *Internet hosts*—computers that are connected directly to the worldwide network.

What is the solution to this global disconnect between the haves and the have-nots? Some people have suggested giving everyone a computer—or at least, everyone who can't afford one.

Another unsettling aspect of technological innovation is the possibility that such advances could eliminate people's jobs. This concern is not new; throughout the 20th century, first machines and then sophisticated robots took the place of human workers. Today, with software becoming steadily more sophisticated and affordable, the pace of technological innovation is increasing. Researchers at Oxford University looked at 702 occupations in the United States in terms of the worker's role in manipulating objects, thinking with originality, negotiating with or persuading others, and gauging others' emotions and reactions. They then used their findings to predict the likelihood that existing or foreseeable technologies could automate those 702 jobs within the next decade or two. Table 60-1 summarizes a portion of their research.

These predictions are by no means airtight; changes in many variables could affect the researchers' probability estimates. For example, even if a technology can be

"We have to move - they're putting in a cell phone tower here."

Finding a place where you can't receive a text message is getting harder and harder.

BOX 60-1

Our Wired World

The Internet's Global Profile

The old notion of an Internet accessed primarily in the United States and dominated by English-only content is passé. In fact, usage patterns are changing so fast, generalizing about global use of the Internet requires careful research and phrasing.

For example, Figure A, Internet Users by World Region, shows an Internet that is dominated by users in Asia and Europe, two relatively populous continents. However, Figure B, Internet Penetration by World Region, shows a dramatically different picture, one in which the *proportion* of people in each region who access the Internet is highest in North America and Australia. That is, numerically, most Internet users live in Asia and Europe, but the likelihood of a person being an Internet user is greatest in North America and Australia. Figure B shows dramatically low Internet use in Africa, where less than 10 percent of residents access the global network.

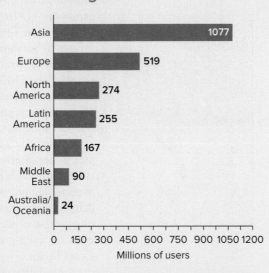

FIGURE A **Internet Users by World Region**

Millions of users

- Asia: 1077
- Europe: 519
- North America: 274
- Latin America: 255
- Africa: 167
- Middle East: 90
- Australia/Oceania: 24

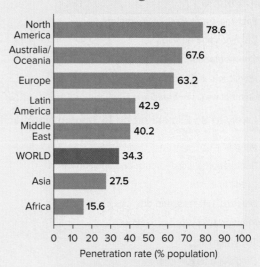

FIGURE B **Internet Penetration by World Region**

Penetration rate (% population)

- North America: 78.6
- Australia/Oceania: 67.6
- Europe: 63.2
- Latin America: 42.9
- Middle East: 40.2
- WORLD: 34.3
- Asia: 27.5
- Africa: 15.6

> The old notion of an Internet accessed primarily in the United States and dominated by English-only content is passé.

Though English is still the primary language of Internet users, as Figure C shows, use of the Chinese language has become much more common. Interestingly, 78 percent of all Japanese speakers use the Internet, compared to 43 percent of all English speakers, though in absolute terms, speakers of Japanese are a significantly smaller group.

FIGURE C **Internet's Top 10 Languages**

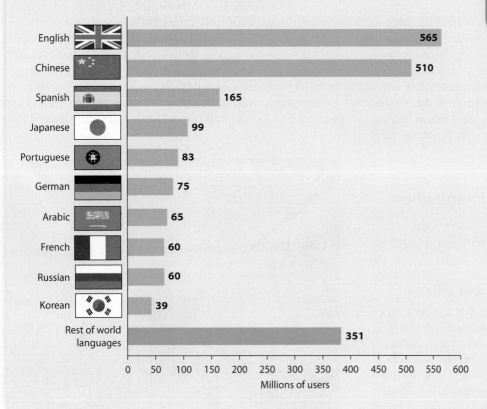

Millions of users

- English: 565
- Chinese: 510
- Spanish: 165
- Japanese: 99
- Portuguese: 83
- German: 75
- Arabic: 65
- French: 60
- Russian: 60
- Korean: 39
- Rest of world languages: 351

LET'S DISCUSS

1. Of the three figures shown here, which do you think presents the most sociologically significant statistics? Explain.

2. Why do you think the use of Chinese on the Internet has increased so dramatically in just a decade? What kind of information would you expect to find in Chinese? Who would use it?

Source: All data taken from Internet World Stats 2014 as of June 30 for Figures A and B and May 31, 2011, for Figure C.

TABLE 60-1 JOBS PROJECTED TO BE ELIMINATED BY COMPUTERIZATION

Unlikely to Be Eliminated by Technology (probability under 0.5 percent)

Emergency management directors

Mental health and substance abuse social workers

Audiologists

First-line supervisors of firefighters

Dietitians and nutritionists

Choreographers

Physicians and surgeons

Elementary school teachers

Likely to Be Eliminated by Technology (probability over 98 percent)

Models

Bookkeepers, accountants, and auditing clerks

Credit analysts

Umpires, referees, and other sports officials

Photographic process workers

Tax preparers

Cargo and freight agents

Watch repairers

Hand embroiderers and sewers

Note: Probability that an occupation could be computerized in the next decade or two. Occupations selected from those extremely likely or unlikely to be computerized on a list of 702 U.S. occupations.

Source: Data from Appendix in Frey and Osborne 2013.

developed to perform a specific skill, access to cheap labor or relatively high technological costs could prevent automation of that skill. Labor organizing could also defer such an outcome. Nevertheless, around 47 percent of total U.S. employment falls into the high-risk category, in danger of being automated within the next decade or two. As Karl Albrecht wrote in the chapter-opening excerpt, technological innovation has a human impact, one that may be difficult or impossible to control given the rapid pace of change.

 use your **sociological imagination**

Have you ever learned about a social movement outside the United States via the Internet?

Privacy and Censorship in a Global Village

Today, new technologies like robots, cars that can park themselves, and smartphones with map applications are bringing about sweeping social change. While much of that change is beneficial, there are some negative effects. Recent advances in computer technology have made it increasingly easy for business firms, government agencies, and even criminals to retrieve and store information about everything from our buying habits to our web-surfing patterns. In public places, at work, and on the Internet, surveillance devices now track our every move, be it a keystroke or an ATM withdrawal. At the same time that these innovations have increased others' power to monitor our behavior, they have raised fears that they might be misused for criminal or undemocratic purposes. In short, new technologies threaten not just our privacy, but our freedom from crime and censorship (O'Harrow Jr. 2005).

In recent years, concern about the criminal misuse of personal information has been underscored by the loss of some huge databases. In the midst of the 2013 holiday shopping season, for example, the credit card records of an estimated 40 million shoppers at Target and other major retailers were compromised.

From a sociological point of view, the complex issues of privacy and censorship can be considered illustrations of culture lag. As usual, the material culture (technology) is changing faster than the nonmaterial culture (norms for controlling the use of technology). Too often, the result is an anything-goes approach to the use of new technologies.

Legislation regarding the surveillance of electronic communications has not always upheld citizens' right to privacy. In 1986, the federal government passed the Electronic Communications Privacy Act, which outlawed the surveillance of telephone calls except with the permission of both the U.S. attorney general and a federal judge. Telegrams, faxes, and e-mail did not receive the same degree of protection, however. Then in 2001, one month after the terrorist attacks of September 11, Congress passed the Patriot Act, which relaxed existing legal checks on surveillance by law enforcement officers. As a result, federal agencies are now freer to gather electronic data, including credit card receipts and banking records. In 2005, Americans learned that the National Security Agency was covertly monitoring phone calls with the cooperation of major U.S. telecommunications companies. Four years later, a federal court ruled that wiretapping without warrants is legal (Eckenwiler 1995; Lichtblau 2009; Vaidhyanathan 2008).

Sociologists' views on the use and abuse of new technologies differ depending on their theoretical perspective. Functionalists take a generally positive view of the Internet, pointing to its manifest function of facilitating communication. From their perspective, the Internet performs the latent function of empowering those with few resources—from hate groups to special-interest organizations—to communicate with the masses. Conflict theorists, in contrast, stress the danger that the most powerful groups in a society will use technology to violate the privacy of the less powerful. Indeed, officials in the People's Republic of China have attempted to censor online discussion groups and web postings that criticize the government. The same abuses can occur in the United States, civil liberties advocates remind us, if citizens are not vigilant in protecting their right to privacy (Magnier 2004).

Another source of controversy is the widespread use of GPS devices to track the location of cars or even people, not to mention the electronic tracking of handheld communications devices. Technology allows you to tweet your whereabouts to your friends, but should others, including the government, be able to home in on you? Put another way, is your location at any given moment covered by the Fourth Amendment to the U.S. Constitution, which protects your right to privacy? Both public opinion and court rulings on this question remain divided. The issue is yet another example of culture lag, or the time it takes for society to reconcile a new technology with traditional cultural values and behavior (Zipp 2009).

If anything, people seem to be less vigilant today about maintaining their privacy than they were before the information age. Young people who have grown up browsing the Internet seem to accept the existence of the cookies and spyware they may pick up while surfing. They have become accustomed to adult surveillance of their conversation in electronic chat rooms. Many see no risk in providing personal information about themselves to the strangers they meet online. Little wonder that college professors find their students do not appreciate the political significance of their right to privacy (Turkle 2004).

 use your **sociological imagination**

Do you hold strong views regarding the privacy of your electronic communications? When using a smartphone or similar device, do you ever suspect you are being watched or your actions monitored?

Biotechnology and the Gene Pool

Another field in which technological advances have spurred global social change is biotechnology. Sex selection of fetuses, genetically engineered organisms, cloning of sheep, cows, and

some small animals—these have been among the significant yet controversial scientific advances in the field of biotechnology. George Ritzer's (2013) concept of McDonaldization applies to the entire area of biotechnology. Just as the fast-food concept has permeated society, no phase of life now seems exempt from therapeutic or medical intervention. In fact, sociologists view many aspects of biotechnology as an extension of the recent trend toward the medicalization of society. Through genetic manipulation, the medical profession is expanding its turf still further (Clarke et al. 2003; Human Genome Project 2012).

One notable success of biotechnology—an unintended consequence of modern warfare—has been progress in the treatment of traumatic injuries. In response to the massive numbers of soldiers who survived serious injury in Iraq and Afghanistan, military doctors and therapists have come up with electronically controlled prosthetic devices. Their innovations include artificial limbs that respond to thought-generated nerve impulses, allowing amputees to move legs, arms, and even individual fingers. These applications of computer science to the rehabilitation of the injured will no doubt be extended to civilians (J. Ellison 2008; Gailey 2007).

One startling biotechnological advance is the possibility of altering human behavior or physical traits through genetic engineering. Fish and plant genes have already been mixed to create frost-resistant potato and tomato crops. More recently, human genes have been implanted in pigs to provide humanlike kidneys for organ transplant. William F. Ogburn probably could not have anticipated such scientific developments when he wrote of culture lag more than 80 years earlier. However, advances like these or even the successful cloning of sheep illustrate again how quickly material culture can change, and how nonmaterial culture moves more slowly in absorbing such changes.

Although today's biotechnology holds itself out as totally beneficial to human beings, it is in constant need of monitoring. Biotechnological advances have raised many difficult ethical and political questions, among them the desirability of tinkering with the gene pool, which could alter our environment in unexpected and unwanted ways. In particular, controversy has been growing concerning genetically modified (GM) food, an issue that arose in Europe but has since spread to other parts of the world, including the United States. The idea behind the technology is to increase food production and make agriculture more economical. But critics use the term *Frankenfood* (as in "Frankenstein") to refer to everything from breakfast cereals made from genetically engineered grains to fresh GM tomatoes. Members of the anti-biotech movement object to tampering with nature, and are concerned about the possible health effects of GM food. Supporters of genetically modified food include not just biotech companies, but those who see the technology as a way to help feed the burgeoning populations of Africa and Asia (Petersen 2009; World Health Organization 2009).

In contrast, less expensive and controversial technologies can further agriculture where it is needed more, in the developing world. Consider cell phones. Unlike most new technologies, the majority of the world's cell phones are used in *less* developed countries. Relatively cheap and not as dependent as computers

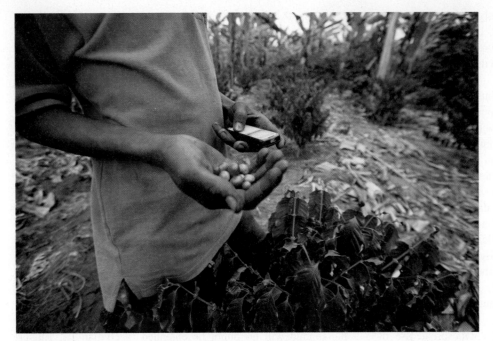

A Ugandan farmer checks the price of coffee beans on his cell phone.

on expensive communications infrastructure, cell phones are common in the world's poorest areas. In Uganda, farmers use them to check weather forecasts and commodity prices. In South Africa, laborers use them to look for work. Researchers at the London Business School have found that in developing countries, a 10 percent increase in cell phone use is correlated with a 0.6 percent rise in GDP (Bures 2011).

While farmers in the developing world use cell phones to improve their incomes, others set out for foreign countries. The Social Policy section that follows considers *transnationals,* immigrants who travel back and forth between the developing and developed worlds, forging human rather than technological links.

social policy and Globalization| Transnationals

Around the world, new communications technologies—cell phones, the World Wide Web—have definitely hastened the process of globalization. Yet without human capital, these innovations would not have spurred the huge increase in global trade and development that occurred over the last several decades. Who are the people behind the trend toward globalization? Often, they are people who see a business opportunity abroad and strike out on their own to take advantage of it. In the process, many of them become migrants.

To facilitate trade and investment with other countries, migrants often exploit their social connections and their familiarity with their home language and culture. In Southeast Asia, for example, Chinese migrants dominate the trade with China; in Africa, Indian migrants dominate. Some migrants invest directly in their home countries to get the manufactured goods they sell abroad. Opportunities abound, and those with capital and good business skills can become quite wealthy (Guest 2011).

The millions of migrant laborers who leave home in search of a better life also play a role in the global economy, filling jobs where there are shortages in the labor market. Although they do not become wealthy working as landscapers or short-order cooks, they consider themselves better off than they were in the old country. Unfortunately, citizens of the host countries often react negatively to the migrants' arrival, worrying that they will take jobs away from the native-born.

Looking at the Issue

As of 2013, 232 million people, or about 3 percent of the world's population, were international migrants. That is more than double the number in 1970. The rest of the world's population were "stayers"—that is, people who continued to live in the countries where they were born (United Nations 2013).

Figure 60-1 shows the worldwide movement of workers with and without the legal right to immigrate. Several areas, such as the European Union, have instituted international agreements that provide for the free movement of laborers. But in most other parts of the world, immigration restrictions give foreign workers only temporary status. Despite such legal restrictions, the labor market has become an increasingly global one. Just as globalization has integrated government policies, cultures, social movements, and financial markets, it has unified what were once discrete national labor markets. So today, for example, immigrants from at least eight different countries work in one small Middle Eastern state, Dubai.

Globalization has changed the immigrant experience as well as the labor market. In generations past, immigrants read foreign language newspapers to keep in touch with events in their home countries. Today, the Internet gives them immediate access to their countries and kinfolk. In this global framework, immigrants are less likely than they were in the past to think of themselves as residents of just one country.

—Continued

MAPPING LIFE WORLDWIDE

FIGURE 60-1 Labor Migration

Income and labor migration
(per capita income in U.S. dollars)

- Greater than $10,000
- $3,000–$10,000
- Less than $3,000
- No data
- Labor migration trend

Source: National Geographic 2005:16.

Transnationals are immigrants who sustain multiple social relationships that link their societies of origin with their societies of settlement (P. Levitt and Jaworsky 2007).

Applying Sociology

As with other issues, sociologists differ in their opinion of transnationals, depending on their theoretical perspective. Functionalists see the free flow of immigrants, even when it is legally restricted, as one way for economies to maximize their use of human labor. Given the law of supply and demand, they note, countries with too few workers will inevitably attract laborers, while those with too many will become unattractive to residents.

Conflict theorists charge that globalization and international migration have increased the economic gulf between developed and developing nations. Today, residents of North America, western Europe, Australia, and Japan consume 32 times more resources than the billions of people who live in developing countries. Through tourism and the global reach of the mass media, people in the poorer countries have become aware of the affluent lifestyle common in developed nations—and of course, many of them now aspire to it (L. Smith 2011).

Interactionists are interested in the day-to-day relationships transnationals have with the people around them, from those of their country of origin to those of the host country and fellow workers from other countries. These scholars are studying transnationals' involvement in local ethnic organizations, to see whether their membership facilitates or retards their integration into the host society. They have discovered that members of global social networks provide one another with mutual support and trust.

Transnationals also participate in social movements. Many transnationals immigrate either to a country with

—Continued

greater political freedom (for example, an Iranian immigrant to Great Britain) or from a more tolerant society (for example, a Filipino worker in Dubai). In these situations, transnational migrants often monitor social movements that interest them via computer. They may also facilitate the growth of a social movement from a distance, by providing information, money, or both (Aunio and Staggenborg 2011).

Another question of interest to interactionists is how transnationals see themselves—how they see their own identities as well as those of their children. In effect, transnationals negotiate their identities, depending on which social network they belong to at the moment. Some sociologists note that while being a transnational can be exhilarating, it can also isolate a person, even in a city of millions. Others worry that transnationals may become so cosmopolitan that they will lose touch with their national identities (Calhoun 2003; Evergeti and Zontini 2006; Plüss 2005; Portes et al. 2008; Rajan and Sharma 2006; Tilly 2007).

Initiating Policy

Although connecting to two societies can be an enriching experience, transnationals face continuing adjustment problems in their new home countries. As we saw with Dubai, immigrant laborers often face difficult living and working conditions. Some sending countries, such as Indonesia and the Philippines, have created national agencies to ensure the protection of their workers abroad. Their objective is ambitious, given that funding for the agencies is limited, and diplomatic and legal challenges complicate their task (United Nations Development Programme 2009:102–104).

Another unresolved transnational issue is voter eligibility. Not all nations allow dual citizenship; even those countries that do may not allow absent nationals to vote. The United States and Great Britain are rather liberal in this regard, permitting dual citizenship and allowing émigrés to continue to vote. Mexico, in contrast, has been reluctant to allow citizens who have emigrated to vote. Mexican politicians worry that the large number of Mexicans who live abroad (especially those in the United States) might vote differently from local voters, causing different outcomes (P. Levitt and Jaworsky 2007; Sellers 2004).

Finally, the controversial issue of illegal immigration has yet to be settled, perhaps because of culture lag. That is, both public attitudes and government policies (nonmaterial culture) have not kept pace with, much less adjusted to, the increasing ease of migration around the globe (material culture). Though globalization has created a global labor market—one that many countries depend on, legal or illegal—the general public's attitude toward illegal immigrants remains hostile, especially in the United States.

TAKE THE ISSUE WITH YOU

1. Suppose you live in an impoverished developing country and have the opportunity to earn a much higher income by immigrating to the United States. Will you do it, even if it means entering the country illegally and working long hours doing menial labor? If so, how will you justify your decision to those who condemn illegal immigration?

2. The U.S. economy depends on the cheap labor that immigrants provide. Should immigrants receive the same social services that U.S. citizens receive? What about their children who are born in the United States (and therefore are U.S. citizens)? Explain your reasoning.

3. Globalization has increased international trade and development at the same time that it has strained nations' social service systems, as migrant workers flow toward countries offering the most extensive social protection. On balance, do you think its overall effect has been beneficial or harmful? What might be done to alleviate the harmful effects of globalization?

MODULE 60 | Recap and Review

Summary

We are living in a time of sweeping social, political, and economic change—change that occurs not just on a local or national basis but on a global scale.

1. Computer technology has made it increasingly easy for any individual, business, or government agency to retrieve more and more information about any of us, thereby infringing on our privacy.

2. Advances in biotechnology have raised difficult ethical questions about genetic engineering.

3. Dubai is a Middle Eastern state that reinvented itself as an information technology hub, in the process undergoing massive social change.

4. Globalization has increased the international migration of laborers, producing a new kind of immigrant. **Transnationals** are immigrants who sustain multiple social relationships that link their societies of origin with their societies of settlement.

Mastering This Chapter

taking sociology with you

1 Choose a social movement that you are interested in and do some research on it. If possible, visit with members of the movement in your local community. Which sociological theory fits this movement better, relative deprivation or resource mobilization? Would you describe the movement as a new social movement? What has been the role of communications in the movement?

2 Try turning off all your electronic devices—phone, laptop, and so on—for a specific period, say a day. Afterward, analyze the experiment from a sociological perspective. What functions did you lose while you were without the devices? Did you gain anything from the experience?

3 Choose a new technology that interests you and analyze it from a sociological point of view. What do you think this technology might contribute to society? What might be some negative effects of the technology? Have you noticed any resistance to it, and if so, on what grounds?

key terms

Assembling perspective A theory of collective behavior introduced by McPhail and Miller that seeks to examine how and why people move from different points in space to a common location.

Collective behavior In the view of sociologist Neil Smelser, the relatively spontaneous and unstructured behavior of a group of people who are reacting to a common influence in an ambiguous situation.

Computer-mediated communication Communicative interaction through two or more networked devices, such as a computer or cell phone. The term applies to a variety of text-based or video interactions, including e-mails, chat rooms, and text messages, some of which may be supported by social media.

Craze An exciting mass involvement that lasts for a relatively long period.

Crowd A temporary gathering of people in close proximity who share a common focus or interest.

Culture lag A period of maladjustment when the nonmaterial culture is still struggling to adapt to new material conditions.

Disaster A sudden or disruptive event or set of events that overtaxes a community's resources, so that outside aid is necessary.

Emergent-norm perspective A theory of collective behavior proposed by Turner and Killian that holds that a collective definition of appropriate or inappropriate behavior emerges during episodes of collective behavior.

Equilibrium model The functionalist view that society tends toward a state of stability or balance.

Evolutionary theory A theory of social change that holds that society is moving in a definite direction.

Fad A temporary pattern of behavior that involves large numbers of people and is independent of preceding trends.

Fashion A pleasurable mass involvement that features a certain amount of acceptance by society and has a line of historical continuity.

False consciousness A term used by Karl Marx to describe an attitude held by members of a class that does not accurately reflect their objective position.

Flash mob A group of people organized by social media to assemble suddenly in a public space, perform some collective activity, and then quickly disperse.

Luddites Rebellious craft workers in 19th-century England who destroyed new factory machinery as part of their resistance to the Industrial Revolution.

New social movement An organized collective activity that addresses values and social identities, as well as improvements in the quality of life.

Nonperiodic assembly A nonrecurring gathering of people that often results from word-of-mouth information.

Panic A fearful arousal or collective flight based on a generalized belief that may or may not be accurate.

Periodic assembly A recurring, relatively routine gathering of people, such as a college class.

Public A dispersed group of people, not necessarily in contact with one another, who share an interest in an issue.

Public opinion Expressions of attitudes on matters of public policy that are communicated to decision makers.

Relative deprivation The conscious feeling of a negative discrepancy between legitimate expectations and present actualities.

Resource mobilization The ways in which a social movement utilizes such resources as money, political influence, access to the media, and personnel.

Rumor A piece of information gathered informally that is used to interpret an ambiguous situation.

Social change Significant alteration over time in behavior patterns and culture, including norms and values.

Social movement An organized collective activity to bring about or resist fundamental change in an existing group or society.

Technology Cultural information about the ways in which the material resources of the environment may be used to satisfy human needs and desires.

Transnational An immigrant who sustains multiple social relationships that link his or her society of origin with the society of settlement.

Value-added model A theory of collective behavior proposed by Neil Smelser to explain how broad social conditions are transformed in a definite pattern into some form of collective behavior.

Vested interests Those people or groups who will suffer in the event of social change, and who have a stake in maintaining the status quo.

self-quiz

Read each question carefully and then select the best answer.

1. In sociological terms, which of the following constitute a crowd?
   a. spectators at a baseball game
   b. participants at a college pep rally
   c. urban rioters
   d. all of the above

2. The least organized and most individualized form of collective behavior is represented by
   a. rumors.
   b. publics.
   c. fashions.
   d. panics.

3. Karl Marx held that leaders of social movements must help workers overcome feelings of
   a. class consciousness.
   b. false consciousness.
   c. socialist consciousness.
   d. surplus value.

4. Organized collective activities that promote autonomy and self-determination, as well as improvements in the quality of life, are referred to as
   a. new social movements.
   b. social revolutions.
   c. resource mobilizations.
   d. crazes.

5. The text cites which of the following as a recognized definition of social change?
   a. tumultuous, revolutionary alternatives that lead to changes in leadership
   b. a significant alteration over time in behavior patterns and culture
   c. regular alteration in a consistent social frame of reference
   d. subtle alterations in any social system

6. Nineteenth-century theories of social change reflect the pioneering work in biological evolution done by
   a. Albert Einstein.
   b. Harriet Martineau.
   c. James Audubon.
   d. Charles Darwin.

7. According to Talcott Parsons's equilibrium model, during which process do social institutions become more specialized in their purposes?
   a. differentiation
   b. adaptive upgrading
   c. inclusion
   d. value generalization

8. Which of the following statements regarding Karl Marx is *not* true?
   a. Marx accepted the evolutionary argument that societies develop along a particular path.
   b. Marx believed that history proceeds through a series of stages, each of which exploits a class of people.
   c. Marx accepted Parsons's equilibrium model, which states that as changes occur in one part of society, there must be adjustments in other parts if stability is to be maintained.
   d. Marx argued that conflict is a normal and desirable aspect of social change.

9. Which of the following terms did William F. Ogburn use to refer to the period of maladjustment during which the nonmaterial culture is still struggling to adapt to new material conditions?
   a. economic shift
   b. political turmoil
   c. social change
   d. culture lag

10. Which sociological perspective sees transnationals as a way for economies to maximize their use of human labor?
    a. functionalist
    b. conflict
    c. interactionist
    d. feminist

11. _____ _____ are organized collective activities to bring about or resist fundamental change in an existing group or society.

12. A person suffering from relative deprivation is dissatisfied because he or she feels downtrodden relative to some appropriate _____ group.

13. Early evolutionary theorists concluded in a(n) _____ fashion that their own behavior and culture were more advanced than those of earlier civilizations.

14. Talcott Parsons used the term _____ to refer to the increasing complexity of social organization.

15. Social economist Thorstein Veblen coined the term _____ _____ to refer to those people or groups who will suffer in the event of social change.

16. The term _____ refers to those who are wary of technological innovations, and who question the incessant expansion of industrialization, the increasing destruction of the natural and agrarian world, and the "throw-it-away" mentality of contemporary capitalism.

17. In 2001, one month after the terrorist attacks of September 11, Congress passed the _____ Act, which relaxed existing legal checks on surveillance by law enforcement officers. Federal agencies are now free to gather data electronically, including credit card receipts and banking records.

18. The _____ is the world's largest computer network.

19. In developing countries, _____ _____ are a less expensive way of furthering agriculture than biotechnology.

20. The _____ perspective would stress the danger that the most powerful groups in a society will use technology to violate the privacy of the less powerful.

Answers

1 (d); 2 (d); 3 (b); 4 (a); 5 (b); 6 (d); 7 (b); 8 (c); 9 (d); 10 (a); 11 Social movements; 12 reference; 13 ethnocentric; 14 differentiation; 15 vested interests; 16 neo-Luddites; 17 Patriot; 18 Internet; 19 cell phones; 20 conflict

glossary

a

Absolute poverty A minimum level of subsistence that no family should be expected to live below.

Achieved status A social position that a person attains largely through his or her own efforts.

Activity theory An interactionist theory of aging that suggests that those elderly people who remain active and socially involved will be best adjusted.

Adoption In a legal sense, the transfer of the legal rights, responsibilities, and privileges of parenthood to a new legal parent or parents.

Affirmative action Positive efforts to recruit minority group members or women for jobs, promotions, and educational opportunities.

Ageism Prejudice and discrimination based on a person's age.

Agrarian society The most technologically advanced form of preindustrial society. Members engage primarily in the production of food, but increase their crop yields through technological innovations such as the plow.

Alienation A condition of estrangement or dissociation from the surrounding society.

Amalgamation The process through which a majority group and a minority group combine to form a new group.

Anomie Durkheim's term for the loss of direction felt in a society when social control of individual behavior has become ineffective.

Anomie theory of deviance Robert Merton's theory of deviance as an adaptation of socially prescribed goals or of the means governing their attainment, or both.

Anticipatory socialization Processes of socialization in which a person rehearses for future positions, occupations, and social relationships.

Anti-Semitism Anti-Jewish prejudice.

Apartheid A former policy of the South African government, designed to maintain the separation of Blacks and other non-Whites from the dominant Whites.

Applied sociology The use of the discipline of sociology with the specific intent of yielding practical applications for human behavior and organizations.

Argot Specialized language used by members of a group or subculture.

Ascribed status A social position assigned to a person by society without regard for the person's unique talents or characteristics.

Assembling perspective A theory of collective behavior introduced by McPhail and Miller that seeks to examine how and why people move from different points in space to a common location.

Assimilation The process through which a person forsakes his or her cultural tradition to become part of a different culture.

Authority Institutionalized power that is recognized by the people over whom it is exercised.

b

Basic sociology Sociological inquiry conducted with the objective of gaining a more profound knowledge of the fundamental aspects of social phenomena. Also known as *pure sociology*.

Big data The rapid collection and analysis of enormous amounts of information by supercomputers.

Bilateral descent A kinship system in which both sides of a person's family are regarded as equally important.

Bilingualism The use of two languages in a particular setting, such as the workplace or schoolroom, treating each language as equally legitimate.

Birthrate The number of live births per 1,000 population in a given year. Also known as the *crude birthrate*.

Black power A political philosophy, promoted by many younger Blacks in the 1960s, that supported the creation of Black-controlled political and economic institutions.

Bourgeoisie Karl Marx's term for the capitalist class, comprising the owners of the means of production.

Brain drain The immigration to the United States and other industrialized nations of skilled workers, professionals, and technicians who are desperately needed in their home countries.

Brass ceiling An invisible barrier that blocks the promotion of a woman in the military because of her official (not necessarily actual) exclusion from combat.

Bureaucracy A component of formal organization that uses rules and hierarchical ranking to achieve efficiency.

Bureaucratization The process by which a group, organization, or social movement becomes increasingly bureaucratic.

c

Capitalism An economic system in which the means of production are held largely in private hands and the main incentive for economic activity is the accumulation of profits.

Caste A hereditary rank, usually religiously dictated, that tends to be fixed and immobile.

Causal logic The relationship between a condition or variable and a particular consequence, with one leading to the other.

Census An enumeration, or counting, of a population.

Charismatic authority Max Weber's term for power made legitimate by a leader's exceptional personal or emotional appeal to his or her followers.

Charter school An experimental school that is developed and managed by individuals, groups of parents, or educational management organizations.

Class A group of people who have a similar level of wealth and income.

Class consciousness In Karl Marx's view, a subjective awareness held by members of a class regarding their common vested interests and the need for collective political action to bring about social change.

Class system A social ranking based primarily on economic position in which achieved characteristics can influence social mobility.

Classical theory An approach to the study of formal organizations that views workers as being motivated almost entirely by economic rewards.

Climate change An observable alteration of the global atmosphere that affects natural weather patterns over several decades or longer.

Clinical sociology The use of the discipline of sociology with the specific intent of altering social relationships or restructuring social institutions.

Closed system A social system in which there is little or no possibility of individual social mobility.

Coalition A temporary or permanent alliance geared toward a common goal.

Code of ethics The standards of acceptable behavior developed by and for members of a profession.

Cognitive theory of development Jean Piaget's theory that children's thought progresses through four stages of development.

Cohabitation The practice of living together as a male–female couple without marrying.

Collective behavior In the view of sociologist Neil Smelser, the relatively spontaneous and unstructured behavior of a group of people who are reacting to a common influence in an ambiguous situation.

Colonialism The maintenance of political, social, economic, and cultural domination over a people by a foreign power for an extended period.

Color-blind racism The use of the principle of race neutrality to defend a racially unequal status quo.

Communism As an ideal type, an economic system under which all property is communally owned and no social distinctions are made on the basis of people's ability to produce.

Computer-mediated communication Communicative interaction through two or more networked devices, such as a computer or cell phone. The term applies to a variety of text-based or video interactions, including e-mails, chat rooms, and text messages, some of which may be supported by social media.

Conflict perspective A sociological approach that assumes that social behavior is best understood in terms of tension between groups over power or the allocation of resources, including housing, money, access to services, and political representation.

Conformity Going along with peers—individuals of our own status who have no special right to direct our behavior.

Conspicuous consumption Purchasing goods not to survive but to flaunt one's superior wealth and social standing.

Contact hypothesis An interactionist perspective which states that in cooperative circumstances, interracial contact between people of equal status will reduce prejudice.

Content analysis The systematic coding and objective recording of data, guided by some rationale.

Control group The subjects in an experiment who are not introduced to the independent variable by the researcher.

Control theory A view of conformity and deviance that suggests that our connection to members of society leads us to systematically conform to society's norms.

Control variable A factor that is held constant to test the relative impact of an independent variable.

Corporate welfare Tax breaks, bailouts, direct payments, and grants that the government gives to corporations.

Correlation A relationship between two variables in which a change in one coincides with a change in the other.

Correspondence principle A term used by Bowles and Gintis to refer to the tendency of schools to promote the values expected of individuals in each social class and to perpetuate social class divisions from one generation to the next.

Counterculture A subculture that deliberately opposes certain aspects of the larger culture.

Craze An exciting mass involvement that lasts for a relatively long period.

Creationism A literal interpretation of the Bible regarding the creation of humanity and the universe, used to argue that evolution should not be presented as established scientific fact.

Credentialism An increase in the lowest level of education needed to enter a field.

Crime A violation of criminal law for which some governmental authority applies formal penalties.

Cross-tabulation A table or matrix that shows the relationship between two or more variables.

Crowd A temporary gathering of people in close proximity who share a common focus or interest.

Crowdsourcing Use of the Internet to seek assistance from the general public in the form of financing, services, or even ideas.

Cultural capital Noneconomic goods, such as family background and education, which are reflected in a knowledge of language and the arts.

Cultural convergence The flow of content across multiple media, and the accompanying migration of media audiences.

Cultural relativism The viewing of people's behavior from the perspective of their own culture.

Cultural transmission A school of criminology that argues that criminal behavior is learned through social interactions.

Cultural universal A common practice or belief found in every culture.

Culture The totality of learned, socially transmitted customs, knowledge, material objects, and behavior.

Culture industry The worldwide media industry that standardizes the goods and services demanded by consumers.

Culture lag A period of maladjustment when the nonmaterial culture is still struggling to adapt to new material conditions.

Culture shock The feeling of surprise and disorientation that people experience when they encounter cultural practices that are different from their own.

Culture war The polarization of society over controversial cultural elements.

Curanderismo Latino folk medicine, a form of holistic health care and healing.

d

Death rate The number of deaths per 1,000 population in a given year. Also known as the *crude death rate.*

Degradation ceremony An aspect of the socialization process within some total institutions, in which people are subjected to humiliating rituals.

Deindustrialization The systematic, widespread withdrawal of investment in basic aspects of productivity, such as factories and plants.

Democracy In a literal sense, government by the people.

Demographic transition A term used to describe the change from high birthrates and death rates to low birthrates and death rates.

Demography The scientific study of population.

Denomination A large, organized religion that is not officially linked to the state or government.

Dependency theory An approach that contends that industrialized nations continue to exploit developing countries for their own gain.

Dependent variable The variable in a causal relationship that is subject to the influence of another variable.

Deviance Behavior that violates the standards of conduct or expectations of a group or society.

Dictatorship A government in which one person has nearly total power to make and enforce laws.

Differential association A theory of deviance proposed by Edwin Sutherland that holds that violation of rules results from exposure to attitudes favorable to criminal acts.

Differential justice Differences in the way social control is exercised over different groups.

Diffusion The process by which a cultural item spreads from group to group or society to society.

Digital divide The relative lack of access to the latest technologies among low-income groups, racial and ethnic minorities, rural residents, and the citizens of developing countries.

Disaster A sudden or disruptive event or set of events that overtaxes a community's resources, so that outside aid is necessary.

Discovery The process of making known or sharing the existence of an aspect of reality.

Discrimination The denial of opportunities and equal rights to individuals and groups because of prejudice or other arbitrary reasons.

Disengagement theory A functionalist theory of aging that suggests that society and the aging individual mutually sever many of their relationships.

Dominant ideology A set of cultural beliefs and practices that helps to maintain powerful social, economic, and political interests.

Double consciousness The division of an individual's identity into two or more social realities.

Downsizing Reductions taken in a company's workforce as part of deindustrialization.

Dramaturgical approach A view of social interaction, popularized by Erving Goffman, in which people are seen as theatrical performers.

Dysfunction An element or process of a society that may disrupt the social system or reduce its stability.

e

Ecclesia A religious organization that claims to include most or all members of a society and is recognized as the national or official religion.

Ecological modernization The alignment of environmentally favorable practices with economic self-interest through constant adaptation and restructuring.

Economic system The social institution through which goods and services are produced, distributed, and consumed.

Education A formal process of learning in which some people consciously teach, while others adopt the social role of learner.

Egalitarian family An authority pattern in which spouses are regarded as equals.

Elite model A view of society as being ruled by a small group of individuals who share a common set of political and economic interests.

Emergent-norm perspective A theory of collective behavior proposed by Turner and Killian that holds that a collective definition of appropriate or inappropriate behavior emerges during episodes of collective behavior.

Endogamy The restriction of mate selection to people within the same group.

Environmental justice A legal strategy based on claims that racial minorities are subjected disproportionately to environmental hazards.

Environmental refugee A person who has been displaced by rising seas, destructive storms, expanding deserts, water shortages, or high levels of toxic pollutants.

Equilibrium model Talcott Parsons's functionalist view that society tends toward a state of stability or balance.

Established sect J. Milton Yinger's term for a religious group that is the outgrowth of a sect, yet remains isolated from society.

Estate system A system of stratification under which peasants were required to work land leased to them by nobles in exchange for military protection and other services. Also known as *feudalism.*

Esteem The reputation that a specific person has earned within an occupation.

Ethnic group A group that is set apart from others primarily because of its national origin or distinctive cultural patterns.

Ethnocentrism The tendency to assume that one's own culture and way of life represent the norm or are superior to all others.

Ethnography The study of an entire social setting through extended systematic fieldwork.

Euthanasia The act of bringing about the death of a hopelessly ill and suffering person in a relatively quick and painless way for reasons of mercy.

Evolutionary theory A theory of social change that holds that society is moving in a definite direction.

Exogamy The requirement that people select a mate outside certain groups.

Experiment An artificially created situation that allows a researcher to manipulate variables.

Experimental group The subjects in an experiment who are exposed to an independent variable introduced by a researcher.

Exploitation theory A Marxist theory that views racial subordination in the United States as a manifestation of the class system inherent in capitalism.

Expressiveness Concern for the maintenance of harmony and the internal emotional affairs of the family.

Extended family A family in which relatives—such as grandparents, aunts, or uncles—live in the same home as parents and their children.

f

Face-work A term used by Erving Goffman to refer to the efforts people make to maintain the proper image and avoid public embarrassment.

Fad A temporary pattern of behavior that involves large numbers of people and is independent of preceding trends.

False consciousness A term used by Karl Marx to describe an attitude held by members of a class that does not accurately reflect their objective position.

Familism (*Familismo*) Pride in the extended family, expressed through the maintenance of close ties and strong obligations to kinfolk outside the immediate family.

Family A set of people related by blood, marriage or some other agreed-on relationship, or adoption, who share the primary responsibility for reproduction and caring for members of society.

Fashion A pleasurable mass involvement that features a certain amount of acceptance by society and has a line of historical continuity.

Feminism An ideology that favors equal rights for women.

Feminist perspective A sociological approach that views inequity in gender as central to all behavior and organization.

Feminization of poverty A trend in which women constitute an increasing proportion of the poor people of both the United States and the world.

Fertility The level of reproduction in a society.

Flash mob A group of people organized by social media to assemble suddenly in a public space, perform some collective activity, and then quickly disperse.

Folkway A norm governing everyday behavior whose violation raises comparatively little concern.

Force The actual or threatened use of coercion to impose one's will on others.

Formal norm A norm that has been written down and that specifies strict punishments for violators.

Formal organization A group designed for a special purpose and structured for maximum efficiency.

Formal social control Social control that is carried out by authorized agents, such as police officers, judges, school administrators, and employers.

Functionalist perspective A sociological approach that emphasizes the way in which the parts of a society are structured to maintain its stability.

Fundamentalism An emphasis on doctrinal conformity and the literal interpretation of sacred texts.

g

Gatekeeping The process by which a relatively small number of people in the media industry control what material eventually reaches the audience.

Gemeinschaft A term used by Ferdinand Tönnies to describe a close-knit community, often found in rural areas, in which strong personal bonds unite members.

Gender role Expectations regarding the proper behavior, attitudes, and activities of males and females.

Generalized other A term used by George Herbert Mead to refer to the attitudes, viewpoints, and expectations of society as a whole that a child takes into account in his or her behavior.

Genocide The deliberate, systematic killing of an entire people or nation.

Gerontology The scientific study of the sociological and psychological aspects of aging and the problems of the aged.

Gesellschaft A term used by Ferdinand Tönnies to describe a community, often urban, that is large and impersonal, with little commitment to the group or consensus on values.

Glass ceiling An invisible barrier that blocks the promotion of a qualified individual in a work environment because of the individual's gender, race, or ethnicity.

Glass escalator The advantage men experience in occupations dominated by women.

Global warming A significant rise in the earth's surface temperatures that occurs when industrial gases like carbon dioxide turn the planet's atmosphere into a virtual greenhouse.

Globalization The worldwide integration of government policies, cultures, social movements, and financial markets through trade and the exchange of ideas.

Goal displacement Overzealous conformity to official regulations of a bureaucracy.

Group Any number of people with similar norms, values, and expectations who interact with one another on a regular basis.

Growth rate The difference between births and deaths, plus the difference between immigrants and emigrants, per 1,000 population.

h

Hate crime A criminal offense committed because of the offender's bias against a race, religion, ethnic group, national origin, or sexual orientation. Also referred to as *bias crime.*

Hawthorne effect The unintended influence that observers of experiments can have on their subjects.

Health As defined by the World Health Organization, a state of complete physical, mental, and social well-being, and not merely the absence of disease and infirmity.

Hidden curriculum Standards of behavior that are deemed proper by society and are taught subtly in schools.

Holistic medicine Therapies in which the health care practitioner considers the person's physical, mental, emotional, and spiritual characteristics.

Homogamy The conscious or unconscious tendency to select a mate with personal characteristics similar to one's own.

Homophobia Fear of and prejudice against homosexuality.

Horizontal mobility The movement of an individual from one social position to another of the same rank.

Horticultural society A preindustrial society in which people plant seeds and crops rather than merely subsist on available foods.

Hospice care Treatment of the terminally ill in their own homes, or in special hospital units or other facilities, with the goal of helping them to die easily, without pain.

Human ecology An area of study that is concerned with the interrelationships between people and their environment.

Human relations approach An approach to the study of formal organizations that emphasizes the role of people, communication, and participation in a bureaucracy and tends to focus on the informal structure of the organization.

Hunting-and-gathering society A preindustrial society in which people rely on whatever foods and fibers are readily available in order to survive.

Hyperconsumerism The practice of buying more than we need or want, and often more than we can afford; a preoccupation of postmodern consumers.

Hyper-local media Reporting that is highly local and typically Internet-based.

Hypothesis A speculative statement about the relationship between two or more variables.

i

Ideal type A construct or model for evaluating specific cases.

Impression management A term used by Erving Goffman to refer to the altering of the presentation of the self in order to create distinctive appearances and satisfy particular audiences.

Incest taboo The prohibition of sexual relationships between certain culturally specified relatives.

Income Salaries and wages.

Independent variable The variable in a causal relationship that causes or influences a change in another variable.

Index crimes The eight types of crime tabulated each year by the FBI in the *Uniform Crime Reports:* murder, rape, robbery, assault, burglary, theft, motor vehicle theft, and arson.

Industrial society A society that depends on mechanization to produce its goods and services.

Infant mortality rate The number of deaths of infants under 1 year old per 1,000 live births in a given year.

Influence The exercise of power through a process of persuasion.

Informal economy Transfers of money, goods, or services that are not reported to the government.

Informal norm A norm that is generally understood but not precisely recorded.

Informal social control Social control that is carried out casually by ordinary people through such means as laughter, smiles, and ridicule.

In-group Any group or category to which people feel they belong.

Innovation The process of introducing a new idea or object to a culture through discovery or invention.

Institutional discrimination The denial of opportunities and equal rights to individuals and groups that results from the normal operations of a society.

Instrumentality An emphasis on tasks, a focus on more distant goals, and a concern for the external relationship between one's family and other social institutions.

Intelligent design (ID) The idea that life is so complex that it could only have been created by intelligent design.

Interactionist perspective A sociological approach that generalizes about everyday forms of social interaction in order to explain society as a whole.

Intergenerational mobility Changes in the social position of children relative to their parents.

Interview A face-to-face, phone, or online questioning of a respondent to obtain desired information.

Intragenerational mobility Changes in social position within a person's adult life.

Invention The combination of existing cultural items into a form that did not exist before.

Iron law of oligarchy A principle of organizational life developed by Robert Michels, under which even a democratic organization will eventually develop into a bureaucracy ruled by a few individuals.

k

Kinship The state of being related to others.

l

Labeling theory An approach to deviance that attempts to explain why certain people are viewed as deviants while others engaged in the same behavior are not.

Labor union Organized workers who share either the same skill or the same employer.

Laissez-faire A form of capitalism under which people compete freely, with minimal government intervention in the economy.

Language An abstract system of word meanings and symbols for all aspects of culture; includes gestures and other nonverbal communication.

Latent function An unconscious or unintended function that may reflect hidden purposes.

Law Governmental social control.

Liberation theology Use of a church, primarily Roman Catholic, in a political effort to eliminate poverty, discrimination, and other forms of injustice from a secular society.

Life chances Max Weber's term for the opportunities people have to provide themselves with material goods, positive living conditions, and favorable life experiences.

Life course approach A research orientation in which sociologists and other social scientists look closely at the social factors that influence people throughout their lives, from birth to death.

Life expectancy The median number of years a person can be expected to live under current mortality conditions.

Living wage A wage that meets workers' basic needs, allowing them to maintain a safe, decent standard of living within their community.

Looking-glass self A concept used by Charles Horton Cooley that emphasizes the self as the product of our social interactions.

Luddites Rebellious craft workers in 19th-century England who destroyed new factory machinery as part of their resistance to the Industrial Revolution.

m

Machismo A sense of virility, personal worth, and pride in one's maleness.

Macrosociology Sociological investigation that concentrates on large-scale phenomena or entire civilizations.

Manifest function An open, stated, and conscious function.

Mass media Print and electronic means of communication that carry messages to widespread audiences.

Master status A status that dominates others and thereby determines a person's general position in society.

Material culture The physical or technological aspects of our daily lives.

Matriarchy A society in which women dominate in family decision making.

Matrilineal descent A kinship system in which only the mother's relatives are significant.

Matrix of domination The cumulative impact of oppression because of race and ethnicity, gender, and social class, as well as religion, sexual orientation, disability, age, and citizenship status.

McDonaldization The process by which the principles of bureaucratization have increasingly shaped organizations worldwide.

Mean A number calculated by adding a series of values and then dividing by the number of values.

Mechanical solidarity A collective consciousness that emphasizes group solidarity, characteristic of societies with minimal division of labor.

Median The midpoint or number that divides a series of values into two groups of equal numbers of values.

Medical model An approach in which medical experts define illness or disease, determine and control the course of treatment, and even affect patients' views of themselves.

Mental illness A disorder of the brain that disrupts a person's thinking, feeling, and ability to interact with others.

Microfinancing Lending small sums of money to the poor so they can work their way out of poverty.

Microsociology Sociological investigation that stresses the study of small groups, often through experimental means.

Midlife crisis A stressful period of self-evaluation that begins at about age 40.

Migration The relatively permanent movement of people, with the purpose of changing their place of residence.

Minority group A subordinate group whose members have significantly less control or power over their own lives than the members of a dominant or majority group have over theirs.

Mode The single most common value in a series of scores.

Model, or ideal, minority A subordinate group whose members supposedly have succeeded economically, socially, and educationally despite past prejudice and discrimination, and without resorting to political and violent confrontations with Whites.

Modernization The far-reaching process through which periphery nations move from traditional or less developed institutions to those characteristic of more developed societies.

Modernization theory A functionalist approach that proposes that modernization and development will gradually improve the lives of people in developing nations.

Monarchy A form of government headed by a single member of a royal family, usually a king, queen, or some other hereditary ruler.

Monogamy A form of marriage in which an individual has only one partner.

Monopoly Control of a market by a single business firm.

Morbidity rate The rate of disease in a given population.

Mores Norms deemed highly necessary to the welfare of a society.

Mortality rate The rate of death in a given population.

Multinational corporation A commercial organization that is headquartered in one country but does business throughout the world.

Multiple masculinities A variety of male gender roles, including nurturing-caring and effeminate-gay roles, that men may play along with their more pervasive traditional role of dominating women.

n

Narcotizing dysfunction The phenomenon in which the media provide such massive amounts of coverage that the audience becomes numb and fails to act on the information, regardless of how compelling the issue.

Natural science The study of the physical features of nature and the ways in which they interact and change.

Naturally occurring retirement community (NORC) An area that has gradually become an informal center for senior citizens.

Neocolonialism Continuing dependence of former colonies on foreign countries.

New religious movement (NRM) or **cult** A small, secretive religious group that represents either a new religion or a major innovation of an existing faith.

New social movement An organized collective activity that addresses values and social identities, as well as improvements in the quality of life.

Nonmaterial culture Ways of using material objects, as well as customs, beliefs, philosophies, governments, and patterns of communication.

Nonperiodic assembly A nonrecurring gathering of people that often results from word-of-mouth information.

Nonverbal communication The sending of messages through the use of gestures, facial expressions, and postures.

Norm An established standard of behavior maintained by a society.

Nuclear family A married couple and their unmarried children living together.

O

Obedience Compliance with higher authorities in a hierarchical structure.

Objective method A technique for measuring social class that assigns individuals to classes on the basis of criteria such as occupation, education, income, and place of residence.

Observation A research technique in which an investigator collects information through direct participation, by closely watching a group or community.

Offshoring The transfer of work to foreign contractors.

Oligarchy A form of government in which a few individuals rule.

Open system A social system in which the position of each individual is influenced by his or her achieved status.

Operational definition An explanation of an abstract concept that is specific enough to allow a researcher to assess the concept.

Opinion leader Someone who influences the opinions and decisions of others through day-to-day personal contact and communication.

Organic solidarity A collective consciousness that rests on mutual interdependence, characteristic of societies with a complex division of labor.

Organized crime The work of a group that regulates relations between criminal enterprises involved in illegal activities, including prostitution, gambling, and the smuggling and sale of illegal drugs.

Out-group A group or category to which people feel they do not belong.

p

Panic A fearful arousal or collective flight based on a generalized belief that may or may not be accurate.

Patriarchy A society in which men dominate in family decision making.

Patrilineal descent A kinship system in which only the father's relatives are significant.

Peace The absence of war, or more broadly, a proactive effort to develop cooperative relations among nations.

Percentage A portion of 100.

Periodic assembly A recurring, relatively routine gathering of people, such as a college class.

Personality A person's typical patterns of attitudes, needs, characteristics, and behavior.

Peter principle A principle of organizational life, originated by Laurence J. Peter, according to which every employee within a hierarchy tends to rise to his or her level of incompetence.

Pluralism Mutual respect for one another's cultures among the various groups in a society, which allows minorities to express their cultures without experiencing prejudice.

Pluralist model A view of society in which many competing groups within the community have access to government, so that no single group is dominant.

Political system The social institution that is founded on a recognized set of procedures for implementing and achieving society's goals.

Politics In Harold Lasswell's words, "who gets what, when, and how."

Polyandry A form of polygamy in which a woman may have more than one husband at the same time.

Polygamy A form of marriage in which an individual may have several husbands or wives simultaneously.

Polygyny A form of polygamy in which a man may have more than one wife at the same time.

Population pyramid A special type of bar chart that shows the distribution of a population by gender and age.

Postindustrial society A society whose economic system is engaged primarily in the processing and control of information.

Postmodern society A technologically sophisticated society that is preoccupied with consumer goods and media images.

Power The ability to exercise one's will over others.

Power elite A term used by C. Wright Mills to refer to a small group of military, industrial, and government leaders who control the fate of the United States.

Precarious work Employment that is poorly paid, and from the worker's perspective, insecure and unprotected.

Prejudice A negative attitude toward an entire category of people, often an ethnic or racial minority.

Prestige The respect and admiration that an occupation holds in a society.

Primary group A small group characterized by intimate, face-to-face association and cooperation.

Profane The ordinary and commonplace elements of life, as distinguished from the sacred.

Professional criminal A person who pursues crime as a day-to-day occupation, developing skilled techniques and enjoying a certain degree of status among other criminals.

Proletariat Karl Marx's term for the working class in a capitalist society.

Protestant ethic Max Weber's term for the disciplined work ethic, this-worldly concerns, and rational orientation to life emphasized by John Calvin and his followers.

Public A dispersed group of people, not necessarily in contact with one another, who share an interest in an issue.

Public opinion Expressions of attitudes on matters of public policy that are communicated to decision makers.

q

Qualitative research Research that relies on what is seen in field or naturalistic settings more than on statistical data.

Quantitative research Research that collects and reports data primarily in numerical form.

Quasi-religion A scholarly category that includes organizations that may see themselves as religious but may be seen by others as "sort of religious."

Queer theory The study of society from the perspective of a broad spectrum of sexual identities, including heterosexuality, homosexuality, and bisexuality.

Questionnaire A printed or written form used to obtain information from a respondent.

r

Racial formation A sociohistorical process in which racial categories are created, inhabited, transformed, and destroyed.

Racial group A group that is set apart from others because of physical differences that have taken on social significance.

Racial profiling Any arbitrary action initiated by an authority based on race, ethnicity, or national origin rather than on a person's behavior.

Racism The belief that one race is supreme and all others are innately inferior.

Random sample A sample for which every member of an entire population has the same chance of being selected.

Rational-legal authority Power made legitimate by law.

Reference group Any group that individuals use as a standard for evaluating themselves and their own behavior.

Relative deprivation The conscious feeling of a negative discrepancy between legitimate expectations and present actualities.

Relative poverty A floating standard of deprivation by which people at the bottom of a society, whatever their lifestyles, are judged to be disadvantaged *in comparison with the nation as a whole.*

Reliability The extent to which a measure produces consistent results.

Religion According to Émile Durkheim, a unified system of beliefs and practices relative to sacred things.

Religious belief A statement to which members of a particular religion adhere.

Religious experience The feeling or perception of being in direct contact with the ultimate reality, such as a divine being, or of being overcome with religious emotion.

Religious ritual A practice required or expected of members of a faith.

Remittances The monies that immigrants return to their families of origin. Also called *migradollars.*

Representative democracy A form of government in which certain individuals are selected to speak for the people.

Research design A detailed plan or method for obtaining data scientifically.

Resocialization The process of discarding former behavior patterns and accepting new ones as part of a transition in one's life.

Resource mobilization The ways in which a social movement utilizes such resources as money, political influence, access to the media, and personnel.

Rites of passage A ritual marking the symbolic transition from one social position to another.

Role conflict The situation that occurs when incompatible expectations arise from two or more social positions held by the same person.

Role exit The process of disengagement from a role that is central to one's self-identity in order to establish a new role and identity.

Role strain The difficulty that arises when the same social position imposes conflicting demands and expectations.

Role taking The process of mentally assuming the perspective of another and responding from that imagined viewpoint.

Rumor A piece of information gathered informally that is used to interpret an ambiguous situation.

s

Sacred Elements beyond everyday life that inspire awe, respect, and even fear.

Sample A selection from a larger population that is statistically representative of that population.

Sanction A penalty or reward for conduct concerning a social norm.

Sandwich generation The generation of adults who simultaneously try to meet the competing needs of their parents and their children.

Sapir-Whorf hypothesis A hypothesis concerning the role of language in shaping our interpretation of reality. It holds that language is culturally determined.

Science The body of knowledge obtained by methods based on systematic observation.

Scientific management approach Another name for the classical theory of formal organizations.

Scientific method A systematic, organized series of steps that ensures maximum objectivity and consistency in researching a problem.

Second shift The double burden—work outside the home followed by child care and housework—that many women face and few men share equitably.

Secondary analysis A variety of research techniques that make use of previously collected and publicly accessible information and data.

Secondary group A formal, impersonal group in which there is little social intimacy or mutual understanding.

Sect A relatively small religious group that has broken away from some other religious organization to renew what it considers the original vision of the faith.

Secularization The process through which religion's influence on other social institutions diminishes.

Segregation The physical separation of two groups of people in terms of residence, workplace, and social events; often imposed on a minority group by a dominant group.

Self According to George Herbert Mead, a distinct identity that sets us apart from others.

Serial monogamy A form of marriage in which a person may have several spouses in his or her lifetime, but only one spouse at a time.

Sexism The ideology that one sex is superior to the other.

Sick role Societal expectations about the attitudes and behavior of a person viewed as being ill.

Significant other A term used by George Herbert Mead to refer to an individual who is most important in the development of the self, such as a parent, friend, or teacher.

Single-parent family A family in which only one parent is present to care for the children.

Slavery A system of enforced servitude in which some people are owned by other people.

Social capital The collective benefit of social networks, which are built on reciprocal trust.

Social change Significant alteration over time in behavior patterns and culture, including norms and values.

Social constructionist perspective An approach to deviance that emphasizes the role of culture in the creation of the deviant identity.

Social control The techniques and strategies for preventing deviant human behavior in any society.

Social disorganization theory The theory that crime and deviance are caused by the absence or breakdown of communal relationships and social institutions.

Social epidemiology The study of the distribution of disease, impairment, and general health status across a population.

Social inequality A condition in which members of society have differing amounts of wealth, prestige, or power.

Social institution An organized pattern of beliefs and behavior centered on basic social needs.

Social interaction The ways in which people respond to one another.

Social mobility Movement of individuals or groups from one position in a society's stratification system to another.

Social movement An organized collective activity to bring about or resist fundamental change in an existing group or society.

Social network A series of social relationships that links a person directly to others, and through them indirectly to still more people.

Social role A set of expectations for people who occupy a given social position or status.

Social science The study of the social features of humans and the ways in which they interact and change.

Social structure The way in which a society is organized into predictable relationships.

Socialism An economic system under which the means of production and distribution are collectively owned.

Socialization The lifelong process in which people learn the attitudes, values, and behaviors appropriate for members of a particular culture.

Societal-reaction approach Another name for *labeling theory*.

Society A fairly large number of people who live in the same territory, are relatively independent of people outside their area, and participate in a common culture.

Sociobiology The systematic study of how biology affects human social behavior.

Sociocultural evolution Long-term social trends resulting from the interplay of continuity, innovation, and selection.

Socioeconomic status (SES) A measure of social class that is based on income, education, and occupation.

Sociological imagination An awareness of the relationship between an individual and the wider society, both today and in the past.

Sociology The scientific study of social behavior and human groups.

Sovereignty movement The effort by the indigenous people of Hawai'i to win self-government, as well as the restoration of—or compensation for—their ancestral lands.

Status A term used by sociologists to refer to any of the full range of socially defined positions within a large group or society.

Status group A term used by Max Weber to refer to people who have the same prestige or lifestyle, independent of their class positions.

Stereotype An unreliable generalization about all members of a group that does not recognize individual differences within the group.

Stigma A label used to devalue members of certain social groups.

Stratification A structured ranking of entire groups of people that perpetuates unequal economic rewards and power in a society.

Subculture A segment of society that shares a distinctive pattern of customs, rules, and traditions that differs from the pattern of the larger society.

Survey A study, generally in the form of an interview or questionnaire, that provides researchers with information about how people think and act.

Symbol A gesture, object, or word that forms the basis of human communication.

Symbolic ethnicity An ethnic identity that emphasizes concerns such as ethnic food or political issues rather than deeper ties to one's ethnic heritage.

t

Teacher-expectancy effect The impact that a teacher's expectations about a student's performance may have on the student's actual achievements.

Technology Cultural information about the ways in which the material resources of the environment may be used to satisfy human needs and desires.

Terrorism The use or threat of violence against random or symbolic targets in pursuit of political aims.

Theory In sociology, a set of statements that seeks to explain problems, actions, or behavior.

Total fertility rate (TFR) The average number of children born alive to any woman, assuming that she conforms to current fertility rates.

Total institution A term coined by Erving Goffman to refer to an institution that regulates all aspects of a person's life under a single authority, such as a prison, the military, a mental hospital, or a convent.

Totalitarianism Virtually complete government control and surveillance over all aspects of a society's social and political life.

Tracking The practice of placing students in specific curriculum groups on the basis of their test scores and other criteria.

Traditional authority Legitimate power conferred by custom and accepted practice.

Trained incapacity The tendency of workers in a bureaucracy to become so specialized that they develop blind spots and fail to notice obvious problems.

Transnational An immigrant who sustains multiple social relationships that link his or her society of origin with the society of settlement.

Transnational crime Crime that occurs across multiple national borders.

Transracial adoption The adoption of a non-White child by White parents or a Hispanic child by non-Hispanics.

u

Underclass The long-term poor who lack training and skills.

v

Validity The degree to which a measure or scale truly reflects the phenomenon under study.

Value A collective conception of what is considered good, desirable, and proper—or bad, undesirable, and improper—in a culture.

Value-added model A theory of collective behavior proposed by Neil Smelser to explain how broad social conditions are transformed in a definite pattern into some form of collective behavior.

Value neutrality Max Weber's term for objectivity of sociologists in the interpretation of data.

Variable A measurable trait or characteristic that is subject to change under different conditions.

Verstehen The German word for "understanding" or "insight"; used by Max Weber to stress the need for sociologists to take into account the subjective meanings people attach to their actions.

Vertical mobility The movement of an individual from one social position to another of a different rank.

Vested interests Veblen's term for those people or groups who will suffer in the event of social change, and who have a stake in maintaining the status quo.

Victimization survey A questionnaire or interview given to a sample of the population to determine whether people have been victims of crime.

Victimless crime A term used by sociologists to describe the willing exchange among adults of widely desired but illegal goods and services.

Visual sociology The use of photographs, film, and video to study sociology.

Vital statistics Records of births, deaths, marriages, and divorces gathered through a registration system maintained by governmental units.

W

War Conflict between organizations that possess trained combat forces equipped with deadly weapons.

Wealth An inclusive term encompassing all a person's material assets, including land, stocks, and other types of property.

White-collar crime Illegal acts committed by affluent, "respectable" individuals in the course of business activities.

White privilege Rights or immunities granted to people as a particular benefit or favor simply because they are White.

World systems analysis The global economy as an interdependent system of economically and politically unequal nations.

Z

Zero population growth (ZPG) The state of a population in which the number of births plus immigrants equals the number of deaths plus emigrants.

references

a

Aaronson, Daniel, and Eric French. 2013. "How Does a Federal Minimum Wage Hike Affect Aggregate Household Spending?" Chicago Fed Letter (August). Accessed December 20 at http://www.chicagofed.org/digital_assets/publications/chicago_fed_letter/2013/cflaugust2013_313.pdf.

AARP. 2011. "Research and Strategic Analysis Integrated Value and Strategy June, 2011." Accessed January 10, 2012 (http://assets.aarp.org/rgcenter/general/boomers-envision-retirement-2011.pdf).

ABC Television. 2013. "Arkansas Schools to Start Moment of Silence when Classes Begin." August 2. Accessed September 8, 2013 at http://www.4029tv.com.

Abercrombie, Nicholas, Bryan S. Turner, and Stephen Hill, eds. 1990. *Dominant Ideologies.* Cambridge, MA: Unwin Hyman.

———, Stephen Hill, and Bryan S. Turner. 1980. *The Dominant Ideology Thesis.* London: Allen and Unwin.

Aberle, David F., A. K. Cohen, A. K. Davis, M. J. Leng, Jr., and F. N. Sutton. 1950. "The Functional Prerequisites of a Society." *Ethics* 60 (January):100–111.

Abramson, David, Irwin Redlener, Tasha Stehling-Ariza, and Elizabeth Fuller. 2007. *The Legacy of Katrina's Children: Estimating the Numbers of At-Risk Children in the Gulf Coast States of Louisiana and Mississippi.* New York: Columbia University Mailman School of Public Health.

ACLU. 2013. "Frank v. Walker: Fighting Voter Suppression in Wisconsin." November 4. Accessed December 30 at https://www.aclu.org/voting-rights/frank-v-walker-fighting-voter-suppression-wisconsin.

———. 2014. "Map of States with Restrictions on Adoption or Fostering by LGB People." Accessed January 18 at https://www.aclu.org/lgbt-rights/map-states-restrictions-adoption-or-fostering-lgb-people.

Adams, Tracey L. 2010. "Gender and Feminization in Health Care Professions." *Sociology Compass* 4 (July):454–465.

Adams, Tyrone L., and Stephen A. Smith. 2008. *Electronic Tribes: The Virtual Worlds of Geeks, Gamas, Shamans, and Scammers.* Austin: University of Texas Press.

Addams, Jane. 1910. *Twenty Years at Hull-House.* New York: Macmillan.

———. 1930. *The Second Twenty Years at Hull-House.* New York: Macmillan.

Adler, Patricia A., and Peter Adler. 2007. "The Demedicalization of Self-Injury: From Psychopathology to Sociological Deviance."

Journal of Contemporary Ethnography 36 (October):537–570.

———, and ———. 2011. *The Tender Cut: Inside the Hidden World of Self-Injury.* New York: New York University Press.

———, ———, and John M. Johnson. 1992. "Street Corner Society Revisited." *Journal of Contemporary Ethnography* 21 (April):3–10.

Adorno, Theodor. [1971] 1991. *The Culture Industry.* London: Routledge.

Agence France-Presse. 2013. "World Watches American TV, Not Always Legally." September 21. Accessed November 23, 2013 at http://www.rawstory.com/rs/2013/09/21/world-watches-american-tv-not-always-legally/.

Aguirre, Benigno E., E. L. Quarantelli, and Jorge L. Mendoza. 1988. "The Collective Behavior of Fads: The Characteristics, Effects, and Career of Streaking." *American Sociological Review* 53 (August):569–584.

Alain, Michel. 1985. "An Empirical Validation of Relative Deprivation." *Human Relations* 38 (8):739–749.

Alba, Richard D. 1990. *Ethnic Identity: The Transformation of White America.* New Haven, CT: Yale University Press.

———. 2009. *Blurring the Color Line: The New Chance for a More Integrated America.* Cambridge, MA: Harvard University Press.

Albas, Cheryl, and Daniel Albas. 1996. "An Invitation to the Ethnographic Study of University Examination Behavior: Concepts, Methodology and Implications." *Canadian Journal of Higher Education* 26 (3):1–26.

Albas, Daniel, and Cheryl Albas. 1988. "Aces and Bombers: The Post-Exam Impression Management Strategies of Students." *Symbolic Interaction* 11 (Fall):289–302.

Albrecht, Gary L. 2004. "Disability: Sociological Perspectives." Pp. 3710–3713 in *International Encyclopedia of the Social and Behavioral Sciences,* edited by Neil J. Smelser and Paul B. Baltes. New York: Elsevier.

Albrecht, Karl. 2014. "The Information Revolution's Broken Promises." *Futurist* (March–April):22–28.

Alderman, Liz. 2010. "Rapid Growth in Dubai Outstrips Its Resources." *New York Times,* October 28, pp. D1, D5.

———. 2012. "Starbucks on the Seine." *New York Times,* March 30, pp. B1, B8.

Alexander, Karl L. 1997. "Public Schools and the Public Good." *Social Forces* 70 (September):1–30.

Ali, Syed. 2010. "Permanent Impermanence." *Contexts* (Spring):26–31.

Allen, Bem P. 1978. *Social Behavior: Fact and Falsehood.* Chicago: Nelson-Hall.

Allen, Greg. 2012. "Mission Diversify: CIA Begins LGBT Recruiting." December 2. Accessible at www.wbur.org.

Alliance for Board Diversity. 2013. *Missing Pieces: Women and Minorities on Fortune 500 Boards. 2012 Alliance for Board Diversity Census.* Accessible at http://theabd.org/2012_ABD%20Missing_Pieces_Final_8_15_13.pdf.

Allport, Gordon W. 1979. *The Nature of Prejudice.* 25th anniversary ed. Reading, MA: Addison-Wesley.

Alon, Sigal. 2009. "The Evolution of Class Inequality in Higher Education: Competition, Exclusion, and Adaptation." *American Sociological Review* 74 (October):731–755.

Alvord, Lori Arviso, and Elizabeth Cohen Van Pelt. 1999. *The Scalpel and the Silver Bear.* New York: Bantam Books.

Alwin, Duane F. 2002. "Generations X, Y, and Z: Are They Changing America?" *Contexts* (Fall–Winter):42–51.

Alzheimer's Association. 2012. *2012 Alzheimer's Disease Facts and Figures.* Accessed March 25 at http://www.alzheimers_disease_facts_and_figures.asp.

American Academy of Cosmetic Surgery. 2010. "New Survey Indicates More than 17 Million Cosmetic Procedures Performed Last Year in U.S." Chicago: AACS.

American Academy of Pediatrics. 2011. "Media Use by Children Younger Than 2 Years." *Pediatrics* 128 (November):1040–1045.

———. 2013. "Children, Adolescents, and the Media." *Pediatrics* 132 (November): 958–959.

American Community Survey. 2011. "American Community Survey 2010." Accessible at www.census.gov/acs/www/.

———. 2013a. "American Community Survey 2012." Data released August 2013 and accessible at www.census.gov.

———. 2013b. "Survey Methodology Main." Accessible at www.census.gov/acs/www/methodology/methodology_main/.

American Jewish Committee. 2005. *2005 Annual Survey of American Jewish Opinion.* New York: AJC.

American Lung Association. 2011. "State of the Air 2011." Accessed March 26, 2012 (www.stateoftheair.org).

American Psychiatric Association. 2013. *Diagnostic and Statistical Manual of Mental Disorders, Fifth Edition (DSM-5(TM)).* Arlington VA: American Psychiatric Publishing.

American Psychological Association. 2008. "Being Gay Is Just as Healthy as Being Straight." Accessed February 25 (www.apa.org).

American Sociological Association. 1999. *Code of Ethics.* Reprinted 2008. Washington, DC: ASA.

———. 2005. "Need Today's Data Yesterday." Accessed December 17 (www.asanet.org).

———. 2009. *21st Century Careers with an Undergraduate Degree in Sociology.* Washington, DC: ASA.

———. 2014. *Current Sections.* Accessed January 2 (www.asanet.org/sections/list.cfm).

Amoss, Pamela, and Stevan Harrell. 1981. *Other Ways of Growing Old.* Stanford, CA: Stanford University Press.

Anatale, Alex, Atsushi Yamanaka, and Didier Nkurikiyimfura. 2013. "The Metamorphosis to a Knowledge-Based Society: Rwanda." Chapter 2.2 in *The Global Information Technology Report 2013: Growth and Jobs in a Hyperconnected World,* edited by Beñat Bilbao-Osorio, Soumitra Dutta, and Bruno Lanvin. April 10. Geneva: World Economic Forum. Accessible at http://www.weforum.org/reports/global-information-technology-report-2013.

Andersen, Margaret. 2007. *Thinking about Women: Sociological Perspectives on Sex and Gender.* 7th ed. New York: Allyn and Bacon.

Anderson, Elijah. 1990. *Streetwise: Race, Class, and Change in an Urban Community.* Chicago: University of Chicago Press.

Anderson, Gretchen. 2009. *Love, Actually: A National Survey of Adults 18+ on Love, Relationships, and Romance.* Washington, DC: AARP.

Anderson, John Ward, and Molly Moore. 1993. "The Burden of Womanhood." *Washington Post National Weekly Edition* 10 (March 22–28):6–7.

Anderson, Warwick. 2003. *The Cultivation of Whiteness: Science, Health and Racial Destiny in Australia.* New York: Perseus.

Andrews, Lori. 2012. "Facebook Is Using You." *New York Times,* February 5, Sunday Review, p. 7.

Angier, Natalie. 1998. "Drugs, Sports, Body Image and G.I. Joe." *New York Times,* December 22, pp. D1, D3.

Angwin, Julia. 2010. "The Web's New Gold Mine: Your Secrets." *Wall Street Journal,* July 31, pp. W1, W2.

———. 2012. "Digital-Privacy Rules Taking Shape." *Wall Street Journal,* March 26. Accessible at http://online.wsj.com/news/articles/SB100014240527023034047045773054730611907 62.

———, and Jennifer Valentino-DeVries. 2010a. "Race Is On to 'Fingerprint' Phones, PCs." *Wall Street Journal,* December 1, pp. A1, A15.

Ansell, Amy E. 2008. "Color Blindness." Pp. 320–321, vol. 1, in *Encyclopedia of Race, Ethnicity, and Society,* edited by Richard T. Schaefer. Thousand Oaks, CA: Sage.

Anti-Defamation League. 2013. *2012 Audit of Anti-Semitic Incidents.* Accessible at http://www.adl.org.

Arab American Institute. 2010. "Demographics." Accessed March 7 (www.aaiusa.org/arab-americans/22/demographics).

Archer, Patrick, and Bryan Orr. 2011. "Class Identification in Review: Past Perspectives and Future Directions." *Sociology Compass* 5 (January):104–115.

Argetsinger, Amy, and Jonathan Krim. 2002. "Stopping the Music." *Washington Post National Weekly Edition* 20 (December 2):20.

Armer, J. Michael, and John Katsillis. 1992. "Modernization Theory." Pp. 1299–1304, vol. 4, in *Encyclopedia of Sociology,* edited by Edgar F. Borgatta and Marie L. Borgatta. New York: Macmillan.

Ash, Timothy Garton. 2007. "Welcome to a Mixed-Up World." *Globe and Mail* (Toronto), July 14, p. A19.

Asi, Maryam, and Daniel Beaulieu. 2013. *Arab Households in the United States 2006–2010.* ACSBR/10-20. Accessible at http://www.census.gov.

Aslanian, Sasha. 2006. "Researchers Still Learning from Romania's Orphans." NPR, September 16. Accessed September 25, 2013 at http://www.npr.org/templates/story/story.php?storyi=6089477.

Association of Theological Schools. 2013. "Annual Data Tables 2012–2013." Table 2-12A. Accessed January 25, 2014 at http://docs.ats.edu/uploads/resources/institutional-data/annual-data-tables/2012-2013-annual-data-tables.pdf.

Atchley, Robert C. 1976. *The Sociology of Retirement.* New York: Wiley.

Atchley, Robert C., and Amanda S. Barusch. 2004. *Social Forces and Agency: An Introduction to Social Gerontology.* 10th ed. Belmont, CA: Thomson.

Attwood, Bain. 2003. *Rights for Aborigines.* Crows Nest, Australia: Allen and Unwin.

Aunio, Anna-Lisa, and Suzanne Staggenborg. 2011. "Transnational Linkages and Movement Communities." *Sociology Compass* 5 (5):364–375.

Austin, Chammie. 2009. *Impression Management.* Accessed January 11, 2012 (www.education.com/reference/article/impression-management).

Australia. 1997. "Bringing Them Home: Report of the National Inquiry into the Separation of Aboriginal and Torres Strait Islander Children from Their Families." Accessible at www.humanrights.gov.au.

———. 2008. "Apology to Australia's Indigenous Peoples, House of Representatives, Parliament House, Canberra." Accessed February 13 (www.pm.gov.au/media/speech/2008/speech_0073.cfm).

Avon. 2013. "Experience Avon's History." Accessed February 26 at http://www.avoncompany.com/aboutavon/history/index.html.

Azumi, Koya, and Jerald Hage. 1972. *Organizational Systems.* Lexington, MA: Heath.

b

Babad, Elisha Y., and P. J. Taylor. 1992. "Transparency of Teacher Expectancies across Language, Cultural Boundaries." *Journal of Educational Research* 86:120–125.

Bacon Lovers' Talk. 2009. "Bacon Lovers' Talk." Accessed February 4 (www.bacontalk.com/).

Bado-Fralick, Nikki, and Rebecca Sachs Norris. 2010. *Toying with God: The World of Religious Games and Dolls.* Waco, TX: Baylor University Press.

Bagby, Ihsam. 2012. *The American Mosque 2011.* Washington, DC: Council on American-Islamic Relations.

Bajaj, Vikas. 2011a. "15 Years in Microcredit Has Suffered a Black Eye." *New York Times,* January 6, p. B3.

———. 2011b. "Luster Dims for a Public Microlender." *New York Times,* May 11, pp. 1, 4.

Baker, Joseph O., and Buster G. Smith. 2009. "The Names: Social Characteristics of the Religiously Unfaithful." *Social Forces* 87 (March):1251–1263.

Baker, Peter. 2009. "Obama Reverses Rules on U.S. Abortion Aid." *New York Times,* January 24.

Baker, Therese L. 1999. *Doing Social Research.* 3rd ed. New York: McGraw-Hill.

Bankston III, Carl I., Christopher Bonastia, Michael J. Petrilli, Diane Ravitch, Linda A. Renzuti, and Maria Paino. 2013. "Charter Schools." *Contexts* 12 (Summer):16–20.

Baran, Stanley. 2014. *Introduction to Mass Communication: Media Literacy and Culture.* 8th ed. New York: McGraw-Hill.

Barnes, Patricia, Barbara Bloom, and Richard Nahin. 2008. "Complementary and Alternative Medicine Use among Adults and Children: United States, 2007." *National Health Statistics Reports,* December 10.

———, Eve Powell-Griner, Ken McFann, and Richard L. Nation. 2004. "Complementary and Alternative Medicine Use among Adults: United States, 2002." *Advance Data from Vital and Health Statistics,* No. 343. Hyattsville, MD: National Center for Health Statistics.

Barnes, Taylor. 2009. "Rise of the Shadow Economy." *Christian Science Monitor,* November 8, pp. 30–31.

Barnett, W. Steven, Megan E. Carolan, Jen Fitzgerald, and James H. Squires. 2013. *The State of Preschool 2012: State Preschool Yearbook.* New Brunswick, NJ: National Institute for Early Education Research.

Barrett, David B., Todd M. Johnson, and Peter F. Crossing. 2008. "The 2007 Annual Megacensus of Religions." Chicago: Encyclopaedia Britannica.

Barron, Milton L. 1953. "Minority Group Characteristics of the Aged in American Society." *Journal of Gerontology* 8:477–482.

Bartlett, Thomas. 2009. "How the International Essay Mill Has Changed Cheating." *Chronicle of Higher Education,* March 20, pp. A1, A22–A25.

———. 2011. "A Database Named Desire: 2 Scientists Examine Online Searches for Sex." *Chronicle of Higher Education* 57 (August 12):A12.

Barton, Bernadette. 2006. *Stripped: Inside the Lives of Exotic Dancers.* New York: New York University Press.

Basulto, Dominic. 2011. "Popping the 'Supercommittee' 'Filter Bubble.'" *Washington Post* (November 3). Accessed November 11 (www.washingtonpost.com/blogs/innovations/post/popping-the-supercommittee-filter-bubble/2010/12/20glQAMfcviM_blog.html).

Battin, Margaret P., Agnes van der Heide, and Bregje D. Onwuleaka-Philipsen. 2007. "Legal Physician-Assisted Dying in Oregon and the Netherlands: Evidence Concerning the Impact on Patients in 'Vulnerable' Groups." *Journal of Medical Ethics* 33 (October):591–597.

Baudrillard, Jean. [1970] 1998. *The Consumers Society.* London: Sage.

Bauerlein, Mark. 2008. "Online Literacy Is a Lesser Kind." *Chronicle of Higher Education,* September 19, pp. B10–B11.

Bauerlein, Monika. 1996. "The Luddites Are Back." *Utne Reader* (March–April):24, 26.

Bauman, Kurt J. 1999. "Extended Measures of Well-Being: Meeting Basic Needs." *Current Population Reports,* ser. P-70, no. 67. Washington, DC: U.S. Government Printing Office.

Bazar, Emily. 2009. "Tent Cities Filling up with Casualties of the Economy." *USA Today,* May 5, pp. 1A–2A.

BBC News. 2005. "Indonesian Village Report: January 12, 2005." Accessed January 19 (www.theworld.org).

Beagan, Brenda L. 2001. " 'Even If I Don't Know What I'm Doing I Can Make It Look Like I Know What I'm Doing': Becoming a Doctor in the 1990s." *Canadian Review of Sociology and Anthropology* 38:275–292.

———, Alana Chiasson, Cheryl Fiske, Stephanie Forseth, Alisha Hosein, Marianne Myers, and Janine Stang. 2013. "Working with Transgender Clients: Learning from Others to Improve Occupational Therapy Practice." *Canadian Journal of Occupational Therapy* 80(2):82–91.

Bearman, Peter S., James Moody, and Katherine Stovel. 2004. "Chains of Affection: The Structure of Adolescent Romantic and Sexual Networks." *American Journal of Sociology* 110 (July):44–91.

Beck, Barbara. 2009. "A Slow-Burning Fuse: A Special Report on Ageing Populations." *The Economist* (June 27).

Becker, Anne E. 2007. "Facets of Acculturation and Their Diverse Relations to Body Shape Concerns in Fiji." *International Journal of Eating Disorders* 40 (1):42–50.

Becker, Howard S. 1952. "Social Class Variations in the Teacher-Pupil Relationship." *Journal of Educational Sociology* 25 (April):451–465.

———. 1963. *The Outsiders: Studies in the Sociology of Deviance.* New York: Free Press.

——— (ed.). 1964. *The Other Side: Perspectives on Deviance.* New York: Free Press.

———. 1974. "Photography and Sociology." *Studies in the Anthropology of Visual Communication* 1:3–26. Accessible by the author at http://lucy.ukc.ac.uk/becker.html. Also reproduced in his 1986 *Doing Things Together: Selected Papers.* Evanston, IN: Northwestern University Press.

———, Blanche Geer, Everett C Hughes, and Anselm Strauss. 1961. *Boys in White: Student Culture in Medical School.* Chicago: University of Chicago Press.

Beddoes, Zanny Milton. 2012. "For Richer, for Poorer." *The Economist* (October 13): Special Report.

Beisel, Nicola, and Tamara Kay. 2004. "Abortion, Race, and Gender in Nineteenth-Century America." *American Sociological Review* 69 (4):498–518.

Belkin, Douglas, and Caroline Porter. 2012. "Web Profiles Haunt Students." *Wall Street Journal,* October 4, p. A3.

Bell, Daniel. 1953. "Crime as an American Way of Life." *Antioch Review* 13 (Summer):131–154.

———. [1973] 1999. *The Coming of Post-Industrial Society: A Venture in Social Forecasting.* With new foreword. New York: Basic Books.

Bell, Wendell. 1981. "Modernization." Pp. 186–187 in *Encyclopedia of Sociology.* Guilford, CT: DPG Publishing.

Beller, Emily. 2009. "Bringing Intergenerational Social Mobility Research into the Twenty-first Century: Why Mothers Matter." *American Sociological Review* 74 (August):507–528.

Bendavid, Naftali. 2013. "For Belgium's Tormented Souls, Euthansia-Made-Easy-Beckons." *Wall Street Journal,* June 15, pp. A1, A12.

Bendick, Marc, Jr., Charles W. Jackson, and J. Horacio Romero. 1993. *Employment Discrimination against Older Workers: An Experimental Study of Hiring Practices.* Washington, DC: Fair Employment Council of Greater Washington.

Benford, Robert D. 1992. "Social Movements." Pp. 1880–1887, vol. 4, in *Encyclopedia of Sociology,* edited by Edgar F. Borgatta and Marie Borgatta. New York: Macmillan.

Bergen, Raquel Kennedy. 2006. *Marital Rape: New Research and Directions.* Harrisburg, PA: VAW Net.

Berger, Peter, and Thomas Luckmann. 1966. *The Social Construction of Reality.* New York: Doubleday.

Berk, Richard A., and Howard E. Aldrich. 1972. "Patterns of Vandalism during Civil Disorders as an Indicator of Selection of Targets." *American Sociological Review* 37 (October):533–547.

Berman, Paul. 2003. *Terror and Liberalism.* New York: Norton.

Bernhardt, Annette, et al. (10 additional co-authors). 2009. *Broken Laws, Unprotected Workers.* New York: Ford, Joyce, Haynes, and Russell Sage Foundations.

Bernstein, Elizabeth. 2007. "Colleges Move Boldly on Student Drinking." *Wall Street Journal,* December 6, pp. D1, D2.

Bernstein, Mary, and Verta Taylor, eds. 2013. *The Marrying Kind?* Minneapolis: University of Minnesota Press.

Bessen-Cassino, Yasemin. 2013. "Cool Store Bad Jobs." *Contexts* (Fall):42–47.

Best, Joel. 2004. *Deviance: Career of a Concept.* Belmont, CA: Wadsworth Thomson.

Bhagat, Chetan. 2007. *One Night at the Call Centre.* London: Black Swan.

Bialik, Carol. 2010. "Seven Careers in a Lifetime? Think Twice, Researchers Say." *Wall Street Journal,* September 4, p. A6.

Bianchi, Suzanne M., and Daphne Spain. 1996. "Women, Work, and Family in America." *Population Bulletin* 51 (December).

Biddlecom, Ann, and Steven Martin. 2006. " Childless in America." *Contexts* 5 (Fall):54.

Bielby, Denise D., and C. Lee Harrington. 2008. *Global TV: Exporting Television and Culture in the World Market.* New York: New York University Press.

Bilbao-Osorio, Beñat, Soumitra Dutta, and Bruno Lanvin, eds. 2013. *The Global Information Technology Report 2013: Growth and Jobs in a Hyperconnected World.* April 10. Geneva: World Economic Forum. Accessible at http://www.weforum.org/reports/global-information-technology-report-2013.

Billboard. 2012. "The Year in Music 2012—Charts, Ringtones." Accessed February 11 at www.billboard.com.

Billitteri, Thomas, J. 2009. "Middle-Class Squeeze." *CQ Researcher* 19 (March 6):201–224.

Birnbaum, Jeffrey H. 2005. "Listen to the Wallet." *Washington Post National Weekly Edition,* April 4, p. 11.

Bishaw, Aleyayehu. 2011. "Areas with Concentrated Poverty: 2006–2010." *American Community Survey Briefs.* Issued December 2011 ACSBR/10-17. Accessible at http://www.census.gov/prod/2011pubs/acsbr10-17.pdf.

Bitler, Marianne, and Hilary W. Hoynes. 2010. "The State of the Safety Net in the Post-Welfare Reform Era." Paper prepared for Brookings Papers on Economic Activity, Washington, DC, September 16–20.

Black, Donald. 1995. "The Epistemology of Pure Sociology." *Law and Social Inquiry* 20 (Summer):829–870.

Blais, Allison, and Lynn Rasic. 2011. *A Place of Remembrance: Official Book of the National September 11 Memorial.* Washington, DC: National Geographic.

Blank, Rebecca M. 2010. "Middle Class in America." *Focus* 27 (Summer):1–8.

———. 2011. *Changing Inequality.* Berkeley: University of California Press.

Blau, Peter M., and Otis Dudley Duncan. 1967. *The American Occupational Structure.* New York: Wiley.

Blauner, Robert. 1972. *Racial Oppression in America.* New York: Harper and Row.

Blumberg, Stephen J., and Julian V. Luke. 2007. "Coverage Bias in Traditional Telephone Surveys of Low-Income and Young Adults." *Public Opinion Quarterly* 71 (5):734–749.

Blumer, Herbert. 1955. "Collective Behavior." Pp. 165–198 in *Principles of Sociology,* 2nd ed., edited by Alfred McClung Lee. New York: Barnes and Noble.

———. 1969. *Symbolic Interactionism: Perspective and Method.* Englewood Cliffs, NJ: Prentice Hall.

Boase, Jeffery, John B. Horrigan, Barry Wellman, and Lee Rainie. 2006. *The Strength of Internet Ties.* Washington, DC: Pew Internet and American Life Project.

Boje, David M. 1995. "Stories of Storytelling Organization: A Postmodern Analysis of Disney as 'Tamara-Land.'" *Academy of Management Journal* 38:997–1035.

Bonilla-Silva, Eduardo. 2004. "From Bi-Racial to Tri-Racial: Towards a New System of Racial Stratification in the USA." *Ethics and Racial Studies* 27 (November):931–950.

———. 2006. *Racism without Racists.* Lanham, MD: Rowman and Littlefield.

Bonus, Rick. 2000. *Locating Filipino Americans: Ethnicity and the Cultural Politics of Space.* Philadelphia: Temple University Press.

Borjas, George S., Jeffrey Grogger, and Gordon H. Hanson. 2006. "Immigration and African-American Employment Opportunities: The Response of Wages, Employment, and Incarceration to Labor Supply Shocks." Working Paper 12518. Cambridge, MA: National Bureau of Economic Research.

Boston Area Research Initiative. 2013. "Housing Issues." Accessible at http://www.bostonarearesearchinitiative.net.

Bottomore, Tom, and Maximilien Rubel, eds. 1956. *Karl Marx: Selected Writings in Sociology and Social Philosophy.* New York: McGraw-Hill.

Bourdieu, Pierre, and Jean-Claude Passerson. 1990. *Reproduction in Education, Society and Culture.* 2nd ed. London. Sage. Originally published as *La reproduction.*

Boushey, Heather. 2005. *Student Debt: Bigger and Bigger.* Washington, DC: Center for Economic and Policy Research.

Bouvier, Leon F. 1980. "America's Baby Boom Generation: The Fateful Bulge." *Population Bulletin* 35 (April).

Bowles, Samuel, and Herbert Gintis. 1976. *Schooling in Capitalist America: Educational Reforms and the Contradictions of Economic Life.* New York: Basic Books.

Bowman, Thomas. 2013. "As Qualified Men Dwindle, Military Looks for a Few Good Women." March 23. Accessible at http://www.npr.org/2013/03/25/174966070/as-qualified-men-dwindle-military-looks-for-a-few-good-women.

Boy Scouts of America. 2010. "2009 Annual Report." Accessed November 10, 2011 (www.scouting.org).

Brabazon, Tara. 2007. *The University of Google: Education in the (post) Information Age.* Burlington, VT: Ashgate.

Brady Campaign. 2013. "2013 State Rankings." Accessed February 16 at www.bradycampaign.org/xshare/stateleg/scorecard/2011/2011_brady_campaign_state_scorecard_rankings.pdf.

Brady, Erik. 2010. "Title IX Model Survey Policy to Be Rescinded." *USA Today,* April 20, p. C1.

Brandchannel.com. 2013. "Browse by Brand or Film." Accessed February 11 at http://www.brandchannel.com/brandcameo_films.asp?movie_year=2-12.

Brannigan, Augustine. 1992. "Postmodernism." Pp. 1522–1525 in *Encyclopedia of Sociology,* vol. 3, edited by Edgar F. Borgatta and Marie L. Borgatta. New York: Macmillan.

Bray, James H., and John Kelly. 1999. *Stepfamilies: Love, Marriage, and Parenting in the First Decade.* New York: Broadway Books.

Brazier, Chris, and Amir Hamed, eds. 2007. *The World Guide.* 11th ed. Oxford, UK: New Internationalist.

Breines, Winifred. 2007. "Struggling to Connect: White and Black Feminism in the Movement Years." *Contexts* 6 (Winter):18–24.

Brennan Center. 2006. *Citizens Without Proof.* New York: Brennan Center for Justice at NYU School of Law.

———. 2013. *Election 2012 Laws Roundup.* Accessed January 13 at http://www.brennancenter.org.

Brewer, Rose M., and Nancy A. Heitzeg. 2008. "The Racialization of Criminal Punishment." *American Behavioral Scientist* 51 (January):625–644.

Brewis, Alexandra, Amber Wutich, Ashlan Falletta-Cowden, and Isa Rodriguez-Soto. 2011. "Body Norms and Fat Stigma in Global Perspective." *Current Anthropology* 52 (April):269–276.

Brint, Steven. 1998. *Schools and Societies.* Thousand Oaks, CA: Pine Forge Press.

Britannica Online. 2011. "Worldwide Adherents of All Religions by Six Continental Areas. Mid-2010." Accessed March 28.

Brown, David. 2009. "Doing a Number on Surveys." *Washington Post National Weekly Edition* 26 (January 19):37.

Brown, David K. 2001. "The Social Sources of Educational Credentialism: Status Cultures, Labor Markets, and Organizations." *Sociology of Education* 74 (Extra issue):19–34.

Brown, Geoff. 2008a. "Cities under Fire." *Johns Hopkins Public Health* (Fall).

———. 2008b. "Building a Safer Gun." *Johns Hopkins Public Health* (Fall).

Brown, Michael, and Amy Goldin. 1973. *Collective Behavior: A Review and Reinterpretation of the Literature.* Pacific Palisades, CA: Goodyear.

Brown, Patricia Leigh. 2004. "For Children of Gays, Marriage Brings Joy." *New York Times,* March 19, p. A13.

Brown, Robert McAfee. 1980. *Gustavo Gutierrez.* Atlanta: John Knox.

Brown, Roger W. 1954. "Mass Phenomena." Pp. 833–873, vol. 2, in *Handbook of Social Psychology,* edited by Gardner Lindzey. Reading, MA: Addison-Wesley.

Browne, Irene, ed. 2001. *Latinas and African American Women at Work: Race, Gender, and Economic Inequality.* New York: Russell Sage Foundation.

Brubaker, Bill. 2008. "Social Insecurity: Many People's Numbers Are Readily Available Online to Identity Thieves." *Washington Post National Weekly Edition,* January 14, p. 34.

Brulle, Robert, and J. Craig Jenkins. 2008. "Fixing the Bungled U.S. Environmental Movement." *Contexts* 7 (Spring):14–18.

Bryman, Alan. 1995. *Disney and His Worlds.* London: Routledge.

Buchmann, Claudia, Thomas A. DiPrete, and Anne McDaniel. 2008. "Gender Inequalities in Education." *Annual Review of Sociology* 34:319–337.

Buckingham, David. 2007. "Selling Childhood? Children and Consumer Culture." *Journal of Children and Media* 1 (1):15–24.

Buddeberg-Fischer, Barbara, Marina Stamm, Claus Buddeberg, Georg Bauer, Oliver Hämmig, Michaela Knecht, and Richard Klafhofer. 2012. "The Impact of Gender and Parenthood on Physicians' Careers—Professional and Personal Situation Seven Years After Graduation." *BMC Health Services Research* 10:40.

Budig, Michelle J. 2002. "Male Advantage and the Gender Composition of Jobs: Who Rides the Glass Escalator?" *Social Problems* 49 (2):258–277.

Bullard, Robert D. 1993. *Dumping in Dixie: Race, Class, and Environmental Quality.* 2nd ed. Boulder, CO: Westview Press.

———, and Beverly Wright. 2009. *Race, Place, and Environmental Justice after Hurricane Katrina.* Boulder, CO: Westview Press.

Burawoy, Michael. 2005. "For Public Sociology." *American Sociological Review* 70 (February):4–28.

Bureau of the Census. 1975. *Historical Statistics of the United States, Colonial Times to 1970.* Washington, DC: U.S. Government Printing Office.

———. 1981. "Statistical Abstract of the United States, 1980." Accessible at www.census.gov/compendia/statlab/.

———. 2004a. *Statistical Abstract of the United States, 2004–2005.* Washington, DC: U.S. Government Printing Office.

———. 2005a. *Florida, California and Texas Future Population Growth,* Census Bureau Reports, CB05-52. Washington, DC: U.S. Government Printing Office.

———. 2005b. "American Fact Finder: Places with United States." Accessed December 12 (http://factfinder.census.gov).

———. 2008a. *Statistical Abstract of the United States, 2008.* Washington, DC: U.S. Government Printing Office.

———. 2008c. "America's Families and Living Arrangements 2008." Accessible at www.census.gov/population/www/socdemo/hh-fam/cps2008.html.

———. 2010. "Record Unemployment among Older Workers Does Not Keep Them Out of the Job Market." *Issues in Labor Statistics.* Accessed May 18 (www.bls.gov/spotlight).

———. 2010b. "America's Families and Living Arrangements: 2010." Released January. Accessible at www.census.gov/population/www/socdemo/hh-fam/cps2010.html.

———. 2010c. "America's Families and Living Arrangements, 2010." Accessible at http://www.census.gov/population/www/socdemo/hh-fam/cps2010.html.

———. 2011a. *Statistical Abstract of the United States, 2012.* Washington, DC: U.S. Government Printing Office.

———. 2011c. "Census Bureau Releases Estimate of Same-Sex Married Couples." Accessible at www.census.gov/newsroom/releases/archives/2010_census/cb11-cn181.html.

———. 2011d. "Current Population Survey, Annual Social and Economic Supplements." Washington, DC: U.S. Government Printing Office.

———. 2011e. "America's Families and Living Arrangements: 2011," November 3. Accessible at www.census.gov/newsroom/releases/archives/families_households/cb11-183.html.

———. 2011f. "Voting and Registration in the Elections of November 2012—Detailed Tables." Accessible at http://www.census.gov/hhes/www/socdemo/voting/publications/p20/2012/tables.html.

———. 2012c. "Graphs on Historical Voting Trends." February 15. Accessible at www.census.gov/newsroom/releases/archives/voting/cb12-tps08.html.

———. 2012e. "Annual Estimates of the Resident Population." Accessible at http://www.census.gov/popest/data/national/asrh/2011/index.html.

———. 2012f. "Age and Sex Composition in the United States: 2012." Accessible at http://www.census.gov/population/age/data/2012comp.html.

———. 2013a. "2012 American Community Survey." Accessible at www.census.gov.

———. 2013b. "Estimated Median Age at First Marriage, by Sex: 1890 to the Present." Accessible at http://www.census.gov/hhes/families/data/marital.html.

———. 2013b. "International Data Base Total Midyear Population for the World: 1950–2050." Accessed May 14 (www.census.gov/population/international/data/idb/worldpoptotal.php).

———. 2013c. "Men in Nursing Occupations." *American Community Survey Highlight Report.* February 2012. Accessible at www.census.gov.

———. 2013d. "America's Families and Living Arrangements: 2013: Children (C table series): tabC3-all." Accessible at www.census.gov.

Bureau of Consular Affairs. 2013. FY 2012 Annual Report on Intercountry Adoption, January 2013. Washington, DC: Bureau of Consular Affairs, U.S. Department of State.

Bureau of Labor Statistics. 2003. "Women at Work: A Visual Essay." *Monthly Labor Review* (October):45.

———. 2010. "Economic News Release: Number of Jobs Held." Accessible at www.bls.gov/news. release/nlsoy.nr0.htm.

———. 2012. "Part-Time Employment Rates by Sex, Selected Countries, 2010." Chart 2.7 in *Charting International Labor Comparisons.* September 2012. Accessible at http://www.bls .gov/fls/chartbook/2012/chartbook2012.pdf.

———. 2012c. "Part-time Employment Rates by Sex, Selected Countries, 2010." Chart 2.7 in *Charting International Labor Comparisons.* September 2012. Accessible at www.bls.gov.

———. 2013a. *Women in the Labor Force: A Databook.* February 2013. Accessible at http://www .bls.gov/cps/wlf-databook-2012.pdf.

———. 2013b. "Labor Force Statistics from the Current Population Survey. Table 11. Employed Persons by Detailed Occupation, Sex, Race, and Hispanic or Latino Ethnicity." February 6. Accessible at http://www.bls.gov/cps/tables.htm.

———. 2014. *Employment Situation—January 2014.* Washington, DC: U.S. Government Printing Office.

Bures, Frank. 2011. "Can You Hear Us Now?" *Utne Reader* (March–April):8–9, 11.

Burger, Jerry M. 2009. "Replicating Milgram: Would People Still Obey Today?" *American Psychologist* 64 (January):1–11.

Burger King. 2009. "Whopper Sacrifice." Accessed February 4 (www.whoppersacrifice.com/).

Burns, Melinda. 2010. "Workfare and the Low-Wage Woman." *Miller-McClune* (November–December):76–81.

Butler, Daniel Allen. 1998. *"Unsinkable": The Full Story.* Mechanicsburg, PA: Stackpole Books.

Byrd-Bredbenner, Carol, and Jessica Murray. 2003. "Comparison of the Anthropometric Measurements of Idealized Female Body Images in Media Directed to Men, Women, and Mixed Gender Audiences." *Topics in Clinical Nutrition* 18 (2):117–129.

C

Calhoun, Craig. 1998. "Community without Propinquity Revisited." *Sociological Inquiry* 68 (Summer):373–397.

———. 2003. "Belonging in the Cosmopolitan Imaginary." *Ethnicities* 3 (December):531–553.

Cali, Billie E., Jill M. Coleman, and Catherine Campbell. 2013. "Stranger Danger? Women's Self-Protection Intent and the Continuing Stigma of Online Dating." *Cyberpsychology, Behavior, and Social Networking* 16 (December):853–857.

Cameron, Deborah. 2007. *The Myth of Mars and Venus.* Oxford: Oxford University Press.

Campbell, Mary, Robert Haveman, Gary Sandefur, and Barbara Wolte. 2005. "Economic Inequality and Educational Attainment across a Generation." *Focus* 23 (Spring):11–15.

Campo-Flores, Arian. 2013. "Street Vendors Battle Limits." *Wall Street Journal,* January 22, p. A3.

Cantril, Hadley. 1940. *The Invasion from Mars: A Study in the Psychology of Panic.* Princeton, NJ: Princeton University Press.

Caplan, Ronald L. 1989. "The Commodification of American Health Care." *Social Science and Medicine* 28 (11):1139–1148.

Caplow, Theodore, and Louis Hicks. 2002. *Systems of War and Peace.* 2nd ed. Lanham, MD: University Press of America.

Carbon Trust. 2012. "About the Carbon Trust." Accessed March 27 (www.carbontrust.co.uk/ about-carbon-trust/pages/default.aspx).

Carey, Anne R., and Karl Gelles. 2010. "What Viewers Enjoy Most about Watching the Super Bowl on TV." *USA Today,* February 5, p. A1; *Gallup Poll* (May):3.

Carlton-Ford, Steve. 2010. "Major Armed Conflicts, Militarization, and Life Chances." *Armed Forces and Society* 36 (October):864–899.

Carr, Nicholas. 2008a. *The Big Switch: Rewiring the World: From Edison to Google.* New York: Norton.

———. 2008b. "Is Google Making Us Stoopid?" *Atlantic* (July/August):56–58, 60, 62–63.

Carr, Nicholas. 2010. "Tracking Is an Assault on Liberty, with Real Dangers." *Wall Street Journal,* August 7, pp. W1, W2.

Carroll, Joseph. 2006. "Public National Anthem Should Be Sung in English." *Gallup Poll* (May):3.

Caruso, Eugene M., Dobromir A. Rahnev, and Mahzarin R. Banaji. 2009. "Using Conjoint Analysis to Detect Discrimination: Revealing Covert Preferences from Overt Choices." *Social Cognition* 27 (1):128–137.

Castells, Manuel. 2001. *The Internet Galaxy: Reflections on the Internet, Business, and Society.* New York: Oxford University Press.

———. 2010a. *The Rise of the Network Society.* 2nd ed. With a new preface. Malden, MA: Wiley-Blackwell.

———. 2010b. *The Power of Identity.* 2nd ed. With a new preface. Malden, MA: Wiley-Blackwell.

———. 2012. *Networks of Outrage and Hope: Social Movements in the Internet Age.* Cambridge, UK: Polity.

Cauchon, Dennis. 2009. "Women Gain in Historic Job Shift." *USA Today,* September 3, p. A1.

CBS News. 1979. Transcript of *Sixty Minutes* segment, "I Was Only Following Orders." March 31, pp. 2–8.

Center for Academic Integrity. 2006. *CAI Research.* Accessed January 10 (www.academicintegrity.org).

Center for Community Initiatives. 2012a. "Northeast Florida Center for Community Initiatives (CCI)." Accessed January 3 (www.unf.edu/coas/ cci/).

———. 2012b. "Magnolia Grant Objectives 2012." Accessed April 11 (htpp://aries.unfcsd.unf.edu/ Magnolia/2012/objectives2012.php).

Centers for Disease Control and Prevention. 2010. "Binge Drinking among High School Students and Adults—United States, 2009." Washington, DC: CDC. Accessible at http://www.cdc .gov/mmwr/preview/mmwrhtml/mm5939a4 .htm?s_cid=mm5939a4_w.

———. 2011b. *Health Disparities and Inequalities Report—United States, 2011.*

———. 2012a. *Vital Signs:* Binge Drinking. January 2012. Accessible at www.cdc.gov/vitalsigns/ BingeDrinking.

———. 2012b. "National Marriage and Divorce Rate Trends." Accessed February 24 (www.cdc .gov/nchs/nvss/marriage_divorce_tables.htm).

———. 2013. "Understanding School Violence." Accessed May 12, 2014 (www.cdec/ VIOLENCEPREVENTION/youthviolence/ schoolviolence/index.html).

Centers for Medicare and Medicaid Services. 2013a. "NHE Historical and Projections 1965–2022." Accessible at http://www.cms.gov/ Research-Statistics-Data-and-Systems/Statistics-Trends-and-Reports/NationalHealthExpendData/ index.html.

———. 2013b. "NHE Projections 2012–2022." Accessible at http://www.cms.gov/Research-Statistics-Data-and-Systems/Statistics-Trends-and-Reports/NationalHealthExpendData/index.html.

Chalfant, H. Paul, Robert E. Beckley, and C. Eddie Palmer. 1994. *Religion in Contemporary Society.* 3rd ed. Itasca, IL: F. E. Peacock.

Chambliss, William. 1973. "The Saints and the Roughnecks." *Society* 11 (November–December): 24–31.

Chan, Sewell. 2009. "City Unveils Facebook Page to Encourage Condom Use." *New York Times,* February 12, p. A32.

Charles, Susan T., and Laura L. Carstensen. 2009. "Social and Emotional Aging." *Annual Review of Psychology* 61:383–409.

Charness, Gary, and Marie-Claire Villeval. 2009. "Cooperation and Competition in International Experiments in the Field and the Laboratory." *American Economic Review* 99 (3):956–978.

Charrad, Mounira M. 2011. "Gender in the Middle East: Islam, State, Agency." *Annual Review of Sociology* 37:417–437

Chase, Randall. 2010. "O'Donnell: 'I'm Not a Witch.'" *Washington Times,* October 4. Accessed March 23 (www.washingtontimes.com/news/2010/oct/4/ odonnell-im-not-witch/?page52).

Chase-Dunn, Christopher, and Peter Grimes. 1995. "World-Systems Analysis." Pp. 387–417 in *Annual Review of Sociology,* 1995, edited by John Hagan. Palo Alto, CA: Annual Reviews.

———, Yukio Kawano, and Benjamin D. Brewer. 2000. "Trade Globalization Since 1795: Waves of Integration in the World System." *American Sociological Review* 65 (February):77–95.

Cheng, Shu-Ju Ada. 2003. "Rethinking the Globalization of Domestic Service." *Gender and Society* 17 (2):166–186.

Cherlin, Andrew J. 2003. "Should the Government Promote Marriage?" *Contexts* 2 (Fall):22–29.

———. 2006. "On Single Mothers 'Doing' Family." *Journal of Marriage and Family* 68 (November):800–803.

———. 2009. *The Marriage-Go-Round: The State of Marriage and the Family in America Today.* New York: Knopf.

———. 2010. *Public and Private Families: An Introduction.* 6th ed. New York: McGraw-Hill.

———. 2011. "The Increasing Complexity of Family Life in the United States." September 8. Accessible at www.prb.org/Articles/2011/us-complex-family-life.aspx?p=1.

Child Welfare Information. 2011. *How Many Children Were Adopted in 2007 and 2008?* Washington, DC: U.S. Government Printing Office.

Chin, Kolin. 1996. *Chinatown Gangs: Extortion, Enterprise, and Ethnicity.* New York: Oxford University Press.

Choney, Suzanne. 2010. "Mobile Giving for Chile Pales Compared to Haiti." MSNBC. March 12, 2010. Accessible at www.msnmb.msn.com/ed/35822836/ns/technology_and_science-wireless/t/mobile-giving-chile-pales-compared-haiti.

Chrisafis, Angelique. 2013. "Faith War Enters Private Spheres." *The Guardian Weekly* (September 8):30–31.

Christakis, Nicholas A., and James H. Fowler. 2007. "The Spread of Obesity in a Large Social Network over 32 Years." *New England Journal of Medicine* 357 (July 26):370–379.

———, and ———. 2009. *Connected: The Amazing Power of Social Networks and How They Shape Our Lives.* New York: Harper.

Chronic Poverty Research Centre. 2009. *The Chronic Poverty Report 2008–09: Escaping Poverty Traps.* Geneva: Chronic Poverty Research Centre.

Chu, Henry. 2005. "Tractors Crush Heart of a Nation." *Los Angeles Times,* July 10, p. A9.

Chu, Kathy. 2010. "Vietnam's Market Grows Up." *USA Today,* August 23, p. B3.

Chubb, Catherine, Simone Melis, Louisa Potter, and Raymond Storry. 2008. *The Global Gender Pay Gap.* London: Incomes Data Services.

Chung, Esther K., Leny Mathew, Amy C. Rothkopf, Irma T. Elo, James C. Cayne, and Jennifer F. Culhane. 2009. "Parenting Attitudes and Infant Spanking: The Influence of Childhood Experiences." *Pediatrics* 124 (August):278–286.

Clark, Burton, and Martin Trow. 1966. "The Organizational Context." Pp. 17–70 in *The Study of College Peer Groups,* edited by Theodore M. Newcomb and Everett K. Wilson. Chicago: Aldine.

Clark, Candace. 1983. "Sickness and Social Control." Pp. 346–365 in *Social Interaction: Readings in Sociology,* 2nd ed., edited by Howard Robboy and Candace Clark. New York: St. Martin's Press.

Clark, Kim. 2010. "Can School Reform Even Really Work?" *US News and World Report.* January 2010. Accessible at www.ihavenet. com/Education-Can-School-Reform-Ever-Really-Work-KC.html.

Clarke, Adele E., Janet K. Shim, Laura Maro, Jennifer Ruth Fusket, and Jennifer R. Fishman. 2003. "Bio Medicalization: Technoscientific Transformations of Health, Illness, and U.S. Biomedicine." *American Sociological Review* 68 (April):161–194.

Clarke, Lee. 2002. "Panic: Myth or Reality?" *Contexts* 1 (Fall):21–26.

Clayton, Mark. 2011. "The New Cyber Arms Race." *Christian Science Monitor,* March 7, pp. 26–71.

Clemmitt, Marcia. 2005. "Intelligent Design." *CQ Researcher* 15 (July 29): 637–660.

Clifford, Stephanie. 2009a. "Teaching Teenagers about Harassment." *New York Times,* January 27, p. B1.

———. 2009b. "Online 'A Reason to Keep On Going.'" *New York Times,* June 2, pp. D5–D6.

Clinard, Marshall B., and Robert F. Miller. 1998. *Sociology of Deviant Behavior.* 10th ed. Fort Worth, TX: Harcourt Brace.

Clymer, Adam. 2000. "College Students Not Drawn to Voting or Politics, Poll Shows." *New York Times,* January 2, p. A14.

Coates, Rodney. 2008. "Covert Racism in the USA and Globally." *Sociology Compass* 2:208–231.

Coca-Cola. 2013. Coca-Cola Rumors & Facts. Accessed May 14 (www.coca-colacompany.com/contact-us/coca-cola-rumors-facts).

Cockerham, William C. 2012. *Medical Sociology.* 12th ed. Upper Saddle River, NJ: Prentice Hall.

Coffman, Katherine B., Lucas C. Coffman, and Keith M. Marzilli Ericson. 2013. "The Size of the LGBT Population and the Magnitude of Anti-Gay Sentiment Are Substantially Underestimated." NBER Working Paper No. 19508. Accessible at http://www.nber.org/papers/w19508.

Cole, Mike. 1988. *Bowles and Gintis Revisited: Correspondence and Contradiction in Educational Theory.* Philadelphia: Falmer.

Coleman, Isobel. 2004. "The Payoff from Women's Rights." *Foreign Affairs* 83 (May–June):80–95.

Coleman, James William. 2006. *The Criminal Elite: Understanding White-Collar Crime.* 6th ed. New York: Worth.

———, and Donald R. Cressey. 1980. *Social Problems.* New York: Harper and Row.

College Board Advocacy and Policy Center. 2012. *Trends in College Pricing.* New York: CBAPC.

Collins, Daryl, Jonathan Morduch, Stuart Rutherford, and Orlanda Ruthven. 2009. *Portfolios of the Poor: How the World's Poor Live on $2 a Day.* Princeton, NJ: Princeton University Press.

Collins, Patricia Hill. 2000. *Black Feminist Thought: Knowledge, Consciousness, and the Politics of Empowerment.* Revised 10th anniv. 2nd ed. New York: Routledge.

Collins, Randall. 1975. *Conflict Sociology: Toward an Explanatory Sociology.* New York: Academic Press.

———. 1980. "Weber's Last Theory of Capitalism: A Systematization." *American Sociological Review* 45 (December):925–942.

———. 1986. *Weberian Sociological Theory.* New York: Cambridge University Press.

———. 1995. "Prediction in Macrosociology: The Case of the Soviet Collapse." *American Journal of Sociology* 100 (May):1552–1593.

Colucci, Jim. 2008. "All the World's a Screen." *Watch!* (June):50–53.

Commission on Civil Rights. 1976. *A Guide to Federal Laws and Regulations Prohibiting Sex Discrimination.* Washington, DC: U.S. Government Printing Office.

———. 1981. *Affirmative Action in the 1980s: Dismantling the Process of Discrimination.* Washington, DC: U.S. Government Printing Office.

Commoner, Barry. 1971. *The Closing Circle.* New York: Knopf.

———. 1990. *Making Peace with the Planet.* New York: Pantheon.

———. 2007. "At 90, an Environmentalist from the 70's Still Has Hope." *New York Times,* June 19, p. D2.

Conley, Dalton. 2010. *Being Black, Living in the Red.* 10th anniversary edition. Berkeley: University of California Press.

Connell, R. W. 1987. *Gendered Power: Society, the Person, and Sexual Politics.* Stanford, CA: Stanford University Press.

———. 2002. *Gender.* Cambridge, UK: Polity Press.

———. 2005. *Masculinities.* 2nd ed. Berkeley: University of California Press.

Conner, Thaddieus, and William A. Taggart. 2009. "The Impact of Gaming on the Indian Nations in New Mexico." *Social Science Quarterly* 90 (March):52–70.

Conrad, Peter, ed. 2009. *The Medicalization of Society: On the Transformation of Human Conditions into Treatable Disorders.* 11th ed. Baltimore, MD: Johns Hopkins University.

———, and Kristin K. Barker. 2010. "The Social Construction of Illness: Key Insights and Policy Implications." *Journal of Health and Social Behavior* 51 (5):567–579.

———, and Valerie Leiter. 2013. *The Sociology of Health and Illness: Critical Perspectives.* 9th ed. New York: Worth.

Cooky, Cheryl, and Nicole M. LaVoi. 2012. "Playing but Losing." *Contexts* (Winter):42–46.

Cooley, Charles. H. 1902. *Human Nature and the Social Order.* New York: Scribner.

Coontz, Stephanie. 2006. "A Pop Quiz on Marriage." *New York Times,* February 19, p. 12.

———. 2012. "The Myth of Male Decline." *New York Times,* September 30 (Section SR), pp. 1, 8.

Cooper, K., S. Day, A. Green, and H. Ward. 2007. "Maids, Migrants and Occupational Health in the London Sex Industry." *Anthropology and Medicine* 14 (April):41–53.

Corbett, Christianne, Catherine Hill, and Andresse St. Rose. 2008. *Where the Girls Are: The Facts about Gender Equity in Education.* Washington, DC: American Association of University Women.

Cord, David C. 2014. *The Decline and Fall of Nokia.* Helsinki: Schildts & Söderströms.

Cornwell, Benjamin, Edward O. Laumann, and L. Philip Schumm. 2008. "The Social Connectedness of Older Adults: A National Profile." *American Sociological Review* 73 (April):185–203.

Coser, Lewis A. 1977. *Masters of Sociological Thought: Ideas in Historical and Social Context.* 2nd ed. New York: Harcourt, Brace and Jovanovich.

Coser, Rose Laub. 1984. "American Medicine's Ambiguous Progress." *Contemporary Sociology* 13 (January):9–13.

Côté, James E. 2000. *Arrested Adulthood: The Changing Nature of Identity and Maturity in the Late World.* New York: New York University.

Couch, Carl J. 1968. "Collective Behavior: An Examination of Some Stereotypes." *Social Problems* 15:310–322.

———. 1996. *Information Technologies and Social Orders.* Edited with an introduction by

David R. Maines and Shing-Ling Chien. New York: Aldine de Gruyter.

Council on Foreign Relations. 2009. "Public Opinion on Global Issues." Accessible at www.cfr.org/public-opinion.

Counts, D. A. 1977. "The Good Death in Kaliai: Preparation for Death in Western New Britain." *Omega* 7:367–372.

Cox, Gerry R. 2010. *Death and the American Indian*. Omaha, NE: Grief Illustrated Press.

Cox, Oliver C. 1948. *Caste, Class, and Race: A Study in Social Dynamics*. Detroit: Wayne State University Press.

Cox, Rachel S. 2003. "Home Schooling Debate." *CQ Researcher* 13 (January 17):25–48.

Crabtree, Steve. 2010. *Religiosity Highest in World's Poorest Nations*. August 31. Accessible at www.gallup.com.

Crosnoe, Robert. 2011. *Fitting in, Standing out: Navigating the Social Challenges of High School to Get an Education*. New York: Cambridge University Press.

Cross, Simon, and Barbara Bagilhole. 2002. "Girls' Jobs for the Boys? Men, Masculinity and Non-Traditional Occupations." *Gender, Work, and Organization* 9 (April):204–226.

Croteau, David, and William Haynes. 2006. *The Business of the Media: Corporate Media and the Public Interest*. 2nd ed. Thousand Oaks, CA: Pine Forge Press.

———, and ———. 2014. *Media/Society: Industries, Images, and Audiences*. 5th ed. Los Angeles: Sage.

Croucher, Sheila L. 2004. *Globalization and Belonging: The Politics of Identity in a Changing World*. Lanham, MD: Rowman and Littlefield.

Crouse, Kelly. 1999. "Sociology of the *Titanic*." *Teaching Sociology Listserv*. May 24.

Crowe, Jerry, and Valli Herman. 2005. "NBA Lists Fashion Do's and Don'ts." *Los Angeles Times*, October 19, pp. A1, A23.

Crump, Andy. 2006. "Suicide in Japan." *Lancet* 367 (April 8):1143.

Cuff, E. C., W. W. Sharrock, and D. W. Francis, eds. 1990. *Perspectives in Sociology*. 3rd ed. Boston: Unwin Hyman.

Currie, Elliott. 1985. *Confronting Crime: An American Challenge*. New York: Pantheon.

———. 1998. *Crime and Punishment in America*. New York: Metropolis Books.

Curry, Timothy Jon. 1993. "A Little Pain Never Hurt Anyone: Athletic Career Socialization and the Normalization of Sports Injury." *Symbolic Interaction* 26 (Fall):273–290.

Cushing-Daniels, Brenda, and Sheila R. Zedlewski. 2008. "Tax and Spending Policy and Economic Mobility." Washington, DC: Economic Mobility Project. Also accessible at www.economic-mobility.org/reports_and_research/literature_reviews?id=0004.

d

Dade, Corey. 2012. "Battles Over Voter ID Laws Intensify." June 2. Accessible at www.wbur.org/npr/154152507/battles-over-voter-id-laws-intensify.

Dahl, Robert A. 1961. *Who Governs?* New Haven, CT: Yale University Press.

Dahrendorf, Ralf. 1958. "Toward a Theory of Social Conflict." *Journal of Conflict Resolution* 2 (June):170–183.

———. 1959. *Class and Class Conflict in Industrial Sociology*. Stanford, CA: Stanford University Press.

Daitz, Ben. 2011. "Navajos Confront Life's End With Poem." *New York Times*, January 25, pp. D5, D6.

Daley, Suzanne. 2013. "Danes Rethink a Welfare State Ample to a Fault." *New York Times*, April 12, pp. 1, 13.

Dalla, Rochelle L., and Wendy C. Gamble. 2001. "Teenage Mothering and the Navajo Reservation: An Examination of Intergovernmental Perceptions and Beliefs." *American Indian Culture and Research Journal* 25 (1):1–19.

Daniel, G. Reginald. 2006. *Race and Multiraciality in Brazil and the United States: Converging Paths?* University Park: Pennsylvania State University Press.

Danziger, Sandra K. 2010. "The Decline of Cash Welfare and Implications for Social Policy and Poverty." *Annual Review of Sociology* 36:523–545.

Darlin, Damon. 2006. "It's O.K. to Fall Behind the Technology Curve." *New York Times*, December 30, p. B6.

Darwin, Charles. 1859. *On the Origin of Species*. London: John Murray.

David, Gary. 2004. "Scholarship on Arab Americans Distorted Past 9/11." *Al Jadid* (Winter–Spring):26–27.

———. 2008. "Arab Americans." Pp. 84–87, vol. 1, in *Encyclopedia of Race, Ethnicity, and Society*, edited by Richard T. Schaefer. Thousand Oaks, CA: Sage.

Davidson, Paul. 2012. "More U.S. Service Jobs Go Overseas." *USA Today*, December 7, p. B1.

———. 2013. "Low-paid Workers March for Fairness." *USA Today*, August 29, p. A1.

Davies, Christie. 1989. "Goffman's Concept of the Total Institution: Criticisms and Revisions." *Human Studies* 12 (June):77–95.

Davis, Darren W., and Brian D. Silver. 2003. "Stereotype Threat and Race of Interviewer Knowledge." *American Journal of Political Science* 47 (January):33–45.

Davis, Gerald. 2003. *America's Corporate Banks Are Separated by Just Four Handshakes*. Accessed March 7 (www.bus.umich.edu/research/davis.html).

———. 2004. "American Cronyism: How Executive Networks Inflated the Corporate Bubble." *Contexts* (Summer):34–40.

Davis, Kingsley. 1947. "A Final Note on a Case of Extreme Isolation." *American Journal of Sociology* 52 (March):432–437.

———, and Wilbert E. Moore. 1945. "Some Principles of Stratification." *American Sociological Review* 10 (April):242–249.

Davis, Martha F. 2010. "Abortion Access in the Global Marketplace." *North Carolina Law Review* 88:1657–1685.

Davis, Paul K., and Kim Cragin, eds. 2009. *Social Science for Counterterrorism: Putting the Pieces Together*. Santa Monica, CA: RAND.

De Anda, Roberto M. 2004. *Chicanas and Chicanos in Contemporary Society*. 2nd ed. Lanham, MD: Rowman and Littlefield.

Death Penalty Information Center. 2014. "Number of Executions by State and Region Since 1976." Updated December 18, 2013. Accessed December 20 at http://www.deathpenaltyinfo.org/number-executions-state-and-region-1976.

Deegan, Mary Jo, ed. 1991. *Women in Sociology: A Bio-Bibliographical Sourcebook*. Westport, CT: Greenwood.

———. 2003. "Textbooks, the History of Sociology, and the Sociological Stock of Knowledge." *Sociological Theory* 21 (November):298–305.

Deflem, Mathieu. 2005. "'Wild Beasts without Nationality': The Uncertain Origins of Interpol, 1898–1910." Pp. 275–285 in *Handbook of Transnational Crime and Justice*, edited by Philip Rerchel. Thousand Oaks, CA: Sage.

Deibert, Ronald J., John Palfrey, Rafal Rohozinski, and Jonathan Zittrain. 2008. *Access Denied: The Practice and Policy of Global Internet Filtering*. Cambridge, MA: MIT Press.

Delaney, Kevin J. 2005. "Big Mother Is Watching." *Wall Street Journal*, November 26, pp. A1, A6.

Della Porta, Donatella, and Sidney Tarrow, eds. 2005. *Transnational Protest and Global Activism*. Lanham, MD: Rowman and Littlefield.

DellaPergola, Sergio. 2012. "Jewish Population of the World." Accessible at www.jewishvirtuallibrary.org.

DeNavas-Walt, Carmen, Bernadette D. Proctor, and Jessica C. Smith. 2011. *Income, Poverty, and Health Insurance Coverage in the United States: 2010*. Washington, DC: U.S. Government Printing Office.

———. 2013. *Income, Poverty, and Health Insurance Coverage in the United States: 2012*. Washington, DC: U.S. Government Printing Office.

Denny, Charlotte. 2004. "Migration Myths Hold No Fears." *Guardian Weekly*, February 26, p. 12.

Denny, Kathleen E. 2011. "Gender in Context, Content, and Approach: Contemporary Gender Measures in Girl Scout and Boy Scout Handbooks." *Gender and Society* 25 (February): 27–47.

Denzin, Norman K. 2004. "Postmodernism." Pp. 581–583 in *Encyclopedia of Social Theory*, edited by George Ritzer. Thousand Oaks, CA: Sage.

DeParle, Jason. 2003. "The 'W' Word, Re-Engaged." *New York Times*, February 8, Week in Review, p. 1.

Department of Education. 1999. *Report on State Implementation of the Gun-Free Schools Act. School Year 1997–98*. Rockville, MD: Westat.

———. 2004. *Crime and Safety in America's Public Schools*. Washington, DC: U.S. Government Printing Office.

Department of Health and Human Services. 2013. "TANF: Total Number of Families." Accessed December 27 at http://www.acf.hhs.gov/sites/default/files/main/2013_family_tan.pdf.

———. 2014. "AFCARS, Report." Accessed January 16 (www.acf.hhs.gov/programs/cb/stats_research/afcars/tar/report20.htm).

Department of Homeland Security. 2010. *Haiti Social Media: Disaster Monitoring Initiative*. January 21. Washington, DC: U.S. Department of Homeland Security.

Department of Justice. 2000. *The Civil Liberties Act of 1988: Redress for Japanese Americans.* Accessed June 29 (www.usdoj.gov/crt/ora/main.html).

———. 2008. "Hate Crime Statistics, 2007." Accessible at www.fbi.gov/ucr/ucr.htm.

———. 2013. "Crime in the United States, 2013." Accessed December 7, 2013 (www.fbi.gov/about-us/cjis/ucr/crime-in-the-u.s/2013/crime-in-the-u.s.-2013).

Department of Labor. 2013a. "Wage and Hour Department." Accessible at www.dol.gov/whd.

Department of State. 2013. "Tier Placements." Accessed December 13, 2013 (www.state.gov/j/tip/rls/tiprpt/2013/index.htm).

Desai, Rani A., Suchitra Krishnan-Sarin, Dana Cavallo, and Marc N. Potenza. 2010. "Video-Gaming among High School Students: Health Correlates, Gender Differences, and Problematic Gaming." *Pediatrics* 126 (November 15):1414–1424.

Deutsch, Francine M. 2007. "Undoing Gender." *Gender and Society* 21 (February):106–127.

Devitt, James. 1999. *Framing Gender on the Campaign Trail: Women's Executive Leadership and the Press.* New York: Women's Leadership Conference.

Dewan, Shaila. 2013. "New, but Not for Sale." *New York Times,* December 5, pp. B1, B9.

Dickler, Jessica. 2011. "Dig Deep to Buy Titanic Visit." *Chicago Tribune,* June 3, p. 25.

Dickson, Martin. 2013. "Lunch with the FT Muhammad Yunnus: Micro-financial Times." *Financial Times,* October 27, p. 3.

Diefenbach, Donald L., and Mark D. West. 2007. "Television and Attitudes toward Mental Health Issues: Cultivation Analysis and the Third Person Effect." *Journal of Community Psychology* 35 (2):181–195.

Dillon, Sam. 2008. "Under 'No Child' Law, Even Solid Schools Falter." *New York Times,* October 15, pp. A1, A14.

Dimrock, Michael, Carroll Doherty, and Rob Suls. 2013. "Uncertainty over Court's Voting Rights Decision, Public Divided over Same-Sex Marriage Rulings." July 1. Accessible at http://www.peoplepress.org.

Disaster Research Center. 2013. "About the DRC." Accessed April 25 (www.udel.edu/DRC/aboutus/about.html).

Dobbin, Frank, and Jiwook Jung. 2010. "Corporate Board Gender Diversity and Stock Performance: The Competence Gap on Institutional Investor Bias?" *North Carolina Law Review* 89.

Dodds, Klaus. 2000. *Geopolitics in a Changing World.* Harlow, UK: Pearson Education.

Domeij, David, and Paul Klein. 2013. "Should Day Care Be Subsidized?" *Review of Economic Studies* 80 (2):568–595.

Domhoff, G. William. 1978. *Who Really Rules? New Haven and Community Power Reexamined.* New Brunswick, NJ: Transaction.

———. 2014. *Who Rules America? The Triumph of the Corporate Rich.* 7th ed. New York: McGraw-Hill.

Domi, Tanya L. 2013. "Women in Combat: Policy Catches up with Reality." *New York Times,* February 8.

Dominick, Joseph R. 2009. *The Dynamics of Mass Communication: Media in the Digital Age.* 10th ed. New York: McGraw-Hill.

Donadio, Rachel. 2012. "'Dear Friends': Pope Takes to Twitter, with an Assist." *New York Times,* December 13, p. A8.

Donnelly, Sally B. 2007. "Growing Younger." *Time* (January bonus section):A13–A14.

Donohue, Elizabeth, Vincent Schiraldi, and Jason Ziedenberg. 1998. *School House Hype: School Shootings and Real Risks Kids Face in America.* New York: Justice Policy Institute.

Doress, Irwin, and Jack Nusan Porter. 1977. *Kids in Cults: Why They Join, Why They Stay, Why They Leave.* Brookline, MA: Reconciliation Associates.

Dougherty, Kevin, and Floyd M. Hammack. 1992. "Education Organization." Pp. 535–541 in *Encyclopedia of Sociology,* vol. 2, edited by Edgar F. Borgatta and Marie L. Borgatta. New York: Macmillan.

Downey, Liam, and Brian Hawkins. 2008. "Race, Income, and Environmental Inequality in the United States." *Sociological Perspectives* 50 (4):759–781.

Dreifus, Claudia. 2003. "A Conversation with Lee Clarke." *New York Times,* May 20, Science Times section, p. 2.

———. 2004. "A Sociologist with an Advanced Degree in Calamity." *New York Times,* September 7, p. D2.

Dube, Arindrajit. 2013a. "The Minimum We Can Do." *New York Times,* December 1 (Section S), p. 5.

———. 2013b. "Minimum Wages and Aggregate Job Growth: Causal Effect or Statistical Artifact?" October 4. Accessible at http://arindube.files.wordpress.com/2013/10/dube_minwagejobgrowth.pdf.

DuBois, W. E. B. [1899] 1995. *The Philadelphia Negro: A Social Study.* Philadelphia: University of Pennsylvania Press.

———. [1900] 1969. "To the Nations of the World." Pp. 19–23 in *An ABC of Color,* edited by W. E. B. DuBois. New York: International Publishers.

———. [1903] 1961. *The Souls of Black Folks: Essays and Sketches.* New York: Fawcett.

———. [1903] 2003. *The Negro Church.* Walnut Creek, CA: AltaMira Press.

———. [1909] 1970. *The Negro American Family.* Atlanta University. Reprinted 1970. Cambridge, MA: MIT Press.

———. [1935] 1962. *Black Reconstruction in America 1860–1880.* New York: Athenaeum.

———. [1940] 1968. *Dusk of Dawn.* New York: Harcourt, Brace. Reprint. New York: Schocken Books.

Duggan, Maeve. 2012. "Politics." November 14. Accessible at http://www.pewinternet.org/Commentary/2012/November/Pew-Internet-Politics.aspx.

Duhigg, Charles, and Keith Bradsher. 2012. "How U.S. Lost Out on iPhone Work." *New York Times,* January 22, p. A1.

Dukić, Vanja, Hedibert F. Lopes, and Nicholas G. Polson. 2011. "Tracking Flu Epidemics Using Google Flu Trends and Particle Learning." Accessible at http://faculty.chicagobooth.edu/nicholas.polson/research/papers/Track.pdf.

Dundas, Susan, and Miriam Kaufman. 2000. "The Toronto Lesbian Family Study." *Journal of Homosexuality* 40 (20):65–79.

Duneier, Mitchell. 1994a. "On the Job, but Behind the Scenes." *Chicago Tribune,* December 26, pp. 1, 24.

———. 1994b. "Battling for Control." *Chicago Tribune,* December 28, pp. 1, 8.

Dunlap, Riley E. 2010. "At 40, Environmental Movement Endures with Less Consensus." April 22. Accessed April 27 (www.gallup.com/poll/127487/Environmental-Movement-Endures-Less-Consensus.aspx?version=print).

———, and Angela G. Mertig. 1991. "The Evolution of the U.S. Environmental Movement from 1970 to 1990: An Overview." *Society of National Resources* 4 (July–September):209–218.

Dunne, Gillian A. 2000. "Opting into Motherhood: Lesbians Blurring the Boundaries and Transforming the Meaning of Parenthood and Kinship." *Gender and Society* 14 (February):11–35.

Durden, T. Elizabeth, and Robert A. Hummer. 2006. "Access to Healthcare among Working-Aged Hispanic Adults in the United States." *Social Science Quarterly* 87 (December):1319–1343.

Durex. 2007. "The Face of Global Sex 2007—First Sex: An Opportunity of a Lifetime." Accessible at http://www.durexnetwork.org/SiteCollectionDocuments/Research%20%20Face%20of%20Global%20Sex%202007.pdf.

Durkheim, Émile. [1893] 1933. *Division of Labor in Society.* Translated by George Simpson. Reprint. New York: Free Press.

———. [1895] 1964. *The Rules of Sociological Method.* Translated by Sarah A. Solovay and John H. Mueller. Reprint. New York: Free Press.

———. [1897] 1951. *Suicide.* Translated by John A. Spaulding and George Simpson. Reprint. New York: Free Press.

———. [1912] 2001. *The Elementary Forms of Religious Life.* A new translation by Carol Cosman. New York: Oxford University Press.

Dwyer, Tim. 2010. *Media Convergence.* New York: McGraw-Hill.

Dyrbye, Liselotte, N. Tait, D. Shanafelt, Charles M. Balch, Daniel Satele, and Julie Freischlag. 2011. "Relationship Between Work-Home Conflicts and Burnout Among American Surgeons." *Archives of Surgery* 146 (February):211–217.

Dzidzienyo, Anani. 1987. "Brazil." In *International Handbook on Race and Race Relations,* edited by Jay A. Sigler. New York: Greenwood Press.

Ebaugh, Helen Rose Fuchs. 1988. *Becoming an Ex: The Process of Role Exit.* Chicago: University of Chicago Press.

Eby, Lillian T., Charleen P. Maher, and Marcus M. Butts. 2010. "The Intersection of Work and Family Life: The Role of Affect." *Annual Review of Psychology* 61:599–622.

Eckenwiler, Mark. 1995. "In the Eyes of the Law." *Internet World* (August):74, 76–77.

Economic Mobility Project. 2009. *Findings from a National Survey and Focus Groups on Economic Mobility.* Washington, DC: Pew Charitable Trusts.

The Economist. 2005b. "We Are Tous Québécois." (January 8):39.

———. 2008b. "Following the Crowd." (September 6):10–11.

———. 2010c. "The Dark Side." (September 11):15.

———. 2011b. "China's Population: The Most Surprising Demographic Crisis." (May 7):43–44.

———. 2011c. "Digging for Victory." (September 24):60.

———. 2011d. "Age Shall Not Wither Them." (April 9):78.

———. 2012. "Digital Diplomacy: Virtual Relations." (September 22):69.

———. 2012u. "Retail in Developing Countries: Selling Sisters." (November 29). Accessed February 26, 2013 at www.economist.com/blogs/schumpeter/2012/11/retail-developing-countries.

———. 2013. "China's Population: Peak Toll." (January 26):41–42.

———. 2013a. "Romania: The Nanny State." (August 17):51–52.

———. 2013b. "A Giant Cage." (April 6):S1–S16.

———. 2013c. "Little Peepers Everywhere." (July 21):23–24.

———. 2013d. "Raising the Floor." (December 16):36.

———. 2013e. "Game, Sex and Match." (September 7):61–62.

———. 2013f. "Here, There and Everywhere." (January 19):S1–S20.

Eggen, Dan. 2009. "AARP's Dual Role." *Washington Post National Weekly Edition* 27 (November 2):11.

Ehrenreich, Barbara. 2001. *Nickel and Dimed: On (Not) Getting By in America.* New York: Metropolitan.

———. 2009. "Is It Now a Crime to Be Poor?" *New York Times,* August 2.

Ehrlich, Paul R. 1968. *The Population Bomb.* New York: Ballantine.

———, and Anne H. Ehrlich. 1990. *The Population Explosion.* New York: Simon and Schuster.

———, and Katherine Ellison. 2002. "A Looming Threat We Won't Face." *Los Angeles Times,* January 20, p. M6.

Eitzen, D. Stanley. 2009. *Fair and Foul: Beyond the Myths and Paradoxes of Sport.* 4th ed. Lanham, MD: Rowman and Littlefield.

El Nasser, Haya, and Paul Overberg. 2011. "Recession Reshapes Life in the USA." *USA Today,* September 12, p. 3A.

Elgan, Mike. 2011. "How to Pop Your Internet 'Filter Bubble.'" *Computer World* (May 7). Accessed November 11 (www.computerworld.com/s/article/9216484/Elgan_How_to_pop_your_Internet_filter_bubble).

Ellison, Brandy. 2008. "Tracking." Pp. 301–304, vol. 2, in *Encyclopedia of Race, Ethnicity, and Society,* edited by Richard T. Schaefer. Thousand Oaks, CA: Sage.

Ellison, Jesse. 2008. "A New Grip on Life." *Newsweek* 152 (December 15):64.

Ellison, Nicole B., Jeffrey T. Hancock, and Catalina L. Toma. 2012. "Profile as Promise: A Framework for Conceptualizing the Veracity of Self Presentation in Online Dating Profiles." *New Media and Society,* 14 (February):45–62.

Ellison, Nicole, Rebecca Heino, and Jennifer Gibbs. 2006. "Managing Impressions Online; Self-Presentation Processes in the Online Dating Environment." *Journal of Computer-Mediated Communication* 11 (2):415–441.

Ellison, Ralph. 1952. *Invisible Man.* New York: Random House.

Ely, Robin J. 1995. "The Power of Demography: Women's Social Construction of Gender Identity at Work." *Academy of Management Journal* 38 (3):589–634.

Engels, Friedrich [1884] 1959. "The Origin of the Family, Private Property, and the State." Pp. 392–394, excerpted in *Marx and Engels: Basic Writings on Politics and Philosophy,* edited by Lewis Feuer. Garden City, NY: Anchor Books.

Ennis, Sharon R., Merarys Rios-Vargas, and Nora G. Albert. 2011. *The Hispanic Population: 2010.* 2010 Census Brief BR-04. Washington, DC: U.S. Government Printing Office.

Entine, Jon, and Martha Nichols. 1996. "Blowing the Whistle on Meaningless 'Good Intentions.'" *Chicago Tribune,* June 20, sec. 1, p. 21.

Environmental Protection Agency. 2012. Global Greenhouse Gas Data, Figure 3 Total Greenhouse Gas Emissions by Region, from Global Anthropogenic Emissions of Non-CO2 Greenhouse Gases 1990-2020, EPA Report 430-R-06-003. June 2006. www.epa.gov/climatechange/emissions/globalghg.html.

———. 2012. Global Greenhouse Gas Data. Accessible at http://epa.gov/climatechange/emissions/globalghg.html.

Epstein, Cynthia Fuchs. 1999. "The Major Myth of the Women's Movement." *Dissent* (Fall):83–111.

Epstein, Robert. 2009. "The Truth about Online Dating." *Scientific American* (Special Edition).

Erikson, Kai. 1966. *Wayward Puritans: A Study in the Sociology of Deviance.* New York: Wiley.

Esbenshade, Jill. 2008. "Giving Up Against the Global Economy: New Developments in the Anti-Sweatshops Movement." *Critical Sociology* 34 (3):453–470.

Etaugh, Claire. 2003. "Witches, Mothers and Others: Females in Children's Books." *Hilltopics* (Winter):10–13.

Etzioni, Amitai. 1964. *Modern Organization.* Englewood Cliffs, NJ: Prentice Hall.

———. 1965. *Political Unification.* New York: Holt, Rinehart and Winston.

European Metalworkers' Federation. 2010. "What Is Precious Work?" Accessed March 1, 2011 (www.emf-fem.org).

European PWN. 2012. "Women on Boards: The Inside Story on Norway's 40% Target." Accessed February 22 (www.europeanpwn.net/index.php?article_id=150).

Evergeti, Venetia, and Elisabetta Zontini. 2006. "Introduction: Some Critical Reflections on Social Capital, Migration and Transnational Families." *Ethnic and Racial Studies* 29 (November):1025–1039.

f

Faiola, Anthony. 2005. "Their Husbands Made Them Sick." *Washington Post National Weekly Edition* 23 (October 24):18.

———. 2006. "Japan's Vulnerable Elderly." *Washington Post National Weekly Edition* 23 (February 27):18.

Fairtrade Foundation. 2010. "Retail Products." Accessed Jan. 5 (www.fairtrade.org.uk/products/retail_products/default.aspx).

Fallows, Deborah. 2006. *Pew Internet Project Data.* Washington, DC: Pew Internet and American Life Project.

Farley, Melissa, and Victor Malarek. 2008. "The Myth of the Victimless Crime." *New York Times,* March 12, p. A27.

Farr, Grant M. 1999. *Modern Iran.* New York: McGraw-Hill.

Farrell, Amy, and Jack McDevitt. 2010. "Identifying and Measuring Racial Profiling by the Police." *Sociology Compass* 4:77–88.

Feagin, Joe R. 1989. *Minority Group Issues in Higher Education: Learning from Qualitative Research.* Norman: Center for Research on Minority Education, University of Oklahoma.

———, Harnán Vera, and Nikitah Imani. 1996. *The Agony of Education: Black Students at White Colleges and Universities.* New York: Routledge.

Featherman, David L., and Robert M. Hauser. 1978. *Opportunity and Change.* New York: Aeodus.

Federal Bureau of Investigation. 2012. "Crime in the United States 2011." Accessible at http://www.fbi.gov/about-us/cjis/ucr/crime-in-the.u.s/2012/crime-in-the.u.s.-2012.

———. 2013. "2012 Hate Crime Statistics." Accessed December 20 at http://www.fbi.gov/about-us/cjis/ucr/hate-crime/2012.

Felson, David, and Akis Kalaitzidis. 2005. "A Historical Overview of Transnational Crime." Pp. 3–19 in *Handbook of Transnational Crime and Justice,* edited by Philip Reichel. Thousand Oaks, CA: Sage.

Ferber, Abby L., and Michael S. Kimmel. 2008. "The Gendered Face of Terrorism." *Sociology Compass* 2:870–887.

Ferree, Myra Marx, and David A. Merrill. 2000. "Hot Movements, Cold Cognition: Thinking about Social Movements in Gendered Frames." *Contemporary Society* 29 (May):454–462.

Feuer, Lewis S. 1989. *Marx and Engels: Basic Writings on Politics and Philosophy.* New York: Anchor Books.

Fields, Jason. 2004. "America's Families and Living Arrangements: 2003." *Current Population Reports,* ser. P-20, no. 553. Washington, DC: U.S. Government Printing Office.

Fieser, Ezra. 2009. "What Price for Good Coffee?" *Time,* October 5, pp. 61–62.

Fiji TV. 2012. Home Page. Accessed January 10 (www.fijitv.com.fj).

File, Thom. 2013. "The Diversifying Electorate-Voting Rates by Race and Hispanic Origin in 2012 (and Other Recent Elections)." Current Population Survey P20-568. Accessible at http://www.census.gov.

Fine, Gary Alan, and Bill Ellis. 2011. *The Global Grapevine: Why Rumors of Terrorism, Immigration, and Trade Matter.* New York: Oxford University Press.

Fine, Gary C. 1987. *With the Boys: Little League Baseball and Preadolescent Culture.* Chicago: University of Chicago Press.

———. 2008. " Robbers Cave." Pp. 1163–1164, vol. 3, in *Encyclopedia of Race, Ethnicity, and Society,* edited by Richard T. Schaefer. Thousand Oaks, CA: Sage.

Finkel, Steven E., and James B. Rule. 1987. "Relative Deprivation and Related Psychological Theories of Civil Violence: A Critical Review." *Research in Social Movements* 9:47–69.

Fiola, Jan. 2008. "Brazil." Pp. 200–204, vol. 2, in *Encyclopedia of Race, Ethnicity, and Society,* edited by Richard T. Schaefer. Thousand Oaks, CA: Sage.

Fishman, Ted C. 2010a. *Shock of Gray.* New York: Scribner.

———. 2010b. "The Old World." *New York Times Magazine* (October 17):48–53.

Fiss, Peer C., and Paul M. Hirsch. 2005. "The Discourse of Globalization: Framing of an Emerging Concept." *American Sociological Review* (February):29–52.

Fitzgerald, Kathleen J. 2008. "White Privilege." Pp. 1403–1405, vol. 3, in *Encyclopedia of Race, Ethnicity, and Society,* edited by Richard T. Schaefer. Thousand Oaks, CA: Sage.

Fjellman, Stephen M. 1992. *Vinyl Leaves: Walt Disney World and America.* Boulder, CO: Westview Press.

Flacks, Richard. 1971. *Youth and Social Change.* Chicago: Markham.

Fletcher, Connie. 1995. "On the Line: Women Cops Speak Out." *Chicago Tribune Magazine,* February 19, pp. 14–19.

Flores, Glenn, M. Abreu, C. P. Barone, R. Bachur, and H. Lin. 2012. "Errors of Medical Interpretation and Their Potential Clinical Consequences: A Comparison of Professional versus Ad Hoc versus No Interpreters." *Annals of Emergency Medicine* 60 (5):545–553.

Florida, Richard. 2011. "Why Crime Is Down in America's Cities." *The Atlantic* (July). Accessible at www.theatlantic.com.

Fonseca, Felicia. 2008. "Dine College on Quest to Rename Navajo Cancer Terms." *News from Indian Country* 22 (January 7):11.

Forbes. 2012. "Leaderboard: Billionaire Box Scores." 189 (March 26):34.

Forte, Maximilian. 2010. "HTS' Other Handlers." May 20. Accessible at http://zeroanthropology.net.

Foucault, Michel. 1978. *The History of Sexuality.* Vol. 1, An Introduction. New York: Vintage.

Fowler, Geoffrey A. 2013. "Woman Leads Prayer at Mormon Event." *Wall Street Journal,* April 8, p. A3.

Fox, Porter. 2014. "The End of Snow?" *New York Times,* February 9 (Section SR), pp. 1, 6.

Francis, David. 2010. "Homeschoolers Seek Asylum in US." *Christian Science Monitor,* March 8, p. 12.

Frandsen, Ronald J., Dave Naglich, Gene A. Lasuver, and Allina D. Lee. 2013. *Background Checks for Firearm Transfers, 2010—Statistical Tables.*

February 2013. NCJ 238226. Washington, DC: Bureau of Justice Statistics.

Franke, Richard Herbert, and James D. Kaul. 1978. "The Hawthorne Experiments: First Statistical Interpretation." *American Sociological Review* 43 (October):623–643.

Franklin, John Hope, and Evelyn Brooks Higginbotham. 2011. *From Slavery to Freedom.* 9th ed. New York: McGraw-Hill.

Freese, Jeremy. 2008. "Genetics and the Social Science Explanation of Individual Outcomes." *American Journal of Sociology* 114 (Suppl.):51–535.

Freidson, Eliot. 1970. *Profession of Medicine.* New York: Dodd, Mead.

French, Howard W. 2004. "China's Textbooks Twist and Omit History." *New York Times,* December 6, p. A10.

Freudenburg, William R. 2005. "Seeing Science, Courting Conclusions: Reexamining the Intersection of Science, Corporate Cash, and the Law." *Sociological Forum* 20 (March):3–33.

Freudenheim, Milt. 2005. "Help Wanted: Oldest Workers Please Apply." *New York Times,* March 23, pp. A1, C3.

Freund, Linda. 2013. "Spontaneity for Hire: Flash Mobs Go Corporate." *Wall Street Journal,* May 9, pp. A1, A16.

Freundlich, Madelyn, and Joy Kim Lieberthal. 2000. "The Gathering of the First Generation of Adult Korean Adoptees: Adoptees' Perceptions of International Adoption." Accessible at www.adoptioninstitute.org/proed/korfindings.html.

Frey, Benedikt, and Michael Osborne. 2013. "The Future of Employment: How Susceptible Are Jobs to Computerisation?" September 17, 2013. Working paper accessible at http://www.oxfordmartin.ox.ac.uk/downloads/academic/The_Future_of_Employment.pdf.

Frey, William H. 2011. *A Demographic Tipping Point among America's Three-Year-Olds.* February 7. Accessible at http://www.brookings.edu/opinions/2011/0207_population_frey.aspx?p=1.

Fridlund, Alan J., Paul Ekman, and Harriet Oster. 1987. "Facial Expressions of Emotion; Review of Literature 1970–1983." Pp. 143–224 in *Nonverbal Behavior and Communication,* 2nd ed., edited by Aron W. Seigman and Stanley Feldstein. Hillsdale, NJ: Erlbaum.

Friedan, Betty. 1963. *The Feminine Mystique.* New York: Dell.

Friedman, Louis. 2010. "NASA's Down-to-Earth Problems." *Star-Telegram* (Fort Worth), March 28. Accessible at http://www.star-telegram.com/2010/03/28/2072608/friedman-nasas-down-to-earth-problem.html.

Friedman, Richard A. 2012. "In Gun Debate, a Misguided Focus on Mental Illness." *New York Times,* December 18, p. D6.

Friends of the Congo. 2011. "Coltan: What You Should Know." Accessed May 21 (www.friendsofthecongo.org/new/coltan.php).

Fry, Richard, D'Vera Cohn, Gretchen Livingston, and Paul Taylor. 2011. "The Rising Age Gap in Economic Well-Being." Accessible at http://pewresearch.org/pubs/2124/age-gap-silent-generation-millennials-wealth-gap.

Fudge, Judy, and Rosemary Owens, eds. 2006. *Precarious Work, Women, and the New Economy: The Challenge to Legal Norms.* Oxford, UK: Hart.

Fuentes-Nieva, Ricardo, and Nicholas Galasso. 2014. *Working for the Few: Political Capture and Economic Inequality.* Accessible at http://www.oxfam.org/en/policy/working-for-the-few-economic-inequality.

Fukase, Atsuko, and Kana Inagaki. 2012. "Japan Insider Penalty: $600." *Wall Street Journal,* March 22, p. C2.

Furstenberg, Frank F. 2007. "The Making of the Black Family: Race and Class in Qualitative Studies in the Twentieth Century." *Annual Review of Sociology* 33:429–448.

———, and Andrew Cherlin. 1991. *Divided Families: What Happens to Children When Parents Part.* Cambridge, MA: Harvard University Press.

g

Gabriel, Trip. 2010. "Despite Push, Success at Charter Schools Is Mixed." *New York Times,* May 1, pp. A1, A24–A25.

Gailey, Robert. 2007. "As History Repeats Itself, Unexpected Developments Move Us Forward." *Journal of Rehabilitation Research and Development* 44 (4):vii–xiv.

Galbraith, John Kenneth. 1977. *The Age of Uncertainty.* Boston: Houghton Mifflin.

Galea, Sandro, Melissa Tracy, Katherine J. Hoggatt, Charles DiMaggio, and Adam Karpati. 2011. "Estimated Deaths Attributed to Social Factors in the United States." *American Journal of Public Health* 101 (August):1456–1465.

Gallagher, Kevin P. 2009. "Economic Globalization and the Environment." *Annual Review of Environmental Resources* 34:279–304.

Gallup. 2011a. *Religion.* Accessed March 27 (www.gallup.com).

———. 2012. "Party Affiliation." Accessed March 8 (www.gallup.com/poll/15370/Party-Affiliation.aspx).

Gallup Opinion Index. 1978. "Religion in America, 1977–1978." 145 (January).

Gans, Herbert J. 1995. *The War against the Poor: The Underclass and Antipoverty Policy.* New York: Basic Books.

Garamone, Jim. 1999. "The Challenge." American Forces Press Service. January 12, 1999. Accessed January 24, 2014 at http://www.defense.gov/specials/basic/.

Garcia-Moreno, Claudia, Henrica A. F. M. Jansen, Mary Ellsberg, Lori Heise, and Charlotte Watts. 2005. *WHO Multi-Country Study on Women's Health and Domestic Violence against Women.* Geneva, Switzerland: WHO.

Garfinkel, Harold. 1956. "Conditions of Successful Degradation Ceremonies." *American Journal of Sociology* 61 (March):420–424.

Garner, Roberta. 1996. *Contemporary Movements and Ideologies.* New York: McGraw-Hill.

———. 1999. "Virtual Social Movements." Presented at Zaldfest: A conference in honor of Mayer Zald. September 17, Ann Arbor, MI.

Garrett-Peters, Raymond. 2009. "'If I Don't Have to Work Anymore, Who Am I?': Job Loss and

Collaborative Self-Concept Repair." *Journal of Contemporary Ethnography* 38 (5):547–583.

Gasparro, Annie, and Julie Jargon. 2012. "McDonald's to Go Vegetarian in India." *Wall Street Journal,* September 5, p. B7.

Gates, Gary J. 2012. "LGBT VOTE 2012." Los Angeles: The Williams Institute. Accessible at www.law.ucla.edu/williamsinstitute.

Gaudin, Sharon. 2009. "Facebook Has Whopper of a Problem with Burger King Campaign." *Computerworld,* January 15.

Gay, Lesbian and Straight Education Network. 2012. "About GLSEN." Accessed March 1 (www.glsen.org).

Gecas, Viktor. 2004. "Socialization, Sociology of." Pp. 14525–14530 in *International Encyclopedia of the Social and Behavioral Sciences,* edited by Neil J. Smelser and Paul B. Baltes. Cambridge, MA: Elsevier.

Gelles, David. 2011. "It's All About the Algorithm." *Financial Times* (July 30).

General Social Survey. 2012. "GSS General Social Survey." Accessed January 25 (www3.norc.org/GSS+Website).

Gentile, Carmen. 2009. "Student Fights Record of 'Cyberbullying.'" *New York Times,* February 8, p. 20.

Gentleman, Amelia. 2006. "Bollywood Captivated by the Call Centre Culture." *Guardian Weekly,* June 2, p. 17.

Gerth, H. H., and C. Wright Mills. 1958. *From Max Weber: Essays in Sociology.* New York: Galaxy.

Gertner, Jon. 2005. "Our Ratings, Ourselves." *New York Times Magazine,* April 10, pp. 34–41, 56, 58, 64–65.

Gibbs, Jennifer L., Nicole B. Ellison, and Chih-Hui Lai. 2011. "First Comes Love, Then Comes Google: An Investigation of Uncertainty Reduction Strategies and Self-Disclosure in Online Dating." *Communication Research* 38. Accessible at https://www.msu.edu/[[sim]]nellison/GibbsEllisonLai_2011_FirstComesLove.pdf.

Gibbs, Nancy. 1993. "Rx for Death." *Time* (May 31):34–39.

———. 2009. "What Women Want Now." *Time* 174 (16):24–33.

Giddens, Anthony. 1991. *Modernity and Self-Identity: Self and Society in the Late Modern Age.* Cambridge, UK: Polity.

Giddings, Paul J. 2008. *Ida: A Sword among Lions.* New York: Amistad.

Gill, Adrian A. 2011. "Dubai on Empty." *Vanity Fair* (April). Accessible at http://www.vanityfair.com/culture/features/2011/04/dubai-201104.

Gilley, Brian Joseph. 2006. *Becoming Two-Spirit: Gay Identity and Social Acceptance in Indian Country.* Lincoln: University of Nebraska Press.

Gillum, Jack. 2011. "How USA Today Analyzed Border Crime Trends." *USA Today,* July 16, p. 7A.

Giordano, Peggy C. 2003. "Relationships in Adolescence." Pp. 257–281 in *Annual Review of Sociology, 2003,* edited by Karen S. Cook and John Hagan. Palo Alto, CA: Annual Reviews.

Girl Scouts of the USA. 2001. *Junior Girl Scout Badge Book.* New York: Girl Scouts of the United States of America.

Giroux, Henry A. 1988. *Schooling and the Struggle for Public Life: Critical Pedagogy in the Modern Age.* Minneapolis: University of Minnesota Press.

Gitlin, Todd. 2002. *Media Unlimited: How the Torrent of Images and Sounds Overwhelms Our Lives.* New York: Henry Holt.

Glazer, Sarah. 2013. "Plagiarism and Cheating: Are They Becoming More Acceptable to the Internet Age?" *CQ Researcher* 23 (January 4).

Glazer, Susan. 2010. "Evaluating Microfinance." *EQ Global Research* 4 (April).

Goering, Laurie. 2008b. "Outsourced to India: Stress." *Chicago Tribune,* April 20, pp. 1, 18.

Goffman, Erving. 1959. *The Presentation of Self in Everyday Life.* New York: Doubleday.

———. 1961. *Asylums: Essays on the Social Situation of Mental Patients and Other Inmates.* Garden City, NY: Doubleday.

———. 1963. *Stigma: Notes on Management of Spoiled Identity.* Englewood Cliffs, NJ: Prentice Hall.

———. 1979. *Gender Advertisements.* Cambridge, MA: Harvard University Press.

Gold, Rachel Benson, and Elizabeth Nash. 2012. "Troubling Trend: More States Hostile to Abortion Rights as Middle Ground Shrinks." *Guttmacher Policy Review* 15 (Winter):14–19

Goldman, David. 2012. "Are Landlines Doomed?" CNN Money. April 10. Accessed April 11 (http://money.cnn.com/2012/04/10/technology/att-verizon-landlines/index.htm).

Gomez, Alan, Jack Gillum, and Kevin Johnson. 2011. "On U.S. Side, Cities Are Havens from Drug Wars." *USA Today,* July 15, pp. 1A, 6A–7A.

Goode, Erica, and Jack Healy. 2013. "Focus on Mental Health Laws to Curb Violence Is Unfair, Some Say." *New York Times,* February 1, p. A13.

Gorney, Cynthia. 2014. "Far from Home." *National Geographic* (February):7–95.

Gottfredson, Michael, and Travis Hirschi. 1990. *A General Theory of Crime.* Palo Alto, CA: Stanford University Press.

Gough, Margaret, and Alexandra Killewald. 2011. "Unemployment in Families: The Case of Housework." *Journal of Marriage and Family* 73 (October):1085–1100.

Gould, Elise. 2007. "The Health-Finance Debate Reaches a Fever Pitch." *Chronicle of Higher Education,* April 13, pp. B14, B15.

Gould, Larry A. 2002. "Indigenous People Policing Indigenous People: The Potential Psychological and Cultural Costs." *Social Science Journal* 39:171–188.

Government Accountability Office. 2003. "Women's Earnings: Work Patterns Partially Explain Difference between Men's and Women's Earnings." Washington, DC: U.S. Government. Printing Office.

Grady, John. 2001. "Becoming a Visual Sociologist." *Sociological Imagination* 38 (1/2):83–118.

———. 2007. "Visual Sociology." Vol. 3 in *21st Century Sociology: A Reference Handbook,* edited by Clifton D. Bryant and Dennis L. Peck. Thousand Oaks, CA: Sage.

Grady, Sarah, Stacy Bielick, and Susan Aud. 2010. *Trends in the Use of School Choice: 1993 to 2010.* Washington, DC: U.S. Government Printing Office.

Graells-Garrido, Eduardo, Mounia Lalmas, and Daniele Quercia. 2013. "Data Portraits: Connecting People of Opposing Views." Submitted

November 19. Accessed December 1 at http://arxiv.org/abs/1311.4658.

Gramsci, Antonio. 1929. *Selections from the Prison Notebooks.* Edited and translated by Quintin Hoare and Geoffrey Nowell Smith. London: Lawrence and Wishort.

Grattet, Ryken. 2011. "Societal Reactions to Deviance." *Annual Review of Sociology* 37:185–204.

Grazian, David. 2010. *Mix It Up: Popular Culture, Mass Media, and Society.* New York: Norton.

Greeley, Andrew M. 1989. "Protestant and Catholic: Is the Analogical Imagination Extinct?" *American Sociological Review* 54 (August):485–502.

Greenhalgh, Susan. 2008. *Just One Child: Science and Policy in Deng's China.* Berkeley: University of California Press.

Greenhouse, Steven. 2008a. "Unions Look for New Life in the World of Obama." *New York Times,* December 29, p. B6.

———. 2008b. "Millions of Jobs of a Different Collar." *New York Times,* March 26.

———. 2009. "In America, Labor Has an Unusually Long Fuse." *New York Times,* April 5, Week in Review News, p. 3.

———. 2013. "On Register's Other Side, Little Money to Spend." *New York Times,* November 29, pp. B1, B4.

Gregor, Alison. 2013. "A NORC, Up Close and Personal." *New York Times,* May 5, p. 8.

Gregory, Katherine. 2007. "Drawing a Virtual Gun?" Pp. 98–111 in *Open Fire: Understanding Global Gun Cultures,* edited by Charles Fruehling Springwood. New York: Berg.

Gross, Lynne Schaefer. 2013. *Electronic Media: An Introduction.* 11th ed. New York: McGraw-Hill.

Groza, Victor, Daniela F. Ileana, and Ivor Irwin. 1999. *A Peacock or a Crow: Stories, Interviews, and Commentaries on Romanian Adoptions.* Euclid, OH: Williams Custom Publishing.

Guarino, Mark. 2009. "New Orleans' 'Katrina Generation' Struggles with Drugs and Depression." *Christian Science Monitor* (May 13).

Guest, Robert. 2011. "Tribes Still Matter." *The Economist* (January 22):17–18.

Guo, Guang, Michael E. Roettger, and Tianji Cai. 2008. "The Integration of Genetic Propensities into Social-Control Models of Delinquency and Violence among Male Youths." *American Sociological Review* 73 (August):543–568.

Gurbuz, Mustafa, and Gulsum Gurbuz-Kucuksari. 2009. "Between Sacred Codes and Secular Consumer Society: The Practice of Headscarf Adoption among American College Girls." *Journal of Muslim Minority Affairs* 29 (September):387–399.

Gutiérrez, Gustavo. 1990. "Theology and the Social Sciences." Pp. 214–225 in *Liberation Theology at the Crossroads: Democracy or Revolution?* edited by Paul E. Sigmund. New York: Oxford University Press.

Guttmacher Institute. 2008. *Facts on Induced Abortion Worldwide.* New York: Guttmacher.

———. 2014. "More State Abortion Restrictions Were Enacted in 2011–2013 than in the Entire Previous Decade." January 2. Accessed at http://www.guttmacher.org/media/inthenews/2014/01/02/index.html?utm_source=feedburner&utm_medium=feed&utm_campaign=Feed%3A+Guttmacher+(New+from+the+Guttmacher+Institute).

h

Haas, Steven A., David R. Schaefer, and Olga Kornienko. 2010. "Health and the Structure of Adolescent Social Networks." *Journal of Health and Social Behavior* 5 (4):424–439.

Hacker, Andrew. 1964. "Power to Do What?" Pp. 134–146 in *The New Sociology*, edited by Irving Louis Horowitz. New York: Oxford University Press.

Hacker, Helen Mayer. 1951. "Women as a Minority Group." *Social Forces* 30 (October):60–69.

———. 1974. "Women as a Minority Group, Twenty Years Later." Pp. 124–134 in *Who Discriminates against Women?* edited by Florence Denmark. Beverly Hills, CA: Sage.

Hall, Jeremiah. 2013. "Charities Latch onto 'Crowdsourcing.'" *Christian Science Monitor Weekly* (November 25):33–34.

Hall, Mimi. 2005. "Senators 'to Demand Answers' on Slow Action." *USA Today,* September 6, p. 4A.

Hallinan, Maureen T. 1997. "The Sociological Study of Social Change." *American Sociological Review* 62 (February):1–11.

Halme, Kimmo, Ilari Lindy, Kalle A. Piirainen, Vesa Salminen, and Justine White. 2014. *Finland as a Knowledge Economy 2.0. Lessons on Policies and Governance.* Washington, DC: The World Bank.

Halualani, Rona Tamiko. 2002. *In the Name of Hawaiians: Native Identities and Cultural Politics.* Minneapolis: University of Minnesota Press.

Hamm, Steve. 2007. "Children of the Web." *BusinessWeek,* July 2, pp. 50–56, 58.

Hani, Yoko. 1998. "Hot Pots Wired to Help the Elderly." *Japan Times Weekly International Edition,* April 13, p. 16.

Haq, Husna. 2011. "How Marriage Is Faring." *Christian Science Monitor,* February 14, p. 21.

Harden, Blaine. 2009. "Revising History: Japan Helps Immigrants Find Work, Realizing that Its Aging Population Can't Support Itself." *Washington Post National Weekly Edition* (February): 20.

Harlow, Harry F. 1971. *Learning to Love.* New York: Ballantine.

Harman, Donna. 2009. "Dubai's Glitz Lost in Grim Life." *Christian Science Monitor,* May 3, p. 8.

Harmon, Katherine. 2011. "How Obesity Spreads in Social Networks." May 5. Accessible at http://www.scientificamerican.com/article.cfm?id=social-spread-obesity.

Harper, Douglas. 1988. "Visual Sociology: Expanding Sociological Vision." *American Sociologist* (Spring):54–70.

Harrington, Michael. 1980. "The New Class and the Left." Pp. 123–138 in *The New Class,* edited by B. Bruce Briggs. Brunswick, NJ: Transaction.

Harrisinteractive. 2008. "Cell Phone Usage Continues to Increase." Accessed January 13 (www.harrisinteractive.com).

Haub, Carl. 2010. "2010 World Population Data Sheet." Washington, DC: Population Reference Bureau.

———. 2013. "Were the Population Alarmists Right or Wrong?" Washington, DC: Population Reference Bureau. Accessed April 24 (demographicsrevealed.org/2013/03/26/were-the-population-alarmists-right-or-wrong/).

———, and Toshiko Kaneda. 2013. *World Population Data Sheet 2013.* Accessible at http://www.prb.org/Publications/Datasheets/2013/2013-world-population-data-sheet.aspx.

Hauser, Orlee. 2011. "'We Rule the Base Because We're Few': 'Lone Girls' in Israel's Military." *Journal of Contemporary Ethnography* 40 (6):623–651.

Haviland, William A., Harald E. L. Prins, Dana Walrath, and Bunny McBride. 2008. *Cultural Anthropology—The Human Challenge.* 12th ed. Belmont, CA: Wadsworth.

Hawdon, James, and John Ryan. 2011. "Social Relations that Generate and Sustain Solidarity after a Mass Tragedy." *Social Forces* 89 (4):1383–1384.

Hay, Andrew. 2009. "Spain's New Middle Classes Slip into Poverty." *Reuters.* April 8. Accessed May 11, 2011 (http://uk.reuters.com/article/email/ioUKTRE537029200904).

Hayden, H. Thomas. 2004. "What Happened at Abu Ghraib." Accessed August 7 (www.military.com).

He, Wan, Manisha Sengupta, Victoria A. Velkoff, and Kimberly A. DeBarros. 2005. "65+ in the United States: 2005." *Current Population Reports,* ser. P-23, no. 209. Washington, DC: U.S. Government Printing Office.

Health Cost Institute. 2013. "The Impact of the Mental Health Parity and Addiction Equity Act on Inpatient Admissions." February. Issue Brief #5. Accessed May 15 at http://www.healthcostinstitute.org/files/HCCI-Mental-Health-Parity-Issue-Brief.pdf.

Heckert, Druann, and Amy Best. 1997. "Ugly Duckling to Swan: Labeling Theory and the Stigmatization of Red Hair." *Symbolic Interaction* 20 (4):365–384.

Hedley, R. Alan. 1992. "Industrialization in Less Developed Countries." Pp. 914–920, vol. 2, in *Encyclopedia of Sociology,* edited by Edgar F. Borgatta and Marie L. Borgatta. New York: Macmillan.

Heilman, Madeline E. 2001. "Description and Prescription: How Gender Stereotypes Prevent Women's Ascent up the Organizational Ladder." *Journal of Social Issues* 57 (4):657–674.

Heisig, Jan Paul. 2011. "Who Does More Housework: Rich or Poor? A Comparison of 33 Countries." *American Sociological Review* 76 (1):74–99.

Hellmich, Nanci. 2001. "TV's Reality: No Vast American Waistlines." *USA Today,* October 8, p. D7.

Helman, Ruth, Mathew Greenwald, Craig Copeland, and Jack VanDerhel. 2012. "The 2012 Retirement Confidence Survey: Job Security, Debt Weigh on Retirement Confidence, Savings." *Employee Benefit Research Institute* Notes 33 (March).

Hendershott, Ann. 2002. *The Politics of Deviance.* San Francisco: Encounter Books.

Henderson, Carter. 1997. *Funny; I Don't Feel Old.* San Francisco: ICS Press.

Hengeveld, Rob. 2012. *Wasted World: How Our Consumption Challenges the Planet.* Chicago: University of Chicago Press.

Hernandez, Elaine M., and Christopher Uggen. 2012. "Institutions, Politics, and Mental Health Parity." *Society and Mental Health* 2 (3):154–171.

Hernandez, Javier C. 2014. "Charters, Public Schools and a Chasm Between." *New York Times,* May 12, pp. A1, A16.

Hersch, Patricia. 1998. *A Tribe Apart: A Journey into the Heart of American Adolescence.* New York: Fawcett Books.

Hertz, Rosanna. 2006. *Single by Chance. Mothers by Choice.* New York: Oxford University Press.

Hewlett, Sylvia Ann, and Carolyn Buck Luce. 2005. "Off-Ramps and On-Ramps: Keeping Talented Women on the Road to Success." *Harvard Business Review* (March):43–53.

Higgins, Chris A., Linda E. Duxbury, and Sean T. Lyons. 2010. "Coping with Overload in Stress: Men and Women in Dual-Earner Families." *Journal of Marriage and Family* 72 (August):847–859.

Hill, Michael R., and Susan Hoecker-Drysdale, eds. 2001. *Harriet Martineau: Theoretical and Methodological Perspectives.* New York: Routledge.

Hillsman, Sally T. 2013. "Gun Violence: Lifting the Shackles on Federal Firearms Research." *Footnotes* (January):2, 4.

Himes, Christine L. 2001. "Elderly Americans." *Population Bulletin* 56 (December).

Hira, Ron. 2008. "An Overview of the Offshoring of U.S. Jobs." Pp. 14–15 in Marlene A. Lee and Mark Mather. "U.S. Labor Force Trends." *Population Bulletin* 63 (June).

Hirschi, Travis. 1969. *Causes of Delinquency.* Berkeley: University of California Press.

Hirst, Paul, and Grahame Thompson. 1996. *Globalization in Question: The International Economy and the Possibilities of Governance.* Cambridge, UK: Polity Press.

Hitlin, Steven, and Jane Allyn Piliavin. 2004. "Values: Reviving a Dormant Concept." Pp. 359–393 in *Annual Review of Sociology, 2004,* edited by Karen S. Cook and John Hagan. Palo Alto, CA: Annual Reviews.

Hixson, Lindsay, Bradford B. Hepler, and Myoung Ouk Kim. 2012. *Islander Population: 2010.* May 2012. C2010BR-12. Washington, DC: U.S. Government Printing Office.

Hochschild, Arlie Russell. 1990. "The Second Shift: Employed Women Are Putting in Another Day of Work at Home." *Utne Reader* 38 (March–April):66–73.

———. 2005. *The Commercialization of Intimate Life: Notes from Home and Work.* Berkeley: University of California Press.

———, with Anne Machung. 2012. *The Second Shift: Working Parents and the Revolution at Home.* Revised with a new Afterword. New York: Penguin.

Hoeffel, Elizabeth M., Sonya Rastogi, Myoung Ouk Kim, and Hasan Shahid. 2012. *The Asian Population: 2010.* C2101BR-11. Washington, DC: U.S. Government Printing Office.

Holden, Constance. 1980. "Identical Twins Reared Apart." *Science* 207 (March 21):1323–1328.

———. 1987. "The Genetics of Personality." *Science* 257 (August 7):598–601.

Hollingshead, August B. 1975. *Elmtown's Youth and Elmtown Revisited.* New York: Wiley.

Holmes, Mary. 2009. "Commuter Couples and Distance Relationships: Living Apart Together." Sloan Work and Family Research Network. Accessible at http://wfnetwork.bc.edu/encyclopedia_entry.php?id=15551&area=all.

Homans, George C. 1979. "Nature versus Nurture: A False Dichotomy." *Contemporary Sociology* 8 (May):345–348.

Home School Legal Defense Association. 2005. "State Laws" and "Academic Statistics on Homeschooling." Accessed May 12 (www.hslda.org).

Hondagneu-Sotelo, Pierrette, ed. 2003. *Gender and U.S. Immigration: Contemporary Trends.* Berkeley: University of California Press.

hooks, bell. 1994. *Feminist Theory: From Margin to Center.* 2nd ed. Boston: South End Press.

Hopper, Nate, and Jen Oritz. 2012. "The Appalling Frequency of the Shooting Spree." *New York* (July 30):7.

Horgan, John. 1993. "Eugenics Revisited." *Scientific American* 268 (June):122–128, 130–133.

Horkheimer, Max, and Theodore Adorno. [1944] 2002. *Dialectic of Enlightenment.* Palo Alto, CA: Stanford University Press.

Horowitz, Helen Lefkowitz. 1987. *Campus Life.* Chicago: University of Chicago Press.

Horwitz, Allan V. 2002. *Creating Mental Illness.* Chicago: University of Chicago Press.

Hosokawa, William K. 1969. *Nisei: The Quiet Americans.* New York: Morrow.

Hospice Association of America. 2010. "Hospice Facts and Statistics." Accessed March 12, 2012 (www.nah.org/facts/HospiceStats/o.pdf).

Houle, Jason N. 2013. "Disparities in Debt: Parents' Socioeconomic Resources and Young Adult Student Loan Debt." *Sociology of Education* 20 (10):1–17.

Houseman, John. 1972. *Run Through.* New York: Simon and Schuster.

Houser, Trevor, Shashank Mohamad, and Robert Heilmayer. 2009. *A Green Global Recovery? Assessing U.S. Economic Stimulus and the Prospects for International Coordination.* Washington, DC: World Resources Institute of Peterson Institute for International Economics.

Howard, Judith A. 1999. "Border Crossings between Women's Studies and Sociology." *Contemporary Sociology* 28 (September):525–528.

Howard, Michael. 2009. *Modern Wicca: A History from Gerald Gardner to the Present.* St. Paul, MN: Llewellyn Books.

Howard, Michael C. 1989. *Contemporary Cultural Anthropology.* 3rd ed. Glenview, IL: Scott, Foresman.

Howard, Russell D., and Reid L. Sawyer. 2003. *Terrorism and Counterterrorism: Understanding the New Security Environment.* Guilford, CT: McGraw-Hill/Dushkin.

Hu, Winnie. 2010. "In a New Role, Teachers Move to Run Schools." *New York Times,* September 7, pp. A1, A20.

Huang, Gary. 1988. "Daily Addressing Ritual: A Cross-Cultural Study." Presented at the annual meeting of the American Sociological Association, Atlanta.

Hughes, Everett. 1945. "Dilemmas and Contradictions of Status." *American Journal of Sociology* 50 (March):353–359.

Human Genome Project. 2012. "Human Genome Project Information." Accessed April 4 (www.ornl.gov/sci/techresources/Human_Genome/home.shtml).

Human Rights Campaign. 2014. "Marriage Center: Marriage Recognition." As of January 2014. Accessible at http://www.hrc.org/campaigns/marriage-center.

Humes, Karen R., Nicholas A. Jones, and Roberto R. Ramirez. 2011. *Overview of Race and Hispanic Origin: 2010.* 2010 Census Brief BR-02. Accessible at http://www.census.gov/prod/cen2010/briefs/c2010br-02.pdf.

Hunt, Darnell. 1997. *Screening the Los Angeles "Riots": Race, Seeing, and Resistance.* New York: Cambridge University Press.

Hunter, Herbert M., ed. 2000. *The Sociology of Oliver C. Cox: New Perspectives: Research in Race and Ethnic Relations,* vol. 2. Stamford, CT: JAI Press.

Hunter, James Davison. 1991. *Culture Wars: The Struggle to Define America.* New York: Basic Books.

Huntington, Samuel P. 1993. "The Clash of Civilizations?" *Foreign Affairs* 72 (Summer):22–49.

Hur, Song-Woo. 2011. "Mapping South Korean Women's Movements During and After Democratization: Shifting Identities." *East Asian Social Movements,* edited by J. Broadbent and V. Brockman.

Hurn, Christopher J. 1985. *The Limits and Possibilities of Schooling.* 2nd ed. Boston: Allyn and Bacon.

Hussar, William J., and Tabitha M. Bailey. 2011. *Projections of Education Statistics to 2019.* Washington, DC: National Center for Education Statistics.

———, and ———. 2013. *Projection of Education Statistics to 2021.* Washington, DC: U.S. Government Printing Office. Accessible at http://nces.ed.gov/programs/projections/projections2021/.

Hyde, Janet Shibley. 2005. "The Gender Similarities Hypothesis." *American Psychologist* 60 (6):581–592.

i

Igo, Sarah E. 2007. *The Average American: Surveys, Citizens, and the Making of a Mass Public.* Cambridge, MA: Harvard University Press.

Immervoll, Herwig, and David Barber. 2005. *Can Parents Afford to Work? Childcare Costs, Tax-Benefit Policies and Work Incentives.* Paris: Organisation for Economic Co-Operation and Development.

Inglehart, Ronald, and Wayne E. Baker. 2000. "Modernization, Cultural Change, and the Persistence of Traditional Values." *American Sociological Review* 65 (February):19–51.

Inoue, Sachiko, Takashi Yorifuji, Soshi Takao, Hiroyuki Doi, and Ichiro Kawachi. 2013. "Social Cohesion and Mortality: A Survival Analysis of Older Adults in Japan." *American Journal of Public Health* 103 (December):e60–e66.

Institute for Economics and Peace. 2014. "Global Peace Index 2013." June 11, 2013. Accessed January 26, 2014 (www.visionofhumanity.org/gpi/results/world-map.php).

Interbrand. 2013. "Best Global Brands 2013." Accessible at http://www.interbrand.com/en/best-global-brands/2013/Best-Global-Brands-2013.aspx.

Interface Group Report (Virginia Tech). 2007. *Presidential Internal Review.* Blacksburg, Virginia Polytechnic Institute and State University.

International Gay and Lesbian Human Rights Commission. 2010. Home Page. Accessed February 11 (www.iglhrc.org).

International Institute for Democracy and Electoral Assistance. 2014. "Voter Turnout Database—Custom Query." Accessed January 26 (http://www.idea.int/vt/viewdata.cfm#).

International Monetary Fund. 2000. *World Economic Outlook: Asset Prices and the Business Cycle.* Washington, DC: International Monetary Fund.

International Telecommunication Union. 2012. Global Technology Development Figures. October 11. Accessed November 14, 2013 at http://www.itu.int/net/pressoffice/press_releases/2012/70.aspx#.UoUJgKW50pE.

International Trade Union Confederation. 2009. "Davos: World Unions Call for Action against Corporate Grand Theft." Accessed January 31 at www.ituc-csi.org/spip.php?article2736.

International Visual Sociology Association. 2013. "About IVSA." Accessible at http://visualsociology.org/about.html.

Internet Crime Complaint Center. 2012. *The 2011 Internet Crime Report.* Washington, DC: The National White Collar Crime Center. Accessible at www.ic3.gov/media/annualreport/2011_IC3Report.pdf.

Inter-Parliamentary Union. 2014. *Women in National Parliaments.* November 1, 2013. Accessed January 26, 2014 (www.ipu.org).

Ironside, Virginia. 2011. "Romania's Orphanages: Locking the Past Away." *The Independent* (UK) (November 29). Accessed September 25, 2012 at http://www.independent.co.uk/life-style/health-and-families/features/romanias-orphanages-locking-the-past-away-6269173.html.

Isaacs, Julia B. 2007b. *Economic Mobility of Men and Women.* Washington, DC: Economic Mobility Project.

———, Isabel V. Sawhill, and Ron Haskins. 2008. *Getting Ahead or Losing Ground: Economic Mobility in America.* Washington, DC: Pew Charitable Trusts.

ITOPF. 2006. "Statistics: International Tanker Owners Pollution Federation Limited." Accessed May 2 (www.itopf.com/stats.html).

j

Jackson, Philip W. 1968. *Life in Classrooms.* New York: Holt.

Jacobs, Andres. 2010. "As China's Economy Grows, Pollution Worsens Despite New Efforts to Control It." *New York Times,* July 29, p. A4.

Jacobs, Tom. 2009. "Hot Men of the Links." *Miller-McCune* (May–June):79.

Jacobsen, Linda A., May Kent, Marlene Lee, and Mark Mather. 2011. "America's Aging Population." *Population Bulletin* 66 (February).

———. Mark Mather, and Genevieve Dupuis. 2012. "Household Change in the United States." *Population Bulletin* 67 (September).

Jaffee, Daniel. 2012. "Weak Coffee: Certification and Co-Optation in the Fair Trade Movement." *Social Problems* 59 (1):94–116.

Jain, Saranga, and Kathleen Kurz. 2007. *New Insights on Preventing Child Marriage: A Global Analysis of Factors and Programs*. Washington, DC: International Center for Research on Women.

Jäntti, Markus. 2009. "Mobility in the United States in Comparative Perspectives." *Focus* 26 (Fall).

Japan Aisaika Organization. 2012. "Aisaika Organization Prospectus." Accessed January 15 (www.aisaika.org/en/prospectus.html).

Jasper, James M. 1997. *The Art of Moral Protest: Culture, Biography, and Creativity in Social Movements*. Chicago: University of Chicago Press.

Jayson, Sharon. 2009. "Holding Up the Value of Marriage." *USA Today,* February 18, pp. D1, D2.

———. 2013. "The End of 'Online Dating.'" *USA Today,* February 14, pp. 1A, 2A.

Jenkins, Henry. 2006. *Convergence Culture: Where Old and New Media Collide*. New York: New York University Press.

Jensen, Gary F. 2005. "Social Organization Theory." In *Encyclopedia of Criminology,* edited by Richard A. Wright and J. Mitchell Miller. Chicago: Fitzrog Dearborn.

Jervis, Rick. 2008. "New Orleans Homicides up 30% over 2006 Level." *USA Today,* January 3, p. 3A.

Jesella, Kara. 2008. "Blogging's Glass Ceiling." *New York Times,* July 27, Style section, pp. 1, 2.

Jian, Ma. "China's Brutal One-Child Policy." *New York Times,* May 22, p. A27.

Joas, Hans, and Wolfgang Knöbl. 2009. *Social Theory: Twenty Introductory Lectures*. Cambridge: Cambridge University Press.

John, Robert. 2012. "The Native American Family." Pp. 361–410 in *Ethnic Families in America: Patterns and Variations*. 5th ed., edited by Roosevelt Wright, Jr., Charles H. Mindel, Thanh Van Tran, and Robert W. Halsenstein. Upper Saddle River, NJ: Pearson.

Johnson, Benton. 1975. *Functionalism in Modern Sociology: Understanding Talcott Parsons*. Morristown, NJ: General Learning.

Johnson, Bobbie. 2010. "Privacy No Longer a Social Norm, Says Facebook Founder." January 10. Accessed December 2, 2013 at http://www.theguardian.com/technology/2010/jan/11/facebook-privacy.

Johnson, Ian. 2012. "A Promise to Tackle China's Problems, but Few Hints of a Shift in Path." *New York Times,* November 16, p. A19.

Johnson, Richard A. 1985. *American Fads*. New York: Beech Tree.

Jones, Jeffrey. 2013. "Americans Still Divided on Energy-Environment Trade-Off." April 10, 2013. Accessible at http://www.gallup.com/poll/161729/americans-divided-energy-environment-trade-off.aspx.

Jones-Puthoff, Alexa. 2013. *Is the U.S. Population Getting Older and More Diverse?* June 14. Accessible at http://www.census.gov/newsroom/cspan/pop_diverse/.

Jordan, Mary. 2007. "The New Face of Global Mormonism." *Washington Post National Weekly Edition* (November 26):20–21.

Jost, Kenneth. 2008. "Women in Politics." *CQ Researcher* 18 (March 21).

Julian, Tiffany, and Robert Kominski. 2011. *Education and Synthetic Work-Life Earnings Estimates*. ACS-14. Washington, DC: U.S. Government Printing Office.

k

Kahn, Joseph. 2006. "Where's Mao? Chinese Revise History Books." *New York Times,* September 1, pp. A1, A6.

Kalleberg, Arne L. 2009. "Precarious Work, Insecure Workers: Employment Relations in Transition." *American Sociological Review* 74 (February):1–22.

———. 2012. "The Social Contract in an Era of Precarious Work." *Pathways* (Fall):3–6.

Kambayashi, Takehiko. 2008. "Japanese Men Shout the Oft-Unsaid 'I love you.'" *Christian Science Monitor,* February 13.

Kamenetz, Anya. 2006. *Generation Debt*. New York: Riverhead.

Kang, K. Connie. 1996. "Filipinos Happy with Life in U.S. but Lack United Voice." *Los Angeles Times,* January 26, pp. A1, A20.

Karides, Marina. 2010. "Theorizing the Rise of Microenterprise Development in Caribbean Context." *Journal of World-Systems Research* 16 (2):192–216.

Katovich, Michael A. 1987. Correspondence. June 1.

Katz, Michael. 1971. *Class, Bureaucracy, and the Schools: The Illusion of Educational Change in America*. New York: Praeger.

Kaufman, Sarah. 2006. "The Criminalization of New Orleanians in Katrina's Wake." Accessed April 4 (www.ssrc.org).

Kaufman, Sharon R., and Lynn M. Morgan. 2005. "The Anthropology of the Beginnings and Ends of Life." *Annual Review of Anthropology* 34:317–341.

Kavada, Anastasia. 2005. "Exploring the Role of the Interest in the 'Movement for Alternative Globalization': The Case of the Paris 2003 European Social Forum." *Westminster Papers in Communication and Culture* 2 (1):72–95.

Keenan, Jillian. 2013. "Legalize Polygamy! No. I Am Not Kidding." April 15. Accessible at http://www.slate.com/articles/double_x/doublex/2013/04/legalize_polygamy_marriage_equality_for_all.html.

Keeter, Scott, and Courtney Kennedy. 2006. "The Cell Phone Challenge to Survey Research." Washington, DC: Pew Research Center.

Kelleher, Jennifer Sinco. 2011. "23 Arrested for Refusing to Leave Iolani Palace." *News from Indian Country,* November, p. 5.

Kellerman, Arthur L., Frederick P. Rivara, Norman B. Rushforth, Joyce G. Banton, Donald T. Reay, Jerry T. Francisco, Ana B. Locci, Janice Prodzinski, Bela B. Hackman, and Grant Somes. 1993. "Gun Ownership as a Risk Factor for Homicide in the Home." *New England Journal of Medicine* 329:1084–1091.

Kelly, Thomas. 2012. "Thomas Kelly on the Nyinba People of Nepal." Accessible at http://www.annenbergspaceforphotography.org/the-shot-blog/thomas-kelly-nyinba-people-nepal.

Kelly, Timothy A. 2009. *Healing the Broken Mind: Transforming America's Failed Mental Health System*. New York: New York University Press.

Kennickell, Arthur B. 2009. *Ponds and Streams: Wealth and Income in the U.S., 1989 to 2007*. Washington, DC: Federal Reserve Board.

Kennicott, Philip. 2011. "Review: 9/11 Memorial in New York." Accessed August 26 (www.washingtonpost.com).

Kenny, Charles. 2009. "Revolution in a Box." *Foreign Policy* (November):68–74.

Kentor, Jeffrey, and Yong Suk Jang. 2004. "Yes, There Is a (Growing) Transnational Business Community." *International Sociology* 19 (September):355–368.

Kerbo, Harold R. 2006. *World Poverty: The Roots of Global Inequality and the World System*. New York: McGraw-Hill.

———. 2012. *Social Stratification and Inequality*. 8th ed. New York: McGraw-Hill.

Kesmodel, David, and Danny Yadron. 2010. "E-Cigarettes Spark New Smoking War." *Wall Street Journal,* August 25, pp. A1, A12.

Kessler, Ronald C., Emil F. Coccaro, Maurizio Fava, Savina Jaeger, Robert Jin, and Ellen Walters. 2006. "The Prevalence and Correlates of DSM-IV Intermittent Explosive Disorder in the National Comorbidity Survey Replication." *Archives of General Psychiatry* 63 (June):669–678.

Khan, Shamus. 2013. "We Are Not All in This Together." *New York Times,* December 15 (Section SR), p. 4.

Kidder, Jeffrey L. 2012. "Parkour, the Affective Appropriation of Urban Space, and the Real/Virtual Dialectic." *City and Community* 11 (September):229–253.

Killian, Caitlin. 2003. "The Other Side of the Veil: North African Women in France Respond to the Headscarf Affair." *Gender and Society* (August 17):576–590.

Kim, Hyun Sik. 2011. "Consequences of Parental Divorce for Child Development." *American Sociological Review* 76 (3):487–511.

Kim, Kwang Chung. 1999. *Koreans in the Hood: Conflict with African Americans*. Baltimore: Johns Hopkins University Press.

Kimmel, Michael S. 2006. "A War against Boys?" *Dissent* (Fall):65–70.

———. 2008. *The Gendered Society*. 3rd ed. New York: State University of New York at Stony Brook.

King, Gary. 2011. "Ensuring the Data-Rich Future of the Social Sciences." *Science* (February 11):719–721.

King, Leslie. 1998. "France Needs Children: Pronatalism, Nationalism, and Women's Equity." *Sociological Quarterly* 39 (Winter):33–52.

King, Meredith L. 2007. *Immigrants in the U.S. Health Care System*. Washington, DC: Center for American Progress.

King, Sharon A. 1999. "Mania for 'Pocket Monsters' Yields Billions for Nintendo." *New York Times,* April 26, pp. A1, A18.

Kingsbury, Alex. 2008. "Q and A: Sudhir Venkatesh." *US News and World Report,* January 21, p. 14.

Kinsey, Alfred C., Wardell B. Pomeroy, and Clyde E. Martin. 1948. *Sexual Behavior in the Human Male.* Philadelphia: Saunders.

———, ———, and Paul H. Gebhard. 1953. *Sexual Behavior in the Human Female.* Philadelphia: Saunders.

Kiser, Edgar. 1992. "War." Pp. 2243–2247 in *Encyclopedia of Sociology,* edited by Edgar F. Borgatta and Marie L. Borgatta. New York: Macmillan.

Kitchener, Richard F. 1991. "Jean Piaget: The Unknown Sociologist." *British Journal of Sociology* 42 (September):421–442.

Klass, Perri. 2003. "This Side of Medicine." P. 319 in *This Side of Doctoring Reflection for Women in Medicine,* edited by Eliza Lo Chin. New York: Oxford University Press.

Klein, Lloyd. 1994. "We're Going to Disney World: Consumers Credit and the Consumption of Social Experience." *Free Inquiry in Creative Sociology* 22 (November):117–124.

Klein, Naomi. 1999. *No Logo: Money, Marketing, and the Growing Anti-Corporate Movement.* New York: Picador (St. Martin's Press).

Kleiner, Art. 2003. "Are You In with the In Crowd?" *Harvard Business Review* 81 (July):86–92.

Kleinknecht, William. 1996. *The New Ethnic Mobs: The Changing Face of Organized Crime in America.* New York: Free Press.

———. 2014. "As the Population Grays, Americans Stay Upbeat." February 12. Accessed March 8 (www.pewreasearch.org).

Klinenberg, Eric. 2002. *Heat Wave: A Social Autopsy of Disaster in Chicago.* Chicago: University of Chicago Press.

———. 2012. Going Solo: *The Extraordinary Rise and Surprising Appeal of Living Alone.* New York: Penguin Press.

Knudsen, Morten. 2010. "Surprised by Method— Functional Method and System Theory." *Forum: Qualitative Social Research* 11 (September): article 12.

Kochhar, Rakesh. 2006. "Growth in the Foreign-Born Workforce and Employment of the Native Born." Washington, DC: Pew Hispanic Center.

———. 2014. "As the Population Grays, Americans Stay Upbeat." February 12. Accessed March 8 (www.pewreasearch.org).

———, Richard Fry, and Paul Taylor. 2011. "Twenty-to-One: Wealth Gaps Rise to Record Highs between Whites, Blacks and Hispanics." July 26. Accessible at http://www.pewsocialtrends.org/files/2011/07/SDT-Wealth-Report_7-26-11_FINAL.pdf.

Koerth-Baker, Maggie. 2012. "Head in the Crowds." *New York Times Magazine* (December 23):12, 14.

Kohut, Andrew, et al. 2005. *American Character Gets Mixed Reviews: 16-Nation Pew Global Attitudes Survey.* Washington, DC: Pew Global Project Attitudes.

———, et al. 2007. *Global Unease with Major World Powers: Rising Environmental Concern in 47-Nation Survey.* Washington, DC: Pew Global Project Attitudes.

Kokmen, Leyla. 2008. "Environmental Justice for All." *Utne Reader* (March–April):42–46.

Koppel, Nathan, and Ashby Jones. 2013. "Firms Balk at Gay Weddings." *Wall Street Journal,* October 2, p. A3.

Korean Women's Association United. 2010. "Republic of Korea: Critical Issues on the Seventh Periodical Report on the Convention on the Elimination of All Forms of Discrimination against Women." November 10. Accessed March 27, 2010 (www2.ohchr.org/English/bodies/cedaw/docs/ngos/Korean_Womens_Association_United(PSWG).pdf).

Kornblum, Janet. 2007. "Meet the 'Tech-No's': People Who Reject Plugging into the Highly Wired World." *USA Today,* January 11, pp. A1, A2.

Kosmin, Barry A., and Ariela Keysar. 2009. *American Religious Identification Survey.* Hartford, CT: Trinity College.

Kotkin, Joel. 2010. "Ready Set Grow." *Smithsonian* (July/August):61–73.

Kottak, Conrad. 2011. *Anthropology: Appreciating Human Diversity.* 14th ed. New York: McGraw-Hill.

Krane, Jim. 2009. *Dubai: The Story of the World's City.* London: Atlantic Books.

———. 2010. "To Spend or Not to Spend." Interviewed on Al Jazeera television, March 26. Accessed April 20 (http://english.aljazeera.net/ programmes/countingthecost/2010/03/201032510494187263.html).

Kratz, Corinne A., and Iman Karp. 1993. "Wonder and Worth: Disney Museums in World Showcase." *Museum Anthropology* 17 (3):32–42.

Kraybill, Donald. 2001. *The Riddle of Amish Culture.* Rev. ed. Baltimore: Johns Hopkins University Press.

Kreider, Rose M. 2010. "Increase in Opposite-Sex Cohabiting Couples from 2009 to 2010 in the Annual Social and Economic Supplement (AEFC) to the Current Population Survey (CPS)." Working Paper. Washington, DC: U.S. Bureau of the Census.

———. 2011. "Contexts of Racial Socialization: Are Transracial Adoptive Families More Like Multiracial or White Monoracial Families?" March 1. Accessible at www.census.gov.

———, and Renee Ellis. 2011. "Living Arrangements of Children: 2009." *Current Population Reports,* ser. P70, no. 126. Washington, DC: U.S. Government Printing Office.

Kriesberg, Louis. 1992. "Peace." Pp. 1432–1436 in *Encyclopedia of Sociology,* edited by Edgar F. Borgatta and Marie L. Borgatta. New York: Macmillan.

Kristof, Nicholas D. 1998. "As Asian Economies Shrink, Women Are Squeezed Out." *New York Times,* June 11, pp. A1, A12.

Kronstadt, Jessica, and Melissa Favreault. 2008. "Families and Economic Mobility." Washington, DC: Economic Mobility Project. Also accessible at www.economicmobility.org/reports_and_research/literature_reviews?id=0004.

Krysan, Maria, Reynolds Farley, and Mick P. Couper. 2008. "In the Eye of the Beholder." *DuBois Review* 5 (1):5–26.

Kübler-Ross, Elisabeth. 1969. *On Death and Dying.* New York: Macmillan.

Kunzig, Robert. 2011. "Seven Billion." *National Geographic* (January):40–69.

Kwong, Jo. 2005. "Globalization's Effects on the Environment." *Society* 42 (January–February): 21–28.

Ladner, Joyce. 1973. *The Death of White Sociology.* New York: Random Books.

Lahey, Joanna. 2006. *Age, Women, and Hiring: An Experimental Study.* Boston: Center

Landtman, Gunnar. [1938] 1968. *The Origin of Inequality of the Social Class.* New York: Greenwood (original edition 1938, Chicago: University of Chicago Press).

Lasswell, Harold D. 1936. *Politics: Who Gets What, When, How.* New York: McGraw-Hill.

Last, Jonathan. 2013. *What to Expect When No One's Expecting: America's Coming Demographic Disaster.* New York: Encounter Books.

Lau, Yvonne M. 2006. "Re-Visioning Filipino American Communities: Evolving Identities, Issues, and Organizations." Pp. 141–153 in *The New Chicago,* edited by John Koval et al. Philadelphia: Temple University Press.

Lauer, Robert H. 1982. *Perspectives on Social Change.* 3rd ed. Boston: Allyn and Bacon.

Laumann, Edward O., John H. Gagnon, and Robert T. Michael. 1994a. "A Political History of the National Sex Survey of Adults." *Family Planning Perspectives* 26 (February):34–38.

———, ———, ———, and Stuart Michaels. 1994b. *The Social Organization of Sexuality: Sexual Practices in the United States.* Chicago: University of Chicago Press.

Lavrakas, Paul J., Charles D. Shuttles, Charlotte Steel, and Howard Fienberg. 2007. "The State of Surveying Cell Phone Numbers in the United States: 2007 and Beyond." *Public Opinion Quarterly* 71 (5):840–854.

Lawson, Sandra. 2008. *Girls Count.* New York: Goldman Sachs.

Lazarsfeld, Paul, Bernard Beretson, and H. Gaudet. 1948. *The People's Choice.* New York: Columbia University Press.

———, and Robert K. Merton. 1948. "Mass Communication, Popular Taste, and Organized Social Action." Pp. 95–118 in *The Communication of Ideas,* edited by Lymon Bryson. New York: Harper and Brothers.

Lazer, David, Ryan Kennedy, Gary King, and Alessandro Vespignani. 2014. "The Parable of Google Flu: Traps in Big Data Analysis." *Science* 343 (March 14):1203–1205.

Leavell, Hugh R., and E. Gurney Clark. 1965. *Preventive Medicine for the Doctor in His Community: An Epidemiologic Approach.* 3rd ed. New York: McGraw-Hill.

Ledgerwood, Joanna, ed. 2013. *The New Microfinance Handbook: A Financial Market Perspective.* Washington, DC: World Bank.

Lee, Alfred McClung. 1983. *Terrorism in Northern Ireland.* Bayside, NY: General Hall.

Lee, Ji Hyun. 2013. "Modern Lessons from Arranged Marriages." *New York Times,* January 18. Accessible at http://www.nytimes.com/2013/01/20/fashion/weddings/parental-involvement-can-help-in-choosing-marriage-partners-experts-say.html?pagewanted=all.

Lee, Ronald D., and David S. Reher. 2011. "Introduction: The Landscape of Demographic Transition and Its Aftermath." *Population and Development Review* 37 (Supplement):1–7.

Lee, Suevon. 2013. "Five Federal Policies on Guns You've Never Heard Of." January 7. Accessed February 25 at http://www.propublica.org.

Lehman, Chris. 2012. "Retirement Communities Find Niche with Gay Seniors." February 16. Accessible at www.wbur.org/npr/146713531/retirement-communities-find=niche-with-gay-seniors.

Lengermann, Patricia Madoo, and Jill Niebrugge-Brantley. 1998. *The Women Founders: Sociology and Social Theory, 1830–1930.* Boston: McGraw-Hill.

Lenski, Gerhard. 1966. *Power and Privilege: A Theory of Social Stratification.* New York: McGraw-Hill.

Leonhardt, David. 2004. "As Wealthy Fill Top Colleges Concerns Grow over Fairness." *New York Times,* April 22, pp. A1, A12.

Levin, Jack, and William C. Levin. 1980. *Ageism.* Belmont, CA: Wadsworth.

Levine, Nancy. 1988. *The Dynamics of Polyandry: Kinship, Domesticity, and Population on the Tibetan Border.* Chicago: University of Chicago Press.

Levinson, Daniel J. 1978. *The Seasons of a Man's Life.* With Charlotte N. Darrow et al. New York: Knopf.

———. 1996. *The Seasons of a Woman's Life.* With Judy D. Levinson. New York: Knopf.

Levitt, Peggy, and B. Nadya Jaworsky. 2007. "Transnational Migration Studies: Past Developments and Future Trends." *Annual Review of Sociology* 33:129–156.

Levitt, Steven D., and Stephen J. Dubner. 2006. *Freakonomics: A Rogue Economist Explores the Hidden Side of Everything.* Revised and expanded edition. New York: Morrow.

———, and Sudhir Venkatesh. 2000. "An Economic Analysis of a Drug-Selling Gang's Finances." *Quarterly Journal of Economics* (August):775–789.

Lewin, Tamar. 2011. "College Graduates' Debt Grew, Yet Again, in 2010." *New York Times,* November 3, p. A20.

Li, Jennifer S., Tracie A. Barnett, Elizabeth Goodman, Richard C. Wasserman, and Alex R. Kemper. 2013. "Approaches to the Prevention and Management of Childhood Obesity: The Role of Social Networks and the Use of Social Media and Related Electronic Technologies: A Scientific Statement from the American Heart Association." *Circulation* 127:260–267.

Lichtblau, Eric. 2009. "Telecom Companies Win Dismissal of Wiretap Suits." *New York Times,* June 4, p. A14.

Light, Donald W. 2004. "Dreams of Success: A New History of the American Health Care System." *Journal of Health and Social Behavior* 45 (Extra issue):1–24.

Light, Paul C. 2005. "Katrina's Lesson in Readiness." *Washington Post,* September 1.

Lindner, Eileen W. 2012. *Yearbook of American and Canadian Churches, 2012.* Nashville: Abingdon Press.

Linn, Susan, and Alvin F. Poussaint. 1999. "Watching Television: What Are Children Learning about Race and Ethnicity?" *Child Care Information Exchange* 128 (July):50–52.

Lino, Mark. 2013. *Expenditures on Children by Families, 2012.* Washington, DC: U.S. Department of Agriculture, Center for Nutrition Policy and Promotion.

Lio, Shoon, Scott Melzer, and Ellen Reese. 2008. "Constructing Threat and Appropriating 'Civil Rights': Rhetorical Strategies of Gun Rights and English Only Leaders." *Symbolic Interaction* 31 (1):5–31.

Lipka, Sara. 2009. "Do Crime Statistics Keep Students Safe?" *Chronicle of Higher Education* 55 (January 30):A15–A17.

Lipson, Karen. 1994. "'Nell' Not Alone in the Wilds." *Los Angeles Times,* December 19, pp. F1, F6.

Liptak, Adam. 2006. "The Ads Discriminate, but Does the Web?" *New York Times,* March 5, p. 16.

———. 2008. "From One Footnote, a Debate over the Tangles of Law, Science and Money." *New York Times,* November 25, p. A13.

Liska, Allen E., and Steven F. Messner. 1999. *Perspectives on Crime and Deviance.* 3rd ed. Upper Saddle River, NJ: Prentice Hall.

Living Goods. 2013. "A Scalable Model for Massive Impact." Accessed May 15 at http://livinggoods.org/what-we-do/micro-franchise-business-model/.

Livingstone, Sonia. 2004. "The Challenge of Changing Audiences." *European Journal of Communication* 19 (March):75–86.

Llana, Sara Miller, and Whitney Eulich. 2013. "Women at War, Worldwide." *Christian Science Monitor Weekly* (February 4):18–20.

Lo Sasso, Anthony T., Michael R. Richards, Chiu-Fang Chou, and Susan E. Gerber. 2011. "The $16,819 Pay Gap for Newly Trained Physicians: The Unexplained Trend of Men Earning More Than Women." *Health Affairs* 30 (February):193–201.

Loeb, Susanna, Bruce Fuller, Sharon Lynn Kagan, and Bidemi Carrol. 2004. "Child Care in Poor Communities: Early Learning Effects of Type, Quality, and Stability." *Child Development* 75 (January–February):47–65.

Loecke, Janet. 2014. "Minimum Wage by State." *USA Today,* February 11, p. 4A.

Lofland, Lyn H. 1975. "The 'Thereness' of Women: A Selective Review of Urban Sociology." Pp. 144–170 in *Another Voice,* edited by M. Millman and R. M. Kanter. New York: Anchor/Doubleday.

Lofland, John. 1981. "Collective Behavior: The Elementary Forms." Pp. 441–446 in *Social Psychology: Sociological Perspectives,* edited by Morris Rosenberg and Ralph Turner. New York: Basic Books.

———. 1985. *Protests: Studies of Collective Behavior and Social Movements.* Rutgers, NJ: Transaction.

Lofquist, Daphne. 2011. *Same-Sex Couple Households.* ACSBR/10-03. Washington, DC: U.S. Government Printing Office.

Logan, John R., Richard D. Alba, and Werquan Zhang. 2002. "Immigrant Enclaves and Ethnic Communities in New York and Los Angeles." *American Sociological Review* 67 (April):299–322.

———, and Brian Stults. 2011. "The Persistence of Segregation in the Metropolis: New Findings from the 2010 Census." Census Brief prepared for Project US2010. http://www.s4.brown.edu/us2010.

Lohr, Steve. 2008. "For a Good Retirement, Find Work. Good Luck." *New York Times,* June 22, p. 3.

Long, Sharon K., and Paul B. Masi. 2009. *Access to and Affordability of Care in Massachusetts as of Fall 2008: Geographic and Racial/Ethnic Differences.* Washington, DC: Urban Institute.

Longhofer, Wesley, and Evan Schofer. 2010. "National and Global Origins of Environmental Association." *American Sociological Review* 75 (4):505–533.

Lopez, Mark Hugo. 2011. *The Latino Electorate in 2010: More Voters, More Non-Voters.* Washington, DC: Pew Hispanic Center.

Lorber, Judith. 2005. *Breaking the Bowls: Degendering and Feminist Change.* New York: Norton.

Loughran, Thomas A., Holly Nguyen, Alex R. Piquero, and Jeffrey Fagan. 2013. "The Returns to Criminal Capital." *American Sociological Review* 78 (6):925–948.

Lubienski, Christopher A., and Peter C. Weitzel. 2012. *The Charter School Experiment Expectations, Evidence, and Implications.* Cambridge MA: Harvard Education Press.

Ludwig, Jens, and Isabel Sawhill. 2007. *Success by Ten: Interviewing Early, Often, and Efficiently in the Education of Young Children.* Washington, DC: Brookings Institution.

Lukacs, Georg. 1923. *History and Class Consciousness.* London: Merlin.

Lundquist, Jennifer Hickes. 2006. "Choosing Single Motherhood." *Contexts* 5 (Fall):64–67.

Luster, Tom, Kelly Rhoades, and Bruce Haas. 1989. "The Relation between Parental Values and Parenting Behavior: A Test of the Kohn Hypothesis." *Journal of Marriage and the Family* 51 (February):139–147.

Luttinger, Nina, and Gregory Dicum. 2006. *The Coffee Book: Anatomy of an Industry from Crop to the Last Drop.* Revised and updated. New York: New Press.

Lyall, Sarah. 2002. "For Europeans, Love, Yes; Marriage, Maybe." *New York Times,* March 24, pp. 1–8.

Lynn, Barry C. 2003. "Trading with a Low-Wage Tiger." *American Prospect* 14 (February):10–12.

m

MacDorman, Marian F., and T. J. Mathews. 2009. "Behind International Rankings of Infant Mortality: How the United States Compares with Europe." *NCHS Date Brief* (No. 23, November).

MacFarquhar, Neil. 2008. "Resolute or Fearful, Many Muslims Turn to Home Schooling." *New York Times,* March 26, p. A1.

Machalek, Richard, and Michael W. Martin. 2010. "Evolution, Biology and Society: A Conversation for the 21st-Century Sociology Classroom." *Teaching Sociology* 38 (1):35–45.

Mack, Mick G. 2003. "Does Exercise Status Influence the Impressions Formed by College Students?" *College Student Journal* 37 (December).

Mack, Raymond W., and Calvin P. Bradford. 1979. *Transforming America: Patterns of Social Change.* 2nd ed. New York: Random House.

Madden, Mary, Amanda Lenhart, Sandra Cortesi, Urs Gasser, Maeve Duggan, Aaron Smith, and Meredith Beaton. 2013. "Teens, Social Media, and Privacy." May 21. Accessible at http://pewinternet.org/Reports/2013/Teens-Social-Media-And Privacy.aspx.

Maestretti, Danielle. 2009. "Information Overload." *Utne Reader* (July–August):22–23.

Magga, Ole Henrik. 2006. "Diversity in Sami Terminology for Reindeer, Snow, and Ice." *International Social Science Journal* 58 (March):25–34.

Magnier, Mark. 2004. "China Clamps Down on Web News Discussion." *Los Angeles Times,* February 26, p. A4.

Malcolm, Andrew H. 1974. "The 'Shortage' of Bathroom Tissue: A Classic Study in Rumor." *New York Times,* February 3, p. 29.

Malcolm X, with Alex Haley. [1964] 1999. *The Autobiography of Malcolm X.* Revised with Epilogue by Alex Haley and Afterword by Ossie Davis. New York: One World, Ballantine Books.

Males, Mike, and Meda Chesney-Lind. 2010. "The Myth of Mean Girls." *New York Times,* April 2, p. A21.

Malhotra, Neil, and Yotam Margalit. 2009. "State of the Nation: Anti-Semitism and the Economic Crisis." *Boston Review* (May–June). Accessible at http://bostonreview.net/BR34.3/malhotra_margalit.php.

Malthus, Thomas Robert, Julian Huxley, and Frederick Osborn. [1824] 1960. *Three Essays on Population.* Reprint. New York: New American Library.

Manza, Jeff, and Clem Brooks. 2012. "How Sociology Lost Public Opinion: A Genealogy of a Missing Concept in the Study of the Political." *Sociological Theory* 30 (2):89–113.

Marable, Manning. 2011. *Malcolm X: A Life of Reinvention.* New York: Viking.

Margolis, Mac. 2009. "The Land of Less Contrast: How Brazil Reined in Inequality." *Newsweek,* November 28.

Marquis, Julie, and Dan Morain. 1999. "A Tortuous Path for the Mentally Ill." *Los Angeles Times,* November 21, pp. A1, A22, A23.

Marshall, Brent K., and J. Steven Picou. 2008. "Postnormal Science, Precautionary Principle, and Worst Cases: The Challenge of Twenty-First-Century Catastrophes." *Sociological Inquiry* 78 (May):230–247.

Martin, Dominique, Jean-Luc Metzger, and Philippe Pierre. 2006. "The Sociology of Globalization: Theoretical and Methodological Reflections." *International Sociology* 21 (July):499–521.

Martin, Joyce A., Brady E. Hamilton, Paul D. Sutton, Stephanie J. Ventura, Fay Menacker, Sharon Kirmeyer, and T. J. Mathews. 2009. "Births: Final Data for 2006." *National Vital Statistics Reports* 57 (January 7).

Martin, Karin A. 2009. "Normalizing Heterosexuality: Mothers' Assumptions, Talk, and Strategies with Young Children." *American Sociological Review* 74 (April):190–207.

Martin, Marvin. 1996. "Sociology Adapting to Changes." *Chicago Tribune,* July 21, sec. 18, p. 20.

Martin, Susan E. 1994. "Outsider within the Station House: The Impact of Race and Gender on Black Women Politics." *Social Problems* 41 (August):383–400.

Martin, Susan F. 2013. "Environmental Change and Migration: What We Know." *Policy Brief of the Migration Policy Institute.* Accessible at http://lawprofessors.typepad.com/files/migration-environmentalchange.pdf.

Martineau, Harriet. [1837] 1962. *Society in America.* Edited, abridged, with an introductory essay by Seymour Martin Lipset. Reprint. Garden City, NY: Doubleday.

———. [1838] 1989. *How to Observe Morals and Manners.* Philadelphia: Leal and Blanchard. Sesquentennial edition, edited by M. R. Hill, Transaction Books.

Martinez, Elizabeth. 1993. "Going Gentle into That Good Night: Is a Rightful Death a Feminist Issue?" *Ms.* 4 (July–August):65–69.

Marubbio, M. Elise. 2006. *Killing the Indian Maiden: Images of Native American Women in Film.* Lexington: University Press of Kentucky.

Marx, Earl. 2009. "How Will Fair Fare?" *Christian Science Monitor,* April 19, pp. 30–31.

Marx, Gary T. 2012. "Looking at Smelser's Theory of Collective Behavior After Almost 50 Years: A Review and Appreciation." *American Sociologist* 43 (June):135–152.

Marx, Karl. [1844] 1964. "Contribution to the Critique of Hegel's Philosophy of Right." In *On Religion,* Karl Marx and Friedrich Engels. New York: Schocker Books.

———, and Friedrich Engels. [1847] 1955. *Selected Work in Two Volumes.* Reprint. Moscow: Foreign Languages Publishing House.

Maryanski, Alexandra R. 2004. "Evolutionary Theory." Pp. 257–263 in *Encyclopedia of Social Theory,* edited by George Ritzer. Thousand Oaks, CA: Sage.

Massey, Douglas S. 2007. *Categorically Unequal: The American Stratification System.* New York: Russell Sage Foundation.

———, and Nancy A. Denton. 1993. *American Apartheid: Segregation and the Making of the Underclass.* Cambridge, MA: Harvard University Press.

———, and Margarita Mooney. 2007. "The Effects of America's Three Affirmative Action Programs on Academic Performance." *Social Problems* 54 (1):99–117.

Masuda, Takahiko, Phoebe C. Ellsworth, Batja Mesquita, Janxin Leu, Shigehito Tanida, and Ellen Van de Veerdonk. 2008. "Attitudes and Social Cognition: Placing the Face in Context: Cultural Differences in the Perception of Facial Emotion." *Journal of Personality and Social Psychology* 94 (3):365–381.

Masud-Piloto, Felix. 2008. "Cuban Americans." Pp. 357–359, vol. 1, in *Encyclopedia of Race, Ethnicity, and Society,* edited by Richard T. Schaefer. Thousand Oaks, CA: Sage.

Mattoni, Alice. 2012. *Media Practices and Protest Politics: How Precarious Workers Mobilise.* Farnham, United Kingdom: Ashgate.

Mazumder, Bhashkar. 2008. *Upward Intergenerational Economic Mobility in the United States.* Washington, DC: Economic Mobility Project.

McCarthy, Justin. 2014. "Same-Sex Marriage Support Reaches New High at 55%." May 21. Accessible at www.gallup.com.

McCormack, Mark. 2010. "Changing Masculinities in Youth Cultures." *Qualitative Sociology* 33:111–115.

McFarland, Andrew S. 2007. "Neopluralism." *Annual Review of Political Science* 10:45–66.

McGirk, Tim. 2009. "Postcard: Dubai." *Time,* October 19, p. 6.

McGuire, Thomas G., and Jeanne Miranda. 2008. "New Evidence Regarding Racial and Ethnic Disparities in Mental Health: Policy Implications." *Health Affairs* 27 (2):393–403.

McGurty, Eileen Maura. 2000. "Warren County, NC, and the Emergence of the Environmental Justice Movement: Unlikely Coalitions and Shared Meanings in Local Collective Action." *Society and Natural Resources* 13:373–387.

McIntosh, Peggy. 1988. "White Privilege and Male Privilege: A Personal Account of Coming to See Correspondence through Work and Women's Studies." Working Paper No. 189, Wellesley College Center for Research on Women, Wellesley, MA.

McKinlay, John B., and Sonja M. McKinlay. 1977. "The Questionable Contribution of Medical Measures to the Decline of Mortality in the United States in the Twentieth Century." *Milbank Memorial Fund Quarterly* 55 (Summer):405–428.

McLanahan, Sara, and Christine Percheski. 2008. "Family Structure and the Reproduction of Inequalities." *Annual Review of Sociology* 38:257–276.

McLane, Daisann. 2013. "Getting Off on the Wrong Foot." *National Geographic Traveler* (January):28.

McLuhan, Marshall. 1964. *Understanding Media: The Extensions of Man.* New York: New American Library.

———. 1967. *The Medium Is the Message: An Inventory of Effects.* New York: Bantam Books.

McNeil, Donald G., Jr. 2002. "W.H.O. Moves to Make AIDS Drugs More Accessible to Poor Worldwide." *New York Times,* August 23, p. D7.

———. 2004. "When Real Food Isn't an Option." *New York Times,* September 3, pp. A1, A5.

McPhail, Clark. 1991. *The Myth of the Madding Crowd.* New York: De Gruyter.

———. 1994. "The Dark Side of Purpose in Riots: Individual and Collective Violence." *Sociological Quarterly* 35 (January):i–xx.

———. 2006. "The Crowd and Collective Behavior: Bringing Symbolic Interaction Back In." *Symbolic Interaction* 29 (4):433–464.

———, and David Miller. 1973. "The Assembling Process: A Theoretical Empirical Examination." *American Sociological Review* 38 (December):721–735.

———. 2008. "Crowd." *Contexts* (Spring):78–79.

Mead, George H. 1934. In *Mind, Self and Society,* edited by Charles W. Morris. Chicago: University of Chicago Press.

———. 1964a. In *On Social Psychology,* edited by Anselm Strauss. Chicago: University of Chicago Press.

————. 1964b. "The Genesis of the Self and Social Control." Pp. 267–293 in *Selected Writings: George Herbert Mead,* edited by Andrew J. Reck. Indianapolis: Bobbs-Merrill.

Mead, Margaret. [1935] 2001. *Sex and Temperament in Three Primitive Societies.* New York: Perennial, HarperCollins.

Mehl, Matthias R., Simine Vazire, Nairán Ramírez-Esparza, Richard B. Slatcher, and James W. Pennebaker. 2007. "Are Women Really More Talkative than Men?" *Science* 317 (July 6):82.

Mendez, Jennifer Bickman. 1998. "Of Mops and Maids: Contradictions and Continuities in Bureaucratized Domestic Work." *Social Problems* 45 (February):114–135.

Merton, Robert. 1948. "The Bearing of Empirical Research upon the Development of Social Theory." *American Sociological Review* 13 (October):505–515.

————. 1968. *Social Theory and Social Structure.* New York Free Press.

————, and Alice S. Kitt. 1950. "Contributions to the Theory of Reference Group Behavior." Pp. 40–105 in *Continuities in Social Research: Studies in the Scope and Methods of the American Soldier,* edited by Robert K. Merton and Paul L. Lazarsfeld. New York: Free Press.

Messner, Michael A. 2002. "Gender Equity in College Sports: 6 Views." *Chronicle of Higher Education* 49 (December 6):B9–B10.

Meston, Cindy M., and David M. Buss. 2007. "Why Humanoids Have Sex." *Archives of Sexual Behavior* 36 (August).

Michals, Jennifer M. 2003. "The Price We Pay to Get Richer: A Look at Student Indebtedness." Unpublished M.A. paper, DePaul University, Chicago, IL.

Michels, Robert. 1915. *Political Parties.* Glencoe, IL: Free Press (reprinted 1949).

Microfinance Information Exchange. 2014. "MIX Market." Accessed January 26 (www.themix.org).

Milgram, Stanley. 1963. "Behavioral Study of Obedience." *Journal of Abnormal and Social Psychology* 67 (October):371–378.

————. 1975. *Obedience to Authority: An Experimental View.* New York: Harper and Row.

Miller, Dan E. 2006. "Rumor: An Examination of Some Stereotypes." *Symbolic Interaction* 28 (4):505–519.

Miller, David L. 2000. *Introduction to Collective Behavior and Collective Action.* 2nd ed. Prospect Heights, IL: Waveland Press.

————. 2014. *Introduction to Collective Behavior and Collective Action.* 3rd ed. Long Grove, IL: Waveland Press.

————, and JoAnne DeRoven Darlington. 2002. "Fearing for the Safety of Others: Disasters and the Small World Problem." Paper presented at Midwest Sociological Society, Milwaukee, WI.

Miller, Jacqueline W., Timothy S. Naimi, Robert D. Brewer, and Sherry Everett Jones. 2007. "Binge Drinking and Associated Health Risk Behaviors among High School Students." *Pediatrics* 119 (January):76–85.

Miller, Laura. 2008. "The Rise of the Superclass." Accessed in *Salon* May 2 (www.salon.com/books/review/2008/03/14/superclass/print.html).

Miller, Reuben. 1988. "The Literature of Terrorism." *Terrorism* 11 (1):63–87.

Mills, C. Wright. [1959] 2000a. *The Sociological Imagination.* 40th anniversary edition. New Afterword by Todd Gitlin. New York: Oxford University Press.

————. [1956] 2000b. *The Power Elite.* New edition. Afterword by Alan Wolfe. New York: Oxford University Press.

Miner, Horace. 1956. "Body Ritual among the Nacirema." *American Anthropologist* 58 (June): 503–507.

Mizruchi, Mark S. 1996. "What Do Interlocks Do? An Analysis, Critique, and Assessment of Research on Interlocking Directorates." Pp. 271–298 in *Annual Review of Sociology, 1996,* edited by John Hagan and Karen Cook. Palo Alto, CA: Annual Reviews.

Moaveni, Azadeh. 2005a. *Lipstick Jihad. A Memoir of Growing Up Iranian in America and American in Iran.* New York: Public Affairs.

————. 2005b. "Fast Times in Tehran." *Time* (June 12):38–42.

————. 2007. "The Unbearable Chic-ness of Jihad." *Time* (April 10).

————. 2009. *Honeymoon in Tehran: Two Years of Love and Danger in Iran.* New York: Random House.

Moeller, Susan D. 1999. *Compassion Fatigue.* London: Routledge.

————, Elia Powers, and Jessica Roberts. 2012. "The World Unplugged and 24 Hours without Media: Media Literacy to Develop Self-Awareness Regarding Media." *Comunicar* 20 (39):45–52.

Mohai, Paul, David Pellow, and J. Timmons Roberts. 2009. "Environmental Justice." *Annual Review of Environmental Research* 34:405–430.

————, and Robin Saha. 2007. "Racial Inequality in the Distribution of Hazardous Waste: A National-Level Reassessment." *Social Problems* 54 (3):343–370.

Mol, A. J. 2010. "Ecological Modernization as a Social Theory of Environmental Reform." Pp. 63–71 in *The International Handbook of Environmental Sociology,* 2nd ed., edited by Michael R. Redcraft and Graham Woodgate. Cheltenham, UK: Edward Elgar.

————, and D. A. Sonnenfeld, eds. 2000. *Ecological Modernization around the World.* Portland, OR: Frank Cass.

————, ————, and G. Spaargaren, eds. 2009. *The Ecological Modernization Reader.* London: Routledge.

Mollen, Milton. 1992. *"A Failure of Responsibility": Report to Mayor David N. Dinkins on the December 28, 1991, Tragedy at City College of New York.* New York: Office of the Deputy Mayor for Public Safety.

Monaghan, Peter. 1993. "Sociologist Jailed Because He 'Wouldn't Snitch' Ponders the Way Research Ought to Be Done." *Chronicle of Higher Education* 40 (September 1):A8, A9.

Monahan, Torin. 2011. "Surveillance as Cultural Practice." *The Sociological Quarterly* 52:495–508.

Moncarz, Roger J., Michael G. Wolf, and Benjamin Wright. 2008. "Service-Providing Occupations, Offshoring, and the Labor Market." *Monthly Labor Review* (December):71–86.

Money. 1987. "A Short History of Shortages." 16 (Fall, Special Issue):42.

Montgomery, Marilyn J., and Gwendolyn T. Sorell. 1997. "Differences in Love Attitudes across Family Life Stages." *Family Relations* 46:55–61.

Moore, Jina. 2013. "'Extreme Poverty' Cut by Half." *Christian Science Monitor Weekly* (January 7):30.

Moore, Malcolm. 2012. "China's New Leader Xi, Jinping Warns Communist Party Forces 'Severe Challenges.'" *Telegraph* (London) (November 15). Accessed at www.telegrapj.co.ul.

Moore, Mignon, and Michael Stambolis-Ruhstorfer. 2013. "LGBT Sexuality and Families at the Start of the Twenty-First Century." *Annual Review of Sociology* 39:491–507.

Moore, Molly. 2006. "Romance, but Not Marriage." *Washington Post National Weekly Edition,* November 27, p. 18.

Moore, Wilbert E. 1967. *Order and Change: Essays in Comparative Sociology.* New York: Wiley.

Morin, Rich, and Seth Motel. 2013. "After a Highly Partisan Election Year, Survey Finds Less Group Conflict." January 10. Accessible at www.pewsocialtrends.org.

Morris, Aldon. 2000. "Reflections on Social Movement Theory: Criticisms and Proposals." *Contemporary Sociology* 29 (May):445–454.

Morrison, Denton E. 1971. "Some Notes toward Theory on Relative Deprivation, Social Movements, and Social Change." *American Behavioral Scientist* 14 (May–June):675–690.

Morse, Arthur D. 1967. *While Six Million Died: A Chronicle of American Apathy.* New York: Ace.

Moskos, Peter. 2008. *Cop in the Hood: My Year Policing Baltimore's Eastern District.* Princeton, NJ: Princeton University Press.

Mosley, J., and E. Thomson. 1995. Pp. 148–165 in *Fatherhood: Contemporary Theory, Research and Social Policy,* edited by W. Marsiglo. Thousand Oaks, CA: Sage.

Motel, Seth, and Eileen Patten. 2012. *The 10 Largest Hispanic Origin Groups: Characteristics, Rankings, and Top Counties.* Washington, DC: Pew Hispanic Center.

Mueller, G. O. 2001. "Transnational Crime: Definitions and Concepts." Pp. 13–21 in *Combating Transnational Crime: Concepts, Activities, and Responses,* edited by P. Williams and D. Vlassis. London: Franklin Cass.

Mulrine, Anna. 2012. "Up in Arms." *Christian Science Monitor Weekly* (July 2): 26–32.

Murdock, George P. 1945. "The Common Denominator of Cultures." Pp. 123–142 in *The Science of Man in the World Crisis,* edited by Ralph Linton. New York: Columbia University Press.

————. 1949. *Social Structure.* New York: Macmillan.

————. 1957. "World Ethnographic Sample." *American Anthropologist* 59 (August):664–687.

Murphy, Dean E. 1997. "A Victim of Sweden's Pursuit of Perfection." *Los Angeles Times,* September 2, pp. A1, A8.

Murray, Velma McBride, Amanda Willert, and Diane P. Stephens. 2001. "The Half-Full Glass: Resilient African American Single Mothers and Their Children." *Family Focus* (June):F4–F5.

Myers, Dowell, and John Pitkin. 2011. *Assimilation Tomorrow: How America's Immigrants Will Integrate by 2030.* Washington, DC: Centers for American Progress.

Myers, Steven Lee, and Nicholas Kulish. 2013. "Growing Clamor about Inequities of Climate Crisis." *New York Times,* November 17, pp. 1, 12.

Myre, Greg. 2013. "Women in Combat: 5 Key Questions." January 24. Accessed March 3 at http://m.npr.org/story/170161752.

n

NAACP. 2008. *Out of Focus—Out of Sync Take 4.* Baltimore: NAACP.

NACCRRA (National Association of Child Care Resource and Referral Agencies). 2010. "Parents and the High Cost of Child Care: 2010 Update." Accessible at http://www.naccrra.org/docs/Cost_Report_073010-final.pdf.

Nakao, Keiko, and Judith Treas. 1994. "Updating Occupational Prestige and Socioeconomic Scores: How the New Measures Measure Up." *Sociological Methodology* 24:1–72.

Nash, Manning. 1962. "Race and the Ideology of Race." *Current Anthropology* 3 (June):285–288.

National Advisory Commission on Criminal Justice. 1976. *Organized Crime.* Washington, DC: U.S. Government Printing Office.

National Alliance for Caregiving. 2009. *Caregiving in the U.S.: Executive Summary.* Washington, DC: NAC and AARP.

National Alliance for Public Charter Schools. 2014. The Public Charter Schools Dashboard School. Accessed May 12 at http://dashboard.publiccharters.org/dashboard/schools/year/2013/.

National Alliance on Mental Illness. 2008. "What Is Mental Illness?" Accessed May 24, 2011 at www.nami.org.

National Alliance to End Homelessness. 2014. "Cost of Homelessness." Accessed April 14 at http://www.endhomelessness.org/pages/cost_of_homelessness.

National Center for Education Statistics. 2009. *Homeschooled Students.* Accessed May 31 (http://nces.ed.gov/programs/coe/2009/section1/indicator06.asp).

———. 2011a. *Average Undergraduate Tuition and Fees.* Accessed March 29 (http://nces.ed.gov/programs/digest/d09/tables/dt09_335.asp).

———. 2012. *Digest of Education Statistics, 2011.* Washington, DC: NCCES.

———. 2013. "Fast Facts." Accessible at http://nces.ed.gov/fastfacts/.

———. 2013. *Health, United States, 2012: With Special Feature on Emergency Care.* Accessible at http://www.cdc.gov/nchs/data/hus/hus12.pdf#018.

National Center for Health Statistics. 2007. *Health, United States 2006.* Washington, DC: U.S. Government Printing Office.

National Center on Addiction and Substance Abuse at Columbia University. 2007. *Wasting the Best and the Brightest: Substance Abuse at America's Colleges and Universities.* New York: NCASA at Columbia University.

National Conference of State Legislatures. 2013. *Voter Identification Requirements.* Accessed August 6, 2013 at http://www.ncsl.org/legislatures-elections/elections/voter-id.aspx.

National Education Association. 2012. "Rankings and Estimates. Rankings of the States 2012 and Estimates of School Statistics 2013." Accessed January 25, 2014 at http://www.nea.org/assets/img/content/NEA_Rankings_And_Estimates-2013_(2).pdf.

National Employment Law Project. 2013. "Living Wage and Minimum Wage." Accessed December 19 at http://www.nelp.org/index.php/content/content_issues/category/living_wage_and_minimum_wage/.

National Geographic. 2005. *Atlas of the World.* 8th ed. Washington, DC: National Geographic.

National Institute of Justice. 2005. *Sexual Assault on Campus: What Colleges and Universities Are Doing about It.* Washington, DC: National Institute of Justice.

National Institute on Aging. 1999. *Early Retirement in the United States.* Washington, DC: U.S. Government Printing Office.

National Oceanic and Atmospheric Administration. 2014. "Climate Information." Accessed February 2, 2014 at http://www.ncdc.noaa.gov/climate-information.

National Organization for Men Against Sexism. 2012. Home Page. Accessed February 22 (www.nomas.org).

National Public Radio. 2013. "Impossible Choice Faces America's First 'Climate Refugees.'" May 18. Accessible at www.wbur.org.

Navarro, Mireya. 2005. "When You Contain Multitudes." *New York Times,* April 24, pp. 1, 2.

Needham, Paul. 2011. "9/11 Memorial Review: At Ground Zero, Staying Above Ground Matters." September 9. Accessible at www.huffingtonpost.com.

Negroni, Lirio K. 2012. "The Puerto Rican American Family." Pp. 129–147 in *Ethnic Families in America: Patterns and Variations.* 5th ed., edited by Roosevelt Wright, Jr., Charles H. Mindel, Thanh Van Tran, and Robert W. Halsenstein. Upper Saddle River, NJ: Pearson.

Nelson, Emily. 2004. "Goodbye, 'Friends'; Hello, New Reality." *Wall Street Journal,* February 9, pp. B6, B10.

Neuman, Lawrence W. 2009. *Understanding Research.* Boston: Allyn and Bacon.

Neumark, David. 2007. *Minimum Wage Effects in the Post-Welfare Reform Era.* Washington, DC: The Employment Policies Institute.

Neves, Barbara Barbosa. 2013. "Social Capital and Internet Use: The Irrelevant, the Bad, and the Good." *Sociology Compass* 7/8:599–611.

New Unionism Network. 2011. "State of the Unions." Accessed February 10, 2011 at http://www.newunionism.net/State_of_the_Unions.htm.

New York Times. 2007. "University Officials Accused of Hiding Campus Homicide." June 24, p. 19.

———. 2008. "Law and Order." *New York Times,* January 6, pp. 10–11.

Newman, Katherine S. 2012. *The Accordion Family: Boomerang Kids, Anxious Parents, and the Private Toll of Global Competition.* Boston: Beacon Press.

Newman, William M. 1973. *American Pluralism: A Study of Minority Groups and Social Theory.* New York: Harper and Row.

Newport, Frank. 2010b. *In U.S., Increasing Number Have No Religious Identity.* Accessed March 28, 2011 (www.gallup.com).

———. 2011a. "For First Time, Majority of Americans Favor Legal Gay Marriage." Accessed February 27, 2012 (www.gallup.com/poll/147662/First-Time-Majority-Americans-Favor-Legal-Gay-Marriage.aspx?version=print).

———. 2012a. "In U.S., 46% Hold Creationist View of Human Origins." June 1. Accessible at http://www.gallup.com/poll/155003/Hold-Creationist-View-Human-Origins.aspx.

———. 2012b. "Americans Want Federal Gov't Out of State Marijuana Laws." December 10. Accessible at www.gallup.com.

Newsday. 1997. "Japan Sterilized 16,000 Women." September 18, p. A19.

NICHD. 2007. "Children Who Complete Intensive Early Childhood Program Show Gains in Adulthood: Greater College Attendance, Lower Crime and Depression." Accessed January 7, 2008 (www.nichd.nih.gov/news.releases/early_interventions_082107.cfm).

Nielsen Company. 2010. "Most Super Bowl Viewers Tune in for the Commercials Nielsen Says." Accessed February 11 at http://www.nielsen.com/us/en/insights/press-room/2010/most_super_bowl_vieqwers.html.

Nielsen, Joyce McCarl, Glenda Walden, and Charlotte A. Kunkel. 2000. "Gendered Heteronormativity: Empirical Illustrations in Everyday Life." *Sociological Quarterly* 41 (2):283–296.

Niemi, Richard G., and Michael J. Hanmer. 2010. "Voter Turnout among College Students: New Data and a Rethinking of Traditional Theories." *Social Science Quarterly* 91 (June):301–323.

Niesse, Mark. 2008. "Hawaiian Sovereignty Seekers Take Over Historic Iolani Palace in Honolulu." *News from Indian Country* (May 12):3.

———. 2011. "Native Hawaiian Self-Government May Be Set Up by State." *News from Indian Country* (March):3.

Niezen, Ronald. 2005. "Digital Identity: The Construction of Virtual Selfhood in the Indigenous Peoples' Movement." *Comparative Studies in Society and History* 47 (3):532–551.

Nixon, Darren. 2009. "'I Can't Put a Smiley Face On': Working-Class Masculinity, Emotional Labor and Service Work in the 'New Economy.'" *Gender, Work and Organization* 16 (3):300–322.

Nocera, Joe. 2012. "Guns and Mental Illness." *New York Times,* December 29, p. A17.

Nolan, Patrick D. 2004. "Ecological-Evolutionary Theory: A Reanalysis and Reassessment of Lenski's Theory for the 21st Century." *Sociological Theory* 22 (June):328–337.

———, and Gerhard Lenski. 2009. *Human Societies: An Introduction to Macrosociology.* 11th ed. Boulder, CO: Paradigm.

Noonan, Rita K. 1995. "Women against the State: Political Opportunities and Collective Action Frames in Chile's Transition to Democracy." *Sociological Forum* 10:81–111.

Nordhaus, Ted, and Michael Shellenberger. 2007. *Break Through: From the Death of Environmentalism to the Politics of Possibility.* Boston: Houghton Mifflin.

NORML. 2013. "State Laws." Accessed June 1 (http://norml.org/laws).

Norris, Poppa, and Ronald Inglehart. 2004. *Sacred and Secular: Religion and Politics Worldwide.* Cambridge: Cambridge University Press.

Norris, Tina, Paula L. Vines, and Elizabeth M. Hoeffel. 2012. *The American Indian and Alaska Native Population: 2010.* C2010BR-10. Accessible at http://www.census.gov.

North Carolina Department of Environmental and Natural Resources. 2008. "Warren County PCB Landfill Fact Sheet." Accessed April 9 (www.wastenotnc.org/WarrenCo_Fact_Sheet.htm).

Northam, Jack. 2014. "As Overseas Costs Rise, More U.S. Companies Are 'Reshoring.'" January 27. Accessed January 28, 2014 at www.wbur.org.

NPD Group. 2008. "Wired Baby Boomers Going Digital, Visiting Social Networks and Watching Videos on the Web." Accessed March (www.npd.com/press/releases/press_080909.html).

O

O'Brien, Daniel Tumminelli, Robert J. Sampson, and Christopher Winship. 2013. *Econometrics in the Age of Big Data: Measuring and Assessing 'Brooklyn Windows' Using Administrative Records.* Cambridge, MA: Radcliffe Institute for Advanced Study, Harvard University.

O'Donnell, Mike. 1992. *A New Introduction to Sociology.* Walton-on-Thames, UK: Thomas Nelson and Sons.

Office for National Statistics. 2013. "Female Male Occupation." Accessed March 3 at www.ons.gov.uk.

Office of Family Assistance. 2014. "Healthy Marriage & Responsible Fatherhood." Accessible at http://www.acf.hhs.gov/programs/ofa/programs/healthy-marriage.

Office of Immigration Statistics. 2013. *2012 Yearbook of Immigration Statistics.* Accessible at http://www.dhs.gov/yearbook-immigration-statistics.

Office of the United States Trade Representative. 2012. "Benefits of Trade." Accessed January 29 (www.ustr.gov/about-us/benefits-trade).

Ogas, Ogi, and Sai Gaddam. 2011. *A Billion Wicked Thoughts: What the World's Largest Experiment Reveals about Human Desire.* New York: Dutton.

Ogburn, William F. 1922. *Social Change with Respect to Culture and Original Nature.* New York: Huebsch (reprinted 1966, New York: Dell).

———, and Clark Tibbits. 1934. "The Family and Its Functions." Pp. 661–708 in *Recent Social Trends in the United States,* edited by Research Committee on Social Trends. New York: McGraw-Hill.

O'Harrow, Jr., Robert. 2005. "Mining Personal Data." *Washington Post National Weekly Edition,* February 6, pp. 8–10.

Okano, Kaori, and Motonori Tsuchiya. 1999. *Education in Contemporary Japan: Inequality and Diversity.* Cambridge: Cambridge University Press.

Okun, Barbara, and Joseph Nowinski. 2011. *Saying Goodbye: How Families Can Find Renewal Through Loss.* Cambridge, MA: Harvard Health Publications.

Oliver, Melvin L., and Thomas M. Shapiro. 2006. *Black Wealth/White Wealth: New Perspectives on Racial Inequality.* 2nd ed. New York: Routledge.

Omi, Michael, and Howard Winant. 1994. *Racial Formation in the United States.* 2nd ed. New York: Routledge.

Onishi, Norimitsu. 2003. "Divorce in South Korea: Striking a New Attitude." *New York Times,* September 21, p. 19.

Orfield, Gary, John Kucsera, and Genevieve Siegel-Hawley. 2012. "E Pluribus . . . Separation: Deepening Double Segregation for More Students." September 19. Accessible at http://civilrightsproject.ucla.edu/research/k-12-education/integration-and-diversity/mlk-national/e-pluribus. . .separation-deepening-double-segregation-for-more-students.

Organisation for Economic Co-Operation and Development. 2008. *Growing Unequal? Income Distribution and Poverty in OECD Countries.* Geneva: OECD.

———. 2009b. "Green at Fifteen? How 15-Year-Olds Perform in Environmental Sciences and Geosciences in PISA 2006." PISA, OECD Publishing. Accessible at http://dx.doi.org/10.1787/9789264063600-en.

———. 2012b. "Gender Equality and Social Institutions in Afghanistan." Accessed February 22 (http://genderindex.org/country/Afghanistan).

———. 2012c. "Education at a Glance 2011: OECD Indicators." Accessible at www.oecd-ilibrary.org/education/education-at-a-glance-2011/how-many-students-finish-tertiary-education_eaf-2011-7-en.

———. 2013a. "Dataset: Income Distribution and Poverty." Accessed February 20 at http://stats.occd.org.

———. 2013b. "Aid Statistics." Table 1. Updated December 23, 2013 at http://www.oecd.org/dac/stats/statisticsonresourceflowstodeveloping-countries.htm.

Ormond, James. 2005. "The McDonaldization of Football." Accessed January 23, 2006 (http://courses.essex.ac.uk/sc/sc111).

Ortman, Jennifer, and Hyon B. Shin. 2011. "Language Projections: 2010 to 2020." Presented at the American Sociological Association.

Ortman, Jennifer M., Victoria A. Velkoff, and Howard Hogan. 2014. "An Aging Nation: The Older Population in the United States: Population Estimates and Projections." P25–1140. Washington, DC: U.S. Government Printing Office.

Ortulay, Barbara. 2013. "Pew: Love Is in the Air and on the Web." Associated Press, October 21, 2013. Accessible at www.pewinternet.org/Media-Mentions/2013.

Orum, Anthony M., and John G. Dale. 2009. *Political Sociology: Power and Participation in the Modern World.* 5th ed. New York: Oxford University Press.

Orwell, George. 1949. *Nineteen Eighty-Four.* London: Secker and Warburg.

Ostling, Richard N., and Joan K. Ostling. 2000. *Mormon America: The Power and the Promise.* San Francisco: HarperCollins.

Outside the Classroom. 2009. "College Students Spend More Time Drinking than Studying." Accessed March 11 (www.outsidetheclassroom.com).

Oxford Poverty and Human Development Initiative. 2012. "Multidimensional Poverty Index." Accessed January 30 (www.ophi.org.uk).

P

Pace, Richard. 1993. "First-Time Televiewing in Amazonia: Television Acculturation in Gurupa, Brazil. *Ethnology* 32:187–205.

———. 1998. "The Struggle for Amazon Town." Boulder, CO: Lynne Rienner.

Padilla, Efren N. 2008. "Filipino Americans." Pp. 493–497 in vol. 1, *Encyclopedia of Race, Ethnicity, and Society,* edited by Richard T. Schaefer. Thousand Oaks, CA: Sage.

Page, Charles H. 1946. "Bureaucracy's Other Face." *Social Forces* 25 (October):89–94.

Page, Jeremy. 2011. "China's One-Child Plan Faces New Fire." *New York Times,* April 29, pp. A1, A12.

Page, Susan. 2012. "Attitudes toward Gays Changing Fast, Poll Finds." *USA Today,* December 6, pp. 1A, 2A.

Pager, Devah. 2007. *Marked: Race, Crime, and Finding Work in an Era of Mass Incarceration.* Chicago: University of Chicago Press.

———, Bruce Western, and Bart Bonikowski. 2009. "Discrimination in a Low-Wage Labor Market: A Field Experiment." *American Sociological Review* 74 (October):777–799.

Pampel, Fred C., Patrick M. Krueger, and Justin T. Denney. 2010. "Socioeconomic Disparities in Health Behaviors." *Annual Review of Sociology* 36:349–370.

Pariser, Ei. 2011a. *The Filter Bubble. What the Internet Is Hiding from You.* New York: Penguin Press.

———. 2011b. "In Our Own Little Internet Bubbles." *Guardian Weekly,* June 24, p. 32.

Park, Robert E. 1922. *The Immigrant Press and Its Control.* New York: Harper.

Parker, Ashley. 2010. "Where Parties Look for an Audience." *New York Times,* October 30.

Parker-Pope, Tara. 2012. "America's Drinking Binge." January 11. Accessed January 18 (http://well.blogs.nytimes.com/2012/01/11/Americas-drinking-binge).

Parkin, Stephen, and Ross Coomber. 2009. "Value in the Visual: On Public Injecting, Visual Methods and Their Potential for Informing Policy (and Change)." *Methodological Innovations Online* 4(2):21–36.

Parsons, Talcott. 1951. *The Social System.* New York: Free Press.

———. 1966. *Societies: Evolutionary and Comparative Perspectives.* Englewood Cliffs, NJ: Prentice Hall.

———. 1975. "The Sick Role and the Role of the Physician Reconsidered." *Milbank Medical Fund Quarterly Health and Society* 53 (Summer):257–278.

———, and Robert Bales. 1955. *Family: Socialization and Interaction Process.* Glencoe, IL: Free Press.

Passel, Jeffrey S., D'Vera Cohn, and Ana Gonzalez-Barrera. 2013. *Population Decline of Unauthorized Immigrants Stalls, May Have Reversed.* September 23. Accessible at http://www.pewresearch.org/hispanic.

Passero, Kathy. 2002. "Global Travel Expert Roger Axtell Explains Why." *Biography* (July):70–73, 97–98.

Patel, Reena. 2010. *Working the Night Shift: Women in India's Call Center Industry.* Stanford, CA: Stanford University Press.

Patterson, Thomas E. 2005. "Young Voters and the 2004 Election." Cambridge, MA: Vanishing Voter Project, Harvard University.

Pattillo-McCoy, Mary. 1999. *Black Picket Fences: Privilege and Peril among the Black Middle Class.* Chicago: University of Chicago Press.

Paul, Brad. 2014. "Dating Questions for Successful Relationships." Accessed January 18, 2014 at http://www.solotopia.com/dating-questions.

Paulson, Amanda. 2013. "*Roe v. Wade* at 40: Six Questions about the State of Abortion Rights Today." *Christian Science Monitor* (January 22). Accessible at www.csmonitor.com.

———. 2013. "Some Charter Schools Gain." *Christian Science Monitor Weekly* (July 8):11.

Pavlik, John V. 2013. "Trends in New Media Research: A Critical Review of Recent Scholarship." *Sociology Compass* 7 (1):1–12.

Pear, Robert. 1997. "Now, the Archenemies Need Each Other." *New York Times,* June 22, sec. 4, pp. 1, 4.

———. 2009. "Congress Relaxes Rules on Suits over Pay Inequity." *New York Times,* January 28, p. A14.

Pellow, David N., and Hollie Nyseth Brehm. 2013. "An Environmental Sociology for the Twenty-First Century." *Annual Review of Sociology* 39:229–250.

Pennington, Bill. 2008. "College Athletic Scholarships: Expectations Lose Out to Reality." *New York Times,* March 10, pp. A1, A15.

Peralta, Eyder. 2011. "Who Are the 1 Percent? Gallup Finds They're a Lot Like the 99 Percent." December 5. Accessed December 12 (www.wbur.org/npr/143143332/who-are-the-1-percent-gallup-finds-theyre-a-lot-like-the-99-percent).

Pescosolido, Bernice A. 2013. "The Public Stigma of Mental Illness: What Do We Think; What Do We Know; What Can We Prove?" *Journal of Health and Social Behavior* 54 (1):1–21.

Peter, Laurence J., and Raymond Hull. 1969. *The Peter Principle.* New York: Morrow.

Petersen, John L. 2009. "How 'Wild Cards' May Reshape Our Future." *Futurist* (May–June): 19–20.

Petersen, William. 1979. *Malthus.* Cambridge, MA: Harvard University Press.

Peterson, Kristina. 2013. "Minimum-Wage Maneuvering Begins." *Wall Street Journal,* February 14, p. A9.

Petrášová, Alexandra. 2006. *Social Protection in the European Union.* Brussels: European Union.

Pew Forum on Religion and Public Life. 2008. *U.S. Religious Landscape Survey.* Washington, DC: Author.

Pew Global Attitudes Project. 2007. *Global Unease with Major World Powers.* Washington, DC: Pew Global.

Pew Hispanic Center. 2011. "The Mexican-American Boom: Births Overtake Immigration." Washington, DC: Pew Hispanic Center.

Pew Internet Project. 2009. "Demographics of Internet Users." Accessed February 4 (www.pewinternet.org/trends/User_Demo_Jan_2009.htm).

Pew Internet and American Life Project. 2012. "Social Media and Political Engagement." October 10. Accessible at http://www.pewinternet.org/~/media//Files/Reports/2012/PIP_SocialMediaAndPoliticalEngagement_PDF.pdf.

Pew Research Center. 2010. "Glenn Beck, Christians and Mormons." Accessed October 4, 2010 at http://pewresearch.org/pubs/1717/glenn-beck-christians-mormons.

———. 2012b. "Fewer, Poorer, Gloomier: The Lost Decade of the Middle Class." August 22. Accessible at http://www.pewsocialtrends.org/files/2012/08/pew-social-trends-lost-decade-of-the-middle-class.pdf.

Pew Research Center Global Attitudes Project. 2012. "Social Networking Popular across Globe: Accessed Arab Publics Most Likely to Express Political Views Online." Accessible at http://www.pewglobal.org/files/2012/12/Pew-Global-Attitudes-Project-Technology-Report-FINAL-December-12-2012.pdf.

Pew Social and Demographic Trends. 2011. "Twenty-to-One: Wealth Caps Rise to Record Highs Between Whites, Black and Hispanics." Washington, DC: Pew Research Center.

Pfeifer, Mark. 2008. "Vietnamese Americans." Pp. 1365–1368, vol. 3, in *Encyclopedia of Race, Ethnicity, and Society,* edited by Richard T. Schaefer. Thousand Oaks, CA: Sage.

Phelan, Jo C., Bruce G. Lint, and Parisha Tehranifar. 2010. "Social Conditions as Fundamental Causes of Health Inequalities: Theory, Evidence, and Policy Implications." *Journal of Health and Social Behavior* 51 (5):528–540.

Phillips, Susan A. 1999. *Wallbangin': Graffiti and Gangs in L.A.* Chicago: University of Chicago Press.

Piaget, Jean. 1954. *Construction of Reality in the Child.* Translated by Margaret Cook. New York: Basic Books.

Picca, Leslie Houts, and Joe R. Feagin. 2007. *Two-Faced Racism: Whites in Backstage and Frontstage.* New York: Routledge.

Pickert, Kate. 2009. "Getting Well While You Shop." *Time,* June 22, pp. 68–70.

———. 2012. "Doing Good by Texting." *Time* (August 27):27.

Pilkington, Ed. 2010. "Right to Bear Arms Upheld." *The Guardian Weekly* (February 7):8.

Pincus, Fred L. 2003. *Reverse Discrimination: Dismantling the Myth.* Boulder, CO: Lynne Rienner.

———. 2008. "Reverse Discrimination." Pp. 1159–1161, vol. 3, in *Encyclopedia of Race, Ethnicity, and Society,* edited by Richard T. Schaefer. Thousand Oaks, CA: Sage.

Pinderhughes, Dianne. 1987. *Race and Ethnicity in Chicago Politics: A Reexamination of Pluralist Theory.* Urbana: University of Illinois Press.

Pinderhughes, Raquel. 2008. "Green Collar Jobs." Accessed June 29 (www.urbanhabitat.org/node/528).

Piturro, Marlene. 2012. "NORCs: Some of the Best Retirement Communities Occur Naturally." May 30. Accessed November 14, 2013 at www.nextavenue.org/article/2012-05/norcs-some-best-retirement-communities-occur-naturally.

Piven, Frances Fox, and Richard A. Cloward. 1996. "Welfare Reform and the New Class War." Pp. 72–86 in *Myths about the Powerless: Contesting Social Inequalities,* edited by M. Brinton Lykes, Ali Banuazizi, Ramsay Liem, and Michael Morris. Philadelphia: Temple University Press.

Plomin, Robert. 1989. "Determinants of Behavior." *American Psychologist* 44 (February):105–111.

Plüss, Caroline. 2005. "Constructing Globalized Ethnicity." *International Sociology* 20 (June):201–224.

Poder, Thomas C. 2011. "What Is Really Social Capital? A Critical Review." *American Sociologist* 42:341–367.

Pogash, Carol. 2008. "Poor Students in High School Suffer Stigma from Lunch Aid." *New York Times,* March 1, pp. A1, A14.

Polletta, Francesca, and James M. Jasper. 2001. "Collective Identity and Social Movements." Pp. 283–305 in *Annual Review of Sociology, 2001,* edited by Karen S. Cook and Leslie Hogan. Palo Alto, CA: Annual Reviews.

Population Reference Bureau. 1996. "Speaking Graphically." *Population Today* 24 (June/July).

Porter, Eduardo. 2013. "In the War on Poverty, a Dogged Adversary." *New York Times,* December 16, pp. B1, B3.

Portes, Alejandro, Cristina Escobar, and Renelinda Arana. 2008. "Bridging the Gap: Transnational and Ethnic Organizations in the Political Incorporation of Immigrants in the United States." *Ethnic and Racial Studies* 31 (September 6):1056–1090.

Powell, Brian, Catherine Bolzendahl, Claudia Geist, and Lola Carr Steelman. 2010. *Counted Out. Same-Sex Relationships and Americans' Definitions of Family.* New York: Russell Sage Foundation.

Powell, Gary N. 2010. *Women and Men in Management.* 4th ed. Thousand Oaks, CA: Sage.

Prahalad, C. K. 2014. *The Fortune at the Bottom of the Pyramid,* Revised and Updated 5th Anniversary Edition. London: Dorling Kindersley Pvt Ltd.

Prehn, John W. 1991. "Migration." Pp. 190–191 in *Encyclopedia of Sociology.* 4th ed. Guilford, CT: Dushkin.

Preston, Jennifer. 2011. "Facebook Page for Jesus with Highly Active Fans." *New York Times,* September 5, p. B3.

———, and Brian Stelter. 2011. "Cellphone Cameras Become World's Eyes and Ears on Protests across the Middle East." *New York Times,* February 19, p. A7.

Price, Tom. 2013. "Big Data and Privacy." *CQ Researcher* 23 (October 25):909–932. Accessible at http://library.cqpress.com.ezproxy1.lib.depaul.edu/cqresearcher/.

Prince, Martin, Vikram Patel, Shekhar Saxena, Mario Maj, Johanna Maselko, Michael Phillips, and Atif Rahman. 2007. "No Health without Mental Health." *The Lancet* 370 (September 8):859–877.

Pryor, John H., Kevin Egan, Laura Palucki Blake, Sylvia Hurtado, Jennifer Berdan, Matthew H. Case, and Linda DeAngelo. 2013. *The American Freshman: National Norms for Fall 2012.* Los Angeles: Higher Education Research Institute, UCLA.

———, Sylvia Hurtado, Victor B. Saenz, José Luis Santos, and William S. Korn. 2007. *The American Freshman: Forty Year Trends.* Los Angeles: Higher Education Research Institute, UCLA.

Purser, Gretchen. 2013. "Precarious Work." *Contexts* 12 (4):74–76.

q

Quadagno, Jill. 2014. *Aging and the Life Course: An Introduction to Social Gerontology.* 6th ed. New York: McGraw-Hill.

Quarantelli, Enrico L. 1957. "The Behavior of Panic Participants." *Sociology and Social Research* 41 (January):187–194.

———, and Russell R. Dynes. 1970. "Property Norms and Looting: Their Patterns in Continuity Crises." *Phylon* (Summer):168–182.

———, and James R. Hundley, Jr. 1975. "A Test of Some Propositions about Crowd Formation and Behavior." Pp. 538–554 in *Readings in Collective Behavior,* edited by Robert R. Evans. Chicago: Rand McNally.

Quillian, Lincoln. 2006. "New Approaches to Understanding Racial Prejudice and Discrimination." *Annual Review of Sociology* 32:299–328.

Quinney, Richard. 1970. *The Social Reality of Crime.* Boston: Little, Brown.

———. 1974. *Criminal Justice in America.* Boston: Little, Brown.

———. 1979. *Criminology.* 2nd ed. Boston: Little, Brown.

———. 1980. *Class, State and Crime.* 2nd ed. New York: Longman.

Quinnipiac University. 2013. "Americans Back Women in Combat 3-1, but Less for Draft." Release Detail February 7. Accessed March 3 at www.quinnipiac.edu.

Quiñones-Hinojosa, Alfredo, with Mim Eichler Rivas. 2011. *Becoming Dr. Q: My Journey from Migrant Farm Worker to Brain Surgeon.* Berkeley: University of California Press.

r

Rabinovitch, Shelley, and James Lewis, eds. 2004. *The Encyclopedia of Modern Witchcraft and New Paganism.* New York: Citadel Press.

Rainie, Lee. 2005. *Sports Fantasy Leagues Online.* Washington, DC: Pew Internet and American Life Project.

Rajan, Gita, and Shailja Sharma. 2006. *New Cosmopolitanisms: South Asians in the US.* Stanford, CA: Stanford University Press.

Ramet, Sabrina. 1991. *Social Currents in Eastern Europe: The Source and Meaning of the Great Transformation.* Durham, NC: Duke University Press.

Ramos, Jorge. 2010. *A Country for All.* New York: Vintage Books.

Ramstad, Evan. 2011. "Studying Too Much Is a New No-No in Upwardly Mobile South Korea." *Wall Street Journal,* October 6, p. A1.

RAND. 2010. "Retail Medical Clinics Perform Well Relative to Other Medical Settings." *RAND Review* (Winter 2009–2010). Accessed January 25 (www.rand.org/publications/randreview/issues/winter2009/news.html#medclinics).

Randolph, Tracey H., and Mellisa Holtzman. 2010. "The Role of Heritage Camps in Identity Development Among Korean Transnational Adoptees: A Relational Dialectics Approach." *Adoption Quarterly* 13:75–91.

Rangaswamy, Padma. 2005. "Asian Indians in Chicago." In *The New Chicago,* edited by John Koval et al. Philadelphia: Temple University Press.

Rasmussen Reports. 2013. "59% Believe Voter ID Laws Do Not Discriminate." Accessed December 30 at http://www.rasmussenreports.com/public_content/politics/general_politics/september_2013/59_believe_voter_id_laws_do_not_discriminate.

Ratnesar, Romesh. 2011. "The Menace Within." *Stanford Magazine* (July/August). Accessible at www.stanfordalumni.org.

Ravitch, Diane. 2010. *The Death and Life of the Great American School System: How Testing and Choice Are Undermining Education.* New York: Basic Books.

Rawlinson, Linnie, and Nick Hunt. 2009. "Jackson Dies, Almost Takes Internet with Him." Accessed July 1 (www.cnn.com/2009/TECH/06/26/michael.jackson.internet/).

Reinharz, Shulamit. 1992. *Feminist Methods in Social Research.* New York: Oxford University Press.

Reitzes, Donald C., and Elizabeth J. Mutran. 2006. "Lingering Identities in Retirement." *Sociological Quarterly* 47:333–359.

Religion News Service. 2003. "New U.S. Guidelines on Prayer in Schools Get Mixed Reaction." *Los Angeles Times,* February 15, p. B24.

Renzulli, Linda A., and Vincent J. Roscigno. 2007. "Charter Schools and Public Good." *Contexts* 6 (Winter):31–36.

Revkin, Andrew C. 2007. "Wealth and Poverty, Drought and Flood: Report from Four Fronts in the War on Warming." *New York Times,* April 3, pp. D4–D5.

Rheingold, Howard. 2003. *Smart Mobs: The Next Social Revolution.* Cambridge, MA: Perseus.

Ridgeway, Cecilia L. 2011. *Framed by Gender: How Gender Inequality Persists in the Modern World.* New York: Oxford University Press.

Riding, Alan. 1998. "Why 'Titanic' Conquered the World." *New York Times,* April 26, sec. 2, pp. 1, 28, 29.

———. 2005. "Unesco Adopts New Plan against Cultural Invasion." *New York Times,* October 21, p. B3.

Rieker, Patricia R., and Chloe E. Bird. 2000. "Sociological Explanations of Gender Differences in Mental and Physical Health." Pp. 98–113 in *Handbook of Medical Sociology,* edited by Chloe Bird, Peter Conrad, and Allan Fremont. New York: Prentice Hall.

Rifkin, Jeremy. 1995. *The End of Work; The Decline of the Global Labor Force and the Dawn of the Post-Market Era.* New York: Tarcher/Putnam.

Riley, Matilda White, Robert L. Kahn, and Anne Foner. 1994a. *Age and Structural Lag.* New York: Wiley InterScience.

———, Robert L. Kahn, and Anne Foner, in association with Karin A. Mock. 1994b. "Introduction: The Mismatch between People and Structures." Pp. 1–36 in *Age and Structural Lag,* edited by Matilda White Riley, Robert L. Kahn, and Anne Foner. New York: Wiley InterScience.

Rimer, Sara. 1998. "As Centenarians Thrive, 'Old' Is Redefined." *New York Times,* June 22, pp. A1, A14.

Ripley, Amanda. 2011. "Teacher, Leave Those Kids Alone." *Time,* December 5, pp. 46–49.

Ritzer, George. 2007. "A 'New' Global Age, but Are There New Perspectives on It?" Pp. 361–370 in *Frontiers of Globalization Research,* edited by Ino Rossi. New York: Springer.

———. 2010. *Enchanting a Disenchanted World: Revolutionizing the Means of Consumption.* 3rd ed. Thousand Oaks, CA: Pine Forge Press.

———. 2013. *The McDonaldization of Society,* 20th Anniversary Edition. Thousand Oaks CA: Sage.

Robertson, Roland. 1988. "The Sociological Significance of Culture: Some General Considerations." *Theory, Culture, and Society* 5 (February):3–23.

Robinson, Kristopher, and Edward M. Crenshaw. 2010. "Reevaluating the Global Digital Divide: Socio-Demographic and Conflict Barriers to the Internet Revolution." *Sociological Inquiry* 80 (February):34–62

Robnett, Belinda, and Cynthia Feliciano. 2011. "Patterns of Racial-Ethnic Exclusion by Internet Daters." *Social Forces* 89 (March):807–828.

Rodman, George. 2011. *Mass Media in a Changing World.* 3rd ed. New York: McGraw-Hill.

Rodriquez, Laura, and Donald Gatlin. 2014. "New Studies Offer Estimates of LGBT Population and Married Same-Sex Couples." September 29. Accessible at http://williamsinstitute.law.ucla.edu.

Rogan, Eugene. 2009. "Sand, Sea and Shopping." *Guardian Weekly,* October 16, pp. 38–39.

Rooks, Gerrit, Frits Tazelaar, and Chris Snijders. 2011. "Gossip and Reputation in Business Networks." *European Sociological Review* 27 (1):90–106. *Times,* April 6.

Rootes, Christopher. 2007. "Environmental Movements." Pp. 608–640 in *The Blackwell Companion to Social Movements,* edited by David A. Snow, Sarah A. Sovle, and Hanspeter Kriesi. Malden, MA: Blackwell.

Roscigno, Vincent J. 2010. "Ageism in the American Workplace." *Contexts* (Winter):15–21.

Rose, Arnold. 1951. *The Roots of Prejudice.* Paris: UNESCO.

Rose, Peter I., Myron Glazer, and Penina Migdal Glazer. 1979. "In Controlled Environments: Four Cases of Intense Resocialization." Pp. 320–338 in *Socialization and the Life Cycle,* edited by Peter I. Rose. New York: St. Martin's Press.

Rosen, Eva, and Sudhir Alladi Venkatesh. 2008. "A Perversion of Choice: Sex Work Offers Just Enough in Chicago's Urban Ghetto." *Journal of Contemporary Ethnography* (August):417–441.

Rosenberg, Douglas H. 1991. "Capitalism." Pp. 33–34 in *Encyclopedic Dictionary of Sociology,* 4th ed., edited by Dushkin Publishing Group. Guilford, CT: Dushkin.

Rosenberg, Tina. 2012. "The 'Avon Ladies' of Africa." *New York Times,* October 14, Week in Review, p. 9.

Rosenbloom, Stephanie. 2011. "Love, Lies, and What They Learned." *New York Times,* November 13, pp. ST1, ST8.

Rosenfeld, Jake. 2010. "Little Labor." *Pathways* (Summer):4–6.

———, and Meredith Klegkamp. 2012. "Organized Labor and Racial Wage Inequality in the United States." *American Journal of Sociology* 117 (March):1460–1502.

Rosenfeld, Michael J., and Reuben J. Thomas. 2012. "Searching for a Mate: The Rise of the Internet as a Social Intermediary." *American Sociological Review* 77 (4):523–547.

Rosenthal, Robert, and Lenore Jacobson. 1968. *Pygmalion in the Classroom.* New York: Holt.

———. 1992. *Pygmalion in the Classroom: Teacher Expectations and Pupils' Intellectual Development.* Newly expanded edition. Bancyfelin, UK: Crown House.

Rossi, Alice S. 1968. "Transition to Parenthood." *Journal of Marriage and the Family* 30 (February): 26–39.

———. 1984. "Gender and Parenthood." *American Sociological Review* 49 (February):1–19.

Rossi, Peter H. 1987. "No Good Applied Social Research Goes Unpunished." *Society* 25 (November–December):73–79.

Rossides, Daniel W. 1997. *Social Stratification: The Interplay of Class, Race, and Gender.* 2nd ed. Upper Saddle River, NJ: Prentice Hall.

Roszak, Theodore. 1969. *The Making of a Counterculture.* Garden City, NY: Doubleday.

Roter, Debra L., Judith A. Hall, and Yutaka Aoki. 2002. "Physician Gender Effects in Medical Communications: A Meta-analytic Review." *Journal of the American Medical Association* 288 (August 14):756–764.

Rothkopf, David. 2008. *Superclass: The Global Power Elite and the World They Are Making.* New York: Farrar, Straus and Giroux.

Rowe, Aimee Carrillo, Sheena Malhotra, and Kimberlee Pérez. 2013. *Answer the Call: Virtual Migration in Indian Call Centers.* Minneapolis: University of Minnesota Press.

Rubin, Alissa J. 2003. "Pat-Down on the Way to Prayer." *Los Angeles Times,* November 25, pp. A1, A5.

———, and Sam Dagher. 2009. "Election Quotas for Iraqi Women Are Weakened, Provoking Anger as Vote Nears." *New York Times,* January 14, p. A13.

Rudel, Thomas K., J. Timmons Roberts, and Jo Ann Carmin. 2011. "Political Economy of the Environment." *Annual Review of Sociology* 37:221–238.

Ruiz, Rebecca. 2010. "Care for the Caregivers." *The American Prospect* (October):A17–A20.

Ryan, Camille. 2013. *Language Use in the United States.* ACS-22. Washington, DC: U.S. Government Printing Office.

Ryan, William. 1976. *Blaming the Victim.* Rev. ed. New York: Random House.

S

Saad, Lydia. 2004. "Divorce Doesn't Last." *Gallup Poll Tuesday Briefing.* March 30. Accessible at www.gallup.com.

———. 2011. "Americans Decry Power of Lobbyists, Corporations, Banks, Feds." April

11. Accessible at http://www.gallup.com/poll/147026/Americans-Decry-Power-Lobbyists-Corporations-Banks-Feds.aspx.

———. 2012. "In U.S., Half of Women Prefer a Job Outside the Home." September 7. Accessible at www.gallup.com.

———. 2013. "Majority of Americans Still Support *Roe v. Wade* Decision." January 22. Accessible at www.gallup.com.

———. 2013b. "Americans' Concerns about Global Warming on the Rise." April 8. Accessible at http://www.gallup.com/poll/161645/americans-concerns-global-warming-rise.aspx?version=print.

Sachs, Jeffrey D. 2005. *The End of Poverty: Economic Possibilities for Our Time.* New York: Penguin.

Sacks, Peter. 2007. *Tearing Down the Gates: Confronting the Class Divide in American Education.* Berkeley: University of California Press.

Saez, Emmanuel. 2013. "Striking It Richer: The Evolution of Top Incomes in the United States." Updated with 2012 preliminary estimates. September 3. Accessible at http://Elsa.berkeley.edu/~Saez/.

SAGE. 2012. "About Us: Services and Advocacy for Gay, Lesbian, Bisexual and Transgender Elders." Accessed March 12 (http://sageusa.org/about).

Saguy, Abigail, and Rene Almeling. 2008. "Fat in the Fire? Science, the News Media, and the 'Obesity Epidemic.'" *Sociological Forum* 23 (March):53–83.

Said, Edward W. 2001. "The Clash of Ignorance." *Nation,* October 22.

Sale, Kirkpatrick. 1996. *Rebels against the Future: The Luddites and Their War on the Industrial Revolution* (with a new preface by the author). Reading, MA: Addison-Wesley.

Salem, Richard, and Stanislaus Grabarek. 1986. "Sociology B.A.s in a Corporate Setting: How Can They Get There and of What Value Are They?" *Teaching Sociology* 14 (October):273–275.

Sampson, Robert. 2011. *Great American City: Chicago and the Enduring Neighborhood Effect.* Chicago: University of Chicago Press.

———, and W. Byron Graves. 1989. "Community Structure and Crime: Testing Social-Disorganization Theory." *American Journal of Sociology* 94 (January):774–802.

Samuelson, Paul A., and William D. Nordhaus. 2010. *Economics.* 19th ed. New York: McGraw-Hill.

Sandefur, Rebecca L. 2008. "Access to Civil Justice and Race, Class, and Gender Inequality." *Annual Review of Sociology* 34:339–358.

Sanders, Edmund. 2004. "Coming of Age in Iraq." *Los Angeles Times,* August 14, pp. A1, A5.

Sanderson, Stephen K., Seth A. Abrutyn, and Kristopher R. Proctor. 2011. "Testing the Protestant Ethic Thesis with Quantitative Historical Data: A Research Note." *Social Forces* 89 (March):905–912.

Sanderson, Warren, and Sergei Scherbov. 2008. "Rethinking Age and Aging." *Population Bulletin* 63 (December).

Santos, José Alcides Figueiredo. 2006. "Class Effects on Racial Inequality in Brazil." *Dados* 2:1–35.

Sanua, Marianne R. 2007. "AJC and Intermarriage: The Complexities of Jewish Continuity, 1960–2006." Pp. 3–32 in *American Jewish Yearbook 2007,* edited by David Singer and Lawrence Grossman. New York: American Jewish Committee.

Sapir, Edward. 1929. "The State of Linguistics as a Science." *Language* 5 (4):207–214.

Sassen, Saskia. 2005. "New Global Classes: Implications for Politics." Pp. 143–170 in *The New Egalitarianism,* edited by Anthony Giddens and Patrick Diamond. Cambridge: Polity.

Satel, Sally. 2013. "Why the Fuss over the D.S.M.-5?" *New York Times,* May 12, Week in the News, p. 5.

Sawhill, Isabel, and Ron Haskins. 2009. "If You Can Make It Here . . ." *Washington Post National Weekly Edition,* November 9, p. 27.

———, and John E. Morton. 2007. *Economic Mobility: Is the American Dream Alive and Well?* Washington, DC: Economic Mobility Project, Pew Charitable Trusts.

———, Scott Winship, and Kerry Searle Grannis. 2012. *Pathways to the Middle Class: Balancing Personal and Public Responsibilities.* Washington, DC: Brookings.

Sayer, Liana C., Suzanne M. Bianchi, and John P. Robinson. 2004. "Are Parents Investing Less in Children? Trends in Mothers' and Fathers' Time with Children." *American Journal of Sociology* 110 (July):1–43.

Scarce, Rik. 2005. "A Law to Protect Scholars." *Chronicle of Higher Education,* August 12, p. 324.

Schaefer, Peter. 2008. "Digital Divide." Pp. 388–389, vol. 1, in *Encyclopedia of Race, Ethnicity, and Society in the United States,* edited by Richard T. Schaefer. Thousand Oaks, CA: Sage.

Schaefer, Richard T. 1998. "Differential Racial Mortality and the 1995 Chicago Heat Wave." Presentation at the annual meeting of the American Sociological Association, August, San Francisco.

———. 2008b. "'Power' and 'Power Elite.'" In *Encyclopedia of Social Problems,* edited by Vincent Parrillo. Thousand Oaks, CA: Sage.

———. 2012. *Racial and Ethnic Groups.* 13th ed. Upper Saddle River, NJ: Pearson.

———. 2014. *Racial and Ethnic Groups in the United States.* 14th ed. Upper Saddle River, NJ: Prentice Hall.

———, and William Zellner. 2011. *Extraordinary Groups.* 9th ed. New York: Worth.

Scharfenberg, David. 2013. "Big Data Comes to Boston's Neighborhoods." Accessible at http://www.wbur.org/2013/07/03/big-data-boston.

Scharnberg, Kirsten. 2007. "Black Market for Midwives Defies Bans." *Chicago Tribune,* November 25, pp. 1, 10.

Scheid, Teresa L. 2013. "A Decade of Critique: Notable Books in the Sociology of Mental Health." *Contemporary Sociology* 42 (2):177–183.

Scherer, Michael. 2011. "Introduction: Taking It to the Streets." Pp. 5–12 in *Occupy: What Is Occupy?* New York: Time Books.

———. 2013. "The Next Gun Fight." *Time* (January 20):25–41.

Scherer, Ron. 2010a. "A Long Struggle to Find Jobs." *Christian Science Monitor,* January 31, pp. 18–19.

———. 2010b. "For Jobless, Online Friends Can Be Lifelines." *Christian Science Monitor,* March 25, p. 21.

———. 2010c. "Jim Bunning Delays Vote; Unemployed Face First Week Without Check." *Christian Science Monitor* (March 2).

Schlesinger, Traci. 2011. "The Failure of Race-Neutral Policies: How Mandatory Terms and Sentencing Enhancements Contribute to Mass Racialized Incarceration." *Crime & Delinquency* 57 (January):56–81.

Schmeeckle, Maria. 2007. "Gender Dynamics in Stepfamilies: Adult Stepchildren's Views." *Journal of Marriage and Family* 69 (February):174–189.

———, Roseann Giarrusso, Du Feng, and Vern L. Bengtson. 2006. "What Makes Someone Family? Adult Children's Perceptions of Current and Former Stepparents." *Journal of Marriage and Family* 68 (August):595–610.

Schnaiberg, Allan. 1994. *Environment and Society: The Enduring Conflict.* New York: St. Martin's Press.

Schneider, Christopher. 2008. "Sexuality." Pp. 847–848 in *Encyclopedia of Social Problems,* edited by Vincent Parrillo. Los Angeles: Sage.

Schneider, Friedrich. 2010. "Dues and Don'ts." *The Economist* (August 14):62.

Schnittker, Jason, Jeremy Freese, and Brian Powell. 2003. "Who Are Feminists and What Do They Believe? The Role of Generations." *American Sociologist Review* 68 (August): 607–622.

Schram, Sanford F., Ruhard C. Fording, Joe Soss, and Linda Houser. 2009. "Deciding to Discipline: Race, Choice and Punishment at the Frontlines of Welfare Reform." *American Sociological Review* 74 (June):398–422.

Schulman, Gary I. 1974. "Race, Sex, and Violence: A Laboratory Test of the Sexual Threat of the Black Male Hypothesis." *American Journal of Sociology* 79 (March):1260–1272.

Schur, Edwin M. 1965. *Crimes without Victims: Deviant Behavior and Public Policy.* Englewood Cliffs, NJ: Prentice Hall.

———. 1968. *Law and Society: A Sociological View.* New York: Random House.

———. 1985. "'Crimes without Victims': A 20-Year Reassessment." Paper presented at the annual meeting of the Society for the Study of Social Problems.

Schwartz, Howard D., ed. 1994. *Dominant Issues in Medical Sociology.* 3rd ed. New York: McGraw-Hill.

Schwartz, Shalom H., and Anat Bardi. 2001. "Value Hierarchies across Cultures: Taking a Similarities Perspective." *Journal of Cross-Cultural Perspective* 32 (May):268–290.

Scott, Alan. 1990. *Ideology and the New Social Movements.* London: Unwin Hyman.

Scott, Gregory. 2001. "Broken Windows behind Bars: Eradicating Prison Gangs through Ecological Hardening and Symbolic Cleansing." *Corrections Management Quarterly* 5 (Winter):23–36.

Scott, W. Richard, and Gerald F. Davis. 2007. *Organizations and Organizing: Rational, Natural and Open Systems Perspectives.* New York: Pearson.

Scoville, David. 2010. "Disneyland Deconstructed: Postmodernism Revealed." April 16. Accessible at http://davidscoville.blogspot.com/2010/04/Disneyland-deconstructed-postmodernism.html.

Search Engine Watch. 2011. "comScore: Bing Grows for Sixth Straight Year." March 16. Accessible at http://searchenginewatch.com/3642049.

Seccombe, Karen. 2011. *So You Think I Drive a Cadillac?* Boston: Allyn and Bacon.

Security on Campus. 2008. "Complying with the Jeanne Clery Act." Accessed January 13 (www.securityoncampus.org/crimestats/index.html).

Sedgwick, Eve Kosofsky. 1990. *Epistemology of the Closet.* Berkeley: University of California Press.

Sefiha, Ophir. 2012. "Bad Sports: Explaining Sport Related Deviance." *Sociology Compass* 6:949–961.

Segal, Nancy L. 2012. *Born Together—Reared Apart. O Brother, Who Art Thou.* Cambridge, MA: Harvard University Press.

Seidman, Steven. 1994. "Heterosexism in America: Prejudice against Gay Men and Lesbians." Pp. 578–593 in *Introduction to Social Problems,* edited by Craig Calhoun and George Ritzer. New York: McGraw-Hill.

Sellers, Frances Stead. 2004. "Voter Globalization." *Washington Post National Weekly Edition,* November 29, p. 22.

Selod, Saher Farooq. 2008a. "Muslim Americans." Pp. 920–923, vol. 2, in *Encyclopedia of Race, Ethnicity, and Society,* edited by Richard T. Schaefer. Thousand Oaks, CA: Sage.

———. 2008b. "Veil." Pp. 1359–1360, vol. 3, in *Encyclopedia of Race, Ethnicity, and Society,* edited by Richard T. Schaefer. Thousand Oaks, CA: Sage.

Sengupta, Somini. 2009. "An Empire for Poor Working Women, Guided by a Gandhian Approach." *New York Times,* March 7, p. A6.

Sernau, Scott. 2001. *Worlds Apart: Social Inequalities in a New Century.* Thousand Oaks, CA: Pine Forge Press.

Settersten, Richard, and Barbara Ray. 2011. *Not Quite Adults: Why 20-Somethings Are Choosing a Slower Path to Adulthood, and Why It's Good for Everyone.* New York: Bantam.

Shachtman, Tom. 2006. *Rumspringa: To Be or Not to Be Amish.* New York: North Point Press.

Shahrani, M. Nazif. 1981. "Growing in Respect: Aging among the Kirghiz of Afghanistan." Pp. 175–192 in *Other Ways of Growing Old,* edited by P. Amoss and S. Harrell. Stanford, CA: Stanford University Press.

Shane, Scott. 2010. "Wars Fought and Wars Googled." *New York Times,* June 27, pp. PWK1–5.

Shapiro, Joseph P. 1993. *No Pity: People with Disabilities Forging a New Civil Rights Movement.* New York: Times Books.

Shapiro, Thomas M., Tatjana Meschede, and Laura Sullivan. 2010. "The Racial Wealth Gap Increases Fourfold." Research and Policy Brief, Institute on Assets and Social Policy, Brandeis University.

Shapley, Dan. 2010. "4 Dirty Secrets of the Exxon Valdez Oil Spill." Accessed May 3 (www.thedailygreen.com).

Sharma, Hari M., and Gerard C. Bodeker. 1998. "Alternative Medicine." Pp. 228–229 in

Britannica Book of the Year 1998. Chicago: Encyclopaedia Britannica.

Sharp, Ansel M., Charles A. Register, and Paul W. Grimes. 2013. *Economics of Social Issues.* 20th ed. New York: McGraw Hill.

Shaw, Clifford R., and Henry D. McKay. 1942. *Juvenile Delinquency and Urban Areas.* Chicago: University of Chicago Press.

Shea, Andrea. 2013. "Facebook Envy: How the Social Network Affects Our Self-Esteem." February 20. Accessed at www.wbur.org.

Sheehan, Charles. 2005. "Poor Seniors Take On Plans of Condo Giant." *Chicago Tribune,* March 22, pp. 1, 9.

Sherman, Arloc. 2007. *Income Inequality Hits Record Levels, New CBO Data Show.* Washington, DC: Center on Budget and Policy Priorities.

Sherman, Jennifer, and Elizabeth Harris. 2012. "Social Class and Parenting: Classic Debates and New Understandings." *Sociology Compass* 6:60–71.

Shibutani, Tamotshu. 1966. *Improvised News: A Sociological Study of Rumor.* Indianapolis, IN: Bobbs-Merrill.

Shogren, Elizabeth. 1994. "Treatment against Their Will." *Los Angeles Times,* August 18, pp. A1, A14–A15.

Short, Kathleen. 2012. *The Research Supplemental: Poverty Measure 2011.* Current Population Reports. P60-244. Washington, DC: U.S. Government Printing Office.

Shostak, Arthur B. 2002. "Clinical Sociology and the Art of Peace Promotion: Earning a World without War." Pp. 325–345 in *Using Sociology: An Introduction from the Applied and Clinical Perspectives,* edited by Roger A. Straus. Lanham, MD: Rowman and Littlefield.

Sieber, Renée E., Daniel Spitzberg, Hannah Muffatt, Kristen Brewer, Blanka Füleki, and Naomi Arbit. 2006. *Influencing Climate Change Policy: Environmental Non-Governmental Organizations (ENGOs) Using Virtual and Physical Activism.* Montreal: McGill University.

Silva, Jennifer M. 2012. "Constructing Adulthood in an Age of Uncertainty." *American Sociological Review* 77 (4):505–522.

Silver, Ira. 1996. "Role Transitions, Objects, and Identity." *Symbolic Interaction* 10 (1):1–20.

Silverman, Rachel Emma. 2009. "As Jobs Grow Scarce, Commuter Marriages Rise." Accessed March 31, 2010 (http://blogs.wsj.com/juggle/2009/01/16/as-jobs-grow-scarce-commuter-marriages-rise/).

———. 2013. "Tracking Sensors Invade the Workplace." *Wall Street Journal,* March 7, pp. B1, B2.

Silverstein, Ken. 2010. "Shopping for Sweat: The Human Cost of a Two-Dollar T-shirt." *Harpers* 320 (January):36–44.

Simpson, Sally S. 2013. "White-collar Crime: A Review of Recent Developments and Promising Directions for Future Research." *Annual Review of Sociology* 39:309–331.

Skocpol, Theda, and Vanessa Williamson. 2012. *The Tea Party and the Remaking of Republican Conservatism.* New York: Oxford University Press.

Slack, Jennifer Daryl, and J. Macgregor Wise. 2007. *Culture + Technology.* New York: Peter Lang.

Slackman, Michael. 2008. "9/11 Rumors That Harden into Conventional Wisdom." *New York Times,* September 9, p. A16.

Slaughter, Chuck. 2011. "Taking the 'Avon' Way to Reach 'The Last Mile.'" October 31. Accessed February 26, 2013 at http://www.huffingtonpost.com/chuck-slaughter/taking-the-avon-way-to re_b_1067840.html.

Slavin, Barbara. 2007. "Child Marriage Rife in Nations Getting U.S. Aid." *USA Today,* July 17, p. 6A.

Slavin, Robert E., and A. Cheung. 2003. *Effective Reading Programs for English Language Learners: A Best-Evidence Synthesis.* Baltimore: Johns Hopkins University, Center for Research on the Education of Students Placed at Risk.

Sloan, Allan. 2009. "What's Still Wrong with Wall Street." *Time,* November 9, pp. 24–29.

Sloop, John M. 2009. "Queer: Approaches to Communication." Pp. 90–100 in *21st Century Communication,* edited by Bill Eadie. Thousand Oaks, CA: Sage.

Slug-Lines.com. 2011. "A Unique Commuter Solution." Accessed November 10, 2011. (www.slug-lines.com).

Smart, Barry. 1990. "Modernity, Postmodernity, and the Present." Pp. 14–30 in *Theories of Modernity and Postmodernity,* edited by Bryan S. Turner. Newbury Park, CA: Sage.

Smelser, Neil. 1962. *Theory of Collective Behavior.* New York: Free Press.

———. 1963. *The Sociology of Economic Life.* Englewood Cliffs, NJ: Prentice Hall.

———. 1981. *Sociology.* Englewood Cliffs, NJ: Prentice Hall.

Smith, Aaron. 2009. *The Internet's Role in Campaign 2000.* Washington, DC: Pew Internet and American Life Project.

———. 2012. *Real Time Charitable Giving.* Washington, DC: Pew Research Center's Internet and American Life Project. Accessible at www.pewinternet.org/Reports/2012/MobileGiving.aspx.

———, and Maeve Duggan. 2012. "Presidential Campaign Donations in the Digital Age." October 25. Accessible at http://www.pewinternet.org/Reports/2012/Election-2012-Donations/Key-Findings/Presidential-Campaign-Donations-in-the-Digital-Age.aspx.

———, and ———. 2013. "Online Dating & Relationships." October 21, 2013. Accessible at http://www.pewinternet.org/Reports/2013/Online-Dating/Summary-of-Findings.aspx.

Smith, Carter, F., Jeffrey P. Rush, Daniel Robinson, and Megan Karmiller. 2012. "Views from the Field: Flashgangs and Flash Gangbanging: How Can Local Police Prepare?" *Journal of Gang Research* 20 (October):33–50.

Smith, Christian. 1991. *The Emergence of Liberation Theology: Radical Religion and Social Movement Theory.* Chicago: University of Chicago Press.

———. 2007. "Getting a Life: The Challenge of Emerging Adulthood." *Books and Culture: A Christian Review* (November–December).

———. 2008. "Future Directions of the Sociology of Religion." *Social Forces* 86 (June):1564–1589.

Smith, Craig S. 2006. "Romania's Orphans Face Widespread Abuse, Group Says." *New York Times,* May 10, p. A3.

Smith, Dan. 1999. *The State of the World Atlas.* 6th ed. London: Penguin.

Smith, Denise, and Hava Tillipman. 2000. *The Older Population in the United States.* U.S. Department of Commerce, Economics and Statistics Administration, U.S. Census Bureau.

Smith, Lawrence C. 2011. *The World in 2050: Four Forces Shaping Civilization's Northern Future.* New York: A Plume Book.

Smith, Tom W. 2003. *Coming of Age in 21st Century America: Public Attitudes toward the Importance and Timing of Transition to Adulthood.* Chicago: National Opinion Research Center.

———. 2009. *Religious Change around the World.* Chicago: NORC/University of Chicago.

Smith, Wesley J. 2011. "Euthanasia Spreads in Europe." October 26. Accessed March 12, 2012 (http://nationalreview.com/articles/281303/euthanasia-spreads-europe-wesley-j-smith?pg=3).

Snyder, Thomas D. 1996. *Digest of Education Statistics 1996.* Washington, DC: U.S. Government Printing Office.

Somaskanda, Sumi. 2012. "European Pensions Targeted." *USA Today,* September 20, p. 2B.

Somavia, Juan. 2008. "The ILO at 90 Working for Social Justice." *World of Work* 64 (December):4–5.

Sorokin, Pitirim A. [1927] 1959. *Social and Cultural Mobility.* New York: Free Press.

Southern Poverty Law Center. 2010. "Active 'Patriot' Groups in the United States in 2009." Accessed November 5 (www.splcenter.org/patriot).

———. 2013. "Patriot Movement." Accessible at http://www.splcenter.org/get-informed/intelligence-files/ideology/patriot-movememnt.

Spalter-Roth, Roberta, Nicole Van Vooren, and Mary S. Senter. 2013. "Using the Bachelor's and Beyond Project to Help Launch Students in Careers." Accessed November 1 at www.asanet.org/documents/research/docs/B%26BLaunchingCareers.pptx.

Spar, Debora. 2001. *Ruling the Waves: Cycles of Discovery, Chaos, and Wealth from the Compass to the Internet.* New York: Harcourt.

Spencer, Nancy. 2008. "Title IX." Pp. 1308–1310, vol. 3, in *Encyclopedia of Race, Ethnicity, and Society,* edited by Richard T. Schaefer. Thousand Oaks, CA: Sage.

Spitzer, Steven. 1975. "Toward a Marxian Theory of Deviance." *Social Problems* 22 (June):641–651.

Sprague, Joey. 2005. *Feminist Methodologies for Critical Research: Bridging Differences.* Lanham, MD: AltaMira Press.

Stacey, Judith. 2011. *Unhitched.* New York: New York University Press.

Stansell, Christine. 2011. *The Feminist Promise: 1792 to the Present.* New York: The Modern Library.

Stark, Rodney. 2004. *Exploring the Religious Life.* Baltimore: Johns Hopkins University Press.

———. 2005. *The Rise of Mormonism,* edited by Reid L. Neilson. New York: Columbia University Press.

———, and William Sims Bainbridge. 1979. "Of Churches, Sects, and Cults: Preliminary Concepts for a Theory of Religious Movements." *Journal for the Scientific Study of Religion* 18 (June):117–131.

———, and ———. 1985. *The Future of Religion.* Berkeley: University of California Press.

Staton, Ron. 2004. "Still Fighting for National Hawaiian Recognition." *Asian Week,* January 22, p. 8.

Steffen, Alex, ed. 2008. *World Changing: A User's Guide for the 21st Century.* New York: Harry N. Abrams.

Stein, Leonard I. 1967. "The Doctor-Nurse Game." *Archives of General Psychology* 16:699–703.

Stevick, Richard A. 2007. *Growing Up Amish: The Teenage Years.* Baltimore: Johns Hopkins University Press.

Stockard, Janice E. 2002. *Marriage in Culture.* Belmont, CA: Thomson Wadsworth.

Stolberg, Sheryl Gay. 2008. "Richest Nations Pledge to Halve Greenhouse Gas." *New York Times,* July 9, pp. A1, A13.

Stray, Jonathan. 2012. "Are We Stuck in Filter Bubbles? Here Are Five Potential Paths Out." July 12. Accessed December 1 at http://www.niemanlab.org/2012/07/are-we-stuck-in-filter-bubbles-here-are-five-potential-paths-out/.

Suárez, Zulema E., and Rose M. Perez. 2012. "The Cuban American Family." Pp. 112–128 in *Ethnic Families in America: Patterns and Variations.* 5th ed., edited by Roosevelt Wright, Jr., Charles H. Mindel, Thanh Van Tran, and Robert W. Halsenstein. Upper Saddle River, NJ: Pearson.

Subramaniam, Mangala. 2006. *The Power of Women's Organization: Gender, Caste, and Class in India.* Lanham, MD: Lexington Books.

Suchar, Charles S. 1997. "Grounding Visual Sociology Research in Shooting Scripts." *Qualitative Sociology* 20 (1):33–55.

Suh, Doowon. 2011. "Institutionalizing Social Movements: The Dual Strategy of the Korean Women's Movement." *Sociological Quarterly* 52:442–471.

Suitor, J. Jill, Staci A. Minyard, and Rebecca S. Carter. 2001. "'Did You See What I Saw?' Gender Differences in Perceptions of Avenues to Prestige among Adolescents." *Sociological Inquiry* 71 (Fall):437–454.

Sullivan, Harry Stack. [1953] 1968. *The Interpersonal Theory of Psychiatry.* Edited by Helen Swick Perry and Mary Ladd Gawel. New York: Norton.

Sullivan, Kevin. 2006. "Bridging the Digital Divide." *Washington Post National Weekly Edition* 25 (July 17):11–12.

Sum, Andrew, Paul Harrington, and Ishwar Khatiwada. 2006. *The Impact of New Immigrants on Young Native-Born Workers, 2000–2005.* Washington, DC: Center for Immigration Studies.

Sumner, William G. 1906. *Folkways.* New York: Ginn.

Sunstein, Cass. 2002. *Republic.com.* Rutgers, NJ: Princeton University Press.

Survival International. 2012. "Brazilian Indians." Accessed January 12 (www.survivalinternational.org/tribes/Brazilian).

SustainAbility. 2006. *Brazil—Country of Diversities and Inequalities.* London: SustainAbility.

Sutch, Richard, and Susan B. Carter. 2006. *Historical Statutes of US: Earliest Time to the Present.* Cambridge: Cambridge University Press.

Sutherland, Edwin H. 1937. *The Professional Thief.* Chicago: University of Chicago Press.

———. 1940. "White-Collar Criminality." *American Sociological Review* 5 (February):1–11.

———. 1949. *White Collar Crime.* New York: Dryden.

———. 1983. *White Collar Crime: The Uncut Version.* New Haven, CT: Yale University Press.

———, Donald R. Cressey, and David F. Luckenbill. 1992. *Principles of Criminology.* 11th ed. New York: Rowman and Littlefield.

Swanson, Emily. 2013. "Poll: Few Identify as Feminists, but Most Believe in Equality of Sexes." *Huffington Post,* April 15. Accessible at www.huffingtonpost.com.

Swartz, Jon. 2012. "Google's Personalized Search Charges Set Off Uproar." *USA Today,* January 12, p. B1.

Swatos, William H., Jr., ed. 1998. *Encyclopedia of Religion and Society.* Lanham, MD: AltaMira.

Sweet, Kimberly. 2001. "Sex Sells a Second Time." *Chicago Journal* 93 (April):12–13.

Swidler, Ann. 1986. "Culture in Action: Symbols and Strategies." *American Sociological Review* 51 (April):273–286.

Szabo, Liz. 2013. "Mental Illness Takes Fall in Gun Laws." *USA Today,* March 12, p. 7D.

Szasz, Andrew. 2007. *Shopping Our Way to Safety: How We Changed from Protecting the Environment to Protecting Ourselves.* Minneapolis: University of Minnesota Press.

Szasz, Thomas. 2010. *The Myth of Mental Illness: Foundations of a Theory of Personal Conduct.* 50th Anniversary Edition. New York: Harper Perennial.

t

Tabuchi, Hiroko. 2013. "Desperate Hunt for Day Care." *New York Times,* February 27, pp. A4, A9.

Tachibana, Judy. 1990. "Model Minority Myth Presents Unrepresentative Portrait of Asian Americans, Many Educators Say." *Black Issues in Higher Education* 6 (March 1):1, 11.

Takei, Isao, and Arthur Sakamoto. 2011. "Poverty Among Asian Americans in the 21st Century." *Sociological Perspectives* 54 (Summer):251–276.

Tanielian, Terri. 2009. "Assessing Combat Exposure and Post-Traumatic Stress Disorder in Troops and Estimating the Costs to Society." Testimony presented before the House Veterans' Affairs Committee, Subcommittee on Disability Assistance and Memorial Affairs (March 24).

Tannen, Deborah. 1990. *You Just Don't Understand: Women and Men in Conversation.* New York: Ballantine.

Tatchell, Jo. 2009. *A Diamond in the Desert: Behind the Scenes in the World's Richest City.* London: Hodder and Stoughton.

Taylor, Rob. 2013. "Australian Court Rejects Same-Sex Marriage." *Wall Street Journal,* December 13, p. A14.

Taylor, Verta. 1999. "Gender and Social Movements: Gender Processes in Women's Self-Help Movements." *Gender and Society* 13:8–33.

———. 2004. "Social Movements and Gender." Pp. 14348–14352 in *International Encyclopedia of the Social and Behavioral Sciences,* edited by Neil J. Smelser and Paul B. Baltes. New York: Elsevier.

———, Leila J. Rupp, and Nancy Whittier. 2009. *Feminist Frontiers.* 8th ed. New York: McGraw-Hill.

Teaching Tolerance. 2012. "LGBT Content Access Denied." Accessed March 29 (www.tollerance.org/blog/lgbt-content-access-denied).

Tedeschi, Bob. 2006. "Those Born to Shop Can Now Use Cellphones." *New York Times,* January 2.

Telles, Edward E. 2004. *Race in America: The Significance of Skin Color in Brazil.* Princeton, NJ: Princeton University Press.

Teranishi, Robert T. 2010. *Asians in the Ivory Tower: Dilemmas of Racial Inequity in American Higher Education.* New York: Teachers College Press.

Themed Entertainment Association. 2012. *Global Attractions Attendance Report 2011.* Burbank, CA: TEA.

Thomas, Evan, and Pat Wingert. 2010. "Understanding Charter Schools." *Newsweek* 155 (June 21):46.

Thomas, Gordon, and Max Morgan Witts. 1974. *Voyage of the Damned.* Greenwich, CT: Fawcett Crest.

Thomas Jr., Landon. 2011. "Money Troubles Take Personal Toll in Greece." *New York Times,* May 16, pp. A1, A2. Accessible at www.nytimes.com/2011/05/16/business/global/16drachma.html?pagewanted=all.

Thomas, R. Murray. 2003. "New Frontiers in Cheating." In *Encyclopaedia Britannica 2003 Book of the Year.* Chicago: Encyclopaedia Britannica.

Thomas, William I. 1923. *The Unadjusted Girl.* Boston: Little, Brown.

Thomasrobb.com. 2007. "WhitePride TV." Accessed May 7 (http://thomasrobb.com).

Thompson, Tony. 2005. "Romanians Are Being Paid to Play Computer Games for Westerners." *Guardian Weekly,* March 25, p. 17.

Threadcraft, Shatema. 2008. "Welfare Queen." In *Encyclopedia of Race, Ethnicity and Society,* edited by Richard T. Schaefer. Thousand Oaks, CA: Sage.

Thurow, Lester. 1984. "The Disappearance of the Middle Class." *New York Times,* February 5, sec. 5, p. 2.

Tibbles, Kevin. 2007. "Web Sites Encourage Eating Disorders." *Today,* February 18. Accessed May 7 (www.msnbc.msn.com).

Tierney, John. 1990. "Betting the Planet." *New York Times Magazine* (December 2):52–53, 71, 74, 76, 78, 80–81.

Tierney, Kathleen J. 1980. "Emergent Norm Theory as 'Theory': An Analysis and Critique of Turner's Formulation." Pp. 42–53 in *Collective Behavior: A Source Book,* edited by Meredith David Pugh. St. Paul, MN: West.

———. 2007. "From the Margins to the Mainstream? Disaster Research at the Crossroads." *Annual Review of Sociology* 33:503–525.

Tierney, William G., and Karri A. Holley. 2008. "Intelligent Design and the Attack on Scientific Inquiry." *Cultural Studies Critical Methodologies* 8 (February):39–49.

Tigay, Chanan. 2011. "Women and Sports." *CQ Researcher* 21 (March 25).

Tilly, Charles. 1964. *The Vendée.* Cambridge, MA: Harvard University Press.

———. 1980. "The Old New Social History and the New Old Social History." October. Center for Research on Social Organization Working Paper No. 218. Accessed December 1, 2013 at http://deepblue.lib.umich.edu/bitstream/handle/2027.42/50992/218.pdf?sequence=1.

———. 1993. *Popular Contention in Great Britain 1758–1834.* Cambridge, MA: Harvard University Press.

———. 2003. *The Politics of Collective Violence.* New York: Cambridge University Press.

———. 2004. *Social Movements, 1768–2004.* Boulder, CO: Paradigm.

———. 2007. "Trust Networks in Transnational Migration." *Sociological Forum* 22 (March):3–24.

Tilly, Chris. 1991. "Reasons for the Continuing Growth of Part-time Employment." *Monthly Labor Review* (March):10–18.

Timmerman, Kelsey. 2009. *Where Am I Wearing?* Hoboken NJ: Wiley.

———. 2013. "Follow the Label: The Odyssey of Our Food and Clothing." *Christian Science Monitor Weekly* (July 22):27–29.

Toensing, Gale Country. 2009. "Akaka Bill Gets Obama Approval." *Indian Country Today* (August 19):1, 2.

Toffler, Alvin. 1970. *Future Shock.* New York: Bantam Books.

———. 1980. *The Third Wave.* New York: Bantam Books.

Toma, Catalina L., and Jeffrey T. Hancock. 2010. "Looks and Lies: The Role of Physical Attractiveness in Online Dating Self-Presentation and Deception." *Community Research* 37 (3):335–351.

———, ———, and Nicole B. Ellison. 2008. "Separating Fact from Fiction: An Examination of Deceptive Self-Presentation in Online Dating Profiles." *Personality and Social Psychology Bulletin* 34:1023–1036.

Tönnies, Ferdinand. [1887] 1988. *Community and Society.* Rutgers, NJ: Transaction.

Toossi, Mitra. 2009. "Employment Outlook: 2008–2018." *Monthly Labor Review* (November):30–51.

———. 2012. "Labor Force Projections to 2020: A More Slowly Growing Labor Force." *Monthly Labor Review* (January):43–64.

———. 2012. "Projections of the Labor Force to 2050: A Visual Essay. *Monthly Labor Review* (October):3–16. Accessible at www.bls.gov/opub/mlr/2012/10/art1full.pdf.

Toppo, Greg. 2011. "The Search for a New Way to Test Schoolkids." *USA Today,* March 18, p. A4.

Torres, Lourdes. 2008. "Puerto Rican Americans" and "Puerto Rico." Pp. 1082–1089, vol. 3, in *Encyclopedia of Race, Ethnicity, and Society,* edited by Richard T. Schaefer. Thousand Oaks, CA: Sage.

Torrey, E. Fuller. 2013. "Fifty Years of Failing America's Mentally Ill." *Wall Street Journal,* February 5, p. A15.

Touraine, Alain. 1974. *The Academic System in American Society.* New York: McGraw-Hill.

Transactional Records Access Clearinghouse. 2009. "TRAC Monthly Bulletins by Topic, September 2009." Accessed February 11, 2010 (www.trac.syr.edu/tracreports/bulletins/white_collar_crime/monthly_sep09/fil).

Trimble, Charles. 2008. "Itheska: Notes from Mixed Blood Country." *Indian Country Today* (May 7):5.

Trimble, Lindsey B., and Julie A. Kmec. 2011. "The Role of Social Networks in Getting a Job." *Sociology Compass* 5 (2):165–178.

Trotter III, Robert T., and Juan Antonio Chavira. 1997. *Curanderismo: Mexican American Folk Healing.* Athens: University of Georgia Press.

Trottman, Melanie, and Kris Maher. 2013. "Organized Labor Loses Members." *Wall Street Journal,* January 24, p. A6.

Truman, Jennifer, Lynn Langton, and Michael Planty. 2013. *Criminal Victimization, 2012.* NCJ243389. October 2013. Accessible at www.bjs.gov.

Trumbull, Mark. 2006. "America's Younger Workers Losing Ground on Income." *Christian Science Monitor,* February 27.

Tuan, Mia, and Jiannbin Lee Shiao. 2011. *Choosing Ethnicity, Negotiating Race: Korean Adoptees in America.* New York: Russell Sage Foundation.

Tuchman, Gaye. 1992. "Feminist Theory." Pp. 695–704 in *Encyclopedia of Sociology,* vol. 2, edited by Edgar F. Borgatta and Marie L. Borgatta. New York: Macmillan.

Tucker, Robert C. (ed.) 1978. *The Marx-Engels Reader.* 2nd ed. New York: Norton.

Ture, Kwame, and Charles Hamilton. 1992. *Black Power: The Politics of Liberation.* With new Afterword by authors. New York: Vintage Books.

Turkle, Sherry. 2004. "How Computers Change the Way We Think." *Chronicle of Higher Education* 50 (January 30):B26–B28.

———. 2011. *Alone Together: Why We Expect More from Technology and Less from Each Other.* New York: Basic Books.

Turner, Bryan S., ed. 1990. *Theories of Modernity and Postmodernity.* Newbury Park, CA: Sage.

Turner, C. F., L. Ku, S. M. Rogers, L. D. Lindberg, H. Pleck, and F. L. Sonenstein. 1998. "Adolescent Sexual Behavior, Drug Use, and Violence: Increased Reporting with Computer Survey Technology." *Science* 280 (May 8):867–873.

Turner, Ralph, and Lewis M. Killian. 1987. *Collective Behavior.* 3rd ed. Englewood Cliffs, NJ: Prentice Hall.

U

Uggen, Christopher. 2012. "The Crime Wave that Wasn't." *Pathways* (Fall):13–18.

UNAIDS. 2013. *AIDS by the Numbers.* November 20, 2013. Accessible at http://www.unaids.org/en/media/unaids/contentassets/images/infographics/2013/20131120aidsbythenumbers01/20131120_aidsbythenumbers_en.pdf.

UNHCR. 2010. *UNHCR Statistical Yearbook 2009.* Geneva: UNHCR.

UNICEF. 2009. *Progress for Children: A Report Card on Child Protection.* September. Vienna: UNICEF.

———. 2010. "Child Marriage." Accessed January 15 (www.unicef.org/progressfprchildren/2007n6/index_41848.htm?q=printme).

United Nations. 2005. *The Millennium Development Goals Report.* Washington, DC: United Nations.

———. 2009. *International Migration Report 2006: A Global Assessment.* New York: United Nations, Economic and Social Affairs.

———. 2013. "Number of International Migrants Rises above 232 Million, UN Reports." September 11. United Nations News Centre. Accessible at www.un.org.

United Nations Development Programme. 1995. *Human Development Report 1995.* New York: Oxford University Press.

———. 2000. *Poverty Report 2000: Overcoming Human Poverty.* Washington, DC: UNDP.

———. 2009. *Overcoming Barriers: Human Mobility and Development.* New York: Palgrave Macmillan.

United Nations Economic and Social Council. 2010. "Review of the Implementation of the Beijing Declaration." New York: Economic and Social Council.

United Nations Office on Drugs and Crime. 2010. *The Globalization of Crime: A Transnational Organized Crime Threat Assessment.* New York: UNODC.

United Nations Population Division. 2013. "World Abortion Policies." Accessed January 15, 2014 at http://www.un.org/en/development/desa/population/publications/policy/world-abortion-policies-2013.shtml.

———. 2013. *Median Age at First Marriage.* Geneva: Department of Economic and Social Affairs.

United Nations Statistics Division. 2009. *Demographic Yearbook 2007.* Accessed April 1, 2010 (http://unstats.un.org/unsd/ demographic/products/dyb/dyb2.htm).

United States Copyright Office. 2012. *Annual Report of the Register of Copyrights.* Accessible at http://www.copyright.gov/reports/annual/2011/ar2011.pdf.

United States Patent and Trademark Office. 2012. *Patenting by Organizations, 2012.* Accessible at http://www.uspto.gov/web/offices/ac/ido/oeip/taf/topo_12.pdf.

University of Michigan. 2003. *Information on Admissions Lawsuits.* Accessed August 8 (www.umich.edu/urel/admissions).

Urban Dictionary. 2012. "Urban Amish." Accessed March 29 (www.urbandictionary.com/define.php?term=urban+20amish).

U.S. English. 2012. "Making English the Official Language." Accessed January 12 (www.us-english.org/inc/).

U.S. Surgeon General. 1999. *Surgeon General's Report on Mental Health.* Washington, DC: U.S. Government Printing Office.

V

Vaidhyanathan, Siva. 2008. "Generational Myth: Not All Young People Are Tech-Savvy." *Chronicle of Higher Education,* September 19, pp. B7–B9.

Vamosi, Robert, Mary Monahan, and Rachel Kim. 2010. *2010 Identity Fraud Survey Report.* Pleasanton, CA: Javelin Strategy.

van den Berghe, Pierre L. 1978. *Race and Racism: A Comparative Perspective.* 2nd ed. New York: Wiley.

van Dijk, Jan, John van Kesteren, and Paul Smit. 2007. *Criminal Victimisation [sic] in International Perspective.* Tilburg, Netherlands: United Nations Office on Drugs and Crime. Accessible at http://www.uncri.it/services/library_documentation/publications/icvs/publicatons/ICVS2004_05report.pdf.

Van Gennep, Arnold. [1909] 1960. *The Rites of Passage.* Translated by Monika B. Vizedom and Gabrielle L. Caffee. Chicago: University of Chicago Press.

van Vucht Tijssen, Lieteke. 1990. "Women between Modernity and Postmodernity." Pp. 147–163 in *Theories of Modernity and Postmodernity,* edited by Bryan S. Turner. London: Sage.

VandenBrook, Tom. 2013. "Army Leaders Warned about Issues with Human Terrain System." September 23. Accessible at http://www.armytimes.com/article/20130923/NEWS/3092230032/.

Vasagar, Jeeran. 2005. "'At Last Rwanda Is Known for Something Positive.'" *Guardian Weekly,* July 22, p. 18.

Vaughan, R. M. 2007. "Cairo's Man Show." *Utne Reader* (March–April):94–95.

Veblen, Thorstein. [1899] 1964. *Theory of the Leisure Class.* New York: Macmillan. New York: Penguin.

———. 1919. *The Vested Interests and the State of the Industrial Arts.* New York: Huebsch.

Venkatesh, Sudhir Alladi. 2006. *Off the Books: The Underground Economy of the Urban Poor.* Cambridge, MA: Harvard University Press.

———. 2008. *Gang Leader for a Day: A Rogue Sociologist Takes to the Streets.* New York: Penguin Press.

Vernon, Glenn. 1962. *Sociology and Religion.* New York: McGraw-Hill.

Vespa, Jonathan, Jamie M. Lewis, and Rose M. Kreider. 2013. "America's Families and Living Arrangements 2012." August 2013. Accessible at http://www.census.gov/prod/2013pubs/p20-570.pdf.

Vigdor, Jacob L. 2011. "Comparing Immigrant Assimilation in North America and Europe." May 2011. Accessible at www.manhattan-institute.org/cgl-bin/apMI/print.cgi.

Violence Policy Center. 2012. *Gun Deaths Outpace Motor Vehicle Deaths in 10 States in 2009.* Washington, DC: VPC.

Viramontes, Helena Maria. 2007. "Loyalty Spoken Here." *Los Angeles Times,* September 23, p. R7.

Visser, Jelle. 2006. "Union Membership Statistics in 24 Countries." *Monthly Labor Review* (January):38–49.

Volti, Rudi. 2010. *Society and Technological Change.* 6th ed. New York: Worth Publishers.

W

Wachtendorf, Tricia. 2002. "A Changing Risk Environment: Lessons Learned from the 9/11 World Trade Center Disaster." Presentation at the Sociological Perspectives on Disasters, Mt. Macedon, Australia, July.

Wages for Housework Campaign. 1999. *Wages for Housework Campaign.* Circular. Los Angeles.

Wagley, Charles, and Marvin Harris. 1958. *Minorities in the New World: Six Case Studies.* New York: Columbia University Press.

Waitzkin, Howard. 1986. *The Second Sickness: Contradictions of Capitalist Health Care.* Chicago: University of Chicago Press.

Walder, Andrew. G. 2009. "Political Sociology and Social Movements." *Annual Review of Sociology* 35:393–412.

———, and Giang Hoang Nguyen. 2008. "Ownership, Organization, and Income Inequality: Market Transition in Rural Vietnam." *American Sociological Review* 73 (April):251–269.

Waldman, Amy. 2004a. "India Takes Economic Spotlight, and Critics Are Unkind." *New York Times,* March 7, p. 3.

———. 2004b. "Low-Tech or High, Jobs Are Scarce in India's Boom." *New York Times,* May 6, p. A3.

———. 2004c. "What India's Upset Vote Reveals: The High Tech Is Skin Deep." *New York Times,* May 15, p. A5.

Walker, Andrea C., and David E. Balk. 2007. "Bereavement Rituals in the Muscogee Creek Tribe." *Death Studies* 31:633–652.

Walker, Edward. 2010. "Activism Industry-Driven." *Contexts* (Spring):43–49.

Wallace, Ruth A., and Alison Wolf. 1980. *Contemporary Sociological Theory.* Englewood Cliffs, NJ: Prentice Hall.

Wallerstein, Immanuel. 1974. *The Modern World System.* New York: Academic Press.

———. 1979a. *Capitalist World Economy.* Cambridge: Cambridge University Press.

———. 1979b. *The End of the World as We Know It: Social Science for the Twenty-First Century.* Minneapolis: University of Minnesota Press.

———. 2000. *The Essential Wallerstein.* New York: New Press.

———. 2012. "Reflections on an Intellectual Adventure." *Contemporary Sociology* 41 (1):6–12.

Wallis, Claudia. 2005. "A Snapshot of Teen Sex." *Time,* February 7, p. 58.

———. 2008. "How to Make Great Teachers." *Time* 171 (February 25):28–34.

Walsh, Anthony. 2000. "Behavior Genetics and Anomie/Strain Theory." *Criminology* (November):1075–1107.

Wang, Esther. 2013. "As Wal-Mart Swallows China's Economy, Workers Fight Back." April 23. Accessed November 16 at http://prospect.org/article/wal-mart-swallows-chinas-economy-workers-fight-back.

Wang, Feng. 2011. "The Future of a Demographic Overachiever: Long-Term Implications of the Demographic Transition in China." *Population and Development Review* 37 (Suppl.):173–190.

———, and Cai Yong. 2011. "China's One-Child Policy at 39." May 31. Washington, DC: Brookings Institution.

Wang, Wendy. 2012. "The Rise of Intermarriage: Rates, Characteristics Vary by Race and Gender." Washington, DC: Pew Social and Demographic Trends.

Warrell, Helen. 2013. "Cost of Malnutrition to Global Economy Put at $125bn by 2030." *Financial Times* (May 28):3.

Wattenberg, Martin P. 2008. *Is Voting for Young People?* New York: Pearson Longman.

Weber, Max. [1904] 1949. *Methodology of the Social Sciences.* Translated by Edward A. Shils and Henry A. Finch. Glencoe, IL: Free Press.

———. [1904] 2011. *The Protestant Ethic and the Spirit of Capitalism.* The Revised 1920 Edition. Translation by Stephen Kalberg. New York: Oxford University Press.

———. [1913–1922] 1947. *The Theory of Social and Economic Organization.* Translated by A. Henderson and T. Parsons. New York: Free Press.

———. [1916] 1958. *The Religion of India: The Sociology of Hinduism and Buddhism.* New York: Free Press.

Wechsler, Henry, J. E. Lee, M. Kuo, M. Seibring, T. F. Nelson, and H. Lee. 2002. "Trends in College Binge Drinking during a Period of Increased Prevention Efforts: Findings from Four Harvard School of Public Health College Alcohol Surveys: 1993–2001." *Journal of American College Health* 50 (5):203–217.

———, Mark Seibring, I- Chao Liu, and Marilyn Ahl. 2004. "Colleges Respond to Student Binge Drinking: Reducing Student Demand or Limiting Access." *Journal of American College Health* 52 (4):159–168.

Weeks, John R. 2012. *Population: An Introduction to Concepts and Issues.* 11th ed. Belmont, CA: Cengage.

Weinberg, Daniel H. 2004. *Evidence from Census 2000 About Earnings by Detailed Occupation for Men and Women.* CENSR-15. Washington, DC: U.S. Government Printing Office.

———. 2007. "Earnings by Gender: Evidence from Census 2000." *Monthly Labor Review* (July–August):26–34.

Weinraub, Bernard. 2004. "UPN Show Is Called Insensitive to Amish." *New York Times,* March 4, pp. B1, B8.

Weitz, Rose. 2009. *The Sociology of Health, Illness, and Heath Care.* 5th ed. Belmont, CA: Cengage.

Welch, William M. 2011. "More Hawaii Residents Identify as Mixed Race." *USA Today,* February 28.

Wells-Barnett, Ida B. 1970. *Crusade for Justice: The Autobiography of Ida B. Wells.* Edited by Alfreda M. Duster. Chicago: University of Chicago Press.

Wentling, Tre, Elroi Windsor, Kristin Schilt, and Betsy Lucal. 2008. "Teaching Transgender." *Teaching Sociology* 36 (January):49–57.

Wesolowski, Amy, Nathan Eagle, Andrew J. Tatem, David L. Smith, Abdisalam M. Noor, Robert W. Snow, and Caroline O. Buckee. 2012. "Quantifying the Impact of Human Mobility on Malaria." *Science* (October 12):267–270.

Wessell, David. 2011. "Untangling the Long-Term-Unemployment Crisis." *Wall Street Journal,* October 20, p. A6.

———. 2012. "Race's Roles in Economic Fate." *Wall Street Journal,* September 20, p. A6.

———, and Stephanie Banchero. 2012. "Education Slowdown Threatens U.S." *Wall Street Journal,* April 26, p. A1.

West, Candace, and Don H. Zimmerman. 1987. "Doing Gender." *Gender and Society* 1 (June):125–151.

Westergaard-Nielsen, Niels. 2008. *Low-Wage Work in Denmark.* New York: Russell Sage Foundation.

Western, Bruce, and Jake Rosenfeld. 2011. "Unions, Norms, and the Rise in U.S. Wage Inequality." *American Sociological Review* 70 (4):513–537.

White House. 2013. "Fact Sheet: The President's Plan to Reward Work by Raising the Minimum Wage." February 13. Accessed February 20 at www.whitehouse.gov.

Whitlock, Craig. 2005. "The Internet as Bully Pulpit." *Washington Post National Weekly Edition* 22 (August 22):9.

Whittaker, Stephanie. 2006. "Who Would You Prefer to Work For?" *Gazette* (Montreal), November 4, p. 1.

Whyte, William Foote. 1981. *Street Corner Society: Social Structure of an Italian Slum.* 3rd ed. Chicago: University of Chicago Press.

Wildsmith, Elizabeth, Nicole R. Steward-Streng, and Jennifer Manlove. 2011. "Childbearing Outside of Marriage: Estimates and Trends in the United States." *Child Trends Research Brief* #2011-29. Accessible at www.childtrends.org.

Wilford, John Noble. 1997. "New Clues Show Where People Made the Great Leap to Agriculture." *New York Times,* November 18, pp. B9, B12.

Wilgoren, Jodi. 2005. "In Kansas, Darwinism Goes on Trial Once More." *New York Times,* May 6, p. A14.

Wilkes, Rima, and John Iceland. 2004. "Hypersegregation in the Twenty-First Century." *Demography* 41 (February):23–36.

Wilkins, Amy C. "Becoming Black Women: 2012. Intimate Stories and Intersectional Identities." *Social Psychological Quarterly* 75 (2):173–196.

Wilkinson, Tracy. 2011. "Cuba: Now Open for Business." *Chicago Tribune,* August 15, p. 14.

Williams, Carol J. 1995. "Taking an Eager Step Back." *Los Angeles Times,* June 3, pp. A1, A14.

Williams, David R., and Chiquita Collins. 2004. "Reparations." *American Behavioral Scientist* 47 (March):977–1000.

Williams, J. Allen, Christopher Podeschi, Nathan Palmer, Philip Schwadel, and Deanna Meyler. 2012. "The Human-Environment Dialog in Award-winning Children's Picture Books." *Sociological Inquiry* 82 (February): 145–159.

Williams, Kristine N., Ruth Herman, Byron Gajewski, and Kristel Wilson. 2009. "Elderspeak Communication: Impact on Dementia Care." *American Journal of Alzheimer's Disease and Other Dementias* 24 (March):11–20.

Williams, Robin M., Jr. 1970. *American Society.* 3rd ed. New York: Knopf.

———, with John P. Dean and Edward A. Suchman. 1964. *Strangers Next Door: Ethnic Relations in American Communities.* Englewood Cliffs, NJ: Prentice Hall.

Wills, Jeremiah B., and Barbara J. Risman. 2006. "The Visibility of Feminist Thought in Family Studies." *Journal of Marriage and Family* 68 (August):690–700.

Wilson, Edward O. 1975. *Sociobiology: The New Synthesis.* Cambridge, MA: Harvard University Press.

———. 1978. *On Human Nature.* Cambridge, MA: Harvard University Press.

————. 2000. *Sociobiology: The New Synthesis.* Cambridge, MA: Belknap Press, Harvard University Press.

Wilson, James Q. 2011. "Hard Times, Fewer Crimes." *Wall Street Journal,* May 28, pp. C1–C2.

Wilson, John. 1973. *Introduction to Social Movements.* New York: Basic Books.

Wilson, William Julius. 1996. *When Work Disappears: The World of the New Urban Poor.* New York: Knopf.

————. 1999. *The Bridge over the Racial Divide: Rising Inequality and Coalition Politics.* Berkeley: University of California Press.

————. 2009. *More Than Just Race: Being Black and Poor in the Inner City.* New York: Norton.

————. 2012a. *The Declining Significance of Race: Blacks and Changing American Institutions.* 3rd ed. Chicago: University of Chicago Press.

————. 2012b. *The Truly Disadvantaged: The Inner City, the Underclass and Public Policy.* 2nd ed. Chicago: University of Chicago Press.

————, J. M. Quane, and B. H. Rankin. 2004. "Underclass." In *International Encyclopedia of Social and Behavioral Sciences.* New York: Elsevier.

————, and Richard P. Taub. 2006. *There Goes the Neighborhood: Racial, Ethnic, and Class Tensions in Four Chicago Neighborhoods and Their Meaning for America.* New York: Alfred A. Knopf.

Winant, Howard B. 1994. *Racial Conditions: Politics, Theory, Comparisons.* Minneapolis: University of Minnesota Press.

————. 2006. "Race and Racism: Towards a Global Future." *Ethnic and Racial Studies* 29 (September):986–1003.

Winickoff, Jonathan P., Joan Friebely, Susanne E. Tanski, Cheryl Sherrod, George E. Matt, Melbourne F. Hovell, and Robert C. McMillen. 2009. "Beliefs about the Health Effects of 'Thirdhand' Smoke and Home Smoking Bans." *Pediatrics* 123 (January):74–79.

Winkler, Adam. 2009. "Heller's Catch-22." *UCLA Law Review* 56 (June).

Winter, J. Allen. 2008. "Symbolic Ethnicity." Pp. 1288–1290, vol. 3, in *Encyclopedia of Race, Ethnicity, and Society,* edited by Richard T. Schaefer. Thousand Oaks, CA: Sage.

Wirth, Louis. 1931. "Clinical Sociology." *American Journal of Sociology* 37 (July):49–60.

Wolf, Naomi. 1992. *The Beauty Myth: How Images of Beauty Are Used against Women.* New York: Anchor Books.

Wolfe, Alan. 2008. "Pew in the Pews." *Chronicle of Higher Education,* March 21, pp. B5–B6.

Women's Sports Foundation. 2011. *Title IX.* Accessed March 29 (http://www.womens sportsfoundation.org/Issues-And-Research/Title-IX.aspx).

Wong, Morrison G. 2006. "Chinese Americans." Pp. 110–145 in *Asian Americans: Contemporary Trends and Issues,* 2nd ed., edited by Pyong Gap Min. Thousand Oaks, CA: Sage.

Wood, Daniel B. 2012. "How Serious Crime Fell in US." *Christian Science Monitor* (January 16):18.

Woon, Lee Kang. 2005. "Socialization of Transracially Adopted Korean Americans: A Self Analysis." *Human Architecture: Journal of the Sociology of Self-Knowledge* 3 (Spring):79–84.

Working Women's Forum. 2012. Home Page. Accessed March 27 (www.workingwomensforum .org).

World Association of Girl Guides and Girl Scouts. 2011. "Our World." Accessed November 10 (www.wagggs.org/en/world).

World Bank. 2011. *Development Indicators 2011.* Washington, DC: World Bank.

————. 2012a. *World Development Indicators 2012.* Washington, DC: World Bank.

————. 2012b. *Gender Equality and Development.* Washington, DC: World Bank

————. 2013. "World Indicators 2013." Accessible online data at http://wdi.worldbank.org/tables.

World Development Forum. 1990. "The Danger of Television." 8 (July 15):4.

World Health Organization. 2000. *The World Health Report 2000. Health Systems: Improving Performance.* Geneva: WHO.

————. 2009. "Biotechnology (GM Foods)." Accessed May 11 (www.who.int/foodsafety/biotech/en/).

————. 2010. "Suicide Prevention." Accessed October 31 (http://www.who.int/mental_health/prevention/en/).

World Stats. 2014. "Internet World Stats." Accessed February 11, 2014 at http://www.internet worldstats.com.

World Unplugged. 2013. "One World Unplugged. 'Comparison Charts.'" Accessible at http://theworldunplugged.wordpress.com/about/comparison-charts-of-reactions/.

Worth, Robert F. 2008. "As Taboos Ease, Saudi Girl Group Dares to Rock." *New York Times,* November 24, pp. A1, A9.

Wortham, Robert A. 2008. "DuBois, William Edward Burghardt." Pp. 423–427, vol. 1, in *Encyclopedia of Race, Ethnicity, and Society,* edited by Richard T. Schaefer. Thousand Oaks CA: Sage.

Wray, Matt, Matthew Miller, Jill Gurvey, Joanna Carroll, and Ichiro Kawachi. 2008. "Leaving Las Vegas: Exposure to Las Vegas and Risk of Suicide." *Social Science and Medicine* 67:1882–1888.

————, Cynthia Colen, and Bernice Pescosolido. 2011. "The Sociology of Suicide." *Annual Review of Sociology* 37:505–528.

Wright, Charles R. 1986. *Mass Communication: A Sociological Perspective.* 3rd ed. New York: Random House.

Wright II, Earl. 2012. "Why, Where, and How to Infuse the Atlanta Sociological Laboratory into the Sociology Curriculum." *Teaching Sociology* 40 (43):257–270.

Wright, Eric R., William P. Gronfein, and Timothy J. Owens. 2000. "Deinstitutionalization, Social Rejection, and the Self-Esteem of Former Mental Patients." *Journal of Health and Social Behavior* (March).

Wright, Erik O. 2011. "The Classical Marxist Theory of the History of Capitalism's Future." October 3. Accessed January 20, 2012 (www .ssc.wisc.edu/~wright/621-2011/lecture%20 8%202011%20--%20Classical%20Theory%20 of%20Capitalisms%20future.pdf).

————, David Hachen, Cynthia Costello, and Joey Sprague. 1982. "The American Class Structure." *American Sociological Review* 47 (December):709–726.

Wyatt, Edward. 2009. "No Smooth Ride on TV Networks' Road to Diversity." *New York Times,* March 18, pp. 1, 5.

Y

Yemma, John. 2013. "Teaching the Freedom to Believe." *Christian Science Monitor* (June 17):5.

Yinger, J. Milton. 1970. *The Scientific Study of Religion.* New York: Macmillan.

York, Richard, Eugene A. Rosa, and Thomas Dietz. 2010. "Ecological Modernization Theory: Theoretical and Empirical Challenges." Pp. 77–90 in *The International Handbook and Environmental Sociology,* 2nd ed., edited by Michael R. Redclift and Graham Woodgate. Cheltenham, UK: Edward Elgar.

Young, Kevin, ed. 2004. *Sporting Bodies, Damaged Selves.* New York: Elsevier.

Yourish, Karen, and Larry Buchanan. 2013. "State Gun Laws Enacted in Year Since Newtown." *New York Times,* December 11, p. A20.

YouTube. [2009] 2013. "Historic Flashmob in Antwerp Train Station, Do Re Mi." Accessed May 13, 2013 (www.youtube.com/watch?v=0UE3CNu_rtY).

Yunus, Muhammad. 2010. *Building Social Business.* New York: Perseus.

Z

Zakaria, Fareed. 2012. "Incarceration Nation." *Time,* April 2, p. 18.

Zarembo, Alan. 2004a. "A Theater of Inquiry and Evil." *Los Angeles Times,* July 15, pp. A1, A24, A25.

Zeitzen, Miriam Koktvedgaard. 2008. *Polygamy: A Cross-Cultural Analysis.* Oxford, UK: Berg.

Zellner, William M. 1995. *Counter Cultures: A Sociological Analysis.* New York: St. Martin's Press.

Zernike, Kate. 2002. "With Student Cheating on the Rise, More Colleges Are Turning to Honor Codes." *New York Times,* November 2, p. A10.

Zhang, Xiaodan. 2009. "Trade Unions under the Modernization of Paternalist Rule in China." *Journal of Labor and Society* 12 (June):193–218.

Zi, Jui-Chung Allen. 2007. *The Kids Are OK: Divorce and Children's Behavior Problems.* Santa Monica, CA: RAND.

Zia, Helen. 2000. *Asian American Dreams: The Emergence of an American People.* New York: Farrar, Straus & Giroux.

Zimbardo, Philip G. 1972. "Pathology of Imprisonment." *Society* 9 (April):4, 6, 8.

————. 2004. "Power Turns Good Soldiers into 'Bad Apples.'" *Boston Globe,* May 9. Also accessible at www.prisonexp.org.

————. 2007. *The Lucifer Effect: Understanding How Good People Turn Evil.* New York: Random House.

————. 2007a. "Revisiting the Stanford Prison Experiment: A Lesson in the Power of the Situation." *Chronicle of Higher Education* 53 (March 20):B6, B7.

————, Craig Haney, W. Curtis Banks, and David Jaffe. 1974. "The Psychology of Imprisonments:

Privation, Power, and Pathology." In *Doing unto Others: Joining, Molding, Conforming, Helping, and Loving,* edited by Zick Rubin. Englewood Cliffs, NJ: Prentice Hall.

———, Robert L. Johnson, and Vivian McCann Hamilton. 2009. *Psychology: Core Concepts.* 6th ed. Upper Saddle River, NJ: Pearson.

———, Ann L. Weber, and Robert Johnson. 2003. *Psychology: Core Concepts.* 4th ed. Boston: Allyn and Bacon.

Zimmerman, Seth. 2008a. "Globalization and Economic Mobility." Washington, DC: Economic Mobility Project. Also accessible at www.economicmobility.org/reports_and_research/literature_reviews?id=0004.

———. 2008b. *Labor Market Institutions and Economic Mobility.* Washington, DC: Pew Charitable Trusts.

Zipp, Yvonne. 2009. "Courts Divided on Police Use of GPS Tracking." *Christian Science Monitor,* May 15.

Zirin, Dave. 2008. "Calling Sports Sociology off the Bench." *Contexts* (Summer):28–31.

Zittrain, Jonathan, and John Palfrey. 2008. "Reluctant Gatekeepers: Corporate Ethics on a Filtered Internet." Pp. 103–122 in *Access Denied,* edited by Ronald Deibert, John Palfrey, Rafal Rohozinski, and Jonathan Zittrain. Cambridge, MA: MIT Press.

Zogby. 2010. "Zogby Interactive: 54% Support Ethnic & Religious Profiling; 71% Favor Full-Body Scans." February 4. Accessed July 2, 2011 (http://www.zogby.com/news/2010/02/04/zogby-interactive-54-support-ethnic-religious profiling-71-favor-full-body-scans/).

Zola, Irving K. 1972. "Medicine as an Institution of Social Control." *Sociological Review* 20 (November):487–504.

———. 1983. *Socio-Medical Inquiries.* Philadelphia: Temple University Press.

Zweigenhaft, Richard L., and G. William Domhoff. 2006. *Diversity in the Power Elite: How It Happened, Why It Matters.* 2nd ed. New York: Rowman and Littlefield.

acknowledgments

Chapter 1

Page 6: Émile Durkheim, *Suicide,* Translated by John A. Spaulding and George Simpson [1897] 1951. Reprint. New York: Free Press; p. 8: Charles Darwin; p. 10: Karl Marx and Friedrich Engels, "The Manifesto of the Communist Party," *The Marx-Engels Reader,* edited by Robert Tucker, NY: Norton, 1978, 473, 500; p. 14: Scott Gregory, "Broken Windows Behind Bars: Eradicating Prison Gangs through Ecological Hardening and Symbolic Cleansing," *Corrections Management Quarterly*, 5, Winter, 2001, 23–36; p. 16: Jerry Crowe and Valli Herman, "NBA Lists Fashion Do's and Don'ts," *Los Angeles Times,* October 19, 2005; p. 21: W.E.B. DuBois, *The Autobiography of W.E.B. DuBois: A Soliloquy on Viewing My Life from the Last Decade of Its First Century*, New York, NY: International Publishers Co. Inc., 1968, pp. 409–423.

Chapter 2

Page 28: Patricia A. Adler and Peter Adler, "The Demedicalization of Self-Injury: From Psychopathology to Sociological Deviance," *Journal of Contemporary Ethnography*, 36, October, 2007, 542; Figure 5-2: American Community Survey in Bureau of the Census 2013a:Table 80201; p. 36: William F. Whyte, *Street Corner Society: The Social Structure of an Italian Slum,* 2nd ed., Chicago: University of Chicago Press, 1955; p. 40: Peter Monaghan, "Sociologist Jailed Because He 'Wouldn't Snitch' Ponders the Way Research Ought to Be Done," *Chronicle of Higher Education,* 1 September 1993, p. A8.

Chapter 3

Page 61: Donald Black, "The Epistemology of Pure Sociology," *Law and Social Inquiry,* 20, Summer, Issue 4, 1995, 829–870; p. 67: Patrick Nolan and Gerhard Lenski, *Human Societies: An Introduction to Macrosociology,* 11th ed., Boulder, Colo.: Paradigm Publishers, 2009, 357.

Chapter 4

Page 77: Jim Garamone, AFPS; p. 94: Hiroko Tabuchi, "Desperate Hunt for Day Care in Japan," *The New York Times,* February 26, 2013, A9.

Chapter 5

Page 98: Philip G. Zimbardo, Robert L. Johnson, and Vivian McCann Hamilton, *Psychology: Core Concepts,* 6th ed. Upper Saddle River, NJ: Pearson, 2009, 516; p. 99: Herbert Blumer, *Symbolic Interactionism: Perspective and Method,* Englewood Cliffs, NJ: Prentice-Hall, Inc., 1969, 79; p. 100: William I. Thomas, *The Unadjusted Girl: With Cases and Standpoint for Behavior Analysis,* Boston: Little, Brown, 1923; p. 108: Patrick Nolan and Gerhard Lenski, *Human Societies: An Introduction to Macrosociology,* 11th ed., Boulder, Colo.: Paradigm Publishers, 2009, 357; p. 113: Robert Merton, *Social Theory and Social Structure,* New York: Free Press, 1968; p. 115: Robin J. Ely, "The Power in Demography: Women's Social Constructions of Gender Identity at Work," *Academy of Management Journal*, 38:3, June 1, 1995, 589–634; p. 116: Karl Marx and Friedrich Engels, "The Manifesto of the Communist Party," *The Marx-Engels Reader,* edited by Robert Tucker, NY: Norton, 1978; Max Weber, *The Theory of Social and Economic Organization,* translated by A. M. Henderson and Talcott Parsons, The Free Press and the Falcon's Bring Press, 1947.

Chapter 6

Page 133: T. Gitlin, *Media Unlimited: How the Torrent of Images and Sounds Overwhelms Our Lives,* New York, NY: Holt, 2002.

Chapter 7

Page 153: Stanley Milgram, *Obedience to Authority: An Experimental View,* Harper & Row, NY, 1974; p. 154: "The Perils of Obedience" as it appeared in *Harper's Magazine*. Abridged and adapted from *Obedience to Authority* by Stanley Milgram, 1974; Milgram, CBS News, *Sixty Minutes,* March 31, 1979; p. 159: Howard Saul Becker, *Outsiders: Studies in the Sociology of Deviance,* Free Press of Glencoe, 1963, 9; p. 164: Federal Bureau of Narcotics, 1930; Figure 25-1: Incidents reported for 2012 in 2013, Federal Bureau of Investigation, 2013.

Chapter 8

Figure 26-1: 2012 census data presented in Bureau of the Census 2013a:Tables R1701, R1901; Table 26-1: Department of State 2013; p. 182: Steve Greenberg/ Rights available from Cartoonstock.com. Reproduced by permission; John Kenneth Galbraith, *The Age of Uncertainty,* Houghton Mifflin, 1977; p. 190: Paul A. Samuelson and William D. Nordhaus, *Economics,* 19th ed., New York: McGraw-Hill, 2010, 324.

Chapter 9

Page 207: Steve Greenberg/Cartoon Movement. Reproduced by permission.

Chapter 10

Page 227: Charles Wagley and Marvin Harris, *Minorities in the New World: Six Case Studies,* New York: Columbia University Press, 1958; p. 228: DuBois, "To the Nations of the World," *An ABC of Color,* edited by W. E. B. DuBois. New York: International Publishers, [1900] 1969, 19–23; Mireya Navarro, "When You Contain Multitudes," *The New York Times,* April 24, 2005, pp. 1, 2; p. 230: William I. Thomas, *The Unadjusted Girl,* Boston: Little, Brown, 1923; p. 233: DuBois, *Black Reconstruction in America 1860–1880,* New York: Athenaeum, [1935] 1962; p. 237: Manning Nash, "Race and the Ideology of Race," *Current Anthropology*, 3, June, 1962, 285–288; Gordon Allport, *The Nature of Prejudice,* 25th anniversary ed. Reading, MA: Addison-Wesley, 1979, 210; Figure 33-1: Jones-Puthoff 2013:slide 5; p. 242: Ralph Ellison, *Invisible Man,* New York: Random House,1952; 33-4: Sharon R. Ennis, Merarys Rios-Vargas, and Nora G. Albert, *The Hispanic Population: 2010,* 2010 Census Brief BR-04. Washington, DC: U.S. Government Printing Office, 2011.

Chapter 11

Page 269: U.S. Commission on Civil Rights. *A Guide to Federal Laws and Regulations Prohibiting Sex Discrimination*, Washington, DC: U.S. Government Printing Office, 1, 1976.

Chapter 12

Page 280: Jill Quadagno, 2014. *Aging and the Life Course: An Introduction to Social Gerontology*. 6th ed. Copyright © 2014 by McGraw-Hill Companies, Inc. Reproduced by permission; Figure 37-2: AARP, 2011. "Baby Boomer Envision What's Next? Research and Strategic Analysis Integrated Value and Strategy June, 2011." Accessed January 10, 2010. Reproduced by permission of GfK Roper; p. 287: Robert C. Atchley, *The Sociology of Retirement,* New York: Wiley, 1976; 38-3: Bureau of the Census 2005a.

Chapter 13

Page 299: Katherine S. Newman, *The Accordion Family: Boomerang Kids, Anxious Parents, and the Private Toll of Global Competition,* Boston: Beacon Press, 2012, xv–xvii, 2012; Figure 39-1: Bureau of the Census 1981:2; Vespa et al. 2013:5, also Table HH1; p. 303: William F. Ogburn and Clark Tibbits, "The Family and Its Functions," *Recent Social Trends in the United States,* edited by Research Committee on Social Trends, New York: McGraw-Hill, 1934, 661–708; p. 305: Verta Taylor, Leila J. Rupp, and Nancy Whittier, *Feminist Frontiers,* 8th ed. New York: McGraw-Hill, 2009; 42-1: 2010 American Community Survey data in Lofquist, "Same-Sex Couple Households," ACSBR/10-03. Washington, DC: U.S. Government Printing Office, 2011, 4.

Chapter 14

Page 325: Diane Ravitch, *The Death and Life of the Great American School System: How Testing and Choice Are Undermining Education.* © 2010 by Basic Books. Reproduced by permission; Figure 43-2: Tiffany Julian and Robert Kominski, *Education and Synthetic Work-Life Earnings Estimates.* ACS-14. Washington, DC: U.S. Government Printing Office, 2011; p. 330: H. H. Gerth and C. Wright Mills, *Max Weber: Essays in Sociology,* New York: Galaxy, 1958, 240–241; 43-3: National Center for Education Statistics, 2013; p. 337: Helen Lefkowitz Horowitz, *Campus Life,* Chicago: University of Chicago Press, 1987; 44-2: William J. Hussar and Tabitha M. Bailey, *Projections of Education Statistics to 2019,* Washington, DC: National Center for Education Statistics, 2011; p. 338: Joe R. Feagin, *Minority Group Issues in Higher Education: Learning from Qualitative Research,* Norman: Center for Research on Minority Education, University of Oklahoma, 1989, 11.

Chapter 15

Page: 346: Émile Durkheim, *The Elementary Forms of Religious Life,* Translated and with an Introduction by Karen E. Fields, New York: The Free Press (Simon & Schuster), 1995 [1912], 39–44; p. 347: Émile Durkheim, *Division of Labor in Society,* Translated by George Simpson. Reprint. New York: Free Press, [1893] 1933; p. 348: Gustavo Gutiérrez, "Theology and the Social Sciences," *Liberation Theology at the Crossroads: Democracy or Revolution?* edited by Paul E. Sigmund, New York: Oxford University Press, 1990, 214–225; p. 354: President Obama's 2009 inaugural address.

Chapter 16

Page 374: Bureau of the Census 2011e:Table 10; p. 385: Bureau of Labor Statistics data cited in Hira 2008; Moncarz et al. 2008.

Chapter 17

Figure 53-2: DeNavas-Walt et al. 2013:Table HI05; p. 409: Cartoon by Manny Francisco © 2008 www.PoliticalCartoons.com. Reproduced by permission; 55-3: Projections updated as of December 2010. Bureau of the Census 2011b; 56-1: Environmental Protection Agency 2012.

Chapter 18

Page 438: Herbert Blumer, "Collective Behavior," *Principles of Sociology,* 2nd ed., edited by Alfred McClung Lee, New York: Barnes and Noble, 1955, 165–198.

photo credits

Press. Reprinted by permission of Princeton University Press; p. 209 (top left): ChinaFotoPress/Getty Images; p. 209 (top right): Steve Morgan/Photofusion Picture Library/Alamy; p. 210: Imaginechina/AP Images; p. 211: Peter Probst/Alamy; p. 212 (left): Frederic Soltan/Corbis; p. 212 (right): PhotoDisc Imaging/Getty Images; p. 213 (top): Photo by Esther Havens. Courtesy, Living Goods; p. 213 (bottom): EyeWire/Getty Images; p. 215: The commercial titled JEANS was done by Springer & Jacoby Werbung advertising agency for AGAINST CHILD LABOUR (a UNICEF campaign) in Germany. Copywriter: Sven Keitel; Art Director: Claudia Todt; Creative Director: Timm Weber/Bettina Olf; p. 219: Stuart Franklin/Magnum Photos; p. 220: Pascal Saez/Alamy.

Chapter 10

Page 225: Ariel Skelley/Blend Images; p. 226: Courtesy of Charles Trimble. Photo by Don Doll SJ; p. 229 (top right): Library of Congress Prints and Photographs Division [LC-USZC2-1745]; p. 229 (bottom right): Ken Usami/Photodisc/Getty Images; p. 230 (top center): Juanmonino/Getty Images; p. 230 (top right): Motofish Images/Corbis; p. 231 (top left): Kevin C. Cox/Getty Images; p. 231 (bottom right): Yellow Dog Productions/The Image Bank/Getty Images; p. 233: Enigma/Alamy; p. 234: Courtesy of Prudence Hannis; p. 236: Library of Congress Prints and Photographs Division Washington, DC 20540 USA[LC-USF33-020522-M2 [P&P]]; p. 238: Tony Savino/The Image Works; p. 239: Gaizka Iroz/AFP/Getty Images; p. 240: Barbara Penoyar/Photodisc/Getty Images; p. 243: Bram Belloni/Hollandse Hoogte/Redux Pictures; p. 244: Michael Jensen/Auscape/The Image Works; p. 245: New Line Cinema/PhotoFest; p. 246: Ariel Skelley/Blend Images/Corbis; p. 247: George Rose/Getty Images; p. 249 (top center): Sigma Pi Alpha Sorority at Sacramento State University; p. 249 (bottom right): The Collection of the Supreme Court of the United States/MCT/Getty Images; p. 250: Rachel Morton/Impact/HIP/The Image Works; p. 251: David L. Moore - OR/Alamy; p. 252: Pixhook/E+/Getty Images; p. 253: Robert Nickelsberg/Getty Images.

Chapter 11

Page 257: Thinkstock/Index Stock; p. 258: Courtesy of Azadeh Moaveni/Diana Finch Literary Agency; p. 260 (top right): Eric Jamison/AP Images; p. 260 (center): Picture provided by Harrison G. Pope, Jr. adapted from THE ADONIS COMPLEX by Harrison G. Pope, Jr., Katherine Phillips, Roberto Olivardia. The Free Press, 2000; p. 261: Gideon Mendel/Corbis; p. 262: Rex Features/AP Images; p. 264 (top left): STR/EPA/Newscom; p. 264 (bottom right): amsteker/Bloomberg/Getty Images; p. 265: Inti St Clair/Getty Images; p. 268: John Birdsall/The Image Works; p. 270: Thinkstock/Index Stock; p. 271: Stefano Lunardi/Alamy.

Chapter 12

Page 279: Purestock/SuperStock; p. 280: Brendan McDermid/Reuters/Corbis; p. 281: Hill Street Studios/Blend Images; p. 282: Strauss/Curtis/CORBIS; p. 285: Rex Moreton/Bubbles Photolibrary/Alamy; p. 287: Gero Breloer/dpa/Corbis; p. 288: Ron Sanford/Corbis; p. 291: Masterfile; p. 292: L. Busacca/Getty Images; p. 293: Stefan Kiefer/imagebroker/Alamy; p. 294: Richard Sheinwald/AP Images; p. 296: Purestock/SuperStock.

Chapter 13

Page 298: Jeff Greenberg/The Image Works; p. 299: Image courtesy of Beacon Press 2012 by Katherine Newman; p. 302: Thomas L. Kelly; p. 303 (top left): ImagesBazaar/Alamy; p. 303 (bottom left): Burke/Triolo Productions/Brand X/Corbis; p. 304: Lumi Images/Alamy; p. 306: Dominique Charriau/WireImage/Getty Images; p. 309: Hill Street Studios/Blend Images/Corbis; p. 310: Lori Waselchuck/New York Times/Redux Pictures; p. 311: Blend Images/Alamy; p. 312: Cheryl Gerber for The New York Times/Redux Pictures; p. 315: Amos Morgan/Photodisc/Getty Images; p. 317: Kevin Winter/Getty Images; p. 318: Image Source/Alamy.

Chapter 14

Page 324: Bob Daemmrich/The Image Works; p. 325: *The Death and Life of the Great American School System* by Diane Ravitch. Publisher: Basic

Books. Jacket design by Ariana Abud. Photo © Darrell Gulin/Getty Images; p. 327: Warner Bros. Pictures/Photofest Warner Bros. Pictures; p. 328: Mark Peterson/Redux Pictures; p. 330: Brand X Pictures/Punchstock; p. 331: Comstock Images/Punchstock; p. 332: Photodisc/Getty Images; p. 333: sozaijiten/Datacraft/Getty Images; p. 334: Andy Sacks/Getty Images; p. 335: Courtesy of Diane Belcher Gray/New River Community College/Workforce Development; p. 338: Andrew Holbrooke/The Image Works; p. 340: Troy Maben/AP Images.

Chapter 15

Page 344: iStockphoto.com/gnomeandi; p. 345: "Book cover," *Toying with God, The World of Religious Games and Dolls* by Nikki Bado-Fralick and Rebecca Sachs Norris. 2010. Reprinted with permission of Baylor University Press; p. 347: JAVIER ROJAS/Landov; p. 348: Fox Broadcasting/Photo: Isabella Vosmikova/Photofest; p. 349: The Star-Ledger/Jennifer Brown/The Image Works; p. 351: Jonathan Nackstrand/AFP/Getty Images; p. 352: Kazuyoshi Nomachi/HAGA/The Image Works; p. 354 (center) Freedom from Religion Foundation, ffrg.org; p. 356: Patrick Frilet/Hemis/Alamy; p. 358: Wes Pope KRT/Newscom.

Chapter 16

Page 363: TIM SLOAN/AFP/Getty Images; p. 364: © McGraw-Hill Education; p. 366 (top center): C Squared Studios/Getty Images; p. 366 (bottom left): Ryan Anson/AFP/Getty Images; p. 367 (top right): Gerhard Joren; p. 367 (bottom center): Frank Micelotta/Getty Images; p. 368: Marco Garcia/AP Images; p. 369: U.S. Army Space and Missile Defense Command; p. 371: Al Bello/Getty Images; p. 373: Win McNamee/Getty Images News/Getty Images; p. 374: Ryan McVay/Photodisc/Getty Images; p. 376: Haraz Ghanbari/AP Images; p. 380 (top): © The McGraw-Hill Companies, Inc./Mark Steinmetz, photographer; p. 380 (bottom): Eric Baccega/AGE Fotostock; p. 384 (bottom left): age fotostock/Superstock; p. 384 (bottom right): ERIN LUBIN/Landov; p. 386: Farjana K. Godhuly/AFP/Getty Images; p. 387: Adeel Halim/Bloomberg via Getty Images.

Chapter 17

Page 391: Imaginechina/Corbis; p. 392: Johannes Kroemer/Getty Images; p. 393: Paul Souders/Corbis; p. 394: Hill Street Studios/Blend Images/Getty Images; p. 395: megastocker/Alamy; p. 396 (top left): Courtesy of Lola Adedokun/Doris Duke Charitable Foundation; p. 396 (bottom center): Photodisc/Getty Images; p. 401 (top left): Comstock Images/Alamy; p. 401 (bottom left): Rubberball/Corbis; p. 402: Nati Harnik/AP Images; p. 403 (top center): Photodisc/Getty Images; p. 403 (bottom center): Anthony Saint James/Photodisc/Getty Images; p. 404 (bottom left): MarioPonta/Alamy; p. 404 (bottom right): John Bazemore/AP Images; p. 406: Andreas Branch/Patrick McMullan.com/Sipa Press/AP Images; p. 407: Doug Schneider/Alamy; p. 409: Mustafa Ozer/AFP/Getty Images; p. 410: Courtesy, Kelsie Lenor Wilson-Dorsett; p. 414: Josef Polleross/The Image Works; p. 415: Goh Chai Hin/AFP/Getty Images; p. 416: Mustafa Ozer/AFP/Getty Images; p. 417: Eduardo Verdugo/AP Images; p. 418: Jeffrey Hamilton/Getty Images; p. 420 (top left): Steve Allen/Brand X Pictures; p. 420 (top right): Richard Wear/DesignPics; p. 421: Ariadne Van Zandbergen/Africa Media Online/The Image Works; p. 423 (top left): Hemera Technologies/dynamicgraphics/Jupiter Images; p. 423 (center right): H. David Seawell/Digital Stock/Corbis.

Chapter 18

Page 427: Fathi/Caro/Alamy; p. 429: AP Photo/Ed Betz; p. 430: Amos Morgan/Getty Images; p. 431 (top left): Brandon Laufenberg/Getty Images RF; p. 431 (bottom right): Jewel Samad/Getty Images; p. 433: Pat Milton/AP Images; p.434: Vincent Laforet/AP Images; p. 435: picturesbyrob/Alamy; p. 436: Raoul Minsart/Superstock; p. 439: Oli Scarff/Getty Images; p. 440: Joshua Roberts/Getty Images; p. 442: Pavel Filatov/Alamy; p. 443: Stockbyte/Getty Images; p. 446 (top): Joseph Rodriguez/Gallery Stock; p. 446 (bottom right): Manjunath Kiran/AFP/Getty Images; p. 449 (top left): Howard Boylan/Getty Images; p. 449 (top right): David Cannon/Getty Images; p. 450: Issei Kato/Reuters/Landov; p. 452: Andre Kudyusov/Photodisc/Alamy; p. 454: Trevor Snapp/Bloomberg via Getty Images.

subject index

attention-deficit/hyperactivity disorder
(ADHD), 338–339
audience, 140–142
Aurora, Colo., theater shootings (2012), 172
Australia, 208*f*, 423*f*
Aboriginal people of, 9, 244, *244*
age at first marriage, 308*f*
child care subsidized in, 93, *93*
college graduation rates, 326*f*
economy of, 379*f*
foreign aid per capita, 212*f*
human sexual behavior in, 47*f*
labor union membership in, 120*f*
nonverbal communication in, 59
poverty in, 194*f*
voter turnout, 372*f*
Austria, 120*f*, 208*f*, 214*f*, 326*f*
authority, 365–366, 371. *See also*
government
charismatic, 366, *366*, 367, 371
hierarchy of, 116, 117*t*, 118, 334
patterns of, in families, 302–303, *303*
rational-legal, 366, 371
traditional, 366, 371
of U.S. Constitution, 366
authority figures, 153–154
Avatar (film), *439*
Avon, 213
Azerbaijan, 208*f*

b

baby boom, 413
baby boomers, 287, 292
"Baby Mama" (song), 312
Baltimore (Md.) Police Department, 151
Bangladesh, 57*f*, 206, 208*f*, 219*f*, 386
basic sociology, 20, 22
beauty myth, 158, *159*, 268
Belarus, 208*f*
Belgium, 208*f*
beliefs
generalized, in social change, 431
religious beliefs, 352–353, 354, 354*t*
shared, collective behavior and, 436
Bell v. Maryland (1964), 250
Beloved Wives Day, 99
Benin, 208*f*
"bereavement symptoms," 407
Betsileo people (Madagascar), 300
Bhutan, 208*f*
BIA (Bureau of Indian Affairs), 243
bias, 42
bias (hate) crimes, 168, 168*f*
Big Brother (TV series), 133
"Big Brother," 146, *146*
big data, 144
Big Toe Crew, 67
bilateral kinship descent, 301, 305
bilingual education, 72–73, 248–249
bilingualism, 71–73, 72*f*, 328
Bill and Melinda Gates Foundation, 340
binge drinking, 155, *155*
biotechnology, 453–454, *454*, 456
bipolar disorder, *406*
birth control, 316, 438, 447
birthrate (crude birthrate), 410

bisexuality, 317–318
Black feminists, 266
Black power, 243
Blacks. *See* African Americans
"blaming the victim," 163, 195, 231–232
blended families, 300, 313, *313*
blogging, 136
B'nai B'rith, 250
boards of directors, 270, 375–376
body image, 54–55, 260, *260*
"Body Ritual Among the Nacirema"
(Miner), 54
Bolivia, 208*f*
Bombers, 84
Book of Mormon, The (play), 356
born-again Christians, 353–354
"Born This Way" (song), *317*
Bororo people, 68
Bosnia-Herzegovina, 208*f*
Botswana, 208*f*
Bourdieu, Pierre, 12
bourgeoisie, 184
Boy Scouts of America, 39, *39*
BP (British Petroleum), 132, 214*f*
Brady Campaign to Prevent Gun
Violence, 172
Brady Handgun Violence Prevention Act
of 1994, 172
brain drain, 395
brass ceiling, 262
Brazil, 208*f*
age at first marriage, 308*f*
cultural survival in, 68
destruction of rain forest, 417
economy of, 379*f*
human sexual behavior in, 47*f*
income distribution in, 219*f*
indigenous groups of, 68
stratification in, 218, *218*
voter turnout in, 372*f*
Breaking Bad (TV series), 133
British Petroleum (BP), 132, 214*f*
"bromance," 263
Brown v. Board of Education
(1950), 329
Buddhism, *344*, 351*t*, 352, *427*
Bulgaria, 208*f*, 285*f*
bureaucracies, 115–117, *116*, 117*t*, 119
division of labor in, 115–116, 117*t*
hierarchy of authority in, 116,
117*t*, 118
as ideal type, 9
impersonality in, 116, *116*, 117*t*, 118
oligarchies, 117
organizational culture and, 117–119
schools as, effect on teachers, *335*,
335–336
written rules and regulations in, 116,
117*t*, 118
bureaucratization
of medical treatment, 118, *118*
of schools, *334*, 334–335
in small-group settings, 117
Bureau of Indian Affairs (BIA), 243
Bureau of Justice Statistics, 170
Bureau of Labor Statistics, 35
Bureau of the Census, 24, 32–33, 72
Burger King, 137

Burj Khalifa, 448
Burkina Faso, 57*f*, 208*f*
burnout, 336
Burundi, 208*f*

C

California Civil Rights Initiative
(Proposition 209), 383
call center subcultures, *69*, 70
Cambodia, 208*f*, 372*f*
Cameroon, 208*f*
Canada, 208*f*, 423*f*
age at first marriage, 308*f*
college graduation rates, 326*f*
economy of, 379*f*
First Nations, 234
foreign aid per capita, 212*f*
global brands of, 130*f*
human sexual behavior in, 47*f*
income distribution in, 219*f*
infant mortality rates, 395*f*
labor union membership in, 120*f*
population growth rate, 411*f*
poverty in, 194*f*
religious participation in, 353*f*
voter turnout, 372*f*
women in government, 375*f*
capital, 12, 58, 136
capitalism, 184, 378–380, *381*, 382
neo-Luddites and, 447
Protestant work ethic and, 348
stratification in, 186–187
tracking in schools and, 331
in Vietnam and Cuba, 380–381
career criminals, 167
careers in sociology, *23*, 23–24, 24*f*
in education, 234, *234*, 335, *335*
ethnography used in, 90, *90*
in health care, 396, *396*
human services, 41, *41*
military careers, 369, *369*
in population studies, 410, *410*
research coordinator, 41, *41*
with Secret Service, 171
small business owners, 103, *103*
social media consulting, 134, *134*
caregiving role, *285*, 285–286, 289, 310
Carnegie Mellon University Data
Truck, *37*
castes (*varnas*), 181, 187
cattle (zebu), 13, *14*
causal logic, 30, 32*f*
CCI (Center for Community Initiatives),
19, *19*
CDC (Centers for Disease Control and
Prevention), 173, 396
cell phones, 36, 90, *90*, 92, 453–454, *454*
census, 410, 416
Center for Community Initiatives (CCI),
19, *19*
Centers for Disease Control and Prevention (CDC), 173, 396
Central African Republic, 57*f*, 208*f*, 395*f*
Central Intelligence Agency (CIA),
116, 319
Chad, 208*f*

charisma, 439
charismatic authority, 366, *366*, 367, 371
charitable giving, 137
charter schools, 339*f*, 339–340, *340*, 341
cheating, culture of, 63, 64
child care, 90, *90*, 92–94, *93*
Child Care Law Center, 90
childless marriage, 315–316
child marriage, 56, 57*f*
child protective services, 311–312
child-rearing patterns, 310–313
adoption, 310–312
in dual-income families, 312, *312*
parents and grandparents, 310, *310*
in single-parent families, 309*f*,
312, 313
stepfamilies, 313, *313*
children. *See also* adolescents
aboriginal, removed from families,
244, *244*
adoption of, 310–312
child pornography, 318
child soldiers, *81*
effects of pollution on, 420
in foster care, 311–312
gender-role socialization of, 260*t*, *260*,
260–261
impact of divorce on, 314
paternal involvement with, 304, *304*
without health insurance, 398, 399*f*
Chile, *91*, 208*f*, 214*f*, 269*f*
China, People's Republic of, 208*f*, 214*f*
air pollution in Beijing, *391*, 419
American factories in, 385
cultural practices in, *55*
cyber-police in, 131
declining poverty in, 211, 217
economy of, 379*f*
female infanticide in, 219
infant mortality rates, 395*f*
labor unions in, 121
media in, *91*, 143*f*
oligarchy in, 367
population growth rate, 411*f*
restrictive population policies,
415, *415*
revision of history curriculum in,
326–327
as semiperipheral nation, 210
value of ethnicity in, 63*f*
women in government, 375*f*
China National Petroleum, 214*f*
Chinese Americans, 237, 244–245
Chinese Exclusion Act of 1882, 245
Christianity, 351, 351*t*, 352
Arab American Christians, 248*f*
born-again Christians, 353–354
Christian Science Church, 350, 357
Chrysler Corporation, 384
Church of Christ, Scientist, 350, 357
Church of Jesus Christ of Latter Day
Saints (LDS), 301, 356, *356*
CIA (Central Intelligence Agency),
116, 319
cities, housing issues in, 44*f*, 45
Civil Liberties Act of 1988, 247
civil marriage, 316, 320
Civil Rights Act of 1964, 236, *236*

civil rights model of disability, 102
civil rights movement, 242–243
Civil Union Act of 2006 (S. Africa), 316
class, 185
class consciousness, 184, 440
class differentiation. *See* stratification
class-domination theory, 364
classical theory of formal
    organizations, 118
Classmates, 132
class systems, 182–184. *See also* social
    class; *specific classes*
class warfare, *183,* 183–184
Clean Air Act, 422
Clean Water Act, 422
Clery Act of 1990, 166
climate change, *420,* 420–421
clinical sociology, 20, 22
closed stratification systems, 196
CMC (computer-mediated communica-
    tion), 442, 443
CMHC program, 407
coal-fired power generation, 421
coalitions, 114, *114,* 115
coal miners, *184*
codes of ethics, 40, 41
coffee trade, 21
cognitive theory of development, 85, 87
cohabitation, 311, 315, 316
collective behavior, 429–438
    assembling perspective of, *431,*
        431–432, 437
    crowds as, 432–433, 437
    disaster behavior, *433,* 433–435, 437
    emergent-norm perspective of,
        429–430, 432, 436, 437
    fads and fashions, 435, *435,* 438
    forms of, 432–437, 437t
    panics and crazes, 435–436, 438
    publics and public opinion,
        436–437, 438
    rumors as, 429, 436, *436,* 438
    theories of, *429,* 429–432
    value-added model of, 430–431, 437
collective consciousness
    of elderly, *292,* 292–293
    of women, emergence of, 272–273
colleges and universities. *See also*
    academia
    affirmative action, 383
    campus crime, 166, *166*
    culture of cheating in, 63, 64
    day without media, 91, *91*
    degrees conferred in sociology,
        23–24, 24f
    financial aid, 196, 197
    Gallaudet University protests, 432, *440*
    graduation rates, 326f
    institutional discrimination by,
        234–235
    Native American, *30*
    sociological research by, *37*
    subcultures in, 337–338
    tuition and fees, 330, 331f
    use of search engines, 327
college students
    binge drinking by, 155, *155*
    impression management by, 84

life goals of, 63f
student safety issue, 166, *166*
subcultures of, 336–338, 338f, *338*
collegiate subculture, 337
Colombia, 208f
colonialism
    effect on Aboriginal people, 244
    legacy of, 209f, *209,* 209–210, *210*
color-blind racism, *231,* 231–232,
    236, 383
"color line," 228
coltan (columbite-tantalite) mining, 380
Columbine High School shootings
    (1999), 113, 131, 172
Columbo (TV series), 133
commercial motives for fads, 435
common sense, 6
communication(s). *See also* language
    computer-mediated, 442, 443
    essential to disaster relief, 434–435
    globalization of social movements
        and, 441, 443
    nonverbal, 16, *59,* 59–60
communications technologies, 20. *See*
        also technology
    cell phone surveys, 36
    computer-mediated communication,
        442, 443
    cultural diffusion and, 67
    deviance and, 159–160
    effect on human relationships, 2
    Internet search filters, 132
    online dating, 44, *45,* 307
    online giving, 137
    privacy issue and, *452,* 452–453
    role in social movements, 442, *442*
    socialization through, 90–91
    use by political figures, 366
communism, 381, 382
Communist League, 10
Communist Manifesto, The (Marx &
    Engels), 10, 10f, 20, 116
Communist Party, 185
Community Mental Health Centers Act
    of 1963, 407
computer crime, 168
computer-mediated communication
    (CMC), 442, 443
computer-mediated instruction, 335
computer technology, 450, *450,* 452,
    452t, 456
Comte, Auguste, 8, 12
conclusions, in research, 29f, 33–34
concrete operational stage of develop-
    ment, 85
confidentiality, 40–41
conflict of interest, *41,* 41–42
conflict perspective, 14–15, 16t, 18. *See*
        also feminist perspective
    on abortion, 275
    on abuse of technologies, 453
    on aging, 283, 283t, 291
    on bilingual education, 72–73
    on bureaucratization of education, 334
    on charter schools, 340
    on cultural variation, 70
    on culture, 64–65, 65t
    in dependency theory, 210, 215, 216t

on deviance, 164, *164,* 165t
on downsizing, 383–384
on education, 329–331, 333, 333t
on environment, 417–418, 418f, 421,
    423, 424
on euthanasia, 295
on family, 302, 304, 304t, 305
feminist view allied with, 15
on feminization of poverty, 195
on gay marriage, 320
on gender stratification, *264,* 264–265,
    266t, 267
on global immigration, 253
on gun control, 173
on health, 394–395, 395f, 397t, 399
on Internet, 145
on malnourishment, 212
Marxist view, *14,* 14–15
on mass media, 131–135, 139, 139t
on minimum wage, 200
on monopolies, 379
on multinational corporations,
    214–215, *215*
on obedience, 154
on postindustrial society, 110
queer theory. *See* queer theory
on race and ethnicity, 237, 238t
on religion, 346, 348, 349, 350t
on schools, 88
on social change, 445, 445t,
    446, *446,* 447
on social control, 153
on social institutions, 105–106, 106t
on sports, 17
on stratification, 186–187, 187t, *187*
on transnational immigration, 455
on welfare, 221
on women in military, 262
on women's poverty, 269
in world systems analysis, 209f,
    209–210, 216t
conformity, 152, 158
    binge drinking as, 155
    cultural transmission of, 161–162, 165
    emergent-norm view of, 430
    obedience and, 153–154
    as opposite of deviance, 160
Congo, Democratic Republic of, 208f,
    380, *381*
conspicuous leisure, *185,* 186
Constellation project (NASA), 446
Constitution, U.S.
    authority of, 366
    First Amendment to, 359
    Fourth Amendment to, 453
    Nineteenth Amendment to, 272
    Second Amendment to, 172
    Twenty-Sixth Amendment to, 374
consumption
    conspicuous, *185,* 185–186
    promoted by media, *128,* 128–129
contact hypothesis, 238, 238t, 241
content analysis, 38, 39, 141
control group, 29f
control theory, 157
control variables, *33,* 33–34
convenience samples, 32
"cookies," 145, 146

Cooley, Charles Horton, 11, 12, 16t, 82,
    83, 84, 85t, 112, 168
*Cop in the Hood: My Year Policing
    Baltimore's Eastern District*
    (Moskos), 151
core nations, 209f, 209–210
corporal punishment, 154
corporate-conservative coalition, 376
corporate crime, 168
corporate culture, 62
corporate restructuring, 383
corporate welfare, 221
corporations
    boards of directors, 270, 375–376
    critique of, 364, 365
    female managerial positions, 270, 271
    multinational. *See* multinational
        corporations
    power of, 364
    scandals, 375
correlations, 30–32
correspondence principle, 331
Cosby Show (TV series), 300
cosmetic surgery, 159, *159*
Costa Rica, 208f, 375f
"Cost of Homelessness" (National Alli-
    ance to End Homelessness), 178, 179
costs of health care, 400, 401f, 404–405
Cote d'Ivoire, 208f
cottage industries, 387, *387*
countercultures, 70, *70,* 71
courtship. *See* mate selection
covens, 358
Craigslist.org, 232
"cram schools," 64
crazes, 435, 437t
creationism, 352, 358–359, 360
credentialism, 330
crime, 166–174. *See also specific crimes*
    biological roots of, 160
    campus crime, 166, *166*
    committed by women, 171
    death penalty for, 155, 156f
    deviant uses of technology, 159–160
    Durkheim's theory of, 160
    feminist perspective on, 166, 169, 171
    following natural disasters, 6
    hate crimes, 168, 168f
    index crimes, 169, 170t
    informal economy and, 381
    misuse of personal information, 452
    organized crime, 167, 169, 174, 249
    professional crime, 167, 174
    profitability of, 162
    statistics on. *See* crime statistics
    transnational crime, 169, 169t, 174
    victimless crimes, 166–167
    violent. *See* violence; violent crime
    white-collar and technology-based,
        167, 167–168, 169, 174
crime statistics, 169–171, 174
    data collection and analysis, 46
    index crimes, 169, 170t
    international rates of, 171
    trends, 170f, 170t, 170–171
    victimization surveys, 170
criminal justice system, 151, 164. *See*
        also prisons

Croatia, 208*f*
cross-tabulation, 49
"cross-talk," 266
crowds, 432–433, 437, 437*t*
crowdsourcing, 137, 432
crude birthrate (birthrate), 410
crude death rate (death rate), 410
CSI: Crime Scene Investigation (TV series), 133
Cuba, 208*f*, 375*f*, 381
Cuban Americans, 249–250
cults, 357, 357*t*, 360
cultural capital, 12, 58
cultural convergence, 127, 215
cultural diffusion, 66–68, *67, 68,* 69
cultural factors in resistance to social change, 446–447
cultural relativism, 56, 57*f*, 58
cultural transmission of conformity, 161–162, 165
cultural universals, 56, 58–59, 345
culture, 53–73
   academic culture of cheating, 63, 64
   aging and, 280, 283
   bilingualism, 71–73, 72*f*, 74
   conflict perspective on, 64–65, 65*t*
   countercultures, 70, *70,* 71
   cross-cultural perspective on gender, 263–264, *264*
   described, *55,* 55–58
   diffusion of, 66–68, *67, 68*
   disseminated by mass media, *133,* 133–135
   ethnocentrism and, 56
   feminist perspective on, 65, 65*t*
   functionalist perspective on, 64, 65*t*, 70
   global culture war, 63–64
   influence on human behavior, 55, *55*
   innovation and, 66–69
   interactionist perspective on, 65*t*
   mass media and, 127–128
   material culture, 68, 145, 446, 447
   "Nacirema" culture, 54
   nonmaterial culture, 68, *68,* 145, 446
   norms and values of, 60–63, 301
   organizational culture, 117–119
   persistence of traditions, 215
   polyandrous cultures, 301, 302, *302*
   role of language in, 58–65
   social policy and, 70, *70*
   sociobiology and, 56–57
   sociological perspectives on, 64–65, 65*t*
   subcultures. *See* subcultures
   transmitted by education, 326–327, *327*
   variation in, 69–71
culture industry, 56
culture lag, 68, *68,* 145
   illegal immigration and, 456
   resistance to social change and, 446, 447
culture shock, 70–71
curanderismo, 398
"cutting," 28–29
CVS, 402
cyberbullying, 128
Czech Republic, 143*f*, 194*f*, 208*f*, 219*f*, 395*f*

d

Dalit (untouchables), 13, 181
Dancing with the Stars (TV series), 140
Das Kapital (Marx), 10*f*, 445
data collection and analysis
   crime statistics, 46
   macro-level analysis, 29
   privacy concerns in, *452,* 452–453
   reading graphs, 48*f*, 48–49, 49*f*
   report writing, 49–50
   in scientific method, 29*f*, 32–33
   study of, 369
   technology in, 44*f*, 44–46
day without media, 91, *91*
death, 289
   crude death rate, 410
   cultural traditions, *287*
   "death control," 412
   Native American traditions, 288, *288*
Death and Life of the Great American School System, The (Ravitch), 325
Death of White Sociology, The (Ladner), 42
death penalty, 155, 156*f*
Death with Dignity Act of 1997, 295
decision making
   lack of coordination in, 434, *434*
   public opinion and, 436
decriminalization, 166–167
Deepwater Horizon oil spill (2010), 420
Defense of Marriage Act (DOMA) of 1996, 320
Defense Security Agency, 116
defining problem, 29*f*, 29–30
degradation ceremony, 86
deindustrialization, 382–384, *384,* 388
deinstitutionalization of mentally ill, 195, 407
democracy, 367, 371
Democratic Party, 140, 253, 422
Democratic Republic of Congo, 208*f*, 380, *381*
demographic transition, 411*t*, 411–412, 412*f*, 416
demography, 408–411
   current studies, 410
   elements of, 410–411, 411*f*
   Malthus and Marx, 409, *409*
Denmark, 208*f*, 214*f*
   aid to developing countries, 211
   child care subsidized in, 94
   religious participation in, 353*f*
   social welfare in, 221
   unemployment assistance in, 193
denominations, religious, 355, 356, 357*t*, 360
Department of Homeland Security, 434
dependency theory, 210, 215, 216, 216*t*
dependent variables, 30
Desi (Asian Indians), 245
Desperate Housewives (TV series), 133
developing nations. *See also* global inequality
   abortion policies in, 276
   aid to, 211
   cell phone use in, 90, *90,* 92, 453–454, *454*

digital divide and, 135
economic exploitation of, 209–210
environmental issues for, 421
environmental problems in, 417
health care in, 395, 395*f*
health of elderly in, 284
impact of globalization on, 210, *210,* 216
life expectancy in, 395
media use in, 144
offshoring to, 384–385, 385*t*
population growth in, 412, 416
poverty in, 206–207
social mobility in, 217
spirituality in, 353
deviance, 150–174
   anomie theory of, 160–161, 161*t*
   binge drinking, 155, *155*
   conflict perspective on, 164, *164,* 165*t*
   crime. *See* crime
   deviant behavior, 12, 152
   differential association and, 161–162, 165
   Durkheim's theory of, 160
   feminist perspective on, 164, 165*t*
   functionalist perspective on, 160–161, 164, 165*t*
   interactionist perspective on, 161–163, 165*t*
   labeling perspective on, 163, 165, 263
   nature of, *158,* 158–159
   sexual behavior as, 317
   social control of, *152,* 152–158
   social disorganization theory of, 162–163, *163,* 165
   sociological perspectives on, 160–164, 165*t*
   stigma and, 159, *159,* 165
   technology and, 159–160
Devoted Husband Organization (Japan), 99
Diagnostic and Statistical Manual of Mental Disorders (DSM), 406–407
dictatorships, 367, *367,* 371
differential association, 161–162, 165
differential justice, 164
differentiation, in social change, 444
diffusion, cultural, 66–68, *67, 68,* 69
digital divide, 135
digital surveillance, 145, 146
direct-selling networks, 212, 213
disability, as master status, 101, 102
disaster behavior, *433,* 433–435, 437, 437*t*
   case studies of, *434,* 434–435
   research, 433
Disaster Research Center, 433
discovery, 66, 69
discrimination, 236. *See also* prejudice; racism
   against Blacks at White schools, 338
   discriminatory behavior, 232*f*, 232–233
   against elderly persons, 283
   institutional. *See* institutional discrimination
   against LGBT people, 319, 320
   "reverse discrimination," 383
   sex discrimination, 267–271, 332

disenchantment phase of retirement, 287
disengagement theory of aging, 282, 283, 283*t*, 284
distributive power, 364
District of Columbia v. Heller (2008), 172
division of labor
   in bureaucracy, 115–116, 117*t*
   housework, 262, 269*f*, 272
   in schools, 334
Division of Labor in Society, The (Durkheim), 10*f*, 107
divorce, 3. *See also* family(ies); marriage
   factors in, 314, 316
   statistical trends, 314, 314*f*
"doctor-nurse game," 402
Doctors Without Borders, 370
"doing gender," 266
DOMA (Defense of Marriage Act) of 1996, 320
domestic violence, 304
Domhoff, G. William, 376, 376*f*
dominant groups
   creation of stereotypes, 230
   gender roles and, 265
   hate crime committed by, 168
   men, challenge to, 273
   White privilege, *233,* 233–234
dominant ideology, 64–65
   of mass media, 132–133, *133,* 139
   stratification and, 187
domination, 364
Dominican Republic, 57*f*, 208*f*
Dongria Kondh people, *439*
"Do Re Mi" flash mob, 433
Do the Right Thing (film), 247
double consciousness, 11
downsizing, 383–384
Dr. Phil (TV series), 140
dramaturgical approach, 83, 371
"drapetomania," 397
dreidel, *351*
dress codes, in sports, 16
Driving While Black (DWB), 163
drug trade, 162, 171
DSM (Diagnostic and Statistical Manual of Mental Disorders), 406–407
dual-income families, 305, 312, *312*
Dubai (UAE), 448–449, *449,* 456
DuBois, W. E. B., 10*f*, 10–11, 12, 16*t*, 19
Durkheim, Émile
   anomie theory of, 160–161, 161*t*
   on religion, 346, 350
   on social structure, 107, 111
   study of suicide, 6–7, 12, 20
   views of, 8–9, 10*f*, 16*t*
DWB (Driving While Black), 163
dysfunctions, 14
   in bureaucracies, 116, 117
   of global immigration, 252–253
   illness as, 393
   of informal economy, 381
   of liberation theology, 348–349
   narcotizing, 130–131, 139
   of racism, 237
   of religion, 347
   in romantic relationships, 314
   social change as, 105–106

e

Earth Day, 422, 424
East Germany, 430–431
East Timor, 208*f*
Ebony magazine, 129*t*
ecclesiae, 355, 357*t*, 360
ecological modernization, 418
economic factors
  in demise of estate system, 182
  effect on labor unions, 120–121
  in intergenerational mobility,
    197–198, 198*f*
  in minimum wage laws, 199–200
  in resistance to social change, 446
economics, 4
economic systems, 365, 378–382, 379*f*
  capitalism. *See* capitalism
  informal economy, 381, 382
  socialism, 380–381, 381*t*, 382
economy. *See also* economic systems
  age bias and, 292
  dual-income families and, 312
  effect on retirement age, 286–287, 292
  global economy, 209
  government and. *See* government
  impact of change in minimum wage, 201
  informal economy, 381, 382
  intergenerational mobility and, 198
  pressure on middle class, 183
  recession. *See* global recession of 2008
  social policy: microfinancing, *386,*
    386–387, *387*
  of United States, 379*f*, 382–388
Economy and Society (Weber), 10*f*
ecotourism, *421*
Ecuador, 208*f*
education, 324–341. *See also* colleges
    and universities; high schools;
    school(s)
  as agent of change, 328, 329*f*
  Asian Americans and, 246
  bestowal of status by, 330–331, 331*f*
  bilingual, 72–73, 248–249
  careers in, 234, *234*, 335, *335*
  for careers in sociology, *23,* 23–24, 24*f*
  completion of, 86
  conflict perspective on, 329–331,
    333, 333*t*
  credentialism and, 330
  culture transmitted by, 326–327, *327*
  debate over Title IX, 331, 332
  effect of global recession on, 5
  feminist perspective on, 331–332, 333*t*
  functionalist perspective on, 326–328,
    333*t*, 334
  hidden curriculum in, 329–330
  impact on social mobility, 198
  inherently conservative nature of,
    105–106
  integrative function of, 327–328, *328*
  interactionist perspective on,
    332–333, 333*t*
  Latino/Hispanic students, 309
  of Native Americans, *30,* 243
  relationship to income, 29–34, 31*f*,
    33*f*, 328, 329*f*

  search engines in, 327
  social control and, 328
  social policy: charter schools, 339*f*,
    339–340, *340*
  social policy: religion in schools,
    358–360, *359*
  sociological perspectives on, 326*f*,
    326–333, 333*t*
Education Act of 1972, 331, 332
egalitarian family, 303, *303,* 304, 305
egocasting, 138–139
Egypt, 59, 85–86, 208*f*, 420
eHarmony, 307
elderly. *See also* aging; retirement
  collective consciousness of, *292,*
    292–293
  health of, 284
  as minority group, 281
  volunteering by, 282–283
"elderspeak," 292
electronic church, 357–358, 360
Electronic Communications Privacy Act
    of 1986, 145, 452
Electronic Media (Gross), 126
Elementary and Secondary Education
    Act (ESEA) of 1965, 73
Elementary Forms of Religious Life
    (Durkheim), 10*f*
elite models of power relations, 367,
    375–376, 376*f*
"Elmtown" study, 337
El Salvador, 208*f*
Emergency Management Center (NYC),
    433, 434
emergent-norm perspective, 429–430,
    432, 436, 437
emigrants, 411
Emirates Golf Club (Dubai), *448*
employment. *See also* unemployment;
    workforce; workplace
  after retirement, 287, 291–292, 292*f*
  age bias in, 292, 293, *293*
  among adolescents, 92
  of Asian Americans, 244
  based on technical qualifications,
    116–117, 117*t*, 118, 334
  competition for, age and, 291–292,
    292*f*, 293
  in developing countries, *219*
  discrimination in hiring, 232, 233–234
  female-dominated occupations,
    261, *261*
  gender bias in, 269, 331
  global immigration and, 251–254,
    252*f*, 253
  green-collar jobs, 422
  minimum wage jobs, 192
  minimum wage laws, 200*t*,
    200–202, *201*
  occupational barriers for women,
    199, *199*
  precarious work, 192
  restrictive leave policies, 234
  shrinking middle class and, 183
  social consequences of, 269*f*, 272, 272*f*
  for sociologists, 23–24, 24*f*
  of women. *See* women in U.S.
    workforce

Endangered Species Act, 422
endogamy, 308, 313
Engle v. Vitale (1962), 350
English language, 58, 328
English-only rules, 234
environment (environmental issues)
  adolescent lack of interest in, 423*f*
  air pollution, 419
  climate change, *420,* 420–421
  conflict perspective on, 417–418, 418*f*,
    421, 423, 424
  in Dubai, 449
  ecological modernization and, 418
  effect of coffee industry on, 21
  environmental justice movement, 19,
    418–419, *419,* 420, 424
  human ecology, 411*t*, 417
  impact of globalization, 421–422
  role in socialization, 81, *81*
  social policy: environmentalism,
    422–424, *423*
  sociological perspectives on, *417,*
    417–424
  water pollution, 419–420, *420*
environmentalism, 392, 423
  effect of global recession on, 5
  social policy on, 422–424, *423*
  values associated with, 62–63
environmental justice, 19, 418–419, *419,*
    420, 424
Environmental Protection Agency
    (EPA), 422
environmental refugees, 421–422
environmental sociology, 19
EPA (Environmental Protection
    Agency), 422
equilibrium model of society, 444
Eritrea, 57*f*, 208*f*
ESEA (Elementary and Secondary
    Education Act) of 1965, 73
Essays on the Principle of Population
    (Mathus), 409
established sects, 355
estate system, 181–182, 188
esteem, 189
Estonia, 208*f*
ethics, 40–42
  academic culture of cheating, 63, 64
  codes of ethics, 40, 41
  confidentiality, 40–41
  conflict of interest, *41,* 41–42
  privacy issues, 46
  Protestant work ethic, 348, 350
  value neutrality, 42
Ethiopia, 57*f*, 208*f*
ethnic city neighborhoods, 241, 245
ethnic groups, 227, 236, 239, *239*
ethnicity, 229*f*, 229–230, *230. See also*
    specific ethnic groups
  conflict perspective on, 237, 238*t*
  cultural values regarding, 63*f*
  family and, 308–310, 309*f*
  functionalist perspective on, 237, 238*t*
  inequality due to. *See* racial and ethnic
    inequality
  interactionist perspective on, 238, 238*t*
  interethnic marriage, 308, *308*
  labeling theory of, 237–238, 238*t*, *238*

  role in social mobility, 198–199
  social epidemiology and, 399
  sociological perspectives on,
    237–238, 238*t*
  symbolic, 251
  value of, 63*f*
  White ethnics, 251, *251*
  women oppressed by, 265–266
ethnic slurs, *231*
ethnic succession, 167
ethnocentric bias, 215
ethnocentrism, 56, 58, 73, 230
ethnography, 35–37, *37,* 38*t,* 39
  careers in sociology and, 90, *90*
  studies of unemployed persons, 83
Europe. *See also specific countries*
  immigration issue in, 414–415
  welfare in, 220, *220,* 221
European Union, 254
euthanasia, *294,* 294–295
"evacuation camps," 247
evolution, controversy over, 358–359, 360
evolutionary theory, 8, 444, 445,
    445*t,* 447
existing sources, in research, 37–38, 38*t*
exogamy, 308, 313
expectations, 101, 332–333
experiment(s)
  Milgram experiment, 153–154, *154*
  mock prison experiment, *98,* 98–99,
    100, 101, 369
  in sociological research, 37, 38*t,* 39
experimental group, 37
exploitation theory, 237, 238*t,* 241
expressiveness, 264
expulsion of ethnic groups, 239, *239*
extended family, 300, 305
ExxonMobil, 214*f*
Exxon *Valdez* oil spill (1989), *41,* 41–42,
    419–420

f

Facebook, 132
Facebook envy, 186
face-to-face socialization, 91, *91*
face-work, 83
fads, 435, *435,* 437*t*
fair trade coffee, 21
false consciousness, 184, 349
familismo (familism), 309
family(ies)
  "accordion families," 299–300
  as agent of socialization, *76,* 87–88,
    88, 89
  alternatives to, 314–316
  authority patterns in, 302–303, *303*
  blended families, 300, 313, *313*
  child-rearing patterns, 310–313
  composition of, 300–301, 301*f*
  conflict perspective on, 302, 304,
    304*t,* 305
  dual-income families, 305, 312, *312*
  egalitarian family, 303, *303,* 304, 305
  ethnicity and, 308–310, 309*f*
  extended family, 300, 305
  family reunions, *298*

feminist perspective on, 304*t*, 304–305

functionalist perspective on, 303, 304*t*

gender roles in, 264

global view of, 300–305

human sexuality and. *See* human sexuality

interactionist perspective on, 304, 304*t*, *304*, 305, 312

kinship patterns, 301

loyalty to *(sa pamilya)*, 246

marriage and. *See* marriage

nuclear family, 300, 305

racial and ethnic differences in, 308–310, 309*f*

single-parent families, 305, 309*f*, 312, 313, 315

social class differences in, 308

as social institution, 304–305

social policy: gay marriage, 319–321, 320*f*

sociological perspectives on, 303–305, 304*t*

stepfamilies, 300, 313, *313*

fashions, 435, 437*f*

fathers, 304, *304*, 312

Federal Bureau of Investigation (FBI), 116, 168, 169

Federal Election Commission, 377

Federal Emergency Management Agency (FEMA), 434

federal government, U.S.

CMHC program, 407

economic and tax policies, 191

funding for sociological research by, 46–47

poverty measures of, 193

role in health care, 404–405, *405*

surveillance by, 452–453

Federal Reserve Bank, 191

Federal Trade Commission, 145

FEMA (Federal Emergency Management Agency), 434

female infanticide, 219

Feminine Mystique, The (Friedan), 273

feminism, 276

Black feminists, 266

challenge to traditional family, 304

collective consciousness, 272–273

feminist perspective, 15, *15*, 18

on child care, 93

on crime, 166, 169, 171

on culture, 65, 65*t*

on deviance, 164, 165*t*

on education, 331–332, 333*t*

on family, 304*t*, 304–305

on gender-related language, 59

on gender stratification, 265, 266*t*

of global immigration, 253

on mass media, 136, 139, 139*t*

methodology, 43, *43*, 48

occupational prestige of women, 189–190

on postmodern society, 110

on religion, *349*, 349–350, 350*t*

research methodology, 43, *43*

on social institutions, 106

of sports, 17, *17*

of violence in schools, 336

feminist theory, 265

feminization of poverty, 194*t*, 194–195, 269, 308

fertility, 408–409

fertility patterns in U.S., 412–414

feudalism (estate system), 181–182, 188

"fiesta politics," 373

fighting attack *(atague)*, 398

Fiji, 54–55

Filipino Americans, 245–246

The Filter Bubble (Pariser), 132

financial aid, 196, 197

Finland, 130*f*, 208*f*, 423*f*

age at first marriage, 308*f*

aging in, 285*f*

college graduation rates, 326*f*

prisons in, *152*

five-stage theory of dying, 289

flash gangs, 433

flash mob, 432–433

folkways, 61, 65

force, 365

Ford Motor Company, 385

foreign adoptions, 310, 311, *311*

foreign aid, 211, 212*f*

foreign investment by multinationals, 215

formal norms, 61, 61*t*, 65, 294

formal operational stage of development, 85

formal organizations, 115, 118, 119, 334–341

formal social control, 155–156, 156*f*

Fort Bethold Community College, *30*

Fort Bethold Reservation, *30*

foster care, 311–312

France, 208*f*, 423*f*

antiforeign sentiments in, 415

child care subsidized in, 94

economy of, 379*f*

global brands of, 130*f*

head scarf banned in, 268

labor union membership in, 120*f*

poverty in, 194*f*

religious participation in, 353*f*

television in, 133

value of ethnicity in, 63*f*

"Frankenfood," 453

Freakonomics (Levitt), 162

"free agent mentality," 384

free enterprise system, 379

Freej (TV series), *133*

free trade, 67

friendship networks, 90, 136

fright sickness *(susto)*, 398

Fulani people (Africa), 281

functionalist perspective, 13–14, 16*t*, 18

on abuse of technologies, 453

on adoption, 310

on aging, 282, 283, 283*t*, 284

on bureaucratization of education, 334

on culture, 64, 65*t*, 70

on deviance, 160–161, 164, 165*t*

on education, 326–328, 333*t*, 334

on education-income relation, 29–34

on ethnicity, 237, 238*t*

on family, 303, 304*t*

on gay marriage, 319–320

on gender stratification, 264, 266*t*, 267

on global immigration, 252–253

on "good death," 289

on health, 393–394, 397*t*

on informal economy, 381

on Internet, 145

on labor unions, 121

on malnourishment, 212

on mass media, 127–131, 139, 139*t*

modernization theory, 215–216, 216*t*

on multinational corporations, 214

on offshoring, 385

on physician-patient relations, 401

on postindustrial society, 110

on poverty, 195

on race and ethnicity, 237, 238*t*

on religion, 346–347, *347*, *348*, 350*t*

on schools, 88, 340

on social change, 444–445, 445*t*, 447

on social control, 153

on social institutions, 104–105, 106*t*

on social movements, 438

on sports, 17

on stratification, 186, 187*t*

on transnational immigration, 455

on women in military, 262

in world systems analysis, 209*f*, 209–210, 216*t*

fundamentalism, 352–353

born-again Christians, 353–354

Islamic, 56, 352, 448

g

Gabon, 208*f*

Gallaudet University, 432, *440*

Gallup poll, 49, 49*f*

Gambia, 208*f*

gambling, 243

game stage of self, 82, 83*t*

gatekeeping, 131, 139, 393–394

gay marriage, 319–321, 320*f*

gay relationships, 318*f*, 318–319

adoption and, 311

demographics of, 318, 318*f*

gay marriage, 319–321, 320*f*

online dating, 307

gay-straight alliances (GSAs), 337

gay teens, 337

Gaza Strip, 208*f*

G8 economic powers, 424

Gemeinschaft, 107, 108*t*, 109, 111

gender

abortion and, 273–274

cross-cultural perspective on, 263–264, *264*

"doing gender," 266

gender messages in scouting, 39, *39*

impact on social mobility, 199, *199*, 217, 219, *219*, 222

in politics, 373, *373*, 375*f*

social class and, 189–190

social construction of, 259–267

social development and, 87–88, *88*

social epidemiology and, 399–400, 405

social movements and, 432*t*, 440, 441

sociological imagination and, 21–22

talkativeness and, 6

Gender Advertisements (Goffman), 141

gender bias, 269, 331, 440

gender differences

in academic achievement, 331

among adolescents, 88, 89*t*, 90

in social mobility, 199, *199*, 217, 219, *219*, 222

gender inequality in housework, 269*f*, 272

gender messages in scouting, 39

gender norms, violation of, 260, 260*t*

gender-related language, 59

gender roles, 259, 267

dominant groups and, 265

in families, 264

human sexuality and, 263

men's roles, 261, *261*, 263

in United States, 259–263

women's roles, 260–261

gender-role socialization, 259–260, 263

of children, 260*t*, *260*, 260–261

in families, 87–88, 94

in schools, 328

gender stratification, 257–276

conflict perspective on, *264*, 264–265, 266*t*, 267

feminist perspective on, 265, 266*t*

functionalist perspective on, 264, 266*t*, 267

interactionist perspective on, 266, 266*t*

matrix of domination and, 265*f*, 265–266, 267

social construction of gender, 259–267

social policy: abortion, 273–276, 274*f*, 275*f*

sociological perspectives on, 264–266, 266*t*

women as oppressed majority, 267–276

General Electric, 385

generalized belief in social change, 431

generalized other, 82, 87

General Motors, 383, 384

genetically modified (GM) food, 453

genetic engineering, 453

gentrification, as threat to NORCs, 288

George Lopez (TV series), 133

Georgia (country), 208*f*

Germany, 208*f*, 423*f*

aging in, 285*f*

antiforeign sentiments in, 415

child care subsidized in, 94

collapse of East Germany, 430–431

college graduation rates, 326*f*

economy of, 379*f*

gender inequality in housework, 269*f*

global brands of, 130*f*

homeschooling illegal in, 339

under Nazi regime, 154, 239, 347

poverty in, 194*f*

religious participation in, 353*f*

voter turnout, 372*f*

gerontology, 281–282, 284

Gesellschaft, 107–108, 108*t*, *108*, 111

Ghana, 208*f*, 287

ghetto, 151

G.I. Joe doll, *260*

Gifted Learning Links, 134

Israel, 208*f*, 262
Italy, 130*f*, 208*f*, 285*f*, 372*f*, 379*f*, 423*f*
"Iyeska: Notes from Mixed-Blood Country" (Trimble), 226

j

Jamaica, 208*f*, 219*f*
Japan, 208*f*, 423*f*
  aging in, 284, 285*f*, 286
  child care issues in, 94
  college graduation rates, 326*f*
  as core nation, 210
  "cram schools" in, 64, *333*
  economy of, 379*f*
  foreign aid per capita, 212*f*
  global brands of, 130*f*
  health practices in, *393*
  infant mortality rates, 395*f*
  labor union membership in, 120*f*
  marriage in, 99
  schools in, 330
  sterilization of the disabled, 102
  television in, 133
  traditional authority in, 366
  women-only public transit, *264*
Japanese Americans, 237, 247
Jehovah's Witnesses, 355
Jewish Americans, 250, *250*
Jews
  Hebrew language, *250*
  Nazi genocide against, 239, 247, 250
  refused immigration by U.S., 252
  religious toys for children, 345, *351*
Jim Crow laws, 242
Jordan, 143*f*, 208*f*, 375*f*
Judaism, 351, 351*t*, 352
Junior Girl Scout Handbook (Girl Scouts), 39

k

Kaliai people (Polynesia), 289
Kazakhstan, 208*f*
Kenya, 63*f*, 208*f*
Kinsey Report, 46
kinship groups, 301, 314
kinship patterns, 301, 305
Kirghiz people (Afghanistan), 280
Kitzmiller v. Dove Area School District (2005), 359
Kiwai Papuan people, 186
Koran (Qur'an), *373*
Korea, 423*f*
Korean Americans, 247
Korean War, 247
Korean Women's Association United (KWAU), 441
Kota rite, 85
Ku Klux Klan, 242
Kurds, 248
Kuwait, 375*f*
KWAU (Korean Women's Association United), 441
Kyoto Protocol (1997), 420–421
Kyrgyzstan, 208*f*

l

labeling, 163, *317,* 317–318
labeling theory
  on aging, 283, 283*t,* 284
  of deviance, 163, 165, 263
  on health, 396–397, 397*t*
  on mental illness, 397, 407
  perceptions in, 163
  of race and ethnicity, 237–238, 238*t,* 238
  on stereotyping of minorities, 332–333
labor. *See also* workforce
  exploitation of, 21, 448
  global immigration, 251–254, 252*f,* 253
  pool of cheap labor, 215
  transnational workers, 454–456, 455*f*
  by women, value of, 190
labor force participation of women, 269–270, 270*t,* 270*f*
labor unions, 118
  as barrier to unemployment, 452
  declining membership in, 120
  employer opposition to, 121
  lacking in charter schools, 340
  Marx's failure to predict, 185
  social policy and, 120*f,* 120–121
laissez-faire principle, 379
language, 65. *See also* communication(s); *specific languages*
  American Sign Language, *59*
  argot, 69–70
  Internet top ten languages, *451*
  nonverbal communication, *59,* 59–60
  role in culture, 58–65
  written and spoken, *58,* 58–59
Laos, 208*f*
Las Vegas, suicide in, 7
latent functions, 14
  of education, 326, 336–337, 341
  of religion, 346
Latin America
  debate over abortion in, 273
  impact of globalization on, 210
  television in, 133
Latinos/Hispanics, 254
  Central and South Americans, 250
  class system and, 199
  Cuban Americans, 249–250
  income-education relation, 329*f*
  income inequality and, 191
  marches for immigration reform, 253
  mental disorders of, 408
  Mexican Americans, 249, 309, 398
  Miss Quinceañera Latina pageant, 85
  poverty among, 195
  Puerto Ricans, 249, *249*
  racial inequality and, 248*f,* 248–250
  social class of, 309–310
  students, 309
  treatment of women, 266
Latvia, 208*f*, 285*f*, 411*f*
law(s), 61
  antitrust legislation, 379
  Arizona's immigration law, 253

  on human sexuality, 316
  Jim Crow laws, 242
  liberal divorce laws, 314
  minimum wage laws, 200*t,* 200–202, *201*
  promoting marriage, 315
  social control, 156–157, 157*f, 157,* 158
law enforcement, 151
LDS (Church of Jesus Christ of Latter Day Saints), 301, 356, *356*
LDs (learning disorders), 338–339
League of Arab States, 247
learning disorders (LDs), 338–339
Lebanon, *91,* 208*f*
Lenski, Gerhard, 99, 108–110, 109*t,* 111, 378
  view of stratification, 187–188
lesbian relationships, 318*f,* 318–319
Lesotho, 208*f*
LGBT persons, 319, 320–321
liberal-labor coalition, 376
liberation theology, 348–349, 350
Liberia, 208*f*
Libya, 208*f*
life chances, 195–196, *196,* 202, 243, 368
life course, *85,* 85–86, 284–289
life course approach, 86
life expectancy, 283, 395, 410–411
life goals, 63*f*
lifestyles, 315–316
LinkedIn, 132
Lipstick Jihad (Moaveni), 258
Lithuania, 208*f*
Living Goods, 213
living wage, 201
LMFAO, *143*
looking-glass self, 82, 87
looting, 432
Los Angeles riots (1992), 140, 142, 431
Los Angeles Times, 128
love relationship, 307
lower class, 182, 308
lower-middle class, 183
Luddites, 447
Luxembourg, 211
lynching, 242

m

Macedonia, 208*f*
machismo, 309
macro-level analysis, 29, 93, 418
macrosociology, 12, 13, 140
Madagascar, 208*f*
Magnolia Project, 19, *19*
Maid in Manhattan (film), 196
Maktoum family, 448
Malawi, 57*f*, 208*f*
Malaysia, 47*f*, 208*f*, 214*f*
Mali, 57*f*, 208*f*
Malthus, Thomas Robert, 409, *409,* 416
malnourishment, 211–212, 410
management, 118, 119
manifest functions, 13–14, 326, 333, 346
man-made disasters
  due to collective behavior, 429, 430, 431

oil spills, *41,* 41–42, 419–420
  "technological disasters," 433
terrorism. *See* September 11, 2001, attacks; terrorism
marijuana, 48, 48*f*, 157, *164*
Marine Corps, 77, 78
marital rape, 164, 318
marriage, 306–313. *See also* divorce; family(ies)
  age at first marriage, 306, 308*f,* 315
  arranged marriages, 307
  attitudes toward, 319
  childless, 315–316
  child marriage, 56, 57*f*
  civil marriage, 316, 320
  courtship, 306–307, 308*f*
  divorce and, 314
  dual-income couples, 305, 312, *312*
  effect of global recession on, 4–5
  "empty shell" marriages, 318
  gay marriage, 319–321, 320*f*
  interracial (interethnic), 228, 240, 308, *308*
  in Japan, 99
  love relationship and, 307
  marital rape, 164, 318
  mate selection, *306,* 306–307
  in minority groups, 227, 281
  monogamy, 300
  polygamous, 300–301, 302, *302,* 356
  remarriage, 314
Martineau, Harriet, 8, *8,* 12
Marx, Karl, 9–10, 10*f,* 12, 16*t*
  conflict perspective and, *14,* 14–15, 16*t*
  elite model of power relations, 375
  on population control, 409, 416
  on stratification, 184–185
  view of labor unions, 121
Marxist class theory, 237, 238*t*
mass media, 125–147
  as agent of socialization, 90, *90,* 92, 127–128
  audience for, 140–142
  conflict perspective on, 131–135, 139, 139*t*
  consumption promoted by, *128,* 128–129
  consumption promoted by media, *128,* 128–129
  cultural convergence in, 127
  culture disseminated by, *133,* 133–135
  of deviant acts, 163
  "digital divide," 135
  dominant ideology of, 132–133, *133,* 139
  as enforcer of social norms, 128
  feminist perspective on, 136, 139, 139*t*
  functionalist perspective on, 127–131, 139, 139*t*
  gatekeeping by, 131, 139
  global reach of, 142–146, 143*f, 143*
  health care information, 400
  interactionist perspective on, 136*f,* 136–139, 138*f,* 139, 139*t*
  media-free days, 91, *91*
  monitoring by interest groups, 131–132

New York State Department of Hygiene, 407

New Zealand, 208f, 214f, 269f

NGOs (nongovernmental organizations), 370

NHSLS (National Health and Social Life Survey), 47, 48

Nicaragua, 57f, 208f, 217

Nickel and Dimed: On (Not) Getting By in America (Ehrenreich), 35

Niger, 57f, 208f

Nigeria, 57f, 208f

NIH (National Institutes of Health), 396, 404

Nike, 215, 433

Nile River, pollution of, 420

NIMBY ("not in my backyard"), 418, 446

Nineteen Eighty-Four (Orwell), 146, *146*

No Child Left Behind Act of 2002, 339

No Kidding, 316

nonconformist subculture, 337

nongovernmental organizations (NGOs), 370

nonmaterial culture, 68, *68*, 145, 446

nonperiodic assemblies, 432

nonreactivity of secondary analysis, 38

nonreligious persons, 354

nonscientific polling, 32, 35

nonverbal communication, 16, *59*, 59–60

NORCs (naturally occurring retirement communities), 287–288

norm(s), 60–63, 65, 65t

acceptance of, 61, 61t, 152–153

collective behavior and, 429–430, 432, 436, 437

enforcement of, 128

family cultural practices and, 301

formal norms, 61, 61t, 65, 294

gender norms, violation of, 260, 260t

on human sexuality, 316

informal norms, 61, 61t, 65

legitimacy of, 195

sanctions and, 61, 61t

social context of, 56, 57f

types of, 61

violation of, as deviance, 158

normative function, 114

North Korea, 133, 208f

Norway, 208f, 269f

aid to developing countries, 211

foreign aid per capita, 212f

Sami people of, 58

"not in my backyard" (NIMBY), 418, 446

NRA (National Rifle Association), 172, 173

NRI (Networked Readiness Index), 139

NRMs (new religious movements), 357, 357t, 360

NSA (National Security Agency), 116, 144, 452–453

nuclear family, 300, 305

nuclear power generation, *68*

"Nuestro Himno," 73

nurse-midwives, 394

nurses, *401*, 401–402, 405

Nyinba people (Nepal and Tibet), 301, 302, *302*

O

obedience, 153–154, *154, 158*

Oberlin College, 331

obesity, 105, 133, 158, *394*

objective method of measuring social class, 188–190, 189t

observation, 35

occupational mobility, 198, *199*

occupational prestige, 189t, 189–190

occupational segregation, 269

Occupy Wall Street movement, 183, *183*, 184, 193, 221, 443

Office of Naval Research, 369

offshoring, 384–385, 385t, 388

Oglala Lakota Sioux, 226

Ohio Defense Force, *70*

oil spills

Deepwater Horizon (2010), 420

Exxon *Valdez* oil spill (1989), *41*, 41–42, 419–420

OKCupid, 45

oligarchy, 117, 367, 371

Olympics, *371*, 419, 420

Oman, 208f

On Death and Dying (Kübler-Ross), 289

"one-drop rule," 228

Oneida Nation, *58*

online communities, 28

online curricula, 335

online dating, 45, *45*, 307

online friendship networks, 90

online giving, 137

online marketing, 136f, 136–137

online politicking, 377

online research, 46, 50

Ontario Place (Chicago), 288

On the Origin of Species (Darwin), 8

openness to ideas, 328

open stratification systems, 196, 202

operational definition, 30, 34

opinion leaders, 140, 142

"opposites attract" rule, 307

oppression of women, 267–276

oral contraceptives, 316

organic solidarity, 107, 111

organization(s), 115–119

bureaucracies. *See* bureaucracies

formal, 115, 118, 119, 334–341

social policy: unions, 120f, 120–121

organizational culture, 117–119

organized crime, 167, 169, 174, 249

organ transplantation, 453

Origin of the Family, Private Property, and the State, The (Engels), 265

The Other America (Harrington), 110

out-groups, 113, *113*, 114, 227

outpatient treatment of mental illness, 407

Oxfam, 365

P

Pakistan, 208f, 214f, 360, 395f

Panama, 208f

Pan-Cordillera Women's Network for Peace and Development, 219

panics, 435–436, 437t

Papua New Guinea, 208f

Paraguay, 208f

parent(s)

as agents of socialization, 88, *88*

child-rearing patterns, 310, *310*

fathers, 304, *304*, 312

gender-role socialization by, 260

monitoring by, 131–132

single-parent families, 305, 309f, 312, 313, 315

stepparents, 304

parenting, 261, 315

parkour, 69–70

Parsons, Talcott, 13, 16t

"partial-birth" abortions, 276

participant observation, 35

Partners in Development Programme (U.N.), 219

passive euthanasia, 294

patients, 396, 401

patriarchy, 302

patrilineal descent, 301, 305

Patriot Act of 2001, 145, 371, 452

Peabody Energy Co., *184*

peace, 369–370, 370f

"Peacemaking," 102

Pearl Harbor attack, 247

pedophilia, 318

peer groups, 62, 88, 89t, 90, 94

People magazine, 128, 129t

per capita gross national income, 208f

percentages, 48

perceptions, 82, 163, 439

periodic assemblies, 432

peripheral nations, 209f, 209–210, 215

personality, 78

Personal Responsibility and Work Opportunity Reconciliation Act of 1996, 220

Peru, 208f

Peter principle, 117

Philadelphia Negro, The (DuBois), 10f

Philippines, 208f, 245, 269f

flash-mob protests in, 432–433

indigenous peoples of, 219

protection of transnational workers, 456

photographs, in visual sociology, 140, 141, *141*

"Photography and Sociology" (Becker), 141

physicians

care of mentally ill and, 407

"doctor-nurse game," 402

dominance of, *401*, 401–402, 405

gatekeeping by, 393–394

occupational role of, 395–396

sociological perspectives on, *401*, 401–403

women as, 401, 402, 403, *403*

Pine Ridge Reservation, 226

Pirates of the Caribbean films, 67

planking, *435*

play stage of self, 82, 83t

Pledge of Allegiance, 360

pluralism, 240–241

pluralist model, *376*, 376–378

Poland, 194f, 214f, 308f, 326f, 353f, *414*

political integration, 327–328, *328*

political participation, 372f, 372–373, 374, *374*

political science, 4

political systems

authority in, 365–366

power in, 365

types of government, 366–367

war and peace, 368–371

politics, 365, 372–378

"fiesta politics," 373

gender in, 373, *373*, 375f

labor union role in, 121

online politicking, 377

participation and apathy, 372f, 372–373, 374, *374*

race in, 373, *373*, 375f, 377

in U.S., 267, 372–378

women in, 267, 373, 375f

polyandry, 300, 301, 302, *302*

polygamy, 300–301, 356

polygyny, 301

Pop Idol (TV series), 133

"popular health movement," 400

population, 408–416, *409*

baby boom, 413

China's restrictive policies, 415, *415*

demographic transitions, 411t, 411–412, 412f

fertility patterns in U.S., 412–414

migration and, 414–416

"population explosion," 411t, 412, 413f

stable growth in, 413f, 413–414

study of (demography), 408–411

world patterns, 411–412

Population Bomb, The (Ehrlich), 409

population control, 409, *409*

population growth rate, 411f

population pyramid, 413, 413f

pornography, 136, 138, 166, 318

Portfolios of the Poor: How the World's Poor Live on $2 a Day (Collins et al.), 206–207

Portugal, 208f, 285f

postindustrial societies, 109t, 110, 447

postmodern societies, 109t, 110–111, *111*

poverty. *See also* income; wealth

absolute or relative, 192, 194f

among Asian Americans, 244

as barrier to medical care, 398, 399f, 405

benefits of, to society, 195

concern for environment and, 423

demographics of, 194, 194t

in developing nations, 206–207

effects of Hurricane Katrina on poor, 196, 434

family life and, 308

feminization of, 194t, 194–195, 269, 308

global recession of 2008 and, 192, 193, 195

precarious work, 193

social mobility and, 192–199

sociological perspectives of, 195, 269

sociological research on, 192–195,
194f, 206–207
stigma of, 332
study of, 192–195, 194f
underclass, 195, 202
worldwide, 208f, 210–212, 211f, 212f
power, 365, 371
of corporations, 364
in environmental organizations, 422
in gender stratification, 264–265
institutionalized. See authority
in political systems, 365
in stratification, 185, 186, 187
unequal distribution in U.S., 377–378
Power Elite, The (Mills), 375
power elite models, 367, 375–376, 376f
Domhoff's model, 376, 376f
Mills's model, 375–376, 376f
power structure
pluralist model of, *376,* 376–378
power elite models of, 367,
375–376, 376f
in U.S., 375–378
prayer in schools, 359–360
precarious work, 192, 193, 384
precipitating factors in social
change, 431
preindustrial societies, 108–109,
109t, 378
prejudice, *231.* See also discrimination;
racism
based on stereotypes, 230, 236
discriminatory behavior and, 232f,
232–233
against mentally ill, 159
slavery and, 242
preoperational stage of development, 85
preparatory stage of self, 82, 83t
preretirement, 287
presentation of self, 83, *84*
preservation of order, 105
prestige, 189, 189t
prestige symbols, 159
primary groups, 112, 112t, 114
PRISM, 144, 145
prisons
Abu Ghraib, 99, 154, 369
comparison of, *152*
degradation ceremony in, 86
mock prison experiment, *98,* 98–99,
100, 101, 369
prison gangs, 14
privacy
communications technology and, *452,*
452–453
ethics of, 46
social policy on right to, *144,*
144–146, *146*
product placement, *128,* 129
profane realm, 346, 359
professional crime, 167, 174
profiteering from microfinancing, 387
Project Head Start, 328
proletariat, 10, 184
pro-life groups, 273
Proposition 209 (California Civil Rights
Initiative), 383
protective function of family, 303

protest(s)
antiwar protests, *431*
flash mobs, 432–433
at Gallaudet University, 432, *440*
over minimum wage, 201
Protestant ethic, 348, 350
*Protestant Ethic and the Spirit of
Capitalism, The* (Weber), 10f, 348
Protestant Reformation, 348
Protestants, 355
psychological approaches to self, 84–85, 85t
psychology, 4
public figures, 129t
public health, 45–46
public opinion, 436–437, 437t
public policy, 23–24, 420–421
publics, 436
public sociology, 19
Puerto Ricans, 249, *249*
Puerto Rico, 208f
pure sociology, 20
Pygmalion in the Classroom (Rosenthal
& Jacobson), 332–333

q

qualitative research, 35
quantitative research, 35
quasi-religions, 358
Québec, 73
Québec Native Women, 234
queer theory, 15, 18
gay marriage, 320
media presentation of
homosexuality, 133
research methodology, 43–44
view of sports, 17
questionnaires, 35, 39, 62
queuing, 429–430, *430*
quinceañera, 85
quota systems, 218, 373
Qur'an (Koran), *373*

r

race, 227–229. See also racial and ethnic
inequality
family and, 308–310, 309f
income disparity and, 218, *218,* 232, 232f
infant mortality rates and, 399
labeling theory of, 237–238, 238t, *238*
as motivation for hate crimes, 168
multiple identities, 228–229, 250
in politics, 373, *373,* 375f, 377
response to Los Angeles riots and,
140, 142
role in social mobility, 198–199
social class as proxy for, 231
social construction of, 218, *218,*
227–228, 229f
social development and, 87
social epidemiology and, 399, 405
sociological imagination and, 21–22
sociological perspectives on, 237,
238, 238t
women oppressed by, 265–266

Race to the Top program, 340
racial and ethnic inequality, 10,
225–254. See also ethnicity; race;
specific ethnicities
Aboriginal people of Australia, 9,
244, *244*
color-blind racism, *231,* 231–232,
236, 383
discrimination. See discrimination;
institutional discrimination
ethnic groups. See ethnic groups
minority groups, 227, 236
prejudice, 230, *231,* 236, 242
research on, 10
social policy: global immigration,
251–254, 252f, *253*
sociological perspectives on,
237–238, 238t
spectrum of intergroup relations. See
intergroup relations
in United States, 229f, 242f, 242–254
White privilege, *233,* 233–234
racial formation, 228–229
racial groups, 227, 236
racial profiling, 163, 237–238, *238,* 241
racism, 230. See also discrimination;
prejudice
"color-blind," *231,* 231–232, 236, 383
functionalist perspective of, 237, 238t
in health care, 399
in Mormon Church, 356
rain forest, destruction of, 417
random sample, 29f, 32
rape, 164, 166, 318
rational-legal authority, 366, 371
rebellion, 161, 161t
Recognition of Customary Marriages
Act of 1998 (S. Africa), 316
recruitment, 440
Red Crescent, 370
Red Cross, 370
reference groups, *113,* 114
"Reflecting Absence" (Arad), 60, *60*
relationship marketing, 137
relationships
effects of technology on, 2
family and, 303
gay. See gay relationships
lesbian, 318f, 318–319
romantic, 104, 307, 314, 318f,
318–319
social, healthy aging and, 282, *282*
relative deprivation approach, 432t,
439, 443
relative poverty, 192
reliability, ensuring, 29f, 32–33, 34
religion, 344–360. See also *specific religions and churches*
as agent of socialization, 92, 94
components of, 352–354, 354t
conflict perspective on, 346, 348,
349, 350t
denominations, 355, 356, 357t, 360
Durkheim's view of, 346, 350
ecclesiae, 355, 357t, 360
electronic church, 357–358
feminist perspective on, *349,*
349–350, 350t

functionalist perspective on, 346–347,
347, 348, 350t
importance of, 9, 10, 346, 347, *347*
integrative function of, 346–347,
347, 350t
interactionist perspective on,
347–348, *348*
liberation theology, 348–349, 350
new religious movements (cults), 357,
357t, 360
nonreligious persons, 354
organization of, 355–360
quasi-religions, 358
religious toys, 345, *351*
rites of passage, 92
sects, 355, 357t, 360
social control and, 349, 350t
in social media, 347–348
social policy: religion in schools,
358–360, *359*
social support and, 347–348,
348, 349
society and, 104
sociological imagination and, 21–22
sociological perspectives on,
346–350, 350t
stem cell research and, *376*
Weberian thesis of, 348
women subordinate in governance of,
349–350
world religions, 351t, *351,*
351–354, *352*
religious beliefs, 352–353, 354, 354t
religious experience, 353–354, 354t
religious ritual, 353, 353f, 354, 354t
remarriage, 314
remittances, 246
reorientation phase of retirement, 287
replacement of personnel, 104
report writing, 49–50
representative democracy, 367, 372
reproduction function of family, 303
Republican Party, 140, 422
research, general. See also sociological
research
online research, 46, 50
sexism in medical research, 400
stem cell research, *376*
research designs, 34–39
ethnography. See ethnography
experiments, 37, 38t, 39
surveys, 34–35, 36t, 38t
use of existing sources, 37–38, 38t
researcher bias, 42
reservation system, 228, 243
reshoring, 385
resistance to social change, 446–447
resistance to technology, *446,* 447
resocialization, 86
resource allocation
differential access, 184
emergence of surplus resources,
187–188
in social institutions, 105
unequal distribution, 409
resource mobilization, 432t, 439–440,
440, 443
"retired-husband syndrome," 286

retirement, *286,* 286–288, 289
  employment following, 287,
    291–292, 292*f*
  NORCs, 287–288
  phases of, 287, 287*f*
  as rite of passage, 286–287
retreatism, 160, 161*t*
"reverse discrimination," 383
review of literature, 29*f,* 30, 31*f*
revolution against bourgeoisie, 184
rewards, 61
right to die, 289, *294,* 294–295
riots
  Los Angeles riots (1992), 140, 142, 431
  urban, looting and, 432
rites of passage
  life course approach to, *85,* 85–86, 87
  military training as, 78, 79
  religious, 92
  retirement as, 286–287
ritualism, 161, 161*t*
Roe v. Wade (1973), 273, 274–275
role conflict, 101
role exit, 102–103, *103*
role strain, 102
role taking, 82
role transitions
  adjusting to retirement, *286,* 286–288
  aging and, 284–289
  sandwich generation, *285,* 285–286
Rolling Stone (magazine), 129*t*
Roma (Gypsies), 239, *239*
Roman Catholic Church, *347,* 355
  on birth control, 447
  fundamentalism in, 352
  liberation theology and, 348–349
  women in, 350
Romania, 79, *79,* 208*f*
romantic relationships, 307. *See also*
    human sexuality; mate selection
  dysfunctional, divorce and, 314
  in high school, 104
  lesbian and gay, 318*f,* 318–319
Roommate.com, 232
Royal Dutch Shell, 214*f*
rules and regulations
  in bureaucracy, 116, 117*t,* 118
  rational-legal authority, 366
  in schools, 329–330, 334
rumors, 429, 436, *436,* 438
rum springa, 87, 89
Russia, 208*f*
  age at first marriage, 308*f*
  economy of, 379*f*
  as former Soviet Union, 185, 262, 448
  media penetration in, 143*f*
  population growth rate, 411*f*
  religious participation in, 353*f*
  value of ethnicity in, 63*f*
Rwanda, 208*f,* 373, 375*f,* 380

S

sabotage, 447
sacred realm, 346, 359
SAGE (Services and Advocacy for
    GLBT Elders), 293

salaries of teachers, 336, 337*f*
same-sex couples. *See* gay relationships
Sami people, 58
sample selection, 29*f,* 32, 34, 437
sanctions, 65, 153
  norms and, 61, 61*t*
  religious rituals and, 353
  in welfare system, 221
sandwich generation, *285,* 285–286, 289
sa pamilya, 246
Sapir-Whorf hypothesis, 59
Saudi Arabia, 59, 208*f, 352,* 353
"Saya" (robot), *450*
Scalpel and the Silver Bear, The (Alvord
    and van Pelt), 401
Scandinavian Festival, *251*
scheduled castes, 181
school(s). *See also* education
  as agents of socialization, 88, 92, 326
  "apartheid schools," 329
  as bureaucracies, *335,* 335–336
  bureaucratization of, *334,* 334–335
  Columbine shootings (1999), 113,
    131, 172
  "cram schools," 64
  as formal organizations, 334–341
  functionalist perspective on, 88, 340
  gender-role socialization in, 328
  high school. *See* high schools
  homeschooling, 338–339, 341
  impersonality of, 334, *334*
  Newtown, Conn., shootings (2012),
    159, 172, 406
  roles of teachers in, *335,*
    335–336, 337*f*
  social organization in, 337–338
  social policy: charter schools, 339*f,*
    339–340, *340,* 341
  social policy: religion in schools,
    358–360, *359*
  student subcultures, 336–338,
    338*f, 338*
  tracking in, 330–331
school choice programs, 334–335, 340
science, 3–4
scientific management approach,
    118, 119
scientific method, 29*f,* 29–34
  data collection and analysis, 32–33
  defining problem in, 29–30
  developing conclusions in, 33–34
  formulating hypotheses, 30–32, 32*f*
  review of literature, 30, 31*f*
SCLC (Southern Christian Leadership
    Conference), 242
Scopes ("monkey") trial, 359
search engines, 327
search filters (Internet), 132
secession, 239
secondary analysis, 37–38, 38*t,* 39
secondary groups, 112*t,* 112–113,
    113, 114
Second Life, 2
Second Sex, The (de Beauvoir), 273
"second shift," 262
Secret Service, 171
sects, 355, 357*t,* 360
secularization, 346

segmented audience, 140
segregation, 236, *236,* 239–240,
    241, 241*t*
self, 82–87
  impression management, 83, 84,
    84, 87
  looking-glass self, 82, 87
  Mead's theory of, 83
  presentation of, 83, *84*
  psychological approaches to,
    84–85, 85*t*
  stages of, 82–83, 83*t*
self-employment, 199
self-evaluation, 114
self-identity
  developing, perceptions in, 82
  role exit and, 102–103, *103*
  transracial adoption and, 311
self-injury, 28–29, 43, 443
semiperipheral nations, 209*f,* 209–210
Seneca Falls Convention (1848), 272
Senegal, 208*f*
"senilicide," 294
sense of purpose, 105
September 11, 2001 attacks, 131
  anti-terrorist efforts following, 371
  bureaucratic division of labor
    and, 116
  collapse of World Trade Center, 434
  economic decline due to, 21
  identity theft as component of, 168
  immigration procedures and, 254
  media coverage of, 128
  Patriot Act and, 145, 371, 452
  racial profiling following, 238, 248
  rumors about, 436
  surveillance following, 156
  as transnational crime, 169
  World Trade Center memorial, 60, *60*
Serbia, 208*f*
serial monogamy, 300
service industries, 213, 261
Services and Advocacy for GLBT Elders
    (SAGE), 293
SES (socioeconomic status), 190, 304
settlement house movement, 11, *11*
Seventh-Day Adventists, 355
sex discrimination, 267–269
  in education, 332
  in wage payments, 270–271
sex education, 328, *328*
sexism, 267–269, 276, 331, 356, 400
sexual behavior
  comparison of, 47*f*
  as deviance, 317
  regulation of, as function of
    family, 303
  singlehood and, 315
  STDs and, 294, 295, 317
sexual harassment in military, 262
sexual identities, 15, 259
sexually transmitted diseases (STDs),
    294, 295, 317
Sexual Politics (Millett), 273
sex workers, global trafficking of, 43, *43*
Shakers, 104, 350
Sherpas (Nepal), 280

shootings
  Aurora, Colo., theater shootings
    (2012), 172
  Columbine High School shootings
    (1999), 113, 131, 172
  Newtown, Conn., school shootings
    (2012), 159, 172, 406
  Virginia Tech (2007), 5, 112, 131,
    155–156, 166, *166*
*Shopping Our Way to Safety: How We
    Changed from Protecting the Envi-
    ronment to Protecting Ourselves*
    (Szasz), 392, 423
*Shoshit, Shetkari, Kashtkari, Kamgar,
    Mukti Sangharsh (SSKKMS),* 441
Shout Your Love from the Middle of a
    Cabbage Patch Day, 99
sick role, 393, 394, 397
Sierra Club, 414
Sierra Leone, 57*f,* 208*f*
significant others, 83, 87, 88
"silver collar economy," 291
Singapore, *157,* 208*f*
singlehood, 315
single-parent families, 305, 309*f,*
    312, 313, 315
Sinopec, 214*f*
skin color, 227
Skype, 138
slave reparations, 242
slavery, 169, 187, 242
  religion and, 349
  runaways, 397
  in stratification systems,
    179–181, 181*t*
  trafficking of sex workers, 43, *43*
Slender Man, 436
Slovakia, *91,* 208*f*
Slovenia, 208*f*
"slugging," 15
smog, *391*
smoking, *33,* 33–34, 163
SNAP (Supplemental Nutrition
    Assistance Program), 193
snow, decline in, 420
snowball samples, 32
Soboa ceremony, 85–86
social capital, 12, 136
social change, 429, 444–447
  conflict perspective on, 445, 445*t,* 446,
    446, 447
  dysfunctional, 105–106
  evolutionary theory of, 444, 445,
    445*t,* 447
  functionalist perspective on, 444–445,
    445*t,* 447
  global. *See* global social change
  liberation theology and, 348–349, 350
  precipitating factors in, 430–431
  resistance to, 446–447
  sociology and, 9
  theories of, 444–445, 445*t*
social characteristics of audience,
    140, 142
social class, 188–192
  achieved statuses. *See* achieved
    statuses
  aging and, 283

South Asia tsunami (2004), 22, 88
Southern Christian Leadership Conference (SCLC), 242
South Korea, 120*f*, 208*f*
  "cram schools" in, 64
  global brands of, 130*f*
  voter turnout, 372*f*
  women's social movements in, 441
sovereignty movement (Hawai'i), 368
Soviet Union (former), 185, 262, 448
Spain, 130*f*, 208*f*, 379*f*
Spanish-American War, 245
Spanish language, 73, 248–249
Spencer, Herbert, 8, 12
SPM (Supplemental Poverty Measure), 193–194
"spoiled identity," 159
sports
  dress codes in, 16
  female athletes, 136
  sociological imagination and, 3
  sociological perspectives on, *17*, 17–18
  Title IX and, 331, 332
squatter settlements, *446*
Sri Lanka, 208*f*
SSKKMS (Shoshit, Shetkari, Kashtkari, Kamgar, Mukti Sangharsh), 441
SS *St. Louis* (ship), 252
stability of society, 444–445
stability phase of retirement, 287
stable population growth, 414
"stained glass ceiling," 349
Starbucks, 214–215
"Star-Spangled Banner," 73
state. *See* government
State Grid (China), 214*f*
statistics, 48*f*, 48–49, 49*f*
statuses, 106
  abortion and, 274–275
  achieved. *See* achieved statuses
  ascribed. *See* ascribed statuses
  bestowed by education, 330–331, 331*f*
  conferred by mass media, 128, 129*t*
  family and, 303, 304
  inequality of women, 268–269, 269*f*
  inherited, 186
  of jobs, 336
  master status, 101, 102, 106, 281, 284
  socioeconomic status, 190, 304
status groups, 185, 188
STDs (sexually transmitted diseases), 294, 295, 317
stem cell research, *376*
stepfamilies, 300, 313, *313*
stepparents, 304
stereotypes (stereotyping)
  criminalization of poor by, 194
  of cults, 350
  following September 11 attacks, 155
  in mass media, 133, 136
  of minorities, 332–333
  prejudice based on, 230, 236
  racial profiling based on, 237–238, *238*
  "unwed mothers," 312
  women's gender roles, *260*, 260–261

stigma
  deviance and, 159, *159*, 165
  disability as, 102
  of homosexuality, 260, 317
  of mental illness, 159, 406, 408
  of poverty, 332
stratification, 177–202
  by age. *See* age stratification
  conflict perspective on, 186–187, 187*t*, *187*
  distribution of wealth and income, 217, 219*f*
  functionalist perspective on, 186, 187*t*
  by gender. *See* gender stratification
  interactionist perspective on, *185*, 185–186, 187*t*
  Lenski's view of, 187–188
  Marxist perspective on, 184–185
  within nations, 217–219
  schooling essential to, 330–331, 331*f*
  by social class. *See* social class
  social mobility and, 217–219
  social policy: minimum wage laws, 200*t*, 200–202, *201*
  sociological perspectives on, 184–186, 187*t*
  systems of. *See* stratification systems
  universality of, 186–188, 187*t*
  Weber's perspective on, 185
  in world system, 207–216, 208*f*, 216*t*
stratification systems, 179–188, 180*f*
  castes, 181
  estates, 181–182
  open v. closed, 196, 202
  slavery, 179–181, 181*t*
Street Corner Society (Whyte), 35–36
stress of teaching, *335*, 335–336
structural conduciveness, 430
structural power, 364
structural strain, 430–431
subcultures, *69*, 69–70, 71
  activist, 422
  Amish as, 89
  environmental activists, 422
  in high schools, 336–337
  in India's call centers, *69*, 70
  self-injurers as, 29
  student subcultures, 336–338, 338*f*, *338*
Subjection of Women, The (Mill), 265
Sudan, 208*f*
suicide
  among Native Americans, 243
  right to die issues, *294*, 294–295
  sociological research on, 6–7, 12, 20
Suicide: A Study in Sociology (Durkheim), 10*f*
"suicide tourism," 295
Sunnah, 347
Supplemental Nutrition Assistance Program (SNAP), 193
Supplemental Poverty Measure (SPM), 193–194
Supreme Court, U.S.
  on abortion, 273, 274–275
  on affirmative action, *383*
  on Affordable Care Act, *404*, 405
  on Arizona immigration law, 253

  on conflict of interest, 42
  on Death with Dignity Act, 295
  on gay marriage, 319, 320
  on gun control, 172
  on Jim Crow laws, 242
  on marijuana, 157
  on Pledge of Allegiance, 360
  on preservation of confidentiality, 40–41
  on restricted membership, 250
  on school prayer, 359
  on segregation, 329
  on teaching creationism, 359
  wiretaps approved by, 145
  women on, *249*, 267
surveys
  by cell phone, 36
  on euthanasia, 294
  Gallup poll, 49, 49*f*
  on groups, 112
  nonscientific polling, 32, 35
  of public opinion, 437
  in sociological research, 34–35, 36*t*, 38*t*
  victimization surveys, 170
Survivor (TV series), 114, *114*, 133
susto (fright sickness), 398
Swaziland, 208*f*
sweatshops, *215*, 245
Sweden, 208*f*
  aging in, 285*f*
  aid to developing countries, 211
  child care subsidized in, 94
  foreign aid per capita, 212*f*
  global brands of, 130*f*
  income distribution in, 219*f*
  infant mortality rates, 395*f*
  labor union membership in, 120*f*
  sterilization of the disabled, 102
  women in government, 375*f*
Switzerland, 130*f*, 208*f*, 241, 295
symbol(s), 16, 60, 65
  learning to use, 82
  prestige v. stigma symbols, 159
  role in global community, 60, *60*
symbolic ethnicity, 251
symbolic interactionism. *See* interactionist perspective
Syria, 208*f*

t

Taiwan, 208*f*
Tajikistan, 208*f*
Taliban, 332
talkativeness, 6
Tanzania, 208*f*
Target, 452
teacher(s)
  roles of, *335*, 335–336, 337*f*, 341
  salaries of, 336, 337*f*
  sexism in employment of, 331
teacher-expectancy effect, 332–333
Tea Party, 183
technical qualifications, 116–117, 117*t*, 118
"technological disasters," 433

technology (technological advances). *See also* communications technologies
  as agent of socialization, *90*, 90–91, 92
  biotechnology, 453–454, *454*, 456
  computer technology, 450, *450*, 452, 452*t*, 456
  consumer technologies, 449
  crime and, 159–160, *167*, 167–168, 169, 174
  "death control" and, 412
  environmental destruction and, 421
  global social change and, 449–454
  intellectual technologies, 327
  Internet's global profile, 451, 451*f*
  in measuring social class, 190
  media penetration and, *143*, 143–144
  privacy and censorship issues, *452*, 452–453
  reproductive, kinship and, 301
  resistance to, *446*, 447
  role in globalization, 66–68, *67*, *68*
  in security measures, 155–156
  social effects of, 428, 429
  in sociological research, 44*f*, 44–46, 48
  speed of cultural diffusion and, 67–68
  unemployment due to, 450, 452*t*
  in visual sociology, 141, *141*
"tech-nos," 449
teenagers. *See* adolescents
telenovelas, 133
televangelists, 357–358
television, 133
  as babysitter, 128, 138
  in gender-role socialization, 260
  portrayals of mental illness, 405
  portrayals of religion, *348*
  viewing habits, 137–138
  worldwide use of, *143*, 143–144
temporary employment, 384, 385*f*
Tender Cut, The: Inside the Hidden World of Self-Injury (Adler & Adler), 28
termination phase of retirement, 287
terrorism, 370–371, *371*
  differential standards and, 113
  use of Internet by extremists, 138
  World Trade Center. *See* September 11, 2001, attacks
TFR (total fertility rate), 410
Thailand, 208*f*, 214*f*, 217
Theology of Liberation, A (Gutiérrez), 348
theoretical perspectives, 13–18
  conflict perspective. *See* conflict perspective
  feminist perspective. *See* feminist perspective
  functionalism. *See* functionalist perspective
  interactionist perspective. *See* interactionist perspective
  in practice, 20
theory(ies), 6–7
Time magazine, 128, 129*t*, 273
Titanic (ship), 196, *196*

women—*Cont.*
  female managerial positions,
    270, 271
  feminization of poverty, 194*t,*
    194–195, 269, 308
  gender and social mobility, 199, *199,*
    217, 219, *219,* 222
  head scarf and veil, 268, *268*
  health of, 399–400
  immigrants, 253
  institutional discrimination against,
    267–268, 276
  in military, *262,* 262–263, 369
  occupational prestige of, 189–190
  oppressed by ethnicity, 265–266
  as oppressed majority, 267–276
  as physicians, 401, 402, 403, *403*
  in politics, 267, 373, 375*f*
  in polyandrous cultures, 301, 302, *302*
  self-images, 115
  sexism and sex discrimination,
    267–269
  social mobility of, 199, *199*
  in social movements, 440, 441
  social policy on abortion and,
    273–276, 274*f,* 275*f*

societal pressure on, 413
"stained glass ceiling," *349,* 350
status of, worldwide, 268–269, 269*f*
stereotyped gender roles, *260,*
  260–261
subordinate, in religious governance,
  349–350
on Supreme Court, *249,* 267
value of labor by, 190
violence against, 153–154
women in U.S. workforce, 269–272, 276
  compensation, 270–272
  labor force participation, 269–270,
    270*t,* 270*f*
  preferences for male boss, 271
  self-employment, 199
  social consequences of employment,
    269*f,* 272, 272*f*
Women's Sports Foundation, 332
"women's work," 304
"workfare," 221
workforce
  affirmative action, 382, *383,* 388, 393
  changing face of, 382–385
  deindustrialization and, 382–384,
    384, 388

dysfunctions of informal
  economy, 381
exploitation of, 21, 448
offshoring and, 384–385, 385*t,* 388
temporary workers, 384, 385*f*
working class, 183, *184,* 283
workplace
  conflict over family policies in, 316
  secondary groups in, 112–113, *113*
  socialization to, 92, 94
World Bank, 210
World Changing (Steffen), 442
World Economic Forum, 135
World Health Organization (WHO),
  393, 404
world population growth rate, 411*f*
world population patterns, 411–412
world religions, 351*t, 351,* 351–354, *352*
world system
  legacy of colonialism, 209*f, 209,*
    209–210, *210*
  stratification in, 207–216, 216*t*
world systems analysis, 209*f,* 209–210,
  216, 216*t*
World Trade Center memorial, 60, *60*
World Trade Organization (WTO), 438

World War II, 239, 247, 250, 413
WTO (World Trade Organization), 438

X

X-Factor, The (TV series), 133
xiao, 280

Y

Yanomami people (Brazil), 300
Yemen, *81,* 208*f*
young people
  interest in environment, 423*f*
  voting patterns among, 374, *374*

Z

Zambia, 57*f,* 208*f,* 211
zero population growth (ZPG), 414
Zimbabwe, 208*f*
Zimbardo, Philip, *98,* 98–99, 100, 101, 369
ZPG (zero population growth), 414

Applications of *Sociology's* Major Theoretical Approaches

Sociology in Modules provides comprehensive coverage of the major sociological perspectives. This summary table includes a sample of the topics in the text that have been explored using the major approaches. "M" indicates the module and the numbers in parentheses indicate the pertinent chapters.

FUNCTIONALIST PERSPECTIVE

- M3 Defined and explained (1)
- M40 Adoption (13)
- M24 Anomie theory of deviance (7)
- M12 Bilingualism (3)
- M43 Bureaucratization of schools (14)
- M44 Charter schools (14)
- M3 Cow worship in India (1)
- M10 M43 Culture (3, 14)
- M26 Davis and Moore's view of stratification (8)
- M23 Death penalty (7)
- M9 Dominant ideology (3)
- M24 Durkheim's view of deviance (7)
- M32 Dysfunctions of racism (10)
- M9 Ethnocentrism (3)
- M39 Family (13)
- M19 Formal organizations (5)
- M32 Functions of racism (10)
- M28 Gans's functions of poverty (8)
- M41 Gay marriage (13)
- M34 Gender stratification (11)
- M33 Global immigration (10)
- M52 Health and illness (17)
- M53 Human ecology (17)
- M18 In-groups and out-groups (5)
- M45 Integrative function of religion (15)
- M22 Internet privacy (6)
- M20 Media and social norms (6)
- M20 Media and socialization (6)
- M20 Media and status conferral (6)
- M22 Media concentration (6)
- M20 Media promotion of consumption (6)
- M29 Modernization theory (9)
- M29 Multinational corporations (9)
- M24 Narcotizing effect of the media (6)
- M32 Racial prejudice and discrimination (10)
- M45 Religion as a source of social support (15)
- M43 M57 Social change (14, 18)
- M23 M43 Social control (7, 14)
- M16 Social institutions (5)
- M45 Socialization function of religion (15)
- M15 M43 Socialization in schools (4, 14)
- M3 Sports (1)
- M11 Subcultures (3)
- M60 Transnationals (18)

CONFLICT PERSPECTIVE

- M3 Defined and explained (1)
- M35 Abortion (11)
- M53 Access to health care (17)
- M60 Access to technology (18)
- M51 Affirmative action (16)
- M36 Age stratification (12)
- M12 Bilingualism (3)
- M44 Bureaucratization of schools (14)
- M50 Capitalism (16)
- M44 Charter schools (14)
- M28 Corporate welfare (8)
- M43 Correspondence principle (14)
- M43 Credentialism (14)
- M10 Culture (3)
- M15 Day care funding (4)
- M25 Death penalty (7)
- M24 Deviance (7)
- M16 Disability as a master status (5)
- M9 M20 M26 Dominant ideology (3, 6, 8)
- M51 Downsizing (16)
- M49 Elite model of the U.S. power structure (16)
- M56 Environmental issues (17)
- M56 Environmentalism (17)
- M28 Executive compensation (8)
- M32 Exploitation theory of discrimination (10)
- M39 Family (13)
- M41 Gay marriage (13)
- M43 Gender equity in education (13)
- M34 Gender stratification (11)
- M33 Global immigration (10)
- M25 Gun control (7)
- M43 Hidden curriculum (14)
- M19 Iron Law of Oligarchy (5)
- M26 Marx's view of stratification (8)
- M34 Matrix of domination (11)
- M22 Media concentration (6)
- M20 Media gatekeeping (6)
- M20 Media stereotypes (6)
- M52 Medicalization of society (17)
- M51 Microfinancing (16)
- M28 Minimum wage laws (8)
- M33 Model minority (10)
- M29 Multinational corporations (9)
- M28 Poverty (8)
- M60 Privacy and technology (18)
- M53 Racism and health (17)
- M45 Religion and social control (15)
- M59 Social change (18)
- M23 Social control (7)
- M16 Social institutions (5)
- M15 Socialization in schools (4)
- M3 Sports (1)
- M12 Subcultures (3)
- M43 Tracking (14)
- M60 Transnationals (18)
- M24 Victimless crimes (7)
- M25 White-collar crime (7)
- M29 M56 World systems analysis (9, 18)

INTERACTIONIST PERSPECTIVE

- M3 Defined and explained (1)
- M36 Activity theory of aging (12)
- M40 Adoption (13)
- M51 Affirmative action (16)
- M48 Charismatic authority (16)
- M3 Commuter behavior (1)
- M26 Conspicuous consumption (8)
- M32 Contact hypothesis (10)
- M10 Culture (3)
- M24 Differential association (7)
- M14 M48 Dramaturgical approach (4, 16)
- M20 Electronic communication (6)
- M28 Executive compensation (8)
- M39 Family relationships (13)
- M41 Gay marriage (13)
- M34 Gender stratification (11)
- M52 Health and illness (17)
- M19 Human relations approach (5)
- M49 Influence of social media sites on politics (16)
- M22 Media concentration (6)
- M51 Microfinancing (16)
- M28 Minimum wage laws (8)
- M23 Obedience (7)
- M14 Presentation of the self (4)
- M24 Routine activities theory (7)
- M24 Social disorganization theory (7)

FEMINIST PERSPECTIVE

- M3 Defined and explained (1)
- M15 Day care funding (4)
- M24 Deviance (7)
- M9 Dominant ideology (3)
- M8 Ethnographic research (2)
- M39 Family (13)
- M43 Gender gap in education (14)
- M34 Gender stratification (11)
- M10 Language (3)
- M34 Matrix of domination (1)
- M20 Media stereotypes (6)
- M51 Microfinancing (16)
- M20 Pornography (6)
- M24 Rape (7)
- M45 Religion and socialization (15)
- M6 Research methodology (2)
- M5 Self-injury (2)
- M3 Sports (1)
- M24 Victimless crimes (7)
- M35 Women's movement (11)

LABELING THEORY

- M3 Defined and explained (1)
- M16 Disabilities and labeling (5)
- M52 Health and illness (17)
- M42 Human sexuality (13)
- M32 Profiling at airports (10)
- M24 Racial profiling (7)
- M24 Sexual deviance (7)
- M24 Societal reaction approach (7)
- M43 Teacher-expectancy effect (14)
- M24 Victimless crimes (7)

QUEER THEORY

- M9 Child rearing (3)
- M42 Gay marriage (13)
- M20 Homosexuality in the mass media (6)
- M42 LGBT households (13)
- M8 Research methodology (2)
- M3 Sports (1)

(Feminist Perspective continued)
- M16 Social institutions (5)
- M3 Sports (1)
- M16 Tattoos and social reality (5)
- M43 Teacher-expectancy effect (14)
- M40 Teenage pregnancy (13)
- M60 Transnationals (18)
- M59 Vested interests in NASA's Constellation Project (18)
- M34 Women in combat (11)